معجم أحاديث الشيعة

Compilation of the Shīʿa Narrations

Syed Maisum

ISBN: 9798755249607

This work is dedicated to as-Ṣādiqayn (The two truthful ones)

Preface

﴿يٰاَيُّهَا الَّذِيْنَ اٰمَنُوْا اَطِيْعُوا اللّٰهَ وَاَطِيْعُوا الرَّسُوْلَ وَاُولِى الْاَمْرِ مِنْكُمْ ۚ فَاِنْ تَنَازَعْتُمْ فِىْ شَىْءٍ فَرُدُّوْهُ اِلَى اللّٰهِ وَالرَّسُوْلِ اِنْ كُنْتُمْ تُؤْمِنُوْنَ بِاللّٰهِ وَالْيَوْمِ الْاٰخِرِ ؕ ذٰلِكَ خَيْرٌ وَّاَحْسَنُ تَاْوِيْلًا﴾

"O you who have believed, obey Allāh and obey the Messenger and the Ulu l-Amr (those vested with authority amongst you). And if you disagree over anything, refer it to Allāh and the Messenger, if you should believe in Allāh and the Last Day. That is the best [way] and best in result." **Surah an-Nisā** (4), **verse 59**

All Praise is due to Allāh (تبارك و طائلة), the First and the Last, the one who cannot be compared to, the one who cannot be described, the one who cannot be imagined, he is the provider for all of creation, nothing can be accomplished without his support, no entity can be guided without his guidance, the one who has no boundaries nor duration, the one who feels neither drowsiness nor sleep, to him belongs whatever is in the Heavens and the Earth, Indeed he is a witness over all of creation.

This work was written for the purpose of gaining al-Qurb (Proximity) to Allāh (تبارك و طائلة), and we hope that this small, but yet brief and humble work is accepted by Allāh (تبارك و طائلة), His Messenger (صلى الله عليه وآله وسلم), and the Ulu l-Amr (عليهم السلام) as a small act of obedience. This work however, would never have been possible without the constant assistance of Allāh, and the guidance of his Messenger and the Ulu l-Amr, and the help of the scholars, my family, friends, teachers, the Thaqalayn library, and especially my younger brother.

Disclaimer: None of the translations or gradings are of my own, I have not provided commentary on any of narrations as I do not believe I am qualified to give any sort of commentary on these blessed narrations, rather this work is simply a compilation of narrations that I have personally been touched by, all of the translations, Arabic text, and gradings used can be found in the following sources:

al-Kāfi, (Translated by Shaykh Muhmmad Sarwar)
Thaqalayn.net
Shia Online Library
Mu'jam al-Aḥādīth al-Mu'tabara by Shaykh Āṣif al-Muḥsinī (Translated by Ammaar Muslim)
Rise of the Qa'im by Bilal Muḥammad
Reviving Al-Islam by Nader Zaveri

All Aḥādīth referenced to al-Kāfi are graded by al-'Allāma Muḥammad Bāqir al-Majlisī, and can be located within his commentary of al-Kafi "Mir'at al 'Uqul".

All Aḥādīth graded as "Mu'tabar" are derived from Shaykh Āṣif al-Muḥsinī's work "Mu'jam al-Aḥādīth al-Mu'tabara".

Aḥādīth found in works other than al-Kāfi are graded by various scholarly personalities.

Islamic Honorifics

تَبَارَكَ وَتَعَالَى (tabāraka wa-ta'ālā)	Blessed and Exalted
صَلَّى ٱللَّهُ عَلَيْهِ وَآلِهِ وَسَلَّمَ (ṣallā -llāhu 'alayhī wa-'ālihī wa-sallam)	Peace and blessings of Allāh be upon him and his progeny
عَلَيْهِ ٱلسَّلَامُ ('alayhi s-salām)	Peace be upon him
عَلَيْهَا ٱلسَّلَامُ ('alayha s-salām)	Peace be upon her
عَلَيْهِم ٱلسَّلَامُ ('alayhim s-salām)	Peace be upon them
عجل الله تعالى فرجه ('ajal a llāhu ta'ālā farajah)	May Allāh hasten his re-appearance
رَضِيَ ٱللَّهُ عَنْهُ (raḍiya -llāhu 'anh)	May Allāh be pleased with him
لعنة الله عليه (La'anatu 'llahi 'alay-hi)	May Allāh curse him

Common Hadīth Terminologies

صحيح (Ṣaḥīḥ)	Commonly used to describe a connected chain going back to one of the infallibles, in which each narrator is *Imami Shi'a* and is proven to be *Adl* (just) and *Thiqa* (Trustworthy).
حسن (Ḥasan)	Commonly used to describe a connected chain going back to one of the infallibles, in which each narrator is *Imami Shi'a*, but one or more narrator(s) have been praised, however, he has not been proven to be *Adl* (just).
موثق (Muwathaq)	Commonly used to describe a connected chain of *thiqat* going back to one of the infallibles, however, one or more narrator(s) are considered to be of corrupt doctrine (non-*Imami Shi'a*).
معتبر (Mu'tabar)	Linguistically means something that is considered, however is often used to term a reliable Hadīth.

مجهول (Majhūl)	Commonly used to describe a chain in which one or more narrator(s) have been declared to be unknown.
مرسل (Mursal)	Commonly used to describe a chain which has a disconnection between either one of the Infallibles, or amongst the chain of narrators themselves.
ضعيف (Ḍa'īf)	Commonly used to describe a chain which contains one or more narrator(s) that have been declared as weak.

بِسْمِ ٱللَّهِ ٱلرَّحْمَٰنِ ٱلرَّحِيمِ

ٱللَّهُمَّ صَلِّ عَلَىٰ مُحَمَّدٍ وَآلِ مُحَمَّدٍ وَعَجِّلْ فَرَجَهُمْ وَٱلْعَنْ أَعْدَاءَهُمْ

Table of Contents

Preliminaries of attributing any statement to the Infallibles

1. Which book/books is this report found in?

2. Who is author of this book?

3. Is the alleged author someone who is reliable in terms of Hadīth? (applies to authors of primary sources like al-Kulaynī, al-Ṣaduq, etc.)

4. Has it been established that this alleged author has actually written said book?

5. The most important question, before even looking into the chain of narrators of this report, does the matn (text) of this report contradict either the Holy Qur'an or the established Sunnah (narrations)? If so then this report would be thrown away and not considered because the A'immah would never say such a thing willingly, only after one confirms that the matn (text) aligns with the Qur'an and established Sunnah, or at the very least doesn't contradict the both, only then may one analyze the chain of narrators in an attempt to authenticate the report and consider it a saying from the Imam.

(**A narration that agrees with the Qur'an and established Sunnah is often accepted regardless of the chain**, **as the matn (text) is correct**.)

6. Who are the narrators narrating the report? Is there any disconnection within the chain? Are all the narrators Thiqa (trustworthy)? Are there any controversies or doubts surrounding the trustworthiness of one or more narrators in the chain? (**It's not always necessary for a Hadīth to have an impeccable chain, often times narrations that are correct are reported by known liars or unknown people**.)

باب التوحيد

Chapter on at-Tawḥīd

We have decided it is best to start off with at-Tawhid itself

1.

مُحَمَّدُ بْنُ يَحْيَى عَنْ مُحَمَّدِ بْنِ الْحُسَيْنِ عَنِ ابْنِ أَبِي عُمَيْرٍ عَنْ هِشَامِ بْنِ سَالِمٍ عَنْ مُحَمَّدِ بْنِ مُسْلِمٍ عَنْ ابي جعفر (عَلَيْهِ السَّلام) قَالَ سَمِعْتُهُ يَقُولُ كَانَ اللهُ عَزَّ وَجَلَّ وَلا شَيْءَ غَيْرُهُ وَلَمْ يَزَلْ عَالِماً بِمَا يَكُونُ فَعِلْمُهُ بِهِ قَبْلَ كَوْنِهِ كَعِلْمِهِ بِهِ بَعْدَ كَوْنِهِ

Muhammad b. Yahya has narrated from Muḥammad b. al-Husayn from b. abu 'Umayr from Hisham b. Salim from Muḥammad b. Muslim who has said the following. "I heard Abi Ja'far (عليه السلام) saying, 'Allāh, to Whom belong Might and Majesty, existed when nothing else existed. He eternally knows whatever comes into being. His knowledge of things before their coming into existence and afterwards is exactly the same. (صحيح)[1]

2.

أَحْمَدُ بْنُ إِدْرِيسَ عَنْ مُحَمَّدِ بْنِ عَبْدِ الْجَبَّارِ عَنْ صَفْوَانَ بْنِ يَحْيَى عَنْ أَبِي أَيُّوبَ عَنْ مُحَمَّدِ بْنِ مُسْلِمٍ عَنْ أَبِي عَبْدِ اللهِ (عَلَيْهِ السَّلام) قَالَ إِنَّ الْيَهُودَ سَأَلُوا رَسُولَ اللهِ (صَلَّى اللهُ عَلَيْهِ وَآلِه) فَقَالُوا انْسِبْ لَنَا رَبَّكَ فَلَبِثَ ثَلاثاً لا يُجِيبُهُمْ ثُمَّ نَزَلَتْ قُلْ هُوَ اللهُ أَحَدٌ إِلَى آخِرِهَا. وَرَوَاهُ مُحَمَّدُ بْنُ يَحْيَى عَنْ أَحْمَدَ بْنِ مُحَمَّدٍ عَنْ عَلِيِّ بْنِ الْحَكَمِ عَنْ أَبِي أَيُّوبَ

Ahmad b. Idris has narrated from Muḥammad b. ‘Abd al-Jabbar from Safwan b. Yahya from abu Ayyub from Muḥammad b. Muslim from Abi ‘AbdAllāh (عليه السلام) who has said the following. “The Jews asked the Messenger of Allāh صلى الله عليه وآله وسلم, ‘Describe for us the genealogy- of your Lord.’” The Prophet waited for three days and gave no reply. Then the following verses were revealed to him: In the Name of Allāh, the Beneficent, the Merciful (Muhammad), say, “He is the only God (112:1). God is Absolute (112:2). He neither begets nor was He begotten (112:3). There is no one equal to Him (112:4). The same Hadīth has been narrated by Muḥammad b. Yahya from Ahmad b. Muḥammad from ‘Alī b. al-Hakam from abu Ayyub. (صحيح)[2]

3.

حدثنا أبي رضي الله عنه، قال: حدثنا محمد بن يحيى العطار، عن أحمد ابن محمد بن عيسى، عن أبي هاشم الجعفري،

---

[1] *al-Kāfi, v1, ch12, h2*

[2] *al-Kāfi, v1, ch7, h1*

قال: سألت أبا جعفر محمد بن علي الثاني عليهما السلام، ما معنى الواحد؟ فقال: المجتمع عليه بجميع الألسن بالوحدانية

My father – Muhammad al-Attar – Ibn Isa – Abi Hashim al-Ja'fari who said: I asked Aba Ja'far the Second عليه السلام - what is the meaning of 'the One'? He said: (One) whose Oneness is united upon in all tongues (languages). (معتبر)[3]

4.

أبي رحمه الله، قال: حدثنا سعد بن عبد الله، قال: حدثنا أحمد بن محمد ابن عيسى، عن ابن فضال، عن الحلبي، وزرارة، عن أبي عبد الله عليه السلام، قال: إن الله تبارك وتعالى أحد، صمد، ليس له جوف، وإنما الروح خلق من خلقه، نصر وتأييد وقوة، يجعله الله في قلوب الرسل والمؤمنين

My father from Sa'd from Ibn Isa from Ibn Fadhal from al-Halabi and Zurara from Abi Abdillahعليه السلام who said: Allah Blessed and Elevated is One, Compact, He does not have any hollowness, while the spirit (al-Ruh) is a creation from among His creations and is an aid, support and power which Allah places in the hearts of the messengers and believers.. (معتبر)[4]

5.

أبي رحمه الله، قال: حدثنا سعد بن عبد الله، عن إبراهيم بن هاشم، و يعقوب بن يزيد جميعا، عن ابن فضال، عن ابن بكير، عن زرارة، عن أبي عبد الله عليه السلام، قال: سمعته يقول في قوله عز وجل: ﴿وله أسلم من في السماوات والأرض طوعا وكرها﴾ قال: هو توحيدهم لله عز وجل

---

[3] *Al-Tawḥīd, ch3, h1*

[4] *Al-Tawḥīd, ch 27, h2*

My father from Sa'd from Ibrahim b. Hashim from Ya'qub b. Yazid from Ibn Fadhal from Ibn Bukayr from Zurara from Abi Abdillah عليه السلام. He (Zurara) said: I heard him (the Imam) saying about His words Mighty and Majestic: "and to Him have submitted whomsoever is in the heavens and the earth whether willingly or unwillingly" (3:83) - this is their acknowledgment of Oneness to Allah Mighty and Majestic. (معتبر)[5]

6.

حدثنا محمد بن الحسن بن أحمد بن الوليد رحمه الله قال: حدثنا محمد بن الحسن الصفار، عن أحمد بن محمد بن عيسى، عن محمد بن أبي عمير، عن هشام بن الحكم، قال: قلت لأبي عبد الله عليه السلام: ما الدليل على أن الله واحد؟ قال: اتصال التدبير وتمام الصنع كما قال عز وجل: ﴿لو كان فيهما آلهة إلا الله لفسدتا﴾

b. al-Walid from al-Saffar from b. Isa from b. Abi Umayr from Hisham b. al-Hakam who said: I said to Abi Abdillah عليه السلام: What is the proof that Allāh is one? He said: the continuing regulation (of the universe) and the perfection in creation, as the Mighty and Majestic said: "If there were in them other gods apart from Allāh then they (the heavens and the earth) would have fallen apart" (21:22) (معتبر)[6]

7.

---

[5] *Al-Tawḥid, ch2, h7*

[6] *Al-Tawḥid, ch36, h2*

ابن إدريس، عن أبيه، عن ابن هاشم، عن ابن أبي عمير، عن هشام بن سالم قال: سئل أبو عبد الله عليه السلام فقيل له: بم عرفت ربك؟ قال: بفسخ العزم ونقض الهم، عزمت ففسخ عزمي، وهممت فنقض همي

b. Idris – his father – b. Hashim – b. Abi Umayr – Hisham b. Salim who said: Abu Abdillah عليه السلام was asked: By what (thing) did you know your Lord? He said: By the dissolution of resolutions and the invalidation of plans. I resolved but He dissolved my resolution and I planned but He invalidated my plan. (معتبر)[7]

8.

محمد بن إسماعيل، عن الفضل بن شاذان، عن صفوان بن يحيى، عن منصور ابن حازم قال: قلت لابي عبدالله عليه السلام: إني ناظرت قوما فقلت لهم: إن الله جل جلاله أجل وأعز وأكرم من أن يعرف بخلقه بل العباد يعرفون بالله، فقال: رحمك الله

Muhammad b. Ismail from al-Fadhl b. Shadhan from Safwan b. Yahya from Mansur b. Hazm who said: I said to Abi Abdillah عليه السلام: I debated a group and said to them: Verily Allāh Majestic is His Majesty is more Majestic, Strong, and Gracious that He be known through His creatures, rather the slaves are known through Allāh. He said: May Allāh have mercy on you. (معتبر)[8]

9.

عِدَّةٌ مِنْ أَصْحَابِنَا عَنْ أَحْمَدَ بْنِ مُحَمَّدِ بْنِ خَالِدٍ عَنْ أَحْمَدَ بْنِ مُحَمَّدِ بْنِ أَبِي نَصْرٍ قَالَ جَاءَ رَجُلٌ إِلَى أَبِي الْحَسَنِ الرِّضَا (عَلَيْهِ السَّلام) مِنْ وَرَاءِ نَهَرِ بَلْخَ فَقَالَ إِنِّي أَسْأَلُكَ عَنْ مَسْأَلَةٍ فَإِنْ أَجَبْتَنِي فِيهَا بِمَا عِنْدِي

[7] *Al-Tawḥīd, ch41, h8*

[8] *Al-Tawḥīd, ch41, h1*

قُلْتُ بِإِمَامَتِكَ فَقَالَ أَبُو الْحَسَنِ (عَلَيْهِ السَّلَام) سَلْ عَمَّا شِئْتَ فَقَالَ أَخْبِرْنِي عَنْ رَبِّكَ مَتَى كَانَ وَكَيْفَ كَانَ

وَعَلَى أَيِّ شَيْءٍ كَانَ اعْتِمَادُهُ فَقَالَ أَبُو الْحَسَنِ (عَلَيْهِ السَّلَام) إِنَّ اللهَ تَبَارَكَ وَتَعَالَى أَيَّنَ الْاَيْنَ بِلَا أَيْنَ

وَكَيَّفَ الْكَيْفَ بِلَا كَيْفَ وَكَانَ اعْتِمَادُهُ عَلَى قُدْرَتِهِ فَقَامَ إِلَيْهِ الرَّجُلُ فَقَبَّلَ رَأْسَهُ وَقَالَ أَشْهَدُ أَنْ لَا إِلَهَ إِلَّا اللهُ

وَأَنَّ مُحَمَّداً رَسُولُ اللهِ وَأَنَّ عَلِيّاً وَصِيُّ رَسُولِ اللهِ (صَلَّى اللهُ عَلَيْهِ وَآلِهِ) وَالْقَيِّمُ بَعْدَهُ بِمَا قَامَ بِهِ رَسُولُ اللهِ

(صَلَّى اللهُ عَلَيْهِ وَآلِهِ) وَأَنَّكُمُ الْاَئِمَّةُ الصَّادِقُونَ وَأَنَّكَ الْخَلَفُ مِنْ بَعْدِهِمْ

A group of our people from Ahmad b. Muḥammad b. Khalid from Ahmad b. Muḥammad b. Abu Nasr who has said the following. A man from Ma Wara' Nahr Balkh (Transoxania) came to abu al-Hassan al-Rida (عليه السلام), and said, 'I have a question for you. If your answer is the same as I already know, I will accept you as my Imam (leader with divine authority).'" Imam abul-Hassan (عليه السلام) replied, "Ask whatever you wish." The man said, "Tell me when did your Lord come into existence, how has He been and on what did He depend?" Imam Abul-Hassan (عليه السلام), replied, "Allāh, the Blessed, the Almighty, is the space maker of space, Who Himself is not subject to the effects of any space. He is the maker of How and Himself is not subject to How. He is Self-sufficient with His own power." The man stood up and kissed the head of the Imam (عليه السلام) and then said, "I testify that there is no god except Allāh and Muḥammad is the Messenger of Allāh and that Imam 'Alī (عليه السلام) is the successor of the Messenger of Allāh and the Guardian and protector of what the Messenger of Allāh has brought from Allāh and that your forefathers are the leaders with divine authority and that you are a successor to them. (صحيح)[9]

10.

أَبِي، عَنْ سَعْدِ بْنِ عَبْدِ اللهِ، عَنْ أَحْمَدَ بْنِ مُحَمَّدِ بْنِ عِيسَى، عَنِ الْحَسَنِ بْنِ مَحْبُوبٍ، عَنْ أَبِي حَمْزَةَ الثَّمَالِيِّ

قَالَ: سَأَلَ نَافِعُ بْنُ الْأَزْرَقِ أَبَا جَعْفَرٍ عَلَيْهِ السَّلَام فَقَالَ: أَخْبِرْنِي عَنِ اللهِ مَتَى كَانَ؟ فَقَالَ لَهُ: وَيْلَكَ،

[9] Al-Kafi, v1, ch6, h2

أخبرني أنت متى لم يكن حتى أخبرك متى كان، سبحان من لم يزل ولا يزال فردا صمدا لم يتخذ صاحبة ولا ولدا

My father from Sa'd b. AbdAllāh from Ahmad b. Muḥammad b. Isa from al-Hasan b. Mahbub from Abi Hamza al-Thumali who said: Na'fi b. al-Azraq asked Aba Ja'far عليه السلام saying: Inform me about Allāh - when was He? He (the Imam) said to Him: Woe be upon you! You inform me when wasn't He then I will inform you when He was. Glory be to the One who is and has always been Singular, Eternal, not betaking to Himself partner nor off-spring. (معتبر)[10]

11.

أبي رحمه الله، قال: حدثنا سعد بن عبد الله، عن محمد بن الحسين عن صفوان بن يحيى، عن عبد الرحمن بن الحجاج، قال: سألت أبا عبد الله عليه السلام عن قول الله عز وجل: (الرحمن على العرش استوى) فقال: استوى من كل شئ، فليس شئ أقرب إليه من شئ، لم يبعد منه بعيد، ولم يقرب منه قريب، استوى من كل شئ

My father from Sa'd from Muḥammad b. al-Husayn from Safwan b. Yahya from Abd al-Rahman b. al-Hajjaj who said: I asked Aba Abdillah عليه السلام about the words of Allāh Mighty and Majestic "The Beneficent who is over the throne" (20:5). He said: He has transcended over all things. Thus, nothing is closer to Him than another thing. The distant is not far from Him and the near is not close to Him. He has transcended over all things. (معتبر)[11]

12.

---

[10] *Al-Tawḥīd, ch28, h1*

[11] *Al-Tawḥīd,ch48, h2*

العطار، عن سعد، عن ابن يزيد، عن الحسن بن علي الخزاز، عن مثنى الحناط، عن أبي جعفر أظنه محمد بن النعمان قال: سألت أبا عبد الله عليه السلام عن قول الله عزوجل: وَهُوَ اللَّهُ فِي السَّمَاوَاتِ وَفِي الْأَرْضِ قال: كذلك هو في كل مكان. قلت: بذاته؟ قال: ويحك إن الاماكن أقدار، فإذا قلت: في مكان بذاته لزمك أن تقول في أقدار وغير ذلك، ولكن هو بائن من خلقه، محيط بما خلق علما وقدرة وإحاطة وسلطانا، وليس علمه بما في الارض باقل مما في السماء، لا يبعد منه شئ، والاشياء له سواء علما وقدرة وسلطانا وملكا وإحاطة

al-Attar from Sa'd from b. Yazid from al-Hasan b. 'Alī al-Khazzaz from Muthanna al-Hannat from Abi Ja'far - I think him to be Muḥammad b. al-Nu'man (al-Ahwal) - who said: I asked Aba Abdillah عليه السلام about the words of Allāh Mighty and Majestic: "and He is Allāh in the heavens and in the earth" (6:3). He said: That is how He is - everywhere. I said: by His essence? He said: Woe be upon you! Physical spaces have limits, so if you were to believe that He is 'in a place by His essence' then it would be necessary for you to also assert that He has limits and other such (deficiencies). Rather He is distinct from his creation. Fully encompassing what He created in terms of (His) knowledge, power, awareness, and authority. His knowledge of what is in the earth is not less than that of which is in heaven. Nothing can become distant from Him. All things are equal to Him in terms of (His) knowledge, power, authority, ownership, and awareness (over them). (صحيح)[12]

13.

حمزة العلوي، عن علي، عن أبيه، عن ابن أبي عمير، عن ابن اذينة، عن أبي عبد الله عليه السلام في قوله عزوجل: مَا يَكُونُ مِن نَّجْوَىٰ ثَلَاثَةٍ إِلَّا هُوَ رَابِعُهُمْ وَلَا خَمْسَةٍ إِلَّا هُوَ سَادِسُهُمْ وَلَا أَدْنَىٰ مِن ذَٰلِكَ وَلَا أَكْثَرَ إِلَّا هُوَ مَعَهُمْ أَيْنَ مَا كَانُوا فقال: هو واحد أحدي الذات، بائن من خلقه، وبذاك وصف نفسه، وهو بكل شئ محيط بالاشراف والاحاطة والقدرة، لا يعزب عنه مثقال ذرة في السماوات ولا في الارض ولا

[12] *Al-Tawḥīd, ch9, h15*

أصغر من ذلك ولا أكبر بالاحاطة والعلم لا بالذات لان الاماكن محدودة تحويها حدود أربعة فإذا كان بالذات لزمه الحواية

Hamza al-Alawi from 'Alī from his father from b. Abi Umayr from b. Udhayna from Abi Abdillah عليه السلام about His words Mighty and Majestic: "there is no private conversation of three except He is the fourth of them, nor of five except He is the sixth of them - and no less than that and no more except that He is with them wherever they are" (58:7). He said: He is One. Unique in Essence. Distinct from His creation. That is how He described Himself. He encompasses everything in terms of supervision, awareness, and power. Nothing escapes Him even the weight of a particle in the Heavens and in the earth nor smaller than that or bigger - in terms of awareness and knowledge not by (His) essence, for locations are bounded, delimited by the four bounds (height, width, depth), so if it was by essence then that would necessarily imply containment. (صحيح)[13]

14.

مُحَمَّدُ بْنُ يَحْيَى عَنْ سَعْدِ بْنِ عَبْدِ اللهِ عَنْ مُحَمَّدِ بْنِ عِيسَى عَنْ أَيُّوبَ بْنِ نُوحٍ أَنَّهُ كَتَبَ إِلَى أَبِي الْحَسَنِ (عَلَيْهِ السَّلام) يَسْأَلُهُ عَنِ اللهِ عَزَّ وَجَلَّ أَكَانَ يَعْلَمُ الاشْيَاءَ قَبْلَ أَنْ خَلَقَ الاشْيَاءَ وَكَوَّنَهَا أَوْ لَمْ يَعْلَمْ ذَلِكَ حَتَّى خَلَقَهَا وَأَرَادَ خَلْقَهَا وَتَكْوِينَهَا فَعَلِمَ مَا خَلَقَ عِنْدَ مَا خَلَقَ وَمَا كَوَّنَ عِنْدَ مَا كَوَّنَ فَوَقَّعَ بِخَطِّهِ لَمْ يَزَلِ اللهُ عَالِماً بِالاشْيَاءِ قَبْلَ أَنْ يَخْلُقَ الاشْيَاءَ كَعِلْمِهِ بِالاشْيَاءِ بَعْدَ مَا خَلَقَ الاشْيَاءَ

Muhammad b. Yahya has narrated from Sa'd b. 'AbdAllāh from Muḥammad b. 'Isa from Ayyub b. Nuh, who wrote to abu al-Hassan (al-Thalith (عليه السلام) asking him about Allāh, the Majestic, the Glorious. "Did He know all things before creating and giving them being, or did He not know until He brought them into existence or until He willed their creation and existence? Did Allāh come to know what He created

[13] *Al-Tawhid, ch9, h13*

during the process of their creation and what He originated during their being originated?" The Imam wrote in reply in his own handwriting, "Eternally Allāh has had full knowledge of all things, before as well as after their creation. (صحيح)[14]

15.

مُحَمَّدُ بْنُ يَحْيَى عَنْ مُحَمَّدِ بْنِ الْحُسَيْنِ عَنْ صَفْوَانَ بْنِ يَحْيَى عَنِ الْكَاهِلِيِّ قَالَ كَتَبْتُ إِلَى أَبِي الْحَسَنِ (عَلَيْهِ السَّلام) فِي دُعَاءٍ الْحَمْدُ لله مُنْتَهَى عِلْمِهِ فَكَتَبَ إِلَيَّ لا تَقُولَنَّ مُنْتَهَى عِلْمِهِ فَلَيْسَ لِعِلْمِهِ مُنْتَهًى وَلَكِنْ قُلْ مُنْتَهَى رِضَاهُ

Muhammad b. Yahya has narrated from Muḥammad b. al-Husayn from Safwan b. Yahya from al-Kahili who has said the following. "I wrote to abu al-Hassan (al-Kazim) (عليه السلام), praising Allāh in my letter as, 'All praise belongs to Allāh to the limit of His knowledge.'" He wrote back to me, "Do not say, "To the limit of His knowledge because there is no limit to His knowledge. Instead say, "All praise belongs to Allāh to the limit of His pleasure. (حسن)[15]

16.

مُحَمَّدُ بْنُ يَحْيَى عَنْ أَحْمَدَ بْنِ مُحَمَّدٍ عَنِ الْحُسَيْنِ بْنِ سَعِيدٍ عَنِ النَّضْرِ بْنِ سُوَيْدٍ عَنْ عَاصِمِ بْنِ حُمَيْدٍ قَالَ قَالَ سُئِلَ عَلِيُّ بن الحسين (عَلَيْهِما السَّلام) عَنِ التَّوْحِيدِ فَقَالَ إِنَّ الله عَزَّ وَجَلَّ عَلِمَ أَنَّهُ يَكُونُ فِي آخِرِ الزَّمَانِ أَقْوَامٌ مُتَعَمِّقُونَ فَأَنْزَلَ الله تَعَالَى قُلْ هُوَ الله أَحَدٌ وَالآيَاتِ مِنْ سُورَةِ الْحَدِيدِ إِلَى قَوْلِهِ وَهُوَ عَلِيمٌ بِذاتِ الصُّدُورِ فَمَنْ رَامَ وَرَاءَ ذَلِكَ فَقَدْ هَلَكَ

---

[14] *al-Kāfi, v1, ch12, h4*

[15] *al-Kāfi, v1, ch12, h3*

Muhammad b. Yahya has narrated from Ahmad b. Muḥammad from al-Husayn b. Sa'id from al-Nadr b. Suwayd from 'Asim b. Hamiyd who has said the following. "I asked Imam 'Alī b. al-Husayn (عليه السلام) about the Oneness of Allāh. The Imam replied, "Allāh the Almighty, the Great, the Exalted knew that in the latter times there will be people who would investigate the issues very deeply in a hair-splitting manner. Therefore, Allāh, the Glorious, has revealed chapter one hundred twelve of the holy Qur'ān that speak of the Oneness of Allāh. He has also revealed the verses of the chapter fifty-seven of the holy Qur'ān In the Name of God, the Beneficent, the Merciful All that is in the heavens and the earth speak of the glory of God. He is Majestic and All-wise (57:1). To Him belongs the Kingdom of the heavens and the earth. He gives life and causes things to die. He has power over all things (57:2). He is the First, the Last, the Manifest, and the Unseen and He knows all things (57:3). It is He who created the heavens and the earth in six days and then established His Dominion over the Throne. He knows whatever enters into the earth, what comes out of it, what descends from the sky, and what ascends to it. He is with you wherever you may be and He is Well Aware of what you do (57:4). To Him belong the heavens and the earth and to Him all things return (57:5). He causes night to enter into day and day into night. He knows best what all hearts contain (57:6). Whoever would accept anything otherwise he is destroyed. (صحيح)[16]

17.

مُحَمَّدُ بْنُ يَحْيَى عَنْ أَحْمَدَ بْنِ مُحَمَّدٍ عَنِ ابْنِ مَحْبُوبٍ عَنْ عَلِيِّ بْنِ رِئَابٍ عَنْ زُرَارَةَ قَالَ سَأَلْتُ أَبَا عَبْدِ اللهِ (عَلَيهِ السَّلام) عَنْ قَوْلِ اللهِ عَزَّ وَجَلَّ فِطْرَتَ اللهِ الَّتِي فَطَرَ النَّاسَ عَلَيْهَا قَالَ فَطَرَهُمْ جَمِيعاً عَلَى التَّوْحِيدِ

Muhammad b. Yahya has narrated from Ahmad b. Muḥammad from b. Mahbub from 'Alī b. Ri'ab from Zurara who has said the following: "Once I asked abu 'Abd

---

[16] *al-Kafi, v1, ch7, h3*

Allāh (عليه السلام) about the words of Allāh, the Majestic, the Glorious, '. . . the creation (and invention) of Allāh (had a certain) nature with which He created all people. . . .' (30:30) The Imam said, 'He created them and placed belief in Oneness of Allāh in the nature of every one of them. (صحيح)[17]

18.

حدثنا محمد بن الحسن بن أحمد بن الوليد رضي الله عنه قال: حدثنا محمد ابن الحسن الصفار، عن محمد بن عيسى بن عبيد، عن عبد الرحمن بن أبي نجران قال: سألت أبا جعفر الثاني عليه السلام عن التوحيد، فقلت: أتوهم شيئا فقال: نعم غير معقول ولا محدود، فما وقع وهمك عليه من شئ فهو خلافه، لا يشبهه شئ، ولا تدركه الأوهام كيف تدركه الأوهام وهو خلاف ما يعقل وخلاف ما يتصور في الأوهام، إنما يتوهم شئ غير معقول ولا محدود

Muhammad b. al-Hasan b. Ahmad b. al-Walid رضي الله عنه said: Muḥammad b. al-Hasan alSaffar, on the authority of Muḥammad b. `Isa b. `Ubayd, on the authority of `Abd al-Rahman b. Abu Najran that I asked Abu Ja`far the Second (عليه السلام) about Divine Unity [Tawhid], so I said: "Is He presumed to be a thing?" Consequently, he (عليه السلام) replied: Yes. However, since He is Incomprehensible, and Unlimited, He is unlike anything you can conceive. Nothing resembles Him. Imagination perceives Him not. And how could imagination perceive Him when He is beyond all imagination? He is an Imagined Thing which is Incomprehensible and Unlimited. (معتبر)[18]

19.

---

[17] *al-Kāfi, v2, ch6, h3*

[18] *Al-Tawḥīd, ch7, h6*

مُحَمَّدُ بْنُ يَحْيَى عَنْ أَحْمَدَ بْنِ مُحَمَّدِ بْنِ عِيسَى عَنْ مُعَمَّرِ بْنِ خَلادٍ قَالَ سَمِعْتُ أَبَا الْحَسَنِ الرِّضَا (عَلَيهِ السَّلام) يَقُولُ لَيْسَ الْعِبَادَةُ كَثْرَةَ الصَّلاةِ وَالصَّوْمِ إِنَّمَا الْعِبَادَةُ التَّفَكُّرُ فِي أَمْرِ اللهِ عَزَّ وَجَلَّ

Muhammad b. Yahya from Ahmad b. Muḥammad b. Isa from Muammar b. Khallad who said: I heard Aba al-Hasan al-Ridha عليه السلام saying: worship is not excessive prayers or fasting, worship is reflecting over the affair of Allāh Mighty and Majestic. (صحيح)[19]

It is only through the doorstep of the Purified People of the House (عليهم السلام) and those righteously chosen by Allāh Himself that one can achieve the true sweet nectar of Tawhid, any other way leads to deviance and misguidance, and this is apparent when one reads the narrations of the pure Tawhid that the People of the House (عليهم السلام) have preached.

[19] *Al-Kāfi, v2, ch28, h4*

باب الأسماء الله

Chapter on the Names of Allāh

1.

عَلِيُّ بْنُ إِبْرَاهِيمَ عَنْ أَبِيهِ عَنِ النَّضْرِ بْنِ سُوَيْدٍ عَنْ هِشَامِ بْنِ الْحَكَمِ أَنَّهُ سَأَلَ أَبَا عَبْدِ اللهِ (عَلَيْهِ السَّلام) عَنْ أَسْمَاءِ اللهِ وَاشْتِقَاقِهَا اللهُ مِمَّا هُوَ مُشْتَقٌّ فَقَالَ يَا هِشَامُ اللهُ مُشْتَقٌّ مِنْ إِلَهٍ وَإِلَهٌ يَقْتَضِي مَأْلُوهاً وَالاسْمُ غَيْرُ الْمُسَمَّى فَمَنْ عَبَدَ الاسْمَ دُونَ الْمَعْنَى فَقَدْ كَفَرَ وَلَمْ يَعْبُدْ شَيْئاً وَمَنْ عَبَدَ الاسْمَ وَالْمَعْنَى فَقَدْ أَشْرَكَ وَعَبَدَ اثْنَيْنِ وَمَنْ عَبَدَ الْمَعْنَى دُونَ الاسْمِ فَذَاكَ التَّوْحِيدُ أَ فَهِمْتَ يَا هِشَامُ قَالَ قُلْتُ زِدْنِي قَالَ للهِ تِسْعَةٌ وَتِسْعُونَ اسْماً فَلَوْ كَانَ الاسْمُ هُوَ الْمُسَمَّى لَكَانَ كُلُّ اسْمٍ مِنْهَا إِلَهاً وَلَكِنَّ اللهَ مَعْنًى يُدَلُّ عَلَيْهِ بِهَذِهِ الاسْمَاءِ وَكُلُّهَا غَيْرُهُ يَا هِشَامُ الْخُبْزُ اسْمٌ لِلْمَأْكُولِ وَالْمَاءُ اسْمٌ لِلْمَشْرُوبِ وَالثَّوْبُ اسْمٌ لِلْمَلْبُوسِ وَالنَّارُ اسْمٌ لِلْمُحْرِقِ أَ فَهِمْتَ يَا هِشَامُ فَهْماً تَدْفَعُ بِهِ وَتُنَاضِلُ بِهِ أَعْدَاءَنَا الْمُتَّخِذِينَ مَعَ اللهِ عَزَّ وَجَلَّ غَيْرَهُ قُلْتُ نَعَمْ فَقَالَ نَفَعَكَ اللهُ بِهِ وَثَبَّتَكَ يَا هِشَامُ قَالَ فَوَ اللهِ مَا قَهَرَنِي أَحَدٌ فِي التَّوْحِيدِ حَتَّى قُمْتُ مَقَامِي هَذَا

Ali b. Ibrahim has narrated from his father from an-Nadr b. Suwayd from Hisham b. al-Hakam who has said that he asked abu 'AbdAllāh (عليه السلام), about the names of Allāh and their derivations and roots. "What is the root from which the word Allāh is derived?" The Imam replied, "O Hisham, the word Allāh is derived from 'ilah, that is, the One Who is worshipped and the One who is worshipped is supposed to be worth worshipping. The name of Allāh is different from His Own self. Whoever worships the name not the meaning has become a heathen and has, in fact, worshipped nothing. Whoever worships the name and it's meaning jointly, he becomes a polytheist because of worshipping two gods. Whoever worships the meaning of the word Allāh only he, in reality, has worshipped the One Allāh (God). O Hisham, did you grasp it?" Hisham requested, "Kindly enlighten me more." The Imam added, "Allāh has ninety-nine names. If each name had a separate meaning then each meaning would have been a god. Allāh is One only and all His names stand for just One reality and all these names are other than Allāh Himself. O Hisham, bread is the name of something to eat. Water is the name of something to drink. Dress is the name of something to wear on. Fire is the name of something that burns. O Hisham, did you fully grasp the point so you can defend your belief and contest successfully against our opponents, who, along with Allāh, the Exalted, the Great, except things other than Him?" Hisham replied, "Yes, I did understand." The Imam said, "O Hisham, may Allāh benefit you thereby and grant you steadfastness." Hisham (the narrator) says, "I swear by Allāh, no one has ever defeated me on the issue of the Oneness of Allāh until now. (حسن)[1]

2.

أَحْمَدُ بْنُ إِدْرِيسَ عَنْ مُحَمَّدِ بْنِ عَبْدِ الْجَبَّارِ عَنْ صَفْوَانَ بْنِ يَحْيَى عَنْ فُضَيْلِ بْنِ عُثْمَانَ عَنِ ابْنِ أَبِي يَعْفُورٍ قَالَ سَأَلْتُ أَبَا عَبْدِ اللهِ (عَلَيْهِ السَّلام) عَنْ قَوْلِ اللهِ عَزَّ وَجَلَّ هُوَ الاوَّلُ وَالاخِرُ وَقُلْتُ أَمَّا الاوَّلُ فَقَدْ عَرَفْنَاهُ وَأَمَّا الاخِرُ فَبَيِّنْ لَنَا تَفْسِيرَهُ فَقَالَ إِنَّهُ لَيْسَ شَيْءٌ إِلا يَبِيدُ أَوْ يَتَغَيَّرُ أَوْ يَدْخُلُهُ التَّغَيُّرُ وَالزَّوَالُ أَوْ يَنْتَقِلُ مِنْ لَوْنٍ إِلَى لَوْنٍ وَمِنْ هَيْئَةٍ إِلَى هَيْئَةٍ وَمِنْ صِفَةٍ إِلَى صِفَةٍ وَمِنْ زِيَادَةٍ إِلَى نُقْصَانٍ وَمِنْ نُقْصَانٍ إِلَى زِيَادَةٍ إِلا رَبَّ الْعَالَمِينَ فَإِنَّهُ لَمْ يَزَلْ وَلا يَزَالُ بِحَالَةٍ وَاحِدَةٍ هُوَ الاوَّلُ قَبْلَ كُلِّ شَيْءٍ وَهُوَ الاخِرُ عَلَى مَا لَمْ يَزَلْ وَلا تَخْتَلِفُ عَلَيْهِ الصِّفَاتُ وَالاسْمَاءُ كَمَا تَخْتَلِفُ عَلَى غَيْرِهِ مِثْلُ الانْسَانِ الَّذِي يَكُونُ تُرَاباً مَرَّةً وَمَرَّةً لَحْماً وَدَماً وَمَرَّةً رُفَاتاً وَرَمِيماً وَكَالْبُسْرِ الَّذِي يَكُونُ مَرَّةً بَلَحاً وَمَرَّةً بُسْراً وَمَرَّةً رُطَباً وَمَرَّةً تَمْراً فَتَتَبَدَّلُ عَلَيْهِ الاسْمَاءُ وَالصِّفَاتُ وَاللهُ جَلَّ وَعَزَّ بِخِلافِ ذَلِكَ

---

[1] *al-Kāfi, v1, ch16, h2*

Ahmad b. Idris has narrated from Muḥammad b. 'Abd al-Jabbar from Safwan b. Yahya from Fudayl b. 'Uthman from b. abu Ya'fur who has said the following. "I asked abu 'AbdAllāh (عليه السلام), about the words of Allāh, The Majestic, the Glorious, 'He (Allāh) is the first and the last.' (57:3) We have understood His being the first but explain for us the meaning of His being the last." The Imam said, "There is nothing in the universe, but that is subject to annihilation, alteration, change, decay, transition from one color to another, from one shape to another and from one quality to another. They increase, decrease and change from decrease to increase, except He, Who is the Lord of the worlds. He alone is eternal and in one state. He is the first, before everything and the last eternally. His attributes and names do not change as they do in the case of others. A man at one time is dust, at other time flesh and blood, then turns into decaying bones and finally becomes dust. A piece of date at one time is raw, at another time ripe, mature and then it dries up. With every change, the names and attributes also change. Allāh, the Majestic, the Glorious is different from all such things. (صحيح)[2]

3.

حدثنا أحمد بن زياد بن جعفر الهمداني رضي الله عنه، قال: حدثنا علي ابن إبراهيم بن هاشم، عن أبيه، عن أبي الصلت عبد السلام بن صالح الهروي، عن علي بن موسى الرضا، عن أبيه، عن آبائه، عن علي عليهم السلام قال: قال رسول الله صلى الله عليه وآله وسلم: لله عز وجل تسعة وتسعون اسما، من دعا الله بها استجاب له، ومن أحصاها دخل الجنة

al-Hamdani from 'Alī from his father from al-Harawi from 'Alī b. Mūsā al-Ridha from his father from his forefathers from 'Alī عليهم السلام who said: The Messenger of Allāh صلى الله عليه واله said: Allāh Mighty and Majestic has ninety-nine names. Whoever

---

[2] *al-Kāfi, v1, ch16, h5*

asks Allāh through them is answered. Whoever enumerates them enters paradise. (صحيح)[3]

(Shaykh as-Saduq explains this narration, however, since it is quite long, it will not be presented here)

4.

حدثنا محمد بن علي ماجيلويه رحمه الله، قال: حدثنا علي بن إبراهيم ابن هاشم، عن المختار بن محمد بن المختار الهمداني، عن الفتح بن يزيد الجرجاني عن أبي الحسن عليه السلام قال: سمعته يقول: هو اللطيف الخبير السميع البصير، الواحد الأحد الصمد إلي لم يلد ولم يولد ولم يكن له كفوا أحد، منشئ الأشياء ومجسم الأجسام ومصور الصور، لو كان كما يقولون لم يعرف الخالق من المخلوق، ولا المنشئ من المنشأ، لكنه المنشئ، فرق بين من جسمه وصوره وأنشأه وبينه إذ كان لا يشبهه شئ ولا يشبه هو شيئا، قلت: أجل، جعلني الله فداك، لكنك قلت: الأحد الصمد، وقلت: لا يشبه هو شيئا، والله واحد والإنسان واحد، ليس قد تشابهت الوحدانية ؟! قال: يا فتح أحلت ثبتك الله، إنما التشبيه في المعاني، فأما في الأسماء فهي واحدة، وهي دلالة على المسمى، وذلك أن الإنسان وإن قيل واحد فإنما يخبر أنه جثة واحدة وليس باثنين، فالإنسان نفسه ليس بواحد، لأن أعضاءه مختلفة وألوانه مختلفة غير واحدة، وهو أجزاء مجزأة ليس بسواء، دمه غير لحمه ولحمه غير دمه، وعصبه غير عروقه، وشعره غير بشره، وسواده غير بياضه وكذلك سائر الخلق، فالإنسان واحد في الاسم لا واحد في المعنى، والله جل جلاله هو واحد في المعنى، لا واحد غيره، لا اختلاف فيه ولا تفاوت ولا زيادة ولا نقصان فأما الإنسان المخلوق المصنوع المؤلف من أجزاء مختلفة وجواهر شتى غير أنه بالاجتماع شئ واحد، قلت: جعلت فداك فرجت عني فرج الله عنك، فقولك: (اللطيف الخبير) فسره لي كما فسرت الواحد، فإني أعلم أن لطفه على خلاف لطف خلقه للفصل، غير أني أحب أن تشرح ذلك لي، فقال: يا فتح إنما قلنا: اللطيف، للخلق اللطيف، ولعلمه بالشئ اللطيف، أولا ترى وفقك الله وثبتك إلى أثر صنعه في النبات اللطيف وغير اللطيف وفي الخلق اللطيف من الحيوان الصغار من البعوض والجرجس وما هو أصغر منها مما لا يكاد تستبينه العيون، بل لا يكاد يستبان لصغره الذكر من الأنثى والحدث المولود من القديم، فلما رأينا صغر ذلك في لطفه، واهتدائه للسفاد، والهرب من الموت، والجمع لما يصلحه مما في لجج البحار وما في لحاء الأشجار والمفاوز والقفار، وفهم بعضها عن بعض منطقها، وما يفهم به أولادها عنها، ونقلها الغذاء إليها، ثم تأليف ألوانها حمرة مع صفرة، وبياض مع حمرة، وما لا تكاد عيوننا

---

[3] *Al-Tawḥīd, ch29, h8*

تستبينه بتمام خلقها ولا تراه عيوننا ولا تلمسه أيدينا. علمنا أن خالق هذا الخلق لطيف، لطف في خلق ما سميناه بلا علاج ولا أداة ولا آله، وإن صانع كل شئ فمن شئ صنع والله الخالق اللطيف الجليل خلق وصنع لا من شيء

Muhammad b. `Ali b. Majilwayh (may Allāh have mercy on him) said: `Ali b. Ibrahim b. Hashim said, on the authority of al-Mukhtar b. Muḥammad b. al-Mukhtar al-Hamdani said, on the authority of al-Fath b. Yazid al-Jurjani, that I say: He is the Subtle, the All-Aware, the All-)عليه السلام(heard Abu al-Hasan al-Rida Hearing, the All-Seeing, the One, the Unique, the Needless, who begets not nor is begotten, and there is none like unto Him. He is the Producer of all Things, the Former of Bodies, and the Maker of Images. If He was as they say, then the Creator . would not be distinguished from the created, nor the Producer from the production However, He is the Producer. The difference between Him and bodes and images I . that he created them, and there is nothing like unto Him. I asked, "By all means ' May Allāh make me your ransom! However, you said: `The Alone, the Needless and you also said: `He is not like anything.' If Allāh is One, and man is one, are they replied, O Fath! You paid attention, may Allāh)عليه السلام(not similar in unity?" He secure you! Verily, the similarity is limited to meaning. Identifiers are merely means of identifying the identified. If it is said that there is one man, it means that there is one body, as opposed to two. However, although we say that man is one, he is not truly one, as he has different body parts and different colors. Although we say that he is one, he is composed of many different parts which are not the same. His blood is other than his flesh, his flesh is other than his blood, his nerves are other than his veins, his hair is other than his skin, and the darkness of his skin is other than the " paleness of his skin. Likewise, is the rest of creation. Thus, the human being is "one in name, but he is other than "one" in meaning. Not only is Allāh, lofty be His . Majesty, One in name, He is also One in meaning as there is none other than Him There is no variation in Him, no contrast, nor any increase or decrease. As a crated being, the human being is composed of different parts and substances. He is one one" in comb.ation. I enquired: "You have relieved me. May Allāh relieve you! As" for your statement: `The Subtle, All-Aware,' could you explain it to me as you explained to me the meaning of 'the One.' I really need to know how His Subtlety is different from the subtlety of His Creation. I would surely appreciate it if you could answered: O Fath! We had said: He is)عليه السلام(explain that to me." Therefore, he the Subtle due to the delicate nature of His Creation, and for His Knowledge of tiny things. Do you not see, may Allāh help you and secure you, the effect of His Making in soft and hard plants? And do you not see in the delicate creation of tiny insects like the mosquito, the gnat, and that which is smaller than these two, and are almost not evident to the (naked) eyes? In fact, due to their small size, it is virtually impossible to . differentiate between the male and the female, and between the young and the old Thus, we come to know that the Creator is Subtle in His Creation when we see the smallness of creatures in their refinement, their guidance out of decay, and their fleeing from death. We come to know that the Creator is Subtle when we contemplate the creatures found teeming in the depths of the ocean, on the branches of trees, and in the deserts and barren lands. We come to know the Creator is Subtle when we contemplate how species communicate with one another using various forms of communication, permitting them to communicate with their offspring. We come to know that the Creator is Subtle when we contemplate how creatures provide food to their offspring, and how they are distinguished by colors, red with yellow, white with red, and with what we can barely see with our eyes due to its small size. We come to know that the Creator is Subtle when we contemplate the creatures that our eyes cannot see, and our hands cannot touch. He created the world in subtlety without planning, without instruments, and without tools. Verily, the , founder of anything founded it on the basis of another. However, Allāh, the Creator (مجهول)[4].the Subtle, and the Sublime, created everything out of nothing

[4] *Al-Tawhīd, ch29, h1*

باب العرش والكرسي

Chapter on the Throne

1.

أَحْمَدُ بْنُ إِدْرِيسَ عَنْ مُحَمَّدِ بْنِ عَبْدِ الْجَبَّارِ عَنْ صَفْوَانَ بْنِ يَحْيَى قَالَ سَأَلَنِي أَبُو قُرَّةَ الْمُحَدِّثُ أَنْ أُدْخِلَهُ عَلَى أَبِي الْحَسَنِ الرِّضَا (عَلَيْهِ السَّلام) فَاسْتَأْذَنْتُهُ فَأَذِنَ لِي فَدَخَلَ فَسَأَلَهُ عَنِ الْحَلالِ وَالْحَرَامِ ثُمَّ قَالَ لَهُ أَ فَتُقِرُّ أَنَّ اللَّهَ مَحْمُولٌ فَقَالَ أَبُو الْحَسَنِ (عَلَيْهِ السَّلام) كُلُّ مَحْمُولٍ مَفْعُولٌ بِهِ مُضَافٌ إِلَى غَيْرِهِ مُحْتَاجٌ وَالْمَحْمُولُ اسْمُ نَقْصٍ فِي اللَّفْظِ وَالْحَامِلُ فَاعِلٌ وَهُوَ فِي اللَّفْظِ مِدْحَةٌ وَكَذَلِكَ قَوْلُ الْقَائِلِ فَوْقَ وَتَحْتَ وَأَعْلَى وَأَسْفَلَ وَقَدْ قَالَ اللَّهُ وَلِلَّهِ الاسْمَاءُ الْحُسْنَى فَادْعُوهُ بِهَا وَلَمْ يَقُلْ فِي كُتُبِهِ إِنَّهُ الْمَحْمُولُ بَلْ قَالَ إِنَّهُ الْحَامِلُ فِي الْبَرِّ وَالْبَحْرِ وَالْمُمْسِكُ السَّمَاوَاتِ وَالارْضَ أَنْ تَزُولا وَالْمَحْمُولُ مَا سِوَى اللَّهِ وَلَمْ يُسْمَعْ أَحَدٌ آمَنَ بِاللَّهِ وَعَظَمَتِهِ قَطُّ قَالَ فِي دُعَائِهِ يَا مَحْمُولُ قَالَ أَبُو قُرَّةَ فَإِنَّهُ قَالَ وَيَحْمِلُ عَرْشَ رَبِّكَ فَوْقَهُمْ يَوْمَئِذٍ ثَمَانِيَةٌ وَقَالَ الَّذِينَ يَحْمِلُونَ الْعَرْشَ فَقَالَ أَبُو الْحَسَنِ (عَلَيْهِ السَّلام) الْعَرْشُ لَيْسَ هُوَ اللَّهَ وَالْعَرْشُ اسْمُ عِلْمٍ وَقُدْرَةٍ وَعَرْشٍ فِيهِ كُلُّ شَيْءٍ ثُمَّ أَضَافَ الْحَمْلَ إِلَى غَيْرِهِ خَلْقٍ مِنْ خَلْقِهِ لانَّهُ اسْتَعْبَدَ خَلْقَهُ بِحَمْلِ عَرْشِهِ وَهُمْ حَمَلَةُ عِلْمِهِ وَخَلْقاً يُسَبِّحُونَ حَوْلَ عَرْشِهِ وَهُمْ يَعْمَلُونَ بِعِلْمِهِ وَمَلائِكَةً يَكْتُبُونَ أَعْمَالَ عِبَادِهِ وَاسْتَعْبَدَ أَهْلَ الارْضِ بِالطَّوَافِ حَوْلَ بَيْتِهِ وَاللَّهُ عَلَى الْعَرْشِ اسْتَوَى كَمَا قَالَ وَالْعَرْشُ وَمَنْ يَحْمِلُهُ وَمَنْ حَوْلَ الْعَرْشِ وَاللَّهُ الْحَامِلُ لَهُمُ الْحَافِظُ لَهُمُ الْمُمْسِكُ الْقَائِمُ عَلَى كُلِّ نَفْسٍ وَفَوْقَ كُلِّ شَيْءٍ وَعَلَى كُلِّ شَيْءٍ وَلا يُقَالُ مَحْمُولٌ وَلا أَسْفَلُ قَوْلاً مُفْرَداً لا يُوصَلُ بِشَيْءٍ فَيَفْسُدُ اللَّفْظُ وَالْمَعْنَى قَالَ أَبُو قُرَّةَ فَتُكَذِّبُ بِالرِّوَايَةِ الَّتِي جَاءَتْ أَنَّ اللَّهَ إِذَا غَضِبَ إِنَّمَا يُعْرَفُ غَضَبُهُ أَنَّ الْمَلائِكَةَ الَّذِينَ يَحْمِلُونَ الْعَرْشَ يَجِدُونَ ثِقْلَهُ عَلَى كَوَاهِلِهِمْ فَيَخِرُّونَ سُجَّداً فَإِذَا ذَهَبَ الْغَضَبُ خَفَّ وَرَجَعُوا إِلَى مَوَاقِفِهِمْ فَقَالَ أَبُو الْحَسَنِ (عَلَيْهِ السَّلام) أَخْبِرْنِي عَنِ اللَّهِ تَبَارَكَ وَتَعَالَى مُنْذُ لَعَنَ إِبْلِيسَ إِلَى يَوْمِكَ هَذَا هُوَ غَضْبَانُ عَلَيْهِ فَمَتَى رَضِيَ وَهُوَ فِي صِفَتِكَ لَمْ يَزَلْ غَضْبَانَ عَلَيْهِ وَعَلَى أَوْلِيَائِهِ وَعَلَى أَتْبَاعِهِ كَيْفَ تَجْتَرِئُ أَنْ

تَصِفَ رَبَّكَ بِالتَّغْيِيرِ مِنْ حَالٍ إِلَى حَالٍ وَأَنَّهُ يَجْرِي عَلَيْهِ مَا يَجْرِي عَلَى الْمَخْلُوقِينَ سُبْحَانَهُ وَتَعَالَى لَمْ يَزَلْ مَعَ الزَّائِلِينَ وَلَمْ يَتَغَيَّرْ مَعَ الْمُتَغَيِّرِينَ وَلَمْ يَتَبَدَّلْ مَعَ الْمُتَبَدِّلِينَ وَمَنْ دُونَهُ فِي يَدِهِ وَتَدْبِيرِهِ وَكُلُّهُمْ إِلَيْهِ مُحْتَاجٌ وَهُوَ غَنِيٌّ عَمَّنْ سِوَاهُ

Ahmad b. Idris from Muḥammad b. ‘Abd al-Jabbar from Safwan b. Yahya who has said the following. “Abu Qurrah, the narrator of Hadīth asked for help to meet Imam ‘Alī abu al-Hassan al-Rida (عليه السلام). I requested the Imam (عليه السلام) to meet him, and he agreed. Abu Qurrah asked the Imam about the lawful and unlawful matters and then said, “Do you affirm that Allāh is carried?” Imam abu al-Hassan (عليه السلام) replied, “Everything in an objective case is related to another thing and is dependent. Being carried is the name for verbal defect. On the other hand, carrier is in a subjective case and it verbally is a word to convey praises and so is the expression of one who says, “Above, below, upper and lower.” Allāh has said, ‘For Him there are beautiful names, thus, call Him through those names.’ He (Allāh) has not said anywhere in His books that He is al-Mahmul (Being carried) He has, in fact, said that He is the carrier in the sea and on land and the preserver of the heavens and earth from banishment. Al-Mahmul, (being carried) are things other than Allāh. It is never heard from anyone who believed in Allāh and His greatness saying in his prayers Ya Mahmul, (O the one being carried,).” Abu Qurrah then said, “He Himself has said, ‘The angels will be around the heavens and on that day eight of them will carry the Throne of your Lord above all the creatures.’ (69:17) Also He has said, “Those who carry the Throne (al-‘Arsh).” Imam abu al-Hassan (عليه السلام) then said, “Al-‘Arsh (the Throne) is not Allāh. Al-‘Arsh is the name of knowledge and power. In al-‘Arsh there is everything. Besides, He has ascribed carrying to things other than His Own self. It is ascribed to a creature among His creatures. This is because He has made His creatures to worship Him through carrying His al-‘Arsh (the Throne) and they are the carrier of His knowledge. There is a creature, who speaks of His praise around His al-‘Arsh (the Throne) and act according to His knowledge and the angels write down the deeds of His servants. He has made those on earth to worship Him in the form of Tawaf (walking around) His house. Allāh has control over al-‘Arsh (the Throne) as He has said, “Allāh carries al-‘Arsh, those who carry it and those around it, preserves them, keeps them together and is the guardian of all souls and above and over all things." It is not permissible to say, "He is carried. He is below." It would be the only expression that would not make any sense. Thus, both the word and meaning would be destroyed." Abu Qurrah than said, "Do you then consider a false Hadīth the Hadīth that says, "When Allāh becomes angry His anger becomes known to the angels who carry al-'Arsh. They at such time feel the weight of His anger on their shoulders. They then bow down in prostration. When Allāh's anger goes away it becomes light and the angels return to their places." Imam abu al-Hassan (عليه السلام) said, "Tell me about Allāh, the Most Holy, the Most High. From the time He condemned Satan until today is He not angry with Satan? When did He become happy with Satan? As you say He is still angry with Satan, his friend, and followers. How would you dare speak of your Lord as undergoing changes from one condition to another condition and that what happens to the creatures happens to Him also? He is the Most Glorious, the Most High. He does not banish with those who banish and does not change with those who change. He is not replaced with those who are replaced. The creatures are under His guardianship and they all are dependent on Him. He is Self-sufficient and independent of others." (صحيح)[1]

2.

مُحَمَّدُ بْنُ إِسْمَاعِيلَ عَنِ الْفَضْلِ بْنِ شَاذَانَ عَنْ حَمَّادِ بْنِ عِيسَى عَنْ رِبْعِيٍّ بْنِ عَبْدِ اللهِ عَنِ الْفُضَيْلِ بْنِ يَسَارٍ قَالَ سَأَلْتُ أَبَا عَبْدِ اللهِ (عَلَيْهِ السَّلام) عَنْ قَوْلِ اللهِ جَلَّ وَعَزَّ وَسِعَ كُرْسِيُّهُ السَّماواتِ وَالارْضَ فَقَالَ يَا فُضَيْلُ كُلُّ شَيْءٍ فِي الْكُرْسِيِّ السَّمَاوَاتُ وَالارْضُ وَكُلُّ شَيْءٍ فِي الْكُرْسِيِّ

Muhammad b. Isma'il has narrated from Fadl b. Shadhan from Hammad b. 'Isa from Rabi'i b. 'AbdAllāh from Fudayl b. Yasar who has said the following. "I asked Imam abu 'AbdAllāh (عليه السلام) about the words of Allāh, the Most Holy, the Most High, "His al-Kursi (the Throne) encompasses the heavens and earth." He said, "O Fudayl

[1] *Al-Kāfi, v1, ch20, h2*

everything is the al-Kursi (the Throne), the heavens and earth everything is in al-Kursi." (كالصحيح)[2]

3.

مُحَمَّدُ بْنُ يَحْيَى عَنْ أَحْمَدَ بْنِ مُحَمَّدِ بْنِ عِيسَى عَنِ الْحَجَّالِ عَنْ ثَعْلَبَةَ بْنِ مَيْمُونٍ عَنْ زُرَارَةَ بْنِ أَعْيَنَ قَالَ سَأَلْتُ أَبَا عَبْدِ اللهِ (عَلَيْهِ السَّلام) عَنْ قَوْلِ اللهِ جَلَّ وَعَزَّ وَسِعَ كُرْسِيُّهُ السَّماواتِ وَالارْضَ السَّمَاوَاتُ وَالارْضُ وَسِعْنَ الْكُرْسِيَّ أَمِ الْكُرْسِيُّ وَسِعَ السَّمَاوَاتِ وَالارْضَ فَقَالَ بَلِ الْكُرْسِيُّ وَسِعَ السَّمَاوَاتِ وَالارْضَ وَالْعَرْشَ وَكُلَّ شَيْءٍ وَسِعَ الْكُرْسِيُّ

Muhammad b. Yahya has narrated from Ahmad b. Muḥammad b. 'Isa from al-Hajjal form Tha'labah b. Maymun from Zurāra b. 'a'yun who has said the following. "I asked Imam abu 'AbdAllāh (عليه السلام), 'The heavens and the earth are (contained in His al-Kursi) under His dominion . .' (2:255) Do the heavens and earth contain the al-Kursi or that the latter contains the former?" He said that it is al-Kursi that contains the heavens and earth and all things are contained in al-Kursi." (صحيح)[3]

4.

مُحَمَّدُ بْنُ يَحْيَى عَنْ أَحْمَدَ بْنِ مُحَمَّدٍ عَنِ الْحُسَيْنِ بْنِ سَعِيدٍ عَنْ فَضَالَةَ بْنِ أَيُّوبَ عَنْ عَبْدِ اللهِ بْنِ بُكَيْرٍ عَنْ زُرَارَةَ بْنِ أَعْيَنَ قَالَ سَأَلْتُ أَبَا عَبْدِ اللهِ (عَلَيْهِ السَّلام) عَنْ قَوْلِ اللهِ عَزَّ وَجَلَّ وَسِعَ كُرْسِيُّهُ السَّماواتِ وَالارْضَ السَّمَاوَاتُ وَالارْضُ وَسِعْنَ الْكُرْسِيَّ أَوِ الْكُرْسِيُّ وَسِعَ السَّمَاوَاتِ وَالارْضَ فَقَالَ إِنَّ كُلَّ شَيْءٍ فِي الْكُرْسِيِّ

Muhammad b. Yahya has narrated from Ahmad b. Muḥammad from al-Hassan b. Sa'id from Fudala b. Ayyub from 'AbdAllāh b. Bukayr from Zurara b. 'Ayun who has

---

[2] *Al-Kāfi, v1, ch20, h3*

[3] *Al-Kāfi, v1, ch20, h4*

said the following. "I asked Imam abu 'AbdAllāh (عليه السلام) about the words of Allāh, 'The heavens and the earth are (contained in His al-Kursi) under His dominion.. .' (2:255) Do the heavens and earth contain the al-Kursi or that the latter contains the former?" He said that all things are contained in al-Kursi." (موثق كالصحيح)[4]

5.

مُحَمَّدُ بْنُ يَحْيَى عَنْ أَحْمَدَ بْنِ مُحَمَّدِ بْنِ عِيسَى عَنْ أَحْمَدَ بْنِ مُحَمَّدِ بْنِ أَبِي نَصْرٍ عَنْ مُحَمَّدِ بْنِ الْفُضَيْلِ عَنْ أَبِي حَمْزَةَ عَنْ أَبِي عَبْدِ اللهِ (عَلَيْهِ السَّلام) قَالَ حَمَلَةُ الْعَرْشِ وَالْعَرْشُ الْعِلْمُ ثَمَانِيَةٌ أَرْبَعَةٌ مِنَّا وَأَرْبَعَةٌ مِمَّنْ شَاءَ اللهُ

Muhammad b. Yahya has narrated from Ahmad b. Muḥammad b. 'Isa from Ahmad b. Muḥammad b. abu Nasr from Muḥammad b. al-Fudayl from abu Hamza from Imam abu 'AbdAllāh (عليه السلام) who said the following. "The carriers of al-'Arsh (the Throne), al-'Arsh and al-'Ilm (knowledge) are eight. Four of these are from us and the rest are whoever Allāh will chose." (مجهول)[5]

6.

حدثنا أبي رضي الله عنه، قال: حدثنا علي بن إبراهيم، عن أبيه، عن ابن أبي عمير، عن عبد الله بن سنان، عن أبي عبد الله عليه السلام في قول الله عز وجل: ((وسع كرسيه السماوات والأرض) فقال: السماوات والأرض وما بينهما في الكرسي، والعرش هو العلم الذي لا يقدر أحد قدره

My father رضي الله عنه said: `Ali b. Ibrahim said, on the authority of his father, on the authority of b. Abu `Umayr, on the authority of `Abd Allāh b. Sinan that Abu `Abd Allāh al-Ṣādiq (عليه السلام) was asked to interpret the Word of Allāh, the Mighty and

[4] *Al-Kāfi, v1, ch20, h5*

[5] *Al-Kāfi, v1, ch20, h6*

High: His knowledge extends over the heaves and the earth.' He (عليه السلام) said: "The heavens and the earth, and whatever is between them, are in the Throne [al-Kursi], and the Empyrean [al-`Arsh] is the Knowledge (of Allāh) over which no one has power." (صحيح)[6]

7.

حدثنا محمد بن الحسن بن أحمد بن الوليد رحمه الله، قال: حدثنا محمد بن الحسن الصفار، قال: حدثنا يعقوب بن يزيد، عن حماد بن عيسى، عن ربعي عن فضيل بن يسار، قال: سألت أبا عبد الله عليه السلام عن قول الله عز وجل: (وسع كرسيه السماوات والأرض) فقال: يا فضيل السماوات والأرض وكل شئ في الكرسي

Muhammad b. al-Hasan b. Ahmad b. al-Walid رضي الله عنه said: Muḥammad b. al-Hasan alSaffar said: Ya`qub b. Yazid said, on the authority of Hammad b. `Isa, on the authority of Rabi`I, on the authority of Fudayl b. Yasar that I asked Abu `Abd Allāh al-Ṣādiq (عليه السلام) about the Word of Allāh, the Mighty and High: His knowledge extends over the heaves and the earth.' Consequently, he (عليه السلام) replied, "O Fudayl! The heavens and the earth and everything between them, are in the Throne." (صحيح)[7]

8.

حدثنا أحمد بن محمد بن يحيى العطار رحمه الله، عن أبيه، عن أحمد بن محمد بن عيسى، عن الحجال، عن ثعلبة بن ميمون، عن زرارة، قال: سألت أبا عبد الله عليه السلام عن قول الله عز وجل: (وسع كرسيه السماوات والأرض) السماوات و الأرض وسعن الكرسي، أم الكرسي وسع السماوات والأرض؟ فقال: بل الكرسي وسع السماوات والأرض والعرش وكل شئ في الكرسي

---

[6] *Al-Tawhīd, ch52, h2*

[7] *Al-Tawhīd, ch52, h3*

Ahmad b. Muḥammad b. Yahya al-`Attar رضي الله عنه said, on the authority of his father, on the authority of Ahmad b. Muḥammad b. `Isa, on the authority of la-0hajjal, on the authority of Thaa`labah b. Maymun, on the authority of Zurāra that I asked Abu `Abd Allāh al-Ṣādiq (عليه السلام) about the Word of Allāh, the Mighty and High His knowledge extends over the heaves and the earth: Are the heavens and the earth greater than the Throne, or is the Throne greater than the heavens and the earth? He replied, "Nay, the Throne is greater than the heavens, the earth, and the sky as the Throne encompasses everything." (مجهول)[8]

9.

حدثنا محمد بن الحسن بن أحمد بن الوليد رحمه الله قال: حدثنا الحسين ابن أبان، عن الحسين بن سعيد، عن فضالة، عن عبد الله بن بكير، عن زرارة، قال: سألت أبا عبد الله عليه السلام عن قول الله عز وجل: (وسع كرسيه السماوات والأرض) السماوات والأرض وسعن الكرسي، أم الكرسي وسع السماوات والأرض؟ فقال: إن كل شئ في الكرسي (١). باب فطرة الله عز وجل الخلق على التوحيد

Muhammad b. al-Hasan b. Ahmad b. al-Walid رضي الله عنه said: al-Hasan b. Aban said, on the authority of al-Husayn b. Sa`id, on the authority of Fadalah, on the authority of `Abd Allāh b. Bukayr, on the authority of Zurāra that I asked Abu `Abd Allāh al-Ṣādiq (عليه السلام) about the Word of Allāh, the Mighty and High His knowledge extends over the heaves and the earth: Are the heavens ad the earth greater than the Throne, or is the Throne greater than the heaves and the earth? He answered, "The Throne encompasses everything." (مجهول)[9]

---

[8] *Al-Tawḥid, ch52, h4*

[9] *Al-Tawḥid, ch52, h5*

باب الرؤية الله

Chapter on Seeing Allāh

1.

مُحَمَّدُ بْنُ أَبِي عَبْدِ اللهِ عَنْ عَلِيِّ بْنِ أَبِي الْقَاسِمِ عَنْ يَعْقُوبَ بْنِ إِسْحَاقَ قَالَ كَتَبْتُ إِلَى أَبِي مُحَمَّدٍ (عَلَيْهِ السَّلام) أَسْأَلُهُ كَيْفَ يَعْبُدُ الْعَبْدُ رَبَّهُ وَهُوَ لا يَرَاهُ فَوَقَّعَ (عَلَيْهِ السَّلام) يَا أَبَا يُوسُفَ جَلَّ سَيِّدِي وَمَوْلايَ وَالْمُنْعِمُ عَلَيَّ وَعَلَى آبَائِي أَنْ يُرَى قَالَ وَسَأَلْتُهُ هَلْ رَأَى رَسُولُ اللهِ (صَلَّى اللهُ عَلَيْهِ وَآلِهِ) رَبَّهُ فَوَقَّعَ (عَلَيْهِ السَّلام) إِنَّ اللهَ تَبَارَكَ وَتَعَالَى أَرَى رَسُولَهُ بِقَلْبِهِ مِنْ نُورِ عَظَمَتِهِ مَا أَحَبَّ

Muhammad b. abu 'AbdAllāh has narrated from 'Alī b. abu al-Qasim from Ya'qub b. Ishaq who wrote to Imam abu Muḥammad al-'Askari and asked. "How can a worshipper worship his Lord, whom he does not see?" The Imam wrote in reply, "O abu Yusuf, my Lord, my Master, and my Benefactor and the Benefactor of my ancestors, is far exalted and is above being seen." I (Ya'qub b. Ishaq) asked him, "Had the Messenger of Allāh seen his Lord?" The Imam replied in writing and signed, "Allāh, the Most Holy, the Most High, showed His Prophet, in his heart, the light of His Greatness as much as He liked." (مجهول)[1]

---

[1] *Al-Kāfi, v1, ch9, h1*

2.

أَحْمَدُ بْنُ إِدْرِيسَ عَنْ مُحَمَّدِ بْنِ عَبْدِ الْجَبَّارِ عَنْ صَفْوَانَ بْنِ يَحْيَى قَالَ سَأَلَنِي أَبُو قُرَّةَ الْمُحَدِّثُ أَنْ أُدْخِلَهُ عَلَى أَبِي الْحَسَنِ الرِّضَا (عَلَيْهِ السَّلام) فَاسْتَأْذَنْتُهُ فِي ذَلِكَ فَأَذِنَ لِي فَدَخَلَ عَلَيْهِ فَسَأَلَهُ عَنِ الْحَلالِ وَالْحَرَامِ وَالاحْكَامِ حَتَّى بَلَغَ سُؤَالُهُ إِلَى التَّوْحِيدِ فَقَالَ أَبُو قُرَّةَ إِنَّا رُوِّينَا أَنَّ اللهَ قَسَمَ الرُّؤْيَةَ وَالْكَلامَ بَيْنَ نَبِيَّيْنِ فَقَسَمَ الْكَلامَ لِمُوسَى وَلِمُحَمَّدٍ الرُّؤْيَةَ فَقَالَ أَبُو الْحَسَنِ (عَلَيْهِ السَّلام) فَمَنِ الْمُبَلِّغُ عَنِ اللهِ إِلَى الثَّقَلَيْنِ مِنَ الْجِنِّ وَالانْسِ لا تُدْرِكُهُ الابْصَارُ وَلا يُحِيطُونَ بِهِ عِلْماً وَلَيْسَ كَمِثْلِهِ شَيْءٌ أَ لَيْسَ مُحَمَّدٌ قَالَ بَلَى قَالَ كَيْفَ يَجِيءُ رَجُلٌ إِلَى الْخَلْقِ جَمِيعاً فَيُخْبِرُهُمْ أَنَّهُ جَاءَ مِنْ عِنْدِ اللهِ وَأَنَّهُ يَدْعُوهُمْ إِلَى اللهِ بِأَمْرِ اللهِ فَيَقُولُ لا تُدْرِكُهُ الابْصَارُ وَلا يُحِيطُونَ بِهِ عِلْماً وَلَيْسَ كَمِثْلِهِ شَيْءٌ ثُمَّ يَقُولُ أَنَا رَأَيْتُهُ بِعَيْنِي وَأَحَطْتُ بِهِ عِلْماً وَهُوَ عَلَى صُورَةِ الْبَشَرِ أَ مَا تَسْتَحُونَ مَا قَدَرَتِ الزَّنَادِقَةُ أَنْ تَرْمِيَهُ بِهَذَا أَنْ يَكُونَ يَأْتِي مِنْ عِنْدِ اللهِ بِشَيْءٍ ثُمَّ يَأْتِي بِخِلافِهِ مِنْ وَجْهٍ آخَرَ قَالَ أَبُو قُرَّةَ فَإِنَّهُ يَقُولُ وَلَقَدْ رَآهُ نَزْلَةً أُخْرَى فَقَالَ أَبُو الْحَسَنِ (عَلَيْهِ السَّلام) إِنَّ بَعْدَ هَذِهِ الايَةِ مَا يَدُلُّ عَلَى مَا رَأَى حَيْثُ قَالَ مَا كَذَبَ الْفُؤَادُ مَا رَأَى يَقُولُ مَا كَذَبَ فُؤَادُ مُحَمَّدٍ مَا رَأَتْ عَيْنَاهُ ثُمَّ أَخْبَرَ بِمَا رَأَى فَقَالَ لَقَدْ رَأَى مِنْ آيَاتِ رَبِّهِ الْكُبْرَى فَآيَاتُ اللهِ غَيْرُ اللهِ وَقَدْ قَالَ اللهُ وَلا يُحِيطُونَ بِهِ عِلْماً فَإِذَا رَأَتْهُ الابْصَارُ فَقَدْ أَحَاطَتْ بِهِ الْعِلْمُ وَوَقَعَتِ الْمَعْرِفَةُ فَقَالَ أَبُو قُرَّةَ فَتُكَذِّبُ بِالرِّوَايَاتِ فَقَالَ أَبُو الْحَسَنِ (عَلَيْهِ السَّلام) إِذَا كَانَتِ الرِّوَايَاتُ مُخَالِفَةً لِلْقُرْآنِ كَذَّبْتُهَا وَمَا أَجْمَعَ الْمُسْلِمُونَ عَلَيْهِ أَنَّهُ لا يُحَاطُ بِهِ عِلْماً وَلا تُدْرِكُهُ الابْصَارُ وَلَيْسَ كَمِثْلِهِ شَيْءٌ

Ahmad b. Idris has narrated from Muḥammad b. 'Abdal Jabbar from Safwan b. Yahya who has said that abu Qurrah (Musa b. Tariq al-Yamani al-Zabudi, d. 203/818), a narrator of Hadīth, asked me to take him to abul Hassan al-Rida (عليه السلام). I sought permission from the Imam (عليه السلام) and an audience was granted. He asked the Imam about what is lawful and unlawful and the rules in Islamic laws. His questions came to Oneness of Allāh (God). Abu Qurrah said, "We (the narrators of Hadīth) narrate that Allāh, the Almighty has divided His being seen al-Ru'yah and His al-kalam, speech between the two prophets. He gave Mūsā (Moses) the opportunity to hear His speech, and Muḥammad the opportunity to see Him." Imam abu al-Hassan (عليه السلام) said, "Who conveyed the message from Allāh to the two heavy communities; mankind and the Jinn that says: 'The eyes cannot comprehend Him.' (6:103) "They cannot limit Him through their knowledge." (20:110) 'There is nothing similar to Him.' (42:11) "Was it not Muḥammad صلى الله عليه وآله وسلم?'" Asked the Imam (عليه السلام).

Abu Qurrah then replied, "Yes, He was Prophet Muḥammad صلى الله عليه وآله وسلم. " The Imam said, "How can a person who brought such messages to all creatures and told them that he has brought such messages from Allāh and called them to Allāh by His commands and said, "The eyes cannot comprehend Him." (6:103) "They cannot limit Him through their knowledge." (20:110) "There is nothing similar to Him." (42:11), then he would say, "I saw Him with my own eyes? I did limit Him in my knowledge and that He is similar to a man? Should you not be ashamed of yourselves? Even the atheist have not said that the Prophet first brought one thing from Allāh and then announced from Him other things contrary to the first." Abu Qurrah then said, "Does Allāh Himself not say, 'And indeed he (the Prophet) saw him in another descent.?" (53: 13) Imam abu al-Hassan (عليه السلام) said, "The other verses point out what the Prophet actually saw. Allāh has said, "His heart did not lie about what he saw" (53: 11) It means that the heart of Muḥammad did not belie what his eyes saw. Therefore, Allāh in the subsequent verse has said, "Indeed he saw of the greatest signs of his Lord." (53:18) The signs of Allāh are different from Allāh Himself. Allāh has also said, "They cannot limit Him in their knowledge." (20:110) If the eyes could see Him, then people might limit Him in their knowledge and He could be fully defined." Abu Qurrah asked, "Do you disregard Hadīth?" Imam abu al-Hassan (عليه السلام) replied, "If AHadīth are contrary to Qur'ān, I disregard them. Besides, all Muslims believe that Allāh cannot be limited by knowledge, that eyes cannot see Him and that nothing is similar to Him." (صحيح)[2]

3.

عِدَّةٌ مِنْ أَصْحَابِنَا عَنْ أَحْمَدَ بْنِ مُحَمَّدِ بْنِ خَالِدٍ عَنْ أَحْمَدَ بْنِ مُحَمَّدِ بْنِ أَبِي نَصْرٍ عَنْ أَبِي الْحَسَنِ الْمَوْصِلِيِّ عَنْ أَبِي عَبْدِ اللهِ (عَلَيْهِ السَّلام) قَالَ جَاءَ حِبْرٌ إِلَى أَمِيرِ الْمُؤْمِنِينَ صَلَوَاتُ اللهِ عَلَيْهِ فَقَالَ يَا أَمِيرَ الْمُؤْمِنِينَ هَلْ رَأَيْتَ رَبَّكَ حِينَ عَبَدْتَهُ قَالَ فَقَالَ وَيْلَكَ مَا كُنْتُ أَعْبُدُ رَبّاً لَمْ أَرَهُ قَالَ وَكَيْفَ رَأَيْتَهُ قَالَ وَيْلَكَ لا تُدْرِكُهُ الْعُيُونُ فِي مُشَاهَدَةِ الابْصَارِ وَلَكِنْ رَأَتْهُ الْقُلُوبُ بِحَقَائِقِ الايمَانِ

[2] *Al-Kāfi, v1, ch9, h2*

A group of our people has narrated from Ahmad b. Muḥammad b. Khalid from Ahmad b. Muḥammad b. abu Nasr from abu al-Hassan al-Muwsali from abu ʻAbdAllāh (عليه السلام) who has said, "Once a rabbi (hibr) came to Imam ʿAlī (عليه السلام) and asked, ʻO Amir al-Mu'minin, have you seen your Lord when worshipping Him?'" Imam ʿAlī (عليه السلام) replied, "This is not a proper question. I would not have worshipped a Lord whom I could not see." He then asked, "How did you see Him?" Imam ʿAlī (عليه السلام) said, "This is not a proper statement. Eyes cannot see Him in eye-witnessing process but hearts see Him in the realities of faith." (مجهول)[3]

4.

مُحَمَّدُ بْنُ يَحْيَى وَغَيْرُهُ عَنْ أَحْمَدَ بْنِ مُحَمَّدِ بْنِ عِيسَى عَنِ ابْنِ أَبِي نَصْرٍ عَنْ أَبِي الْحَسَنِ الرِّضَا (عَلَيْهِ السَّلام) قَالَ قَالَ رَسُولُ اللهِ (صَلَّى اللهُ عَلَيْهِ وَآلِه) لَمَّا أُسْرِيَ بِي إِلَى السَّمَاءِ بَلَغَ بِي جَبْرَئِيلُ مَكَاناً لَمْ يَطَأْهُ قَطُّ جَبْرَئِيلُ فَكَشَفَ لَهُ فَأَرَاهُ اللهُ مِنْ نُورِ عَظَمَتِهِ مَا أَحَبَّ. فِي قَوْلِهِ تَعَالَى لا تُدْرِكُهُ الابْصارُ وَهُوَ يُدْرِكُ الابْصارَ

Muhammad b. Yahya and others have narrated from Ahmad b. Muḥammad b. ʻIsa from b. abu Nasr from abu al-Hassan al-Rida (عليه السلام) who has said that the holy Prophet said, "When Jibril took me for a visit to the heavens we reached a place where he had never sat foot there before. Then it was unveiled to him and Allāh showed him of the light of His greatness that which he loved." On the words of Allāh " No mortal eyes can see Him, but He can see all eyes. He is All-kind and All-aware. (6:103)(صحيح)[4]

5.

---

[3] *Al-Kāfi, v1, ch9, h6*

[4] *Al-Kāfi, v1, ch9, h8*

مُحَمَّدُ بْنُ يَحْيَى عَنْ أَحْمَدَ بْنِ مُحَمَّدِ بْنِ عِيسَى عَنِ ابْنِ أَبِي نَجْرَانَ عَنْ عَبْدِ اللّٰه بْنِ سِنَانٍ عَنْ أَبِي عَبْدِ اللّٰه (عَلَيْهِ السَّلام) فِي قَوْلِهِ لا تُدْرِكُهُ الابْصارُ قَالَ إِحَاطَةُ الْوَهْمِ أَ لا تَرَى إِلَى قَوْلِهِ قَدْ جاءَكُمْ بَصائِرُ مِنْ رَبِّكُمْ لَيْسَ يَعْنِي بَصَرَ الْعُيُونِ فَمَنْ أَبْصَرَ فَلِنَفْسِهِ لَيْسَ يَعْنِي مِنَ الْبَصَرِ بِعَيْنِهِ وَمَنْ عَمِيَ فَعَلَيْها لَيْسَ يَعْنِي عَمَى الْعُيُونِ إِنَّمَا عَنَى إِحَاطَةَ الْوَهْمِ كَمَا يُقَالُ فُلانٌ بَصِيرٌ بِالشِّعْرِ وَفُلانٌ بَصِيرٌ بِالْفِقْهِ وَفُلانٌ بَصِيرٌ بِالدَّرَاهِمِ وَفُلانٌ بَصِيرٌ بِالثِّيَابِ اللّٰه أَعْظَمُ مِنْ أَنْ يُرَى بِالْعَيْنِ

Muhammad b. Yahya has narrated from Ahmad b. Muḥammad b. ‘Isa from b. abu Najran from ‘AbdAllāh b. Sinan from Imam abu ‘AbdAllāh (عليه السلام) who has said the following about the words of Allāh. "No mortal eyes can see Him, but He can see all eyes. He is All-kind and All-aware." (6:103) It means within what is called al-Wahm which in terms of the degrees of knowledge is less than fifty percent. Consider the words of Allāh in: "Clear proofs have certainly come to you from your Lord... ." (6:104) It does not mean eye-witnessed knowledge. Also consider, "Whosoever sees clearly, it is to his own gain." (ibid) does not mean seeing with the eyes and in "Whosoever is blind, it is to his own loss' (ibid). Blindness does not mean deprivation of eyesight. It means within the range of Wahm (mentioned above). As is commonly said, so and so is very keen-sighted in matters of poetry, and so and so is very keen-sighted in religion and jurisprudence. So and so has a keen eye for money, and so and so an eye for clothes. Allāh is far great and above being eye-witnessed by people." (صحيح)[5]

6.

مُحَمَّدُ بْنُ يَحْيَى عَنْ أَحْمَدَ بْنِ مُحَمَّدٍ عَنْ أَبِي هَاشِمٍ الْجَعْفَرِيِّ عَنْ أَبِي الْحَسَنِ الرِّضَا (عَلَيْهِ السَّلام) قَالَ سَأَلْتُهُ عَنِ اللّٰه هَلْ يُوصَفُ فَقَالَ أَ مَا تَقْرَأُ الْقُرْآنَ قُلْتُ بَلَى قَالَ أَ مَا تَقْرَأُ قَوْلَهُ تَعَالَى لا تُدْرِكُهُ الابْصارُ وَهُوَ يُدْرِكُ الابْصارَ قُلْتُ بَلَى قَالَ فَتَعْرِفُونَ الابْصَارَ قُلْتُ بَلَى قَالَ مَا هِيَ قُلْتُ أَبْصَارُ الْعُيُونِ فَقَالَ إِنَّ أَوْهَامَ الْقُلُوبِ أَكْبَرُ مِنْ أَبْصَارِ الْعُيُونِ فَهُوَ لا تُدْرِكُهُ الاوْهَامُ وَهُوَ يُدْرِكُ الاوْهَامَ

[5] *Al-Kāfi, v1, ch9, h9*

Muhammad b. Yahya has narrated from Ahmad b. Muḥammad from Abu Hashim al-Ja'fari who has said the following. "I asked Imam abul Hassan al-Rida (عليه السلام), about Allāh if He can be described (defined in words). The Imam (عليه السلام) said, "Have you not read the Qur'ān?" I replied, "Yes, I do read the Qur'ān." He then said, "Have you not read the words of Allāh, the Most High, "No mortal eyes can see Him, but He can see all eyes. He is All-kind and All-aware." (6:103) I replied, "Yes, I have read them." The Imam (عليه السلام) said, "Do they know the meaning of the eyes?" I replied, "Yes, they do." The Imam (عليه السلام) said, "What is it?" I replied, " It means seeing with the eyes." Then the Imam said, the Awham (mentioned above) of the heart is far greater comprehensive in knowledge than eye-witnessing. It is not able to comprehend Him but He comprehends all things." (صحيح)[6]

7.

أَحْمَدُ بْنُ إِدْرِيسَ عَنْ مُحَمَّدِ بْنِ عَبْدِ الْجَبَّارِ عَنْ صَفْوَانَ بْنِ يَحْيَى عَنْ عَلِيِّ بْنِ أَبِي حَمْزَةَ قَالَ قُلْتُ لابِي عَبْدِ اللهِ (عَلَيْهِ السَّلام) سَمِعْتُ هِشَامَ بْنَ الْحَكَمِ يَرْوِي عَنْكُمْ أَنَّ اللهَ جِسْمٌ صَمَدِيٌّ نُورِيٌّ مَعْرِفَتُهُ ضَرُورَةٌ يَمُنُّ بِهَا عَلَى مَنْ يَشَاءُ مِنْ خَلْقِهِ فَقَالَ (عَلَيْهِ السَّلام) سُبْحَانَ مَنْ لا يَعْلَمُ أَحَدٌ كَيْفَ هُوَ إِلا هُوَ لَيْسَ كَمِثْلِهِ شَيْءٌ وَهُوَ السَّمِيعُ الْبَصِيرُ لا يُحَدُّ وَلا يُحَسُّ وَلا يُجَسُّ وَلا تُدْرِكُهُ الابْصَارُ وَلا الْحَوَاسُّ وَلا يُحِيطُ بِهِ شَيْءٌ وَلا جِسْمٌ وَلا صُورَةٌ وَلا تَخْطِيطٌ وَلا تَحْدِيدٌ

Ahmad b. Idris has narrated from Muḥammad b. 'Abd al-Jabbar from Safwan b. Yahya from 'Alī b. abu Hamzah, who has said the following. "I stated before abu 'AbdAllāh (عليه السلام) that I have heard Hisham b. al-Hakam quoting you that Allāh is a body of Self-subsisting nature and is from light. He can very clearly be recognized and He bestows such knowledge to whoever among His creatures He wills." The Imam said, "Glorious is He, whom no one knows how He is except He Himself. There is no one similar to Him and He is All-hearing, All-seeing. He cannot be limited, nor can He be felt or touched or moved. Eyes cannot see Him nor any of the

---

[6] *Al-Kāfi, ch9, h10*

senses can comprehend Him. He cannot be contained in anything, nor has He anybody or form or figure or confine." (موثق)[7]

8.

حدثنا محمد بن الحسن بن أحمد بن الوليد رضي الله عنه قال: حدثنا محمد ابن الحسن الصفار، عن محمد بن عيسى بن عبيد، عن عبد الرحمن بن أبي نجران قال: سألت أبا جعفر الثاني عليه السلام عن التوحيد، فقلت: أتوهم شيئا فقال: نعم غير معقول ولا محدود، فما وقع وهمك عليه من شئ فهو خلافه، لا يشبهه شئ، ولا تدركه الأوهام كيف تدركه الأوهام وهو خلاف ما يعقل وخلاف ما يتصور في الأوهام، إنما يتوهم شئ غير معقول ولا محدود

Muhammad b. al-Hasan b. Ahmad b. al-Walid رضي الله عنه said: Muḥammad b. al-Hasan alSaffar, on the authority of Muḥammad b. `Isa b. `Ubayd, on the authority of `Abd al-Rahman b. Abu Najran that I asked Abu Ja`far the Second (عليه السلام) about Divine Unity [Tawhid], so I said: "Is He presumed to be a thing?" Consequently, he (عليه السلام) replied: Yes. However, since He is Incomprehensible, and Unlimited, He is unlike anything you can conceive. Nothing resembles Him. Imagination perceives Him not. And how could imagination perceive Him when He is beyond all imagination? He is an Imagined Thing which is Incomprehensible and Unlimited. (معتبر)[8]

9.

حدثنا محمد بن الحسن بن أحمد بن الوليد رضي الله عنه، قال: حدثنا إبراهيم بن هاشم، عن ابن أبي عمير، عن مرازم، عن أبي عبد الله عليه السلام قال: سمعته يقول: رأى رسول الله صلى الله عليه وآله ربه عز وجل يعني بقلبه (١). وتصديق ذلك:

---

[7] *Al-Kāfi, v1, ch11, h1*

[8] *Al-Tawḥīd, ch7, h6*

Muhammad b. al-Hasan b. Ahmad b. al-Walid رضي الله عنه said: Ibrahim b. Hashim said on the authority of b. Abu `Umayr, on the authority of Murazim, that Abu `Abd Allāh al-Ṣādiq (عليه السلام) said: "The Messenger of Allāh saw his Lord, the Mighty and High, by means of his heart." The confirmation of this is found in the following tradition. (صحيح)[9]

10.

وَعَنْهُ عَنْ أَحْمَدَ بْنِ إِسْحَاقَ قَالَ كَتَبْتُ إِلَى أَبِي الْحَسَنِ الثَّالِثِ (عَلَيْهِ السَّلام) أَسْأَلُهُ عَنِ الرُّؤْيَةِ وَمَا اخْتَلَفَ فِيهِ النَّاسُ فَكَتَبَ لا تَجُوزُ الرُّؤْيَةُ مَا لَمْ يَكُنْ بَيْنَ الرَّائِي وَالْمَرْئِيِّ هَوَاءٌ لَمْ يَنْفُذْهُ الْبَصَرُ فَإِذَا انْقَطَعَ الْهَوَاءُ عَنِ الرَّائِي وَالْمَرْئِيِّ لَمْ تَصِحَّ الرُّؤْيَةُ وَكَانَ فِي ذَلِكَ الاشْتِبَاهُ لانَّ الرَّائِيَ مَتَى سَاوَى الْمَرْئِيَّ فِي السَّبَبِ الْمُوجِبِ بَيْنَهُمَا فِي الرُّؤْيَةِ وَجَبَ الاشْتِبَاهُ وَكَانَ ذَلِكَ التَّشْبِيهُ لانَّ الاسْبَابَ لا بُدَّ مِنِ اتِّصَالِهَا بِالْمُسَبَّبَاتِ

It is narrated from the same narrator (Ahmad b. Idris) from Ahmad b. Ishaq who has said the following. "I wrote to Imam abul Hassan the 3rd and asked him about eye-witnessing Allāh's self and the differences among people about this issue. The Imam (عليه السلام) answered in writing." "Eye-witnessing Allāh's self is not possible until there is air (light-carrier medium) that would let the light reach the eye. If air is removed from (space between) the viewer and the object, no eye-witnessing will take place. In this is ground for similarity. When the viewer and the object in view would have the same medium that make eye-witnessing possible a similarity must exist therein. (When applying this to the case of Allāh) it is an analogy and similarity. The means must have a connection with the source. (صحيح)[10]

---

[9] *Al-Tawḥīd, ch8, h16*

[10] *Al-Kāfi, v1, ch9, h4*

باب التجسيم

Chapter on Anthropomorphism

1.

أَحْمَدُ بْنُ إِدْرِيسَ عَنْ مُحَمَّدِ بْنِ عَبْدِ الْجَبَّارِ عَنْ صَفْوَانَ بْنِ يَحْيَى عَنْ عَلِيِّ بْنِ أَبِي حَمْزَةَ قَالَ قُلْتُ لِأَبِي عَبْدِ اللهِ (عَلَيْهِ السَّلام) سَمِعْتُ هِشَامَ بْنَ الْحَكَمِ يَرْوِي عَنْكُمْ أَنَّ اللهَ جِسْمٌ صَمَدِيٌّ نُورِيٌّ مَعْرِفَتُهُ ضَرُورَةٌ يَمُنُّ بِهَا عَلَى مَنْ يَشَاءُ مِنْ خَلْقِهِ فَقَالَ (عَلَيْهِ السَّلام) سُبْحَانَ مَنْ لَا يَعْلَمُ أَحَدٌ كَيْفَ هُوَ إِلا هُوَ لَيْسَ كَمِثْلِهِ شَيْءٌ وَهُوَ السَّمِيعُ الْبَصِيرُ لَا يُحَدُّ وَلَا يُحَسُّ وَلَا يُجَسُّ وَلَا تُدْرِكُهُ الابْصَارُ وَلَا الْحَوَاسُّ وَلَا يُحِيطُ بِهِ شَيْءٌ وَلَا جِسْمٌ وَلَا صُورَةٌ وَلَا تَخْطِيطٌ وَلَا تَحْدِيدٌ

Ahmad b. Idris has narrated from Muḥammad b. ‘Abd al-Jabbar from Safwan b. Yahya from ‘Alī b. abu Hamzah, who has said the following. "I stated before abu ‘AbdAllāh (عليه السلام) that I have heard Hisham b. al-Hakam quoting you that Allāh is a body of Self-subsisting nature and is from light. He can very clearly be recognized and He bestows such knowledge to whoever among His creatures He wills." The Imam said, "Glorious is He, whom no one knows how He is except He Himself. There is no one similar to Him and He is All-hearing, All-seeing. He cannot be limited, nor can He be felt or touched or moved. Eyes cannot see Him nor any of the senses can comprehend Him. He cannot be contained in anything, nor has He anybody or form or figure or confine." (موثق)[1]

2.

مُحَمَّدُ بْنُ أَبِي عَبْدِ اللهِ عَنْ عَلِيِّ بْنِ أَبِي الْقَاسِمِ عَنْ يَعْقُوبَ بْنِ إِسْحَاقَ قَالَ كَتَبْتُ إِلَى أَبِي مُحَمَّدٍ (عَلَيْهِ السَّلام) أَسْأَلُهُ كَيْفَ يَعْبُدُ الْعَبْدُ رَبَّهُ وَهُوَ لا يَرَاهُ فَوَقَّعَ (عَلَيْهِ السَّلام) يَا أَبَا يُوسُفَ جَلَّ سَيِّدِي وَمَوْلايَ وَالْمُنْعِمُ عَلَيَّ وَعَلَى آبَائِي أَنْ يُرَى قَالَ وَسَأَلْتُهُ هَلْ رَأَى رَسُولُ اللهِ (صَلَّى اللهُ عَلَيْهِ وَآلِهِ) رَبَّهُ فَوَقَّعَ (عَلَيْهِ السَّلام) إِنَّ اللهَ تَبَارَكَ وَتَعَالَى أَرَى رَسُولَهُ بِقَلْبِهِ مِنْ نُورِ عَظَمَتِهِ مَا أَحَبَّ

Muhammad b. abu 'AbdAllāh has narrated from 'Alī b. abu al-Qasim from Ya'qub b. Ishaq who wrote to Imam abu Muḥammad al-'Askari and asked. "How can a worshipper worship his Lord, whom he does not see?" The Imam wrote in reply, "O abu Yusuf, my Lord, my Master, and my Benefactor and the Benefactor of my ancestors, is far exalted and is above being seen." I (Ya'qub b. Ishaq) asked him, "Had the Messenger of Allāh seen his Lord?" The Imam replied in writing and signed, "Allāh, the Most Holy, the Most High, showed His Prophet, in his heart, the light of His Greatness as much as He liked." (مجهول)[2]

3.

حدثنا محمد بن الحسن بن أحمد بن الوليد رضي الله عنه قال: حدثنا محمد ابن الحسن الصفار، عن محمد بن عيسى بن عبيد، عن عبد الرحمن بن أبي نجران قال: سألت أبا جعفر الثاني عليه السلام عن التوحيد، فقلت: أتوهم شيئا فقال: نعم غير معقول ولا محدود، فما وقع وهمك عليه من شئ فهو خلافه، لا يشبهه شئ، ولا تدركه الأوهام كيف تدركه الأوهام وهو خلاف ما يعقل وخلاف ما يتصور في الأوهام، إنما يتوهم شئ غير معقول ولا محدود

---

[1] *Al-Kāfi, v1, ch11, h1*

[2] *Al-Kāfi, v1, ch9, h1*

Muhammad b. al-Hasan b. Ahmad b. al-Walid رضي الله عنه said: Muḥammad b. al-Hasan alSaffar, on the authority of Muḥammad b. `Isa b. `Ubayd, on the authority of `Abd al-Rahman b. Abu Najran that I asked Abu Ja`far the Second (عليه السلام) about Divine Unity [Tawhid], so I said: "Is He presumed to be a thing?" Consequently, he (عليه السلام) replied: Yes. However, since He is Incomprehensible, and Unlimited, He is unlike anything you can conceive. Nothing resembles Him. Imagination perceives Him not. And how could imagination perceive Him when He is beyond all imagination? He is an Imagined Thing which is Incomprehensible and Unlimited. (معتبر)[3]

4.

حدثنا محمد بن الحسن بن أحمد بن الوليد رضي الله عنه، قال: حدثنا إبراهيم بن هاشم، عن ابن أبي عمير، عن مرازم، عن أبي عبد الله عليه السلام قال: سمعته يقول: رأى رسول الله صلى الله عليه وآله ربه عز وجل يعني بقلبه (١). وتصديق ذلك:

Muhammad b. al-Hasan b. Ahmad b. al-Walid رضي الله عنه said: Ibrahim b. Hashim said on the authority of b. Abu `Umayr, on the authority of Murazim, that Abu `Abd Allāh al-Ṣādiq (عليه السلام) said: "The Messenger of Allāh saw his Lord, the Mighty and High, by means of his heart." The confirmation of this is found in the following tradition. (صحيح)[4]

5.

---

[3] *Al-Tawḥīd, ch7, h6*

[4] *Al-Tawḥīd, ch8, h16*

ابن الوليد، عن الصفار، عن ابن معروف، عن علي بن مهزيار قال: كتبت إلى أبي جعفر الثاني عليه السلام: جعلت فداك اصلي خلف من يقول بالجسم، ومن يقول بقول يونس - يعني ابن عبد الرحمن؟ فكتب عليه السلام لا تصلوا خلفهم ولا تعطوهم من الزكاة وابرؤوا منهم، برأ الله منهم

b. al-Walid from al-Saffar from b. Ma'ruf from 'Alī b. Mahziyar who said: I wrote to Abi Ja'far the Second عليه السلام: May I be made your ransom - should I pray behind the one who asserts (the doctrine of) 'the body' (God is corporeal) or the one who subscribes to the doctrine of Yunus - that is the son of Abd al-Rahman? He عليه السلام wrote: Do not pray behind them nor not give them anything of the Zakat. Disassociate from them. Allāh has disassociated from them. (صحيح)[5]

6.

ابن الوليد، عن الصفار، عن البرقي، عن أبي هاشم الجعفري قال: سمعت علي بن موسى الرضا عليه السلام يقول: إلهي بدت قدرتك ولم تبد هيئتك فجهلوك و به قدروك والتقدير على غير ما وصفوك، وإني برئ يا إلهي من الذين بالتشبيه طلبوك، ليس كمثلك شئ، إلهي ولن يدركوك، وظاهر ما بهم من نعمك دليلهم عليك لو عرفوك، وفي خلقك يا إلهي مندوحة أن يتناولوك، بل سووك بخلقك فمن ثم لم يعرفوك، واتخذوا بعض آياتك ربا فبذلك وصفوك، تعاليت ربي عما به المشبهون نعتوك

b. al-Walid from al-Saffar from al-Barqi from Abi Hashim al-Ja'fari who said: I heard 'Alī b. Mūsā al-Ridha عليه السلام saying: My God, your power is manifest, but your form is not. Because of this they became ignorant of you and with that (ignorance) estimated you. While the (true) estimation is other than how they described you. O My God, I am disassociated from those who seek you by likening you (to your creatures). There is nothing like you. My God, they will never reach you. What is apparent of your blessings around them is an indicator towards you. If only they recognized you. And in your creation - O my God - there is ample to understand you. However, they equated you to your creation and because of that did not attain

---

[5] *Amālī al-Ṣaduq 1/329*

recognition of you. They took some of your signs as Lord (instead of you) and with that (imperfect attributes) described you. Elevated are you My Lord from that which the Likeners impute to you. (صحيح)[6]

7.

وبهذا الإسناد، عن الحسن بن محبوب، عن حماد، قال: قال أبو عبد الله عليه السلام: كذب من زعم أن الله عز وجل من شئ أو في شئ أو على شئ

And with this chain of transmission, on the authority of al-Hasan b. Mahbub, on the authority of Hammid that Abu `Abd Allāh al-Ṣādiq (عليه السلام) said: "Whoever claims that Allāh, the Mighty and High, is from something, in something, or on something, has surely lied." (صحيح)[7]

8.

عِدَّةٌ مِنْ أَصْحَابِنَا عَنْ أَحْمَدَ بْنِ مُحَمَّدِ بْنِ خَالِدٍ عَنْ أَحْمَدَ بْنِ مُحَمَّدِ بْنِ أَبِي نَصْرٍ عَنْ صَفْوَانَ الْجَمَّالِ عَنْ أَبِي عَبْدِ اللهِ (عَلَيْهِ السَّلام) فِي قَوْلِ اللهِ عَزَّ وَجَلَّ كُلُّ شَيْءٍ هالِكٌ إِلا وَجْهَهُ قَالَ مَنْ أَتَى اللهَ بِمَا أُمِرَ بِهِ مِنْ طَاعَةِ مُحَمَّدٍ (صَلَّى اللهُ عَلَيْهِ وَآلِه) فَهُوَ الْوَجْهُ الَّذِي لا يَهْلِكُ وَكَذَلِكَ قَالَ مَنْ يُطِعِ الرَّسُولَ فَقَدْ أَطاعَ اللهَ

A number of our companions from Ahmad b. Muḥammad b. Khalid from Ahmad b. Muḥammad b. Abi Nasr from Safwan al-Jammal from Abi Abdillah عليه السلام about the words of Allāh Mighty and Majestic: "Everything is to perish except His face" (28:88). He said: Whoever comes to Allāh with what he had been ordered (to do) in terms of obeying Muḥammad صلى الله عليه وآله then he is the 'face' who will not perish. In

---

[6] *Amālī al-Ṣaduq 2/330*

[7] *Al-Tawḥīd, ch48, h8*

a similar vein Did He say: "whoever obeys the Messenger has obeyed Allāh" (4:80). (صحيح)[8]

9.

أبي رحمه الله، قال: حدثنا سعد بن عبد الله، قال حدثنا أحمد بن محمد بن عيسى عن الحسن بن علي الخزاز، عن أبي الحسن الرضا عليه السلام قال: إن رسول الله يوم القيامة آخذ بحجزة الله، ونحن آخذون بحجزة نبينا، وشيعتنا آخذون بحجزتنا ثم قال: والحجزة النو

My father from Sa'd from b. Isa from al-Hasan b. 'Alī al-Khazzaz from Abi al-Hasan al-Ridha عليه السلام who said: The Messenger of Allāh صلى الله عليه واله will hold on to the waist-knot of Allāh on the Day of Judgment, we will hold on to the waist-knot of our prophet, and our Shia (followers) will hold on to our waist-knot. Then he said: waist-knot means light. (صحيح)[9]

10.

حدثنا محمد بن موسى بن المتوكل رضي الله عنه قال: حدثنا علي بن إبراهيم بن هاشم، قال: حدثنا أبي، عن الريان بن الصلت، عن علي بن موسى الرضا عليهما السلام، عن أبيه، عن آبائه، عن أمير المؤمنين عليهم السلام، قال: قال رسول الله صلى الله عليه وآله: قال الله جل جلاله، ما آمن بي من فسر برأيه كلامي، وما عرفني من شبهني بخلقي، وما على ديني من استعمل القياس في ديني

b. al-Mutawakkil from 'Alī from his father from al-Rayyan from al-Ridha from his forefathers from The Commander of the Faithful عليهم السلام who said: The Messenger of Allāh صلى الله عليه واله said: Allāh Majestic is His Majesty said: He has not believed in Me the one who interprets My words by his opinion. He has not known Me the one

---

[8] *Al-Kāfi, ch23, h2*

[9] *Al-Tawḥīd, ch23, h2*

who likens Me to My creatures. He is not upon My religion the one who uses analogy in My religion. (صحيح)[10]

11.

حدثني محمد بن موسى بن المتوكل رحمه الله، قال: حدثنا عبد الله بن جعفر الحميري، عن أحمد بن محمد بن عيسى، عن الحسن بن محبوب، عن يعقوب السراج، قال: قلت لأبي عبد الله عليه السلام: إن بعض أصحابنا يزعم أن لله صورة مثل صورة الإنسان، وقال آخر: إنه في صورة أمرد جعد قطط، فخر أبو عبد الله ساجدا، ثم رفع رأسه، فقال: سبحان الله الذي ليس كمثله شئ، ولا تدركه الأبصار، ولا يحيط به علم، لم يلد لأن الولد يشبه أباه، ولم يولد فيشبه من كان قبله، ولم يكن له من خلقه كفوا أحد، تعالى عن صفة من سواه علوا كبيرا

b. al-Mutawakkil from al-Himyari from b. Isa from b. Mahbub from Ya'qub al-Sarraj who said: I said to Abi Abdillah عليه السلام: One of our companions claims that Allāh has a form like that of a human and another says that He is in the form of a beardless youth with very curly hair! Abu Abdillah عليه السلام fell down in prostration then he raised his head and said: Glory be to Allāh whom there is nothing like Him. Vision cannot reach Him. Knowledge cannot encompass Him. He does not give birth for an off spring resembles his parent. He was not born so that He could resemble one who came before Him. He will never have among His creatures any rival. Elevated is He from the description of the one who equates Him - a great elevation. (معتبر)[11]

12.

[10] *Al-Tawḥid, ch2, h23*

[11] *Al-Tawḥid, ch6, h19*

محمد بن محمد بن عصام، عن الكليني، عن علان، عن محمد بن الفرج الرخجي قال: كتبت إلى أبي الحسن علي بن محمد عليهما السلام أسأله عما قال هشام بن الحكم في الجسم، وهشام بن سالم في الصورة. فكتب عليه السلام: دع عنك حيرة الحيران واستعذ بالله من الشيطان، ليس القول ما قال الهشامان

Muhammad b. Muḥammad b. Assam from al-Kulayni from Allan from Muḥammad b. al-Faraj al-Rukhaji who said: I wrote to Abi al-Hasan ʿAlī b. Muḥammad عليهما السلام asking him about the position of Hisham b. al-Hakam regarding 'the body' and the position of Hisham b. Salim regarding 'the human form'. He wrote: Leave the confusion of the confused, seek refuge in Allāh from the Shaytan, the (true) position is not what was said by the two Hishams. (صحيح)[12]

13.

حدثنا محمد بن محمد بن عصام الكليني رضي الله عنه، قال: حدثنا محمد بن يعقوب الكليني، قال: حدثنا علي بن محمد المعروف بعلان الكليني، قال: حدثنا محمد بن عيسى بن عبيد، قال: سألت أبا الحسن علي بن محمد العسكري عليهما السلام، عن قول الله عز وجل: (والأرض جميعا قبضته يوم القيمة والسماوات مطويات بيمينه) فقال: ذلك تعيير الله تبارك وتعالى لمن شبهه بخلقه، ألا ترى أنه، قال: (وما قدروا الله حق قدره) ومعناه إذ قالوا: إن الأرض جميعا قبضته يوم القيمة والسماوات مطويات بيمينه، كما قال عز وجل: (وما قدروا الله حق قدره) إذ قالوا: ﴿ما أنزل الله على بشر من شئ﴾ (١) ثم نزه عز وجل نفسه عن القبضة واليمين فقال: (سبحانه وتعالى عما يشركون) (٢).

I asked Aba al-Hasan ʿAlī b. Muḥammad al-Askari عليهما السلام about the words of Allāh Mighty and Majestic: "the entire earth will be His grip on the Day of Resurrection and the Heavens will be folded in His right hand" (39:67). He said: That is a rebuke of Allāh Blessed and Elevated against the one who likens Him to his creation. Don't you see that He said (in the same verse): "they have not estimated Allāh His true estimate" (39:67). The meaning of this is (a reply to) when they said: 'the entire earth will be His grip on the Day of Resurrection and the heavens will be

---

[12] *Al-Tawḥīd, ch4, h9*

folded in His right hand'. This is just as He Mighty and Majestic said: "they have not estimated Allāh His true estimate" (6:91) when they said: "Allāh has not sent down anything to a human" (6:91). Then He Mighty and Majestic declared Himself free of (possessing attributes such as) 'gripping' and 'right hand' by saying: "Glorified is He and Elevated above what they associate (with Him)" (39:67). (صحيح)[13]

---

[13] *Al-Tawḥīd, ch17, h1*

باب الولاية

Chapter on al-Wilāyah

1.

عَلِيُّ بْنُ إِبْرَاهِيمَ عَنْ أَبِيهِ وَعَبْدِ اللهِ بْنِ الصَّلْتِ جَمِيعاً عَنْ حَمَّادِ بْنِ عِيسَى عَنْ حَرِيزِ بْنِ عَبْدِ اللهِ عَنْ زُرَارَةَ
عَنْ أَبِي جَعْفَرٍ (عَلَيهِ السَّلام) قَالَ بُنِيَ الإِسْلامُ عَلَى خَمْسَةِ أَشْيَاءَ عَلَى الصَّلاةِ وَالزَّكَاةِ وَالْحَجِّ وَالصَّوْمِ وَالْوَلايَةِ
قَالَ زُرَارَةُ فَقُلْتُ وَأَيُّ شَيْءٍ مِنْ ذَلِكَ أَفْضَلُ فَقَالَ الْوَلايَةُ أَفْضَلُ لأَنَّهَا مِفْتَاحُهُنَّ وَالْوَالِي هُوَ الدَّلِيلُ عَلَيْهِنَّ قُلْتُ
ثُمَّ الَّذِي يَلِي ذَلِكَ فِي الْفَضْلِ فَقَالَ الصَّلاةُ إِنَّ رَسُولَ اللهِ (صَلَّى اللهُ عَلَيْهِ وآلِه) قَالَ الصَّلاةُ عَمُودُ دِينِكُمْ قَالَ
قُلْتُ ثُمَّ الَّذِي يَلِيهَا فِي الْفَضْلِ قَالَ الزَّكَاةُ لأَنَّهُ قَرَنَهَا بِهَا وَبَدَأَ بِالصَّلاةِ قَبْلَهَا وَقَالَ رَسُولُ اللهِ (صَلَّى اللهُ عَلَيْهِ
وآلِه) الزَّكَاةُ تُذْهِبُ الذُّنُوبَ قُلْتُ وَالَّذِي يَلِيهَا فِي الْفَضْلِ قَالَ الْحَجُّ قَالَ اللهُ عَزَّ وَجَلَّ وَللهِ عَلَى النَّاسِ حِجُّ
الْبَيْتِ مَنِ اسْتَطَاعَ إِلَيْهِ سَبِيلاً وَمَنْ كَفَرَ فَإِنَّ اللهَ غَنِيٌّ عَنِ الْعَالَمِينَ وَقَالَ رَسُولُ اللهِ (صَلَّى اللهُ عَلَيْهِ وآلِه)
لَحَجَّةٌ مَقْبُولَةٌ خَيْرٌ مِنْ عِشْرِينَ صَلاةً نَافِلَةً وَمَنْ طَافَ بِهَذَا الْبَيْتِ طَوَافاً أَحْصَى فِيهِ أُسْبُوعَهُ وَأَحْسَنَ رَكْعَتَيْهِ
غَفَرَ اللهُ لَهُ وَقَالَ فِي يَوْمِ عَرَفَةَ وَيَوْمِ الْمُزْدَلِفَةِ مَا قَالَ قُلْتُ فَمَا ذَا يَتْبَعُهُ قَالَ الصَّوْمُ قُلْتُ وَمَا بَالُ الصَّوْمِ صَارَ
آخِرَ ذَلِكَ أَجْمَعَ قَالَ قَالَ رَسُولُ اللهِ (صَلَّى اللهُ عَلَيْهِ وآلِه) الصَّوْمُ جُنَّةٌ مِنَ النَّارِ قَالَ ثُمَّ قَالَ إِنَّ أَفْضَلَ
الأَشْيَاءِ مَا إِذَا فَاتَكَ لَمْ تَكُنْ مِنْهُ تَوْبَةٌ دُونَ أَنْ تَرْجِعَ إِلَيْهِ فَتُؤَدِّيَهُ بِعَيْنِهِ إِنَّ الصَّلاةَ وَالزَّكَاةَ وَالْحَجَّ وَالْوَلايَةَ لَيْسَ
يَقَعُ شَيْءٌ مَكَانَهَا دُونَ أَدَائِهَا وَإِنَّ الصَّوْمَ إِذَا فَاتَكَ أَوْ قَصَّرْتَ أَوْ سَافَرْتَ فِيهِ أَدَّيْتَ مَكَانَهُ أَيَّاماً غَيْرَهَا
وَجَزَيْتَ ذَلِكَ الذَّنْبَ بِصَدَقَةٍ وَلا قَضَاءَ عَلَيْكَ وَلَيْسَ مِنْ تِلْكَ الأَرْبَعَةِ شَيْءٌ يُجْزِيكَ مَكَانَهُ غَيْرُهُ قَالَ ثُمَّ قَالَ
ذِرْوَةُ الأَمْرِ وَسَنَامُهُ وَمِفْتَاحُهُ وَبَابُ الأَشْيَاءِ وَرِضَا الرَّحْمَنِ الطَّاعَةُ لِلإِمَامِ بَعْدَ مَعْرِفَتِهِ إِنَّ اللهَ عَزَّ وَجَلَّ يَقُولُ
مَنْ يُطِعِ الرَّسُولَ فَقَدْ أَطَاعَ اللهَ وَمَنْ تَوَلَّى فَمَا أَرْسَلْنَاكَ عَلَيْهِمْ حَفِيظاً أَمَا لَوْ أَنَّ رَجُلاً قَامَ لَيْلَهُ وَصَامَ نَهَارَهُ

وَتَصَدَّقَ بِجَمِيعِ مَالِهِ وَحَجَّ جَمِيعَ دَهْرِهِ وَلَمْ يَعْرِفْ وَلايَةَ وَلِيِّ اللهِ فَيُوَالِيَهُ وَيَكُونَ جَمِيعُ أَعْمَالِهِ بِدَلالَتِهِ إِلَيْهِ مَا كَانَ لَهُ عَلَى اللهِ جَلَّ وَعَزَّ حَقٌّ فِي ثَوَابِهِ وَلا كَانَ مِنْ أَهْلِ الإِيمَانِ ثُمَّ قَالَ أُولَئِكَ الْمُحْسِنُ مِنْهُمْ يُدْخِلُهُ اللهُ الْجَنَّةَ بِفَضْلِ رَحْمَتِهِ

Ali b. Ibrahim has narrated from his father and 'Abd Allāh b. al-Salt all of them from Hammad b. 'Isa from Hariz b. 'Abd Allāh from Zurara from abu Ja'far (عليه السلام) who has said the following: "Abu Ja'far (عليه السلام) has said, **'Islam is based on five issues. It is based on prayer, charity (al- Zakat), Hajj, Fasting and al-Wilāya.**" Zurara has said, 'I then asked the Imam, "Which of these is more important than the others?"' The Imam said, **'Al-Wilāya is more important**. It is the key to the others. The person who possesses Divine Authority is the guide to the other principles.' I then asked, 'Which is the next important?' The Imam said, **'Thereafter is prayer**. The Messenger of Allāh has said, "Prayer is the pillar of your religion."' I then asked, 'Which is the next important among them?' The Imam said, **'Al-Zakat is the one thereafter**. Allāh has mentioned it next to prayer but He has mentioned prayer first. The Messenger of Allāh has said, "Al-Zakat removes sins."' I then asked, 'Which one is important thereafter?' The Imam said, **'Hajj is important thereafter**. Allāh, the Most Majestic, the Most Holy, has said, "It is a duty of the people to Allāh to perform Hajj of the House if they are capable to do so. Whoever rejects it should know that Allāh does not need anyone in the world." (3:97) The messenger of Allāh has said, "Performing Hajj that is accepted is more virtuous than twenty Rak'at optional prayer. Whoever walks around the House seven times and performs the two Rak'at prayers thereafter properly Allāh will grant him cover." He (The Messenger of Allāh) did say on the ninth of the month of Dil Hajj and on the tenth of the month of Dil Hajj in Muzdalifa (a place in Makka), what he wanted to say.' I then asked, 'Which one is important thereafter?' The Imam said, **'It is fasting**.' "I then asked, 'Why is fasting the last of all in importance?' The Imam said, 'The Messenger of Allāh has said, "Fasting is a shield against the fire."' The narrator has said that the Imam said, **'The best of all things is that for which, if you miss, you do not find an alternative accept going back to achieve it. Prayer, al-Wilāya and Hajj are**

not of matters replaceable with their own kind. On the other hand if fasting is missed on a journey one has the choice to fast on other days as remedy or compensate for the sin with expiation and no fasting is necessary as a remedy. In the cases of the other four issues there is no alternative for them.' The narrator has said that the Imam then said, **'The topmost, the peak of the issue, the key and the door to it and the pleasure of the Beneficent (Lord) is to obey the Imam properly after knowing him clearly**. Allāh, the Most Majestic, the Most Holy, says, "Whoever obeys the Messenger he has obeyed Allāh and whoever turns away from such obedience then you should know that We have not sent you to guard them." (4:80) **'Without recognizing the Divine Authority of the Imam, the deputy of Allāh, no one has the right to receive any reward from Allāh**, the Most Majestic, the Most Holy. This is true even though in his lifetime he may stand up in worship the whole night, fast during the day, give all his belongings in charity and perform Hajj every year. So also it is if he does not acknowledge the Divine Authority of his Imam with which all of one's deeds can take place with the guidance of the Imam. **Without al- Wilāya, one is not considered of the people of belief**.' Thereafter the Imam said, 'Allāh will admit, those of them who do good deeds into paradise through His extra mercy. (صحيح)[1]

2.

أَبُو عَلِيٍّ الْأَشْعَرِيُّ عَنِ الْحَسَنِ بْنِ عَلِيٍّ الْكُوفِيِّ عَنْ عَبَّاسِ بْنِ عَامِرٍ عَنْ أَبَانِ بْنِ عُثْمَانَ عَنْ فُضَيْلِ بْنِ يَسَارٍ عَنْ أَبِي جَعْفَرٍ (عَلَيهِ السَّلام) قَالَ بُنِيَ الإِسْلامُ عَلَى خَمْسٍ عَلَى الصَّلاةِ وَالزَّكَاةِ وَالصَّوْمِ وَالْحَجِّ وَالْوَلايَةِ وَلَمْ يُنَادَ بِشَيْءٍ كَمَا نُودِيَ بِالْوَلايَةِ فَأَخَذَ النَّاسُ بِأَرْبَعٍ وَتَرَكُوا هَذِهِ يَعْنِي الْوَلايَةَ

Abu 'Alī al-Ash'ari has narrated from al-Hassan b. 'Alī al-Kufi from 'Abbas b. 'Amir from Aban b. 'Uthman from Fudayl b. Yasar from abu Ja'far (عليه السلام) who has said

---

[1] *Al-Kāfi, v2, ch13, h5*

the following: "Abu Ja'far (عليه السلام) has said, 'Islam is based on **five principles**. They are: Prayer, al-Zakat (charity) fasting, Hajj and al-Wilāya. The call to none of the other principles has been so emphatic as it has been to **al- Wilāya**. People accepted the other four, but they **left aside this [al-Wilāya]**. (موثق كالصحيح)[2]

3.

مُحَمَّدُ بْنُ يَحْيَى عَنْ أَحْمَدَ بْنِ مُحَمَّدٍ عَنْ صَفْوَانَ بْنِ يَحْيَى عَنْ عِيسَى بْنِ السَّرِيِّ أَبِي الْيَسَعِ قَالَ قُلْتُ لأَبِي عَبْدِ اللهِ (عَلَيهِ السَّلام) أَخْبِرْنِي بِدَعَائِمِ الإِسْلامِ الَّتِي لا يَسَعُ أَحَداً التَّقْصِيرُ عَنْ مَعْرِفَةِ شَيْءٍ مِنْهَا الَّذِي مَنْ قَصَّرَ عَنْ مَعْرِفَةِ شَيْءٍ مِنْهَا فَسَدَ دِينُهُ وَلَمْ يَقْبَلِ [الله] مِنْهُ عَمَلَهُ وَمَنْ عَرَفَهَا وَعَمِلَ بِهَا صَلَحَ لَهُ دِينُهُ وَقَبِلَ مِنْهُ عَمَلَهُ وَلَمْ يَضِقْ بِهِ مِمَّا هُوَ فِيهِ لِجَهْلِ شَيْءٍ مِنَ الأُمُورِ جَهْلُهُ فَقَالَ شَهَادَةُ أَنْ لا إِلَهَ إِلا اللهُ وَالإِيمَانُ بِأَنَّ مُحَمَّداً رَسُولُ اللهِ (صَلَّى اللهُ عَلَيْهِ وآلِه) وَالإِقْرَارُ بِمَا جَاءَ بِهِ مِنْ عِنْدِ اللهِ وَحَقٌّ فِي الأَمْوَالِ الزَّكَاةُ وَالْوَلايَةُ الَّتِي أَمَرَ اللهُ عَزَّ وَجَلَّ بِهَا وَلايَةُ آلِ مُحَمَّدٍ (صَلَّى اللهُ عَلَيْهِ وآلِه) قَالَ فَقُلْتُ لَهُ هَلْ فِي الْوَلايَةِ شَيْءٌ دُونَ شَيْءٍ فَضْلٌ يُعْرَفُ لِمَنْ أَخَذَ بِهِ قَالَ نَعَمْ قَالَ اللهُ عَزَّ وَجَلَّ يا أَيُّهَا الَّذِينَ آمَنُوا أَطِيعُوا اللهَ وَأَطِيعُوا الرَّسُولَ وَأُولِي الأَمْرِ مِنْكُمْ وَقَالَ رَسُولُ اللهِ (صَلَّى اللهُ عَلَيْهِ وآلِه) مَنْ مَاتَ وَلا يَعْرِفُ إِمَامَهُ مَاتَ مِيتَةً جَاهِلِيَّةً وَكَانَ رَسُولَ اللهِ (صَلَّى اللهُ عَلَيْهِ وآلِه) وَكَانَ عَلِيّاً (عَلَيهِ السَّلام) وَقَالَ الآخَرُونَ كَانَ مُعَاوِيَةَ ثُمَّ كَانَ الْحَسَنَ (عَلَيهِ السَّلام) ثُمَّ كَانَ الْحُسَيْنَ (عَلَيهِ السَّلام) وَقَالَ الآخَرُونَ يَزِيدَ بْنَ مُعَاوِيَةَ وَحُسَيْنَ بْنَ عَلِيٍّ وَلا سَوَاءَ وَلا سَوَاءَ قَالَ ثُمَّ سَكَتَ ثُمَّ قَالَ أَزِيدُكَ فَقَالَ لَهُ حَكَمٌ الأَعْوَرُ نَعَمْ جُعِلْتُ فِدَاكَ قَالَ ثُمَّ كَانَ عَلِيَّ بْنَ الْحُسَيْنِ ثُمَّ كَانَ مُحَمَّدَ بْنَ عَلِيٍّ أَبَا جَعْفَرٍ وَكَانَتِ الشِّيعَةُ قَبْلَ أَنْ يَكُونَ أَبُو جَعْفَرٍ وَهُمْ لا يَعْرِفُونَ مَنَاسِكَ حَجِّهِمْ وَحَلالَهُمْ وَحَرَامَهُمْ حَتَّى كَانَ أَبُو جَعْفَرٍ فَفَتَحَ لَهُمْ وَبَيَّنَ لَهُمْ مَنَاسِكَ حَجِّهِمْ وَحَلالَهُمْ وَحَرَامَهُمْ حَتَّى صَارَ النَّاسُ يَحْتَاجُونَ إِلَيْهِمْ مِنْ بَعْدِ مَا كَانُوا يَحْتَاجُونَ إِلَى النَّاسِ وَهَكَذَا يَكُونُ الأَمْرُ وَالأَرْضُ لا تَكُونُ إِلا بِإِمَامٍ وَمَنْ مَاتَ لا يَعْرِفُ إِمَامَهُ مَاتَ مِيتَةً جَاهِلِيَّةً وَأَحْوَجُ مَا تَكُونُ إِلَى مَا أَنْتَ عَلَيْهِ إِذْ بَلَغَتْ نَفْسُكَ هَذِهِ وَأَهْوَى بِيَدِهِ إِلَى حَلْقِهِ وَانْقَطَعَتْ عَنْكَ الدُّنْيَا تَقُولُ لَقَدْ كُنْتُ عَلَى أَمْرٍ حَسَنٍ. أَبُو عَلِيٍّ الأَشْعَرِيُّ عَنْ مُحَمَّدِ بْنِ عَبْدِ الْجَبَّارِ عَنْ صَفْوَانَ عَنْ عِيسَى بْنِ السَّرِيِّ أَبِي الْيَسَعِ عَنْ أَبِي عَبْدِ اللهِ (عَلَيهِ السَّلام) مِثْلَهُ

Muhammad b. Yahya has narrated from Ahmad b. Muḥammad from Safwan b. Yahya from 'Isa b. al-Sariyy abu al-Yasa' who has said the following: "Once I said to

---

[2] *Al-Kafi v2, ch13, h3*

abu ‘Abd Allāh (عليه السلام) ‘Teach me, please, the basic principles of Islam that are necessary for everyone to know to his limits of understanding, and if he fails to learn them to the necessary levels his religion is destroyed and Allāh does not accept his deeds. What is the limit of learning about the deeds with which someone’s religion can take proper shape and Allāh may accept his deeds? What are the limits and degrees of the permissible level of ignorance and lack of knowledge of certain aspects of these principles?’ “The Imam said, ‘The matters necessary to learn are to testify that no one deserves to be worshipped except Allāh, that Muḥammad (عليه السلام) is the Messenger of Allāh, that whatever he has brought from Allāh is the truth and to affirm that paying Zakat (charity) is a right. (Of such necessary matters is) to affirm al-Wilāya (Divine Authority of ‘ A’immah) that Allāh, the Most Majestic, the Most Holy, has made obligatory upon the other people to obey and acknowledge the Divine Authority of certain members of the family of Prophet Muhammad, recipient of divine supreme covenant.’ I (the narrator) then asked the Imam, ‘Is al-Wilāya of an exclusive nature?’ The Imam said, ‘Yes, Allāh, the Most Majestic, the Most Holy, has said, “O believers, obey Allāh, obey the Messenger and those among you who possess Divine Authority.” (4:59) The Merssenger of Allāh has said, “Whoever dies without knowing who the Imam of his time is, he is considered as a person dying in the time of ignorance (as an unbeliever).” There was the Messenger of Allāh and there was ‘Alī (عليه السلام) but others said there was Mu’awiyah. Then there was al-Hassan (عليه السلام) and then there was al-Husayn, recipient of divine supreme covenant. Others said that there were Yazid b. Mu’awiyah and Husayn b. Ali. They were not equals and certainly they were not equals, meaning thereby Ali, al-Hassan and al-Husayn with Mu’awiyah and his son Yazid.’ He has said that the Imam remained calm for a while and then said, ‘Do you want me to tell you additional facts?’ Hakam b. al-’A’War said, ‘Yes, may Allāh keep my soul in service to your cause.’ The Imam said, ‘Then there was ‘Alī b. al-Husayn (عليه السلام) then there was Muḥammad b. Ali, abu Ja’far. The Shi’a before abu Ja’far did not know the rules of Hajj, the lawful matters and the unlawful matters until there was abu Ja’far, recipient of divine supreme covenant. He opened it (system of religion) for them and explained to them the rules of their Hajj, the lawful and unlawful matters. People began to realize that they needed him very much while before they would ask other people for what they needed. This is how the facts are. The earth does not remain without an Imam and one who dies without knowing, who his Imam is, he is as though he was of the people of the dark ages of ignorance. The time when you need al-Wilāya most urgently is the time when your soul reaches here (pointing to his throat) and the world is cut off from you and then you say, 'I have certainly been on the good side of the affairs, (a supporter of al-Wilāya).''" Abu 'Alī al-Ash'ari has narrated from Muḥammad b. 'Abd al-Jabbar from Safwan from 'Isa b. al-Sariyy abu al-Yasa' from abu 'Abd Allāh (عليه السلام) a similar Hadīth. (صحيح)[3]

4.

عَلِيُّ بْنُ إِبْرَاهِيمَ عَنْ مُحَمَّدِ بْنِ عِيسَى عَنْ يُونُسَ عَنْ حَمَّادِ بْنِ عُثْمَانَ عَنْ عِيسَى بْنِ السَّرِيِّ قَالَ قُلْتُ لأَبِي عَبْدِ اللهِ (عَلَيهِ السَّلام) حَدِّثْنِي عَمَّا بُنِيَتْ عَلَيْهِ دَعَائِمُ الإِسْلامِ إِذَا أَنَا أَخَذْتُ بِهَا زَكَى عَمَلِي وَلَمْ يَضُرَّنِي جَهْلُ مَا جَهِلْتُ بَعْدَهُ فَقَالَ شَهَادَةُ أَنْ لا إِلَهَ إِلا اللهُ وَأَنَّ مُحَمَّداً رَسُولُ اللهِ (صَلَّى اللهُ عَلَيْهِ وآلِه) وَالإِقْرَارُ بِمَا جَاءَ بِهِ مِنْ عِنْدِ اللهِ وَحَقٌّ فِي الأَمْوَالِ مِنَ الزَّكَاةِ وَالْوَلايَةُ الَّتِي أَمَرَ اللهُ عَزَّ وَجَلَّ بِهَا وَلايَةُ آلِ مُحَمَّدٍ (صَلَّى اللهُ عَلَيْهِ وآلِه) فَإِنَّ رَسُولَ اللهِ (صَلَّى اللهُ عَلَيْهِ وآلِه) قَالَ مَنْ مَاتَ وَلا يَعْرِفُ إِمَامَهُ مَاتَ مِيتَةً جَاهِلِيَّةً قَالَ اللهُ عَزَّ وَجَلَّ أَطِيعُوا اللهَ وَأَطِيعُوا الرَّسُولَ وَأُولِي الأَمْرِ مِنْكُمْ فَكَانَ عَلِيٌّ (عَلَيهِ السَّلام) ثُمَّ صَارَ مِنْ بَعْدِهِ الْحَسَنُ ثُمَّ مِنْ بَعْدِهِ الْحُسَيْنُ ثُمَّ مِنْ بَعْدِهِ عَلِيُّ بْنُ الْحُسَيْنِ ثُمَّ مِنْ بَعْدِهِ مُحَمَّدُ بْنُ عَلِيٍّ ثُمَّ هَكَذَا يَكُونُ الأَمْرُ إِنَّ الأَرْضَ لا تَصْلُحُ إِلا بِإِمَامٍ وَمَنْ مَاتَ لا يَعْرِفُ إِمَامَهُ مَاتَ مِيتَةً جَاهِلِيَّةً وَأَحْوَجُ مَا يَكُونُ أَحَدُكُمْ إِلَى مَعْرِفَتِهِ إِذَا بَلَغَتْ نَفْسُهُ هَاهُنَا قَالَ وَأَهْوَى بِيَدِهِ إِلَى صَدْرِهِ يَقُولُ حِينَئِذٍ لَقَدْ كُنْتُ عَلَى أَمْرٍ حَسَنٍ

Ali b. Ibrahim has narrated from Muḥammad b. 'Isa from Yunus from Hammad b. 'Uthman from 'Isa al-Sariyy who has said the following: "Once I asked abu 'Abd Allāh (عليه السلام) to teach me the principles of Islam in such a way that on holding to them my deeds can take pure and correct form and thereafter the ignorance of whatever I am ignorant of cannot harm me. The Imam said, 'Of the principles of Islam are to testify and acknowledge that no one deserves to be worshipped except

---

[3] *Al-Kāfi, v2, ch13, h6*

Allāh, and that Muḥammad (عليه السلام) is the Messenger of Allāh. Of such principles is to affirm and acknowledge that whatever he has brought is from Allāh, to pay al-Zakat (charity) is a right and that al-Wilāya which Allāh, the Most Majestic, the Most Holy, has commanded to accept and acknowledge is al-Wilāya (Divine Authority) of Ahl al-Bayt of Muhammad, recipient of divine supreme covenant. The Messenger of Allāh has said, "Whoever dies while he does not know who his Imam is, he is considered as one who has died in the darkness of ignorance." Allāh, the Most Majestic, the Most Holy, has said, "Obey Allāh, obey the Messenger of Allāh and the persons among you who possess Divine Authority." (4:59). Imam ʿAlī was there (possessed Divine Authority) and after him were Imam Hassan, Imam Husayn and ʿAlī b. al-Husayn and after them was Muḥammad b. Ali, recipients of divine supreme covenant, successively and thus it will continue. The land will not take an ideal shape without an Imam. Whoever dies while he does not know who his Imam is, he is considered as one who has died in the darkness of ignorance. What everyone of you will need very urgently when his soul will reach here (pointing to his chest) is to know him (the Imam) so that he can say it is certain that I have been holding to a genuinely good matter. (صحيح)[4]

5.

عَلِيُّ بْنُ إِبْرَاهِيمَ عَنْ أَبِيهِ وَأَبُو عَلِيٍّ الأَشْعَرِيُّ عَنْ مُحَمَّدِ بْنِ عَبْدِ الْجَبَّارِ جَمِيعاً عَنْ صَفْوَانَ عَنْ عَمْرِو بْنِ حُرَيْثٍ قَالَ دَخَلْتُ عَلَى أَبِي عَبْدِ اللهِ (عَلَيهِ السَّلام) وَهُوَ فِي مَنْزِلِ أَخِيهِ عَبْدِ اللهِ بْنِ مُحَمَّدٍ فَقُلْتُ لَهُ جُعِلْتُ فِدَاكَ مَا حَوَّلَكَ إِلَى هَذَا الْمَنْزِلِ قَالَ طَلَبُ النُّزْهَةِ فَقُلْتُ جُعِلْتُ فِدَاكَ أَ لا أَقُصُّ عَلَيْكَ دِينِي فَقَالَ بَلَى قُلْتُ أَدِينُ اللهَ بِشَهَادَةِ أَنْ لا إِلَهَ إِلا اللهُ وَحْدَهُ لا شَرِيكَ لَهُ وَأَنَّ مُحَمَّداً عَبْدُهُ وَرَسُولُهُ وَأَنَّ السَّاعَةَ آتِيَةٌ لا رَيْبَ فِيهَا وَأَنَّ اللهَ يَبْعَثُ مَنْ فِي الْقُبُورِ وَإِقَامِ الصَّلاةِ وَإِيتَاءِ الزَّكَاةِ وَصَوْمِ شَهْرِ رَمَضَانَ وَحِجِّ الْبَيْتِ وَالْوَلايَةِ لِعَلِيٍّ أَمِيرِ الْمُؤْمِنِينَ بَعْدَ رَسُولِ اللهِ (صَلَّى اللهُ عَلَيْهِ وآلِه) وَالْوَلايَةِ لِلْحَسَنِ وَالْحُسَيْنِ وَالْوَلايَةِ لِعَلِيِّ بْنِ الْحُسَيْنِ وَالْوَلايَةِ لِمُحَمَّدِ بْنِ عَلِيٍّ وَلَكَ مِنْ بَعْدِهِ صَلَوَاتُ اللهِ عَلَيْهِمْ أَجْمَعِينَ وَأَنَّكُمْ أَئِمَّتِي عَلَيْهِ أَحْيَا وَعَلَيْهِ أَمُوتُ وَأَدِينُ اللهَ بِهِ فَقَالَ يَا عَمْرُو هَذَا وَاللهِ دِينُ اللهِ وَدِينُ آبَائِيَ الَّذِي أَدِينُ اللهَ بِهِ فِي السِّرِّ وَالْعَلانِيَةِ فَاتَّقِ اللهَ وَكُفَّ

---

[4] *Al-Kāfi, v2, ch13, h9*

لِسَانَكَ إِلا مِنْ خَيْرٍ وَلا تَقُلْ إِنِّي هَدَيْتُ نَفْسِي بَلِ اللهُ هَدَاكَ فَأَدِّ شُكْرَ مَا أَنْعَمَ اللهُ عَزَّ وَجَلَّ بِهِ عَلَيْكَ وَلا تَكُنْ مِمَّنْ إِذَا أَقْبَلَ طُعِنَ فِي عَيْنِهِ وَإِذَا أَدْبَرَ طُعِنَ فِي قَفَاهُ وَلا تَحْمِلِ النَّاسَ عَلَى كَاهِلِكَ فَإِنَّكَ أَوْشَكَ إِنْ حَمَلْتَ النَّاسَ عَلَى كَاهِلِكَ أَنْ يُصَدِّعُوا شَعْبَ كَاهِلِكَ

Ali b. Ibrahim has narrated from his father and abu ʻAlī al-Ash'ari from Muḥammad b. 'Abd al-Jabbar all of them from Safwan from 'Amr b. Harith who has said the following: "Once I went to see abu 'Abd Allāh (عليه السلام) and he was in the house of his brother, 'Abd Allāh b. Muhammad, and I said, 'May Allāh keep my soul in service for your cause, what has brought you to this house?' 'Seeking privacy,' said the Imam. I said, 'May Allāh keep my soul in service for your cause, can I state before you my religion?' The Imam said, 'Yes, you may do so.' I then said, 'I follow a religion (that requires me) to obey Allāh and testify that no one else deserves to be worshipped except Allāh Who has no partners. That Muḥammad (عليه السلام) is His servant and messenger, that the Hour (of reckoning) will certainly come, that Allāh will bring all people from their graves, that it is obligatory to pray, pay Zakat (charity), fast in the month of Ramadan and perform Hajj of the House. I affirm and acknowledge the Divine Authority of ʻAlī b. abu Talib after the Messenger of Allāh, the Divine Authority of al-Hassan, al- Husayn, the Divine Authority of ʻAlī b. al-Husayn, the Divine Authority of Muḥammad b. ʻAlī and your Divine Authority after him (your father), recipients of divine supreme covenant. You are my Imam. With such beliefs I live and with them I will die and such is my religion before Allāh.' The Imam said, 'Such, O 'Amr, I swear by Allāh, is the religion of Allāh and the religion of my ancestors and such is the religion that 1 follow to obey Allāh in private and in public. Maintain piety before Allāh and hold your tongue except from good and do not say, "I have guided myself." In fact, Allāh has guided you. Give thanks to Allāh, the Most Majestic, the Most Holy, for the favor that He has done to you. Do not be of those who on their moving forward are hit in the eyes or when moving backwards are hit from the back. Do not allow people ride on your shoulders for if you do so they cause injury to your shoulders. (صحيح)[5]

---

[5] *Al-Kafi, v2, ch13, h14*

6.

عَنْهُ عَنْ أَبِيهِ رَفَعَهُ قَالَ قَالَ أَبُو عَبْدِ اللهِ (عَلَيْهِ السَّلام) يُسْأَلُ الْمَيِّتُ فِي قَبْرِهِ عَنْ خَمْسٍ عَنْ صَلاتِهِ وَزَكَاتِهِ وَحَجِّهِ وَصِيَامِهِ وَوَلايَتِهِ إِيَّانَا أَهْلَ الْبَيْتِ فَتَقُولُ الْوَلايَةُ مِنْ جَانِبِ الْقَبْرِ لِلأَرْبَعِ مَا دَخَلَ فِيكُنَّ مِنْ نَقْصٍ فَعَلَيَّ تَمَامُهُ

It is narrated from him (narrator of the above Hadīth) from his father in a marfu' manner who has said the following: "Abu 'Abd Allāh, (عليه السلام), has said that a deceased is asked in his grave about five issues. He is asked about his prayer, Zakat (paying charity), his Hajj, his fasting and about our, Ahl al-Bayt's Wilāya (guardianship) over him. Wilāya then from one side of the grave says to the others, 'If you face any deficiency in your task (of protecting him), leave it for me to suffice? (صحيح)[6]

7.

يَحْيَى الْحَلَبِيُّ عَنْ عَبْدِ اللَّهِ بْنِ مُسْكَانَ عَنْ أَبِي بَصِيرٍ قَالَ قُلْتُ جُعِلْتُ فِدَاكَ أَ رَأَيْتَ الرَّادَّ عَلَيَّ هَذَا الأَمْرَ فَهُوَ كَالرَّادِّ عَلَيْكُمْ فَقَالَ يَا أَبَا مُحَمَّدٍ مَنْ رَدَّ عَلَيْكَ هَذَا الأَمْرَ فَهُوَ كَالرَّادِّ عَلَى رَسُولِ اللَّهِ (صلى الله عليه وآله) وَ عَلَى اللَّهِ تَبَارَكَ وَ تَعَالَى يَا أَبَا مُحَمَّدٍ إِنَّ الْمَيِّتَ مِنْكُمْ عَلَى هَذَا الأَمْرِ شَهِيدٌ قَالَ قُلْتُ وَ إِنْ مَاتَ عَلَى فِرَاشِهِ قَالَ إِي وَ اللَّهِ وَ إِنْ مَاتَ عَلَى فِرَاشِهِ حَيٌّ عِنْدَ رَبِّهِ يُرْزَقُ

Yahya Al-Halby, from 'Abd Allāh b. Muskaan, from Abu Baseer who said: I said to him, 'May I be sacrificed for you, do you see the one who rejects this matter (Al-Wilāya) to me as if he has rejected you?' He said: 'O Abu Muhammad! The one who rejects this matter to you, so he has rejected against the Messenger of Allāh (صلى الله عليه وآله وسلم), and against Allāh (تبارك و طائلة) Blessed and High. O Abu Muhammad! The dead

[6] *Al-Kāfi, v3, ch88, h15*

ones from among you who were upon this matter (Al-Wilāya) is the martyr'. I said, 'Even if he died upon his bed?' He said: 'Yes, by Allāh (تبارك و طائلة), even if he died upon his bed, he is alive in the Presence of his Lord being given Sustenance (صحيح)[7]

8.

عَلِيُّ بْنُ إِبْرَاهِيمَ عَنْ أَبِيهِ عَنِ ابْنِ أَبِي عُمَيْرٍ عَنْ هِشَامِ بْنِ سَالِمٍ قَالَ قَالَ أَبُو عَبْدِ اللَّهِ (عليه السلام) إِنَّ مِمَّنْ يَنْتَحِلُ هَذَا الْأَمْرَ لَيَكْذِبُ حَتَّى إِنَّ الشَّيْطَانَ لَيَحْتَاجُ إِلَى كَذِبِهِ

Ali b. Ibrahim, from his father, from b. Abu Umeyr, from Hashaam b. Saalim who said: Abu 'AbdAllāh (عليه السلام) said: 'Whosoever (other than us) claims to posses this Command (Wilāya), he has lied to the extent that the Satan (لعنة الله عليه) would be needy of his lie'. (حسن)[8]

9.

أَبُو عَلِيٍّ الْأَشْعَرِيُّ عَنْ مُحَمَّدِ بْنِ عَبْدِ الْجَبَّارِ عَنِ الْحَسَنِ بْنِ عَلِيِّ بْنِ فَضَّالٍ عَنْ ثَعْلَبَةَ بْنِ مَيْمُونٍ عَنْ أَبِي أُمَيَّةَ يُوسُفَ بْنِ ثَابِتِ بْنِ أَبِي سَعِيدَةَ عَنْ أَبِي عَبْدِ اللَّهِ (عليه السلام) أَنَّهُمْ قَالُوا حِينَ دَخَلُوا عَلَيْهِ إِنَّمَا أَحْبَبْنَاكُمْ لِقَرَابَتِكُمْ مِنْ رَسُولِ اللَّهِ (صلى الله عليه وآله) وَ لَمَّا أَوْجَبَ اللَّهُ عَزَّ وَ جَلَّ مِنْ حَقِّكُمْ مَا أَحْبَبْنَاكُمْ لِلدُّنْيَا نُصِيبُهَا مِنْكُمْ إِلَّا لِوَجْهِ اللَّهِ وَ الدَّارِ الْآخِرَةِ وَ لِيُصْلِحَ لِامْرِئٍ مِنَّا دِينَهُ فَقَالَ أَبُو عَبْدِ اللَّهِ (عليه السلام) صَدَقْتُمْ صَدَقْتُمْ ثُمَّ قَالَ مَنْ أَحَبَّنَا كَانَ مَعَنَا أَوْ جَاءَ مَعَنَا يَوْمَ الْقِيَامَةِ هَكَذَا ثُمَّ جَمَعَ بَيْنَ السَّبَّابَتَيْنِ ثُمَّ قَالَ وَ اللَّهِ لَوْ أَنَّ رَجُلًا صَامَ النَّهَارَ وَ قَامَ اللَّيْلَ ثُمَّ لَقِيَ اللَّهَ عَزَّ وَ جَلَّ بِغَيْرِ وَلَايَتِنَا أَهْلَ الْبَيْتِ لَلَقِيَهُ وَ هُوَ عَنْهُ غَيْرُ رَاضٍ أَوْ سَاخِطٌ عَلَيْهِ ثُمَّ قَالَ وَ ذَلِكَ قَوْلُ اللَّهِ عَزَّ وَ جَلَّ وَ مَا مَنَعَهُمْ أَنْ تُقْبَلَ مِنْهُمْ نَفَقَاتُهُمْ إِلَّا أَنَّهُمْ كَفَرُوا بِاللَّهِ وَ بِرَسُولِهِ وَ لَا يَأْتُونَ الصَّلَاةَ إِلَّا وَ هُمْ كُسَالَى وَ لَا يُنْفِقُونَ إِلَّا وَ هُمْ كَارِهُونَ فَلَا تُعْجِبْكَ أَمْوَالُهُمْ وَ لَا أَوْلَادُهُمْ إِنَّمَا يُرِيدُ اللَّهُ لِيُعَذِّبَهُمْ بِهَا فِي الْحَيَاةِ الدُّنْيَا وَ تَزْهَقَ أَنْفُسُهُمْ وَ هُمْ كَافِرُونَ ثُمَّ قَالَ وَ كَذَلِكَ الْإِيمَانُ لَا يَضُرُّ مَعَهُ الْعَمَلُ وَ كَذَلِكَ الْكُفْرُ لَا يَنْفَعُ مَعَهُ الْعَمَلُ ثُمَّ قَالَ إِنْ تَكُونُوا وَحْدَانِيِّينَ فَقَدْ كَانَ رَسُولُ اللَّهِ (صلى الله عليه وآله) وَحْدَانِيّاً يَدْعُو النَّاسَ فَلَا يَسْتَجِيبُونَ لَهُ وَ كَانَ أَوَّلَ مَنِ اسْتَجَابَ لَهُ عَلِيُّ بْنُ أَبِي طَالِبٍ (عليه السلام) وَ قَدْ قَالَ

[7] Al-Kāfi, v8, ch120

[8] Al-Kāfi, v8, ch362

رَسُولُ اللَّهِ (صلى الله عليه وآله) أَنْتَ مِنِّي بِمَنْزِلَةِ هَارُونَ مِنْ مُوسَى إِلَّا أَنَّهُ لَا نَبِيَّ بَعْدِي. لِيُّ بْنُ إِبْرَاهِيمَ عَنْ مُحَمَّدِ بْنِ عِيسَى بْنِ عُبَيْدٍ عَنْ يُونُسَ قَالَ قَالَ أَبُو عَبْدِ اللَّهِ (عليه السلام) لِعَبَّادِ بْنِ كَثِيرٍ الْبَصْرِيِّ الصُّوفِيِّ وَيْحَكَ يَا عَبَّادُ غَرَّكَ أَنْ عَفَّ بَطْنُكَ وَ فَرْجُكَ إِنَّ اللَّهَ عَزَّ وَ جَلَّ يَقُولُ فِي كِتَابِهِ يَا أَيُّهَا الَّذِينَ آمَنُوا اتَّقُوا اللَّهَ وَ قُولُوا قَوْلاً سَدِيداً يُصْلِحْ لَكُمْ أَعْمالَكُمْ اعْلَمْ أَنَّهُ لَا يَتَقَبَّلُ اللَّهُ مِنْكَ شَيْئاً حَتَّى تَقُولَ قَوْلاً عَدْلَ

Abu ʿAlī Al-Ashary, from Muḥammad b. Abdul Jabbaar, from Al-Hassan b. ʿAlī b. Fazzaal, from Tha'albat b. Maymoun, from Aby Amiyya Yusuf b. Sabit b. Abu Saeeda, who has narrated the following: Abu 'AbdAllāh (عليه السلام) having said when they came up to him and said, 'But rather, we love you due to your nearness to the Messenger of Allāh (صلى الله عليه وآله وسلم) ,and for what Allāh (تبارك و طائلة) Mighty and Majestic has Obligated from your rights. We do not love you for the sake of the world for getting a share of it from you. But (we love you) only for the Sake of Allāh (تبارك و طائلة) and the House of the Hereafter and that the man from among us would be able to correct his Religion'. So Abu 'AbdAllāh (عليه السلام) said: 'You have spoken the truth, you have spoken the truth'. Then he said: 'The one who loves us is as if he is with us, or will come with us on the Day of Judgement like this' – then he joined the two forefingers, then said – 'By Allāh (تبارك و طائلة)! If the man were to Fast during the day, and stand up (for Prayer) during the night, then meets Allāh (تبارك و طائلة) Mighty and Majestic without our Wilāya, (the People of the Household) he then would be facing Him (in such that) Allāh (تبارك و طائلة) would either be Unhappy with him or Angry against him'. Then he said: 'And that is the Statement of Allāh (تبارك و طائلة) Mighty and Majestic: "[9:54] The only reasons why their contributions are not accepted are: that they reject Allāh and His Rasool; that they come to prayer without earnestness; and that they offer contributions unwillingly [9:55] Let not then their property and their children excite your admiration; Allāh only wishes to chastise them with these in this world's life and (that) their souls may depart while they are unbelievers" Then he said: 'And such is that belief that the (bad) deed neither had affected it adversely nor is that disbelief that the (good) deed had provided any profit to it'. Then he said; 'You should become (believers in) Oneness (of Allāh (تبارك و طائلة)) for the Messenger of Allāh (صلى الله عليه وآله وسلم) Allāh (تبارك و طائلة) had called the people to the Oneness (of Allāh (تبارك و طائلة)) but they did not answer him, and the first one who had came forward to him was 'Alī (عليه السلام) b. Abu Talib (عليه السلام), and the Messenger of Allāh (صلى الله عليه وآله وسلم) Allāh (تبارك و طائلة) said: 'You are from me of the status which Haroun (عليه السلام) had from Mūsā (عليه السلام) except that there is no Prophet (عليه السلام) after me'. (موثق)[9]

10.

مُحَمَّدُ بْنُ يَحْيَى عَنْ أَحْمَدَ بْنِ مُحَمَّدِ بْنِ عِيسَى عَنِ ابْنِ مَحْبُوبٍ عَنْ جَمِيلِ بْنِ صَالِحٍ عَنْ أَبِي خَالِدٍ الْكَابُلِيِّ عَنْ أَبِي جَعْفَرٍ)عليه السلام (قَالَ ضَرَبَ اللَّهُ مَثَلًا رَجُلًا فِيهِ شُرَكَاءُ مُتَشَاكِسُونَ وَ رَجُلًا سَلَماً لِرَجُلٍ هَلْ يَسْتَوِيانِ مَثَلًا قَالَ أَمَّا الَّذِي فِيهِ شُرَكَاءُ مُتَشَاكِسُونَ فَلِأَنَّ الْأَوَّلَ يَجْمَعُ الْمُتَفَرِّقُونَ وَلَايَتَهُ وَ هُمْ فِي ذَلِكَ يَلْعَنُ بَعْضُهُمْ بَعْضاً وَ يَبْرَأُ بَعْضُهُمْ مِنْ بَعْضٍ فَأَمَّا رَجُلٌ سَلَمٌ رَجُلٍ فَإِنَّهُ الْأَوَّلُ حَقّاً وَ شِيعَتُهُ ثُمَّ قَالَ إِنَّ الْيَهُودَ تَفَرَّقُوا مِنْ بَعْدِ مُوسَى)عليه السلام (عَلَى إِحْدَى وَ سَبْعِينَ فِرْقَةً مِنْهَا فِرْقَةٌ فِي الْجَنَّةِ وَ سَبْعُونَ فِرْقَةً فِي النَّارِ وَ تَفَرَّقَتِ النَّصَارَى بَعْدَ عِيسَى)عليه السلام (عَلَى اثْنَتَيْنِ وَ سَبْعِينَ فِرْقَةً فِرْقَةٌ مِنْهَا فِي الْجَنَّةِ وَ إِحْدَى وَ سَبْعُونَ فِي النَّارِ وَ تَفَرَّقَتْ هَذِهِ الْأُمَّةُ بَعْدَ نَبِيِّهَا)صلى الله عليه وآله (عَلَى ثَلَاثٍ وَ سَبْعِينَ فِرْقَةً اثْنَتَانِ وَ سَبْعُونَ فِرْقَةً فِي النَّارِ وَ فِرْقَةٌ فِي الْجَنَّةِ وَ مِنَ الثَّلَاثِ وَ سَبْعِينَ فِرْقَةً ثَلَاثَ عَشْرَةَ فِرْقَةً تَنْتَحِلُ وَلَايَتَنَا وَ مَوَدَّتَنَا اثْنَتَا عَشْرَةَ فِرْقَةً مِنْهَا فِي النَّارِ وَ فِرْقَةٌ فِي الْجَنَّةِ وَ سِتُّونَ فِرْقَةً مِنْ سَائِرِ النَّاسِ فِي النَّارِ

Muhammad b. yahya, from Ahmad b. Muḥammad b. Isa, from b. Mahboub, from Jameel b. Salih, from Abu Khalid Al-Kabuly, who has narrated the following: Abu Ja'far (عليه السلام) having said: "[39:29] Allāh sets forth an example: There is a slave in whom are (several) partners differing with one another, and there is another slave wholly owned by one man. Are the two alike in condition?" He said: 'But rather it is the one who has associates with regards to whom they doubt because he was the first one who gathered them for his leadership, so they differed regarding it and some of them cursed each other for that, and some of them distanced themselves from each other. As for the man of peace, he is the first one for the 'حَقّاً' Just and his Shittes'. Then he said: 'The Jews differed, from after Mūsā (عليه السلام) and separated into seventy-one sects, one of which will be in the Paradise and seventy sects would be in

---

[9] *Al-Kāfi, v8, ch80*

the Fire. And the Christians separated, from after Isa (عليه السلام) into seventy-two sects, one of which would be in the Paradise and seventy-one of the sects would be in the Fire. And this community will separate after its Prophet (صلى الله عليه وآله وسلم) into seventy-three sects. Seventy-two sects would be in the Fire and one sect would be in the Paradise. **And from these seventy-three sects, thirteen would be of those who claim to be in our Wilāya and show affection to us**. Twelve sects from these would be in the Fire and one sect would be in the Paradise. And sixty sects from the rest of the people would be in the Fire'. (حسن)[10]

11.

عَلِ مُحَمَّدُ بْنُ يَحْيَى عَنْ أَحْمَدَ بْنِ مُحَمَّدِ بْنِ عِيسَى عَنِ ابْنِ مَحْبُوبٍ عَنْ جَمِيلِ بْنِ صَالِحٍ عَنْ أَبِي خَالِدٍ الْكَابُلِيِّ عَنْ أَبِي جَعْفَرٍ (عليه السلام) قَالَ ضَرَبَ اللَّهُ مَثَلًا رَجُلًا فِيهِ شُرَكَاءُ مُتَشَاكِسُونَ وَ رَجُلًا سَلَماً لِرَجُلٍ هَلْ يَسْتَوِيَانِ مَثَلًا قَالَ أَمَّا الَّذِي فِيهِ شُرَكَاءُ مُتَشَاكِسُونَ فَلِأَنَّ الْأَوَّلَ يَجْمَعُ الْمُتَفَرِّقُونَ وَلَايَتَهُ وَ هُمْ فِي ذَلِكَ يَلْعَنُ بَعْضُهُمْ بَعْضاً وَ يَبْرَأُ بَعْضُهُمْ مِنْ بَعْضٍ فَأَمَّا رَجُلٌ سَلَمُ رَجُلٍ فَإِنَّهُ الْأَوَّلُ حَقّاً وَ شِيعَتُهُ ثُمَّ قَالَ إِنَّ الْيَهُودَ تَفَرَّقُوا مِنْ بَعْدِ مُوسَى (عليه السلام) عَلَى إِحْدَى وَ سَبْعِينَ فِرْقَةً مِنْهَا فِرْقَةٌ فِي الْجَنَّةِ وَ سَبْعُونَ فِرْقَةً فِي النَّارِ وَ تَفَرَّقَتِ النَّصَارَى بَعْدَ عِيسَى (عليه السلام) عَلَى اثْنَتَيْنِ وَ سَبْعِينَ فِرْقَةً فِرْقَةٌ مِنْهَا فِي الْجَنَّةِ وَ إِحْدَى وَ سَبْعُونَ فِي النَّارِ وَ تَفَرَّقَتْ هَذِهِ الْأُمَّةُ بَعْدَ نَبِيِّهَا (صلى الله عليه وآله) عَلَى ثَلَاثٍ وَ سَبْعِينَ فِرْقَةً اثْنَتَانِ وَ سَبْعُونَ فِرْقَةً فِي النَّارِ وَ فِرْقَةٌ فِي الْجَنَّةِ وَ مِنَ الثَّلَاثِ وَ سَبْعِينَ فِرْقَةً ثَلَاثَ عَشْرَةَ فِرْقَةً تَنْتَحِلُ وَلَايَتَنَا وَ مَوَدَّتَنَا اثْنَتَا عَشْرَةَ فِرْقَةً مِنْهَا فِي النَّارِ وَ فِرْقَةٌ فِي الْجَنَّةِ وَ سِتُّونَ فِرْقَةً مِنْ سَائِرِ النَّاسِ فِي النَّارِ

\`Ali b. Ibrahim from his father from b. Abi \`Umayr from \`Umar b. Udhayna from Zurara, al-Fudayl b. Yasar, Bukayr b. A\`yan, Muḥammad b. Muslim, Burayd b. Mu\`awiya and Abu'l Jarud together from Abu Ja\`far عليه السلام.

He said: The Wilāya of \`Ali was an order from Allāh عز وجل to His messenger, and He revealed upon him, "**Verily your guardian is Allāh**, **His messenger**, **and those**

---

[10] *Al-Kāfi, v8, ch283*

who believed – who stand in prayer and give the zakat..." (5:55). And He made the Wilāya of the Possessors of the Command (ulu 'l-amr) obligatory, and they did not understand what it was; so Allāh ordered Muḥammad صلى الله عليه وآله to interpret [and clarify] the Wilāya to them, just as he interpreted salat, zakat, sawm, and Hajj. When Allāh gave that [order] to him, the chest of the Messenger of Allāh صلى الله عليه وآله tightened, and he feared that they would apostatize from their religion and bely him – so his chest tightened. He consulted his Lord عز وجل, so Allāh عز وجل inspired to him, "O Messenger, preach what is revealed to you from your Lord. If you do not preach, it will be as though you have not conveyed My Message, and Allāh will protect you from the people". (5:67) So he executed the command of Allāh تعالى ذكره and declared the Wilāya of `Ali عليه السلام on the day of Ghadeer Khumm. He called for a congregational prayer and commanded the people to bear testimony and inform the absent. `Umar b. Udhayna said: All except Abu'l Jarud said:

And Abu Ja`far عليه السلام said: And an obligation would be revealed after the other, and the Wilāya was the final obligation, so Allāh عز وجل revealed, "Today I have perfected for you your religion and completed my favour..." (5:3). Abu Ja`far عليه السلام said: Allāh عز وجل says: I will not reveal to you any obligation after this – I have completed for you the obligations(حسن)[11]

12.

عَلِيُّ بْنُ إِبْرَاهِيمَ عَنْ أَبِيهِ عَنْ عَبْدِ الْعَزِيزِ بْنِ الْمُهْتَدِي عَنْ عَبْدِ اللهِ بْنِ جُنْدَبٍ أَنَّهُ كَتَبَ إِلَيْهِ الرِّضَا (عَلَيْهِ السَّلام) أَمَّا بَعْدُ فَإِنَّ مُحَمَّداً (صَلَّى اللهُ عَلَيْهِ وَآلِه) كَانَ أَمِينَ اللهِ فِي خَلْقِهِ فَلَمَّا قُبِضَ (صَلَّى اللهُ عَلَيْهِ وَآلِه) كُنَّا أَهْلَ الْبَيْتِ وَرَثَتَهُ فَنَحْنُ أُمَنَاءُ اللهِ فِي أَرْضِهِ عِنْدَنَا عِلْمُ الْبَلايَا وَالْمَنَايَا وَأَنْسَابُ الْعَرَبِ وَمَوْلِدُ الاسْلامِ وَإِنَّا لَنَعْرِفُ الرَّجُلَ إِذَا رَأَيْنَاهُ بِحَقِيقَةِ الايمَانِ وَحَقِيقَةِ النِّفَاقِ وَإِنَّ شِيعَتَنَا لَمَكْتُوبُونَ بِأَسْمَائِهِمْ وَأَسْمَاءِ آبَائِهِمْ أَخَذَ اللهُ عَلَيْنَا وَعَلَيْهِمُ الْمِيثَاقَ يَرِدُونَ مَوْرِدَنَا وَيَدْخُلُونَ مَدْخَلَنَا لَيْسَ عَلَى مِلَّةِ الاسْلامِ غَيْرُنَا وَغَيْرُهُمْ نَحْنُ النُّجَبَاءُ النُّجَاةُ وَنَحْنُ أَفْرَاطُ الانْبِيَاءِ وَنَحْنُ أَبْنَاءُ الاوْصِيَاءِ وَنَحْنُ الْمَخْصُوصُونَ فِي كِتَابِ اللهِ عَزَّ وَجَلَّ وَنَحْنُ أَوْلَى النَّاسِ بِكِتَابِ اللهِ وَنَحْنُ أَوْلَى النَّاسِ بِرَسُولِ اللهِ (صَلَّى اللهُ عَلَيْهِ وَآلِه) وَنَحْنُ الَّذِينَ شَرَعَ اللهُ لَنَا دِينَهُ فَقَالَ

---

[11] *Al-Kāfi, v1, ch64, h4*

فِي كِتَابِهِ شَرَعَ لَكُمْ يَا آلَ مُحَمَّدٍ مِنَ الدِّينِ ما وَصَّى بِهِ نُوحاً قَدْ وَصَّانَا بِمَا وَصَّى بِهِ نُوحاً وَالَّذِي أَوْحَيْنا إِلَيْكَ يَا مُحَمَّدُ وَما وَصَّيْنا بِهِ إِبْراهِيمَ وَمُوسى وَعِيسى فَقَدْ عَلَّمَنَا وَبَلَّغَنَا عِلْمَ مَا عَلِمْنَا وَاسْتَوْدَعَنَا عِلْمَهُمْ نَحْنُ وَرَثَةُ أُولِي الْعَزْمِ مِنَ الرُّسُلِ أَنْ أَقِيمُوا الدِّينَ يَا آلَ مُحَمَّدٍ وَلا تَتَفَرَّقُوا فِيهِ وَكُونُوا عَلَى جَمَاعَةٍ كَبُرَ عَلَى الْمُشْرِكِينَ مَنْ أَشْرَكَ بِوَلايَةِ عَلِيٍّ ما تَدْعُوهُمْ إِلَيْهِ مِنْ وَلايَةِ عَلِيٍّ إِنَّ اللهَ يَا مُحَمَّدُ يَهْدِي إِلَيْهِ مَنْ يُنِيبُ مَنْ يُجِيبُكَ إِلَى وَلايَةِ عَلِيٍّ (عَلَيْهِ السَّلام)

`Ali b. Ibrahim from his father from `Abd al-`Azeez b. al-Muhtadi from `Abdillah b. Jundub that ar-Rida عليه السلام wrote to him:

Thereafter, Muḥammad صلى الله عليه وآله was the trustee of Allāh in His creation. So when he صلى الله عليه وآله passed away, we, the Ahl al-Bayt, inherited from him. Thus, we are the trustees of Allāh in His Earth – with us is the knowledge of suffering and death, the lineages of the Arabs, and the birth of Islam. We know upon seeing a man if he upheld the truth of belief or hypocrisy. Our Shi`a are written [with us] by their names and the names of their fathers; Allāh has taken a covenant upon us and upon them. They respond by our responses and they enter by our entrances; none are upon the creed of Islam besides us and besides them. We are the saviours of salvation and we are the descendants of the prophets. We are the children of the successors and we are the specialists in the Book of Allāh عز وجل. We are the first (i.e. in closeness) of the people to the Book of Allāh and we are the first of the people to the Messenger of Allāh صلى الله عليه وآله. For us He stipulated His religion, as He says in His Book: "He has stipulated for you" – O family of Muḥammad – "the religion which He commended unto Nuh" – we have been given what Nuh was given – "and that which We inspire in you" – O Muḥammad – "and that which We commended unto Ibrahim, Musa, and `Isa" – we have learned and we have been made to know the knowledge that we have and we have been entrusted with their knowledge; we have inherited from the Possessors of Constancy (*ulu 'l `azm*) from the messengers – "Establish the religion" – O family of Muḥammad – "and be not divided therein" – and be upon the majority – "Dreadful for the mushrikeen" – those who associated partners in the *Wilāya* of `Ali – "is that unto which you call them to" – from the *Wilāya* of `Ali – "Verily, Allāh" –

O Muḥammad – "chooses for Himself whom He will" (42:13) – who obey you to [acknowledge] **the *Wilāya* of `Ali** عليه السلام. (حسن)[12]

13.

وَعَنْهُ عَنْ هِشَامِ بْنِ سَالِمٍ عَنْ حَبِيبٍ السِّجِسْتَانِيِّ عَنْ ابي جعفر (عَلَيْهِ السَّلام) قَالَ قَالَ الله تَبَارَكَ وَتَعَالَى لاعَذِّبَنَّ كُلَّ رَعِيَّةٍ فِي الاسْلام دَانَتْ بِوَلايَةِ كُلِّ إِمَامٍ جَائِرٍ لَيْسَ مِنَ الله وَإِنْ كَانَتِ الرَّعِيَّةُ فِي أَعْمَالِهَا بَرَّةً تَقِيَّةً وَلاعْفُوَنَّ عَنْ كُلِّ رَعِيَّةٍ فِي الاسْلامِ دَانَتْ بِوَلايَةِ كُلِّ إِمَامٍ عَادِلٍ مِنَ الله وَإِنْ كَانَتِ الرَّعِيَّةُ فِي أَنْفُسِهَا ظَالِمَةً مُسِيئَةً.

And from him from Hisham b. Salim from HAbib as-Sijistani from Abu Ja`far عليه السلام. He said: Allāh تبارك وتعالى said: I will punish every subject of Islam that commits to the Wilāya of all unjust Imams who are not from Allāh, even if the deeds of the subject are virtuous and pious. And I will forgive every subject of Islam who commits to the Wilāya of all just Imams from Allāh, even if the subject in its nafs was unjust and harmful.
(صحيح)[13]

14.

مُحَمَّدُ بْنُ يَحْيَى عَنْ أَحْمَدَ بْنِ مُحَمَّدِ بْنِ عِيسَى عَنِ ابْنِ مَحْبُوبٍ عَنِ الاحْوَلِ عَنْ سَلامِ بْنِ الْمُسْتَنِيرِ عَنْ ابي جعفر (عَلَيْهِ السَّلام) فِي قَوْلِهِ تَعَالَى قُلْ هذِهِ سَبِيلِي أَدْعُوا إِلَى الله عَلى بَصِيرَةٍ أَنَا وَمَنِ اتَّبَعَنِي قَالَ ذَاكَ رَسُولُ الله (صَلَّى اللهُ عَلَيْهِ وَآلِهِ) وَأَمِيرُ الْمُؤْمِنِينَ (عَلَيْهِ السَّلام) وَالاوْصِيَاءُ مِنْ بَعْدِهِمْ

Muhammad b. Yahya has narrated from Ahmad b. Muḥammad b. 'Isa from b. Mahbub from al-Ahwal from Salam b. al-Mustanir from abu Ja'far (عليه السلام) about the

---

[12] *Al-Kāfi, v1, ch33, h1*

[13] *Al-Kāfi, v1, ch86, h4*

words of Allāh, the Most High. " (Muhammad), say, 'This is my way. I and all my followers invite you to God with proper understanding.. ." (12:108) The Imam (عليه السلام) said, "They are the Messenger of Allāh and Amir al-Mu'minin 'Alī (عليه السلام). (مجهول كالصحيح)[14]

15.

مُحَمَّدُ بْنُ إِسْمَاعِيلَ عَنِ الْفَضْلِ بْنِ شَاذَانَ عَنْ حَمَّادِ بْنِ عِيسَى عَنْ رِبْعِيِّ بْنِ عَبْدِ اللهِ عَنْ ابي جعفر (عَلَيْهِ السَّلام) فِي قَوْلِ اللهِ عَزَّ وَجَلَّ وَلَوْ أَنَّهُمْ أَقامُوا التَّوْراةَ وَالانْجِيلَ وَما أُنْزِلَ إِلَيْهِمْ مِنْ رَبِّهِمْ قَالَ الْوَلايَةُ

Muhammad b. Isma'il has narrated from al-Fadl b. Shadhan from Hammad b. 'Isa from RibIsma'il b. 'AbdAllāh from abu Ja'far (عليه السلام) about the words of Allāh, the Most Majestic, the Most Gracious, "Had they followed the Laws of the Old and New Testaments and what was revealed to them from their Lord,. ." (5:66) The Imam (عليه السلام) said, "It refers to Wilāya, (Leadership with Divine Authority). (مجهول كالصحيح)[15]

16.

مُحَمَّدُ بْنُ يَحْيَى عَنْ أَحْمَدَ بْنِ مُحَمَّدٍ عَنِ ابْنِ مَحْبُوبٍ عَنِ الْحُسَيْنِ بْنِ نُعَيْمٍ الصَّحَّافِ قَالَ سَأَلْتُ أَبَا عَبْدِ اللهِ (عَلَيْهِ السَّلام) عَنْ قَوْلِ اللهِ عَزَّ وَجَلَّ فَمِنْكُمْ كافِرٌ وَمِنْكُمْ مُؤْمِنٌ فَقَالَ عَرَفَ اللهُ إِيمَانَهُمْ بِوَلايَتِنَا وَكُفْرَهُمْ بِهَا يَوْمَ أَخَذَ عَلَيْهِمُ الْمِيثَاقَ فِي صُلْبِ آدَمَ (عَلَيْهِ السَّلام) وَهُمْ ذَرٌّ

Muhammad b. Yahya has narrated from from Ahmad b. Muḥammad from b. Mahbub from al-Hassan b. Nu'aym al-Sahhaf who has said the following. "I asked abu 'AbdAllāh (عليه السلام) about the words of Allāh, the Most Majestic, the Most gracious. ". some of you have accepted the faith and some of you have not.. ." (64:2)

---

[14] *Al-Kāfi, v1, ch 108, h65*

[15] *Al-Kāfi, v1, ch108, h6*

The Imam (عليه السلام) said, "On the day that Allāh made all the offspring of Adam to make a covenant with Him when **they were just small particles He made faith our Wilāya**, (Leadership with Divine Authority) the standard for faith and disbelief. (حسن)[16]

17.

مُحَمَّدُ بْنُ يَحْيَى عَنْ أَحْمَدَ بْنِ مُحَمَّدٍ عَنْ أَحْمَدَ بْنِ مُحَمَّدِ بْنِ أَبِي نَصْرٍ قَالَ سَأَلْتُ أَبَا الْحَسَنِ الرِّضَا (عَلَيهِ السَّلام) عَنْ مَسْأَلَةٍ فَأَبَى وَأَمْسَكَ ثُمَّ قَالَ لَوْ أَعْطَيْنَاكُمْ كُلَّمَا تُرِيدُونَ كَانَ شَرّاً لَكُمْ وَأُخِذَ بِرَقَبَةِ صَاحِبِ هَذَا الأَمْرِ قَالَ أَبُو جَعْفَرٍ (عَلَيهِ السَّلام) وَلايَةُ اللهِ أَسَرَّهَا إِلَى جَبْرَئِيلَ (عَلَيهِ السَّلام) وَأَسَرَّهَا جَبْرَئِيلُ إِلَى مُحَمَّدٍ (صَلَّى اللهُ عَلَيْهِ وآلِه) وَأَسَرَّهَا مُحَمَّدٌ إِلَى عَلِيٍّ (عَلَيهِ السَّلام) وَأَسَرَّهَا عَلِيٌّ إِلَى مَنْ شَاءَ اللهُ ثُمَّ أَنْتُمْ تُذِيعُونَ ذَلِكَ مَنِ الَّذِي أَمْسَكَ حَرْفاً سَمِعَهُ قَالَ أَبُو جَعْفَرٍ (عَلَيهِ السَّلام) فِي حِكْمَةِ آلِ دَاوُدَ يَنْبَغِي لِلْمُسْلِمِ أَنْ يَكُونَ مَالِكاً لِنَفْسِهِ مُقْبِلاً عَلَى شَأْنِهِ عَارِفاً بِأَهْلِ زَمَانِهِ فَاتَّقُوا اللهَ وَلا تُذِيعُوا حَدِيثَنَا فَلَوْ لا أَنَّ اللهَ يُدَافِعُ عَنْ أَوْلِيَائِهِ وَيَنْتَقِمُ لأَوْلِيَائِهِ مِنْ أَعْدَائِهِ أَ مَا رَأَيْتَ مَا صَنَعَ اللهُ بِآلِ بَرْمَكَ وَمَا انْتَقَمَ اللهُ لأَبِي الْحَسَنِ (عَلَيهِ السَّلام) وَقَدْ كَانَ بَنُو الأَشْعَثِ عَلَى خَطَرٍ عَظِيمٍ فَدَفَعَ اللهُ عَنْهُمْ بِوَلايَتِهِمْ لأَبِي الْحَسَنِ (عَلَيهِ السَّلام) وَأَنْتُمْ بِالْعِرَاقِ تَرَوْنَ أَعْمَالَ هَؤُلاءِ الْفَرَاعِنَةِ وَمَا أَمْهَلَ اللهُ لَهُمْ فَعَلَيْكُمْ بِتَقْوَى اللهِ وَلا تَغُرَّنَّكُمُ الْحَيَاةُ الدُّنْيَا وَلا تَغْتَرُّوا بِمَنْ قَدْ أُمْهِلَ لَهُ فَكَأَنَّ الأَمْرَ قَدْ وَصَلَ إِلَيْكُمْ

Muhammad b. Yahya from Ahmad b. Muḥammad from Ahmad b. Muḥammad b. Abi Nasr. He said: I asked Abu'l Hasan ar-Rida a question, so he refrained silently. Then, he said: If I were to give you all that you want, it would be evil for you and it would take the Patron of this Affair by his neck. Abu Ja`far عليه السلام said:

The *Wilāya* of Allāh was discretely told to Jibra'il عليه السلام, Jibra'il discretely told it to Muḥammad صلى الله عليه وآله , Muḥammad discretely told it to `Ali, and `Ali discretely told it to whoever Allāh willed. Then, you publicize it! Who is he that has withheld a letter of that which he had heard? Abu Ja`far عليه السلام said: It is in the wisdom of the Family of Dawud. It is necessary for a Muslim to have control over his self, to be attentive to what concerns him, and to have knowledge of the people of his

---

[16] *Al-Kāfi, v1, ch108, h4*

time; so fear Allāh and do not publicize our Hadīth (i.e. to the point of endangering Ahl al-Bayt and their message). Verily, Allāh defends His awliyya' and exacts recompense for His *awliyya'* upon His enemies. Have you not seen how Allāh dealt with the Family of Barmak, and how He recompensed for Abu'l Hasan عليه السلام when the Banu al-Ash`ath faced the great danger and Allāh defended them for their support of Abu'l Hasan عليه السلام? And in Iraq you are aware of the actions of these Pharaohs and the respite that Allāh has given to them. So, you must fear Allāh, and do not allow the worldly life to deceive you. And do not be confused about those who have been given respite. It is as if the Affair has [almost] arrived to you (صحيح)[17]

18.

عِدَّةٌ مِنْ أَصْحَابِنَا عَنْ أَحْمَدَ بْنِ مُحَمَّدِ بْنِ عِيسَى عَنِ ابْنِ مَحْبُوبٍ عَنْ هِشَامِ بْنِ سَالِمٍ عَنْ يَزِيدَ الْكُنَاسِيِّ قَالَ سَأَلْتُ أَبَا جَعْفَرٍ (عَلَيْهِ السَّلام) أَ كَانَ عِيسَى ابْنُ مَرْيَمَ (عَلَيْهِ السَّلام) حِينَ تَكَلَّمَ فِي الْمَهْدِ حُجَّةَ اللهِ عَلَى أَهْلِ زَمَانِهِ فَقَالَ كَانَ يَوْمَئِذٍ نَبِيّاً حُجَّةَ اللهِ غَيْرَ مُرْسَلٍ أَ مَا تَسْمَعُ لِقَوْلِهِ حِينَ قَالَ إِنِّي عَبْدُ اللهِ آتانِيَ الْكِتابَ وَجَعَلَنِي نَبِيًّا. وَجَعَلَنِي مُبارَكاً أَيْنَ ما كُنْتُ وَأَوْصانِي بِالصَّلاةِ وَالزَّكاةِ ما دُمْتُ حَيًّا قُلْتُ فَكَانَ يَوْمَئِذٍ حُجَّةً لله عَلَى زَكَرِيَّا فِي تِلْكَ الْحَالِ وَهُوَ فِي الْمَهْدِ فَقَالَ كَانَ عِيسَى فِي تِلْكَ الْحَالِ آيَةً لِلنَّاسِ وَرَحْمَةً مِنَ اللهِ لِمَرْيَمَ حِينَ تَكَلَّمَ فَعَبَّرَ عَنْهَا وَكَانَ نَبِيّاً حُجَّةً عَلَى مَنْ سَمِعَ كَلَامَهُ فِي تِلْكَ الْحَالِ ثُمَّ صَمَتَ فَلَمْ يَتَكَلَّمْ حَتَّى مَضَتْ لَهُ سَنَتَانِ وَكَانَ زَكَرِيَّا الْحُجَّةَ لله عَزَّ وَجَلَّ عَلَى النَّاسِ بَعْدَ صَمْتِ عِيسَى بِسَنَتَيْنِ ثُمَّ مَاتَ زَكَرِيَّا فَوَرِثَهُ ابْنُهُ يَحْيَى الْكِتَابَ وَالْحِكْمَةَ وَهُوَ صَبِيٌّ صَغِيرٌ أَ مَا تَسْمَعُ لِقَوْلِهِ عَزَّ وَجَلَّ يا يَحْيى خُذِ الْكِتابَ بِقُوَّةٍ وَآتَيْناهُ الْحُكْمَ صَبِيًّا فَلَمَّا بَلَغَ عِيسَى (عَلَيْهِ السَّلام) سَبْعَ سِنِينَ تَكَلَّمَ بِالنُّبُوَّةِ وَالرِّسَالَةِ حِينَ أَوْحَى اللهُ تَعَالَى إِلَيْهِ فَكَانَ عِيسَى الْحُجَّةَ عَلَى يَحْيَى وَعَلَى النَّاسِ أَجْمَعِينَ وَلَيْسَ تَبْقَى الارْضُ يَا أَبَا خَالِدٍ يَوْماً وَاحِداً بِغَيْرِ حُجَّةٍ لله عَلَى النَّاسِ مُنْذُ يَوْمَ خَلَقَ اللهُ آدَمَ (عَلَيْهِ السَّلام) وَأَسْكَنَهُ الارْضَ فَقُلْتُ جُعِلْتُ فِدَاكَ أَ كَانَ عَلِيٌّ (عَلَيْهِ السَّلام) حُجَّةً مِنَ اللهِ وَرَسُولِهِ عَلَى هَذِهِ الامَّةِ فِي حَيَاةِ رَسُولِ اللهِ (صَلَّى اللهُ عَلَيْهِ وَآلِه) فَقَالَ نَعَمْ يَوْمَ أَقَامَهُ لِلنَّاسِ وَنَصَبَهُ عَلَماً وَدَعَاهُمْ إِلَى وَلَايَتِهِ وَأَمَرَهُمْ بِطَاعَتِهِ قُلْتُ وَكَانَتْ طَاعَةُ عَلِيٍّ (عَلَيْهِ السَّلام) وَاجِبَةً عَلَى النَّاسِ فِي حَيَاةِ رَسُولِ اللهِ (صَلَّى اللهُ عَلَيْهِ وَآلِه) وَبَعْدَ وَفَاتِهِ فَقَالَ نَعَمْ وَلَكِنَّهُ صَمَتَ فَلَمْ يَتَكَلَّمْ مَعَ رَسُولِ اللهِ (صَلَّى اللهُ عَلَيْهِ وَآلِه) وَكَانَتِ الطَّاعَةُ لِرَسُولِ اللهِ (صَلَّى اللهُ عَلَيْهِ وَآلِه) عَلَى أُمَّتِهِ وَعَلَى عَلِيٍّ (عَلَيْهِ السَّلام) فِي حَيَاةِ رَسُولِ اللهِ

---

[17] *Al-Kāfi, v2, ch98, h10*

(صَلَّى اللهُ عَلَيْهِ وَآلِه) وَكَانَتِ الطَّاعَةُ مِنَ اللهِ وَمِنْ رَسُولِهِ عَلَى النَّاسِ كُلِّهِمْ لِعلي (عَلَيْهِ السَّلام) بَعْدَ وَفَاةِ رَسُولِ الله (صَلَّى اللهُ عَلَيْهِ وَآلِه) وَكَانَ علي (عَلَيْهِ السَّلام) حَكِيماً عَالِماً

Several of our companions from Ahmad b. Muhammad b. `Isa from b. Mahbub from Hisham b. Salim from Yazid al-Kunasi. He said: I asked Abu Ja`far عليه السلام: Was `Isa b. Maryam عليه السلام like you (i.e. a hujja) in the cradle over the people of his era? So he said: On that day, he was a prophet and a hujja of Allāh, but not a messenger. Have you not heard His saying, when he said, "I am the slave of Allāh, He has given me the Book and has appointed me to be a prophet" (19:30)? I said: So on that day he was the hujja of Allāh over Zakariyya in that state, and he was in the cradle? So he said: In that state, `Isa was a sign to the people, and a mercy from Allāh to Maryam when he spoke on her behalf. He was a prophet and a hujja over whoever heard his words in that state. Then he went silent and did not speak until he was two years of age. And Zakariyya was the hujja of Allāh عزوجل over the people after `Isa went silent for two years. Then, Zakariyya died, and his son Yahya inherited the Book and wisdom whilst he was a small boy. Have you not heard His عزوجل saying, "O Yahya, take the Book with strength; and We gave him wisdom as a child" (19:12). When `Isa عليه السلام became seven years of age, he spoke by prophethood and messengership when Allāh تعالى divinely inspired him, and so `Isa became the hujja over Yahya and over all people. And the Earth does not remain, O Abu Khalid, for one day without a hujja of Allāh over the people from the day Allāh created Adam عليه السلام and settled him on the Earth. So I said: May I be your ransom, was `Ali عليه السلام a hujja from Allāh and His Messenger above this Umma during the lifetime of the Messenger of Allāh صلى الله عليه وآله? So he said: Yes, on the day he (i.e. the Prophet) raised him before the people, and appointed him and called them to his Wilāya and commanded them to his obedience. I said: And was obedience to `Ali عليه السلام obligatory upon the people in the lifetime of the Messenger of Allāh صلى الله عليه وآله and after his passing? So he said: Yes, but he was silent and did not speak alongside the Messenger of Allāh صلى الله عليه وآله, as the obedience to the Messenger of Allāh صلى الله عليه وآله was over his Umma and over `Ali عليه السلام in the lifetime of the Messenger of Allāh صلى الله عليه وآله. And the obedience of Allāh and of His Messenger over all the people went to `Ali عليه السلام

after the passing of the Messenger of Allāh صلى الله عليه وآله; and `Ali عليه السلام was wise and knowledgeable. (كالصحيح)[18]

(The last two Hadīths of this chapter will be dedicated to Hadīth al-Thaqalayn(Two weighty things), the Hadīth that makes up the core of our madhab and paves the way to our salvation)

19.

حدثنا محمد بن الحسن بن أحمد بن الوليد رضي الله عنه قال :حدثنا محمد بن الحسن الصفار، عن محمد بن الحسين بن أبي الخطاب، ويعقوب بن يزيد جميعا، عن محمد بن أبي عمير، عن عبد الله بن سنان، عن معروف بن خربوذ، عن أبيالطفيل عامر بن واثلة، عن حذيفة بن أسيد الغفاري قال :لما رجع رسول الله صلى الله عليه وآله من حجة الوداع ونحن معه أقبل حتى انتهى إلى الجحفة فأمر أصحابه بالنزول فنزل القوم منازلهم، ثم نودي بالصلاة فصلى بأصحابه ركعتين، ثم أقبل بوجهه إليهم فقال لهم :إنه قد نبأني اللطيف الخبير أني ميت وأنكم ميتون، وكأني قد دعيت فاجبت وأني مسؤول عما ارسلت به إليكم، وعما خلفت فيكم من كتاب الله وحجته وأنكم مسؤولون، فما أنتم قائلون لربكم؟ قالوا :نقول :قد بلغت ونصحت وجاهدت فجزاك الله عنا أفضل الجزاء ثم قال لهم :ألستم تشهدون أن لا إله إلا الله وأني رسول الله إليكم وأن الجنة حق؟ وأن النار حق؟ وأن البعث بعد الموت حق؟ فقالوا :نشهد بذلك، قال :اللهم اشهد على ما يقولون، ألا وإني اشهدكم أني أشهد أن الله مولاي، وأنا مولى كل مسلم، وأنا أولى بالمؤمنين من أنفسهم، فهل تقرون لي ،بذلك، وتشهدون لي به؟ فقالوا :نعم نشهد لك بذلك، فقال: ألا من كنت مولاه فإن عليا مولاه وهو هذا ثم أخذ بيد علي عليه السلام فرفعها مع يده حتى بدت آباطهما :ثم: قال :اللهم وال من والاه، وعاد من عاداه، وانصر من نصره واخذل من خذله، ألا وإني فرطكم وأنتم واردون علي الحوض، حوضي غدا وهو حوض عرضه ما بين بصرى وصنعاء فيه أقداح من فضة عدد نجوم السماء، ألا وإني سائلكم غدا ماذا صنعتم فيما أشهدت الله به عليكم في يومكم هذا إذا وردتم علي حوضي، وماذا صنعتم بالثقلين من بعدي فانظروا كيف تكونون خلفتموني فيهما حين تلقوني؟ قالوا :وما هذان الثقلان يا رسول الله؟ قال :أما الثقل الاكبر فكتاب الله عز وجل، سبب ممدود من الله ومني في أيديكم، طرفه بيد الله والطرف الآخر بأيديكم، فيه علم ما مضى وما بقي إلى أن تقوم الساعة، وأما الثقل الاصغر فهو حليف القرآن وهو علي بن أبي طالب وعترته عليهم السلام، وإنهما لن يفترقا حتى يردا علي الحوضقال معروف بن خربوذ :فعرضت هذا الكلام

---

[18] *Al-Kāfi, v1, ch91, h1*

على أبي جعفر عليه السلام فقال :صدق أبوالطفيل - رحمه الله - هذا الكلام وجدناه في كتاب علي عليه السلام وعرفناهوحدثنا أبي رضي الله عنه قال :حدثنا علي بن إبراهيم، عن أبيه، عن محمد بن أبي عمير. وحدثنا جعفر بن محمد بن مسرور رضي الله عنه قال :حدثنا الحسين بن محمد ابن عامر، عن عمه عبد الله بن عامر، عن محمد بن أبي عمير .وحدثنا محمد بن موسى بن المتوكل رضي الله عنه قال :حدثنا علي بن الحسين السعد آبادي، عن أحمد بن أبي عبد الله البرقي، عن أبيه، عن محمد بن أبي عمير، عن عبد الله بن سنان، عن معروف بن خربوذ، عن أبي الطفيل عامر بن واثلة، عن حذيفة بن أسيد الغفاري بمثل هذا الحديث سواءقال مصنف هذا الكتاب أدام الله عزه :الاخبار في هذا المعنى كثيرة وقد أخرجتها في كتاب المعرفة في الفضائل

Muhammad b. al-Hasan b. Ahmad b. al-Walid from Muḥammad b. al-Hasan al-Saffar from Muḥammad b. al-Husayn b. Abi al-Khattab and Ya`qub b. Yazid from Muḥammad b. Abi Umayr from AbdAllāh b. Sinan from Ma`ruf b. Kharrabudh from Abi Tufayl `Amir b. Wathila from Hudhayfa b. Asid al-Ghiffari who said: We were with the messenger of Allāh صلى الله عليه وآله when he was returning from his farewell pilgrimage. He went forth until he reached Juhfa where he ordered his companions to decamp. The call for prayer was made and he led his companions in a two-unit prayer. After that he turned his face to them and said: The Kind and All-Aware has informed me that I am to die and you too will one day die. It is as though I have been called and have responded. I am to be asked about that which I was sent with for you and also what I leave behind in your midst including the Book of Allāh and His proof – and you too shall be asked – so what are you going to reply to your Lord? They said: we will say 'you have conveyed, counselled and struggled, so may Allāh reward you on our behalf the best of rewards'. Then he said to them: do you bear witness that there is no God but Allāh and that I am the messenger of Allāh? that the Paradise is a reality, the Fire is a reality and the resurrection after death is reality? They said: we bear witness to that, he said: O Allāh witness what they say. **Behold! I make you witnesses that I myself bear witness that Allāh is my Mawla, and that I am the Mawla of every Muslim, and that I have a greater claim over the believers than their own selves, do you admit to that and bear witness to it about me?**

They said: yes, we witness that to be true about you. He said: Behold! To whomsoever I am a Mawla then ʿAlī is also his Mawla, and he is this one, and he took ʿAlī by the hand and raised it with his own hand until their armpits became visible, then he said: **O Allāh – be a guardian to whomever takes him to be a guardian, and be an enemy to whomever takes him to be an enemy, aid the one who aids him and abandon the one who abandons him**. Behold! I will proceed you but you will catch up with me at the reservoir – my Lake-fount – tomorrow. It is a Lake-fount whose breadth is like the distance between Busra and San`a. In it are goblets made of silver like the number of stars in the sky. Behold! I will ask you tomorrow about what you did in regards that which I made Allāh bear witness to – over you – in this day of yours when you reach my Lake-fount. And also about what you did with regards the 'Two Weighty Things' after me, so take care of how you will preserve my legacy in them when you meet me. They said: and **what are these 'Two Weighty Things'** O the messenger of Allāh? he said: as for **the greater weighty thing then it is the Book of Allāh Mighty and Majestic**, a rope extending from Allāh and myself in your hands, one end of it is by the hand of Allāh and the other end is in your hands, in it is the knowledge of what has passed and what is left until the Hour comes. As for **the smaller weighty thing it is the ally of the Qur`an, and that is ʿAlī b. Abi Talib and his descendants عليهم السلام – the two will not separate until they return to me at the Lake-fount**. Ma`ruf b. Kharrabudh said: I relayed these words to Abi Ja`far عليه السلام so he said: Abu Tufayl has spoken the truth – may Allāh have mercy on him – we have found this speech in the book of ʿAlī and do recognize it. (صحيح)[19]

20.

[19] *Al-Khiṣāl, ch81, h1*

قال رسول الله صلى الله عليه وآله :إني تارك فيكم الثقلين ما إن تمسكتم بهما لن تضلوا بعدي :كتاب الله وعترتي

The messenger of Allāh صلى الله عليه وآله said: I leave behind in your midst the **two weighty things**, as long you hold on to them you will not go astray after me: **the Book of Allāh** and **my descendants(Ahl al-Bayt)**. (صحيح)[20]

I pray that Allāh raises us all under the banner of the Ahl al-Bayt, and keeps us steadfast upon their Wilāyah

---

[20] *Kitāb al-Irshād(Mufid)*

باب القرآن الكريم

Chapter on the Holy Qur'ān

1.

عَلِيٌّ عَنْ أَبِيهِ عَنْ عَبْدِ اللهِ بْنِ الْمُغِيرَةِ عَنْ سَمَاعَةَ بْنِ مِهْرَانَ قَالَ قَالَ أَبُو عَبْدِ اللهِ (عَلَيهِ السَّلام) إِنَّ الْعَزِيزَ الْجَبَّارَ أَنْزَلَ عَلَيْكُمْ كِتَابَهُ وَهُوَ الصَّادِقُ الْبَارُّ فِيهِ خَبَرُكُمْ وَخَبَرُ مَنْ قَبْلَكُمْ وَخَبَرُ مَنْ بَعْدَكُمْ وَخَبَرُ السَّمَاءِ وَالْأَرْضِ وَلَوْ أَتَاكُمْ مَنْ يُخْبِرُكُمْ عَنْ ذَلِكَ لَتَعَجَّبْتُمْ

Ali b. Ibrahim has narrated from his father from 'Abd Allāh b. al-Mughirah from Sama'a b. Mehran who has said the following: "Abu 'Abd (عليه السلام) has said, the Majestic, the Almighty, has revealed to you His book. It is truthful and virtuous. In it there is news about you, the news of those before you, the news about those after you, the news about the heaven and earth and if one brings you such news, you are astonished. (حسن أو موثق) [1]

2.

---

[1] *Al-Kāfi, v2, ch1, h3*

حُمَيْدُ بْنُ زِيَادٍ عَنِ الْحَسَنِ بْنِ مُحَمَّدٍ عَنْ وُهَيْبِ بْنِ حَفْصٍ عَنْ أَبِي بَصِيرٍ قَالَ سَمِعْتُ أَبَا عَبْدِ اللهِ (عَلَيهِ السَّلام) يَقُولُ إِنَّ الْقُرْآنَ زَاجِرٌ وَآمِرٌ يَأْمُرُ بِالْجَنَّةِ وَيَزْجُرُ عَنِ النَّارِ

Hamid has narrated from al-Hassan b. m h from Wuhayb b. Hafs from abu Basir who has said the following: "I heard abu 'Abd Allāh (عليه السلام) saying, 'The Holy Qur'ān forbids and commands, it commands (people to go) to paradise and prohibits (people from going) to the fire. (موثق)[2]

3.

عَلِيُّ بْنُ إِبْرَاهِيمَ عَنْ أَبِيهِ عَنِ ابْنِ أَبِي عُمَيْرٍ عَنْ إِبْرَاهِيمَ بْنِ عَبْدِ الْحَمِيدِ عَنْ إِسْحَاقَ بْنِ غَالِبٍ قَالَ قَالَ أَبُو عَبْدِ اللهِ (عَلَيهِ السَّلام) إِذَا جَمَعَ اللهُ عَزَّ وَجَلَّ الْأَوَّلِينَ وَالْآخِرِينَ إِذَا هُمْ بِشَخْصٍ قَدْ أَقْبَلَ لَمْ يُرَ قَطُّ أَحْسَنُ صُورَةً مِنْهُ فَإِذَا نَظَرَ إِلَيْهِ الْمُؤْمِنُونَ وَهُوَ الْقُرْآنُ قَالُوا هَذَا مِنَّا هَذَا أَحْسَنُ شَيْءٍ رَأَيْنَا فَإِذَا انْتَهَى إِلَيْهِمْ جَازَهُمْ ثُمَّ يَنْظُرُ إِلَيْهِ الشُّهَدَاءُ حَتَّى إِذَا انْتَهَى إِلَى آخِرِهِمْ جَازَهُمْ فَيَقُولُونَ هَذَا الْقُرْآنُ فَيَجُوزُهُمْ كُلَّهُمْ حَتَّى إِذَا انْتَهَى إِلَى الْمُرْسَلِينَ فَيَقُولُونَ هَذَا الْقُرْآنُ فَيَجُوزُهُمْ حَتَّى يَنْتَهِيَ إِلَى الْمَلَائِكَةِ فَيَقُولُونَ هَذَا الْقُرْآنُ فَيَجُوزُهُمْ ثُمَّ يَنْتَهِي حَتَّى يَقِفَ عَنْ يَمِينِ الْعَرْشِ فَيَقُولُ الْجَبَّارُ وَعِزَّتِي وَجَلَالِي وَارْتِفَاعِ مَكَانِي لَأُكْرِمَنَّ الْيَوْمَ مَنْ أَكْرَمَكَ وَلَأُهِينَنَّ مَنْ أَهَانَكَ

Ali b. Ibrahim has narrated from his father b. abu 'Umayr from Ibrahim b. 'Abd al-Hamid from Ishaq b. Ghalib who has said the following: "Abu 'Abd Allāh (عليه السلام) has said, 'When Allāh, the Most Majestic, the Most Holy, will gather together all the people of the past and later generation, a person the like of whom in beauty has never been seen will appear. The believing people will look at him (the Holy Qur'ān) and say, 'This is one of us, the best that we have ever seen. He will come to them and pass them. The martyrs will look at him, and he will pass them until the last one among them and they will say, 'This is the Holy Qur'ān.' He will pass all of them toward the messengers who will say, 'This is the Holy Qur'ān,' he will pass them toward the angels who will say, 'This is the Holy Qur'ān,' and he will pass them until he will

---

[2] *Al-Kāfi, v2, ch1, h9*

approach the right side of the Throne and stand up at that point. The Almighty will say, 'I swear by my Majesty and Glory, and High status, this day I will honor those who had honored him and bring low those who had disregarded him (حسن أو موثق)[3]

4.

عِدَّةٌ مِنْ أَصْحَابِنَا عَنْ أَحْمَدَ بْنِ مُحَمَّدٍ وَسَهْلِ بْنِ زِيَادٍ جَمِيعاً عَنِ ابْنِ مَحْبُوبٍ عَنْ جَمِيلِ بْنِ صَالِحٍ عَنِ الْفُضَيْلِ بْنِ يَسَارٍ عَنْ أَبِي عَبْدِ اللهِ (عَلَيهِ السَّلام) قَالَ الْحَافِظُ لِلْقُرْآنِ الْعَامِلُ بِهِ مَعَ السَّفَرَةِ الْكِرَامِ الْبَرَرَةِ

A number of our people have narrated from Ahmad b. Muḥammad from Sahl b. Ziyad all from b. Mahbub from Jamil b. Salih from al-Fudayl b. Yasar from abu 'Abd Allāh (عليه السلام) who has said the following: "One who has memorized the Holy Qur'ān and follows its laws will be with the honorable angels who carry Allāh's messages. (صحيح)[4]

5.

وَبِإِسْنَادِهِ عَنْ أَبِي عَبْدِ اللهِ (عَلَيهِ السَّلام) قَالَ قَالَ رَسُولُ اللهِ (صَلَّى اللهُ عَلَيهِ وآلِه) تَعَلَّمُوا الْقُرْآنَ فَإِنَّهُ يَأْتِي يَوْمَ الْقِيَامَةِ صَاحِبَهُ فِي صُورَةِ شَابٍّ جَمِيلٍ شَاحِبِ اللَّوْنِ فَيَقُولُ لَهُ الْقُرْآنُ أَنَا الَّذِي كُنْتُ أَسْهَرْتُ لَيْلَكَ وَأَظْمَأْتُ هَوَاجِرَكَ وَأَجْفَفْتُ رِيقَكَ وَأَسَلْتُ دَمْعَتَكَ أَؤُولُ مَعَكَ حَيْثُمَا أُلْتَ وَكُلُّ تَاجِرٍ مِنْ وَرَاءِ تِجَارَتِهِ وَأَنَا الْيَوْمَ لَكَ مِنْ وَرَاءِ تِجَارَةِ كُلِّ تَاجِرٍ وَسَيَأْتِيكَ كَرَامَةٌ مِنَ اللهِ عَزَّ وَجَلَّ فَأَبْشِرْ فَيُؤْتَى بِتَاجٍ فَيُوضَعُ عَلَى رَأْسِهِ وَيُعْطَى الأَمَانَ بِيَمِينِهِ وَالْخُلْدَ فِي الْجِنَانِ بِيَسَارِهِ وَيُكْسَى حُلَّتَيْنِ ثُمَّ يُقَالُ لَهُ اقْرَأْ وَارْقَهْ فَكُلَّمَا قَرَأَ آيَةً صَعِدَ دَرَجَةً وَيُكْسَى أَبَوَاهُ حُلَّتَيْنِ إِنْ كَانَا مُؤْمِنَيْنِ ثُمَّ يُقَالُ لَهُمَا هَذَا لِمَا عَلَّمْتُمَاهُ الْقُرْآنَ

Through the same chain of narrators it is narrated from abu 'Abd Allāh (عليه السلام) who has said the following: "The Messenger of Allāh has said, 'Learn the Holy Qur'ān; on

---

[3] *Al-Kafi, v2, ch1,h14*

[4] *Al-Kafi, v2, ch2, h2*

the Day of Judgment it will come to his friends in the form of a most beautiful young person of pale complexion and will speak to his friend saying, "I am the Qur'ān for which you kept awake so often and endured thirst during the heat of midday, dried up your mouth and let your tears flow. I will be with you whenever you will go. Every trader is after his trade. Today I look after the trade of everyone who had a deal with me. Honor will come to you from Allāh, the Most Majestic, the Most Holy, as good news for you. The man will receive a crown and peace will be placed on his right hand and eternal life in paradise in his left hand and he will be dressed with two dresses of paradise, then he will be told, 'Read and climb.' For each verse that he will read he will climb up one degree and his parents, if they are of the believers, will each receive two dresses of paradise and they will be told that this is for your teaching the Holy Qur'ān to your child. (صحيح)[5]

6.

عِدَّةٌ مِنْ أَصْحَابِنَا عَنْ أَحْمَدَ بْنِ مُحَمَّدٍ وَسَهْلِ بْنِ زِيَادٍ جَمِيعاً عَنِ ابْنِ مَحْبُوبٍ عَنْ جَمِيلِ بْنِ صَالِحٍ عَنِ الْفُضَيْلِ بْنِ يَسَارٍ عَنْ أَبِي عَبْدِ اللهِ (عَلَيهِ السَّلام) قَالَ سَمِعْتُهُ يَقُولُ إِنَّ الَّذِي يُعَالِجُ الْقُرْآنَ وَيَحْفَظُهُ بِمَشَقَّةٍ مِنْهُ وَقِلَّةِ حِفْظٍ لَهُ أَجْرَانِ

A number of our people have narrated from Ahmad b. Muḥammad and Sahl b. Ziyad all from b. Mahbub from Jamil b. Salih from al-Fudayl b. Yasar who has said the following: "I heard abu 'Abd Allāh (عليه السلام) saying, 'Those who face difficulty memorizing the Holy Qur'ān due to lesser ability of memorization will be rewarded twofold. (صحيح)[6]

7.

[5] *al-Kāfi, v2, ch2, h3*

[6] *Al-Kāfi, v2, ch3, h1*

مُحَمَّدُ بْنُ يَحْيَى عَنْ أَحْمَدَ بْنِ مُحَمَّدِ بْنِ عِيسَى عَنْ مُحَمَّدِ بْنِ خَالِدٍ وَالْحُسَيْنِ بْنِ سَعِيدٍ جَمِيعاً عَنِ النَّضْرِ بْنِ سُوَيْدٍ عَنْ يَحْيَى الْحَلَبِيِّ عَنْ عَبْدِ اللهِ بْنِ مُسْكَانَ عَنْ يَعْقُوبَ الأَحْمَرِ قَالَ قُلْتُ لأَبِي عَبْدِ اللهِ (عَلَيهِ السَّلام) جُعِلْتُ فِدَاكَ إِنَّهُ أَصَابَتْنِي هُمُومٌ وَأَشْيَاءُ لَمْ يَبْقَ شَيْءٌ مِنَ الْخَيْرِ إِلا وَقَدْ تَفَلَّتَ مِنِّي مِنْهُ طَائِفَةٌ حَتَّى الْقُرْآنِ لَقَدْ تَفَلَّتَ مِنِّي طَائِفَةٌ مِنْهُ قَالَ فَفَزِعَ عِنْدَ ذَلِكَ حِينَ ذَكَرْتُ الْقُرْآنَ ثُمَّ قَالَ إِنَّ الرَّجُلَ لَيَنْسَى السُّورَةَ مِنَ الْقُرْآنِ فَتَأْتِيهِ يَوْمَ الْقِيَامَةِ حَتَّى تُشْرِفَ عَلَيْهِ مِنْ دَرَجَةٍ مِنْ بَعْضِ الدَّرَجَاتِ فَتَقُولُ السَّلامُ عَلَيْكَ فَيَقُولُ وَعَلَيْكِ السَّلامُ مَنْ أَنْتِ فَتَقُولُ أَنَا سُورَةُ كَذَا وَكَذَا ضَيَّعْتَنِي وَتَرَكْتَنِي أَمَا لَوْ تَمَسَّكْتَ بِي بَلَغْتُ بِكَ هَذِهِ الدَّرَجَةَ ثُمَّ أَشَارَ بِإِصْبَعِهِ ثُمَّ قَالَ عَلَيْكُمْ بِالْقُرْآنِ فَتَعَلَّمُوهُ فَإِنَّ مِنَ النَّاسِ مَنْ يَتَعَلَّمُ الْقُرْآنَ لِيُقَالَ فُلانٌ قَارِئٌ وَمِنْهُمْ مَنْ يَتَعَلَّمُهُ فَيَطْلُبُ بِهِ الصَّوْتَ فَيُقَالُ فُلانٌ حَسَنُ الصَّوْتِ وَلَيْسَ فِي ذَلِكَ خَيْرٌ وَمِنْهُمْ مَنْ يَتَعَلَّمُهُ فَيَقُومُ بِهِ فِي لَيْلِهِ وَنَهَارِهِ لا يُبَالِي مَنْ عَلِمَ ذَلِكَ وَمَنْ لَمْ يَعْلَمْهُ

Muhammad b. Yahya has narrated from Ahmad b. Muḥammad b. 'Isa from Muḥammad b. Khalid and al-Husayn b. Sa'id all from al-Nadr b. Suwayd from Yahya al-Halabi from 'Abd Allāh b. Muskan from Ya'qub al-Ahmar who has said the following: "Once I said to abu 'Abd Allāh (عليه السلام) 'May Allāh keep my soul in service for your cause, I am facing such problems and difficulties that I forget so many good things even some of the Holy Qur'ān.' The Imam was shocked upon my mentioning the Holy Qur'ān and said, 'If a man forgets a chapter of the Holy Qur'ān, on the Day of Judgment that chapter will appear to him with a certain rank and offers him the greeting of peace. The man will ask, 'Who are you?' The chapter of the Holy Qur'ān will say, 'I am chapter so and so of the Holy Qur'ān which you forgot, and I wish you had not forgotten me; today I could have taken you to such and such high ranks. He will point to a certain rank.' The Imam then said, 'You must hold fast to the Holy Qur'ān and learn it. Certain people learn the Holy Qur'ān so that others call him a very good reader of the Holy Qur'ān. Others learn the Holy Qur'ān so that people praise him for his vocal attractiveness in reciting the Holy Qur'ān. There is nothing good in all of this. Certain people learn the Holy Qur'ān and at night they stand upon their feet with the Holy Qur'ān as well as during the day and they are not concerned whether others know this about them or not. (صحيح)[7]

---

[7] *Al-Kāfi, v2, ch4, h6*

8.

عَلِيٌّ عَنْ أَبِيهِ عَنْ حَمَّادٍ عَنْ حَرِيزٍ عَنْ أَبِي عَبْدِ اللهِ (عَلَيهِ السَّلام) قَالَ الْقُرْآنُ عَهْدُ اللهِ إِلَى خَلْقِهِ فَقَدْ يَنْبَغِي لِلْمَرْءِ الْمُسْلِمِ أَنْ يَنْظُرَ فِي عَهْدِهِ وَأَنْ يَقْرَأَ مِنْهُ فِي كُلِّ يَوْمٍ خَمْسِينَ آيَةً

Ali has narrated from his father from Hammad from Hariz from abu 'Abd Allāh (عليه السلام) who has said the following: "The Holy Qur'ān is a covenant of Allāh with His creatures. A Muslim must look at his covenant and read fifty verses every day. (حسن)[8]

9.

مُحَمَّدُ بْنُ يَحْيَى عَنْ أَحْمَدَ بْنِ مُحَمَّدِ بْنِ عِيسَى عَنْ مُحَمَّدِ بْنِ خَالِدٍ وَالْحُسَيْنِ بْنِ سَعِيدٍ جَمِيعاً عَنِ النَّضْرِ بْنِ سُوَيْدٍ عَنْ يَحْيَى بْنِ عِمْرَانَ الْحَلَبِيِّ عَنْ عَبْدِ الأَعْلَى مَوْلَى آلِ سَامٍ عَنْ أَبِي عَبْدِ اللهِ (عَلَيهِ السَّلام) قَالَ إِنَّ الْبَيْتَ إِذَا كَانَ فِيهِ الْمَرْءُ الْمُسْلِمُ يَتْلُو الْقُرْآنَ يَتَرَاءَاهُ أَهْلُ السَّمَاءِ كَمَا يَتَرَاءَى أَهْلُ الدُّنْيَا الْكَوْكَبَ الدُّرِّيَّ فِي السَّمَاءِ

Muhammad b. Yahya has narrated from Ahmad b. Muḥammad b. 'Isa from Muḥammad b. Khalid and al-Husayn b. Sa'id all from al-Nadr b. Suwayd from Yahya b. 'Imran al-Halabi from 'Abd al-'Ala' Mawla 'Ale (family) S'am from abu 'Abd Allāh (عليه السلام) who has said the following: "A house wherein a Muslim reads the Holy Qur'ān is looked upon by the inhabitants of heavens, just as the inhabitants of earth like to look at a shining star in the skies (حسن أو مجهول)[9]

10.

[8] *Al-Kafi, v2, ch5, h1*

[9] *Al-Kāfi, v2, ch6, h2*

ابْنُ مَحْبُوبٍ عَنْ جَمِيلِ بْنِ صَالِحٍ عَنِ الْفُضَيْلِ بْنِ يَسَارٍ عَنْ أَبِي عَبْدِ اللهِ (عَلَيهِ السَّلام) قَالَ مَا يَمْنَعُ التَّاجِرَ مِنْكُمُ الْمَشْغُولَ فِي سُوقِهِ إِذَا رَجَعَ إِلَى مَنْزِلِهِ أَنْ لا يَنَامَ حَتَّى يَقْرَأَ سُورَةً مِنَ الْقُرْآنِ فَتُكْتَبَ لَهُ مَكَانَ كُلِّ آيَةٍ يَقْرَؤُهَا عَشْرُ حَسَنَاتٍ وَيُمْحَى عَنْهُ عَشْرُ سَيِّئَاتٍ

b. Mahbub has narrated from Jamil b. Salih from al-Fudayl b. Yasar from abu 'Abd Allāh (عليه السلام) who has said the following: "Why should any thing prevent a business man working in the market place from reading one chapter from the Holy Qur'ān before going to sleep when he is home? For the reading of each verse the reward for ten good deeds will be written down for him and ten of his evil deeds will be deleted. (صحيح)[10]

11.

عَلِيُّ بْنُ إِبْرَاهِيمَ عَنْ أَبِيهِ عَنِ ابْنِ أَبِي عُمَيْرٍ عَمَّنْ ذَكَرَهُ عَنْ أَبِي عَبْدِ اللهِ (عَلَيهِ السَّلام) قَالَ إِنَّ الْقُرْآنَ نَزَلَ بِالْحُزْنِ فَاقْرَءُوهُ بِالْحُزْنِ

Ali b. Ibrahim has narrated from his father from b. abu 'Umayr from those whom he has mentioned (in his book) from abu 'Abd Allāh who has said the following: "The Holy Qur'ān has come down with sadness, thus, you should read it with sadness. (حسن)[11]

12.

[10] *Al-Kāfi, v2, ch7, h2*

[11] *Al-Kāfi, v2, ch9, h2*

سَهْلُ بْنُ زِيَادٍ عَنِ الْحَجَّالِ عَنْ عَلِيِّ بْنِ عُقْبَةَ عَنْ رَجُلٍ عَنْ أَبِي عَبْدِ اللهِ (عَلَيهِ السَّلام) قَالَ كَانَ عَلِيُّ بْنُ الْحُسَيْنِ (صَلَّى اللهُ عَلَيْهِ وآلِه) أَحْسَنَ النَّاسِ صَوْتاً بِالْقُرْآنِ وَكَانَ السَّقَّاءُونَ يَمُرُّونَ فَيَقِفُونَ بِبَابِهِ يَسْمَعُونَ قِرَاءَتَهُ وَكَانَ أَبُو جَعْفَرٍ (عَلَيهِ السَّلام) أَحْسَنَ النَّاسِ صَوْتاً

Sahl b. Ziyad has narrated from al-Hajjal from 'Alī b. 'Aqabah from a man from abu 'Abd Allāh (عليه السلام) who has said the following: "Ali b. al-Husayn (عليه السلام) was the best among the people for his attractive voice in reading the Holy Qur'ān. The water carrier would stop in front of his door to listen to his reading and abu Ja'far (عليه السلام) was the best among the people for his attractive voice. (موثق)[12]

13.

عَلِيُّ بْنُ إِبْرَاهِيمَ عَنْ أَبِيهِ عَنِ ابْنِ مَحْبُوبٍ عَنْ عَلِيِّ بْنِ أَبِي حَمْزَةَ عَنْ أَبِي بَصِيرٍ قَالَ قُلْتُ لأَبِي جَعْفَرٍ (عَلَيهِ السَّلام) إِذَا قَرَأْتُ الْقُرْآنَ فَرَفَعْتُ بِهِ صَوْتِي جَاءَنِي الشَّيْطَانُ فَقَالَ إِنَّمَا تُرَائِي بِهَذَا أَهْلَكَ وَالنَّاسَ قَالَ يَا أَبَا مُحَمَّدٍ اقْرَأْ قِرَاءَةً مَا بَيْنَ الْقِرَاءَتَيْنِ تُسْمِعُ أَهْلَكَ وَرَجِّعْ بِالْقُرْآنِ صَوْتَكَ فَإِنَّ اللهَ عَزَّ وَجَلَّ يُحِبُّ الصَّوْتَ الْحَسَنَ يُرَجَّعُ فِيهِ تَرْجِيعاً

Ali b. Ibrahim has narrated from his father from b. Mahbub from 'Alī b. abu Hamza from abu Basir who has said the following: "Once I said to abu Ja'far (عليه السلام) 'When I read the Holy Qur'ān, I raise my voice. Satan comes and says, "You are only showing this off to people and your family."' The Imam said, 'O abu Muhammad, read in a middle of the way reading, so your family may hear. Give turns to your voice in reading the Holy Qur'ān; Allāh, the Most Majestic, the Most Holy, loves an attractive voice in which there is fluctuations and oscillations. (صحيح)[13]

14.

---

[12] *Al-Kāfi, v2, ch9, h11*

[13] *Al-Kāfi, v2, ch9, h13*

عَلِيُّ بْنُ إِبْرَاهِيمَ عَنْ أَبِيهِ عَنْ حَمَّادٍ عَنِ الْحُسَيْنِ بْنِ الْمُخْتَارِ عَنْ مُحَمَّدِ بْنِ عَبْدِ اللهِ قَالَ قُلْتُ لأَبِي عَبْدِ اللهِ (عَلَيهِ السَّلام) أَقْرَأُ الْقُرْآنَ فِي لَيْلَةٍ قَالَ لا يُعْجِبُنِي أَنْ تَقْرَأَهُ فِي أَقَلَّ مِنْ شَهْرٍ

Ali b. Ibrahim has narrated from his father from Hammad from al-Husayn b. al-Mukhtar from Muḥammad b. 'Abd Allāh who has said the following: "Once I asked abu 'Abd Allāh (عليه السلام) 'Can I read the Holy Qur'ān in one night?' The Imam said, 'I do not like your reading it in less than a month's time. (حسن أو موثق على **الظاهر**)[14]

15.

حُمَيْدُ بْنُ زِيَادٍ عَنِ الْحُسَيْنِ بْنِ مُحَمَّدٍ عَنْ أَحْمَدَ بْنِ الْحَسَنِ الْمِيثَمِيِّ عَنْ يَعْقُوبَ بْنِ شُعَيْبٍ عَنْ أَبِي عَبْدِ اللهِ (عَلَيهِ السَّلام) قَالَ لَمَّا أَمَرَ اللهُ عَزَّ وَجَلَّ هَذِهِ الآيَاتِ أَنْ يَهْبِطْنَ إِلَى الأَرْضِ تَعَلَّقْنَ بِالْعَرْشِ وَقُلْنَ أَيْ رَبِّ إِلَى أَيْنَ تُهْبِطُنَا إِلَى أَهْلِ الْخَطَايَا وَالذُّنُوبِ فَأَوْحَى اللهُ عَزَّ وَجَلَّ إِلَيْهِنَّ أَنِ اهْبِطْنَ فَوَ عِزَّتِي وَجَلالِي لا يَتْلُوكُنَّ أَحَدٌ مِنْ آلِ مُحَمَّدٍ وَشِيعَتِهِمْ فِي دُبُرِ مَا افْتَرَضْتُ عَلَيْهِ مِنَ الْمَكْتُوبَةِ فِي كُلِّ يَوْمٍ إِلا نَظَرْتُ إِلَيْهِ بِعَيْنِيَ الْمَكْنُونَةِ فِي كُلِّ يَوْمٍ سَبْعِينَ نَظْرَةً أَقْضِي لَهُ فِي كُلِّ نَظْرَةٍ سَبْعِينَ حَاجَةً وَقَبِلْتُهُ عَلَى مَا فِيهِ مِنَ الْمَعَاصِي وَهِيَ أُمُّ الْكِتَابِ وَشَهِدَ اللهُ أَنَّهُ لا إِلَهَ إِلا هُوَ وَالْمَلائِكَةُ وَأُولُوا الْعِلْمِ وَآيَةُ الْكُرْسِيِّ وَآيَةُ الْمُلْكِ

Hamid b. Ziyad has narrated from al-Husayn b. Muḥammad from Ahmad b. al-Hassan al-Maythami from Ya'qub b. Shu'ayb from abu 'Abd Allāh (عليه السلام) who has said the following: "When Allāh, the Most Majestic, the Most Holy, commanded certain verses of the Holy Qur'ān to descend to earth, they clung to the Throne asking, 'O Lord, why are You sending us to people of sins and evil deeds.' Allāh, the Most Majestic, the Most Holy, inspired them to descend saying, 'I swear by My Majesty and Glory that any Shi'a (followers) of Ahl al-Bciyt (family of Muhammad, recipients of divine supreme covenant), who reads you after an obligatory prayer every day I will look at him with My hidden eyes (special favor) everyday seventy times and in every look fulfill his seventy wishes and accept him with whatever sins he

---

[14] *Al-Kāfi, v2, ch11, h1*

may have. The verses are Chapter One of the Holy Qur'ān, verses 18-19 and 26-27 of Chapter 3 and verse 255 of Chapter 2 of the Holy Qur'ān. (موثق)[15]

16.

أَبُو عَلِيٍّ الأَشْعَرِيُّ عَنْ مُحَمَّدِ بْنِ عَبْدِ الْجَبَّارِ عَنْ صَفْوَانَ بْنِ يَحْيَى عَنْ يَعْقُوبَ بْنِ شُعَيْبٍ عَنْ أَبِي عَبْدِ اللهِ (عَلَيهِ السَّلام) قَالَ كَانَ أَبِي (صَلَّى اللهُ عَلَيْهِ وآلِه) يَقُولُ قُلْ هُوَ اللهُ أَحَدٌ ثُلُثُ الْقُرْآنِ وَقُلْ يَا أَيُّهَا الْكَافِرُونَ رُبُعُ الْقُرْآنِ

Abu 'Alī al-Ash'ari has narrated from Muḥammad b. 'Abd al-Jabbar from Safwan b. Yahya from Ya'qub b. Shu'ayb from abu 'Abd Allāh (عليه السلام) who has said the following: "My father (عليه السلام) would say, 'Chapter 112 of the Holy Qur'ān is one third and Chapter 109 is one forth of the Holy Qur'ān. (صحيح)[16]

17.

عَلِيُّ بْنُ إِبْرَاهِيمَ عَنْ أَبِيهِ عَنِ ابْنِ أَبِي عُمَيْرٍ عَنْ عُمَرَ بْنِ أُذَيْنَةَ عَنِ الْفُضَيْلِ بْنِ يَسَارٍ قَالَ قُلْتُ لأَبِي عَبْدِ اللهِ (عَلَيهِ السَّلام) إِنَّ النَّاسَ يَقُولُونَ إِنَّ الْقُرْآنَ نَزَلَ عَلَى سَبْعَةِ أَحْرُفٍ فَقَالَ كَذَبُوا أَعْدَاءُ اللهِ وَلَكِنَّهُ نَزَلَ عَلَى حَرْفٍ وَاحِدٍ مِنْ عِنْدِ الْوَاحِدِ

Ali b. Ibrahim has narrated from his father from b. abu 'Umayr from 'Umar b. 'Udhaynah from al-Fudayl b. Yasar who has said the following: "Once, I said to abu 'Abd Allāh (عليه السلام) 'People say that the Holy Qur'ān was revealed upon seven letters.' The Imam said, 'They, the enemies of Allāh, lie. It was revealed upon one letter from One source. (حسن)[17]

---

[15] *Al-Kāfi, v2, ch13, h2*

[16] *Al-Kāfi, v2, ch13, h7*

[17] *Al-Kāfi, v2, ch14, h13*

18.

عِدَّةٌ مِنْ أَصْحَابِنَا عَنْ أَحْمَدَ بْنِ مُحَمَّدِ بْنِ خَالِدٍ عَنْ أَبِيهِ عَنِ النَّضْرِ بْنِ سُوَيْدٍ عَنْ يَحْيَى الْحَلَبِيِّ عَنْ أَيُّوبَ بْنِ الْحُرِّ قَالَ سَمِعْتُ أَبَا عَبْدِ اللهِ (عَلَيْهِ السَّلام) يَقُولُ كُلُّ شَيْءٍ مَرْدُودٌ إِلَى الْكِتَابِ وَالسُّنَّةِ وَكُلُّ حَدِيثٍ لا يُوَافِقُ كِتَابَ اللهِ فَهُوَ زُخْرُفٌ

A number of our people has narrated from Ahmad b. Muḥammad b. Khalid from his father from al-Nadr b. Suwayd from Yahya al-Halab from Ayyub b. al-Hurr who has said the following. "Abu 'AbdAllāh (عليه السلام) has said, 'Everything must be referred to the holy Qur'ān and the Sunnah, the noble traditions of the holy Prophet and any Hadīth that does not agree with the holy Qur'ān it is a useless statement. (صحيح)[18]

19.

مُحَمَّدُ بْنُ إِسْمَاعِيلَ عَنِ الْفَضْلِ بْنِ شَاذَانَ عَنِ ابْنِ أَبِي عُمَيْرٍ عَنْ هِشَامِ بْنِ الْحَكَمِ وَغَيْرِهِ عَنْ أَبِي عَبْدِ اللهِ (عَلَيْهِ السَّلام) قَالَ خَطَبَ النَّبِيُّ (صَلَّى اللهُ عَلَيْهِ وَآلِهِ) بِمِنًى فَقَالَ أَيُّهَا النَّاسُ مَا جَاءَكُمْ عَنِّي يُوَافِقُ كِتَابَ اللهِ فَأَنَا قُلْتُهُ وَمَا جَاءَكُمْ يُخَالِفُ كِتَابَ اللهِ فَلَمْ أَقُلْهُ

Muhammad b. Ismail from al-Fadhl b. Shadhan from b. Abi Umayr from Hisham b. al-Hakam and other than him from Abi Abdillah عليه السلام who said: the Prophet صلى الله عليه وآله addressed the people in Mina and said: O people, whatever comes to you attributed to me which agrees with the Book of Allāh then I have indeed said it, and whatever comes to you opposing the book of Allāh then I never said it. (مجهول كالصحيح)[19]

20.

[18] *Al-Kafi, v1, ch22, h3*

[19] *Al-Kafi, v1, ch22, h5*

أَبُو عَلِيٍّ الأَشْعَرِيُّ عَنْ مُحَمَّدِ بْنِ عَبْدِ الْجَبَّارِ عَنْ صَفْوَانَ عَنْ إِسْحَاقَ بْنِ عَمَّارٍ عَنْ أَبِي بَصِيرٍ عَنْ أَبِي جَعْفَرٍ (عَلَيهِ السَّلام) قَالَ نَزَلَ الْقُرْآنُ أَرْبَعَةَ أَرْبَاعٍ رُبُعٌ فِينَا وَرُبُعٌ فِي عَدُوِّنَا وَرُبُعٌ سُنَنٌ وَأَمْثَالٌ وَرُبُعٌ فَرَائِضُ وَأَحْكَامٌ

Abu 'Alī al-Ash'ari has narrated from Muḥammad b. 'Abd al-Jabbar from Safwan from Ishaq b. 'Ammar from abu Basir from abu Ja'far (عليه السلام) who has said the following: "The Holy Qur'ān came in four parts: One fourth is about us (Ahl al-Bayt) one fourth about our enemies, one about traditions and axioms and one fourth about obligations and laws. (موثق)[20]

---

[20] *Al-Kāfi, v2, ch14, h4*

باب الفضائل أهل البيت

Chapter on the virtues of the Ahl al-Bayt

Given that this chapter is the lengthiest chapter in the book (for obvious reasons), it will be separated into 13 sub-chapters, the first will be exclusive to The Prophet (صلى الله عليه وآله وسلم) and Amir al-Mu'minin (عليه السلام), the second will be about the virtues of Lady Fatimah tuz-Zahra (عليها السلام), the third will be a mix of virtues of Imam al-Hasan (عليه السلام) and Imam al-Husayn (عليه السلام), the fourth part is about Ahl al-Kisa together (Muhammad, Ali, Fatimah, Hasan, Husayn), and the remaining sub-chapters will be about the rest of the A'immah (عليهم السلام) from ʿAlī b. Husayn as-Sajjad (عليه السلام) to al-Qa'im min A'l Muhammad (عجل الله تعالى فرجه)

Virtues of The Prophet (صلى الله عليه وآله وسلم) and Amir al-Mu'minin (عليه السلام)

1.

أَحْمَدُ بْنُ مُحَمَّدٍ عَنْ مُحَمَّدِ بْنِ الْحَسَنِ عَنْ عَلِيِّ بْنِ إِسْمَاعِيلَ عَنْ صَفْوَانَ بْنِ يَحْيَى عَنِ ابْنِ مُسْكَانَ عَنِ الْحَارِثِ بْنِ الْمُغِيرَةِ عَنْ أَبِي عَبْدِ الله (عَلَيْهِ السَّلام) قَالَ سَمِعْتُهُ يَقُولُ قَالَ رَسُولُ الله (صَلَّى اللهُ عَلَيْهِ وَآلِهِ) نَحْنُ فِي الامْرِ وَالْفَهْمِ وَالْحَلالِ وَالْحَرَامِ نَجْرِي مَجْرًى وَاحِداً فَأَمَّا رَسُولُ الله (صَلَّى اللهُ عَلَيْهِ وَآلِهِ) وَعلي (عَلَيْهِ السَّلام) فَلَهُمَا فَضْلُهُمَا

Ahmad b. Muḥammad has narrated from Muḥammad b. al-Hassan from 'Alī b. Isma'il from Safwan b. Yahya from b. Muskan from al-Harith b. al-Mughirah who has narrated the following from abu 'AbdAllāh (عليه السلام). "We in the matters of commands, understanding, lawful and unlawful all are alike and the same. However, the Messenger of Allāh and 'Alī (عليه السلام) have their own virtue and excellence. (حسن)[1]

2.

عَلِيُّ بْنُ إِبْرَاهِيمَ عَنْ أَبِيهِ وَمُحَمَّدُ بْنُ يَحْيَى عَنْ مُحَمَّدِ بْنِ الْحَسَنِ عَمَّنْ ذَكَرَهُ جَمِيعاً عَنِ ابْنِ أَبِي عُمَيْرٍ عَنِ ابْنِ أُذَيْنَةَ عَنْ بُرَيْدِ بْنِ مُعَاوِيَةَ قَالَ قُلْتُ لابي جعفر (عَلَيْهِ السَّلام) قُلْ كَفى بِاللهِ شَهِيداً بَيْنِي وَبَيْنَكُمْ وَمَنْ عِنْدَهُ عِلْمُ الْكِتابِ قَالَ إِيَّانَا عَنَى وَعَلِيٌّ أَوَّلُنَا وَأَفْضَلُنَا وَخَيْرُنَا بَعْدَ النَّبِيِّ (صَلَّى اللهُ عَلَيْهِ وَآلِهِ)

Ali b. Ibrahim has narrated from his father and Muḥammad b. Yahya from Muḥammad b. al-Hassan from those he mentioned, both of them from b. abu 'Umayr from b. 'Udhayna from Burayd b. Mu'awiya who has said that he asked abu Ja'far (عليه السلام) about the meaning of the following verse. ". . Say, 'God and those who have the knowledge of the Book are sufficient witness (to my prophet-hood).'" (13:43) The Imam (عليه السلام) said, "It is a reference to us. 'Alī (عليه السلام) is the first among us and the most virtuous and the best among us after the Holy Prophet (حسن كالصحيح)[2]

3.

[1] *Al-Kāfi, v1, ch58, h3*

[2] *Al-Kāfi, v1, ch35, h6*

عَلِيٌّ عَنْ أَبِيهِ عَنِ ابْنِ أَبِي عُمَيْرٍ عَنِ ابْنِ أُذَيْنَةَ عَنْ زُرَارَةَ عَنْ ابي جعفر (عَلَيْهِ السَّلام) قَالَ نَزَلَ جَبْرَئِيلُ (عَلَيْهِ السَّلام) عَلَى رَسُولِ الله (صَلَّى اللهُ عَلَيْهِ وَآلِه) بِرُمَّانَتَيْنِ مِنَ الْجَنَّةِ فَأَعْطَاهُ إِيَّاهُمَا فَأَكَلَ وَاحِدَةً وَكَسَرَ الاخْرَى بِنِصْفَيْنِ فَأَعْطَى عَلِيّاً (عَلَيْهِ السَّلام) نِصْفَهَا فَأَكَلَهَا فَقَالَ يَا عَلِيُّ أَمَّا الرُّمَّانَةُ الاولَى الَّتِي أَكَلْتُهَا فَالنُّبُوَّةُ لَيْسَ لَكَ فِيهَا شَيْءٌ وَأَمَّا الاخْرَى فَهُوَ الْعِلْمُ فَأَنْتَ شَرِيكِي فِيهِ

Ali has narrated from his father from b. abu ‘Umayr from b. ‘Udhaynah from Zurāra from abu Ja‘far (عليه السلام) who has said the following. “Once Jibril brought from Paradise two pieces of pomegranate to the Messenger of Allāh and brought him two pieces of pomegranates. The Messenger of Allāh ate one of them and broke the other one into two pieces. He then ate one half and gave the other half to ‘Alī (عليه السلام) who also ate it (عليه السلام). The Messenger of Allāh said, “The first one that I ate was prophet-hood. There is no share in it for you. The other one is knowledge in which you are my partner. (حسن)[3]

4.

عَلِيُّ بْنُ إِبْرَاهِيمَ عَنْ أَبِيهِ عَنْ مُحَمَّدِ بْنِ أَبِي عُمَيْرٍ عَنِ ابْنِ أُذَيْنَةَ عَنْ بُرَيْدٍ الْعِجْلِيِّ عَنْ ابي جعفر (عَلَيْهِ السَّلام) فِي قَوْلِ اللهِ عَزَّ وَجَلَّ إِنَّمَا أَنْتَ مُنْذِرٌ وَلِكُلِّ قَوْمٍ هادٍ فَقَالَ رَسُولُ الله (صَلَّى اللهُ عَلَيْهِ وَآلِه) الْمُنْذِرُ وَلِكُلِّ زَمَانٍ مِنَّا هَادٍ يَهْدِيهِمْ إِلَى مَا جَاءَ بِهِ نَبِيُّ الله (صَلَّى اللهُ عَلَيْهِ وَآلِه) ثُمَّ الْهُدَاةُ مِنْ بَعْدِهِ عَلِيٌّ ثُمَّ الاوْصِيَاءُ وَاحِدٌ بَعْدَ وَاحِدٍ

Ali b. Ibrahim has narrated from his father from Muḥammad b. abu ‘Umayr from b. ’Udhayna from Buray al-‘Ijli from Ima abu Ja’far (عليه السلام) who has said the following about the words of Allāh. “ (Muhammad), you are only a Warner. For every nation there is a guide. (13:7)” The Imam (عليه السلام) said that at all times there is a guide from us who guides people to the teachings of the Holy Prophet Of the guides who possess

---

[3] *Al-Kāfi, v1, ch49, h2*

Divine authority after the holy Prophet is Amir al-Mu'minin (عليه السلام) and his successors one after the other. (حسن)[4]

5.

عَلِيُّ بْنُ إِبْرَاهِيمَ عَنْ أَبِيهِ عَنِ ابْنِ أَبِي عُمَيْرٍ عَنْ عُمَرَ بْنِ أُذَيْنَةَ عَنْ زُرَارَةَ وَالْفُضَيْلِ بْنِ يَسَارٍ وَبُكَيْرِ بْنِ أَعْيَنَ وَمُحَمَّدِ بْنِ مُسْلِمٍ وَبُرَيْدِ بْنِ مُعَاوِيَةَ وَأَبِي الْجَارُودِ جَمِيعاً عَنْ ابي جعفر (عَلَيْهِ السَّلام) قَالَ أَمَرَ اللهُ عَزَّ وَجَلَّ رَسُولَهُ بِوَلايَةِ عَلِيٍّ وَأَنْزَلَ عَلَيْهِ إِنَّمَا وَلِيُّكُمُ اللهُ وَرَسُولُهُ وَالَّذِينَ آمَنُوا الَّذِينَ يُقِيمُونَ الصَّلاةَ وَيُؤْتُونَ الزَّكَاةَ وَفَرَضَ وَلايَةَ أُولِي الامْرِ فَلَمْ يَدْرُوا مَا هِيَ فَأَمَرَ اللهُ مُحَمَّداً (صَلَّى اللهُ عَلَيْهِ وَآلِهِ) أَنْ يُفَسِّرَ لَهُمُ الْوَلايَةَ كَمَا فَسَّرَ لَهُمُ الصَّلاةَ وَالزَّكَاةَ وَالصَّوْمَ وَالْحَجَّ فَلَمَّا أَتَاهُ ذَلِكَ مِنَ اللهِ ضَاقَ بِذَلِكَ صَدْرُ رَسُولِ اللهِ (صَلَّى اللهُ عَلَيْهِ وَآلِهِ) وَتَخَوَّفَ أَنْ يَرْتَدُّوا عَنْ دِينِهِمْ وَأَنْ يُكَذِّبُوهُ فَضَاقَ صَدْرُهُ وَرَاجَعَ رَبَّهُ عَزَّ وَجَلَّ فَأَوْحَى اللهُ عَزَّ وَجَلَّ إِلَيْهِ يا أَيُّهَا الرَّسُولُ بَلِّغْ ما أُنْزِلَ إِلَيْكَ مِنْ رَبِّكَ وَإِنْ لَمْ تَفْعَلْ فَمَا بَلَّغْتَ رِسالَتَهُ وَاللهُ يَعْصِمُكَ مِنَ النَّاسِ فَصَدَعَ بِأَمْرِ اللهِ تَعَالَى ذِكْرُهُ فَقَامَ بِوَلايَةِ علي (عَلَيْهِ السَّلام) يَوْمَ غَدِيرِ خُمٍّ فَنَادَى الصَّلاةَ جَامِعَةً وَأَمَرَ النَّاسَ أَنْ يُبَلِّغَ الشَّاهِدُ الْغَائِبَ قَالَ عُمَرُ بْنُ أُذَيْنَةَ قَالُوا جَمِيعاً غَيْرَ أَبِي الْجَارُودِ وَقَالَ أَبُو جَعْفَرٍ (عَلَيْهِ السَّلام) وَكَانَتِ الْفَرِيضَةُ تَنْزِلُ بَعْدَ الْفَرِيضَةِ الاخْرَى وَكَانَتِ الْوَلايَةُ آخِرَ الْفَرَائِضِ فَأَنْزَلَ اللهُ عَزَّ وَجَلَّ الْيَوْمَ أَكْمَلْتُ لَكُمْ دِينَكُمْ وَأَتْمَمْتُ عَلَيْكُمْ نِعْمَتِي قَالَ أَبُو جَعْفَرٍ (عَلَيْهِ السَّلام) يَقُولُ اللهُ عَزَّ وَجَلَّ لا أُنْزِلُ عَلَيْكُمْ بَعْدَ هَذِهِ فَرِيضَةً قَدْ أَكْمَلْتُ لَكُمُ الْفَرَائِضَ

`Ali b. Ibrahim from his father from b. Abi `Umayr from `Umar b. Udhayna from Zurara, al-Fudayl b. Yasar, Bukayr b. A`yan, Muḥammad b. Muslim, Burayd b. Mu`awiya and Abu'l Jarud together from Abu Ja`far عليه السلام.

He said: The Wilāya of `Ali was an order from Allāh عز وجل to His messenger, and He revealed upon him, "**Verily your guardian is Allāh, His messenger, and those who believed – who stand in prayer and give the zakat...**" (5:55). And He made the Wilāya of the Possessors of the Command (ulu 'l-amr) obligatory, and they did not understand what it was; so Allāh ordered Muḥammad صلى الله عليه وآله to interpret [and clarify] the Wilāya to them, just as he interpreted salat, zakat, sawm, and Hajj.

---

[4] *Al-Kāfi, v1, ch10, h2*

When Allāh gave that [order] to him, the chest of the Messenger of Allāh صلى الله عليه وآله tightened, and he feared that they would apostatize from their religion and bely him – so his chest tightened. He consulted his Lord عز وجل, so Allāh عز وجل inspired to him, "O Messenger, preach what is revealed to you from your Lord. If you do not preach, it will be as though you have not conveyed My Message, and Allāh will protect you from the people". (5:67) So he executed the command of Allāh تعالى ذكره and declared the Wilāya of `Ali عليه السلام on the day of Ghadeer Khumm. He called for a congregational prayer and commanded the people to bear testimony and inform the absent. `Umar b. Udhayna said: All except Abu'l Jarud said:

And Abu Ja`far عليه السلام said: And an obligation would be revealed after the other, and the Wilāya was the final obligation, so Allāh عز وجل revealed, "Today I have perfected for you your religion and completed my favour..." (5:3). Abu Ja`far عليه السلام said: Allāh عز وجل says: I will not reveal to you any obligation after this – I have completed for you the obligations (حسن)[5]

6.

وَ قَدْ قَالَ رَسُولُ اللَّهِ (صلى الله عليه وآله) أَنْتَ مِنِّي بِمَنْزِلَةِ هَارُونَ مِنْ مُوسَى إِلَّا أَنَّهُ لَا نَبِيَّ بَعْدِي

Messenger of Allāh (صلى الله عليه وآله وسلم) Allāh (تبارك و طائلة) said: 'You are from me of the status which Haroun (عليه السلام) had from Mūsā (عليه السلام) except that there is no Prophet (عليه السلام) after me'. (موثق)[6]

7.

[5] *Al-Kāfi, v1, ch64, h4*

[6] *Al-Kāfi, v8, ch80*

وَبِإِسْنادِهِ عَنْ عَلِي عَلَيْهِ السَّلامُ قالَ :قالَرَسُولَ اللَّهِ صَلَّى اللهُ عَلَيْهِ وَآلِهِ :أَنَا مَدِينَةُ العِلْمِ وَعَلِيٌّ بابُها]فَمَنْ أَرادَ العِلْمَ فَلْيَاتِ الباب

According to the same documentation on the authority of ʿAlī (عليه السلام), God's Prophet (صلى الله عليه وآله وسلم) said, "I am the city of knowledge and ʿAlī is its portal. (Whoever wishes to gain knowledge should go through that gate.[7]

8.

عِدَّةٌ مِنْ أَصْحَابِنَا عَنْ أَحْمَدَ بْنِ مُحَمَّدٍ عَنِ ابْنِ أَبِي نَصْرٍ عَنْ مُثَنًّى عَنْ زُرَارَةَ قَالَ كُنْتُ عِنْدَ ابي جعفر (عَلَيْهِ السَّلام) فَقَالَ لَهُ رَجُلٌ مِنْ أَهْلِ الْكُوفَةِ يَسْأَلُهُ عَنْ قَوْلِ أَمِيرِ الْمُؤْمِنِينَ (عَلَيْهِ السَّلام) سَلُونِي عَمَّا شِئْتُمْ فَلا تَسْأَلُونِّي عَنْ شَيْءٍ إِلا أَنْبَأْتُكُمْ بِهِ قَالَ إِنَّهُ لَيْسَ أَحَدٌ عِنْدَهُ عِلْمُ شَيْءٍ إِلا خَرَجَ مِنْ عِنْدِ أَمِيرِ الْمُؤْمِنِينَ (عَلَيْهِ السَّلام) فَلْيَذْهَبِ النَّاسُ حَيْثُ شَاءُوا فَوَ الله لَيْسَ الامْرُ إِلا مِنْ هَاهُنَا وَأَشَارَ بِيَدِهِ إِلَى بَيْتِهِ

A number of our people has narrated from Ahmad b. Muḥammad from b. abu Basir from Muthanna from Zurara who has said the following. "Once I was in the presence of abu Ja'far (عليه السلام). A man from Kufa asked him about the words of Amir al-Mu'minin (عليه السلام), "Ask me whatever you would like. Whatever you may ask I will give you the answer." The Imam (عليه السلام) said, "No one has any piece of knowledge of anything that has not come through Amir al-Mu'minin (عليه السلام) People may go wherever they may like, however, by Allāh, the truth comes from no where else except from here, he pointed out with his hand towards his house. (حسن)[8]

9.

---

[7] *'Uyūn Akhbār al-Riḍā, v1, ch1, h299*

[8] *Al-Kāfi, v1, ch101, h2*

عَلِيُّ بْنُ إِبْرَاهِيمَ عَنْ أَبِيهِ عَنِ ابْنِ أَبِي عُمَيْرٍ عَنْ حَمَّادٍ عَنْ مَنْصُورِ بْنِ حَازِمٍ عَنْ أَبِي عَبْدِ اللَّهِ (عَلَيْهِ السَّلام) قَالَ لَمَّا هَبَطَ جَبْرَئِيلُ (عَلَيْهِم السَّلام) بِالأَذَانِ عَلَى رَسُولِ اللَّهِ (صلّى اللَّهُ عَلَيْهِ وَآلِه) كَانَ رَأْسُهُ فِي حِجْرِ عَلِيٍّ (عَلَيْهِ السَّلام) فَأَذَّنَ جَبْرَئِيلُ (عَلَيْهِم السَّلام) وَأَقَامَ فَلَمَّا انْتَبَهَ رَسُولُ اللَّهِ (صلّى اللَّهُ عَلَيْهِ وَآلِه) قَالَ يَا عَلِيُّ سَمِعْتَ قَالَ نَعَمْ قَالَ حَفِظْتَ قَالَ نَعَمْ قَالَ ادْعُ بِلالاً فَعَلِّمْهُ فَدَعَا عَلِيٌّ (عَلَيْهِ السَّلام) بِلالاً فَعَلَّمَهُ

Ali b. Ibrahim has narrated from his father from b. abu ‘Umayr from Hammad from Mansur b. Hazim who has said the following: “Abu ‘Abd Allāh, (عليه السلام), has said that when Jibril (Gabriel) descended with Adhan to the Messenger of Allāh, he was resting and his head was on Amir al-Mu’minin Ali’s lap. Jibril then read Adhan and Iqamah. When the Messenger of Allāh woke up he asked, ‘O Ali, did you hear it?’ He replied, ‘Yes, I did.’ He (the Messenger of Allāh) asked, ‘Do you remember it?’ He (Ali) replied, ‘Yes, I remember.’ He (the Messenger of Allāh) then said, ‘Call Bilal and teach him.’ ‘Alī then called Bilal and taught him Adhan and Iqamah. (حسن)[9]

10.

عَلِيُّ بْنُ إِبْرَاهِيمَ عَنْ أَبِيهِ عَنِ ابْنِ أَبِي عُمَيْرٍ عَنْ عُمَرَ بْنِ أُذَيْنَةَ عَنْ زُرَارَةَ وَالْفَضْلِ عَنْ أَبِي جَعْفَرٍ (عَلَيْهِ السَّلام) قَالَ لَمَّا أُسْرِيَ بِرَسُولِ اللَّهِ (صلّى اللَّهُ عَلَيْهِ وَآلِه) إِلَى السَّمَاءِ فَبَلَغَ الْبَيْتَ الْمَعْمُورَ وَحَضَرَتِ الصَّلاةُ فَأَذَّنَ جَبْرَئِيلُ وَأَقَامَ فَتَقَدَّمَ رَسُولُ اللَّهِ (صلّى اللَّهُ عَلَيْهِ وَآلِه) وَصَفَّ الْمَلائِكَةُ وَالنَّبِيُّونَ خَلْفَ مُحَمَّدٍ (صلّى اللَّهُ عَلَيْهِ وَآلِه)

Ali b. Ibrahim has narrated from his father from b. abu ‘Umayr from ‘Umar b. ’Udhaynah from Zurāra from and al-Fadl who has said the following: “Abu Ja’far, (عليه السلام), has said, ‘When the Messenger of Allāh was taken to the heaven upon his arrival in Bayt al-Ma‘mur at the time of Salah (prayer), Jibril (Gabriel) said Adhan and Iqamah. The Messenger of Allāh went ahead to lead and the angels and prophets lined up behind Prophet Muḥammad for prayer. (حسن)[10]

---

[9] *Al-Kāfi, v3, ch18, h2*

[10] *Al-Kāfi, v3, ch18, h1*

11.

أحمد بن زياد بن جعفر الهمداني، عن علي بن إبراهيم بن هاشم، عن أبيه، عن أحمد بن محمد بن أبي نصر البزنطي ومحمد بن أبي عمير، عن أبان بن عثمان، عن أبي عبد الله عليه السلام قال :لما كان يوم أحد انهزم أصحاب رسول الله حتى لم يبق معه إلا علي بن أبي طالب عليه السلام وأبو دجانة سماك بن خرشة فقال له النبي صلى الله عليه وآله :يا أبا دجانة أما ترى قومك؟ قال :بلى قال :الحق بقومك قال :ما على هذا بايعت الله ورسوله قال :أنت في حل قال :والله لا تتحدث قريش بأني خذلتك وفررت حتى أذوق ما تذوق فجزاه النبي خيرا .وكان علي عليه السلام كلما حملت طائفة على رسول الله صلى الله عليه وآله استقبلهم وردهم حتى أكثر فيهم القتل والجراحات حتى انكسر سيفه فجاء إلى النبي صلى الله عليه وآله فقال :يا رسول الله إن الرجل يقاتل بسلاحه وقد انكسر سيفي فأعطاه سيفه ذا الفقار فما زال يدفع به عن رسول الله صلى الله عليه وآله حتى أثر وانكر فنزل عليه جبرئيل وقال :يا محمد إن هذه لهي المواساة من علي لك فقال النبي صلى الله عليه وآله :إنه مني وأنا منه فقال جبرئيل :وأنا منكما وسمعوا دويا من السماء لا سيف إلا ذو الفقار ولا فتى إلا علي

Ahmad b. Ziyad b. Ja`far al-Hamdani from 'Alī b. Ibrahim b. Hashim from his father from Ahmad b. Muḥammad b. Abi Nasr al-Bazanti and Muḥammad b. Abi Umayr from Aban b. Uthman from Abi Abdillah عليه السلام who said: All the companions of the messenger of Allāh ran away on the day of Uhud – no one was left among them except 'Alī b. Abi Talib عليه السلام and Abu Dujana Simak b. Kharasha. The prophet صلى الله عليه وآله said to him: O Aba Dujana – don't you see your people? he said: I do, he said: join up with them, he said: this is not what I gave my pledge of allegiance to Allāh and His messenger for! he said: you are released [from your pledge], he said: by Allāh the Quraysh will never get the opportunity to say that I abandoned you and ran away until I taste what you taste! Then the prophet صلى الله عليه وآله prayed for a good recompense for him. Whenever a group used to attack the messenger of Allāh – 'Alī عليه السلام would face them and repel them until he had killed a large number of them and injured others. He continued this way until his sword broke so he came to the prophet صلى الله عليه وآله and said: O messenger of Allāh – a man can only fight with his weapon but my sword has broken! So he (the prophet) gave him his sword Dhu al-

Fiqar and he (Ali) kept on defending the prophet using it until marks [wound traces] were inflicted on him and he became unrecognizable [because of a multitude of injuries]. Jibril descended and said: O Muḥammad this is an incomparable support from 'Alī to you! so the prophet said: he is from me and I am from him, Jibril said: and I am from you both, and they heard a voice from heaven saying: there is no sword but Dhu al-Fiqar and the there is no young champion except Ali. (صحيح)[11]

12.

مُحَمَّدُ بْنُ يَحْيَى عَنْ أَحْمَدَ بْنِ مُحَمَّدٍ عَنِ ابْنِ فَضَّالٍ عَنْ عَبْدِ اللهِ بْنِ مُحَمَّدٍ بْنِ أَخِي حَمَّادٍ الْكَاتِبِ عَنِ الْحُسَيْنِ بْنِ عَبْدِ اللهِ قَالَ قُلْتُ لابِي عَبْدِ اللهِ (عَلَيْهِ السَّلام) كَانَ رَسُولُ اللهِ (صَلَّى اللهُ عَلَيْهِ وَآلِهِ) سَيِّدَ وُلْدِ آدَمَ فَقَالَ كَانَ وَاللهِ سَيِّدَ مَنْ خَلَقَ اللهُ وَمَا بَرَأَ اللهُ بَرِيَّةً خَيْراً مِنْ مُحَمَّدٍ (صَلَّى اللهُ عَلَيْهِ وَآلِهِ)

Muhammad b. Yahya has narrated from Ahmad b. Muḥammad from b. Faddal from 'AbdAllāh b. Muḥammad son of the brother of Hammad al-Katib from al-Husayn b. 'AbdAllāh who has said the following. "I asked abu 'AbdAllāh (عليه السلام), 'Was the Messenger of Allāh the mater of the children of Adam?" The Imam (عليه السلام) said, 'By Allāh, he was the master of all whom Allāh has created. Allāh has not created any creature better than Muḥammad صلى الله عليه وآله وسلم. (مجهول)[12]

13.

مُحَمَّدُ بْنُ يَحْيَى عَنْ أَحْمَدَ بْنِ مُحَمَّدٍ عَنِ الْحَجَّالِ عَنْ حَمَّادٍ عَنْ أَبِي عَبْدِ اللهِ (عَلَيْهِ السَّلام) وَذَكَرَ رَسُولَ اللهِ (صَلَّى اللهُ عَلَيْهِ وَآلِهِ) فَقَالَ قَالَ أَمِيرُ الْمُؤْمِنِينَ (عَلَيْهِ السَّلام) مَا بَرَأَ اللهُ نَسَمَةً خَيْراً مِنْ مُحَمَّدٍ (صَلَّى اللهُ عَلَيْهِ وَآلِهِ)

---

[11] *Ilal al-Sharai, v1, ch7, h3*

[12] *Al-Kafi, v1, ch111, h1*

Ahmad b. Muḥammad from al-Hajjal from Hammad from abu 'AbdAllāh (عليه السلام) who has said the following. When mentioning the the Messenger of Allāh he said, "Amir al-Mu'minin 'Alī (عليه السلام) has said, "Allāh has not created any creature better than Muḥammad صلى الله عليه وآله وسلم. (صحيح)[13]

14.

عَلِيُّ بْنُ إِبْرَاهِيمَ عَنْ أَبِيهِ عَنْ أَحْمَدَ بْنِ مُحَمَّدِ بْنِ أَبِي نَصْرٍ عَنْ حَمَّادِ بْنِ عُثْمَانَ عَنْ أَبِي بَصِيرٍ عَنْ أَبِي عَبْدِ اللهِ (عَلَيْهِ السَّلام) قَالَ لَمَّا عُرِجَ بِرَسُولِ اللهِ (صَلَّى اللهُ عَلَيْهِ وَآلِه) انْتَهَى بِهِ جَبْرَئِيلُ إِلَى مَكَانٍ فَخَلَّى عَنْهُ فَقَالَ لَهُ يَا جَبْرَئِيلُ تُخَلِّينِي عَلَى هَذِهِ الْحَالَةِ فَقَالَ امْضِهْ فَوَ اللهِ لَقَدْ وَطِئْتَ مَكَاناً مَا وَطِئَهُ بَشَرٌ وَمَا مَشَى فِيهِ بَشَرٌ قَبْلَكَ

Ali b. Ibrahim has narrated from from his father from Ahmad b. Muḥammad b. abu Nasr from Hammad b. 'Uthman from abu Basir from abu 'AbdAllāh (عليه السلام) who has said the following. "When the Messenger of Allāh was taken for the ascension Jibril took him to place and left him there alone. He said, "Jibril, How would leave me in such a condition?" Jibril said, "Go on. By Allāh, you have stepped at a place whereat no human has ever stepped and no human had ever walked on before you. (حسن)[14]

15.

مُحَمَّدُ بْنُ يَحْيَى عَنْ أَحْمَدَ بْنِ مُحَمَّدِ بْنِ عِيسَى عَنِ الْحَسَنِ بْنِ مَحْبُوبٍ عَنْ إِسْحَاقَ بْنِ غَالِبٍ عَنْ أَبِي عَبْدِ اللهِ (عَلَيْهِ السَّلام) فِي خُطْبَةٍ لَهُ خَاصَّةً يَذْكُرُ فِيهَا حَالَ النَّبِيِّ وَالائِمَّةِ (عَلَيْهِ السَّلام) وَصِفَاتِهِمْ فَلَمْ يَمْنَعْ رَبَّنَا لِحِلْمِهِ وَأَنَاتِهِ وَعَطْفِهِ مَا كَانَ مِنْ عَظِيمِ جُرْمِهِمْ وَقَبِيحِ أَفْعَالِهِمْ أَنِ انْتَجَبَ لَهُمْ أَحَبَّ أَنْبِيَائِهِ إِلَيْهِ وَأَكْرَمَهُمْ عَلَيْهِ مُحَمَّدَ بْنَ عَبْدِ اللهِ (عَلَيْهِ السَّلام) فِي حَوْمَةِ الْعِزِّ مَوْلِدُهُ وَفِي دَوْمَةِ الْكَرَمِ مَحْتِدُهُ غَيْرَ مَشُوبٍ حَسَبُهُ وَلا

---

[13] *Al-Kāfi, v1, ch111, h2*

[14] *Al-Kāfi, c1, ch111, h12*

مَمْزُوجٍ نَسَبُهُ وَلا مَجْهُولٍ عِنْدَ أَهْلِ الْعِلْمِ صِفَتُهُ بَشَّرَتْ بِهِ الانْبِيَاءُ فِي كُتُبِهَا وَنَطَقَتْ بِهِ الْعُلَمَاءُ بِنَعْتِهَا وَتَأَمَّلَتْهُ الْحُكَمَاءُ بِوَصْفِهَا مُهَذَّبٌ لا يُدَانَى هَاشِمِيٌّ لا يُوَازَى أَبْطَحِيٌّ لا يُسَامَى شِيمَتُهُ الْحَيَاءُ وَطَبِيعَتُهُ السَّخَاءُ مَجْبُولٌ عَلَى أَوْقَارِ النُّبُوَّةِ وَأَخْلاقِهَا مَطْبُوعٌ عَلَى أَوْصَافِ الرِّسَالَةِ وَأَحْلامِهَا إِلَى أَنِ انْتَهَتْ بِهِ أَسْبَابُ مَقَادِيرِ اللهِ إِلَى أَوْقَاتِهَا وَجَرَى بِأَمْرِ اللهِ الْقَضَاءُ فِيهِ إِلَى نِهَايَاتِهَا أَدَّاهُ مَحْتُومُ قَضَاءِ اللهِ إِلَى غَايَاتِهَا تُبَشِّرُ بِهِ كُلُّ أُمَّةٍ مَنْ بَعْدَهَا وَيَدْفَعُهُ كُلُّ أَبٍ إِلَى أَبٍ مِنْ ظَهْرٍ إِلَى ظَهْرٍ لَمْ يَخْلِطْهُ فِي عُنْصُرِهِ سِفَاحٌ وَلَمْ يُنَجِّسْهُ فِي وِلادَتِهِ نِكَاحٌ مِنْ لَدُنْ آدَمَ إِلَى أَبِيهِ عَبْدِ اللهِ فِي خَيْرِ فِرْقَةٍ وَأَكْرَمِ سِبْطٍ وَأَمْنَعِ رَهْطٍ وَأَكْلا حَمْلٍ وَأَوْدَعِ حَجْرٍ اصْطَفَاهُ اللهُ وَارْتَضَاهُ وَاجْتَبَاهُ وَآتَاهُ مِنَ الْعِلْمِ مَفَاتِيحَهُ وَمِنَ الْحُكْمِ يَنَابِيعَهُ ابْتَعَثَهُ رَحْمَةً لِلْعِبَادِ وَرَبِيعاً لِلْبِلادِ وَأَنْزَلَ اللهُ إِلَيْهِ الْكِتَابَ فِيهِ الْبَيَانُ وَالتِّبْيَانُ قُرْآناً عَرَبِيّاً غَيْرَ ذِي عِوَجٍ لَعَلَّهُمْ يَتَّقُونَ قَدْ بَيَّنَهُ لِلنَّاسِ وَنَهَجَهُ بِعِلْمٍ قَدْ فَصَّلَهُ وَدِينٍ قَدْ أَوْضَحَهُ وَفَرَائِضَ قَدْ أَوْجَبَهَا وَحُدُودٍ حَدَّهَا لِلنَّاسِ وَبَيَّنَهَا وَأُمُورٍ قَدْ كَشَفَهَا لِخَلْقِهِ وَأَعْلَنَهَا فِيهَا دَلالَةٌ إِلَى النَّجَاةِ وَمَعَالِمُ تَدْعُو إِلَى هُدَاهُ فَبَلَّغَ رَسُولُ اللهِ (صَلَّى اللهُ عَلَيْهِ وَآلِهِ) مَا أُرْسِلَ بِهِ وَصَدَعَ بِمَا أُمِرَ وَأَدَّى مَا حُمِّلَ مِنْ أَثْقَالِ النُّبُوَّةِ وَصَبَرَ لِرَبِّهِ وَجَاهَدَ فِي سَبِيلِهِ وَنَصَحَ لامَّتِهِ وَدَعَاهُمْ إِلَى النَّجَاةِ وَحَثَّهُمْ عَلَى الذِّكْرِ وَدَلَّهُمْ عَلَى سَبِيلِ الْهُدَى بِمَنَاهِجَ وَدَوَاعٍ أَسَّسَ لِلْعِبَادِ أَسَاسَهَا وَمَنَارٍ رَفَعَ لَهُمْ أَعْلامَهَا كَيْلا يَضِلُّوا مِنْ بَعْدِهِ وَكَانَ بِهِمْ رَءُوفاً رَحِيماً

Muhammad b. Yahya has narrated from Ahmad b. Muḥammad b. ‘Isa from al-Hassan b. Mahbub from Ishaq b. Ghalib from abu ‘AbdAllāh (عليه السلام) who has said the following in a special sermon in which he has described the The Holy Prophet (s.a) and the Imams (عليه السلام) and their qualities. “Despite the great sins and their bad deeds it did not prevent Our Lord due to His forbearance, considerate and kindness to chose for them the best of His prophets and most respectable to Him who is Muḥammad b. ‘AbdAllāh who was born in an honorable environment and a noble family. His association was suspicious and his lineage was not unknown to the people of knowledge to describe. The glad news of his coming was mentioned in the books of the prophets and spoken of in the words of the scholars and whose qualities were discussed in the thinking of the people of wisdom. No person of Hashimit descent has ever reached the level of his discipline to become parallel to him and no person of the inhabitants of Abtah has ever climbed to his high position. Restraint was of his attributes and generosity was part of his nature. He was made with the dignity of prophet-hood and its discipline. His nature was formed out of the qualities of Divine messenger and its wisdom. The means and measures of Allāh brought him to the appointed time and the decree by the commands of Allāh continued to their goals. The determined decision of Allāh delivered him to their objects. Every nation would gave the glad news about him to the one thereafter and every father would deliver to the next one from one generation to the next. No indecency ever mixed his element and no conjugal relation ever made him unclean from Adam to his father 'AbdAllāh. He was in the best group and most honorable descent, the tribe of glory, in the well preserved womb and in the best protective hands. Allāh had chosen him as it pleased Him, selected him, gave him the keys to knowledge and the sources of wisdom. He raised as the mercy and blessings for His servants and as the season of spring for His lands. Allāh sent to him the Book in which there is communication and explanations. It is a reading in Arabic free of complexities so that they may perhaps observe piety (before Allāh). He has explained to people. He has arranged it into a system with the knowledge that explains in details and a religion that he has clarified its obligations, determined his limits for the people and has clarified them. There are matters that He has stated to His servants openly. In it there is guidance to salvation and evidence to show the right guidance. The Messenger of Allāh has preached the message that he had brought and demanded obedience to what he was ordered to preach and delivered the responsibilities of a prophet towards his followers. He exercised patience for the sake of his Lord and strove hard in the way of the Lord. He gave good advise to his followers and called them to salvation. He exhorted them in the matters of al-Dhikr (reminder) and showed them the right guidance. He did so with systems and potentials that he established on certain foundations for the servants (of Allāh) and with the sources of light for which he raised proper beacons. He did so, so that they will not be mislead after him and he was very compassionate and kind to them." for warned made clear e in accordance with His been a parallel of him. (صحيح)[15].

16.

عَلِيُّ بْنُ إِبْرَاهِيمَ عَنْ مُحَمَّدِ بْنِ عِيسَى عَنْ يُونُسَ عَنْ خَالِدِ بْنِ عُمَارَةَ عَنْ أَبِي بَصِيرٍ قَالَ قَالَ أَبُو عَبْدِ اللَّه (عَلَيْهِ السَّلَام) إِذَا حِيلَ بَيْنَهُ وَبَيْنَ الْكَلَامِ أَتَاهُ رَسُولُ اللَّه (صَلَّى اللَّهُ عَلَيْهِ وَآلِهِ) وَمَنْ شَاءَ اللَّهُ فَجَلَسَ رَسُولُ اللَّه

[15] Al-Kāfi, v1, ch111, h17

(صلّى اللهُ عَلَيْهِ وَآلِه) عَنْ يَمِينِهِ وَالآخَرُ عَنْ يَسَارِهِ فَيَقُولُ لَهُ رَسُولُ الله (صلّى اللهُ عَلَيْهِ وَآلِه) أَمَّا مَا كُنْتَ تَرْجُو فَهُوَ ذَا أَمَامَكَ وَأَمَّا مَا كُنْتَ تَخَافُ مِنْهُ فَقَدْ أَمِنْتَ مِنْهُ ثُمَّ يُفْتَحُ لَهُ بَابٌ إِلَى الْجَنَّةِ فَيَقُولُ هَذَا مَنْزِلُكَ مِنَ الْجَنَّةِ فَإِنْ شِئْتَ رَدَدْنَاكَ إِلَى الدُّنْيَا وَلَكَ فِيهَا ذَهَبٌ وَفِضَّةٌ فَيَقُولُ لاَ حَاجَةَ لِي فِي الدُّنْيَا فَعِنْدَ ذَلِكَ يَبْيَضُّ لَوْنُهُ وَيَرْشَحُ جَبِينُهُ وَتَقَلَّصُ شَفَتَاهُ وَتَنْتَشِرُ مَنْخِرَاهُ وَتَدْمَعُ عَيْنُهُ الْيُسْرَى فَأَيَّ هَذِهِ الْعَلاَمَاتِ رَأَيْتَ فَاكْتَفِ بِهَا فَإِذَا خَرَجَتِ النَّفْسُ مِنَ الْجَسَدِ فَيُعْرَضُ عَلَيْهَا كَمَا عُرِضَ عَلَيْهِ وَهِيَ فِي الْجَسَدِ فَتَخْتَارُ الآخِرَةَ فَتُغَسِّلُهُ فِيمَنْ يُغَسِّلُهُ وَتُقَلِّبُهُ فِيمَنْ يُقَلِّبُهُ فَإِذَا أُدْرِجَ فِي أَكْفَانِهِ وَوُضِعَ عَلَى سَرِيرِهِ خَرَجَتْ رُوحُهُ تَمْشِي بَيْنَ أَيْدِي الْقَوْمِ قُدُماً وَتَلْقَاهُ أَرْوَاحُ الْمُؤْمِنِينَ يُسَلِّمُونَ عَلَيْهِ وَيُبَشِّرُونَهُ بِمَا أَعَدَّ اللهُ لَهُ جَلَّ ثَنَاؤُهُ مِنَ النَّعِيمِ فَإِذَا وُضِعَ فِي قَبْرِهِ رُدَّ إِلَيْهِ الرُّوحُ إِلَى وَرِكَيْهِ ثُمَّ يُسْأَلُ عَمَّا يَعْلَمُ فَإِذَا جَاءَ بِمَا يَعْلَمُ فُتِحَ لَهُ ذَلِكَ الْبَابُ الَّذِي أَرَاهُ رَسُولُ الله (صلّى اللهُ عَلَيْهِ وَآلِه) فَيَدْخُلُ عَلَيْهِ مِنْ نُورِهَا وَضَوْئِهَا وَبَرْدِهَا وَطِيبِ رِيحِهَا قَالَ قُلْتُ جُعِلْتُ فِدَاكَ فَأَيْنَ ضَغْطَةُ الْقَبْرِ فَقَالَ هَيْهَاتَ مَا عَلَى الْمُؤْمِنِينَ مِنْهَا شَيْءٌ وَالله إِنَّ هَذِهِ الأَرْضَ لَتَفْتَخِرُ عَلَى هَذِهِ فَيَقُولُ وَطِئَ عَلَى ظَهْرِي مُؤْمِنٌ وَلَمْ يَطَأْ عَلَى ظَهْرِكِ مُؤْمِنٌ وَتَقُولُ لَهُ الأَرْضُ وَالله لَقَدْ كُنْتُ أُحِبُّكَ وَأَنْتَ تَمْشِي عَلَى ظَهْرِي فَأَمَّا إِذَا وُلِّيتُكَ فَسَتَعْلَمُ مَا ذَا أَصْنَعُ بِكَ فَتَفْسَحُ لَهُ مَدَّ بَصَرِهِ

Ali b. Ibrahim has narrated from Muḥammad 'Isa from Yunus from Khalid b. 'Umarah from abu Basir who has said the following: "Abu 'Abd Allāh, (عليه السلام), has said that when a dying person loses the ability to speak, the Messenger of Allāh comes to him along with whomever Allāh wants. The Messenger of Allāh sits near his right side and the other on his left side. The Messenger of Allāh then says, 'What you hoped for is in front of you, you are safe from that of which you were afraid.' Then he opens for him a door to paradise saying, 'This is your dwelling place in paradise. However, if you like I can send you back to the worldly life where you can have gold and silver.' He will then say, 'I do not want the worldly things.' At this time his color whitens, his forehead sweats, his lips shrink, his nostrils expand and his left eye tears up (moistons with tears). Whichever of these signs you see is enough. When the soul departs the body, it is given the choice again as when in the body but it chooses the life hereafter. He is then washed among those who wash him and is turned side to side among those who turn him side to side. When he is wrapped up in the shroud and is placed on the stretcher, his spirit comes out and begins to walk before the people. The spirits of believing people meet him with greetings of peace and good news of whatever bounties Allāh, to whom belongs the Glorious praise, has prepared for him. When he is placed in his grave his spirit is returned to him down to his thighs and is asked of what he knows. If he then comes up with what he knows, that door which the Messenger of Allāh had shown to him is opened, light, brightness, coolness, goodness and sweet smelling fragrance comes to him from there.' The narrator has said that I then asked, 'What about the strong pressure that grave applies?' The Imam replied, 'Never, a thing as such ever happens to believing people. By Allāh, this earth feels proud of him saying, "Look, a believing person walks upon me but no believing person walks upon you." The earth says to him, "I loved you when you walked upon my back and when I love, you can see what I will do for you." It opens up as far and wide as his eyes can see. (مجهول)[16]

17.

مُحَمَّدُ بْنُ يَحْيَى عَنْ أَحْمَدَ بْنِ مُحَمَّدِ بْنِ عِيسَى عَنِ ابْنِ فَضَّالٍ عَنْ يُونُسَ بْنِ يَعْقُوبَ عَنْ سَعِيدِ بْنِ يَسَارٍ أَنَّهُ حَضَرَ أَحَدَ ابْنَيْ سَابُورَ وَكَانَ لَهُمَا فَضْلٌ وَوَرَعٌ وَإِخْبَاتٌ فَمَرِضَ أَحَدُهُمَا وَمَا أَحْسَبُهُ إِلاَّ زَكَرِيَّا بْنَ سَابُورَ قَالَ فَحَضَرْتُهُ عِنْدَ مَوْتِهِ فَبَسَطَ يَدَهُ ثُمَّ قَالَ ابْيَضَّتْ يَدِي يَا عَلِيُّ قَالَ فَدَخَلْتُ عَلَى أَبِي عَبْدِ اللهِ (عَلَيْهِ السَّلام) وَعِنْدَهُ مُحَمَّدُ بْنُ مُسْلِمٍ قَالَ فَلَمَّا قُمْتُ مِنْ عِنْدِهِ ظَنَنْتُ أَنَّ مُحَمَّداً يُخْبِرُهُ بِخَبَرِ الرَّجُلِ فَأَتْبَعَنِي بِرَسُولٍ فَرَجَعْتُ إِلَيْهِ فَقَالَ أَخْبِرْنِي عَنْ هَذَا الرَّجُلِ الَّذِي حَضَرْتَهُ عِنْدَ الْمَوْتِ أَيَّ شَيْءٍ سَمِعْتَهُ يَقُولُ قَالَ قُلْتُ بَسَطَ يَدَهُ ثُمَّ قَالَ ابْيَضَّتْ يَدِي يَا عَلِيُّ فَقَالَ أَبُو عَبْدِ اللهِ (عَلَيْهِ السَّلام) وَاللهِ رَآهُ وَاللهِ رَآهُ وَاللهِ رَآهُ

Muhammad b. Yahya has narrated from Ahmad b. Muḥammad b. 'Isa from b. Faddal from Yunus b. Ya'qub from Sa'id b. Yasar who has said the following: "I was present at the time of the death of one of the sons of Sabur - both being people of merits, piety and great sincerity in their belief. One of them became ill and I think he was Zachariah b. Sabur. I visited him in his dying condition. He stretched his hand and then said, 'O Ali, my hands have become white.' I then visited abu 'Abd Allāh, (عليه السلام), when Muḥammad b. Muslim was also there. When I stood up to leave, thinking that Muḥammad would inform him about the case of the man (Zachariah b. Sabur), he sent someone after me and I returned. He said, 'Tell me about the man in

---

[16] *Al-Kāfi, v3, ch13, h2*

whose dying condition you were present. What did you hear from him?' I replied, 'He stretched his hand and then said, "O Ali, my hands have become white!" Abu 'Abd Allāh, (عليه السلام), then said, 'By Allāh he saw him, by Allāh he saw him, by Allāh he saw him! (موثق)[17]

18.

مُحَمَّدُ بْنُ يَحْيَى عَنْ أَحْمَدَ بْنِ مُحَمَّدٍ عَنْ عَلِيِّ بْنِ الْحَكَمِ عَنْ مُعَاوِيَةَ بْنِ وَهْبٍ عَنْ يَحْيَى بْنِ سَابُورٍ قَالَ سَمِعْتُ أَبَا عَبْدِ اللهِ (عَلَيْهِ السَّلام) يَقُولُ فِي الْمَيِّتِ تَدْمَعُ عَيْنُهُ عِنْدَ الْمَوْتِ فَقَالَ ذَلِكَ عِنْدَ مُعَايَنَةِ رَسُولِ اللهِ (صلّى اللهُ عَلَيْهِ وَآلِه) فَيَرَى مَا يَسُرُّهُ ثُمَّ قَالَ أَ مَا تَرَى الرَّجُلَ يَرَى مَا يَسُرُّهُ وَمَا يُحِبُّ فَتَدْمَعُ عَيْنُهُ لِذَلِكَ وَيَضْحَكُ

Muhammad b. Yahya has narrated from Ahmad b. Muhammad from 'Alī b. al-Hakam from Mu'awiyah b. Wahab from Yahya b. Sabur who has said the following: "I heard abu 'Abd Allāh, (عليه السلام), say about a dying person, 'His eye tears up (moistens with tears) at the time of his death.' He then said, 'This happens upon seeing the Messenger of Allāh. He sees what makes him happy.' He then said, 'Is it not a fact that when a person sees someone whom he loves his eye tears up (moistens with tears) and he laughs (حسن)[18]

19.

أَبَانُ بْنُ عُثْمَانَ عَنْ عُقْبَةَ أَنَّهُ سَمِعَ أَبَا عَبْدِ اللهِ (عَلَيْهِ السَّلام) يَقُولُ إِنَّ الرَّجُلَ إِذَا وَقَعَتْ نَفْسُهُ فِي صَدْرِهِ يَرَى قُلْتُ جُعِلْتُ فِدَاكَ وَمَا يَرَى قَالَ يَرَى رَسُولَ اللهِ (صلّى اللهُ عَلَيْهِ وَآلِه) فَيَقُولُ لَهُ رَسُولُ اللهِ أَنَا رَسُولُ اللهِ أَبْشِرْ ثُمَّ يَرَى عَلِيَّ بْنَ أَبِي طَالِبٍ (عَلَيْهِ السَّلام) فَيَقُولُ أَنَا عَلِيُّ بْنُ أَبِي طَالِبٍ الَّذِي كُنْتَ تُحِبُّهُ تُحِبُّ أَنْ أَنْفَعَكَ الْيَوْمَ قَالَ قُلْتُ لَهُ أَ يَكُونُ أَحَدٌ مِنَ النَّاسِ يَرَى هَذَا ثُمَّ يَرْجِعُ إِلَى الدُّنْيَا قَالَ قَالَ لَا إِذَا رَأَى هَذَا أَبَداً

---

[17] *Al-Kāfi, v3, ch13, h3*

[18] *Al-Kāfi, v3, ch13, h6*

مَاتَ وَأَعْظَمَ ذَلِكَ قَالَ وَذَلِكَ فِي الْقُرْآنِ قَوْلُ اللهِ عَزَّ وَجَلَّ الَّذِينَ آمَنُوا وَكَانُوا يَتَّقُونَ. لَهُمُ الْبُشْرَى فِي الْحَيَاةِ الدُّنْيَا وَفِي الآخِرَةِ لا تَبْدِيلَ لِكَلِمَاتِ اللهِ

Aban b. 'Uthman has narrated from 'Uqbah who had heard abu 'Abd Allāh, (عليه السلام), saying the following: "I heard abu 'Abd Allāh, (عليه السلام), say, 'When a man's soul reaches his chest he then sees.' I then asked, 'May Allāh keep my soul in the service of your cause, what does he see?' The Imam said, 'He sees the Messenger of Allāh and he says, "I am the Messenger of Allāh. I have good news for you." He then sees 'Alī b. abu Talib, (عليه السلام), who says, "I am 'Alī b. abu Talib, whom you loved. He loves to benefit you today."' I then asked, 'Can anyone who sees them come back to this life?' He said, 'No, when one sees them, he then can never return back to this life.' He considered it a great thing. He said this is in the Qur'ān in the words of Allāh, the Majestic, the Glorious, 'Those who believe, who were faithful to their belief, receive good news in this world and in the next life and there is no change in the words of Allāh.'" (10:64) (مرسل كالحسن)[19]

20.

الْحُسَيْنُ بْنُ مُحَمَّدٍ عَنْ مُعَلَّى بْنِ مُحَمَّدٍ عَنْ مُحَمَّدِ بْنِ جُمْهُورٍ عَنْ إِسْمَاعِيلَ بْنِ سَهْلٍ عَنِ الْقَاسِمِ بْنِ عُرْوَةَ عَنْ أَبِي السَّفَاتِجِ عَنْ زُرَارَةَ عَنْ ابي جعفر (عَلَيْهِ السَّلام) فِي قَوْلِهِ تَعَالَى فَلَمَّا رَأَوْهُ زُلْفَةً سِيئَتْ وُجُوهُ الَّذِينَ كَفَرُوا وَقِيلَ هذَا الَّذِي كُنْتُمْ بِهِ تَدَّعُونَ قَالَ هَذِهِ نَزَلَتْ فِي أَمِيرِ الْمُؤْمِنِينَ وَأَصْحَابِهِ الَّذِينَ عَمِلُوا مَا عَمِلُوا يَرَوْنَ أَمِيرَ الْمُؤْمِنِينَ (عَلَيْهِ السَّلام) فِي أَغْبَطِ الاماكِنِ لَهُمْ فَيُسِيءُ وُجُوهَهُمْ وَيُقَالُ لَهُمْ هذَا الَّذِي كُنْتُمْ بِهِ تَدَّعُونَ الَّذِي انْتَحَلْتُمُ اسْمَهُ

Al-Husayn b. Muhammad has narrated from Mu'alla b. Muhammad from Muhammad b. Jumhur from 'Isma'il b. Sahl from al-Qasim b. 'Urwa from abu al-Safatij from Zurara from abu Ja'far (عليه السلام) about the words of Allāh, the Most High. "When they see the torment approaching, the faces of the unbelievers will blacken

---

[19] *Al-Kāfi, v3, ch13, h8*

and they will be told, "This is what you wanted to (experience)" (67:27). The Imam (عليه السلام) said, "This was revealed about Amir al-Mu'minin (عليه السلام) and his contemporaries who did what they to him. They will see Amir al-Mu'minin (عليه السلام) in such a position that will make them envious. This will cause their faces to show miserable. It will be said to them, "This is the one whose title 'Amir al-Mu'minin' you had assumed. (موثق)[20]

21.

مُحَمَّدُ بْنُ يَحْيَى عَنْ أَحْمَدَ بْنِ مُحَمَّدٍ وَعَلِيُّ بْنُ مُحَمَّدٍ عَنْ سَهْلِ بْنِ زِيَادٍ جَمِيعاً عَنِ ابْنِ مَحْبُوبٍ عَنْ أَبِي حَمْزَةَ عَنْ ابي جعفر (عَلَيْهِ السَّلام) قَالَ لَمَّا قُبِضَ أَمِيرُ الْمُؤْمِنِينَ (عَلَيْهِ السَّلام) قَامَ الْحَسَنُ بن علي (عَلَيْهِما السَّلام) فِي مَسْجِدِ الْكُوفَةِ فَحَمِدَ اللهَ وَأَثْنَى عَلَيْهِ وَصَلَّى عَلَى النَّبِيِّ (صَلَّى اللهُ عَلَيْهِ وَآلِه) ثُمَّ قَالَ أَيُّهَا النَّاسُ إِنَّهُ قَدْ قُبِضَ فِي هَذِهِ اللَّيْلَةِ رَجُلٌ مَا سَبَقَهُ الاوَّلُونَ وَلا يُدْرِكُهُ الاخِرُونَ إِنَّهُ كَانَ لَصَاحِبَ رَايَةِ رَسُولِ الله (صَلَّى اللهُ عَلَيْهِ وَآلِه) عَنْ يَمِينِهِ جَبْرَئِيلُ وَعَنْ يَسَارِهِ مِيكَائِيلُ لا يَنْثَنِي حَتَّى يَفْتَحَ اللهُ لَهُ وَاللهِ مَا تَرَكَ بَيْضَاءَ وَلا حَمْرَاءَ إِلا سَبْعَمِائَةِ دِرْهَمٍ فَضَلَتْ عَنْ عَطَائِهِ أَرَادَ أَنْ يَشْتَرِيَ بِهَا خَادِماً لاهْلِهِ وَاللهِ لَقَدْ قُبِضَ فِي اللَّيْلَةِ الَّتِي فِيهَا قُبِضَ وَصِيُّ مُوسَى يُوشَعُ بْنُ نُونٍ وَاللَّيْلَةِ الَّتِي عُرِجَ فِيهَا بِعِيسَى ابْنِ مَرْيَمَ وَاللَّيْلَةِ الَّتِي نُزِّلَ فِيهَا الْقُرْآنُ

Muhammad b. Yahya has narrated from Ahmad b. Muḥammad and 'Alī b. mmd from Sahl b. Ziyad all from kbn Mahbub from abu Hamza from abu Ja'far (عليه السلام) who has said the following. "When Amir al-Mu'minin 'Alī (عليه السلام) passed away, al-Hassan b. 'Alī stoop up in the Mosque if Kufa. He praises Allāh and spoke of His Glory prayed to Allāh to grant blessings up on the Holy Prophet (s.a) and then he said this. People tonight a man has passed away the like whom cannot be found in previous and the coming generations. He was the standard bearer of the Messenger of Allāh, with Jibril on his right micha'il on his left. He would not turn back until Allāh would grant him victory. All that he has left of the worldly belongings is a seven hundred Dirham extra from his gifts with which he wanted to buy (hire) a servant for his household. By Allāh, he died during a night in which the executor of the will of

---

[20] *Al-Kafi, v1, ch108, h67*

Mūsā (Moses) Yusha' b. Nun had passed away, the night in which Jesus son of Mary was taken to heavens and the night in which the Holy Qur'ān was revealed. (صحيح)[21]

22.

عَنْهُ عَنْ أَبِيهِ عَنْ أَحْمَدَ بْنِ مُحَمَّدٍ عَنْ أَبَانٍ عَنْ أَبِي بَصِيرٍ عَنْ أَبِي جَعْفَرٍ (عليه السلام) قَالَ لَمَّا وُلِدَ النَّبِيُّ (صلى الله عليه وآله) جَاءَ رَجُلٌ مِنْ أَهْلِ الْكِتَابِ إِلَى مَلَإٍ مِنْ قُرَيْشٍ فِيهِمْ هِشَامُ بْنُ الْمُغِيرَةِ وَ الْوَلِيدُ بْنُ الْمُغِيرَةِ وَ الْعَاصُ بْنُ هِشَامٍ وَ أَبُو وَجْزَةَ بْنُ أَبِي عَمْرِو بْنِ أُمَيَّةَ وَ عُتْبَةُ بْنُ رَبِيعَةَ فَقَالَ أَ وُلِدَ فِيكُمْ مَوْلُودٌ اللَّيْلَةَ فَقَالُوا لَا قَالَ فَوُلِدَ إِذاً بِفِلَسْطِينَ غُلَامٌ اسْمُهُ أَحْمَدُ بِهِ شَامَةٌ كَلَوْنِ الْخَزِّ الْأَدْكَنِ وَ يَكُونُ هَلَاكُ أَهْلِ الْكِتَابِ وَ الْيَهُودِ عَلَى يَدَيْهِ قَدْ أَخْطَأَكُمْ وَ اللَّهِ يَا مَعْشَرَ قُرَيْشٍ فَتَفَرَّقُوا وَ سَأَلُوا فَأُخْبِرُوا أَنَّهُ وُلِدَ لِعَبْدِ اللَّهِ بْنِ عَبْدِ الْمُطَّلِبِ غُلَامٌ فَطَلَبُوا الرَّجُلَ فَلَقُوهُ فَقَالُوا إِنَّهُ قَدْ وُلِدَ فِينَا وَ اللَّهِ غُلَامٌ قَالَ قَبْلَ أَنْ أَقُولَ لَكُمْ أَوْ بَعْدَ مَا قُلْتُ لَكُمْ قَالُوا قَبْلَ أَنْ تَقُولَ لَنَا قَالَ فَانْطَلِقُوا بِنَا إِلَيْهِ حَتَّى نَنْظُرَ إِلَيْهِ فَانْطَلَقُوا حَتَّى أَتَوْا أُمَّهُ فَقَالُوا أَخْرِجِي ابْنَكِ حَتَّى نَنْظُرَ إِلَيْهِ فَقَالَتْ إِنَّ ابْنِي وَ اللَّهِ لَقَدْ سَقَطَ وَ مَا سَقَطَ كَمَا يَسْقُطُ الصِّبْيَانُ لَقَدِ اتَّقَى الْأَرْضَ بِيَدَيْهِ وَ رَفَعَ رَأْسَهُ إِلَى السَّمَاءِ فَنَظَرَ إِلَيْهَا ثُمَّ خَرَجَ مِنْهُ نُورٌ حَتَّى نَظَرْتُ إِلَى قُصُورِ بُصْرَى وَ سَمِعْتُ هَاتِفاً فِي الْجَوِّ يَقُولُ لَقَدْ وَلَدْتِيهِ سَيِّدَ الْأُمَّةِ فَإِذَا وَضَعْتِيهِ فَقُولِي أُعِيذُهُ بِالْوَاحِدِ مِنْ شَرِّ كُلِّ حَاسِدٍ وَ سَمِّيهِ مُحَمَّداً قَالَ الرَّجُلُ فَأَخْرِجِيهِ فَأَخْرَجَتْهُ فَنَظَرَ إِلَيْهِ ثُمَّ قَلَّبَهُ وَ نَظَرَ إِلَى الشَّامَةِ بَيْنَ كَتِفَيْهِ فَخَرَّ مَغْشِيّاً عَلَيْهِ فَأَخَذُوا الْغُلَامَ فَأَدْخَلُوهُ إِلَى أُمِّهِ وَ قَالُوا بَارَكَ اللَّهُ لَكِ فِيهِ فَلَمَّا خَرَجُوا أَفَاقَ فَقَالُوا لَهُ مَا لَكَ وَيْلَكَ قَالَ ذَهَبَتْ نُبُوَّةُ بَنِي إِسْرَائِيلَ إِلَى يَوْمِ الْقِيَامَةِ هَذَا وَ اللَّهِ مَنْ يُبِيرُهُمْ فَفَرِحَتْ قُرَيْشٌ بِذَلِكَ فَلَمَّا رَآهُمْ قَدْ فَرِحُوا قَالَ قَدْ فَرِحْتُمْ أَمَا وَ اللَّهِ لَيَسْطُوَنَّ بِكُمْ سَطْوَةً يَتَحَدَّثُ بِهَا أَهْلُ الْمَشْرِقِ وَ الْمَغْرِبِ وَ كَانَ أَبُو سُفْيَانَ يَقُولُ يَسْطُو بِمِصْرِهِ.

From Abī Baṣīr from Abī Ja`far (عليه السلام) said: 'When the Prophet (صلى الله عليه وآله وسلم) was born, a man from the people of the Book came to a group from the Quraysh, in them were Hishām b. al-Mughīrah, al-Walīd b. al-Mughīrah, al-Āṣ b. Hishām, Abū Wajzah b. Abī `Amr b. Umayyah and `Utbah b. Rabī`ah. So he (the man from the people of the book) said: 'Has a child been born among you at night?' They said: 'No' He (the man) said: 'Therefore a child must have been born in Palenstine, his name is Aḥmad, with him is a dark silky color mole. The destruction of the people of the book and the Jews will be by his hands, this has come to pass you

---

[21] *Al-Kāfi, v1, ch113, h8*

up, by Allāh, O gathering of Quraysh!' They dispersed, and they asked (around), and they were told that a boy was born to `Abd Allāh b. `Abd al-Muṭalib. They searched for the man, and found him. They said: 'By Allāh, a boy has been born among us.' He (the man) said: '(Was he born) before what I said to you, or after what I said to you?' They said: 'Before what you said to us'. He (the man) said: 'They must hurry to him until they see him, so they hurried until they came to his (صلى الله عليه وآله وسلم) mother (Āminah b.t Wahab), So they said: 'Give me your son, so we can see him. She (Āminah) said: 'By Allāh, my son dropped (to the ground), but he did not drop like what other children drop. When he dropped, he supported from the ground with his hand, and he raised his head to the sky and looked at it, then a light came from him until the castles of Baṣrah could see, and I heard a caller in the air say: 'You have given birth to the master of the nation (*Sayyid al-Ummah*), and when place him, you must say: 'I seek refuge by the One from every jealousy, and name him is Muḥammad'. The man said: 'Bring him', so she brought him (صلى الله عليه وآله وسلم) to him and he saw him, then he (the man) turned him (صلى الله عليه وآله وسلم) over and saw the mole (mark) between his shoulders, then he collapsed and (fell) unconscious. They took the child and brought him to his mother and they said: 'May Allāh bless you with him' .When they left, he (the man) woke up, and they said to him (the man): 'Woe unto you, what happened to you?' He (the man) said: 'Prophethood has left the Banī Isrā`īl until the day of Judgment, this, by Allāh, will destroy them.' The Quraysh were happy by this, when he saw them happy he (the man) said: 'You are happy, by Allāh, he will rule over you and he will speak to the people of the east and the west. And Abū Sufyān said: 'Will he rule his region?' (حسن أو موثق)[22]

23.

حُمَيْدُ بْنُ زِيَادٍ عَنْ مُحَمَّدِ بْنِ أَيُّوبَ عَنْ مُحَمَّدِ بْنِ زِيَادٍ عَنْ أَسْبَاطِ بْنِ سَالِمٍ عَنْ أَبِي عَبْدِ اللَّهِ (عليه السلام) قَالَ كَانَ حَيْثُ طُلِقَتْ آمِنَةُ بِنْتُ وَهْبٍ وَ أَخَذَهَا الْمَخَاضُ بِالنَّبِيِّ (صلى الله عليه وآله) حَضَرَتْهَا فَاطِمَةُ بِنْتُ

[22] *Al-Kāfi, v8, h458*

أَسَدٍ امْرَأَةُ أَبِي طَالِبٍ فَلَمْ تَزَلْ مَعَهَا حَتَّى وَضَعَتْ فَقَالَتْ إِحْدَاهُمَا لِلْأُخْرَى هَلْ تَرَيْنَ مَا أَرَى فَقَالَتْ وَ مَا تَرَيْنَ قَالَتْ هَذَا النُّورَ الَّذِي قَدْ سَطَعَ مَا بَيْنَ الْمَشْرِقِ وَ الْمَغْرِبِ فَبَيْنَمَا هُمَا كَذَلِكَ إِذْ دَخَلَ عَلَيْهِمَا أَبُو طَالِبٍ فَقَالَ لَهُمَا مَا لَكُمَا مِنْ أَيِّ شَيْءٍ تَعْجَبَانِ فَأَخْبَرَتْهُ فَاطِمَةُ بِالنُّورِ الَّذِي قَدْ رَأَتْ فَقَالَ لَهَا أَبُو طَالِبٍ أَ لَا أُبَشِّرُكِ فَقَالَتْ بَلَى فَقَالَ أَمَا إِنَّكِ سَتَلِدِينَ غُلَاماً يَكُونُ وَصِيَّ هَذَا الْمَوْلُودِ

Humeyd b. Ziyad, from Muḥammad b. Ayyub, from Muḥammad b. Ziyad, from Asbaat b. Saalim, who has narrated the following: Abu 'AbdAllāh (عليه السلام) having said: 'When Aamina b. Wahab (عليها السلام) went behind the curtain, and was taken before the 'nazool' of the Prophet (صلى الله عليه وآله وسلم), Fatima b. Asad (عليها السلام) the wife of Abu Talib (عليه السلام) was present with her (عليه السلام). She (عليه السلام) did not cease to be with her (عليه السلام) until she (عليها السلام) was blessed. So one of them (عليه السلام) said to the other (عليه السلام), 'Did you (عليه السلام) see what I (عليه السلام) saw?' She (عليه السلام) said, 'And what did you (عليه السلام) see?' She (عليه السلام) said, 'This light which has brightened up what is in between the East and the West and what is in between the two as well'. Then Abu Talib (عليه السلام) came up to them (عليه السلام) and said to them (عليه السلام) both, 'What is the matter with you (عليه السلام) two? Which thing has astounded you (عليه السلام) two?' So Fatima (عليه السلام) informed him (عليه السلام) of the light which she (عليه السلام) had seen. So Abu Talib (عليه السلام) said to her (عليه السلام), 'Indeed! I (عليه السلام) give you (عليه السلام) good news!' She (عليه السلام) said, 'Yes'. So he (عليه السلام) said, 'You (عليه السلام) will be blessed with the one who will be the successor of this newborn'. (حسن أو موثق)[23]

24.

أَبَانٌ عَنْ أَبِي بَصِيرٍ عَنْ أَبِي عَبْدِ اللَّهِ (عليه السلام) نَزَلَ رَسُولُ اللَّهِ (صلى الله عليه وآله) فِي غَزْوَةِ ذَاتِ الرِّقَاعِ تَحْتَ شَجَرَةٍ عَلَى شَفِيرِ وَادٍ فَأَقْبَلَ سَيْلٌ فَحَالَ بَيْنَهُ وَ بَيْنَ أَصْحَابِهِ فَرَآهُ رَجُلٌ مِنَ الْمُشْرِكِينَ وَ الْمُسْلِمُونَ قِيَامٌ عَلَى شَفِيرِ الْوَادِي يَنْتَظِرُونَ مَتَى يَنْقَطِعُ السَّيْلُ فَقَالَ رَجُلٌ مِنَ الْمُشْرِكِينَ لِقَوْمِهِ أَنَا أَقْتُلُ مُحَمَّداً فَجَاءَ وَ شَدَّ عَلَى رَسُولِ اللَّهِ (صلى الله عليه وآله) بِالسَّيْفِ ثُمَّ قَالَ مَنْ يُنْجِيكَ مِنِّي يَا مُحَمَّدُ فَقَالَ رَبِّي وَ رَبُّكَ فَنَسَفَهُ جَبْرَئِيلُ (عليه السلام) عَنْ فَرَسِهِ فَسَقَطَ عَلَى ظَهْرِهِ فَقَامَ رَسُولُ اللَّهِ (صلى الله عليه وآله) وَ أَخَذَ

---

[23] *Al-Kafi, v8, h459*

السَّيْفَ وَ جَلَسَ عَلَى صَدْرِهِ وَ قَالَ مَنْ يُنْجِيكَ مِنِّي يَا غَوْرَثُ فَقَالَ جُودُكَ وَ كَرَمُكَ يَا مُحَمَّدُ فَتَرَكَهُ فَقَامَ وَ هُوَ يَقُولُ وَ اللَّهِ لَأَنْتَ خَيْرٌ مِنِّي وَ أَكْرَمُ

Abaan, from Abu Baseer has narrated the following: Abu 'AbdAllāh (عليه السلام) has said that the Messenger of Allāh (صلى الله عليه وآله وسلم) Allāh (تبارك و طائلة) encamped under a tree on the edge of the valley during the (military) expedition of Zaat Al-Raqa'a. A flooding came in between him and his companions. A man from the Polytheists saw it, and the Muslims were standing upon the edge of the valley waiting for the flood to be cut-off (subside). So a man from the Polytheists said to his people, 'I will kill Messenger of Allāh (صلى الله عليه وآله وسلم)'. So he came and pulled out his sword against the Messenger of Allāh (صلى الله عليه وآله وسلم) Allāh (تبارك و طائلة) then said, 'Who is going to save you from me, O Messenger of Allāh (صلى الله عليه وآله وسلم)?' He said: 'My Lord , and your Lord '. So Jibraeel (عليه السلام) blew him off his horse and he fell upon his back. The Messenger of Allāh (صلى الله عليه وآله وسلم) stood up and took the sword, and sat upon his chest and said: 'Who is the one who will rescue you from me, O Gowras?' He said, 'Your benevolence and your generosity, O Messenger of Allāh (صلى الله عليه وآله وسلم)'. So he left him. He stood up and he was saying, 'By Allāh (تبارك و طائلة), you are better than me and more generous'. (صحيح)[24]

25.

حدثنا أبي رضي الله عنه قال: حدثنا علي بن إبراهيم بن هاشم، عن أبيه، عن محمد بن أبي عمير، عن أبان الاحمر، عن الصادق أبي عبد الله جعفر بن محمد عليهما السلام قال: جاء رجل إلى رسول الله صلى الله عليه وآله وقد بلي ثوبه فحمل إليّ اثني عشر درهما فقال عليه السلام: يا علي خذ هذه الدراهم فاشتر لي بها ثوبا ألبسه. قال علي عليه السلام: فجئت إلى السوق فاشتريت له قميصاً باثني عشر درهما وجئت به إلى رسول الله صلى الله عليه وآله. فنظر إليّ فقال: يا علي، غير هذا أحب إليّ. أترى صاحبه يقيلنا؟ فقلت: لا أدري. فقال: انظر. فجئت إلى صاحبه فقلت: إن رسول الله صلى الله عليه وآله قد كره هذا يريد غيره فأقلنا فيه، فرد علي الدراهم وجئت بها إلى رسول الله صلى الله عليه وآله فمشى معه إلى السوق ليبتاع قميصا

[24] *Al-Kāfi, v8, h97*

فنظر إلى جارية قاعدة على الطريق تبكي، فقال لها رسول الله صلى الله عليه وآله: وما شأنك: قالت: يا رسول الله إن أهلي أعطوني أربعة دراهم لاشتري لهم حاجة فضاعت، فلا أجسر أن أرجع إليهم فأعطاها، رسول الله صلى الله عليه وآله أربعة دراهم وقال: ارجعي إلى أهلك ومضى رسول الله صلى الله عليه وآله إلى السوق فاشترى قميصا بأربعة دراهم ولبسه وحمد الله عز وجل فرأى رجلا عريانا يقول: من كساني كساه الله من ثياب الجنة، فخلع رسول الله صلى الله عليه وآله قميصه الذي اشتراه وكساه السائل،ثم رجع عليه السلام إلى السوق فاشترى بالاربعة التي بقيت قميصا آخر فلبسه وحمد الله عز وجل ورجع إلى منزله فإذا الجارية قاعدة على الطريق تبكي فقال لها رسول الله صلى الله عليه وآله: مالك لا تأتين أهلك؟ قالت: يا رسول الله إني قد أبطأت عليهم أخاف أن يضربوني، فقال رسول الله صلى الله عليه وآله: مري بين يدي وليني على أهلك، وجاء رسول الله صلى الله عليه وآله حتى وقف على باب دراهم، ثم قال: السلام عليكم يا أهل الدار، فلم يجيبوه فأعاد السلام فلم يجيبوه، فأعاد السلام فقالوا: وعليكم السلام يا رسول الله ورحمة الله وبركاته، فقال عليه الصلاة والسلام: ما لكم تركتم إجابتي في أول السلام والثاني؟ فقالوا: يا رسول الله سمعنا كلامك فأحببنا أن نستكثر منه، فقال رسول الله صلى الله عليه وآله: إن هذه الجارية أبطأت عليكم فلا تؤذوها، فقالوا: يا رسول الله هي حرة لممشاك، فقال رسول الله صلى الله عليه وآله: الحمد لله ما رأيت اثني عشر درهما أعظم بركة من هذه، كسا الله بها عاريين، وأعتق نسمة

(The compiler of the book narrated) that his father - may God be pleased with him - narrated that 'Alī b. Ibrahim b. Hashim quoted his father, on the authority of Muḥammad b. Abi Umayr, on the authority of Aban al-Ahmar, on the authority of As-Ṣādiq Aba 'Abd Allāh Ja'far b. Muḥammad (عليه السلام), "A man went to see God's Prophet (صلى الله عليه وآله وسلم). When he saw that the Prophet's shirt was old, he gave him twelve Dirhams. The Prophet (صلى الله عليه وآله وسلم) said, "O Ali! Take this money and buy me a shirt with it."Ali (عليه السلام) said, "I went to the store and bought the Prophet (صلى الله عليه وآله وسلم) a shirt with twelve Dirhams and took it to the Prophet (صلى الله عليه وآله وسلم). He (عليه السلام) looked at it and said, 'O Ali! I like a different shirt! Do you think that the seller would take it back?' 'Alī (عليه السلام) replied, 'I do not know.' The Prophet (صلى الله عليه وآله وسلم) said, 'Then try it.'Ali (عليه السلام) went back to the store and told the store-keeper, 'The Prophet of God (صلى الله عليه وآله وسلم) doesn't like this shirt. He wants another shirt. Please take it back and return the money.' Then he (عليه السلام) returned the money to the Prophet (صلى الله عليه وآله وسلم). The Prophet (صلى الله عليه وآله وسلم) accompanied 'Alī (عليه السلام) to the shop to buy another shirt. They ran into a slave girl who was sitting there and crying. The Prophet (صلى الله عليه وآله وسلم) asked her, 'Why are you crying?' She said, 'O Prophet of God! My master gave me four Dirhams with which to buy things from the market. I don't know where that money got lost. Now, I don't have the courage to go back home.' The Prophet (صلى الله عليه وآله وسلم) gave her four Dirhams and told her, 'Buy whatever you had to buy and go back home.'Then the Prophet (صلى الله عليه وآله وسلم) went to the market to buy a shirt for himself for four Dirhams. He (صلى الله عليه وآله وسلم) put it on, praised the Honorable the Exalted God and returned. On his way back from the market, the Prophet (صلى الله عليه وآله وسلم) saw an undressed man who kept on saying, 'God will put on a Heavenly attire on whoever dresses me up.' Then the Prophet (صلى الله عليه وآله وسلم) took off his shirt and put it on the needy man.'Then the Prophet (صلى الله عليه وآله وسلم) himself went to the market to buy another shirt for himself with the last four Dirhams. He (صلى الله عليه وآله وسلم) put it on, praised the Honorable the Exalted God and returned. On his way back, he (صلى الله عليه وآله وسلم) ran into the slave-girl again who was sitting there and crying. The Prophet (صلى الله عليه وآله وسلم) asked her, "Why didn't you go home?" She replied, "O Prophet of God! It is too late for me to return and I am afraid that they might beat me up." The Prophet of God (صلى الله عليه وآله وسلم) said, "Walk ahead of me and take me to your house." The Prophet (صلى الله عليه وآله وسلم) walked with her until they reached her house. He stopped at the door and said, "O residents of this house! Peace be upon you." There was no response. He (صلى الله عليه وآله وسلم) greeted again, but they did not respond. So he (صلى الله عليه وآله وسلم) greeted for the third time. Then they said, "O Prophet of God (صلى الله عليه وآله وسلم)! Peace, blessings and His Mercy be upon you!" The Prophet (صلى الله عليه وآله وسلم) asked, "Then what was the reason why you did not respond to my greeting the first and the second time?" They said, "O Prophet of God (صلى الله عليه وآله وسلم)! Yes! After hearing your voice for the first time itself, we came to know that it was you. However, we loved to hear your voice over and over again." God's Prophet (صلى الله عليه وآله وسلم) said, "Your slave-girl has taken a long time to come back. Hence, I have come to request that you do not punish her." They said, "O Prophet of God! By the blessing of your gracious coming over to our place, we have set this slave-girl free." The Prophet (صلى الله عليه وآله وسلم) said, "Praise be to God. How blessed were these twelve Dirhams with which two undressed persons got dressed in and a slave-girl was freed. (موثق)[25]

26.

عَلِيُّ بْنُ إِبْرَاهِيمَ عَنْ أَبِيهِ عَنْ أَحْمَدَ بْنِ مُحَمَّدِ بْنِ أَبِي نَصْرٍ عَنْ أَبَانِ بْنِ عُثْمَانَ عَنْ زُرَارَةَ عَنْ أَبِي جَعْفَرٍ (عليه السلام) أَنَّ ثُمَامَةَ بْنَ أُثَالٍ أَسَرَتْهُ خَيْلُ النَّبِيِّ (صلى الله عليه وآله) وَ قَدْ كَانَ رَسُولُ اللَّهِ (صلى الله عليه وآله) قَالَ اللَّهُمَّ أَمْكِنِّي مِنْ ثُمَامَةَ فَقَالَ لَهُ رَسُولُ اللَّهِ (صلى الله عليه وآله) إِنِّي مُخَيِّرُكَ وَاحِدَةً مِنْ ثَلَاثٍ أَقْتُلُكَ قَالَ إِذاً تَقْتُلَ عَظِيماً أَوْ أُفَادِيكَ قَالَ إِذاً تَجِدَنِي غَالِياً أَوْ أَمُنُّ عَلَيْكَ قَالَ إِذاً تَجِدَنِي شَاكِراً قَالَ فَإِنِّي قَدْ مَنَنْتُ عَلَيْكَ قَالَ فَإِنِّي أَشْهَدُ أَنْ لَا إِلَهَ إِلَّا اللَّهُ وَ أَنَّكَ مُحَمَّدٌ رَسُولُ اللَّهِ وَ قَدْ وَ اللَّهِ عَلِمْتُ أَنَّكَ رَسُولُ اللَّهِ حَيْثُ رَأَيْتُكَ وَ مَا كُنْتُ لِأَشْهَدَ بِهَا وَ أَنَا فِي الْوَثَاقِ

Ali b. Ibrahim, from his father, from Ahmad b. Muḥammad b. Abu Nasr, from Abaan b. Usmaan, from Zurara, who has narrated the following: Abu Ja'far (عليه السلام) that: 'Thumamah b. Asaal was captured by the cavalry of the Prophet (صلى الله عليه وآله وسلم) and the Messenger of Allāh (صلى الله عليه وآله وسلم) had said; 'Our Allāh (تبارك و طائلة)! Make me to overcome Thumamah!' So the Messenger of Allāh (صلى الله عليه وآله وسلم) said to him: 'I give you one of three choices. I could kill you'. He said, 'Then you would have killed a great person'. He said: 'I could ransom you'. He said, 'Then you would find me to be expensive'. He said: 'Or I give safety to you'. He said, 'Then you would find me to be thankful'. He said: 'So I give safety to you'. He said, 'I hereby testify that there is no god except Allāh (تبارك و طائلة), and you Messenger of Allāh (صلى الله عليه وآله وسلم) are the Messenger of Allāh (صلى الله عليه وآله وسلم), and by Allāh (تبارك و طائلة), I knew you were the Messenger of Allāh (صلى الله عليه وآله وسلم) when I saw you, and I did not testify by it whilst I was in bondage'. (حسن أو موثاق)[26]

---

[25] *Al-Khiṣāl, ch15, h1*

[26] *Al-Kāfi, v8, h457*

27.

مُحَمَّدُ بْنُ يَحْيَى عَنْ أَحْمَدَ بْنِ مُحَمَّدٍ عَنِ الْوَشَّاءِ عَنْ جَمِيلِ بْنِ دَرَّاجٍ عَنْ أَبِي عَبْدِ اللهِ (عَلَيهِ السَّلام) قَالَ كَانَ رَسُولُ اللهِ (صَلَّى اللهُ عَلَيْهِ وآلِه) يَقْسِمُ لَحَظَاتِهِ بَيْنَ أَصْحَابِهِ فَيَنْظُرُ إِلَى ذَا وَيَنْظُرُ إِلَى ذَا بِالسَّوِيَّةِ قَالَ وَلَمْ يَبْسُطْ رَسُولُ اللهِ (صَلَّى اللهُ عَلَيْهِ وآلِه) رِجْلَيْهِ بَيْنَ أَصْحَابِهِ قَطُّ وَإِنْ كَانَ لَيُصَافِحُهُ الرَّجُلُ فَمَا يَتْرُكُ رَسُولُ اللهِ (صَلَّى اللهُ عَلَيْهِ وآلِه) يَدَهُ مِنْ يَدِهِ حَتَّى يَكُونَ هُوَ التَّارِكَ فَلَمَّا فَطَنُوا لِذَلِكَ كَانَ الرَّجُلُ إِذَا صَافَحَهُ قَالَ بِيَدِهِ فَنَزَعَهَا مِنْ يَدِهِ

Muhammad b. Yahya has narrated from Ahmad b. Muḥammad from al- Washsha' from Jamil b. Darraj from abu 'Abd Allāh (عليه السلام) who has said the following: "The Messenger of Allāh would look to every one of his companions in equal proportions of time. He would look to this and then to that person. The Messenger of Allāh was never seen stretching his legs in a gathering of his companions. When he would shake hands, with a person, the Messenger of Allāh would not pull back his hand before the other man. When they noticed it thereafter a man shaking hands with him would pull his hand away quickly. (صحيح)[27]

28.

حَدَّثنا مُحَمَّدِ بْنِ عَلِي ماجِيلوَيْه وَأَحْمَدِ بْنِ عَلِيِّ بْنِ إِبراهِيمِ بْنِ هاشِمٍ وَأَحْمَد بْنِ جَعْفَرِ الْهَمَذانِيِّ - رَضِيَ اللَّهُ عَنْهُمْ - قالُوا: حَدَّثنا عَلِيّ بْنِ إبراهِيم بْنِ هاشِمٍ، عَنْ أَبِيهِ، عَنْ مَعبَدٍ عَنِ الْحُسَيْنِ بْنِ خالِدٍ عَنِ الرِّضا عَلِيِّ بْنِ مُوسَى، عَنْ أَبِيهِ مُوسَى بْنِ جَعْفَر، عَنْأَبِيهِ جَعْفَرِ بْنِ مُحَمَّد، عَنْ أَبِيهِ مُحَمَّدِ بْنِ عَلِيٍّ، عَنْ أَبِيهِ عَلِيِّ بْنِ الْحُسَيْنِ، عَنْ أَبِيهِ الْحُسَيْنُ بْنُ عَلِيٍّ، عَنْ أَبِيهِ عَلِيِّ بْنِ أَبِي طالِب عَلَيْهِمُ السَّلاَمُ قالَ: قالَ رَسُولَ اللَّهِ صَلَّى اللَّهُ عَلَيْهِ وَآلِهِ: لِكُلِّ أُمَّةٍ صِدِّيقٌ وَفارُوقٌ وَصِدِّيقُ هَذِهِ الأُمَّةِ وَفارُوقُها عَلِيُّ بْنُ أَبِي طالِبٍ إِنَّ عَلِيّاً سَفِينَةُ نَجاتِها وَبابُ حِطَّتِها إِنَّهُ يُوشَعُها وَشَمْعُونُها وَذُو قَرْنَيْها مَعاشِرَ النّاسِ إِنَّ عَلِيّاً خَلِيفَةُ اللَّهِ وَخَلِيفَتِي عَلَيْكُمْ بَعْدِي وَإِنَّهُ لاميرُ الْمُؤْمِنِينَ وَخَيْرُ الْوَصِيِّينَ مَنْ نازَعَهُ فَقَدْ نازَعَنِي وَمَنْ ظَلَمَهُ فَقَدْ ظَلَمَنِي وَمَنْ غالَبَهُ فَقَدْ غالَبَنِي وَمَنْ بَرَّهُ فَقَدْ بَرَّنِي وَمَنْ جَفاهُ فَقَدْ جَفانِي وَمَنْ عاداهُ فَقَدْ عادانِي وَمَنْ والاهُ فَقَدْ والانِي وَذَلِكَ أَنَّهُ أَخِي وَوَزِيرِي وَمَخْلُوقٌ مِنْ طِينَتِي وَكُنْتُ أَنَا وَإِيّاهُ نُوراً واحِداً

---

[27] *Al-Kāfi, v2, ch28, h1*

Muhammad b. 'Alī Majiluwayh, Ahmad b. 'Alī b. Ibrahim b. Hashem, and Ahmad b. Ziyad b. Ja'far al-Hamadani - may God be pleased with them - narrated that 'Alī b. Ibrahim b. Hashem quoted on the authority of his father, on the authority of 'Alī b. Ma'bad, on the authority of Al-Hussein b. Khalid, on the authority of Al-Ridha 'Alī b. Mūsā (عليه السلام), on the authority of his father Mūsā b. Ja'far (عليه السلام), on the authority of his father Ja'far b. Muḥammad (عليه السلام), on the authority of hisfather Muḥammad b. 'Alī (عليه السلام), on the authority of 'Alī b. Al-Hussein (عليه السلام), on the authority of his father Al-Hussein b. 'Alī (عليه السلام), on the authority of his father 'Alī b. Abi Talib (عليه السلام), "God's Prophet (صلى الله عليه وآله وسلم) said, There is a companion and one who distinguishes truth from falsehood for every nation. The one for this nation is 'Alī b. Abi Talib. He is the ship of salvation. He is its gate of repentance. He is like its Yosha', Sham'oon, and Thul-Qarnayn. O people! 'Alī is God's vicegerent and my Caliph after me. He is the Commander of the Faithful. He is the best of the Trustees. Whoever fights with him has indeed fought with me. Whoever oppresses him has indeed oppressed me. Whoever overcomes him has indeed overcome me. Whoever does him good has indeed done good to me. Whoever mistreats him has indeed mistreated me. Whoever is his enemy is indeed my enemy. Whoever is his friend is indeed my friend, since he is my brother and Vizier. He has been created from the same essence that I have been created from. He and I are but one and the same light. (مجهول)[28]

29.

عَلِيُّ بْنُ إِبْرَاهِيمَ عَنْ أَبِيهِ عَنْ أَحْمَدَ بْنِ مُحَمَّدِ بْنِ أَبِي نَصْرٍ عَنْ مُعَاوِيَةَ بْنِ عَمَّارٍ عَنْ أَبِي عَبْدِ اللهِ (عَلَيْهِ السَّلام) قَالَ شِعَارُنَا يَا مُحَمَّدُ يَا مُحَمَّدُ وَشِعَارُنَا يَوْمَ بَدْرٍ يَا نَصْرَ اللهِ اقْتَرِبْ اقْتَرِبْ وَشِعَارُ الْمُسْلِمِينَ يَوْمَ أُحُدٍ يَا نَصْرَ اللهِ اقْتَرِبْ وَيَوْمَ بَنِي النَّضِيرِ يَا رُوحَ الْقُدُسِ أَرِحْ وَيَوْمَ بَنِي قَيْنُقَاعَ يَا رَبَّنَا لا يَغْلِبَنَّكَ وَيَوْمَ الطَّائِفِ يَا رِضْوَانُ وَشِعَارُ يَوْمِ حُنَيْنٍ يَا بَنِي عَبْدِ اللهِ [يَا بَنِي عَبْدِ اللهِ] وَيَوْمِ الأَحْزَابِ حم لا يُبْصِرُونَ وَيَوْمِ بَنِي قُرَيْظَةَ

[28] *'Uyūn Akhbār al-Riḍa, v1, ch30, h30*

يَا سَلامُ أَسْلِمْهُمْ وَيَوْمِ الْمُرَيْسِيعِ وَهُوَ يَوْمُ بَنِي الْمُصْطَلِقِ أَلا إِلَى اللهِ الأَمْرُ وَيَوْمِ الْحُدَيْبِيَةِ أَلا لَعْنَةُ اللهِ عَلَى الظَّالِمِينَ وَيَوْمِ خَيْبَرَ يَوْمِ الْقَمُوصِ يَا عَلِيُّ آتِهِمْ مِنْ عَلُ وَيَوْمِ الْفَتْحِ نَحْنُ عِبَادُ اللهِ حَقّاً حَقّاً وَيَوْمِ تَبُوكَ يَا أَحَدُ يَا صَمَدُ وَيَوْمِ بَنِي الْمَلُوحِ أَمِتْ أَمِتْ وَيَوْمِ صِفِّينَ يَا نَصْرَ اللهِ وَشِعَارُ الْحُسَيْنِ (عَلَيْهِ السَّلام) يَا مُحَمَّدُ وَشِعَارُنَا يَا مُحَمَّدُ

Ali b. Ibrahim has narrated from his father from Ahmad b. Muḥammad b. abu Nasr from Mu'awiyah b. 'Ammar who has said the following: "Abu ' Abd Allāh, (عليه السلام), has said that our slogan on the day Badr was, 'O victory of Allāh, come close! come close!' The slogan of Muslims on the day of 'Uhud was, O victory of Allāh, come close! ' On the day of banu al-Nadir it was, 'O Holy Spirit, bring comfort! ' On the day of banu Qaynaqa' it was, 'O our Lord, no one is able to defeat You!' On the day of Taef it was, 'O Ridwan! (name of a certain angel)' Our slogan on the day of Hunayn was, 'O banu ' Abd Allāh! O banu 'Abd Allāh! ' On the day of al-Ahzab it was, 'Ha Mim, They cannot see! ' On the day of banu Quraydah it was, 'O Peace Giver, make them surrender!' On the day of al-Muraysi' which is also called the day of banu al-Mustliq it was, 'Is the matter not in the hands of Allāh! ' On the day of al-Hudaybiyah it was, 'May Allāh condemn the unjust!' On the day of al-Khaybar, also called the day of al-Qamus it was, 'O Ali, come upon them from on high! ' On the day of victory it was, 'We are the servants of Allāh, indeed, indeed!' On the day of Tabuk it was, 'O the One! O self-sufficient!' On the day of banu al- Maluh it was, 'Higher, higher!' On the day of Siffin it was, 'O Assistance of Allāh!' The slogan of al- Husayn, (عليه السلام), was, 'O Muhammad!' Our slogan is, 'O Muhammad! (حسن)[29]

30.

حُمَيْدُ بْنُ زِيَادٍ عَنِ الْحَسَنِ بْنِ مُحَمَّدٍ الْكِنْدِيِّ عَنْ غَيْرِ وَاحِدٍ عَنْ أَبَانِ بْنِ عُثْمَانَ عَنِ الْفُضَيْلِ عَنْ زُرَارَةَ عَنْ أَبِي جَعْفَرٍ (عليه السلام) قَالَ إِنَّ النَّاسَ لَمَّا صَنَعُوا مَا صَنَعُوا إِذْ بَايَعُوا أَبَا بَكْرٍ لَمْ يَمْنَعْ أَمِيرَ الْمُؤْمِنِينَ (عليه السلام) مِنْ أَنْ يَدْعُوَ إِلَى نَفْسِهِ إِلَّا نَظَراً لِلنَّاسِ وَتَخَوُّفاً عَلَيْهِمْ أَنْ يَرْتَدُّوا عَنِ الْإِسْلَامِ فَيَعْبُدُوا الْأَوْثَانَ وَ لَا

[29] *Al-Kāfi, v5, ch21, h1*

يَشْهَدُوا أَنْ لَا إِلَهَ إِلَّا اللَّهُ وَ أَنَّ مُحَمَّداً رَسُولُ اللَّهِ (صلى الله عليه وآله) وَ كَانَ الْأَحَبَّ إِلَيْهِ أَنْ يُقِرَّهُمْ عَلَى مَا صَنَعُوا مِنْ أَنْ يَرْتَدُّوا عَنْ جَمِيعِ الْإِسْلَامِ وَ إِنَّمَا هَلَكَ الَّذِينَ رَكِبُوا مَا رَكِبُوا فَأَمَّا مَنْ لَمْ يَصْنَعْ ذَلِكَ وَ دَخَلَ فِيمَا دَخَلَ فِيهِ النَّاسُ عَلَى غَيْرِ عِلْمٍ وَ لَا عَدَاوَةٍ لِأَمِيرِ الْمُؤْمِنِينَ (عليه السلام) فَإِنَّ ذَلِكَ لَا يُكَفِّرُهُ وَ لَا يُخْرِجُهُ مِنَ الْإِسْلَامِ وَ لِذَلِكَ كَتَمَ عَلِيٌّ (عليه السلام) أَمْرَهُ وَ بَايَعَ مُكْرَهاً حَيْثُ لَمْ يَجِدْ أَعْوَاناً

Humeyd b. Ziyad, from Al-Hassan b. Muḥammad Al-Kindy, from someone else, from Abaan b. Usmaan, from Al-Fazel, from Zurara, who has narrated the following: Abu Ja'far (عليه السلام) has said that: 'The people, when they did what they did, they pledged their allegiances to Abu Bakr, nothing prevented Amir al- Mu'minin (عليه السلام) calling the people to himself except that he looked around at the people and feared for them that they would renege from Al-Islam, and resort to worshipping the idols and not testify that there is no god except Allāh (تبارك و طائلة) and that Muḥammad (صلى الله عليه وآله وسلم) is the Messenger of Allāh (صلى الله عليه وآله وسلم), and it was more beloved to him than he should agree with them upon what they had done rather than them reneging against the whole of Al-Islam. But rather, destroyed is the one who does what they did. So, as for the one who did not do that, and entered into what the people had entered into without knowledge or enmity against Amir al- Mu'minin (عليه السلام), so for that they have neither blasphemed nor exited from Al-Islam, and it is for that reason that 'Alī (عليه السلام) concealed his matter, and had to pledge allegiance unwillingly, when he did not find any helpers'. (صحيح)[30]

31.

[قال:] حدثنا أبو جعفر محمد بن علي بن الحسين قال: حدثني أبي قال: حدثني محمد بن يحيى العطار قال: حدثنا أحمد بن محمد بن عيسى، عن علي بن الحكم، عن هشام بن سالم، عن سليمان بن خالد، عن أبي عبد الله جعفر بن محمد الصادق، عن آبائه عليهم السلام قال: قال رسول الله صلى الله عليه وآله لعلي عليه السلام: يا علي أنت مني وأنا منك: وليك وليي ووليي ولي الله، وعدوك عدوي وعدوي عدو الله. يا علي أنا حرب لمن حاربك، وسلم لمن سالمك. يا علي لك كنز في الجنة وأنت ذو قرنيها . يا علي أنت قسيم الجنة

[30] *Al-Kāfi, v8, ch453*

والنار، لا يدخل الجنة إلا من عرفك وعرفته ، ولا يدخل النار إلا من أنكرك وأنكرته. يا علي أنت والأئمة من ولدك على الأعراف يوم القيامة تعرف المجرمين بسيماهم، والمؤمنين بعلاماتهم. يا علي لولاك لم يعرف المؤمنون بعدي

He said: Abu Ja'far Muḥammad b. 'Ali b. al-Husayn reported to me from his father, who reported from Muḥammad b. Yahya al-Attar, who reported from Ahmad b. Muḥammad b. Isa, from 'Ali b. Al-Hakam, from Hisham b. Salim, from Sulaiman b. Khalid, from Abu Abdillah Ja'far b. Muḥammad al-Ṣādiq, (عليه السلام) him, from his forefathers, (عليهم السلام), who said: The Prophet, (صلى الله عليه وآله وسلم) and his progeny, told 'Ali, (عليه السلام): "O 'Ali, you are from me and I from you. Your friend is my friend and my friend is Allāh's friend. And your enemy is my enemy and my enemy is the enemy of Allāh. O 'Ali, I am at war with the one who fights you and at peace with one who is at peace with you. O 'Ali, you have a treasure in the Heaven and you are the master of its both sides. O 'Ali, you are the divider of heaven and hell. None shall enter the heaven unless he has recognized you, and you have recognized him! And none shall enter hell unless he has rejected you and you have rejected him. O 'Ali, you and your descendants shall be on the heights (al-A'araaf) on the Day of Judgment, recognizing the sinners by their marks, and the believers by their signs. O 'Ali, the believers would not have been distinguished, after I have departed, if you were not there. (صحيح)[31]

32.

قال: أخبرني أبو جعفر محمد بن علي بن الحسين بن بابويه رحمه الله عن أبيه، عن محمد بن الحسن الصفار، عن أحمد بن محمد بن عيسى، عن علي بن النعمان ، عن عامر بن معقل عن أبي حمزة الثمالي قال: قال أبو جعفر محمد بن علي الباقر عليهما السلام: يا أبا حمزة لا تضعوا عليا دون ما رفعه الله، ولا ترفعوا عليا فوق ما جعله الله، كفى عليا أن يقاتل أهل الكرة وأن يزوج أهل الجنة

[31] *Al-Amālī (Mufīd), ch4, h1*

He said: Abu Ja'far Muḥammad b. 'Ali b. Al-Husayn b. Babawayh, may Allāh bless him with mercy, reported to me from his father who reported from Muḥammad b. al-Hasan al-Saffar, from Ahmad b. Muḥammad b. Isa, from 'Ali b. al-Nu'man, from Amir b. Ma'qal, from Abu Hamza al-Thumali, that Abu Ja'far Muḥammad b. 'Ali al-Baqir ((عليه السلام)) said: "O Abu Hamza, do not place 'Ali (عليه السلام) below the level to which Allāh has raised him, and do not elevate him above the level where Allāh has kept him. It is enough (excellence) for 'Ali that he is the one who fought the apostates and he is the one who will pair off the inmates of Paradise. (مجهول)[32]

33.

ما في كتاب الله عز و جل آية إلا و أنا أعرف تفسيرها و في أي مكان نزلت من سهل أو جبل و في أي وقت نزلت من ليل أو نهار و أن هاهنا لعلما جما و أشار إلى صدره و لكن طلابه يسيرة و عن قليل يندمون لو قد يفقدوني

(Excerpt from a long narration) Imām `Alī (عليه السلام)said: "There is not an *ayah* in the Book of Allāh (عَزَّ وَ جَلَّ)except that I know its *tafsīr*, and in whichever place it was revealed, on a plain or a mountain, and in whatever time it was revealed, in the night or the day.' – Pointing to his chest – 'here there is abundant knowledge, but the seekers of it are few, and from the few they will regret when they lose me. (صحيح)[33]

34.

قال: حدثنا أبو جعفر محمد بن علي بن الحسين بن بابويه رحمه الله قال: حدثني أبي قال: حدثنا سعد بن عبد الله، عن أيوب بن نوح، عن صفوان ابن يحيى، عن أبان بن عثمان، عن أبي عبد الله جعفر بن محمد عليهما السلام قال: إذا كان يوم القيامة نادى مناد من بطنان العرش: أين خليفة الله في أرضه؟ فيقوم داود النبي

---

[32] *Al-Amālī (Mufid), ch6, h1*

[33] *'Ilal al-Sharā'ī', v1, ch38, h1*

عليه السلام، فيأتي النداء من عند الله عز وجل: لسنا إياك أردنا وإن كنت لله خليفة، ثم ينادي ثانية: أين خليفة الله في أرضه؟ فيقوم أمير المؤمنين علي بن أبي طالب عليه السلام، فيأتي النداء من قبل الله عز وجل: يا معشر الخلائق هذا علي بن أبي طالب خليفة الله في أرضه وحجته على عباده، فمن تعلق بحبله في دار الدنيا فليتعلق بحبله في هذا اليوم ليستضئ بنوره، وليتبعه إلى الدرجات العلى من الجنان. قال: فيقوم أناس قد تعلقوا بحبله في الدنيا فيتبعونه إلى الجنة، ثم يأتي النداء من عند الله جل جلاله: ألا من ائتم بإمام في دار الدنيا فليتبعه إلى حيث [شاء و] يذهب به، فحينئذ " يتبرأ الذين اتبعوا من الذين اتبعوا ورأوا العذاب وتقطعت بهم الأسباب * وقال الذين اتبعوا لو أن لنا كرة فنتبرأ منهم كما تبرأوا منا كذلك يريهم الله أعمالهم حسرات عليهم وما هم بخارجين من النار

From Abi `Abd Allāh Ja`far b. Muḥammad (عليه السلام): "On the Day of Judgment, a caller will call from inside the `Arsh (throne): "Where is the Khalifah of Allāh on His earth?" So Dawood, the Prophet (عليه السلام) will stand up. And a voice from Allāh will say: "We did not mean you, even though you are a khalifah*". Then he (the caller) will call again, "Where is the Khalifah of Allāh on His earth?" Then Ameer Al-Mu'mineen `Ali bn Abi Taalib (عليه السلام)will stand up. Then a call by Allāh will come: "O gathering of creations, this is `Ali b. Abi Taalib, khalifah of Allāh on His earth, and His hujjah (proof) upon His servants, so whoever hung on to His rope (`Ali) in this life, so hang on to His rope in this day. Illuminate with his light, and follow him to the highest stages (darajaat) of jannah. He (عليه السلام)said: So a group of people who followed His rope (`Ali) in this world will follow him to Jannah. Then a call from Allāh (جل جلاله)will come "O those who following a leader (imaam) while living in this world, following him to wherever he goes, and go with him at that time" « those that were followed disown their followers, and they see the chastisement, and their cords are cut asunder (166) And those who followed say: 'If only we might return (to the world) and disown them, as they have disowned us.' Thus does Allāh show them their deeds in a manner that will cause them bitter regrets. Never will they come out of the Fire. (167) »" [Surah Al-Baqarah (2) : 166-167] (موثق)[34]

---

[34] *Al-Amali (Mufid), ch34, h3*

35.

مُحَمَّدُ بْنُ يَحْيَى عَنْ أَحْمَدَ بْنِ مُحَمَّدٍ وَعَلِيُّ بْنُ مُحَمَّدٍ عَنْ سَهْلِ بْنِ زِيَادٍ جَمِيعاً عَنِ ابْنِ مَحْبُوبٍ عَنْ أَبِي حَمْزَةَ عَنْ ابي جعفر (عَلَيْهِ السَّلام) قَالَ لَمَّا قُبِضَ أَمِيرُ الْمُؤْمِنِينَ (عَلَيْهِ السَّلام) قَامَ الْحَسَنُ بن علي (عَلَيْهِما السَّلام) فِي مَسْجِدِ الْكُوفَةِ فَحَمِدَ اللهَ وَأَثْنَى عَلَيْهِ وَصَلَّى عَلَى النَّبِيِّ (صَلَّى اللهُ عَلَيْهِ وَآلِه) ثُمَّ قَالَ أَيُّهَا النَّاسُ إِنَّهُ قَدْ قُبِضَ فِي هَذِهِ اللَّيْلَةِ رَجُلٌ مَا سَبَقَهُ الاوَّلُونَ وَلا يُدْرِكُهُ الاخِرُونَ إِنَّهُ كَانَ لَصَاحِبَ رَايَةِ رَسُولِ اللهِ (صَلَّى اللهُ عَلَيْهِ وَآلِه) عَنْ يَمِينِهِ جَبْرَئِيلُ وَعَنْ يَسَارِهِ مِيكَائِيلُ لا يَنْثَنِي حَتَّى يَفْتَحَ اللهُ لَهُ وَاللهِ مَا تَرَكَ بَيْضَاءَ وَلا حَمْرَاءَ إِلا سَبْعَمِائَةِ دِرْهَمٍ فَضَلَتْ عَنْ عَطَائِهِ أَرَادَ أَنْ يَشْتَرِيَ بِهَا خَادِماً لاهْلِهِ وَاللهِ لَقَدْ قُبِضَ فِي اللَّيْلَةِ الَّتِي فِيهَا قُبِضَ وَصِيُّ مُوسَى يُوشَعُ بْنُ نُونٍ وَاللَّيْلَةِ الَّتِي عُرِجَ فِيهَا بِعِيسَى ابْنِ مَرْيَمَ وَاللَّيْلَةِ الَّتِي نُزِّلَ فِيهَا الْقُرْآنُ

Muhammad b. Yahya has narrated from Ahmad b. Muḥammad and 'Alī b. mmd from Sahl b. Ziyad all from kbn Mahbub from abu Hamza from abu Ja'far (عليه السلام) who has said the following. "When Amir al-Mu'minin 'Alī (عليه السلام) passed away, al-Hassan b. 'Alī stoop up in the Mosque if Kufa. He praises Allāh and spoke of His Glory prayed to Allāh to grant blessings up on the Holy Prophet (s.a) and then he said this. People tonight a man has passed away the like whom cannot be found in previous and the coming generations. He was the standard bearer of the Messenger of Allāh, with Jibril on his right micha'il on his left. He would not turn back until Allāh would grant him victory. All that he has left of the worldly belongings is a seven hundred Dirham extra from his gifts with which he wanted to buy (hire) a servant for his household. By Allāh, he died during a night in which the executor of the will of Mūsā (Moses) Yusha' b. Nun had passed away, the night in which Jesus son of Mary was taken to heavens and the night in which the Holy Qur'ān was revealed. (صحيح)[35]

36.

[35] *Al-Kafi, v1, ch113, h8*

مُحَمَّدُ بْنُ يَحْيَى عَنْ أَحْمَدَ بْنِ مُحَمَّدِ بْنِ عِيسَى عَنْ عَلِيِّ بْنِ النُّعْمَانِ عَنْ مُعَاوِيَةَ بْنِ عَمَّارٍ قَالَ سَمِعْتُ أَبَا عَبْدِ اللَّهِ (عليه السلام) يَقُولُ كَانَ فِي وَصِيَّةِ النَّبِيِّ (صلى الله عليه وآله) لِعَلِيٍّ (عليه السلام) أَنْ قَالَ يَا عَلِيُّ أُوصِيكَ فِي نَفْسِكَ بِخِصَالٍ فَاحْفَظْهَا عَنِّي ثُمَّ قَالَ اللَّهُمَّ أَعِنْهُ أَمَّا الْأُولَى فَالصِّدْقُ وَ لَا تَخْرُجَنَّ مِنْ فِيكَ كَذِبَةٌ أَبَداً وَ الثَّانِيَةُ الْوَرَعُ وَ لَا تَجْتَرِئْ عَلَى خِيَانَةٍ أَبَداً وَ الثَّالِثَةُ الْخَوْفُ مِنَ اللَّهِ عَزَّ ذِكْرُهُ كَأَنَّكَ تَرَاهُ وَ الرَّابِعَةُ كَثْرَةُ الْبُكَاءِ مِنْ خَشْيَةِ اللَّهِ يُبْنَى لَكَ بِكُلِّ دَمْعَةٍ أَلْفُ بَيْتٍ فِي الْجَنَّةِ وَ الْخَامِسَةُ بَذْلُكَ مَالَكَ وَ دَمَكَ دُونَ دِينِكَ وَ السَّادِسَةُ الْأَخْذُ بِسُنَّتِي فِي صَلَاتِي وَ صَوْمِي وَ صَدَقَتِي أَمَّا الصَّلَاةُ فَالْخَمْسُونَ رَكْعَةً وَ أَمَّا الصِّيَامُ فَثَلَاثَةُ أَيَّامٍ فِي الشَّهْرِ الْخَمِيسُ فِي أَوَّلِهِ وَ الْأَرْبِعَاءُ فِي وَسَطِهِ وَ الْخَمِيسُ فِي آخِرِهِ وَ أَمَّا الصَّدَقَةُ فَجُهْدَكَ حَتَّى تَقُولَ قَدْ أَسْرَفْتُ وَ لَمْ تُسْرِفْ وَ عَلَيْكَ بِصَلَاةِ اللَّيْلِ وَ عَلَيْكَ بِصَلَاةِ الزَّوَالِ وَ عَلَيْكَ بِصَلَاةِ الزَّوَالِ وَ عَلَيْكَ بِصَلَاةِ الزَّوَالِ وَ عَلَيْكَ بِتِلَاوَةِ الْقُرْآنِ عَلَى كُلِّ حَالٍ وَ عَلَيْكَ بِرَفْعِ يَدَيْكَ فِي صَلَاتِكَ وَ تَقْلِيبِهِمَا وَ عَلَيْكَ بِالسِّوَاكِ عِنْدَ كُلِّ وُضُوءٍ وَ عَلَيْكَ بِمَحَاسِنِ الْأَخْلَاقِ فَارْكَبْهَا وَ مَسَاوِي الْأَخْلَاقِ فَاجْتَنِبْهَا فَإِنْ لَمْ تَفْعَلْ فَلَا تَلُومَنَّ إِلَّا نَفْسَكَ

Muhammad b. Yahya, from Ahmad b. Muḥammad b. Isa, from ʿAlī b. Al-No'man, from Muawiya b. Ammar who said: 'I heard Abu ʿAbd Allāh say: 'There was in the bequest of the Prophet (صلى الله عليه وآله وسلم) to ʿAlī (عليه السلام) that he said: 'O ʿAlī (عليه السلام), I hereby bequeath you with regards to yourself of qualities, so preserve them from me'. Then he said: 'Our Allāh (تبارك و طائلة), Support him. As for the first one is to be truthful, and do not let lies to come out from you ever. And the second is the piety and do not let yourself be treacherous ever. And the third is the fear of Allāh (تبارك و طائلة), Mighty is His Mention, as if you can actually see Him . And the fourth is the excessive weeping for the fear of Allāh (تبارك و طائلة). There will be built for you, for every tear drop, a thousand houses in the Paradise. And the fifth is that your wealth and your blood is not for other than your Religion. And the sixth is to take to my Sunnah with regards to my Prayer, and my Fast, and my charity. As for the Prayer, so it is of fifty Rakaat, and as for the Fasts, so that is for three days in the month, the Thursday in the first part of it, and the Wednesday in the middle of it, and the Thursday in the last part of it. And as for the charity, so you strive in it to the extent that you would say: 'I have been excessive', but you would not have been excessive. And it is on you to perform the Night Prayer, and it is on you to perform the Noon Prayer, and it is on you to perform the Noon Prayer, and it is on you to perform the Noon Prayer. And it is on you to recite the Qurʾān in every condition. And it is on you to raise your hands in your Prayer and turn them both. And it is on you to brush (your teeth) during every ablution. And it is on you to observe the most excellent morals and to abstain from evil manners, for it you do not do it, so you should not blame anyone except for yourself'. (صحيح)[36]

37.

عَلِيُّ بْنُ إِبْرَاهِيمَ عَنْ أَبِيهِ عَنِ ابْنِ أَبِي عُمَيْرٍ عَنْ هِشَامِ بْنِ سَالِمٍ عَنْ أَبِي عَبْدِ اللهِ (عَلَيهِ السَّلام) قَالَ لا يَزَالُ الدُّعَاءُ مَحْجُوباً حَتَّى يُصَلَّى عَلَى مُحَمَّدٍ وَآلِ مُحَمَّدٍ

'Alī b. Ibrahim has narrated from his father from b. abu 'Umayr from Hisham b. Salim from abu 'Abd Allāh (عليه السلام) who has said the following: "A prayer remains barred until one asks favors (in the form of al-Salat (the special expression called al-Salat ' Ala al-Nabiyy) from Allāh for Muḥammad and his family, recipient of divine supreme covenant. (حسن كالصحيح)[37]

38.

مُحَمَّدُ بْنُ يَحْيَى عَنْ أَحْمَدَ بْنِ مُحَمَّدٍ عَنْ عَلِيِّ بْنِ الْحَكَمِ وَعَبْدِ الرَّحْمَنِ بْنِ أَبِي نَجْرَانَ جَمِيعاً عَنْ صَفْوَانَ الْجَمَّالِ عَنْ أَبِي عَبْدِ اللهِ (عَلَيهِ السَّلام) قَالَ كُلُّ دُعَاءٍ يُدْعَى اللهُ عَزَّ وَجَلَّ بِهِ مَحْجُوبٌ عَنِ السَّمَاءِ حَتَّى يُصَلَّى عَلَى مُحَمَّدٍ وَآلِ مُحَمَّدٍ

Muhammad b. Yahya has narrated from Ahmad b. Muḥammad from 'Alī b. al-Hakam and 'Abd al-Rahman b. abu Najran all from Safwan al-Jammal from abu 'Abd Allāh (عليه السلام) who has said the following: "Every prayer to Allāh, the Most

---

[36] *Al-Kāfi, v8, ch33*

[37] *Al-Kāfi, v2, ch20, h1*

Majestic, the Most Holy, remains on hold and barred from heavens until he asks from Allāh favors (in the form of al-Salat) for the Holy Prophet and his family. (صحيح)[38]

Virtues of Lady Fatimah (عليها السلام)

39.

مُحَمَّدُ بْنُ يَحْيَى عَنِ الْعَمْرَكِيِّ بْنِ عَلِيٍّ عَنْ عَلِيِّ بْنِ جَعْفَرٍ عَنْ أَخِيهِ أَبِي الْحَسَنِ (عَلَيْهِ السَّلام) قَالَ إِنَّ فَاطِمَةَ (عليها السلام) صِدِّيقَةٌ شَهِيدَةٌ وَإِنَّ بَنَاتِ الانْبِيَاءِ لا يَطْمَثْنَ

Muhammad in Yahya has narrated from al-'Amrakiy b. 'Alī from 'Alī b. Ja'far from his brother from abu al-Hassan (عليه السلام) who has said the following. "Fatima is truthful and a martyr. The daughter of the prophet do not experience menses. (صحيح)[39]

40.

أَحْمَدُ بْنُ مِهْرَانَ رَحِمَهُ اللهُ رَفَعَهُ وَأَحْمَدُ بْنُ إِدْرِيسَ عَنْ مُحَمَّدِ بْنِ عَبْدِ الْجَبَّارِ الشَّيْبَانِيِّ قَالَ حَدَّثَنِي الْقَاسِمُ بْنُ مُحَمَّدٍ الرَّازِيُّ قَالَ حَدَّثَنَا عَلِيُّ بْنُ مُحَمَّدٍ الْهُرْمُزَانِيُّ عَنْ أَبِي عَبْدِ اللهِ الْحُسَيْنِ بن علي (عَلَيْهِما السَّلام) قَالَ لَمَّا قُبِضَتْ فَاطِمَةُ (عليها السلام) دَفَنَهَا أَمِيرُ الْمُؤْمِنِينَ سِرّاً وَعَفَا عَلَى مَوْضِعِ قَبْرِهَا ثُمَّ قَامَ فَحَوَّلَ وَجْهَهُ إِلَى قَبْرِ رَسُولِ اللهِ (صَلَّى اللهُ عَلَيْهِ وَآلِهِ) فَقَالَ السَّلامُ عَلَيْكَ يَا رَسُولَ اللهِ عَنِّي وَالسَّلامُ عَلَيْكَ عَنِ ابْنَتِكَ وَزَائِرَتِكَ وَالْبَائِتَةِ فِي الثَّرَى بِبُقْعَتِكَ وَالْمُخْتَارِ اللهُ لَهَا سُرْعَةَ اللِّحَاقِ بِكَ قَلَّ يَا رَسُولَ اللهِ عَنْ صَفِيَّتِكَ صَبْرِي وَعَفَا عَنْ سَيِّدَةِ نِسَاءِ الْعَالَمِينَ تَجَلُّدِي إِلا أَنَّ لِي فِي التَّأَسِّي بِسُنَّتِكَ فِي فُرْقَتِكَ مَوْضِعَ تَعَزٍّ فَلَقَدْ وَسَّدْتُكَ فِي مَلْحُودَةِ قَبْرِكَ وَفَاضَتْ نَفْسُكَ بَيْنَ نَحْرِي وَصَدْرِي بَلَى وَفِي كِتَابِ اللهِ لِي أَنْعَمُ الْقَبُولِ إِنَّا للهِ وَإِنَّا إِلَيْهِ رَاجِعُونَ قَدِ اسْتُرْجِعَتِ الْوَدِيعَةُ وَأُخِذَتِ الرَّهِينَةُ وَأُخْلِسَتِ الزَّهْرَاءُ فَمَا أَقْبَحَ الْخَضْرَاءَ وَالْغَبْرَاءَ يَا رَسُولَ اللهِ أَمَّا حُزْنِي فَسَرْمَدٌ وَأَمَّا لَيْلِي فَمُسَهَّدٌ وَهَمٌّ لا يَبْرَحُ مِنْ قَلْبِي أَوْ يَخْتَارَ اللهُ لِي دَارَكَ الَّتِي أَنْتَ فِيهَا مُقِيمٌ كَمَدٌ مُقَيِّحٌ وَهَمٌّ مُهَيِّجٌ سَرْعَانَ مَا فَرَّقَ بَيْنَنَا وَإِلَى اللهِ أَشْكُو وَسَتُنْبِئُكَ ابْنَتُكَ بِتَظَافُرِ أُمَّتِكَ عَلَى هَضْمِهَا فَأَحْفِهَا السُّؤَالَ وَاسْتَخْبِرْهَا

[38] *Al-Kāfi, v2, ch20, h10*

[39] *Al-Kāfi, v1, ch114, h2*

الْحَالَ فَكَمْ مِنْ غَلِيلٍ مُعْتَلِجٍ بِصَدْرِهَا لَمْ تَجِدْ إِلَى بَثِّهِ سَبِيلاً وَسَتَقُولُ وَيَحْكُمُ اللهُ وَهُوَ خَيْرُ الْحَاكِمِينَ سَلامَ مُوَدِّعٍ لا قَالٍ وَلا سَئِمٍ فَإِنْ أَنْصَرِفْ فَلا عَنْ مَلالَةٍ وَإِنْ أُقِمْ فَلا عَنْ سُوءِ ظَنٍّ بِمَا وَعَدَ اللهُ الصَّابِرِينَ وَاهَ وَاهاً وَالصَّبْرُ أَيْمَنُ وَأَجْمَلُ وَلَوْ لا غَلَبَةُ الْمُسْتَوْلِينَ لَجَعَلْتُ الْمُقَامَ وَاللَّبْثَ لِزَاماً مَعْكُوفاً وَلاعْوَلْتُ إِعْوَالَ الثَّكْلَى عَلَى جَلِيلِ الرَّزِيَّةِ فَبِعَيْنِ اللهِ تُدْفَنُ ابْنَتُكَ سِرّاً وَتُهْضَمُ حَقَّهَا وَتُمْنَعُ إِرْثَهَا وَلَمْ يَتَبَاعَدِ الْعَهْدُ وَلَمْ يَخْلَقْ مِنْكَ الذِّكْرُ وَإِلَى اللهِ يَا رَسُولَ اللهِ الْمُشْتَكَى وَفِيكَ يَا رَسُولَ اللهِ أَحْسَنُ الْعَزَاءِ صَلَّى اللهُ عَلَيْكَ وَعَلَيْهَا السَّلامُ وَالرِّضْوَانُ

Ahmad b. Mihran, may Allāh grant him blessing, has narrated from narrated in a in a marfu‘ manner and Ahmad b. Idris has narrated from Muḥammad b. ‘Abd al-Jabbar al-Shaybani has said that narrated to me al-Qasim b. Muḥammad al-Razi who has said that narrated to him ‘Alī b. Muḥammad al-Hurmuzi from abu ‘AbdAllāh al-Husayn b. ‘Alī (عليه السلام) who has said the following. "When Fatima (عليه السلام) passed away Amir al-Mu'minin ‘Alī (عليه السلام) buried her secretly, camouflaged her grave site he then stood up facing the grave of the Messenger of Allāh said, "O the Messenger of Allāh may He grant you blessings on behalf of me the on behalf of your daughter who is visiting you and will pass this night in the soil in your location whom Allāh chose to make join you the fastest. O the Messenger of Allāh of my patience has reached to the brims and I miss so much your chosen one (daughter) and my self-control is banished for the departure of the leader of the ladies of the worlds. The only solace for me is to follow your tradition and be mournful for your own departure from us. A little while ago I placed you in your grave and your spirit left your body between my own throat and chest. Yes, in the book of Allāh (for me) there is the best form to express acceptance of Allāh's decision ""We are the servants of God and to Him we shall all return." (2:156) The trust is returned and the commit is recalled amd al-Zahra' is taken away from us. How sad, O the Messenger of Allāh, the green skies and the dusty earth seem to us. My sadness has become perpetual and my night have become sleepless. There is an anxiety that will not relieve my heart until Allāh will chose for me the dwelling like that where you are. I have a heart bleeding sorrow and a restless anxiety. How quickly the separation took place? To Allāh I raise my complains and your own daughter will explain to you how your 'Umma (followers) succeeded in committing injustice against her. You may ask her questions and find information about the case from her. How great was the sorrow that she will find a place and an ear to express to. She would say Allāh will judge because he is the best judge. I offer my prayer to Allāh to grant you blessings as a note of farewell but not because of disappointment and despaired. If I return it is not that I have become tired and if I will stand up it will not be because of pessimism in the promise of Allāh to those who exercise patience. Indeed to exercise patience is more safe and fruitful. Had not been for the mischief of the enemies I would have turned the place a place of worship andd would have kept my worship continuous and would cried like the mothers for the death of their son for the great loss. In the sight of Allāh your daughter is buried secretly, her rights are taken away unjustly, her inheritance is withheld for no valid reason. It all has happen just after you left and your memories are still fresh. To Allāh O the Messenger of Allāh we complain and from youu O the Messenger of Allāh we seek condolences. May Allāh grant blessings to you and to her. May the peace and happiness of Allāh be with you. (مجهول)[40]

41.

قال: حدثنا أبو جعفر محمد بن علي بن موسى قال: حدثنا أبي قال: حدثنا علي بن إبراهيم بن هاشم، عن أبيه، عن ابن أبي عمير، عن أبان بن عثمان، عن أبي عبد الله جعفر بن محمد عليهما السلام قال: إذا كان يوم القيامة جمع الله الأولين والآخرين في صعيد واحد ثم أمر مناديا فنادى : غضوا أبصاركم ونكسوا رؤوسكم حتى تجوز فاطمة ابنة محمد الصراط. قال: فتغض الخلائق أبصارهم فتأتي فاطمة عليها السلام على نجيب من نجب الجنة يشيعها سبعون ألف ملك، فتقف موقفا شريفا من مواقف القيامة، ثم تنزل عن نجيبها فتأخذ قميص الحسين بن علي عليهما السلام بيدها مضمخا بدمه، وتقول: يا رب هذا قميص ولدي وقد علمت ما صنع به. فيأتيها النداء من قبل الله عز وجل: يا فاطمة لك عندي الرضا، فتقول: يا رب انتصر لي من قاتله، فيأمر الله تعالى عنقا من النار فتخرج من جهنم فتلتقط قتلة الحسين بن علي عليهما السلام كما يلتقط الطير الحب، ثم يعود العنق بهم إلى النار فيعذبون فيها بأنواع العذاب، ثم تركب فاطمة عليها السلام نجيبها حتى تدخل الجنة، ومعها الملائكة المشيعون لها، وذريتها بين يديها، وأولياءهم من الناس عن يمينها وشمالها

---

[40] *Al-Kāfi, v1, ch114, h3*

He said: Abu Ja'far Muḥammad b. 'Ali b. Mūsā reported from his father, who reported from 'Ali b. Ibrahim b. Hashim, from his father, from b. Abi Umayr, from Aban b. Uthman, that: Abu Abdillah Ja'far b. Muhammad, (عليه السلام), said: On the Day of Judgement, Allāh will bring together the first and the last people on one plane and then He will cause an announcement to be made: "Cast down your glances and lower your heads, so that Fatimah(peace be upon her), daughter of Muhammad, (صلى الله عليه وآله وسلم), crosses the Bridge (al-Sirat)." He said: "People will cast down their glances and then Fatimah, peace be upon her, will arrive seated on one of the highbred animals of Paradise, followed by 70 thousand angels. Then she will make a distinguished pause at one of the high stations on the Day of Judgement, dismount and take the blood soiled shirt of al-Husayn b. 'Ali (عليه السلام), in her hands, saying: "O Allāh! This shirt belongs to my son, and You know what was done to him." There will be proclamation from Allāh, Most High: "O Fatimah, you have My pleasure." She will say: "Help me avenge from those who killed him." Allāh will then command a flame from hellfire to leap forth and devour all the killers of al-Husayn b. 'Ali, (عليه السلام), the way a bird devours a seed. The flame will take them back into the hellpit, subjecting them to various chastisements. Then Fatimah, peace be upon her, will ride again and proceed to enter Paradise, accompanied by the angels following her, her descendants before her and her friends and partisans on her right and on her left. (صحيح)[41]

42.

وسأله بعض المتكلمين وهو المعروف بترك الهروي فقال له: كم بنات رسول الله ؟. فقال: أربع، قال: فأيهن أفضل ؟ فقال: فاطمة فقال: ولم صارت أفضل، وكانت أصغرهن سنا وأقلهن صحبة لرسول الله ؟ !. قال: لخصلتين خصها الله بهما تطولا عليها وتشريفا وإكراما لها. إحداهما أنها ورثت رسول الله ولم يرث غيرها من ولده. والاخرى أن الله تعالى أبقى نسل رسول الله منها ولم يبقه من غيرها، ولم يخصصها بذلك إلا لفضل

[41] *Al-Amāli (Mufid), ch15, h6*

إخلاص عرفه من نيتها. قال الهروي: فما رأيت أحدا تكلم وأجاب في هذا الباب بأحسن ولا أوجز من جوابه.

And one of the theologians asked him (i.e. Shaykh al-Hasan b. Ruh رضي الله عنه) – and he is known by Tirk al-Harawi– so he said to him: How many daughters did the Messenger of Allāh have? So he said: Four.[1] He said: So which of them is preferred? So he said: Fatima. So he said: And why did she become preferred while she was the youngest of them in age and the one from them to spend the least amount of time in the company of the Messenger of Allāh صلى الله عليه وآله وسلم?! He said: For having two special traits, which Allāh characterized her by, favoring her and conferring her honor and respect. One of them is that she inherited from the Messenger of Allāh صلى الله عليه وآله وسلم, and none other than her inherited from his children; and the other is that Allāh maintained the progeny of the Messenger of Allāh from her and it did not remain from other than her. And He did not qualify her with that except due to the virtue of sincerity which He had distinguished of her intention. (صحيح)[42]

43.

أخبرني جماعة، عن أبي محمد هارون، عن أبي علي محمد بن همام، قال أبو علي: وعلى خاتم أبي جعفر السمان رضي الله عنه لا إله إلا الله الملك الحق المبين، فسألته عنه فقال: حدثني أبو محمد يعني صاحب العسكر عليه السلام، عن آبائه عليهم السلام (أنهم) (4) قالوا: كان لفاطمة عليها السلام خاتم فصه عقيق، فلما حضرتها الوفاة دفعته إلى الحسن عليه السلام، فلما حضرته الوفاة دفعه إلى الحسين عليه السلام. قال الحسين عليه السلام فاشتهيت أن أنقش عليه شيئا، فرأيت في النوم المسيح عيسى بن مريم على نبينا وآله وعليه السلام، فقلت له: يا روح الله ما أنقش على خاتمي هذا ؟ قال: انقش عليه لا إله إلا الله الملك الحق المبين، فإنه أول التوراة وآخر الانجيل

A group narrated from Abu Muḥammad Harun from Abu `Ali Muḥammad b. Himam. He said: On the ring of Abu Ja`far al-Samman رضي الله عنه it said, "There is no

---

[42] *Al-Ghayba (Tusi), v1, ch60*

god except Allāh, the True and Manifest King", so I asked him about it and he said: Abu Muḥammad Sahib al-'Askar السلام عليه [narrated] from his his forefathers عليهم السلام that they said: Fatima عليها السلام had a ring with an agate gem. When she passed away, she gave it to al-Hasan عليه السلام, and when he passed away, he gave it to al-Husayn عليه السلام. al-Husayn عليه السلام said: I wanted to engrave something on it, so I saw the Messiah 'Isa b. Maryam على نبينا وآله وعليه السلام in my sleep, so I said to him, "O Spirit of Allāh, what shall I engrave on this ring?" He said, "Engrave 'There is no god except Allāh, the True and Manifest King' upon it, for that is [at] the beginning of the Torah and the end of the Gospel. (صحيح)[43]

44.

أحمد بن محمد بن يحيى العطار، عن أبي، عن محمد بن الحسين بن أبي الخطاب، عن الحسن بن محبوب، عن أبي الجارود، عن أبي جعفر، عن جابر بن عبد الله الانصاري قال: دخلت على فاطمه عليها السلام وبين يديها لوح فيه اسماء الاوصياء فعددت اثنا عشر آخرهم القائم ثلاثه منهم محمد واربعه منهم على عليهم السلامالسلام

Ahmad b. Muḥammad b. Yahya al-Attar from his father from Muḥammad b. al-Husayn b. Abi al-Khattab from al-Hasan b. Mahbub from Abi al-Jarud from Abi Ja'far from Jabir b. AbdAllāh al-Ansari who said: I entered to meet Fatima السلام عليها and found a tablet in front of her which had the names of the Awsiya (Heirs). I counted twelve [names] the last of them being the Qa'im, three of them were Muḥammad and four of them had names of 'Alī السلام عليهم(صحيح)[44]

45.

[43] Al-Ghayba (Tusi), v1, ch50

[44] 'Uyūn Akhbār al-Riḍā, ch6, h6

حَدَّثَنا أَبو الحَسَن مُحمَّدِ بْن عَلِيّ بْن لِشاه بِمَرْوَرُودَ قالَ: حَدَّثَنا أَبُوالعَبّاس أَحْمَد بْنِ المُظَفَّرُ بْن الحُسَيْن قالَ: حَدَّثَنا أَبُوعَبْدِ اللّه مُحمَّدِ بْن زَكَرِيَّا البَصْرِيّ قالَ: حَدَّثَني مُحمَّدِ بْن سابِق قالَ: حَدَّثَنا عَلِيّ بْن مُوسَى بْن جَعْفَر عَلَيْهِ السَّلامُ قالَ: حَدَّثَني أَبي، عَن أَبيهِ جَعْفَرِ بْن مُحمَّد عَلَيْهِ السَّلامُ عَنْ أَبيهِ، عَن جَدِّهِ عَلَيْهِ السَّلامُ قالَ: قالَ عَلِيّ بْن أَبِي طالب عَلَيْهِ السَّلامُ: لَقَدْ هَمَمْتُ بِتَزْوِيجِ فاطِمَةَ ابْنَةَ مُحمَّدٍ صَلَّى اللهُ عَلَيْهِ وَآلِهِ وَلَمْ أَتَجَرَّأْ أَنْ أَذْكُرَ ذٰلِكَ لِلنَّبِيِّ وَإِنَّ ذٰلِكَ لَيَخْتَلِجُ فِي صَدْرِي لَيْلِي وَنَهارِي حَتَّى دَخَلْتُ عَلى رَسُولِ اللّهِ صَلَّى اللهُ عَلَيْهِ وَآلِهِ فَقالَ: يا عَلِيُّ. قُلْتُ: لَبَّيْكَ يا رَسُولَ اللّهِ. قالَ: هَلْ لَكَ فِي التَّزْوِيجِ؟ قُلْتُ: رَسُولُ اللّهِ أَعْلَمُ. وَإِذا هُوَ يُرِيدُ أَنْ يُزَوِّجَني بَعْضَ نِساءِ قُرَيْشٍ، وَإِنِّي لَخائِفٌ عَلى فَوْتِ فاطِمَةَ، فَما شَعَرْتُ بِشَيْءٍ إِذْ أَتاني رَسُولُ رَسُولِ اللّهِ صَلَّى اللهُ عَلَيْهِ وَآلِهِ فَقالَ لِي: أَجِبِ النَّبِيَّ صَلَّى اللهُ عَلَيْهِ وَآلِهِ وَأَسْرِعْ، فَما رَأَيْنا رَسُولَ اللّهِ صَلَّى اللهُ عَلَيْهِ وَآلِهِ أَشَدَّ فَرَحاً مِنْهُ الْيَوْمَ. قالَ: فَأَتَيْتُهُ مُسْرِعاً، فَإِذا هُوَ فِي حُجْرَةِ أُمِّ سَلَمَةَ. فَلَمَّا نَظَرَ إِلَيَّ تَهَلَّلَ وَجْهُهُ فَرَحاً وَتَبَسَّمَ حَتَّى نَظَرْتُ إِلى بَياضِ أَسْنانِهِ يَبْرُقُ. فَقالَ: أَبْشِرْ يا عَلِيُّ، فَإِنَّ اللّهَ عَزَّ وَجَلَّ قَدْ كَفاني ما قَدْ كانَ أَهَمَّني مِنْ أَمْرِ تَزْوِيجِكَ. فَقُلْتُ: وَكَيْفَ ذٰلِكَ يا رَسُولَ اللّهِ؟ قالَ: أَتاني جَبْرَئِيلُ وَمَعَهُ مِنْ سُنْبُلِ الْجَنَّةِ وَقَرَنْفُلِها فَناوَلَنِيهِما فَأَخَذْتُهُما وَشَمَمْتُهُما فَقُلْتُ: ما سَبَبُ هٰذا السُّنْبُلِ وَالْقَرَنْفُلِ؟ فَقالَ: إِنَّ اللّهَ تَبارَكَ وَتَعالى أَمَرَ سُكّانَ الْجِنانِ مِنَ الْمَلائِكَةِ وَمَنْ فِيها أَنْ يُزَيِّنُوا الْجِنانَ كُلَّها بِمَغارِسِها وَأَشْجارِها وَثِمارِها وَقُصُورِها، وَأَمَرَ رِيحَها فَهَبَّتْ بِأَنْواعِ الْعِطْرِ وَالطِّيبِ، وَأَمَرَ حُورَ عِينِها بِالْقِراءَةِ فِيها بِسُورَةِ طه وَطَواسِينَ وَيس وَحمعسق. ثُمَّ نادى مُنادٍ مِنْ تَحْتِ الْعَرْشِ أَلا إِنَّ الْيَوْمَ يَوْمُ وَلِيمَةِ عَلِيِّ بْن أَبِي طالِبِ عَلَيْهِ السَّلامُ. أَلا إِنِّي أُشْهِدُكُمْ أَنِّي قَدْ زَوَّجْتُ فاطِمَةَ بِنْتَ مُحَمَّدٍ مِنْ عَلِيِّ بْنِ أَبِي طالِبٍ رِضًى مِنِّي بَعْضُهُما لِبَعْضٍ.ثُمَّ بَعَثَ اللّهُ تَبارَكَ وَتَعالى سَحابَةً بَيْضاءَ فَقَطَرَتْ عَلَيْهِمْ مِنْ لُؤْلُئِها وَزَبَرْجَدِها وَيَواقِيتِها وَقامَتِ الْمَلائِكَةُ فَنَثَرَتْ مِنْ سُنْبُلِ الْجَنَّةِ وَقَرَنْفُلِها هٰذا مِمَّا نَثَرَتِ الْمَلائِكَةُ ثُمَّ أَمَرَ اللّهُ تَبارَكَ وَتَعالى مَلَكاً مِنْ مَلائِكَةِ الْجَنَّةِ يُقالُ لَهُ راحِيلُ وَلَيْسَ فِي الْمَلائِكَةِ أَبْلَغُ مِنْهُ فَقالَ اخْطُبْ يا راحِيلُ فَخَطَبَ بِخُطْبَةٍ لَمْ يَسْمَعْ بِمِثْلِها أَهْلُ السَّماءِ وَلا أَهْلُ الأَرْضِ ثُمَّ نادى مُنادٍ أَلا يا مَلائِكَتِي وَسُكّانَ جَنَّتِي بارِكُوا عَلى عَلِيِّ بْنِ أَبِي طالِبٍ حَبِيبِ مُحَمَّدٍ وَفاطِمَةَ بِنْتِ مُحَمَّدٍ فَقَدْ بارَكْتُ عَلَيْهِما أَلا إِنِّي قَدْ زَوَّجْتُ أَحَبَّ النِّساءِ إِلَيَّ مِنْ أَحَبِّ الرِّجالِ إِلَيَّ بَعْدَ النَّبِيِّينَ وَالْمُرْسَلِينَ فَقالَ راحِيلُ الْمَلَكُ يا رَبِّ وَما بَرَكَتُكَ فِيهِما بِأَكْثَرَ مِمّا رَأَيْنا لَهُما فِي جِنانِكَ وَدارِكَ فَقالَ عَزَّ وَجَلَّ يا راحِيلُ إِنَّ مِنْ بَرَكَتِي عَلَيْهِما أَنْ أَجْمَعَهُما عَلى مَحَبَّتِي وَأَجْعَلَهُما حُجَّةً عَلى خَلْقِي وَعِزَّتِي وَجَلالِي لَأَخْلُقَنَّ مِنْهُما خَلْقاً وَلَأُنْشِئَنَّ مِنْهُما ذُرِّيَّةً أَجْعَلُهُمْ خُزّانِي فِي أَرْضِي وَمَعادِنَ لِعِلْمِي وَدُعاةً إِلى دِينِي بِهِمْ أَحْتَجُّ عَلى خَلْقِي بَعْدَ النَّبِيِّينَ وَالْمُرْسَلِينَ فَأَبْشِرْ يا عَلِيُّ فَإِنَّ اللّهَ عَزَّ وَجَلَّ أَكْرَمَكَ كَرامَةً لَمْ يُكْرِمْ بِمِثْلِها أَحَداً وَقَدْ زَوَّجْتُكَ ابْنَتِي فاطِمَةَ عَلى ما زَوَّجَكَ الرَّحْمٰنُ وَقَدْ رَضِيتُ لَها بِما رَضِيَ اللّهُ لَها فَدُونَكَ أَهْلَكَ فَإِنَّكَ أَحَقُّ بِها مِنِّي وَلَقَدْ أَخْبَرَنِي جَبْرَئِيلُ عَلَيْهِ السَّلامُ أَنَّ الْجَنَّةَ مُشْتاقَةٌ إِلَيْكُما وَلَوْ لا أَنَّ اللّهَ عَزَّ وَجَلَّ قَدَّرَ أَنْ يُخْرِجَ مِنْكُما ما يَتَّخِذُهُ عَلى الْخَلْقِ حُجَّةً لَأَجابَ فِيكُما الْجَنَّةُ وَأَهْلُها فَنِعْمَ الأَخُ أَنْتَ وَنِعْمَ الْخَتَنُ أَنْتَ وَنِعْمَ الصّاحِبُ أَنْتَ وَكَفاكَ بِرِضَى اللّهِ رِضًى قالَ عَلِيٌّ عَلَيْهِ السَّلامُ فَقُلْتُ يا رَسُولَ اللّهِ بَلَغَ مِنْ قَدْرِي حَتَّى إِنِّي ذُكِرْتُ فِي الْجَنَّةِ وَزَوَّجَنِي اللّهُ فِي مَلائِكَتِهِ فَقالَ إِنَّ اللّهَ عَزَّ وَجَلَّ إِذا أَكْرَمَ وَلِيَّهُ وَأَحَبَّهُ أَكْرَمَهُ بِما لا عَيْنٌ رَأَتْ وَلا أُذُنٌ سَمِعَتْ فَحَباها اللّهُ لَكَ يا عَلِيُّ فَقالَ عَلِيٌّ عَلَيْهِ السَّلامُ رَبِّ أَوْزِعْنِي أَنْ

أَشْكُرَ نِعْمَتَكَ الَّتِي أَنْعَمْتَ عَلَيَّ فَقَالَ رَسُولُ اللَّهِ صَلَّى اللهُ عَلَيْهِ وَآلِهِ آمِينَ.حَدَّثَنِي بِهَذَا الْحَدِيث عَلِيّ بْنِ أَحْمَدِ بْنِ مُحَمَّدِ بْنِ عِمْرانِ الدَّقَّاق رَضِيَ اللهُ عَنْهُ قالَ: حَدَّثَنا أَحْمَدِ بْنِ يَحْيَى بن زَكَرِيَّا القَطَّانُ قالَ: حَدَّثَنا أَبُو مُحَمَّد بَكْرِ بْنِ عَبْدِاللَّه بْنِ حَبِيبٍ قالَ: حَدَّثَنا أَحْمَدِ بْنِ الحارِثِ قالَ: حَدَّثَنا أَبُو مُعاوِيَة، عَنِ الأَعْمَشِ، عَن جَعْفَرِ بْنِ مُحَمَّد، عَن أَبِيهِ عَنْ جَدِّهِ، عَن أَبِيهِ، عَن عَلِيِّ بْنِ أَبِي طالِب عَلَيْهِ السَّلامُ قـالَ لَقَدْ هممتهممت بتزويج فاطِمَة عَلَيْهَا السَّلاَمُ وَلامْ○جتر؟ أَن أذكر ذلِكَ لرسول اللَّه وَذكر الْحَدِيث مِثْلَهُ سَواء. وَلِهذا الْحَدِيث طَرِيق آخِرَ قَدْ أَخْرَجْتُه فِي مَدِينَة العِلْمُ

Abul Hassan Muḥammad b. ʿAlī b. al-Shah in Marvrood narrated that Abul Abbas Ahmad b. Al-Mudhaffar b. Al-Hussein quoted on the authority of Abu ʿAbd Allāh Muḥammad b. Zakariya al-Basri, on the authority of Muḥammad b. Sabiq, on the authority of ʿAlī b. Mūsā b. Ja'far (al-Reza) (عليه السلام) on the authority of his father (Imam Kazim) (عليه السلام), on the authority of his grandfather (عليه السلام), on the authority of ʿAlī b. Abi Talib (عليه السلام), "When I decided to get married, I did not dare to tell God's Prophet (صلى الله عليه وآله وسلم). This issue was on my mind for many days and nights until one day I went to see God's Prophet (صلى الله عليه وآله وسلم) and he (صلى الله عليه وآله وسلم) said, "O Ali!" I said, "Prophet of God! Yes." He (صلى الله عليه وآله وسلم) said, "Are you interested in getting married?" I said, "God's Prophet (صلى الله عليه وآله وسلم) knows best." I thought that God's Prophet (صلى الله عليه وآله وسلم) would marry off one of the women from the Quraysh tribe to me. I was worried that I might lose the chance to marry (the Blessed Lady) Fatima. I did not understand what happened and God's Prophet (صلى الله عليه وآله وسلم) called me in. I went to see him in the house of Umm Salama. When he (صلى الله عليه وآله وسلم) saw me his face got bright and he smiled such that his white teeth were shining. He (صلى الله عليه وآله وسلم) told me, "O Ali! Here are the glad tidings. The Blessed the Sublime God took care of the issue of your marriage which was on my mind." I asked, "O Prophet of God! What is the result?" He (صلى الله عليه وآله وسلم) said, "Gabriel descended to me and gave me some heavenly hyacinth and clove gillyflower. I took them and smelled them and said, O Gabriel! What is the occasion for bringing me this hyacinth and gillyflower? He (صلى الله عليه وآله وسلم) said, "The Blessed the Sublime God has ordered all the angels and others residing in Paradise to decorate all the trees, rivers, fruits and palaces in Heaven. He has ordered the winds to blow there with the scent of various perfumes. He has ordered the houri-eyed ones to recite the Chapters of Ta-Ha (No. 20) the three chapters beginning with Ta-Sin (al-Shu'ara, al-Naml, and al-Qasas -No. 26,27,28-) and the chapter of Ya-Sin (No. 36) and the chapter of Ha Mim Ayn Sin Qaf (al-Shura, No.42). The Honorable the Exalted God has ordered the callers to call out, 'Verily, today is the banquet of 'Alī b. Abi-Talib. Bear witness that I marry off (the Blessed Lady) Fatima, the daughter of Muhammad, to 'Alī b. Abi Talib. I am pleased with this. These two are one from the other.'"Then, Almighty God sent a white cloud to pour down some of its pearls, aquamarine, and corundum. The angels then dispersed hyacinth and gillyflower of Paradise. Then, the Blessed the Sublime God ordered one of the angels of Paradise called Rahil -who has no other equal in eloquence among the angels- to read the marriage contract. Then Rahil recited such a marriage contract which no one from the heavens and the Earth had recited before. Then God ordered one of the angels to call out, 'O My angels and the residents of My Paradise! Express congratulations to the beloved friend of Muḥammad 'Alī b. Abi Talib and the daughter of Muḥammad - (the Blessed Lady) Fatima. I have established Blessings for them.'" Rahil said, "O Lord! Are not Your Blessings for them more than what we saw for them in Paradise and considering their rank?" The Honorable the Exalted God said, "O Rahil! Amongst My Blessings for them is My own Love with which I unite them, and establish them as My Proofs for My creatures. I swear by My Honor and Majesty that I will create from them descendants whom I will make My Treasures on My Earth, and as Mines of My Wisdom. By them I will provide My Proofs after My Prophets and Messengers.""O Ali! Then give me glad tidings! I will marry off my daughter (the Blessed Lady) Fatima to you as the Merciful God did. For her I am pleased with what God is pleased with. Now take the hands of your spouse as you deserve her more than I do. Gabriel informed me that Paradise and its residents are eager to see you two. Had not the Blessed the Sublime God planned to create Proofs for His creatures from your generation, He would have fulfilled the request of the residents of Paradise regarding you. How good a brother, a groom and a companion you are. God's Pleasure suffices for you. It is better than anyone else's pleasure." Then 'Alī (عليه السلام) said, "O my Lord! Enable me to be grateful for Thy favours, which thou hast bestowed on me..." Then God's Prophet (صلى الله عليه وآله وسلم) said, "Amin!"The same tradition was narrated by ʿAlī b. Ahmad b. Muḥammad b. Imran ad-Daqqaq - may God be pleased with him, on the authority of Ahmad b. Yahya al-Zakariya al-Qattan, on the authority of Abu Muḥammad Bakr b. ʿAbd Allāh b. HAbib on the authority of Ahmad b. al-Harith, on the authority of Abu Mo'awiya, on the authority of al-A'amesh, on the authority of Ja'far b. Muḥammad (as-Ṣādiq) (عليه السلام), on the authority of his father (عليه السلام), on the authority of his grandfather (عليه السلام), on the authority of his father (عليه السلام) that ʿAlī b. Abi Talib (عليه السلام) said, "I had decided to marry (the Blessed Lady) Fatima (عليها السلام) but did not dare tell this to God's Prophet (صلى الله عليه وآله وسلم)." The rest is as it was narrated before. This tradition has also been narrated in a different way which I have stated in my book Madinatul-Ilm. (معتبر)[45]

46.

حَدَّثنا أَحْمَدُ بْنُ زِيادِ بْنِ جَعْفَر الْهَمَذانِيُ رَضِيَ اللهُ عَنْهُ قالَ: حَدَّثَنا عَلِيُّ بْنُ إِبراهِيمَ بْنِ هاشِمٍ، عَنْ أَبِيهِ، عَن إِبْراهِيمَ بْنِ هاشِمٍ، عَنْ عَبْدِ السَّلامِ بْنِ صالِحِ الهَرَوِيِّ قالَ: قُلْتُ لِعَلِيِّ بْنِ مُوسَى الرِّضا عَلَيْهِمَا السَّلاَمُ: يا ابْنَ رَسُولَ اللَّهِ ما تَقُول فِي الْحَدِيثِ الَّذِي يَروِيهِ أَهْلُ الْحَدِيثِ: أَنَّ الْمُؤْمِنِينَ يَزُورُونَ رَبَّهُمْ مِن مَنازِلِهِمْ فِي الجَنَّةِ؟ فَقالَ عَلَيْهِ السَّلامُ: يا أَبَا الصَّلْتِ إِنَّ اللَّهَ تبارَكَ وَتَعالى فَضَّلَ نَبِيِّهِ مُحَمَّداً عَلَى جَمِيعِ خَلقِهِ مِنَ النَبِيِّينَ وَالمَلائِكَةِ، وَجعَلَ طاعَتَهُ طاعَتَهُ، وَمَتابِعَتَهُ مُتابِعَتَهُ، وَزِيارَتَهُ فِي الدُّنْيا وَالآخِرَةِ زِيارَتَهُ فَقالَ عَزَّ وَجَلَّ: «مَن يُطِعِ الرَّسُولَ فَقَدْ أَطاعَ اللَّهَ» قالَ: «إِنَّ الَّذِينَ يُبايِعُونَ كَأَنَّما يُبايِعُونَ اللَّهَ يَدُ اللهِ فَوْقَ أَيْدِيهِمْ» وَقالَ النَّبِيُّ صَلَّى اللهُ عَلَيْهِ وَآلِهِ «مَن زارَنِي فِي حَياتِي أَوْ بَعْدَ مَوْتِي فَقَدْ زارَ اللَّهَ تَعالى» وَدَرَجَةُ النَّبِي صَلَّى اللهُ عَلَيْهِ وَآلِهِ فِي الجَنَّةِ أَرْفَعُ الدَّرَجاتِ.فَمَنْ زارَهُ فِي دَرَجَتِهِ الجَنَّةِ مِن مَنْزِلِهِ فَقَدْ زارَ اللَّهُ تبارَكَ وَتَعالى. قالَ: فَقُلْتُ لَهُ: يا ابْنِ رَسُولَ اللَّهِ فَما مَعْنَى الخَبَرِ الَّذِي رَوَوهُ: «أَنَّ ثَوَابَ لا إِلَهَ إِلاّ اللَّهُ النَّظَرُ إِلى وَجْهِ اللَّهِ تَعالى» فَقالَ عَلَيْهِ السَّلامُ: يا أَبَا الصَّلْتِ مَن وَصَفَ اللَّهَ تَعالى بِوَجهٍ كَالوُجُوهِ فَقَدْ كَفَرَ ،وَلكِن وَجْهُ اللَّهِ تَعالى أَنْبِياؤُهُ وَرُسُلِهِ وَحُجَجُهُ صَلَواتُ اللَّهِ عَلَيهِم، هُمُ الَّذِينَ بِهِم يَتَوَجَّهُ إِلَى اللَّهِ عَزَّ وَجَلَّ وَإِلى دِينِهِ وَمَعْرِفَتِهِ و قالَ اللَّه تَعالى: «كُلُّ مَنْ عَلَيْها فانٍ وَيَبْقى وَجْهُ رَبِّكَ ذُو الْجَلالِ وَالْإِكْرامِ» وَقالَ عَزَّ وَجَلَّ: «كُلُّ شَيْءٍ هالِكٌ إِلَّا وَجْهَهُ» فَالنَّظَرُ إِلى أَنْبِياءَ اللَّه تَعالى وَرُسُلِهِ وَحُجَجِهِ عَلَيْهِمُ السَّلاَمُ فِي دَرَجاتِهِمْ ثَوابٌ عَظِيمٌ لِلمُؤمِنِينَ يَوْمَ القِيامَةِ وَقَدْ قالَ النَّبِي صَلَّى اللهُ عَلَيْهِ وَآلِهِ: «مَن أَبغَضَ أَهْلَ بَيْتِي وَعِتْرَتِي لَمْ يَرنِي وَلَمْ أَرَهُ يَوْمَ القِيامَةِ» وَقالَ: «إِنَّ فِيكُم مَنْ لا يَرانِي بَعْدَ أَن يُفارِقَنِي»، يا أَبَا الصَّلْتِ إِنَّ اللَّهَ تبارَكَ وَتَعالى لا يُوصَفُ بِمَكانٍ، وَلا يُدْرِكُ بِالأَبصارِ وَالأَوهامِ.قالَ:.

---

[45] *'Uyūn Akhbār al-Riḍā, v1, ch21, h1*

قُلْتُ لَهُ يا ابْنَ رَسُولَ اللّهِ أَخبرني عَنِ الجَنَّةِ وَالنَّارِ أهما الْيَوْمَ مَخْلُوقتانِ ؟ فقال: نعم، وَإِنَّ رَسُولَ اللّهِ صَلَّى اللهُ عَلَيْهِ وَآلِهِ قَدْ دَخَلَ الجَنَّةَ وَرأى النَّارَ لَمّا عُرِجَ بِهِ إِلى السَّماءِ، قالَ: فَقُلْتُ لَهُ: إنَّ قَوْماً يقُولُونَ: إِنَّهُما الْيَوْمَ مُقَدَّرتانِ غَيْرِ مَخلُوقتَيْنِ، فقالَ عَلَيْهِ السَّلامُ لا هُمْ مِنّا وَلا نَحْنُ مِنْهُمْ، مَنْ أَنْكَر خَلق الجَنَّةِ وَالنّارِ فَقَدْ كَذَّبَ النَّبِي صَلَّى اللّهُ عَلَيْهِ وَآلِهِ وَكذبنا وَكَذَّبَنا وَلَيْسَ مِن وِلايَتِنا عَلى شَيءٍ وَيُخلَّدُ في نارِ جَهَنَّمَ، قالَ اللّهُ تعالى: «هذهِ جَهَنَّمُ الَّتي يُكَذِّبُ بِها الْمُجْرِمُونَ يَطُوفُونَ بَيْنَها وَبَيْنَ حَمِيمٍ آنٍ» وَقالَ النَّبي صَلَّى اللّهُ عَلَيْهِ وَآلِهِ: «لَمّا عُرِجَ بي إِلى السَّماءِ أَخَذَ بِيَدِي جِبْرَئِيلُ عَلَيْهِ السَّلامُ فَأَدخلَني الجَنَّةَ، فناولَني مِن رُطَبِها، فأَكَلْتُهُ فتَحَوَّلَ ذلِكَ نُطْفَةً في صُلْبي، فَلَمّا هَبَطْتُ إِلى الأَرْضِ واقعتُ خَدِيجَةَ، فَحَمَلَت بِفاطِمَةَ عَلَيْها السَّلامُ فَفاطِمَةُ حَوراءٌ إِنسِيَّةٌ، فَكُلَّما اشتَقتُ إِلى رائِحَةِ الجَنَّةِ شَمَمتُ رائِحَةَ ابنَتي فاطِمَةَ عَلَيْها السَّلامُ

Ahmad b. Ziyad b. Ja'far al-Hamadani - may God be pleased with him - narrated that 'Alī b. Ibrahim b. Hashem quoted on the authority of his father, on the authority of Abdul Salam b. Salih al-Harawi , "I asked 'Alī b. Mūsā Al-Ridha (عليه السلام), 'O son of the Prophet of God! What is your opinion on the following traditions which the narrators of traditions narrate: 'The believers visit their Lord from their homes in Paradise.' Al-Ridha (عليه السلام) replied, 'O Aba Salt! Indeed the Blessed the Sublime God has honored His Prophet Muḥammad over all His creatures - even the Prophets and the angels. He has established obeying him equal to obeying God, following him equal to following God, and visiting him equal to visiting God. The Honorable the Exalted God said, 'He who obeys the Apostle, obeys God...' God also said, 'Verily those who plight their fealty to thee do no less than plight their fealty to God: the Hand of God is over their hands...' Moreover, the Prophet (صلى الله عليه وآله وسلم) has said, 'Whoever comes to visit me during my life or after my death has indeed visited the Sublime God. The rank of the Prophet (صلى الله عليه وآله وسلم) in Heaven is the highest rank of all. Therefore, whoever visits the Prophet (صلى الله عليه وآله وسلم) in the Prophet's (صلى الله عليه وآله وسلم) own rank and position in Heaven has indeed visited the Blessed the Sublime God.''"Aba Salt (Abdul Salam b. Salih al-Harawi) added, "I asked, 'O son of the Prophet of God (صلى الله عليه وآله وسلم)! What is the meaning of the following tradition, 'The reward of saying There is no god but God is looking at the Face of the Sublime God?' The Imam (صلى الله عليه وآله وسلم) replied, 'Whoever considers the Sublime God as having a face similar to that of the creatures is an atheist.However, the Sublime God's Face is His Prophets (صلى الله عليه وآله وسلم), His Messengers (عليه السلام) and His Proofs (عليه

السلام). They are the people by whom the people are directed towards the Honorable the Exalted God, His Religion and His Recognition. The Sublime God said, 'All that is on earth will perish. But will abide (forever) the Face of thy Lord, full of Majesty, Bounty and Honor.' The Honorable the Exalted God also said, '...Everything (that exists) will perish except His own Face..' . Therefore, looking at the Sublime God's Prophets (عليه السلام), Messengers (عليه السلام) and Proofs (عليه السلام) in their respective ranks has a great reward for the believers on the Resurrection Day. The Prophet (صلى الله عليه وآله وسلم) has also said, 'On the Resurrection Day whoever despises the members of my Holy Household and my 'Itra will not see me. I will not see him either.' The Prophet (صلى الله عليه وآله وسلم) has also said, 'Among you there are some people who will never again see me after they depart from me.' O Aba Salt! Indeed the Blessed the Sublime God cannot be described by position, cannot be perceived by the eyes or imaginations.'"Aba Salt said, "I asked, 'Please tell me whether Heaven and Hell have been created?' Imam Al-Ridha (عليه السلام) answered, 'Yes. When the Prophet of God (صلى الله عليه وآله وسلم) was taken for the Ascension to the heavens he entered Paradise, and saw the Fire.'"Aba Salt said, "I asked, 'Some people believe that these two have been destined to be, but have not been created yet.' The Imam (عليه السلام) replied, 'Neither do they belong to us, nor do we belong to them. Whoever denies Heaven and Hell has indeed denied the Prophet (صلى الله عليه وآله وسلم) and us. He is not controlled by any part of our Mastery. He will abide in the Fire for eternity. The Sublime God has said, 'This is the Hell which the sinners deny. In its midst and in the midst of boiling hot water will they wander around! ' **The Prophet (صلى الله عليه وآله وسلم) said, 'When I was taken for Ascension to the heavens Gabriel took my hands and took me into Paradise. They he gave me some Heavenly Dates from which I ate. The date turned into sperms in my loin. Once I returned to the Earth I made love with Khadija and she got pregnant with (the Blessed Baby) Fatima (عليها السلام). Therefore, Fatima is a human houri. Whenever I wish to smell Paradise, I smell the scent of my daughter Fatima (عليها السلام).** (حسن)[46]

[46] *'Uyūn Akhbār al-Riḍā, v1, ch11, h3*

47.

عَلِيُّ بْنُ مُحَمَّدِ بْنِ عَبْدِ اللهِ عَنْ بَعْضِ أَصْحَابِنَا أَظُنُّهُ السَّيَّارِيَّ عَنْ عَلِيِّ بْنِ أَسْبَاطٍ قَالَ لَمَّا وَرَدَ أَبُو الْحَسَنِ مُوسَى (عَلَيْهِ السَّلام) عَلَى الْمَهْدِيِّ رَآهُ يَرُدُّ الْمَظَالِمَ فَقَالَ يَا أَمِيرَ الْمُؤْمِنِينَ مَا بَالُ مَظْلِمَتِنَا لا تُرَدُّ فَقَالَ لَهُ وَمَا ذَاكَ يَا أَبَا الْحَسَنِ قَالَ إِنَّ اللهَ تَبَارَكَ وَتَعَالَى لَمَّا فَتَحَ عَلَى نَبِيِّهِ (صَلَّى اللهُ عَلَيْهِ وَآلِه) فَدَكاً وَمَا وَالاهَا لَمْ يُوجَفْ عَلَيْهِ بِخَيْلٍ وَلا رِكَابٍ فَأَنْزَلَ اللهُ عَلَى نَبِيِّهِ (صَلَّى اللهُ عَلَيْهِ وَآلِه) وَآتِ ذَا الْقُرْبى حَقَّهُ فَلَمْ يَدْرِ رَسُولُ اللهِ (صَلَّى اللهُ عَلَيْهِ وَآلِه) مَنْ هُمْ فَرَاجَعَ فِي ذَلِكَ جَبْرَئِيلَ وَرَاجَعَ جَبْرَئِيلُ (عَلَيْهِ السَّلام) رَبَّهُ فَأَوْحَى اللهُ إِلَيْهِ أَنِ ادْفَعْ فَدَكاً إِلَى فَاطِمَةَ (عليها السلام) فَدَعَاهَا رَسُولُ اللهِ (صَلَّى اللهُ عَلَيْهِ وَآلِه) فَقَالَ لَهَا يَا فَاطِمَةُ إِنَّ اللهَ أَمَرَنِي أَنْ أَدْفَعَ إِلَيْكِ فَدَكاً فَقَالَتْ قَدْ قَبِلْتُ يَا رَسُولَ اللهِ مِنَ اللهِ وَمِنْكَ فَلَمْ يَزَلْ وُكَلاؤُهَا فِيهَا حَيَاةَ رَسُولِ اللهِ (صَلَّى اللهُ عَلَيْهِ وَآلِه) فَلَمَّا وُلِّيَ أَبُو بَكْرٍ أَخْرَجَ عَنْهَا وُكَلاءَهَا فَأَتَتْهُ فَسَأَلَتْهُ أَنْ يَرُدَّهَا عَلَيْهَا فَقَالَ لَهَا ائْتِينِي بِأَسْوَدَ أَوْ أَحْمَرَ يَشْهَدُ لَكِ بِذَلِكِ فَجَاءَتْ بِأَمِيرِ الْمُؤْمِنِينَ (عَلَيْهِ السَّلام) وَأُمِّ أَيْمَنَ فَشَهِدَا لَهَا فَكَتَبَ لَهَا بِتَرْكِ التَّعَرُّضِ فَخَرَجَتْ وَالْكِتَابُ مَعَهَا فَلَقِيَهَا عُمَرُ فَقَالَ مَا هَذَا مَعَكِ يَا بِنْتَ مُحَمَّدٍ قَالَتْ كِتَابٌ كَتَبَهُ لِي ابْنُ أَبِي قُحَافَةَ قَالَ أَرِينِيهِ فَأَبَتْ فَانْتَزَعَهُ مِنْ يَدِهَا وَنَظَرَ فِيهِ ثُمَّ تَفَلَ فِيهِ وَمَحَاهُ وَخَرَقَهُ فَقَالَ لَهَا هَذَا لَمْ يُوجِفْ عَلَيْهِ أَبُوكِ بِخَيْلٍ وَلا رِكَابٍ فَضَعِي الْحِبَالَ فِي رِقَابِنَا فَقَالَ لَهُ الْمَهْدِيُّ يَا أَبَا الْحَسَنِ حُدَّهَا لِي فَقَالَ حَدٌّ مِنْهَا جَبَلُ أُحُدٍ وَحَدٌّ مِنْهَا عَرِيشُ مِصْرَ وَحَدٌّ مِنْهَا سِيفُ الْبَحْرِ وَحَدٌّ مِنْهَا دُومَةُ الْجَنْدَلِ فَقَالَ لَهُ كُلُّ هَذَا قَالَ نَعَمْ يَا أَمِيرَ الْمُؤْمِنِينَ هَذَا كُلُّهُ إِنَّ هَذَا كُلَّهُ مِمَّا لَمْ يُوجِفْ عَلَى أَهْلِهِ رَسُولُ اللهِ (صَلَّى اللهُ عَلَيْهِ وَآلِه) بِخَيْلٍ وَلا رِكَابٍ فَقَالَ كَثِيرٌ وَأَنْظُرُ فِيهِ

Ali b. Muḥammad b. 'AbdAllāh has narrated from Certain persons of our people that I thinks is al-Sayyari from 'Alī b. Asbat who has said the following. "In one of the meetings of abu al-Hassan Mūsā (عليه السلام) with al-Mahdi (one of 'Abbassid ruler) the Imam found him paying reparations (for the damages caused to people). The Imam (عليه السلام) said, "O Amir al-Mu'minin, what has happened to the reparations due to us?" He then asked, "What damage is caused to you O abu al-Hassan ?" He (the Imam (عليه السلام) said, "Allāh, the Holy, the Most High, granted victory to His Holy Prophet (s.a) and the land of Fadak and its surrounding areas came under his control without any armed struggle Allāh sent a message to His the Holy Prophet (s.a). It said, "Give the relatives their rights." The Messenger of Allāh did not know who they were. He turned to Jibril to find out and Jibril turned to his Lord for the answer.

Allāh then sent revelation to him to give possession of Fadak to Fatima (عليه السلام). Thereupon, the Messenger of Allāh called Fatima and said to her. "O Fatima (عليه السلام) Allāh has commanded me to give possession of Fadak to you. She then said, " O the Messenger of Allāh, I have accepted the offer from Allāh and from you." Thereafter her representatives lived there during the life time of the Messenger of Allāh. When abu Bakr took control he expelled her representatives therefrom. She went to abu Bakr and asked him to reverse his decision and return Fadak to her but he said to Fatima (عليه السلام), "Bring to a black or white to testify that Fadak belonged to you." Fatima (عليه السلام) brought Amir al-Mu'minin 'Alī (عليه السلام) and 'Umm Ayman who both testified in favor of Fatima (عليه السلام). He then wrote, "Fatima must not be disturbed in the matters of Fadak." Fatima then left with the document. On the way 'Umar came from the opposite direction and asked, "What is it in your hand O daughter of Muhammad?" Fatima (عليه السلام) said, "It is a document that b. abu Quhafa has written for me." He said, "Show it to me." Fatima refused to hand it over to him but he snatched it away from her hand and read it. He then spit on it wiped out its writing and tore it into pieces. He said, "This was not captured by forces of the camels and horses of your father so that you can tie the rope around our necks." Al-Mahdi said, "O abu al-Hassan define for me the boundaries of Fadak." The Imam (عليه السلام) said, "On one side it borders the mountain of 'Uhud. On the other side is 'Arish Misr. Also it borders Sayf al-Bahr and on one of its sides is Dawmat al-Jandal." Then he asked the Imams, "Is that all?" He said, "Yes, O Amir al-Mu'minin, this is all that came to the Messenger of Allāh without the use of the forces of the camels and horses." He said, "This is a large area but I will look into it. (مجهول)[47]

48.

عِدَّةٌ مِنْ أَصْحَابِنَا عَنْ أَحْمَدَ بْنِ مُحَمَّدٍ عَنْ عَبْدِ اللهِ بْنِ الْحَجَّالِ عَنْ أَحْمَدَ بْنِ عُمَرَ الْحَلَبِيِّ عَنْ أَبِي بَصِيرٍ قَالَ دَخَلْتُ عَلَى أَبِي عَبْدِ اللهِ (عَلَيْهِ السَّلام) فَقُلْتُ لَهُ جُعِلْتُ فِدَاكَ إِنِّي أَسْأَلُكَ عَنْ مَسْأَلَةٍ هَاهُنَا أَحَدٌ يَسْمَعُ

[47] *Al-Kāfi, v1, ch130, h5*

كَلامِي قَالَ فَرَفَعَ أَبُو عَبْدِ الله (عَلَيْهِ السَّلام) سِتْراً بَيْنَهُ وَبَيْنَ بَيْتٍ آخَرَ فَاطَّلَعَ فِيهِ ثُمَّ قَالَ يَا أَبَا مُحَمَّدٍ سَلْ عَمَّا بَدَا لَكَ قَالَ قُلْتُ جُعِلْتُ فِدَاكَ إِنَّ شِيعَتَكَ يَتَحَدَّثُونَ أَنَّ رَسُولَ الله (صَلَّى اللهُ عَلَيْهِ وَآلِه) عَلَّمَ عَلِيّاً (عَلَيْهِ السَّلام) بَاباً يُفْتَحُ لَهُ مِنْهُ أَلْفُ بَابٍ قَالَ فَقَالَ يَا أَبَا مُحَمَّدٍ عَلَّمَ رَسُولُ الله (صَلَّى اللهُ عَلَيْهِ وَآلِه) عَلِيّاً (عَلَيْهِ السَّلام) أَلْفَ بَابٍ يُفْتَحُ مِنْ كُلِّ بَابٍ أَلْفُ بَابٍ قَالَ قُلْتُ هَذَا وَالله الْعِلْمُ قَالَ فَنَكَتَ سَاعَةً فِي الارْضِ ثُمَّ قَالَ إِنَّهُ لَعِلْمٌ وَمَا هُوَ بِذَاكَ قَالَ ثُمَّ قَالَ يَا أَبَا مُحَمَّدٍ وَإِنَّ عِنْدَنَا الْجَامِعَةَ وَمَا يُدْرِيهِمْ مَا الْجَامِعَةُ قَالَ قُلْتُ جُعِلْتُ فِدَاكَ وَمَا الْجَامِعَةُ قَالَ صَحِيفَةٌ طُولُهَا سَبْعُونَ ذِرَاعاً بِذِرَاعِ رَسُولِ الله (صَلَّى اللهُ عَلَيْهِ وَآلِه) وَإِمْلائِهِ مِنْ فَلْقِ فِيهِ وَخَطُّ عَلِيٍّ بِيَمِينِهِ فِيهَا كُلُّ حَلالٍ وَحَرَامٍ وَكُلُّ شَيْءٍ يَحْتَاجُ النَّاسُ إِلَيْهِ حَتَّى الارْشُ فِي الْخَدْشِ وَضَرَبَ بِيَدِهِ إِلَيَّ فَقَالَ تَأْذَنُ لِي يَا أَبَا مُحَمَّدٍ قَالَ قُلْتُ جُعِلْتُ فِدَاكَ إِنَّمَا أَنَا لَكَ فَاصْنَعْ مَا شِئْتَ قَالَ فَغَمَزَنِي بِيَدِهِ وَقَالَ حَتَّى أَرْشُ هَذَا كَأَنَّهُ مُغْضَبٌ قَالَ قُلْتُ هَذَا وَالله الْعِلْمُ قَالَ إِنَّهُ لَعِلْمٌ وَلَيْسَ بِذَاكَ ثُمَّ سَكَتَ سَاعَةً ثُمَّ قَالَ وَإِنَّ عِنْدَنَا الْجَفْرَ وَمَا يُدْرِيهِمْ مَا الْجَفْرُ قَالَ قُلْتُ وَمَا الْجَفْرُ قَالَ وِعَاءٌ مِنْ أَدَمٍ فِيهِ عِلْمُ النَّبِيِّينَ وَالْوَصِيِّينَ وَعِلْمُ الْعُلَمَاءِ الَّذِينَ مَضَوْا مِنْ بَنِي إِسْرَائِيلَ قَالَ قُلْتُ إِنَّ هَذَا هُوَ الْعِلْمُ قَالَ إِنَّهُ لَعِلْمٌ وَلَيْسَ بِذَاكَ ثُمَّ سَكَتَ سَاعَةً ثُمَّ قَالَ وَإِنَّ عِنْدَنَا لَمُصْحَفَ فَاطِمَةَ (عليها السلام) وَمَا يُدْرِيهِمْ مَا مُصْحَفُ فَاطِمَةَ (عليها السلام) قَالَ قُلْتُ وَمَا مُصْحَفُ فَاطِمَةَ (عليها السلام) قَالَ مُصْحَفٌ فِيهِ مِثْلُ قُرْآنِكُمْ هَذَا ثَلاثَ مَرَّاتٍ وَالله مَا فِيهِ مِنْ قُرْآنِكُمْ حَرْفٌ وَاحِدٌ قَالَ قُلْتُ هَذَا وَالله الْعِلْمُ قَالَ إِنَّهُ لَعِلْمٌ وَمَا هُوَ بِذَاكَ ثُمَّ سَكَتَ سَاعَةً ثُمَّ قَالَ إِنَّ عِنْدَنَا عِلْمَ مَا كَانَ وَعِلْمَ مَا هُوَ كَائِنٌ إِلَى أَنْ تَقُومَ السَّاعَةُ قَالَ قُلْتُ جُعِلْتُ فِدَاكَ هَذَا وَالله هُوَ الْعِلْمُ قَالَ إِنَّهُ لَعِلْمٌ وَلَيْسَ بِذَاكَ قَالَ قُلْتُ جُعِلْتُ فِدَاكَ فَأَيُّ شَيْءٍ الْعِلْمُ قَالَ مَا يَحْدُثُ بِاللَّيْلِ وَالنَّهَارِ الامْرُ مِنْ بَعْدِ الامْرِ وَالشَّيْءُ بَعْدَ الشَّيْءِ إِلَى يَوْمِ الْقِيَامَةِ

A number of our people has narrated from Ahmad b. Muḥammad from 'AbdAllāh b. al-Hajjal from Ahmad b. 'Umar al-Halabi from abu Basir who has said the following. "I went to abu 'AbdAllāh (عليه السلام) and said, "May Allāh take my soul in service for your cause, I like to ask you a question. Is there anyone else in this house who may hear my words?" The Imams (عليه السلام) then folded the curtain between his room and the other room next to it and looked into it. Then the Imams (عليه السلام) said, "O abu Muhammad, ask whatever you wish." I said, "May Allāh take my soul in service for your cause, your followers say that the Messenger of Allāh taught 'Alī (عليه السلام) a thousand chapter of knowledge and from each chapter there opens a thousand chapter. I then said, 'This, I swear by Allāh, is knowledge.'" He would mark the ground with his staff (a sign of thinking in normal people) for a while and said, "That is knowledge but it is not that." The narrators has said that The Imam (عليه السلام) then said, "O abu Muhammad, with us there is al-Jami'a. What do they know what al-

Jami' is?" I then asked, "May Allāh take my soul in service for your cause, what is al-Jami'a? The Imam (عليه السلام) said, it is a parchment seventy yards by the yards of the Messenger of Allāh long that contains his dictations that is in graved in to with the right hand writing of 'Alī (عليه السلام). It contains all the lawful and unlawful and all matters that people need, even the law to of compensation for A number of our people has narrated from scratch caused to a person. He then stretched his hand to me and asked, 'May I, O abu Muhammad?' I then replied, "May Allāh take my soul in service for your cause, I am all at your disposal." He pinched me with his hand and said, "Even there is the law of compensation for this." He seemed angry. The narrator has said, "I then said, "This, I swear by Allāh is knowledge." The Imams (عليه السلام) said, "It certainly is knowledge but not that one." The Imams (عليه السلام) remained silent for a while and then said, "With us there is al-Jafr (the parchment). What do they know what al-Jafr is? I then asked, "What is al-Jafr (the parchment or a container) ?" The Imams (عليه السلام) said, "It is a container made of skin that contains the knowledge of the prophets and the executors of their wills and the knowledge of the scholars in the past from the Israelites." The narrator has said that he then said, "This certainly, is the knowledge." The Imam (عليه السلام) said, "It certainly is knowledge but not that knowledge." The Imams (عليه السلام) remained silent for a while and then said, "With us there is the book (Mushaf) of Fatima, (عليه السلام). What do they know what Mushaf of Fatima is? The Imam (عليه السلام) said, "Mushaf of Fatima is three times bigger than your Qur'ān. There is not even a single letter therein from your Qur'ān." The narrator has said, "I then said, "This, I swear by Allāh, is the knowledge." The Imam (عليه السلام) said, "This certainly is knowledge, but it is not that." The Imam (عليه السلام) remained silent for a while and then said, "With us there is the knowledge of whatever has been and the knowledge of whatever will come into being to the Day of Judgment." The narrator has said that he then said, "May Allāh take my soul in service for your cause, this, I swear by Allāh is, certainly, knowledge." The Imam (عليه السلام) said, "It certainly is knowledge but not that." The narrator has said that he then asked, "May Allāh take my soul in service for your cause, What then is knowledge?" The Imam (عليه السلام) said, "Whatever takes place during the night and during the day, one matter after the other matter and one thing after the other thing to the Day of Judgment. (صحيح)[48]

49.

مُحَمَّدُ بْنُ يَحْيَى عَنْ أَحْمَدَ بْنِ مُحَمَّدٍ عَنِ ابْنِ مَحْبُوبٍ عَنِ ابْنِ رِئَابٍ عَنْ أَبِي عُبَيْدَةَ قَالَ سَأَلَ أَبَا عَبْدِ اللهِ (عَلَيْهِ السَّلَام) بَعْضُ أَصْحَابِنَا عَنِ الْجَفْرِ فَقَالَ هُوَ جِلْدُ ثَوْرٍ مَمْلُوءٌ عِلْماً قَالَ لَهُ فَالْجَامِعَةُ قَالَ تِلْكَ صَحِيفَةٌ طُولُهَا سَبْعُونَ ذِرَاعاً فِي عَرْضِ الادِيمِ مِثْلُ فَخِذِ الْفَالِجِ فِيهَا كُلُّ مَا يَحْتَاجُ النَّاسُ إِلَيْهِ وَلَيْسَ مِنْ قَضِيَّةٍ إِلا وَهِيَ فِيهَا حَتَّى أَرْشُ الْخَدْشِ قَالَ فَمُصْحَفُ فَاطِمَةَ (عليها السلام) قَالَ فَسَكَتَ طَوِيلاً ثُمَّ قَالَ إِنَّكُمْ لَتَبْحَثُونَ عَمَّا تُرِيدُونَ وَعَمَّا لا تُرِيدُونَ إِنَّ فَاطِمَةَ مَكَثَتْ بَعْدَ رَسُولِ اللهِ (صَلَّى اللهُ عَلَيْهِ وَآلِه) خَمْسَةً وَسَبْعِينَ يَوْماً وَكَانَ دَخَلَهَا حُزْنٌ شَدِيدٌ عَلَى أَبِيهَا وَكَانَ جَبْرَئِيلُ (عَلَيْهِ السَّلَام) يَأْتِيهَا فَيُحْسِنُ عَزَاءَهَا عَلَى أَبِيهَا وَيُطَيِّبُ نَفْسَهَا وَيُخْبِرُهَا عَنْ أَبِيهَا وَمَكَانِهِ وَيُخْبِرُهَا بِمَا يَكُونُ بَعْدَهَا فِي ذُرِّيَّتِهَا وَكَانَ علي (عَلَيْهِ السَّلَام) يَكْتُبُ ذَلِكَ فَهَذَا مُصْحَفُ فَاطِمَةَ (عليها السلام)

Muhammad b. Yahya has narrated from Ahmad b. Muḥammad from b. Mahbub from b. Ri'ab from abu 'Ubaydah who has said that the people from our group asked abu 'AbdAllāh (عليه السلام) about Jafr and the Imam (عليه السلام) said the following. "It is the skin of a bull which is full of knowledge." Then they asked the Imam (عليه السلام) about al-Jami'a. The Imam (عليه السلام) replied, "It is a parchment that is seventy yards long with a width of hide like that of the leg of a huge camel. It contains all that people may need. There is no case for there is a rule in it. In it there is the law to settle the compensation for a scratch caused to a person." The narrator has said that he asked the Imams (عليه السلام), "What is Mushaf of Fatima?" The Imam (عليه السلام) waited for quite a while. Then he said, "You ask about what you really mean and what you do not mean. Fatima (عليه السلام) lived after the Messenger of Allāh for seventy-five days. She was severely depressed because of the death of her father. Jibril (عليه السلام) would come to provide her solace because of the death of her father. Jibril would comfort her soul. Jibril would inform her about her father and his place and of the

[48] *Al-Kafi, v1, ch40, h1*

future events and about what will happen to her children. At the same time 'Alī (عليه السلام) would write all of them down and thus is Mushaf of Fatima (عليه السلام). (صحيح)[49]

Virtues of Imam al-Hasan (عليه السلام) and Imam al-Husayn (عليه السلام)

50.

حدثنا محمد بن إبراهيم بن إسحاق رضي الله عنه قال : أخبرنا أحمد بن محمد الهمداني قال : حدثنا علي بن الحسن بن علي بن فضال ، عن أبيه ، عن هشام بن سالم قال : قلت للصادق جعفر بن محمد عليهما السلام : الحسن أفضل أم الحسين ؟ فقال : الحسن أفضل من الحسين . [قال :] قلت : فكيف صارت الإمامة من بعد الحسين في عقبه دون ولد الحسن ؟ فقال : إن الله تبارك وتعالى أحب أن يجعل (3) سنة موسى وهارون جارية في الحسن والحسين عليهما السلام ، ألا ترى أنهما كانا شريكين في النبوة كما كان الحسن والحسين شريكين في الإمامة وإن الله عز وجل جعل النبوة في ولد هارون ولم يجعلها في ولد موسى وإن كان موسى أفضل من هارون عليهما السلام ، قلت : فهل يكون إمامان في وقت واحد ؟ قال : لا إلا أن يكون أحدهما صامتا مأموما لصاحبه ، والآخر ناطقا إماما لصاحبه ، فأما أن يكونا إمامين ناطقين في وقت واحد فلا . قلت : فهل تكون الإمامة في أخوين بعد الحسن والحسين عليهما السلام ؟ قال : لا إنما هي جارية في عقب الحسين عليه السلام كما قال الله عز وجل : " وجعلها كلمة باقية في عقبة " ثم هي جارية في الأعقاب وأعقاب الأعقاب إلى يوم القيامة

Muhammad b. Ibrahim b. Is`haq رضي الله عنه narrated. He said: Ahmad b. Muḥammad al-Hamadani informed us. He said: `Ali b. al-Hasan b. `Ali b. Faddal narrated from his father from Hisham b. Salim.

He said: I said to as-Ṣādiq Ja`far b. Muḥammad عليهما السلام: Who is superior: al-Hasan or al-Husayn? So he said: al-Hasan is superior to al-Husayn. He said: I said: Then why did the Imamate go to the descendents of al-Husayn rather than the loins of al-Hasan? So he said: Allāh تبارك وتعالى loved to apply the sunna of Mūsā and Harun to al-

[49] *Al-Kāfi, v1, ch40, h5*

Hasan and al-Husayn عليهما السلام. Have you not seen that the two were partners in prophethood, just as al-Hasan and al-Husayn were partners in Imamate? And Allāh عز وجل caused prophethood to come from the loins of Harun and did not cause it to come from to loins of Musa, even though Mūsā was superior to Harun عليهما السلام. I said: So can there be two Imams at the same time? He said: No, unless one of them is silent, following the leadership of his companion, and the other is a speaking Imam for his companion. But as to whether there can be two speaking Imams at the same time – then no. I said: So can the Imamate go to two brothers after al-Hasan and al-Husayn عليهما السلام? He said: No, rather, it will transfer through descendents of al-Husayn عليه السلام, just as Alllah عز وجل says, "And he made it a word to continue in his posterity." (43:28), then it will transfer from descendent to descendent to descendent until the Day of Judgment.[50]

51.

مُحَمَّدُ بْنُ يَحْيَى وَأَحْمَدُ بْنُ مُحَمَّدٍ عَنْ مُحَمَّدِ بْنِ الْحَسَنِ عَنِ الْقَاسِمِ النَّهْدِيِّ عَنْ إِسْمَاعِيلَ بْنِ مِهْرَانَ عَنِ الْكُنَاسِيِّ عَنْ أَبِي عَبْدِ اللهِ (عَلَيْهِ السَّلام) قَالَ خَرَجَ الْحَسَنُ بن علي (عَلَيْهِمَا السَّلام) فِي بَعْضِ عُمَرِهِ وَمَعَهُ رَجُلٌ مِنْ وُلْدِ الزُّبَيْرِ كَانَ يَقُولُ بِإِمَامَتِهِ فَنَزَلُوا فِي مَنْهَلٍ مِنْ تِلْكَ الْمَنَاهِلِ تَحْتَ نَخْلٍ يَابِسٍ قَدْ يَبِسَ مِنَ الْعَطَشِ فَفُرِشَ لِلْحَسَنِ (عَلَيْهِ السَّلام) تَحْتَ نَخْلَةٍ وَفُرِشَ لِلزُّبَيْرِيِّ بِحِذَاهُ تَحْتَ نَخْلَةٍ أُخْرَى قَالَ فَقَالَ الزُّبَيْرِيُّ وَرَفَعَ رَأْسَهُ لَوْ كَانَ فِي هَذَا النَّخْلِ رُطَبٌ لَأَكَلْنَا مِنْهُ فَقَالَ لَهُ الْحَسَنُ وَإِنَّكَ لَتَشْتَهِي الرُّطَبَ فَقَالَ الزُّبَيْرِيُّ نَعَمْ قَالَ فَرَفَعَ يَدَهُ إِلَى السَّمَاءِ فَدَعَا بِكَلَامٍ لَمْ أَفْهَمْهُ فَاخْضَرَّتِ النَّخْلَةُ ثُمَّ صَارَتْ إِلَى حَالِهَا فَأَوْرَقَتْ وَحَمَلَتْ رُطَباً فَقَالَ الْجَمَّالُ الَّذِي اكْتَرَوْا مِنْهُ سِحْرٌ وَاللهِ قَالَ فَقَالَ الْحَسَنُ (عَلَيْهِ السَّلام) وَيْلَكَ لَيْسَ بِسِحْرٍ وَلَكِنْ دَعْوَةُ ابْنِ نَبِيٍّ مُسْتَجَابَةٌ قَالَ فَصَعِدُوا إِلَى النَّخْلَةِ فَصَرَمُوا مَا كَانَ فِيهِ فَكَفَاهُمْ

Muhammad b. Yahya and Ahmad b. Muḥammad have narrated from Muḥammad b. al-Hassan from al-Qasim al-Nahdi from 'Isma'il b. Mihran from al-Kunasi from abu 'AbdAllāh (عليه السلام) who has said the following. "Once al-Hassan (عليه السلام) went out side the town with a man from the children of al-Zubayr who believed al-Hassan to

[50] *Kamal ad-Deen (Ṣaduq), v1, ch40, h9*

be the Imam. They stopped for rest on one of the oasis under a palm tree that had dried up because of lack of water. A furnishing was spread for Imam al-Hassan (عليه السلام) under that tree and for al-Zubayri the furnishings were arranged under a tree just next to it. The narrator has said that al-Zubayri looked up the tree and said, "It had fruits so we could eat from them." Al-Hassan (عليه السلام) asked, "Do you wish to have dates?" He said, "Yes, I do wish to have dates." He (al-Hassan (عليه السلام) raised his hands to the sky and spoke certain words that I did not understand. The tree turned green then it returned to its normal condition and its leaves grew and it became loaded with dates. The man from they had hired camels begun to say, "It by Allāh, is magic." Al-Hassan (عليه السلام) said, woe is you. It is not magic but it is a prayer of the son of a prophet that is answered." They climbed the tree and picked the dates that were there and it provided enough for their needs. (صحيح)[51]

52.

مُحَمَّدُ بْنُ يَحْيَى عَنِ الْحُسَيْنِ بْنِ إِسْحَاقَ عَنْ عَلِيِّ بْنِ مَهْزِيَارَ عَنِ الْحُسَيْنِ بْنِ سَعِيدٍ عَنِ النَّضْرِ بْنِ سُوَيْدٍ عَنْ عَبْدِ اللهِ بْنِ سِنَانٍ عَمَّنْ سَمِعَ أَبَا جَعْفَرٍ (عَلَيْهِ السَّلام) يَقُولُ لَمَّا حَضَرَتِ الْحَسَنَ (عَلَيْهِ السَّلام) الْوَفَاةُ بَكَى فَقِيلَ لَهُ يَا ابْنَ رَسُولِ اللهِ تَبْكِي وَمَكَانُكَ مِنْ رَسُولِ اللهِ (صَلَّى اللهُ عَلَيْهِ وَآلِه) الَّذِي أَنْتَ بِهِ وَقَدْ قَالَ فِيكَ مَا قَالَ وَقَدْ حَجَجْتَ عِشْرِينَ حَجَّةً مَاشِياً وَقَدْ قَاسَمْتَ مَالَكَ ثَلاثَ مَرَّاتٍ حَتَّى النَّعْلَ بِالنَّعْلِ فَقَالَ إِنَّمَا أَبْكِي لِخَصْلَتَيْنِ لِهَوْلِ الْمُطَّلَعِ وَفِرَاقِ الاحِبَّةِ

Muhammad b. Yahya has narrated from al-Husayn b. Ishaq from 'Alī b. Mahziyar from al-Husayn b. Sa'id from al-Nadr b. Suwayd from 'AbdAllāh b. Sinan from the one who heard from abu Ja'far (عليه السلام) who said, "When al-Hassan was about to die he wept. "He was asked, "O son of the Messenger of Allāh, why would you weep, when you have such a position with the Messenger of Allāh such as you have? And all the (good things) said about you. You have performed Hajj twenty times on foot and distributed all of your belongings among the needy three times exactly." He replied,

---

[51] *Al-Kāfi, v1, ch115, h4*

"I weep for two reasons, It is the fear of resurrection and separation from the loved ones. (مجهول)[52]

53.

عِدَّةٌ مِنْ أَصْحَابِنَا عَنْ أَحْمَدَ بْنِ مُحَمَّدٍ عَنْ عَلِيِّ بْنِ النُّعْمَانِ عَنْ سَيْفِ بْنِ عَمِيرَةَ عَنْ أَبِي بَكْرٍ الْحَضْرَمِيِّ قَالَ إِنَّ جَعْدَةَ بِنْتَ أَشْعَثَ بْنِ قَيْسٍ الْكِنْدِيِّ سَمَّتِ الْحَسَنَ بْنَ عَلِيٍّ وَسَمَّتْ مَوْلَاةً لَهُ فَأَمَّا مَوْلَاتُهُ فَقَاءَتِ السَّمَّ وَأَمَّا الْحَسَنُ فَاسْتَمْسَكَ فِي بَطْنِهِ ثُمَّ انْتَفَطَ بِهِ فَمَاتَ

A number of our people has narrated has narrated from Ahmad b. Muḥammad from 'Alī b. al-Ni'man from Sayf b. 'Amira from abu Bakr al-Hadrami has said that Jumhu'ada daughter of 'Ash'th b. Qays al-Kidi poisoned al-Hassan b. 'Alī (عليه السلام) and a female servant of the Imam (عليه السلام). The female servant, however, vomited the poison but in the case of al-Hassan (عليه السلام) the poison remained his digestive system and caused swelling that killed him. (حسن)[53]

54.

أَحْمَدُ بْنُ مُحَمَّدٍ وَمُحَمَّدُ بْنُ يَحْيَى عَنْ مُحَمَّدِ بْنِ الْحَسَنِ عَنْ يَعْقُوبَ بْنِ يَزِيدَ عَنِ ابْنِ أَبِي عُمَيْرٍ عَنْ رِجَالِهِ عَنْ أَبِي عَبْدِ اللهِ (عَلَيْهِ السَّلام) قَالَ إِنَّ الْحَسَنَ (عَلَيْهِ السَّلام) قَالَ إِنَّ للهِ مَدِينَتَيْنِ إِحْدَاهُمَا بِالْمَشْرِقِ وَالاخْرَى بِالْمَغْرِبِ عَلَيْهِمَا سُورٌ مِنْ حَدِيدٍ وَعَلَى كُلِّ وَاحِدٍ مِنْهُمَا أَلْفُ أَلْفِ مِصْرَاعٍ وَفِيهَا سَبْعُونَ أَلْفَ أَلْفِ لُغَةٍ يَتَكَلَّمُ كُلُّ لُغَةٍ بِخِلَافِ لُغَةِ صَاحِبِهَا وَأَنَا أَعْرِفُ جَمِيعَ اللُّغَاتِ وَمَا فِيهِمَا وَمَا بَيْنَهُمَا وَمَا عَلَيْهِمَا حُجَّةٌ غَيْرِي وَغَيْرُ الْحُسَيْنِ أَخِي

Ahmad b. Muḥammad and Muḥammad b. Yahya have narrated from Muḥammad b. al-Hassan from ya'qub b. Yazid from b. abu 'Umayr from his people from abu

---

[52] Al-Kāfi, v1, ch115, h1

[53] Al-Kāfi, v1, ch115, h3

'AbdAllāh (عليه السلام) who has said the following. "Al-Hassan (عليه السلام) has said, 'Allāh has two cities. One is in the east and the other is in the west. They have a boundary around them that is made of iron and each one has a million doors. Seven thousand different languages exist therein and know all those languages and all that is therein. There is no one who would possess Leadership with Divine Authority except me and my brother, al-Husayn (عليه السلام). (صحيح)[54]

55.

عَلِيُّ بْنُ إِبْرَاهِيمَ عَنْ أَبِيهِ عَنْ حَمَّادِ بْنِ عِيسَى عَنْ إِبْرَاهِيمَ بْنِ عُمَرَ الْيَمَانِيِّ وَعُمَرَ بْنِ أُذَيْنَةَ عَنْ أَبَانٍ عَنْ سُلَيْمِ بْنِ قَيْسٍ قَالَ شَهِدْتُ وَصِيَّةَ أَمِيرِ الْمُؤْمِنِينَ (عَلَيْهِ السَّلام) حِينَ أَوْصَى إِلَى ابْنِهِ الْحَسَنِ (عَلَيْهِ السَّلام) وَأَشْهَدَ عَلَى وَصِيَّتِهِ الْحُسَيْنَ (عَلَيْهِ السَّلام) وَمُحَمَّداً وَجَمِيعَ وُلْدِهِ وَرُؤَسَاءَ شِيعَتِهِ وَأَهْلَ بَيْتِهِ ثُمَّ دَفَعَ إِلَيْهِ الْكِتَابَ وَالسِّلاحَ وَقَالَ لابْنِهِ الْحَسَنِ (عَلَيْهِ السَّلام) يَا بُنَيَّ أَمَرَنِي رَسُولُ اللهِ (صَلَّى اللهُ عَلَيْهِ وَآلِه) أَنْ أُوصِيَ إِلَيْكَ وَأَنْ أَدْفَعَ إِلَيْكَ كُتُبِي وَسِلاحِي كَمَا أَوْصَى إِلَيَّ رَسُولُ اللهِ (صَلَّى اللهُ عَلَيْهِ وَآلِه) وَدَفَعَ إِلَيَّ كُتُبَهُ وَسِلاحَهُ وَأَمَرَنِي أَنْ آمُرَكَ إِذَا حَضَرَكَ الْمَوْتُ أَنْ تَدْفَعَهَا إِلَى أَخِيكَ الْحُسَيْنِ (عَلَيْهِ السَّلام) ثُمَّ أَقْبَلَ عَلَى ابْنِهِ الْحُسَيْنِ (عَلَيْهِ السَّلام) فَقَالَ وَأَمَرَكَ رَسُولُ اللهِ (صَلَّى اللهُ عَلَيْهِ وَآلِه) أَنْ تَدْفَعَهَا إِلَى ابْنِكَ هَذَا ثُمَّ أَخَذَ بِيَدِ عَلِيِّ بْن الحسين (عَلَيْهِمَا السَّلام) ثُمَّ قَالَ لِعَلِيِّ بْنِ الْحُسَيْنِ وَأَمَرَكَ رَسُولُ اللهِ (صَلَّى اللهُ عَلَيْهِ وَآلِه) أَنْ تَدْفَعَهَا إِلَى ابْنِكَ مُحَمَّدِ بْنِ عَلِيٍّ وَأَقْرِئْهُ مِنْ رَسُولِ اللهِ (صَلَّى اللهُ عَلَيْهِ وَآلِه) وَمِنِّي السَّلامَ

Ali b. Ibrahim has narrated from his father from Hammad b. 'Isa from Ibrahim b. 'Umar al-Yamani and 'Umar b. 'Udhayna from Sulaym b. Qays who has said the following. "I witnessed Amir al-Mu'minin Ali's (عليه السلام) will made before me in which he appointed his, al-Hassan (عليه السلام) as the executor. He called al-Husayn (عليه السلام), Muḥammad and all his other sons, all the leaders among his followers and his whole family to bear testimony to his will. He then delivered the Book and the Armament to his son al-Hassan (عليه السلام) and said, "My son, the Messenger of Allāh commanded me to appoint you as the executor of my will. (He commanded me) to deliver to you my books and my Armament just as the Messenger of Allāh did. He

---

[54] *Al-Kāfi, v1, ch115, h5*

made his will in which he appointed me as the executor, delivered to me his books and his Armament and commanded me to command you to deliver them to al-Husayn (عليه السلام) when you will be about to leave this world. Then he turned to his son, al-Husayn (عليه السلام) and said, "The Messenger of Allāh has commanded you to deliver them to your son, this one. Then he held with his hand 'Alī b. al-Husayn (عليه السلام) and said to him, "The Messenger of Allāh has commanded you to deliver them to your son, Muḥammad b. 'Alī and convey to him the Islamic greeting of the Messenger of Allāh and my Islamic greeting. (حسن على الظاهر)[55]

56.

عَلِيُّ بْنُ إِبْرَاهِيمَ عَنْ أَبِيهِ عَنِ ابْنِ أَبِي عُمَيْرٍ عَنْ جَمِيلِ بْنِ دَرَّاجٍ عَنْ يُونُسَ بْنِ ظَبْيَانَ وَ حَفْصِ بْنِ غِيَاثٍ عَنْ أَبِي عَبْدِ اللَّهِ (عليه السلام) قَالَا قُلْنَا جُعِلْنَا فِدَاكَ أَ يُكْرَهُ أَنْ يَكْتُبَ الرَّجُلُ فِي خَاتَمِهِ غَيْرَ اسْمِهِ وَ اسْمِ أَبِيهِ فَقَالَ فِي خَاتَمِي مَكْتُوبٌ اللَّهُ خَالِقُ كُلِّ شَيْءٍ وَ فِي خَاتَمِ أَبِي مُحَمَّدِ بْنِ عَلِيٍّ (عليه السلام) وَ كَانَ خَيْرَ مُحَمَّدِيٍّ رَأَيْتُهُ بِعَيْنِي الْعِزَّةُ لِلَّهِ وَ فِي خَاتَمِ عَلِيِّ بْنِ الْحُسَيْنِ (عليه السلام) الْحَمْدُ لِلَّهِ الْعَلِيِّ الْعَظِيمِ وَ فِي خَاتَمِ الْحَسَنِ وَ الْحُسَيْنِ (عليه السلام) حَسْبِيَ اللَّهُ وَ فِي خَاتَمِ أَمِيرِ الْمُؤْمِنِينَ (عليه السلام) اللَّهُ الْمَلِكُ

Ali b. Ibrahim has narrated from his father from b. abu 'Umayr from Jamil b. Darraj from Yunus b. Zabayan and Hafs b. Ghiyath who has said the following: "Once we asked abu 'Abd Allāh, (عليه السلام), saying, 'We pray to Allāh to keep our souls in service for your cause, is it undesirable to write on one's ring something other than one's name and the name of one's father?' He (the Imam) said, 'The writing on my ring says, 'Allāh is the Creator of all things'. On the ring of my father, Muḥammad b. Ali, (عليه السلام), who was the best Muhammadi, I saw with my own eyes, the writing said, 'All glory belongs to Allāh. ' On the ring of 'Alī b. al-Husayn, (عليه السلام), the writing said, 'All praise belongs to Allāh, the most High, the most Great.' On the ring of al-Hassan and al-Husayn, (عليه السلام), the writing said, 'Allāh is sufficient for me.' On the

---

[55] *Al-Kāfi, v1, ch66, h1*

ring of 'Amir al-Mu'minin, (عليه السلام), the writing said, 'Allāh is the owner'. (حسن أو موثق)[56]

57.

عِدَّةٌ مِنْ أَصْحَابِنَا عَنْ أَحْمَدَ بْنِ مُحَمَّدٍ الْبَرْقِيِّ عَنْ أَبِي هَاشِمٍ دَاوُدَ بْنِ الْقَاسِمِ الْجَعْفَرِيِّ عَنْ أَبِي جَعْفَرٍ الثَّانِي (عَلَيْهِ السَّلام) قَالَ أَقْبَلَ أَمِيرُ الْمُؤْمِنِينَ (عَلَيْهِ السَّلام) وَمَعَهُ الْحَسَنُ بن علي (عَلَيْهِما السَّلام) وَهُوَ مُتَّكِئٌ عَلَى يَدِ سَلْمَانَ فَدَخَلَ الْمَسْجِدَ الْحَرَامَ فَجَلَسَ إِذْ أَقْبَلَ رَجُلٌ حَسَنُ الْهَيْئَةِ وَاللِّبَاسِ فَسَلَّمَ عَلَى أَمِيرِ الْمُؤْمِنِينَ فَرَدَّ عَلَيْهِ السَّلامَ فَجَلَسَ ثُمَّ قَالَ يَا أَمِيرَ الْمُؤْمِنِينَ أَسْأَلُكَ عَنْ ثَلاثِ مَسَائِلَ إِنْ أَخْبَرْتَنِي بِهِنَّ عَلِمْتُ أَنَّ الْقَوْمَ رَكِبُوا مِنْ أَمْرِكَ مَا قُضِيَ عَلَيْهِمْ وَأَنْ لَيْسُوا بِمَأْمُونِينَ فِي دُنْيَاهُمْ وَآخِرَتِهِمْ وَإِنْ تَكُنِ الاخْرَى عَلِمْتُ أَنَّكَ وَهُمْ شَرَعٌ سَوَاءٌ فَقَالَ لَهُ أَمِيرُ الْمُؤْمِنِينَ (عَلَيْهِ السَّلام) سَلْنِي عَمَّا بَدَا لَكَ قَالَ أَخْبِرْنِي عَنِ الرَّجُلِ إِذَا نَامَ أَيْنَ تَذْهَبُ رُوحُهُ وَعَنِ الرَّجُلِ كَيْفَ يَذْكُرُ وَيَنْسَى وَعَنِ الرَّجُلِ كَيْفَ يُشْبِهُ وَلَدُهُ الاعْمَامَ وَالاخْوَالَ فَالْتَفَتَ أَمِيرُ الْمُؤْمِنِينَ (عَلَيْهِ السَّلام) إِلَى الْحَسَنِ فَقَالَ يَا أَبَا مُحَمَّدٍ أَجِبْهُ قَالَ فَأَجَابَهُ الْحَسَنُ (عَلَيْهِ السَّلام) فَقَالَ الرَّجُلُ أَشْهَدُ أَنْ لا إِلَهَ إِلا الله وَلَمْ أَزَلْ أَشْهَدُ بِهَا وَأَشْهَدُ أَنَّ مُحَمَّداً رَسُولُ الله وَلَمْ أَزَلْ أَشْهَدُ بِذَلِكَ وَأَشْهَدُ أَنَّكَ وَصِيُّ رَسُولِ الله (صَلَّى اللهُ عَلَيْهِ وَآلِه) وَالْقَائِمُ بِحُجَّتِهِ وَأَشَارَ إِلَى أَمِيرِ الْمُؤْمِنِينَ وَلَمْ أَزَلْ أَشْهَدُ بِهَا وَأَشْهَدُ أَنَّكَ وَصِيُّهُ وَالْقَائِمُ بِحُجَّتِهِ وَأَشَارَ إِلَى الْحَسَنِ (عَلَيْهِ السَّلام) وَأَشْهَدُ أَنَّ الْحُسَيْنَ بْنَ عَلِيٍّ وَصِيُّ أَخِيهِ وَالْقَائِمُ بِحُجَّتِهِ بَعْدَهُ وَأَشْهَدُ عَلَى عَلِيِّ بْنِ الْحُسَيْنِ أَنَّهُ الْقَائِمُ بِأَمْرِ الْحُسَيْنِ بَعْدَهُ وَأَشْهَدُ عَلَى مُحَمَّدِ بْنِ عَلِيٍّ أَنَّهُ الْقَائِمُ بِأَمْرِ عَلِيِّ بْنِ الْحُسَيْنِ وَأَشْهَدُ عَلَى جَعْفَرِ بْنِ مُحَمَّدٍ بِأَنَّهُ الْقَائِمُ بِأَمْرِ مُحَمَّدٍ وَأَشْهَدُ عَلَى مُوسَى أَنَّهُ الْقَائِمُ بِأَمْرِ جَعْفَرِ بْنِ مُحَمَّدٍ وَأَشْهَدُ عَلَى عَلِيِّ بْنِ مُوسَى أَنَّهُ الْقَائِمُ بِأَمْرِ مُوسَى بْنِ جَعْفَرٍ وَأَشْهَدُ عَلَى مُحَمَّدِ بْنِ عَلِيٍّ أَنَّهُ الْقَائِمُ بِأَمْرِ عَلِيِّ بْنِ مُوسَى وَأَشْهَدُ عَلَى عَلِيِّ بْنِ مُحَمَّدٍ بِأَنَّهُ الْقَائِمُ بِأَمْرِ مُحَمَّدِ بْنِ عَلِيٍّ وَأَشْهَدُ عَلَى الْحَسَنِ بْنِ عَلِيٍّ بِأَنَّهُ الْقَائِمُ بِأَمْرِ عَلِيِّ بْنِ مُحَمَّدٍ وَأَشْهَدُ عَلَى رَجُلٍ مِنْ وُلْدِ الْحَسَنِ لا يُكَنَّى وَلا يُسَمَّى حَتَّى يَظْهَرَ أَمْرُهُ فَيَمْلاهَا عَدْلاً كَمَا مُلِئَتْ جَوْراً وَالسَّلامُ عَلَيْكَ يَا أَمِيرَ الْمُؤْمِنِينَ وَرَحْمَةُ الله وَبَرَكَاتُهُ ثُمَّ قَامَ فَمَضَى فَقَالَ أَمِيرُ الْمُؤْمِنِينَ يَا أَبَا مُحَمَّدٍ اتْبَعْهُ فَانْظُرْ أَيْنَ يَقْصِدُ فَخَرَجَ الْحَسَنُ بن علي (عَلَيْهِما السَّلام) فَقَالَ مَا كَانَ إِلا أَنْ وَضَعَ رِجْلَهُ خَارِجاً مِنَ الْمَسْجِدِ فَمَا دَرَيْتُ أَيْنَ أَخَذَ مِنْ أَرْضِ الله فَرَجَعْتُ إِلَى أَمِيرِ الْمُؤْمِنِينَ (عَلَيْهِ السَّلام) فَأَعْلَمْتُهُ فَقَالَ يَا أَبَا مُحَمَّدٍ أَ تَعْرِفُهُ قُلْتُ الله وَرَسُولُهُ وَأَمِيرُ الْمُؤْمِنِينَ أَعْلَمُ قَالَ هُوَ الْخَضِرُ (عَلَيْهِ السَّلام)

A number of our people has narrated Ahmad b. Muḥammad al-Barqi from abu Hashim Dawud b. al-Qasim al-Ja'fari from abu Ja'far al-Thani who has said the

[56] *Al-Kāfi, v6, ch26, h2*

following. "Once Amir al-Mu'minin 'Alī (عليه السلام) came with al-Hassan and al-Husayn and he was holding the hand of Salman for support. He entered the sacred Mosque in Makka and sat down. Then a good looking and well dressed man came. He offered the greeting of peace to Amir al-Mu'minin 'Alī (عليه السلام) who answered his greetings likewise and he sat down. He then said, "I will ask you three questions. If you would answer them I will acknowledge that the people who have acted against you in the matters of leadership after the Holy Prophet (s.a) they have acted against their own selves. Their actions have taken away peace from them in this world as well in the next life. If it would be otherwise, (you can answer) then you and those people will be the same." Amir al-Mu'minin 'Alī (عليه السلام) said, "Ask whatever you would like." He said, "Tell about the man who sleeps. Where does his spirit go?" Tell about the man, how he remembers and forgets? Tell me about the man how do his children become similar to the aunts and uncles.?" Amir al-Mu'minin 'Alī (عليه السلام) turned to al-Hassan and said, "O abu Muhammad, answer him." The narrator has said that al-Hassan answered his questions. The man then said, "I testify that there is no lord besides Allāh and I continue to testify to this fact. I testify that Muḥammad is the Messenger of Allāh and I continue to testify to this fact I testify that you are the executor of the will of the Messenger of Allāh and that you are the in charge of this task ((Leadership with Divine Authority) with His authorization." He pointed out to Amir al-Mu'minin (عليه السلام) with his hand. He then said, "I continue to testify to this fact." "I testify that you are the executor of his (Amir al-Mu'minin's (عليه السلام) will and the in charge of this task ((Leadership with Divine Authority) by His authorization after him (Amir al-Mu'minin (عليه السلام) " He pointed out with his hand to al-Hassan (عليه السلام). Then He then said, "I continue to testify to this fact." "I testify that al-Husayn b. 'Alī (عليه السلام) will be the executor of the will of his brother and the in charge of this task ((Leadership with Divine Authority) with His authorization after him. "I testify in support of 'Alī b. al-Husayn (عليه السلام) that he will be the in charge of the task of al-Husayn after him. "I testify that Muḥammad b. 'Alī will be the in charge of the task of 'Alī b. al-Husayn (عليه السلام) after him. "I testify that Ja'far b. Muḥammad (عليه السلام) will be the in charge of the task of Muḥammad b. 'Alī (عليه السلام). "I testify that Mūsā will be the in charge of the task of Ja'far b. Muḥammad after him. "I testify that 'Alī b. Mūsā will be the in charge of the task of Mūsā b. Ja'far (عليه السلام). "I testify that Muḥammad b. 'Alī (عليه السلام) will be the in charge of the task of 'Alī b. Mūsā (عليه السلام) after him. "I testify that 'Alī b. Muḥammad will be the in charge of the task of Muḥammad b. 'Alī (عليه السلام) after him. "I testify that al-Hassan b. 'Alī (عليه السلام) will be the in charge of the task of 'Alī b. Muḥammad (عليه السلام) after him. "I testify in support of a man from the children of al-Hassan who will not be mentioned by his Kunya (father or son of so and so) or his name until he will rise with Divine authority to fill the earth with justice after being filled with injustice. "I offer you my greeting of peace O Amir al-Mu'minin (عليه السلام) and praay to Allāh to grant you blessings and holiness." He then stood up and left. Amir al-Mu'minin (عليه السلام) said, "O abu Muḥammad follow him and see where went." Al-Hassan b. 'Alī (عليه السلام) went out to find out (and came back) and said, "As soon as he stepped out of the Mosque I could not figure out in which direction of the earth of Allāh ddid he disappear. I returned to Amir al-Mu'minin (عليه السلام) and informed him." He said, "O abu Muhammad, do you know him?" I said, Allāh, the Messenger of Allāh and Amir al-Mu'minin (عليه السلام) know best." He said, "He was al-Khidr (عليه السلام)" (صحيح)[57]

58.

روى ذلك جماعة، منهم أحمد بن صالح التميمي، عن عبد الله بن عيسى، عن جعفر بن محمد عليهما السلام وكان الحسن أشبه الناس برسول الله صلى الله عليهما خلقا وسؤددا وهديا.

[It is reported by a group (of authorities), including Aḥmad b. Ṣāliḥ al-Tamīmī, on the authority of 'Abd Allāh b 'Īsa on the authority of Ja'far al-Ṣādiq b. Muḥammed, peace be on him:] Al-Ḥasan, (عليه السلام), was the most similar person to Apostle of Allāh, may Allāh bless Him and His Family, in form, manner and nobility (مجهول)[58]

---

[57] *Al-Kāfī, v1, ch126, h1*

[58] *Al-Irshad(Mufid), v2, pg. 5*

59.

أَحْمَدُ بْنُ مُحَمَّدٍ عَنْ مُحَمَّدِ بْنِ الْحَسَنِ عَنْ مُحَمَّدِ بْنِ عِيسَى بْنِ عُبَيْدٍ عَنْ عَلِيِّ بْنِ أَسْبَاطٍ عَنْ سَيْفِ بْنِ عَمِيرَةَ عَنْ مُحَمَّدِ بْنِ حُمْرَانَ قَالَ قَالَ أَبُو عَبْدِ اللهِ (عَلَيْهِ السَّلام) لَمَّا كَانَ مِنْ أَمْرِ الْحُسَيْنِ (عَلَيْهِ السَّلام) مَا كَانَ ضَجَّتِ الْمَلائِكَةُ إِلَى اللهِ بِالْبُكَاءِ وَقَالَتْ يُفْعَلُ هَذَا بِالْحُسَيْنِ صَفِيِّكَ وَابْنِ نَبِيِّكَ قَالَ فَأَقَامَ اللهُ لَهُمْ ظِلَّ الْقَائِمِ (عَلَيْهِ السَّلام) وَقَالَ بِهَذَا أَنْتَقِمُ لِهَذَا

Ahmad b. Muḥammad has narrated from Muḥammad b. al-Hassan from Muḥammad b. 'Isa b. 'Ubayd from 'Alī b. Asbat from Sayf b. 'Amira from Muḥammad b. humran who has said the following. "Abu 'AbdAllāh (عليه السلام) has said, 'When all that happened to al-Husayn had happened, the angels wept and cried before Allāh and said, "How such thing would happen to al-Husayn Your chosen one and the grand son of Your Prophet?" The Imam (عليه السلام) has said that Allāh then showed to them the shadow of Al-Qa'im (the one who will rise with Divine Authority) and said, "Through him I will take My revenge." (موثق كالصحيح)[59]

60.

حَدَّثَنِي أَبِي (رحمه الله) تَعَالَى قَالَ حَدَّثَنِي سَعْدُ بْنُ عَبْدِ اللَّهِ بْنِ أَبِي خَلَفٍ عَنْ أَحْمَدَ بْنِ مُحَمَّدِ بْنِ عِيسَى عَنِ الْحُسَيْنِ بْنِ سَعِيدٍ عَنِ النَّضْرِ بْنِ سُوَيْدٍ عَنْ يَحْيَى الْحَلَبِيِّ عَنْ هَارُونَ بْنِ خَارِجَةَ عَنْ أَبِي بَصِيرٍ عَنْ أَبِي عَبْدِ اللَّهِ (ع) قَالَ إِنَّ جَبْرَئِيلَ (ع) أَتَى رَسُولَ اللَّهِ (ص) وَ الْحُسَيْنُ (ع) يَلْعَبُ بَيْنَ يَدَيْهِ فَأَخْبَرَهُ أَنَّ أُمَّتَهُ سَتَقْتُلُهُ قَالَ فَجَزِعَ رَسُولُ اللَّهِ (ص) فَقَالَ أَ لَا أُرِيكَ التُّرْبَةَ الَّتِي يُقْتَلُ فِيهَا قَالَ فَخَسَفَ مَا بَيْنَ مَجْلِسِ رَسُولِ اللَّهِ (ص) إِلَى الْمَكَانِ الَّذِي قُتِلَ فِيهِ الْحُسَيْنُ (ع) حَتَّى الْتَقَتَا الْقِطْعَتَانِ فَأَخَذَ مِنْهَا وَ دُحِيَتْ فِي أَسْرَعَ مِنْ طَرْفَةِ عَيْنٍ فَخَرَجَ وَ هُوَ يَقُولُ طُوبَى لَكِ مِنْ تُرْبَةٍ وَ طُوبَى لِمَنْ يُقْتَلُ حَوْلَكِ قَالَ وَ كَذَلِكَ صَنَعَ صَاحِبُ سُلَيْمَانَ تَكَلَّمَ بِاسْمِ اللهِ الْأَعْظَمِ فَخَسَفَ مَا بَيْنَ سَرِيرِ سُلَيْمَانَ وَ بَيْنَ الْعَرْشِ مِنْ سُهُولَةِ الْأَرْضِ وَ حُزُونَتِهَا- حَتَّى الْتَقَتِ الْقِطْعَتَانِ فاجْتَرَّ الْعَرْشَ قَالَ سُلَيْمَانُ يُخَيَّلُ إِلَيَّ أَنَّهُ خَرَجَ مِنْ تَحْتِ سَرِيرِي- قَالَ وَ دُحِيَتْ فِي أَسْرَعَ مِنْ طَرْفَةِ الْعَيْنِ

---

[59] *Al-Kāfi, v1, ch116, h6*

My father narrated to me from Sa'd b. 'Abdillāh b. Abī Khalaf, from Aĥmad b. Muĥammad b. 'Isā, from Ĥusain b. Sa'īd, from Nad'r b. Suwayd, from Yaĥyā Al-Ĥalabi, from Hārūn b. Khārijah, from Abī Bašīr, who said: Abū 'Abdillāh (Imam Šādiq (عليه السلام)) said: (One day) Jabra`īl came to the Messenger of Allāh (صلى الله عليه وآله وسلم) while Ĥusain (عليه السلام) was playing in front of him. Jabra`īl informed him that his nation would kill Ĥusain (عليه السلام), so the Messenger of Allāh (صلى الله عليه وآله وسلم) became restless. Jabra`īl said, "Should I not show you the land on which he will be killed?" Then the land (between Karbalā and Madīnah) sunk within the ground and the place where the Messenger of Allāh (صلى الله عليه وآله وسلم) was sitting (in Madīnah) and the land on which Ĥusain (عليه السلام) was killed became attached to one another. Then Jabra`īl took some of the dust (of Karbalā). Thereafter, the earth returned to the way it (originally) was in less than a blink of an eye. The Prophet (صلى الله عليه وآله وسلم) left while saying, "Bliss for you, O dust! And bliss for those who will be killed 0n you!" Imam (عليه السلام) continued: The companion of Sulaymān (عليه السلام) (Āšaf b. Barkhiyā) also did the same thing. He mentioned the Great Name of Allāh and the earth between Sulaymān's bed and the throne (of Bilqīs) sank within the ground. The earth and all of its flexible and inflexible parts sank within the ground, and Āšif lifted the throne (of Bilqīs) before the two pieces of land were attached. So Sulaymān (عليه السلام) said, "It looks like it (the throne of Bilqīs) came out from under my bed." Imam (عليه السلام) added: Thereafter, the earth returned to the way it (originally) was in less than a blink of an eye. (صحيح)[60]

61.

حَدَّثَنِي أَبِي (رحمه الله) تَعَالَى عَنْ سَعْدٍ عَنْ عَلِيِّ بْنِ إِسْمَاعِيلَ بْنِ عِيسَى وَ مُحَمَّدِ بْنِ الْحُسَيْنِ بْنِ أَبِي الْخَطَّابِ وَ إِبْرَاهِيمَ بْنِ هَاشِمٍ عَنْ عُثْمَانَ بْنِ عِيسَى عَنْ سَمَاعَةَ بْنِ مِهْرَانَ عَنْ أَبِي عَبْدِ اللَّهِ (ع) مِثْلَهُ وَ زَادَ فِيهِ فَلَمْ تَزَلْ عِنْدَ أُمِّ سَلَمَةَ حَتَّى مَاتَتْ رَحِمَهَا اللَّهُ

[60] *Kāmil az-Ziyārāt, ch17, h1*

My father narrated to me from Sa'd (b. 'Abdillāh), from 'Ali b. Ismā'īl b. 'Isā, Muĥammad b. Ĥusain b. Abil Khaťťāb, and Ibrāhīm b. Hāshim, from 'Uthmān b. 'Isā, from Samā'ah b. Mihrān, who said: Abū 'Abdillāh (Imam Šādiq (عليه السلام)) said: Jabra`īl announced the news of the killing of Ĥusain (عليه السلام) to the Messenger of Allāh (صلى الله عليه وآله وسلم) in the house of Um Salamah. While Jabra`īl was with the Messenger of Allāh (صلى الله عليه وآله وسلم), Ĥusain (عليه السلام) entered. Jabra`īl said to the Prophet (صلى الله عليه وآله وسلم), "Verily your nation will kill him." The Messenger of Allāh (صلى الله عليه وآله وسلم) said, "Show me the dust on which his blood will be shed." Therefore, Jabra`īl took a handful of that dust and it was a red-coloured dust. Um Salamah kept that dust until she died. (موثق)[61]

62.

حَدَّثَنِي أَبِي (رحمه الله) عَنْ سَعْدِ بْنِ عَبْدِ اللَّهِ عَنْ أَحْمَدَ بْنِ مُحَمَّدِ بْنِ عِيسَى عَنِ الْحَسَنِ بْنِ عَلِيٍّ الْوَشَّاءِ عَنْ أَحْمَدَ بْنِ عَائِذٍ عَنْ أَبِي خَدِيجَةَ سَالِمِ بْنِ مُكْرَمٍ الْجَمَّالِ عَنْ أَبِي عَبْدِ اللَّهِ (ع) قَالَ لَمَّا وَلَدَتْ فَاطِمَةُ الْحُسَيْنَ (ع) جَاءَ جَبْرَئِيلُ إِلَى رَسُولِ اللَّهِص فَقَالَ لَهُ إِنَّ أُمَّتَكَ تَقْتُلُ الْحُسَيْنَ (ع) مِنْ بَعْدِكَ ثُمَّ قَالَ أَ لَا أُرِيكَ مِنْ تُرْبَتِهِ فَضَرَبَ بِجَنَاحِهِ فَأَخْرَجَ مِنْ تُرْبَةِ كَرْبَلَاءَ وَ أَرَاهَا إِيَّاهُ ثُمَّ قَالَ هَذِهِ التُّرْبَةُ الَّتِي يُقْتَلُ عَلَيْهَا

My father narrated to me from Sa'd b. 'Abdillāh, from Aĥmad b. Muĥammad b. 'Isā, from Ĥasan b. 'Ali Al-Washā`, from Aĥmad b. 'Ā`idh, from Abī Khadījah Sālim b. Mukram Al-Jammāl, who said: Abū 'Abdillāh (Imam Šādiq (عليه السلام)) said: When Fāťimah gave birth to Ĥusain (عليه السلام), Jabra`īl came to the Messenger of Allāh (صلى الله عليه وآله وسلم) and said, "Your nation will kill Ĥusain after you. Should I not show you some of his dust (the dust on which he will be killed)?" Then Jabra`īl hit the land of Karbalā with his wing, took some of its dust, showed it to the Prophet (صلى الله عليه وآله وسلم), and said, "This is the dust on which he will be killed." (صحيح)[62]

---

[61] *Kāmil az-Ziyārāt, ch17, h3*

[62] *Kāmil az-Ziyārāt, ch17, h6*

63.

حَدَّثَنِي أَبِي (رحمه الله) وَ جَمَاعَةُ مَشَايِخِي عَنْ سَعْدِ بْنِ عَبْدِ اللَّهِ عَنْ أَحْمَدَ بْنِ مُحَمَّدِ بْنِ عِيسَى عَنِ الْحَسَنِ [الْحُسَيْنِ] بْنِ سَعِيدٍ عَنْ حَمَّادِ بْنِ عِيسَى عَنْ رِبْعِيِّ بْنِ عَبْدِ اللَّهِ عَنِ الْفُضَيْلِ بْنِ يَسَارٍ عَنْ أَبِي عَبْدِ اللَّهِ (ع) قَالَ مَا لَكُمْ لَا تَأْتُونَهُ يَعْنِي قَبْرَ الْحُسَيْنِ (ع) فَإِنَّ أَرْبَعَةَ آلَافِ مَلَكٍ يَبْكُونَ [يَبْكُونَهُ] عِنْدَ قَبْرِهِ إِلَى يَوْمِ الْقِيَامَةِ

My father and all of my scholars narrated to me from Sa'd b. 'Abdillāh, from Aĥmad b. Muĥammad b. 'Isā, from Ĥusain b. Sa'īd, from Ĥammād b. 'Isā, from Rib'i b. 'Abdillāh, from Fuďayl b. Yasār, who said: Abū 'Abdillāh (Imam Šādiq (عليه السلام)) said: What is wrong with you (people)?! Why do you not go to him? – This refers to the Ziyārah of the grave of Ĥusain (عليه السلام). Verily four thousand angels cry by his grave (and will continue to do so) until the Day of Judgment. (صحيح)[63]

64.

حَدَّثَنِي مُحَمَّدُ بْنُ الْحَسَنِ عَنْ مُحَمَّدِ بْنِ الْحَسَنِ الصَّفَّارِ عَنْ مُحَمَّدِ بْنِ الْحُسَيْنِ بْنِ أَبِي الْخَطَّابِ عَنْ صَفْوَانَ بْنِ يَحْيَى عَنْ حَرِيزٍ عَنِ الْفُضَيْلِ عَنْ أَحَدِهِمَا قَالَ إِنَّ عَلَى قَبْرِ الْحُسَيْنِ (ع) أَرْبَعَةَ آلَافِ مَلَكٍ- شُعْثٌ غُبْرٌ [شُعْثاً غُبْراً يَبْكُونَهُ إِلَى يَوْمِ الْقِيَامَةِ قَالَ مُحَمَّدُ بْنُ مُسْلِمٍ يَحْرُسُونَهُ

Muĥammad b. Ĥasan narrated to me from Muĥammad b. Ĥasan Al-Šaffār, from Muĥammad b. Ĥusain b. Abil Khaťťāb, from Šafwān b. Yaĥyā, from Ĥarīz, from Fuďayl (b. Yasār) who said: Imam Bāqir or Imam Šādiq (عليه السلام) said: There are four thousand disheveled angels who are covered with dust on the grave of Ĥusain (عليه السلام) and they cry over him (and will continue to do so) until the Day of Judgment. (صحيح)[64]

[63] *Kāmil az-Ziyārāt, ch27, h1*

[64] *Kāmil az-Ziyārāt, ch27, h8*

65.

حَدَّثَنَا مُحَمَّدُ بْنُ مُوسَى بْنِ الْمُتَوَكِّلِ قَالَ حَدَّثَنَا عَبْدُ اللَّهِ بْنُ جَعْفَرٍ الْحِمْيَرِيُّ عَنْ أَحْمَدَ وَ عَبْدِ اللَّهِ ابْنَيْ مُحَمَّدِ بْنِ عِيسَى عَنِ الْحَسَنِ بْنِ مَحْبُوبٍ عَنِ الْعَلَاءِ بْنِ رَزِينٍ عَنْ مُحَمَّدِ بْنِ مُسْلِمٍ عَنْ أَبِي جَعْفَرٍ ع قَالَ كَانَ عَلِيُّ بْنُ الْحُسَيْنِ ع يَقُولُ أَيُّمَا مُؤْمِنٍ دَمَعَتْ عَيْنَاهُ لِقَتْلِ الْحُسَيْنِ ع حَتَّى تَسِيلَ عَلَى خَدِّهِ بَوَّأَهُ اللَّهُ تَعَالَى بِهَا فِي الْجَنَّةِ غُرَفاً يَسْكُنُهَا أَحْقَاباً وَ أَيُّمَا مُؤْمِنٍ دَمَعَتْ عَيْنَاهُ حَتَّى تَسِيلَ عَلَى خَدَّيْهِ فِيمَا مَسَّنَا مِنَ الْأَذَى مِنْ عَدُوِّنَا فِي الدُّنْيَا بَوَّأَهُ اللَّهُ مَنْزِلَ صِدْقٍ وَ أَيُّمَا مُؤْمِنٍ مَسَّهُ أَذًى فِينَا فَدَمَعَتْ عَيْنَاهُ حَتَّى تَسِيلَ عَلَى خَدِّهِ مِنْ مَضَاضَةِ أَوْ أَذًى فِينَا صَرَفَ اللَّهُ مِنْ وَجْهِهِ الْأَذَى وَ آمَنَهُ يَوْمَ الْقِيَامَهِ مِنْ سَخَطِ النَّارِ

Imam Muḥammad Baqir (عليه السلام) narrates that Imam Zainul Abideen (عليه السلام) said, "One who cries for Imam Husain (عليه السلام) and his tears flow from the eyes and fall on his cheeks Almighty Allāh would give him a place on a high apartment where he would live in peace for years. One who cries on the troubles given to us by our enemies in this world and his tears fall on his cheeks, the Almighty Allāh would grant him a place in Maqam-e-Sidq. If a believer bears difficulties and becomes aggrieved for the calamities, which we have suffered, his eyes become wet, tears flow on cheeks, Allāh would remove sufferings from his face and keep him safe from difficulties and chastisement on the Day of Judgment." (صحيح)[65]

66.

حدثنا محمد بن محمد، قال: حدثنا أبو القاسم جعفر بن محمد بن قولويه (رحمه الله)، قال: حدثني أبي، قال: حدثني سعد بن عبد الله، عن أحمد بن محمد ابن عيسى، عن الحسن بن محبوب الزراد، عن أبي محمد الأنصاري، عن معاوية بن وهب، قال: كنت جالسا عند جعفر بن محمد (عليهما السلام) إذ جاء شيخ قد انحنى من الكبر، فقال: السلام عليك و رحمة الله و بركاته. فقال له أبو عبد الله: و عليك السلام و رحمة الله و بركاته، يا شيخ ادن مني، فدنا منه فقبل يده فبكى، فقال له أبو عبد الله (عليه السلام): و ما يبكيك

[65] *Thawāb al-A'māl wa 'iqāb al-A'māl, ch145, h1*

يا شيخ قال له: يا ابن رسول الله، أنا مقيم على رجاء منكم منذ نحو من مائة سنة، أقول هذه السنة و هذا الشهر و هذا اليوم، و لا أراه فيكم، فتلومني أن أبكي

قال: فبكى أبو عبد الله (عليه السلام) ثم قال: يا شيخ، إن أخرت منيتك كنت معنا، و إن عجلت كنت يوم القيامة مع ثقل رسول الله (صلى الله عليه و آله). فقال الشيخ: ما أبالي ما فاتني بعد هذا يا ابن رسول الله.

فقال له أبو عبد الله (عليه السلام): يا شيخ، إن رسول الله (صلى الله عليه و آله) قال: إني تارك فيكم الثقلين ما إن تمسكتم بهما لن تضلوا: كتاب الله المنزل، و عترتي أهل بيتي، تجيء و أنت معنا يوم القيامة.

قال: يا شيخ، ما أحسبك من أهل الكوفة. قال: لا. قال: فمن أين أنت قال: من سوادها جعلت فداك.

قال: أين أنت من قبر جدي المظلوم الحسين (عليه السلام) قال: إني لقريب منه.

قال: كيف إتيانك له قال: إني لآتيه و أكثر .

قال: يا شيخ، ذاك دم يطلب الله (تعالى) به، ما أصيب ولد فاطمة و لا يصابون بمثل الحسين (عليه السلام)، و لقد قتل (عليه السلام) في سبعة عشر من أهل بيته، نصحوا لله و صبروا في جنب الله، فجزاهم أحسن جزاء الصابرين،

إنه إذا كان يوم القيامة أقبل رسول الله (صلى الله عليه و آله) و معه الحسين (عليه السلام) و يده على رأسه يقطر دما فيقول: يا رب، سل أمتي فيم قتلوا ولدي.

و قال (عليه السلام): كل الجزع و البكاء مكروه سوى الجزع و البكاء على الحسين (عليه السلام.(

From Mu`aawiyah b. Wahab said: "I was sitting with Ja`far b. Muḥammad (عليه السلام) when a shaykh (an old man) who was bent from being old came. So he (the old man said) said: 'Assalaamu `alayka wa raHmatullaahi wa barakaatuh' So Aboo `Abd Allāh (عليه السلام) said to him: 'Wa `Alayka Assalaam wa raHmatullaahi wa barakaatuh, O Shaykh come to me'. So the old man came to him (عليه السلام) and kissed his (عليه السلام) hand and cried. So Aboo `Abd Allāh (عليه السلام) said to him: 'O Shaykh, why are you crying?' He (the old man) said to him: 'O son of the Messenger of Allāh, I have been wishing to be with you for about 100 years. I (kept) saying (to myself): 'This is the year, this is the month, this is the day, and I did not see you. And (now) you censure/stop me from crying?!' He (the narrator) said: Aboo `Abd Allāh (عليه السلام) started to cry and then said:'O Shaykh, You will be with us. And that you will hurry to be with the weight *(thaqal)* of the Messenger of Allāh (صلى الله عليه وآله وسلم) on the Day of Judgment. So the shaykh said: 'I will take heed and after today I wlll not (cry) O son of the Messenger of Allāh (صلى الله عليه وآله وسلم)', So Aboo `Abd Allāh (عليه

السلام)said: 'O Shaykh, The Messenger of Allāh (صلى الله عليه وآله وسلم)said: 'Verily, I am leaving with you two weight things (*thaqalayn*), and if you hold on to them you will NEVER go astray: (they are) The Book of Allāh revealed, and My `itratee, the Ahl Al-Bayt. I will come and you will be with us on the Day of Judgment.' He (عليه السلام)said: "O Shaykh, I do not think that you are of the people of Koofa? He (the shaykh) said: 'No'. He (عليه السلام)said: 'Then where are you from?' He (the shaykh) said: "May I be sacrificed for you, from Sawaaduhaa. He (عليه السلام)said: "Where are you (in regards) to my oppressed grandfather's grave, Al-Hussayn (عليه السلام)" He (the shaykh): "I am close to it (the grave)." He (عليه السلام)said: 'How (often) do you go to him (grave of Al-Hussayn)' He (the shaykh) said: "I go there frequently", He (عليه السلام)said: "O Shaykh, Allāh (سبحانه و تعالى)will seek the blood of him (Al-Hussayn), there is no calamity for the children of FaaTimah (عليها السلام)like the calamity of Al-Hussayn (عليه السلام). And 17 members of his Ahl Al-Bayt (i.e. family) were killed. They have patiently (strove) on the side of Allāh. And He (سبحانه و تعالى)has rewarded them the best of rewards for the patient ones. 'And when the day of judgment (arrives), the Messenger of Allāh (صلى الله عليه وآله وسلم) will come with Al-Hussayn (عليه السلام), and his (صلى الله عليه وآله وسلم) hand on his (عليه السلام) head dripping with blood. Then he (صلى الله عليه وآله وسلم)will say: 'O Lord! Ask my ummah (nation) why did they kill my son?!' And He (عليه السلام)said: "Every grief/sadness and crying is makrooh (disliked) except the grief/sadness and crying upon Al-Hussayn (حسن))[66]

67.

عَلِيُّ بْنُ إِبْرَاهِيمَ عَنْ أَبِيهِ عَنْ حَمَّادِ بْنِ عِيسَى عَنْ إِبْرَاهِيمَ بْنِ عُمَرَ الْيَمَانِيِّ وَعُمَرَ بْنِ أُذَيْنَةَ عَنْ أَبَانٍ عَنْ سُلَيْمِ بْنِ قَيْسٍ قَالَ شَهِدْتُ وَصِيَّةَ أَمِيرِ الْمُؤْمِنِينَ (عَلَيْهِ السَّلام) حِينَ أَوْصَى إِلَى ابْنِهِ الْحَسَنِ (عَلَيْهِ السَّلام) وَأَشْهَدَ عَلَى وَصِيَّتِهِ الْحُسَيْنَ (عَلَيْهِ السَّلام) وَمُحَمَّداً وَجَمِيعَ وُلْدِهِ وَرُؤَسَاءَ شِيعَتِهِ وَأَهْلَ بَيْتِهِ ثُمَّ دَفَعَ إِلَيْهِ الْكِتَابَ وَالسِّلاحَ وَقَالَ لابْنِهِ الْحَسَنِ (عَلَيْهِ السَّلام) يَا بُنَيَّ أَمَرَنِي رَسُولُ الله (صَلَّى اللهُ عَلَيْهِ وَآلِه) أَنْ أُوصِيَ إِلَيْكَ وَأَنْ أَدْفَعَ إِلَيْكَ كُتُبِي وَسِلاحِي كَمَا أَوْصَى إِلَيَّ رَسُولُ الله (صَلَّى اللهُ عَلَيْهِ وَآلِه) وَدَفَعَ إِلَيَّ كُتُبَهُ وَسِلاحَهُ

[66] *Al-Amālī(Tusi), pg. 161*

وَأَمَرَنِي أَنْ آمُرَكَ إِذَا حَضَرَكَ الْمَوْتُ أَنْ تَدْفَعَهَا إِلَى أَخِيكَ الْحُسَيْنِ (عَلَيْهِ السَّلام) ثُمَّ أَقْبَلَ عَلَى ابْنِهِ الْحُسَيْنِ (عَلَيْهِ السَّلام) فَقَالَ وَأَمَرَكَ رَسُولُ الله (صَلَّى اللهُ عَلَيْهِ وَآلِه) أَنْ تَدْفَعَهَا إِلَى ابْنِكَ هَذَا ثُمَّ أَخَذَ بِيَدِ عَلِيِّ بن الحسين (عَلَيْهِمَا السَّلام) ثُمَّ قَالَ لِعَلِيِّ بْنِ الْحُسَيْنِ وَأَمَرَكَ رَسُولُ الله (صَلَّى اللهُ عَلَيْهِ وَآلِه) أَنْ تَدْفَعَهَا إِلَى ابْنِكَ مُحَمَّدِ بْنِ عَلِيٍّ وَأَقْرِئْهُ مِنْ رَسُولِ الله (صَلَّى اللهُ عَلَيْهِ وَآلِه) وَمِنِّي السَّلامَ

Ali b. Ibrahim has narrated from his father from Hammad b. 'Isa from Ibrahim b. 'Umar al-Yamani and 'Umar b. 'Udhayna from Sulaym b. Qays who has said the following. "I witnessed Amir al-Mu'minin Ali's (عليه السلام) will made before me in which he appointed his, al-Hassan (عليه السلام) as the executor. He called al-Husayn (عليه السلام), Muḥammad and all his other sons, all the leaders among his followers and his whole family to bear testimony to his will. He then delivered the Book and the Armament to his son al-Hassan (عليه السلام) and said, "My son, the Messenger of Allāh commanded me to appoint you as the executor of my will. (He commanded me) to deliver to you my books and my Armament just as the Messenger of Allāh did. He made his will in which he appointed me as the executor, delivered to me his books and his Armament and commanded me to command you to deliver them to al-Husayn (عليه السلام) when you will be about to leave this world. Then he turned to his son, al-Husayn (عليه السلام) and said, "The Messenger of Allāh has commanded you to deliver them to your son, this one. Then he held with his hand 'Alī b. al-Husayn (عليه السلام) and said to him, "The Messenger of Allāh has commanded you to deliver them to your son, Muḥammad b. 'Alī and convey to him the Islamic greeting of the Messenger of Allāh and my Islamic greeting. (حسن على الظاهر)[67]

68.

حكيم بن داود بن حكيم، عن سلمة، عن علي بن الحسين، عن معمر بن خلاد، عن أبي الحسن الرضا عليه السلام قال: بينا الحسين عليه السلام يسير في جوف الليل وهو متوجه إلى العراق وإذا رجل يرتجز ويقول: وحدثني أبي، عن سعد عن ابن عيسى، عن معمر بن خلاد، عن الرضا عليه السلام مثل ألفاظ سلمة قال:

[67] *Al-Kāfi, v1, ch66, h1*

وهو يقول :يا ناقتي لا تذعري من زجري وشمري قبل طلوع الفجر بخير ركبان وخير سفر حتى تحلى بكريم
البحر بماجد الجد رحيب الصدر أثابه الله لخير أمر ثمت أبقاه بقاء الدهر فقال الحسين بن علي عليه
السلام: سأمضي وما بالموت عار على الفتى إذا ما نوى حقا وجاهد مسلما وواسى الرجال الصالحين
بنفسه وفارق مثبورا وخالف مجرما فان عشت لم أندم وإن مت لم ألم كفى بك موتا أن تذل وتغرما
وحدثني أبي، عن سعد عن ابن عيسى، عن معمر بن خلاد، عن الرضا عليه السلام مثل

Ĥukaym b. Dāwūd b. Ĥukaym narrated to me from Salamah, from 'Ali b. Ĥusain, from Mu'ammar b. Khallād, who said: Abul Ĥasan (Imam Rid'ā (عليه السلام)) said: As Ĥusain (عليه السلام) was traveling toward Iraq, he heard a man recite this poem in the middle of the night: O my camel! Do not be frightened by my scolding and break out before the rising of dawn. (Carry me to) the best of riders on the best of journeys until you arrive at the most honourable place. (Carry me to Ĥusain (عليه السلام)) whose grandfather is the most glorious grandfather and Ĥusain (عليه السلام) is the most magnanimous one. Verily Allāh has chosen him for the best of affairs. May he remain until the end of time! So Ĥusain (عليه السلام) replied by reciting the following poem: I shall go toward death and there is no shame for a man in death as long as his intentions are based on the truth and he fights (for Allāh) as a Muslim. (There is no shame in death for men) as long as they support the righteous ones, fight the criminals, and abandon the sinners. (I shall fight) and if I live, I shall not have any regrets. And if I am killed, I will not be blamed. Nothing is more humiliating than living under the humiliation of the oppressors. The above Ĥadīth has also been narrated to me through the following chain: My father, from Sa'd b. 'Abdillāh, from Aĥmad b. Muĥammad b. 'Isā, from Mu'ammar b. Khallād, from Imam Rid'ā (عليه السلام). (صحيح)[68]

69.

حَدَّثَنِي أَبِي (رحمه الله) عَنْ سَعْدِ بْنِ عَبْدِ اللَّهِ عَنْ مُحَمَّدِ بْنِ حَمَّادٍ عَنْ أَخِيهِ أَحْمَدَ بْنِ حَمَّادٍ عَنْ مُحَمَّدِ بْنِ
عَبْدِ اللَّهِ عَنْ أَبِيهِ قَالَ سَمِعْتُ أَبَا عَبْدِ اللَّهِ (ع) يَقُولُ أَتَى جَبْرَئِيلُ (ع) إِلَى رَسُولِ اللَّهِ (ص) فَقَالَ لَهُ السَّلَامُ

[68] *Kāmil az-Ziyārāt, ch29, h7*

عَلَيْكَ يَا مُحَمَّدُ أَ لَا أُبَشِّرُكَ بِغُلَامٍ تَقْتُلُهُ أُمَّتُكَ مِنْ بَعْدِكَ فَقَالَ لَا حَاجَةَ لِي فِيهِ قَالَ فَانْتَهَضَ إِلَى السَّمَاءِ ثُمَّ عَادَ إِلَيْهِ الثَّانِيَةَ فَقَالَ لَهُ مِثْلَ ذَلِكَ فَقَالَ لَا حَاجَةَ لِي فِيهِ فَانْعَرَجَ إِلَى السَّمَاءِ ثُمَّ انْقَضَّ إِلَيْهِ الثَّالِثَةَ فَقَالَ مِثْلَ ذَلِكَ فَقَالَ لَا حَاجَةَ لِي فِيهِ فَقَالَ إِنَّ رَبَّكَ جَاعِلٌ الْوَصِيَّةَ فِي عَقِبِهِ فَقَالَ نَعَمْ أَوْ قَالَ ذَلِكَ ثُمَّ قَامَ رَسُولُ اللَّهِ (ص) فَدَخَلَ عَلَى فَاطِمَةَ (ع) فَقَالَ لَهَا إِنَّ جَبْرَئِيلَ (ع) أَتَانِي فَبَشَّرَنِي بِغُلَامٍ تَقْتُلُهُ أُمَّتِي مِنْ بَعْدِي فَقَالَتْ لَا حَاجَةَ لِي فِيهِ فَقَالَ لَهَا إِنَّ رَبِّي جَاعِلٌ الْوَصِيَّةَ فِي عَقِبِهِ فَقَالَتْ نَعَمْ إِذَنْ قَالَ فَأَنْزَلَ اللَّهُ تَعَالَى عِنْدَ ذَلِكَ هَذِهِ الْآيَةَ- حَمَلَتْهُ أُمُّهُ كُرْهاً وَ وَضَعَتْهُ كُرْهاً لِمَوْضِعِ إِعْلَامِ جَبْرَئِيلَ إِيَّاهَا بِقَتْلِهِ فَحَمَلَتْهُ كُرْهاً بِأَنَّهُ مَقْتُولٌ وَ وَضَعَتْهُ كُرْهاً لِأَنَّهُ مَقْتُولٌ

My father narrated to me from Sa'd b. 'Abdillāh, from Muĥammad b. Ĥammād, from his brother Aĥmad b. Ĥammād, from Muĥammad b. 'Abdillāh, from his father, who said: I heard Abā 'Abdillāh (Imam Sādiq (عليه السلام)) say: Jabra`īl came to the Messenger of Allāh (صلى الله عليه وآله وسلم) and said, "Salām to you, O Muĥammad! Should I give you glad tidings of a son who will be killed by your nation after you?" The Messenger of Allāh (صلى الله عليه وآله وسلم) replied, "I do not need such a son." Jabra`īl ascended to the heavens and then came back to him again, repeating what he had said. The Messenger of Allāh (صلى الله عليه وآله وسلم) replied, "I do not need such a son." Jabra`īl ascended to the heavens (yet) again and then came back to him for the third time, repeating what he had said. The Messenger of Allāh (صلى الله عليه وآله وسلم) replied, "I do not need such a son." Jabra`īl said, "Verily your Lord has placed the succession in his progeny." The Messenger of Allāh (صلى الله عليه وآله وسلم) said, "Yes, (I accept)." Then the Prophet (صلى الله عليه وآله وسلم) went to Fāťimah and said, "Jabra`īl came to me and gave me glad tidings of a son who will be killed by my nation after me." Fāťimah replied, "I do not need such a son." The Messenger of Allāh (صلى الله عليه وآله وسلم) said to her, "Verily my Lord has placed the succession in his progeny." Fāťimah replied, "In this case, yes (I will accept)." Therefore, Allāh revealed this verse, "His mother bears him with aversion, and with aversion she gives birth to him" (46:15) because Jabra`īl informed her that he would be killed. So "his mother bears him with aversion" because he would be killed. "And with aversion she gives birth to him" because (she knew) he would be killed. (صحيح)[69]

---

[69] *Kāmil az-Ziyārāt, ch16, h3*

70.

حَدَّثَنِي أَبِي وَ جَمَاعَةُ مَشَايِخِي رَحِمَهُمُ اللَّهُ عَنْ سَعْدِ بْنِ عَبْدِ اللَّهِ عَنْ أَحْمَدَ بْنِ مُحَمَّدِ بْنِ عِيسَى عَنْ جَعْفَرِ بْنِ مُحَمَّدِ بْنِ عُبَيْدِ اللَّهِ عَنْ عَبْدِ اللَّهِ بْنِ مَيْمُونٍ الْقَدَّاحِ عَنْ أَبِي عَبْدِ اللَّهِ (ع) قَالَ مَرَّ أَمِيرُ الْمُؤْمِنِينَ (ع) بِكَرْبَلَاءَ فِي أُنَاسٍ مِنْ أَصْحَابِهِ فَلَمَّا مَرَّ بِهَا اغْرَوْرَقَتْ عَيْنَاهُ بِالْبُكَاءِ ثُمَّ قَالَ هَذَا مُنَاخُ رِكَابِهِمْ وَ هَذَا مُلْقَى رِحَالِهِمْ- وَ هُنَا تُهَرَقُ دِمَاؤُهُمْ طُوبَى لَكِ مِنْ تُرْبَةٍ عَلَيْكِ تُهَرَقُ دِمَاءُ الْأَحِبَّةِ

My father and all of my scholars narrated to me from Sa'd b. 'Abdillāh, from Aĥmad b. Muĥammad b. 'Isā, from Ja'far b. Muĥammad b. 'Ubaydillāh, from 'Abdillāh b. Maymūn Al-Qaddāĥ, who said: Abū 'Abdillāh (Imam Šādiq (عليه السلام)) said: The Commander of the Believers (عليه السلام) and some of his companions passed by Karbalā. When he (عليه السلام) passed by it, his eyes became filled with tears and he said: This is where they will descend from their sumpters. This is where they will unpack. This is where their blood will be spilled. Bliss be for you, O land! The blood of the loved ones will be spilled on your grounds. (حسن)[70]

71.

عِدَّةٌ مِنْ أَصْحَابِنَا عَنْ أَحْمَدَ بْنِ مُحَمَّدٍ عَنِ الْحُسَيْنِ بْنِ سَعِيدٍ عَنِ النَّضْرِ بْنِ سُوَيْدٍ عَنِ الْقَاسِمِ بْنِ سُلَيْمَانَ عَنْ سَمَاعَةَ بْنِ مِهْرَانَ عَنْ أَبِي عَبْدِ الله (عَلَيْهِ السَّلام) فِي قَوْلِ الله عَزَّ وَجَلَّ يُؤْتِكُمْ كِفْلَيْنِ مِنْ رَحْمَتِهِ قَالَ الْحَسَنُ وَالْحُسَيْنُ وَيَجْعَلْ لَكُمْ نُوراً تَمْشُونَ بِهِ قَالَ إِمَامٌ تَأْتَمُّونَ بِهِ

A number of our people has narrated from Ahmad b. Muḥammad from al-Husayn b. Sa'id from al-Nadr b. Suwayd from al-Qasim b. Sulayman from Sama'a from abu 'AbdAllāh (عليه السلام) about the words of Allāh, the Most Majestic, the Most gracious. ". . God will grant you a double share of mercy, (al-Hassan and al-Husayn) a light by

[70] *Kāmil az-Ziyārāt, ch88, h10*

which you can walk. ." (57:28) The Imam (عليه السلام) said, "Light means the Imam that you would follow." (صحيح)[71]

72.

مُحَمَّدُ بْنُ يَحْيَى عَنْ أَحْمَدَ بْنِ مُحَمَّدٍ عَنِ ابْنِ مَحْبُوبٍ عَنِ ابْنِ رِئَابٍ عَنْ ضُرَيْسٍ الْكُنَاسِيِّ عَنْ ابي جعفر (عَلَيْهِ السَّلام) قَالَ قَالَ لَهُ حُمْرَانُ جُعِلْتُ فِدَاكَ أَ رَأَيْتَ مَا كَانَ مِنْ أَمْرِ عَلِيٍّ وَالْحَسَنِ وَالْحُسَيْنِ (عَلَيْهِ السَّلام) وَخُرُوجِهِمْ وَقِيَامِهِمْ بِدِينِ اللهِ عَزَّ وَجَلَّ وَمَا أُصِيبُوا مِنْ قَتْلِ الطَّوَاغِيتِ إِيَّاهُمْ وَالظَّفَرِ بِهِمْ حَتَّى قُتِلُوا وَغُلِبُوا فَقَالَ أَبُو جَعْفَرٍ (عَلَيْهِ السَّلام) يَا حُمْرَانُ إِنَّ اللهَ تَبَارَكَ وَتَعَالَى قَدْ كَانَ قَدَّرَ ذَلِكَ عَلَيْهِمْ وَقَضَاهُ وَأَمْضَاهُ وَحَتَمَهُ ثُمَّ أَجْرَاهُ فَبِتَقَدُّمِ عِلْمِ ذَلِكَ إِلَيْهِمْ مِنْ رَسُولِ اللهِ قَامَ عَلِيٌّ وَالْحَسَنُ وَالْحُسَيْنُ وَبِعِلْمٍ صَمَتَ مَنْ صَمَتَ مِنَّا

Muhammad b. Yahya has narrated from Ahmad b. Muḥammad from b. Mahbub from b. Ri'ab from Durays al-Kunasi from Humran who has said that once Humran asked abu Ja'far (عليه السلام) the following. "May Allāh take my soul in service for your cause, 'Why the cases of 'Alī al-Hassan and al-Husayn (عليه السلام) come about the way they did? Their rising and coming out for the religion of Allāh, the Most Holy, the Most High their suffering and being murdered at the hands of the rebellious devils and their defeat until they all were murdered and defeated.'" Abu Ja'far (عليه السلام) then said, "O Humran, Allāh, the Most Holy, the Most High had destined it for them. So it was decreed, approved and was made unavoidable. Then He executed it but it all happened with the prior knowledge of the same through the Messenger of Allāh. Ali, al-Hassan and al-Husayn (عليه السلام) all rose for the cause of Allāh with knowledge of the consequences remained silent whoever of us that remained silent." (صحيح)[72]

73.

---

[71] *Al-Kāfi, v1, ch108, h83*

[72] *Al-Kāfi, v1, ch61, h3*

مُحَمَّدُ بْنُ يَحْيَى عَنْ أَحْمَدَ بْنِ مُحَمَّدٍ عَنِ ابْنِ مَحْبُوبٍ عَنِ ابْنِ رِئَابٍ عَنْ ضُرَيْسٍ الْكُنَاسِيِّ قَالَ سَمِعْتُ أَبَا جَعْفَرٍ (عَلَيْهِ السَّلام) يَقُولُ وَعِنْدَهُ أُنَاسٌ مِنْ أَصْحَابِهِ عَجِبْتُ مِنْ قَوْمٍ يَتَوَلَّوْنَا وَيَجْعَلُونَا أَئِمَّةً وَيَصِفُونَ أَنَّ طَاعَتَنَا مُفْتَرَضَةٌ عَلَيْهِمْ كَطَاعَةِ رَسُولِ اللهِ (صَلَّى اللهُ عَلَيْهِ وَآلِه) ثُمَّ يَكْسِرُونَ حُجَّتَهُمْ وَيَخْصِمُونَ أَنْفُسَهُمْ بِضَعْفِ قُلُوبِهِمْ فَيَنْقُصُونَا حَقَّنَا وَيَعِيبُونَ ذَلِكَ عَلَى مَنْ أَعْطَاهُ اللهُ بُرْهَانَ حَقِّ مَعْرِفَتِنَا وَالتَّسْلِيمَ لامْرِنَا أَ تَرَوْنَ أَنَّ اللهَ تَبَارَكَ وَتَعَالَى افْتَرَضَ طَاعَةَ أَوْلِيَائِهِ عَلَى عِبَادِهِ ثُمَّ يُخْفِي عَنْهُمْ أَخْبَارَ السَّمَاوَاتِ وَالارْضِ وَيَقْطَعُ عَنْهُمْ مَوَادَّ الْعِلْمِ فِيمَا يَرِدُ عَلَيْهِمْ مِمَّا فِيهِ قِوَامُ دِينِهِمْ فَقَالَ لَهُ حُمْرَانُ جُعِلْتُ فِدَاكَ أَ رَأَيْتَ مَا كَانَ مِنْ أَمْرِ قِيَامِ عَلِيِّ بْنِ أَبِي طَالِبٍ وَالْحَسَنِ وَالْحُسَيْنِ (عَلَيْهِ السَّلام) وَخُرُوجِهِمْ وَقِيَامِهِمْ بِدِينِ اللهِ عَزَّ ذِكْرُهُ وَمَا أُصِيبُوا مِنْ قَتْلِ الطَّوَاغِيتِ إِيَّاهُمْ وَالظَّفَرِ بِهِمْ حَتَّى قُتِلُوا وَغُلِبُوا فَقَالَ أَبُو جَعْفَرٍ (عَلَيْهِ السَّلام) يَا حُمْرَانُ إِنَّ اللهَ تَبَارَكَ وَتَعَالَى قَدْ كَانَ قَدَّرَ ذَلِكَ عَلَيْهِمْ وَقَضَاهُ وَأَمْضَاهُ وَحَتَمَهُ عَلَى سَبِيلِ الاخْتِيَارِ ثُمَّ أَجْرَاهُ فَبِتَقَدُّمِ عِلْمٍ إِلَيْهِمْ مِنْ رَسُولِ اللهِ (صَلَّى اللهُ عَلَيْهِ وَآلِه) قَامَ عَلِيٌّ وَالْحَسَنُ وَالْحُسَيْنُ (عَلَيْهِ السَّلام) وَبِعِلْمٍ صَمَتَ مَنْ صَمَتَ مِنَّا وَلَوْ أَنَّهُمْ يَا حُمْرَانُ حَيْثُ نَزَلَ بِهِمْ مَا نَزَلَ مِنْ أَمْرِ اللهِ عَزَّ وَجَلَّ وَإِظْهَارِ الطَّوَاغِيتِ عَلَيْهِمْ سَأَلُوا اللهَ عَزَّ وَجَلَّ أَنْ يَدْفَعَ عَنْهُمْ ذَلِكَ وَأَلَحُّوا عَلَيْهِ فِي طَلَبِ إِزَالَةِ مُلْكِ الطَّوَاغِيتِ وَذَهَابِ مُلْكِهِمْ إِذاً لاجَابَهُمْ وَدَفَعَ ذَلِكَ عَنْهُمْ ثُمَّ كَانَ انْقِضَاءُ مُدَّةِ الطَّوَاغِيتِ وَذَهَابُ مُلْكِهِمْ أَسْرَعَ مِنْ سِلْكٍ مَنْظُومٍ انْقَطَعَ فَتَبَدَّدَ وَمَا كَانَ ذَلِكَ الَّذِي أَصَابَهُمْ يَا حُمْرَانُ لِذَنْبٍ اقْتَرَفُوهُ وَلا لِعُقُوبَةِ مَعْصِيَةٍ خَالَفُوا اللهَ فِيهَا وَلَكِنْ لِمَنَازِلَ وَكَرَامَةٍ مِنَ اللهِ أَرَادَ أَنْ يَبْلُغُوهَا فَلا تَذْهَبَنَّ بِكَ الْمَذَاهِبُ فِيهِمْ

Muhammad b. Yahya has narrated from Ahmad b. Muḥammad from b. Mahbub from b. Ri'ab from Durays al-Kunasi who has said that he heard abu Ja'far (عليه السلام) the following to an audience of his companions. "What an strange case is the case with a group of followers! They acknowledge us as the Divine authority over themselves, accept us as their Imam and say that obedience to us is obligatory just as is the case with the Messenger of Allāh. They then destroy the veracity of their belief as such and dispute against their own selves due to weakness of their hearts. They then diminish our right and blame those whom Allāh has granted evidence to know us as it should be and the (abulity) to submit themselves to our Divine authority. Do you not consider that how would Allāh, the Most Holy, the Most High, make it obligatory to obey those who possess Divine authority over his servants and then hide from them (people who possess Divine authority) `the new of the heaves and the earth? How would He cut them off of the sources of knowledge that might come to them to maintain their religion?" Humran then said to the Imam (عليه السلام), "May Allāh, take my soul in service for your cause, how would you explain the case of the uprising of

ʿAlī b. abu Talib, al-Hassan and al-Husayn (عليه السلام)? They came out and rose up for the cause of Allāh, Whose mention is so Majestic. How much they suffered and how mercilessly were they murdered at the hands of the rebels? They were defeated, murdered and over powered." Abu Jaʿfar (عليه السلام) then said, "O Humran, Allāh, the Most Holy, the Most High, had determined it on them. He had decreed, approved and made it unavoidable though the voluntary manner. He then allowed to take place. It, thus, happened with a pre-existing knowledge that had come to them from the Messenger of Allāh. ʿAlī al-Hassan and al-Husayn (عليه السلام) rose up for the cause of Allāh with full knowledge of the consequences and remained silent from us those who remained silent. Had they, O Humran, when facing what Allāh, the Most Holy, the Most High, made them to face and suffer defeat at the hands of the rebels, asked Allāh, the Most Holy, the Most High, to remove their suffering and would implore Him to destroy the government and kingdom of the rebels He would have answered their prayers and would grant them relief. In such case the destruction of the governments of the rebels and the ending of their time would take place quicker than the dispersal under a great pressure, of beads threaded together. The suffering, O Humran, that befell them, because of the sins that they might have committed or the punishment for their opposition to Allāh. It was because of the high marvelous position that Allāh had prepared and wanted them to reach Do not let people's opinions take you away from the right path." (صحيح)[73]

74.

عِدَّةٌ مِنْ أَصْحَابِنَا عَنْ أَحْمَدَ بْنِ مُحَمَّدٍ عَنْ عَلِيِّ بْنِ الْحَكَمِ عَنْ سَيْفِ بْنِ عَمِيرَةَ عَنْ عَبْدِ الْمَلِكِ بْنِ أَعْيَنَ عَنْ ابي جعفر (عَلَيْهِ السَّلام) قَالَ أَنْزَلَ الله تَعَالَى النَّصْرَ عَلَى الْحُسَيْنِ (عَلَيْهِ السَّلام) حَتَّى كَانَ مَا بَيْنَ السَّمَاءِ وَالارْضِ ثُمَّ خُيِّرَ النَّصْرَ أَوْ لِقَاءَ الله فَاخْتَارَ لِقَاءَ الله تَعَالَ

---

[73] *Al-Kāfi, v1, ch48, h4*

A number of our people has narrated from Ahmad b. Muḥammad from ʿAlī b. al-Hakam from Sayf b. ʻUmayra from ʻAbd al-Malik b. Aʻyan from abu Jaʻfar (عليه السلام) who has said the following. "Allāh, the Most Holy, the Most High, sent support for Imam al-Husayn (عليه السلام) up to the fill between the heavens and earth. Then he was let to choose either victory or meeting Allāh. He, however, chose the meeting of Allāh the Most High." (حسن)[74]

75.

حدثنا الشيخ الجليل أبو جعفر محمد بن علي بن الحسين بن موسى ابن بابويه القمي (رضي الله عنه) ، قال : حدثنا أبي (رحمه الله) ، قال : حدثنا سعد بن عبد الله ، عن أحمد بن محمد بن عيسى ، عن أبي عبد الله محمد بن خالد البرقي ، عن داود بن أبي يزيد ، عن أبي الجارود وابن بكير وبريد بن معاوية العجلي ، عن أبي جعفر الباقر (عليه السلام) ، قال : أصيب الحسين بن علي (عليهما السلام) ووجد به ثلاثمائة وبضعة وعشرون طعنة برمح أو ضربة بسيف أو رمية بسهم ، فروي أنها كانت كلها في مقدمه لأنه (عليه السلام) كان لا يولي

Shaikh Sadooq (رضي الله عنه) said narrated to me: my father (رضي الله عنه) who said: narrated to me Sa'd b. ʿAbd Allāh, from Ahmad b. Muḥammad b. Isa, from Abi Abdillah Muḥammad b. Khalid al Barqi, from Dawud b. Abi Yazid, from Abi al Jarud and b. Bukair and Buraid b. Muawiya al Ajli, from Abi Ja'far al Baqir (عليه السلام), who said:

"When Imam Hussain (عليه السلام) was wounded in Karbala, more than three hundred and twenty wounds were found on him, resulting from javelin/lance shot, or sword strikes or arrow shots. It has been reported that all the wounds were on the front of his body because he did not turn around/show his back (i.e. to run away from the enemy)."[75]

---

[74] *Al-Kāfi, v1, ch47, h8*

[75] *Al-Amāli(Ṣaduq), pg.228*

ابْنُ مَحْبُوبٍ عَنْ عَبْدِ اللَّهِ بْنِ سِنَانٍ قَالَ سَمِعْتُ أَبَا عَبْدِ اللَّهِ (عليه السلام) يَقُولُ ثَلَاثٌ هُنَّ فَخْرُ الْمُؤْمِنِ وَ زَيْنُهُ فِي الدُّنْيَا وَ الْآخِرَةِ الصَّلَاةُ فِي آخِرِ اللَّيْلِ وَ يَأْسُهُ مِمَّا فِي أَيْدِي النَّاسِ وَ وَلَايَتُهُ الْإِمَامَ مِنْ آلِ مُحَمَّدٍ (عليهم السلام) قَالَ وَ ثَلَاثَةٌ هُمْ شِرَارُ الْخَلْقِ ابْتُلِيَ بِهِمْ خِيَارُ الْخَلْقِ أَبُو سُفْيَانَ أَحَدُهُمْ قَاتَلَ رَسُولَ اللَّهِ (صلى الله عليه وآله) وَ عَادَاهُ وَ مُعَاوِيَةُ قَاتَلَ عَلِيّاً (عليه السلام) وَ عَادَاهُ وَ يَزِيدُ بْنُ مُعَاوِيَةَ لَعَنَهُ اللَّهُ قَاتَلَ الْحُسَيْنَ بْنَ عَلِيٍّ (عليه السلام) وَ عَادَاهُ حَتَّى قَتَلَهُ

b. Mahboub, from ʿAbd Allāh b. Sinan who said: I heard Abu ʻAbdAllāh (عليه السلام) saying; ʻThree things are a matter of pride for the Believer and an adornment of him in the world and the Hereafter – The Prayer during the last part of the night, and his dejection from what is in the hands of the people, and his Wilāya of the Imam (عليه السلام) from the Progeny of Messenger of Allāh (صلى الله عليه وآله وسلم). And the three who are the most evil of the creatures by whom the people were plagued, are Abu Sufyan who fought against the Messenger of Allāh (صلى الله عليه وآله وسلم) during his era and was inimical to him, and Muawiya fought against ʿAlī (عليه السلام) and was inimical to him, and Yazeed b. Muawiya, may Allāh (تبارك و طائلة) Curse him (لعنة الله عليه), fought against Al-Husayn b. ʿAlī (عليه السلام), and was inimical to him until he (لعنة الله عليه) killed him'. (حسن)[76]

77.

حَدَّثَنِي أَبِي (رحمه الله) عَنْ سَعْدِ بْنِ عَبْدِ اللَّهِ عَنْ أَحْمَدَ بْنِ مُحَمَّدِ بْنِ عِيسَى عَنِ الْحَسَنِ بْنِ عَلِيِّ بْنِ فَضَّالٍ عَنِ ابْنِ بُكَيْرٍ عَنْ زُرَارَةَ عَنْ عَبْدِ الْخَالِقِ بْنِ عَبْدِ رَبِّهِ قَالَ سَمِعْتُ أَبَا عَبْدِ اللَّهِ (ع) يَقُولُ لَمْ يَجْعَلِ اللَّهُ لَهُ مِنْ قَبْلُ سَمِيّاً الْحُسَيْنُ بْنُ عَلِيٍّ لَمْ يَكُنْ لَهُ مِنْ قَبْلُ سَمِيّاً وَ يَحْيَى بْنُ زَكَرِيَّا (ع) لَمْ يَكُنْ لَهُ مِنْ قَبْلُ سَمِيّاً وَ لَمْ تَبْكِ السَّمَاءُ إِلَّا عَلَيْهِمَا أَرْبَعِينَ صَبَاحاً قَالَ قُلْتُ مَا بُكَاؤُهَا قَالَ كَانَتْ تَطْلُعُ حَمْرَاءَ وَ تَغْرُبُ حَمْرَاءَ

My father narrated to me from Sa'd b. ʻAbdillāh, from Aĥmad b. Muĥammad b. ʻIsā, from Ĥasan b. ʻAli b. Fad'd'āl, from b. Bukayr, from Zurārah, from ʻAbdil Khāliq b.

[76] Al-Kāfi, v8, ch311

‘Abd Rabbih, who said: I heard Abā ‘Abdillāh (Imam Šādiq (عليه السلام)) say: “We have not given that name to anyone before (him)” (19:7). Ĥusain b. ‘Ali’s name was not given to anyone before him and Yaĥyā b. Zakariyyā’s name was also not given to anyone before him. And the heavens have never wept over anyone for forty days except for the two of them. I asked, “How did the heavens weep?” Imam (عليه السلام) replied, “The heavens became red at the time of sunrise and sunset.” (معتبر)[77]

78.

حَدَّثَنِي أَبِي (رحمه الله) وَ عَلِيُّ بْنُ الْحُسَيْنِ عَنْ سَعْدِ بْنِ عَبْدِ اللَّهِ عَنْ أَحْمَدَ بْنِ مُحَمَّدِ بْنِ عِيسَى عَنْ مُوسَى بْنِ الْفَضْلِ عَنْ حَنَانٍ قَالَ قُلْتُ لِأَبِي عَبْدِ اللَّهِ (ع) مَا تَقُولُ فِي زِيَارَةِ قَبْرِ أَبِي عَبْدِ اللَّهِ الْحُسَيْنِ (ع) فَإِنَّهُ بَلَغَنَا عَنْ بَعْضِهِمْ أَنَّهَا تَعْدِلُ حِجَّةً وَ عُمْرَةً- قَالَ لَا تَعْجَبْ [مَا أَصَابَ مَا يَقُولُ] بِالْقَوْلِ هَذَا كُلِّهِ وَ لَكِنْ زُرْهُ وَ لَا تَجْفُهُ فَإِنَّهُ سَيِّدُ الشُّهَدَاءِ وَ سَيِّدُ شَبَابِ أَهْلِ الْجَنَّةِ وَ شَبِيهُ يَحْيَى بْنِ زَكَرِيَّا وَ عَلَيْهِمَا بَكَتِ السَّمَاءُ وَ الْأَرْضُ حَدَّثَنِي أَبِي وَ مُحَمَّدُ بْنُ الْحَسَنِ بْنِ الْوَلِيدِ عَنْ مُحَمَّدِ بْنِ الْحَسَنِ الصَّفَّارِ عَنْ عَبْدِ الصَّمَدِ بْنِ مُحَمَّدٍ عَنْ حَنَانِ بْنِ سَدِيرٍ عَنْ أَبِي عَبْدِ اللَّهِ (ع) مِثْلَهُ سَوَاءً حَدَّثَنِي أَبِي (رحمه الله) تَعَالَى وَ جَمَاعَةُ مَشَايِخِي عَنْ سَعْدِ بْنِ عَبْدِ اللَّهِ عَنْ أَحْمَدَ بْنِ مُحَمَّدِ بْنِ عِيسَى عَنْ مُحَمَّدِ بْنِ إِسْمَاعِيلَ بْنِ بَزِيعٍ عَنْ حَنَانِ بْنِ سَدِيرٍ عَنْ أَبِي عَبْدِ اللَّهِ (ع) مِثْلَهُ

My father and ‘Ali b. Ĥusain both narrated to me from Sa’d b. ‘Abdillāh, from Aĥmad b. Muĥammad b. ‘Isā, from Mūsā b. Fad’l, from Ĥanān (b. Sadǐr), who said: I asked Abā ‘Abdillāh (Imam Šādiq (عليه السلام)), “What do you say about (the reward for) the Ziyārah of the grave of Abǐ ‘Abdillāh Al-Ĥusain (عليه السلام)? Some people have informed us that it is equal to one Hajj and one ‘Umrah.” Imam (عليه السلام) replied: Do not be surprised by all of these rewards. Rather, go to his Ziyārah and do not abandon him, for verily he is the Master of the Martyrs and he is the Master of the Youth of Paradise. Yaĥyā b. Zakariyyā (عليه السلام) is similar to Ĥusain (عليه السلام) and the heavens and the earth wept (only) over the two of them. The above Ĥadǐth has also been narrated to me through the following chains: A) My father, and Muĥammad b. Ĥasan

---

[77] *Kāmil az-Ziyārāt, ch28, h8*

b. Walīd, both from Muĥammad b. Ĥasan Al-Šaffār, from ‘Abdil Šamad b. Muĥammad, from Ĥanān b. Sadīr, from Abī ‘Abdillāh (عليه السلام). B) My father, and all of my scholars, from Sa’d b. ‘Abdillāh, from Aĥmad b. Muĥammad b. ‘Isā, from Muĥammad b. Ismā’īl b. Bazī’, from Ĥanān b. Sadīr, from Abī ‘Abdillāh (عليه السلام). (معتبر)[78]

79.

حدثنا أبي رضي الله عنه قال: حدثنا علي بن إبراهيم بن هاشم، عن أبيه عن عبدالرحمن بن أبي نجران، عن عاصم بن حميد، عن محمد بن قيس، عن أبي جعفر عليه السلام قال: بينما أمير المؤمنين عليه السلام في الرحبة والناس عليه متراكمون فمن بين مستفت ومن بين مستعد إذ قام إليه رجل فقال: السلام عليك يا أمير المؤمنين ورحمة الله وبركاتهفنظر إليه أمير المؤمنين عليه السلام بعينيه هاتيك العظيمتين ثم قال: وعليك السلام ورحمة الله وبركاته. من أنت؟فقال: أنا رجل من رعيتك وأهل بلادكقال: ما أنت من رعيتي وأهل بلادي، ولو سلمت علي يوما واحدا ماخفيت عليفقال: الامان يا أمير المؤمنينفقال أمير المؤمنين عليه السلام: هل أحدثت في مصري هذا حدثا منذ دخلتهقال: لاقال: فعلك من رجال الحرب؟قال: نعمقال: إذا وضعت الحرب أوزارها فلا بأسقال: أنا رجل بعثني إليك معاوية متغفلا لك أسألك عن شيء بعث فيه ابن الاصفر وقال له: إن كنت أنت أحق بهذا الامر والخليفة بعد محمد فأجبني عما أسألك فإنك إذا فعلت ذلك اتبعتك وأبعث إليك بالجائزة فلم يكن عنده جواب،وقد أقلقه ذلك فبعثني إليك لاسألك عنهافقال أمير المؤمنين عليه السلام: قاتل الله ابن آكلة الاكباد ماأضله وأعماه ومن معه. والله لقد أعتق جارية فما أحسن أن يتزوج بها. حكم الله بيني وبين هذه الامة، قطعوا رحمي، واضاعوا أيامي، ودفعوا حقي وصغروا عظيم منزلتي وأجمعوا على منازعتي. يا قنبر، عليّ بالحسن والحسين ومحمدفاحضروا، فقال: ياشامي هذان ابنا رسول الله وهذا ابني فسأل أيهم أحببت؟فقال: أسأل ذا الوفرة، يعني الحسن عليه السلام، وكان صبيافقال له الحسن عليه السلام: سلني عما بدا لكفقال الشامي: كم بين الحق والباطل، وكم بين السماء والارض، وكم بين المشرق والمغرب، وماقوس قزح، وما العين التي تأوي إليها أرواح المشركين، وما العين التي تأوي إليها أرواح المؤمنين، وما المؤنث، وما عشرة أشياء بعضها أشد من بعض؟فقال الحسن بن علي عليهما السلام: بين الحق والباطل أربع أصابع فما رأيته بعينك فهو الحق، وقد تسمع باذنيك باطلا كثيراقال الشامي صدقتقال: وبين السماء والارض دعوة المظلوم ومد البصر، فمن قال لك غير هذا فكذبهقال: صدقت يا بن رسول اللهقال: وبين المشرق والمغرب مسيرة يوم للشمس تنظر إليها حين تطلع من مشرقها وحين تغيب من مغربهاقال

---

[78] *Kāmil az-Ziyārāt, ch28, h13*

الشامي: صدقت. فما قوس قزح ؟قال عليه السلام: ويحك، لا تقل قوس قزح، فإن قزح اسم شيطان، وهو قوس الله وعلامة الخصب وأمان لاهل الارض من الغرق. وأما العين التي تأوي إليها أرواح المشركين فهي عين يقال لها برهوت، وأما العين التي تأوي إليها أرواح المؤمنين وهي يقال لها سلمى، وأما المؤنث فهو الذي لا يدري أذكر هو أم انثى، فإنه ينتظر به فإن كان ذكرا احتلم وإن كانت انثى حاضت وبدا ثديها، وإلا قيل له بُل علىالحائط فان أصاب بوله الحائط فهو ذكر وإن انتكص بوله كما انتكص بول البعير فهي امرأةوأما عشرة أشياء بعضها أشد من بعض فأشد شيء خلقه الله عز وجل الحجر، وأشد من الحجر الحديد الذي يقطع به الحجر، وأشد من الحديد النار تذيب الحديد وأشد من النار الماء يطفئ النار، وأشد من الماء السحاب يحمل الماء، وأشد من السحاب الريح تحمل السحاب، واشد من الريح الملك الذي يرسلها، وأشد من الملك ملك الموت الذي يميت الملك، وأشد من ملك الموت الموت الذي يميت ملك الموت، وأشد من الموت أمر الله رب العالمين يميت الموتفقال الشامي: أشهد أنك ابن رسول الله صلى الله عليه وآله حقا وأن عليا أولى بالامر من معاويةثم كتب هذه الجوابات وذهب بها ألى معاوية، فبعثها معاوية ألى ابن الاصفر فكتب أليه ابن الاصفر: يا معاوية، لم تكلمني بغير كلامك وتجيبني بغير جوابك؟ اقسم بالمسيح ما هذا جوابك وما هو إلا من معدن النبوة وموضع الرسالة. وأما أنت فلو سألتني درهما ما أعطيتك

(The compiler of the book narrated) that his father - may God be pleased with him - narrated that 'Alī b. Ibrahim b. Hashim quoted on the authority of his father, on the authority of Abdul Rahman b. Abi Najran, on the authority of Asim b. Hamid, on the authority of Muḥammad b. Qays that Abi Ja'far al-Baqir (عليه السلام) said, "Once when the Commander of the Faithful Imam 'Alī (عليه السلام) was in a courtyard, the people had gathered around him (عليه السلام). Someone wanted to ask about a decree, another one had a complaint, and was expressing his conditions. Suddenly a man came to him and said, 'O Commander of the Faithful! Peace be upon you as well as God's Mercy and His Blessings.' Then the Commander of the Faithful (عليه السلام) looked at him with his two big eyes and replied, 'And peace be upon you as well as God's Mercy and His Blessings. Who are you?' The man said, 'A man and I are from your people, and I am a resident of one of your towns.'The Commander of the Faithful (عليه السلام) said, 'You are not one of my people and are not a resident of one of our towns. I would not have forgotten it, even if you had greeted me once.'Then the man said, "O Commander of the Faithful! Please grant me immunity.' Then the Commander of the Faithful (عليه السلام) asked, 'Have you committed a crime in my town since you came here?'The man replied, 'No.' The Commander of the Faithful

(عليه السلام) asked him, 'Then are you a soldier?' The man replied, 'Yes.' Then the Commander of the Faithful (عليه السلام) said, 'Now that there is a peace treaty in effect, it doesn't matter.'The man said, 'I am one of the agents of Muawiyah. I was sent here in a disguise in order to ask you questions which b. al-Asfar (who is the Emperor of Rome) asked Muawiyah. The Emperor replied that if Muawiyah is the real ruler and the Caliph after Muḥammad (صلى الله عليه وآله وسلم), he should be able to answer these questions. Then the Emperor would pledge allegiance to Muawiyah and pay him remuneration. Since Muawiyah could not answer thequestions he has dispatched me to ask them from you.' Then the Commander of the Faithful ʿAlī (عليه السلام) said, 'May God kill the offspring of the liver-eater Hind. How deviated and blind he and his companions are! I swear by God that he freed his female slave and did not understand how to join her in marriage. God will rule between me and this nation. They cut off my bonds of relationship; wasted my time; usurped my rights; belittled my grand position and united against me. O Qanbar! Bring Al-Hassan (عليه السلام), Al-Hussein (عليه السلام) and Muḥammad (عليه السلام) to me.' The sons came by him. Then the Commander of the Faithful (عليه السلام) said, 'O Syrian man! These two are the (grand)sons of God's Prophet (صلى الله عليه وآله وسلم) and this one is my own son. Ask your questions from any of them as you wish.' The Syrian man said, 'I will ask my questions from the long-haired one that is Al-Hassan (عليه السلام) who is young. Then Al-Hassan (عليه السلام) told him, 'Ask me whatever you wish to ask.'Then the Syrian fellow asked, 'What is the distance between right and wrong? How much is the distance between the heavens and the Earth? How much is the distance between the East and the West? What is Qus and Qazah (the bow and the rainbow)? Where is the place in which the unbelievers' souls reside? Where is the place in which the believers' souls reside? What does Al-Mo'anas refer to? What are the ten things each of which is harder than the other?' Then Al-Hassan b. ʿAlī (عليه السلام) said, 'The distance between right and wrong is just four fingers. Whatever you yourself see is right, but most of whatever you hear may be wrong.' The Syrian fellow said, 'You are right!' Al-Hassan (عليه السلام) said, 'The distance between the heavens and the Earth is the supplication of the oppressed one and the closing of the eyes. Anyone who says anything else has lied.' The Syrian fellow said, 'O (grand)son of the Prophet! You are right!' Al-Hassan (عليه السلام) said, 'The distance between the East and the West is just the duration of time needed for the rotation of the sun from where it rises to where it sets during one day.' The Syrian man said, 'You are right! Then what is Qus and Qazah (the bow and the rainbow)?' Al-Hassan b. 'Alī (عليه السلام) said, 'Shame on you! Do not say Qus and Qazah since Qazah is the name of Satan. It is Qus Allāh and it is a sign of abundance and immunity of the people of the Earth from drowning. The place in which the unbelievers' souls shall reside is called Barahut. And the place in which the believers' souls shall reside is called Salma. And Al-Mo'anas refers to one whose gender cannot be recognized. Once he or she grows up, it is a male if he ejaculates and it would be a female if she menstruates and the nipples grow. If its gender is still not distinguishable with these two signs, it should be asked to urinate towards a wall. It would be a male, if the urinationis fast flowing and it reaches the wall, while it would be a female if the urination just flows out like that of a camel. The ten things each of which is harder than the other are as follows. The hardest thing which the Honorable the Exalted God has created is the stone. However, iron is even harder than stone since it cuts the stone. Fire is even harder than iron since it can melt the iron. Water is even harder than fire since it can extinguish it. Clouds are even harder than water since they move it around. Winds are even harder than clouds since they move the clouds around. Yet the angel who dispatches the winds is harder than the wind itself. And the angel of death is even harder than the angel which dispatches the winds since it can take away its life. And death is even harder than the angel of death, since it takes away the angel of death. Yet harder than all of these is the order of God - the Lord of the Two Worlds - which can take away death itself. Then the Syrian fellow said, 'I bear witness that you are the (grand)son of God's Prophet (صلى الله عليه وآله وسلم). You are right! And I bear witness that 'Alī more deserves to rule than Muawiyah.'Then the Syrian fellow wrote down these answers and went to Muawiyah with them. Muawiyah wrote these answers to (b. Al-Asfar) the Emperor of Rome. Then b. al-Safar wrote the following back to Muawiyah, 'O Muawiyah! Why do you use other people's sayings and answer me with other people's responses? I swear by Jesus that these are not your answers. Rather they have come from the treasury of

Prophethood and the seat of messengership. And I will not even give you one Dirham if you ask for it.'" (صحيح)[79]

80.

حَدَّثَنِي أَبِي (رحمه الله) وَ عَلِيُّ بْنُ الْحُسَيْنِ وَ مُحَمَّدُ بْنُ الْحَسَنِ رَحِمَهُمُ اللَّهُ جَمِيعاً عَنْ سَعْدِ بْنِ عَبْدِ اللَّهِ عَنْ أَحْمَدَ بْنِ مُحَمَّدِ بْنِ عِيسَى عَنْ سَعِيدِ بْنِ جَنَاحٍ عَنْ أَبِي يَحْيَى الْحَذَّاءِ عَنْ بَعْضِ أَصْحَابِنَا عَنْ أَبِي عَبْدِ اللَّهِ (ع) قَالَ نَظَرَ أَمِيرُ الْمُؤْمِنِينَ (ع) إِلَى الْحُسَيْنِ فَقَالَ يَا عَبْرَةَ كُلِّ مُؤْمِنٍ فَقَالَ أَنَا يَا أَبَتَاهْ قَالَ نَعَمْ يَا بُنَيَّ

My father, 'Ali b. Ĥusain, and Muĥammad b. Ĥasan all narrated to me from Sa'd b. 'Abdillāh, from Aĥmad b. Muĥammad b. 'Isā, from Sa'ĭd b. Janāĥ (Al-Azdi), from Abĭ Yaĥyā Al-Ĥadhā, from some of our companions, who said: Abū 'Abdillāh (Imam Šādiq (عليه السلام)) said: The Commander of the Believers (عليه السلام) looked at Ĥusain (عليه السلام) and said, "O 'ABRAH (tear) of every believer!" Ĥusain (عليه السلام) asked, "O father! Are you referring to me?" The Commander of the Believers (عليه السلام) replied, "Yes! O my son!"[80]

Virtues of Ahl al-Kisa (عليهم السلام)

81.

عَلِيُّ بْنُ إِبْرَاهِيمَ عَنْ مُحَمَّدِ بْنِ عِيسَى عَنْ يُونُسَ وَعَلِيُّ بْنُ مُحَمَّدٍ عَنْ سَهْلِ بْنِ زِيَادٍ أَبِي سَعِيدٍ عَنْ مُحَمَّدِ بْنِ عِيسَى عَنْ يُونُسَ عَنِ ابْنِ مُسْكَانَ عَنْ أَبِي بَصِيرٍ قَالَ سَأَلْتُ أَبَا عَبْدِ اللهِ (عَلَيْهِ السَّلام) عَنْ قَوْلِ اللهِ عَزَّ وَجَلَّ أَطِيعُوا اللهَ وَأَطِيعُوا الرَّسُولَ وَأُولِي الامْرِ مِنْكُمْ فَقَالَ نَزَلَتْ فِي عَلِيِّ بْنِ أَبِي طَالِبٍ وَالْحَسَنِ وَالْحُسَيْنِ (عَلَيْهِم السَّلام) فَقُلْتُ لَهُ إِنَّ النَّاسَ يَقُولُونَ فَمَا لَهُ لَمْ يُسَمِّ عَلِيّاً وَأَهْلَ بَيْتِهِ (عَلَيْهِم السَّلام) فِي كِتَابِ اللهِ عَزَّ وَجَلَّ قَالَ فَقَالَ قُولُوا لَهُمْ إِنَّ رَسُولَ اللهِ (صَلَّى اللهُ عَلَيْهِ وَآلِهِ) نَزَلَتْ عَلَيْهِ الصَّلاةُ وَلَمْ يُسَمِّ اللهُ لَهُمْ ثَلاثاً وَلا

---

[79] *Al-Khişāl, ch25, h1*

[80] *Kāmil az-Ziyārāt, ch36, h1*

أَرْبَعاً حَتَّى كَانَ رَسُولُ اللهِ (صَلَّى اللهُ عَلَيْهِ وَآلِهِ) هُوَ الَّذِي فَسَّرَ ذَلِكَ لَهُمْ وَنَزَلَتْ عَلَيْهِ الزَّكَاةُ وَلَمْ يُسَمِّ لَهُمْ مِنْ كُلِّ أَرْبَعِينَ دِرْهَماً دِرْهَمٌ حَتَّى كَانَ رَسُولُ اللهِ (صَلَّى اللهُ عَلَيْهِ وَآلِهِ) هُوَ الَّذِي فَسَّرَ ذَلِكَ لَهُمْ وَنَزَلَ الْحَجُّ فَلَمْ يَقُلْ لَهُمْ طُوفُوا أُسْبُوعاً حَتَّى كَانَ رَسُولُ اللهِ (صَلَّى اللهُ عَلَيْهِ وَآلِهِ) هُوَ الَّذِي فَسَّرَ ذَلِكَ لَهُمْ وَنَزَلَتْ أَطِيعُوا اللهَ وَأَطِيعُوا الرَّسُولَ وَأُولِي الامْرِ مِنْكُمْ وَنَزَلَتْ فِي عَلِيٍّ وَالْحَسَنِ وَالْحُسَيْنِ فَقَالَ رَسُولُ اللهِ (صَلَّى اللهُ عَلَيْهِ وَآلِهِ) فِي عَلِيٍّ مَنْ كُنْتُ مَوْلاهُ فَعَلِيٌّ مَوْلاهُ وَقَالَ (صَلَّى اللهُ عَلَيْهِ وَآلِهِ) أُوصِيكُمْ بِكِتَابِ اللهِ وَأَهْلِ بَيْتِي فَإِنِّي سَأَلْتُ اللهَ عَزَّ وَجَلَّ أَنْ لا يُفَرِّقَ بَيْنَهُمَا حَتَّى يُورِدَهُمَا عَلَيَّ الْحَوْضَ فَأَعْطَانِي ذَلِكَ وَقَالَ لا تُعَلِّمُوهُمْ فَهُمْ أَعْلَمُ مِنْكُمْ وَقَالَ إِنَّهُمْ لَنْ يُخْرِجُوكُمْ مِنْ بَابِ هُدًى وَلَنْ يُدْخِلُوكُمْ فِي بَابِ ضَلالَةٍ فَلَوْ سَكَتَ رَسُولُ اللهِ (صَلَّى اللهُ عَلَيْهِ وَآلِهِ) فَلَمْ يُبَيِّنْ مَنْ أَهْلُ بَيْتِهِ لادَّعَاهَا آلُ فُلانٍ وَآلُ فُلانٍ وَلَكِنَّ اللهَ عَزَّ وَجَلَّ أَنْزَلَهُ فِي كِتَابِهِ تَصْدِيقاً لِنَبِيِّهِ (صَلَّى اللهُ عَلَيْهِ وَآلِهِ) إِنَّمَا يُرِيدُ اللهُ لِيُذْهِبَ عَنْكُمُ الرِّجْسَ أَهْلَ الْبَيْتِ وَيُطَهِّرَكُمْ تَطْهِيراً فَكَانَ عَلِيٌّ وَالْحَسَنُ وَالْحُسَيْنُ وَفَاطِمَةُ (عَلَيْهِم السَّلام) فَأَدْخَلَهُمْ رَسُولُ اللهِ (صَلَّى اللهُ عَلَيْهِ وَآلِهِ) تَحْتَ الْكِسَاءِ فِي بَيْتِ أُمِّ سَلَمَةَ ثُمَّ قَالَ اللَّهُمَّ إِنَّ لِكُلِّ نَبِيٍّ أَهْلاً وَثَقَلاً وَهَؤُلاءِ أَهْلُ بَيْتِي وَثَقَلِي فَقَالَتْ أُمُّ سَلَمَةَ أَ لَسْتُ مِنْ أَهْلِكَ فَقَالَ إِنَّكِ إِلَى خَيْرٍ وَلَكِنَّ هَؤُلاءِ أَهْلِي وَثِقْلِي فَلَمَّا قُبِضَ رَسُولُ اللهِ (صَلَّى اللهُ عَلَيْهِ وَآلِهِ) كَانَ عَلِيٌّ أَوْلَى النَّاسِ بِالنَّاسِ لِكَثْرَةِ مَا بَلَّغَ فِيهِ رَسُولُ اللهِ (صَلَّى اللهُ عَلَيْهِ وَآلِهِ) وَإِقَامَتِهِ لِلنَّاسِ وَأَخْذِهِ بِيَدِهِ فَلَمَّا مَضَى عَلِيٌّ لَمْ يَكُنْ يَسْتَطِيعُ عَلِيٌّ وَلَمْ يَكُنْ لِيَفْعَلَ أَنْ يُدْخِلَ مُحَمَّدَ بْنَ عَلِيٍّ وَلا الْعَبَّاسَ بْنَ عَلِيٍّ وَلا وَاحِداً مِنْ وُلْدِهِ إِذاً لَقَالَ الْحَسَنُ وَالْحُسَيْنُ إِنَّ اللهَ تَبَارَكَ وَتَعَالَى أَنْزَلَ فِينَا كَمَا أَنْزَلَ فِيكَ فَأَمَرَ بِطَاعَتِنَا كَمَا أَمَرَ بِطَاعَتِكَ وَبَلَّغَ فِينَا رَسُولُ اللهِ (صَلَّى اللهُ عَلَيْهِ وَآلِهِ) كَمَا بَلَّغَ فِيكَ وَأَذْهَبَ عَنَّا الرِّجْسَ كَمَا أَذْهَبَهُ عَنْكَ فَلَمَّا مَضَى علي (عَلَيْهِ السَّلام) كَانَ الْحَسَنُ (عَلَيْهِ السَّلام) أَوْلَى بِهَا لِكِبَرِهِ فَلَمَّا تُوُفِّيَ لَمْ يَسْتَطِعْ أَنْ يُدْخِلَ وُلْدَهُ وَلَمْ يَكُنْ لِيَفْعَلَ ذَلِكَ وَاللهُ عَزَّ وَجَلَّ يَقُولُ وَأُولُوا الارْحامِ بَعْضُهُمْ أَوْلى بِبَعْضٍ فِي كِتابِ اللهِ فَيَجْعَلَهَا فِي وُلْدِهِ إِذاً لَقَالَ الْحُسَيْنُ أَمَرَ اللهُ بِطَاعَتِي كَمَا أَمَرَ بِطَاعَتِكَ وَطَاعَةِ أَبِيكَ وَبَلَّغَ فِيَّ رَسُولُ اللهِ (صَلَّى اللهُ عَلَيْهِ وَآلِهِ) كَمَا بَلَّغَ فِيكَ وَفِي أَبِيكَ وَأَذْهَبَ اللهُ عَنِّي الرِّجْسَ كَمَا أَذْهَبَ عَنْكَ وَعَنْ أَبِيكَ فَلَمَّا صَارَتْ إِلَى الْحُسَيْنِ (عَلَيْهِ السَّلام) لَمْ يَكُنْ أَحَدٌ مِنْ أَهْلِ بَيْتِهِ يَسْتَطِيعُ أَنْ يَدَّعِيَ عَلَيْهِ كَمَا كَانَ هُوَ يَدَّعِي عَلَى أَخِيهِ وَعَلَى أَبِيهِ لَوْ أَرَادَا أَنْ يَصْرِفَا الامْرَ عَنْهُ وَلَمْ يَكُونَا لِيَفْعَلا ثُمَّ صَارَتْ حِينَ أَفْضَتْ إِلَى الْحُسَيْنِ (عَلَيْهِ السَّلام) فَجَرَى تَأْوِيلُ هَذِهِ الايَةِ وَأُولُوا الارْحامِ بَعْضُهُمْ أَوْلى بِبَعْضٍ فِي كِتابِ اللهِ ثُمَّ صَارَتْ مِنْ بَعْدِ الْحُسَيْنِ لِعَلِيِّ بْنِ الْحُسَيْنِ ثُمَّ صَارَتْ مِنْ بَعْدِ عَلِيِّ بْنِ الْحُسَيْنِ إِلَى مُحَمَّدِ بن علي (عَلَيْهِما السَّلام) وَقَالَ الرِّجْسُ هُوَ الشَّكُّ وَاللهِ لا نَشُكُّ فِي رَبِّنَا أَبَداً

Ali b. Ibrahim has narrated from Muḥammad b. ‘Isa from Yunus and ‘Alī b. Muḥammad from Sahl b. Ziyad, abu Sa‘id from Muḥammad b. ‘Isa from Yunus from b. Muskan from abu Basir who has said that he asked abu ‘AbdAllāh (عليه السلام) about the following words of Allāh, the Most Holy, the Most High. “Believers, obey God,

His Messenger, and your leaders (who possess Divine authority). . ." (4:59) The Imam (عليه السلام) said, "This was sent from heavens about 'Alī b. abu talib al-Hassan and al-Husayn (عليه السلام)." I then said, "People say, "Why did He not specify 'Alī and his family by their names in the book of Allāh, the Most Holy, the Most High?'" The Imam (عليه السلام) said, "Say to them, 'The command for prayer came to the Messenger of Allāh but He has not specified (the number of the Rak'ats) for them three nor four. It, in fact, was the Messenger of Allāh who explained to them this matter. The command for Zakat (a form of income tax) came to the Messenger of Allāh and there was no specific taxable number such as one Dirham on every forty Dirham. It was the Messenger of Allāh who explained it for them. The command for Hajj came to the Messenger of Allāh. It did not say walk senven times around the Ka'ba It was the Messenger of Allāh who explained it for them. The verse about obedience came "Believers, obey God, His Messenger, and your leaders (who possess Divine authority). . ." (4:59) It came to declare that Ali, al-Hassan and al-Husayn (عليه السلام) were the leards who possessed Divine authority. The Messenger of Allāh then said about 'Alī (عليه السلام), "On whoever I have Divine Authority, then 'Alī (عليه السلام) has Divne Authority over him also." He also has said, "I enjoin you to follow the book of Allāh and my family because have prayed to Allāh, the Most Holy, the Most High not to separate these two from eachother until He will make them arrive al-Kawthar (at the pool of Paradise) to meet me. He has granted my prayer as suCh" The Holy Prophet has said, "Do not try to teach them (The Imam (عليه السلام) becaue they are far more knowledgeable than you." The Holy Prophet has said, "The Imam (عليه السلام) will never take you out of the gate of guidance and they never make you enter the gate of misguidance." Had the Messenger of Allāh remained silent and would not explain anything about his Ahl al-Bayt (family) the family of so and so would have advanced their claim for Imamat (Leadership with Divine Authority). However, Allāh, the Most Holy, the Most High, has revealed it in His book to confirm the explanantions of His Prophet about Ahl al-Bayt (in the following verse), "People of the house, God wants to remove all kinds of uncleanliness from you and to purify you thoroughly." (33:33) Ali, Fatima, al-Hassan andlhy (عليه السلام) were there and the Holy Prophet made them to enter under al-Kisa' (the Cloak) in the house of 'Umm Salama and then said, "O Lord, every prophet has a family and a gravity, and these are my family and gravity." 'Umm Salama at this point said, "Am I not of your family?" The Holy Prophet said, "You are in goodness but these are my family and my gravity." Whe the Messenger of Allāh passed away 'Alī (عليه السلام) had the utmost priority and guardianship of the people all because of what the Messenger of Allāh had preached about him. It was because of raising him up for the people and holding his hand in his hand. When 'Alī (عليه السلام) (was about to) passed away he could not (and would not) enter Muḥammad b. 'Alī or al-'Abbass b. 'Alī or anyone of his other sons in the position of Imamt. Otherewise, al-Hassan and al-Husayn (عليه السلام) would have said, "Allāh, the Most Holy, the Most High, has revealed about us jus as He has done so about you, and He has commaned people to obey us just as He has commanded people to obey you. The Messenger of Allāh has preached to people about us just as he has done so about you. Allāh has removed al-Rijs uncleanliness from us just as He has done so to you. When 'Alī (عليه السلام) left this world, al-Hassan had the utmost priority for Imamat (Leadership with Divine Authority) because he was the eldest. When was about to die he could not, and would not, enter his sons in the position of Imamat.It is because ;Allāh, the Most Holy, the Most High, says, ". . The relatives are closer to each other, according to the Book of God, than the believers and the emigrants. ." (33:6) He then places Imamat (Leadership with Divine Authority) in his sons. If so, al-Husayn (عليه السلام) would have said, "Allāh has commanded people to obey me just as He has commanded people to obey you and to obey your father. The Messenger of Allāh has preached to people about me just as he has preached to people about you and your father. Allāh has removed al-Rijs (unleanliness) from me just as He has removed from you and your father. When the Imamat (Leadership with Divine Authority) was infull force with al-Husayn (عليه السلام) there was no one in his family to who could claim against him as he could calim against his brother and father, had they wanted to diver it from him and they would not do so. After them it found its place with al-Husayn (عليه السلام) and the interpretation of this verse continued, ". . The relatives are closer to each other, according to the Book of God, than the believers and the emigrants. . ." (33:6) After al-Husayn (عليه السلام) Imamat (Leadership with Divine Authority) found its place with 'Alī b. al-Husayn (عليه السلام). After 'Alī b.

al-Husayn (عليه السلام) it (Leadership with Divine Authority) found its place with Muḥammad b. ʿAlī (عليه السلام)." The Imam (عليه السلام) said, "Al-Rijs means doubts, I swear by Allāh that we never doubt in our Lord." Muḥammad b. Yahya has narrated from Ahmad b. Muḥammad b. 'Isa from Muḥammad b. Khalid and al-Husayn b. Sa'id from al-Nadr b. Suwayd from Yahya b. 'Imran al-Halabi from Ayyub b. al-Hurr and 'Imran b. ʿAlī al-Halabi from abu 'AbdAllāh (عليه السلام) a similar Hadīth. (صحيح)[81]

82.

مُحَمَّدُ بْنُ يَحْيَى عَنْ أَحْمَدَ بْنِ مُحَمَّدِ بْنِ عِيسَى عَنْ عَلِيِّ بْنِ الْحَكَمِ عَنْ إِسْمَاعِيلَ بْنِ عَبْدِ الْخَالِقِ قَالَ سَمِعْتُ أَبَا عَبْدِ اللَّهِ (عليه السلام) يَقُولُ لِأَبِي جَعْفَرٍ الْأَحْوَلِ وَ أَنَا أَسْمَعُ أَتَيْتَ الْبَصْرَةَ فَقَالَ نَعَمْ قَالَ كَيْفَ رَأَيْتَ مُسَارَعَةَ النَّاسِ إِلَى هَذَا الْأَمْرِ وَ دُخُولَهُمْ فِيهِ قَالَ وَ اللَّهِ إِنَّهُمْ لَقَلِيلٌ وَ لَقَدْ فَعَلُوا وَ إِنَّ ذَلِكَ لَقَلِيلٌ فَقَالَ عَلَيْكَ بِالْأَحْدَاثِ فَإِنَّهُمْ أَسْرَعُ إِلَى كُلِّ خَيْرٍ ثُمَّ قَالَ مَا يَقُولُ أَهْلُ الْبَصْرَةِ فِي هَذِهِ الْآيَةِ قُلْ لا أَسْئَلُكُمْ عَلَيْهِ أَجْراً إِلَّا الْمَوَدَّةَ فِي الْقُرْبى قُلْتُ جُعِلْتُ فِدَاكَ إِنَّهُمْ يَقُولُونَ إِنَّهَا لِأَقَارِبِ رَسُولِ اللَّهِ (صلى الله عليه وآله) فَقَالَ كَذَبُوا إِنَّمَا نَزَلَتْ فِينَا خَاصَّةً فِي أَهْلِ الْبَيْتِ فِي عَلِيٍّ وَ فَاطِمَةَ وَ الْحَسَنِ وَ الْحُسَيْنِ أَصْحَابِ الْكِسَاءِ (عليهم السلام)

Muhammad b. Yahya, from Ahmad b. Muḥammad b. Isa, from ʿAlī b. Al-Hakam, from Ismail b. Abd Al-Khaliq who said: 'I heard Abu 'AbdAllāh (عليه السلام) saying to Abu Ja'far Al-Ahwal, and I was listening: 'Did you go to Al-Basra?' He said, 'Yes'. He said: 'How did you see the hastening of the people to this matter and their entering in it to be?' He said, 'By Allāh (تبارك و طائلة), they are few, and they have done it but that is little'. He said: 'It is on you to (approach) the juveniles for they are quick to every good'. Then he said: 'What are the people of Al-Basra saying regarding this Verse: '[42:23] Say: I do not ask of you any reward for it but love for my near relatives''. I said, 'May I be sacrificed for you, they are saying that it is for the near relatives of the Messenger of Allāh (صلى الله عليه وآله وسلم) of Allāh (تبارك و طائلة)'. He said: 'They lie. But rather it Descended with regards to us especially, regarding the People

---

[81] *Al-Kāfi, v1, ch64, h1*

of the Household, regarding 'Alī (عليه السلام), and Fatimah (عليها السلام), and Al-Hasan (عليه السلام), and Al-Husayn (عليه السلام) the ones of the Cloak (As'haab Al-Kisaa)'. (صحيح)[82]

83.

مُحَمَّدُ بْنُ الْحَسَنِ عَنْ سَهْلِ بْنِ زِيَادٍ عَنْ مُحَمَّدِ بْنِ عِيسَى عَنْ صَفْوَانَ بْنِ يَحْيَى عَنْ صَبَّاحٍ الازْرَقِ عَنْ أَبِي بَصِيرٍ قَالَ قُلْتُ لابِي جعفر (عَلَيْهِ السَّلام) إِنَّ رَجُلاً مِنَ الْمُخْتَارِيَّةِ لَقِيَنِي فَزَعَمَ أَنَّ مُحَمَّدَ بْنَ الْحَنَفِيَّةِ إِمَامٌ فَغَضِبَ أَبُو جَعْفَرٍ (عَلَيْهِ السَّلام) ثُمَّ قَالَ أَ فَلا قُلْتَ لَهُ قَالَ قُلْتُ لا وَاللهِ مَا دَرَيْتُ مَا أَقُولُ قَالَ أَ فَلا قُلْتَ لَهُ إِنَّ رَسُولَ اللهِ (صَلَّى اللهُ عَلَيْهِ وَآلِه) أَوْصَى إِلَى عَلِيٍّ وَالْحَسَنِ وَالْحُسَيْنِ فَلَمَّا مَضَى علي (عَلَيْهِ السَّلام) أَوْصَى إِلَى الْحَسَنِ وَالْحُسَيْنِ وَلَوْ ذَهَبَ يَزْوِيهَا عَنْهُمَا لَقَالا لَهُ نَحْنُ وَصِيَّانِ مِثْلُكَ وَلَمْ يَكُنْ لِيَفْعَلَ ذَلِكَ وَأَوْصَى الْحَسَنُ إِلَى الْحُسَيْنِ وَلَوْ ذَهَبَ يَزْوِيهَا عَنْهُ لَقَالَ أَنَا وَصِيٌّ مِثْلُكَ مِنْ رَسُولِ اللهِ (صَلَّى اللهُ عَلَيْهِ وَآلِه) وَمِنْ أَبِي وَلَمْ يَكُنْ لِيَفْعَلَ ذَلِكَ قَالَ اللهُ عَزَّ وَجَلَّ وَأُولُوا الارْحَامِ بَعْضُهُمْ أَوْلَى بِبَعْضٍ هِيَ فِينَا وَفِي أَبْنَائِنَا

Muhammad b. al-Hassan from Sahl b. Ziyad from Muḥammad b. 'Isa from Safwan b. Yahya from Sabbah al-Azraq that Abu Basir said: "I said to Abu Ja'far (عليه السلام): 'A man from the Mukhtariyyah met me and claimed that Muḥammad b. al-Hanafiyyah (one of the sons of 'Alī b. Abu Talib—was an Imam.' Abu Ja'far (عليه السلام) became angry, then he said: 'Did you not say anyone. i.e. the Kaysaniyyah —Nlukhtar b. Abu 'Ubayd ath-Thaqafi (1/622 — 67/687) was the leader of the uprising to avenge the slaying of al-Husayn (عليه السلام) at Karbala' and Kaysan Abu 'Amra was then his leading supporter among the rnaw~li thing to him?' " He said: "I said: 'No, by Allāh! I did not know what to say.' He said: 'Did you not say to him: "The Messenger of Allāh (صلى الله عليه وآله وسلم) appointed Ali, al-Hassan and al-Husayn as his successors. When 'Alī (عليه السلام) passed away, he appointed al-Hassan and al-Husayn as his successors, and if he (Ali) had tried to withhold it from them, they would have said to him: 'We are successors like you.' But he would never have done this. al-Hasan appointed al-Husayn as his successor, and if he had tried to withhold it from him, he would have said: 'I am a successor like you of the Messenger of Allāh (صلى الله عليه وآله وسلم) and of my

[82] *Al-Kāfi, v8, ch66*

father.' But he would not have done this. Allāh, to Whom belong Might and Majesty, said: Some of those bound by blood are nearer (to each other) than others (al-Anfal,8:75; al-Ahzab, 33 :6)." This is about us and about our sons.' (صحيح)[83]

Virtues of Imam 'Alī b. al-Husayn az-Zayn al- Abideen (عليه السلام)

84.

عِدَّةٌ مِنْ أَصْحَابِنَا عَنْ أَحْمَدَ بْنِ مُحَمَّدٍ عَنِ ابْنِ فَضَّالٍ عَنِ ابْنِ بُكَيْرٍ عَنْ زُرَارَةَ قَالَ سَمِعْتُ أَبَا جَعْفَرٍ (عَلَيْهِ السَّلام) يَقُولُ كَانَ لِعَلِيِّ بن الحسين (عَلَيْهِما السَّلام) نَاقَةٌ حَجَّ عَلَيْهَا اثْنَتَيْنِ وَعِشْرِينَ حَجَّةً مَا قَرَعَهَا قَرْعَةً قَطُّ قَالَ فَجَاءَتْ بَعْدَ مَوْتِهِ وَمَا شَعَرْنَا بِهَا إِلا وَقَدْ جَاءَنِي بَعْضُ خَدَمِنَا أَوْ بَعْضُ الْمَوَالِي فَقَالَ إِنَّ النَّاقَةَ قَدْ خَرَجَتْ فَأَتَتْ قَبْرَ عَلِيِّ بْنِ الْحُسَيْنِ فَانْبَرَكَتْ عَلَيْهِ فَدَلَكَتْ بِجِرَانِهَا الْقَبْرَ وَهِيَ تَرْغُو فَقُلْتُ أَدْرِكُوهَا وَجِيئُونِي بِهَا قَبْلَ أَنْ يَعْلَمُوا بِهَا أَوْ يَرَوْهَا قَالَ وَمَا كَانَتْ رَأَتِ الْقَبْرَ قَطُّ

A number of our people has narrated from Ahmad b. Muḥammad from b. al-Faddal from b. Bukayr from Zurara who has said the following. "I heard abu Ja'far (عليه السلام) say, 'Ali b. al-Husayn (عليه السلام) had a she camel. He had taken this camel twenty two times to Hajj (pilgrimage to Makka) and had not used the whip against not even once. The Imam (عليه السلام) has said that the camel came after he passed away and we were not aware but we noticed only when one of the servants or slaves came and said, "The she camel has went out all the way to the grave of 'Alī b. al-Husayn (عليه السلام) and sat on the grave. She rubs her neck against the grave and moans. I then asked them to quickly get to her before they would know about her or see her. The Imam (عليه السلام) has said, "She had never seen the grave before." (صحيح)[84]

85.

---

[83] *Al-Kāfi, v1, ch64, h7*

[84] *Al-Kāfi, v1, ch117, h2*

الْحُسَيْنُ بْنُ مُحَمَّدِ بْنِ عَامِرٍ عَنْ أَحْمَدَ بْنِ إِسْحَاقَ بْنِ سَعْدٍ عَنْ سَعْدَانَ بْنِ مُسْلِمٍ عَنْ أَبِي عُمَارَةَ عَنْ رَجُلٍ عَنْ أَبِي عَبْدِ اللهِ (عَلَيْهِ السَّلام) قَالَ لَمَّا كَانَ فِي اللَّيْلَةِ الَّتِي وُعِدَ فِيهَا عَلِيُّ بن الحسين (عَلَيْهِما السَّلام) قَالَ لِمُحَمَّدٍ (عَلَيْهِ السَّلام) يَا بُنَيَّ ابْغِنِي وَضُوءاً قَالَ فَقُمْتُ فَجِئْتُهُ بِوَضُوءٍ قَالَ لا أَبْغِي هَذَا فَإِنَّ فِيهِ شَيْئاً مَيِّتاً قَالَ فَخَرَجْتُ فَجِئْتُ بِالْمِصْبَاحِ فَإِذَا فِيهِ فَأْرَةٌ مَيْتَةٌ فَجِئْتُهُ بِوَضُوءٍ غَيْرِهِ فَقَالَ يَا بُنَيَّ هَذِهِ اللَّيْلَةُ الَّتِي وُعِدْتُهَا فَأَوْصَى بِنَاقَتِهِ أَنْ يُحْظَرَ لَهَا حِظَارٌ وَأَنْ يُقَامَ لَهَا عَلَفٌ فَجُعِلَتْ فِيهِ قَالَ فَلَمْ تَلْبَثْ أَنْ خَرَجَتْ حَتَّى أَتَتِ الْقَبْرَ فَضَرَبَتْ بِجِرَانِهَا وَرَغَتْ وَهَمَلَتْ عَيْنَاهَا فَأُتِيَ مُحَمَّدُ بْنُ عَلِيٍّ فَقِيلَ لَهُ إِنَّ النَّاقَةَ قَدْ خَرَجَتْ فَأَتَاهَا فَقَالَ صَهْ الان قُومِي بَارَكَ اللهُ فِيكِ فَلَمْ تَفْعَلْ فَقَالَ وَإِنْ كَانَ لَيَخْرُجُ عَلَيْهَا إِلَى مَكَّةَ فَيُعَلِّقُ السَّوْطَ عَلَى الرَّحْلِ فَمَا يَقْرَعُهَا حَتَّى يَدْخُلَ الْمَدِينَةَ قَالَ وَكَانَ عَلِيُّ بن الحسين (عَلَيْهِما السَّلام) يَخْرُجُ فِي اللَّيْلَةِ الظَّلْمَاءِ فَيَحْمِلُ الْجِرَابَ فِيهِ الصُّرَرُ مِنَ الدَّنَانِيرِ وَالدَّرَاهِمِ حَتَّى يَأْتِيَ بَاباً بَاباً فَيَقْرَعُهُ ثُمَّ يُنِيلُ مَنْ يَخْرُجُ إِلَيْهِ فَلَمَّا مَاتَ عَلِيُّ بن الحسين (عَلَيْهِما السَّلام) فَقَدُوا ذَاكَ فَعَلِمُوا أَنَّ عَلِيّاً (عَلَيْهِ السَّلام) كَانَ يَفْعَلُهُ

al-Husayn b. Muḥammad b. ‘Amir has narrated from Ahmad b. Ishaq b. Sa‘d from Su‘dan b. Muslim from abu ‘Imara from a man from abu ‘AbdAllāh (عليه السلام) who has said the following. "When it was the night wherein ‘Alī b.hy (عليه السلام) would pass away he asked his Muḥammad (عليه السلام), his son, "Son bring me water for Wudu (cleaning for prayer). Muḥammad has said, "I then brought water for him." He said, "I do not like this water. There is something dead in it." I then brought the water in the light and found a dead mouse in it. I then brought him other water. He said, "Son this is the night in which I am promise to be taken out of this world. He explained his recommendations about his she camel and that a stable be prepared for her and that she is fed properly and I personally did so. Very shortly there after she came out of the stable and reached the grave, placed her neck on it, rolled her bodyon the ground and her eyes had become full of tears. Muḥammad b. ‘Alī (عليه السلام) was informed that the she camel had gone. He came to her and said, "Control your emotion and get up, may Allāh grant you good fortune. She would not do so. The Imam (عليه السلام) has said, "When he would take the camel to Makka, he would hang the whip from the luggage and would not use it until he would return to Madina." The Imam (عليه السلام) has said, "Ali b. al-Husayn (عليه السلام) would come out in the dark night with a sack containing Darahim and Dananir (units of money) and would go door to door, knock them and gave a certain amount to the person that would come. When ‘Alī b. al-

Husayn died these people would see the person with money and then they realized that 'Alī b. al-Husayn (عليه السلام) must have been the distributor of money among them." (مجهول)[85]

86.

مُحَمَّدُ بْنُ أَحْمَدَ عَنْ عَمِّهِ عَبْدِ اللهِ بْنِ الصَّلْتِ عَنِ الْحَسَنِ بْنِ عَلِيِّ بْنِ بِنْتِ إِلْيَاسَ عَنْ أَبِي الْحَسَنِ (عَلَيْهِ السَّلام) قَالَ سَمِعْتُهُ يَقُولُ إِنَّ عَلِيَّ بن الحسين (عَلَيْهِما السَّلام) لَمَّا حَضَرَتْهُ الْوَفَاةُ أُغْمِيَ عَلَيْهِ ثُمَّ فَتَحَ عَيْنَيْهِ وَقَرَأَ إِذَا وَقَعَتِ الْوَاقِعَةُ وَإِنَّا فَتَحْنَا لَكَ وَقَالَ الْحَمْدُ لله الَّذِي صَدَقَنَا وَعْدَهُ وَأَوْرَثَنَا الارْضَ نَتَبَوَّأُ مِنَ الْجَنَّةِ حَيْثُ نَشَاءُ فَنِعْمَ أَجْرُ الْعَامِلِينَ ثُمَّ قُبِضَ مِنْ سَاعَتِهِ وَلَمْ يَقُلْ شَيْئاً.

Muhammad b. Ahmad has narrated from his uncle, 'AbdAllāh b. al-Salt from al-Hassan b. 'Alī b. b.t al-Yahya's who has said the following. "I hear abu al-Hassan (عليه السلام) say, 'When 'Alī b. al-Husayn (عليه السلام) was about 'Uthman pass away he passed out then he opened his eyes and recited chapters 48 and 56 from the Holy Qur'ān and said, "All praise belongs to Allāh Who has fulfilled His promise to us and made us to inherit the earth passed out and chose from Paradise whatever we would like and thus, is the reward for those who work. Within the hour he passed away and did not say any thing." (حسن)[86]

87.

سَهْلُ بْنُ زِيَادٍ عَنِ الْحَجَّالِ عَنْ عَلِيِّ بْنِ عُقْبَةَ عَنْ رَجُلٍ عَنْ أَبِي عَبْدِ الله (عَلَيهِ السَّلام) قَالَ كَانَ عَلِيُّ بْنُ الْحُسَيْنِ (صَلَّى اللهُ عَلَيْهِ وآلِه) أَحْسَنَ النَّاسِ صَوْتاً بِالْقُرْآنِ وَكَانَ السَّقَّاءُونَ يَمُرُّونَ فَيَقِفُونَ بِبَابِهِ يَسْمَعُونَ قِرَاءَتَهُ وَكَانَ أَبُو جَعْفَرٍ (عَلَيهِ السَّلام) أَحْسَنَ النَّاسِ صَوْتاً

[85] *Al-Kāfi, v1, ch117, h4*

[86] *Al-Kāfi, v1, ch117, h5*

Sahl b. Ziyad has narrated from al-Hajjal from 'Alī b. 'Aqabah from a man from abu 'Abd Allāh (عليه السلام) who has said the following: "Ali b. al-Husayn (عليه السلام) was the best among the people for his attractive voice in reading the Holy Qur'ān. The water carrier would stop in front of his door to listen to his reading and abu Ja'far (عليه السلام) was the best among the people for his attractive voice." (موثق)[87]

88.

وَ فِي خَاتَمِ عَلِيِّ بْنِ الْحُسَيْنِ (عليه السلام) الْحَمْدُ لِلَّهِ الْعَلِيِّ الْعَظِيمِ

On the ring of 'Alī b. al-Husayn, (عليه السلام), the writing said, 'All praise belongs to Allāh, the most High, the most Great.'(حسن أو موثق)[88]

89.

(Another variation of the Hadīth above)

عَلِيُّ بْنُ إِبْرَاهِيمَ عَنْ أَبِيهِ عَنْ عَلِيِّ بْنِ مَعْبَدٍ عَنِ الْحُسَيْنِ بْنِ خَالِدٍ عَنْ أَبِي الْحَسَنِ (عليه السلام) قَالَ كَانَ عَلَى خَاتَمِ عَلِيِّ بْنِ الْحُسَيْنِ (عليه السلام) خَزِيَ وَ شَقِيَ قَاتِلُ الْحُسَيْنِ بْنِ عَلِيٍّ (عليه السلام)

Ali b. Ibrahim has narrated from his father from Afi b. Ma'bad from af-Husayn b. Khafid who has said the following: "Abu al-Hassan, (عليه السلام), has said, 'On the ring of 'Alī b. al-Husayn, (عليه السلام), the writing said, 'Disgraced and destroyed are murderers of al-Husayn b. Ah' (عليه السلام).''' (مجهول)[89]

90.

---

[87] *Al-Kāfi, v1, ch9, h11*

[88] *Al-Kāfi, v6, ch26, h2*

[89] *Al-Kāfi, v6, ch26, h6*

عَلِيُّ بْنُ إِبْرَاهِيمَ عَنْ أَبِيهِ عَنْ حَمَّادِ بْنِ عِيسَى عَنْ إِبْرَاهِيمَ بْنِ عُمَرَ الْيَمَانِيِّ وَعُمَرَ بْنِ أُذَيْنَةَ عَنْ أَبَانٍ عَنْ سُلَيْمِ بْنِ قَيْسٍ قَالَ شَهِدْتُ وَصِيَّةَ أَمِيرِ الْمُؤْمِنِينَ (عَلَيْهِ السَّلام) حِينَ أَوْصَى إِلَى ابْنِهِ الْحَسَنِ (عَلَيْهِ السَّلام) وَأَشْهَدَ عَلَى وَصِيَّتِهِ الْحُسَيْنَ (عَلَيْهِ السَّلام) وَمُحَمَّداً وَجَمِيعَ وُلْدِهِ وَرُؤَسَاءَ شِيعَتِهِ وَأَهْلَ بَيْتِهِ ثُمَّ دَفَعَ إِلَيْهِ الْكِتَابَ وَالسِّلاحَ وَقَالَ لابْنِهِ الْحَسَنِ (عَلَيْهِ السَّلام) يَا بُنَيَّ أَمَرَنِي رَسُولُ اللهِ (صَلَّى اللهُ عَلَيْهِ وَآلِهِ) أَنْ أُوصِيَ إِلَيْكَ وَأَنْ أَدْفَعَ إِلَيْكَ كُتُبِي وَسِلاحِي كَمَا أَوْصَى إِلَيَّ رَسُولُ اللهِ (صَلَّى اللهُ عَلَيْهِ وَآلِهِ) وَدَفَعَ إِلَيَّ كُتُبَهُ وَسِلاحَهُ وَأَمَرَنِي أَنْ آمُرَكَ إِذَا حَضَرَكَ الْمَوْتُ أَنْ تَدْفَعَهَا إِلَى أَخِيكَ الْحُسَيْنِ (عَلَيْهِ السَّلام) ثُمَّ أَقْبَلَ عَلَى ابْنِهِ الْحُسَيْنِ (عَلَيْهِ السَّلام) فَقَالَ وَأَمَرَكَ رَسُولُ اللهِ (صَلَّى اللهُ عَلَيْهِ وَآلِهِ) أَنْ تَدْفَعَهَا إِلَى ابْنِكَ هَذَا ثُمَّ أَخَذَ بِيَدِ عَلِيِّ بْنِ الحسين (عَلَيْهِما السَّلام) ثُمَّ قَالَ لِعَلِيِّ بْنِ الْحُسَيْنِ وَأَمَرَكَ رَسُولُ اللهِ (صَلَّى اللهُ عَلَيْهِ وَآلِهِ) أَنْ تَدْفَعَهَا إِلَى ابْنِكَ مُحَمَّدِ بْنِ عَلِيٍّ وَأَقْرِئْهُ مِنْ رَسُولِ اللهِ (صَلَّى اللهُ عَلَيْهِ وَآلِهِ) وَمِنِّي السَّلامَ

Ali b. Ibrahim has narrated from his father from Hammad b. 'Isa from Ibrahim b. 'Umar al-Yamani and 'Umar b. 'Udhayna from Sulaym b. Qays who has said the following. "I witnessed Amir al-Mu'minin Ali's (عليه السلام) will made before me in which he appointed his, al-Hassan (عليه السلام) as the executor. He called al-Husayn (عليه السلام), Muḥammad and all his other sons, all the leaders among his followers and his whole family to bear testimony to his will. He then delivered the Book and the Armament to his son al-Hassan (عليه السلام) and said, "My son, the Messenger of Allāh commanded me to appoint you as the executor of my will. (He commanded me) to deliver to you my books and my Armament just as the Messenger of Allāh did. He made his will in which he appointed me as the executor, delivered to me his books and his Armament and commanded me to command you to deliver them to al-Husayn (عليه السلام) when you will be about to leave this world. Then he turned to his son, al-Husayn (عليه السلام) and said, "The Messenger of Allāh has commanded you to deliver them to your son, this one. Then he held with his hand 'Alī b. al-Husayn (عليه السلام) and said to him, "The Messenger of Allāh has commanded you to deliver them to your son, Muḥammad b. 'Alī and convey to him the Islamic greeting of the Messenger of Allāh and my Islamic greeting. (حسن على الظاهر)[90]

---

[90] *Al-Kafi, v1, ch66, h1*

91.

مُحَمَّدُ بْنُ يَحْيَى عَنْ أَحْمَدَ بْنِ مُحَمَّدٍ عَنِ ابْنِ مَحْبُوبٍ عَنْ عَلِيِّ بْنِ رِئَابٍ عَنْ أَبِي عُبَيْدَةَ وَزُرَارَةَ جَمِيعاً عَنْ ابي جعفر (عَلَيْهِ السَّلام) قَالَ لَمَّا قُتِلَ الْحُسَيْنُ (عَلَيْهِ السَّلام) أَرْسَلَ مُحَمَّدُ بْنُ الْحَنَفِيَّةِ إِلَى عَلِيِّ بن الحسين (عَلَيْهِما السَّلام) فَخَلا بِهِ فَقَالَ لَهُ يَا ابْنَ أَخِي قَدْ عَلِمْتَ أَنَّ رَسُولَ الله (صَلَّى اللهُ عَلَيْهِ وَآلِه) دَفَعَ الْوَصِيَّةَ وَالامَامَةَ مِنْ بَعْدِهِ إِلَى أَمِيرِ الْمُؤْمِنِينَ (عَلَيْهِ السَّلام) ثُمَّ إِلَى الْحَسَنِ (عَلَيْهِ السَّلام) ثُمَّ إِلَى الْحُسَيْنِ (عَلَيْهِ السَّلام) وَقَدْ قُتِلَ أَبُوكَ رَضِيَ الله عَنْهُ وَصَلَّى عَلَى رُوحِهِ وَلَمْ يُوصِ وَأَنَا عَمُّكَ وَصِنْوُ أَبِيكَ وَوِلادَتِي مِنْ علي (عَلَيْهِ السَّلام) فِي سِنِّي وَقَدِيمِي أَحَقُّ بِهَا مِنْكَ فِي حَدَاثَتِكَ فَلا تُنَازِعْنِي فِي الْوَصِيَّةِ وَالامَامَةِ وَلا تُحَاجَّنِي فَقَالَ لَهُ عَلِيُّ بن الحسين (عَلَيْهِما السَّلام) يَا عَمِّ اتَّقِ الله وَلا تَدَّعِ مَا لَيْسَ لَكَ بِحَقٍّ إِنِّي أَعِظُكَ أَنْ تَكُونَ مِنَ الْجَاهِلِينَ إِنَّ أَبِي يَا عَمِّ صَلَوَاتُ الله عَلَيْهِ أَوْصَى إِلَيَّ قَبْلَ أَنْ يَتَوَجَّهَ إِلَى الْعِرَاقِ وَعَهِدَ إِلَيَّ فِي ذَلِكَ قَبْلَ أَنْ يُسْتَشْهَدَ بِسَاعَةٍ وَهَذَا سِلاحُ رَسُولِ الله (صَلَّى اللهُ عَلَيْهِ وَآلِه) عِنْدِي فَلا تَتَعَرَّضْ لِهَذَا فَإِنِّي أَخَافُ عَلَيْكَ نَقْصَ الْعُمُرِ وَتَشَتُّتَ الْحَالِ إِنَّ الله عَزَّ وَجَلَّ جَعَلَ الْوَصِيَّةَ وَالامَامَةَ فِي عَقِبِ الْحُسَيْنِ (عَلَيْهِ السَّلام) فَإِذَا أَرَدْتَ أَنْ تَعْلَمَ ذَلِكَ فَانْطَلِقْ بِنَا إِلَى الْحَجَرِ الاسْوَدِ حَتَّى نَتَحَاكَمَ إِلَيْهِ وَنَسْأَلَهُ عَنْ ذَلِكَ قَالَ أَبُو جَعْفَرٍ (عَلَيْهِ السَّلام) وَكَانَ الْكَلامُ بَيْنَهُمَا بِمَكَّةَ فَانْطَلَقَا حَتَّى أَتَيَا الْحَجَرَ الاسْوَدَ فَقَالَ عَلِيُّ بْنُ الْحُسَيْنِ لِمُحَمَّدِ بْنِ الْحَنَفِيَّةِ ابْدَأْ أَنْتَ فَابْتَهِلْ إِلَى الله عَزَّ وَجَلَّ وَسَلْهُ أَنْ يُنْطِقَ لَكَ الْحَجَرَ ثُمَّ سَلْ فَابْتَهَلَ مُحَمَّدٌ فِي الدُّعَاءِ وَسَأَلَ الله ثُمَّ دَعَا الْحَجَرَ فَلَمْ يُجِبْهُ فَقَالَ عَلِيُّ بن الحسين (عَلَيْهِما السَّلام) يَا عَمِّ لَوْ كُنْتَ وَصِيّاً وَإِمَاماً لاجَابَكَ قَالَ لَهُ مُحَمَّدٌ فَادْعُ الله أَنْتَ يَا ابْنَ أَخِي وَسَلْهُ فَدَعَا الله عَلِيُّ بن الحسين (عَلَيْهِما السَّلام) بِمَا أَرَادَ ثُمَّ قَالَ أَسْأَلُكَ بِالَّذِي جَعَلَ فِيكَ مِيثَاقَ الانْبِيَاءِ وَمِيثَاقَ الاوْصِيَاءِ وَمِيثَاقَ النَّاسِ أَجْمَعِينَ لَمَّا أَخْبَرْتَنَا مَنِ الْوَصِيُّ وَالامَامُ بَعْدَ الْحُسَيْنِ بن علي (عَلَيْهِما السَّلام) قَالَ فَتَحَرَّكَ الْحَجَرُ حَتَّى كَادَ أَنْ يَزُولَ عَنْ مَوْضِعِهِ ثُمَّ أَنْطَقَهُ الله عَزَّ وَجَلَّ بِلِسَانٍ عَرَبِيٍّ مُبِينٍ فَقَالَ اللهمَّ إِنَّ الْوَصِيَّةَ وَالامَامَةَ بَعْدَ الْحُسَيْنِ بن علي (عَلَيْهِما السَّلام) إِلَى عَلِيِّ بْنِ الْحُسَيْنِ بْنِ عَلِيِّ بْنِ أَبِي طَالِبٍ وَابْنِ فَاطِمَةَ بِنْتِ رَسُولِ الله (صَلَّى اللهُ عَلَيْهِ وَآلِه) قَالَ فَانْصَرَفَ مُحَمَّدُ بْنُ عَلِيٍّ وَهُوَ يَتَوَلَّى عَلِيَّ بْنَ الْحُسَيْنِ (عَلَيْهِما السَّلام)

Muhammad b. Yahya has narrated from Ahmad b. Muḥammad from b. Mahbub from ʻAlī b. Ri'ab from abu ʻUbayda and Zurara from abu Ja'far (عليه السلام) who has said the following. "When al-Husayn (عليه السلام) was martyred, Muḥammad b. al-Hanafiya asked ʻAlī b. al-Husayn (عليه السلام) for a private meeting. In the meeting he said, "O son of my brother, you know that the Messenger of Allāh (s.a) delivered the task of al-Wasiyya, (the executor-ship of the will) and al-Imamat, (Leadership with

Divine Authority) thereafter it was delivered to al-Hassan (عليه السلام) and then to al-Husayn (عليه السلام). Your father, may Allāh be pleased with him has been murdered, may Allāh grant blessing up on his soul, and he did make any will. I am your uncle and equal in status to your father and I am a son of 'Alī (عليه السلام). Because of being older in age I am more deserving of the the position of Imamat considering that you are younger than me. Therefore, you should not dispute with me about al-Wasiyya, the will and Imamat, leadership and should argue with me about it." 'Alī b. al-Husayn (عليه السلام) said, "O uncle, be pious before Allāh and do not claim in what you have no right. I advise not to be of the ignorant people. In fact, my father (عليه السلام), O my uncle, appointed me as the executor of his will before his leaving for Iraq. He made such covenant with me just an hour before his becoming a martyr. This is the Armament of the Messenger of Allāh with me. You then should not dislocate them. I am afraid for you of a shorter life and quandary of conditions. Allāh, the Most Majestic, the Most gracious, has placed al-Wasiyya, and Imamat in the descendants of al-Husayn (عليه السلام). If you would like to know it we can go near the Blackstone and fro judgment and ask it about the issue." Abu Ja'far (عليه السلام) has said that the issue came up between them in Makka and they went near the Blackstone. 'Alī b. al-Husayn (عليه السلام) said to Muḥammad al-Hanafiya, "You begin first and pray to Allāh, the Most Majestic, the Most gracious, and ask Him to make the Blackstone speak to you and then ask your question." Muḥammad then pleaded in his prayer and asked Allāh and then ask the Blackstone about the disputed issue but there was no answer. 'Alī b. al-Husayn (عليه السلام) said, "O uncle, had you been the Executor of the will and the Imam it would have answered your question. Muḥammad then said, "Now you pray to Allāh, O son of my brother and ask your question. Alin b. al-Husayn (عليه السلام) prayed to Allāh for what he wanted then addressing the Blackstone said, "I ask you for the sake of the One Who placed the covenant of the prophets in you, as well as the covenant of the executors of the will and the covenant of all the peole. You must tell us who the Wasiyy and Imam after al-Husayn (عليه السلام)?" The narrator has said that the Blackstone began to shake so much that it almost camme out of its place. Allāh, the Most Majestic, the Most gracious, then made it to speak in clear Arabic language and said, "O Lord, al-Wasiyya and Imamat after al-Husayn (عليه السلام) b. 'Alī is for ʿAlī b. al-Husayn b. ʿAlī ab. abu Talib and b. Fatima (عليه السلام) daughter of the the Messenger of Allāh." The narrator has said that Muḥammad ʿAlī (عليه السلام) returned back and he acknowledged ʿAlī b. al-Husayn (عليه السلام) to be his Wali (Leadership with Divine Authority)." ʿAlī b. Ibrahim has narrated from his father from Hammad b. 'Isa from Hariz from Zurara from abu Ja'far (عليه السلام) the same Hadīth. (صحيح)[91]

92.

علي بن إبراهيم، عن أبيه، عن ابن أبي عمير، عن محمد بن أبي حمزة، عن أبيه قال: رأيت علي بن الحسين (عليهما السلام) في فناء الكعبة في الليل وهو يصلي فأطال القيام حتى جعل مرة يتوكأ على رجله اليمنى ومرة على رجله اليسرى ثم سمعته يقول بصوت كأنه باك: " يا سيدي تعذبني وحبك في قلبي ؟ أما وعزتك لئن فعلت لتجمعن بيني وبين قوم طال ما عاديتهم فيك

Ali b. Ibrahim has narrated from his father from b. abu 'Umayr from Muḥammad b. abu Hamza from his father who has said the following: "Once I saw ʿAlī b. al-Husayn (عليه السلام) praying in the vicinity of al-Ka'bah in the night. He prolonged in standing so much so that he would lean on his right leg once and then on the left leg. Then I heard him saying with a crying voice, 'O my Master, will You punish me while there is Your love in my heart? If You will do so You will be placing me together with the people with whom, just for Your sake, I had been enemies all along.'" (حسن)[92]

Virtues of Imam Abu Ja'far Muḥammad b. ʿAlī al-Baqir (عليه السلام)

93.

---

[91] *Al-Kāfi, v1, ch81, h5*

[92] *Al-Kāfi, v2, ch60, h10*

عِدَّةٌ مِنْ أَصْحَابِنَا عَنْ أَحْمَدَ بْنِ مُحَمَّدٍ عَنْ عَلِيِّ بْنِ الْحَكَمِ عَنْ مُثَنًّى الْحَنَّاطِ عَنْ أَبِي بَصِيرٍ قَالَ دَخَلْتُ عَلَى ابي جعفر (عَلَيْهِ السَّلام) فَقُلْتُ لَهُ أَنْتُمْ وَرَثَةُ رَسُولِ الله (صَلَّى اللهُ عَلَيْهِ وَآلِه) قَالَ نَعَمْ قُلْتُ رَسُولُ الله (صَلَّى اللهُ عَلَيْهِ وَآلِه) وَارِثُ الانْبِيَاءِ عَلِمَ كُلَّ مَا عَلِمُوا قَالَ لِي نَعَمْ قُلْتُ فَأَنْتُمْ تَقْدِرُونَ عَلَى أَنْ تُحْيُوا الْمَوْتَى وَتُبْرِءُوا الاكْمَهَ وَالابْرَصَ قَالَ نَعَمْ بِإِذْنِ الله ثُمَّ قَالَ لِيَ ادْنُ مِنِّي يَا أَبَا مُحَمَّدٍ فَدَنَوْتُ مِنْهُ فَمَسَحَ عَلَى وَجْهِي وَعَلَى عَيْنَيَّ فَأَبْصَرْتُ الشَّمْسَ وَالسَّمَاءَ وَالارْضَ وَالْبُيُوتَ وَكُلَّ شَيْءٍ فِي الْبَلَدِ ثُمَّ قَالَ لِي أَ تُحِبُّ أَنْ تَكُونَ هَكَذَا وَلَكَ مَا لِلنَّاسِ وَعَلَيْكَ مَا عَلَيْهِمْ يَوْمَ الْقِيَامَةِ أَوْ تَعُودَ كَمَا كُنْتَ وَلَكَ الْجَنَّةُ خَالِصاً قُلْتُ أَعُودُ كَمَا كُنْتُ فَمَسَحَ عَلَى عَيْنَيَّ فَعُدْتُ كَمَا كُنْتُ قَالَ فَحَدَّثْتُ ابْنَ أَبِي عُمَيْرٍ بِهَذَا فَقَالَ أَشْهَدُ أَنَّ هَذَا حَقٌّ كَمَا أَنَّ النَّهَارَ حَقٌّ

A number of our people has narrated from Ahmad b. Muḥammad from ʿAlī b. al-Hakam from al-Muthanna al-Hannat from abu Basir who has said the following. "Once I went to see abu Jaʿfar (عليه السلام) and asked him, "Are you the heirs of the Messenger of Allāh?" He said, "Yes, we are his heirs." I then asked, "Was the Messenger of Allāh the heir of the prophets and knew all that they knew?" He said to me, "Yes, it is true." I then asked, "Do you have the power to bring the dead back to life and cure the lepers, and the blind?" He said, "Yes, we do have such powers by the permission of Allāh." The he said to me, "Come closer to me, O abu Muhammad." I went closer to him and he rubbed my face and my eyes and saw the sun, the skies, the earth, the houses and all things in the town. Then he said to me, "Do you like to live this way and will have what others have and be responsible for whatever they will be held responsible on the Day of Judgment or like to live as before and will have paradise purely?" I said, "I would like to live as I lived before." He rubbed my eyes and I found myself as before." The narrator has said that he told it to b. abu 'Umayr who said, "I testify that this is true just as the day is true." (حسن)[93]

94.

مُحَمَّدُ بْنُ يَحْيَى عَنْ مُحَمَّدِ بْنِ أَحْمَدَ عَنْ مُحَمَّدِ بْنِ الْحُسَيْنِ عَنْ مُحَمَّدِ بْنِ عَلِيٍّ عَنْ عَاصِمِ بْنِ حُمَيْدٍ عَنْ مُحَمَّدِ بْنِ مُسْلِمٍ عَنْ ابي جعفر (عَلَيْهِ السَّلام) قَالَ كُنْتُ عِنْدَهُ يَوْماً إِذْ وَقَعَ زَوْجُ وَرَشَانٍ عَلَى الْحَائِطِ وَهَدَلا

[93] *Al-Kāfi, v1, ch118, h3*

هَدِيلَهُمَا فَرَدَّ أَبُو جَعْفَرٍ (عَلَيْهِ السَّلام) عَلَيْهِمَا كَلامَهُمَا سَاعَةً ثُمَّ نَهَضَا فَلَمَّا طَارَا عَلَى الْحَائِطِ هَدَلَ الذَّكَرُ عَلَى الانْثَى سَاعَةً ثُمَّ نَهَضَا فَقُلْتُ جُعِلْتُ فِدَاكَ مَا هَذَا الطَّيْرُ قَالَ يَا ابْنَ مُسْلِمٍ كُلُّ شَيْءٍ خَلَقَهُ الله مِنْ طَيْرٍ أَوْ بَهِيمَةٍ أَوْ شَيْءٍ فِيهِ رُوحٌ فَهُوَ أَسْمَعُ لَنَا وَأَطْوَعُ مِنِ ابْنِ آدَمَ إِنَّ هَذَا الْوَرَشَانَ ظَنَّ بِامْرَأَتِهِ فَحَلَفَتْ لَهُ مَا فَعَلَتْ فَقَالَتْ تَرْضَى بِمُحَمَّدِ بْنِ عَلِيٍّ فَرَضِيَا بِي فَأَخْبَرْتُهُ أَنَّهُ لَهَا ظَالِمٌ فَصَدَّقَهَا

Muhammad b. Yahya has narrated from Muḥammad b. Ahmad from Muḥammad b. al-Husayn from Muḥammad b. ʿAlī from ʻAsim b. Hamid from Muḥammad b. Muslim who has said the following. "One day I was in the presence of abu Ja'far (عليه السلام) that a pair of turtledove came and sat on the wall and exchanged voices as they usually do. Abu Ja'far (عليه السلام) then also exchanged voices with them for a while. They then flew away and on the other wall the male sounded to the fame for a while and then both of them flew away. I then asked The Imam (عليه السلام), "May Allāh take my soul in service for your cause, "What were these birds?" The Imam (عليه السلام) said, "O b. Muslim, all that Allāh has created, such as birds, animals or other things that have life they obey us better than people. The male dove was suspicious about the female and she denied it on oath which the male did not accept. Then she asked if he would abide by the decision of Muḥammad b. Ali? He agreed and told him that he had wronged his pair then he believed her." (مجهول)[94]

95.

مُحَمَّدُ بْنُ يَحْيَى عَنْ عِمْرَانَ بْنِ مُوسَى عَنْ مُحَمَّدِ بْنِ الْحُسَيْنِ عَنْ مُحَمَّدِ بْنِ عَبْدِ الله عَنْ عِيسَى بْنِ عَبْدِ الله عَنْ أَبِيهِ عَنْ جَدِّهِ قَالَ الْتَفَتَ عَلِيُّ بن الحسين (عَلَيْهِمَا السَّلام) إِلَى وُلْدِهِ وَهُوَ فِي الْمَوْتِ وَهُمْ مُجْتَمِعُونَ عِنْدَهُ ثُمَّ الْتَفَتَ إِلَى مُحَمَّدِ بْنِ عَلِيٍّ فَقَالَ يَا مُحَمَّدُ هَذَا الصُّنْدُوقُ اذْهَبْ بِهِ إِلَى بَيْتِكَ قَالَ أَمَا إِنَّهُ لَمْ يَكُنْ فِيهِ دِينَارٌ وَلا دِرْهَمٌ وَلَكِنْ كَانَ مَمْلُوءاً عِلْماً

Muhammad b. Yahya has narrated from 'Imran b. Mūsā from Muḥammad b. al-Husayn from Muḥammad b. 'AbdAllāh from 'Isa b. 'AbdAllāh from his father that his

---

[94] *Al-Kāfi, v1, ch118, h4*

grandfather who has said the following. "Ali b. al-Husayn looked at his sons when he was about to leave this world and they had all gathered around him. He then looked at his son, Muḥammad b. 'Alī and said, "O Muhammad, take this box to your house." He said, "It was not full of Dirhams and Dinars (valuable properties), it, however, was full of knowledge." (مجهول)[95]

96.

عَلِيُّ بْنُ إِبْرَاهِيمَ عَنْ أَبِيهِ عَنْ حَمَّادِ بْنِ عِيسَى عَنْ إِبْرَاهِيمَ بْنِ عُمَرَ الْيَمَانِيِّ وَعُمَرَ بْنِ أُذَيْنَةَ عَنْ أَبَانٍ عَنْ سُلَيْمِ بْنِ قَيْسٍ قَالَ شَهِدْتُ وَصِيَّةَ أَمِيرِ الْمُؤْمِنِينَ (عَلَيْهِ السَّلام) حِينَ أَوْصَى إِلَى ابْنِهِ الْحَسَنِ (عَلَيْهِ السَّلام) وَأَشْهَدَ عَلَى وَصِيَّتِهِ الْحُسَيْنَ (عَلَيْهِ السَّلام) وَمُحَمَّداً وَجَمِيعَ وُلْدِهِ وَرُؤَسَاءَ شِيعَتِهِ وَأَهْلَ بَيْتِهِ ثُمَّ دَفَعَ إِلَيْهِ الْكِتَابَ وَالسِّلاحَ وَقَالَ لابْنِهِ الْحَسَنِ (عَلَيْهِ السَّلام) يَا بُنَيَّ أَمَرَنِي رَسُولُ اللهِ (صَلَّى اللهُ عَلَيْهِ وَآلِهِ) أَنْ أُوصِيَ إِلَيْكَ وَأَنْ أَدْفَعَ إِلَيْكَ كُتُبِي وَسِلاحِي كَمَا أَوْصَى إِلَيَّ رَسُولُ اللهِ (صَلَّى اللهُ عَلَيْهِ وَآلِهِ) وَدَفَعَ إِلَيَّ كُتُبَهُ وَسِلاحَهُ وَأَمَرَنِي أَنْ آمُرَكَ إِذَا حَضَرَكَ الْمَوْتُ أَنْ تَدْفَعَهَا إِلَى أَخِيكَ الْحُسَيْنِ (عَلَيْهِ السَّلام) ثُمَّ أَقْبَلَ عَلَى ابْنِهِ الْحُسَيْنِ (عَلَيْهِ السَّلام) فَقَالَ وَأَمَرَكَ رَسُولُ اللهِ (صَلَّى اللهُ عَلَيْهِ وَآلِهِ) أَنْ تَدْفَعَهَا إِلَى ابْنِكَ هَذَا ثُمَّ أَخَذَ بِيَدِ عَلِيِّ بن الحسين (عَلَيْهِمَا السَّلام) ثُمَّ قَالَ لِعَلِيِّ بْنِ الْحُسَيْنِ وَأَمَرَكَ رَسُولُ اللهِ (صَلَّى اللهُ عَلَيْهِ وَآلِهِ) أَنْ تَدْفَعَهَا إِلَى ابْنِكَ مُحَمَّدِ بْنِ عَلِيٍّ وَأَقْرِئْهُ مِنْ رَسُولِ اللهِ (صَلَّى اللهُ عَلَيْهِ وَآلِهِ) وَمِنِّي السَّلامَ

Ali b. Ibrahim has narrated from his father from Hammad b. 'Isa from Ibrahim b. 'Umar al-Yamani and 'Umar b. 'Udhayna from Sulaym b. Qays who has said the following. "I witnessed Amir al-Mu'minin Ali's (عليه السلام) will made before me in which he appointed his, al-Hassan (عليه السلام) as the executor. He called al-Husayn (عليه السلام), Muḥammad and all his other sons, all the leaders among his followers and his whole family to bear testimony to his will. He then delivered the Book and the Armament to his son al-Hassan (عليه السلام) and said, "My son, the Messenger of Allāh commanded me to appoint you as the executor of my will. (He commanded me) to deliver to you my books and my Armament just as the Messenger of Allāh did. He made his will in which he appointed me as the executor, delivered to me his books

---

[95] *Al-Kāfi, v1, ch69, h2*

and his Armament and commanded me to command you to deliver them to al-Husayn (عليه السلام) when you will be about to leave this world. Then he turned to his son, al-Husayn (عليه السلام) and said, "The Messenger of Allāh has commanded you to deliver them to your son, this one. Then he held with his hand ʿAlī b. al-Husayn (عليه السلام) and said to him, "The Messenger of Allāh has commanded you to deliver them to your son, Muḥammad b. ʿAlī and convey to him the Islamic greeting of the Messenger of Allāh and my Islamic greeting. (حسن على الظاهر)[96]

97.

عِدَّةٌ مِنْ أَصْحَابِنَا عَنْ أَحْمَدَ بْنِ مُحَمَّدٍ عَنْ مُحَمَّدِ بْنِ سِنَانٍ عَنْ أَبَانِ بْنِ تَغْلِبَ عَنْ أَبِي عَبْدِ اللهِ (عَلَيْهِ السَّلام) قَالَ إِنَّ جَابِرَ بْنَ عَبْدِ اللهِ الانْصَارِيَّ كَانَ آخِرَ مَنْ بَقِيَ مِنْ أَصْحَابِ رَسُولِ اللهِ وَكَانَ رَجُلاً مُنْقَطِعاً إِلَيْنَا أَهْلَ الْبَيْتِ وَكَانَ يَقْعُدُ فِي مَسْجِدِ رَسُولِ اللهِ (صَلَّى اللهُ عَلَيْهِ وَآلِه) وَهُوَ مُعْتَجِرٌ بِعِمَامَةٍ سَوْدَاءَ وَكَانَ يُنَادِي يَا بَاقِرَ الْعِلْمِ يَا بَاقِرَ الْعِلْمِ فَكَانَ أَهْلُ الْمَدِينَةِ يَقُولُونَ جَابِرٌ يَهْجُرُ فَكَانَ يَقُولُ لا وَاللهِ مَا أَهْجُرُ وَلَكِنِّي سَمِعْتُ رَسُولَ اللهِ (صَلَّى اللهُ عَلَيْهِ وَآلِه) يَقُولُ إِنَّكَ سَتُدْرِكُ رَجُلاً مِنِّي اسْمُهُ اسْمِي وَشَمَائِلُهُ شَمَائِلِي يَبْقُرُ الْعِلْمَ بَقْراً فَذَاكَ الَّذِي دَعَانِي إِلَى مَا أَقُولُ قَالَ فَبَيْنَا جَابِرٌ يَتَرَدَّدُ ذَاتَ يَوْمٍ فِي بَعْضِ طُرُقِ الْمَدِينَةِ إِذْ مَرَّ بِطَرِيقٍ فِي ذَاكَ الطَّرِيقِ كُتَّابٌ فِيهِ مُحَمَّدُ بْنُ عَلِيٍّ فَلَمَّا نَظَرَ إِلَيْهِ قَالَ يَا غُلامُ أَقْبِلْ فَأَقْبَلَ ثُمَّ قَالَ لَهُ أَدْبِرْ فَأَدْبَرَ ثُمَّ قَالَ شَمَائِلُ رَسُولِ اللهِ (صَلَّى اللهُ عَلَيْهِ وَآلِه) وَالَّذِي نَفْسِي بِيَدِهِ يَا غُلامُ مَا اسْمُكَ قَالَ اسْمِي مُحَمَّدُ بْنُ عَلِيِّ بْنِ الْحُسَيْنِ فَأَقْبَلَ عَلَيْهِ يُقَبِّلُ رَأْسَهُ وَيَقُولُ بِأَبِي أَنْتَ وَأُمِّي أَبُوكَ رَسُولُ اللهِ (صَلَّى اللهُ عَلَيْهِ وَآلِه) يُقْرِئُكَ السَّلامَ وَيَقُولُ ذَلِكَ قَالَ فَرَجَعَ مُحَمَّدُ بْنُ عَلِيِّ بْنِ الْحُسَيْنِ إِلَى أَبِيهِ وَهُوَ ذَعِرٌ فَأَخْبَرَهُ الْخَبَرَ فَقَالَ لَهُ يَا بُنَيَّ وَقَدْ فَعَلَهَا جَابِرٌ قَالَ نَعَمْ قَالَ الْزَمْ بَيْتَكَ يَا بُنَيَّ فَكَانَ جَابِرٌ يَأْتِيهِ طَرَفَيِ النَّهَارِ وَكَانَ أَهْلُ الْمَدِينَةِ يَقُولُونَ وَا عَجَبَاهْ لِجَابِرٍ يَأْتِي هَذَا الْغُلامَ طَرَفَيِ النَّهَارِ وَهُوَ آخِرُ مَنْ بَقِيَ مِنْ أَصْحَابِ رَسُولِ اللهِ (صَلَّى اللهُ عَلَيْهِ وَآلِه) فَلَمْ يَلْبَثْ أَنْ مَضَى عَلِيُّ بن الحسين (عَلَيْهِما السَّلام) فَكَانَ مُحَمَّدُ بْنُ عَلِيٍّ يَأْتِيهِ عَلَى وَجْهِ الْكَرَامَةِ لِصُحْبَتِهِ لِرَسُولِ اللهِ (صَلَّى اللهُ عَلَيْهِ وَآلِه) قَالَ فَجَلَسَ (عَلَيْهِ السَّلام) يُحَدِّثُهُمْ عَنِ اللهِ تَبَارَكَ وَتَعَالَى فَقَالَ أَهْلُ الْمَدِينَةِ مَا رَأَيْنَا أَحَداً أَجْرَأَ مِنْ هَذَا فَلَمَّا رَأَى مَا يَقُولُونَ حَدَّثَهُمْ عَنْ رَسُولِ اللهِ (صَلَّى اللهُ عَلَيْهِ وَآلِه) فَقَالَ أَهْلُ الْمَدِينَةِ مَا رَأَيْنَا أَحَداً قَطُّ أَكْذَبَ مِنْ هَذَا يُحَدِّثُنَا عَمَّنْ لَمْ يَرَهُ فَلَمَّا رَأَى مَا يَقُولُونَ حَدَّثَهُمْ عَنْ جَابِرِ بْنِ عَبْدِ اللهِ قَالَ فَصَدَّقُوهُ وَكَانَ جَابِرُ بْنُ عَبْدِ اللهِ يَأْتِيهِ فَيَتَعَلَّمُ مِنْهُ

---

[96] *Al-Kafi, v1, ch66, h1*

A number of our people has narrated from Ahmad b. Muḥammad from Muḥammad b. Sinan from Aban b. Taghlib from abu 'AbdAllāh (عليه السلام) who has said the following. "Jabir b.'AbdAllāh al-Ansari was last surviving of the companions of the Messenger of Allāh. He was a devoted follower of us, Ahl al-Bayt. He would sit in the Mosque of the Messenger of Allāh, wearing a black turban. He would call, "O Baqir al-'Ilm, O Baqir al-'Ilm, (a person of deep knowledge)" The people of Madina would say, "Jabir is hallucinating." He would say, "No, by Allāh, I do not hallucinate, but I heard the Messenger of Allāh say, "You will soon meet a man from me whose name will be as my name and his manners would be as my manners. He will dig very deep in knowledge"' This is what maakes me say what I say." The Imam (عليه السلام) has said, "Jabir would still come and go and one day in one of the roads of Madina when passing he found a few of the school children among who Muḥammad b. 'Alī (عليه السلام) was also present (for a reason other than schooling. Imams are not heard of as attending schools). He looked at him and called him (Muhammad b. Ali) to himself. The boy came to him and then he said, "Go back." The boy went back. Then he said, "I swear by the One in Whose hand is my life, (that I see) manners as the manners of the Messenger of Allāh. O boy, What is your name?" He replied, "My name is Muḥammad b. 'Alī b. al-Husayn (عليه السلام). Jabir came forwards and began to kiss his head and say, "May Allāh take my soul and the souls of my parents in service for your cause, your great-great grandfather told me to convey his greetings and Salam to you and would say all of that. The Imam (عليه السلام) has said, "Muhammad b. 'Alī b. al-Husayn came to his father and he was anxious. He explained to him about Jabir. His father asked, "Did Jabir really do this?" He replied, "Yes, he did so." The Imam (عليه السلام) said, "My son, stay home (and do not expose yourself to the enemy because Jabir will maintain secrecy)." Jabir thereafter would come to him mornings and evenings and the people of Madina would say, "It is so strange that Jabir, the only surving companion of the Messenger of Allāh would come to a boy on both ends of the day everyday." Very shortly 'Alī b. al-Husayn (عليه السلام) passed away Muḥammad b. 'Alī (عليه السلام) would go to visit Jabir out of respect for his being a companion of the Messenger of Allāh and would speak to people from Allāh, the Most Holy, the Most High. The people of madina would say, "We have not seen anyone as bold as he is." On hearing this from them he began to speak to them from the Messenger of Allāh. The people of Madina began to say, "We have not seen a greater liar as he is because he speaks from one whom he has never seen." On hearing this from them he began to narrate to them from Jabir. The Imam (عليه السلام) has said, "They would accept what he would narrate from Jabir b. 'AbdAllāh. However, Jabir would come to him and would from him (Muhammad b. 'Alī b. al-Husayn (عليه السلام))." (ضعيف)[97]

98.

حدثنا محمد بن الحسن (رضي الله عنه)، قال: حدثنا عبد الله بن جعفر الحميري، قال: حدثنا يعقوب بن يزيد، قال: حدثنا محمد بن أبي عمير، عن أبان بن عثمان، عن الصادق جعفر بن محمد (عليهما السلام)، قال: إن رسول الله (صلى الله عليه وآله) قال ذات يوم لجابر بن عبد الله الانصاري: يا جابر، إنك ستبقى حتى تلقى ولدي محمد بن علي بن الحسين بن علي بن أبي طالب، المعروف في التوراة بالباقر فإذا لقيته فأقرئه مني السلام. فدخل جابر إلى علي بن الحسين (عليهما السلام) فوجد محمد بن علي (عليهما السلام) عنده غلاما، فقال له، يا غلام، أقبل. فأقبل، ثم قال له: أدبر. فأدبر، فقال جابر: شمائل رسول الله ورب الكعبة، ثم أقبل على علي بن الحسين (عليهما السلام) فقال له، من هذا ؟ قال: هذا ابني، وصاحب الامر بعدي محمد الباقر. فقام جابر فوقع على قدميه يقبلهما، ويقول: نفسي لنفسك الفداء يا بن رسول الله، اقبل سلام أبيك، إن رسول الله (صلى الله عليه وآله) يقرأ عليك السلام. قال: فدمعت عينا أبي جعفر (عليه السلام)، ثم قال: يا جابر، على أبي رسول الله (صلى الله عليه وآله) السلام ما دامت السماوات والارض، وعليك - يا جابر - بما بلغت السلام

Muhammad b. al-Hasan (may Allāh be pleased with him) narrated from 'Abd Allāh b. Ja'far Hameeri, who narrated from Yaqub b. Yazid from Muḥammad b. Abi Amir, from Aban b. 'Uthman, from Imam Ja'far Ṣādiq (عليه السلام) who narrates that one day Prophet Muḥammad (صلى الله عليه وآله وسلم) said to Jabir b. 'Abd Allāh Ansari "you will stay alive until you meet my son Muḥammad b. 'Alī b. Hosein b. 'Alī b. Abi Talib (عليه السلام)who is mentioned in the Torah as baqir. Give him my salutation (salam)

---

[97] *Al-Kāfi, v1, ch118, h2*

when you meet him". One day when Jabir visited Imam Zain-ul-Abideen (عليه السلام), he saw the young boy sitting next to the Imam (عليه السلام). He addressed the young boy and asked him to come closer and show his back. Then he proclaimed that by God, that young boy had the features and traits of the Prophet Muḥammad (صلى الله عليه وآله وسلم). Then he asked Imam Sajjad (عليه السلام) who the young boy was and Imam (عليه السلام) replied that he was his son and the successor to the Imamate and his name was Muḥammad Baqir (عليه السلام). Hearing this, Jabir rose up and kissed the young Imam and said "Son of Prophet (صلى الله عليه وآله وسلم), may I be taken ransom for you, accept the salutation (salam) of Prophet (صلى الله عليه وآله وسلم). He asked me to convey it to you". Imam Ja'far Ṣādiq (عليه السلام) states that his father burst into tears on hearing this and said "Jabir my salutation to my grand father until this sky and earth survives. You conveyed the salam of my grandfather to me so I convey my salam to you as well" (صحيح)[98]

99.

عِدَّةٌ مِنْ أَصْحَابِنَا عَنْ أَحْمَدَ بْنِ مُحَمَّدٍ عَنِ الْوَشَّاءِ عَنْ ثَعْلَبَةَ بْنِ مَيْمُونٍ عَنْ أَبِي مَرْيَمَ قَالَ قَالَ أَبُو جَعْفَرٍ (عَلَيْهِ السَّلام) لِسَلَمَةَ بْنِ كُهَيْلٍ وَالْحَكَمِ بْنِ عُتَيْبَةَ شَرِّقَا وَغَرِّبَا فَلا تَجِدَانِ عِلْماً صَحِيحاً إِلا شَيْئاً خَرَجَ مِنْ عِنْدِنَا أَهْلَ الْبَيْتِ

A number of our people has narrated Ahmad b. Muḥammad from al-Washsha' from Tha'laba b. Maymun from b. abu Mayam who has said the following. "Abu Ja'far (عليه السلام) said to Salma b. Kuhayl and al-Hakam b. 'Utayba, 'Easternize or westernize you two will find not find correct knowledge except that which has come to light through Ahl al-Bayt (members of the family of Prophet Muhammad)." (صحيح)[99]

---

[98] *Al-Amālī(Ṣaduq), pg. 434*

[99] *Al-Kāfi, v1, ch101, h3*

100.

مُحَمَّدُ بْنُ يَحْيَى عَنْ أَحْمَدَ بْنِ مُحَمَّدٍ عَنِ ابْنِ أَبِي عُمَيْرٍ عَنْ هِشَامِ بْنِ سَالِمٍ عَنْ أَبِي عَبْدِ اللهِ (عَلَيْهِ السَّلام) قَالَ لَمَّا حَضَرَتْ أَبِي (عَلَيْهِ السَّلام) الْوَفَاةُ قَالَ يَا جَعْفَرُ أُوصِيكَ بِأَصْحَابِي خَيْراً قُلْتُ جُعِلْتُ فِدَاكَ وَاللهِ لَادَعَنَّهُمْ وَالرَّجُلُ مِنْهُمْ يَكُونُ فِي الْمِصْرِ فَلَا يَسْأَلُ أَحَداً

Muhammad b. Yahya has narrated from Ahmad b. Muḥammad from b. abu ‘Umayr from Hisham b. Salim from abu ‘AbdAllāh (عليه السلام) who has said the following. “When my father was about to leave this world he said, “O Ja‘far, I recommend you to be good to my companions.” I then said, “May Allāh take my soul in service for your cause, by Allāh, I will educated them as such that in any city where any of them would live he would not need to ask others for knowledge (of religion).” (صحيح)[100]

101.

عَلِيُّ بْنُ إِبْرَاهِيمَ عَنْ أَبِيهِ عَنِ ابْنِ أَبِي عُمَيْرٍ عَنْ هِشَامِ بْنِ الْمُثَنَّى عَنْ سَدِيرٍ الصَّيْرَفِيِّ قَالَ سَمِعْتُ أَبَا جَعْفَرٍ (عَلَيْهِ السَّلام) يَقُولُ إِنَّ مِنْ سَعَادَةِ الرَّجُلِ أَنْ يَكُونَ لَهُ الْوَلَدُ يُعْرَفُ فِيهِ شِبْهُ خَلْقِهِ وَخُلُقِهِ وَشَمَائِلِهِ وَإِنِّي لَاعْرِفُ مِنِ ابْنِي هَذَا شِبْهَ خَلْقِي وَخُلُقِي وَشَمَائِلِي يَعْنِي أَبَا عَبْدِ اللهِ (عَلَيْهِ السَّلام)

Ali b. Ibrahim has narrated from his father from b. abu ‘Umayr from Hisham b. al-Muthanna from Sadir al-Sayrafi who has said that he heard abu Ja‘far (عليه السلام) say the following. “It is part of the success of a man to have a child who is similar to his father physically, ethically and in good characters. I do not know anyone more similar to me

---

[100] *Al-Kāfi, v1, ch70, h2*

physically, ethically and in good characters than this son of mine, (meaning thereby abu ‘AbdAllāh (عليه السلام). (حسن على الظاهر)[101]

102.

عِدَّةٌ مِنْ أَصْحَابِنَا عَنْ أَحْمَدَ بْنِ مُحَمَّدٍ عَنْ عَلِيِّ بْنِ الْحَكَمِ عَنْ طَاهِرٍ قَالَ كُنْتُ عِنْدَ ابي جعفر (عَلَيْهِ السَّلام) فَأَقْبَلَ جَعْفَرٌ (عَلَيْهِ السَّلام) فَقَالَ أَبُو جَعْفَرٍ (عَلَيْهِ السَّلام) هَذَا خَيْرُ الْبَرِيَّةِ أَوْ أَخْيَرُ

A number of our people has narrated from Ahmad b. Muḥammad from ‘Alī b. al-Hakam from Tahir who has said the following. “Once I was in the presence of abu Ja‘far (عليه السلام) when Ja‘far (عليه السلام) came. Abu Ja‘far (عليه السلام) said, “This (Ja‘far) is the best of the people or the best of best among them.” (مجهول)[102]

103.

مُحَمَّدُ بْنُ يَحْيَى عَنْ أَحْمَدَ بْنِ مُحَمَّدٍ عَنِ ابْنِ مَحْبُوبٍ عَنْ هِشَامِ بْنِ سَالِمٍ عَنْ جَابِرِ بْنِ يَزِيدَ الْجُعْفِيِّ عَنْ ابي جعفر (عَلَيْهِ السَّلام) قَالَ سُئِلَ عَنِ الْقَائِمِ (عَلَيْهِ السَّلام) فَضَرَبَ بِيَدِهِ عَلَى أَبِي عَبْدِ الله (عَلَيْهِ السَّلام) فَقَالَ هَذَا وَالله قَائِمُ آلِ مُحَمَّدٍ (صَلَّى اللهُ عَلَيْهِ وَآلِه) قَالَ عَنْبَسَةُ فَلَمَّا قُبِضَ أَبُو جَعْفَرٍ (عَلَيْهِ السَّلام) دَخَلْتُ عَلَى أَبِي عَبْدِ الله (عَلَيْهِ السَّلام) فَأَخْبَرْتُهُ بِذَلِكَ فَقَالَ صَدَقَ جَابِرٌ ثُمَّ قَالَ لَعَلَّكُمْ تَرَوْنَ أَنْ لَيْسَ كُلُّ إِمَامٍ هُوَ الْقَائِمَ بَعْدَ الامَامِ الَّذِي كَانَ قَبْلَهُ

Muhammad b. Yahya has narrated from Ahmad b. Muḥammad from b. Mahbub from Hisham b. Salim from Jabur b. Yazid al-Ju‘fiy who has said the following. “A question was asked (from abu Ja‘far (عليه السلام) about al-Qa’im (the twelfth Imam (عليه السلام). He (abu Ja‘far) tapped (at the shoulder of) abu ‘AbdAllāh (عليه السلام) and said, “This, by Allāh, is the Qa’im (one who will establish the kingdom of Allāh) of the family of Muḥammad صلى الله عليه وآله وسلم.” ‘Anbasa has said, “when abu Ja‘far passed

---

[101] *Al-Kafi, v1, ch70, h3*

[102] *Al-Kāfi, v1, ch70, h4*

away, went to see abu 'AbdAllāh (عليه السلام) and told him of what I had heard (from Jabur). The Imam (عليه السلام) said, "Jabur has spoken the truth." He then said, "You perhaps think that the every succeeding Imam after a preceding Imam is not al-Qa'im (also meaning the one who obeys and serves Allāh)." (صحيح)[103]

104.

عِدَّةٌ مِنْ أَصْحَابِنَا عَنْ أَحْمَدَ بْنِ أَبِي عَبْدِ اللَّهِ عَنْ عَبْدِ اللَّهِ بْنِ مُحَمَّدٍ النَّهِيكِيِّ عَنْ إِبْرَاهِيمَ بْنِ عَبْدِ الْحَمِيدِ قَالَ مَرَّ بِي مُعَتِّبٌ وَ مَعَهُ خَاتَمٌ فَقُلْتُ لَهُ أَيُّ شَيْءٍ هَذَا فَقَالَ خَاتَمُ أَبِي عَبْدِ اللَّهِ (عليه السلام) فَأَخَذْتُ لِأَقْرَأَ مَا فِيهِ فَإِذَا فِيهِ اللَّهُمَّ أَنْتَ ثِقَتِي فَقِنِي شَرَّ خَلْقِكَ

A number of our people have narrated from Ahmad b. abu 'Abd Allāh from 'Abd Allāh b. Muḥammad al-Nuhaykiy from Ibrahim b. 'Abd al-Hamid who has said that:Mu'attib passed by me and there was a ring with him and I asked him what it was? He replied, 'It is the ring of abu 'Abd Allāh, (عليه السلام).' I took it to read what was written on it and it said, 'O Lord, You are my protector so protect me from the mischief of Your creatures.'" (This may not be consider a Hadīth directly from an Imam, but it speaks what was written on the ring of the Imam) (موثق)[104]

105.

(Another variation of the Hadīth above)

عَنْهُ عَنْ أَحْمَدَ بْنِ مُحَمَّدِ بْنِ أَبِي نَصْرٍ قَالَ كُنْتُ عِنْدَ أَبِي الْحَسَنِ الرِّضَا (عليه السلام) فَأَخْرَجَ إِلَيْنَا خَاتَمَ أَبِي عَبْدِ اللَّهِ (عليه السلام) وَ خَاتَمَ أَبِي الْحَسَنِ (عليه السلام) وَ كَانَ عَلَى خَاتَمِ أَبِي عَبْدِ اللَّهِ (عليه السلام) أَنْتَ ثِقَتِي فَاعْصِمْنِي مِنَ النَّاسِ وَ نَقْشُ خَاتَمِ أَبِي الْحَسَنِ (عليه السلام) حَسْبِيَ اللَّهُ وَ فِيهِ وَرْدَةٌ وَ هِلَالٌ فِي أَعْلَاهُ

---

[103] *Al-Kāfi, v1, ch70, h7*

[104] *Al-Kāfi, v6, ch26, h3*

It is narrated from the narrator of the previous Hadīth from Ahmad b. Muḥammad from b. abu Nasr who has said the following: "I once was with abu al-Hassan, al-Rida', (عليه السلام), and he (the Imam) showed us the ring of abu 'Abd Allāh, and abu al-Hassan, (عليه السلام). On the ring of abu 'Abd Allāh, (عليه السلام), it said, 'You are my trusty so protect me from people. ' The engraving on the ring of abu al- Hassan, (عليه السلام), said, 'Allāh is sufficient for me' and there was a flower and a crescent on its upper part.''' (صحيح)[105]

106.

مُحَمَّدُ بْنُ يَحْيَى عَنْ أَحْمَدَ بْنِ مُحَمَّدٍ عَنِ الْحُسَيْنِ بْنِ سَعِيدٍ عَنِ النَّضْرِ بْنِ سُوَيْدٍ عَنْ يَحْيَى الْحَلَبِيِّ عَنْ مُعَلَّى بْنِ عُثْمَانَ عَنْ أَبِي بَصِيرٍ قَالَ قَالَ لِي إِنَّ الْحَكَمَ بْنَ عُتَيْبَةَ مِمَّنْ قَالَ اللهُ وَمِنَ النَّاسِ مَنْ يَقُولُ آمَنَّا بِاللهِ وَبِالْيَوْمِ الاخِرِ وَما هُمْ بِمُؤْمِنِينَ فَلْيُشَرِّقِ الْحَكَمُ وَلْيُغَرِّبْ أَمَا وَاللهِ لا يُصِيبُ الْعِلْمَ إِلا مِنْ أَهْلِ بَيْتٍ نَزَلَ عَلَيْهِمْ جَبْرَئِيلُ

Muhammad b. Yahya from Ahmad b. Muḥammad from al-Husayn b. Sa'id from al-Nadr b. Suwayd from Yahya al-Halabi from Mu'alla b. 'Uthman who has said the following. " Abu Basir said to me, 'Al-Hakam b. 'Utayba is of those people about whom Allāh has said, "Some people say, "We believe in God and the Day of Judgment," but they are not true believers." (2:8) Al-Hakam may easternize or westernize, he, by Allāh, will not find the true knowledge in no other source except from Ahl al-Bayt to whom Jibril came (with knowledge)." (صحيح)[106]

107.

---

[105] *Al-Kāfi, v6, ch26, h4*

[106] *Al-Kāfi, v1, ch101, h4*

عَلِيُّ بْنُ إِبْرَاهِيمَ عَنْ أَبِيهِ عَنِ ابْنِ أَبِي عُمَيْرٍ عَنِ الْحُسَيْنِ بْنِ أَبِي الْعَلاءِ قَالَ قَالَ أَبُو عَبْدِ الله (عَلَيْهِ السَّلام) إِنَّمَا الْوُقُوفُ عَلَيْنَا فِي الْحَلالِ وَالْحَرَامِ فَأَمَّا النُّبُوَّةُ فَلا

Ali b. Ibrahim has narrated from his father from b. abu 'Umayrfrom al-Husayn b. abu al-'Ala' from abu 'AbdAllāh (عليه السلام) who has said the following. "To refer to us (as the Divine authorities) is valid only in finding the lawful and unlawful matters. To refer to us as prophet-hood is not valid." (حسن)[107]

108.

مُحَمَّدُ بْنُ يَحْيَى عَنْ أَحْمَدَ بْنِ مُحَمَّدٍ عَنِ الْبَرْقِيِّ عَنْ أَبِي طَالِبٍ عَنْ سَدِيرٍ قَالَ قُلْتُ لابِي عَبْدِ الله (عَلَيْهِ السَّلام) إِنَّ قَوْماً يَزْعُمُونَ أَنَّكُمْ آلِهَةٌ يَتْلُونَ بِذَلِكَ عَلَيْنَا قُرْآناً وَهُوَ الَّذِي فِي السَّماءِ إِلَهٌ وَفِي الارْضِ إِلَهٌ فَقَالَ يَا سَدِيرُ سَمْعِي وَبَصَرِي وَبَشَرِي وَلَحْمِي وَدَمِي وَشَعْرِي مِنْ هَؤُلاءِ بَرَاءٌ وَبَرِئَ الله مِنْهُمْ مَا هَؤُلاءِ عَلَى دِينِي وَلا عَلَى دِينِ آبَائِي وَالله لا يَجْمَعُنِي الله وَإِيَّاهُمْ يَوْمَ الْقِيَامَةِ إِلا وَهُوَ سَاخِطٌ عَلَيْهِمْ قَالَ قُلْتُ وَعِنْدَنَا قَوْمٌ يَزْعُمُونَ أَنَّكُمْ رُسُلٌ يَقْرَءُونَ عَلَيْنَا بِذَلِكَ قُرْآناً يَا أَيُّهَا الرُّسُلُ كُلُوا مِنَ الطَّيِّباتِ وَاعْمَلُوا صالِحاً إِنِّي بِما تَعْمَلُونَ عَلِيمٌ فَقَالَ يَا سَدِيرُ سَمْعِي وَبَصَرِي وَشَعْرِي وَبَشَرِي وَلَحْمِي وَدَمِي مِنْ هَؤُلاءِ بَرَاءٌ وَبَرِئَ الله مِنْهُمْ وَرَسُولُهُ مَا هَؤُلاءِ عَلَى دِينِي وَلا عَلَى دِينِ آبَائِي وَالله لا يَجْمَعُنِي الله وَإِيَّاهُمْ يَوْمَ الْقِيَامَةِ إِلا وَهُوَ سَاخِطٌ عَلَيْهِمْ قَالَ قُلْتُ فَمَا أَنْتُمْ قَالَ نَحْنُ خُزَّانُ عِلْمِ الله نَحْنُ تَرَاجِمَةُ أَمْرِ الله نَحْنُ قَوْمٌ مَعْصُومُونَ أَمَرَ الله تَبَارَكَ وَتَعَالَى بِطَاعَتِنَا وَنَهَى عَنْ مَعْصِيَتِنَا نَحْنُ الْحُجَّةُ الْبَالِغَةُ عَلَى مَنْ دُونَ السَّمَاءِ وَفَوْقَ الارْضِ

Muhammad b. Yahya has narrated from Ahmad b. Muḥammad from al-Barqi from abu Talib from Sadir who has said that he asked abu 'AbdAllāh (عليه السلام) the following. "A certain group of people believe that you are gods. They read to us from the Qur'ān about it. And it is He Who in heaven is God and in earth is God." (43:84). The Imam (عليه السلام) said, "O Sadir, my hearing, my sight, my skin, my flesh, my blood and my hair are (all) disdain such people, and Allāh also disdains them. They do not follow my religion and the religion of my forefathers. I swear by Allāh, Allāh will not place me with them on the Day of Resurrection. The only thing from

[107] *Al-Kafi, v1, ch53, h2*

Allāh to them will be His anger." The narrator has said that he said, "Among us there is a group of people who believe that you are messenger and read to from the Holy Qur'ān. "O Messengers, eat of the good things and do righteousness; surely I know the things you do (23:51). The Imam (عليه السلام) said, "O Sadir, my hearing, my sight, my skin, my flesh, my blood and my hair are (all) disdain such people, and Allāh and Hid Messenger also disdains them. They do not follow my religion and the religion of my forefathers. Allāh will not place me with them on the Day of Judgment. The only thing from Allāh towards them will be His anger." The narrator has said that he then asked, "What are you then?" the Imam (عليه السلام) said, "We are the treasuries of the knowledge of Allāh. We are the translators of the commands of Allāh. We are infallible people. Allāh, the Most Holy, the Most High, has commanded people to obey us and prohibited them to disobey us. We are the complete Divine authority over all that is below the heavens and above the earth." (حسن)[108]

109.

مُحَمَّدُ بْنُ يَحْيَى عَنْ أَحْمَدَ بْنِ مُحَمَّدِ بْنِ عِيسَى عَنِ الْحَسَنِ بْنِ مَحْبُوبٍ عَنْ إِسْحَاقَ بْنِ غَالِبٍ عَنْ أَبِي عَبْدِ اللهِ (عَلَيْهِ السَّلام) فِي خُطْبَةٍ لَهُ يَذْكُرُ فِيهَا حَالَ الائِمَّةِ (عَلَيْهِ السَّلام) وَصِفَاتِهِمْ إِنَّ اللهَ عَزَّ وَجَلَّ أَوْضَحَ بِأَئِمَّةِ الْهُدَى مِنْ أَهْلِ بَيْتِ نَبِيِّنَا عَنْ دِينِهِ وَأَبْلَجَ بِهِمْ عَنْ سَبِيلِ مِنْهَاجِهِ وَفَتَحَ بِهِمْ عَنْ بَاطِنِ يَنَابِيعِ عِلْمِهِ فَمَنْ عَرَفَ مِنْ أُمَّةِ مُحَمَّدٍ (صَلَّى اللهُ عَلَيْهِ وَآلِهِ) وَاجِبَ حَقِّ إِمَامِهِ وَجَدَ طَعْمَ حَلاوَةِ إِيمَانِهِ وَعَلِمَ فَضْلَ طُلاوَةِ إِسْلامِهِ لانَّ اللهَ تَبَارَكَ وَتَعَالَى نَصَبَ الامَامَ عَلَماً لِخَلْقِهِ وَجَعَلَهُ حُجَّةً عَلَى أَهْلِ مَوَادِّهِ وَعَالَمِهِ وَأَلْبَسَهُ اللهُ تَاجَ الْوَقَارِ وَغَشَّاهُ مِنْ نُورِ الْجَبَّارِ يَمُدُّ بِسَبَبٍ إِلَى السَّمَاءِ لا يَنْقَطِعُ عَنْهُ مَوَادُّهُ وَلا يُنَالُ مَا عِنْدَ اللهِ إِلا بِجِهَةِ أَسْبَابِهِ وَلا يَقْبَلُ اللهُ أَعْمَالَ الْعِبَادِ إِلا بِمَعْرِفَتِهِ فَهُوَ عَالِمٌ بِمَا يَرِدُ عَلَيْهِ مِنْ مُلْتَبِسَاتِ الدُّجَى وَمُعَمِّيَاتِ السُّنَنِ وَمُشَبِّهَاتِ الْفِتَنِ فَلَمْ يَزَلِ اللهُ تَبَارَكَ وَتَعَالَى يَخْتَارُهُمْ لِخَلْقِهِ مِنْ وُلْدِ الْحُسَيْنِ (عَلَيْهِ السَّلام) مِنْ عَقِبِ كُلِّ إِمَامٍ يَصْطَفِيهِمْ لِذَلِكَ وَيَجْتَبِيهِمْ وَيَرْضَى بِهِمْ لِخَلْقِهِ وَيَرْتَضِيهِمْ كُلَّ مَا مَضَى مِنْهُمْ إِمَامٌ نَصَبَ لِخَلْقِهِ مِنْ عَقِبِهِ إِمَاماً عَلَماً بَيِّناً وَهَادِياً نَيِّراً وَإِمَاماً قَيِّماً وَحُجَّةً عَالِماً أَئِمَّةً مِنَ اللهِ يَهْدُونَ بِالْحَقِّ وَبِهِ يَعْدِلُونَ حُجَجُ اللهِ وَدُعَاتُهُ وَرُعَاتُهُ عَلَى خَلْقِهِ يَدِينُ بِهَدْيِهِمُ الْعِبَادُ وَتَسْتَهِلُّ بِنُورِهِمُ الْبِلادُ وَيَنْمُو بِبَرَكَتِهِمُ التِّلادُ جَعَلَهُمُ اللهُ حَيَاةً لِلانَامِ وَمَصَابِيحَ لِلظَّلامِ وَمَفَاتِيحَ لِلْكَلامِ وَدَعَائِمَ لِلاسْلامِ جَرَتْ بِذَلِكَ فِيهِمْ مَقَادِيرُ اللهِ عَلَى مَحْتُومِهَا فَالامَامُ هُوَ الْمُنْتَجَبُ الْمُرْتَضَى وَالْهَادِي

---

[108] *Al-Kafi, v1, ch53, h6*

الْمُنْتَجى وَالْقَائِمُ الْمُرْتَجى اصْطَفَاهُ اللهُ بِذَلِكَ وَاصْطَنَعَهُ عَلى عَيْنِهِ فِي الذَّرِّ حِينَ ذَرَأَهُ وَفِي الْبَرِيَّةِ حِينَ بَرَأَهُ ظِلاً قَبْلَ خَلْقِ نَسَمَةٍ عَنْ يَمِينِ عَرْشِهِ مَحْبُوّاً بِالْحِكْمَةِ فِي عِلْمِ الْغَيْبِ عِنْدَهُ اخْتَارَهُ بِعِلْمِهِ وَانْتَجَبَهُ لِطُهْرِهِ بَقِيَّةً مِنْ آدَمَ (عَلَيْهِ السَّلام) وَخِيَرَةً مِنْ ذُرِّيَّةِ نُوحٍ وَمُصْطَفًى مِنْ آلِ إِبْرَاهِيمَ وَسُلالَةً مِنْ إِسْمَاعِيلَ وَصَفْوَةً مِنْ عِتْرَةِ مُحَمَّدٍ (صَلَّى اللهُ عَلَيْهِ وَآلِهِ) لَمْ يَزَلْ مَرْعِيّاً بِعَيْنِ اللهِ يَحْفَظُهُ وَيَكْلَؤُهُ بِسِتْرِهِ مَطْرُوداً عَنْهُ حَبَائِلُ إِبْلِيسَ وَجُنُودِهِ مَدْفُوعاً عَنْهُ وُقُوبُ الْغَوَاسِقِ وَنُفُوثُ كُلِّ فَاسِقٍ مَصْرُوفاً عَنْهُ قَوَارِفُ السُّوءِ مُبْرَأً مِنَ الْعَاهَاتِ مَحْجُوباً عَنِ الافَاتِ مَعْصُوماً مِنَ الزَّلاتِ مَصُوناً عَنِ الْفَوَاحِشِ كُلِّهَا مَعْرُوفاً بِالْحِلْمِ وَالْبِرِّ فِي يَفَاعِهِ مَنْسُوباً إِلَى الْعَفَافِ وَالْعِلْمِ وَالْفَضْلِ عِنْدَ انْتِهَائِهِ مُسْنَداً إِلَيْهِ أَمْرُ وَالِدِهِ صَامِتاً عَنِ الْمَنْطِقِ فِي حَيَاتِهِ فَإِذَا انْقَضَتْ مُدَّةُ وَالِدِهِ إِلَى أَنِ انْتَهَتْ بِهِ مَقَادِيرُ اللهِ إِلَى مَشِيئَتِهِ وَجَاءَتِ الارَادَةُ مِنَ اللهِ فِيهِ إِلَى مَحَبَّتِهِ وَبَلَغَ مُنْتَهَى مُدَّةِ وَالِدِهِ (عَلَيْهِ السَّلام) فَمَضَى وَصَارَ أَمْرُ اللهِ إِلَيْهِ مِنْ بَعْدِهِ وَقَلَّدَهُ دِينَهُ وَجَعَلَهُ الْحُجَّةَ عَلَى عِبَادِهِ وَقَيِّمَهُ فِي بِلادِهِ وَأَيَّدَهُ بِرُوحِهِ وَآتَاهُ عِلْمَهُ وَأَنْبَأَهُ فَصْلَ بَيَانِهِ وَاسْتَوْدَعَهُ سِرَّهُ وَانْتَدَبَهُ لِعَظِيمِ أَمْرِهِ وَأَنْبَأَهُ فَضْلَ بَيَانِ عِلْمِهِ وَنَصَبَهُ عَلَماً لِخَلْقِهِ وَجَعَلَهُ حُجَّةً عَلَى أَهْلِ عَالَمِهِ وَضِيَاءً لاهْلِ دِينِهِ وَالْقَيِّمَ عَلَى عِبَادِهِ رَضِيَ اللهُ بِهِ إِمَاماً لَهُمُ اسْتَوْدَعَهُ سِرَّهُ وَاسْتَحْفَظَهُ عِلْمَهُ وَاسْتَخْبَأَهُ حِكْمَتَهُ وَاسْتَرْعَاهُ لِدِينِهِ وَانْتَدَبَهُ لِعَظِيمِ أَمْرِهِ وَأَحْيَا بِهِ مَنَاهِجَ سَبِيلِهِ وَفَرَائِضَهُ وَحُدُودَهُ فَقَامَ بِالْعَدْلِ عِنْدَ تَحَيُّرِ أَهْلِ الْجَهْلِ وَتَحْيِيرِ أَهْلِ الْجَدَلِ بِالنُّورِ السَّاطِعِ وَالشِّفَاءِ النَّافِعِ بِالْحَقِّ الابْلَجِ وَالْبَيَانِ اللائِحِ مِنْ كُلِّ مَخْرَجٍ عَلَى طَرِيقِ الْمَنْهَجِ الَّذِي مَضَى عَلَيْهِ الصَّادِقُونَ مِنْ آبَائِهِ (عَلَيْهِم السَّلام) فَلَيْسَ يَجْهَلُ حَقَّ هَذَا الْعَالِمِ إِلا شَقِيٌّ وَلا يَجْحَدُهُ إِلا غَوِيٌّ وَلا؛"11 يَصُدُّ عَنْهُ إِلا جَرِيٌّ عَلَى اللهِ جَلَّ وَعَلا

Muhammad b. Yahya has narrated from Ahmad b. Muḥammad b. ’Isa from al-Hasan b. Mahbub from Ishaq b. Ghalib from abu ’AbdAllāh (عليه السلام) who has described the condition of the Imams (عليه السلام) and their attributes in one of his sermons. “Allāh, the Most Holy, the Most High, has explained His religion through the Imams of (true) guidance from the family of our Prophet the Ahlul Bayt (عليه السلام), and has clear through them the path of His system and plan. He has opened through them the inside of the springs of His knowledge. Whoever of the followers of Muḥammad has recognized his obligation towards the rights of his Imam he has realized the taste of the sweetness of his faith and the superior beauty of his Islam. It is because Allāh, the Most Holy, the Most High, has appointed the Imam the torchbearer for His creatures and authority over those who receive His blessings of His world. He has crowned him with dignity and has encompassed him in the Light of His Omnipotence. He extends a means to the heavens. The blessings do not discontinue from him. Nothing from what is with Allāh is achieved except through its right means. Allāh does not accept the good deeds of His servants without one’s recognition of the Imam (عليه السلام). The

Imam (عليه السلام) knows how to sort out the dark confusing matters and whatever obscures the Sunnah (tradition of the Holy Prophet and the confounding matters in mischievous conditions. Allāh, the Most Holy, the Most High, has always been choosing the Imams from the descendants of al-Husayn (عليه السلام) one after the other Imam. He would select and choose them for the leadership of His creatures delightfully and well satisfied with them. Whenever one Imam would leave this world He would appoint for His creatures his successor as a clear beacon and a shining guide, a guarding leader, a knowledgeable Divine authority. The Imams from Allāh guide people with the truth and with the truth they judge. They are Allāh's authority calling people to Him and as shepherds of His creatures. With their guidance people follow the religion and from them the land receive light. Through their holiness the bounties increase. Allāh has made them life for the people and the torches in the darkness, the keys to communication and the strongholds for Islam. Thus, has the measures of Allāh continued in them towards His final decision. "The Imam is the outstanding amicable person, the most trusted guide and the guardian who can make hopes come true. Allāh has chosen him with such distinctions. He choose him as such in the realm when all things were in the form of particles in the instance that He made him made him a particle and in the realm in which all things were designed as He had designed him (well-protected) as a shadow??, before He made the organisms, on the right side of His throne, gifted with wisdom in the unseen knowledge with Him. He chose him in His knowledge and granted him outstanding nobility for his purity. He is a heir of Adam, the best one among the descendents, the chosen one of the family of Abraham, a descendent of Ismael and of the most preferred ones in the family of Prophet Muḥammad صلى الله عليه وآله وسلم. He has always been looked after by the watchful eyes of Allāh Who would provide him security and guard him with His shield, well protected against the evil nets of Satan and his armies. He is well defended against the approaching dark nights and the false accusations of the evil doers. All wickedness is kept away from him and he kept safe against all forms of defects and flaws. He is veiled against all the scourge and infallible in the case of sins. He is kept safe and sound against all indecencies. He is well known for his forbearance and virtuousness in the early days of his life and great knowledge, chastity and excellence are ascribed to him towards the end of his life. The task of Imamt (leadership) of his father rests with him while in the lifetime of his father he remained silent. When the time of the Imamat (leadership) of his father ends it is the time when the measures of Allāh ends up with him to His wish, the will from Allāh brings him to His love, thus, the end of the Imamat of his father comes and he passes away. The authority from Allāh shifts to him after his father. He then is made in charge of His religion and the Divine authority over His servants, the guardian over His lands, supported with His spirit and is given of His knowledge. He raises him as a beacon for His creatures, makes him to have His authority over the people of his world and as the light for the people of His religion and a guardian for His servants. Allāh will agree to have him as Imam of the people, entrust him with His secret, makes him a safe-keeper of His knowledge, and makes him to hide His wisdom in him. He protects him for His religion calls up on him to serve His great task, revives through him the phases of His system (of religion) and the obligations in His laws. The Imam then enforces justice, when the people of ignorance are confused and the disputing and quarrelling people are frustrated, with shining light, the beneficial cure and radiant truth. He would do so with clear explanations of all aspects and just in the manner and practice his truthful father and forefathers would do before him. No one would ignore the rights of such scholar except the wicked ones. No one would struggle against him except those who have strayed away from the right path. No one would keep away from him except those who keep a bold face against Allāh, the Most Holy, the Most High. (صحيح)[109]

110.

حدثنا أبي رضي الله عنه قال: حدثنا سعد بن عبد الله، عن يعقوب بن يزيد، عن محمد بن أبي عمير، عن غير واحد، عن أبي عبد الله عليه السلام قال: السبت لنا، والاحد لشيعتنا، والاثنين لاعدائنا، والثلثاء لبني امية، والاربعاء يوم شرب الدواء، والخميس تقضى فيه الحوائج، والجمعة للتنظف والتطيب، وهو عيد المسلمين وهو أفضل من الفطر والاضحى، ويوم الغدير أفضل الاعياد، وهو ثامن عشر من ذي الحجة

[109] Al-Kāfi, v1, ch15, h2

وكان يوم الجمعة، ويخرج قائمنا أهل البيت يوم الجمعة، ويقوم القيامة يوم الجمعة، وما من عمل يوم الجمعة أفضل من الصلاة على محمد وآله

(The compiler of the book narrated) that his father - may God be pleased with him - narrated that Sa'ed b. 'Abd Allāh quoted Yaqoob b. Yazid, on the authority of Muḥammad b. Abi Umayr, on the authority of some other people that Aba 'Abd Allāh as-Ṣādiq (عليه السلام) said, "Saturdays are for us. Sundays are for our followers. Mondays are for our enemies. Tuesdays are for the Umayyads. Wednesdays are the days for taking medicine. Thursdays are for taking care of your needs. Fridays are for leaning up and putting on perfume. Fridays are the holidays for the Muslims. They are even better than the Eid ul-Fitr and Eid ul-Azha. The Day of Eid ul-Qadir is the noblest of the holidays. It is on the eighteenth day of the month of Dhul-Hijja. Our Riser (عجل الله تعالى فرجه) - the Riser (عجل الله تعالى فرجه) from the Members of the Holy Household - will rise on a Friday. The Resurrection Day will be on a Friday. No deeds are better on Fridays than sending God's Blessings upon Muḥammad (صلى الله عليه وآله وسلم) and his Household." (صحيح)[110]

111.

عَنْهُ عَنْ أَحْمَدَ عَنْ عَلِيِّ بْنِ الْمُسْتَوْرِدِ النَّخَعِيِّ عَمَّنْ رَوَاهُ عَنْ أَبِي عَبْدِ اللَّهِ (عليه السلام) قَالَ إِنَّ مِنَ الْمَلَائِكَةِ الَّذِينَ فِي سَمَاءِ الدُّنْيَا لَيَطَّلِعُونَ عَلَى الْوَاحِدِ وَ الِاثْنَيْنِ وَ الثَّلَاثَةِ وَ هُمْ يَذْكُرُونَ فَضْلَ آلِ مُحَمَّدٍ (عليهم السلام) فَيَقُولُونَ أَ مَا تَرَوْنَ هَؤُلَاءِ فِي قِلَّتِهِمْ وَ كَثْرَةِ عَدُوِّهِمْ يَصِفُونَ فَضْلَ آلِ مُحَمَّدٍ (عليهم السلام) فَتَقُولُ الطَّائِفَةُ الْأُخْرَى مِنَ الْمَلَائِكَةِ ذَلِكَ فَضْلُ اللَّهِ يُؤْتِيهِ مَنْ يَشَاءُ وَ اللَّهُ ذُو الْفَضْلِ الْعَظِيمِ

From him, from Ahmad, from 'Alī b. Al-Mustawarad Al-Nakha'ie, from the one who reported it: Abu 'AbdAllāh (عليه السلام) has said; 'From the Angels who are in the sky of the world, they come to one, and two, and three when they are mentioning the virtues of the Progeny of Messenger of Allāh (صلى الله عليه وآله وسلم), so they say: 'But

[110] *Al-Khiṣāl, ch49, h5*

did you see those in their scarcity (of numbers) and the abundance of their enemies, describ.g the virtues of the Progeny of Messenger of Allāh (صلى الله عليه وآله وسلم)?' So the other group of Angels say: "[62:4] That is Allāh's grace; He grants it to whom He pleases, and Allāh is the Lord of mighty grace". (موثق)[111]

112.

مُحَمَّدُ بْنُ يَحْيَى عَنْ أَحْمَدَ بْنِ مُحَمَّدٍ عَنْ مُحَمَّدِ بْنِ إِسْمَاعِيلَ عَنْ أَبِي إِسْمَاعِيلَ السَّرَّاجِ عَنِ ابْنِ مُسْكَانَ عَنْ أَبِي بَصِيرٍ قَالَ قَالَ أَبُو الْحَسَنِ الأَوَّلُ (عَلَيْهِ السَّلام) إِنَّهُ لَمَّا حَضَرَ أَبِيَ الْوَفَاةُ قَالَ لِي يَا بُنَيَّ إِنَّهُ لاَ يَنَالُ شَفَاعَتَنَا مَنِ اسْتَخَفَّ بِالصَّلاَةِ

Muhammad b. Yahya has narrated from Ahmad b. Muḥammad from Muḥammad b. 'Isma'il from abu 'Isma'il al-Sarraj from b. Muskan from abu Basir who has said the following: "Abu al-Hassan the first, (عليه السلام), has said, 'When my father was about to pass away he said, "My son, those who consider Salah (prayers) insignificant will not be able to benefit from our intercession. (صحيح على الظاهر)[112]

113.

عِدَّةٌ مِنْ أَصْحَابِنَا عَنْ أَحْمَدَ بْنِ مُحَمَّدٍ عَنْ عَلِيِّ بْنِ سَيْفٍ عَنْ أَبِيهِ عَنْ عَمْرِو بْنِ حُرَيْثٍ قَالَ سَأَلْتُ أَبَا عَبْدِ اللهِ (عَلَيْهِ السَّلام) عَنْ قَوْلِ اللهِ كَشَجَرَةٍ طَيِّبَةٍ أَصْلُها ثابِتٌ وَفَرْعُها فِي السَّماءِ قَالَ فَقَالَ رَسُولُ اللهِ (صَلَّى اللهُ عَلَيْهِ وَآلِه) أَصْلُهَا وَأَمِيرُ الْمُؤْمِنِينَ (عَلَيْهِ السَّلام) فَرْعُهَا وَالائِمَّةُ مِنْ ذُرِّيَّتِهِمَا أَغْصَانُهَا وَعِلْمُ الائِمَّةِ ثَمَرَتُهَا وَشِيعَتُهُمُ الْمُؤْمِنُونَ وَرَقُهَا هَلْ فِيهَا فَضْلٌ قَالَ قُلْتُ لا وَاللهِ قَالَ وَاللهِ إِنَّ الْمُؤْمِنَ لَيُولَدُ فَتُورِقُ وَرَقَةٌ فِيهَا وَإِنَّ الْمُؤْمِنَ لَيَمُوتُ فَتَسْقُطُ وَرَقَةٌ مِنْهَا

---

[111] *Al-Kāfi, v8, ch520*

[112] *Al-Kāfi, v3, ch2, h15*

A number of our people has narrated from Ahmad b. Muḥammad from ʿAlī b. Sayf from his father from ʿAmr b. Harith who has said the following. "I asked abu ʿAbdAllāh (عليه السلام) about the words of Allāh. ". . a blessed tree which has firm roots and branches rising up into the sky." (14:24) The Imam (عليه السلام) said that the The Holy Prophet (s.a) said, "The root is Amir al-Mu'minin ʿAlī (عليه السلام) and the branches are the Imams from their (Amir al-Mu'minin (عليه السلام) and The Holy Prophet (s.a) descendants and the knowledge of Imams stand for the fruits. Their faithful followers represent the leaves of such tree." The Imam (عليه السلام) asked, "Is there anything else in the tree?" I said, "No, there is nothing else there. The Imam (عليه السلام) then said, "By Allāh, when a faithful is given a child a leave grows in the tree and when a faithful dies a leave falls off the tree." (صحيح)[113]

Virtues of Imam Abul Hasan Mūsā b. Ja'far al-Kadhim (عليه السلام)

114.

عِدَّةٌ مِنْ أَصْحَابِنَا عَنْ أَحْمَدَ بْنِ مُحَمَّدٍ عَنْ عَلِيِّ بْنِ الْحَكَمِ عَنْ أَبِي أَيُّوبَ الْخَزَّازِ عَنْ ثُبَيْتٍ عَنْ مُعَاذِ بْنِ كَثِيرٍ عَنْ أَبِي عَبْدِ اللهِ (عَلَيْهِ السَّلام) قَالَ قُلْتُ لَهُ أَسْأَلُ اللهَ الَّذِي رَزَقَ أَبَاكَ مِنْكَ هَذِهِ الْمَنْزِلَةَ أَنْ يَرْزُقَكَ مِنْ عَقِبِكَ قَبْلَ الْمَمَاتِ مِثْلَهَا فَقَالَ قَدْ فَعَلَ اللهُ ذَلِكَ قَالَ قُلْتُ مَنْ هُوَ جُعِلْتُ فِدَاكَ فَأَشَارَ إِلَى الْعَبْدِ الصَّالِحِ وَهُوَ رَاقِدٌ فَقَالَ هَذَا الرَّاقِدُ وَهُوَ غُلَامٌ

A number of our people has narrated Ahmad b. Muḥammad from ʿAlī b. al-Hakam from abu Ayyub al-Khazzaz from Thubayt from that Mu'dh b. Kathir who has said the following. "I said to abu ʿAbdAllāh (عليه السلام), 'I pray to Allāh who has granted your father because of you such a high position to grant you also such high position through your successor before you will leave this world." He then said, "Allāh has already granted such favor." The narrator has said that he then asked the Imam (عليه السلام), "Who is he, 'May Allāh take my soul in service for your cause?" He pointed

---

[113] *Al-Kafi, v1, ch108, h78*

out towards the pious servant (of Allāh), who was asleep, saying this man(Imam Musa) who is asleep." He was a young boy." (حسن)[114]

115.

عَلِيُّ بْنُ إِبْرَاهِيمَ عَنْ أَبِيهِ عَنِ ابْنِ أَبِي نَجْرَانَ عَنْ صَفْوَانَ الْجَمَّالِ عَنْ أَبِي عَبْدِ اللهِ (عَلَيْهِ السَّلام) قَالَ قَالَ لَهُ مَنْصُورُ بْنُ حَازِمٍ بِأَبِي أَنْتَ وَأُمِّي إِنَّ الانْفُسَ يُغْدَى عَلَيْهَا وَيُرَاحُ فَإِذَا كَانَ ذَلِكَ فَمَنْ فَقَالَ أَبُو عَبْدِ اللهِ (عَلَيْهِ السَّلام) إِذَا كَانَ ذَلِكَ فَهُوَ صَاحِبُكُمْ وَضَرَبَ بِيَدِهِ عَلَى مَنْكِبِ أَبِي الْحَسَنِ (عَلَيْهِ السَّلام) الايْمَنِ فِي مَا أَعْلَمُ وَهُوَ يَوْمَئِذٍ خُمَاسِيٌّ وَعَبْدُ اللهِ بْنُ جَعْفَرٍ جَالِسٌ مَعَنَا

Ali b. Ibrahim has narrated from his father from b. abu Najran from Safwan al-Jammal from abu 'AbdAllāh (عليه السلام). Safwan has said the following. "Mansur b. Hazim said to him, 'May Allāh take my soul in service for your cause, the (human) souls pass through mornings and evenings if that (death for you) comes then who (will be the Imam)?" Abu 'AbdAllāh (عليه السلام) then said, "If that happens then he is your companion." He tapped the right shoulder of abu al-Hassan with his hand, as I know. He was five (feet tall or years old) at that time and 'AbdAllāh b. Ja'far was also present with us." (حسن)[115]

116.

مُحَمَّدُ بْنُ يَحْيَى وَأَحْمَدُ بْنُ إِدْرِيسَ عَنْ مُحَمَّدِ بْنِ عَبْدِ الْجَبَّارِ عَنِ الْحَسَنِ بْنِ الْحُسَيْنِ عَنْ أَحْمَدَ بْنِ الْحَسَنِ الْمِيثَمِيِّ عَنْ فَيْضِ بْنِ الْمُخْتَارِ فِي حَدِيثٍ طَوِيلٍ فِي أَمْرِ أَبِي الْحَسَنِ (عَلَيْهِ السَّلام) حَتَّى قَالَ لَهُ أَبُو عَبْدِ اللهِ (عَلَيْهِ السَّلام) هُوَ صَاحِبُكَ الَّذِي سَأَلْتَ عَنْهُ فَقُمْ إِلَيْهِ فَأَقِرَّ لَهُ بِحَقِّهِ فَقُمْتُ حَتَّى قَبَّلْتُ رَأْسَهُ وَيَدَهُ وَدَعَوْتُ اللهَ عَزَّ وَجَلَّ لَهُ فَقَالَ أَبُو عَبْدِ اللهِ (عَلَيْهِ السَّلام) أَمَا إِنَّهُ لَمْ يُؤْذَنْ لَنَا فِي أَوَّلَ مِنْكَ قَالَ قُلْتُ جُعِلْتُ فِدَاكَ فَأُخْبِرُ بِهِ أَحَداً فَقَالَ نَعَمْ أَهْلَكَ وَوُلْدَكَ وَكَانَ مَعِي أَهْلِي وَوُلْدِي وَرُفَقَائِي وَكَانَ يُونُسُ بْنُ ظَبْيَانَ مِنْ رُفَقَائِي

[114] *Al-Kāfi, v1, ch71, h2*

[115] *Al-Kāfi, v1, ch71, h6*

فَلَمَّا أَخْبَرْتُهُمْ حَمِدُوا اللهَ عَزَّ وَجَلَّ وَقَالَ يُونُسُ لا وَاللهِ حَتَّى أَسْمَعَ ذَلِكَ مِنْهُ وَكَانَتْ بِهِ عَجَلَةٌ فَخَرَجَ فَاتَّبَعْتُهُ فَلَمَّا انْتَهَيْتُ إِلَى الْبَابِ سَمِعْتُ أَبَا عَبْدِ اللهِ (عَلَيْهِ السَّلام) يَقُولُ لَهُ وَقَدْ سَبَقَنِي إِلَيْهِ يَا يُونُسُ الامْرُ كَمَا قَالَ لَكَ فَيْضٌ قَالَ فَقَالَ سَمِعْتُ وَأَطَعْتُ فَقَالَ لِي أَبُو عَبْدِ اللهِ (عَلَيْهِ السَّلام) خُذْهُ إِلَيْكَ يَا فَيْضُ

Muhammad b. Yahya and Ahmad b. Idris have narrated from Muḥammad b. 'Abd al-Jabbar from al-Hassan b. al-Husayn from Ahmad b. al-Hassan al-Maythami from Fayd b. al-Mukhtar, in a lengthy Hadīth on the affair of abu al-Hassan (عليه السلام). In it abu 'AbdAllāh (عليه السلام) has said to the narrator. "He is your Master of who you asked. Stand up for him and acknowledge his rights." I then stood up and kissed his head and hand and prayed to Allāh, the Most Holy, the Most High, for him." Abu 'AbdAllāh (عليه السلام) then said, "Keep in mind that permission is not given to us to speak about him to anyone before you." The narrator has said that he then said to the Imam (عليه السلام), "'May Allāh take my soul in service for your cause, can I inform any one about him?" The Imam (عليه السلام) said, "Yes, you may inform your family (wife) and sons." With me there were my family (wife), sons and friends and of my friends there was Yunus b. al_Zabyan. When I informed them they all thanked Allāh, the Most Holy, the Most High. Yunus said, "No, by Allāh, I must hear that from him. He was in a hurry. He went and I followed him. When I reached the door I heard abu 'AbdAllāh (عليه السلام) say to him,- he had reached him before I-, "What Fayd has said to you is true." The narrator has said that he (Yunus) then said, "I have heard it and I have obeyed." Abu 'AbdAllāh (عليه السلام) then said, "Take him with you, O Fayd." (موثق)[116]

117.

أَحْمَدُ بْنُ إِدْرِيسَ عَنْ مُحَمَّدِ بْنِ عَبْدِ الْجَبَّارِ عَنْ صَفْوَانَ عَنِ ابْنِ مُسْكَانَ عَنْ سُلَيْمَانَ بْنِ خَالِدٍ قَالَ دَعَا أَبُو عَبْدِ اللهِ (عَلَيْهِ السَّلام) أَبَا الْحَسَنِ (عَلَيْهِ السَّلام) يَوْماً وَنَحْنُ عِنْدَهُ فَقَالَ لَنَا عَلَيْكُمْ بِهَذَا فَهُوَ وَاللهِ صَاحِبُكُمْ بَعْدِي

[116] *Al-Kāfi, v1, ch71, h9*

Ahmad b. Idris has narrated from Muḥammad b. 'Abd al-Jabbar from Safwan from b. Muskan from Sulayman b. Khalid who has said the following. "Abu 'AbdAllāh (عليه السلام) one day called abu al-Hassan (عليه السلام) while we were in his presence and said to us, "You must take hold of this man. He, by Allāh, will be your Master after me." (صحيح)[117]

118.

عِدَّةٌ مِنْ أَصْحَابِنَا عَنْ أَحْمَدَ بْنِ مُحَمَّدٍ عَنْ عَلِيِّ بْنِ الْحَكَمِ عَنْ عَبْدِ اللهِ بْنِ الْمُغِيرَةِ قَالَ مَرَّ الْعَبْدُ الصَّالِحُ بِامْرَأَةٍ بِمِنًى وَهِيَ تَبْكِي وَصِبْيَانُهَا حَوْلَهَا يَبْكُونَ وَقَدْ مَاتَتْ لَهَا بَقَرَةٌ فَدَنَا مِنْهَا ثُمَّ قَالَ لَهَا مَا يُبْكِيكِ يَا أَمَةَ اللهِ قَالَتْ يَا عَبْدَ اللهِ إِنَّ لَنَا صِبْيَاناً يَتَامَى وَكَانَتْ لِي بَقَرَةٌ مَعِيشَتِي وَمَعِيشَةُ صِبْيَانِي كَانَ مِنْهَا وَقَدْ مَاتَتْ وَبَقِيتُ مُنْقَطَعاً بِي وَبِوُلْدِي لا حِيلَةَ لَنَا فَقَالَ يَا أَمَةَ اللهِ هَلْ لَكِ أَنْ أُحْيِيَهَا لَكِ فَأُلْهِمَتْ أَنْ قَالَتْ نَعَمْ يَا عَبْدَ اللهِ فَتَنَحَّى وَصَلَّى رَكْعَتَيْنِ ثُمَّ رَفَعَ يَدَهُ هُنَيْئَةً وَحَرَّكَ شَفَتَيْهِ ثُمَّ قَامَ فَصَوَّتَ بِالْبَقَرَةِ فَنَخَسَهَا نَخْسَةً أَوْ ضَرَبَهَا بِرِجْلِهِ فَاسْتَوَتْ عَلَى الارْضِ قَائِمَةً فَلَمَّا نَظَرَتِ الْمَرْأَةُ إِلَى الْبَقَرَةِ صَاحَتْ وَقَالَتْ عِيسَى ابْنُ مَرْيَمَ وَرَبِّ الْكَعْبَةِ فَخَالَطَ النَّاسَ وَصَارَ بَيْنَهُمْ وَمَضَى (عَلَيْهِ السَّلام)

Some of our companions, from Ahmad b. Muḥammad from 'Alī b. al-Hakam from 'AbdAllāh b. al-Mughira who has said the following. "The pious servant of Allāh passed in Mina by a woman who was weeping and her children around her also were weeping because her cow was dead. He went close to her and asked, "What has caused you t weep O slave of Allāh ?" She said, "O servant of Allāh, we have orphan children. Our cow that was them means for our living has died and we are left without any means of living." He said, "Will you be happy if will bring your cow back to kife?" She was just inspired to say, "Yes, O servant of Allāh I will be very happy.." He stepped aside and said two Rak'at prayers. He then raised his hands gently has said the following and moved his lips. He then stood up and called the cow to get up. He pushed the cow with his foot or a staff and she was up straight and

---

[117] *Al-Kāfi, v1, ch71, h12*

standing. When the woman looked at the cow she cried and said, "Jesus, son of Mary, I swear by the Lord of the Ka'ba. Many people gathered around and he disappeared among them and went." (صحيح)[118]

119.

حَدَّثَنا مُحَمَّدُ بْنُ الحَسَنِ بْنِ أَحْمَدَ بْنِ الوَلِيدِ رَضِيَ اللهُ عَنْهُ قالَ: حَدَّثَنا مُحَمَّدُ بْنُ الحَسَنِ الصَّفَّارُ وَسَعْدُ بْنُ عَبْدِاللهِ جَمِيعاً، عَنْ أَحْمَدَ بْنِ مُحَمَّدِ بْنِ عِيسَى، عَنِ الحَسَنِ بْنِ عَلِيِّ بْنِ يَقْطِينٍ، عَنْ أَخِيهِ الحُسَيْنِ، عَنْ أَبِيهِ عَلِيِّ بْنِ يَقْطِينٍ، قالَ: اسْتَدْعَى الرَّشِيدُ رَجُلاً يُبْطِلُ بِهِ أَمْرَ أَبِي الحَسَنِ مُوسَى بْنِ جَعْفَرٍ عَلَيْهِمَا السَّلامُ يُخْجِلُهُ وَيَقْطَعُهُ فِي المَجْلِسِ، فَانْتَدَبَ لَهُ رَجُلٌ مُعَزِّمٌ فَلَمَّا أُحْضِرَتِ المائِدَةُ عَمِلَ ناموساً عَلَى الْخُبْزِ، فَكانَ كُلَّما رامَ أَبُو الحَسَنِ تَناوُلَ رَغِيفٍ مِنَ الْخُبْزِ طارَ مِنْ بَيْنِ يَدَيْهِ وَاسْتَفَزَّ مِنْ هارُونَ الفَرَحُ وَالضَّحِكُ لِذلِكَ فَلَمْ يَلْبَثْ أَبُو الحَسَنِ عَلَيْهِ السَّلامُ أَنْ رَفَعَ رَأْسَهُ إِلَى أَسَدٍ مُصَوَّرٍ عَلَى بَعْضِ السُّتُورِ فَقالَ لَهُ: يا أَسَدُ خُذْ عَدُوَّ اللهِ، قالَ: فَوَثَبَتْ تِلْكَ الصُّورَةُ كَأَعْظَمِ ما يَكُونُ مِنَ السِّباعِفافْتَرَسَتْ ذلِكَ المُعَزِّمَ، فَخَرَّ هارُونُ وَنُدَماؤُهُ عَلَى وُجُوهِهِمْ مَغْشِيّاً عَلَيْهِمْ فَطارَتْ عُقُولُهُمْ خَوْفاً مِنْ هَوْلِ ما رَأَوْهُ فَلَمَّا أَفاقُوا مِنْ ذلِكَ، قالَ هارُونُ لِأَبِي الحَسَنِ عَلَيْهِ السَّلامُ: سَأَلْتُكَ بِحَقِّي عَلَيْكَ لَمّا سَأَلْتَ الصُّورَةَ أَنْ تَرُدَّ الرَّجُلَ، فَقالَ: إِنْ كانَتْ عَصا مُوسَى رَدَّتْ ما ابْتَلَعَتْهُ مِنْ حِبالِ القَوْمِ وَعِصِيِّهِمْ، فَأَنَّ هذِهِ الصُّورَةَ تَرُدُّ ما ابْتَلَعَتْهُ مِنْ هذا الرَّجُلِ، فَكانَ ذلِكَ أَعْمَلَ الأَشْياءِ فِي إِفاتَةِ نَفْسِهِ

Muhammad b. Al-Hassan b. Ahmad b. al-Waleed - may God be pleased with him - narrated that Muḥammad b. Al-Hassan al-Saffar and Sa'd b. 'Abd Allāh quoted on the authority of Ahmad b. Muḥammad b. Isa, on the authority of Al-Hassan b. 'Alī b. Yaqteen, on the authority of his brother Al-Hussein, on the authority of his father 'Alī b. Yaqteen, "Harun Ar-Rashid was looking for someone who could make fun of Abil Hassan Mūsā b. Ja'far (عليه السلام), belittle him and defeat him in arguments in a meeting. A magician volunteered to do so. When they spread the table to eat, the magician put a spell on the bread so that whenever Abul Hassan wanted to grab a piece of bread to eat, it would fly away from his hands. Harun was very pleased and laughed a lot at this. Then Abul Hassan turned to the picture of a lion which was on a portrait and said, "O Lion! Seize this enemy of God!" The narrator of the tradition

---

[118] *Al-Kāfi, v1, ch120, h6*

added, "Then the picture of the lion turned into a big lion, jumped on the magician, and tore him up."Then Harun and all his companions who were present were watching got scared, fainted and fell down. When they regained consciousness, Harun told Abil Hassan (عليه السلام), "I beg you by the right I have over you to ask the picture to return that man." Then the Imam (عليه السلام) said, "If the Cane of Moses (عليه السلام) returned the canes and the ropes which it swallowed, this picture will also return that man." The narrator of this tradition added, "This was one of the most important reasons why the Imam (عليه السلام) was martyred." (معتبر)[119]

120.

عَنْهُ عَنْ أَحْمَدَ بْنِ مُحَمَّدِ بْنِ أَبِي نَصْرٍ قَالَ كُنْتُ عِنْدَ أَبِي الْحَسَنِ الرِّضَا (عليه السلام) فَأَخْرَجَ إِلَيْنَا خَاتَمَ أَبِي عَبْدِ اللَّهِ (عليه السلام) وَ خَاتَمَ أَبِي الْحَسَنِ (عليه السلام) وَ كَانَ عَلَى خَاتَمِ أَبِي عَبْدِ اللَّهِ (عليه السلام) أَنْتَ ثِقَتِي فَاعْصِمْنِي مِنَ النَّاسِ وَ نَقْشُ خَاتَمِ أَبِي الْحَسَنِ (عليه السلام) حَسْبِيَ اللَّهُ وَ فِيهِ وَرْدَةٌ وَ هِلَالٌ فِي أَعْلَاهُ

It is narrated from the narrator of the previous Hadīth from Ahmad b. Muḥammad from b. abu Nasr who has said the following: "I once was with abu al-Hassan, al-Rida', (عليه السلام), and he (the Imam) showed us the ring of abu 'Abd Allāh, and abu al-Hassan, (عليه السلام). On the ring of abu 'Abd Allāh, (عليه السلام), it said, 'You are my trusty so protect me from people. ' The engraving on the ring of abu al- Hassan, (عليه السلام), said, 'Allāh is sufficient for me' and there was a flower and a crescent on its upper part.''' (صحيح)[120]

121.

---

[119] *'Uyūn Akhbār al-Riḍā, v1, ch8, h1*

[120] *Al-Kāfi, v6, ch26, h4*

مُحَمَّدُ بْنُ يَحْيَى عَنْ مُحَمَّدِ بْنِ الْحُسَيْنِ عَنْ مُحَمَّدِ بْنِ إِسْمَاعِيلَ عَنِ الْحِمْيَرِيِّ عَنِ الْحُسَيْنِ بْنِ مُحَمَّدٍ الْقُمِّيِّ قَالَ قَالَ الرِّضَا (عَلَيْهِ السَّلاَمُ) مَنْ زَارَ قَبْرَ أَبِي بِبَغْدَادَ كَمَنْ زَارَ قَبْرَ رَسُولِ اللهِ (صلى اللهُ عَلَيْهِ وَآلِهِ) وَقَبْرَ أَمِيرِ الْمُؤْمِنِينَ صَلَوَاتُ اللهِ عَلَيْهِ إِلاَّ أَنَّ لِرَسُولِ اللهِ وَلأَمِيرِ الْمُؤْمِنِينَ صَلَوَاتُ اللهِ عَلَيْهِمَا فَضْلَهُمَا

Muhammad b. Yahya has narrated from Muḥammad b. al-Husayn from Muḥammad b. Isma'il from al-Himyariy from al-Husayn b. Muḥammad al-Qummiy who has said the following: "Al-Rida', (عليه السلام), has said, 'Whoever visits my father in Baghdad is like one who has visited the Messenger of Allāh, (صلى الله عليه وآله وسلم), and the grave of 'Amir al-Mu'minin. O Allāh, I appeal before You to grant salawat (favors and compensation to Muḥammad and his family worthy of their services to Your cause). Except, however, the Messenger of Allāh and 'Amir al-Mu'minin have their own special merits.'" (مجهول)[121]

122.

مُحَمَّدُ بْنُ يَحْيَى عَنْ أَحْمَدَ بْنِ مُحَمَّدٍ عَنِ الْحَسَنِ بْنِ عَلِيٍّ الْوَشَّاءِ عَنِ الرِّضَا (عَلَيْهِ السَّلاَمُ) قَالَ سَأَلْتُهُ عَنْ زِيَارَةِ قَبْرِ أَبِي الْحَسَنِ (عَلَيْهِ السَّلاَمُ) مِثْلُ قَبْرِ الْحُسَيْنِ (عَلَيْهِ السَّلاَمُ) قَالَ نَعَمْ

Muhammad b. Yahya has narrated from Ahmad b. Muḥammad from al-Hassan b. 'Alī al-Washsha' who has said the following: "I once asked al-Rida', (عليه السلام), 'Is visiting the grave of abu al-Hassan, (عليه السلام), like visiting the grave of al-Husayn, (عليه السلام)?' He (the Imam) replied, 'Yes, it is so.'" (صحيح)[122]

Virtues of Imam Abul Hasan 'Alī b. Mūsā ar-Rida (عليه السلام)

123.

---

[121] *Al-Kāfi, v4, ch234, h1*

[122] *Al-Kāfi, v4, ch234, h2*

عِدَّةٌ مِنْ أَصْحَابِنَا عَنْ أَحْمَدَ بْنِ مُحَمَّدٍ عَنْ مُعَاوِيَةَ بْنِ حُكَيْمٍ عَنْ نُعَيْمٍ الْقَابُوسِيِّ عَنْ أَبِي الْحَسَنِ (عَلَيْهِ السَّلام) أَنَّهُ قَالَ إِنَّ ابْنِي عَلِيّاً أَكْبَرُ وُلْدِي وَأَبَرُّهُمْ عِنْدِي وَأَحَبُّهُمْ إِلَيَّ وَهُوَ يَنْظُرُ مَعِي فِي الْجَفْرِ وَلَمْ يَنْظُرْ فِيهِ إِلا نَبِيٌّ أَوْ وَصِيُّ نَبِيٍّ

A number of our people has narrated from Ahmad b. Muḥammad from Mu'awiya b. Hakim from Nu'aym al-Qabusi from abu al-Hassan (عليه السلام) who has said the following. "My son, 'Alī is the eldest of my sons and the most virtuous among them to me and the most beloved of them to me. He looks into the Jafr (a secret source of knowledge) with me. No one looks into it except a prophet or the executor of the will of a prophet." (موثق)[123]

124.

أَحْمَدُ بْنُ إِدْرِيسَ عَنْ مُحَمَّدِ بْنِ عَبْدِ الْجَبَّارِ عَنِ الْحَسَنِ بْنِ الْحُسَيْنِ اللُّؤْلُؤِيِّ عَنْ يَحْيَى بْنِ عَمْرٍو عَنْ دَاوُدَ الرَّقِّيِّ قَالَ قُلْتُ لابِي الْحَسَنِ مُوسَى (عَلَيْهِ السَّلام) إِنِّي قَدْ كَبِرَتْ سِنِّي وَدَقَّ عَظْمِي وَإِنِّي سَأَلْتُ أَبَاكَ (عَلَيْهِ السَّلام) فَأَخْبَرَنِي بِكَ فَأَخْبِرْنِي مَنْ بَعْدَكَ فَقَالَ هَذَا أَبُو الْحَسَنِ الرِّضَا

Ahmad b. Idris has narrated from Muḥammad b. 'Abd al-Jabbar from al-Hassan b. al-Husayn al-Lu'lu'i from Yahya b. 'Amr from Dawud al-Raqqi who has said the following. "I said to abu al-Hassan aMusa (عليه السلام), 'I have grown old and my bones are weakening. I asked your father (عليه السلام) and he informed me about you. Would you also inform me (about the Imam after you)." The Imam (عليه السلام) said, "This abu al-Hassan al-Rida." (مجهول)[124]

125.

[123] *Al-Kāfi, v1, ch72, h2*

[124] *Al-Kāfi, v1, ch72, h5*

عِدَّةٌ مِنْ أَصْحَابِنَا عَنْ أَحْمَدَ بْنِ مُحَمَّدٍ عَنْ عَلِيِّ بْنِ الْحَكَمِ عَنْ عَبْدِ اللهِ بْنِ الْمُغِيرَةِ عَنِ الْحُسَيْنِ بْنِ الْمُخْتَارِ قَالَ خَرَجَ إِلَيْنَا مِنْ أَبِي الْحَسَنِ (عَلَيْهِ السَّلام) بِالْبَصْرَةِ أَلْوَاحٌ مَكْتُوبٌ فِيهَا بِالْعَرْضِ عَهْدِي إِلَى أَكْبَرِ وُلْدِي يُعْطِي فُلانٌ كَذَا وَفُلانٌ كَذَا وَفُلانٌ لا يُعْطَى حَتَّى أَجِيءَ أَوْ يَقْضِيَ اللهُ عَزَّ وَجَلَّ عَلَيَّ الْمَوْتَ إِنَّ اللهَ يَفْعَلُ مَا يَشَاءُ

A number of our people has narrated from Ahmad b. Muḥammad from 'Alī b. al-Hakam from 'AbdAllāh b. al-Mughirah from al-Husayn b. al-Mukhtar who has said the following. "In Basra (wherein the Imam (عليه السلام) was imprisoned) certain tablets came out to us from abu al-Hassan (عليه السلام) on which, it was written horizontally, 'My instructions and directives to the my eldest son (Ali b. Mūsā al-Rida (عليه السلام) who should give such and such to so and so. As far so and so is concerned do not give him anything until I will come or Allāh, the Most Holy, the Most High, will decree that I must die, Allāh certainly does what He wills." (موثق)[125]

126.

مُحَمَّدُ بْنُ يَحْيَى عَنْ أَحْمَدَ بْنِ مُحَمَّدٍ عَنِ ابْنِ مَحْبُوبٍ عَنْ هِشَامِ بْنِ أَحْمَرَ قَالَ قَالَ لِي أَبُو الْحَسَنِ الاوَّلُ هَلْ عَلِمْتَ أَحَداً مِنْ أَهْلِ الْمَغْرِبِ قَدِمَ قُلْتُ لا قَالَ بَلَى قَدْ قَدِمَ رَجُلٌ فَانْطَلِقْ بِنَا فَرَكِبَ وَرَكِبْتُ مَعَهُ حَتَّى انْتَهَيْنَا إِلَى الرَّجُلِ فَإِذَا رَجُلٌ مِنْ أَهْلِ الْمَدِينَةِ مَعَهُ رَقِيقٌ فَقُلْتُ لَهُ اعْرِضْ عَلَيْنَا فَعَرَضَ عَلَيْنَا سَبْعَ جَوَارٍ كُلَّ ذَلِكَ يَقُولُ أَبُو الْحَسَنِ (عَلَيْهِ السَّلام) لا حَاجَةَ لِي فِيهَا ثُمَّ قَالَ اعْرِضْ عَلَيْنَا فَقَالَ مَا عِنْدِي إِلا جَارِيَةٌ مَرِيضَةٌ فَقَالَ لَهُ مَا عَلَيْكَ أَنْ تَعْرِضَهَا فَأَبَى عَلَيْهِ فَانْصَرَفَ ثُمَّ أَرْسَلَنِي مِنَ الْغَدِ فَقَالَ قُلْ لَهُ كَمْ كَانَ غَايَتُكَ فِيهَا فَإِذَا قَالَ كَذَا وَكَذَا فَقُلْ قَدْ أَخَذْتُهَا فَأَتَيْتُهُ فَقَالَ مَا كُنْتُ أُرِيدُ أَنْ أَنْقُصَهَا مِنْ كَذَا وَكَذَا فَقُلْتُ قَدْ أَخَذْتُهَا فَقَالَ هِيَ لَكَ وَلَكِنْ أَخْبِرْنِي مَنِ الرَّجُلُ الَّذِي كَانَ مَعَكَ بِالامْسِ فَقُلْتُ رَجُلٌ مِنْ بَنِي هَاشِمٍ قَالَ مِنْ أَيِّ بَنِي هَاشِمٍ فَقُلْتُ مَا عِنْدِي أَكْثَرُ مِنْ هَذَا فَقَالَ أُخْبِرُكَ عَنْ هَذِهِ الْوَصِيفَةِ إِنِّي اشْتَرَيْتُهَا مِنْ أَقْصَى الْمَغْرِبِ فَلَقِيَتْنِي امْرَأَةٌ مِنْ أَهْلِ الْكِتَابِ فَقَالَتْ مَا هَذِهِ الْوَصِيفَةُ مَعَكَ قُلْتُ اشْتَرَيْتُهَا لِنَفْسِي فَقَالَتْ مَا يَكُونُ يَنْبَغِي أَنْ تَكُونَ هَذِهِ عِنْدَ مِثْلِكَ إِنَّ هَذِهِ الْجَارِيَةَ يَنْبَغِي أَنْ تَكُونَ عِنْدَ خَيْرِ أَهْلِ الارْضِ فَلا تَلْبَثُ عِنْدَهُ إِلا قَلِيلاً حَتَّى تَلِدَ مِنْهُ غُلاماً مَا يُولَدُ بِشَرْقِ الارْضِ وَلا غَرْبِهَا مِثْلُهُ قَالَ فَأَتَيْتُهُ بِهَا فَلَمْ تَلْبَثْ عِنْدَهُ إِلا قَلِيلاً حَتَّى وَلَدَتِ الرِّضَا (عَلَيْهِ السَّلام)

---

[125] *Al-Kāfi, v1, ch72, h9*

Muhammad b. Yahya has narrated from Ahmad b. Muḥammad from b. Mahbub from Hisham b. Ahmar who has said the following. "Once abu al-Hassan, the second asked me, "Do you know if anyone from Morocco (or the west) has arrived?" I replied, "No, no one has come." He said, "Yes, a man has come. Come with us." He rode and also rode and went until we reached the man. He was a man from Madina who had a few slaves with him for sale. I asked him to show the slaves for sale and he showed me seven slave-girls. Abu al-Hassan (عليه السلام) said, "I do not need any of these." Then he asked, "Show us more." The man said, "There is no more except one who is ill." The Imam (عليه السلام) said, "Why do you not show her to us?" The man refused and the Imam (عليه السلام) returned. The next day he sent me and said to ask him for how much is the girl who is ill and if he said for so and so amount say, "I pay." I went to him and he said, "I will not accept less than so and so amount for her." I said, "I take her." He said, "She is yours but tell me who was the man with you yesterday?" I said, "A man from the clan of banu Hashim." He asked from which family is he?" I said, "That is all I have." He said, "I like to tell you about this girl. I bought her in the far corner of the west (or Morocco). A woman from the followers of the Bible came and said, "What is she doing with you?" I said, "I have purchased her for my self." She said, "This girl should not be with one like you. This girl should be with the best of the people on earth. With such a one she will not live very long before giving birth to a boy whose like will not be born in the west or east of the earth." The narrator has said, "I brought her to the Imam (عليه السلام) and shortly afterwards she became the mother of Imam al-Rida (عليه السلام)." (صحيح)[126]

127.

عَلِيُّ بْنُ إِبْرَاهِيمَ عَنْ يَاسِرٍ الْخَادِمِ وَالرَّيَّانِ بْنِ الصَّلْتِ جَمِيعاً قَالَ لَمَّا انْقَضَى أَمْرُ الْمَخْلُوعِ وَاسْتَوَى الامْرُ لِلْمَأْمُونِ كَتَبَ إِلَى الرِّضَا (عَلَيْهِ السَّلام) يَسْتَقْدِمُهُ إِلَى خُرَاسَانَ فَاعْتَلَّ عَلَيْهِ أَبُو الْحَسَنِ (عَلَيْهِ السَّلام) بِعِلَلٍ

[126] *Al-Kāfi, v1, ch121, h1*

فَلَمْ يَزَلِ الْمَأْمُونُ يُكَاتِبُهُ فِي ذَلِكَ حَتَّى عَلِمَ أَنَّهُ لا مَحِيصَ لَهُ وَأَنَّهُ لا يَكُفُّ عَنْهُ فَخَرَجَ (عَلَيْهِ السَّلام) وَلابي جعفر (عَلَيْهِ السَّلام) سَبْعُ سِنِينَ فَكَتَبَ إِلَيْهِ الْمَأْمُونُ لا تَأْخُذْ عَلَى طَرِيقِ الْجَبَلِ وَقُمْ وَخُذْ عَلَى طَرِيقِ الْبَصْرَةِ وَالاهْوَازِ وَفَارِسَ حَتَّى وَافَى مَرْوَ فَعَرَضَ عَلَيْهِ الْمَأْمُونُ أَنْ يَتَقَلَّدَ الامْرَ وَالْخِلافَةَ فَأَبَى أَبُو الْحَسَنِ (عَلَيْهِ السَّلام) قَالَ فَوِلايَةَ الْعَهْدِ فَقَالَ عَلَى شُرُوطٍ أَسْأَلُكَهَا قَالَ الْمَأْمُونُ لَهُ سَلْ مَا شِئْتَ فَكَتَبَ الرِّضَا (عَلَيْهِ السَّلام) إِنِّي دَاخِلٌ فِي وِلايَةِ الْعَهْدِ عَلَى أَنْ لا آمُرَ وَلا أَنْهَى وَلا أُفْتِيَ وَلا أَقْضِيَ وَلا أُوَلِّيَ وَلا أَعْزِلَ وَلا أُغَيِّرَ شَيْئاً مِمَّا هُوَ قَائِمٌ وَتُعْفِيَنِي مِنْ ذَلِكَ كُلِّهِ فَأَجَابَهُ الْمَأْمُونُ إِلَى ذَلِكَ كُلِّهِ قَالَ فَحَدَّثَنِي يَاسِرٌ قَالَ فَلَمَّا حَضَرَ الْعِيدُ بَعَثَ الْمَأْمُونُ إِلَى الرِّضَا (عَلَيْهِ السَّلام) يَسْأَلُهُ أَنْ يَرْكَبَ وَيَحْضُرَ الْعِيدَ وَيُصَلِّيَ وَيَخْطُبَ فَبَعَثَ إِلَيْهِ الرِّضَا (عَلَيْهِ السَّلام) قَدْ عَلِمْتَ مَا كَانَ بَيْنِي وَبَيْنَكَ مِنَ الشُّرُوطِ فِي دُخُولِ هَذَا الامْرِ فَبَعَثَ إِلَيْهِ الْمَأْمُونُ إِنَّمَا أُرِيدُ بِذَلِكَ أَنْ تَطْمَئِنَّ قُلُوبُ النَّاسِ وَيَعْرِفُوا فَضْلَكَ فَلَمْ يَزَلْ (عَلَيْهِ السَّلام) يُرَادُّهُ الْكَلامَ فِي ذَلِكَ فَأَلَحَّ عَلَيْهِ فَقَالَ يَا أَمِيرَ الْمُؤْمِنِينَ إِنْ أَعْفَيْتَنِي مِنْ ذَلِكَ فَهُوَ أَحَبُّ إِلَيَّ وَإِنْ لَمْ تُعْفِنِي خَرَجْتُ كَمَا خَرَجَ رَسُولُ الله (صَلَّى اللهُ عَلَيْهِ وَآلِهِ) وَأَمِيرُ الْمُؤْمِنِينَ (عَلَيْهِ السَّلام) فَقَالَ الْمَأْمُونُ اخْرُجْ كَيْفَ شِئْتَ وَأَمَرَ الْمَأْمُونُ الْقُوَّادَ وَالنَّاسَ أَنْ يُبَكِّرُوا إِلَى بَابِ أَبِي الْحَسَنِ قَالَ فَحَدَّثَنِي يَاسِرٌ الْخَادِمُ أَنَّهُ قَعَدَ النَّاسُ لابِي الْحَسَنِ (عَلَيْهِ السَّلام) فِي الطُّرُقَاتِ وَالسُّطُوحِ الرِّجَالُ وَالنِّسَاءُ وَالصِّبْيَانُ وَاجْتَمَعَ الْقُوَّادُ وَالْجُنْدُ عَلَى بَابِ أَبِي الْحَسَنِ (عَلَيْهِ السَّلام) فَلَمَّا طَلَعَتِ الشَّمْسُ قَامَ (عَلَيْهِ السَّلام) فَاغْتَسَلَ وَتَعَمَّمَ بِعِمَامَةٍ بَيْضَاءَ مِنْ قُطْنٍ أَلْقَى طَرَفاً مِنْهَا عَلَى صَدْرِهِ وَطَرَفاً بَيْنَ كَتِفَيْهِ وَتَشَمَّرَ ثُمَّ قَالَ لِجَمِيعِ مَوَالِيهِ افْعَلُوا مِثْلَ مَا فَعَلْتُ ثُمَّ أَخَذَ بِيَدِهِ عُكَّازاً ثُمَّ خَرَجَ وَنَحْنُ بَيْنَ يَدَيْهِ وَهُوَ حَافٍ قَدْ شَمَّرَ سَرَاوِيلَهُ إِلَى نِصْفِ السَّاقِ وَعَلَيْهِ ثِيَابٌ مُشَمَّرَةٌ فَلَمَّا مَشَى وَمَشَيْنَا بَيْنَ يَدَيْهِ رَفَعَ رَأْسَهُ إِلَى السَّمَاءِ وَكَبَّرَ أَرْبَعَ تَكْبِيرَاتٍ فَخُيِّلَ إِلَيْنَا أَنَّ السَّمَاءَ وَالْحِيطَانَ تُجَاوِبُهُ وَالْقُوَّادُ وَالنَّاسُ عَلَى الْبَابِ قَدْ تَهَيَّئُوا وَلَبِسُوا السِّلاحَ وَتَزَيَّنُوا بِأَحْسَنِ الزِّينَةِ فَلَمَّا طَلَعْنَا عَلَيْهِمْ بِهَذِهِ الصُّورَةِ وَطَلَعَ الرِّضَا (عَلَيْهِ السَّلام) وَقَفَ عَلَى الْبَابِ وَقْفَةً ثُمَّ قَالَ اللهُ أَكْبَرُ اللهُ أَكْبَرُ اللهُ أَكْبَرُ اللهُ أَكْبَرُ عَلَى مَا هَدَانَا اللهُ أَكْبَرُ عَلَى مَا رَزَقَنَا مِنْ بَهِيمَةِ الانْعَامِ وَالْحَمْدُ للهِ عَلَى مَا أَبْلانَا نَرْفَعُ بِهَا أَصْوَاتَنَا قَالَ يَاسِرٌ فَتَزَعْزَعَتْ مَرْوُ بِالْبُكَاءِ وَالضَّجِيجِ وَالصِّيَاحِ لَمَّا نَظَرُوا إِلَى أَبِي الْحَسَنِ (عَلَيْهِ السَّلام) وَسَقَطَ الْقُوَّادُ عَنْ دَوَابِّهِمْ وَرَمَوْا بِخِفَافِهِمْ لَمَّا رَأَوْا أَبَا الْحَسَنِ (عَلَيْهِ السَّلام) حَافِياً وَكَانَ يَمْشِي وَيَقِفُ فِي كُلِّ عَشْرِ خُطُوَاتٍ وَيُكَبِّرُ ثَلاثَ مَرَّاتٍ قَالَ يَاسِرٌ فَتُخُيِّلَ إِلَيْنَا أَنَّ السَّمَاءَ وَالارْضَ وَالْجِبَالَ تُجَاوِبُهُ وَصَارَتْ مَرْوُ ضَجَّةً وَاحِدَةً مِنَ الْبُكَاءِ وَبَلَغَ الْمَأْمُونَ ذَلِكَ فَقَالَ لَهُ الْفَضْلُ بْنُ سَهْلٍ ذُو الرِّئَاسَتَيْنِ يَا أَمِيرَ الْمُؤْمِنِينَ إِنْ بَلَغَ الرِّضَا الْمُصَلَّى عَلَى هَذَا السَّبِيلِ افْتَتَنَ بِهِ النَّاسُ وَالرَّأْيُ أَنْ تَسْأَلَهُ أَنْ يَرْجِعَ فَبَعَثَ إِلَيْهِ الْمَأْمُونُ فَسَأَلَهُ الرُّجُوعَ فَدَعَا أَبُو الْحَسَنِ (عَلَيْهِ السَّلام) بِخُفِّهِ فَلَبِسَهُ وَرَكِبَ وَرَجَعَ

Ali b. Ibrahim has narrated from from Yasir al-Khadim and al-Rayyan b. al-Salt all have said the following. "When the matter of the deposed Caliph (Amin) ended and it was established for al-Ma'mun he wrote to al-Rida asking to come to Khurasan. Abu al-Hassan (عليه السلام) in reply presented certain reason to justify his disagreement to the proposal but al-Ma'mun continued writing until The Imam (عليه السلام) found it out to be unavoidable and that will not leave him alone. He (عليه السلام) then left for Khurasan when abu Ja'far was only seven years old. Al-Ma'mun wrote to him, "do not travel through the mountains and Qum. Take the road through Basra, al-Ahwaz and Persia. The Imam (عليه السلام) arrived at Marw. Al-Ma'mun offered him to command and lead the task of Khilafat (Leadership) but abu al-Hassan (عليه السلام) declined. He then offered the Imam (عليه السلام) to accept the post of the crown prince The Imam (عليه السلام) said that he may accept it under certain conditions. Al-Ma'mun said, "Say whatever conditions you like." The Imam (عليه السلام) wrote, "I will assume this post with the conditions that I will nor issue any order or prohibitions nor issue any fatwa or judgment nor any appointment or dismissal of officers or change anything in the current system. You must excuse me in all such matters. Al-Ma'mun agreed to all such conditions. The narrator has said that Yasir narrated to me saying, "When it was 'Id (the holiday) al-Ma'mun asked al-Rida to attend the program, lead the prayer and deliver the sermon. Al-Rida (عليه السلام) replied him saying, "You know the conditions between us. They did not consist of any such matters. Al-Ma'mun sent the message, "I only want there by to build confidence in the people and they would know your distinction." He continued insisting until the Imam (عليه السلام) said, "O Amir al-Mu'minin, I would appreciate much if you would excuse me from such task and if you would still insist then I will out for this task in the manner that the Messenger of Allāh and Amir al-Mu'minin 'Alī (عليه السلام) would do." Al-Ma'mun then said, "You may do as you would chose. Al-Ma'mun ordered the servants guides to lead a procession to the door of abu al-Hassan (عليه السلام) saying 'Allāhu Akbar' Allāh is great. The narrator has said that Yasir al-Khadim narrated to me this. "People lined up waiting for the Imam (عليه السلام) on the roads and roof tops, men women and children. The guides and people from the army gathered at the door of abu al-Hassan (عليه السلام). At sun rise the Imam (عليه السلام) took a shower, wore a white turban made of cotton. He let one end of the turban hang over his chest and the other end between his shoulder on his back. He tied his belt and asked his followers, "Do as I have done." He picked up an arrow shaped staff and came out and we were along with him. He was bare foot and his gown was raised half way between his feet and knees and so were his other (long) clothes. When he walked and we walked along with him he raised his head towards the sky and Allāhu Akbar (Allāh is great) four times. It seemed to us as if the sky and the walls responded to him. the guides and the people at the door were ready and armed and decorated with the best dresses. When we appeared before them in such fashion and al-Rida (عليه السلام) appeared to them he stood at the door shortly and then said, "Allāhu Akbar (Allāh is great). Allāhu Akbar (Allāh is great). Allāhu Akbar (Allāh is great). Allāhu Akbar (Allāh is great) for guidance that He has granted us. Allāhu Akbar (Allāh is great) that has granted us the cattle. All praise belongs to Allāh that He has granted us blessings. We all would raise our voices. Yasir al-Khadim has said that the whole Maw shock with the weeping, cries and shouts when they looked at abu al-Hassan (عليه السلام). Many of the guides fell from their horses who would kick and throw their boots when they saw abu al-Hassan barefoot. He would walk about ten steps and pause and say Allāhu Akbar three times. **Yasir al-Khadim has said that to us it seemed as if the sky, earth and mountains would respond to him**. The whole Marw had become one voice loud and tearful. Information of this was reported to al-Ma'mun and Sahl b. al-Fadl, who had two official posts, said to him, "Amir al-Mu'minin, if al-Rida would reach the place of prayer in this manner people will into his devotees. Ask him to return home." Al-Ma'mun sent his people to ask abu al-Hassan to return home. He asked to bring his shoes and wore them and rode back home." (صحيح)[127]

128.

عَنْهُ عَنْ أَبِيهِ عَنْ يُونُسَ بْنِ عَبْدِ الرَّحْمَنِ قَالَ سَأَلْتُ أَبَا الْحَسَنِ الرِّضَا (عليه السلام) عَنْ نَقْشِ خَاتَمِهِ وَ خَاتَمِ أَبِيهِ (عليه السلام) قَالَ نَقْشُ خَاتَمِي مَا شَاءَ اللَّهُ لَا قُوَّةَ إِلَّا بِاللَّهِ وَ نَقْشُ خَاتَمِ أَبِي حَسْبِيَ اللَّهُ وَ هُوَ الَّذِي كُنْتُ أَتَخَتَّمُ بِهِ

---

[127] *Al-Kāfi, v1, ch121, h7*

It is narrated from the narrator of the previous Hadīth from Yunus b. 'Abd al-Rahman who has said the following: "I once asked abu al-Hassan, al-Rida', (عليه السلام), about the engraving on his ring and the ring of his father. He (the Imam) said, 'The engraving on my ring says, 'It is whatever Allāh wants and there is no power except the power of Allāh' and the engraving on the ring of my father said, 'Allāh is sufficient for me' and it is what I used for my ring.'" (صحيح)[128]

129.

عَلِيُّ بْنُ إِبْرَاهِيمَ عَنْ أَبِيهِ عَنْ عَلِيِّ بْنِ مَهْزِيَارَ قَالَ قُلْتُ لأَبِي جَعْفَرٍ (عَلَيْهِ السَّلام) جُعِلْتُ فِدَاكَ زِيَارَةُ الرِّضَا (عَلَيْهِ السَّلاَم) أَفْضَلُ أَمْ زِيَارَةُ أَبِي عَبْدِ اللهِ الْحُسَيْنِ (عَلَيْهِ السَّلاَم) فَقَالَ زِيَارَةُ أَبِي أَفْضَلُ وَذَلِكَ أَنَّ أَبَا عَبْدِ اللهِ (عَلَيْهِ السَّلاَم) يَزُورُهُ كُلُّ النَّاسِ وَأَبِي لا يَزُورُهُ إِلاَّ الْخَوَاصُّ مِنَ الشِّيعَةِ

Ali b. Ibrahim has narrated from his father from 'Alī b. Mahziyar who has said the following: "I once asked abu Ja'far, (عليه السلام), saying, 'I pray to Allāh to keep my soul in service for your cause, Is visiting al-Rida, (عليه السلام), more virtuous or that of abu 'Abd Allāh, al-Husayn, (عليه السلام), more virtuous?' He (the Imam) replied, 'Visiting my father is more virtuous; all people visit abu 'Abd Allāh, al-Husayn, (عليه السلام), but only very special people of our followers visit my father.'" (حسن)[129]

130.

مُحَمَّدُ بْنُ يَحْيَى عَنْ عَلِيِّ بْنِ إِبْرَاهِيمَ الْجَعْفَرِيِّ عَنْ حَمْدَانَ بْنِ إِسْحَاقَ قَالَ سَمِعْتُ أَبَا جَعْفَرٍ (عَلَيْهِ السَّلاَم) أَوْ حُكِيَ لِي عَنْ رَجُلٍ عَنْ أَبِي جَعْفَرٍ (عَلَيْهِ السَّلاَم) الشَّكُّ مِنْ عَلِيِّ بْنِ إِبْرَاهِيمَ قَالَ قَالَ أَبُو جَعْفَرٍ (عَلَيْهِ السَّلاَم) مَنْ زَارَ قَبْرَ أَبِي بِطُوسَ غَفَرَ اللهُ لَهُ مَا تَقَدَّمَ مِنْ ذَنْبِهِ وَمَا تَأَخَّرَ قَالَ فَحَجَجْتُ بَعْدَ الزِّيَارَةِ فَلَقِيتُ أَيُّوبَ بْنَ نُوحٍ فَقَالَ لِي قَالَ أَبُو جَعْفَرٍ الثَّانِي (عَلَيْهِ السَّلاَم) مَنْ زَارَ قَبْرَ أَبِي بِطُوسَ غَفَرَ اللهُ لَهُ مَا تَقَدَّمَ مِنْ

---

[128] *Al-Kāfi, v6, ch26, h5*

[129] *Al-Kāfi, v4, ch235, h1*

ذَنْبِهِ وَمَا تَأَخَّرَ وَبَنَى اللهُ لَهُ مِنْبَراً فِي حِذَاءِ مِنْبَرِ مُحَمَّدٍ وَعَلِيٍّ (عَلَيْهِمَا السَّلاَم) حَتَّى يَفْرُغَ اللهُ مِنْ حِسَابِ الْخَلاَئِقِ فَرَأَيْتُهُ وَقَدْ زَارَ فَقَالَ جِئْتُ أَطْلُبُ الْمِنْبَرَ

Muhammad b. Yahya has narrated from ʿAlī b. Ibrahim al-Ja'fariy from Hamdan b. Ishaq who has said the following: "I heard abu Ja'far, or it was narrated to me from abu Ja'far, (عليه السلام)", -uncertainty is from ʿAlī b. Ibrahim- "that abu Ja'far, (عليه السلام), has said, 'Whoever visits my father in Tus (Iran), Allāh forgives his sins of the past and those that comes later on.' He (the narrator) has said, 'I then performed al-Hajj after Ziyarat (visit). Thereafter, I met Ayyub b. Nuh who said to me, 'Abu Ja'far, the 2nd, (عليه السلام), has said, "Whoever visits the grave of my father in Tus, Allāh forgives his sins of the past and that which come later. Allāh builds for his use a pulpit, parallel to those for Muḥammad and Ali, (عليه السلام), until He will complete all creatures, accounting.'" I (the narrator) saw him when he already had visited and said, 'I have come to claim my pulpit.'" (مجهول)[130]

131.

مُحَمَّدُ بْنُ يَحْيَى عَنْ عَلِيِّ بْنِ الْحُسَيْنِ النَّيْسَابُورِيِّ عَنْ إِبْرَاهِيمَ بْنِ أَحْمَدَ عَنْ عَبْدِ الرَّحْمَنِ بْنِ سَعِيدٍ الْمَكِّيِّ عَنْ يَحْيَى بْنِ سُلَيْمَانَ الْمَازِنِيِّ عَنْ أَبِي الْحَسَنِ مُوسَى (عَلَيْهِ السَّلاَم) قَالَ مَنْ زَارَ قَبْرَ وَلَدِي عَلِيٍّ كَانَ لَهُ عِنْدَ اللهِ كَسَبْعِينَ حَجَّةً مَبْرُورَةً قَالَ قُلْتُ سَبْعِينَ حَجَّةً قَالَ نَعَمْ وَسَبْعِينَ أَلْفَ حَجَّةٍ قَالَ قُلْتُ سَبْعِينَ أَلْفَ حَجَّةٍ قَالَ رُبَّ حَجَّةٍ لاَ تُقْبَلُ مَنْ زَارَهُ وَبَاتَ عِنْدَهُ لَيْلَةً كَانَ كَمَنْ زَارَ اللهَ فِي عَرْشِهِ قَالَ نَعَمْ إِذَا كَانَ يَوْمُ الْقِيَامَةِ كَانَ عَلَى عَرْشِ الرَّحْمَنِ أَرْبَعَةٌ مِنَ الْأَوَّلِينَ وَأَرْبَعَةٌ مِنَ الْآخِرِينَ فَأَمَّا الْأَرْبَعَةُ الَّذِينَ هُمْ مِنَ الْأَوَّلِينَ فَنُوحٌ وَإِبْرَاهِيمُ وَمُوسَى وَعِيسَى (عَلَيْهِم السَّلاَم) وَأَمَّا الْأَرْبَعَةُ مِنَ الْآخِرِينَ فَمُحَمَّدٌ وَعَلِيٌّ وَالْحَسَنُ وَالْحُسَيْنُ صَلَوَاتُ اللهِ عَلَيْهِمْ ثُمَّ يُمَدُّ الْمِضْمَارُ فَيَقْعُدُ مَعَنَا مَنْ زَارَ قُبُورَ الْأَئِمَّةِ (عَلَيْهِم السَّلاَم) إِلاَّ أَنَّ أَعْلاَهُمْ دَرَجَةً وَأَقْرَبَهُمْ حَبْوَةً زُوَّارُ قَبْرِ وَلَدِي عَلِيٍّ (عَلَيْهِ السَّلاَم)

Muhammad b. Yahya has narrated from ʿAlī b. al-Husayn al-Naysaburiy from Ibrahim b. Ahmad from 'Abd al-Rahman b. Sa'id al-Makkiy from Yahya' b.

---

[130] *Al-Kāfi, v4, ch235, h3*

Sulayman al-Mazeniy who has said the following: "Abu al-Hassan, Musa, (عليه السلام), has said, 'Whoever visits the grave of my son, 'Alī it is before Allāh like performing seventy thousand well-performed accepted Hajjah.' He (the narrator) said, I asked, 'Is it seventy well-performed Hajjah?' He (the Imam) said, 'Yes, and it is seventy thousand Hajjah.' I then said, 'Seventy thousand Hajjah!' He (the Imam) said, 'A Hajjah perhaps is not accepted. One who visits him and spends the night near his grave is as if one's visiting Allāh in His Throne. He (the Imam) said, 'Yes, on the Day of Judgment, on the Throne of the Beneficent there will be four from those of the earlier times and four from the latter generations. The four from the earlier generations are Nuh, Ibrahim, Moses and Jesus, (عليه السلام). The four from the later generations are Muhammad, Ali, al-Hassan and al-Husayn, (عليه السلام). Thereafter, the leveling tool is applied and along with us will sit those who have visited the graves of 'A'immah, and among them of the highest degree and the first to receive gifts are those who have visited the grave of my son, Ali, (عليه السلام).'" (مجهول)[131]

132.

حَدَّثَنَا مُحَمَّد بن الحَسَن بن أَحمَد بن الوليد رَضِيَ اللهُعَنْهُ قالَ حَدَّثَنَا مُحَمَّد بن الحَسَن الصفار عَن أَحمَد بن مُحَمَّد بن عيسى عَن أَحمَد بن مُحَمَّد بن أبي نصر البزنطي قالَ قَرَأْتُ كِتَابَ أَبِي الْحَسَنِ الرِّضَا عَلَيْهِ السَّلامُ أَبْلِغْ شِيعَتِي أَنَّ زِيَارَتِي تَعْدِلُ عِنْدَ اللَّهِ عَزَّ وَجَلَّ أَلْفَ حَجَّةٍ قَالَ فَقُلْتُ لابِي جَعْفَرٍ عَلَيْهِ السَّلامُ أَلْفَ حَجَّةٍ قَالَ عَلَيْهِ السَّلامُ إِي وَاللَّهِ أَلْفَ أَلْفِ حَجَّةٍ لِمَنْ زَارَهُ عَارِفاً بِحَقِّهِ

Muhammad b. Al-Hassan b. Ahmad b. al-Waleed - may God be pleased with him - narrated that Muḥammad b. Al-Hassan al-Saffar quoted on the authority of Ahmad b. Muḥammad b. Isa, on the authority of Ahmad b. Muḥammad b. Abi Nasr al-Bezanti according to which Abi Nasr narrated that he had read a letter from Imam Ar-Ridha' (عليه السلام) in which it was written, "Let my followers know that God considers visiting my shrine to be like one thousand pilgrimages (to the Kaaba)." Then Abi Nasr went

---

[131] Al-Kāfi, v4, ch235, h4

to Imam Muḥammad Taqi (عليه السلام) and asked the Imam (عليه السلام) about this issue. The Imam (عليه السلام) said, "Yes, by God! There is the reward of one million pilgrimages to the Kaaba for anyone who visits his shrine and recognizes his rightfulness." (صحيح)[132]

133.

حَدَّثَنَا أَبِي و مُحَمَّد بن مُوسَى بن المُتَوَكِّل رَضِيَ اللهُ عَنْهُ قالا حَدَّثَنا عَلِيٌّ بن إبراهِيم بن هاشِم عَن أَبِيهِ عَن سعد بن سعد قالَ سَأَلْتُ أَبَا الحَسَنِ الرِّضَا عَلَيْهِ السَّلامُ عَن زِيَارَةِ فاطِمَةَ بِنتِ مُوسَى بنِ جعفر عَلَيْهِ السَّلامُ فقَالَ مَن زَارَها فَلَهُ الجَنَّة

My father and Muḥammad b. Mūsā b. al-Motawakkil - may God be pleased with them - quoted on the authority of 'Alī b. Ibrahim b. Hashem, on the authority of his father Sa'd b. Sa'd to have said, "I asked Abal Hassan Ar-Ridha' (عليه السلام) about visiting the shrine of Fatima - the daughter of Imam Mūsā b. Ja'far. Imam Ar-Ridha' (عليه السلام) said, "The reward of whomever visits her shrine is Heaven." (صحيح)[133]

134.

أَبِي ره قَالَ حَدَّثَنَا سَعْدُ بْنُ عَبْدِ اللَّهِ عَنْ أَحْمَدَ بْنِ أَبِي عَبْدِ اللَّهِ الْبَرْقِيِّ عَنِ الْحَسَنِ بْنِ عَلِيٍّ الْوَشَّاءِ قَالَ: قُلْتُ لِلرِّضَا ع مَا لِمَنْ أَتَى قَبْرَ أَحَدٍ مِنَ الْأَئِمَّهِ ع قَالَ لَهُ مِثْلُ مَا لِمَنْ أَتَى قَبْرَ أَبِي عَبْدِ اللَّهِ ع قَالَ فَقُلْتُ مَا لِمَنْ زَارَ قَبْرَ أَبِي الْحَسَنِ ع قَالَ لَهُ مِثْلُ مَا لِمَنْ زَارَ قَبْرَ أَبِي عَبْدِ اللَّهِ ع

From al-Ḥasan b. `Alī al-Washshā' said, I said to al-Riḍā (عليه السلام), 'What is (the reward) for one who comes to the grave of one of the A'immah (عليهم السلام)?' He (عليه السلام) said to him: 'Like what is (the reward) of the one who comes to the grave of Abī

---

[132] *'Uyūn Akhbār al-Riḍā, v2, ch36, h10*

[133] *'Uyūn Akhbār al-Riḍā, v2, ch27, h1*

`Abd Allāh (al-Ḥussayn).' I (al-Washshā') said: 'What is (the reward) for the one who visits the grave of Abī al-Ḥasan (Mūsa al-Kādhim)?' He (عليه السلام) said: 'Like what is (the reward) of the one who comes to the grave of Abī `Abd Allāh (al-Ḥusayn)' (صحیح)[134]

135.

حَدَّثَنَا الْحَاكِمُ أَبُو جَعْفَرٍ بْنِ نُعَيْمِ بْنِ شَاذان رَضِيَ اللهُ عَنْهُ قالَ: حَدَّثَنَا أَحْمَدُ بْنُ إِدْرِيس، عَنْ إِبْرَاهِيمَ بْنِ هاشِمٍ، عَنْ إِبْرَاهِيمَ بْنِ الْعَبَّاسِ قالَ: مَا رَأَيْتُ أَبَا الْحَسَنِ الرِّضَا عَلَيْهِ السَّلامُ جَفَا أَحَداً بِكَلامِهِ قَطُّ وَمَا رَأَيْتُ قَطَعَ عَلَى أَحَدٍ كَلامَهُ حَتَّى يَفْرُغَ مِنْهُ وَمَا رَدَّ أَحَداً، عَنْ حَاجَةٍ يَقْدِرُ عَلَيْهَا وَلا مَدَّ رِجْلَيْهِ بَيْنَ يَدَيْ جَلِيسٍ لَهُ قَطُّ وَلا اتَّكَأَ بَيْنَ يَدَيْ جَلِيسٍ لَهُ قَطُّ وَلا رَأَيْتُهُ شَتَمَ أَحَداً مِنْ مَوالِيهِ وَمَمَالِيكِهِ قَطُّ وَلا رَأَيْتُهُ تَفَلَ قَطُّ وَلا رَأَيْتُهُ يَقْهَقِهُ فِي ضَحِكِهِ قَطُّ بَلْ كَانَ ضَحِكُهُ التَّبَسُّمَ وَكَانَ إِذَا خَلا وَنُصِبَتْ مَائِدَتُهُ أَجْلَسَ مَعَهُ عَلَى مَائِدَتِهِ مَمَالِيكَهُ حَتَّى الْبَوَّابَ وَالسَّائِسَ وَكَانَ عَلَيْهِ السَّلامُ قَلِيلَ النَّوْمِ بِاللَّيْلِ كَثِيرَ السَّهَرِ يُحْيِي أَكْثَرَ لَيَالِيهِ مِنْ أَوَّلِهَا إِلَى الصُّبْحِ وَكَانَ كَثِيرَ الصِّيامِ فَلا يَفُوتُهُ صِيامُ ثَلاثَةِ أَيَّامٍ فِي الشَّهْرِ وَيَقُولُ ذلِكَ صَوْمُ الدَّهْرِ وَكَانَ عَلَيْهِ السَّلامُ كَثِيرَ الْمَعْرُوفِ وَالصَّدَقَةِ فِي السِّرِّ وَأَكْثَرُ ذلِكَ يَكُونُ مِنْهُ فِي اللَّيَالِي الْمُظْلِمَةِ فَمَنْ زَعَمَ أَنَّهُ رَأَى مِثْلَهُ فِي فَضْلِهِ فَلا تُصَدِّقُوهُ

Al-Hakim Abu Muḥammad Ja'far b. No'aym b. Shathan – may God be pleased with him – narrated that Ahmad b. Idris quoted on the authority of Ibrahim b. Hashem, on the authority of Ibrahim b. Al-Abbas, "I never saw Abal Hassan Ar-Ridha' (عليه السلام) be verbally crude with anyone under any circumstances. I never saw him interrupt anyone. He always waited for them to finish talking. I never saw him refuse to fulfill anyone's needs that he was capable of fulfilling. He never stretched his legs out in front of anyone. He never leaned back in front of anyone. I never saw him reproach any of his servants or agents. I never saw him spit. I never saw him burst into loud laughter. Rather he (عليه السلام) would smile gently. When everyone left and they spread the tablecloth out for him to dine on, he (عليه السلام) called every one of his servants and agents – even the door-keeper to dine with him. He (عليه السلام) slept very

---

[134] *Thawāb al-A'māl wa 'iqāb al-A'māl, ch148, h1*

little in the daytime. He (عليه السلام) was awake most of the time. He (عليه السلام) stayed up a lot at night - from the beginning of the night till early morning. He fasted a lot. He (عليه السلام) always fasted for at least three days each month. He (عليه السلام) used to say, "This fasting is like fasting all year long." He (عليه السلام) often did good deeds and gave charity in secret. He (عليه السلام) did most of this in the darkness of the night. If anyone claims that he has seen anyone as noble as him (عليه السلام), do not believe him."[135]

136.

حَدَّثَنَا أَحْمَدِ بْنِ زِيادِ بْنِ جَعْفَر الهَمْدانِيِّ رَضِيَ اللهُ عَنْهُ قالَ حَدَّثَنَا عَلِيِّ بْنِ إبراهِيم بْنِ هاشِم عَنْ أَبِي الصَّلْتِ الهَرَوِيِّ قالَ كَانَ الرِّضَا عَلَيْهِ السَّلامُ يُكَلِّمُ النَّاسَ بِلُغَاتِهِمْ وَكَانَ وَاللَّهِ أَفْصَحَ النَّاسِ وَأَعْلَمَهُمْ بِكُلِّ لِسَانٍ وَلُغَةٍ فَقُلْتُ لَهُ يَوْماً يَا ابْنَ رَسُولِ اللَّهِ إِنِّي لَأَعْجَبُ مِنْ مَعْرِفَتِكَ بِهَذِهِ اللُّغَاتِ عَلَى اخْتِلَافِهَا فَقَالَ يَا أَبَا الصَّلْتِ أَنَا حُجَّةُ اللَّهِ عَلَى خَلْقِهِ وَمَا كَانَ اللَّهُ لِيَتَّخِذَ حُجَّةً عَلَى قَوْمٍ وَهُوَ لَا يَعْرِفُ لُغَاتِهِمْ أَوَمَا بَلَغَكَ قَوْلُ أَمِيرِ الْمُؤْمِنِينَ عَلَيْهِ السَّلَامُ أُوتِينَا فَصْلَ الْخِطَابِ فَهَلْ فَصْلُ الْخِطَابِ إِلَّا مَعْرِفَةُ اللُّغَاتِ

Ahmad b. Ziyad al-Hamadani - may God be pleased with him - narrated that 'Alī b. Ibrahim b. Hashem quoted on the authority of his father, on the authority of Aba Salt al-Harawi, "Ar-Ridha' (عليه السلام) spoke with people in their own languages. By God, he was the most eloquent and the most knowledgeable person in any language. One day I told him, 'O son of the Prophet of God! I am amazed at your mastery over all these various languages.' Ar-Ridha' (عليه السلام) said, 'O Aba Salt! I am the Proof of God for His creatures. God would not designate a Proof for Himself to any nation who does not know their language. Have you not heard that 'Alī - the Commander of the Faithful (عليه السلام) said?, 'We have been granted elaborate speech.' Then how can this be without mastery of all the languages?''' (صحيح)[136]

---

[135] *'Uyūn Akhbār al-Riḍā., v1, ch14, h7*

[136] *'Uyūn Akhbār al-Riḍā, v2, ch24, h3*

137.

مُحَمَّدُ بْنُ يَحْيَى عَنْ أَحْمَدَ بْنِ مُحَمَّدٍ عَنِ ابْنِ أَبِي نَصْرٍ عَنْ أَبِي الْحَسَنِ الرِّضَا (عَلَيْهِ السَّلام) قَالَ سَأَلْتُهُ عَنْ قَوْلِ اللهِ عَزَّ وَجَلَّ يا أَيُّهَا الَّذِينَ آمَنُوا اتَّقُوا اللهَ وَكُونُوا مَعَ الصَّادِقِينَ قَالَ الصَّادِقُونَ هُمُ الائِمَّةُ وَالصِّدِّيقُونَ بِطَاعَتِهِمْ

Muhammad b. Yahya has narrated from Ahmad b. Muḥammad from b. abu Nasr who has said that he asked abu al-Hassan al-Rida (عليه السلام) about the meaning of the words of Allāh, the Most Holy, the Most High, in the following verse. "Believers, be pious before God and always be friends with the truthful ones." (9:119) The Imams (عليه السلام) said, "The truthful ones are the Imams (عليه السلام) who, are truthful in their obedience (to Allāh)." (صحيح)[137]

138.

حَدَّثَنَا عَلِيّ بْنِ عَبْدِ اللَّه بْنِ الوَرَّاق وَالحُسَيْنَيْنِ إِبْراهِيم بْنِ أَحْمَدِ بْنِ هِشام الْمُؤَدِّبُ حَمْزَة بْنِ مُحَمَّدِ بْنِ أَحْمَد العَلَوِي وَأَحْمَد بْنِ زِيادِ بْنِ جَعْفَر الْهَمَذانِيّ رَضِيَ اللَّهُ عَنْهُمْ أَخْبَرنا عَلِيّ بْنِ إِبراهِيم بْنِ هاشِم، عَن أَبِيهِ، عَن عَبْد السَّلَامُ بْنِ صالِح الْهَرَوِيّ وَحَدَّثَنَا مُحَمَّد جَعْفَرِ بْنِ نُعَيْم بن شاذان رَضِىَ اللَّهُ عَنْهُ، عَن أَحْمَدِ بْنِ إِدْرِيس، عَن إِبْراهِيم بْنِ هاشِم، عَن عَبْد السَّلامُ بْنِ صالِح الهَرَوِيّ قالَ: رُفِعَ إِلَى الْمَأْمُونِ أَنَّ أَبَا الْحَسَنِ عَلِيَّ بْنَ مُوسَى الرِّضَا عَلَيْهِ السَّلامُ يَعْقِدُ مَجالِسَ الْكَلام وَالنَّاسُ يَفْتَتِنُونَ بِعِلْمِهِ فَأَمَرَ مُحَمَّدَ بْنَ عَمْرِو الطُّوسِيَّ حاجِبَ الْمَأْمُونِ فَطَرَدَ النَّاسَ، عَن مَجْلِسِهِ وَأَحْضَرَهُ فَلَمَّا نَظَرَ إِلَيْهِ زَبَرَهُ وَاسْتَخَفَّ بِهِ فَخَرَجَ أَبُو الْحَسَنِ الرِّضَا عَلَيْهِ السَّلامُ مَنْ عِنْدِهِ مُغْضَباً وَهُوَ يُدَمْدِمُ بِشَفَتَيْهِ وَيَقُولُ: وَحَقِّ الْمُصْطَفَى وَالْمُرْتَضَى وَسَيِّدَةِ النِّسَاءِ لأَسْتَنْزِلَنَّ مِنْ حَوْلِ اللهِ عَزَّ وَجَلَّبِدُعَائِي عَلَيْهِ مَا يَكُونُ سَبَباً لِطَرْدِ كِلَابِ أَهْلِ هَذِهِ الْكُورَةِ إِيَّاهُ وَاسْتِخْفَافِهِمْ بِهِ وَبِخَاصَّتِهِ وَعَامَّتِهِ ثُمَّ إِنَّهُ عَلَيْهِ السَّلامُ انْصَرَفَ إِلَى مَرْكَزِهِ وَاسْتَحْضَرَ الْمِيضَاةَ وَتَوَضَّأَ وَصَلَّى رَكْعَتَيْنِ وَقَنَتَ فِي الثَّانِيَةِ فَقَالَ اللَّهُمَّ يَا ذَا الْقُدْرَةِ الْجَامِعَةِ وَالرَّحْمَةِ الْوَاسِعَةِ وَالْمِنَنِ الْمُتَتَابِعَةِ وَالآلاءِ الْمُتَوَالِيَةِ وَالأَيَادِي الْجَمِيلَةِ وَالْمَوَاهِبِ الْجَزِيلَةِ يَا مَنْ لا يُوصَفُ بِتَمْثِيلٍ وَلا يُمَثَّلُ بِنَظِيرٍ وَلا يُغْلَبُ بِظَهِيرٍ يَا مَنْ خَلَقَ فَرَزَقَ وَأَلْهَمَ فَأَنْطَقَ وَابْتَدَعَ فَشَرَعَ وَعَلا فَارْتَفَعَ وَقَدَّرَ فَأَحْسَنَ وَصَوَّرَ فَأَتْقَنَ وَاحْتَجَّ فَأَبْلَغَ وَأَنْعَمَ فَأَسْبَغَ وَأَعْطَى فَأَجْزَلَ يَا مَنْ سَمَا فِي الْعِزِّ فَفَاتَ خَوَاطِرَ الأَبْصَارِ وَدَنَا فِي اللُّطْفِ فَجَازَ هَوَاجِسَ الأَفْكَارِ يَا مَنْ تَفَرَّدَ بِالْمُلْكِ فَلا نِدَّ لَهُ فِي مَلَكُوتِ

---

[137] *Al-Kāfi, v1, ch19, h2*

سُلْطَانِهِ وَتَوَحَّدَ بِالْكِبْرِيَاءِ فَلا ضِدَّ لَهُ فِي جَبَرُوتِ شَأْنِهِ يَا مَنْ حَارَتْ فِي كِبْرِيَاءِ هَيْبَتِهِ دَقَائِقُ لَطَائِفِ الأَوْهَامِ وَحَسَرَتْ دُونَ إِدْرَاكِ عَظَمَتِهِ خَطَائِفُ أَبْصَارِ الأَنَامِ يَا عَالِمَ خَطَرَاتِ قُلُوبِ الْعَالَمِينَ وَيَا شَاهِدَ لَحَظَاتِ أَبْصَارِ النَّاظِرِينَ يَا مَنْ عَنَتِ الْوُجُوهُ لِهَيْبَتِهِ وَخَضَعَتِ الرِّقَابُ لِجَلالَتِهِ وَوَجِلَتِ الْقُلُوبُ مِنْ خِيفَتِهِ وَارْتَعَدَتِ الْفَرَائِصُ مِنْ فَرَقِهِ يَا بَدِيءُ يَا بَدِيعُ يَا قَوِيُّ يَا مَنِيعُ يَا عَلِيُّ يَا رَفِيعُ صَلِّ عَلَى مَنْ شَرَّفْتَ الصَّلاةَ بِالصَّلاةِ عَلَيْهِ وَانْتَقِمْ لِي مِمَّنْ ظَلَمَنِي وَاسْتَخَفَّ بِي وَطَرَدَ الشِّيعَةَ عَنْ بَابِي وَأَذِقْهُ مَرَارَةَ الذُّلِّ وَالْهَوَانِ كَمَا أَذَاقَنِيهَا وَاجْعَلْهُ طَرِيدَ الأَرْجَاسِ وَشَرِيدَ الأَنْجَاسِ قَالَ أَبُو الصَّلْتِ عَبْدُ السَّلامِ بْنُ صَالِحٍ الْهَرَوِيُّ فَمَا اسْتَتَمَّ مَوْلايَ عَلَيْهِ السَّلامُ دُعَاءَهُ حَتَّى وَقَعَتِ الرَّجْفَةُ فِي الْمَدِينَةِ وَارْتَجَّ الْبَلَدُ وَارْتَفَعَتِ الزَّعْقَةُ وَالصَّيْحَةُ وَاسْتَفْحَلَتِ النَّعْرَةُ وَثَارَتِ الْغَبَرَةُ وَهَاجَتِ الْقَاعَةُ فَلَمْ أُزَايِلْ مَكَانِي إِلَى أَنْ سَلَّمَ مَوْلايَ عَلَيْهِ السَّلامُ فَقَالَ لِي يَا أَبَا الصَّلْتِ اصْعَدِ السَّطْحَ فَإِنَّكَ سَتَرَى امْرَأَةً بَغِيَّةً عُثَّةً رَثَّةً مُهَيِّجَةَ الأَشْرَارِ مُتَّسِخَةَ الأَطْمَارِ يُسَمِّيهَا أَهْلُ هَذِهِ الْكُورَةِ سَمَانَةَ لِغَبَاوَتِهَا وَتَهَتُّكِهَا قَدْ أَسْنَدَتْ مَكَانَ الرُّمْحِ إِلَى نَحْرِهَا قَصَباً وَقَدْ شَدَّتْ وِقَايَةً لَهَا حَمْرَاءَ إِلَى طَرَفِهِ مَكَانَ اللِّوَاءِ فَهِيَ تَقُودُ جُيُوشَ الْقَاعَةِ وَتَسُوقُ عَسَاكِرَ الطَّغَامِ إِلَى قَصْرِ الْمَأْمُونِ وَمَنَازِلِ قُوَّادِهِ فَصَعِدْتُ السَّطْحَ فَلَمْ أَرَ إِلا نُفُوساً تَنْتَزِعُ بِالْعَصَا وَهَامَّاتٍ تُرْضَخُ بِالأَحْجَارِ وَلَقَدْ رَأَيْتُ الْمَأْمُونَ مُتَدَرِّعاً قَدْ بَرَزَ مِنْ قَصْرِ الشَّاهْجَانِ مُتَوَجِّهاً لِلْهَرَبِ فَمَا شَعَرْتُ إِلا بِشَاجِرْدِ الْحَجَّامِ قَدْ رَمَى مِنْ بَعْضِ أَعَالِي السُّطُوحِ بِلَبِنَةٍ ثَقِيلَةٍ فَضَرَبَ بِهَا رَأْسَ الْمَأْمُونِ فَأَسْقَطَتْ بَيْضَتَهُ بَعْدَ أَنْ شَقَّتْ جِلْدَةَ هَامَّتِهِ فَقَالَ لِقَاذِفِ اللَّبِنَةِ بَعْضُ مَنْ عَرَفَ الْمَأْمُونَ وَيْلَكَ أَمِيرَ الْمُؤْمِنِينَ فَسَمِعْتُ سَمَانَةَ تَقُولُ اسْكُتْ لا أُمَّ لَكَ لَيْسَ هَذَا يَوْمَ التَّمَيُّزِ وَالْمُحَابَاةِ وَلا يَوْمَ إِنْزَالِ النَّاسِ عَلَى طَبَقَاتِهِمْ فَلَوْ كَانَ هَذَا أَمِيرَ الْمُؤْمِنِينَ لَمَا سَلَّطَ ذُكُورَ الْفُجَّارِ عَلَى فُرُوجِ الأَبْكَارِ وَطُرِدَ الْمَأْمُونُ وَجُنُودُهُ أَسْوَأَ طَرْدٍ بَعْدَ إِذْلالٍ وَاسْتِخْفَافٍ شَدِيدٍ

The following was narrated by ʻAlī b. ʻAbd Allāh b. al-Warraq, Al-Husayn b. Ibrahim b. Ahmad b. Hisham al-Mo'addib, Hamza b. Ahmad al-Alawi and Ahmad b. Ziyad b. Ja'far al-Hamadani - may God be pleased with them - on the authority of ʻAlī b. Ibrahim b. Hashem quoted on the authority of his father, on the authority of Abdul Salam b. Salih al-Harawi. The following was also narrated by Abu Muḥammad Ja'far b. Nu'aym b. Shathan - may God be pleased with him - on the authority of Ahmad b. Idris, on the authority of Ibrahim b. Hashem, on the authority of Abdul Salam b. Salih al-Harawi.Al-Ma'mun was informed that Abal Hassan ʻAlī b. Mūsā Ar-Ridha' (عليه السلام) had held speech meetings, and the people were fascinated by his knowledge. Then Al-Ma'mun ordered his commissionaire Muḥammad b. Amr al-Toosi to fend off the people from attending the Imam's (عليه السلام) meetings. He also called Ar-Ridha' (عليه السلام) in. When Al-Ma'mun saw Ar-Ridha' (عليه السلام), he scolded and belittled him. Abul Hassan Ar-Ridha' (عليه السلام) left there in an angry state. He (عليه السلام) was moving his lips and saying, "I swear by the right of al-Mustafa (referring to the Prophet Muḥammad (صلى الله عليه وآله وسلم)), al-Murtadha (referring to 'Alī b. Abi Talib (عليه السلام)) and the Principal of all Ladies (referring to the Blessed Lady Fatima (عليه السلام)) that I will curse him in such a way so as to remove the Honorable the Exalted God's protection andsupport from him so much that the dogs of this town will throw him out of here and belittle him and the chosen, the regular members of his court. Then Ar-Ridha' (عليه السلام) went home and asked for some water to make ablutions. He made ablutions and said two units of prayers. Then in the second unit when it was time to say the hands raised-up supplications (Qunut), he said, "O God! O the Possessor of the Absolute Power, Extensive Mercy, Consecutive Blessings and Continued Good! O the One for whose characteristics there can be no examples cited! O the One for whose similitude there can be no examples cited! O the One whom no assisted ones can overcome! O the One who has created and provided sustenance; revealed and made eloquent; created and guided; destined and honored; organized and perfected; designed and beautified! O the One who has provided for proofs so perfect; blessings so complete; rewards so plentiful! O the One who is at such a zenith of Grandeur that it is beyond the ability of the viewers to see! O the One who is at such a deep level of Delicacy that it is beyond the ability of the thoughts to understand! O the One who is the Only one to rule, and there is no one to compete with You in the Domain of Thy Kingdom; O the One who is Unique in Greatness and there is no one to compete with His Almightiness! O the One due to whose Grandeur the minds of the intelligent ones are at a loss, and the eyes of the onlookers have lost their sight before seeing Him! O the Knower of the thoughts of the mystics! O the Witness to the viewing of those who see! O the One for whom the faces have fallen down in prostration due to His Might; and the heads have bowed down due to His Majesty; and the hearts have beaten fearing His appalling presence; and the veins of the neck strongly pulsate due to fearing Him. O the Initiator! O the Innovator! O the Powerful! O the Impenetrable! O the Sublime! Send Blessings upon the Prophet (صلى الله عليه وآله وسلم) as You honored the prayers for sending blessings upon him. Take my revenge against those who have oppressed me, belittled me, and have fended off the Shiites from my door. Make him taste the bitterness of humiliation and abasement as they made me taste it. Fend him off from the Threshold of Mercy as filth and contamination is fended off!"Abu Salt Abdul Salam b. Salih al-Harawi said, "The quake shook the town before he had finished saying his prayers. The whole town was in turmoil. There was loud screaming and crying heard. There was a lot of dirt and dust. I did not move until my Master (عليه السلام) had finished saying hisprayers. Then Ar-Ridha' (عليه السلام) told me, "O Aba Salt! Go to the roof and look around. There you will see a hustler who incites the rebels. She is wearing dirty clothes. The people of this town call her Samanah since she is dumb and rude. She is using a piece of cane on which she has tied a piece of red cloth and uses it as her flag. She tries to make an army out of the rebels, lead them and guide the rebels to attack Al-Ma'mun's palace and the houses of the army heads."I went up onto the roof and looked around. I could only see people with sticks in their hands and others with broken heads. I saw Al-Ma'mun leave the Shahjan Palace wearing armor and running away. I saw nothing more but noted that the apprentice of the phlebotomist threw a rock from the roof hitting Al-Ma'mun on the head. His helmet fell off and his head broke. His skull got so much injured that it seemed as if his brain was about to fall out. One of those who recognized Al-Ma'mun told the person who had thrown the rock, "Woe be to you! This is the Commander of the Faithful!" I heard Samanah tell him, "Shut up you bastard! Today is not the day to treat the people according to their ranks. If he was really the Commander of the Faithful, he would not have made pimps masters of virgins. Then they forced Al-Ma'mun and his troops out of town with the utmost degradation. (معتبر)[138]

139.

حَدَّثَنَا مُحَمَّدِ بْنِ عَلِي ماجِيلوَيْه رَضِىَ اللهُ عَنْهُ قالَ: حَدَّثَنَا عَلِيّ بْنِ إبراهِيم بْنِ هاشِم، عَن أَبيهِ، عَن الرَّيانِ بْنِ شَبِيبٍ قالَ دَخَلْتُ عَلَى الرِّضَا عَلَيْهِ السَّلامُ فِي أَوَّلِ يَوْمٍ مِنَ الْ◌ُمحَرَّم فَقَالَ لِي يَا ابْنَ شَبِيبٍ أَصَائِمٌ أَنْتَ؟ فَقُلْتُ لا. فَقَالَ إِنَّ هَذَا الْيَوْمَ هُوَ الْيَوْمُ الَّذِي دَعَا فِيهِ زَكَرِيَّا رَبَّهُ عَزَّ وَجَلَّ فَقَالَ: (رَبِّ هَبْ لِي مِنْ لَدُنْكَ ذُرِّيَّةً

---

[138] *'Uyūn Akhbār al-Riḍā, v2, ch12, h1*

طَيِّبَةً إِنَّكَ سَمِيعُ الدُّعَاءِ).فَاسْتَجَابَ اللَّهُ لَهُ وَأَمَرَ الْمَلَائِكَةَ فَنَادَتْ زَكَرِيَّا وَهُوَ قَائِمٌ يُصَلِّي فِي الْ◯مِحْرَابِ أَنَّ اللَّهَ يُبَشِّرُكَ بِيَحْيَى. فَمَنْ صَامَ هَذَا الْيَوْمَ ثُمَّ دَعَا اللَّهَ عَزَّ وَجَلَّ اسْتَجَابَ اللَّهُ لَهُ كَمَا اسْتَجَابَ لِزَكَرِيَّا عَلَيْهِ السَّلَامُ.ثُمَّ قَالَ يَا ابْنَ شَبِيبٍ إِنَّ الْ◯مُحَرَّمَ هُوَ الشَّهْرُ الَّذِي كَانَ أَهْلُ الْجَاهِلِيَّةِ فِيمَا مَضَى يُحَرِّمُونَ فِيهِ الظُّلْمَ وَالْقِتَالَ لِحُرْمَتِهِ. فَمَا عَرَفَتْ هَذِهِ الْأُمَّةُ حُرْمَةَ شَهْرِهَا وَلَا حُرْمَةَ نَبِيِّهَا. لَقَدْ قَتَلُوا فِي هَذَا الشَّهْرِ ذُرِّيَّتَهُ وَسَبَوْا نِسَاءَهُ وَانْتَهَبُوا ثَقَلَهُ، فَلَا غَفَرَ اللَّهُ لَهُمْ ذَلِكَ أَبَداً يَا ابْنَ شَبِيبٍ إِنْ كُنْتَ بَاكِياً لِشَيْءٍ فَابْكِ لِلْحُسَيْنِ بْنِ عَلِيِّ بْنِ أَبِي طَالِبٍ عَلَيْهِ السَّلَامُ، فَإِنَّهُ ذُبِحَ كَمَا يُذْبَحُ الْكَبْشُ، وَقُتِلَ مَعَهُ مِنْ أَهْلِ بَيْتِهِ ثَمَانِيَةَ عَشَرَ رَجُلاً مَا لَهُمْ فِي الْأَرْضِ شَبِيهُونَ، وَلَقَدْ بَكَتِ السَّمَاوَاتُ السَّبْعُ وَالْأَرَضُونَ لِقَتْلِهِ، وَلَقَدْ نَزَلَ إِلَى الْأَرْضِ مِنَ الْمَلَائِكَةِ أَرْبَعَةُ آلَافٍ لِنَصْرِهِ فَوَجَدُوهُ قَدْ قُتِلَ، فَهُمْ عِنْدَ قَبْرِهِ شُعْثٌ غُبْرٌ إِلَى أَنْ يَقُومَ الْقَائِمُ فَيَكُونُونَ مِنْ أَنْصَارِهِ وَشِعَارُهُمْ يَا لَثَارَاتِ الْحُسَيْنِ.يَا ابْنَ شَبِيبٍ لَقَدْ حَدَّثَنِي أَبِي، عَنْ أَبِيهِ، عَنْ جَدِّهِ أَنَّهُ لَمَّا قُتِلَ جَدِّي الْحُسَيْنُ أَمْطَرَتِ السَّمَاءُ دَماً وَتُرَاباً أَحْمَرَ.يَا ابْنَ شَبِيبٍ إِنْ بَكَيْتَ عَلَى الْحُسَيْنِ حَتَّى تَصِيرَ دُمُوعُكَ عَلَى خَدَّيْكَ غَفَرَ اللَّهُ لَكَ كُلَّ ذَنْبٍ أَذْنَبْتَهُ صَغِيراً كَانَ أَوْ كَبِيراً قَلِيلاً كَانَ أَوْ كَثِيراً.يَا ابْنَ شَبِيبٍ إِنْ سَرَّكَ أَنْ تَلْقَى اللَّهَ عَزَّ وَجَلَّ وَلَا ذَنْبَ عَلَيْكَ فَزُرِ الْحُسَيْنَ عَلَيْهِ السَّلَامُ.يَا ابْنَ شَبِيبٍ إِنْ سَرَّكَ أَنْ تَسْكُنَ الْغُرَفَ الْمَبْنِيَّةَ فِي الْجَنَّةِ مَعَ النَّبِي صَلَّى اللَّهُ عَلَيْهِ وَآلِهِ فَالْعَنْ قَتَلَةَ الْحُسَيْنِ.يَا ابْنَ شَبِيبٍ إِنْ سَرَّكَ أَنْ يَكُونَ لَكَ مِنَ الثَّوَابِ مِثْلَ مَا لِمَنِ اسْتُشْهِدَ مَعَ الْحُسَيْنِ فَقُلْ مَتَى مَا ذَكَرْتَهُ يَا لَيْتَنِي كُنْتُ مَعَهُمْ فَأَفُوزَ فَوْزاً عَظِيماً.يَا ابْنَ شَبِيبٍ إِنْ سَرَّكَ أَنْ تَكُونَ مَعَنَا فِي الدَّرَجَاتِ الْعُلَى مِنَ الْجِنَانِ فَاحْزَنْ لِحُزْنِنَا وَافْرَحْ لِفَرَحِنَا وَعَلَيْكَ بِوَلَايَتِنَا فَلَوْ أَنَّ رَجُلاً تَوَلَّى حَجَراً لَحَشَرَهُ اللَّهُ مَعَهُ يَوْمَ الْقِيَامَةِ

Muhammad b. ʿAlī Majiluwayh – may God be pleased with him –narrated that ʿAlī b. Ibrahim b. Hashem quoted on the authority of his father, on the authority of al-Rayyan b. ShAbib, "I went to see Al-Ridha (عليه السلام) on the first day of the (Arabic) month of Muharram. The Imam (عليه السلام) said, 'O b. ShAbib! Are you fasting?' I answered, 'No.' The Imam (عليه السلام) said, 'Today is the day on which Zakariya prayed to his Lord – the Honorable the Exalted, 'There did Zakariya pray to his Lord, saying, 'O my Lord! Grant unto me from Thee a progeny that is pure: for Thou art He that heareth prayer!'' And God fulfilled his prayer and ordered theangels to call Zakariya 'While he was standing in prayer in the chamber, the angels called unto him, '(Allāh) doth give thee glad tidings of Yahya, witnessing the truth of a Word from Allāh, and (be besides) noble, chaste, and a Prophet, of the (goodly) company of the righteous.'' Therefore, just as God fulfilled the prayers of Zakariya, the Honorable the Exalted God will fulfill the prayers of whoever fasts on this day, and asks God for something.'The Imam (عليه السلام) then added, 'O b. Shabayb! Muharram is the month in which the people of the Age of Ignorance had forbidden committing any oppression and fighting in. However, this nation did not recognize the honor of this month or the honor of their own Prophet (صلى الله عليه وآله وسلم). In this month, they killed the Prophet's offspring, they enslaved the women, and took their belongings as booty. God will never forgive them.O b. Shabayb! If you wish to cry, then cry for Al-Hussein b. 'Alī b. Abi Talib (عليه السلام) who was slaughtered like a sheep, and was killed along with the members of his household. Eighteen people were martyred along with Al-Hussein (عليه السلام) who had no equal on Earth. The seven heavens and the Earths mourned for his martyrdom. Four thousand angels descended to the Earth to assist him (Imam Hussein) (عليه السلام). However, Al-Hussein (عليه السلام) was destined to be martyred. They will remain at his shrine with wrinkled hair until the Riser (Imam al-Mahdi) (عليه السلام) rises. Then they will be among those who will assist him (عليه السلام). Their slogan will be Ya li tharat Al-Hussein (Revenge for Al-Hussein's blood!)O b. ShAbib! My father narrated that his father (عليه السلام) quoted on the authority of his grandfather (عليه السلام) that when they murdered my grandfather Al-Hussein (عليه السلام), the heavens cried (dark) red blood and dirt.O b. ShAbib! If you cry for Al-Hussein (عليه السلام) in such a way that tears flow down your cheeks, then God will forgive all the sins that you have committed whether they be minor or major, whether they be a few instances or a lot.O b. ShAbib! If you would like to meet the Honorable the Exalted God without having any sins then go to visit (the Shrine of) Al-Hussein (عليه السلام).O b. ShAbib! If you would like to accompany the Prophet (صلى الله عليه وآله وسلم) in the rooms of Paradise, then damn the murderers of Al-Hussein (عليه السلام).O b. ShAbib! If you would like to be rewarded just as those who were martyred along with Al-Hussein b. 'Alī (عليه السلام), whenever you remember Al-Hussein (عليه السلام) say, 'I wish I was with them and could achieve the great prosperity.'O b. ShAbib! If you would like to be in the same high ranks in Paradise with us, then be sad when we are sad and be happy when we are happy, and I advise you to have us since the Honorable the Exalted God will resurrect whoever even likes a rock with that same rock on the Resurrection Day. (صحيح)[139]

---

[139] *'Uyūn Akhbār al-Riḍā, v1, ch28, h53*

140.

عِدَّةٌ مِنْ أَصْحَابِنَا عَنْ أَحْمَدَ بْنِ مُحَمَّدِ بْنِ خَالِدٍ عَنْ أَحْمَدَ بْنِ مُحَمَّدِ بْنِ أَبِي نَصْرٍ قَالَ جَاءَ رَجُلٌ إِلَى أَبِي الْحَسَنِ الرِّضَا (عَلَيْهِ السَّلام) مِنْ وَرَاءِ نَهَرِ بَلْخَ فَقَالَ إِنِّي أَسْأَلُكَ عَنْ مَسْأَلَةٍ فَإِنْ أَجَبْتَنِي فِيهَا بِمَا عِنْدِي قُلْتُ بِإِمَامَتِكَ فَقَالَ أَبُو الْحَسَنِ (عَلَيْهِ السَّلام) سَلْ عَمَّا شِئْتَ فَقَالَ أَخْبِرْنِي عَنْ رَبِّكَ مَتَى كَانَ وَكَيْفَ كَانَ وَعَلَى أَيِّ شَيْءٍ كَانَ اعْتِمَادُهُ فَقَالَ أَبُو الْحَسَنِ (عَلَيْهِ السَّلام) إِنَّ اللهَ تَبَارَكَ وَتَعَالَى أَيَّنَ الايْنَ بِلا أَيْنٍ وَكَيَّفَ الْكَيْفَ بِلا كَيْفٍ وَكَانَ اعْتِمَادُهُ عَلَى قُدْرَتِهِ فَقَامَ إِلَيْهِ الرَّجُلُ فَقَبَّلَ رَأْسَهُ وَقَالَ أَشْهَدُ أَنْ لا إِلَهَ إِلا اللهُ وَأَنَّ مُحَمَّداً رَسُولُ اللهِ وَأَنَّ عَلِيّاً وَصِيُّ رَسُولِ اللهِ (صَلَّى اللهُ عَلَيْهِ وَآلِهِ) وَالْقَيِّمُ بَعْدَهُ بِمَا قَامَ بِهِ رَسُولُ اللهِ (صَلَّى اللهُ عَلَيْهِ وَآلِهِ) وَأَنَّكُمُ الائِمَّةُ الصَّادِقُونَ وَأَنَّكَ الْخَلَفُ مِنْ بَعْدِهِمْ

A group of our people from Ahmad b. Muḥammad b. Khalid from Ahmad b. Muḥammad b. Abu Nasr who has said the following. A man from Ma Wara' Nahr Balkh (Transoxania) came to abu al-Hassan al-Rida (عليه السلام), and said, 'I have a question for you. If your answer is the same as I already know, I will accept you as my Imam (leader with divine authority).'" Imam abul-Hassan (عليه السلام) replied, "Ask whatever you wish." The man said, "Tell me when did your Lord come into existence, how has He been and on what did He depend?" Imam Abul-Hassan (عليه السلام), replied, "Allāh, the Blessed, the Almighty, is the space maker of space, Who Himself is not subject to the effects of any space. He is the maker of How and Himself is not subject to How. He is Self-sufficient with His own power." The man stood up and kissed the head of the Imam (عليه السلام) and then said, "I testify that there is no god except Allāh and Muḥammad is the Messenger of Allāh and that Imam 'Alī (عليه السلام) is the successor of the Messenger of Allāh and the Guardian and protector of what the Messenger of Allāh has brought from Allāh and that your forefathers are the leaders with divine authority and that you are a successor to them. (صحيح)[140]

[140] *Al-Kafi, v1, ch6, h2*

141.

حَدَّثَنَا أَحمد بن زياد بن جعفر الهمداني رَضِيَ اللهُ عَنهُقَالَ حَدَّثَنَا عَلِيٌّ بن إبراهيم بن هاشِمٍ عَنْ أَبِيهِ عَنْ عَبدِ السلام بن صالح الهروي قالَ سَمِعتُ دعبل بن عَلِيٍّ الخزاعي يَقُولُ: لَمَا أَنْشَدْتُ مَوْلايَ عَلِيَّ بْنَ مُوسَى الرِّضَا عَلَيْهِ السَّلامُ قَصِيدَتِي الَّتِي أَوَّلُهَا:مَدَارِسُ آيَاتٍ خَلَتْ عَنْ تِلاوَةٍوَمَنْزِلُ وَحْيٍ مُقْفِرُ الْعَرَصَاتِفَلَمَّا انْتَهَيْتُ إِلَى قَوْلِي:خُرُوجُ إِمَامٍ لا مَحَالَةَ خَارِجٌيَقُومُ عَلَى اسْمِ اللَّهِ وَالْبَرَكَاتِيُمَيِّزُ فِينَا كُلَّ حَقٍّ وَبَاطِلٍوَيُجْزِي عَلَى النَّعْمَاءِ وَالنَّقِمَاتِبَكَى الرِّضَا عَلَيْهِ السَّلامُ بُكَاءً شَدِيداً ثُمَّ رَفَعَ رَأْسَهُ إِلَيَّ فَقَالَ لِي يَا خُزَاعِيُّ نَطَقَ رُوحُ الْقُدُسِ عَلَى لِسَانِكَ بِهَذَيْنِ الْبَيْتَيْنِ فَهَلْ تَدْرِي مَنْ هَذَا الإِمَامُ وَمَتَى يَقُومُ فَقُلْتُ لا يَا مَوْلايَ إِلا أَنِّي سَمِعْتُ بِخُرُوجِ إِمَامٍ مِنْكُمْ يُطَهِّرُ الأَرْضَ مِنَ الْفَسَادِ وَيَمْلَؤُهَا عَدْلاً.فَقَالَ يَا دِعْبِلُ الإِمَامُ بَعْدِي مُحَمَّدٌ ابْنِي وَبَعْدَ مُحَمَّدٍ ابْنُهُ عَلِيٌّ وَبَعْدَ عَلِيٍّ ابْنُهُ الْحَسَنُ وَبَعْدَ الْحَسَنِ ابْنُهُ الْحُجَّةُ الْقَائِمُ الْمُنْتَظَرُ فِي غَيْبَتِهِ الْمُطَاعُ فِي ظُهُورِهِ وَلَوْ لَمْ يَبْقَ مِنَ الدُّنْيَا إِلا يَوْمٌ وَاحِدٌ لَطَوَّلَ اللَّهُ ذَلِكَ الْيَوْمَ حَتَّى يَخْرُجَ فَيَمْلَاهَا عَدْلاً كَمَا مُلِئَتْ جَوْراً وَأَمَّا مَتَى فَإِخْبَارٌ عَنِ الْوَقْتِ وَلَقَدْ حَدَّثَنِي أَبِي عَنْ أَبِيهِ عَنْ آبَائِهِ عَنْ عَلِيٍّ عَلَيْهِمُ الصَّلاةُ وَالسَّلامُ أَنَّ النَّبِيَّ صَلَّى اللهُ عَلَيْهِ وَآلِهِ قِيلَ لَهُ يَا رَسُولَ اللَّهِ مَتَى يَخْرُجُ الْقَائِمُ مِنْ ذُرِّيَّتِكَ فَقَالَ مَثَلُهُ مَثَلُ السَّاعَةِ لا يُجَلِّيهَا لِوَقْتِهَا إِلا هُوَ ثَقُلَتْ فِي السَّمَاوَاتِ وَالأَرْضِ لا تَأْتِيكُمْ إِلا بَغْتَةً.خبر دعبل عند وفاته

Ahmad b. Ziyad b. Ja'far al-Hamazani - may God be pleased with him - narrated that 'Alī b. Ibrahim b. Hashem quoted on the authority of his father, on the authority of Abdul Salam b. Saleh al-Harawi, "I heard De'bel b. 'Alī al-Khoza'ee say, 'I recited this poem for my Master Ar-Ridha' (عليه السلام) which starts with: The schools for the Qur'anic verses are void of reciting nowand the landing site of revelations is left like a barren desert!Then I reached the following verses:A Divine Leader shall rise - surely he is to riseIn God's name and His Blessing he shall riseHe will distinguish between right and wrong for usHe will reward the good-doers and the bad-doers he shall chastise.Then Ar-Ridha' (عليه السلام) cried hard. He (عليه السلام) raised up his head towards me and said, 'O De'bel Khoza'ee! It was the Holy Spirit who made these verses flow out from your tongue. Do you know who that Divine Leader is? When will he rise?'Then De'bel said, 'No my Master! I have only heard that a Divine Leader from your progeny shall rise and cleanse the earth of corruption. He shall fill it with justice.'Then the Imam (عليه السلام) said, 'O De'bel! The Divine Leader coming after me is my son Muhammad; then after Muḥammad his son Ali; then his son Hassan; and then his son al-Hujjat the Riser the Awaited one (Imam al-Mahdi) who will come during his absence (Ghayba). He will be obeyed when he appears. God shall prolong time even if there is only one day left for him to rise and fill the earth with justice, since it has been filled with oppression and injustice. But when will it be? This is like informing the people about the time of the arrival of the Resurrection Day. My father quoted on the authority of his father, on the authority of his forefathers, on the authority of 'Alī (عليه السلام) who narrated that God's Prophet (صلى الله عليه وآله وسلم) was asked, 'O Prophet of God! When shall the Riser who is from your progeny rise?' The Prophet (صلى الله عليه وآله وسلم) replied, 'The similitude of that is like the similitude of the Hour (of Resurrection), 'None but He can reveal as to when it will occur. Heavy were its burden through the heavens and the earth. Only, all of a sudden will it come to you. (7:187) (مجهول كال موثق)[141]

142.

حَدَّثَنَا الحُسَين بن إِبراهِيم بن أَحَمد بن هِشام المُوَدَّب وعَلِيِّ بن عَبدُ اللَّه الوَرَّاقِ رضي الله عنهما قالا حَدَّثَنا عَلِيِّ بن إِبراهِيم بن هاشِمِ عَن أَبِيهِ إِبراهِيم بن هاشِمِ عَن عَبد السلام بن صالح الهروي قالَ دَخلَ دِعْبِلُ بْنُ عَلِيِّ الْخُزاعِيُّ رَحِمَهُ اللَّهُ عَلَى أَبِي الْحَسَنِ عَلِيِّ بْنِ مُوسَى الرِّضَا عَلَيْهِ السَّلامُ بِمَرْوَ فَقَالَ لَهُ يَا ابْنَ رَسُولِ اللَّهِ إِنِّي قَدْ قُلْتُ فِيكَ قَصِيدَةً وَآلَيْتُ عَلَى نَفْسِي أَنْ لا أُنْشِدَهَا أَحَداً قَبْلَكَ فَقَالَ عَلَيْهِ السَّلامُ هَاتِهَا
فَأَنْشَدَهُ:مَدارِسُ آيَاتٍ خَلَتْ عَنْ تِلاوَةٍوَمَنْزِلُ وَحْيٍ مُقْفِرُ الْعَرَصَاتِفَلَمَّا بَلَغَ إِلَى قَوْلِهِ:أَرَى فَيْئَهُمْ فِي غَيْرِهِمْ مُتَقَسَّماًوَأَيْدِيهُمْ مِنْ فَيْئِهِمْ صِفْرَاتِفَلَمَّا بَلَغَ إِلَى قَوْلِهِ هَذَا ، بَكَى أَبُو الْحَسَنِ الرِّضَا عَلَيْهِ السَّلامُ وَقَالَ لَهُ: صَدَقْتَ يَا خُزَاعِيُّ فَلَمَّا بَلَغَ إِلَى قَوْلِهِ:إِذَا وُتِرُوا مَدُّوا إِلَى وَاتِرِيهِمْأَكُفّاً عَنِ الأَوْتَارِ مُنْقَبِضَاتِجَعَلَ أَبُو الْحَسَنِ عَلَيْهِ السَّلامُ يُقَلِّبُ كَفَّيْهِ وَيَقُولُ أَجَلْ وَاللَّهِ مُنْقَبِضَاتٍ فَلَمَّا بَلَغَ إِلَى قَوْلِهِ:لَقَدْ خِفْتُ فِي الدُّنْيَا وَأَيَّامَ سَعْيِهَاوَإِنِّي لأَرْجُو الأَمْنَ بَعْدَ وَفَاتِيقَالَ الرِّضَا عَلَيْهِ السَّلامُ: آمَنَكَ اللَّهُ يَوْمَ الْفَزَعِ الأَكْبَرِ.فَلَمَّا انْتَهَى إِلَى قَوْلِهِ:وَقَبْرٌ بِبَغْدَادَ لِنَفْسٍ زَكِيَّةٍتَضَمَّنَهَا الرَّحْمَنُ فِي الْغُرُفَاتِقَالَ لَهُ الرِّضَا عَلَيْهِ السَّلامُ أَفَلا أُلْحِقُ لَكَ بِهَذَا الْمَوْضِعِ بَيْتَيْنِ بِهِمَا تَمَامُ قَصِيدَتِكَ. فَقَالَ بَلَى يَا بْنَ رَسُولِ اللَّهِ. فَقَالَ عليه السلام:وَقَبْرٌ بِطُوسَ يَا لَهَا مِنْ مُصِيبَةٍتَوَقَّدُ بِالأَحْشَاءِ فِي

---

[141] *'Uyūn Akhbār al-Riḍā, v2,ch36, h35*

الْحُرُقَاتِإِلَى الْحَشْرِ حَتَّى يَبْعَثَ اللَّهُ قَائِماًيُفَرِّجُ عَنَّا الْهَمَّ وَالْكُرُبَاتِفَقَالَ دِعْبِلٌ يَا ابْنَ رَسُولِ اللَّهِ هَذَا الْقَبْرُ الَّذِي بِطُوسَ قَبْرُ مَنْ هُوَ فَقَالَ الرِّضَا عَلَيْهِ السَّلَامُ قَبْرِي وَلا تَنْقَضِي الْأَيَّامُ وَاللَّيَالِي حَتَّى يَصِيرَ طُوسُ مُخْتَلَفَ شِيعَتِي وَزُوَّارِي أَلا فَمَنْ زَارَنِي فِي غُرْبَتِي بِطُوسَ كَانَ مَعِي فِي دَرَجَتِي يَوْمَ الْقِيَامَةِ مَغْفُوراً لَهُ ثُمَّ نَهَضَ الرِّضَا عَلَيْهِ السَّلَامُ بَعْدَ فَرَاغِ دِعْبِلٍ مِنْ إِنْشَادِ الْقَصِيدَةِ وَأَمَرَهُ أَنْ لا يَبْرَحَ مِنْ مَوْضِعِهِ وَدَخَلَ الدَّارَ فَلَمَّا كَانَ بَعْدَ سَاعَةٍ خَرَجَ الْخَادِمُ إِلَيْهِ بِمِائَةِ دِينَارٍ رَضَوِيَّةٍ [الرَّضَوِيَّةُ مَنْسُوبَةٌ إِلَى الرَّضِيِّ وَالرِّضَوِيَّةُ مَنْسُوبَةٌ إِلَى الرِّضَا] فَقَالَ لَهُ يَقُولُ لَكَ مَوْلَايَ اجْعَلْهَا فِي نَفَقَتِكَ فَقَالَ دِعْبِلٌ وَاللَّهِ مَا لِهَذَا جِئْتُ وَلا قُلْتُ هَذِهِ الْقَصِيدَةَ طَمَعاً فِي شَيْءٍ يَصِلُ إِلَيَّ وَرَدَّ الصُّرَّةَ وَسَأَلَ ثَوْباً مِنْ ثِيَابِ الرِّضَا عَلَيْهِ السَّلَامُ لِيَتَبَرَّكَ بِهِ وَيَتَشَرَّفَ بِهِ فَأَنْفَذَ إِلَيْهِ الرِّضَا عَلَيْهِ السَّلَامُ جُبَّةَ خَزٍّ مَعَ الصُّرَّةِ وَقَالَ لِلْخَادِمِ قُلْ لَهُ خُذْ هَذِهِ الصُّرَّةَ فَإِنَّكَ سَتَحْتَاجُ إِلَيْهَا وَلا تُرَاجِعْنِي فِيهَا فَأَخَذَ دِعْبِلٌ الصُّرَّةَ وَالْجُبَّةَ وَانْصَرَفَ وَصَارَ مِنْ مَرْوٍ فِي قَافِلَةٍ فَلَمَّا بَلَغَ ميان قوهان وَقَعَ عَلَيْهِمُ اللُّصُوصُ فَأَخَذُوا الْقَافِلَةَ بِأَسْرِهَا وَكَتَفُوا أَهْلَهَا وَكَانَ دِعْبِلٌ فِيمَنْ كُتِفَ وَمَلَكَ اللُّصُوصُ الْقَافِلَةَ وَجَعَلُوا يَقْسِمُونَهَا بَيْنَهُمْ فَقَالَ رَجُلٌ مِنَ الْقَوْمِ مُتَمَثِّلاً بِقَوْلِ دِعْبِلٍ فِي قَصِيدَتِهِ:أَرَى فَيْئَهُمْ فِي غَيْرِهِمْ مُتَقَسَّماًوَأَيْدِيَهُمْ مِنْ فَيْئِهِمْ صِفْرَاتِفَسَمِعَهُ دِعْبِلٌ فَقَالَ لَهُمْ دِعْبِلٌ لِمَنْ هَذَا الْبَيْتُ فَقَالَ لِرَجُلٍ مِنْ خُزَاعَةَ يُقَالُ لَهُ دِعْبِلُ بْنُ عَلِيٍّ قَالَ دِعْبِلٌ فَأَنَا دِعْبِلٌ قَائِلُ هَذِهِ الْقَصِيدَةِ الَّتِي مِنْهَا هَذَا الْبَيْتُ فَوَثَبَ الرَّجُلُ إِلَى رَئِيسِهِمْ وَكَانَ يُصَلِّي عَلَى رَأْسِ تَلٍّ وَكَانَ مِنَ الشِّيعَةِ وَأَخْبَرَهُ فَجَاءَ بِنَفْسِهِ حَتَّى وَقَفَ عَلَى دِعْبِلٍ وَقَالَ لَهُ أَنْتَ دِعْبِلٌ فَقَالَ نَعَمْ فَقَالَ لَهُ أَنْشِدِ الْقَصِيدَةَ فَأَنْشَدَهَا فَحَلَّ كِتَافَهُ وَكِتَافَ جَمِيعِ أَهْلِ الْقَافِلَةِ وَرَدَّ إِلَيْهِمْ جَمِيعَ مَا أَخَذُوا مِنْهُمْ لِكَرَامَةِ دِعْبِلٍ وَسَارَ دِعْبِلٌ حَتَّى وَصَلَ إِلَى قُمَّ فَسَأَلَهُ أَهْلُ قُمَّ أَنْ يُنْشِدَهُمُ الْقَصِيدَةَ فَأَمَرَهُمْ أَنْ يَجْتَمِعُوا فِي الْمَسْجِدِ الْجَامِعِ فَلَمَّا اجْتَمَعُوا صَعِدَ الْمِنْبَرَ فَأَنْشَدَهُمُ الْقَصِيدَةَ فَوَصَلَهُ النَّاسُ مِنَ الْمَالِ وَالْخِلَعِ بِشَيْءٍ كَثِيرٍ وَاتَّصَلَ بِهِمْ خَبَرُ الْجُبَّةِ فَسَأَلُوهُ أَنْ يَبِيعَهَا مِنْهُمْ بِأَلْفِ دِينَارٍ فَامْتَنَعَ مِنْ ذَلِكَ فَقَالُوا لَهُ فَبِعْنَا شَيْئاً مِنْهَا بِأَلْفِ دِينَارٍ فَأَبَى عَلَيْهِمْ وَسَارَ عَنْ قُمَّ فَلَمَّا خَرَجَ مِنْ رُسْتَاقِ الْبَلَدِ لَحِقَ بِهِ قَوْمٌ مِنْ أَحْدَاثِ الْعَرَبِ وَأَخَذُوا الْجُبَّةَ مِنْهُ فَرَجَعَ دِعْبِلٌ إِلَى قُمَّ وَسَأَلَهُمْ رَدَّ الْجُبَّةِ عَلَيْهِ فَامْتَنَعَ الْأَحْدَاثُ مِنْ ذَلِكَ وَعَصَوُا الْمَشَايِخَ فِي أَمْرِهَا فَقَالُوا لِدِعْبِلٍ لا سَبِيلَ لَكَ إِلَى الْجُبَّةِ فَخُذْ ثَمَنَهَا أَلْفَ دِينَارٍ فَأَبَى عَلَيْهِمْ فَلَمَّا يَئِسَ مِنْ رَدِّهِمُ الْجُبَّةَ عَلَيْهِ سَأَلَهُمْ أَنْ يَدْفَعُوا إِلَيْهِ شَيْئاً مِنْهَا فَأَجَابُوهُ إِلَى ذَلِكَ وَأَعْطَوْهُ بَعْضَهَا وَدَفَعُوا إِلَيْهِ ثَمَنَ بَاقِيهَا أَلْفَ دِينَارٍ وَانْصَرَفَ دِعْبِلٌ إِلَى وَطَنِهِ فَوَجَدَ اللُّصُوصَ قَدْ أَخَذُوا جَمِيعَ مَا كَانَ فِي مَنْزِلِهِ فَبَاعَ الْمِائَةَ دِينَارٍ الَّتِي كَانَ الرِّضَا عَلَيْهِ السَّلَامُ وَصَلَهُ بِهَا مِنَ الشِّيعَةِ كُلَّ دِينَارٍ بِمِائَةِ دِرْهَمٍ فَحَصَلَ فِي يَدِهِ عَشَرَةُ آلافِ دِرْهَمٍ فَذَكَرَ قَوْلَ الرِّضَا عَلَيْهِ السَّلَامُ إِنَّكَ سَتَحْتَاجُ إِلَى الدَّنَانِيرِ وَكَانَتْ لَهُ جَارِيَةٌ لَهَا مِنْ قَلْبِهِ مَحَلٌّ فَرَمِدَتْ رَمَداً عَظِيماً.فَأَدْخَلَ أَهْلَ الطِّبِّ عَلَيْهَا فَنَظَرُوا إِلَيْهَا فَقَالُوا أَمَّا الْعَيْنُ الْيُمْنَى فَلَيْسَ لَنَا فِيهَا حِيلَةٌ وَقَدْ ذَهَبَتْ وَأَمَّا الْيُسْرَى فَنَحْنُ نُعَالِجُهَا وَنَجْتَهِدُ وَنَرْجُو أَنْ تَسْلَمَ فَاغْتَمَّ لِذَلِكَ دِعْبِلٌ غَمّاً شَدِيداً وَجَزِعَ عَلَيْهَا جَزَعاً عَظِيماً ثُمَّ ذَكَرَ مَا كَانَ مَعَهُ مِنْ فَضْلَةِ الْجُبَّةِ فَمَسَحَهَا عَلَى عَيْنَيِ الْجَارِيَةِ وَعَصَبَهَا بِعِصَابَةٍ مِنْهَا مِنْ أَوَّلِ اللَّيْلِ فَأَصْبَحَتْ وَعَيْنَاهَا أَصَحُّ مِمَّا كَانَتَا قَبْلُ بِبَرَكَةِ أَبِي الْحَسَنِ الرِّضَا عَلَيْهِ السَّلَامُقال مصنف هذا الكتاب رحمة الله عليه إنما ذكرت هذا الحديث في هذا الكتاب و في هذا الباب لما فيه من ثواب زيارة الرِّضا عَلَيْهِ

السَّلامُ. و لدعبل بن عَلِيٍّ خبر عَن الرِّضا عَلَيْهِ السَّلامُ في النص على القائم عَلَيْهِ السَّلامُ أحببت إيراده على أثر هذَا الحديث

Al-Husayn b. Ibrahim b. Ahmad b. Hisham al-Mo'addib and 'Alī b. 'Abd Allāh al-Warraq - may God be pleased with them - narrated that 'Alī b. Ibrahim b. Hashem quoted on the authority of his father Ibrahim b. Hashem, on the authority of Abdul Salam b. Saleh al-Harawi, 'De'bel b. 'Alī al-Khoza'ee - may God forgive him - went to see 'Alī b. Mūsā Ar-Ridha' (عليه السلام) in Marv and said, 'O son of God's Prophet (صلى الله عليه وآله وسلم)! I have recited some poems for you and have promised myself not to recite them for anyone, before I recite them for you.' The Imam (عليه السلام) said, 'Then recite them.' De'bel recited his poems which started with:The schools for the Qur'anic verses are void of reciting nowand the landing site of revelations is left like a barren desert!Then De'bel went on until he got to this couplet:I find others share their share,Their hands of what is theirs are bare...;Abul Hassan Ar-Ridha' (عليه السلام) cried and said, 'O Khoza'ee! You have told the truth.' Then De'bel continued until he got to this couplet:When they were pulled taut, they did stretchTense hands that couldn't their muscles touch,Abul Hassan Ar-Ridha' (عليه السلام) kept rubb.g the palms of his hands against each other and said, 'Yes. Tense, indeed; they are tense...' Then De'bel continued reciting his poems until he got to the following:I have been frightened in the worldand the days of its effort,and I hope to be saved after I dieAr-Ridha' (عليه السلام) said, 'May God save you from the Day of the Great Dread!'De'bel continued on. When De'bel reached the end of his poems and he said,And the tomb in Baghdad is for a purified soulTo whom the Merciful has guaranteed one of the Chambers (in Heaven)Ar-Ridha' (عليه السلام) told him, 'Do I have the right to add two couplets to your poem at this point?' De'bel replied, 'O son of God's Prophet! Of course.' Then the Imam (عليه السلام) said,And woe be to the shrine in ToosFrom its calamities the giblets burnUntil Resurrection lest it is the Riser's turnTo overcome all grief and pain.Then De'bel asked Ar-Ridha' (عليه السلام), 'O son of God's Prophet! Whose shrine is this one in Toos?' Then Ar-Ridha' (عليه السلام) replied, 'It is mine. Very soon, however, Toos will become the place where my visitors and followers will travel to go on pilgrimage to my shrine. Indeed, whoever visits me in my loneliness in

Toos will be with me in the same rank on the Resurrection Day. He will be forgiven.' Then Ar-Ridha' (عليه السلام) stood up after De'bel had finished reciting his poem, and asked him to stay in his place. He (عليه السلام) went into the house. After an hour, the servant came out with a bag having one hundred Razawi Dinars in it, and said, 'My master has said, 'Take these for your expenses.' De'bel said, 'By God! I have not recited these poems being greedy for anything.' He refused the bag and asked for one of Ar-Ridha''s (عليه السلام) attires to be blessed and honored by him. Then Ar-Ridha' (عليه السلام) granted him a fur cloak plus the bag, and told his servant, 'Tell De'bel to take this bag, since he will need it. Tell him not to return it.' Then De'bel accepted the bag and the cloak and left. He left Marv along with a caravan. When they reached 'Meyan Qawhan', they were attacked by thieves who took all the travelers as captives and tied up their hands. De'bel was among those whose hands were tied. The thieves took all the caravan's goods and started to divide them up amongst themselves. Then one of the thieves started striking a similitude using one of De'bel's poems:I find others share their share,Their hands of what is theirs are bare...;De'bel heard him recite these verses and asked him who had composed it. He replied, 'It was said by a man from the Khoza'ee tribe who is called De'bel b. Ali.' Then De'bel said, 'Indeed, I am De'bel who said this poem. You recited only one of its couplets.' Then the man immediately rushed to their chief - a Shiite who was praying on top of a hill. The man informed the chief of what had happened. Then the chief went to De'bel in person, stopped near De'bel and asked, 'Are you De'bel?' He said, 'Yes.' Then the chief said, 'Then recite the entire poem.' Then he recited the entire poem. The chief untied his hands and ordered that all the travelers from that caravan be freed. Out of respect for De'bel, the chief also ordered that all their belongings be returned to them. Then they continued on until De'bel reached Qum. Then the people of Qum asked him to recite his poems. De'bel asked all of them to come (along with him) to the Jami'a Mosque. When they all got together in the mosque, De'bel climbed up the pulpit and recited his poems for them. The people gave him many gifts.Then they found out about the cloak. They asked him to sell it to them for one-thousand Dinars. De'bel refused to do so. They asked him to sell them just a piece of it for one-thousand Dinars, but he refused. Then he left

Qum.When De'bel left the town, a group of young Arab fellows arrived from behind him and took away his cloak. De'bel had to return to Qum and beg them to return the cloak to him. But they refused and even denied their elders' requests to return the cloak. However, they told De'bel, 'There is no way that you can take back your cloak. Then just take one-thousand Dinars for it.' De'bel did not accept, and they kept on insisting, but it was no use. So finally he lost hopes of getting it back. He asked them to give him just a piece of it. The young fellows accepted this. They gave him a piece of it plus one-thousand Dinars.De'bel set out towards his hometown. When he arrived home, he realized that the thieves had stolen everything he had there. Thus he exchanged the one-hundred Razavi Dinars that Ar-Ridha' (عليه السلام) had given to him. He exchanged each Dinar for one hundred Dirhams and obtained ten-thousand Dirhams. Then De'bel remembered that Ar-Ridha' (عليه السلام) had said, 'You will need these Dinars.' De'bel had a maid whom he dearly loved. She got bad pains in her eyes.Then the doctors came, examined her and said, 'Her right eye cannot be treated. It has become blind. However, her left eye can be treated and there is hope that it may be saved.' Then De'bel got really sorry and upset. He remembered that he had a piece of the cloak. He tied it around her eyes one night. When the morning came, her eyes were treated and were even better than before due to the blessing of Abil Hassan Ar-Ridha'(عليه السلام)."The author of this book (a.s.heikh Sadooq) - may God have mercy upon him - said, "I included this tradition in this chapter of the book since it is related to the rewards for going on pilgrimage to Ar-Ridha' (عليه السلام). There is also another tradition from De'bel b. 'Alī related to Ar-Ridha' (عليه السلام) that is related to the coming of the Riser (عجل الله تعالى فرجه) that I would like to narrate after this tradition." (مجهول كال موثق)[142]

143.

[142] *'Uyūn Akhbār al-Riḍā, v2,ch36, h34*

مُحَمَّدُ بْنُ يَحْيَى عَنْ أَحْمَدَ بْنِ مُحَمَّدٍ عَنْ إِبْرَاهِيمَ بْنِ أَبِي مَحْمُودٍ قَالَ رَأَيْتُ أَبَا الْحَسَنِ (عَلَيْهِ السَّلاَم) وَدَّعَ الْبَيْتَ فَلَمَّا أَرَادَ أَنْ يَخْرُجَ مِنْ بَابِ الْمَسْجِدِ خَرَّ سَاجِداً ثُمَّ قَامَ فَاسْتَقْبَلَ الْكَعْبَةَ فَقَالَ اللهُمَّ إِنِّي أَنْقَلِبُ عَلَى أَلاَّ إِلَهَ إِلاَّ أَنْتَ

Muhammad b. Yahya has narrated from Ahmad b. Muḥammad from Ibrahim b. abu Mahmud who has said the following: "I saw abu al-Hassan, (عليه السلام), when leaving through the door of Masjid. He bowed down in prostration. He then stood up and turned his face to al-Ka'bah and said, 'O Allāh, I go back with my affirmation that no one deserves worship except you. (صحيح)[143]

144.

حَدَّثَنا أَبِي وَمُحَمَّدُ بْنُ مُوسَى بْنِ الْمُتَوَكِّل؛ وَمُحَمَّدُ بْنِ عَلِيّ ماجِيلَوَيْه؛ وَأَحْمَدُ بْنِ على بن إِبْراهيمَ بْنِ هاشِمٍ؛ وَالْحُسَيْنُ بْنُ إِبْراهيم ناتانَة؛ وَأَحْمَدُ بْنِ زِيادِ بْنِ جَعْفَر الْهَمَذانيُّ؛ وَالْحُسَيْنُ بْنِ إِبْراهيمَ بْنِ هشام الْمُكَتِّبُ؛ وَعَلِيُّ بْنِ عَبْدِاللهِ الْوَرَّاق - رَضِيَ اللَّهُ عَنْهُمْ جَمِيعاً - قالُوا: حَدَّثَنا عَلِيُّ بْنُ إِبراهيمَ بْنِ هاشِمٍ، عَنْ أَبِيه، عَنْ أَحْمَدَ بْنِ مُحَمَّدِ بْنِ أَبِي نَصْرِ الْبِزَنْطِيّ قالَ: قُلتُ لأَبِي جَعْفَرٍ مُحَمَّدِ بْنِ مُوسَى عَلَيْهِمُ السَّلامُ: إِنَّ قَوْماً مِنْ مُخالِفِيكُمْ يَزْعُمُونَ أَنَّ أَباكَ إِنَّما سَمّاهُ الْمَأْمُون الرِّضا عَلَيْهِ السَّلامُ لَمّا رَضِيَهُ لِوِلايَةِ عَهْدِهِ فَقالَ: كَذَبُوا وَاللهِ وَفَجَرُوا، بَلِ اللهُ تَبارَكَ وَتَعالى سَمّاهُ الرِّضا عَلَيْهِ السَّلامُ ، لأَنَّهُ كانَ رِضى لِلَّهِ عَزَّ وَجَلَّ فِي سَمائِهِ، وَرِضى لِرَسُولِهِ وَالأَئِمَّةِ مِنْ بَعْدِهِ - صَلَواتُ اللهِ عَلَيْهِم - فِي أَرْضِهِ، قالَ فَقُلْتُ لَهُ: أَلَمْ يَكُنْ كُلُّ واحِدٍ مِنْ آبائِكَ الْماضِينَ عَلَيْهِمُ السَّلامُ رَضِىَ لِلَّهِ تَعالى وَلِرَسُولِهِ وَالأَئِمَّةِ عَلَيْهِمُ السَّلامُ فَقالَ: بَلى، فَقُلْتُ: فَلِمَ سُمِّيَ أَبُوكَ مِنْ بَيْنِهِمُ الرِّضا عَلَيْهِ السَّلامُ ؟ قالَ: لأَنَّهُ رَضِيَ بِهِ الْمُخالِفُونَ مِنْ أَعْدائِهِ كَما رَضِيَ بِهِ الْمُوافِقُونَ مِنْ أَوْلِيائِهِ وَلَمْ يَكُنْ ذلِكَ لأَحَدٍ مِنْ آبائِهِ عَلَيْهِمُ السَّلامُ، فَلِذلِكَ سُمِّيَ مِنْ بَيْنِهِمْ عَلَيْهِمُ السَّلامُ الرِّضا

My father, Muḥammad b. Mūsā b. al-Motawakkil, Muḥammad b. 'Alī b. Majiluwayh, Ahmad b. 'Alī b. Ibrahim b. Hashem; Al-Hussein b. Ibrahim Natanat; Ahmad b. Ziyad b. Ja'far al-Hamadani; Al-Hussein b. Ibrahim b. Hisham al-Mokattib, and 'Alī b. 'Abd Allāh - may God be pleased with them all - narrated that 'Alī b. Ibrahim b. Hashem quoted on the authority of his father that Ahmad b.

---

[143] *Al-Kāfi, v1, ch203, h2*

Muḥammad b. Abi Nasr al-Bezanti told Abi Ja'far Muḥammad b. 'Alī b. Mūsā (عليه السلام), "Some of your opponents think that Al-Ma'mun called your father Al-Ridha (عليه السلام) that means 'acceptable' or 'liked' since he liked your father and chose him to be his crown-prince. Imam Al-Jawad (عليه السلام) said, "No, by God, they are liars. God the Almighty the Sublime named him Al-Ridha (عليه السلام) since he was accepted by God the Almighty in His Heavens , and he was accepted by his Prophet (عليه السلام) and the Imams (عليه السلام) that followed the Prophet (عليه السلام) on His Earth." Al-Bezanti said, "Were not your father and grandfathers accepted by God, the Prophet and the Imams?" Imam Al-Jawad (عليه السلام) said, "Yes, they were." He then asked, "Why then only was your father called Al-Ridha and they were not?" Then Imam Al-Jawad (عليه السلام) said, "That is because his friends and followers as well as his opponents accepted him, while this was never the case for my forefathers. Therefore, he is the only one who is called Al-Ridha."[144]

Virtues of Imam Abu Ja'far al-Thani Muḥammad b. 'Alī al-Jawad (عليه السلام)

145.

عَلِيُّ بْنُ إِبْرَاهِيمَ عَنْ أَبِيهِ قَالَ اسْتَأْذَنَ عَلَى ابي جعفر (عَلَيْهِ السَّلام) قَوْمٌ مِنْ أَهْلِ النَّوَاحِي مِنَ الشِّيعَةِ فَأَذِنَ لَهُمْ فَدَخَلُوا فَسَأَلُوهُ فِي مَجْلِسٍ وَاحِدٍ عَنْ ثَلاثِينَ أَلْفَ مَسْأَلَةٍ فَأَجَابَ (عَلَيْهِ السَّلام) وَلَهُ عَشْرُ سِنِينَ

Ali b. Ibrahim has narrated from his father who has said the following. "Once a group of Shi'a from the suburbs asked permission to meet abu Ja'far(عليه السلام)(Imam al-Jawad). He granted them permission and they came in his presence. In one meeting they asked him thirty thousand questions. He answered them all and at that time he was ten years old." (حسن كالصحيح)[145]

---

[144] *'Uyūn Akhbār al-Riḍā, v1, ch1, h1*

[145] *Al-Kāfi, v1, ch122, h7*

146.

عِدَّةٌ مِنْ أَصْحَابِنَا عَنْ أَحْمَدَ بْنِ مُحَمَّدٍ عَنِ الْحَجَّالِ وَعَمْرِو بْنِ عُثْمَانَ عَنْ رَجُلٍ مِنْ أَهْلِ الْمَدِينَةِ عَنِ الْمُطَرِّفِيِّ قَالَ مَضَى أَبُو الْحَسَنِ الرِّضَا (عَلَيْهِ السَّلام) وَلِي عَلَيْهِ أَرْبَعَةُ آلافِ دِرْهَمٍ فَقُلْتُ فِي نَفْسِي ذَهَبَ مَالِي فَأَرْسَلَ إِلَيَّ أَبُو جَعْفَرٍ (عَلَيْهِ السَّلام) إِذَا كَانَ غَداً فَأْتِنِي وَلْيَكُنْ مَعَكَ مِيزَانٌ وَأَوْزَانٌ فَدَخَلْتُ عَلَى ابي جعفر (عَلَيْهِ السَّلام) فَقَالَ لِي مَضَى أَبُو الْحَسَنِ وَلَكَ عَلَيْهِ أَرْبَعَةُ آلافِ دِرْهَمٍ فَقُلْتُ نَعَمْ فَرَفَعَ الْمُصَلَّى الَّذِي كَانَ تَحْتَهُ فَإِذَا تَحْتَهُ دَنَانِيرُ فَدَفَعَهَا إِلَيَّ

A number of our people has narrated from Ahmad b. Muḥammad from Ali-Hajjal and ‘Amr b. ‘Uthman from a man of the people of al-Madina from Ali-Mutrifiy who has said the following. “Abu al-Hassan al-Rida (عليه السلام) passed away and owed my four thousand dirhams. I said to myself, “My money is lost.” Abu Ja‘far (عليه السلام) sent me a message to come to him the next day and bring with me a balance and weighing stones.” I went to see hiom and he said, “Abu al-Hassan has passed away. Did he owe you four thousand Dirhams?” I said, “Yes, he did.” He then lifted up his prayer rug on which was sitting and there were Dinars and he give them to me.” (مجهول)[146]

147.

مُحَمَّدُ بْنُ يَحْيَى عَنْ أَحْمَدَ بْنِ مُحَمَّدٍ عَنْ مُعَمَّرِ بْنِ خَلادٍ قَالَ سَمِعْتُ الرِّضَا (عَلَيْهِ السَّلام) وَذَكَرَ شَيْئاً فَقَالَ مَا حَاجَتُكُمْ إِلَى ذَلِكَ هَذَا أَبُو جَعْفَرٍ قَدْ أَجْلَسْتُهُ مَجْلِسِي وَصَيَّرْتُهُ مَكَانِي وَقَالَ إِنَّا أَهْلُ بَيْتٍ يَتَوَارَثُ أَصَاغِرُنَا عَنْ أَكَابِرِنَا الْقُذَّةَ بِالْقُذَّةِ

Muhammad b. Yahya has narrated from Ahmad b. Muḥammad from Mu‘ammar b. Khallad who has said the following. “I heard (abu al-Hassan) al-Rida who said something (leadership with Divine Authority) and then said, “I do not think you need

[146] *Al-Kāfi, v1, ch122, h11*

what I just said. This is abu Ja'far (عليه السلام). I have placed him in my own place to assume my position. We are of the family Ahl al-Bayt whose younger ones inherit from elder everything exactly measure to measure." (صحيح)[147]

148.

مُحَمَّدُ بْنُ يَحْيَى عَنْ أَحْمَدَ بْنِ مُحَمَّدِ بْنِ عِيسَى عَنْ أَبِيهِ مُحَمَّدِ بْنِ عِيسَى قَالَ دَخَلْتُ عَلَى أَبِي جَعْفَرٍ الثَّانِي (عَلَيْهِ السَّلام) فَنَاظَرَنِي فِي أَشْيَاءَ ثُمَّ قَالَ لِي يَا أَبَا عَلِيٍّ ارْتَفَعَ الشَّكُّ مَا لابِي غَيْرِي

Muhammad b. Yahya has narrated from Ahmad b. Muḥammad b. 'Isa from his father, Muḥammad b. 'Isa who has said the following. "Once I went to see abu Ja'far al-Thani's (عليه السلام). He debated me in several issues. He then said, "O abu Ali, there is no (reason for) doubt; I am the only son that my father had." (صحيح)[148]

149.

عِدَّةٌ مِنْ أَصْحَابِنَا عَنْ أَحْمَدَ بْنِ مُحَمَّدٍ عَنْ جَعْفَرِ بْنِ يَحْيَى عَنْ مَالِكِ بْنِ أَشْيَمَ عَنِ الْحُسَيْنِ بْنِ بَشَّارٍ قَالَ كَتَبَ ابْنُ قِيَامَا إِلَى أَبِي الْحَسَنِ (عَلَيْهِ السَّلام) كِتَاباً يَقُولُ فِيهِ كَيْفَ تَكُونُ إِمَاماً وَلَيْسَ لَكَ وَلَدٌ فَأَجَابَهُ أَبُو الْحَسَنِ الرِّضَا (عَلَيْهِ السَّلام) شِبْهَ الْمُغْضَبِ وَمَا عَلَّمَكَ أَنَّهُ لا يَكُونُ لِي وَلَدٌ وَاللهِ لا تَمْضِي الايَّامُ وَاللَّيَالِي حَتَّى يَرْزُقَنِي اللهُ وَلَداً ذَكَراً يَفْرُقُ بِهِ بَيْنَ الْحَقِّ وَالْبَاطِلِ

A number of our people has narrated from Ahmad b. Muḥammad from Ja'far b. Yahya from Malik b. Ashyam from al-Husayn b. Bashshar who has said the following. "b. Qiyaman wrote a letter to abu al-Hassan (عليه السلام) in which he had said the following. 'How can you be an Imam when you do not have a son?" Abu al-Hassan al-Rida (عليه السلام) replied him with signs of anger, "How do you know that I will not

---

[147] *Al-Kāfi, v1, ch73, h2*

[148] *Al-Kāfi, v1, ch73, h3*

have a son? By Allāh, not many days and nights will pass before Allāh will grant me a male child through who He will make the truth distinct from falsehood." (مجهول)[149]

150.

مُحَمَّدُ بْنُ يَحْيَى عَنْ أَحْمَدَ بْنِ مُحَمَّدٍ عَنْ صَفْوَانَ بْنِ يَحْيَى قَالَ قُلْتُ لِلرِّضَا (عَلَيْهِ السَّلام) قَدْ كُنَّا نَسْأَلُكَ قَبْلَ أَنْ يَهَبَ اللهُ لَكَ أَبَا جَعْفَرٍ (عَلَيْهِ السَّلام) فَكُنْتَ تَقُولُ يَهَبُ اللهُ لِي غُلاماً فَقَدْ وَهَبَهُ اللهُ لَكَ فَأَقَرَّ عُيُونَنَا فَلا أَرَانَا اللهُ يَوْمَكَ فَإِنْ كَانَ كَوْنٌ فَإِلَى مَنْ فَأَشَارَ بِيَدِهِ إِلَى ابي جعفر (عَلَيْهِ السَّلام) وَهُوَ قَائِمٌ بَيْنَ يَدَيْهِ فَقُلْتُ جُعِلْتُ فِدَاكَ هَذَا ابْنُ ثَلاثِ سِنِينَ فَقَالَ وَمَا يَضُرُّهُ مِنْ ذَلِكَ فَقَدْ قَامَ عِيسَى (عَلَيْهِ السَّلام) بِالْحُجَّةِ وَهُوَ ابْنُ ثَلاثِ سِنِينَ

Muhammad b. Yahya has narrated from Ahmad b. Muhammad from Safwan b. Yahya who has said the following. "Once I said to al-Rida (عليه السلام), before Allāh's granting you the blessing of the birth of abu Ja'far (عليه السلام) we would ask you and you would say, "Allāh will grant me a son and He has granted you one. His birth is the delight of our eyes. May Allāh spare us from showing your (sad) day. However, if something will happen to who then (will leadership with Divine Authority) will go?" The Imam (عليه السلام) pointed out with his hand towards abu Ja'far (عليه السلام) and he was standing before him. I then asked, " May Allāh take my soul in service for your cause, a child of three years?" The Imam (عليه السلام) said, "That will be of no harm to him. Jesus rose with Divine authority when he was a three years old child." (صحيح)[150]

151.

الْحُسَيْنُ بْنُ مُحَمَّدٍ عَنِ الْخَيْرَانِيِّ عَنْ أَبِيهِ قَالَ كُنْتُ وَاقِفاً بَيْنَ يَدَيْ أَبِي الْحَسَنِ (عَلَيْهِ السَّلام) بِخُرَاسَانَ فَقَالَ لَهُ قَائِلٌ يَا سَيِّدِي إِنْ كَانَ كَوْنٌ فَإِلَى مَنْ قَالَ إِلَى أَبِي جَعْفَرٍ ابْنِي فَكَأَنَّ الْقَائِلَ اسْتَصْغَرَ سِنَّ ابي جعفر (عَلَيْهِ

---

[149] *Al-Kafi, v1, ch73, h4*

[150] *Al-Kafi, v1, ch73, h10*

السَّلام) فقَالَ أَبُو الْحَسَنِ (عَلَيْهِ السَّلام) إِنَّ اللهَ تَبَارَكَ وَتَعَالَى بَعَثَ عِيسَى ابْنَ مَرْيَمَ رَسُولاً نَبِيّاً صَاحِبَ شَرِيعَةٍ مُبْتَدَأَةٍ فِي أَصْغَرَ مِنَ السِّنِّ الَّذِي فِيهِ أَبُو جَعْفَرٍ (عَلَيْهِ السَّلام)

Al-Husayn b. Muḥammad has narrated from al-Khayrani, from his father who has said the following. "Once I was standing before abu al-Hassan (عليه السلام) in Khurasan and someone said tp him, "O my master, if something will happen to who (will go Leadership with Divine Authority)?" The Imam (عليه السلام) said, "It will go to abu Ja'far (عليه السلام), my son." The person asking the question thought of abu Ja'far (عليه السلام) as very young for such task. Abu al-Hassan (عليه السلام) said, "Allāh, the Most Holy, the Most High, sent Jesus, son of Mary as a messenger prophet, the owner of a whole legal system. He began his task when he was smaller in age than abu Ja'far (عليه السلام)." (مجهول)[151]

152.

عَلِيُّ بْنُ إِبْرَاهِيمَ عَنْ أَبِيهِ وَعَلِيِّ بْنِ مُحَمَّدٍ الْقَاسَانِيِّ جَمِيعاً عَنْ زَكَرِيَّا بْنِ يَحْيَى بْنِ النُّعْمَانِ الصَّيْرَفِيِّ قَالَ سَمِعْتُ عَلِيَّ بْنَ جَعْفَرٍ يُحَدِّثُ الْحَسَنَ بْنَ الْحُسَيْنِ بْنِ عَلِيِّ بْنِ الْحُسَيْنِ فَقَالَ وَاللهِ لَقَدْ نَصَرَ اللهُ أَبَا الْحَسَنِ الرِّضَا (عَلَيْهِ السَّلام) فَقَالَ لَهُ الْحَسَنُ إِي وَاللهِ جُعِلْتُ فِدَاكَ لَقَدْ بَغَى عَلَيْهِ إِخْوَتُهُ فَقَالَ عَلِيُّ بْنُ جَعْفَرٍ إِي وَاللهِ وَنَحْنُ عُمُومَتُهُ بَغَيْنَا عَلَيْهِ فَقَالَ لَهُ الْحَسَنُ جُعِلْتُ فِدَاكَ كَيْفَ صَنَعْتُمْ فَإِنِّي لَمْ أَحْضُرْكُمْ قَالَ قَالَ لَهُ إِخْوَتُهُ وَنَحْنُ أَيْضاً مَا كَانَ فِينَا إِمَامٌ قَطُّ حَائِلَ اللَّوْنِ فَقَالَ لَهُمُ الرِّضَا (عَلَيْهِ السَّلام) هُوَ ابْنِي قَالُوا فَإِنَّ رَسُولَ اللهِ (صَلَّى اللهُ عَلَيْهِ وَآلِه) قَدْ قَضَى بِالْقَافَةِ فَبَيْنَنَا وَبَيْنَكَ الْقَافَةُ قَالَ ابْعَثُوا أَنْتُمْ إِلَيْهِمْ فَأَمَّا أَنَا فَلا وَلا تُعْلِمُوهُمْ لِمَا دَعَوْتُمُوهُمْ وَلْتَكُونُوا فِي بُيُوتِكُمْ فَلَمَّا جَاءُوا أَقْعَدُونَا فِي الْبُسْتَانِ وَاصْطَفَّ عُمُومَتُهُ وَإِخْوَتُهُ وَأَخَوَاتُهُ وَأَخَذُوا الرِّضَا (عَلَيْهِ السَّلام) وَأَلْبَسُوهُ جُبَّةَ صُوفٍ وَقَلَنْسُوَةً مِنْهَا وَوَضَعُوا عَلَى عُنُقِهِ مِسْحَاةً وَقَالُوا لَهُ ادْخُلِ الْبُسْتَانَ كَأَنَّكَ تَعْمَلُ فِيهِ ثُمَّ جَاءُوا بِابِي جعفر (عَلَيْهِ السَّلام) فَقَالُوا أَلْحِقُوا هَذَا الْغُلامَ بِأَبِيهِ فَقَالُوا لَيْسَ لَهُ هَاهُنَا أَبٌ وَلَكِنَّ هَذَا عَمُّ أَبِيهِ وَهَذَا عَمُّهُ وَهَذِهِ عَمَّتُهُ وَإِنْ يَكُنْ لَهُ هَاهُنَا أَبٌ فَهُوَ صَاحِبُ الْبُسْتَانِ فَإِنَّ قَدَمَيْهِ وَقَدَمَيْهِ وَاحِدَةٌ فَلَمَّا رَجَعَ أَبُو الْحَسَنِ (عَلَيْهِ السَّلام) قَالُوا هَذَا أَبُوهُ قَالَ عَلِيُّ بْنُ جَعْفَرٍ فَقُمْتُ فَمَصَصْتُ رِيقَ ابي جعفر (عَلَيْهِ السَّلام) ثُمَّ قُلْتُ لَهُ أَشْهَدُ أَنَّكَ إِمَامِي عِنْدَ اللهِ فَبَكَى الرِّضَا (عَلَيْهِ السَّلام) ثُمَّ قَالَ يَا عَمِّ أَ لَمْ تَسْمَعْ أَبِي وَهُوَ يَقُولُ قَالَ رَسُولُ اللهِ (صَلَّى اللهُ عَلَيْهِ وَآلِه) بِأَبِي ابْنُ خِيَرَةِ الامَاءِ ابْنُ النُّوبِيَّةِ الطَّيِّبَةِ الْفَمِ

---

[151] *Al-Kafi, v1, ch73, h13*

الْمُنْتَجَبَةِ الرَّحِمِ وَيْلَهُمْ لَعَنَ اللهُ الاعَيْبِسَ وَذُرِّيَّتَهُ صَاحِبَ الْفِتْنَةِ وَيَقْتُلُهُمْ سِنِينَ وَشُهُوراً وَأَيَّاماً يَسُومُهُمْ خَسْفاً وَيَسْقِيهِمْ كَأْساً مُصْبِرَةً وَهُوَ الطَّرِيدُ الشَّرِيدُ الْمَوْتُورُ بِأَبِيهِ وَجَدِّهِ صَاحِبُ الْغَيْبَةِ يُقَالُ مَاتَ أَوْ هَلَكَ أَيَّ وَادٍ سَلَكَ أَ فَيَكُونُ هَذَا يَا عَمِّ إِلا مِنِّي فَقُلْتُ صَدَقْتَ جُعِلْتُ فِدَاكَ

Ali b. Ibrahim has narrated from his father and ʿAlī b. Muḥammad al-Qasani from Zakariyya b. Yahya b. al-Nu'man al-Sayrafi who has said the following. "I heard ʿAlī b. Ja'far speaking to al-Hassan b. al-Husayn b. ʿAlī b. al-Husayn as, "By Allāh, Allāh has supported abu al-Hassan al-Rida (عليه السلام)." Al-Hassan then said, "Yes, by Allāh, may Allāh take my souls in service for your cause, his brothers have rebelled against him." ʿAlī b. Ja'far then said, "Yes, by Allāh, and we, his uncles, rebelled against him." Al-Hassan said to him, "May Allāh take my souls in service for your cause, how did you dealt it, I was not present with you." He said, "His brothers said to him and so did we, "there has never been a blackish Imam from us" The Imam (عليه السلام) al-Rida said to them, "He is my son." They said," Messenger of Allāh did judge on the basis of physiognomy , thus, we can also have a judgment on the basis of physiognomy ." The Imam (عليه السلام) said, "You may call one who has said the following knows physiognomy but I will not do so. You should not give information as to for what reason you have called them. You must stay home. When they will come, we should, all of us, be in the garden. His uncles, brothers and sisters should all line up. They dressed al-Rida (عليه السلام) in a gown made of wool with a hat of wool on his head and a shovel in his hand. The Imam should be asked to act as the gardener in the garden. Then abu Ja'far should be brought in and they should be asked to find his father in the people present. They said, "His father is not present among these people, but this is his uncle, this is the uncle of his father, this is his uncle and this is his aunt. If his father is here he is the gardener because his foot print and his foot print matCh" When abu al-Hassan (عليه السلام) returned, they said, "This is his father." ʿAlī b. Ja'far has said, "I stood up and kissed abu Ja'far and his saliva came in my mouth. Then I said, "I testify that you are my Imam before Allāh. Al-Rida (عليه السلام) wept and said, "O uncle, did not hear my father say, "The Messenger of Allāh has said, "May Allāh take my souls and the souls of my father in service for the cause of the son of the best slave girl, the son of al-Nawbiya (a town in Sudan) lady with a fresh smelling mouth, the lady of who will give birth to a purified one. May Allāh condemn the 'U'aybiss (the 'Abbassides) and their descendents, the mischief makers who murder them (the Imams) for years, months and days, cause them huge sufferings and cause them to endure bitter frustrations. He (abu Ja'far (عليه السلام) he live exiled, away from home and suffering the pain of the murder of his father and grandfather. One who is has disappeared (from the eyes of his loved ones). About whom it will be said, "His is dead or perished. No one will in which valleys he will travel. Can such a person, O uncle, be anyone other than my own son?" I then said, "You have spoken the truth, may Allāh take my souls in service for your cause." (مجهول)[152]

153.

حَدَّثَنَا أَحْمَد بن زياد بن جعفر الهمداني رَضِيَ اللهُ عَنْهُقَالَ حَدَّثَنَا عَلِيٌّ بن إبراهيم بن هاشِمٍ عَنْ أَبِيهِ عَنْ عَبد السلام بن صالح الهروي قالَ سَمِعتُ دعبل بن عَلِيٍّ الخزاعي يَقُولُ: لَمَا أَنْشَدْتُ مَوْلايَ عَلِيَّ بْنَ مُوسَى الرِّضَا عَلَيْهِ السَّلامُ قَصِيدَتِيَ الَّتِي أَوَّلُهَا:مَدَارِسُ آيَاتٍ خَلَتْ عَنْ تِلاوَةٍوَمَنْزِلُ وَحْيٍ مُقْفِرُ الْعَرَصَاتِفَلَمَّا انْتَهَيْتُ إِلَى قَوْلِي:خُرُوجُ إِمَامٍ لا مَحَالَةَ خَارِجٌيَقُومُ عَلَى اسْمِ اللَّهِ وَالْبَرَكَاتِيُمَيِّزُ فِينَا كُلَّ حَقٍّ وَبَاطِلٍوَيُجْزِي عَلَى النَّعْمَاءِ وَالنَّقِمَاتِبَكَى الرِّضَا عَلَيْهِ السَّلامُ بُكَاءً شَدِيداً ثُمَّ رَفَعَ رَأْسَهُ إِلَيَّ فَقَالَ لِي يَا خُزَاعِيٌّ نَطَقَ رُوحُ الْقُدُسِ عَلَى لِسَانِكَ بِهَذَيْنِ الْبَيْتَيْنِ فَهَلْ تَدْرِي مَنْ هَذَا الإِمَامُ وَمَتَى يَقُومُ فَقُلْتُ لا يَا مَوْلايَ إِلا أَنِّي سَمِعْتُ بِخُرُوجِ إِمَامٍ مِنْكُمْ يُطَهِّرُ الأَرْضَ مِنَ الْفَسَادِ وَيَمْلَؤُهَا عَدْلاً.فَقَالَ يَا دِعْبِلُ الإِمَامُ بَعْدِي مُحَمَّد ابْنِي وَبَعْدَ مُحَمَّد ابْنُهُ عَلِيٌّ وَبَعْدَ عَلِيٍّ ابْنُهُ الْحَسَنُ وَبَعْدَ الْحَسَنِ ابْنُهُ الْحُجَّةُ الْقَائِمُ الْمُنْتَظَرُ فِي غَيْبَتِهِ الْمُطَاعُ فِي ظُهُورِهِ وَلَوْ لَمْ يَبْقَ مِنَ الدُّنْيَا إِلا يَوْمٌ وَاحِدٌ لَطَوَّلَ اللَّهُ ذَلِكَ الْيَوْمَ حَتَّى يَخْرُجَ فَيَمْلاهَا عَدْلاً كَمَا مُلِئَتْ جَوْراً وَأَمَّا مَتَى فَإِخْبَارٌ عَنِ الْوَقْتِ وَلَقَدْ حَدَّثَنِي أَبِي عَنْ أَبِيهِ عَنْ آبَائِهِ عَنْ عَلِيٍّ عَلَيْهِمُ الصَّلاةُ وَالسَّلامُ أَنَّ النَّبِيَ صَلَّى اللهُ عَلَيْهِ وَآلِهِ قِيلَ لَهُ يَا رَسُولَ اللَّهِ مَتَى يَخْرُجُ الْقَائِمُ مِنْ ذُرِّيَّتِكَ فَقَالَ مَثَلُهُ مَثَلُ السَّاعَةِ لا يُجَلِّيهَا لِوَقْتِهَا إِلا هُوَ ثَقُلَتْ فِي السَّمَاوَاتِ وَالأَرْضِ لا تَأْتِيكُمْ إِلا بَغْتَةً.خبر دعبل عند وفاته

Ahmad b. Ziyad b. Ja'far al-Hamazani - may God be pleased with him - narrated that 'Alī b. Ibrahim b. Hashem quoted on the authority of his father, on the authority of Abdul Salam b. Saleh al-Harawi, "I heard De'bel b. 'Alī al-Khoza'ee say, 'I recited

[152] *Al-Kāfi, v1, ch73, h14*

this poem for my Master Ar-Ridha' (عليه السلام) which starts with: The schools for the Qur'anic verses are void of reciting now and the landing site of revelations is left like a barren desert! Then I reached the following verses: A Divine Leader shall rise - surely he is to rise In God's name and His Blessing he shall rise He will distinguish between right and wrong for us He will reward the good-doers and the bad-doers he shall chastise. Then Ar-Ridha' (عليه السلام) cried hard. He (عليه السلام) raised up his head towards me and said, 'O De'bel Khoza'ee! It was the Holy Spirit who made these verses flow out from your tongue. Do you know who that Divine Leader is? When will he rise? Then De'bel said, 'No my Master! I have only heard that a Divine Leader from your progeny shall rise and cleanse the earth of corruption. He shall fill it with justice. Then the Imam (عليه السلام) said, 'O De'bel! The Divine Leader coming after me is my son Muhammad; then after Muḥammad his son Ali; then his son Hassan; and then his son al-Hujjat the Riser the Awaited one (Imam al-Mahdi) who will come during his absence (Ghayba). He will be obeyed when he appears. God shall prolong time even if there is only one day left for him to rise and fill the earth with justice, since it has been filled with oppression and injustice. But when will it be? This is like informing the people about the time of the arrival of the Resurrection Day. My father quoted on the authority of his father, on the authority of his forefathers, on the authority of 'Alī (عليه السلام) who narrated that God's Prophet (صلى الله عليه وآله وسلم) was asked, 'O Prophet of God! When shall the Riser who is from your progeny rise?' The Prophet (صلى الله عليه وآله وسلم) replied, 'The similitude of that is like the similitude of the Hour (of Resurrection), 'None but He can reveal as to when it will occur. Heavy were its burden through the heavens and the earth. Only, all of a sudden will it come to you. (7:187) (مجهول كال موثق)[153]

Virtues of Imam Abul Hasan 'Alī b. Muḥammad al-Hadi (عليه السلام)

154.

[153] *'Uyūn Akhbār al-Riḍā, v2.ch36, h35*

بَعْضُ أَصْحَابِنَا عَنْ مُحَمَّدِ بْنِ عَلِيٍّ قَالَ أَخْبَرَنِي زَيْدُ بْنُ عَلِيِّ بْنِ الْحُسَيْنِ بْنِ زَيْدٍ قَالَ مَرِضْتُ فَدَخَلَ الطَّبِيبُ عَلَيَّ لَيْلاً فَوَصَفَ لِي دَوَاءً بِلَيْلٍ آخُذُهُ كَذَا وَكَذَا يَوْماً فَلَمْ يُمَكِّنِّي فَلَمْ يَخْرُجِ الطَّبِيبُ مِنَ الْبَابِ حَتَّى وَرَدَ عَلَيَّ نَصْرٌ بِقَارُورَةٍ فِيهَا ذَلِكَ الدَّوَاءُ بِعَيْنِهِ فَقَالَ لِي أَبُو الْحَسَنِ يُقْرِئُكَ السَّلامَ وَيَقُولُ لَكَ خُذْ هَذَا الدَّوَاءَ كَذَا وَكَذَا يَوْماً فَأَخَذْتُهُ فَشَرِبْتُهُ فَبَرَأْتُ قَالَ مُحَمَّدُ بْنُ عَلِيٍّ قَالَ لِي زَيْدُ بْنُ عَلِيٍّ يَأْبَى الطَّاعِنُ أَيْنَ الْغُلاةُ عَنْ هَذَا الْحَدِيثِ

Certain persons of our people have narrated from Muḥammad b. ʿAlī who has said the following. "Zayd b. ʿAlī b. al-Husayn b. Zayd narrated to me as follows. "I became ill and a doctor came to see me at night. He prescribed a medicine for me to be taken at night for so and so many days. I could not find the medicine that night. The physician was still there that Nasr came in with a bottle that contained the medicine that the physician had prescribed for me and said, "Abu al-Hassan (عليه السلام) sends you the greeting of peace and has asked you to take this medicine for so and so many days." I took the medicine and recovered from my illness." Muḥammad b. ʿAlī has said that Zayd b. ail told me, "The critics would refuse to accept this Hadīth saying, "Wherefrom the extremist have brought this Hadīth?" (مجهول)[154]

155.

عَلِيُّ بْنُ إِبْرَاهِيمَ عَنْ أَبِيهِ عَنْ إِسْمَاعِيلَ بْنِ مِهْرَانَ قَالَ لَمَّا خَرَجَ أَبُو جَعْفَرٍ (عَلَيْهِ السَّلام) مِنَ الْمَدِينَةِ إِلَى بَغْدَادَ فِي الدَّفْعَةِ الاولَى مِنْ خَرْجَتَيْهِ قُلْتُ لَهُ عِنْدَ خُرُوجِهِ جُعِلْتُ فِدَاكَ إِنِّي أَخَافُ عَلَيْكَ فِي هَذَا الْوَجْهِ فَإِلَى مَنِ الامْرُ بَعْدَكَ فَكَرَّ بِوَجْهِهِ إِلَيَّ ضَاحِكاً وَقَالَ لَيْسَ الْغَيْبَةُ حَيْثُ ظَنَنْتَ فِي هَذِهِ السَّنَةِ فَلَمَّا أُخْرِجَ بِهِ الثَّانِيَةَ إِلَى الْمُعْتَصِمِ صِرْتُ إِلَيْهِ فَقُلْتُ لَهُ جُعِلْتُ فِدَاكَ أَنْتَ خَارِجٌ فَإِلَى مَنْ هَذَا الامْرُ مِنْ بَعْدِكَ فَبَكَى حَتَّى اخْضَلَّتْ لِحْيَتُهُ ثُمَّ الْتَفَتَ إِلَيَّ فَقَالَ عِنْدَ هَذِهِ يُخَافُ عَلَيَّ الامْرُ مِنْ بَعْدِي إِلَى ابْنِي عَلِيٍّ

Ali b. Ibrahim has narrated from his father that 'Isma'il b. Mihran who has said the following. "When abu Ja'far (عليه السلام) left Madina for Baghdad the first time of his two journeys on his leaving I said to him, "May Allāh take my souls in service for

---

[154] *Al-Kāfi, v1, ch123, h9*

your cause, I am afraid about you in this condition. To who, after you, will belong the task (Leadership with Divine Authority)?" He turned to me laughing and said, "The disappearance, as have thought, will not take place this year. When he was about to be taken to al-Mu'tasam (179/795 —became caliph 218/833 — 227/841), for the second time I went to him and said, "May Allāh take my souls in service for your cause. You are leaving. To who, after you, will go this task Leadership with Divine Authority)?" He wept until his beard become soaked. He then turned to me and said, "This time you should be afraid about my life. The task (Leadership with Divine Authority) after me will go to my son 'Alī (عليه السلام)." (حسن)[155]

Virtues of Imam Abu Muḥammad al-Hasan b. 'Alī az-Zaki al-Askari (عليه السلام)

156.

عَلِيُّ بْنُ مُحَمَّدٍ عَنْ مُحَمَّدِ بْنِ إِبْرَاهِيمَ الْمَعْرُوفِ بِابْنِ الْكُرْدِيِّ عَنْ مُحَمَّدِ بْنِ عَلِيِّ بْنِ إِبْرَاهِيمَ بْنِ مُوسَى بْنِ جَعْفَرٍ قَالَ ضَاقَ بِنَا الامْرُ فَقَالَ لِي أَبِي امْضِ بِنَا حَتَّى نَصِيرَ إِلَى هَذَا الرَّجُلِ يَعْنِي أَبَا مُحَمَّدٍ فَإِنَّهُ قَدْ وُصِفَ عَنْهُ سَمَاحَةٌ فَقُلْتُ تَعْرِفُهُ فَقَالَ مَا أَعْرِفُهُ وَلا رَأَيْتُهُ قَطُّ قَالَ فَقَصَدْنَاهُ فَقَالَ لِي أَبِي وَهُوَ فِي طَرِيقِهِ مَا أَحْوَجَنَا إِلَى أَنْ يَأْمُرَ لَنَا بِخَمْسِمِائَةِ دِرْهَمٍ مِائَتَا دِرْهَمٍ لِلْكِسْوَةِ وَمِائَتَا دِرْهَمٍ لِلدَّيْنِ وَمِائَةٌ لِلنَّفَقَةِ فَقُلْتُ فِي نَفْسِي لَيْتَهُ أَمَرَ لِي بِثَلاثِمِائَةِ دِرْهَمٍ مِائَةٌ أَشْتَرِي بِهَا حِمَاراً وَمِائَةٌ لِلنَّفَقَةِ وَمِائَةٌ لِلْكِسْوَةِ وَأَخْرُجَ إِلَى الْجَبَلِ قَالَ فَلَمَّا وَافَيْنَا الْبَابَ خَرَجَ إِلَيْنَا غُلامُهُ فَقَالَ يَدْخُلُ عَلِيُّ بْنُ إِبْرَاهِيمَ وَمُحَمَّدٌ ابْنُهُ فَلَمَّا دَخَلْنَا عَلَيْهِ وَسَلَّمْنَا قَالَ لابِي يَا عَلِيُّ مَا خَلَّفَكَ عَنَّا إِلَى هَذَا الْوَقْتِ فَقَالَ يَا سَيِّدِي اسْتَحْيَيْتُ أَنْ أَلْقَاكَ عَلَى هَذِهِ الْحَالِ فَلَمَّا خَرَجْنَا مِنْ عِنْدِهِ جَاءَنَا غُلامُهُ فَنَاوَلَ أَبِي صُرَّةً فَقَالَ هَذِهِ خَمْسُمِائَةِ دِرْهَمٍ مِائَتَانِ لِلْكِسْوَةِ وَمِائَتَانِ لِلدَّيْنِ وَمِائَةٌ لِلنَّفَقَةِ وَأَعْطَانِي صُرَّةً فَقَالَ هَذِهِ ثَلاثُمِائَةِ دِرْهَمٍ اجْعَلْ مِائَةً فِي ثَمَنِ حِمَارٍ وَمِائَةً لِلْكِسْوَةِ وَمِائَةً لِلنَّفَقَةِ وَلا تَخْرُجْ إِلَى الْجَبَلِ وَصِرْ إِلَى سُورَاءَ فَصَارَ إِلَى سُورَاءَ وَتَزَوَّجَ بِامْرَأَةٍ فَدَخْلُهُ الْيَوْمَ أَلْفُ دِينَارٍ وَمَعَ هَذَا يَقُولُ بِالْوَقْفِ فَقَالَ مُحَمَّدُ بْنُ إِبْرَاهِيمَ فَقُلْتُ لَهُ وَيْحَكَ أَ تُرِيدُ أَمْراً أَبْيَنَ مِنْ هَذَا قَالَ فَقَالَ هَذَا أَمْرٌ قَدْ جَرَيْنَا عَلَيْهِ

---

[155] *Al-Kafi, v1, ch74, h1*

Ali b. Muḥammad has narrated from Muḥammad b. Ibrahim, known as b. al-Kurdiy, from Muḥammad b. ʿAlī b. Ibrahim b. Mūsā b. Ja'far (عليه السلام) who has said the following. "We were under pressure and constraint. My father said, "Let us go to abu Muḥammad (عليه السلام). People describe him as very generous and considerate." I asked, "Do you know him?" He said, "No, I do not know him and I have not seen him before." We decided to go and meet him. My father said on the way, "I wish he would grant us five hundred Dirhams. Two hundred for clothes, two hundred for to pay the debts and two hundred for expenses. We need this much very badly." I then said to myself, "I wish he will grant me three hundred Dirhams, one hundred to buy a donkey, one hundred for expenses and one hundred for clothes to go to the mountains." The narrator has said that when we arrived at the door a slave came out and said, "Ali b. Ibrahim and his son Muḥammad come inside." When we were in his (the Imam's (عليه السلام) presence we offered the greeting of peace and said to my father. "O Ali, what held you back from coming to us until now?" He said, "My master, I felt shy to come to you in this condition." When we left him his slave came to us and gave a bag of money to my father saying, "This is five hundred Dirhams, two hundred for clothes, two hundred to pay debts and two hundred for expenses." He gave me a bag and said, "This is three hundred Dirhams, one hundred for the donkey, one hundred for clothes and one hundred for expenses. Do not go to the mountains. Go to Sawra'. He then went to Sawra' and marriage a woman and now his income from properties is a thousand Dinar despite this he belongs to the waqifi sect in matters of beliefs. Muḥammad b. Ibrahim has said that I said to him, "Woe is you! What more clear proof do you want to believe in him as your Imam?" He said, "This (belief in Waqifi sect) is habit that has been with us (and it does not go away)." (مجهول)[156]

157.

[156] *Al-Kāfi, v1, ch124, h3*

عَلِيٌّ عَنْ أَبِي أَحْمَدَ بْنِ رَاشِدٍ عَنْ أَبِي هَاشِمٍ الْجَعْفَرِيِّ قَالَ شَكَوْتُ إِلَى أَبِي مُحَمَّدٍ (عَلَيْهِ السَّلام) الْحَاجَةَ فَحَكَّ بِسَوْطِهِ الارْضَ قَالَ وَأَحْسَبُهُ غَطَّاهُ بِمِنْدِيلٍ وَأَخْرَجَ خَمْسَمِائَةِ دِينَارٍ فَقَالَ يَا أَبَا هَاشِمٍ خُذْ وَأَعْذِرْنَا

Ali has narrated from abu Ahmad b. Rashid from abu Hashim al-Ja'fari who has said the following. "I requested abu Muḥammad for something that I needed. He scratched the earth with his whip. The narrator has said that I think he then covered it with a handkerchief and then took out five hundred Dinars. He then said, "O abu Hashim take it and grants us pardon." (مجهول)[157]

158.

عَلِيُّ بْنُ مُحَمَّدٍ عَنْ أَبِي عَبْدِ اللهِ بْنِ صَالِحٍ عَنْ أَبِيهِ عَنْ أَبِي عَلِيٍّ الْمُطَهَّرِ أَنَّهُ كَتَبَ إِلَيْهِ سَنَةَ الْقَادِسِيَّةِ يُعْلِمُهُ انْصِرَافَ النَّاسِ وَأَنَّهُ يَخَافُ الْعَطَشَ فَكَتَبَ (عَلَيْهِ السَّلام) امْضُوا فَلا خَوْفٌ عَلَيْكُمْ إِنْ شَاءَ اللهُ فَمَضَوْا سَالِمِينَ وَالْحَمْدُ للهِ رَبِّ الْعَالَمِينَ

Ali b. Muḥammad has narrated from abu 'AbdAllāh b. Salih from his father from abu 'Alī al-Mutahhar the following. "He wrote to him (abu Muḥammad (عليه السلام) in the year of Qadisiyya, the year of draught that forced people to returned home without performing Hajj for fear of thirst. He wrote back in reply, "continue your journey and you will have no fear by the will of Allāh." They continued their journey to Hajj safely and thanks to Allāh." (مجهول)[158]

159.

---

[157] *Al-Kāfi, v1, ch124, h5*

[158] *Al-Kāfi, v1, ch124, h6*

عَلِيُّ بْنُ مُحَمَّدٍ عَنْ عَلِيِّ بْنِ الْحَسَنِ بْنِ الْفَضْلِ الْيَمَانِيِّ قَالَ نَزَلَ بِالْجَعْفَرِيِّ مِنْ آلِ جَعْفَرٍ خَلْقٌ لا قِبَلَ لَهُ بِهِمْ فَكَتَبَ إِلَى أَبِي مُحَمَّدٍ يَشْكُو ذَلِكَ فَكَتَبَ إِلَيْهِ تُكْفَوْنَ ذَلِكَ إِنْ شَاءَ الله تَعَالَى فَخَرَجَ إِلَيْهِمْ فِي نَفَرٍ يَسِيرٍ وَالْقَوْمُ يَزِيدُونَ عَلَى عِشْرِينَ أَلْفاً وَهُوَ فِي أَقَلَّ مِنْ أَلْفٍ فَاسْتَبَاحَهُمْ

Ali b. Muḥammad has narrated from ʻAlī b. al-Hassan b. al-Fadl al-Yamani who has said the following. " Al-Jaʻfari from the family of Jaʻfar was attacked by such a large number of people that seemed impossible for them to defend themselves. He wrote to abu Muḥammad (عليه السلام) about his dangerous condition. He wrote back to him in reply, "You will be adequately defended by the will of Allāh, the Most High. He came out with just a few people to defend themselves against the attackers who were in excess of twenty thousand while on his side there were fewer than a thousand but the attackers were all vanished." (مجهول)[159]

160.

عَلِيُّ بْنُ مُحَمَّدٍ عَنْ مُحَمَّدِ بْنِ إِسْمَاعِيلَ الْعَلَوِيِّ قَالَ حُبِسَ أَبُو مُحَمَّدٍ عِنْدَ عَلِيِّ بْنِ نَارْمَشَ وَهُوَ أَنْصَبُ النَّاسِ وَأَشَدُّهُمْ عَلَى آلِ أَبِي طَالِبٍ وَقِيلَ لَهُ افْعَلْ بِهِ وَافْعَلْ فَمَا أَقَامَ عِنْدَهُ إِلا يَوْماً حَتَّى وَضَعَ خَدَّيْهِ لَهُ وَكَانَ لا يَرْفَعُ بَصَرَهُ إِلَيْهِ إِجْلالاً وَإِعْظَاماً فَخَرَجَ مِنْ عِنْدِهِ وَهُوَ أَحْسَنُ النَّاسِ بَصِيرَةً وَأَحْسَنُهُمْ فِيهِ قَوْلاً

Ali b. Muḥammad has narrated from Muḥammad b. 'Ismaʻil al-ʻAlawi who has said the following. "Abu Muḥammad (عليه السلام) was imprisoned under the supervision of ʻAlī b. Narmasha who was extremely hostile towards the descendants of abu Talib. He was told to treat him (abu Muḥammad (عليه السلام) as he (the guard) wished. He stayed with him only for day and the guard who was hostile towards him became so submissive before him that he would not even dare to look up into his face out of glorification and reverence. He (abu Muḥammad (عليه السلام) came out from his prison

---

159 *Al-Kāfi, v1, ch124, h7*

and he (the guard) had turned into having the highest degree of understanding of him and would speak the best words about him." (مجهول)[160]

161.

عَلِيُّ بْنُ مُحَمَّدٍ عَنْ مُحَمَّدِ بْنِ إِسْمَاعِيلَ بْنِ إِبْرَاهِيمَ بْنِ مُوسَى بْنِ جَعْفَرِ بْنِ مُحَمَّدٍ عَنْ عَلِيِّ بْنِ عَبْدِ الْغَفَّارِ قَالَ دَخَلَ الْعَبَّاسِيُّونَ عَلَى صَالِحِ بْنِ وَصِيفٍ وَدَخَلَ صَالِحُ بْنُ عَلِيٍّ وَغَيْرُهُ مِنَ الْمُنْحَرِفِينَ عَنْ هَذِهِ النَّاحِيَةِ عَلَى صَالِحِ بْنِ وَصِيفٍ عِنْدَ مَا حَبَسَ أَبَا مُحَمَّدٍ (عَلَيْهِ السَّلام) فَقَالَ لَهُمْ صَالِحٌ وَمَا أَصْنَعُ قَدْ وَكَّلْتُ بِهِ رَجُلَيْنِ مِنْ أَشَرِّ مَنْ قَدَرْتُ عَلَيْهِ فَقَدْ صَارَا مِنَ الْعِبَادَةِ وَالصَّلاةِ وَالصِّيَامِ إِلَى أَمْرٍ عَظِيمٍ فَقُلْتُ لَهُمَا مَا فِيهِ فَقَالا مَا تَقُولُ فِي رَجُلٍ يَصُومُ النَّهَارَ وَيَقُومُ اللَّيْلَ كُلَّهُ لا يَتَكَلَّمُ وَلا يَتَشَاغَلُ وَإِذَا نَظَرْنَا إِلَيْهِ ارْتَعَدَتْ فَرَائِصُنَا وَيُدَاخِلُنَا مَا لا نَمْلِكُهُ مِنْ أَنْفُسِنَا فَلَمَّا سَمِعُوا ذَلِكَ انْصَرَفُوا خَائِبِينَ

Ali b. Muḥammad has narrated from Muḥammad b. 'Isma'il b. Ibrahim b. Mūsā b. Ja'far b. Muḥammad (عليه السلام) from 'Alī b. 'Abd al-Ghaffar who has said the following. "When abu Muḥammad (عليه السلام) was imprisoned, the 'Abbassids, Salih b. Wasif, Salih b. 'Alī and others who were not Shi'as all came to Salih b. Wasif asking him to exert more pressure on abu Muḥammad (عليه السلام).Salih told them, "What should I do? I managed to find two people who were of the harshest manners and appointed them to guard him they both turned into most assiduous worshippers in prayers and fasting. When I asked them about their behaviors they replied, "What would you say about a man who fasts every day, worships the whole night and does not speak or busy himself with anything? When we look at him a feeling of trembling and shivering over takes us and we lose control over our own selves." When they heard this they returned in despair." (مجهول)[161]

162.

[160] *Al-Kāfi, v1, ch124, h8*

[161] *Al-Kāfi, v1, ch124, h23*

عَلِيُّ بْنُ مُحَمَّدٍ عَنْ بَعْضِ أَصْحَابِنَا قَالَ سُلِّمَ أَبُو مُحَمَّدٍ (عَلَيْهِ السَّلام) إِلَى نِحْرِيرٍ فَكَانَ يُضَيِّقُ عَلَيْهِ وَيُؤْذِيهِ قَالَ فَقَالَتْ لَهُ امْرَأَتُهُ وَيْلَكَ اتَّقِ اللهَ لا تَدْرِي مَنْ فِي مَنْزِلِكَ وَعَرَّفَتْهُ صَلاحَهُ وَقَالَتْ إِنِّي أَخَافُ عَلَيْكَ مِنْهُ فَقَالَ لارْمِيَنَّهُ بَيْنَ السِّبَاعِ ثُمَّ فَعَلَ ذَلِكَ بِهِ فَرُئِيَ (عَلَيْهِ السَّلام) قَائِماً يُصَلِّي وَهِيَ حَوْلَهُ

Ail Muḥammad has narrated from certain persons of our people saying as follows. "Abu Muḥammad (عليه السلام) was placed under the supervision of a zoo-keeper who would cause constraints suffering to him. He has said that his wife told him, "woe is you, be pious before Allāh. Do you not know who is in your house?" She then explained to him the good manners of the Imam (عليه السلام) and said, "I am afraid for you from him." He then said, "I can throw him to the beasts." He inf act, did so and the Imam (عليه السلام) was seeing standing among them for prayer and the beast circled around him." (مرسل)[162]

163.

مُحَمَّدُ بْنُ يَحْيَى عَنْ أَحْمَدَ بْنِ إِسْحَاقَ قَالَ دَخَلْتُ عَلَى أَبِي مُحَمَّدٍ (عَلَيْهِ السَّلام) فَسَأَلْتُهُ أَنْ يَكْتُبَ لانْظُرَ إِلَى خَطِّهِ فَأَعْرِفَهُ إِذَا وَرَدَ فَقَالَ نَعَمْ ثُمَّ قَالَ يَا أَحْمَدُ إِنَّ الْخَطَّ سَيَخْتَلِفُ عَلَيْكَ مِنْ بَيْنِ الْقَلَمِ الْغَلِيظِ إِلَى الْقَلَمِ الدَّقِيقِ فَلا تَشُكَّنَّ ثُمَّ دَعَا بِالدَّوَاةِ فَكَتَبَ وَجَعَلَ يَسْتَمِدُّ إِلَى مَجْرَى الدَّوَاةِ فَقُلْتُ فِي نَفْسِي وَهُوَ يَكْتُبُ أَسْتَوْهِبُهُ الْقَلَمَ الَّذِي كَتَبَ بِهِ فَلَمَّا فَرَغَ مِنَ الْكِتَابَةِ أَقْبَلَ يُحَدِّثُنِي وَهُوَ يَمْسَحُ الْقَلَمَ بِمِنْدِيلِ الدَّوَاةِ سَاعَةً ثُمَّ قَالَ هَاكَ يَا أَحْمَدُ فَنَاوَلَنِيهِ فَقُلْتُ جُعِلْتُ فِدَاكَ إِنِّي مُغْتَمٌّ لِشَيْءٍ يُصِيبُنِي فِي نَفْسِي وَقَدْ أَرَدْتُ أَنْ أَسْأَلَ أَبَاكَ فَلَمْ يُقْضَ لِي ذَلِكَ فَقَالَ وَمَا هُوَ يَا أَحْمَدُ فَقُلْتُ يَا سَيِّدِي رُوِيَ لَنَا عَنْ آبَائِكَ أَنَّ نَوْمَ الانْبِيَاءِ عَلَى أَقْفِيَتِهِمْ وَنَوْمَ الْمُؤْمِنِينَ عَلَى أَيْمَانِهِمْ وَنَوْمَ الْمُنَافِقِينَ عَلَى شَمَائِلِهِمْ وَنَوْمَ الشَّيَاطِينِ عَلَى وُجُوهِهِمْ فَقَالَ (عَلَيْهِ السَّلام) كَذَلِكَ هُوَ فَقُلْتُ يَا سَيِّدِي فَإِنِّي أَجْهَدُ أَنْ أَنَامَ عَلَى يَمِينِي فَمَا يُمْكِنُنِي وَلا يَأْخُذُنِي النَّوْمُ عَلَيْهَا فَسَكَتَ سَاعَةً ثُمَّ قَالَ يَا أَحْمَدُ ادْنُ مِنِّي فَدَنَوْتُ مِنْهُ فَقَالَ أَدْخِلْ يَدَكَ تَحْتَ ثِيَابِكَ فَأَدْخَلْتُهَا فَأَخْرَجَ يَدَهُ مِنْ تَحْتِ ثِيَابِهِ وَأَدْخَلَهَا تَحْتَ ثِيَابِي فَمَسَحَ بِيَدِهِ الْيُمْنَى عَلَى جَانِبِي الايْسَرِ وَبِيَدِهِ الْيُسْرَى عَلَى جَانِبِي الايْمَنِ ثَلاثَ مَرَّاتٍ فَقَالَ أَحْمَدُ فَمَا أَقْدِرُ أَنْ أَنَامَ عَلَى يَسَارِي مُنْذُ فَعَلَ ذَلِكَ بِي (عَلَيْهِ السَّلام) وَمَا يَأْخُذُنِي نَوْمٌ عَلَيْهَا أَصْلاً

---

[162] *Al-Kāfi, v1, ch124, h26*

Muhammad b. Yahya has narrated from Ahmad b. Ishaq who has said the following. "Once I went to see abu Muḥammad (عليه السلام) and asked him to write for me few lines so that whenever I would see his hand writing I would recognize it. The Imam (عليه السلام) said, "Yes, and then said, "O Ahmad the writing with a fine pen and with thick pen will look different to you. Do not have doubts He then asked for a pen and ink pot and began writing. He would make the pen to have ink from the bottom of the ink pot. I thought to myself when he was writing, "I will request him to gift me the pen with which he is writing." When he finished writing he turned to me and began speaking while he was wiping the pen with the handkerchief of the ink pot for a while and then said, "Here, O Ahmad it is for you." He gave it to me. I then said, may Allāh take my soul in service for your cause, I am sad about something that is in my soul. I wanted to ask your father about it but I did not have the chance. He asked, "What is it, O Ahmad?" I said, "My master, it is narrated to us from your holy ancestors that the prophet sleep on their backs, the true believers sleep on their right side, the hypocrites sleep on their left side and Satan's sleep on their belly." He (عليه السلام) said, "That is how it is." I then said, "My master I struggle to sleep on my right side abut I cannot do so and I do not go to sleep on my right side." He remained quite for a while and then said, "O Ahmad, come close to me." I went close to him and he said, "put your hand hand under your clothes." I did so. He then took his hand from under his clothes and place under my clothes. He wiped with his right hand my left side and with his left hand my right side three times. Ahmad has said that ever since I have not been able to sleep on my left side and cannot go to sleep on my left side." (صحيح)[163]

164.

عَلِيُّ بْنُ مُحَمَّدٍ عَنْ مُحَمَّدِ بْنِ أَحْمَدَ النَّهْدِيِّ عَنْ يَحْيَى بْنِ يَسَارٍ الْقَنْبَرِيِّ قَالَ أَوْصَى أَبُو الْحَسَنِ (عَلَيْهِ السَّلام) إِلَى ابْنِهِ الْحَسَنِ قَبْلَ مُضِيِّهِ بِأَرْبَعَةِ أَشْهُرٍ وَأَشْهَدَنِي عَلَى ذَلِكَ وَجَمَاعَةً مِنَ الْمَوَالِي

[163] *Al-Kafi, v1, ch124, h27*

Ali b. Muḥammad has narrated from Muḥammad b. Ahmad al-Nahdi from Yahya b. Yasar al-Qanbar who has said the following. "Abu al-Hassan (عليه السلام) prepared his directive will to his son, al-Hassan four months before his leaving this world. He appointed me to bear testimony to his will as well as a group of the follower friends." (مجهول)[164]

165.

عَلِيُّ بْنُ مُحَمَّدٍ عَنْ جَعْفَرِ بْنِ مُحَمَّدٍ الْكُوفِيِّ عَنْ بَشَّارِ بْنِ أَحْمَدَ الْبَصْرِيِّ عَنْ عَلِيِّ بْنِ عُمَرَ النَّوْفَلِيِّ قَالَ كُنْتُ مَعَ أَبِي الْحَسَنِ (عَلَيْهِ السَّلام) فِي صَحْنِ دَارِهِ فَمَرَّ بِنَا مُحَمَّدٌ ابْنُهُ فَقُلْتُ لَهُ جُعِلْتُ فِدَاكَ هَذَا صَاحِبُنَا بَعْدَكَ فَقَالَ لا صَاحِبُكُمْ بَعْدِيَ الْحَسَنُ

Ali b. Muḥammad has narrated from Ja'far b. Muḥammad al-Kufi from Bashshar b. Ahmad al-Basri from 'Alī b. 'Umar al-Nawfali who has said the following. "Once I was with abu al-Hassan in the compound of his house and at that time his son, Muḥammad passed by. I said to him, "may Allāh take my souls in service for your cause, will he be our master, Imam, after you?" The Imam (عليه السلام) said, " No, your master, Imam, after me will be al-Hassan (عليه السلام)." * This abu Ja'far Muḥammad b. Ali, is the eldest son of the Imam al-Hadi (عليه السلام).He died before his father (230/845 - 252/866). His shrine is near Balad which is near Baghdad, and the place is now known as al-Sayyid Muhammad. In the following aHadīth his name is frequently mentioned. (مجهول)[165]

166.

---

[164] *Al-Kāfi, v1, ch75, h1*

[165] *Al-Kāfi, v1, ch75, h2*

عَنْهُ عَنْ بَشَّارِ بْنِ أَحْمَدَ عَنْ عَبْدِ اللهِ بْنِ مُحَمَّدٍ الاصْفَهَانِيِّ قَالَ قَالَ أَبُو الْحَسَنِ (عَلَيْهِ السَّلام) صَاحِبُكُمْ بَعْدِيَ الَّذِي يُصَلِّي عَلَيَّ قَالَ وَلَمْ نَعْرِفْ أَبَا مُحَمَّدٍ قَبْلَ ذَلِكَ قَالَ فَخَرَجَ أَبُو مُحَمَّدٍ فَصَلَّى عَلَيْهِ

From him has narrated from Bashshar b. Ahmad from ‘AbdAllāh b. Muḥammad al-Isfahani who has said the following. “Abu al-Hassan (عليه السلام) said, “Your master (Imam) after me will be the one who will perform prayer for me (prayer for burial).” The narrator has said that we did not know abu Muḥammad (عليه السلام) before this. Abu Muḥammad came out and prayed (for his burial).” (مجهول)[166]

167.

وَعَنْهُ عَنْ مُوسَى بْنِ جَعْفَرِ بْنِ وَهْبٍ عَنْ عَلِيِّ بْنِ جَعْفَرٍ قَالَ كُنْتُ حَاضِراً أَبَا الْحَسَنِ (عَلَيْهِ السَّلام) لَمَّا تُوُفِّيَ ابْنُهُ مُحَمَّدٌ فَقَالَ لِلْحَسَنِ يَا بُنَيَّ أَحْدِثْ لله شُكْراً فَقَدْ أَحْدَثَ فِيكَ أَمْراً

From him who has narrated from Mūsā b. Ja‘far b. Wahab from ‘Alī b. Ja‘far who has said the following. “I was present with abu al-Hassan (عليه السلام) when his son Muḥammad died. The Imam (عليه السلام) said this to (his son) al-Hassan (عليه السلام), “Son renew your thanks to Allāh because He has just granted you the matter (Leadership with Divine Authority).” (مجهول)[167]

168.

عَلِيُّ بْنُ مُحَمَّدٍ عَنْ أَبِي مُحَمَّدٍ الاسْبَارِقِينِيِّ عَنْ عَلِيِّ بْنِ عَمْرٍو الْعَطَّارِ قَالَ دَخَلْتُ عَلَى أَبِي الْحَسَنِ الْعَسْكَرِيِّ (عَلَيْهِ السَّلام) وَأَبُو جَعْفَرٍ ابْنُهُ فِي الاحْيَاءِ وَأَنَا أَظُنُّ أَنَّهُ هُوَ فَقُلْتُ لَهُ جُعِلْتُ فِدَاكَ مَنْ أَخُصُّ مِنْ وُلْدِكَ فَقَالَ لا تَخُصُّوا أَحَداً حَتَّى يَخْرُجَ إِلَيْكُمْ أَمْرِي قَالَ فَكَتَبْتُ إِلَيْهِ بَعْدُ فِيمَنْ يَكُونُ هَذَا الامْرُ قَالَ فَكَتَبَ إِلَيَّ فِي الْكَبِيرِ مِنْ وَلَدَيَّ قَالَ وَكَانَ أَبُو مُحَمَّدٍ أَكْبَرَ مِنْ أَبِي جَعْفَرٍ

---

[166] *Al-Kāfi, v1, ch75, h3*

[167] *Al-Kāfi, v1, ch75, h4*

Ali b. Muḥammad has narrated from abu Muḥammad al-Asbarqiniy from ʿAlī b. ‘Amr al-‘Attar who has said the following. “Once I went to see al-Hassan al-‘Askari (عليه السلام) when his son abu Ja‘far (Muhammad) was still alive and I thought he will be the Imam after his father. I then asked the Imam (عليه السلام), “May Allāh take my souls in service for your cause, which of your sons I will consider (my Imam)?” The Imam (عليه السلام) said, “do not consider any of them (your Imam) until my command will come to you.” The narrator has said, “I wrote to him afterwards asking, ‘To who will go this task (Leadership with Divine Authority)” The narrator has said, “He wrote to me, “ (It will go) to my eldest son.” The narrator has said, “Abu Muḥammad (عليه السلام) was older then abu Ja‘far.” (مجهول)[168]

169.

مُحَمَّدُ بْنُ يَحْيَى وَغَيْرُهُ عَنْ سَعْدِ بْنِ عَبْدِ اللهِ عَنْ جَمَاعَةٍ مِنْ بَنِي هَاشِمٍ مِنْهُمُ الْحَسَنُ بْنُ الْحَسَنِ الافْطَسُ أَنَّهُمْ حَضَرُوا يَوْمَ تُوُفِّيَ مُحَمَّدُ بْنُ عَلِيِّ بْنِ مُحَمَّدٍ بَابَ أَبِي الْحَسَنِ يُعَزُّونَهُ وَقَدْ بُسِطَ لَهُ فِي صَحْنِ دَارِهِ وَالنَّاسُ جُلُوسٌ حَوْلَهُ فَقَالُوا قَدَّرْنَا أَنْ يَكُونَ حَوْلَهُ مِنْ آلِ أَبِي طَالِبٍ وَبَنِي هَاشِمٍ وَقُرَيْشٍ مِائَةٌ وَخَمْسُونَ رَجُلاً سِوَى مَوَالِيهِ وَسَائِرِ النَّاسِ إِذْ نَظَرَ إِلَى الْحَسَنِ بْنِ عَلِيٍّ قَدْ جَاءَ مَشْقُوقَ الْجَيْبِ حَتَّى قَامَ عَنْ يَمِينِهِ وَنَحْنُ لا نَعْرِفُهُ فَنَظَرَ إِلَيْهِ أَبُو الْحَسَنِ (عَلَيْهِ السَّلام) بَعْدَ سَاعَةٍ فَقَالَ يَا بُنَيَّ أَحْدِثْ للهِ عَزَّ وَجَلَّ شُكْراً فَقَدْ أَحْدَثَ فِيكَ أَمْراً فَبَكَى الْفَتَى وَحَمِدَ اللهَ وَاسْتَرْجَعَ وَقَالَ الْحَمْدُ للهِ رَبِّ الْعَالَمِينَ وَأَنَا أَسْأَلُ اللهَ تَمَامَ نِعَمِهِ لَنَا فِيكَ وَإِنَّا للهِ وَإِنَّا إِلَيْهِ رَاجِعُونَ فَسَأَلْنَا عَنْهُ فَقِيلَ هَذَا الْحَسَنُ ابْنُهُ وَقَدَّرْنَا لَهُ فِي ذَلِكَ الْوَقْتِ عِشْرِينَ سَنَةً أَوْ أَرْجَحَ فَيَوْمَئِذٍ عَرَفْنَاهُ وَعَلِمْنَا أَنَّهُ قَدْ أَشَارَ إِلَيْهِ بِالامَامَةِ وَأَقَامَهُ مَقَامَهُ

Muhammad b. Yahya and others have narrated from Sa‘id b. ‘AbdAllāh from a group of banu Hashim, among whom was al-Hassan b. al-Hassan al-Aftas, the following. “They were present on the day Muḥammad b. ʿAlī b. Muhammad, at the door of abu al-Hassan to offer condolences. A place in the compound of his house was prepared for him and people were sitting around him. They said, “We estimated that at that

[168] *Al-Kāfi, v1, ch75, h7*

time from the descendents of abu Talib, Hashim and Quraysh there were about fifty men besides his slaves and other people. At such time he look at al-Hassan b. 'Alī coming and the front of his shirt was torn. He stood at the right of his father and we did not know him. Abu al-Hassan (عليه السلام) looked at him after a while and said, "My son, renew your thanks to Allāh, the Most Majestic, the Most gracious, because He has granted you a new task (Leadership with Divine Authority)." The young man wept, praised Allāh, and said, "We are for Allāh and to Him we shall return. He then said, "All praise belongs to Allāh, Lord of the worlds. I pray to Allāh for completion the blessings for us in you. "We are for Allāh and to Him we shall return." We asked about him and it was said that he was al-Hassan, the son of the Imam. We estimated his age at that time around twenty years or more. On that day we learned and came to know that he had tacitly made a statement about the succeeding Imam and (the Leader with Divine Authority)." (مجهول كالصحيح)[169]

170.

عَلِيُّ بْنُ مُحَمَّدٍ عَنْ إِسْحَاقَ بْنِ مُحَمَّدٍ عَنْ مُحَمَّدِ بْنِ يَحْيَى بْنِ دَرْيَابَ قَالَ دَخَلْتُ عَلَى أَبِي الْحَسَنِ (عَلَيْهِ السَّلام) بَعْدَ مُضِيِّ أَبِي جَعْفَرٍ فَعَزَّيْتُهُ عَنْهُ وَأَبُو مُحَمَّدٍ (عَلَيْهِ السَّلام) جَالِسٌ فَبَكَى أَبُو مُحَمَّدٍ (عَلَيْهِ السَّلام) فَأَقْبَلَ عَلَيْهِ أَبُو الْحَسَنِ (عَلَيْهِ السَّلام) فَقَالَ لَهُ إِنَّ اللهَ تَبَارَكَ وَتَعَالَى قَدْ جَعَلَ فِيكَ خَلَفاً مِنْهُ فَاحْمَدِ اللهَ

Ali b. Muḥammad has narrated from Ishaq b. Muḥammad from Muḥammad b. Yahya b. Daryab who has said the following. "I went to see abu al-Hassan (عليه السلام) after the death of abu Ja'far and offered condolences for this reason. Abu Muḥammad (عليه السلام) was also present. He wept and abu al-Hassan (عليه السلام) turned to him and said, "Allāh, the Most Holy, the Most High, has made you to succeed (the Imam) instead of him. You must thanks Allāh." (مجهول)[170]

---

[169] *Al-Kāfi, v1, ch75, h8*

[170] *Al-Kāfi, v1, ch75, h9*

171.

عَلِيُّ بْنُ مُحَمَّدٍ عَمَّنْ ذَكَرَهُ عَنْ مُحَمَّدِ بْنِ أَحْمَدَ الْعَلَوِيِّ عَنْ دَاوُدَ بْنِ الْقَاسِمِ قَالَ سَمِعْتُ أَبَا الْحَسَنِ (عَلَيْهِ السَّلام) يَقُولُ الْخَلَفُ مِنْ بَعْدِيَ الْحَسَنُ فَكَيْفَ لَكُمْ بِالْخَلَفِ مِنْ بَعْدِ الْخَلَفِ فَقُلْتُ وَلِمَ جَعَلَنِيَ اللهُ فِدَاكَ فَقَالَ إِنَّكُمْ لا تَرَوْنَ شَخْصَهُ وَلا يَحِلُّ لَكُمْ ذِكْرُهُ بِاسْمِهِ فَقُلْتُ فَكَيْفَ نَذْكُرُهُ فَقَالَ قُولُوا الْحُجَّةُ مِنْ آلِ مُحَمَّدٍ عَلَيْهِم السَّلام

Ali b. Muḥammad has narrated from the person he mentioned from Muḥammad b. Ahmad al-'Alawi from Dawud b. al-Qasim who has said the following. "I heard abu al-Hassan (عليه السلام) saying, 'The succeeding (Imam) after me will be al-Hassan. How will your dealing be with the succeeding (Imam) of the succeeding (Imam)?" I then said, "Why will that be so, may Allāh take my souls in service for your cause?" He said, "You will not see him in person. It will not lawful for you to pronounce his name." I then asked, "How then will we speak of him?" He said, "Say, 'The Divine Authority from the family of Muḥammad (s.a.w)." (مجهول)[171]

Virtues of Al-Qa'im min A'l Muḥammad (عجل الله تعالى فرجه)

172.

أَحْمَدُ بْنُ مُحَمَّدٍ عَنْ مُحَمَّدِ بْنِ الْحَسَنِ عَنْ مُحَمَّدِ بْنِ عِيسَى بْنِ عُبَيْدٍ عَنْ عَلِيِّ بْنِ أَسْبَاطٍ عَنْ سَيْفِ بْنِ عَمِيرَةَ عَنْ مُحَمَّدِ بْنِ حُمْرَانَ قَالَ قَالَ أَبُو عَبْدِ اللهِ (عَلَيْهِ السَّلام) لَمَّا كَانَ مِنْ أَمْرِ الْحُسَيْنِ (عَلَيْهِ السَّلام) مَا كَانَ ضَجَّتِ الْمَلائِكَةُ إِلَى اللهِ بِالْبُكَاءِ وَقَالَتْ يُفْعَلُ هَذَا بِالْحُسَيْنِ صَفِيِّكَ وَابْنِ نَبِيِّكَ قَالَ فَأَقَامَ اللهُ لَهُمْ ظِلَّ الْقَائِمِ (عَلَيْهِ السَّلام) وَقَالَ بِهَذَا أَنْتَقِمُ لِهَذَا

Ahmad b. Muḥammad has narrated from Muḥammad b. al-Hassan from Muḥammad b. 'Isa b. 'Ubayd from 'Alī b. Asbat from Sayf b. 'Amira from Muḥammad b. humran who has said the following. "Abu 'AbdAllāh (عليه السلام) has said, 'When all that

[171] *Al-Kāfi, v1, ch75, h13*

happened to al-Husayn had happened, the angels wept and cried before Allāh and said, "How such thing would happen to al-Husayn Your chosen one and the grand son of Your Prophet?" The Imam (عليه السلام) has said that Allāh then showed to them the shadow of Al-Qa'im (the one who will rise with Divine Authority) and said, "Through him I will take My revenge." (موثق كالصحيح)[172]

173.

حَدَّثَنا أَحْمَدُ بْنُ زِيادِ بْنِ جَعْفَرٍ الْهَمَذانِيُّ رَضِيَ اللهُ عَنْهُ قالَ: حَدَّثَنا عَلِيُّ بْنُ هاشِمٍ، عَنْ أَبِيهِ، عَنْ مُحَمَّدِ بْنِ أَبِي عُمَيْرٍ، عَنْ غِياثِ بْنِ إِبْراهِيمَ، عَنِ الصَّادِقِ جَعْفَرِ بْنِ مُحَمَّدٍ، عَنْ أَبِيهِ مُحَمَّدِ بْنِ عَلِيٍّ، عَنْ أَبِيهِ عَلِيِّ بْنِ الْحُسَيْنِ؛ عَنْ أَبِيهِ الْحُسَيْنِ بْنِ عَلِيٍّ عَلَيْهِ السَّلامُ قالَ: سُئِلَ أَمِيرُ الْمُؤْمِنِينَ عَلَيْهِ السَّلامُ عَنْ مَعْنى قَوْلِ رَسُولِ اللهِ صَلَّى اللهُ عَلَيْهِ وَآلِهِ: «إِنِّي مُخَلِّفٌ فِيكُمُ الثَّقَلَيْنِ كِتابَ اللهِ وَعِتْرَتِي» مَنِ العِتْرَةُ؟ فَقالَ: أَنَا وَالْحَسَنُ وَالْحُسَيْنُ وَالأَئِمَّةُ التِّسْعَةُ مِنْ وُلْدِ الْحُسَيْنِ، تاسِعُهُمْ مَهْدِيُّهُمْ وَقائِمُهُمْ، لا يُفارِقُونَ كِتابَ اللهِ، وَلا يُفارِقُهُمْ حَتَّى يَرِدُوا عَلَى رَسُولِ اللهِ صَلَّى اللهُ عَلَيْهِ وَآلِهِ حَوْضَهُ

Ahmad b. Ziyad b. Ja'far al-Hamadani - may God be pleased with him - narrated that 'Alī b. Ibrahim b. Hashem quoted on the authority of his father, on the authority of Muḥammad b. Abi Omayr, on the authority of Ghiyath b. Ibrahim, on the authority of As-Ṣādiq Ja'far b. Muḥammad (عليه السلام), on the authority of his father Muḥammad b. 'Alī (عليه السلام), on the authority of his father 'Alī b. Al-Hussein (عليه السلام), on the authority of his father Al-Hussein b. 'Alī (عليه السلام) that the Commander of the Faithful (عليه السلام) was questioned about the meaning of what God's Prophet (صلى الله عليه وآله وسلم) said, "I will leave behind two heavy things with you: God's Book and my 'Itra." He (صلى الله عليه وآله وسلم) was asked, "What does "my 'Itra" mean?" He (صلى الله عليه وآله وسلم) replied, "It is I, Al-Hassan, Al-Hussein and the other nine Divine Leaders from the descendants of Al-Hussein. The ninth of them is their Al-Mahdi (Divinely Guided One) who is their Riser. They will not separate themselves from God's Book

---

[172] *Al-Kafi, v1, ch116, h6*

and God's Book will not separate from them until they meet God's Prophet (صلى الله
عليه وآله وسلم) at his Pool." (معتبر)[173]

174.

حدثنا أبي رضي الله عنه قال: حدثنا علي بن إبراهيم بن هاشم، عن أبيه، عن محمد بن أبي عمير. عن سعيد
بن غزوان، عن أبي بصير، عن أبي جعفر عليه السلام قال: يكون تسعة أئمة بعد الحسين بن علي تاسعهم
قائمهم عليهم السلام

(The compiler of the book narrated) that his father - may God be pleased with him -
narrated that 'Alī b. Ibrahim b. Hashim quoted his father, on the authority of
Muḥammad b. Abi Umayr, on the authority of Sa'ed b. Qazvan, on the authority of
Abi Basir that Abi Ja'far al-Baqir (عليه السلام) said, "There are nine Divine Leaders after
al-Hussein b. 'Alī (عليه السلام), the ninth of whom shall be the Riser (عجل الله تعالى فرجه)."
(مجهول كالصحيح)[174]

175.

حَدَّثَنَا أَحْمَدُ بْنُ مُحَمَّدِ بْنِ يَحْيَى الْعَطَّارِ قَالَ: حَدَّثَنَا أَبِي، عَنْ مُحَمَّدِ بْنِ عَبْدِ الْجَبَّارِ، عَنْ أَبِي أَحْمَدَ مُحَمَّدِ بْنِ
زِيَادٍ الأَزْدِيِّ، عَنْ أَبَانِ بْنِ عُثْمَانَ، عَنْ ثَابِتِ بْنِ دِينَارٍ، عَنْ سَيِّدِ الْعَابِدِينَ عَلِيِّ بْنِ الْحُسَيْنِ، عَنْ سَيِّدِ
الشُّهَدَاءِ الْحُسَيْنِ بْنِ عَلِيٍّ، عَنْ سَيِّدِ الأَوْصِيَاءِ أَمِيرَ الْمُؤْمِنِينَ عَلِيِّ بْنِ أَبِي طَالِبٍ عَلَيْهِمُ السَّلَامُ قَالَ: قَالَ لِي
رَسُولُ اللَّهِ صَلَّى اللهُ عَلَيْهِ وَآلِهِ: الأَئِمَّةُ مِنْ بَعْدِي اثْنَا عَشَرَ أَوَّلُهُمْ أَنْتَ يَا عَلِيُّ، وَآخِرُهُمُ الْقَائِمُ الَّذِي يَفْتَحُ اللهُ
- تَبَارَكَ وَتَعَالَى ذِكْرُهُ - عَلَى يَدَيْهِ مَشَارِقَ الأَرْضِ وَمَغَارِبَهَا

Ahmad b. Muḥammad b. Yahya al-Attar narrated that his father quoted on the
authority of Muḥammad b. Abdul Jabbar, on the authority of Abi Ahmad

---

[173] 'Uyūn Akhbār al-Riḍā, v1, ch6, h25
[174] Al-Khiṣāl, ch5, h46

Muḥammad b. Ziyad al-Azedi, on the authority of Aban b. Uthman, on the authority of Abi Ahmad Muḥammad b. Ziyad al-Azedi, on the authority of Aban b. Uthman, on the authority of Thabit b. Dinar, on the authority of the Master of the Worshippers ʿAlī b. Al-Hussein (عليه السلام), on the authority of the Master of the Martyrs Al-Hussein b. Ali, on the authority of the Master of the Trustees the Commander of the Faithful ʿAlī b. Abi Talib (عليه السلام) that God's Prophet (صلى الله عليه وآله وسلم) told him, "There are twelve Divine Leaders after me. O Ali! You are the first one. Their last one is the Riser with whose hands God - whose mentioning is Blessed and High - will conquer the East and the West of the Earth" (مجهول كالصحيح)[175]

176.

عِدَّةٌ مِنْ أَصْحَابِنَا عَنْ أَحْمَدَ بْنِ مُحَمَّدٍ الْبَرْقِيِّ عَنْ أَبِي هَاشِمٍ دَاوُدَ بْنِ الْقَاسِمِ الْجَعْفَرِيِّ عَنْ أَبِي جَعْفَرٍ الثَّانِي (عَلَيْهِ السَّلام) قَالَ أَقْبَلَ أَمِيرُ الْمُؤْمِنِينَ (عَلَيْهِ السَّلام) وَمَعَهُ الْحَسَنُ بن علي (عَلَيْهِما السَّلام) وَهُوَ مُتَّكِئٌ عَلى يَدِ سَلْمَانَ فَدَخَلَ الْمَسْجِدَ الْحَرَامَ فَجَلَسَ إِذْ أَقْبَلَ رَجُلٌ حَسَنُ الْهَيْئَةِ وَاللِّبَاسِ فَسَلَّمَ عَلَى أَمِيرِ الْمُؤْمِنِينَ فَرَدَّ عَلَيْهِ السَّلامَ فَجَلَسَ ثُمَّ قَالَ يَا أَمِيرَ الْمُؤْمِنِينَ أَسْأَلُكَ عَنْ ثَلاثِ مَسَائِلَ إِنْ أَخْبَرْتَنِي بِهِنَّ عَلِمْتُ أَنَّ الْقَوْمَ رَكِبُوا مِنْ أَمْرِكَ مَا قُضِيَ عَلَيْهِمْ وَأَنْ لَيْسُوا بِمَأْمُونِينَ فِي دُنْيَاهُمْ وَآخِرَتِهِمْ وَإِنْ تَكُنِ الاخْرَى عَلِمْتُ أَنَّكَ وَهُمْ شَرَعٌ سَوَاءٌ فَقَالَ لَهُ أَمِيرُ الْمُؤْمِنِينَ (عَلَيْهِ السَّلام) سَلْنِي عَمَّا بَدَا لَكَ قَالَ أَخْبِرْنِي عَنِ الرَّجُلِ إِذَا نَامَ أَيْنَ تَذْهَبُ رُوحُهُ وَعَنِ الرَّجُلِ كَيْفَ يَذْكُرُ وَيَنْسَى وَعَنِ الرَّجُلِ كَيْفَ يُشْبِهُ وَلَدُهُ الاعْمَامَ وَالاخْوَالَ فَالْتَفَتَ أَمِيرُ الْمُؤْمِنِينَ (عَلَيْهِ السَّلام) إِلَى الْحَسَنِ فَقَالَ يَا أَبَا مُحَمَّدٍ أَجِبْهُ قَالَ فَأَجَابَهُ الْحَسَنُ (عَلَيْهِ السَّلام) فَقَالَ الرَّجُلُ أَشْهَدُ أَنْ لا إِلَهَ إِلا اللهُ وَلَمْ أَزَلْ أَشْهَدُ بِهَا وَأَشْهَدُ أَنَّ مُحَمَّداً رَسُولُ اللهِ وَلَمْ أَزَلْ أَشْهَدُ بِذَلِكَ وَأَشْهَدُ أَنَّكَ وَصِيُّ رَسُولِ اللهِ (صَلَّى اللهُ عَلَيْهِ وَآله) وَالْقَائِمُ بِحُجَّتِهِ وَأَشَارَ إِلَى أَمِيرِ الْمُؤْمِنِينَ وَلَمْ أَزَلْ أَشْهَدُ بِهَا وَأَشْهَدُ أَنَّكَ وَصِيُّهُ وَالْقَائِمُ بِحُجَّتِهِ وَأَشَارَ إِلَى الْحَسَنِ (عَلَيْهِ السَّلام) وَأَشْهَدُ أَنَّ الْحُسَيْنَ بْنَ عَلِيٍّ وَصِيُّ أَخِيهِ وَالْقَائِمُ بِحُجَّتِهِ بَعْدَهُ وَأَشْهَدُ عَلَى عَلِيِّ بْنِ الْحُسَيْنِ أَنَّهُ الْقَائِمُ بِأَمْرِ الْحُسَيْنِ بَعْدَهُ وَأَشْهَدُ عَلَى مُحَمَّدِ بْنِ عَلِيٍّ أَنَّهُ الْقَائِمُ بِأَمْرِ عَلِيِّ بْنِ الْحُسَيْنِ وَأَشْهَدُ عَلَى جَعْفَرِ بْنِ مُحَمَّدٍ بِأَنَّهُ الْقَائِمُ بِأَمْرِ مُحَمَّدٍ وَأَشْهَدُ عَلَى مُوسَى أَنَّهُ الْقَائِمُ بِأَمْرِ جَعْفَرِ بْنِ مُحَمَّدٍ وَأَشْهَدُ عَلَى عَلِيِّ بْنِ مُوسَى أَنَّهُ الْقَائِمُ بِأَمْرِ مُوسَى بْنِ جَعْفَرٍ وَأَشْهَدُ عَلَى مُحَمَّدِ بْنِ عَلِيٍّ أَنَّهُ الْقَائِمُ بِأَمْرِ عَلِيِّ بْنِ مُوسَى وَأَشْهَدُ عَلَى عَلِيِّ بْنِ مُحَمَّدٍ بِأَنَّهُ الْقَائِمُ بِأَمْرِ مُحَمَّدِ بْنِ عَلِيٍّ وَأَشْهَدُ عَلَى الْحَسَنِ بْنِ عَلِيٍّ بِأَنَّهُ الْقَائِمُ بِأَمْرِ عَلِيِّ بْنِ مُحَمَّدٍ وَأَشْهَدُ عَلَى رَجُلٍ مِنْ وُلْدِ الْحَسَنِ لا يُكَنَّى وَلا يُسَمَّى حَتَّى يَظْهَرَ أَمْرُهُ

---

[175] *ʿUyūn Akhbār al-Riḍā, v1, ch6, h34*

فَيَمْلاهَا عَدْلاً كَمَا مُلِئَتْ جَوْراً وَالسَّلامُ عَلَيْكَ يَا أَمِيرَ الْمُؤْمِنِينَ وَرَحْمَةُ اللهِ وَبَرَكَاتُهُ ثُمَّ قَامَ فَمَضَى فَقَالَ أَمِيرُ الْمُؤْمِنِينَ يَا أَبَا مُحَمَّدٍ اتْبَعْهُ فَانْظُرْ أَيْنَ يَقْصِدُ فَخَرَجَ الْحَسَنُ بن علي (عَلَيْهِما السَّلام) فَقَالَ مَا كَانَ إِلا أَنْ وَضَعَ رِجْلَهُ خَارِجاً مِنَ الْمَسْجِدِ فَمَا دَرَيْتُ أَيْنَ أَخَذَ مِنْ أَرْضِ اللهِ فَرَجَعْتُ إِلَى أَمِيرِ الْمُؤْمِنِينَ (عَلَيْهِ السَّلام) فَأَعْلَمْتُهُ فَقَالَ يَا أَبَا مُحَمَّدٍ أَ تَعْرِفُهُ قُلْتُ اللهِ وَرَسُولُهُ وَأَمِيرُ الْمُؤْمِنِينَ أَعْلَمُ قَالَ هُوَ الْخَضِرُ (عَلَيْهِ السَّلام)

A number of our people has narrated Ahmad b. Muḥammad al-Barqi from abu Hashim Dawud b. al-Qasim al-Ja'fari from abu Ja'far al-Thani who has said the following. "Once Amir al-Mu'minin 'Alī (عليه السلام) came with al-Hassan and al-Husayn and he was holding the hand of Salman for support. He entered the sacred Mosque in Makka and sat down. Then a good looking and well dressed man came. He offered the greeting of peace to Amir al-Mu'minin 'Alī (عليه السلام) who answered his greetings likewise and he sat down. He then said, "I will ask you three questions. If you would answer them I will acknowledge that the people who have acted against you in the matters of leadership after the Holy Prophet (s.a) they have acted against their own selves. Their actions have taken away peace from them in this world as well in the next life. If it would be otherwise, (you can answer) then you and those people will be the same." Amir al-Mu'minin 'Alī (عليه السلام) said, "Ask whatever you would like." He said, "Tell about the man who sleeps. Where does his spirit go?" Tell about the man, how he remembers and forgets? Tell me about the man how do his children become similar to the aunts and uncles.?" Amir al-Mu'minin 'Alī (عليه السلام) turned to al-Hassan and said, "O abu Muhammad, answer him." The narrator has said that al-Hassan answered his questions. The man then said, "I testify that there is no lord besides Allāh and I continue to testify to this fact. I testify that Muḥammad is the Messenger of Allāh and I continue to testify to this fact I testify that you are the executor of the will of the Messenger of Allāh and that you are the in charge of this task ((Leadership with Divine Authority) with His authorization." He pointed out to Amir al-Mu'minin (عليه السلام) with his hand. He then said, "I continue to testify to this fact." "I testify that you are the executor of his (Amir al-Mu'minin's (عليه السلام) will and the in charge of this task ((Leadership with Divine Authority) by His authorization after him (Amir al-Mu'minin (عليه السلام) " He pointed out with his hand to al-Hassan (عليه السلام). Then He then said, "I continue to testify to this fact." "I testify that al-Husayn b. ʻAlī (عليه السلام) will be the executor of the will of his brother and the in charge of this task ((Leadership with Divine Authority) with His authorization after him. "I testify in support of ʻAlī b. al-Husayn (عليه السلام) that he will be the in charge of the task of al-Husayn after him. "I testify that Muḥammad b. ʻAlī will be the in charge of the task of ʻAlī b. al-Husayn (عليه السلام) after him. "I testify that Ja'far b. Muḥammad (عليه السلام) will be the in charge of the task of Muḥammad b. ʻAlī (عليه السلام). "I testify that Mūsā will be the in charge of the task of Ja'far b. Muḥammad after him. "I testify that ʻAlī b. Mūsā will be the in charge of the task of Mūsā b. Ja'far (عليه السلام). "I testify that Muḥammad b. ʻAlī (عليه السلام) will be the in charge of the task of ʻAlī b. Mūsā (عليه السلام) after him. "I testify that ʻAlī b. Muḥammad will be the in charge of the task of Muḥammad b. ʻAlī (عليه السلام) after him. "I testify that al-Hassan b. ʻAlī (عليه السلام) will be the in charge of the task of ʻAlī b. Muḥammad (عليه السلام) after him. "I testify in support of a man from the children of al-Hassan who will not be mentioned by his Kunya (father or son of so and so) or his name until he will rise with Divine authority to fill the earth with justice after being filled with injustice. "I offer you my greeting of peace O Amir al-Mu'minin (عليه السلام) and praay to Allāh to grant you blessings and holiness." He then stood up and left. Amir al-Mu'minin (عليه السلام) said, "O abu Muḥammad follow him and see where went." Al-Hassan b. ʻAlī (عليه السلام) went out to find out (and came back) and said, "As soon as he stepped out of the Mosque I could not figure out in which direction of the earth of Allāh ddid he disappear. I returned to Amir al-Mu'minin (عليه السلام) and informed him." He said, "O abu Muhammad, do you know him?" I said, Allāh, the Messenger of Allāh and Amir al-Mu'minin (عليه السلام) know best." He said, "He was al-Khidr (عليه السلام)" (صحيح)[176]

177.

حَدَّثَنا أَحْمَدُ بْنُ مُحَمَّدِ بْنِ يَحْيَى العَطَّارُ رَضِيَ اللهُ عَنْهُ قالَ: حَدَّثَنا أَبِي، عَنْ مُحَمَّدِ بْنِ الحُسَيْنِ بْنِ أَبِي الخَطَّابِ، عَنِ الحَسَنِ بْنِ مَحْبُوبٍ، عَنْ أَبِي الجارُودِ، عَنْ أَبِي جَعْفَرٍ عَلَيْهِ السَّلامُ، عَنْ جابِرِ بْنِ عَبْدِ اللهِ

[176] Al-Kāfi, v1, ch126, h1

الأَنْصَارِيّ قَالَ: دَخَلْتُ عَلَى فَاطِمَةَ عَلَيْهَا السَّلاَمُ وَبَيْنَ يَدَيْهَا لَوْحٌ فِيهِ أَسْمَاءُ الأَوْصِيَاءِ فَعَدَدْتُ اثْنَي عَشَرَ، آخِرُهُمُ الْقَائِمُ، ثَلاَثَةٌ مِنْهُمْ مُحَمَّدٌ، وَأَرْبَعَةٌ مِنْهُمْ عَلِيٌّ عَلَيْهِمُ السَّلاَمُ

Ahmad b. Muḥammad b. Yahya al-Attar – may God be pleased with him – narrated that his father quoted on the authority of Muḥammad b. Al-Hussein b. Abil Khattab, on the authority of Al-Hassan b. Mahboob, on the authority of Abil Jarood, on the authority of Abi Ja'far (عليه السلام), on the authority of Jabir b. 'Abd Allāh Al-Ansari, "I went to see (the Blessed Lady) Fatima (عليها السلام). There was a tablet in front of her in which there were the names of the Trustees. There were twelve names – the last one of which is the Riser. Three of them were Muḥammad (صلى الله عليه وآله وسلم) and four of them were 'Alī (عليه السلام)." (معتبر)[177]

178.

حَدَّثَنَا الْحُسَيْنَ بْنُ أَحْمَدَ بْنِ إِدْرِيسَ رَضِيَ اللهُ عَنْهُ قَالَ: حَدَّثَنَا أَبِي، عَنْ أَحْمَدَ بْنِ مُحَمَّدِ بْنِ عِيسَى، وَإِبْرَاهِيمَ بْنِ هَاشِمٍ جَمِيعاً، عَنِ الْحَسَنِ بْنِ مَحْبُوبٍ، عَنْ أَبِي الْجَارُودِ، عَنْ أَبِي جَعْفَرٍ عَلَيْهِ السَّلاَمُ عَنْ جَابِرِ بْنِ عَبْدِ اللهِ الأَنْصَارِيّ قَالَ: دَخَلْتُ عَلَى فَاطِمَةَ عَلَيْهَا السَّلاَمُ وَبَيْنَ يَدَيْهَا لَوْحٌ فِيهِ أَسْمَاءُ الأَوْصِيَاءِ، فَعَدَدْتُ اثْنَي عَشَرَ، آخِرُهُمُ الْقَائِمُ عَلَيْهِ السَّلاَمُ، ثَلاَثَةٌ مِنْهُمْ مُحَمَّدٌ، وَأَرْبَعَةٌ مِنْهُمْ عَلِيٌّ عَلَيْهِمُ السَّلاَمُ

Al-Hussein b. Ahmad b. Idris – may God be pleased with him – narrated that his father quoted on the authority of Ahmad b. Muḥammad b. Isa and Ibrahim b. Hashem, on the authority of Al-Hassan b. Mahboob, on the authority of Abil Jarood, on the authority of Abi Ja'far (s), on the authority of Jabir b. 'Abd Allāh Al-Ansari, "I went to see (the Blessed Lady) Fatima (عليها السلام). There was a tablet in front of her in which there were the names of the Trustees. There were twelve names – the last one of which is the Riser. Three of them were Muḥammad (صلى الله عليه وآله وسلم) and four of them were 'Alī (عليها السلام)." (معتبر)[178]

---

[177] *'Uyūn Akhbār al-Riḍā*, v1, ch6, h6
[178] *'Uyūn Akhbār al-Riḍā*, v1, ch6, h7

179.

عَلِيُّ بْنُ مُحَمَّدٍ قَالَ حَدَّثَنِي مُحَمَّدٌ وَالْحَسَنُ ابْنَا عَلِيِّ بْنِ إِبْرَاهِيمَ فِي سَنَةِ تِسْعٍ وَسَبْعِينَ وَمِائَتَيْنِ قَالا حَدَّثَنَا مُحَمَّدُ بْنُ عَلِيِّ بْنِ عَبْدِ الرَّحْمَنِ الْعَبْدِيُّ مِنْ عَبْدِ قَيْسٍ عَنْ ضَوْءِ بْنِ عَلِيٍّ الْعِجْلِيِّ عَنْ رَجُلٍ مِنْ أَهْلِ فَارِسَ سَمَّاهُ قَالَ أَتَيْتُ سُرَّ مَنْ رَأَى وَلَزِمْتُ بَابَ أَبِي مُحَمَّدٍ (عَلَيْهِ السَّلام) فَدَعَانِي مِنْ غَيْرِ أَنْ أَسْتَأْذِنَ فَلَمَّا دَخَلْتُ وَسَلَّمْتُ قَالَ لِي يَا أَبَا فُلانٍ كَيْفَ حَالُكَ ثُمَّ قَالَ لِي اقْعُدْ يَا فُلانُ ثُمَّ سَأَلَنِي عَنْ جَمَاعَةٍ مِنْ رِجَالٍ وَنِسَاءٍ مِنْ أَهْلِي ثُمَّ قَالَ لِي مَا الَّذِي أَقْدَمَكَ قُلْتُ رَغْبَةٌ فِي خِدْمَتِكَ قَالَ فَقَالَ فَالْزَمِ الدَّارَ قَالَ فَكُنْتُ فِي الدَّارِ مَعَ الْخَدَمِ ثُمَّ صِرْتُ أَشْتَرِي لَهُمُ الْحَوَائِجَ مِنَ السُّوقِ وَكُنْتُ أَدْخُلُ عَلَيْهِ مِنْ غَيْرِ إِذْنٍ إِذَا كَانَ فِي دَارِ الرِّجَالِ فَدَخَلْتُ عَلَيْهِ يَوْماً وَهُوَ فِي دَارِ الرِّجَالِ فَسَمِعْتُ حَرَكَةً فِي الْبَيْتِ فَنَادَانِي مَكَانَكَ لا تَبْرَحْ فَلَمْ أَجْسُرْ أَنْ أَخْرُجَ وَلا أَدْخُلَ فَخَرَجَتْ عَلَيَّ جَارِيَةٌ مَعَهَا شَيْءٌ مُغَطًّى ثُمَّ نَادَانِي ادْخُلْ فَدَخَلْتُ وَنَادَى الْجَارِيَةَ فَرَجَعَتْ فَقَالَ لَهَا اكْشِفِي عَمَّا مَعَكِ فَكَشَفَتْ عَنْ غُلامٍ أَبْيَضَ حَسَنِ الْوَجْهِ وَكَشَفَتْ عَنْ بَطْنِهِ فَإِذَا شَعْرٌ نَابِتٌ مِنْ لَبَّتِهِ إِلَى سُرَّتِهِ أَخْضَرُ لَيْسَ بِأَسْوَدَ فَقَالَ هَذَا صَاحِبُكُمْ ثُمَّ أَمَرَهَا فَحَمَلَتْهُ فَمَا رَأَيْتُهُ بَعْدَ ذَلِكَ حَتَّى مَضَى أَبُو مُحَمَّدٍ (عَلَيْهِ السَّلام) فَقَالَ ضَوْءُ بْنُ عَلِيٍّ فَقُلْتُ لِلْفَارِسِيِّ كَمْ كُنْتَ تُقَدِّرُ لَهُ مِنَ السِّنِينَ قَالَ سَنَتَيْنِ قَالَ الْعَبْدِيُّ فَقُلْتُ لِضَوْءٍ كَمْ تُقَدِّرُ لَهُ أَنْتَ قَالَ أَرْبَعَ عَشْرَةَ سَنَةً قَالَ أَبُو عَلِيٍّ وَأَبُو عَبْدِ اللهِ وَنَحْنُ نُقَدِّرُ لَهُ إِحْدَى وَعِشْرِينَ سَنَةً

Ali b. Muḥammad has said that narrated to me Muḥammad and al-Hassan sons of 'Alī b. Ibrahim in the year two hundred seventy nine saying that narrated to them Muḥammad b. 'Alī b. 'Abd al-Rahman al-'Abdi of 'Abd Qays from Daw' b. 'Alī al-'Ijli from a man from Persia, whose name he mentioned, who has said the following. "I went to the city of Surra man Ra'a and kept myself at the door of abu Muḥammad (عليه السلام). He called me inside without any request from me. When I went inside and offered greeting of peace he said to me, "How are you, O father of so and so?" Then he told me, "Sit down O so and so." He then asked me about a group of men and ladies from my family. He then said to me, "What brings you here?" I said, "The desire to serve you." The narrator has said that he said, "All right, be around the house." I then remained in the house with the servants. Then I would do the purchases for them from the market. I would go in his presence without first requesting permission when he would haven been present in the man's quarters One day I went to him when he was in the men's quarters. I heard the sound of movement in the house and he said, "Do not move from your place." I could not dare to go out or inside. Then a female servant came out to me who had something with her which was covered. He then called me inside and I went inside. He called the female servant and she came back. He told her to uncover what she had with her. She uncovered the very good looking face of a white baby boy. And she uncovered his chest. A line of hairs had grown from his neck down to his bellybutton which seemed to be greenish color and not totally black. He said, "This is your Leader with Divine Authority." He then ordered her to take the baby inside and ever since I could not see him until abu Muḥammad (عليه السلام) passed away." Daw' b. 'Alī has said, "I asked the man from Persia, 'How old do you think he was?" He said, "Two years old." Al-'Abdi has said, "I asked Daw', "How old do you think he was?" He said, "Fourteen years old." Abu 'Alī and abu 'AbdAllāh have said that we think he is twenty one years old." (مجهول)[179]

180.

مُحَمَّدُ بْنُ يَحْيَى عَنْ أَحْمَدَ بْنِ إِسْحَاقَ عَنْ أَبِي هَاشِمٍ الْجَعْفَرِيِّ قَالَ قُلْتُ لِأَبِي مُحَمَّدٍ (عَلَيْهِ السَّلام) جَلَالَتُكَ تَمْنَعُنِي مِنْ مَسْأَلَتِكَ فَتَأْذَنُ لِي أَنْ أَسْأَلَكَ فَقَالَ سَلْ قُلْتُ يَا سَيِّدِي هَلْ لَكَ وَلَدٌ فَقَالَ نَعَمْ فَقُلْتُ فَإِنْ حَدَثَ بِكَ حَدَثٌ فَأَيْنَ أَسْأَلُ عَنْهُ قَالَ بِالْمَدِينَةِ

Muhammad b. Yahya has narrated from Ahmad b. Ishaq from abu Hashim al-Ja'fari who has said the following. "I said to abu Muḥammad (عليه السلام), 'Your grace causes shyness to me to ask you questions. May I ask you a question?" He said, "Yes, you may ask." I said, "My master, do you have a son?" He said, "Yes, I do have a son." I then said, "If anything will happen to you, where would I ask him (about my religion)?" He replied, "Ask him in Madina." (صحيح)[180]

---

[179] *Al-Kāfi, v1, ch125, h2*

[180] *Al-Kāfi, v1, ch76, h2*

181.

حدثنا أبي رضي الله عنه قال: حدثنا سعد بن عبد الله، عن يعقوب بن يزيد، عن محمد بن أبي عمير، عن غير واحد، عن أبي عبد الله عليه السلام قال: السبت لنا، والاحد لشيعتنا، والاثنين لاعدائنا، والثلثاء لبني امية، والاربعاء يوم شرب الدواء، والخميس تقضى فيه الحوائج، والجمعة للتنظف والتطيب، وهو عيد المسلمين وهو أفضل من الفطر والاضحى، ويوم الغدير أفضل الاعياد، وهو ثامن عشر من ذي الحجة وكان يوم الجمعة، ويخرج قائمنا أهل البيت يوم الجمعة، ويقوم القيامة يوم الجمعة، وما من عمل يوم الجمعة أفضل من الصلاة على محمد وآله

(The compiler of the book narrated) that his father - may God be pleased with him - narrated that Sa'ed b. 'Abd Allāh quoted Yaqoob b. Yazid, on the authority of Muḥammad b. Abi Umayr, on the authority of some other people that Aba 'Abd Allāh as-Ṣādiq (عليه السلام) said, "Saturdays are for us. Sundays are for our followers. Mondays are for our enemies. Tuesdays are for the Umayyads. Wednesdays are the days for taking medicine. Thursdays are for taking care of your needs. Fridays are for leaning up and putting on perfume. Fridays are the holidays for the Muslims. They are even better than the Eid ul-Fitr and Eid ul-Azha. The Day of Eid ul-Qadir is the noblest of the holidays. It is on the eighteenth day of the month of Dhul-Hijja. Our Riser (عجل الله تعالى فرجه) - the Riser (عجل الله تعالى فرجه) from the Members of the Holy Household - will rise on a Friday. The Resurrection Day will be on a Friday. No deeds are better on Fridays than sending God's Blessings upon Muḥammad (صلى الله عليه وآله وسلم) and his Household." (صحيح)[181]

182.

حدثنا أحمد بن زياد بن جعفر الهمداني رضي الله عنه قال حدثنا علي بن إبراهيم بن هاشم عن أبيه عن محمد بن أبي عمير عن غياث بن إبراهيم عن الصادق جعفر بن محمد عن أبيه عن آبائه عليهم السلام قال قال رسول الله من أنكر القائم من ولدي فقد أنكرني

[181] *Al-Khiṣāl, ch49, h5*

Ahmad b. Ziyad b. Ja`far al-Hamadani رضي الله عنه narrated. He said: `Ali b. Ibrahim b. Hashim narrated from his father from Muḥammad b. Abi `Umayr from Ghiyath b. Ibrahim from as-Ṣādiq Ja`far b. Muḥammad from his father from his forefathers عليهم السلام.

They said: The Messenger of Allāh said: Whoever denies the Qa'im from my offspring will have denied me. (صحيح)[182]

183.

وعنه، عن عبد الله بن ميمون القداح، عن جعفر، عن أبيه قال: " قال علي بن ابي طالب عليه السلام: منا سبعة خلقهم الله عزوجل لم يخلق في الارض مثلهم: منا رسول الله صلى الله عليه وآله سيد الاولين والآخرين وخاتم النبيين، ووصيه خير الوصيين، وسبطاه خير الاسباط حسنا وحسينا، وسيد الشهداء حمزة عمه، ومن قد طار مع الملائكة جعفر، والقائم

And from him from `Abdillah b. Maymun al-Qadah from Ja`far from his father.

He said: `Ali b. Abi Talib عليه السلام said: From us there are seven that Allāh عزوجل has created that He did not create in their likeness in the world: from us is the Messenger of Allāh صلى الله عليه وآله, the master of the firsts and the lasts and the seal of prophets, and his deputy is the best of deputies, and his tribe is the best of tribes – Hasan, Husayn, his uncle Hamza [who is] the master of martyrs, Ja`far [who is] the one who soared with the angels, and the Qa'im. (صحيح)[183]

184.

---

[182] *Kamal ad-Deen, pg. 440*

[183] *Qurb al-Isnad, pg. 25*

الطالقاني، عن أبي علي بن همام قال: سمعت محمد بن عثمان العمري قدس الله روحه يقول: سمعت أبي يقول: سئل أبو محمد الحسن بن علي (ع) وأنا عنده عن الخبر الذي روي عن آبائه (ع) أن الارض لا تخلو من حجة الله على خلقه إلى يوم القيامة وأن من مات ولم يعرف إمام زمانه مات ميتة جاهلية (فقال (ع): إن هذا حق كما أن النهار حق. فقيل له: يابن رسول الله فمن الحجة والامام بعدك؟ فقال: ابني محمد وهو الامام والحجة بعدي، من مات ولم يعرفه مات ميتة جاهلية) . أما إن له غيبة يحار فيها الجاهلون، ويهلك فيها المبطلون، ويكذب فيها الوقاتون ثم يخرج فكأني أنظر إلى الاعلام البيض تخفق فوق رأسه بنجف الكوفة

at-Talaqani from Abu `Ali b. Himam. He said: I heard Muḥammad b. `Uthman al-`Amri قدس الله روحه say: I heard my father[5] say:

Abu Muḥammad al-Hasan b. `Ali عليه السلام was asked, while I was with him, about a tradition that was narrated from his forefathers عليه السلام that the Earth does not remain without Allāh's hujja over His creation until the Day of Judgment, and if one were to die without recognizing the Imam of his time, he would die the death of jahiliyya. He عليه السلام said: Verily, this is true just as daytime is true. It was said to him: O son of the Messenger of Allāh, who then is the hujja and the Imam after you? So he said: My son MHMD,[6] he is the Imam and hujja after me, whoever dies without recognizing him dies the death of jahiliyya. Behold, he will certainly have an occultation regarding which the ignorant (jahiloon) will be perplexed, the invalidators will be destroyed, and the time-assigners will lie. Then, he will appear. It is as if I am looking at the white banners waving over his head in the Najaf of Kufa. (مجهول كالصحيح)[184]

185.

حدثنا محمد بن الحسن بن أحمد بن الوليد رضي الله عنه قال حدثنا محمد بن الحسن الصفار قال حدثنا أحمد بن محمد بن عيسى ومحمد بن الحسين بن أبي الخطاب والهيثم بن أبي مسروق النهدي عن الحسن بن محبوب السراد عن علي بن رئاب عن أبي حمزة الثمالي عن أبي جعفر عليه السلام قال سمعته يقول إن أقرب الناس

[184] *Kamal ad-Deen (Ṣaduq), v1, pg. 437*

إلى الله عز وجل وأعلمهم به وأرأفهم بالناس محمد والائمة عليهم السلام فادخلوا أين دخلوا وفارقوا من فارقوا عنى بذلك حسينا وولده عليه السلام فإن الحق فيهم وهم الأوصياء ومنهم الأئمة فأينما رأيتموهم فاتبعوهم وإن أصبحتم يوما لا ترون منهم أحدا فاستغيثوا بالله عز وجل وانظروا السنة التي كنتم عليها واتبعوها وأحبوا من كنتم تحبون وأبغضوا من كنتم تبغضون فما أسرع ما يأتيكم الفرج

Muhammad b. al-Hasan b. Ahmad b. al-Walid رضي الله عنه narrated. He said: Muḥammad b. al-Hasan as-Saffar narrated. He said: Ahmad b. Muḥammad b. `Isa, Muḥammad b. Husayn b. Abu'l Khattab, and Haytham b. Abi Masruq an-Nahdi narrated from al-Hasan b. Mahbub as-Sarrad from `Ali b. Ri'aab from Abu Hamza ath-Thumali.

He said: I heard Abu Ja`far عليه السلام say: The closest of people to Allāh عز وجل, the most knowledgeable about Him and the most kind to the people are Muḥammad and the Imams عليهم السلام, so enter where they enter and disassociate from whom they disassociate with. It denotes Husayn and his descendants, as the truth is with them and they are the successors; the Imams عليهم السلام are amongst them. So wherever you see them follow them, and when the day comes when you no longer see one from them, beseech Allāh عز وجل and remain on the sunna you are upon. Love those whom you love and hate those whom you hate, for what comes to you of the relief will not be expedited. (صحيح)[185]

186.

أخبرنا أحمد بن محمد بن سعيد ابن عقدة قال حدثنا محمد بن المفضل بن قيس بن رمانة الأشعري و سعدان بن إسحاق بن سعيد و أحمد بن الحسين بن عبد الملك و محمد بن الحسن القطواني قالوا جميعا حدثنا الحسن بن محبوب الزراد عن هشام بن سالم عن يزيد الكناسي قال سمعت أبا جعفر محمد بن علي الباقر ع يقول إن صاحب هذا الأمر فيه شبه من يوسف ابن أمة سوداء يصلح الله عز و جل له أمره في ليلة واحدة

[185] *Kamal ad-Deen (Ṣaduq), v1, pg. 356*

Ahmad b. Muḥammad b. Sa'eed b. Oqda narrated from Muḥammad b. al-Mufadhdhal b. Qayss b. Rummana al-Ash'ari, Sa'dan b. Iss'haq b. Sa'eed, Ahmad b. al-Husayn b. Abdul Melik and Muḥammad b. al-Hasan al-Qatawani all from al-Hasan b. Mahboob az-Zarrad from Hisham b. Salim from Durays al-Kunaasee said, I heard Abaa Ja`far (عليه السلام) he said: "Verily, the Master of this affair (i.e. al-Qaa'im) in him is the tradition of Yoosuf (عليه السلام), he is the son of a black bondswoman (female slave), and Allāh (عزَّ وَ جَلَّ) will reform his affair in one night (موثق)[186]

187.

عِدَّةٌ مِنْ أَصْحَابِنَا عَنْ سَعْدِ بْنِ عَبْدِ اللهِ عَنْ أَيُّوبَ بْنِ نُوحٍ قَالَ قُلْتُ لابِي الْحَسَنِ الرِّضَا (عَلَيْهِ السَّلام) إِنِّي أَرْجُو أَنْ تَكُونَ صَاحِبَ هَذَا الامْرِ وَأَنْ يَسُوقَهُ اللهُ إِلَيْكَ بِغَيْرِ سَيْفٍ فَقَدْ بُويِعَ لَكَ وَضُرِبَتِ الدَّرَاهِمُ بِاسْمِكَ فَقَالَ مَا مِنَّا أَحَدٌ اخْتَلَفَتْ إِلَيْهِ الْكُتُبُ وَأُشِيرَ إِلَيْهِ بِالاصَابِعِ وَسُئِلَ عَنِ الْمَسَائِلِ وَحُمِلَتْ إِلَيْهِ الامْوَالُ إِلا اغْتِيلَ أَوْ مَاتَ عَلَى فِرَاشِهِ حَتَّى يَبْعَثَ اللهُ لِهَذَا الامْرِ غُلاماً مِنَّا خَفِيَّ الْوِلادَةِ وَالْمَنْشَإِ غَيْرَ خَفِيٍّ فِي نَسَبِهِ

A number of our people has narrated from Sa'd b. 'AbdAllāh from Ayyub b. Nuh who has said the following. "I said to abu al-Hassan al-Rida (عليه السلام), 'Isma'il hope that you will become the inchrge of this task (Leadership with Divine Authority). Allāh will drive it to your control with the sword now that the pledge of allegiance is offered to you and currency coins are printed in your name." The Imam (عليه السلام) said, "There has been no one from us with whom letters had been exchanged, being pointed out with the gesture of fingers, questions asked and properties delivered to him but that he was murdered or died in his bed. (It will be as such) until Allāh will raise for this task (Leadership with Divine Authority) a young boy from us whose birth place and upbringing would be unknown (to people) but not his ancestors." (مرسل كالصحيح)[187]

---

[186] *Al-Ghayba (Nu'māni), ch13, h8*

[187] *Al-Kafi, v1, ch80, h25*

188.

عَلِيُّ بْنُ إِبْرَاهِيمَ عَنْ مُحَمَّدِ بْنِ الْحُسَيْنِ عَنِ ابْنِ أَبِي نَجْرَانَ عَنْ فَضَالَةَ بْنِ أَيُّوبَ عَنْ سَدِيرٍ الصَّيْرَفِيِّ قَالَ سَمِعْتُ أَبَا عَبْدِ اللهِ (عَلَيْهِ السَّلام) يَقُولُ إِنَّ فِي صَاحِبِ هَذَا الامْرِ شَبَهاً مِنْ يُوسُفَ (عَلَيْهِ السَّلام) قَالَ قُلْتُ لَهُ كَأَنَّكَ تَذْكُرُهُ حَيَاتَهُ أَوْ غَيْبَتَهُ قَالَ فَقَالَ لِي وَمَا يُنْكَرُ مِنْ ذَلِكَ هَذِهِ الامَّةُ أَشْبَاهُ الْخَنَازِيرِ إِنَّ إِخْوَةَ يُوسُفَ (عَلَيْهِ السَّلام) كَانُوا أَسْبَاطاً أَوْلادَ الانْبِيَاءِ تَاجَرُوا يُوسُفَ وَبَايَعُوهُ وَخَاطَبُوهُ وَهُمْ إِخْوَتُهُ وَهُوَ أَخُوهُمْ فَلَمْ يَعْرِفُوهُ حَتَّى قَالَ أَنَا يُوسُفُ وَهَذَا أَخِي فَمَا تُنْكِرُ هَذِهِ الامَّةُ الْمَلْعُونَةُ أَنْ يَفْعَلَ اللهُ عَزَّ وَجَلَّ بِحُجَّتِهِ فِي وَقْتٍ مِنَ الاوْقَاتِ كَمَا فَعَلَ بِيُوسُفَ إِنَّ يُوسُفَ (عَلَيْهِ السَّلام) كَانَ إِلَيْهِ مُلْكُ مِصْرَ وَكَانَ بَيْنَهُ وَبَيْنَ وَالِدِهِ مَسِيرَةُ ثَمَانِيَةَ عَشَرَ يَوْماً فَلَوْ أَرَادَ أَنْ يُعْلِمَهُ لَقَدَرَ عَلَى ذَلِكَ لَقَدْ سَارَ يَعْقُوبُ (عَلَيْهِ السَّلام) وَوُلْدُهُ عِنْدَ الْبِشَارَةِ تِسْعَةَ أَيَّامٍ مِنْ بَدْوِهِمْ إِلَى مِصْرَ فَمَا تُنْكِرُ هَذِهِ الامَّةُ أَنْ يَفْعَلَ اللهُ جَلَّ وَعَزَّ بِحُجَّتِهِ كَمَا فَعَلَ بِيُوسُفَ أَنْ يَمْشِيَ فِي أَسْوَاقِهِمْ وَيَطَأَ بُسُطَهُمْ حَتَّى يَأْذَنَ اللهُ فِي ذَلِكَ لَهُ كَمَا أَذِنَ لِيُوسُفَ قَالُوا أَ إِنَّكَ لانْتَ يُوسُفُ قَالَ أَنَا يُوسُفُ

Ali b. Ibrahim has narrated from Muḥammad b. al-Husayn from b. Abi Najran from Fadalah b. Ayyub from Sadir al-Sayrafi who has said that he heard abu ‘AbdAllāh (عليه السلام) say the following. “In the (case) of the person in charge of this task (Leadership with Divine Authority, the twelfth Imam (عليه السلام)) there is a similarity to Yusuf (Joseph) (عليه السلام).” I then said, “Are you, O Imam, speaking of his life time or his disappearance.” The narrator has said that the Imam (عليه السلام) then said, “ What then is it that certain swine-like people of this nation refuse to acknowledge? The brothers of Yusuf were grand children of the prophets. They did business with Yusus, conducted traded with him and spoke to him. They were his brothers and he was their brother but they could not recognize him until he said, I am Yusu and this is my brother.” Why should then (certain people of) this condemned nation refuse to accept if Allāh, the Most Majestic, the Most Gracious, in a certain time would do to the possessor of His authority what He did to Yusuf? Yusuf was the in charge of Egypt and there was a distance of twenty eight days of journey between him and his father. If he wanted to inform him (his father) he could have done so. Jacob and his sons journeyed after they heard the good new for nine days from their Bedouin home to Egypt. Why then this nation would refuse to accept if Allāh, the Most Majestic, the

Most Gracious, would do to the person who possess His authority what He did to Yusuf? That he would walk in their market place and step on their furnishings until Allāh will grant him permission to reappear in public as He did to Yusuf as they said, "Are you really Yusuf?" He said, "Yes, I am Yusuf. (حسن)[188]

189.

عِدَّةٌ مِنْ أَصْحَابِنَا عَنْ جَعْفَرِ بْنِ مُحَمَّدٍ عَنِ ابْنِ فَضَّالٍ عَنِ الرَّيَّانِ بْنِ الصَّلْتِ قَالَ سَمِعْتُ أَبَا الْحَسَنِ الرِّضَا (عَلَيْهِ السَّلام) يَقُولُ وَسُئِلَ عَنِ الْقَائِمِ فَقَالَ لا يُرَى جِسْمُهُ وَلا يُسَمَّى اسْمُهُ

A number of our people has narrated from Ja'far b. Muhammad from b. Faddal from al-Rayyan b. as-Salt who has said the following. "I heard abu al-Hassan al-Rida (عليه السلام) say, when asked al-Qa'im (the one who will establish the kingdom of All), 'He will not be seen physically nor his very name will particularly be mentioned." (موثق)[189]

190.

عَلِيُّ بْنُ إِبْرَاهِيمَ عَنْ أَبِيهِ عَنْ حَنَانِ بْنِ سَدِيرٍ عَنْ مَعْرُوفِ بْنِ خَرَّبُوذَ عَنْ ابي جعفر (عَلَيْهِ السَّلام) قَالَ إِنَّمَا نَحْنُ كَنُجُومِ السَّمَاءِ كُلَّمَا غَابَ نَجْمٌ طَلَعَ نَجْمٌ حَتَّى إِذَا أَشَرْتُمْ بِأَصَابِعِكُمْ وَمِلْتُمْ بِأَعْنَاقِكُمْ غَيَّبَ الله عَنْكُمْ نَجْمَكُمْ فَاسْتَوَتْ بَنُو عَبْدِ الْمُطَّلِبِ فَلَمْ يُعْرَفْ أَيٌّ مِنْ أَيٍّ فَإِذَا طَلَعَ نَجْمُكُمْ فَاحْمَدُوا رَبَّكُمْ

Ali b. Ibrahim has narrated from his father from Hannan b. Sadir from Ma'ruf b. Kharrabudh from abu Ja'far (عليه السلام) who has said the following. "We are only like the stars in the heavens. Whenever one star disappears (from sight) another one comes in view until you will point out with your fingers and make a gesture with your

---

[188] *Al-Kāfi, v1, ch80, h4*

[189] *Al-Kāfi, v1, ch78, h3*

necks. Allāh will cause your star to disappear from your sight. The descendants of 'Abd al-Muttalib will all look similar as such that one would not know which is which When your star will reappear then you must give thanks to Allāh." (موثق حسن)[190]

191.

حَدَّثَنَا أَحْمَدُ بْنُ زِيَادِ بْنِ جَعْفَرٍ الْهَمَدَانِيُّ رَضِيَ اللَّهُ عَنْهُ قَالَ حَدَّثَنَا عَلِيُّ بْنُ إِبْرَاهِيمَ بْنِ هَاشِمٍ عَنْ أَبِيهِ عَنْ أَبِي أَحْمَدَ مُحَمَّدِ بْنِ زِيَادٍ الْأَزْدِيِّ قَالَ: سَأَلْتُ سَيِّدِي مُوسَى بْنَ جَعْفَرٍ ع عَنْ قَوْلِ اللَّهِ عَزَّ وَ جَلَ وَ أَسْبَغَ عَلَيْكُمْ نِعَمَهُ ظاهِرَةً وَ باطِنَةً فَقَالَ ع النِّعْمَةُ الظَّاهِرَةُ الْإِمَامُ الظَّاهِرُ وَ الْبَاطِنَةُ الْإِمَامُ الْغَائِبُ فَقُلْتُ لَهُ وَ يَكُونُ فِي الْأَئِمَّةِ مَنْ يَغِيبُ قَالَ نَعَمْ يَغِيبُ عَنْ أَبْصَارِ النَّاسِ شَخْصُهُ وَ لَا يَغِيبُ عَن قُلُوبِ الْمُؤْمِنِينَ ذِكْرُهُ وَ هُوَ الثَّانِي عَشَرَ مِنَّا يُسَهِّلُ اللَّهُ لَهُ كُلَّ عَسِيرٍ وَ يُذَلِّلُ لَهُ كُلَّ صَعْبٍ وَ يُظْهِرُ لَهُ كُنُوزَ الْأَرْضِ وَ يُقَرِّبُ لَهُ كُلَّ بَعِيدٍ وَ يُبِيرُ بِهِ كُلَّ جَبَّارٍ عَنِيدٍ وَ يُهْلِكُ عَلَى يَدِهِ كُلَّ شَيْطَانٍ مَرِيدٍ ذَلِكَ ابْنُ سَيِّدَةِ الْإِمَاءِ الَّذِي تَخْفَى عَلَى النَّاسِ وِلَادَتُهُ وَ لَا يَحِلُّ لَهُمْ تَسْمِيَتُهُ حَتَّى يُظْهِرَهُ اللَّهُ عَزَّ وَ جَلَّ فَيَمْلَأَ الْأَرْضَ قِسْطاً وَ عَدْلًا كَمَا مُلِئَتْ جَوْراً وَ ظُلْما

Ahmad b. Ziyad b. Ja`far al-Hamadani رضي الله عنه narrated. He said: `Ali b. Ibrahim b. Hashim narrated from his father from Abu Ahmad Muḥammad b. Ziyad al-Azidi.

He said: I asked my master Mūsā b. Ja`far عليه السلام about the saying of Allāh عز و جل, "...and He lavished upon you His favours, both apparent (*thahir*) and hidden (*batin*)..." (31:20). He عليه السلام said: The apparent favour is an apparent Imam, and the hidden favour is an occulted Imam. So I said to him: And will there be any [Imam] who is occulted from amongst the Imams? He said: Yes, his person will be occulted from the people's sight, but his remembrance will not be occulted from the believers' hearts. And he is the twelfth from us. Allāh eases all difficulties for him, helps him overcome all adversities, makes apparent to him the treasures of the Earth, brings close to him all that is remote, eradicates the immensely arrogant through him, and with his hand destroys every disciple of Satan. He is the child of the master of slave women; he is whose birth will be concealed from the people, and whose name is not permissible

---

[190] *Al-Kāfi, v1, ch80, h8*

to be named until Allāh عز و جل makes him apparent and fills the Earth with equity and justice as it would have been fraught with injustice and oppression. (صحيح)[191]

192.

حدثنا محمد بن همام قال: حدثنا عبد الله بن جعفر الحميري، قال: حدثنا الحسن بن محبوب، عن علي بن رئاب، عن محمد بن مسلم، عن أبي عبد الله جعفر بن محمد أنه قال: إنّ قدّام قيام القائم علامات: بلوى من الله تعالى لعباده المؤمنين. قلت: وما هي؟ قال: ذلك قول الله وَلَنَبْلُوَنَّكُمْ بِشَيْءٍ مِنَ الْخَوْفِ وَالْجُوعِ وَنَقْصٍ مِنَ الْأَمْوَالِ وَالْأَنْفُسِ وَالثَّمَرَاتِ ۗ وَبَشِّرِ الصَّابِرِينَ قال: (لنبلونكم) يعني المؤمنين، (بشيء من الخوف) من ملوك بني فلان في آخر سلطانهم، (والجوع) بغلاء أسعارهم، (ونقص من الأموال) فساد التجارات وقلة الفضل فيها، (والأنفس) موت ذريع (والثمرات) قلة ريع ما يزرع وقلة بركة الثمار، (وبشر الصابرين) عند ذلك بخروج القائم . ثم قال لي: يا محمد، هذا تأويله. إن الله يقول هُوَ الَّذِي أَنْزَلَ عَلَيْكَ الْكِتَابَ مِنْهُ آيَاتٌ مُحْكَمَاتٌ هُنَّ أُمُّ الْكِتَابِ وَأُخَرُ مُتَشَابِهَاتٌ ۖ فَأَمَّا الَّذِينَ فِي قُلُوبِهِمْ زَيْغٌ فَيَتَّبِعُونَ مَا تَشَابَهَ مِنْهُ ابْتِغَاءَ الْفِتْنَةِ وَابْتِغَاءَ تَأْوِيلِهِ ۗ وَمَا يَعْلَمُ تَأْوِيلَهُ إِلَّا اللَّهُ ۗ وَالرَّاسِخُونَ فِي الْعِلْمِ يَقُولُونَ آمَنَّا بِهِ كُلٌّ مِنْ عِنْدِ رَبِّنَا ۗ وَمَا يَذَّكَّرُ إِلَّا أُولُو الْأَلْبَابِ

Muhammad b. Hammam narrated from ʿAbd Allāh b. Ja'far al-Himyari from al-Hasan b. Mahboob from ʿAlī b. Ri'ab that Muḥammad b. Muslim had said: "Abu ʿAbd Allāh as-Ṣādiq (عليه السلام) had said: "Before the rising of al-Qa'im there will be some signs, with which Allāh tries His faithful people." I said: "What are they?" He said: "It is the saying of Allāh, "And We will most certainly try you with somewhat of fear and hunger and loss of property and lives and fruits; and give good news to the patient." When Allāh says (We will try you) He means the believers, when He says (with somewhat of fear), He refers to the fright that is caused at the end of the rule of the family of so-and-so, (hunger) is because of expensive prices, (loss of property) is corruption of trade and littleness of profits, (lives) is quick deaths, (fruits) is little production of plants and little blessing of fruits and (give good news to the patient) when al-Qa'im appears." Then he said to me: "O Muhammad, this is the

[191] *Kamal ad-Deen (Ṣaduq), v1, pg. 396*

interpretation of the verse. Allāh says, "But none knows its interpretation except Allāh and those who are firmly rooted in knowledge." (3:7) (صحيح)[192]

193.

عَلِيُّ بْنُ إِبْرَاهِيمَ عَنْ أَبِيهِ عَنِ ابْنِ أَبِي عُمَيْرٍ عَنْ أَبِي أَيُّوبَ الْخَزَّازِ عَنْ مُحَمَّدِ بْنِ مُسْلِمٍ قَالَ سَمِعْتُ أَبَا عَبْدِ اللهِ (عَلَيْهِ السَّلام) يَقُولُ إِنْ بَلَغَكُمْ عَنْ صَاحِبِ هَذَا الامْرِ غَيْبَةٌ فَلا تُنْكِرُوهَا

Ali b. Ibrahim has narrated from from his father from b. abu "Umayr from abu Ayyub al-Khazzaz from Muḥammad b. Muslim who has said the following. "I heard abu 'AbdAllāh (عليه السلام) say, "I the person in charge of this task (Leadership with Divine Authority) will disappear from public sight you must not reject it." (حسن)[193]

194.

مُحَمَّدُ بْنُ يَحْيَى عَنْ أَحْمَدَ بْنِ مُحَمَّدِ بْنِ عِيسَى عَنِ ابْنِ مَحْبُوبٍ عَنْ هِشَامِ بْنِ سَالِمٍ عَنْ أَبِي خَالِدٍ الْكَابُلِيِّ عَنْ ابي جعفر (عَلَيْهِ السَّلام) قَالَ وَجَدْنَا فِي كِتَابِ علي (عَلَيْهِ السَّلام) إِنَّ الارْضَ لله يُورِثُهَا مَنْ يَشَاءُ مِنْ عِبَادِهِ وَالْعَاقِبَةُ لِلْمُتَّقِينَ أَنَا وَأَهْلُ بَيْتِي الَّذِينَ أَوْرَثَنَا اللهُ الارْضَ وَنَحْنُ الْمُتَّقُونَ وَالارْضُ كُلُّهَا لَنَا فَمَنْ أَحْيَا أَرْضاً مِنَ الْمُسْلِمِينَ فَلْيَعْمُرْهَا وَلْيُؤَدِّ خَرَاجَهَا إِلَى الامَامِ مِنْ أَهْلِ بَيْتِي وَلَهُ مَا أَكَلَ مِنْهَا فَإِنْ تَرَكَهَا أَوْ أَخْرَبَهَا وَأَخَذَهَا رَجُلٌ مِنَ الْمُسْلِمِينَ مِنْ بَعْدِهِ فَعَمَرَهَا وَأَحْيَاهَا فَهُوَ أَحَقُّ بِهَا مِنَ الَّذِي تَرَكَهَا يُؤَدِّي خَرَاجَهَا إِلَى الامَامِ مِنْ أَهْلِ بَيْتِي وَلَهُ مَا أَكَلَ مِنْهَا حَتَّى يَظْهَرَ الْقَائِمُ مِنْ أَهْلِ بَيْتِي بِالسَّيْفِ فَيَحْوِيَهَا وَيَمْنَعَهَا وَيُخْرِجَهُمْ مِنْهَا كَمَا حَوَاهَا رَسُولُ اللهِ (صَلَّى اللهُ عَلَيْهِ وَآلِهِ) وَمَنَعَهَا إِلا مَا كَانَ فِي أَيْدِي شِيعَتِنَا فَإِنَّهُ يُقَاطِعُهُمْ عَلَى مَا فِي أَيْدِيهِمْ وَيَتْرُكُ الارْضَ فِي أَيْدِيهِمْ

Muhammad b. Yahya has narrated from Ahmad b. Muḥammad b. 'Isa from b. Mahbub from Hisham b. Salim from abu Khalid al-Kabuli from abu Ja'far (عليه السلام)

[192] *Al-Ghayba (Nu'mānī), ch14, h5*

[193] *al-Kāfi, v1, ch80, h10*

who has said the following. "We found in the book of Amir al-Mu'minin (عليه السلام) this. "The earth belongs to Allāh and He gives it in inheritance to whoever of His servants that He wishes. The good end is for those who are pious before Allāh', I and my Ahl al-Bayt are the people to whom Allāh has given the earth in inheritance and we are the ones who are pious before Allāh. The whole earth belongs to us. Thus, whoever of the Muslims would revive a land, he must establish it, pay taxes to the Imam from my Ahl al-Bayt. Whatever he has used would be his. If he would abandon or allow to become barren and another Muslim would revive and re establish it he will have more right to it than the one who have abandoned. This person will now pay the taxes to the Imam from my Ahl al-Bayt and whatever he would use thereafter is his until Al-Qa'im from my Ahl al-Bayt will rise with Divine Authority and with the sword. He will control and protect them and will remove from them just as the Messenger of Allāh had controlled and protected it, except, however, for what would be in the hands of our followers. He will form a contract with them and will leave the land to them." (حسن)[194]

195.

حَدَّثَنَا مُحَمَّدُ بْنُ الْحَسَنِ بْنِ أَحْمَدَ بْنِ الْوَلِيدِ رَضِيَ اللَّهُ عَنْهُ قَالَ حَدَّثَنَا مُحَمَّدُ بْنُ الْحَسَنِ الصَّفَّارُ عَنْ يَعْقُوبَ بْنِ يَزِيدَ عَنْ مُحَمَّدِ بْنِ أَبِي عُمَيْرٍ عَنْ أَبَانِ بْنِ عُثْمَانَ عَنْ أَبَانِ بْنِ تَغْلِبَ قَالَ قَالَ أَبُو عَبْدِ اللَّهِ ع أَوَّلُ مَنْ يُبَايِعُ الْقَائِمَ ع جَبْرَئِيلُ يَنْزِلُ فِي صُورَةِ طَيْرٍ أَبْيَضَ فَيُبَايِعُهُ ثُمَّ يَضَعُ رِجْلًا عَلَى بَيْتِ اللَّهِ الْحَرَامِ وَ رِجْلًا عَلَى بَيْتِ الْمَقْدِسِ ثُمَّ يُنَادِي بِصَوْتٍ طَلِقٍ تَسْمَعُهُ الْخَلَائِقُ أَتَى أَمْرُ اللَّهِ فَلَا تَسْتَعْجِلُوهُ

Muhammad b. al-Hasan b. Ahmad b. al-Walid رضي الله عنه narrated. He said: Muḥammad b. al-Hasan as-Saffar narrated from Ya`qub b. Yazid from Muḥammad b. Abi `Umayr from Aban b. `Uthman from Aban b. Taghlib.

He said: Abu `Abdillah عليه السلام said: The first to give allegiance to the Qa'im عليه السلام

---

[194] *Al-Kafi, v1, ch105, h1*

will be Jibra'il, who will descend in the form of a white bird and pay allegiance to him. Then he will place one foot upon the Sacred House of Allāh (i.e. the Ka`ba) and one foot upon the Bayt al-Maqdus. Then, he will call with a distinct voice, "Allāh's commandment has come, therefore do not desire to hasten it" (16:1). (صحيح)[195]

196.

عَلِيُّ بْنُ إِبْرَاهِيمَ عَنْ أَبِيهِ عَنِ ابْنِ أَبِي عُمَيْرٍ عَنْ مَنْصُورِ بْنِ يُونُسَ عَنْ إِسْمَاعِيلَ بْنِ جَابِرٍ عَنْ أَبِي خَالِدٍ عَنْ أَبِي جَعْفَرٍ ع فِي قَوْلِ اللَّهِ عَزَّ وَ جَلَّ فَاسْتَبِقُوا الْخَيْرَاتِ أَيْنَ ما تَكُونُوا يَأْتِ بِكُمُ اللَّهُ جَمِيعاً قَالَ الْخَيْرَاتُ الْوَلَايَةُ وَ قَوْلُهُ تَبَارَكَ وَ تَعَالَى أَيْنَ ما تَكُونُوا يَأْتِ بِكُمُ اللَّهُ جَمِيعاً يَعْنِي أَصْحَابَ الْقَائِمِ الثَّلَاثَمِائَةِ وَ الْبِضْعَةَ عَشَرَ رَجُلًا قَالَ وَ هُمْ وَ اللَّهِ الْأُمَّةُ الْمَعْدُودَةُ قَالَ يَجْتَمِعُونَ وَ اللَّهِ فِي سَاعَةٍ وَاحِدَةٍ قَزَعٌ كَقَزَعِ الْخَرِيفِ

From Abī Khālid (al-Kābūlī) from Abī Ja`far (عليه السلام)about the words of Allāh (عزَّ و جلّ): "Hasten to *al-khayrāt*, wherever you are, Allāh will bring you together" (2:148). He (عليه السلام)said: "*al-Khayrāt* means *al-Wilāyah.* And His (تبارك و تعالى)saying, "Wherever you are, Allāh will bring you together" means the companions of al-Qā'im who will be a few (over) three hundred and ten men. He (عليه السلام): 'By Allāh they are the nation of an insignificant amount.' He (عليه السلام)said: 'By Allāh, He will gather them in one hour like the cirrus clouds of autumn'" (حسن أو موثق)[196]

197.

مُحَمَّدُ بْنُ يَحْيَى عَنْ مُحَمَّدِ بْنِ الْحُسَيْنِ عَنِ ابْنِ مَحْبُوبٍ عَنْ إِسْحَاقَ بْنِ عَمَّارٍ قَالَ قَالَ أَبُو عَبْدِ اللهِ (عَلَيْهِ السَّلام) لِلْقَائِمِ غَيْبَتَانِ إِحْدَاهُمَا قَصِيرَةٌ وَالاخرَى طَوِيلَةٌ الْغَيْبَةُ الاولَى لا يَعْلَمُ بِمَكَانِهِ فِيهَا إِلا خَاصَّةُ شِيعَتِهِ وَالاخْرَى لا يَعْلَمُ بِمَكَانِهِ فِيهَا إِلا خَاصَّةُ مَوَالِيهِ

---

[195] *Kamal ad-Deen (Ṣaduq), v1, pg. 699*

[196] *Al-Kāfi, v8, h487*

Muhammad b. Yahya has narrated from Muḥammad b. al-Husayn from b. Mahbub from Ishaq b. 'Ammar who has said the following. "Abu 'AbdAllāh (عليه السلام) has said, Al-Qa'im ((the one who will rise with Divine Authority) will have two disappearances. One of them will be for a short time and the other for a longer time. No one would know his place during the shorter disappearance except the special persons from his Shi'a. During his longer disappearance no one will see him except very special persons from his friends." (موثق)[197]

198.

عِدَّةٌ مِنْ أَصْحَابِنَا عَنْ أَحْمَدَ بْنِ مُحَمَّدٍ عَنْ عُثْمَانَ بْنِ عِيسَى عَنْ بَكْرِ بْنِ مُحَمَّدٍ عَنْ سَدِيرٍ قَالَ قَالَ أَبُو عَبْدِ اللَّهِ (عليه السلام) يَا سَدِيرُ الْزَمْ بَيْتَكَ وَ كُنْ حِلْساً مِنْ أَحْلَاسِهِ وَ اسْكُنْ مَا سَكَنَ اللَّيْلُ وَ النَّهَارُ فَإِذَا بَلَغَكَ أَنَّ السُّفْيَانِيَّ قَدْ خَرَجَ فَارْحَلْ إِلَيْنَا وَ لَوْ عَلَى رِجْلِكَ

A number of our companions, from Ahmad b. Muhammad, from Usmaan b. Isa, from Bakr b. Muhammad, from Sudeyr who said: Abu 'AbdAllāh (عليه السلام) said: 'O Sudeyr! Be seated in your houses and remain calm, and stay like that overnight, and when the day arrives, and Al-Sufyani has come out, so get out to come to us even if you have to walk on your feet'. (حسن أو موثق)[198]

199.

مُحَمَّدُ بْنُ يَحْيَى عَنْ مُحَمَّدِ بْنِ الْحُسَيْنِ عَنْ عَبْدِ الرَّحْمَنِ بْنِ أَبِي هَاشِمٍ عَنِ الْفَضْلِ الْكَاتِبِ قَالَ كُنْتُ عِنْدَ أَبِي عَبْدِ اللَّهِ (عليه السلام) فَأَتَاهُ كِتَابُ أَبِي مُسْلِمٍ فَقَالَ لَيْسَ لِكِتَابِكَ جَوَابٌ اخْرُجْ عَنَّا فَجَعَلْنَا يُسَارُّ بَعْضُنَا بَعْضاً فَقَالَ أَيَّ شَيْءٍ تُسَارُّونَ يَا فَضْلُ إِنَّ اللَّهَ عَزَّ ذِكْرُهُ لَا يَعْجَلُ لِعَجَلَةِ الْعِبَادِ وَ لَإِزَالَةُ جَبَلٍ عَنْ مَوْضِعِهِ أَيْسَرُ مِنْ زَوَالِ مُلْكٍ لَمْ يَنْقَضِ أَجَلُهُ ثُمَّ قَالَ إِنَّ فُلَانَ بْنَ فُلَانٍ حَتَّى بَلَغَ السَّابِعَ مِنْ وُلْدِ فُلَانٍ قُلْتُ فَمَا الْعَلَامَةُ فِيمَا بَيْنَنَا

[197] *al-Kāfi, v1, ch80, h19*

[198] *Al-Kāfi, v8, h383*

وَ بَيْنَكَ جُعِلْتُ فِدَاكَ قَالَ لَا تَبْرَحِ الْأَرْضَ يَا فَضْلُ حَتَّى يَخْرُجَ السُّفْيَانِيُّ فَإِذَا خَرَجَ السُّفْيَانِيُّ فَأَجِيبُوا إِلَيْنَا
يَقُولُهَا ثَلَاثاً وَ هُوَ مِنَ الْمَحْتُومِ

Muhammad b. Yahya, from Muḥammad b. Al-Husayn, from Abdul Rahmaan b. Abu Hashim, from Al-Fazl Al-Katib who said: I was in the presence of Abu 'AbdAllāh (عليه السلام) when a letter of Abu Muslim came to him'. So he said: 'There is no answer to your letter. Exit from us'. So some of us left the others. He said: 'Which thing are you walking upon, O Fazl? Allāh (تبارك و طائلة) does not Make Haste due to the hastiness of the servants. And removing a mountain from its place is easier than toppling a government whose term has not ended'. Then said: 'So and so, son of so and so' – until he reached seven from the sons of so and so'. I said, 'May I be sacrificed for you, so what are the signs with regards to what is in between us and you?' He said: 'The earth will not depart (end), O Fazl, until the Sufyani comes out. So if the Sufyani comes out, so answer to us (to our call)'. And he said it thrice: 'And it is inevitable'. (موثق)[199]

200.

عَلِيُّ بْنُ إِبْرَاهِيمَ عَنْ أَبِيهِ عَنْ صَفْوَانَ بْنِ يَحْيَى عَنْ عِيصِ بْنِ الْقَاسِمِ قَالَ سَمِعْتُ أَبَا عَبْدِ اللَّهِ (عليه السلام)
يَقُولُ عَلَيْكُمْ بِتَقْوَى اللَّهِ وَحْدَهُ لَا شَرِيكَ لَهُ وَ انْظُرُوا لِأَنْفُسِكُمْ فَوَ اللَّهِ إِنَّ الرَّجُلَ لَيَكُونُ لَهُ الْغَنَمُ فِيهَا الرَّاعِي
فَإِذَا وَجَدَ رَجُلًا هُوَ أَعْلَمُ بِغَنَمِهِ مِنَ الَّذِي هُوَ فِيهَا يُخْرِجُهُ وَ يَجِيءُ بِذَلِكَ الرَّجُلِ الَّذِي هُوَ أَعْلَمُ بِغَنَمِهِ مِنَ الَّذِي
كَانَ فِيهَا وَ اللَّهِ لَوْ كَانَتْ لِأَحَدِكُمْ نَفْسَانِ يُقَاتِلُ بِوَاحِدَةٍ يُجَرِّبُ بِهَا ثُمَّ كَانَتِ الْأُخْرَى بَاقِيَةً فَعَمِلَ عَلَى مَا قَدِ
اسْتَبَانَ لَهَا وَ لَكِنْ لَهُ نَفْسٌ وَاحِدَةٌ إِذَا ذَهَبَتْ فَقَدْ وَ اللَّهِ ذَهَبَتِ التَّوْبَةُ فَأَنْتُمْ أَحَقُّ أَنْ تَخْتَارُوا لِأَنْفُسِكُمْ إِنْ أَتَاكُمْ
آتٍ مِنَّا فَانْظُرُوا عَلَى أَيِّ شَيْءٍ تَخْرُجُونَ وَ لَا تَقُولُوا خَرَجَ زَيْدٌ فَإِنَّ زَيْداً كَانَ عَالِماً وَ كَانَ صَدُوقاً وَ لَمْ يَدْعُكُمْ
إِلَى نَفْسِهِ إِنَّمَا دَعَاكُمْ إِلَى الرِّضَا مِنْ آلِ مُحَمَّدٍ (عليهم السلام) وَ لَوْ ظَهَرَ لَوَفَى بِمَا دَعَاكُمْ إِلَيْهِ إِنَّمَا خَرَجَ إِلَى
سُلْطَانٍ مُجْتَمِعٍ لِيَنْقُضَهُ فَالْخَارِجُ مِنَّا الْيَوْمَ إِلَى أَيِّ شَيْءٍ يَدْعُوكُمْ إِلَى الرِّضَا مِنْ آلِ مُحَمَّدٍ (عليهم السلام)
فَنَحْنُ نُشْهِدُكُمْ أَنَّا لَسْنَا نَرْضَى بِهِ وَ هُوَ يَعْصِينَا الْيَوْمَ وَ لَيْسَ مَعَهُ أَحَدٌ وَ هُوَ إِذَا كَانَتِ الرَّايَاتُ وَ الْأَلْوِيَةُ
أَجْدَرُ أَنْ لَا يَسْمَعَ مِنَّا إِلَّا مَعَ مَنِ اجْتَمَعَتْ بَنُو فَاطِمَةَ مَعَهُ فَوَ اللَّهِ مَا صَاحِبُكُمْ إِلَّا مَنِ اجْتَمَعُوا عَلَيْهِ إِذَا كَانَ

---

[199] *Al-Kāfi, v8, h412*

رَجَبٌ فَأَقْبِلُوا عَلَى اسْمِ اللَّهِ عَزَّ وَ جَلَّ وَ إِنْ أَحْبَبْتُمْ أَنْ تَتَأَخَّرُوا إِلَى شَعْبَانَ فَلَا ضَيْرَ وَ إِنْ أَحْبَبْتُمْ أَنْ تَصُومُوا فِي أَهَالِيكُمْ فَلَعَلَّ ذَلِكَ أَنْ يَكُونَ أَقْوَى لَكُمْ وَ كَفَاكُمْ بِالسُّفْيَانِيِّ عَلَامَةً

Ali b. Ibrahim, from his father, from Safwaan b. Yahya, from Ays b. Al-Qasim who said: I heard Abu 'AbdAllāh (عليه السلام) saying: 'It is upon you to fear Allāh (تبارك و طائلة), One with no associates to Him , and look into yourselves, for, by Allāh (تبارك و طائلة), the man who has sheep and the shepherd for it, if he finds a man who is more knowledgeable about the sheep than him, would let him go and come to that man who is more knowledgeable about his sheep. By Allāh (تبارك و طائلة)! If one of you had two souls, he could have fought with one, experimenting by it, then he would have worked with the other one with what has been clarified for it. But, for him there is only one soul, if it goes, by Allāh (تبارك و طائلة), the repentance goes (with it). So you are more deserving that you should choose for yourselves the one who comes to you from us, and upon which matter you are coming out, and do not go around saying that Zayd has come out, for Zayd was a scholar, and he was truthful, and he did not call you for himself. But rather he called to the pleasure (Al-Reza) from the Progeny of Messenger of Allāh (صلى الله عليه وآله وسلم), and had he made an appearance he would have been loyal to what he called you to. But rather, he came out against an authority to break it. So the one who comes out from us today for anything, he will call you to the pleasure (Al-Reza) from the Progeny of Messenger of Allāh (صلى الله عليه وآله وسلم). So we are testifying to you that we are not happy with it, and he has disobeyed us today. And there is no one with him and he with the banners and the flags, more worthy that he should listen from us except that with him would be gathered the children of Fatimah (عليها السلام). By Allāh (تبارك و طائلة)! What is your Master (Al-Qa'im (عجل الله تعالى فرجه)) except that there will be gathered around him in the month of Rajab. So go towards him in the Name of Allāh (تبارك و طائلة), and if you would like to delay it to the month of Shabaan, so it is not harmful, and if you would like to Fast in your situations so that would be more strengthening for you, and let Al-Sufyani suffice for you as a sign'. (حسن)[200]

---

[200] *Al-Kāfi, v8, h381*

201.

أخبرنا أحمد بن محمد بن سعيد، قال: حدثنا محمد بن المفضل بن إبراهيم ابن قيس، قال: حدثنا الحسن بن علي بن فضال، قال: حدثنا ثعلبة بن ميمون عن معمر بن يحيى، عن داود الدجاجي، عن أبي جعفر محمد بن علي ، قال: سئل أمير المؤمنين عن قوله تعالى فَاخْتَلَفَ الْأَحْزَابُ مِنْ بَيْنِهِمْ فَوَيْلٌ لِلَّذِينَ كَفَرُوا مِنْ مَشْهَدِ يَوْمٍ عَظِيمٍ فقال: إنتظروا الفرج من ثلاث. فقيل: يا أمير المؤمنين وما هن؟ فقال: اختلاف أهل الشام بينهم، والرايات السود من خراسان، والفزعة في شهر رمضان. فقيل: وما الفزعة في شهر رمضان؟ فقال: أوما سمعتم قول الله في القرآن إِنْ نَشَأْ نُنَزِّلْ عَلَيْهِمْ مِنَ السَّمَاءِ آيَةً فَظَلَّتْ أَعْنَاقُهُمْ لَهَا خَاضِعِينَ هي آية تخرج الفتاة من خدرها، وتوقظ النائم، وتفزع اليقظان

Ahmad b. Muhammad b. Sa'eed narrated from Muhammad b. al-Mufadhdhal b. Ibraheem b. Qays from al-Hasan b. 'Alī b. Fadhdhal from Tha'laba b. Maymoon from Ma'mar b. Yahya from Dawood ad-Dajaji that Abu Ja'far al-Baqir (عليه السلام) had said: "Once Amirul Mo'mineen (عليه السلام) was asked about (the meaning of) this Qur'anic verse, "The sects among them disagreed." He said: "Expect deliverance when three signs appear." He was asked: "What are they?" He said: "Disagreement among the people of Sham, the black banners coming from Khurasan and terror in the month of Ramadan." He was asked: "What terror is in Ramadan?" He said: "Have you not heard the saying of Allāh in the Qur'an, "If We please, We should send down upon them a sign from the heaven so that their necks should stoop to it?" It is a sign that will bring the girls out of their veils, awaken the sleepers and terrify the awake." (مجهول)[201]

202.

[201] *Al-Ghayba (Nu'mānī), ch14, h8*

حدثنا أحمد بن محمد بن سعيد، قال: حدثنا علي بن الحسن التيملي، عن علي بن مهزيار، عن حماد بن عيسى، عن الحسين بن المختار، عن أبي بصير، قال: قلت لأبي عبد الله قول الله ﴿فَلَوْلَا كَانَتْ قَرْيَةٌ آمَنَتْ فَنَفَعَهَا إِيمَانُهَا إِلَّا قَوْمَ يُونُسَ لَمَّا آمَنُوا كَشَفْنَا عَنْهُمْ عَذَابَ الْخِزْيِ فِي الْحَيَاةِ الدُّنْيَا وَمَتَّعْنَاهُمْ إِلَى حِينٍ﴾ {98} ما هو عذاب خزي الدنيا؟ فقال: وأيّ خزي أخزى، يا أبا بصير، من أن يكون الرجل في بيته وبجهاله وعلى إخوانه وسط عياله إذ شق أهله الجيوب عليه وصرخوا، فيقول الناس: ما هذا؟ فيقال مُسخ فلان الساعة! فقلت: قبل قيام القائم أو بعده؟ قال: لا، بل قبله.

Ahmad b. Muḥammad b. Sa'eed narrated from 'Alī b. al-Hasan at-Taymali from 'Alī b. Mahziyar from Hammad b. Eessa from al-Husayn b. al-Mukhtar that Abu Baseer had said: I said to Abu 'Abd Allāh as-Ṣādiq (عليه السلام): Allāh has said, 'The chastisement of disgrace in this world's life.' What is the chastisement of disgrace in this life?" He said: "O Abu Baseer, is there a disgrace worse than that when a man is in his house and among his family and then his family begins to cry and weep and people ask what the matter is to be said to them that that man is metamorphosed?" I said: "Will that happen before or after the appearance of al-Qa'im (عجل الله تعالى فرجه)؟" He said: "It will happen before the appearance of al-Qa'im (عجل الله تعالى فرجه)."(موثق)[202]

203.

حَدَّثَنَا أَحْمَدُ بْنُ زِيَادِ بْنِ جَعْفَرِ الْهَمَدَانِي رَضِيَ اللهُ عَنْهُ قَالَ حَدَّثَنَا عَلِيُّ بْنُ إِبْرَاهِيمَ عَنْ أَبِيهِ عَنْ عَبْدِ السَّلَامِ بْنِ صَالِحٍ الْهَرَوِي قَالَ سَمِعْتُ دِعْبِلَ بْنَ عَلِيٍّ الْخُزَاعِي يَقُولُ: لَمَّا أَنْشَدْتُ مَوْلَايَ عَلِيَّ بْنَ مُوسَى الرِّضَا عَلَيْهِ السَّلَامُ قَصِيدَتِيَ الَّتِي أَوَّلُهَا:مَدَارِسُ آيَاتٍ خَلَتْ عَنْ تِلَاوَةٍوَمَنْزِلُ وَحْيٍ مُقْفِرُ الْعَرَصَاتِفَلَمَّا انْتَهَيْتُ إِلَى قَوْلِي:خُرُوجُ إِمَامٍ لَا مَحَالَةَ خَارِجٌيَقُومُ عَلَى اسْمِ اللهِ وَالْبَرَكَاتِيُمَيِّزُ فِينَا كُلَّ حَقٍّ وَبَاطِلٍوَيُجْزِي عَلَى النَّعْمَاءِ وَالنَّقِمَاتِبَكَى الرِّضَا عَلَيْهِ السَّلَامُ بُكَاءً شَدِيداً ثُمَّ رَفَعَ رَأْسَهُ إِلَيَّ فَقَالَ لِي يَا خُزَاعِيُّ نَطَقَ رُوحُ الْقُدُسِ عَلَى لِسَانِكَ بِهَذَيْنِ الْبَيْتَيْنِ فَهَلْ تَدْرِي مَنْ هَذَا الْإِمَامُ وَمَتَى يَقُومُ فَقُلْتُ لَا يَا مَوْلَايَ إِلَّا أَنِّي سَمِعْتُ بِخُرُوجِ إِمَامٍ مِنْكُمْ يُطَهِّرُ الْأَرْضَ مِنَ الْفَسَادِ وَيَمْلَؤُهَا عَدْلاً.فَقَالَ يَا دِعْبِلُ الْإِمَامُ بَعْدِي مُحَمَّدٌ ابْنِي وَبَعْدَ مُحَمَّدٍ ابْنُهُ عَلِيٌّ وَبَعْدَ عَلِيٍّ ابْنُهُ الْحَسَنُ وَبَعْدَ الْحَسَنِ ابْنُهُ الْحُجَّةُ الْقَائِمُ الْمُنْتَظَرُ فِي غَيْبَتِهِ الْمُطَاعُ فِي ظُهُورِهِ وَلَوْ لَمْ يَبْقَ مِنَ الدُّنْيَا إِلَّا يَوْمٌ وَاحِدٌ لَطَوَّلَ اللهُ ذَلِكَ الْيَوْمَ حَتَّى يَخْرُجَ فَيَمْلَأَهَا عَدْلاً كَمَا مُلِئَتْ جَوْراً وَأَمَّا مَتَى فَإِخْبَارٌ عَنِ

[202] Al-Ghayba (Nu'māni), ch14, h41

الْوَقْتِ وَلَقَدْ حَدَّثَنِي أَبِي عَنْ أَبِيهِ عَنْ آبَائِهِ عَنْ عَلِيٍّ عَلَيْهِمُ الصَّلاةُ وَالسَّلامُ أَنَّ النَّبِيَ صَلَّى اللهُ عَلَيْهِ وَآلِهِ قِيلَ لَهُ يَا رَسُولَ اللَّهِ مَتَى يَخْرُجُ الْقَائِمُ مِنْ ذُرِّيَّتِكَ فَقَالَ مَثَلُهُ مَثَلُ السَّاعَةِ لا يُجَلِّيهَا لِوَقْتِهَا إِلا هُوَ ثَقُلَتْ فِي السَّمَاوَاتِ وَالأَرْضِ لا تَأْتِيكُمْ إِلا بَغْتَةً.خبر دعبل عند وفاته

Ahmad b. Ziyad b. Ja'far al-Hamazani - may God be pleased with him - narrated that 'Alī b. Ibrahim b. Hashem quoted on the authority of his father, on the authority of Abdul Salam b. Saleh al-Harawi, "I heard De'bel b. 'Alī al-Khoza'ee say, 'I recited this poem for my Master Ar-Ridha' (عليه السلام) which starts with: The schools for the Qur'anic verses are void of reciting nowand the landing site of revelations is left like a barren desert!Then I reached the following verses:A Divine Leader shall rise - surely he is to riseIn God's name and His Blessing he shall riseHe will distinguish between right and wrong for usHe will reward the good-doers and the bad-doers he shall chastise.Then Ar-Ridha' (عليه السلام) cried hard. He (عليه السلام) raised up his head towards me and said, 'O De'bel Khoza'ee! It was the Holy Spirit who made these verses flow out from your tongue. Do you know who that Divine Leader is? When will he rise?'Then De'bel said, 'No my Master! I have only heard that a Divine Leader from your progeny shall rise and cleanse the earth of corruption. He shall fill it with justice.'Then the Imam (عليه السلام) said, 'O De'bel! The Divine Leader coming after me is my son Muhammad; then after Muḥammad his son Ali; then his son Hassan; and then his son al-Hujjat the Riser the Awaited one (Imam al-Mahdi) who will come during his absence (Ghayba). He will be obeyed when he appears. God shall prolong time even if there is only one day left for him to rise and fill the earth with justice, since it has been filled with oppression and injustice. But when will it be? This is like informing the people about the time of the arrival of the Resurrection Day. My father quoted on the authority of his father, on the authority of his forefathers, on the authority of 'Alī (عليه السلام) who narrated that God's Prophet (صلى الله عليه وآله وسلم) was asked, 'O Prophet of God! When shall the Riser who is from your progeny rise?' The Prophet (صلى الله عليه وآله وسلم) replied, 'The similitude of that is like the similitude of the Hour (of Resurrection), 'None but He can reveal as to when it will occur. Heavy were its burden through the heavens and the earth. Only, all of a sudden will it come to you. (7:187) (مجهول كال موثق)[203]

204.

حَدَّثَنا الحُسَين بن إبراهِيم بن أَحمد بن هِشام المُوَدَّب وعَلِيٍّ بن عَبدُ الله الوَرَّاقِ رضي الله عنهما قالا حَدَّثَنا عَلِيٍّ بن إبراهِيم بن هاشِم عَن أَبيهِ إبراهِيم بن هاشِمٍ عَن عَبد السلام بن صالح الهروي قال دَخَلَ دِعْبِلُ بْنُ عَلِيٍّ الْخُزَاعِيُّ رَحِمَهُ اللَّهُ عَلَى أَبِي الْحَسَنِ عَلِيِّ بْنِ مُوسَى الرِّضَا عَلَيْهِ السَّلامُ بِمَرْوٍ فَقَالَ لَهُ يَا ابْنَ رَسُولِ اللَّهِ إِنِّي قَدْ قُلْتُ فِيكَ قَصِيدَةً وَآلَيْتُ عَلَى نَفْسِي أَنْ لا أُنْشِدَهَا أَحَداً قَبْلَكَ فَقَالَ عَلَيْهِ السَّلامُ هَاتِهَا فَأَنْشَدَهُ:مَدَارِسُ آيَاتٍ خَلَتْ عَنْ تِلاوَةٍوَمَنْزِلُ وَحْيٍ مُقْفِرُ الْعَرَصَاتِفَلَمَّا بَلَغَ إِلَى قَوْلِهِ:أَرَى فَيْئَهُمْ فِي غَيْرِهِمْ مُتَقَسَّماًوَأَيْدِيَهُمْ مِنْ فَيْئِهِمْ صِفِرَاتٍفَلَمَّا بَلَغَ إِلَى قَوْلِهِ هَذَا ، بَكَى أَبُو الْحَسَنِ الرِّضَا عَلَيْهِ السَّلامُ وَقَالَ لَهُ: صَدَقْتَ يَا خُزَاعِيُّ فَلَمَّا بَلَغَ إِلَى قَوْلِهِ:إِذَا وُتِرُوا مَدُّوا إِلَى وَاتِرِيهِمأَكُفّاً عَنِ الأَوْتَارِ مُنْقَبِضَاتٍجَعَلَ أَبُو الْحَسَنِ عَلَيْهِ السَّلامُ يُقَلِّبُ كَفَّيْهِ وَيَقُولُ أَجَلْ وَاللَّهِ مُنْقَبِضَاتٍ فَلَمَّا بَلَغَ إِلَى قَوْلِهِ:لَقَدْ خِفْتُ فِي الدُّنْيَا وَأَيَّامَ سَعْيِهَاوَإِنِّي لأَرْجُو الأَمْنَ بَعْدَ وَفَاتِيقَالَ الرِّضَا عَلَيْهِ السَّلامُ: آمَنَكَ اللَّهُ يَوْمَ الْفَزَعِ الأَكْبَرِ.فَلَمَّا انْتَهَى إِلَى قَوْلِهِ:وَقَبْرٌ بِبَغْدَادَ لِنَفْسٍ زَكِيَّةٍتَضَمَّنَهَا الرَّحْمَنُ فِي الْغُرُفَاتِقَالَ لَهُ الرِّضَا عَلَيْهِ السَّلامُ أَفَلا أُلْحِقُ لَكَ بِهَذَا الْمَوْضِعِ بَيْتَيْنِ بِهِمَا تَمَامُ قَصِيدَتِكَ. فَقَالَ بَلَى يَا بْنَ رَسُولِ اللَّهِ. فَقَالَ عليه السلام:وَقَبْرٌ بِطُوسَ يَا لَهَا مِنْ مُصِيبَةٍتَوَقَّدُ بِالأَحْشَاءِ فِي الْحُرُقَاتِإِلَى الْحَشْرِ حَتَّى يَبْعَثَ اللَّهُ قَائِماًيُفَرِّجُ عَنَّا الْهَمَّ وَالْكُرُبَاتِفَقَالَ دِعْبِلٌ يَا ابْنَ رَسُولِ اللَّهِ هَذَا الْقَبْرُ الَّذِي بِطُوسَ قَبْرُ مَنْ هُوَ فَقَالَ الرِّضَا عَلَيْهِ السَّلامُ قَبْرِي وَلا تَنْقَضِي الأَيَّامُ وَاللَّيَالِي حَتَّى يَصِيرَ طُوسُ مُخْتَلَفَ شِيعَتِي وَزُوَّارِي أَلا فَمَنْ زَارَنِي فِي غُرْبَتِي بِطُوسَ كَانَ مَعِي فِي دَرَجَتِي يَوْمَ الْقِيَامَةِ مَغْفُوراً لَهُ ثُمَّ نَهَضَ الرِّضَا عَلَيْهِ السَّلامُ بَعْدَ فَرَاغِ دِعْبِلٍ مِنْ إِنْشَادِ الْقَصِيدَةِ وَأَمَرَهُ أَنْ لا يَبْرَحَ مِنْ مَوْضِعِهِ وَدَخَلَ الدَّارَ فَلَمَّا كَانَ بَعْدَ سَاعَةٍ خَرَجَ الْخَادِمُ إِلَيْهِ بِمِائَةِ دِينَارٍ رَضَوِيَّةٍ [الرَّضَوِيَّةُ مَنْسُوبَةٌ إِلَى الرَّضِيِّ وَالرِّضَوِيَّةُ مَنْسُوبَةٌ إِلَى الرِّضَا] فَقَالَ لَهُ يَقُولُ لَكَ مَوْلايَ اجْعَلْهَا فِي نَفَقَتِكَ فَقَالَ دِعْبِلٌ وَاللَّهِ مَا لِهَذَا جِئْتُ وَلا قُلْتُ هَذِهِ الْقَصِيدَةَ طَمَعاً فِي شَيْءٍ يَصِلُ إِلَيَّ وَرَدَّ الصُّرَّةَ وَسَأَلَ ثَوْباً مِنْ ثِيَابِ الرِّضَا عَلَيْهِ السَّلامُ لِيَتَبَرَّكَ بِهِ وَيَتَشَرَّفَ بِهِ فَأَنْفَذَ إِلَيْهِ الرِّضَا عَلَيْهِ السَّلامُ جُبَّةَ خَزٍّ مَعَ الصُّرَّةِ وَقَالَ لِلْخَادِمِ قُلْ لَهُ خُذْ هَذِهِ الصُّرَّةَ فَإِنَّكَ سَتَحْتَاجُ إِلَيْهَا وَلا تُرَاجِعْنِي فِيهَا فَأَخَذَ دِعْبِلٌ الصُّرَّةَ وَالْجُبَّةَ وَانْصَرَفَ وَصَارَ مِنْ مَرْوٍ فِي قَافِلَةٍ فَلَمَّا بَلَغَ ميان قوهان وَقَعَ عَلَيْهِمُ اللُّصُوصُ فَأَخَذُوا الْقَافِلَةَ بِأَسْرِهَا وَكَتَفُوا أَهْلَهَا وَكَانَ دِعْبِلٌ فِيمَنْ كُتِفَ وَمَلَكَ اللُّصُوصُ الْقَافِلَةَ وَجَعَلُوا يَقْسِمُونَهَا بَيْنَهُمْ فَقَالَ رَجُلٌ مِنَ الْقَوْمِ مُتَمَثِّلاً بِقَوْلِ دِعْبِلٍ فِي قَصِيدَتِهِ:أَرَى فَيْئَهُمْ فِي غَيْرِهِمْ مُتَقَسَّماًوَأَيْدِيَهُمْ مِنْ فَيْئِهِمْ صِفِرَاتٍفَسَمِعَهُ دِعْبِلٌ فَقَالَ لَهُمْ دِعْبِلٌ لِمَنْ هَذَا الْبَيْتُ فَقَالَ لِرَجُلٍ مِنْ خُزَاعَةَ يُقَالُ لَهُ دِعْبِلُ بْنُ عَلِيٍّ قَالَ دِعْبِلٌ فَأَنَا دِعْبِلٌ قَائِلُ

---

[203] *'Uyun Akhbar al-Rida, v2,ch36, h35*

هَذِهِ الْقَصِيدَةِ الَّتِي مِنْهَا هَذَا الْبَيْتُ فَوَثَبَ الرَّجُلُ إِلَى رَئِيسِهِمْ وَكَانَ يُصَلِّي عَلَى رَأْسِ تَلٍّ وَكَانَ مِنَ الشِّيعَةِ وَأَخْبَرَهُ فَجَاءَ بِنَفْسِهِ حَتَّى وَقَفَ عَلَى دِعْبِلٍ وَقَالَ لَهُ أَنْتَ دِعْبِلٌ فَقَالَ نَعَمْ فَقَالَ لَهُ أَنْشِدِ الْقَصِيدَةَ فَأَنْشَدَهَا فَحَلَّ كِتَافَهُ وَكِتَافَ جَمِيعِ أَهْلِ الْقَافِلَةِ وَرَدَّ إِلَيْهِمْ جَمِيعَ مَا أَخَذُوا مِنْهُمْ لِكَرَامَةِ دِعْبِلٍ وَسَارَ دِعْبِلٌ حَتَّى وَصَلَ إِلَى قُمَّ فَسَأَلَهُ أَهْلُ قُمَّ أَنْ يُنْشِدَهُمُ الْقَصِيدَةَ فَأَمَرَهُمْ أَنْ يَجْتَمِعُوا فِي الْمَسْجِدِ الْجَامِعِ فَلَمَّا اجْتَمَعُوا صَعِدَ الْمِنْبَرَ فَأَنْشَدَهُمُ الْقَصِيدَةَ فَوَصَلَهُ النَّاسُ مِنَ الْمَالِ وَالْخِلَعِ بِشَيْءٍ كَثِيرٍ وَاتَّصَلَ بِهِمْ خَبَرُ الْجُبَّةِ فَسَأَلُوهُ أَنْ يَبِيعَهَا مِنْهُمْ بِأَلْفِ دِينَارٍ فَامْتَنَعَ مِنْ ذَلِكَ فَقَالُوا لَهُ فَبِعْنَا شَيْئاً مِنْهَا بِأَلْفِ دِينَارٍ فَأَبَى عَلَيْهِمْ وَسَارَ عَنْ قُمَّ فَلَمَّا خَرَجَ مِنْ رُسْتَاقِ الْبَلَدِ لَحِقَ بِهِ قَوْمٌ مِنْ أَحْدَاثِ الْعَرَبِ وَأَخَذُوا الْجُبَّةَ مِنْهُ فَرَجَعَ دِعْبِلٌ إِلَى قُمَّ وَسَأَلَهُمْ رَدَّ الْجُبَّةِ عَلَيْهِ فَامْتَنَعَ الْأَحْدَاثُ مِنْ ذَلِكَ وَعَصَوُا الْمَشَايِخَ فِي أَمْرِهَا فَقَالُوا لِدِعْبِلٍ لا سَبِيلَ لَكَ إِلَى الْجُبَّةِ فَخُذْ ثَمَنَهَا أَلْفَ دِينَارٍ فَأَبَى عَلَيْهِمْ فَلَمَّا يَئِسَ مِنْ رَدِّهِمُ الْجُبَّةَ عَلَيْهِ سَأَلَهُمْ أَنْ يَدْفَعُوا إِلَيْهِ شَيْئاً مِنْهَا فَأَجَابُوهُ إِلَى ذَلِكَ وَأَعْطَوْهُ بَعْضَهَا وَدَفَعُوا إِلَيْهِ ثَمَنَ بَاقِيهَا أَلْفَ دِينَارٍ وَانْصَرَفَ دِعْبِلٌ إِلَى وَطَنِهِ فَوَجَدَ اللُّصُوصَ قَدْ أَخَذُوا جَمِيعَ مَا كَانَ فِي مَنْزِلِهِ فَبَاعَ الْمِائَةَ دِينَارٍ الَّتِي كَانَ الرِّضَا عَلَيْهِ السَّلامُ وَصَلَهُ بِهَا مِنَ الشِّيعَةِ كُلَّ دِينَارٍ بِمِائَةِ دِرْهَمٍ فَحَصَلَ فِي يَدِهِ عَشَرَةُ آلافِ دِرْهَمٍ فَذَكَرَ قَوْلَ الرِّضَا عَلَيْهِ السَّلامُ إِنَّكَ سَتَحْتَاجُ إِلَى الدَّنَانِيرِ وَكَانَتْ لَهُ جَارِيَةٌ لَهَا مِنْ قَلْبِهِ مَحَلٌّ فَرَمِدَتْ رَمَداً عَظِيماً.فَأَدْخَلَ أَهْلَ الطِّبِّ عَلَيْهَا فَنَظَرُوا إِلَيْهَا فَقَالُوا أَمَّا الْعَيْنُ الْيُمْنَى فَلَيْسَ لَنَا فِيهَا حِيلَةٌ وَقَدْ ذَهَبَتْ وَأَمَّا الْيُسْرَى فَنَحْنُ نُعَالِجُهَا وَنَجْتَهِدُ وَنَرْجُو أَنْ تَسْلَمَ فَاغْتَمَّ لِذَلِكَ دِعْبِلٌ غَمّاً شَدِيداً وَجَزِعَ عَلَيْهَا جَزَعاً عَظِيماً ثُمَّ ذَكَرَ مَا كَانَ مَعَهُ مِنْ فَضْلَةِ الْجُبَّةِ فَمَسَحَهَا عَلَى عَيْنَيِ الْجَارِيَةِ وَعَصَبَهَا بِعِصَابَةٍ مِنْهَا مِنْ أَوَّلِ اللَّيْلِ فَأَصْبَحَتْ وَعَيْنَاهَا أَصَحُّ مِمَّا كَانَتَا قَبْلُ بِبَرَكَةِ أَبِي الْحَسَنِ الرِّضَا عَلَيْهِ السَّلامُ.قال مصنف هذا الكتاب رحمة الله عليه إنما ذكرت هذا الحديث في هذا الكتاب و في هذا الباب لما فيه من ثواب زيارة الرِّضا عَلَيْهِ السَّلامُ. و لدعبل بن عَلِيٍّ خبر عَنِ الرِّضا عَلَيْهِ السَّلامُ في النص على القائم عَلَيْهِ السَّلامُ أحببت إيراده على أثر هذا الحديث

Al-Husayn b. Ibrahim b. Ahmad b. Hisham al-Mo'addib and 'Alī b. 'Abd Allāh al-Warraq - may God be pleased with them - narrated that 'Alī b. Ibrahim b. Hashem quoted on the authority of his father Ibrahim b. Hashem, on the authority of Abdul Salam b. Saleh al-Harawi, 'De'bel b. 'Alī al-Khoza'ee - may God forgive him - went to see 'Alī b. Mūsā Ar-Ridha' (عليه السلام) in Marv and said, 'O son of God's Prophet (صلى الله عليه وآله وسلم)! I have recited some poems for you and have promised myself not to recite them for anyone, before I recite them for you.' The Imam (عليه السلام) said, 'Then recite them.' De'bel recited his poems which started with:The schools for the Qur'anic verses are void of reciting nowand the landing site of revelations is left like a barren desert!Then De'bel went on until he got to this couplet:I find others share their share,Their hands of what is theirs are bare...;Abul Hassan Ar-Ridha' (عليه السلام)

cried and said, 'O Khoza'ee! You have told the truth.' Then De'bel continued until he got to this couplet: When they were pulled taut, they did stretch Tense hands that couldn't their muscles touch, Abul Hassan Ar-Ridha' (عليه السلام) kept rubbing the palms of his hands against each other and said, 'Yes. Tense, indeed; they are tense...' Then De'bel continued reciting his poems until he got to the following: I have been frightened in the worldand the days of its effort,and I hope to be saved after I die Ar-Ridha' (عليه السلام) said, 'May God save you from the Day of the Great Dread!'De'bel continued on. When De'bel reached the end of his poems and he said, And the tomb in Baghdad is for a purified soul To whom the Merciful has guaranteed one of the Chambers (in Heaven) Ar-Ridha' (عليه السلام) told him, 'Do I have the right to add two couplets to your poem at this point?' De'bel replied, 'O son of God's Prophet! Of course.' Then the Imam (عليه السلام) said, And woe be to the shrine in Toos From its calamities the giblets burn Until Resurrection lest it is the Riser's turn To overcome all grief and pain. Then De'bel asked Ar-Ridha' (عليه السلام), 'O son of God's Prophet! Whose shrine is this one in Toos?' Then Ar-Ridha' (عليه السلام) replied, 'It is mine. Very soon, however, Toos will become the place where my visitors and followers will travel to go on pilgrimage to my shrine. Indeed, whoever visits me in my loneliness in Toos will be with me in the same rank on the Resurrection Day. He will be forgiven.' Then Ar-Ridha' (عليه السلام) stood up after De'bel had finished reciting his poem, and asked him to stay in his place. He (عليه السلام) went into the house. After an hour, the servant came out with a bag having one hundred Razawi Dinars in it, and said, 'My master has said, 'Take these for your expenses.' De'bel said, 'By God! I have not recited these poems being greedy for anything.' He refused the bag and asked for one of Ar-Ridha''s (عليه السلام) attires to be blessed and honored by him. Then Ar-Ridha' (عليه السلام) granted him a fur cloak plus the bag, and told his servant, 'Tell De'bel to take this bag, since he will need it. Tell him not to return it.' Then De'bel accepted the bag and the cloak and left.He left Marv along with a caravan. When they reached 'Meyan Qawhan', they were attacked by thieves who took all the travelers as captives and tied up their hands. De'bel was among those whose hands were tied. The thieves took all the caravan's goods and started to divide them up amongst themselves. Then one of the thieves started striking a similitude using one of De'bel's poems:I find others share their share, Their hands of what is theirs are bare...;De'bel heard him recite these verses and asked him who had composed it. He replied, 'It was said by a man from the Khoza'ee tribe who is called De'bel b. Ali.' Then De'bel said, 'Indeed, I am De'bel who said this poem. You recited only one of its couplets.' Then the man immediately rushed to their chief - a Shiite who was praying on top of a hill. The man informed the chief of what had happened. Then the chief went to De'bel in person, stopped near De'bel and asked, 'Are you De'bel?' He said, 'Yes.' Then the chief said, 'Then recite the entire poem.' Then he recited the entire poem. The chief untied his hands and ordered that all the travelers from that caravan be freed. Out of respect for De'bel, the chief also ordered that all their belongings be returned to them. Then they continued on until De'bel reached Qum. Then the people of Qum asked him to recite his poems. De'bel asked all of them to come (along with him) to the Jami'a Mosque. When they all got together in the mosque, De'bel climbed up the pulpit and recited his poems for them. The people gave him many gifts. Then they found out about the cloak. They asked him to sell it to them for one-thousand Dinars. De'bel refused to do so. They asked him to sell them just a piece of it for one-thousand Dinars, but he refused. Then he left Qum. When De'bel left the town, a group of young Arab fellows arrived from behind him and took away his cloak. De'bel had to return to Qum and beg them to return the cloak to him. But they refused and even denied their elders' requests to return the cloak. However, they told De'bel, 'There is no way that you can take back your cloak. Then just take one-thousand Dinars for it.' De'bel did not accept, and they kept on insisting, but it was no use. So finally he lost hopes of getting it back. He asked them to give him just a piece of it. The young fellows accepted this. They gave him a piece of it plus one-thousand Dinars.De'bel set out towards his hometown. When he arrived home, he realized that the thieves had stolen everything he had there. Thus he exchanged the one-hundred Razavi Dinars that Ar-Ridha' (عليه السلام) had given to him. He exchanged each Dinar for one hundred Dirhams and obtained ten-thousand Dirhams. Then De'bel remembered that Ar-Ridha' (عليه السلام) had said, 'You will need these Dinars.' De'bel had a maid whom he dearly loved. She got bad pains in her eyes. Then the doctors came, examined her and said, 'Her right eye cannot be treated. It has become blind. However, her left eye can be treated and there is hope that it may be saved.' Then De'bel got really sorry and upset. He remembered that he had a piece of the cloak. He tied it around her eyes one night. When the morning came, her eyes were treated and were even better than before due to the blessing of Abil Hassan Ar-Ridha'(عليه السلام)."The author of this book (Shaykh Sadooq) - may God have mercy upon him - said, "I included this tradition in this chapter of the book since it is related to the rewards for going on pilgrimage to Ar-Ridha' (عليه السلام). There is also another tradition from De'bel b. 'Alī related to Ar-Ridha' (عليه السلام) that is related to the coming of the Riser (عجل الله تعالى فرجه) that I would like to narrate after this tradition."

(مجهول كال موثق)[204]

205.

وَ عَنْهُ عَنْ أَحْمَدَ بْنِ مُحَمَّدٍ عَنِ ابْنِ مَحْبُوبٍ عَنْ يَعْقُوبَ السَّرَّاجِ قَالَ قُلْتُ لِأَبِي عَبْدِ اللَّهِ (عليه السلام) مَتَى فَرَجُ شِيعَتِكُمْ قَالَ فَقَالَ إِذَا اخْتَلَفَ وُلْدُ الْعَبَّاسِ وَ وَهَى سُلْطَانُهُمْ وَ طَمِعَ فِيهِمْ مَنْ لَمْ يَكُنْ يَطْمَعُ فِيهِمْ وَ خَلَعَتِ الْعَرَبُ أَعِنَّتَهَا وَ رَفَعَ كُلُّ ذِي صِيصِيَةٍ صِيصِيَتَهُ وَ ظَهَرَ الشَّامِيُّ وَ أَقْبَلَ الْيَمَانِيُّ وَ تَحَرَّكَ الْحَسَنِيُّ وَ خَرَجَ صَاحِبُ هَذَا الْأَمْرِ مِنَ الْمَدِينَةِ إِلَى مَكَّةَ بِتُرَاثِ رَسُولِ اللَّهِ (صلى الله عليه وآله) فَقُلْتُ مَا تُرَاثُ رَسُولِ اللَّهِ (صلى الله عليه وآله) قَالَ سَيْفُ رَسُولِ اللَّهِ وَ دِرْعُهُ وَ عِمَامَتُهُ وَ بُرْدُهُ وَ قَضِيبُهُ وَ رَايَتُهُ وَ لَامَتُهُ وَ سَرْجُهُ حَتَّى يَنْزِلَ مَكَّةَ فَيُخْرِجَ السَّيْفَ مِنْ غِمْدِهِ وَ يَلْبَسَ الدِّرْعَ وَ يَنْشُرَ الرَّايَةَ وَ الْبُرْدَةَ وَ الْعِمَامَةَ وَ يَتَنَاوَلَ الْقَضِيبَ بِيَدِهِ وَ يَسْتَأْذِنَ اللَّهَ فِي ظُهُورِهِ فَيَطَّلِعُ عَلَى ذَلِكَ بَعْضُ مَوَالِيهِ فَيَأْتِي الْحَسَنِيَّ فَيُخْبِرُهُ الْخَبَرَ فَيَبْتَدِرُ الْحَسَنِيُّ إِلَى الْخُرُوجِ فَيَثِبُ عَلَيْهِ أَهْلُ مَكَّةَ فَيَقْتُلُونَهُ وَ يَبْعَثُونَ بِرَأْسِهِ إِلَى الشَّامِيِّ فَيَظْهَرُ عِنْدَ ذَلِكَ صَاحِبُ هَذَا الْأَمْرِ فَيُبَايِعُهُ النَّاسُ وَ يَتَّبِعُونَهُ وَ يَبْعَثُ الشَّامِيُّ عِنْدَ ذَلِكَ جَيْشاً إِلَى الْمَدِينَةِ فَيُهْلِكُهُمُ اللَّهُ عَزَّ وَ جَلَّ دُونَهَا وَ يَهْرُبُ يَوْمَئِذٍ مَنْ كَانَ بِالْمَدِينَةِ مِنْ وُلْدِ عَلِيٍّ (عليه السلام) إِلَى مَكَّةَ فَيَلْحَقُونَ بِصَاحِبِ هَذَا الْأَمْرِ وَ يُقْبِلُ صَاحِبُ هَذَا الْأَمْرِ نَحْوَ الْعِرَاقِ وَ يَبْعَثُ جَيْشاً إِلَى الْمَدِينَةِ فَيَأْمَنُ أَهْلُهَا وَ يَرْجِعُونَ إِلَيْهَا

From Ya`qūb al-Sarrāj said, I said to Abī `Abd Allāh (عليه السلام): 'When do your Shī`ahs get relief?' So he (عليه السلام)said: 'When there will be *ikhtilāf* (disagreement) with the children of al-`Abbās about their authority and greed among them. And

---

[204] *'Uyūn Akhbār al-Riḍā, v2,ch36, h34*

those who did not show interest in them will show (interest). The `arabs will leave their reign lose, and whoever has a spur raises it. When the appearance of al-Shāmī, the drawing near of al-Yamānī, the movement of al-Hasanī, and the rise of the owner of this command (i.e. al-Qā'im) from al-Madīnah to Makkah with the legacy of the Messenger of Allāh (صلى الله عليه وآله وسلم).' So I (narrator) said: 'What legacy of the Messenger of Allāh (صلى الله عليه وآله وسلم)?' He (عليه السلام)said: 'The Messenger of Allāh's (صلى الله عليه وآله وسلم)sword, his armor, his turban, his garment, his staff, his banner, his helmet and his saddle. He (عليه السلام)reaches Makkah, then he takes the sword from its sheath, and he wears the armor and hoists the banner. He (dresses) in the gown and turban, and he takes the staff with his hand, and seeks Allāh's permission about his appearance. And he gets acquainted with few of his supporters, and al-Hasanī comes and informs him of the news. So al-Hasanī rushes to come out, but he is jumped by the people of Makkah, they kill him, and send his head to al-Shāmī. That is when the owner of this command (i.e. al-Qā'im) appears, the people do *bay'ah* (allegiance) to him, and they follow him. Al-Shāmī at that time sends an army to al-Madīnah, and Allāh (عزّ و جلّ)destroys them before reaching it. On that day the children of `Alī (عليه السلام)will flee from al-Madīnah to Makkah and stick with the owner of this command (i.e. al-Qā'im). The owner of this command (i.e. al-Qā'im) will approach near Iraq, and he (عليه السلام)will send an army to al-Madīnah whose people will believe in him, and return to it (al-Madīnah)" (صحيح)[205]

206.

أَحْمَدُ بْنُ مُحَمَّدٍ عَنْ مُحَمَّدِ بْنِ يَحْيَى عَنْ حَمَّادِ بْنِ عُثْمَانَ قَالَ كُنْتُ حَاضِراً عِنْدَ أَبِي عَبْدِ اللَّهِ (عليه السلام) إِذْ قَالَ لَهُ رَجُلٌ أَصْلَحَكَ اللَّهُ ذَكَرْتَ أَنَّ عَلِيَّ بْنَ أَبِي طَالِبٍ (عليه السلام) كَانَ يَلْبَسُ الْخَشِنَ يَلْبَسُ الْقَمِيصَ بِأَرْبَعَةِ دَرَاهِمَ وَ مَا أَشْبَهَ ذَلِكَ وَ نَرَى عَلَيْكَ اللِّبَاسَ الْجَيِّدَ قَالَ فَقَالَ لَهُ إِنَّ عَلِيَّ بْنَ أَبِي طَالِبٍ (عليه السلام) كَانَ يَلْبَسُ ذَلِكَ فِي زَمَانٍ لَا يُنْكَرُ وَ لَوْ لَبِسَ مِثْلَ ذَلِكَ الْيَوْمَ لَشُهِرَ بِهِ فَخَيْرُ لِبَاسِ كُلِّ زَمَانٍ لِبَاسُ أَهْلِهِ غَيْرَ أَنَّ قَائِمَنَا إِذَا قَامَ لَبِسَ لِبَاسَ عَلِيٍّ (عليه السلام) وَ سَارَ بِسِيرَتِهِ

[205] *al-Kāfi, v8, h285*

Ahmad b. Muḥammad has narrated from Muḥammad b. Yahya from Hammad b. 'Uthaman who has said the following: "Once I was with abu 'Abd Allāh, (عليه السلام), when a man said, 'I pray to Allāh to keep you well, you have mentioned that 'Alī b. abu Talib wore very rough-textured clothes. He wore a shirt valued at four dirham and similar items and we see you wear fine clothes.' Abu 'Abd Allāh, (عليه السلام), said to him, 'Ali b. abu Talib wore that kind of clothes in a time when it was not disliked. Were he to wear such clothes today he would have been defamed. The best dress in every period of time is what the people of that time use, however, when our al-Qa'im will rise, he will wear the kind of dress Ali, (عليه السلام), wore and follow his way of life.'" (موثق)[206]

207.

عَلِيُّ بْنُ إِبْرَاهِيمَ عَنْ أَبِيهِ عَنْ حَنَانِ بْنِ سَدِيرٍ وَ مُحَمَّدُ بْنُ يَحْيَى عَنْ أَحْمَدَ بْنِ مُحَمَّدٍ عَنْ مُحَمَّدِ بْنِ إِسْمَاعِيلَ عَنْ حَنَانِ بْنِ سَدِيرٍ عَنْ أَبِيهِ قَالَ سَأَلْتُ أَبَا جَعْفَرٍ (عليه السلام) عَنْهُمَا فَقَالَ يَا أَبَا الْفَضْلِ مَا تَسْأَلُنِي عَنْهُمَا فَوَ اللَّهِ مَا مَاتَ مِنَّا مَيِّتٌ قَطُّ إِلَّا سَاخِطاً عَلَيْهِمَا وَ مَا مِنَّا الْيَوْمَ إِلَّا سَاخِطاً عَلَيْهِمَا يُوصِي بِذَلِكَ الْكَبِيرُ مِنَّا الصَّغِيرَ إِنَّهُمَا ظَلَمَانَا حَقَّنَا وَ مَنَعَانَا فَيْئَنَا وَ كَانَا أَوَّلَ مَنْ رَكِبَ أَعْنَاقَنَا وَ بَثَقَا عَلَيْنَا بَثْقاً فِي الْإِسْلَامِ لَا يُسْكَرُ أَبَداً حَتَّى يَقُومَ قَائِمُنَا أَوْ يَتَكَلَّمَ مُتَكَلِّمُنَا ثُمَّ قَالَ أَمَا وَ اللَّهِ لَوْ قَدْ قَامَ قَائِمُنَا أَوْ تَكَلَّمَ مُتَكَلِّمُنَا لَأَبْدَى مِنْ أُمُورِهِمَا مَا كَانَ يُكْتَمُ وَ لَكَتَمَ مِنْ أُمُورِهِمَا مَا كَانَ يُظْهَرُ وَ اللَّهِ مَا أُسِّسَتْ مِنْ بَلِيَّةٍ وَ لَا قَضِيَّةٍ تَجْرِي عَلَيْنَا أَهْلَ الْبَيْتِ إِلَّا هُمَا أَسَّسَا أَوَّلَهَا فَعَلَيْهِمَا لَعْنَةُ اللَّهِ وَ الْمَلَائِكَةِ وَ النَّاسِ أَجْمَعِينَ

Ali b. Ibrahim, from his father, from hanaan b. Sudeyr, and Muḥammad b. Yahya, from Ahmad b. Muhammad, from Muḥammad b. Ismail, from Hanaan b. Sudeyr, from his father who said: I asked Abu Ja'far (عليه السلام) about the two (Abu Bakr and Umar), so he said: 'O Abu Al-Fazl, don't ask me about these two, for by Allāh (تبارك و طائلة), no one from among us passes away at all except being angry against these two, and there is none from us today except that he is angry at them. The old ones

---

[206] *Al-Kāfi, v6, ch2, h15*

bequeath it to the young ones from us. These two have been unjust to us for our rights, and prevented us from our Fey (Spoils of War – Khums), and first one rode upon our necks, and caused damage to us with a damage in Al-Islam which can never be repaired ever until our Qa'im (عجل الله تعالى فرجه) makes a stand and speaks our speech'. Then he said; 'But, by Allāh (تبارك و طائلة), when our Qa'im (عجل الله تعالى فرجه) makes a stand, or speaks our speech, he will expose the matters of these two of what they had concealed, and conceal from their matters what they used to make apparent. By Allāh (تبارك و طائلة), nothing has afflicted us from the afflictions, and what has passed of the difficulties against us, the People of the Household, except that these two laid the foundations of it at first place, so against these two are the Curses of Allāh (تبارك و طائلة), and the Angels, and the people altogether'. (حسن)[207]

208.

مُحَمَّدُ بْنُ يَحْيَى عَنْ أَحْمَدَ بْنِ مُحَمَّدٍ عَنِ الْحُسَيْنِ بْنِ سَعِيدٍ عَنِ ابْنِ أَبِي عُمَيْرٍ عَنْ هِشَامِ بْنِ سَالِمٍ عَنْ أَبِي عَبْدِ اللهِ (عَلَيْهِ السَّلام) قَالَ يَقُومُ الْقَائِمُ وَلَيْسَ لاحَدٍ فِي عُنُقِهِ عَهْدٌ وَلا عَقْدٌ وَلا بَيْعَةٌ

Muhammad b. Yahya has narrated from Ahmad b. Muḥammad from al-Husayn b. Sa'id from b. abu 'Umayr from Hisham b. Salim from abu 'AbdAllāh (عليه السلام) who has said the following. "Al-Qa'im (the one who will rise with Divine Authority) will rise and he will not be obliged to any one under any covenant, agreement or oath of allegiance." (صحيح)[208]

209.

[207] *Al-Kāfi, v8, h340*

[208] *al-Kāfi, v1, ch80, h27*

الهمداني، عن علي بن إبراهيم، عن محمد بن عيسى، عن سليمان بن داود، عن أبي بصير، وحدثنا ابن عصام، عن الكليني، عن القاسم بن العلا، عن إسماعيل بن علي، عن علي بن إسماعيل، عن عاصم بن حميد، عن محمد بن مسلم قال: دخلت على أبي جعفر (ع) وأنا اريد أن أسأله عن القائم من آل محمد(ص) فقال لي مبتدئا: يا محمد بن مسلم إن في القائم من آل محمد(ص) شبها من خمسة من الرسل: يونس بن متى، ويوسف بن يعقوب، وموسى، وعيسى، ومحمد صلوات الله عليهم، فأما شبهه من يونس فرجوعه من غيبته وهو شاب بعد كبر السن وأما شبهه من يوسف بن يعقوب فالغيبة من خاصته وعامته، واختفاؤه من إخوته وإشكال أمره على أبيه يعقوب)ع) مع قرب المسافة بينه وبين أبيه وأهله وشيعته.

وأما شبهه من موسى فدوام خوفه وطول غيبته وخفاء ولادته وتعب شيعته من بعده بما لقوا من الاذى والهوان إلى أن أذن الله(عز و جل) في ظهوره ونصره وأيده على عدوه وأما شبهه من عيسى فاختلاف من اختلف فيه حتى قالت طائفة منهم ما ولد وقالت طائفة مات وقالت طائفة قتل وصلب. وأما شبهه من جده المصطفى (ص) فخروجه بالسيف وقتله أعداء الله وأعداء رسوله (ص) والجبارين والطواغيت وأنه ينصر بالسيف والرعب وأنه لاترد له رأية وأن من علامات خروجه خروج السفياني من الشام وخروج اليماني وصيحة من السماء في شهر رمضان ومناد ينادي باسمه واسم أبيه

al-Hamadani from `Ali b. Ibrahim from Muḥammad b. `Isa from Sulayman b. Dawud from Abu Baseer. And b. `Asam narrated from al-Kulayni from al-Qasim b. al-`Alaa' from Isma`il b. `Ali from `Ali b. Isma`il from `Asim b. Humayd from Muḥammad b. Muslim. He said:

I entered upon Abu Ja`far عليه السلام while I had the intention of asking him about the Qa'im from the Family of Muḥammad صلوات الله عليهم. So he began [the conversation first] by telling me: O Muḥammad b. Muslim, verily in the Qa'im from the Family of Muḥammad صلوات الله عليهم are similarities to five messengers: Yunus b. Matta, Yusuf b. Ya`qub, Musa, `Isa, and Muḥammad صلوات الله عليهم. As for his similarity to Yunus, it is his return from occultation as a youth after being of old age. As for his similarity to Yusuf b. Ya`qub, it is occultation from his special and common [associates] (i.e. occultation from his people), his disappearance from his brothers, and his father Ya`qub's عليه السلام confusion regarding his affair despite the close proximity between him and his father, his family, and his followers (i.e. his Shi`a).

As for his similarity to Musa, it is the continuity of his fear, the length of his occultation, the secrecy of his birth, and the weariness of his followers (i.e. his Shi`a) from the pains and disregard they saw after him until Allāh عز و جل allowed him to appear. He then supported him, and He reinforced him over his enemies. As for his similarity to `Isa, it is the schisms of the disputers about him until one sect from them said, "he was not born", another sect said, "he is dead", and another sect said, "he was killed and crucified". As for his similarity to our grandfather al-Mustafa صلى الله عليه وآله وسلم, it is his appearance with the sword, the killing of the enemies of Allāh, the enemies of His Messenger صلى الله عليه وآله وسلم, the arrogant, and the tyrants; and that he will succeed through the sword and fear; no standard of his will return in defeat. From the signs of his appearance is the appearance of the Sufyani in Sham, the appearance of the Yamani, the cry from the sky in the month of Ramadan, and a Caller will call his and his father's names. (موثق على ظاهر)[209]

210.

أبي وابن الوليد وابن المتوكل جميعاً، عن سعد والحميري ومحمد العطار جميعا، عن ابن عيسى وابن هاشم والبرقي وابن أبي الخطاب جميعا، عن ابن محبوب، عن داود بن الحصين، عن أبي بصير، عن الصادق، عن آبائه (ع) قال: قال رسول الله (ص (المهدي من ولدي اسمه اسمي وكنيته كنيتي أشبه الناس بي خلقا وخلقا تكونه له غيبة وحيرة حتى يضل الخلق عن أديانهم فعند ذلك يقبل كالشهاب الثاقب فيملأها عدلا وقسطا كما ملئت ظلماً وجوراً.

My father and b. al-Walid and b. al-Mutawakkil together narrated from Sa`d and al-Himyari and Muhamad al-`Attar together from b. `Isa and b. Hashim and al-Barqi and b. Abu'l Khattab together from b. Mahbub from Dawud b. al-Hussayn from Abu Baseer from as-Ṣādiq from his forefathers عليهم السلام.

---

[209] *Kamal ad-Deen (Ṣaduq), pg. 355*

He said: The Messenger of Allāh said: The Mahdi is from my sons, his name is my name and his kunya is my kunya. He is, of all people, the most similar to me in his form and his character. There will be an occultation and a perplexity regarding him until the people go astray from their religions. At that time, he will then appear like a shooting star and fill the Earth with equity and justice as it would be fraught with injustice and oppression. (موثق)[210]

211.

حدثنا إبراهيم بن هاشم عن أبي عبد الله البرقي عن أحمد بن محمد بن أبي نصرو غيره عن أبي أيوب الحذاء عن أبي بصير عن أبي عبد الله ع قال قلت له جعلت فداك إني أريد أن ألمس صدرك فقال افعل فمسست صدره و مناكبه فقال و لم يا أبا محمد فقلت جعلت فداك إني سمعت أباك و هو يقول إن القائم واسع الصدر مسترسل المنكبين عريض ما بينهما فقال يا محمد إن أبي لبس درع رسول الله ص و كانت تستخب على الأرض و أنا لبستها فكانت و كانت و إنها تكون من القائم كما كانت من رسول الله ص مشمرة كأنه ترفع نطاقها بحلقتين و ليس هذا الأمر من جاز أربعين

Ibrahim b. Hashim narrated from Abu `Abdillah al-Barqi from Ahmad b. Muḥammad b. Abi Nasr and other than him from Abu Ayyub al-Hadha'[2] from Abu Baseer from Abu `Abdillah عليه السلام.

He said: I said to him: May I be your ransom, I would like to touch your chest. So he said: Do so. So I touched his chest and his shoulders. So he said: And for what, O Abu Muhammad? So I said: May I be your ransom, I have heard your father saying, "The Qa'im has a broad chest, upright shoulders, and what is in between is wide". So he said: O [Abu] Muhammad, my father wore the shield of the Messenger of Allāh صلى الله عليه وآله and it would drag upon the ground, and I wore it and it was [the same], and it will be upon the Qa'im as it was upon the Messenger of Allāh صلى الله عليه وآله –

---

[210] *Kamal ad-Deen (Ṣaduq), pg. 315*

spread as if its belt is held with two rings. And this affair is not for one who has surpassed [the age of] forty. (صحيح)[211]

212.

عَلِيُّ بْنُ إِبْرَاهِيمَ عَنْ أَبِيهِ عَنِ ابْنِ أَبِي عُمَيْرٍ عَنْ مَنْصُورٍ عَنْ فَضْلٍ الاعْوَرِ عَنْ أَبِي عُبَيْدَةَ الْحَذَّاءِ قَالَ كُنَّا زَمَانَ ابي جعفر (عَلَيْهِ السَّلام) حِينَ قُبِضَ نَتَرَدَّدُ كَالْغَنَمِ لا رَاعِيَ لَهَا فَلَقِينَا سَالِمَ بْنَ أَبِي حَفْصَةَ فَقَالَ لِي يَا أَبَا عُبَيْدَةَ مَنْ إِمَامُكَ فَقُلْتُ أَئِمَّتِي آلُ مُحَمَّدٍ فَقَالَ هَلَكْتَ وَأَهْلَكْتَ أَ مَا سَمِعْتُ أَنَا وَأَنْتَ أَبَا جَعْفَرٍ (عَلَيْهِ السَّلام) يَقُولُ مَنْ مَاتَ وَلَيْسَ عَلَيْهِ إِمَامٌ مَاتَ مِيتَةً جَاهِلِيَّةً فَقُلْتُ بَلَى لَعَمْرِي وَلَقَدْ كَانَ قَبْلَ ذَلِكَ بِثَلاثٍ أَوْ نَحْوِهَا دَخَلْتُ عَلَى أَبِي عَبْدِ اللهِ (عَلَيْهِ السَّلام) فَرَزَقَ اللهُ الْمَعْرِفَةَ فَقُلْتُ لابِي عَبْدِ اللهِ (عَلَيْهِ السَّلام) إِنَّ سَالِماً قَالَ لِي كَذَا وَكَذَا قَالَ فَقَالَ يَا أَبَا عُبَيْدَةَ إِنَّهُ لا يَمُوتُ مِنَّا مَيِّتٌ حَتَّى يُخَلِّفَ مِنْ بَعْدِهِ مَنْ يَعْمَلُ بِمِثْلِ عَمَلِهِ وَيَسِيرُ بِسِيرَتِهِ وَيَدْعُو إِلَى مَا دَعَا إِلَيْهِ يَا أَبَا عُبَيْدَةَ إِنَّهُ لَمْ يُمْنَعْ مَا أُعْطِيَ دَاوُدَ أَنْ أُعْطِيَ سُلَيْمَانَ ثُمَّ قَالَ يَا أَبَا عُبَيْدَةَ إِذَا قَامَ قَائِمُ آلِ مُحَمَّدٍ (صَلَّى اللهُ عَلَيْهِ وَآلِهِ) حَكَمَ بِحُكْمِ دَاوُدَ وَسُلَيْمَانَ لا يَسْأَلُ بَيِّنَةً

Ali b. Ibrahim has narrated from his father from b. abu'Umayr from Mansur from al-Fadl al-A 'al-A 'war from abu 'ubayda al-Hadhdha' who has said the following. "We lived during the times of abu Ja'far (عليه السلام). When he passed away we were left like sheep without shepherd. We met Salim b. abu Hafs and he said to me, "O abu 'Ubayda, who is your Imam?" I said, "My Imams are A'l (family) of Muḥammad (s.a)." He said, "Did not I and you hear abu Ja'far (عليه السلام) say, "Whoever would die without an Imam above him he has died as the death of the age ignorance." I said, "Yes, that is very true. I can swear by my own life." It was only about three days before my meeting with abu 'AbdAllāh (عليه السلام) in which meeting Allāh granted to me the blessing of recognizing him as my Imam. I said to abu 'AbdAllāh (عليه السلام) that Salim said to me so and so." The narrator has said that the Imam (عليه السلام) said, "O abu 'Ubayda, no one of us passes away before appointing a successor that would act and behave just as the preceding Imam and call people to what the Imam before him did. O abu 'Ubayda what was given to David did not bar Sulayman from receiving

---

[211] *Basa'ir ad-Darajat, pg. 209*

(Allāh's blessings)." Then he said, "O abu 'Ubayda, when Al-Qa'im (the one who will rise with Divine Authority) will rise he will judge among people the way David and Sulayman had been judging among people. He will call any witness to testify in a case." (حسن موثق)[212]

213.

مُحَمَّدٌ عَنْ أَحْمَدَ بْنِ مُحَمَّدٍ عَنِ ابْنِ مَحْبُوبٍ عَنْ هِشَامِ بْنِ سَالِمٍ عَنْ عَمَّارٍ السَّابَاطِيِّ قَالَ قُلْتُ لابِي عَبْدِ اللهِ (عَلَيْهِ السَّلام) بِمَا تَحْكُمُونَ إِذَا حَكَمْتُمْ قَالَ بِحُكْمِ اللهِ وَحُكْمِ دَاوُدَ فَإِذَا وَرَدَ عَلَيْنَا الشَّيْءُ الَّذِي لَيْسَ عِنْدَنَا تَلَقَّانَا بِهِ رُوحُ الْقُدُسِ

Muhammad has narrated from Ahmad b. Muḥammad from b. Mahbub from Hisahm b. Salim from 'Ammar al-Sabati who has said the following. "Once I asked abu 'AbdAllāh (عليه السلام), "By what means do you judge when you would judge?" He said, "We judge by the laws of Allāh and in the manner of David. If an issue would come before us for which there is nothing with us the Holy Spirit provides us inspiration." (موثق)[213]

214.

مُحَمَّدُ بْنُ يَحْيَى عَنْ أَحْمَدَ بْنِ مُحَمَّدٍ وَعَلِيُّ بْنُ إِبْرَاهِيمَ عَنْ أَبِيهِ جَمِيعاً عَنِ ابْنِ مَحْبُوبٍ عَنِ ابْنِ رِئَابٍ عَنْ أَبِي بَصِيرٍ عَنْ أَبِي عَبْدِ اللهِ (عَلَيْهِ السَّلام) قَالَ إِنَّ اللهَ تَعَالَى أَوْحَى إِلَى عِمْرَانَ أَنِّي وَاهِبٌ لَكَ ذَكَراً سَوِيّاً مُبَارَكاً يُبْرِئُ الاكْمَهَ وَالابْرَصَ وَيُحْيِي الْمَوْتَى بِإِذْنِ اللهِ وَجَاعِلُهُ رَسُولاً إِلَى بَنِي إِسْرَائِيلَ فَحَدَّثَ عِمْرَانُ امْرَأَتَهُ حَنَّةَ بِذَلِكَ وَهِيَ أُمُّ مَرْيَمَ فَلَمَّا حَمَلَتْ كَانَ حَمْلُهَا بِهَا عِنْدَ نَفْسِهَا غُلامٌ فَلَمَّا وَضَعَتْهَا قَالَتْ رَبِّ إِنِّي وَضَعْتُهَا أُنْثَى... وَلَيْسَ الذَّكَرُ كَالانْثَى أَيْ لا يَكُونُ الْبِنْتُ رَسُولاً يَقُولُ اللهُ عَزَّ وَجَلَّ وَاللهُ أَعْلَمُ بِمَا وَضَعَتْ فَلَمَّا وَهَبَ اللهُ

[212] *Al-Kāfi, v1, ch99, h1*

[213] *Al-Kāfi,v1, ch99, h3*

تَعَالَى لِمَرْيَمَ عِيسَى كَانَ هُوَ الَّذِي بَشَّرَ بِهِ عِمْرَانَ وَوَعَدَهُ إِيَّاهُ فَإِذَا قُلْنَا فِي الرَّجُلِ مِنَّا شَيْئاً وَكَانَ فِي وَلَدِهِ أَوْ وَلَدِ وَلَدِهِ فَلا تُنْكِرُوا ذَلِكَ

Muhammad b. Yahya has narrated from Ahmad b. Muḥammad and ʿAlī b. Ibrahim his father all from b. Mahbub from al-Ri'ab from abu Basir from abu 'AbdAllāh (عليه السلام) who has said the following. "Allāh sent revelation to 'Imran saying, "I will grant you a perfect and holy son who would cure the blind and the lepers and bring the dead back to life by Allāh, the permission of Allāh and I make him a messenger to the israelites." 'Iran than told it to his wife, Hanna, mother of Mary all about it When she conceive with the baby Mary and she thought to herself that the baby will be a boy. When she give birth to Mary she said, "Lord, I have given birth to a girl and boys are not like girls. A girl cannot be a messenger. Allāh, the Most Majestic, the Most gracious, has said, "Allāh knows to who have you given birth. When Allāh, the Most High, granted Jesus to Mary he was the boy promised to 'Imran. He promised Jesus to 'Imran. When we would say something about a man from us and that thing would be fount in his sons or grand sons then you must not deny it." (صحيح)[214]

215.

حَدَّثَنَا مُحَمَّدُ بْنُ إِبْرَاهِيمَ بْنِ إِسْحَاقَ رَضِيَ اللهُ عَنْهُ قَالَ: حَدَّثَنَا مُحَمَّدُ بْنُ أَحْمَدَ الْهَمْدَانِيُّ قَالَ عَلِيُّ بْنُ الْحَسَنِ بْنِ عَلِيِّ بْنِ فضال، عَنْ أَبِيهِ، عَنْ أَبِي الْحَسَنِ عَلِيِّ بْنِ مُوسَى الرِّضَا عَلَيْهِ السَّلَامُ أَنَّهُ كَأَنِّي بِالشِّيعَةِ عِنْدَ فَقْدِهِمُ الثَّالِثَ مِنْ وُلْدِي يَطْلُبُونَ الْمَرْعَى فَلَا يَجِدُونَهُ قُلْتُ لَهُ وَلِمَ ذَلِكَ يَا ابْنَ رَسُولِ اللَّهِ قَالَ لأَنَّ إِمَامَهُمْ يَغِيبُ عَنْهُمْ فَقُلْتُ وَلِمَ قَالَ لِئَلا يَكُونَ فِي عُنُقِهِ لأَحَدٍ بَيْعَةٌ إِذَا قَامَ بِالسَّيْفِ

Muhammad b. Ibrahim b. Ishaq - may God be pleased with him - narrated that Muḥammad b. Ahmad al-Hamdani quoted on the authority of ʿAlī b. Al-Hassan b. ʿAlī b. Fadhdhal, on the authority of his father that Abil Hassan ʿAlī b. Mūsā Al-Ridha (عليه السلام) said, "I see my followers when they will not find the third from my

---

[214] *Al-Kāfi, v1, ch127, h1*

progeny. They will be looking for someone to take charge of their affairs, but they will find no one to do so." I asked, "O son of the Prophet of God! Why?" The Imam (عليه السلام) said, "That is because their Divine Leader will become absent." I asked, "Why?" The Imam (عليه السلام) said, "That is because when he (عليه السلام) rises with the sword, no one's pledge of allegiance is b.ding upon him." (مجهول كالموثق)[215]

216.

حدثنا محمد بن يعقوب قال: حدثنا علي بن إبراهيم، عن أبيه، عن بن محبوب، عن يعقوب السراج وعن علي بن رئاب، عن أبي عبد الله أنه قال: لما بويع لأمير المؤمنين بعد مقتل عثمان صعد المنبر وخطب خطبة ذكرها يقول فيها: ألا إنّ بليّتكم قد عادت كهيئتها يوم بعث الله نبيه . والذي بعثه بالحق لتبلبلُنّ بلبلةً ولتغربلُنّ غربلة حتى يعود أسفلكم أعلاكم وأعلاكم أسفلكم، وليسبقنّ سابقون كانوا قصّروا، وليقصرنّ سبّاقون كانوا سبقوا، والله ما كتمت وسمة ولا كذبت كذبة، ولقد نُبّئت بهذا المقام وهذا اليوم

Muhammad b. Ya'qoob narrated from ʿAlī b. Ibraheem from his father from b. Mahboob from Ya'qoob as-Sarraj and ʿAlī b. Ri'ab that Abu ʿAbd Allāh as-Ṣādiq (عليه السلام) had said: When Amirul Mo'mineen (عليه السلام) was paid homage as the caliph after Uthman had been killed, he ascended the minbar and made a speech. He said: "Your affliction became as it had been when Allāh had sent His messenger Muḥammad (عليه السلام). I swear by Him, Who has sent His messenger with the truth, that you will be confused and will be sifted until your notables become low and your lows become notable. Some of you, who have been indecent, will be virtuous and some, who have been virtuous, will be indecent. By Allāh I have not hidden a truth nor have I told a lie. I have been inspired with this position and this day." (صحيح)[216]

217.

---

[215] *ʿUyūn Akhbār al-Riḍā, v1, ch28, h6*

[216] *Al-Ghayba (Nuʿmānī), ch12, h1*

حدثنا محمد بن موسى بن المتوكل رضي الله عنه قال: حدثنا علي بن إبراهيم عن أبيه إبراهيم بن هاشم، عن عبد الله بن حماد الأنصاري، ومحمد بن سنان جميعا، عن أبي الجارود زياد بن المنذر، عن أبي جعفر محمد بن علي الباقر عليهما السلام قال: قال لي: يا أبا الجارود إذا دارت الفلك، وقال الناس :مات القائم أو هلك، بأي واد سلك، وقال الطالب: أنى يكون ذلك وقد بليت عظامه فعند ذلك فارجوه، فإذا سمعتم به فأتوه ولو حبوا على الثلج

Narrated to us Muḥammad b. Mūsā b. Mutawakkil رضي الله عنه: Narrated to us 'Alī b. Ibrahim from his father Ibrahim b. Hashim from 'Abd Allāh b. Hammad Ansari and Muḥammad b. Sinan, all of them from Abil Jarud Ziyad b. Mundhir from Abi Ja'far Muḥammad b. 'Alī al-Baqir (عليه السلام) that he said to me: "O Aba Jarud, when the time of occultation will prolong, people will begin to say: The Qa'im is dead or he has been killed. And in which valley does he reside? And the opponents will say: Where does a Qa'im exist? His bones must also have decayed. At that time remain hopeful for his reappearance and when you hear his call harken to it. You should go to join him even if you have to crawl on snow." (حسن)[217]

218.

عَلِيُّ بْنُ مُحَمَّدٍ عَنْ مُحَمَّدِ بْنِ عَلِيِّ بْنِ إِبْرَاهِيمَ عَنْ أَبِي عَبْدِ اللهِ بْنِ صَالِحٍ أَنَّهُ رَآهُ عِنْدَ الْحَجَرِ الاسْوَدِ وَالنَّاسُ يَتَجَاذَبُونَ عَلَيْهِ وَهُوَ يَقُولُ مَا بِهَذَا أُمِرُوا

Ali b. Muḥammad has narrated from Muḥammad b. 'Alī b. Ibrahim from abu 'AbdAllāh b. Salih who has said the following. "I saw him (the twelfth Imam) near the Black Stone while people were clinging over it. The Imam (عليه السلام) would say, "They are not commanded in this condition (to kiss the Black Stone.)" (صحيح على الظاهر)[218]

---

[217] *Kamal ad-Deen, pg. 354*

[218] *Al-Kāfi, v1, ch77, h7*

219.

حدثنا محمد بن موسى بن المتوكل رضي الله عنه قال: حدثنا عبد الله بن جعفر الحميري، عن محمد بن عثمان العمري رضي الله عنه قال: سمعته يقول: والله إن صاحب هذا الامر ليحضر الموسم كل سنة فيرى الناس ويعرفهم ويرونه ولا يعرفونه

Narrated to us Muḥammad b. Mūsā b. Mutawakkil رضي الله عنه: Narrated to us ʿAbd Allāh b. Ja'far Himyari from Muḥammad b. Uthman al-Amari رضي الله عنه that he said: "The master of this affair shall perform the Hajj rituals every year. Thus he shall see the people and recognize them and they shall (also) see him but will not recognize him." (صحيح)[219]

220.

حدثنا محمد بن موسى بن المتوكل رضي الله عنه قال: حدثنا عبد الله بن جعفر الحميري قال: سألت محمد بن عثمان العمري رضي الله عنه فقلت له: أرأيت صاحب هذا الامر؟ فقال: نعم وآخر عهدي به عند بيت الله الحرام وهو يقول: " اللهم أنجز لي ما وعدتني."

Narrated to us Muḥammad b. Mūsā b. Mutawakkil رضي الله عنه: Narrated to us ʿAbd Allāh b. Ja'far Himyari that:
I asked Muḥammad b. Uthman Amari: "Have you the seen the master of this affair?" He replied: "Yes, and the last time I saw him, he was besides the Holy House of Allāh and praying: O my Lord, fulfill the promise that You made to me." (صحيح)[220]

221.

[219] *Kamal ad-Deen (Ṣaduq), pg. 468*

[220] *Kamal ad-Deen (Ṣaduq), pg. 468*

حدثنا محمد بن موسى بن المتوكل رضي الله عنه قال: حدثنا عبد الله بن جعفر الحميري قال: سمعت محمد بن عثمان العمري رضي الله عنه يقول: رأيته صلوات الله عليه متعلقا بأستار الكعبة في المستجار وهو يقول: " اللهم انتقم لي من أعدائي."

Narrated to us Muḥammad b. Mūsā b. Mutawakkil رضي الله عنه: Narrated to us ʿAbd Allāh b. Ja'far Himyari that:
I heard Muḥammad b. Uthman Amari رضي الله عنه say: "I saw His Eminence (عليه السلام) holding the curtain of the Kaaba below the spout and praying: O my Lord, take revenge from my enemies." (صحيح)[221]

222.

أخبرنا أحمد بن محمد بن سعيد قال: حدثنا علي بن الحسن، عن العباس بن عامر، عن عبد الله بن بكير، عن زرارة بن أعين، عن عبد الملك بن أعين، قال: كنت عند أبي جعفر فجرى ذكر القائم ، فقلت له: أرجو أن يكون عاجلاً ولا يكون سفياني. فقال: لا والله، إنه لمن المحتوم الذي لا بد منه

Ahmad b. Muḥammad b. Sa'eed narrated from ʿAlī b. al-Hasan from al-Abbas b. Aamir from ʿAbd Allāh b. Bukayr from Zurara b. A'yun that Abdul Melik b. A'yun had said: "Once I was with Abu Ja'far al-Baqir (عليه السلام) when al-Qa'im (عجل الله تعالى فرجه) was mentioned before him. I said to him: "I hope that he (al-Qa'im) appears sooner without being preceded by the rising of as-Sufyani." He said: "By Allāh, that will not be! It is an inevitable thing." (حسن موثق)[222]

223.

---

[221] *Kamal ad-Deen (Ṣaduq), pg. 468*

[222] *Al-Ghayba (Nuʿmānī), ch18, h4*

أخبرنا أحمد بن محمد بن سعيد قال: حدثنا علي بن الحسن، عن العباس ابن عامر بن رباح الثقفي، عن عبد الله بن بكير، عن زرارة بن أعين، قال: سمعت أبا عبد الله يقول: ينادي منادٍ من السماء: إن فلاناً هو الأمير. وينادي منادٍ: إن علياً وشيعته هم الفائزون. قلت: فمن يقاتل المهدي بعد هذا؟ فقال: إن الشيطان ينادي: إن فلاناً وشيعته هم الفائزون. (لرجل من بني أمية) قلت: فمن يعرف الصادق من الكاذب؟ قال: يعرفه الذين كانوا يروون حديثنا ويقولون إنه يكون قبل أن يكون، ويعلمون أنهم هم المحقون الصادقون

Ahmad b. Muḥammad b. Sa'eed narrated from ʿAlī b. al-Hasan from al-Abbas b. Aamir b. Rabah ath-Thaqafi from ʿAbd Allāh b. Bukayr that Zurara b. A'yun had said: "I heard Abu ʿAbd Allāh as-Ṣādiq (عليه السلام) saying: "A caller will call out from the Heaven that so-and-so is the emir and that ʿAlī and his followers are the triumphants." I said: "Then who will fight al-Mahdi after that?" He said: "The Satan will call out that so-and-so and his followers are the triumphants-a man of the Umayyads (Uthman)." I said: "Then who will know which the truthful is and which the liar is?" He said: "Those, who used to narrate our traditions, will know that and will know that they are with the truth." (موثق)[223]

224.

أخبرنا أحمد بن محمد بن سعيد بهذا الإسناد عن هشام بن سالم، قال: سمعت أبا عبد الله يقول: هما صيحتان صيحة في أول الليل، وصيحة في آخر اللية الثانية. قال: فقلت: كيف ذلك؟ فقال: واحدة من السماء، وواحدة من إبليس. فقلت: وكيف تعرف هذه من هذه؟ فقال: يعرفها من كان سمع بها قبل أن تكون

Ahmad b. Muḥammad b. Sa'eed narrated that Hisham b. Salim had said: I heard Abu ʿAbd Allāh as-Ṣādiq (عليه السلام) saying: "There will be two cries; one at the beginning of night and the other will be at the end of the second night." I asked: "How will that be?" He said: "One will be from the Heaven and the other will be from Iblis." I said:

---

[223] *Al-Ghayba (Nu'mani), ch14, h28*

"How one will be distinguished from the other?" He said: "He, who has known about them before they occur, will know which of them is from the Heaven." (موثق)[224]

225.

حدثنا أبي رضي الله عنه قال حدثنا سعد بن عبد الله قال حدثنا محمد بن الحسين بن أبي الخطاب عن جعفر بن بشير عن هشام بن سالم عن زرارة عن أبي عبد الله عليه السلام قال ينادي مناد باسم القائم عليه السلام قلت خاص أو عام قال عام يسمع كل قوم بلسانهم قلت فمن يخالف القائم عليه السلام وقد نودي باسمه قال لا يدعهم إبليس حتى ينادي في آخر الليل ويشكك الناس

Narrated to us my father: Narrated to us Saad b. ʿAbd Allāh: Narrated to us Muḥammad b. Husain b. Abil Khattab from Ja'far b. Basheer from Hisham b. Saalim from Zurāra from Abi ʿAbd Allāh (عليه السلام) that he said: "A caller will call out in the name of the Qa'im." I asked: "Will it be for some people or for all?" He replied: "It would be for all. And every community will hear it in its own language." I asked: "Would the opponents of Qa'im be also called in his name?" "No," he said, "For them Iblees will call out at the end of the night and put suspicion in the hearts of the people." (صحيح)[225]

226.

حدثنا أحمد بن زياد بن جعفر الهمداني رضي الله عنه قال: حدثنا علي ابن إبراهيم، عن أبيه، عن الريان بن الصلت قال: قلت للرضا عليه السلام :أنت صاحب هذا الامر ؟ فقال: أنا صاحب هذا الامر ولكني لست بالذي أملاها عدلا كما ملئت جورا، وكيف أكون ذلك على ما ترى من ضعف بدني، وإن القائم هو الذي إذا خرج كان في سن الشيوخ ومنظر الشبان، قويا في بدنه حتى لو مد يده إلى أعظم شجرة على وجه الأرض لقلعها، ولو صاح بين الجبال لتدكدكت صخورها، يكون معه عصا موسى، وخاتم سليمان عليهما السلام .ذلك

---

[224] *Al-Ghayba (Nu'mani), ch14, h31*

[225] *Kamal ad-Deen (Ṣaduq), pg. 678*

الرابع من ولدي، يغيبه الله في ستره ما شاء، ثم يظهره فيملأ [به] الأرض قسطا وعدلا كما ملئت جورا وظلما

Narrated to us Ahmad b. Ziyad b. Ja'far Hamadani رضي الله عنه: Narrated to us 'Alī b. Ibrahim from his father from Rayyan b. Salt that he said: I asked ar-Reza (عليه السلام): "Are you the Sahibul Amr (Master of Affair)? He replied: I am also Sahibul Amr but not the Sahibul Amr who will fill the earth with justice as it would have been fraught with tyranny and oppression. And how can I be that person? While you can see that I am physically weak. Whereas the Qa'im is the one who at the time of his reappearance will be senior in age but have the appearance of the youth. His body shall be so strong that if he catches hold of the biggest tree of the earth he shall be able to uproot it and if he shouts between the mountains, their stones will roll down. The staff of Prophet Mūsā and the seal ring of Prophet Sulayman (عليه السلام) are with him. He is my fourth descendent. The Almighty Allāh will keep him in occultation as long as Divine wisdom dictates. Then He will reveal him so that he may fill the earth with justice and equity just as it would fraught with injustice and oppression." (صحيح)[226]

227.

أخبرنا أحمد بن محمد بن سعيد قال: حدثنا علي بن الحسن التيملي، قال حدثنا الحسن ومحمد ابنا علي بن يوسف، عن سعدان بن مسلم، عن عمر بن أبان الكلبي عن أبان بن تغلب، قال: سمعت أبا عبد الله يقول: كأني أنظر إلى القائم على نجف الكوفة، عليه خوخة من استبرق، ويلبس درع رسول الله فإذا لبسها انتفضت به حتى تستدير عليه، ثم يركب فرساً له أدهم أبلق، بين عينيه شمراخ بيّن، معه راية رسول الله . قلت: مخبوة أو يؤتى بها؟ قال: بل يأتيه بها جبرئيل، عمودها من عمد عرش الله، وسائرها من نصر الله، لا يهوي بها إلى شيء إلاّ أهلكه الله، يهبط بها تسعة آلاف ملك وثلاثمائة وثلاثة عشر ملكاً. فقلت له: جعلت فداك، كل هؤلاء معه؟ قال: نعم، هم الذين كانوا مع نوح في السفينة، والذين كانوا مع إبراهيم حيث أُلقي في النار، وهم الذين كانوا مع موسى لما فلق له البحر، والذين كانوا مع عيسى لما رفعه الله إليه، وأربعة آلاف مسومين كانوا مع رسول الله ، وثلاثمائة وثلاثة عشر ملكاً كانوا معه يوم بدر، ومعهم أربعة آلاف صعدوا إلى

[226] *Kamal ad-Deen (Ṣaduq), pg. 404*

السماء يستأذنون في القتال مع الحسين فهبطوا إلى الأرض وقد قتل، فهم عند قبره شعث غبر يبكونه إلى يوم القيامة، وهم ينتظرون خروج القائم

Ahmad b. Muḥammad b. Sa'eed narrated from 'Alī b. al-Hasan at-Taymali from al-Hasan and Muhammad, the sons of 'Alī b. Yousuf, from Sa'dan b. Muslim from Umar b. Abban al-Kalbi that Abban b. Taghlub had said: "I heard Abu 'Abd Allāh as-Ṣādiq (عليه السلام) saying: "As if I see al-Qa'im on the hill of Kufa wearing a dress of brocade and the armor of the Prophet (صلى الله عليه وآله وسلم), riding a black horse and holding the banner of the Prophet (صلى الله عليه وآله وسلم)." I said: "Has the banner been kept somewhere or it will be brought then?" He said: "Gabriel will bring it. Its pole is from the poles of the Throne of Allāh and the rest of it is from the assistance of Allāh. Everything that he swoops on with this banner Allāh will make it perish. Nine thousand and three hundred and thirteen angels will come down with the banner." I said: "May I die for you! Will all these angels be with him?" He said: "Yes, they will. It is they, who have been with Prophet Noah (عليه السلام) in the Ark, with Abraham (عليه السلام) when he has been thrown into the fire, with Moses (عليه السلام) when the sea has been cleft to him, with Jesus Christ (عليه السلام) when he has been raised to the Heaven and four thousand angels, who have been with Prophet Muḥammad (عليه السلام) and three hundred and thirteen angels, who have fought with him in the battle of Badr besides four thousands that have ascended to the Heaven asking permission to fight with al-Husayn (عليه السلام) but when they have descended they find that al-Husayn (عليه السلام) has been martyred. They have remained near his tomb weeping for him until the Day of Resurrection. They are waiting for the appearance of al-Qa'im (عجل الله تعالى فرجه)." (موثق)[227]

228.

[227] *Al-Ghayba (Nu'mānī), ch19, h4*

حَدَّثَنا مُحَمَّدِ بْنِ عَلِي ماجيلوَيْه رَضِيَ اللهُ عَنْهُ قالَ: حَدَّثَنا عَلِيّ بْنِ إبراهِيمِ بْنِ هاشِم، عَنْ أبِيهِ، عَنِ الرَّيانِ بْنِ شَبِيبٍ قالَ دَخَلْتُ عَلى الرِّضا عَلَيْهِ السَّلامُ فِي أَوَّلِ يَوْمٍ مِنَ الْمُحَرَّمِ فَقالَ لِي يا ابْنَ شَبِيبٍ أَصائِمٌ أَنْتَ؟ فَقُلْتُ لا. فَقالَ إنَّ هَذا الْيَوْمَ هُوَ الْيَوْمُ الَّذِي دَعا فِيهِ زَكَرِيَّا رَبَّهُ عَزَّ وَجَلَّ فَقالَ: (رَبِّ هَبْ لِي مِنْ لَدُنْكَ ذُرِّيَّةً طَيِّبَةً إِنَّكَ سَمِيعُ الدُّعاءِ).فَاسْتَجابَ اللهُ لَهُ وَأَمَرَ الْمَلائِكَةَ فَنادَتْ زَكَرِيَّا وَهُوَ قائِمٌ يُصَلِّي فِي الْمِحْرابِ أَنَّ اللهَ يُبَشِّرُكَ بِيَحْيى. فَمَنْ صامَ هَذا الْيَوْمَ ثُمَّ دَعا اللهَ عَزَّ وَجَلَّ اسْتَجابَ اللهُ لَهُ كَما اسْتَجابَ لِزَكَرِيَّا عَلَيْهِ السَّلامُ.ثُمَّ قالَ يا ابْنَ شَبِيبٍ إِنَّ الْمُحَرَّمَ هُوَ الشَّهْرُ الَّذِي كانَ أَهْلُ الْجاهِلِيَّةِ فِيما مَضى يُحَرِّمُونَ فِيهِ الظُّلْمَ وَالْقِتالَ لِحُرْمَتِهِ. فَما عَرَفَتْ هَذِهِ الأُمَّةُ حُرْمَةَ شَهْرِها وَلا حُرْمَةَ نَبِيِّها. لَقَدْ قَتَلُوا فِي هَذا الشَّهْرِ ذُرِّيَّتَهُ وَسَبَوْا نِساءَهُ وَانْتَهَبُوا ثِقْلَهُ، فَلا غَفَرَ اللهُ لَهُمْ ذَلِكَ أَبَداً.يا ابْنَ شَبِيبٍ إِنْ كُنْتَ باكِياً لِشَيْءٍ فَابْكِ لِلْحُسَيْنِ بْنِ عَلِيِّ بْنِ أَبِي طالِبٍ عَلَيْهِ السَّلامُ، فَإِنَّهُ ذُبِحَ كَما يُذْبَحُ الْكَبْشُ، وَقُتِلَ مَعَهُ مِنْ أَهْلِ بَيْتِهِ ثَمانِيَةَ عَشَرَ رَجُلاً ما لَهُمْ فِي الأَرْضِ شَبِيهُونَ، وَلَقَدْ بَكَتِ السَّماواتُ السَّبْعُ وَالأَرَضُونَ لِقَتْلِهِ، وَلَقَدْ نَزَلَ إِلَى الأَرْضِ مِنَ الْمَلائِكَةِ أَرْبَعَةُ آلافٍ لِنَصْرِهِ فَوَجَدُوهُ قَدْ قُتِلَ، فَهُمْ عِنْدَ قَبْرِهِ شُعْثٌ غُبْرٌ إِلَى أَنْ يَقُومَ الْقائِمُ فَيَكُونُونَ مِنْ أَنْصارِهِ وَشِعارُهُمْ يا لَثاراتِ الْحُسَيْنِ.يا ابْنَ شَبِيبٍ لَقَدْ حَدَّثَنِي أَبِي، عَنْ أَبِيهِ، عَنْ جَدِّهِ أَنَّهُ لَمَّا قُتِلَ جَدِّيَ الْحُسَيْنُ أَمْطَرَتِ السَّماءُ دَماً وَتُراباً أَحْمَرَ.يا ابْنَ شَبِيبٍ إِنْ بَكَيْتَ عَلَى الْحُسَيْنِ حَتَّى تَصِيرَ دُمُوعُكَ عَلَى خَدَّيْكَ غَفَرَ اللهُ لَكَ كُلَّ ذَنْبٍ أَذْنَبْتَهُ صَغِيراً كانَ أَوْ كَبِيراً قَلِيلاً كانَ أَوْ كَثِيراً.يا ابْنَ شَبِيبٍ إِنْ سَرَّكَ أَنْ تَلْقَى اللهَ عَزَّ وَجَلَّ وَلا ذَنْبَ عَلَيْكَ فَزُرِ الْحُسَيْنَ عَلَيْهِ السَّلامُ.يا ابْنَ شَبِيبٍ إِنْ سَرَّكَ أَنْ تَسْكُنَ الْغُرَفَ الْمَبْنِيَّةَ فِي الْجَنَّةِ مَعَ النَّبِي صَلَّى اللهُ عَلَيْهِ وَآلِهِ فَالْعَنْ قَتَلَةَ الْحُسَيْنِ.يا ابْنَ شَبِيبٍ إِنْ سَرَّكَ أَنْ يَكُونَ لَكَ مِنَ الثَّوابِ مِثْلُ ما لِمَنِ اسْتُشْهِدَ مَعَ الْحُسَيْنِ فَقُلْ مَتَى ما ذَكَرْتَهُ يا لَيْتَنِي كُنْتُ مَعَهُمْ فَأَفُوزَ فَوْزاً عَظِيماً.يا ابْنَ شَبِيبٍ إِنْ سَرَّكَ أَنْ تَكُونَ مَعَنا فِي الدَّرَجاتِ الْعُلَى مِنَ الْجِنانِ فَاحْزَنْ لِحُزْنِنا وَافْرَحْ لِفَرَحِنا وَعَلَيْكَ بِوَلايَتِنا فَلَوْ أَنَّ رَجُلاً تَوَلَّى حَجَراً لَحَشَرَهُ اللهُ مَعَهُ يَوْمَ الْقِيامَةِ

Muhammad b. 'Alī Majiluwayh - may God be pleased with him -narrated that 'Alī b. Ibrahim b. Hashem quoted on the authority of his father, on the authority of al-Rayyan b. ShAbib, "I went to see Al-Ridha (عليه السلام) on the first day of the (Arabic) month of Muharram. The Imam (عليه السلام) said, 'O b. ShAbib! Are you fasting?' I answered, 'No.' The Imam (عليه السلام) said, 'Today is the day on which Zakariya prayed to his Lord - the Honorable the Exalted, 'There did Zakariya pray to his Lord, saying, 'O my Lord! Grant unto me from Thee a progeny that is pure: for Thou art He that heareth prayer!'' And God fulfilled his prayer and ordered theangels to call Zakariya 'While he was standing in prayer in the chamber, the angels called unto him, '(Allāh) doth give thee glad tidings of Yahya, witnessing the truth of a Word from Allāh, and (be besides) noble, chaste, and a Prophet, of the (goodly) company of the righteous." Therefore, just as God fulfilled the prayers of Zakariya, the Honorable the Exalted God will fulfill the prayers of whoever fasts on this day, and asks God for something.'The Imam (عليه السلام) then added, 'O b. Shabayb! Muharram is the month in which the people of the Age of Ignorance had forbidden committing any oppression and fighting in. However, this nation did not recognize the honor of this month or the honor of their own Prophet (صلى الله عليه وآله وسلم). In this month, they killed the Prophet's offspring, they enslaved the women, and took their belongings as booty. God will never forgive them.O b. Shabayb! If you wish to cry, then cry for Al-Hussein b. 'Alī b. Abi Talib (عليه السلام) who was slaughtered like a sheep, and was killed along with the members of his household. Eighteen people were martyred along with Al-Hussein (عليه السلام) who had no equal on Earth. The seven heavens and the Earths mourned for his martyrdom. Four thousand angels descended to the Earth to assist him (Imam Hussein) (عليه السلام). However, Al-Hussein (عليه السلام) was destined to be martyred. They will remain at his shrine with wrinkled hair until the Riser (Imam al-Mahdi) (عليه السلام) rises. Then they will be among those who will assist him (عليه السلام). Their slogan will be Ya li tharat Al-Hussein (Revenge for Al-Hussein's blood!)O b. ShAbib! My father narrated that his father (عليه السلام) quoted on the authority of his grandfather (عليه السلام) that when they murdered my grandfather Al-Hussein (عليه السلام), the heavens cried (dark) red blood and dirt.O b. ShAbib! If you cry for Al-Hussein (عليه السلام) in such a way that tears flow down your cheeks, then God will forgive all the sins that you have committed whether they be minor or major, whether they be a few instances or a lot.O b. ShAbib! If you would like to meet the Honorable the Exalted God without having any sins then go to visit (the Shrine of) Al-Hussein (عليه السلام).O b. ShAbib! If you would like to accompany the Prophet (صلى الله عليه وآله وسلم) in the rooms of Paradise, then damn the murderers of Al-Hussein (عليه السلام).O b. ShAbib! If you would like to be rewarded just as those who were martyred along with Al-Hussein b. 'Alī (عليه السلام), whenever you remember Al-Hussein (عليه السلام) say, 'I wish I was with them and could achieve the great prosperity.'O b. ShAbib! If you would like to be in the same high ranks in Paradise with us, then be sad when we are sad and be happy when we are happy, and I advise you to have us since the Honorable the Exalted God will resurrect whoever even likes a rock with that same rock on the Resurrection Day. (صحيح)[228]

229.

عَلِيُّ بْنُ إِبْرَاهِيمَ عَنْ أَبِيهِ عَنِ ابْنِ مَحْبُوبٍ عَنْ إِسْحَاقَ بْنِ عَمَّارٍ عَنْ أَبِي عَبْدِ اللَّهِ (عليه السلام) قَالَ لَا تَرَوْنَ مَا تُحِبُّونَ حَتَّى يَخْتَلِفَ بَنُو فُلَانٍ فِيمَا بَيْنَهُمْ فَإِذَا اخْتَلَفُوا طَمِعَ النَّاسُ وَ تَفَرَّقَتِ الْكَلِمَةُ وَ خَرَجَ السُّفْيَانِيُّ

Ali b. Ibrahim, from his father, from b. Mahboub, from Is'haq b. Ammar, who has said: Abu 'AbdAllāh (عليه السلام) said: 'You will not be seeing what you would love to (appearance of Al-Qa'im (عجل الله تعالى فرجه)) until the Clan of so and so (Clan of Abbas) differing in what is between them. So when they differ, the people would become greedy and the words would be separated, and Al-Sufyani would come out'. (حسن أو موثق)[229]

230.

مُحَمَّدُ بْنُ يَحْيَى عَنْ أَحْمَدَ بْنِ مُحَمَّدٍ عَنِ ابْنِ فَضَّالٍ عَنْ أَبِي جَمِيلَةَ عَنْ مُحَمَّدِ بْنِ عَلِيٍّ الْحَلَبِيِّ قَالَ سَمِعْتُ أَبَا عَبْدِ اللَّهِ (عليه السلام) يَقُولُ اخْتِلَافُ بَنِي الْعَبَّاسِ مِنَ الْمَحْتُومِ وَ النِّدَاءُ مِنَ الْمَحْتُومِ وَ خُرُوجُ الْقَائِمِ مِنَ الْمَحْتُومِ قُلْتُ وَ كَيْفَ النِّدَاءُ قَالَ يُنَادِي مُنَادٍ مِنَ السَّمَاءِ أَوَّلَ النَّهَارِ أَلَا إِنَّ عَلِيّاً وَ شِيعَتَهُ هُمُ الْفَائِزُونَ قَالَ وَ يُنَادِي مُنَادٍ فِي آخِرِ النَّهَارِ أَلَا إِنَّ عُثْمَانَ وَ شِيعَتَهُ هُمُ الْفَائِزُونَ

Muhammad b. Yahya, from Ahmad b. Muhammad, from b. Fazzaal, from Abu Jameela, from Muḥammad b. 'Alī Al-Halby who said: I heard Abu 'AbdAllāh (عليه السلام) saying: 'The differing of the Clan of Abbas is from the inevitable, and the Call is from the inevitable, and the coming out of Al-Qa'im (عجل الله تعالى فرجه) is from the

[228] *'Uyūn Akhbār al Riḍā, v1, ch28, h53*

[229] *Al-Kāfi, v8, h254*

inevitable'. I said, 'And How would be the Call?' He said: 'A Caller will Call out from the sky at the beginning of the day: 'Indeed! ʿAlī (عليه السلام) and his Shites, they are the winners'. He said: 'And a Caller will Call out at the end of the day: 'Indeed! Usman and his Shites, they are the winners'. (حسن كالصحيح)[230]

231.

عِدَّةٌ مِنْ أَصْحَابِنَا عَنْ أَحْمَدَ بْنِ مُحَمَّدِ بْنِ خَالِدٍ عَنْ مُحَمَّدِ بْنِ عَلِيٍّ عَنْ عَبْدِ الرَّحْمَنِ بْنِ أَبِي هَاشِمٍ عَنْ سُفْيَانَ الْجَرِيرِيِّ عَنْ أَبِي مَرْيَمَ الْأَنْصَارِيِّ عَنْ هَارُونَ بْنِ عَنْتَرَةَ عَنْ أَبِيهِ قَالَ سَمِعْتُ أَمِيرَ الْمُؤْمِنِينَ (عليه السلام) مَرَّةً بَعْدَ مَرَّةٍ وَ هُوَ يَقُولُ وَ شَبَّكَ أَصَابِعَهُ بَعْضَهَا فِي بَعْضٍ ثُمَّ قَالَ تَفَرَّجِي تَضَيَّقِي وَ تَضَيَّقِي تَفَرَّجِي ثُمَّ قَالَ هَلَكَتِ الْمَحَاضِيرُ وَ نَجَا الْمُقَرَّبُونَ وَ ثَبَتَ الْحَصَى عَلَى أَوْتَادِهِمْ أُقْسِمُ بِاللَّهِ قَسَماً حَقّاً إِنَّ بَعْدَ الْغَمِّ فَتْحاً عَجَباً

A number of our companions, from Ahmad b. Muḥammad b. Khalid, from Muḥammad b. Ali, from Abdul Rahmaan b. Abu Hashim, from Sufyan Al-Jariry, from Abu Maryam Al-Ansary, from Haroun b. Antara, from his father who said: I heard Amir al- Mu'minin (عليه السلام) again and again, and he was saying with his fingers clasped at each other: 'My ease is my constraint, and my constraint is my ease'. Then said; 'Destroyed are the expectants who expect it now, and rescued are the expectants who expect it soon and are steadfast upon their pegs. I swear by Allāh (تبارك و طائلة) by a true oath that after the grief would be a wonderful victory (Al-Qa'im (عجل الله تعالى فرجه))'. (حسن)[231]

232.

مُحَمَّدُ بْنُ يَحْيَى عَنْ أَحْمَدَ بْنِ مُحَمَّدِ بْنِ عِيسَى عَنْ عَلِيِّ بْنِ الْحَكَمِ عَنْ أَبِي أَيُّوبَ الْخَزَّازِ عَنْ عُمَرَ بْنِ حَنْظَلَةَ قَالَ سَمِعْتُ أَبَا عَبْدِ اللَّهِ (عليه السلام) يَقُولُ خَمْسُ عَلَامَاتٍ قَبْلَ قِيَامِ الْقَائِمِ الصَّيْحَةُ وَ السُّفْيَانِيُّ وَ الْخَسْفُ

---

[230] *Al-Kafi, v8, h483*

[231] *Al-Kāfi, v8, h449*

وَ قَتْلُ النَّفْسِ الزَّكِيَّةِ وَ الْيَمَانِيُّ فَقُلْتُ جُعِلْتُ فِدَاكَ إِنْ خَرَجَ أَحَدٌ مِنْ أَهْلِ بَيْتِكَ قَبْلَ هَذِهِ الْعَلَامَاتِ أَ نَخْرُجُ مَعَهُ قَالَ لَا فَلَمَّا كَانَ مِنَ الْغَدِ تَلَوْتُ هَذِهِ الْآيَةَ إِنْ نَشَأْ نُنَزِّلْ عَلَيْهِمْ مِنَ السَّماءِ آيَةً فَظَلَّتْ أَعْناقُهُمْ لَها خاضِعِينَ فَقُلْتُ لَهُ أَ هِيَ الصَّيْحَةُ فَقَالَ أَمَا لَوْ كَانَتْ خَضَعَتْ أَعْنَاقُ أَعْدَاءِ اللَّهِ عَزَّ وَ جَلَّ

Muhammad b. Yahya, from Ahmad b. Muḥammad b. Isa, from ʿAlī b. Al-Hakam, from Abu Ayyub Al-Khazaz, from Umar b. Hanzala who said: I heard Abu ʻAbdAllāh (عليه السلام) saying: 'There are five signs before the rising of Al-Qa'im (عجل الله تعالى فرجه) – The scream, and the Sufyani, and the sinking (of the earth), and the killing of the pure soul (Al-Nafs Al-Zakkiyya) and Al-Yamany'. So I said, 'May I be sacrificed for you, if someone from your Household comes out (in revolt) before these signs, shall we come out (revolt) with him?' He said: 'No'. So when it was the next morning, I recited this Verse: "[26:4] If We please, We should send down upon them a sign from the heaven so that their necks should stoop to it". I said, 'Is this the scream?' He said: 'If that was, then the necks of the enemies of Allāh (تبارك و طائلة) Mighty and Majestic would stoop down in humility'. (حسن أو موثق)[232]

233.

عَنْهُ عَنْ أَحْمَدَ بْنِ مُحَمَّدٍ عَنْ عَبْدِ الْعَزِيزِ بْنِ الْمُهْتَدِي عَنْ يُونُسَ بْنِ عَبْدِ الرَّحْمَنِ عَنْ دَاوُدَ بْنِ زُرْبِيٍّ قَالَ مَرِضْتُ بِالْمَدِينَةِ مَرَضاً شَدِيداً فَبَلَغَ ذَلِكَ أَبَا عَبْدِ اللَّهِ (عليه السلام) فَكَتَبَ إِلَيَّ قَدْ بَلَغَنِي عِلَّتُكَ فَاشْتَرِ صَاعاً مِنْ بُرٍّ ثُمَّ اسْتَلْقِ عَلَى قَفَاكَ وَ انْثُرْهُ عَلَى صَدْرِكَ كَيْفَمَا انْتَثَرَ وَ قُلِ اللَّهُمَّ إِنِّي أَسْأَلُكَ بِاسْمِكَ الَّذِي إِذَا سَأَلَكَ بِهِ الْمُضْطَرُّ كَشَفْتَ مَا بِهِ مِنْ ضُرٍّ وَ مَكَّنْتَ لَهُ فِي الْأَرْضِ وَ جَعَلْتَهُ خَلِيفَتَكَ عَلَى خَلْقِكَ أَنْ تُصَلِّيَ عَلَى مُحَمَّدٍ وَ عَلَى أَهْلِ بَيْتِهِ وَ أَنْ تُعَافِيَنِي مِنْ عِلَّتِي ثُمَّ اسْتَوِ جَالِساً وَ اجْمَعِ الْبُرَّ مِنْ حَوْلِكَ وَ قُلْ مِثْلَ ذَلِكَ وَ اقْسِمْهُ مُدّاً مُدّاً لِكُلِّ مِسْكِينٍ وَ قُلْ مِثْلَ ذَلِكَ قَالَ دَاوُدُ فَفَعَلْتُ مِثْلَ ذَلِكَ فَكَأَنَّمَا نُشِطْتُ مِنْ عِقَالٍ وَ قَدْ فَعَلَهُ غَيْرُ وَاحِدٍ فَانْتَفَعَ بِهِ

From him, from Ahmad b. Muhammad, from Abdul Aziz b. Al-Muhtady, from Yunus b. Abdul Rahmaan, from Dawood b. Zurby who said: 'I fell ill in Al-Medina

[232] *Al-Kāfi, v8, h482*

with intense illness, and that (news) reached Abu 'AbdAllāh (عليه السلام). So he wrote to me: 'It has reached me (news of) your illness. Buy one Sa'a of wheat, then lie down on your back and scatter it upon your chest a scattering and say, 'Our Allāh (تبارك و طائلة)! I hereby ask You by Your Name which the restless (Al-Muztar i.e. Al-Qa'im (عجل الله تعالى فرجه)) asks You to Remove the adversities, and Enable him in the earth and Make him as Your Caliph upon Your creatures, and send greetings upon Messenger of Allāh (صلى الله عليه وآله وسلم) and upon the People of his Household, and Cure me from my illness'. Then sit straight and gather the wheat which is around you and say the like of that (again) and distribute one Mudd by one Mudd to each of the poor and say the like of that (again)'. Dawood said, 'I did the like of that and I was as if I had been disentangled from a knot, and more than one person did that, so they all benefitted by it'. (صحيح)[233]

234.

عَلِيُّ بْنُ إِبْرَاهِيمَ عَنْ أَبِيهِ عَنْ حَمَّادِ بْنِ عِيسَى عَنْ حَرِيزٍ عَنْ زُرَارَةَ قَالَ قَالَ أَبُو عَبْدِ اللهِ (عَلَيْهِ السَّلام) اعْرِفْ إِمَامَكَ فَإِنَّكَ إِذَا عَرَفْتَ لَمْ يَضُرَّكَ تَقَدَّمَ هَذَا الامْرُ أَوْ تَأَخَّرَ

Ali b. Ibrahim has narrated from his father from Hammad b. 'Isa from Hariz from Zurara who has said the following. "Abu 'AbdAllāh (عليه السلام) has said, 'Learn who your Imam is. When you learn who he is then it will have no affect on you whether this matter (the rise of al-Mahdi with Divine Authority) will take place earlier or later." (صحيح)[234]

235.

[233] *Al-Kāfi, v8, h54*

[234] *Al-Kāfi, v1, ch84, h1*

عِدَّةٌ مِنْ أَصْحَابِنَا عَنْ أَحْمَدَ بْنِ مُحَمَّدٍ عَنْ عَلِيِّ بْنِ النُّعْمَانِ عَنْ مُحَمَّدِ بْنِ مَرْوَانَ عَنْ فُضَيْلِ بْنِ يَسَارٍ قَالَ سَمِعْتُ أَبَا جَعْفَرٍ (عَلَيْهِ السَّلام) يَقُولُ مَنْ مَاتَ وَلَيْسَ لَهُ إِمَامٌ فَمِيتَتُهُ مِيتَةُ جَاهِلِيَّةٍ وَمَنْ مَاتَ وَهُوَ عَارِفٌ لِامَامِهِ لَمْ يَضُرَّهُ تَقَدَّمَ هَذَا الامْرُ أَوْ تَأَخَّرَ وَمَنْ مَاتَ وَهُوَ عَارِفٌ لِامَامِهِ كَانَ كَمَنْ هُوَ مَعَ الْقَائِمِ فِي فُسْطَاطِهِ

A number of our people has narrated from Ahmad b. Muḥammad from ʿAlī b. al-Niʿman from Muḥammad b. Marwan from al-Fudayl b. Yasar who has said the following. "I heard abu ʻAbdAllāh (عليه السلام) say, 'One who would die without having an Imam his death would like the death of ignorance. One who would die and would know who his Imam is then the coming of this matter (the rise of al-Mahdi with Divine Authority) earlier or later will not affect him at all. One who would knowing who his Imam is he would be like the one present with Al-Qa'im in his tents."

(مجهول)[235]

May Allāh curse anyone who rejects any of the infallible individuals mentioned above, after knowing their exalted status.

[235] *Al-Kāfi, v1, ch84, h5*

باب الصلاة

Chapter on as-Ṣalāh (Prayer)

1.

عَلِيُّ بْنُ إِبْرَاهِيمَ عَنْ أَبِيهِ وَعَبْدِ اللهِ بْنِ الصَّلْتِ جَمِيعاً عَنْ حَمَّادِ بْنِ عِيسَى عَنْ حَرِيزِ بْنِ عَبْدِ اللهِ عَنْ زُرَارَةَ عَنْ أَبِي جَعْفَرٍ (عَلَيهِ السَّلام) قَالَ بُنِيَ الإِسْلامُ عَلَى خَمْسَةِ أَشْيَاءَ عَلَى الصَّلاةِ وَالزَّكَاةِ وَالْحَجِّ وَالصَّوْمِ وَالْوَلايَةِ قَالَ زُرَارَةُ فَقُلْتُ وَأَيُّ شَيْءٍ مِنْ ذَلِكَ أَفْضَلُ فَقَالَ الْوَلايَةُ أَفْضَلُ لأَنَّهَا مِفْتَاحُهُنَّ وَالْوَالِي هُوَ الدَّلِيلُ عَلَيْهِنَّ قُلْتُ ثُمَّ الَّذِي يَلِي ذَلِكَ فِي الْفَضْلِ فَقَالَ الصَّلاةُ إِنَّ رَسُولَ اللهِ (صَلَّى اللهُ عَلَيْهِ وآلِه) قَالَ الصَّلاةُ عَمُودُ دِينِكُمْ قَالَ قُلْتُ ثُمَّ الَّذِي يَلِيهَا فِي الْفَضْلِ قَالَ الزَّكَاةُ لأَنَّهُ قَرَنَهَا بِهَا وَبَدَأَ بِالصَّلاةِ قَبْلَهَا وَقَالَ رَسُولُ اللهِ (صَلَّى اللهُ عَلَيْهِ وآلِه) الزَّكَاةُ تُذْهِبُ الذُّنُوبَ قُلْتُ وَالَّذِي يَلِيهَا فِي الْفَضْلِ قَالَ الْحَجُّ قَالَ اللهُ عَزَّ وَجَلَّ وَللهِ عَلَى النَّاسِ حِجُّ الْبَيْتِ مَنِ اسْتَطَاعَ إِلَيْهِ سَبِيلاً وَمَنْ كَفَرَ فَإِنَّ اللهَ غَنِيٌّ عَنِ الْعَالَمِينَ وَقَالَ رَسُولُ اللهِ (صَلَّى اللهُ عَلَيْهِ وآلِه) لَحَجَّةٌ مَقْبُولَةٌ خَيْرٌ مِنْ عِشْرِينَ صَلاةً نَافِلَةً وَمَنْ طَافَ بِهَذَا الْبَيْتِ طَوَافاً أَحْصَى فِيهِ أُسْبُوعَهُ وَأَحْسَنَ رَكْعَتَيْهِ غَفَرَ اللهُ لَهُ وَقَالَ فِي يَوْمِ عَرَفَةَ وَيَوْمِ الْمُزْدَلِفَةِ مَا قَالَ قُلْتُ فَمَا ذَا يَتْبَعُهُ قَالَ الصَّوْمُ قُلْتُ وَمَا بَالُ الصَّوْمِ صَارَ آخِرَ ذَلِكَ أَجْمَعَ قَالَ قَالَ رَسُولُ اللهِ (صَلَّى اللهُ عَلَيْهِ وآلِه) الصَّوْمُ جُنَّةٌ مِنَ النَّارِ قَالَ ثُمَّ قَالَ إِنَّ أَفْضَلَ الأَشْيَاءِ مَا إِذَا فَاتَكَ لَمْ تَكُنْ مِنْهُ تَوْبَةٌ دُونَ أَنْ تَرْجِعَ إِلَيْهِ فَتُؤَدِّيَهُ بِعَيْنِهِ إِنَّ الصَّلاةَ وَالزَّكَاةَ وَالْحَجَّ وَالْوَلايَةَ لَيْسَ يَقَعُ شَيْءٌ مَكَانَهَا دُونَ أَدَائِهَا وَإِنَّ الصَّوْمَ إِذَا فَاتَكَ أَوْ قَصَّرْتَ أَوْ سَافَرْتَ فِيهِ أَدَّيْتَ مَكَانَهُ أَيَّاماً غَيْرَهَا وَجَزَيْتَ ذَلِكَ الذَّنْبَ بِصَدَقَةٍ وَلا قَضَاءَ عَلَيْكَ وَلَيْسَ مِنْ تِلْكَ الأَرْبَعَةِ شَيْءٌ يُجْزِيكَ مَكَانَهُ غَيْرُهُ قَالَ ثُمَّ قَالَ ذِرْوَةُ الأَمْرِ وَسَنَامُهُ وَمِفْتَاحُهُ وَبَابُ الأَشْيَاءِ وَرِضَا الرَّحْمَنِ الطَّاعَةُ لِلإِمَامِ بَعْدَ مَعْرِفَتِهِ إِنَّ اللهَ عَزَّ وَجَلَّ يَقُولُ مَنْ يُطِعِ الرَّسُولَ فَقَدْ أَطَاعَ اللهَ وَمَنْ تَوَلَّى فَمَا أَرْسَلْنَاكَ عَلَيْهِمْ حَفِيظاً أَمَا لَوْ أَنَّ رَجُلاً قَامَ لَيْلَهُ وَصَامَ نَهَارَهُ وَتَصَدَّقَ بِجَمِيعِ مَالِهِ وَحَجَّ جَمِيعَ دَهْرِهِ وَلَمْ يَعْرِفْ وَلايَةَ وَلِيِّ اللهِ فَيُوَالِيَهُ وَيَكُونَ جَمِيعُ أَعْمَالِهِ بِدَلالَتِهِ إِلَيْهِ مَا كَانَ

لَهُ عَلَى اللهِ جَلَّ وَعَزَّ حَقٌّ فِي ثَوَابِهِ وَلا كَانَ مِنْ أَهْلِ الإِيمَانِ ثُمَّ قَالَ أُولَئِكَ الْمُحْسِنُ مِنْهُمْ يُدْخِلُهُ اللهُ الْجَنَّةَ بِفَضْلِ رَحْمَتِهِ

Ali b. Ibrahim has narrated from his father and 'Abd Allāh b. al-Salt all of them from Hammad b. 'Isa from Hariz b. 'Abd Allāh from Zurara from abu Ja'far (عليه السلام) who has said the following: "Abu Ja'far (عليه السلام) has said, **'Islam is based on five issues. It is based on prayer, charity (al- Zakat), Hajj, Fasting and al-Wilāya**." Zurara has said, 'I then asked the Imam, "Which of these is more important than the others?"' The Imam said, 'Al-Wilāya is more important. It is the key to the others. The person who possesses Divine Authority is the guide to the other principles.' I then asked, 'Which is the next important?' The Imam said, **'Thereafter is prayer**. The Messenger of Allāh has said, "Prayer is the pillar of your religion."' I then asked, 'Which is the next important among them?' The Imam said, 'Al-Zakat is the one thereafter. Allāh has mentioned it next to prayer but He has mentioned prayer first. The Messenger of Allāh has said, "Al-Zakat removes sins."' I then asked, 'Which one is important thereafter?' The Imam said, 'Hajj is important thereafter. Allāh, the Most Majestic, the Most Holy, has said, "It is a duty of the people to Allāh to perform Hajj of the House if they are capable to do so. Whoever rejects it should know that Allāh does not need anyone in the world." (3:97) The messenger of Allāh has said, "Performing Hajj that is accepted is more virtuous than twenty Rak'at optional prayer. Whoever walks around the House seven times and performs the two Rak'at prayers thereafter properly Allāh will grant him cover." He (The Messenger of Allāh) did say on the ninth of the month of Dil Hajj and on the tenth of the month of Dil Hajj in Muzdalifa (a place in Makka), what he wanted to say.' I then asked, 'Which one is important thereafter?' The Imam said, 'It is fasting.' "I then asked, 'Why is fasting the last of all in importance?' The Imam said, 'The Messenger of Allāh has said, "Fasting is a shield against the fire."' The narrator has said that the Imam said, **'The best of all things is that for which, if you miss, you do not find an alternative accept going back to achieve it. Prayer, al-Wilāya and Hajj are not of matters replaceable with their own kind**. On the other hand if fasting is missed on a journey one has the choice to fast on other days as remedy, or compensate for the sin with expiation and no fasting is necessary as a remedy. In the cases of the other four issues there is no alternative for them.' The narrator has said that the Imam then said, 'The topmost, the peak of the issue, the key and the door to it and the pleasure of the Beneficent (Lord) is to obey the Imam properly after knowing him clearly. Allāh, the Most Majestic, the Most Holy, says, "Whoever obeys the Messenger he has obeyed Allāh and whoever turns away from such obedience then you should know that We have not sent you to guard them." (4:80) 'Without recognizing the Divine Authority of the Imam, the deputy of Allāh, no one has the right to receive any reward from Allāh, the Most Majestic, the Most Holy. This is true even though in his lifetime he may stand up in worship the whole night, fast during the day, give all his belongings in charity and perform Hajj every year. So also it is if he does not acknowledge the Divine Authority of his Imam with which all of one's deeds can take place with the guidance of the Imam. Without al- Wilāya, one is not considered of the people of belief.' Thereafter the Imam said, 'Allāh will admit, those of them who do good deeds into paradise through His extra mercy. (صحيح)[1]

2.

مُحَمَّدُ بْنُ يَحْيَى عَنْ أَحْمَدَ بْنِ مُحَمَّدٍ عَنْ مُحَمَّدِ بْنِ إِسْمَاعِيلَ عَنْ أَبِي إِسْمَاعِيلَ السَّرَّاجِ عَنِ ابْنِ مُسْكَانَ عَنْ أَبِي بَصِيرٍ قَالَ قَالَ أَبُو الْحَسَنِ الأَوَّلُ (عَلَيْهِ السَّلام) إِنَّهُ لَمَّا حَضَرَ أَبِيَ الْوَفَاةُ قَالَ لِي يَا بُنَيَّ إِنَّهُ لاَ يَنَالُ شَفَاعَتَنَا مَنِ اسْتَخَفَّ بِالصَّلاَةِ

Muhammad b. Yahya has narrated from Ahmad b. Muḥammad from Muḥammad b. 'Isma'il from abu 'Isma'il al-Sarraj from b. Muskan from abu Basir who has said the following: "Abu al-Hassan the first, (عليه السلام), has said, 'When my father was about to

[1] *Al-Kāfi, v2, ch13, h5*

pass away he said, "My son, those who consider Salah (prayers) insignificant will not be able to benefit from our intercession. (صحيح على الظاهر)[2]

3.

قَالَ مُحَمَّدُ بْنُ يَعْقُوبَ الْكُلَيْنِيُّ مُصَنِّفُ هَذَا الْكِتَابِ رَحِمَهُ الله حَدَّثَنِي مُحَمَّدُ بْنُ يَحْيَى عَنْ أَحْمَدَ بْنِ مُحَمَّدِ بْنِ عِيسَى عَنِ الْحَسَنِ بْنِ مَحْبُوبٍ عَنْ مُعَاوِيَةَ بْنِ وَهْبٍ قَالَ سَأَلْتُ أَبَا عَبْدِ الله (عَلَيْهِ السَّلام) عَنْ أَفْضَلِ مَا يَتَقَرَّبُ بِهِ الْعِبَادُ إِلَى رَبِّهِمْ وَأَحَبِّ ذَلِكَ إِلَى الله عَزَّ وَجَلَّ مَا هُوَ فَقَالَ مَا أَعْلَمُ شَيْئاً بَعْدَ الْمَعْرِفَةِ أَفْضَلَ مِنْ هَذِهِ الصَّلَاةِ أَ لَا تَرَى أَنَّ الْعَبْدَ الصَّالِحَ عِيسَى ابْنَ مَرْيَمَ (عَلَيْهِما السَّلام) قَالَ وَأَوْصَانِي بِالصَّلاةِ وَالزَّكَاةِ مَا دُمْتُ حَيّاً

The compiler of this book, Muḥammad b. Ya'qub al-Kulayni, has said that Muḥammad b. Yahya has narrated from Ahmad b. Muḥammad b. 'Isa from al-Hassan b. Mahbub from Mu'awiyah b. Wahab who has said the following: "I asked abu 'Abd Allāh, (عليه السلام), 'What is the best thing through which a servant of Allāh may become closer to his Lord that is also most beloved to Allāh, the Most Majestic, the Most Glorious?' The Imam replied, I do not know anything after knowing (knowing Allāh and His religion) more excellent than this prayer. Consider what the pious servant of Allāh, Jesus son of Mary has said, "He (the Lord) has advised me to pray and pay Zakat as long as I live.' (صحيح)[3]

4.

عَلِيُّ بْنُ إِبْرَاهِيمَ عَنْ مُحَمَّدِ بْنِ عِيسَى عَنْ يُونُسَ عَنْ هَارُونَ بْنِ خَارِجَةَ عَنْ زَيْدٍ الشَّحَّامِ عَنْ أَبِي عَبْدِ الله (عَلَيْهِ السَّلام) قَالَ سَمِعْتُهُ يَقُولُ أَحَبُّ الْأَعْمَالِ إِلَى الله عَزَّ وَجَلَّ الصَّلَاةُ وَهِيَ آخِرُ وَصَايَا الْأَنْبِيَاءِ (عَلَيْهِم

---

[2] *Al-Kāfi, v3, ch2, h15*

[3] *Al-Kāfi, v3, ch 1, h1*

السَّلام) فَمَا أَحْسَنَ الرَّجُلَ يَغْتَسِلُ أَوْ يَتَوَضَّأُ فَيُسْبِغُ الْوُضُوءَ ثُمَّ يَتَنَحَّى حَيْثُ لاَ يَرَاهُ أَنِيسٌ فَيُشْرِفُ عَلَيْهِ وَهُوَ رَاكِعٌ أَوْ سَاجِدٌ إِنَّ الْعَبْدَ إِذَا سَجَدَ فَأَطَالَ السُّجُودَ نَادَى إِبْلِيسُ يَا وَيْلاَهْ أَطَاعَ وَعَصَيْتُ وَسَجَدَ وَأَبَيْتُ

Ali b. Ibrahim has narrated from Muḥammad b. Tsa from Yunus from Harun b. Kharijah from Zayd al-Shahham who has said the following: "I heard abu 'Abd Allāh, (عليه السلام), say, 'The most beloved deed in the sight of Allāh, the Most Majestic, the Most Glorious, is Salah (prayer). Prayer is the last item in the wills of the prophets. How nice it is of a man who takes a shower or Wudu' properly and then moves away where no one cannotice his presence when he is in Ruku' or Sajdah! When a servant of Allāh is in Sajdah which he prolongs, Iblis (Satan) will say crying, "Woe is on me, he (this servant of Allāh) obeys Him but I disobeyed, he is doing Sajdah but I refused to do so.' (صحيح)[4]

5.

أَبُو دَاوُدَ عَنِ الْحُسَيْنِ بْنِ سَعِيدٍ عَنْ مُحَمَّدِ بْنِ الْفُضَيْلِ عَنْ أَبِي الْحَسَنِ الرِّضَا (عَلَيْهِ السَّلام) قَالَ الصَّلاَةُ قُرْبَانُ كُلِّ تَقِيٍّ

Abu Dawud has narrated from al-Husayn b. Sa'id from Muḥammad b. al-Fudayl who has said the following: "Abu al-Hassan al-Rida, (عليه السلام), has said, 'Salah (prayer) is a means for every pious person to getting nearer to Allāh.'" (مجهول)[5]

6.

جَمَاعَةٌ مِنْ أَصْحَابِنَا عَنْ أَحْمَدَ بْنِ مُحَمَّدِ بْنِ عِيسَى عَنِ الْحُسَيْنِ بْنِ سَعِيدٍ عَنْ فَضَالَةَ عَنْ عَبْدِ اللهِ بْنِ سِنَانٍ عَنْ أَبِي عَبْدِ اللهِ (عَلَيْهِ السَّلام) أَنَّهُ قَالَ مَرَّ بِالنَّبِيِّ (صلّى اللهُ عَلَيْهِ وَآلِه) رَجُلٌ وَهُوَ يُعَالِجُ بَعْضَ حُجُرَاتِهِ

[4] *Al-Kāfi, v3, ch 1, h2*

[5] *Al-Kāfi, v3, ch1, h6*

فَقَالَ يَا رَسُولَ اللهِ أَ لاَ أَكْفِيكَ فَقَالَ شَأْنَكَ فَلَمَّا فَرَغَ قَالَ لَهُ رَسُولُ اللهِ (صلّى اللهُ عَلَيْهِ وَآلِهِ) حَاجَتُكَ قَالَ الْجَنَّةُ فَأَطْرَقَ رَسُولُ اللهِ (صلّى اللهُ عَلَيْهِ وَآلِهِ) ثُمَّ قَالَ نَعَمْ فَلَمَّا وَلَّى قَالَ لَهُ يَا عَبْدَ اللهِ أَعِنَّا بِطُولِ السُّجُودِ

A group of our people has narrated from Ahmad b. Muḫammad b. 'Isa from al-Husayn b. Sa'id from Fadalah from 'Abd Allāh b. Sinan who has said the following: "Abu 'Abd Allāh, (عليه السلام), has said that once a man passed by the Holy Prophet while he was doing some work around one of his rooms. He asked, 'O Messenger of Allāh, can I help you?' He (the Holy Prophet) replied, 'If you like, you may do so.' When the work finished the Messenger of Allāh asked, 'Can I do anything for you?' 'Paradise, the man pleaded. The Messenger of Allāh looked into the sky then said, 'Yes, (paradise is your reward). When he was leaving the Messenger of Allāh said, 'O servant of Allāh, you must assist us by prolonging your Sajdah. (صحيح)[6]

7.

أَحْمَدُ بْنُ إِدْرِيسَ عَنْ مُحَمَّدِ بْنِ عَبْدِ الْجَبَّارِ عَنْ صَفْوَانَ عَنْ حَمْزَةَ بْنِ حُمْرَانَ عَنْ عُبَيْدِ بْنِ زُرَارَةَ عَنْ أَبِي عَبْدِ اللهِ (عَلَيْهِ السَّلاَم) قَالَ قَالَ رَسُولُ اللهِ (صلّى اللهُ عَلَيْهِ وَآلِهِ) مَثَلُ الصَّلاَةِ مَثَلُ عَمُودِ الْفُسْطَاطِ إِذَا ثَبَتَ الْعَمُودُ نَفَعَتِ الأَطْنَابُ وَالأَوْتَادُ وَالْغِشَاءُ وَإِذَا انْكَسَرَ الْعَمُودُ لَمْ يَنْفَعْ طُنُبٌ وَلاَ وَتِدٌ وَلاَ غِشَاءٌ

Ahmad b. Idris has narrated from Muḫammad b. 'Abd al-Jabbar from Safwan from Hamzah b. Humran from 'Ubayd b. Zurāra from abu 'Abd Allāh, who has said the following: "The Messenger of Allāh has said, 'Salah (prayer) is like the poles of a tent. If the poles are established then the ropes, pegs and the covering work, but if the poles break, none of the ropes, pegs and covering work. (مجهول)[7]

8.

[6] *Al-Kafi, v3, ch1, h8*

[7] *Al-Kafi, v3, ch1, h9*

عَلِيُّ بْنُ إِبْرَاهِيمَ عَنْ مُحَمَّدِ بْنِ عِيسَى عَنْ يُونُسَ بْنِ عَبْدِ الرَّحْمَنِ عَنْ عَبْدِ الرَّحْمَنِ بْنِ الْحَجَّاجِ عَنْ أَبَانِ بْنِ تَغْلِبَ قَالَ كُنْتُ صَلَّيْتُ خَلْفَ أَبِي عَبْدِ اللَّهِ (عَلَيْهِ السَّلام) بِالْمُزْدَلِفَةِ فَلَمَّا انْصَرَفَ الْتَفَتَ إِلَيَّ فَقَالَ يَا أَبَانُ الصَّلَوَاتُ الْخَمْسُ الْمَفْرُوضَاتُ مَنْ أَقَامَ حُدُودَهُنَّ وَحَافَظَ عَلَى مَوَاقِيتِهِنَّ لَقِيَ اللَّهَ يَوْمَ الْقِيَامَةِ وَلَهُ عِنْدَهُ عَهْدٌ يُدْخِلُهُ بِهِ الْجَنَّةَ وَمَنْ لَمْ يُقِمْ حُدُودَهُنَّ وَلَمْ يُحَافِظْ عَلَى مَوَاقِيتِهِنَّ لَقِيَ اللَّهَ وَلاَ عَهْدَ لَهُ إِنْ شَاءَ عَذَّبَهُ وَإِنْ شَاءَ غَفَرَ لَهُ

Ali b. Ibrahim has narrated from Muḥammad b. ‘Isa from Yunus b. ‘Abd al-Rahman from ‘Abd al-Rahman b. af-Hajjaj from Aban b. Taghlib who has said the following: “Once I performed Salah (prayer) with abu ‘Abd Allāh, (عليه السلام), in Muzdalifah (a place in Makkah). When he completed Salah (prayer) he turned to me and said, ‘O Aban, the five times Salah (prayer) every day is obligatory. Those who properly observe the rules about these prayers and perform them in their designated times they, on the Day of Judgment, will come in the presence of Allāh with their established covenant before Him, because of which they will be admitted in paradise. Those who ignore the rules about Salah (prayer) and ignore the times designated for them, they will come in the presence of Allāh without having any established covenant with Him. He then will decide about them. He may punish or forgive them as He will wish.’” (صحيح)[8]

9.

جَمَاعَةٌ عَنْ أَحْمَدَ بْنِ مُحَمَّدِ بْنِ عِيسَى عَنِ الْحُسَيْنِ بْنِ سَعِيدٍ عَنْ فَضَالَةَ عَنْ حُسَيْنِ بْنِ عُثْمَانَ عَنْ سَمَاعَةَ عَنْ أَبِي بَصِيرٍ قَالَ سَمِعْتُ أَبَا جَعْفَرٍ (عَلَيْهِ السَّلام) يَقُولُ كُلُّ سَهْوٍ فِي الصَّلاَةِ يُطْرَحُ مِنْهَا غَيْرَ أَنَّ اللَّهَ تَعَالَى يُتِمُّ بِالنَّوَافِلِ إِنَّ أَوَّلَ مَا يُحَاسَبُ بِهِ الْعَبْدُ الصَّلاَةُ فَإِنْ قُبِلَتْ قُبِلَ مَا سِوَاهَا إِنَّ الصَّلاَةَ إِذَا ارْتَفَعَتْ فِي أَوَّلِ وَقْتِهَا رَجَعَتْ إِلَى صَاحِبِهَا وَهِيَ بَيْضَاءُ مُشْرِقَةٌ تَقُولُ حَفِظْتَنِي حَفِظَكَ اللَّهُ وَإِذَا ارْتَفَعَتْ فِي غَيْرِ وَقْتِهَا بِغَيْرِ حُدُودِهَا رَجَعَتْ إِلَى صَاحِبِهَا وَهِيَ سَوْدَاءُ مُظْلِمَةٌ تَقُولُ ضَيَّعْتَنِي ضَيَّعَكَ اللَّهُ

[8] *Al-Kāfi, v3, ch2, h1*

A group of our people has narrated from Ahmad b. Muḥammad b. ‘Isa from al-Husayn b. Sa‘id from Fadalah from Husayn b. ‘Uthman from Sama‘ah from abu Basir who has said the following: “I heard abu Ja’far, (عليه السلام), say, ‘Every mistake in Salah (prayer) is dropped thereby except that Allāh, the Most High, completes it with optional prayers. The first item of deeds with which one is judged is Salah (prayer). If Salah (prayer) is accepted, other deeds are also accepted. If Salah (prayer) is raised in the beginning of its designated time, it comes to the person prayed it all white and radiant, saying, “You preserved me, may Allāh protect you.” If Salah (prayer) is raised in other times without observance of the rules about it Salah (prayer) returns back to the person who has performed it, all black and dark, saying, “You wasted me away, may Allāh lay you waste.”’ (موثق)[9]

10.

عَلِيُّ بْنُ إِبْرَاهِيمَ عَنْ أَبِيهِ عَنِ ابْنِ أَبِي عُمَيْرٍ عَنْ عُمَرَ بْنِ أُذَيْنَةَ عَنْ زُرَارَةَ عَنْ أَبِي جَعْفَرٍ (عَلَيْهِ السَّلام) قَالَ بَيْنَا رَسُولُ الله (صلّى اللهُ عَلَيْهِ وَآلِهِ) جَالِسٌ فِي الْمَسْجِدِ إِذْ دَخَلَ رَجُلٌ فَقَامَ يُصَلِّي فَلَمْ يُتِمَّ رُكُوعَهُ وَلاَ سُجُودَهُ فَقَالَ (صلّى اللهُ عَلَيْهِ وَآلِه) نَقَرَ كَنَقْرِ الْغُرَابِ لَئِنْ مَاتَ هَذَا وَهَكَذَا صَلاَتُهُ لَيَمُوتَنَّ عَلَى غَيْرِ دِينِي

Ali b. Ibrahim has narrated from his father from b. abu ‘Umayr from ‘Umar b. ’Udhaynah from Zurāra who has said the following: “A man entered the Masjid when the Messenger of Allāh was present. He began to perform Salah (prayer) without properly doing Ruku‘ and Sajdah. He (the Messenger of Allāh) said, ‘He acted like a crow picking up grain from the ground. If he dies with his Salah (prayer) of such condition he dies in a religion other than my religion.’” (حسن)[10]

11.

[9] *Al-Kafi, v3,ch2, h4*

[10] *Al-Kafi, v3, ch2, h6*

عَنْهُ عَنْ أَبِيهِ عَنْ حَمَّادٍ عَنْ حَرِيزٍ عَنْ زُرَارَةَ عَنْ أَبِي جَعْفَرٍ (عَلَيْهِ السَّلام) قَالَ قَالَ لاَ تَتَهَاوَنْ بِصَلاَتِكَ فَإِنَّ النَّبِيَّ (صلّى اللهُ عَلَيْهِ وَآلِه) قَالَ عِنْدَ مَوْتِهِ لَيْسَ مِنِّي مَنِ اسْتَخَفَّ بِصَلاَتِهِ لَيْسَ مِنِّي مَنْ شَرِبَ مُسْكِراً لاَ يَرِدُ عَلَيَّ الْحَوْضَ لاَ وَاللهِ

It is a narration from him (narrator of previous Hadīth) by his father from Hammad from Hariz from Zurāra who has said the following: "Abu Ja'far, (عليه السلام), has said, 'You must not consider your Salah (prayer) insignificant; the Holy Prophet said when he was about to pass away, "Those who consider their Salah (prayer) insignificant are not of my people, as well as those who drink intoxicating liquor. They will not be able to come to me at the pond of al-Kawthar, no by Allāh (they will not be able to do so). (حسن)[11]

12.

مُحَمَّدُ بْنُ يَحْيَى عَنْ أَحْمَدَ بْنِ مُحَمَّدٍ عَنْ عَلِيِّ بْنِ الْحَكَمِ عَنْ هِشَامِ بْنِ سَالِمٍ عَنْ أَبِي عَبْدِ اللهِ (عَلَيْهِ السَّلام) قَالَ إِذَا قَامَ الْعَبْدُ فِي الصَّلاَةِ فَخَفَّفَ صَلاَتَهُ قَالَ اللهُ تَبَارَكَ وَتَعَالَى لِمَلاَئِكَتِهِ أَ مَا تَرَوْنَ إِلَى عَبْدِي كَأَنَّهُ يَرَى أَنَّ قَضَاءَ حَوَائِجِهِ بِيَدِ غَيْرِي أَ مَا يَعْلَمُ أَنَّ قَضَاءَ حَوَائِجِهِ بِيَدِي

Muhammad b. Yahya has narrated from Ahmad b. Muḥammad from 'Alī b. al-Hakam from Hisham b. Salim who has said the following: "Abu 'Abd Allāh, (عليه السلام), has said that when a man stands up for Salah (prayer) but considers it insignificant, Allāh, the Most Holy, the Most High, says to His angels, 'Look at this servant of Mine. It seems as if he thinks someone other than Me is a person in charge of fulfilling his needs. Does he not know that I am the One who fulfills all of his needs by My own hand?''' (صحيح)[12]

---

[11] *Al-Kāfi, v3, ch2, h7*

[12] *Al-Kāfi, v3, ch2, h10*

13.

عَلِيُّ بْنُ إِبْرَاهِيمَ عَنْ أَبِيهِ عَنْ حَمَّادٍ وَمُحَمَّدُ بْنُ يَحْيَى عَنْ أَحْمَدَ بْنِ مُحَمَّدٍ عَنْ حَمَّادِ بْنِ عِيسَى عَنْ حَرِيزٍ عَنْ زُرَارَةَ عَنْ أَبِي جَعْفَرٍ (عَلَيْهِ السَّلام) قَالَ إِذَا مَا أَدَّى الرَّجُلُ صَلاَةً وَاحِدَةً تَامَّةً قُبِلَتْ جَمِيعُ صَلاَتِهِ وَإِنْ كُنَّ غَيْرَ تَامَّاتٍ وَإِنْ أَفْسَدَهَا كُلَّهَا لَمْ يُقْبَلْ مِنْهُ شَيْءٌ مِنْهَا وَلَمْ يُحْسَبْ لَهُ نَافِلَةٌ وَلاَ فَرِيضَةٌ وَإِنَّمَا تُقْبَلُ النَّافِلَةُ بَعْدَ قَبُولِ الْفَرِيضَةِ وَإِذَا لَمْ يُؤَدِّ الرَّجُلُ الْفَرِيضَةَ لَمْ يُقْبَلْ مِنْهُ النَّافِلَةُ وَإِنَّمَا جُعِلَتِ النَّافِلَةُ لِيَتِمَّ بِهَا مَا أُفْسِدَ مِنَ الْفَرِيضَةِ

Ali b. Ibrahim has narrated from his father from Hammad and Muḥammad b. Yahya from Ahmad b. Muḥammad from Hammad b. 'Isa from Hariz from Zurāra who has said the following: "Abu Ja'far, (عليه السلام), has said, 'When a man completes one Salah (prayer) properly, all of his other prayers are accepted; even though they may not be complete. If he loses them, altogether, none of his Salah (prayer) is accepted, and not even his optional or obligatory prayers are counted. Optional Salah (prayer) are accepted only after obligatory prayers are accepted. If one does not perform obligatory prayers, optional prayers are not accepted; they are to complete therewith the shortcomings of the obligatory ones." (صحيح)[13]

14.

وَبِهَذَا الإِسْنَادِ عَنْ حَرِيزٍ عَنِ الْفُضَيْلِ قَالَ سَأَلْتُ أَبَا جَعْفَرٍ (عَلَيْهِ السَّلام) عَنْ قَوْلِ الله عَزَّ وَجَلَّ الَّذِينَ هُمْ عَلى صَلَواتِهِمْ يُحافِظُونَ قَالَ هِيَ الْفَرِيضَةُ قُلْتُ الَّذِينَ هُمْ عَلى صَلاتِهِمْ دائِمُونَ قَالَ هِيَ النَّافِلَةُ

It narrated through the same chain of narrators from Hariz from af-Fudayl who has said the following: "I asked abu Ja'far, (عليه السلام), about the words of Allāh, the Most Majestic, the Most Glorious, 'Those who are protective of their Salah (prayers)" (23:9). The Imam said, It means obligatory prayer.' I then asked about, 'Those who

[13] *Al-Kāfi, v3, ch2, h11*

are ever observing their prayer' (70:23). The Imam said, It means optional prayers.'" (صحيح)[14]

15.

مُحَمَّدُ بْنُ يَحْيَى عَنْ أَحْمَدَ بْنِ مُحَمَّدٍ عَنِ الْحُسَيْنِ بْنِ سَعِيدٍ عَنْ فَضَالَةَ بْنِ أَيُّوبَ عَنْ دَاوُدَ بْنِ فَرْقَدٍ قَالَ قُلْتُ لِأَبِي عَبْدِ اللهِ (عَلَيْهِ السَّلام) قَوْلُهُ تَعَالَى إِنَّ الصَّلاةَ كَانَتْ عَلَى الْمُؤْمِنِينَ كِتَاباً مَوْقُوتاً قَالَ كِتَاباً ثَابِتاً وَلَيْسَ إِنْ عَجَّلْتَ قَلِيلاً أَوْ أَخَّرْتَ قَلِيلاً بِالَّذِي يَضُرُّكَ مَا لَمْ تُضَيِّعْ تِلْكَ الإِضَاعَةَ فَإِنَّ اللهَ عَزَّ وَجَلَّ يَقُولُ لِقَوْمٍ أَضَاعُوا الصَّلاةَ وَاتَّبَعُوا الشَّهَوَاتِ فَسَوْفَ يَلْقَوْنَ غَيّاً

Muhammad b. Yahya has narrated from Ahmad b. Muḥammad from al-Husayn b. Sa'id from Fadalah b. Ayyub from Dawud b. Farqad who has said the following: "I asked abu 'Abd Allāh, (عليه السلام), about the words of Allāh, 'Salah (prayer) was made obligatory in designated times' (4:105). The Imam replied, It is an established obligation. If you performed earlier or delayed a little, it is not harmful as long as you did not lose them altogether. Allāh, the Most Majestic, the Most Glorious, says about a people, "They lost Salah (prayer) and followed their lustful desires so they face deviation" (19:60).'" (صحيح)[15]

16.

عَلِيُّ بْنُ إِبْرَاهِيمَ عَنْ أَبِيهِ عَنِ ابْنِ أَبِي عُمَيْرٍ عَنْ حَمَّادٍ عَنِ الْحَلَبِيِّ عَنْ أَبِي عَبْدِ اللهِ (عَلَيْهِ السَّلام) قَالَ الصَّلاةُ ثَلاثَةُ أَثْلاثٍ ثُلُثٌ طَهُورٌ وَثُلُثٌ رُكُوعٌ وَثُلُثٌ سُجُودٌ

Ali b. Ibrahim has narrated from his father from b. abu 'Umayr from Hammad from al-Halabiy who has said the following: "Abu 'Abd Allāh, (عليه السلام), has said, 'Acts of

[14] *Al-Kāfi, v3, ch2, h12*

[15] *Al-Kāfi, v3, ch2, h13*

Salah (prayer) fall in three categories; They are Tahur (cleansing), Ruku' (bowing down on one's knees), and Sujud (prostration).'" (حسن)[16]

17.

عَلِيُّ بْنُ إِبْرَاهِيمَ عَنْ أَبِيهِ وَمُحَمَّدُ بْنُ إِسْمَاعِيلَ عَنِ الْفَضْلِ بْنِ شَاذَانَ جَمِيعاً عَنْ حَمَّادِ بْنِ عِيسَى عَنْ حَرِيزٍ عَنْ زُرَارَةَ قَالَ قَالَ أَبُو جَعْفَرٍ (عَلَيْهِ السَّلام) إِذَا قُمْتَ فِي الصَّلاَةِ فَعَلَيْكَ بِالإِقْبَالِ عَلَى صَلاَتِكَ فَإِنَّمَا يُحْسَبُ لَكَ مِنْهَا مَا أَقْبَلْتَ عَلَيْهِ وَلاَ تَعْبَثْ فِيهَا بِيَدِكَ وَلاَ بِرَأْسِكَ وَلاَ بِلِحْيَتِكَ وَلاَ تُحَدِّثْ نَفْسَكَ وَلاَ تَتَثَاءَبْ وَلاَ تَتَمَطَّ وَلاَ تُكَفِّرْ فَإِنَّمَا يَفْعَلُ ذَلِكَ الْمَجُوسُ وَلاَ تَلَثَّمْ وَلاَ تَحْتَفِزْ وَلاَ تَفَرَّجْ كَمَا يَتَفَرَّجُ الْبَعِيرُ وَلاَ تُقْعِ عَلَى قَدَمَيْكَ وَلاَ تَفْتَرِشْ ذِرَاعَيْكَ وَلاَ تُفَرْقِعْ أَصَابِعَكَ فَإِنَّ ذَلِكَ كُلَّهُ نُقْصَانٌ مِنَ الصَّلاَةِ وَلاَ تَقُمْ إِلَى الصَّلاَةِ مُتَكَاسِلاً وَلاَ مُتَنَاعِساً وَلاَ مُتَثَاقِلاً فَإِنَّهَا مِنْ خِلاَلِ النِّفَاقِ فَإِنَّ اللهَ سُبْحَانَهُ نَهَى الْمُؤْمِنِينَ أَنْ يَقُومُوا إِلَى الصَّلاَةِ وَهُمْ سُكَارَى يَعْنِي سُكْرَ النَّوْمِ وَقَالَ لِلْمُنَافِقِينَ وَإِذَا قَامُوا إِلَى الصَّلاَةِ قَامُوا كُسَالَى يُرَاؤُنَ النَّاسَ وَلاَ يَذْكُرُونَ اللهَ إِلاَّ قَلِيلاً

Ali b. Ibrahim has narrated from his father and Muḥammad b. 'Isma'il from Fadl b. Shadhan all from Hammad b. 'Isa from Hariz from Zurāra who has said the following: "Abu Ja'far, (عليه السلام), has said, 'When you stand up for Salah (prayer) you should be prepared (attentive) for prayer; what will be counted in your favor of prayer will be only that in which you were attentive. You should not play during Salah (prayer) with your hands, head and beard, and do not speak in your soul. You should not yawn, stretch or fold your hands one over the other; this is what the Zoroastrians would do. You should not mask your face, feel urged (for urination), keep your feet far apart from each other like camels do, should not sit on your heels, place your arms flat on the ground, crack your fingers; anyone of such things causes a defect in Salah (prayer). You should not stand for Salah (prayer) in a lazy mode, slumbering or feeling burdened; each one of such things is of behaviors of hypocrites. Allāh, the Most Glorious, has forbidden the believers to stand up for prayer in a lazy mode, that is, feeling sleepy. He has said about the hypocrites, "When they stand up for Salah

[16] *Al-Kafi, v3, ch3, h8*

(prayer) they do so in a lazy mode and just to show off to people and they do not speak of (remember) Allāh but very little" (4:141).'" (حسن كالصحيح)[17]

18.

عَلِيُّ بْنُ إِبْرَاهِيمَ عَنْ أَبِيهِ عَنِ ابْنِ أَبِي عُمَيْرٍ عَنْ حَمَّادٍ عَنِ الْحَلَبِيِّ عَنْ أَبِي عَبْدِ اللهِ (عَلَيْهِ السَّلام) قَالَ إِذَا كُنْتَ دَخَلْتَ فِي صَلاَتِكَ فَعَلَيْكَ بِالتَّخَشُّعِ وَالإِقْبَالِ عَلَى صَلاَتِكَ فَإِنَّ اللهَ عَزَّ وَجَلَّ يَقُولُ الَّذِينَ هُمْ فِي صَلاتِهِمْ خاشِعُونَ

Ali b. Ibrahim has narrated from his father from b. abu 'Umayr from Hammad from al-Halabiy who has said the following: "Abu 'Abd Allāh, (عليه السلام), has said that when you are in your Salah (prayer), you must be humble and attentive in it; Allāh, the Most Majestic, the Most Glorious, has said, 'Those who are humble during their Salah (prayer) (are of the true believers)' (23:3)." (حسن)[18]

19.

عِدَّةٌ مِنْ أَصْحَابِنَا عَنْ أَحْمَدَ بْنِ مُحَمَّدٍ وَأَبُو دَاوُدَ جَمِيعاً عَنِ الْحُسَيْنِ بْنِ سَعِيدٍ عَنْ عَلِيِّ بْنِ أَبِي جَهْمَةَ عَنْ جَهْمِ بْنِ حُمَيْدٍ عَنْ أَبِي عَبْدِ اللهِ (عَلَيْهِ السَّلام) قَالَ كَانَ أَبِي (عَلَيْهِ السَّلام) يَقُولُ كَانَ عَلِيُّ بْنُ الْحُسَيْنِ (صلّى الله عَلَيْهِ وَآلِه) إِذَا قَامَ فِي الصَّلاَةِ كَأَنَّهُ سَاقُ شَجَرَةٍ لاَ يَتَحَرَّكُ مِنْهُ شَيْءٌ إِلاَّ مَا حَرَّكَهُ الرِّيحُ مِنْهُ

A number of our people have narrated from Ahmad b. Muhammad and abu Dawud all from al-Husayn b. Sa'id from 'Alī b. abu Jahmah from Jahm b. Hamid who has said the following: "Abu 'Abd Allāh, (عليه السلام), has said that his (Imam's) father has said that when 'Alī b. al- Husayn, (عليه السلام), would stand up for Salah (prayer), he

---

[17] *Al-Kāfi, v3, ch16, h1*

[18] *Al-Kāfi, v3, ch16, h3*

seemed like the trunk of a tree. Not anything of his body would move except what the wind would move.'" (مجهول)[19]

20.

مُحَمَّدُ بْنُ إِسْمَاعِيلَ عَنِ الْفَضْلِ بْنِ شَاذَانَ عَنْ حَمَّادِ بْنِ عِيسَى عَنْ رِبْعِيٍّ بْنِ عَبْدِ اللهِ عَنِ الْفُضَيْلِ بْنِ يَسَارٍ عَنْ أَبِي عَبْدِ اللهِ (عَلَيْهِ السَّلام) قَالَ كَانَ عَلِيُّ بْنُ الْحُسَيْنِ (صلّى اللهُ عَلَيْهِ وَآلِهِ) إِذَا قَامَ فِي الصَّلاَةِ تَغَيَّرَ لَوْنُهُ فَإِذَا سَجَدَ لَمْ يَرْفَعْ رَأْسَهُ حَتَّى يَرْفَضَّ عَرَقاً

Muhammad b. Isma'il has narrated from al-Fadl b. Shadhan from Hammad b. Isa from Rib'i b. 'Abd Allāh from al-Fudayl b. Yasar who has said the following: "Abu 'Abd Allāh, (عليه السلام), has said that when 'Alī b. al-Husayn, (عليه السلام), would stand up for Salah (prayer), the color of his face change and in sajdah he remained so long until (his face) became drenched with perspiration (and tears)." (مجهول كالصحيح)[20]

21.

عَلِيُّ بْنُ إِبْرَاهِيمَ عَنْ أَبِيهِ عَنِ ابْنِ أَبِي عُمَيْرٍ عَنْ حَمَّادٍ عَنِ الْحَلَبِيِّ عَنْ أَبِي عَبْدِ اللهِ (عَلَيْهِ السَّلام) قَالَ سَأَلْتُهُ عَنِ الرَّجُلِ يَكُونُ مَعَ الإِمَامِ فَيَمُرُّ بِالْمَسْأَلَةِ أَوْ بِآيَةٍ فِيهَا ذِكْرُ جَنَّةٍ أَوْ نَارٍ قَالَ لاَ بَأْسَ بِأَنْ يَسْأَلَ عِنْدَ ذَلِكَ وَيَتَعَوَّذَ فِي الصَّلاَةِ مِنَ النَّارِ وَيَسْأَلَ اللهَ الْجَنَّةَ

Ali b. Ibrahim has narrated from his father from b. abu 'Umayr from Hammad from al-Halabiy who has said the following: "I asked abu 'Abd Allāh, (عليه السلام), 'What should a man who performs Salah (prayer) with an Imam do if they come across a

[19] *Al-Kāfi, v3, ch16, h4*

[20] *Al-Kāfi, v3, ch16, h5*

verse that speaks of paradise or fire?' The Imam said, 'In such case (during prayer) he may ask Allāh for protection against fire or for admission in paradise.'" (حسن)[21]

22.

عَلِيُّ بْنُ إِبْرَاهِيمَ عَنْ أَبِيهِ وَمُحَمَّدُ بْنُ إِسْمَاعِيلَ عَنِ الْفَضْلِ بْنِ شَاذَانَ جَمِيعاً عَنْ حَمَّادِ بْنِ عِيسَى عَنْ زُرَارَةَ عَنْ أَبِي جَعْفَرٍ (عَلَيْهِ السَّلام) قَالَ قُلْتُ لَهُ أَسْجُدُ عَلَى الزِّفْتِ يَعْنِي الْقِيرَ فَقَالَ لاَ وَلاَ عَلَى الثَّوْبِ الْكُرْسُفِ وَلاَ عَلَى الصُّوفِ وَلاَ عَلَى شَيْءٍ مِنَ الْحَيَوَانِ وَلاَ عَلَى طَعَامٍ وَلاَ عَلَى شَيْءٍ مِنْ ثِمَارِ الأَرْضِ وَلاَ عَلَى شَيْءٍ مِنَ الرِّيَاشِ

Ali b. Ibrahim has narrated from his father from and Muḥammad b. 'Isma'il from al-Fadl b. Shadhan all from Hammad b. 'Isa from Zurāra who has said the following: "I once asked abu Ja'far, (عليه السلام), 'Can I perform Sajdah (prostration) on asphalt? He (the Imam) said, 'No, also not on cotton, wool, anything from animals, food, fruits of earth and not on anything of clothing. (مجهول كالصحيح)[22]

23.

مُحَمَّدُ بْنُ يَحْيَى عَنْ أَحْمَدَ بْنِ مُحَمَّدٍ عَنِ الْحُسَيْنِ بْنِ سَعِيدٍ عَنْ فَضَالَةَ عَنْ جَمِيلِ بْنِ دَرَّاجٍ عَنْ أَبِي عَبْدِ اللهِ (عَلَيْهِ السَّلام) أَنَّهُ كَرِهَ أَنْ يُسْجَدَ عَلَى قِرْطَاسٍ عَلَيْهِ كِتَابَةٌ

Muhammad b. Yahya has narrated from Ahmad b. Muḥammad from al-Husayn b. Sa'id from Fadalah from Jamil b. Darraj who has said the following: "Abu 'Abd Allāh, (عليه السلام), disliked performing Sajdah (prostration) on a piece of paper with writing on it.'" (صحيح)[23]

---

[21] *Al-Kāfi, v3, ch17, h3*

[22] *Al-Kāfi, v3, ch27, h2*

[23] *Al-Kāfi, v3, ch27, h12*

24.

عَلِيُّ بْنُ إِبْرَاهِيمَ عَنْ أَبِيهِ عَنِ ابْنِ أَبِي عُمَيْرٍ عَنْ جَمِيلِ بْنِ دَرَّاجٍ عَنْ زُرَارَةَ عَنْ أَحَدِهِمَا (عَلَيْهَا السَّلام) قَالَ تَرْفَعُ يَدَيْكَ فِي افْتِتَاحِ الصَّلَاةِ قُبَالَةَ وَجْهِكَ وَلَا تَرْفَعْهُمَا كُلَّ ذَلِكَ

Ali b. Ibrahim has narrated from his father from b. abu 'Umayr from Jamil b. Darraj from Zurāra who has said the following: "One of the two Imam, (عليه السلام), has said, 'Raise your hands when commencing Salah (prayer) on the sides of your face and do not raise them all the way farther.'" (حسن)[24]

25.

وَعَنْهُ عَنْ أَبِيهِ عَنْ حَمَّادٍ عَنْ حَرِيزٍ عَنْ زُرَارَةَ عَنْ أَبِي جَعْفَرٍ (عَلَيْهِ السَّلام) قَالَ إِذَا قُمْتَ فِي الصَّلَاةِ فَكَبَّرْتَ فَارْفَعْ يَدَيْكَ وَلَا تُجَاوِزْ بِكَفَّيْكَ أُذُنَيْكَ أَيْ حِيَالَ خَدَّيْكَ

It is a narration from him (narrator of previous Hadīth) by his father from Hammad from Hariz from Zurāra who has said the following: "Abu Ja'far, (عليه السلام), has said, 'When you stand up for Salah (prayer) say Takbir (Allāh is great beyond description) and raise your hands. Do not allow your palms (hands) to rise higher than your ears. Keep them on the sides of your face.'" (حسن)[25]

26.

---

[24] Al-Kāfi, v3, ch20, h1
[25] Al-Kāfi, v3, ch20, h2

عَلِيُّ بْنُ إِبْرَاهِيمَ عَنْ أَبِيهِ عَنْ حَمَّادِ بْنِ عِيسَى قَالَ قَالَ لِي أَبُو عَبْدِ اللَّه (عَلَيْهِ السَّلام) يَوْماً يَا حَمَّادُ تُحْسِنُ أَنْ تُصَلِّيَ قَالَ فَقُلْتُ يَا سَيِّدِي أَنَا أَحْفَظُ كِتَابَ حَرِيزٍ فِي الصَّلَاةِ فَقَالَ لَا عَلَيْكَ يَا حَمَّادُ قُمْ فَصَلِّ قَالَ فَقُمْتُ بَيْنَ يَدَيْهِ مُتَوَجِّهاً إِلَى الْقِبْلَةِ فَاسْتَفْتَحْتُ الصَّلَاةَ فَرَكَعْتُ وَسَجَدْتُ فَقَالَ يَا حَمَّادُ لَا تُحْسِنُ أَنْ تُصَلِّيَ مَا أَقْبَحَ بِالرَّجُلِ مِنْكُمْ يَأْتِي عَلَيْهِ سِتُّونَ سَنَةً أَوْ سَبْعُونَ سَنَةً فَلَا يُقِيمُ صَلَاةً وَاحِدَةً بِحُدُودِهَا تَامَّةً قَالَ حَمَّادٌ فَأَصَابَنِي فِي نَفْسِي الذُّلُّ فَقُلْتُ جُعِلْتُ فِدَاكَ فَعَلِّمْنِي الصَّلَاةَ فَقَامَ أَبُو عَبْدِ اللَّه (عَلَيْهِ السَّلام) مُسْتَقْبِلَ الْقِبْلَةِ مُنْتَصِباً فَأَرْسَلَ يَدَيْهِ جَمِيعاً عَلَى فَخِذَيْهِ قَدْ ضَمَّ أَصَابِعَهُ وَقَرَّبَ بَيْنَ قَدَمَيْهِ حَتَّى كَانَ بَيْنَهُمَا قَدْرُ ثَلَاثِ أَصَابِعَ مُنْفَرِجَاتٍ وَاسْتَقْبَلَ بِأَصَابِعِ رِجْلَيْهِ جَمِيعاً الْقِبْلَةَ لَمْ يُحَرِّفْهُمَا عَنِ الْقِبْلَةِ وَقَالَ بِخُشُوعٍ اللَّه أَكْبَرُ ثُمَّ قَرَأَ الْحَمْدَ بِتَرْتِيلٍ وَقُلْ هُوَ اللَّه أَحَدٌ ثُمَّ صَبَرَ هُنَيَّةً بِقَدْرِ مَا يَتَنَفَّسُ وَهُوَ قَائِمٌ ثُمَّ رَفَعَ يَدَيْهِ حِيَالَ وَجْهِهِ وَقَالَ اللَّه أَكْبَرُ وَهُوَ قَائِمٌ ثُمَّ رَكَعَ وَمَلَأَ كَفَّيْهِ مِنْ رُكْبَتَيْهِ مُنْفَرِجَاتٍ وَرَدَّ رُكْبَتَيْهِ إِلَى خَلْفِهِ حَتَّى اسْتَوَى ظَهْرُهُ حَتَّى لَوْ صُبَّ عَلَيْهِ قَطْرَةٌ مِنْ مَاءٍ أَوْ دُهْنٍ لَمْ تَزُلْ لِاسْتِوَاءِ ظَهْرِهِ وَمَدَّ عُنُقَهُ وَغَمَّضَ عَيْنَيْهِ ثُمَّ سَبَّحَ ثَلَاثاً بِتَرْتِيلٍ فَقَالَ سُبْحَانَ رَبِّيَ الْعَظِيمِ وَبِحَمْدِهِ ثُمَّ اسْتَوَى قَائِماً فَلَمَّا اسْتَمْكَنَ مِنَ الْقِيَامِ قَالَ سَمِعَ اللَّه لِمَنْ حَمِدَهُ ثُمَّ كَبَّرَ وَهُوَ قَائِمٌ وَرَفَعَ يَدَيْهِ حِيَالَ وَجْهِهِ ثُمَّ سَجَدَ وَبَسَطَ كَفَّيْهِ مَضْمُومَتَيِ الْأَصَابِعِ بَيْنَ يَدَيْ رُكْبَتَيْهِ حِيَالَ وَجْهِهِ فَقَالَ سُبْحَانَ رَبِّيَ الْأَعْلَى وَبِحَمْدِهِ ثَلَاثَ مَرَّاتٍ وَلَمْ يَضَعْ شَيْئاً مِنْ جَسَدِهِ عَلَى شَيْءٍ مِنْهُ وَسَجَدَ عَلَى ثَمَانِيَةِ أَعْظُمٍ الْكَفَّيْنِ وَالرُّكْبَتَيْنِ وَأَنَامِلِ إِبْهَامَيِ الرِّجْلَيْنِ وَالْجَبْهَةِ وَالْأَنْفِ وَقَالَ سَبْعَةٌ مِنْهَا فَرْضٌ يُسْجَدُ عَلَيْهَا وَهِيَ الَّتِي ذَكَرَهَا اللَّه فِي كِتَابِهِ فَقَالَ وَأَنَّ الْمَساجِدَ لِلَّهِ فَلا تَدْعُوا مَعَ اللَّهِ أَحَداً وَهِيَ الْجَبْهَةُ وَالْكَفَّانِ وَالرُّكْبَتَانِ وَالْإِبْهَامَانِ وَوَضْعُ الْأَنْفِ عَلَى الْأَرْضِ سُنَّةٌ ثُمَّ رَفَعَ رَأْسَهُ مِنَ السُّجُودِ فَلَمَّا اسْتَوَى جَالِساً قَالَ اللَّه أَكْبَرُ ثُمَّ قَعَدَ عَلَى فَخِذِهِ الْأَيْسَرِ وَقَدْ وَضَعَ ظَاهِرَ قَدَمِهِ الْأَيْمَنِ عَلَى بَطْنِ قَدَمِهِ الْأَيْسَرِ وَقَالَ أَسْتَغْفِرُ اللَّه رَبِّي وَأَتُوبُ إِلَيْهِ ثُمَّ كَبَّرَ وَهُوَ جَالِسٌ وَسَجَدَ السَّجْدَةَ الثَّانِيَةَ وَقَالَ كَمَا قَالَ فِي الْأُولَى وَلَمْ يَضَعْ شَيْئاً مِنْ بَدَنِهِ عَلَى شَيْءٍ مِنْهُ فِي رُكُوعٍ وَلَا سُجُودٍ وَكَانَ مُجَنِّحاً وَلَمْ يَضَعْ ذِرَاعَيْهِ عَلَى الْأَرْضِ فَصَلَّى رَكْعَتَيْنِ عَلَى هَذَا وَيَدَاهُ مَضْمُومَتَا الْأَصَابِعِ وَهُوَ جَالِسٌ فِي التَّشَهُّدِ فَلَمَّا فَرَغَ مِنَ التَّشَهُّدِ سَلَّمَ فَقَالَ يَا حَمَّادُ هَكَذَا صَلِّ

Ali b. Ibrahim has narrated from his father from Hammad b. 'Isa who has said the following: "Abu 'Abd Allāh, (عليه السلام), one day asked me, 'Do you know how to perform Salah (prayer) properly?' I said, 'I keep the book of Hariz with me in Salah (prayer).' The Imam said, 'Nevermind, O Hammad. Stand up and perform Salah (prayer).' The narrator has said, 'I then stood up in his presence, facing the direction of Qiblah (Makkah). I began performing Salah (prayer), with Ruku' and Sajdah.' He then said, "O Hammad, you do not know how to perform Salah (prayer) properly. It is a shame for a man of your people who at the age of sixty or seventy cannot even perform one Salah (prayer) according to its complete rules and manners.' Hammad has said, 'I belittled myself very much at this point. I then asked him saying, "I pray to Allāh to keep my soul in service for your cause teach me how to perform Salah (prayer) properly."' Abu 'Abd Allāh, (عليه السلام), stood up straight facing the direction of Qiblah. He allowed his hands to rest on his thighs, with his fingers close side by side, kept his feet near each other, only leaving between them a distance of three fingers opened up, with his toes facing the direction of Qiblah without allowing them to deviate from this direction and with humbleness said, 'Allāh is great.' He then recited al-Hamd (the first Chapter of the Holy Qur'ān) with clarity and fluency and Chapter 112 of the Holy Qur'ān. He then paused for a breath while still standing and raised his hands up to the sides of his face and said, 'Allāh is great,' while still standing. He then bent down for Ruku' (kneeling). He then placed his palms over his knees allowing them to be filled up with his knees that were separate from each other, and pressed them backward until his back became so straightly level that even if there had been a drop of water or oil it would not flow to any side. He stretched his neck forward, lowered his eyes and then said with clarity and fluency three times, 'I praise my Lord, the Great, Who is free of all defects.' He then stood up straight. While standing straight he said, 'Allāh hears all those who praise Him.' He then while standing raised his hands up to the sides of his face and said, 'Allāh is great.' Then he bowed down for sajdah. He opened his palms with his fingers close side by side, placed them near his knees on the sides next to his face and said, 'I praise my Lord, the most High who is free of all defects,' three times. He did not place any other part of his body on any other part thereof. He performed sajdah on eight parts of his bones: his palms, knees, big toes of his feet, his forehead and his nose. He (the Imam) said, 'Placing seven parts of these bones on the ground is obligatory during sajdah but one of them (the nose) is not obligatory. This is what Allāh has spoken of in the Qur'ān, "The parts of the body to be placed on the ground during sajdah belong to Allāh, you then must not worship anyone other than Allāh." (72:17) Such parts are forehead, palms, knees and big toes of feet. Placing one's nose on the ground is optional.' He then raised his head from sajdah. When he sat up straight, he then said, 'Allāh is great.' He then sat on his left thigh placing the back of his right foot over the sole of his left foot and then said, 'I seek forgiveness from Allāh, my Lord and turn to Him in repentance.' He then said, 'Allāh is great.' Then he bowed down for second sajdah, saying therein what he said in the first sajdah. He did not place any other part of his body on any other part during Ruku' or sajdah. He spread his elbows and did not place his arms on the ground. In this way, he performed two Rak'ats of Salah (prayer). He (the Imam) kept the fingers of his hands close side by side when saying the two testimonies in a sitting position. When he finished saying the testimonies, he then read Sal am and said, 'O Hammad, you must perform Salah (prayer) like this.' (حسن)[26]

27.

عَلِيٌّ عَنْ أَبِيهِ عَنْ حَمَّادِ بْنِ عِيسَى وَمُحَمَّدُ بْنُ إِسْمَاعِيلَ عَنِ الْفَضْلِ بْنِ شَاذَانَ عَنْ حَمَّادِ بْنِ عِيسَى وَمُحَمَّدُ بْنُ يَحْيَى عَنْ أَحْمَدَ بْنِ مُحَمَّدٍ عَنْ حَمَّادِ بْنِ عِيسَى عَنْ حَرِيزٍ عَنْ زُرَارَةَ عَنْ أَبِي جَعْفَرٍ (عَلَيْهِ السَّلام) قَالَ إِذَا قُمْتَ فِي الصَّلاَةِ فَلاَ تُلْصِقْ قَدَمَكَ بِالأُخْرَى دَعْ بَيْنَهُمَا فَصْلاً إِصْبَعاً أَقَلَّ ذَلِكَ إِلَى شِبْرٍ أَكْثَرُهُ وَاسْدِلْ مَنْكِبَيْكَ وَأَرْسِلْ يَدَيْكَ وَلاَ تُشَبِّكْ أَصَابِعَكَ وَلْتَكُونَا عَلَى فَخِذَيْكَ قُبَالَةَ رُكْبَتَيْكَ وَلْيَكُنْ نَظَرُكَ إِلَى مَوْضِعِ سُجُودِكَ فَإِذَا رَكَعْتَ فَصُفَّ فِي رُكُوعِكَ بَيْنَ قَدَمَيْكَ تَجْعَلُ بَيْنَهُمَا قَدْرَ شِبْرٍ وَتُمَكِّنُ رَاحَتَيْكَ مِنْ رُكْبَتَيْكَ وَتَضَعُ يَدَكَ الْيُمْنَى عَلَى رُكْبَتِكَ الْيُمْنَى قَبْلَ الْيُسْرَى وَبَلِّغْ أَطْرَافَ أَصَابِعِكَ عَيْنَ الرُّكْبَةِ وَفَرِّجْ أَصَابِعَكَ إِذَا وَضَعْتَهَا عَلَى رُكْبَتَيْكَ فَإِذَا وَصَلَتْ أَطْرَافُ أَصَابِعِكَ فِي رُكُوعِكَ إِلَى رُكْبَتَيْكَ أَجْزَأَكَ ذَلِكَ وَأَحَبُّ إِلَيَّ أَنْ تُمَكِّنَ كَفَّيْكَ مِنْ رُكْبَتَيْكَ فَتَجْعَلَ أَصَابِعَكَ فِي عَيْنِ الرُّكْبَةِ وَتُفَرِّجَ بَيْنَهُمَا وَأَقِمْ صُلْبَكَ وَمُدَّ عُنُقَكَ وَلْيَكُنْ نَظَرُكَ إِلَى مَا بَيْنَ قَدَمَيْكَ فَإِذَا أَرَدْتَ أَنْ تَسْجُدَ فَارْفَعْ يَدَيْكَ بِالتَّكْبِيرِ وَخِرَّ سَاجِداً وَابْدَأْ بِيَدَيْكَ فَضَعْهُمَا عَلَى الأَرْضِ قَبْلَ رُكْبَتَيْكَ تَضَعُهُمَا مَعاً وَلاَ تَفْتَرِشْ ذِرَاعَيْكَ افْتِرَاشَ السَّبُعِ ذِرَاعَيْهِ وَلاَ تَضَعَنَّ ذِرَاعَيْكَ عَلَى رُكْبَتَيْكَ وَفَخِذَيْكَ وَلَكِنْ تَجَنَّحْ بِمِرْفَقَيْكَ وَلاَ تُلْصِقْ كَفَّيْكَ بِرُكْبَتَيْكَ وَلاَ تُدْنِهِمَا مِنْ وَجْهِكَ بَيْنَ ذَلِكَ حِيَالَ مَنْكِبَيْكَ وَلاَ تَجْعَلْهُمَا بَيْنَ يَدَيْ رُكْبَتَيْكَ وَلَكِنْ تُحَرِّفُهُمَا عَنْ ذَلِكَ شَيْئاً وَابْسُطْهُمَا عَلَى الأَرْضِ بَسْطاً وَاقْبِضْهُمَا إِلَيْكَ قَبْضاً وَإِنْ كَانَ تَحْتَهُمَا ثَوْبٌ فَلاَ يَضُرُّكَ وَإِنْ أَفْضَيْتَ بِهِمَا إِلَى الأَرْضِ فَهُوَ أَفْضَلُ وَلاَ تُفَرِّجَنَّ بَيْنَ أَصَابِعِكَ فِي سُجُودِكَ وَلَكِنْ ضُمَّهُنَّ جَمِيعاً قَالَ وَإِذَا قَعَدْتَ فِي تَشَهُّدِكَ فَأَلْصِقْ رُكْبَتَيْكَ بِالأَرْضِ وَفَرِّجْ بَيْنَهُمَا شَيْئاً وَلْيَكُنْ ظَاهِرُ قَدَمِكَ الْيُسْرَى عَلَى الأَرْضِ وَظَاهِرُ قَدَمِكَ الْيُمْنَى عَلَى بَاطِنِ قَدَمِكَ الْيُسْرَى وَأَلْيَتَاكَ عَلَى الأَرْضِ وَطَرَفُ إِبْهَامِكَ الْيُمْنَى عَلَى الأَرْضِ وَإِيَّاكَ وَالْقُعُودَ عَلَى قَدَمَيْكَ فَتَتَأَذَّى بِذَلِكَ وَلاَ تَكُنْ قَاعِداً عَلَى الأَرْضِ فَتَكُونَ إِنَّمَا قَعَدَ بَعْضُكَ عَلَى بَعْضٍ فَلاَ تَصْبِرَ لِلتَّشَهُّدِ وَالدُّعَاءِ

[26] *Al-Kāfi, v3, ch20, h8*

Ali has narrated from his father from Hammad b. 'Isa and Muḥammad b. Isma'il from al-Fadl b. Shadhan from Hammad b. 'Isa and Muḥammad b. Yahya from Ahmad b. Muḥammad from Hammad b. 'Isa from Hariz from Zurāra who has said the following: "Abu Ja'far, (عليه السلام), has said, 'When you stand up for Salah (prayer) do not allow one foot to touch the other, leave between them a distance of one finger at the least and one Shibr (about 8 inches) at most. Allow your shoulders to relax and leave your hands alone. Do not crisscross your fingers. Instead they should be kept on your thighs on its front side and your eyes should look at the place for prostration. During Ruku' position line up your feet with a distance of one shibr in between them, allow your fingers to hold on to your knees. Place your right palm on your right knee before placing the left palm on your left knee. Allow your fingers to reach to the sides of your knees and stretch your fingers when placed on your knees. If during Ruku' the tips of your fingers reach your knees it is sufficient but I like that your palm should rest on your knees so you can allow your finger to hold to your knees while they (knees) are kept apart. Your back should be straight, your neck stretched forward and your looks should be kept between your feet. "When you are ready for prostration, raise your hands for saying "Allāh is great", then bow down for prostration. First your hands should be placed on the ground, before your knees, together but do not place your forearms on the ground as beasts do. You must not place your forearms on your knees or thighs but open them up as wings with your elbows. You must not touch your knees with your palms and do not place them very close to your face. Place them in between level with your shoulders. You must not place them in front of your knees. Place them a little out, extend them on the ground and keep them a little toward you. If there is some cloth underneath, it does not matter, and if you allow them to be placed on the ground it is better. You must not keep your fingers apart from each other during your sajdah but keep them close side by side.' The Imam said, 'When you sit up straight for reading the testimonies, keep your knees touching the ground and a little apart from each other. The back of your left foot should be on the ground, the back of you right foot should be placed on the bottom of your left foot and both hips should be placed on the ground as well as the tip of the big toe of your right foot. You should never sit on both your feet; it may hurt you. You should not sit on the ground; in this way some parts of you are sitting on the others and you cannot bear sitting this way for reading the testimonies and supplications.'" (حسن)[27]

28.

عَلِيُّ بْنُ إِبْرَاهِيمَ عَنْ أَبِيهِ عَنْ حَمَّادِ بْنِ عِيسَى عَنْ حَرِيزٍ عَنْ زُرَارَةَ عَنْ أَبِي جَعْفَرٍ (عَلَيْهِ السَّلام) قَالَ الْجَبْهَةُ كُلُّهَا مِنْ قُصَاصِ شَعْرِ الرَّأْسِ إِلَى الْحَاجِبَيْنِ مَوْضِعُ السُّجُودِ فَأَيُّمَا سَقَطَ مِنْ ذَلِكَ إِلَى الأَرْضِ أَجْزَأَكَ مِقْدَارُ الدِّرْهَمِ وَمِقْدَارُ طَرَفِ الأَنْمُلَةِ

Ali b. Ibrahim has narrated from his father from Hammad b. 'Isa from Hariz from Zurāra who has said the following: "Abu Ja'far, (عليه السلام), has said, 'The entire forehead, from the hairline to the eyebrows is for Sajdah (prostration). Whatever of this area falls on the ground of the size of a dirham or of the size of a finger's tip is sufficient.'" (حسن)[28]

29.

جَمَاعَةٌ عَنْ أَحْمَدَ بْنِ مُحَمَّدِ بْنِ عِيسَى عَنِ الْحُسَيْنِ بْنِ سَعِيدٍ عَنْ أَخِيهِ الْحَسَنِ عَنْ زُرْعَةَ عَنْ سَمَاعَةَ قَالَ سَأَلْتُهُ عَنِ الضَّحِكِ هَلْ يَقْطَعُ الصَّلاَةَ قَالَ أَمَّا التَّبَسُّمُ فَلاَ يَقْطَعُ الصَّلاَةَ وَأَمَّا الْقَهْقَهَةُ فَهِيَ تَقْطَعُ الصَّلاَةَ. وَرَوَاهُ أَحْمَدُ بْنُ مُحَمَّدٍ عَنْ عُثْمَانَ بْنِ عِيسَى عَنْ سَمَاعَةَ

A group has narrated from Ahmad b. Muḥammad b. 'Isa, from al-Husayn b. Sa'id, from his brother al-Hassan, from Zur'ah, from Sama'ah who has said the following: "I once asked him (the Imam), (عليه السلام), about laughing if it destroys Salah (prayer). He (the Imam) said, 'Smiling does not destroy Salah (prayer) but laughing loudly

---

[27] *Al-Kāfi, v3, ch29, h1*

[28] *Al-Kāfi, v3, ch28, h1*

destroys it.'" It (the above Hadīth) also is narrated from Ahmad b. Muḥammad from 'Uthman b. 'Isa from Sama'ah." (موثق)[29]

30.

عَلِيُّ بْنُ إِبْرَاهِيمَ عَنْ أَبِيهِ عَنِ ابْنِ أَبِي عُمَيْرٍ عَنْ جَمِيلِ بْنِ دَرَّاجٍ عَنْ زُرَارَةَ عَنْ أَبِي عَبْدِ اللهِ (عَلَيْهِ السَّلام) قَالَ الْقَهْقَهَةُ لاَ تَنْقُضُ الْوُضُوءَ وَتَنْقُضُ الصَّلاَةَ

Ali b. Ibrahim has narrated from his father from b. abu 'Umayr from Jamil b. Darraj from Zurāra who has said the following: "Abu 'Abd Allāh, (عليه السلام), has said, 'Laughing does not invalidate Wudu' but it invalidates Salah (prayer).'" (حسن)[30]

31.

وَبِهَذَا الإِسْنَادِ عَنْ أَبِي إِسْمَاعِيلَ السَّرَّاجِ عَنِ ابْنِ مُسْكَانَ عَنْ شُرَحْبِيلَ الْكِنْدِيِّ عَنْ أَبِي جَعْفَرٍ (عَلَيْهِ السَّلام) قَالَ إِذَا أَرَدْتَ أَمْراً تَسْأَلُهُ رَبَّكَ فَتَوَضَّأْ وَأَحْسِنِ الْوُضُوءَ ثُمَّ صَلِّ رَكْعَتَيْنِ وَعَظِّمِ اللهَ وَصَلِّ عَلَى النَّبِيِّ (صلّى اللهُ عَلَيْهِ وَآلِه) وَقُلْ بَعْدَ التَّسْلِيمِ اللهمَّ إِنِّي أَسْأَلُكَ بِأَنَّكَ مَلِكٌ وَأَنَّكَ عَلَى كُلِّ شَيْءٍ قَدِيرٌ مُقْتَدِرٌ وَبِأَنَّكَ مَا تَشَاءُ مِنْ أَمْرٍ يَكُونُ اللهمَّ إِنِّي أَتَوَجَّهُ إِلَيْكَ بِنَبِيِّكَ مُحَمَّدٍ نَبِيِّ الرَّحْمَةِ (صلّى اللهُ عَلَيْهِ وَآلِه) يَا مُحَمَّدُ يَا رَسُولَ اللهِ إِنِّي أَتَوَجَّهُ بِكَ إِلَى اللهِ رَبِّكَ وَرَبِّي لِيُنْجِحَ لِي طَلِبَتِي اللهمَّ بِنَبِيِّكَ أَنْجِحْ لِي طَلِبَتِي بِمُحَمَّدٍ ثُمَّ سَلْ حَاجَتَكَ

Through the same chain of narrators as the previous Hadīth, it is narrated from abu Isma'il al-Sarraj from b. Muskan from Sharahbil al-Kindiy who has said the following: "Abu Ja' far, (عليه السلام), has said that if you want to ask your Lord for something, take Wudu' properly, perform two Rak'at Salah (prayer), speak of the greatness of Allāh. Say, 'Allāhumma Salli 'Ala Muḥammad wa 'Ali Muḥammad (O Allāh grant

---

[29] *Al-Kāfi, v3, ch45, h1*

[30] *Al-Kāfi, v3, ch45, h6*

Muḥammad and his family a compensation worthy of their serving Your cause). 5 After Salam say, ‘O Allāh, I appeal before You, You are the Owner and the King and have power over all things. You are dominant and whatever You want it comes into existence. O Allāh I turn to You through Your prophet, Muhammad, the prophet of mercy. O Muhammad, O Messenger of Allāh, I turn to you before Allāh, Your Cherisher and my Cherisher so that He makes my wish to come true. O Allāh, through Your prophet, Muhammad, make my wish come true. Then ask for your needs.” (مجهول)[31]

32.

عِدَّةٌ مِنْ أَصْحَابِنَا عَنْ أَحْمَدَ بْنِ مُحَمَّدٍ عَنِ ابْنِ فَضَّالٍ عَنْ ثَعْلَبَةَ بْنِ مَيْمُونٍ عَنِ الْحَارِثِ بْنِ الْمُغِيرَةِ عَنْ أَبِي عَبْدِ اللهِ (عَلَيْهِ السَّلام) قَالَ إِذَا أَرَدْتَ حَاجَةً فَصَلِّ رَكْعَتَيْنِ وَصَلِّ عَلَى مُحَمَّدٍ وَآلِ مُحَمَّدٍ وَسَلْ تُعْطَهُ

A number of our people have narrated from Ahmad b. Muḥammad from b. Faddal from Tha’labah b. Maymun from al-Flarith b. al-Mughirah who has said the following: “Abu ‘Abd Allāh, (عليه السلام), has said, ‘If you need something, perform two Rak‘at Salah (prayer) and say, “Allāhumma Salli ‘Ala Muḥammad wa ‘Ali Muḥammad (O Allāh grant Muḥammad and his family a compensation worthy of their serving Your cause).” Ask for your needs. They will be fulfilled.’” (موثق)[32]

33.

وَعَنْهُ عَنْ أَبِيهِ عَنِ الْحُسَيْنِ بْنِ سَعِيدٍ عَنْ فَضَالَةَ عَنْ أَبَانٍ وَمُعَاوِيَةَ بْنِ وَهْبٍ قَالاَ قَالَ أَبُو عَبْدِ اللهِ (عَلَيْهِ السَّلام) إِذَا قُمْتَ إِلَى الصَّلاَةِ فَقُلِ اللهُمَّ إِنِّي أُقَدِّمُ إِلَيْكَ مُحَمَّداً (صلّى اللهُ عَلَيْهِ وَآلِهِ) بَيْنَ يَدَيْ حَاجَتِي

---

[31] *Al-Kafi, v3, ch95, h7*

[32] *Al-Kafi, v3, ch95, h10*

وَأَتَوَجَّهُ بِهِ إِلَيْكَ فَاجْعَلْنِي بِهِ وَجِيهاً عِنْدَكَ فِي الدُّنْيَا وَالآخِرَةِ وَمِنَ الْمُقَرَّبِينَ اجْعَلْ صَلاَتِي بِهِ مَقْبُولَةً وَذَنْبِي بِهِ مَغْفُوراً وَدُعَائِي بِهِ مُسْتَجَاباً إِنَّكَ أَنْتَ الْغَفُورُ الرَّحِيمُ

It is a narration from him (narrator of previous Hadīth) by his father from al-Husayn b. Sa'id from Fadalah from Aban and Mu'awiyah b. Wahab who have said the following: "Abu 'Abd Allāh, (عليه السلام), has said that when you stand up for Salah (prayer), say this: 'O Allāh, I consider Muhammad, O Allāh grant compensation to Muḥammad and his family worthy of their services to Your cause, to be in front of me in Your presence along with my wishes and needs and I turn to You through him. For the sake of his position before You, grant me honor in this and the next world and include me among those near You. Make my Salah (prayer) accepted through him, my sins forgiven and my prayer and wishes granted. You are forgiving and merciful. (حسن)[33]

34.

عَلِيُّ بْنُ إِبْرَاهِيمَ عَنْ أَبِيهِ عَنِ ابْنِ أَبِي عُمَيْرٍ عَنِ ابْنِ أُذَيْنَةَ عَنْ أَبِي عَبْدِ اللهِ (عَلَيْهِ السَّلام) قَالَ قَالَ مَا تَرْوِي هَذِهِ النَّاصِبَةُ فَقُلْتُ جُعِلْتُ فِدَاكَ فِيمَا ذَا فَقَالَ فِي أَذَانِهِمْ وَرُكُوعِهِمْ وَسُجُودِهِمْ فَقُلْتُ إِنَّهُمْ يَقُولُونَ إِنَّ أُبَيَّ بْنَ كَعْبٍ رَآهُ فِي النَّوْمِ فَقَالَ كَذَبُوا فَإِنَّ دِينَ اللهِ عَزَّ وَجَلَّ أَعَزُّ مِنْ أَنْ يُرَى فِي النَّوْمِ قَالَ فَقَالَ لَهُ سَدِيرٌ الصَّيْرَفِيُّ جُعِلْتُ فِدَاكَ فَأَحْدِثْ لَنَا مِنْ ذَلِكَ ذِكْراً فَقَالَ أَبُو عَبْدِ اللهِ (عَلَيْهِ السَّلام) إِنَّ اللهَ عَزَّ وَجَلَّ لَمَّا عَرَجَ بِنَبِيِّهِ (صلّى اللهُ عَلَيْهِ وَآلِه) إِلَى سَمَاوَاتِهِ السَّبْعِ أَمَّا أُولاَهُنَّ فَبَارَكَ عَلَيْهِ وَالثَّانِيَةَ عَلَّمَهُ فَرْضَهُ فَأَنْزَلَ اللهُ مَحْمِلاً مِنْ نُورٍ فِيهِ أَرْبَعُونَ نَوْعاً مِنْ أَنْوَاعِ النُّورِ كَانَتْ مُحْدِقَةً بِعَرْشِ اللهِ تَغْشَى أَبْصَارَ النَّاظِرِينَ أَمَّا وَاحِدٌ مِنْهَا فَأَصْفَرُ فَمِنْ أَجْلِ ذَلِكَ اصْفَرَّتِ الصُّفْرَةُ وَوَاحِدٌ مِنْهَا أَحْمَرُ فَمِنْ أَجْلِ ذَلِكَ احْمَرَّتِ الْحُمْرَةُ وَوَاحِدٌ مِنْهَا أَبْيَضُ فَمِنْ أَجْلِ ذَلِكَ ابْيَضَّ الْبَيَاضُ وَالْبَاقِي عَلَى سَائِرِ عَدَدِ الْخَلْقِ مِنَ النُّورِ وَالأَلْوَانِ فِي ذَلِكَ الْمَحْمِلِ حَلَقٌ وَسَلاَسِلُ مِنْ فِضَّةٍ ثُمَّ عَرَجَ بِهِ إِلَى السَّمَاءِ فَنَفَرَتِ الْمَلاَئِكَةُ إِلَى أَطْرَافِ السَّمَاءِ وَخَرَّتْ سُجَّداً وَقَالَتْ سُبُّوحٌ قُدُّوسٌ مَا أَشْبَهَ هَذَا النُّورَ بِنُورِ رَبِّنَا فَقَالَ جَبْرَئِيلُ (عَلَيْهِم السَّلام) اللهُ أَكْبَرُ اللهُ أَكْبَرُ ثُمَّ فُتِحَتْ أَبْوَابُ السَّمَاءِ وَاجْتَمَعَتِ الْمَلاَئِكَةُ فَسَلَّمَتْ عَلَى النَّبِيِّ (صلّى اللهُ عَلَيْهِ وَآلِه) أَفْوَاجاً وَقَالَتْ يَا مُحَمَّدُ كَيْفَ أَخُوكَ إِذَا نَزَلْتَ فَأَقْرِئْهُ السَّلاَمَ قَالَ النَّبِيُّ (صلّى اللهُ عَلَيْهِ وَآلِه) أَ فَتَعْرِفُونَهُ قَالُوا وَكَيْفَ لاَ نَعْرِفُهُ وَقَدْ أُخِذَ مِيثَاقُكَ وَمِيثَاقُهُ مِنَّا وَمِيثَاقُ

---

[33] *Al-Kafi, v3, ch19, h3*

شيعَتِهِ إِلَى يَوْمِ الْقِيَامَةِ عَلَيْنَا وَإِنَّا لَنَتَصَفَّحُ وُجوهَ شِيعَتِهِ فِي كُلِّ يَوْمٍ وَلَيْلَةٍ خَمْساً يَعْنُونَ فِي كُلِّ وَقْتِ صَلاَةٍ وَإِنَّا لَنُصَلِّي عَلَيْكَ وَعَلَيْهِ قَالَ ثُمَّ زَادَنِي رَبِّي أَرْبَعِينَ نَوْعاً مِنْ أَنْوَاعِ النُّورِ لاَ يُشْبِهُ النُّورَ الأَوَّلَ وَزَادَنِي حَلَقاً وَسَلاَسِلَ وَعَرَجَ بِي إِلَى السَّمَاءِ الثَّانِيَةِ فَلَمَّا قَرِبْتُ مِنْ بَابِ السَّمَاءِ الثَّانِيَةِ نَفَرَتِ الْمَلاَئِكَةُ إِلَى أَطْرَافِ السَّمَاءِ وَخَرَّتْ سُجَّداً وَقَالَتْ سُبُّوحٌ قُدُّوسٌ رَبُّ الْمَلاَئِكَةِ وَالرُّوحِ مَا أَشْبَهَ هَذَا النُّورَ بِنُورِ رَبِّنَا فَقَالَ جَبْرَئِيلُ (عَلَيْهِم السَّلام) أَشْهَدُ أَنْ لاَ إِلَهَ إِلاَّ اللهُ أَشْهَدُ أَنْ لاَ إِلَهَ إِلاَّ اللهُ فَاجْتَمَعَتِ الْمَلاَئِكَةُ وَقَالَتْ يَا جَبْرَئِيلُ مَنْ هَذَا مَعَكَ قَالَ هَذَا مُحَمَّدٌ (صلّى اللهُ عَلَيْهِ وَآلِه) قَالُوا وَقَدْ بُعِثَ قَالَ نَعَمْ قَالَ النَّبِيُّ (صلّى اللهُ عَلَيْهِ وَآلِه) فَخَرَجُوا إِلَيَّ شِبْهَ الْمَعَانِيقِ فَسَلَّمُوا عَلَيَّ وَقَالُوا أَقْرِئْ أَخَاكَ السَّلاَمَ قُلْتُ أَ تَعْرِفُونَهُ قَالُوا وَكَيْفَ لاَ نَعْرِفُهُ وَقَدْ أُخِذَ مِيثَاقُكَ وَمِيثَاقُهُ وَمِيثَاقُ شِيعَتِهِ إِلَى يَوْمِ الْقِيَامَةِ عَلَيْنَا وَإِنَّا لَنَتَصَفَّحُ وُجُوهَ شِيعَتِهِ فِي كُلِّ يَوْمٍ وَلَيْلَةٍ خَمْساً يَعْنُونَ فِي كُلِّ وَقْتِ صَلاَةٍ قَالَ ثُمَّ زَادَنِي رَبِّي أَرْبَعِينَ نَوْعاً مِنْ أَنْوَاعِ النُّورِ لاَ تُشْبِهُ الأَنْوَارَ الأُولَى ثُمَّ عَرَجَ بِي إِلَى السَّمَاءِ الثَّالِثَةِ فَنَفَرَتِ الْمَلاَئِكَةُ وَخَرَّتْ. سُجَّداً وَقَالَتْ سُبُّوحٌ قُدُّوسٌ رَبُّ الْمَلاَئِكَةِ وَالرُّوحِ مَا هَذَا النُّورُ الَّذِي يُشْبِهُ نُورَ رَبِّنَا فَقَالَ جَبْرَئِيلُ (عَلَيْهِم السَّلام) أَشْهَدُ أَنَّ مُحَمَّداً رَسُولُ اللهِ أَشْهَدُ أَنَّ مُحَمَّداً رَسُولُ اللهِ فَاجْتَمَعَتِ الْمَلاَئِكَةُ وَقَالَتْ مَرْحَباً بِالأَوَّلِ وَمَرْحَباً بِالآخِرِ وَمَرْحَباً بِالْحَاشِرِ وَمَرْحَباً بِالنَّاشِرِ مُحَمَّدٌ خَيْرُ النَّبِيِّينَ وَعَلِيٌّ خَيْرُ الْوَصِيِّينَ قَالَ النَّبِيُّ (صلّى اللهُ عَلَيْهِ وَآلِه) ثُمَّ سَلَّمُوا عَلَيَّ وَسَأَلُونِي عَنْ أَخِي قُلْتُ هُوَ فِي الأَرْضِ أَ فَتَعْرِفُونَهُ قَالُوا وَكَيْفَ لاَ نَعْرِفُهُ وَقَدْ نَحُجُّ الْبَيْتَ الْمَعْمُورَ كُلَّ سَنَةٍ وَعَلَيْهِ رَقٌّ أَبْيَضُ فِيهِ اسْمُ مُحَمَّدٍ وَاسْمُ عَلِيٍّ وَالْحَسَنِ وَالْحُسَيْنِ وَالأَئِمَّةِ (عَلَيْهِم السَّلام) وَشِيعَتِهِمْ إِلَى يَوْمِ الْقِيَامَةِ وَإِنَّا لَنُبَارِكُ عَلَيْهِمْ كُلَّ يَوْمٍ وَلَيْلَةٍ خَمْساً يَعْنُونَ فِي وَقْتِ كُلِّ صَلاَةٍ وَيَمْسَحُونَ رُءُوسَهُمْ بِأَيْدِيهِمْ قَالَ ثُمَّ زَادَنِي رَبِّي أَرْبَعِينَ نَوْعاً مِنْ أَنْوَاعِ النُّورِ لاَ تُشْبِهُ تِلْكَ الأَنْوَارَ الأُولَى ثُمَّ عَرَجَ بِي حَتَّى انْتَهَيْتُ إِلَى السَّمَاءِ الرَّابِعَةِ فَلَمْ تَقُلِ الْمَلاَئِكَةُ شَيْئاً وَسَمِعْتُ دَوِيّاً كَأَنَّهُ فِي الصُّدُورِ فَاجْتَمَعَتِ الْمَلاَئِكَةُ فَفُتِحَتْ أَبْوَابُ السَّمَاءِ وَخَرَجَتْ إِلَيَّ شِبْهَ الْمَعَانِيقِ فَقَالَ جَبْرَئِيلُ (عَلَيْهِم السَّلام) حَيَّ عَلَى الصَّلاَةِ حَيَّ عَلَى الصَّلاَةِ حَيَّ عَلَى الْفَلاَحِ حَيَّ عَلَى الْفَلاَحِ فَقَالَتِ الْمَلاَئِكَةُ صَوْتَانِ مَقْرُونَانِ مَعْرُوفَانِ فَقَالَ جَبْرَئِيلُ (عَلَيْهِم السَّلام) قَدْ قَامَتِ الصَّلاَةُ قَدْ قَامَتِ الصَّلاَةُ فَقَالَتِ الْمَلاَئِكَةُ هِيَ لِشِيعَتِهِ إِلَى يَوْمِ الْقِيَامَةِ ثُمَّ اجْتَمَعَتِ الْمَلاَئِكَةُ وَقَالَتْ كَيْفَ تَرَكْتَ أَخَاكَ فَقُلْتُ لَهُمْ وَتَعْرِفُونَهُ قَالُوا نَعْرِفُهُ وَشِيعَتَهُ وَهُمْ نُورٌ حَوْلَ عَرْشِ اللهِ وَإِنَّ فِي الْبَيْتِ الْمَعْمُورِ لَرَقّاً مِنْ نُورٍ فِيهِ كِتَابٌ مِنْ نُورٍ فِيهِ اسْمُ مُحَمَّدٍ وَعَلِيٍّ وَالْحَسَنِ وَالْحُسَيْنِ وَالأَئِمَّةِ وَشِيعَتِهِمْ إِلَى يَوْمِ الْقِيَامَةِ لاَ يَزِيدُ فِيهِمْ رَجُلٌ وَلاَ يَنْقُصُ مِنْهُمْ رَجُلٌ وَإِنَّهُ لَمِيثَاقُنَا وَ إِنَّهُ لَيُقْرَأُ عَلَيْنَا كُلَّ يَوْمِ جُمُعَةٍ ثُمَّ قِيلَ لِي ارْفَعْ رَأْسَكَ يَا مُحَمَّدُ فَرَفَعْتُ رَأْسِي فَإِذَا أَطْبَاقُ السَّمَاءِ قَدْ خُرِقَتْ وَالْحُجُبُ قَدْ رُفِعَتْ ثُمَّ قَالَ لِي طَأْطِئْ رَأْسَكَ انْظُرْ مَا تَرَى فَطَأْطَأْتُ رَأْسِي فَنَظَرْتُ إِلَى بَيْتٍ مِثْلِ بَيْتِكُمْ هَذَا وَحَرَمٍ مِثْلِ حَرَمِ هَذَا الْبَيْتِ لَوْ أَلْقَيْتُ شَيْئاً مِنْ يَدِي لَمْ يَقَعْ إِلاَّ عَلَيْهِ فَقِيلَ لِي يَا مُحَمَّدُ إِنَّ هَذَا الْحَرَمُ وَأَنْتَ الْحَرَامُ وَلِكُلٍّ مِثْلٌ مِثَالٌ ثُمَّ أَوْحَى اللهُ إِلَيَّ يَا مُحَمَّدُ ادْنُ مِنْ صَادٍ فَاغْسِلْ مَسَاجِدَكَ وَطَهِّرْهَا وَصَلِّ لِرَبِّكَ فَدَنَا رَسُولُ اللهِ (صلّى اللهُ عَلَيْهِ وَآلِه) مِنْ صَادٍ وَهُوَ مَاءٌ يَسِيلُ مِنْ سَاقِ الْعَرْشِ الأَيْمَنِ فَتَلَقَّى رَسُولُ اللهِ (صلّى اللهُ عَلَيْهِ وَآلِه) الْمَاءَ بِيَدِهِ الْيُمْنَى فَمِنْ أَجْلِ ذَلِكَ صَارَ الْوُضُوءُ بِالْيَمِينِ ثُمَّ أَوْحَى اللهُ عَزَّ وَجَلَّ إِلَيْهِ أَنِ اغْسِلْ وَجْهَكَ فَإِنَّكَ تَنْظُرُ إِلَى عَظَمَتِي ثُمَّ اغْسِلْ ذِرَاعَيْكَ الْيُمْنَى وَالْيُسْرَى فَإِنَّكَ تَلَقَّى بِيَدِكَ كَلاَمِي ثُمَّ امْسَحْ رَأْسَكَ

بِفَضْلِ مَا بَقِيَ فِي يَدَيْكَ مِنَ الْمَاءِ وَرِجْلَيْكَ إِلَى كَعْبَيْكَ فَإِنِّي أُبَارِكُ عَلَيْكَ وَأُوطِئُكَ مَوْطِئاً لَمْ يَطَأْهُ أَحَدٌ غَيْرُكَ فَهَذَا عِلَّةُ الأَذَانِ وَالْوُضُوءِ ثُمَّ أَوْحَى اللهُ عَزَّ وَجَلَّ إِلَيْهِ يَا مُحَمَّدُ اسْتَقْبِلِ الْحَجَرَ الأَسْوَدَ وَكَبِّرْنِي عَلَى عَدَدِ حُجُبِي فَمِنْ أَجْلِ ذَلِكَ صَارَ التَّكْبِيرُ سَبْعاً لأَنَّ الْحُجُبَ سَبْعٌ فَافْتَتِحْ عِنْدَ انْقِطَاعِ الْحُجُبِ فَمِنْ أَجْلِ ذَلِكَ صَارَ الافْتِتَاحُ سُنَّةً وَالْحُجُبُ مُتَطَابِقَةٌ بَيْنَهُنَّ بِحَارُ النُّورِ وَذَلِكَ النُّورُ الَّذِي أَنْزَلَهُ اللهُ عَلَى مُحَمَّدٍ (صلّى اللهُ عَلَيْهِ وَآلِهِ) فَمِنْ أَجْلِ ذَلِكَ صَارَ الافْتِتَاحُ ثَلاثَ مَرَّاتٍ لافْتِتَاحِ الْحُجُبِ ثَلاثَ مَرَّاتٍ فَصَارَ التَّكْبِيرُ سَبْعاً وَالافْتِتَاحُ ثَلاثاً فَلَمَّا فَرَغَ مِنَ التَّكْبِيرِ وَالافْتِتَاحِ أَوْحَى اللهُ إِلَيْهِ سَمِّ بِاسْمِي فَمِنْ أَجْلِ ذَلِكَ جُعِلَ بِسْمِ اللهِ الرَّحْمنِ الرَّحِيمِ فِي أَوَّلِ السُّورَةِ ثُمَّ أَوْحَى اللهُ إِلَيْهِ أَنِ احْمَدْنِي فَلَمَّا قَالَ الْحَمْدُ للهِ رَبِّ الْعَالَمِينَ قَالَ النَّبِيُّ فِي نَفْسِهِ شُكْراً فَأَوْحَى اللهُ عَزَّ وَجَلَّ إِلَيْهِ قَطَعْتَ حَمْدِي فَسَمِّ بِاسْمِي فَمِنْ أَجْلِ ذَلِكَ جُعِلَ فِي الْحَمْدِ الرَّحْمنِ الرَّحِيمِ مَرَّتَيْنِ فَلَمَّا بَلَغَ وَلاَ الضَّالِّينَ قَالَ النَّبِيُّ (صلّى اللهُ عَلَيْهِ وَآلِهِ) الْحَمْدُ للهِ رَبِّ الْعَالَمِينَ شُكْراً فَأَوْحَى اللهُ إِلَيْهِ قَطَعْتَ ذِكْرِي فَسَمِّ بِاسْمِي فَمِنْ أَجْلِ ذَلِكَ جُعِلَ بِسْمِ اللهِ الرَّحْمنِ الرَّحِيمِ فِي أَوَّلِ السُّورَةِ ثُمَّ أَوْحَى اللهُ عَزَّ وَجَلَّ إِلَيْهِ اقْرَأْ يَا مُحَمَّدُ نِسْبَةَ رَبِّكَ تَبَارَكَ وَتَعَالَى قُلْ هُوَ اللهُ أَحَدٌ. اللهُ الصَّمَدُ. لَمْ يَلِدْ وَلَمْ يُولَدْ. وَلَمْ يَكُنْ لَهُ كُفُواً أَحَدٌ ثُمَّ أَمْسَكَ عَنْهُ الْوَحْيَ فَقَالَ رَسُولُ اللهِ (صلّى اللهُ عَلَيْهِ وَآلِهِ) الْوَاحِدُ الأَحَدُ الصَّمَدُ فَأَوْحَى اللهُ إِلَيْهِ لَمْ يَلِدْ وَلَمْ يُولَدْ. وَلَمْ يَكُنْ لَهُ كُفُواً أَحَدٌ. ثُمَّ أَمْسَكَ عَنْهُ الْوَحْيَ فَقَالَ رَسُولُ اللهِ (صلّى اللهُ عَلَيْهِ وَآلِهِ) كَذَلِكَ اللهُ كَذَلِكَ اللهُ رَبُّنَا فَلَمَّا قَالَ ذَلِكَ أَوْحَى اللهُ إِلَيْهِ ارْكَعْ لِرَبِّكَ يَا مُحَمَّدُ فَرَكَعَ فَأَوْحَى اللهُ إِلَيْهِ وَهُوَ رَاكِعٌ قُلْ سُبْحَانَ رَبِّيَ الْعَظِيمِ فَفَعَلَ ذَلِكَ ثَلاثاً ثُمَّ أَوْحَى اللهُ إِلَيْهِ أَنِ ارْفَعْ رَأْسَكَ يَا مُحَمَّدُ فَفَعَلَ رَسُولُ اللهِ (صلّى اللهُ عَلَيْهِ وَآلِهِ) فَقَامَ مُنْتَصِباً فَأَوْحَى اللهُ عَزَّ وَجَلَّ إِلَيْهِ أَنِ اسْجُدْ لِرَبِّكَ يَا مُحَمَّدُ فَخَرَّ رَسُولُ اللهِ (صلّى اللهُ عَلَيْهِ وَآلِهِ) سَاجِداً فَأَوْحَى اللهُ عَزَّ وَجَلَّ إِلَيْهِ قُلْ سُبْحَانَ رَبِّيَ الأَعْلَى فَفَعَلَ ذَلِكَ ثَلاثاً ثُمَّ أَوْحَى اللهُ إِلَيْهِ اسْتَوِ جَالِساً يَا مُحَمَّدُ فَفَعَلَ فَلَمَّا رَفَعَ رَأْسَهُ مِنْ سُجُودِهِ وَاسْتَوَى جَالِساً نَظَرَ إِلَى عَظَمَتِهِ تَجَلَّتْ لَهُ فَخَرَّ سَاجِداً مِنْ تِلْقَاءِ نَفْسِهِ لاَ لأَمْرٍ أُمِرَ بِهِ فَسَبَّحَ أَيْضاً ثَلاثاً فَأَوْحَى اللهُ إِلَيْهِ انْتَصِبْ قَائِماً فَفَعَلَ فَلَمْ يَرَ مَا كَانَ رَأَى مِنَ الْعَظَمَةِ فَمِنْ أَجْلِ ذَلِكَ صَارَتِ الصَّلاَةُ رَكْعَةً وَسَجْدَتَيْنِ ثُمَّ أَوْحَى اللهُ عَزَّ وَجَلَّ إِلَيْهِ اقْرَأْ بِالْحَمْدِ للهِ فَقَرَأَهَا مِثْلَ مَا قَرَأَ أَوَّلاً ثُمَّ أَوْحَى اللهُ عَزَّ وَجَلَّ إِلَيْهِ اقْرَأْ إِنَّا أَنْزَلْنَاهُ فَإِنَّهَا نِسْبَتُكَ وَنِسْبَةُ أَهْلِ بَيْتِكَ إِلَى يَوْمِ الْقِيَامَةِ وَفَعَلَ فِي الرُّكُوعِ مِثْلَ مَا فَعَلَ فِي الْمَرَّةِ الأُولَى ثُمَّ سَجَدَ سَجْدَةً وَاحِدَةً فَلَمَّا رَفَعَ رَأْسَهُ تَجَلَّتْ لَهُ الْعَظَمَةُ فَخَرَّ سَاجِداً مِنْ تِلْقَاءِ نَفْسِهِ لاَ لأَمْرٍ أُمِرَ بِهِ فَسَبَّحَ أَيْضاً ثُمَّ أَوْحَى اللهُ إِلَيْهِ ارْفَعْ رَأْسَكَ يَا مُحَمَّدُ ثَبَّتَكَ رَبُّكَ فَلَمَّا ذَهَبَ لِيَقُومَ قِيلَ يَا مُحَمَّدُ اجْلِسْ فَجَلَسَ فَأَوْحَى اللهُ إِلَيْهِ يَا مُحَمَّدُ إِذَا مَا أَنْعَمْتُ عَلَيْكَ فَسَمِّ بِاسْمِي فَأُلْهِمَ أَنْ قَالَ بِسْمِ اللهِ وَبِاللهِ وَلاَ إِلَهَ إِلاَّ اللهُ وَالأَسْمَاءُ الْحُسْنَى كُلُّهَا للهِ ثُمَّ أَوْحَى اللهُ إِلَيْهِ يَا مُحَمَّدُ صَلِّ عَلَى نَفْسِكَ وَعَلَى أَهْلِ بَيْتِكَ فَقَالَ صَلَّى اللهُ عَلَيَّ وَعَلَى أَهْلِ بَيْتِي وَقَدْ فَعَلَ ثُمَّ الْتَفَتَ فَإِذَا بِصُفُوفٍ مِنَ الْمَلاَئِكَةِ وَالْمُرْسَلِينَ وَالنَّبِيِّينَ فَقِيلَ يَا مُحَمَّدُ سَلِّمْ عَلَيْهِمْ فَقَالَ السَّلاَمُ عَلَيْكُمْ وَرَحْمَةُ اللهِ وَبَرَكَاتُهُ فَأَوْحَى اللهُ إِلَيْهِ أَنَّ السَّلاَمَ وَالتَّحِيَّةَ وَالرَّحْمَةَ وَالْبَرَكَاتِ أَنْتَ وَذُرِّيَّتُكَ ثُمَّ أَوْحَى اللهُ إِلَيْهِ أَنْ لاَ يَلْتَفِتَ يَسَاراً وَأَوَّلُ آيَةٍ سَمِعَهَا بَعْدَ قُلْ هُوَ اللهُ أَحَدٌ وَإِنَّا أَنْزَلْنَاهُ آيَةُ أَصْحَابِ الْيَمِينِ وَأَصْحَابِ الشِّمَالِ فَمِنْ أَجْلِ ذَلِكَ كَانَ السَّلاَمُ وَاحِدَةً تُجَاهَ الْقِبْلَةِ وَمِنْ أَجْلِ ذَلِكَ كَانَ التَّكْبِيرُ فِي السُّجُودِ شُكْراً وَقَوْلُهُ سَمِعَ اللهُ لِمَنْ حَمِدَهُ لأَنَّ النَّبِيَّ (صلّى اللهُ عَلَيْهِ

وَآلِهِ) سَمِعَ ضَجَّةَ الْمَلاَئِكَةِ بِالتَّسْبِيحِ وَالتَّحْمِيدِ وَالتَّهْلِيلِ فَمِنْ أَجْلِ ذَلِكَ قَالَ سَمِعَ اللهُ لِمَنْ حَمِدَهُ وَمِنْ أَجْلِ ذَلِكَ صَارَتِ الرَّكْعَتَانِ الأُولَيَانِ كُلَّمَا أَحْدَثَ فِيهِمَا حَدَثاً كَانَ عَلَى صَاحِبِهِمَا إِعَادَتُهُمَا فَهَذَا الْفَرْضُ الأَوَّلُ فِي صَلاَةِ الزَّوَالِ يَعْنِي صَلاَةَ الظُّهْرِ

Ali b. Ibrahim has narrated from his father from b. abu ‘Umayr from b. ’Udhaynah who has said the following: “Abu ’Abd Allāh, (عليه السلام), asked me, ‘What does the enemy narrate?’ I then asked, ‘I pray to Allāh to keep my soul in service for your cause, what kind of narration do you mean?’ He said, ‘It is about their Adhan, Ruku‘, and sajdah?’ I then said, ‘They say, “Ubay b. Ka‘b has seen them in a dream.”’ The Imam said, ‘They have spoken a lie. The religion of Allāh, the Most Majestic, the Most Glorious, is by far more exalted than being seen in a dream.’ The narrator has said that Sadir al- Sayrafiy then said, ‘I pray to Allāh to keep my soul in service for your cause, please enlighten us about it.’ Abu ‘Abd Allāh, (عليه السلام), then said, ‘When Allāh, the most Majestic, the most Glorious, took His prophet for a journey to His seven heavens, in the first heaven He granted him blessing and in the second one He taught him his obligations. Allāh sent down a carriage that was made of light with forty kinds of the kinds of light therein, surrounded by the Throne of Allāh that covers the eyesight of the on-lookers. One of those lights is yellow from which yellowness is yellow. Another one is red because of which redness is red, yet another one is white because of which whiteness is white. The rest of them are like the number of the creatures in the form of light and colors. In that carriage, there are rings and chains of silver. Thereafter He took him up in the heaven. The angels moved in all directions of the heaven and fell down in prostration saying, “He is free of all defects and Most Holy. How similar is this light to the light of our Lord!”’ Jibril (Gabriel) then said, ‘Allāh is greater than can be described, Allāh is greater than can be described.’ Then the doors of the heaven opened, the angels gathered and saluted to the Holy Prophet in large groups saying, “O Muhammad, how is your brother? When you go back to earth tell that we salute him.” The Holy Prophet asked them, “Do you know him?” They replied, “How can we forget him. We were made (by Allāh) to establish a covenant and commitment to (follow and) support him; support you and his followers until the Day of Judgment. We look on the faces of his followers five times every day - meaning thereby during the five times Salah (prayer). We say, 'Allāhumma Salli 'Ala Muḥammad wa 'Ali Muḥammad (O Allāh grant Muḥammad and his family a compensation worthy of their serving Your cause).'" The Messenger of Allāh thereafter has said, "Then my Lord granted me forty kinds of kinds of light of which no one resembled the ones given to me before. He gave me more rings and chains and took me to the second heaven. When I arrived near the second heaven's door, the angels moved to all directions of the heaven and fell down in prostration saying, 'Free of all defects and Most Holy is the Lord of the angels and the spirit. How similar is this light to the light of our Lord!' Jibril then said, 'I testify that no one, other than Allāh, deserves to be worshipped.' The angels then gathered asking, 'O Jibril, who is this with you?' He replied, 'This is Muhammad.' They then asked, 'Is he already commissioned to serve as the Messenger of Allāh?' He replied, 'Yes, he is commissioned.'" The Holy Prophet has said that they then came to me, welcoming with salutations and saying, "Tell your brother we salute him." I asked them, "Do you know him?" They replied, "How can we forget him? We were made (by Allāh) to establish a covenant and commitment to (follow and) support him; support you and his followers until the Day of Judgment. We look on the faces of his followers five times every day" - meaning thereby during the five times Salah (prayer). "The Messenger of Allāh has said, "My Lord then gave me another forty kinds of the kinds of light of which no one was similar to the light given to me before, and increased the number of rings and chains. Then He took me up to the second heaven. The angels moved to all directions in the heaven and fell down in prostration saying, 'Free of all defects and Most Holy is the Lord of the angels and the spirit. What is this light that is so similar to the light of our Lord?' Jibril then said twice, 'I testify that only Allāh deserves worship. The angels gathered and said, 'O Jibril, who is he with you?' He (Jibril) replied, 'He is Muhammad.' They asked, 'Is he commissioned (as messenger of Allāh)?' Jibril answered, 'Yes, he is commissioned.'" The Holy prophet, has said, "They (angels) came to me as if wanting to hold me in their arms and saluted me and said, 'Convey our salutations to you brother.' I asked, 'Do you know him?' They replied, 'Why we would not know him? We are made to establish a solemn covenant of support in your favor, in his favor and in favor of his followers until the Day of Judgment. We look at the faces of his followers five times every day and night.' They meant thereby the times of each of five daily Salah (prayer)." The Messenger of Allāh has said, "My Lord then gave me another forty kinds of the kinds of light of which no one was similar to the light given to me before. Then He took me up to the third heaven. The angels moved to all directions in the heaven and fell down in prostration saying, 'Free of all defects and Most Holy is the Lord of the angels and the spirit. What is this light that is so similar to the light of our Lord?' Jibril then said twice, 'I testify that Muḥammad is the Messenger of Allāh.' The angels all gathered and said, 'Welcome, we greet you, O the first. Welcome, O the last, welcome, O the one who brings about resurrection and welcome the one who brings about distribution (distributor of heavens and hell (one of the title of Imam AJi)), Muḥammad is the best of the prophets and 'Alī is the best of the executors of the wills of the prophets of Allāh.'" "The Holy Prophet has said, "They then saluted me and asked about my brother and I said, 'He is on earth. Do you know him?' They replied, 'How can we forget him? We every year perform Hajj of Bayt al-Ma'mur where there is a white board on which there are the names of Muhammad, Ali, al-Hassan, al-Husayn, all A'immah and their followers till the Day of Judgment. We congratulate them every day and night five times' - meaning thereby the five times Salah (prayer) - 'and they wipe their heads with their hands.'" The Holy Prophet has said, "My Lord then increased the number of the kinds of lights for me by another forty kinds of light of which no one resembled the ones given to me before. He then took me higher until I reached the fourth heaven where the angels did not say anything. I heard a low intensity sound as if vibrating inside the chests. The angels then gathered, the doors of the heaven opened and they came to welcome me. Jibril then said, 'Come for Salah (prayer), come for Salah (prayer). Come to wellbeing, come to wellbeing.' The angels then said, 'They are two very familiar sounds.' Jibril then said, 'Salah (prayer) is about to be performed, Salah (prayer) is about to be performed.' The angels said, 'It is for his followers until the Day of Judgment.' The angels then gathered and asked, 'How is your brother?' I replied, 'Do you know him?' They replied, 'We know him and his followers. They are lights around the Throne of Allāh and in al-Bayt al-Ma'mur, there is a board of light [on which there is a writing of light] and in this writing there are the names of Muhammad, Ali, al-Hassan, al-Husayn, all 'A'immah and their followers until the Day of Judgment from whom not even one man is increased or decreased. This (written document) is our covenant and a document of commitment which is read to us every Friday.' Thereafter it was said to me, 'Raise your head, O Muhammad.' I raised my head, I saw the levels of the heaven opened up, and the curtains rose. I then was told, 'Look downward.' I looked downward and I saw a house like your house, this one, a sacred precinct like this holy precinct. If I were to drop something down from my hand, it would only fall on this house but not on another place. It then was said to me, 'O Muhammad, this is the holy place and you are the Holy person; for every similitude there is something similar.' Allāh then sent Wahy to me, 'O Muḥammad go near the S' ad (a fountain at the foot of the Throne) wash the parts of your body that are used during sajdah, cleanse them and perform Salah (prayer) for the sake of your Lord.'" The Messenger of Allāh then went near the S' ad, water that flows at the right foot of the Throne. The Messenger of Allāh touched the water with his right hand and for this reason Wudu' is with the right hand. Allāh, the Most Majestic, the Most Glorious, then sent Wahy to him (Muhammad), "Wash your face; you look to My greatness, then wash your right arm and then your left arm; you receive My words (book) in your hand. Thereafter wipe your head with your hand while still moist with the water of Wudu' and your feet up to your ankles; I like to bless you and allow you to step where no one, other than you, has ever stepped." This is the reason for Adhan and Wudu'. Then Allāh, the Most Majestic, the Most Glorious, sent Wahy to him, "O Muhammad, face the direction of the black-stone and speak of My greatness an equal number of times as the number of My curtains." For this reason, the number of Takbir is seven, equal to the number of seven curtains. At the end of the curtains, he commenced Salah (prayer) and for this reason, commencement became a Sunnah (a noble tradition). The curtains are of parallel levels and in between every two level, there are oceans of light. This is the light, which Allāh sent to Muhammad, O Allāh grant compensation to Muḥammad and his family worthy of their services to Your cause. For this reason, the number of (Takbir for) commencement is three because of the opening of the curtains three times. The number of Takbir, (altogether before commencement), are seven and the number of commencement three times. When he completed all Takbir and (takbir of) commencement, Allāh sent him Wahy to call Him by His name and for this reason, the phrase "In the name of Allāh, the Beneficent, the Merciful" is placed before every Chapter of the Holy Qur'ān. Then Allāh sent him Wahy to praise Him. When he said, "All praise belongs to Allāh, Lord of the worlds," the Holy Prophet to himself said, "My thanks (to Allāh)." Allāh, the Most Majestic, the Most Glorious, sent him Wahy saying, "You just discontinued My praise. Call Me by My name." For this reason the phrase "most Beneficent, most Merciful" has come twice in al-Hamd (Chapter 1 of the Qur'ān). When the Holy Prophet reached the last word in al-Hamd' he said, "All praise belongs to Allāh, Lord of the worlds and all thanks." Allāh then sent him Wahy, "You discontinued speaking of Me. Call Me by My name." For this reason, at the beginning of every Chapter there is the phrase, "In the name of Allāh, the Beneficent, the Merciful." Thereafter Allāh, the Most Majestic, the Most Glorious, sent him Wahy, "O Muhammad, read about the relationship of your Lord, the most Holy, the most High. " (I begin) in the Name of Allāh, the Beneficent, the Merciful. (112:1) (O Muhammad,) you must say, "He is Allāh, Who is one only (112:2). Allāh is Absolute (112:3). He does not have any child nor is He a child of others (112:4). There is no one equal to Him. (112:5)." "Then Wahy was held back from him and the Messenger of Allāh said, "One the only One who is self-sufficient." Allāh then sent him Wahy, "He does not have any child nor is He a child of others (112:4). There is no one equal to Him. (112:5)." Then Wahy was held back from him and the Messenger of Allāh said, "Thus is Allāh. Thus is Allāh, our Lord." When he said this Allāh sent him Wahy, "Kneel down for Ruku' for the sake of your Lord, O Muhammad." He knelt down for RukuL Allāh then sent Wahy, while he was in Ruku' position, to say, "My Lord, the great, is free of all defects." He said this three times, Then Allāh sent him Wahy, "Raise your head, O Muhammad." The Messenger of Allāh did as he was told to do and stood up straight. Allāh, the Most Majestic, the Most Glorious, sent Wahy, "Bow down in prostration for the sake of your Lord, O Muhammad." The Messenger of Allāh bowed down in prostration, then Allāh, the Most Majestic, the Most Glorious, sent Wahy, say, "My Lord, the most High, is free of all defects." He said it three times. Then Allāh sent Wahy, "Sit upright, O Muhammad." He did as he was told. When he sat upright he looked at (signs of) His greatness that appeared to him, then, on his own he bowed down in prostration without anyone's command. He said three times, "Allāh is free of all defects." Allāh then sent Wahy that said, "Stand up straight." He obeyed but he did not see (of the signs) of greatness that had seen before and for this reason in Salah (prayer) every Rak'at has one Ruku' and two sajdah. Allāh, the Most Majestic, the Most Glorious, then sent Wahy, "Read All praise belong to Allāh, Cherisher of the worlds" (the first Chapter of the Holy Qur'ān) and he read as he had done before. Allāh, the Most Majestic, the Most Glorious, then sent Wahy, "Read Chapter 97 of the Holy Qur'ān; this Chapter speaks, of your relationship and the relationship of your family, until the Day of Judgment." In Ruku' he did just as he had done before, then he did one sajdah. When he raised his head (signs of) greatness appeared to him, he then bowed down in prostration by his own choice, without anyone's command and again he said, "Allāh is free of all defects." Allāh sent Wahy, "Raise your head, O Muhammad, your Lord has made you steadfast." When he wanted to stand up, he was told, "Sit down in your place, O Muhammad." He then sat down. Allāh sent Wahy, "O Muhammad, when I grant you a favor, you should call Me by My name." He was inspired to say, "In the name of Allāh, with (the help of) Allāh, no one, other than Allāh, deserves to be worshipped, and all beautiful names belong to Allāh." Then Allāh sent Wahy, "O Muhammad, ask compensation for yourself and say, ' Allāhumma Salli 'Ala Muḥammad wa 'Ali Muḥammad (O Allāh grant Muḥammad and his family a compensation worthy of their serving Your cause),'" which he did as he was told. He then noticed rows of angels and messenger and prophets of Allāh and it was said to him, "O Muhammad, salute them." He then said, "I pray to Allāh to grant you peace, mercy and blessings." Allāh then sent Wahy, "You and your descendants are the peace, salutations, mercy and blessing." Allāh then sent Wahy, "Do not pay any attention to the left." The first verse that he heard after Chapter 112 and 97 of the Holy Qur'ān was the verse about the people of the right hand and people of the left hand. For this reason one salutation is toward the direction of Qiblah and for this reason there is Shukr (expression of thanks) in sajdah for Takbir and his saying, "Allāh listens to all those who praise Him" because the Holy Prophet heard a great deal of voices of angels saying al- Tasbih, al-Tahmid and al-Tahlil. For this reason he said, "Allāh listens to all of those who praise Him." For this reason, in the first and second Rak'at if something invalidating Wudu' takes place, one needs to perform them all over again. This is the first obligation in the prayer at noontime, that is, Salah (prayer) at noontime. (حسن)[34]

35.

مُحَمَّدُ بْنُ يَحْيَى عَنْ أَحْمَدَ بْنِ مُحَمَّدٍ عَنْ مُحَمَّدِ بْنِ إِسْمَاعِيلَ عَنْ أَبِي إِسْمَاعِيلَ السَّرَّاجِ عَنْ هَارُونَ بْنِ خَارِجَةَ قَالَ ذَكَرْتُ لِأَبِي عَبْدِ اللهِ (عَلَيْهِ السَّلام) رَجُلاً مِنْ أَصْحَابِنَا فَأَحْسَنْتُ عَلَيْهِ الثَّنَاءَ فَقَالَ لِي كَيْفَ صَلاتُهُ

Muhammad b. Yahya has narrated from Ahmad b. Muḥammad from Muḥammad b. Isma'if from abu Isma'if af-Sarraj from Harun b. Kharijah who has said the following: "Once I spoke before abu 'Abd Allāh, (عليه السلام), about a man of our people and I praised him well. The Imam asked, 'How is his Salah (prayer)?'" (صحيح)[35]

36.

عِدَّةٌ مِنْ أَصْحَابِنَا عَنْ أَحْمَدَ بْنِ مُحَمَّدٍ عَنِ ابْنِ أَبِي نَجْرَانَ عَنْ عَبْدِ اللهِ بْنِ سِنَانٍ عَنْ أَبِي عَبْدِ اللهِ (عَلَيْهِ السَّلام) قَالَ إِنَّ الْعَبْدَ يَقُومُ فَيَقْضِي النَّافِلَةَ فَيَعْجَبُ الرَّبُّ مَلائِكَتَهُ مِنْهُ فَيَقُولُ يَا مَلائِكَتِي عَبْدِي يَقْضِي مَا لَمْ أَفْتَرِضْ عَلَيْهِ

A number of our people have narrated from Ahmad b. Muḥammad from b. abu Najran from 'Abd Allāh b. Sinan who has said the following: "Abu 'Abd Allāh, (عليه السلام), has said that a servant of Allāh may rise to perform Qada' (compensatory prayer

[34] *Al-Kāfi, v3, ch100, h1*

[35] *Al-Kāfi, v3, ch100, h4*

for) an optional Salah (prayer) that was missed in its proper time. The Lord then expresses surprise before the angels saying, 'My angels, look at My servant who makes up for the optional Salah (prayer) missed in time, when I have not even made it obligatory for him.''' (صحيح)[36]

37.

مُحَمَّدُ بْنُ يَحْيَى عَنْ أَحْمَدَ بْنِ إِسْحَاقَ عَنْ سَعْدَانَ بْنِ مُسْلِمٍ عَنْ عَبْدِ اللهِ بْنِ سِنَانٍ عَنْ أَبِي عَبْدِ اللهِ (عَلَيْهِ السَّلام) قَالَ شَرَفُ الْمُؤْمِنِ صَلاتُهُ بِاللَّيْلِ وَعِزُّ الْمُؤْمِنِ كَفُّهُ عَنْ أَعْرَاضِ النَّاسِ

Muhammad b. Yahya has narrated from Ahmad b. Ishaq from Sa'dan b. Muslim from 'Abd Allāh b. Sinan who has said the following: "Abu 'Abd Allāh, (عليه السلام), has said that nobility of a man is in his Salah (prayer) during the night and his honor is in his keeping away from unsettling people's confidentiality." (مجهول)[37]

38.

أَبُو عَلِيٍّ الأَشْعَرِيُّ عَنْ مُحَمَّدِ بْنِ عَبْدِ الْجَبَّارِ عَنْ صَفْوَانَ بْنِ يَحْيَى عَنْ هَارُونَ بْنِ خَارِجَةَ عَنْ أَبِي عَبْدِ اللهِ (عَلَيْهِ السَّلام) قَالَ الصَّلاةُ وُكِّلَ بِهَا مَلَكٌ لَيْسَ لَهُ عَمَلٌ غَيْرُهَا فَإِذَا فُرِغَ مِنْهَا قَبَضَهَا ثُمَّ صَعِدَ بِهَا فَإِنْ كَانَتْ مِمَّا تُقْبَلُ قُبِلَتْ وَإِنْ كَانَتْ مِمَّا لا تُقْبَلُ قِيلَ لَهُ رُدَّهَا عَلَى عَبْدِي فَيَنْزِلُ بِهَا حَتَّى يَضْرِبَ بِهَا وَجْهَهُ ثُمَّ يَقُولُ أُفٍّ لَكَ مَا يَزَالُ لَكَ عَمَلٌ يُعْنِينِي

Abu 'Alī al-Ash'ariy has narrated from Muḥammad b. 'Abd al-Jabbar from Safwan b. Yahya from Harun b. Kharijah who has said the following: "Abu 'Abd Allāh, (عليه السلام), has said that for Salah (prayer) an angel is assigned and he has no other task to perform. When one completes a Salah (prayer), the angel takes it and ascends to

---

[36] *Al-Kāfi, v3, ch100, h8*

[37] *Al-Kāfi, v3, ch100, h9*

heaven. If it is of the kind that is accepted, it then is accepted, but if it is of unacceptable kind, it then is said to him, 'Return it to My servant.' He then descends down with that Salah (prayer) and strikes it against his face saying, "Woe is upon you. You continue to have such deeds that make me tired."''' (صحيح)[38]

39.

عِدَّةٌ مِنْ أَصْحَابِنَا عَنْ أَحْمَدَ بْنِ مُحَمَّدٍ عَنِ ابْنِ أَبِي عُمَيْرٍ عَنْ جَابِرٍ عَنْ أَبِي جَعْفَرٍ (عَلَيْهِ السَّلام) قَالَ قَالَ رَسُولُ اللهِ (صلّى اللهُ عَلَيْهِ وَآلِهِ) لِجَبْرَئِيلَ (عَلَيْهِ السَّلام) يَا جَبْرَئِيلُ أَيُّ الْبِقَاعِ أَحَبُّ إِلَى اللهِ عَزَّ وَجَلَّ قَالَ الْمَسَاجِدُ وَأَحَبُّ أَهْلِهَا إِلَى اللهِ أَوَّلُهُمْ دُخُولاً وَآخِرُهُمْ خُرُوجاً مِنْهَا

A number of our people have narrated from Ahmad b. Muhammad from b. abu 'Umayr from Jabir who has said the following: "Abu Ja'far, (عليه السلام), has said, 'The Messenger of Allāh asked Jibril (Gabriel), "Which places are more beloved to Allāh, the Most Majestic, the Most Glorious?" He replied, "It is Masjids and most beloved to Allāh of its people are those who enter them first and leave last.' (صحيح)[39]

40.

مُحَمَّدُ بْنُ يَحْيَى عَنْ أَحْمَدَ بْنِ مُحَمَّدِ بْنِ عِيسَى عَنْ عَلِيِّ بْنِ النُّعْمَانِ عَنْ مُعَاوِيَةَ بْنِ عَمَّارٍ قَالَ سَمِعْتُ أَبَا عَبْدِ اللَّهِ (عليه السلام) يَقُولُ كَانَ فِي وَصِيَّةِ النَّبِيِّ (صلى الله عليه وآله) لِعَلِيٍّ (عليه السلام) أَنْ قَالَ يَا عَلِيُّ أُوصِيكَ فِي نَفْسِكَ بِخِصَالٍ فَاحْفَظْهَا عَنِّي ثُمَّ قَالَ اللَّهُمَّ أَعِنْهُ أَمَّا الْأُولَى فَالصِّدْقُ وَ لَا تَخْرُجَنَّ مِنْ فِيكَ كَذِبَةٌ أَبَداً وَ الثَّانِيَةُ الْوَرَعُ وَ لَا تَجْتَرِئْ عَلَى خِيَانَةٍ أَبَداً وَ الثَّالِثَةُ الْخَوْفُ مِنَ اللَّهِ عَزَّ ذِكْرُهُ كَأَنَّكَ تَرَاهُ وَ الرَّابِعَةُ كَثْرَةُ الْبُكَاءِ مِنْ خَشْيَةِ اللَّهِ يُبْنَى لَكَ بِكُلِّ دَمْعَةٍ أَلْفُ بَيْتٍ فِي الْجَنَّةِ وَ الْخَامِسَةُ بَذْلُكَ مَالَكَ وَ دَمَكَ دُونَ دِينِكَ وَ السَّادِسَةُ الْأَخْذُ بِسُنَّتِي فِي صَلَاتِي وَ صَوْمِي وَ صَدَقَتِي أَمَّا الصَّلَاةُ فَالْخَمْسُونَ رَكْعَةً وَ أَمَّا الصِّيَامُ فَثَلَاثَةُ أَيَّامٍ فِي الشَّهْرِ الْخَمِيسُ فِي أَوَّلِهِ وَ الْأَرْبِعَاءُ فِي وَسَطِهِ وَ الْخَمِيسُ فِي آخِرِهِ وَ أَمَّا الصَّدَقَةُ فَجُهْدَكَ حَتَّى تَقُولَ قَدْ

---

[38] *Al-Kāfi, v3, ch100, h10*

[39] *Al-Kāfi, v3, ch100, h14*

أَسْرَفْتُ وَ لَمْ تُسْرِفْ وَ عَلَيْكَ بِصَلَاةِ اللَّيْلِ وَ عَلَيْكَ بِصَلَاةِ الزَّوَالِ وَ عَلَيْكَ بِصَلَاةِ الزَّوَالِ وَ عَلَيْكَ بِصَلَاةِ الزَّوَالِ وَ عَلَيْكَ بِتِلَاوَةِ الْقُرْآنِ عَلَى كُلِّ حَالٍ وَ عَلَيْكَ بِرَفْعِ يَدَيْكَ فِي صَلَاتِكَ وَ تَقْلِيبِهِمَا وَ عَلَيْكَ بِالسِّوَاكِ عِنْدَ كُلِّ وُضُوءٍ وَ عَلَيْكَ بِمَحَاسِنِ الْأَخْلَاقِ فَارْكَبْهَا وَ مَسَاوِي الْأَخْلَاقِ فَاجْتَنِبْهَا فَإِنْ لَمْ تَفْعَلْ فَلَا تَلُومَنَّ إِلَّا نَفْسَكَ

Muhammad b. Yahya, from Ahmad b. Muḥammad b. Isa, from 'Alī b. Al-No'man, from Muawiya b. Ammar who said: 'I heard Abu 'Abd Allāh say: 'There was in the bequest of the Prophet (صلى الله عليه وآله وسلم) to 'Alī (عليه السلام) that he said: 'O 'Alī (عليه السلام), I hereby bequeath you with regards to yourself of qualities, so preserve them from me'. Then he said: 'Our Allāh (تبارك و طائلة), Support him. As for the first one is to be truthful, and do not let lies to come out from you ever. And the second is the piety and do not let yourself be treacherous ever. And the third is the fear of Allāh (تبارك و طائلة), Mighty is His Mention, as if you can actually see Him . And the fourth is the excessive weeping for the fear of Allāh (تبارك و طائلة). There will be built for you, for every tear drop, a thousand houses in the Paradise. And the fifth is that your wealth and your blood is not for other than your Religion. **And the sixth is to take to my Sunnah with regards to my Prayer**, and my Fast, and my charity. **As for the Prayer, so it is of fifty Rakaat**, and as for the Fasts, so that is for three days in the month, the Thursday in the first part of it, and the Wednesday in the middle of it, and the Thursday in the last part of it. And as for the charity, so you strive in it to the extent that you would say: 'I have been excessive', but you would not have been excessive. **And it is on you to perform the Night Prayer, and it is on you to perform the Noon Prayer, and it is on you to perform the Noon Prayer, and it is on you to perform the Noon Prayer**. And it is on you to recite the Qur'ān in every condition. And it is on you to raise your hands in your Prayer and turn them both. And it is on you to brush (your teeth) during every ablution. And it is on you to observe the most excellent morals and to abstain from evil manners, for it you do not do it, so you should not blame anyone except for yourself'. (صحيح)[40]

[40] *Al-Kāfi, v8, h33*

باب الزكاة

Chapter on az-Zakāt

1.

عَلِيُّ بْنُ إِبْرَاهِيمَ عَنْ أَبِيهِ وَعَبْدِ اللهِ بْنِ الصَّلْتِ جَمِيعاً عَنْ حَمَّادِ بْنِ عِيسَى عَنْ حَرِيزِ بْنِ عَبْدِ اللهِ عَنْ زُرَارَةَ عَنْ أَبِي جَعْفَرٍ (عَلَيهِ السَّلام) قَالَ بُنِيَ الإِسْلامُ عَلَى خَمْسَةِ أَشْيَاءَ عَلَى الصَّلاةِ وَالزَّكَاةِ وَالْحَجِّ وَالصَّوْمِ وَالْوَلايَةِ قَالَ زُرَارَةُ فَقُلْتُ وَأَيُّ شَيْءٍ مِنْ ذَلِكَ أَفْضَلُ فَقَالَ الْوَلايَةُ أَفْضَلُ لأَنَّهَا مِفْتَاحُهُنَّ وَالْوَالِي هُوَ الدَّلِيلُ عَلَيْهِنَّ قُلْتُ ثُمَّ الَّذِي يَلِي ذَلِكَ فِي الْفَضْلِ فَقَالَ الصَّلاةُ إِنَّ رَسُولَ اللهِ (صَلَّى اللهُ عَلَيْهِ وآلِه) قَالَ الصَّلاةُ عَمُودُ دِينِكُمْ قَالَ قُلْتُ ثُمَّ الَّذِي يَلِيهَا فِي الْفَضْلِ قَالَ الزَّكَاةُ لأَنَّهُ قَرَنَهَا بِهَا وَبَدَأَ بِالصَّلاةِ قَبْلَهَا وَقَالَ رَسُولُ اللهِ (صَلَّى اللهُ عَلَيْهِ وآلِه) الزَّكَاةُ تُذْهِبُ الذُّنُوبَ قُلْتُ وَالَّذِي يَلِيهَا فِي الْفَضْلِ قَالَ الْحَجُّ قَالَ اللهُ عَزَّ وَجَلَّ وَللهِ عَلَى النَّاسِ حِجُّ الْبَيْتِ مَنِ اسْتَطَاعَ إِلَيْهِ سَبِيلاً وَمَنْ كَفَرَ فَإِنَّ اللهَ غَنِيٌّ عَنِ الْعَالَمِينَ وَقَالَ رَسُولُ اللهِ (صَلَّى اللهُ عَلَيْهِ وآلِه) لَحَجَّةٌ مَقْبُولَةٌ خَيْرٌ مِنْ عِشْرِينَ صَلاةً نَافِلَةً وَمَنْ طَافَ بِهَذَا الْبَيْتِ طَوَافاً أَحْصَى فِيهِ أُسْبُوعَهُ وَأَحْسَنَ رَكْعَتَيْهِ غَفَرَ اللهُ لَهُ وَقَالَ فِي يَوْمِ عَرَفَةَ وَيَوْمِ الْمُزْدَلِفَةِ مَا قَالَ قُلْتُ فَمَا ذَا يَتْبَعُهُ قَالَ الصَّوْمُ قُلْتُ وَمَا بَالُ الصَّوْمِ صَارَ آخِرَ ذَلِكَ أَجْمَعَ قَالَ قَالَ رَسُولُ اللهِ (صَلَّى اللهُ عَلَيْهِ وآلِه) الصَّوْمُ جُنَّةٌ مِنَ النَّارِ قَالَ ثُمَّ قَالَ إِنَّ أَفْضَلَ الأَشْيَاءِ مَا إِذَا فَاتَكَ لَمْ تَكُنْ مِنْهُ تَوْبَةٌ دُونَ أَنْ تَرْجِعَ إِلَيْهِ فَتُؤَدِّيَهُ بِعَيْنِهِ إِنَّ الصَّلاةَ وَالزَّكَاةَ وَالْحَجَّ وَالْوَلايَةَ لَيْسَ يَقَعُ شَيْءٌ مَكَانَهَا دُونَ أَدَائِهَا وَإِنَّ الصَّوْمَ إِذَا فَاتَكَ أَوْ قَصَّرْتَ أَوْ سَافَرْتَ فِيهِ أَدَّيْتَ مَكَانَهُ أَيَّاماً غَيْرَهَا وَجَزَيْتَ ذَلِكَ الذَّنْبَ بِصَدَقَةٍ وَلا قَضَاءَ عَلَيْكَ وَلَيْسَ مِنْ تِلْكَ الأَرْبَعَةِ شَيْءٌ يُجْزِيكَ مَكَانَهُ غَيْرُهُ قَالَ ثُمَّ قَالَ ذِرْوَةُ الأَمْرِ وَسَنَامُهُ وَمِفْتَاحُهُ وَبَابُ الأَشْيَاءِ وَرِضَا الرَّحْمَنِ الطَّاعَةُ لِلإِمَامِ بَعْدَ مَعْرِفَتِهِ إِنَّ اللهَ عَزَّ وَجَلَّ يَقُولُ مَنْ يُطِعِ الرَّسُولَ فَقَدْ أَطَاعَ اللهَ وَمَنْ تَوَلَّى فَمَا أَرْسَلْنَاكَ عَلَيْهِمْ حَفِيظاً أَمَا لَوْ أَنَّ رَجُلاً قَامَ لَيْلَهُ وَصَامَ نَهَارَهُ وَتَصَدَّقَ بِجَمِيعِ مَالِهِ وَحَجَّ جَمِيعَ دَهْرِهِ وَلَمْ يَعْرِفْ وَلايَةَ وَلِيِّ اللهِ فَيُوَالِيَهُ وَيَكُونَ جَمِيعُ أَعْمَالِهِ بِدَلالَتِهِ إِلَيْهِ مَا كَانَ

لَهُ عَلَى اللهِ جَلَّ وَعَزَّ حَقٌّ فِي ثَوَابِهِ وَلاَ كَانَ مِنْ أَهْلِ الإِيمَانِ ثُمَّ قَالَ أُولَئِكَ الْمُحْسِنُ مِنْهُمْ يُدْخِلُهُ اللهُ الْجَنَّةَ بِفَضْلِ رَحْمَتِهِ

Ali b. Ibrahim has narrated from his father and 'Abd Allāh b. al-Salt all of them from Hammad b. 'Isa from Hariz b. 'Abd Allāh from Zurara from abu Ja'far (عليه السلام) who has said the following: "Abu Ja'far (عليه السلام) has said, **'Islam is based on five issues. It is based on prayer, charity (al- Zakat), Hajj, Fasting and al-Wilāya**." Zurara has said, 'I then asked the Imam, "Which of these is more important than the others?"' The Imam said, 'Al-Wilāya is more important. It is the key to the others. The person who possesses Divine Authority is the guide to the other principles.' I then asked, 'Which is the next important?' The Imam said, 'Thereafter is prayer. The Messenger of Allāh has said, "Prayer is the pillar of your religion."' I then asked, 'Which is the next important among them?' The Imam said, **'Al-Zakat is the one thereafter. Allāh has mentioned it next to prayer but He has mentioned prayer first. The Messenger of Allāh has said, "Al-Zakat removes sins.'"** I then asked, 'Which one is important thereafter?' The Imam said, 'Hajj is important thereafter. Allāh, the Most Majestic, the Most Holy, has said, "It is a duty of the people to Allāh to perform Hajj of the House if they are capable to do so. Whoever rejects it should know that Allāh does not need anyone in the world." (3:97) The messenger of Allāh has said, "Performing Hajj that is accepted is more virtuous than twenty Rak'at optional prayer. Whoever walks around the House seven times and performs the two Rak'at prayers thereafter properly Allāh will grant him cover." He (The Messenger of Allāh) did say on the ninth of the month of Dil Hajj and on the tenth of the month of Dil Hajj in Muzdalifa (a place in Makka), what he wanted to say.' I then asked, 'Which one is important thereafter?' The Imam said, 'It is fasting.' "I then asked, 'Why is fasting the last of all in importance?' The Imam said, 'The Messenger of Allāh has said, "Fasting is a shield against the fire."' The narrator has said that the Imam said, 'The best of all things is that for which, if you miss, you do not find an alternative accept going back to achieve it. Prayer, al-Wilāya and Hajj are not of matters replaceable with their own kind. On the other hand if fasting is missed on a journey one has the choice to fast on other days as remedy, or compensate for the sin with expiation and no fasting is necessary as a remedy. In the cases of the other four issues there is no alternative for them.' The narrator has said that the Imam then said, 'The topmost, the peak of the issue, the key and the door to it and the pleasure of the Beneficent (Lord) is to obey the Imam properly after knowing him clearly. Allāh, the Most Majestic, the Most Holy, says, "Whoever obeys the Messenger he has obeyed Allāh and whoever turns away from such obedience then you should know that We have not sent you to guard them." (4:80) 'Without recognizing the Divine Authority of the Imam, the deputy of Allāh, no one has the right to receive any reward from Allāh, the Most Majestic, the Most Holy. This is true even though in his lifetime he may stand up in worship the whole night, fast during the day, give all his belongings in charity and perform Hajj every year. So also it is if he does not acknowledge the Divine Authority of his Imam with which all of one's deeds can take place with the guidance of the Imam. Without al- Wilāya, one is not considered of the people of belief.' Thereafter the Imam said, 'Allāh will admit, those of them who do good deeds into paradise through His extra mercy. (صحيح)[1]

2.

عَلِيُّ بْنُ إِبْرَاهِيمَ عَنْ أَبِيهِ عَنْ حَمَّادِ بْنِ عِيسَى عَنْ حَرِيزٍ عَنْ زُرَارَةَ وَمُحَمَّدِ بْنِ مُسْلِمٍ أَنَّهُمَا قَالاَ لأَبِي عَبْدِ اللهِ (عَلَيْهِ السَّلام) أَ رَأَيْتَ قَوْلَ اللهِ عَزَّ وَجَلَّ إِنَّمَا الصَّدَقَاتُ لِلْفُقَرَاءِ وَالْمَسَاكِينِ وَالعَامِلِينَ عَلَيْهَا وَالْمُؤَلَّفَةِ قُلُوبُهُمْ وَفِي الرِّقَابِ وَالْغَارِمِينَ وَفِي سَبِيلِ اللهِ وَابْنِ السَّبِيلِ فَرِيضَةً مِنَ اللهِ أَ كُلُّ هَؤُلاَءِ يُعْطَى وَإِنْ كَانَ لاَ يَعْرِفُ فَقَالَ إِنَّ الإِمَامَ يُعْطِي هَؤُلاَءِ جَمِيعاً لأَنَّهُمْ يُقِرُّونَ لَهُ بِالطَّاعَةِ قَالَ قُلْتُ فَإِنْ كَانُوا لاَ يَعْرِفُونَ فَقَالَ يَا زُرَارَةُ لَوْ كَانَ يُعْطِي مَنْ يَعْرِفُ دُونَ مَنْ لاَ يَعْرِفُ لَمْ يُوجَدْ لَهَا مَوْضِعٌ وَإِنَّمَا يُعْطِي مَنْ لاَ يَعْرِفُ لِيَرْغَبَ فِي الدِّينِ فَيَثْبُتَ عَلَيْهِ فَأَمَّا الْيَوْمَ فَلاَ تُعْطِهَا أَنْتَ وَأَصْحَابُكَ إِلاَّ مَنْ يَعْرِفُ فَمَنْ وَجَدْتَ مِنْ هَؤُلاَءِ الْمُسْلِمِينَ عَارِفاً فَأَعْطِهِ دُونَ النَّاسِ ثُمَّ قَالَ سَهْمُ الْمُؤَلَّفَةِ قُلُوبُهُمْ وَسَهْمُ الرِّقَابِ عَامٌّ وَالْبَاقِي خَاصٌّ قَالَ قُلْتُ فَإِنْ لَمْ يُوجَدُوا قَالَ لاَ تَكُونُ فَرِيضَةٌ فَرَضَهَا اللهُ عَزَّ وَجَلَّ لاَ يُوجَدُ لَهَا أَهْلٌ قَالَ قُلْتُ فَإِنْ لَمْ تَسَعْهُمُ الصَّدَقَاتُ فَقَالَ إِنَّ اللهَ فَرَضَ لِلْفُقَرَاءِ

[1] *Al-Kāfi, v2, ch13, h5*

فِي مَالِ الأَغْنِيَاءِ مَا يَسَعُهُمْ وَلَوْ عَلِمَ أَنَّ ذَلِكَ لاَ يَسَعُهُمْ لَزَادَهُمْ إِنَّهُمْ لَمْ يُؤْتَوْا مِنْ قِبَلِ فَرِيضَةِ اللهِ وَلَكِنْ أُتُوا مِنْ مَنْعِ مَنْ مَنَعَهُمْ حَقَّهُمْ لاَ مِمَّا فَرَضَ اللهُ لَهُمْ وَلَوْ أَنَّ النَّاسَ أَدَّوْا حُقُوقَهُمْ لَكَانُوا عَائِشِينَ بِخَيْرٍ

Ali b. Ibrahim has narrated from his father from Hammad b. 'Isa from Hariz from Zurāra and Muḥammad b. Muslim who has said the following: "Once we both asked abu 'Abd Allāh, (عليه السلام), about the words of Allāh, most Majestic, most Glorious, in the following verse of the Holy Qur'ān. 'Charity funds (zakat) are only for the poor, the destitute, and the tax collectors. (It is also for the) people whose hearts are inclined (toward Islam), the slaves, those who cannot pay their debts, for the cause of Allāh, and for those who have become needy on a journey. Paying zakat is an obligation that Allāh has decreed. Allāh is All-knowing and All-wise. '(9:60) 'Can all the people and cases mentioned in this verse receive zakat even though they may not believe (in Divine Authority of 'A'immah)?' He replied, 'The Imam gives charity to all of them; they announce their obedience to him.' I (the narrator) then asked, 'Even if they do not acknowledge (his Divine Authority)?' He then said, 'O Zurāra, were he to give charity only to those who acknowledge (his Divine Authority) and not to others, there would remain no one or cases as recipient of (zakat) charity. He gives charity to those who do not acknowledge (his divine authority) so they incline to religion to become strong (in faith). However, today you and your friends give zakat only to those who acknowledge (our Divine Authority) if you find one who believes (in our Divine Authority).' He then said, 'The share of those who show interest in Islam and the share of slaves to be emancipated are of general nature and other shares in a charity are for certain people but not for everyone.' I (the narrator) then asked, 'What happens if there is no recipient of zakat?' He replied, 'Allāh, the Most Majestic, the Most Glorious, has not made any charity compulsory without any recipient.' I (the narrator) then asked, 'What happens if charity is not enough?' He replied, 'The amount of compulsory charity Allāh has sanctioned in the properties of affluent people for the poor ones is enough. If He knew that it is not enough, He would sanction a greater amount. Shortages do not come from the amount Allāh has made compulsory but it comes from non-payment. There are those who do not pay what belongs to the needy, thus, shortages are not due to the degree of Allāh's sanctioned charity for the needy. Had people paid the rights of the needy, they would have lived happy.'" (حسن)[2]

3.

عِدَّةٌ مِنْ أَصْحَابِنَا عَنْ سَهْلِ بْنِ زِيَادٍ وَأَحْمَدَ بْنِ مُحَمَّدٍ جَمِيعاً عَنِ ابْنِ مَحْبُوبٍ عَنْ عَبْدِ اللهِ بْنِ سِنَانٍ قَالَ قَالَ أَبُو عَبْدِ اللهِ (عَلَيْهِ السَّلام) لَمَّا أُنْزِلَتْ آيَةُ الزَّكَاةِ خُذْ مِنْ أَمْوالِهِمْ صَدَقَةً تُطَهِّرُهُمْ وَتُزَكِّيهِمْ بِها وَأُنْزِلَتْ فِي شَهْرِ رَمَضَانَ فَأَمَرَ رَسُولُ اللهِ (صلّى اللهُ عَلَيْهِ وَآلِه) مُنَادِيَهُ فَنَادَى فِي النَّاسِ أَنَّ اللهَ فَرَضَ عَلَيْكُمُ الزَّكَاةَ كَمَا فَرَضَ عَلَيْكُمُ الصَّلاَةَ فَفَرَضَ اللهُ عَزَّ وَجَلَّ عَلَيْهِمْ مِنَ الذَّهَبِ وَالْفِضَّةِ وَفَرَضَ الصَّدَقَةَ مِنَ الإِبِلِ وَالْبَقَرِ وَالْغَنَمِ وَمِنَ الْحِنْطَةِ وَالشَّعِيرِ وَالتَّمْرِ وَالزَّبِيبِ فَنَادَى فِيهِمْ بِذَلِكَ فِي شَهْرِ رَمَضَانَ وَعَفَا لَهُمْ عَمَّا سِوَى ذَلِكَ قَالَ ثُمَّ لَمْ يَفْرِضْ لِشَيْءٍ مِنْ أَمْوَالِهِمْ حَتَّى حَالَ عَلَيْهِمُ الْحَوْلُ مِنْ قَابِلٍ فَصَامُوا وَأَفْطَرُوا فَأَمَرَ مُنَادِيَهُ فَنَادَى فِي الْمُسْلِمِينَ أَيُّهَا الْمُسْلِمُونَ زَكُّوا أَمْوَالَكُمْ تُقْبَلْ صَلاتُكُمْ قَالَ ثُمَّ وَجَّهَ عُمَّالَ الصَّدَقَةِ وَعُمَّالَ الطَّسُوقِ

A number of our people have narrated from Sahl b. Ziyad and Ahmad b. Muḥammad all from b. Mahbub from 'Abd Allāh b. Sinan who has said the following: "Abu 'Abd Allāh, has said that once this verse of the Holy Qur'ān was revealed to the Messenger of Allāh. 'Collect religious tax (zakat) from them to purify and cleanse them . . .' (9:103) It was revealed in the month of Ramadan, the Messenger of Allāh commanded his announcer to announce among people that Allāh has made it compulsory on you to pay zakat (charity) just as He has made obligatory upon you to perform Salah (prayer). Allāh, the Most Majestic, the Most Glorious, has made it compulsory to pay zakat on gold and silver; and on cattle: camel, cows, sheep; and on grains: wheat, barley, dates and raisins. The announcer announced it in the month of Ramadan. He exempted them from payment of zakat on other forms of properties.' The Imam then said, 'Besides, He did not make it compulsory to pay zakat on their properties before the end of the year. They completed fasting. He then commanded his announcer to announce among the Muslims, "O Muslims, pay zakat on your properties; your Salah (prayer) will be accepted."' He said, 'Then he (the Messenger

---

[2] *Al-Kāfi, v3, ch1, h1*

of Allāh) sent his land assessor and tax collectors among people to collect zakat.'" (صحيح)[3]

4.

عَلِيُّ بْنُ إِبْرَاهِيمَ عَنْ أَبِيهِ عَنْ عَبْدِ اللهِ بْنِ الْمُغِيرَةِ عَنِ ابْنِ مُسْكَانَ وَغَيْرِ وَاحِدٍ عَنْ أَبِي عَبْدِ اللهِ (عَلَيْهِ السَّلام) قَالَ إِنَّ اللهَ جَلَّ وَعَزَّ جَعَلَ لِلْفُقَرَاءِ فِي أَمْوَالِ الأَغْنِيَاءِ مَا يَكْفِيهِمْ وَلَوْ لاَ ذَلِكَ لَزَادَهُمْ وَإِنَّمَا يُؤْتَوْنَ مِنْ مَنْعِ مَنْ مَنَعَهُمْ

Ali b. Ibrahim has narrated from his father from 'Abd Allāh b. al-Mughirah from b. Muskan and more than one person who have said the following: "Abu 'Abd Allāh, (عليه السلام), has said that Allāh, the Most Majestic, the Most Glorious, has assigned in properties of affluent people a share for the needy that is sufficient to meet their need; otherwise, He would have increased such share. Shortages come from non-payment of those who do not pay." (حسن)[4]

5.

عَلِيُّ بْنُ إِبْرَاهِيمَ عَنْ أَبِيهِ عَنْ حَمَّادِ بْنِ عِيسَى عَنْ حَرِيزٍ عَنْ مُحَمَّدِ بْنِ مُسْلِمٍ وَأَبِي بَصِيرٍ وَبُرَيْدٍ وَفُضَيْلٍ عَنْ أَبِي جَعْفَرٍ وَأَبِي عَبْدِ اللهِ (عَلَيْهِ السَّلام) قَالاَ فَرَضَ اللهُ الزَّكَاةَ مَعَ الصَّلاَةِ

Ali b. Ibrahim has narrated from his father from Hammad b. 'Isa from Hariz from Muḥammad b. Muslim and abu Basir, Burayd and Fudayl who have said the following: "Abu Ja'far and abu 'Abd Allāh, (عليه السلام), have said that Allāh has made zakat obligatory along with Salah (prayer)." (حسن)[5]

---

[3] *Al-Kāfi, v3, ch1, h2*

[4] *Al-Kāfi, v3, ch1, h4*

[5] *Al-Kāfi, v3, ch1, h5*

6.

عَلِيُّ بْنُ إِبْرَاهِيمَ عَنْ أَبِيهِ عَنْ إِسْمَاعِيلَ بْنِ مَرَّارٍ عَنْ مُبَارَكِ الْعَقَرْقُوفِيِّ قَالَ قَالَ أَبُو الْحَسَنِ (عَلَيْهِ السَّلَام) إِنَّ اللهَ عَزَّ وَجَلَّ وَضَعَ الزَّكَاةَ قُوتاً لِلْفُقَرَاءِ وَتَوْفِيراً لِأَمْوَالِكُمْ

Ali b. Ibrahim has narrated from his father from Isma'il b. Marrar from Mubarak al-'Aqarqufiy who has said the following: "Abu al-Hassan, (عليه السلام), has said, 'Allāh, the Most Majestic, the Most Glorious, has made zakat as means of living for the needy and to increase your properties.'" (مجهول)[6]

7.

عِدَّةٌ مِنْ أَصْحَابِنَا عَنْ أَحْمَدَ بْنِ مُحَمَّدٍ عَنِ الْحُسَيْنِ بْنِ سَعِيدٍ عَنِ النَّضْرِ بْنِ سُوَيْدٍ عَنْ عَبْدِ اللهِ بْنِ سِنَانٍ عَنْ أَبِي عَبْدِ اللهِ (عَلَيْهِ السَّلَام) قَالَ إِنَّ اللهَ عَزَّ وَجَلَّ فَرَضَ الزَّكَاةَ كَمَا فَرَضَ الصَّلَاةَ وَلَوْ أَنَّ رَجُلاً حَمَلَ الزَّكَاةَ فَأَعْطَاهَا عَلَانِيَةً لَمْ يَكُنْ عَلَيْهِ فِي ذَلِكَ عَيْبٌ وَذَلِكَ أَنَّ اللهَ عَزَّ وَجَلَّ فَرَضَ فِي أَمْوَالِ الْأَغْنِيَاءِ لِلْفُقَرَاءِ مَا يَكْتَفُونَ بِهِ الْفُقَرَاءُ وَلَوْ عَلِمَ أَنَّ الَّذِي فَرَضَ لَهُمْ لَا يَكْفِيهِمْ لَزَادَهُمْ وَإِنَّمَا يُؤْتَى الْفُقَرَاءُ فِيمَا أُتُوا مِنْ مَنْعِ مَنْ مَنَعَهُمْ حُقُوقَهُمْ لَا مِنَ الْفَرِيضَةِ

A number of our people have narrated from Ahmad b. Muḥammad from al-Husayn b. Sa'id from al-Nadr b. al-Suwayd from 'Abd Allāh b. Sinan who has said the following: "Abu 'Abd Allāh, (عليه السلام), has said that Allāh, the Most Majestic, the Most Glorious, has made paying zakat compulsory as He has made performing of Salah (prayer) obligatory. If a man pays zakat publicly, it is not a blamable thing to do. It is because Allāh, the Most Majestic, the Most Glorious, has assigned a share in the properties of affluent people for the needy enough to meet their needs. If it were in His knowledge that such share is not enough for them, He would have increased it. What the needy people face is because of withholding payment of zakat which is

---

denying the rights of the needy, not because of the degree of the amount made compulsory." (صحيح)[7]

8.

عَلِيُّ بْنُ إِبْرَاهِيمَ عَنْ أَبِيهِ عَنِ ابْنِ أَبِي عُمَيْرٍ عَنْ إِسْحَاقَ بْنِ عَمَّارٍ عَنْ أَبِي عَبْدِ الله (عَلَيْهِ السَّلام) فِي قَوْلِ الله عَزَّ وَجَلَّ وَإِنْ تُخْفُوها وَتُؤْتُوهَا الْفُقَراءَ فَهُوَ خَيْرٌ لَكُمْ فَقَالَ هِيَ سِوَى الزَّكَاةِ إِنَّ الزَّكَاةَ عَلانِيَةٌ غَيْرُ سِرٍّ

Ali b. Ibrahim has narrated from his father from b. abu 'Umayr from Ishaq b. 'Ammar who has said the following: "Abu 'Abd Allāh, (عليه السلام), about the words of Allāh, the Most Majestic, the Most Glorious, '. . . If you pay it privately to the needy, it is better for you. . . .' (2:273), has said, 'This payment is a payment other than compulsory zakat which is paid publicly and not privately.'" (حسن أو موثق)[8]

9.

مُحَمَّدُ بْنُ يَحْيَى عَنْ مُحَمَّدِ بْنِ الْحَسَنِ عَنْ صَفْوَانَ بْنِ يَحْيَى عَنِ الْعَلاءِ بْنِ رَزِينٍ عَنْ مُحَمَّدِ بْنِ مُسْلِمٍ عَنْ أَحَدِهِمَا (عَلَيْهِما السَّلام) أَنَّهُ سَأَلَهُ عَنِ الْفَقِيرِ وَالْمِسْكِينِ فَقَالَ الْفَقِيرُ الَّذِي لاَ يَسْأَلُ وَالْمِسْكِينُ الَّذِي هُوَ أَجْهَدُ مِنْهُ الَّذِي يَسْأَلُ.

Muhammad b. Yahya has narrated from Muḥammad b. al-Hassan from Safwan b. Yahya from al-'Ala' b. Razin from Muḥammad b. Muslim from one of them (the two Imam): "Someone asked the Imam, (عليه السلام), about poor and destitute. He replied, 'Poor is one who does not ask for help. Destitute is of a worse condition and he asks for help. (صحيح)[9]

---

[7] *Al-Kāfi, v3, ch1, h7*

[8] *Al-Kāfi, v3, ch1, h17*

[9] *Al-Kāfi, v3, ch1, h18*

10.

عِدَّةٌ مِنْ أَصْحَابِنَا عَنْ أَحْمَدَ بْنِ مُحَمَّدِ بْنِ عِيسَى عَنْ أَحْمَدَ بْنِ مُحَمَّدِ بْنِ أَبِي نَصْرٍ قَالَ ذَكَرْتُ لِلرِّضَا (عَلَيْهِ السَّلام) شَيْئاً فَقَالَ اصْبِرْ فَإِنِّي أَرْجُو أَنْ يَصْنَعَ اللهُ لَكَ إِنْ شَاءَ اللهُ ثُمَّ قَالَ فَوَ اللهِ مَا أَخَّرَ اللهُ عَنِ الْمُؤْمِنِ مِنْ هَذِهِ الدُّنْيَا خَيْرٌ لَهُ مِمَّا عَجَّلَ لَهُ فِيهَا ثُمَّ صَغَّرَ الدُّنْيَا وَقَالَ أَيَّ شَيْءٍ هِيَ ثُمَّ قَالَ إِنَّ صَاحِبَ النِّعْمَةِ عَلَى خَطَرٍ إِنَّهُ يَجِبُ عَلَيْهِ حُقُوقُ اللهِ فِيهَا وَاللهِ إِنَّهُ لَتَكُونُ عَلَيَّ النِّعَمُ مِنَ اللهِ عَزَّ وَجَلَّ فَمَا أَزَالُ مِنْهَا عَلَى وَجَلٍ وَحَرَّكَ يَدَهُ حَتَّى أَخْرُجَ مِنَ الْحُقُوقِ الَّتِي تَجِبُ لِلهِ عَلَيَّ فِيهَا فَقُلْتُ جُعِلْتُ فِدَاكَ أَنْتَ فِي قَدْرِكَ تَخَافُ هَذَا قَالَ نَعَمْ فَأَحْمَدُ رَبِّي عَلَى مَا مَنَّ بِهِ عَلَيَّ

A number of our people have narrated from Ahmad b. Muḥammad b. 'Isa from Ahmad b. Muḥammad b. abu Nasr who has said the following: "I mentioned something before al-Rida, (عليه السلام), and he said, 'Exercise patience. I hope Allāh will do something good for you if He so wills.' He then said, 'By Allāh, He does not delay anything from a believer of the worldly things unless it is better for him than to do it for him quickly.' He then belittled worldly things and said, 'It is worthless.' He then said, 'An affluent person faces the danger of owing compulsory payments of the rights of Allāh. By Allāh, I may receive bounties from Allāh, most Majestic, most Glorious, and I continue to be afraid' - moving his hand- 'until I pay off what Allāh has made compulsory upon me to pay.' I then said, 'I pray to Allāh to keep my soul in service for your cause, why you fear with such a prominent position before Allāh?' He replied, 'Yes, I do and I am thankful to Allāh for what He has granted me.' (صحيح)[10]

11.

عَلِيُّ بْنُ إِبْرَاهِيمَ عَنْ أَبِيهِ عَنِ ابْنِ أَبِي عُمَيْرٍ عَنْ عَبْدِ اللهِ بْنِ مُسْكَانَ عَنْ مُحَمَّدِ بْنِ مُسْلِمٍ قَالَ سَأَلْتُ أَبَا عَبْدِ اللهِ (عَلَيْهِ السَّلام) عَنْ قَوْلِ اللهِ عَزَّ وَجَلَّ سَيُطَوَّقُونَ ما بَخِلُوا بِهِ يَوْمَ الْقِيامَةِ فَقَالَ يَا مُحَمَّدُ مَا مِنْ أَحَدٍ يَمْنَعُ

[10] *Al-Kāfi, v3, ch1, h19*

مِنْ زَكَاةِ مَالِهِ شَيْئاً إِلاَّ جَعَلَ اللَّهُ عَزَّ وَجَلَّ ذَلِكَ يَوْمَ الْقِيَامَةِ ثُعْبَاناً مِنْ نَارٍ مُطَوَّقاً فِي عُنُقِهِ يَنْهَشُ مِنْ لَحْمِهِ حَتَّى يَفْرُغَ مِنَ الْحِسَابِ ثُمَّ قَالَ هُوَ قَوْلُ اللَّهِ عَزَّ وَجَلَّ سَيُطَوَّقُونَ ما بَخِلُوا بِهِ يَوْمَ الْقِيامَةِ يَعْنِي مَا بَخِلُوا بِهِ مِنَ الزَّكَاةِ

Ali b. Ibrahim has narrated from his father from b. abu 'Umayr from 'Abd Allāh b. Muskan from Muḥammad b. Muslim who has said the following: "Once I asked abu 'Abd Allāh, (عليه السلام), about the following words of Allāh, most Majestic, most Glorious, '. . . whatever they are avaricious about will be tied to their necks on the Day of Judgment. . (3:180) The Imam said, 'O abu Muhammad, if one refuses to pay zakat Allāh, the Most Majestic, the Most Glorious, on the Day of Judgment will make a serpent of fire to curl around his neck and bite his flesh until He completes His judging all people.' He then said, 'The words of Allāh, most Majestic, most Glorious, "Whatever they are avaricious about will be tied to their necks" is a reference to their avarice in paying zakat." (حسن)[11]

12.

عَلِيُّ بْنُ إِبْرَاهِيمَ عَنْ أَبِيهِ عَنِ ابْنِ أَبِي عُمَيْرٍ عَنْ أَبِي أَيُّوبَ عَنْ أَبِي بَصِيرٍ عَنْ أَبِي عَبْدِ اللَّهِ (عَلَيْهِ السَّلام) قَالَ قَالَ رَسُولُ اللَّهِ (صلّى اللَّهُ عَلَيْهِ وَآلِه) مَلْعُونٌ مَلْعُونٌ مَالٌ لاَ يُزَكَّى

Afi b. Ibrahim has narrated from his father from b. abu ' Umayr from abu Ayyub from abu Basır who has said the following: "Abu 'Abd Allāh, (عليه السلام), has said that the Messenger of Allāh has said, 'Condemned and condemned indeed is one who refuses to pay zakat.'" (حسن)[12]

13.

---

[11] *Al-Kāfi, v3, ch2, h1*

[12] *Al-Kāfi, v3, ch2, h8*

عَلِيُّ بْنُ إِبْرَاهِيمَ عَنْ أَبِيهِ عَنْ حَمَّادٍ عَنْ حَرِيزٍ عَنْ عُمَرَ بْنِ يَزِيدَ قَالَ قُلْتُ لأَبِي عَبْدِ اللهِ (عَلَيْهِ السَّلام) رَجُلٌ فَرَّ بِمَالِهِ مِنَ الزَّكَاةِ فَاشْتَرَى بِهِ أَرْضاً أَوْ دَاراً أَ عَلَيْهِ فِيهِ شَيْءٌ فَقَالَ لاَ وَلَوْ جَعَلَهُ حُلِيّاً أَوْ نُقَراً فَلاَ شَيْءَ عَلَيْهِ فِيهِ وَمَا مَنَعَ نَفْسَهُ مِنْ فَضْلِهِ أَكْثَرُ مِمَّا مَنَعَ مِنْ حَقِّ اللهِ بِأَنْ يَكُونَ فِيهِ

Ali b. Ibrahim has narrated from his father from Hammad from Hariz from 'Umar b. Yazid who has said the following: "I once asked abu 'Abd Allāh, (عليه السلام), about a man who runs away from paying Zakat by means of buying a piece of land or a house, if he still owes any Zakat. He (the Imam) said, 'No, he does not owe any Zakat even if he turns his asset into jewelries and silver; there is not anything on him. However, what he has denied his soul by the virtue of paying Zakat is much more than what he has saved by means of holding back the right of Allāh that could have existed in his asset.''' (صحيح)[13]

14.

عَلِيُّ بْنُ إِبْرَاهِيمَ عَنْ أَبِيهِ عَنِ ابْنِ فَضَّالٍ عَنْ عَلِيِّ بْنِ عُقْبَةَ عَنْ أَبِي الْحَسَنِ (عَلَيْهِ السَّلام) يَعْنِي الأَوَّلَ قَالَ سَمِعْتُهُ يَقُولُ مَنْ أَخْرَجَ زَكَاةَ مَالِهِ تَامَّةً فَوَضَعَهَا فِي مَوْضِعِهَا لَمْ يُسْأَلْ مِنْ أَيْنَ اكْتَسَبَ مَالَهُ.

Ali b. Ibrahim has narrated from his father from b. Faddal from 'Alī b. 'Uqbah from abu al-Hassan, the first, (عليه السلام), who has said the following: "If one pays, completely, the amount of zakat which is due on his wealth to the proper recipient, he is not asked how he has earned his wealth." (حسن أو موثق)[14]

15.

---

[13] *Al-Kāfi, v3, ch41, h1*

[14] *Al-Kāfi, v3, ch2, h9*

مُحَمَّدُ بْنُ يَحْيَى عَنْ أَحْمَدَ بْنِ مُحَمَّدِ بْنِ عِيسَى عَنِ الْحَسَنِ بْنِ مَحْبُوبٍ عَنْ مَالِكِ بْنِ عَطِيَّةَ عَنْ أَبِي حَمْزَةَ عَنْ أَبِي جَعْفَرٍ (عَلَيْهِ السَّلام) قَالَ وَجَدْنَا فِي كِتَابِ عَلِيٍّ (عَلَيْهِ السَّلام) قَالَ رَسُولُ الله (صلّى اللهُ عَلَيْهِ وَآلِه) إِذَا مُنِعَتِ الزَّكَاةُ مَنَعَتِ الأَرْضُ بَرَكَاتِهَا

Muhammad b. Yahya has narrated from Ahmad b. Muḥammad b. 'Isa from al-Hassan b. Mahbub from Malik b. 'Atiyyah from abu Hamzah who has said the following: "Abu Ja'far, (عليه السلام), has said, 'We have found in the book of Ali, (عليه السلام), that the Messenger of Allāh said, 'When paying zakat is refused, the land withholds her blessings.''' (صحيح)[15]

---

[15] *Al-Kafi, v3, ch2, h17*

باب الحج

Chapter on al-Ḥajj

1.

عَلِيُّ بْنُ إِبْرَاهِيمَ عَنْ أَبِيهِ وَعَبْدِ اللهِ بْنِ الصَّلْتِ جَمِيعاً عَنْ حَمَّادِ بْنِ عِيسَى عَنْ حَرِيزِ بْنِ عَبْدِ اللهِ عَنْ زُرَارَةَ عَنْ أَبِي جَعْفَرٍ (عَلَيهِ السَّلام) قَالَ بُنِيَ الإِسْلامُ عَلَى خَمْسَةِ أَشْيَاءَ عَلَى الصَّلاةِ وَالزَّكَاةِ وَالْحَجِّ وَالصَّوْمِ وَالْوَلايَةِ قَالَ زُرَارَةُ فَقُلْتُ وَأَيُّ شَيْءٍ مِنْ ذَلِكَ أَفْضَلُ فَقَالَ الْوَلايَةُ أَفْضَلُ لأَنَّهَا مِفْتَاحُهُنَّ وَالْوَالِي هُوَ الدَّلِيلُ عَلَيْهِنَّ قُلْتُ ثُمَّ الَّذِي يَلِي ذَلِكَ فِي الْفَضْلِ فَقَالَ الصَّلاةُ إِنَّ رَسُولَ اللهِ (صَلَّى اللهُ عَلَيْهِ وآلِه) قَالَ الصَّلاةُ عَمُودُ دِينِكُمْ قَالَ قُلْتُ ثُمَّ الَّذِي يَلِيهَا فِي الْفَضْلِ قَالَ الزَّكَاةُ لأَنَّهُ قَرَنَهَا بِهَا وَبَدَأَ بِالصَّلاةِ قَبْلَهَا وَقَالَ رَسُولُ اللهِ (صَلَّى اللهُ عَلَيْهِ وآلِه) الزَّكَاةُ تُذْهِبُ الذُّنُوبَ قُلْتُ وَالَّذِي يَلِيهَا فِي الْفَضْلِ قَالَ الْحَجُّ قَالَ اللهُ عَزَّ وَجَلَّ وَللهِ عَلَى النَّاسِ حِجُّ الْبَيْتِ مَنِ اسْتَطاعَ إِلَيْهِ سَبِيلاً وَمَنْ كَفَرَ فَإِنَّ اللهَ غَنِيٌّ عَنِ الْعالَمِينَ وَقَالَ رَسُولُ اللهِ (صَلَّى اللهُ عَلَيْهِ وآلِه) لَحَجَّةٌ مَقْبُولَةٌ خَيْرٌ مِنْ عِشْرِينَ صَلاةً نَافِلَةً وَمَنْ طَافَ بِهَذَا الْبَيْتِ طَوَافاً أَحْصَى فِيهِ أُسْبُوعَهُ وَأَحْسَنَ رَكْعَتَيْهِ غَفَرَ اللهُ لَهُ وَقَالَ فِي يَوْمِ عَرَفَةَ وَيَوْمِ الْمُزْدَلِفَةِ مَا قَالَ قُلْتُ فَمَا ذَا يَتْبَعُهُ قَالَ الصَّوْمُ قُلْتُ وَمَا بَالُ الصَّوْمِ صَارَ آخِرَ ذَلِكَ أَجْمَعَ قَالَ قَالَ رَسُولُ اللهِ (صَلَّى اللهُ عَلَيْهِ وآلِه) الصَّوْمُ جُنَّةٌ مِنَ النَّارِ قَالَ ثُمَّ قَالَ إِنَّ أَفْضَلَ الأَشْيَاءِ مَا إِذَا فَاتَكَ لَمْ تَكُنْ مِنْهُ تَوْبَةٌ دُونَ أَنْ تَرْجِعَ إِلَيْهِ فَتُؤَدِّيَهُ بِعَيْنِهِ إِنَّ الصَّلاةَ وَالزَّكَاةَ وَالْحَجَّ وَالْوَلايَةَ لَيْسَ يَقَعُ شَيْءٌ مَكَانَهَا دُونَ أَدَائِهَا وَإِنَّ الصَّوْمَ إِذَا فَاتَكَ أَوْ قَصَّرْتَ أَوْ سَافَرْتَ فِيهِ أَدَّيْتَ مَكَانَهُ أَيَّاماً غَيْرَهَا وَجَزَيْتَ ذَلِكَ الذَّنْبَ بِصَدَقَةٍ وَلا قَضَاءَ عَلَيْكَ وَلَيْسَ مِنْ تِلْكَ الأَرْبَعَةِ شَيْءٌ يُجْزِيكَ مَكَانَهُ غَيْرُهُ قَالَ ثُمَّ قَالَ ذِرْوَةُ الأَمْرِ وَسَنَامُهُ وَمِفْتَاحُهُ وَبَابُ الأَشْيَاءِ وَرِضَا الرَّحْمَنِ الطَّاعَةُ لِلإِمَامِ بَعْدَ مَعْرِفَتِهِ إِنَّ اللهَ عَزَّ وَجَلَّ يَقُولُ مَنْ يُطِعِ الرَّسُولَ فَقَدْ أَطاعَ اللهَ وَمَنْ تَوَلَّى فَما أَرْسَلْناكَ عَلَيْهِمْ حَفِيظاً أَمَا لَوْ أَنَّ رَجُلاً قَامَ لَيْلَهُ وَصَامَ نَهَارَهُ وَتَصَدَّقَ بِجَمِيعِ مَالِهِ وَحَجَّ جَمِيعَ دَهْرِهِ وَلَمْ يَعْرِفْ وَلايَةَ وَلِيِّ اللهِ فَيُوَالِيَهُ وَيَكُونَ جَمِيعُ أَعْمَالِهِ بِدَلالَتِهِ إِلَيْهِ مَا كَانَ لَهُ عَلَى

اللهِ جَلَّ وَعَزَّ حَقٌّ فِي ثَوَابِهِ وَلا كَانَ مِنْ أَهْلِ الإِيمَانِ ثُمَّ قَالَ أُولَئِكَ الْمُحْسِنُ مِنْهُمْ يُدْخِلُهُ اللهُ الْجَنَّةَ بِفَضْلِ رَحْمَتِهِ

Ali b. Ibrahim has narrated from his father and 'Abd Allāh b. al-Salt all of them from Hammad b. 'Isa from Hariz b. 'Abd Allāh from Zurara from abu Ja'far (عليه السلام) who has said the following: "Abu Ja'far (عليه السلام) has said, **'Islam is based on five issues. It is based on prayer, charity (al- Zakat), Hajj, Fasting and al-Wilāya**." Zurara has said, 'I then asked the Imam, "Which of these is more important than the others?"' The Imam said, 'Al-Wilāya is more important. It is the key to the others. The person who possesses Divine Authority is the guide to the other principles.' I then asked, 'Which is the next important?' The Imam said, 'Thereafter is prayer. The Messenger of Allāh has said, "Prayer is the pillar of your religion."' I then asked, 'Which is the next important among them?' The Imam said, 'Al-Zakat is the one thereafter. Allāh has mentioned it next to prayer but He has mentioned prayer first. The Messenger of Allāh has said, "Al-Zakat removes sins."' I then asked, **'Which one is important thereafter?'** The Imam said, **'Hajj is important thereafter**. Allāh, the Most Majestic, the Most Holy, has said, "**It is a duty of the people to Allāh to perform Hajj of the House if they are capable to do so. Whoever rejects it should know that Allāh does not need anyone in the world**." (3:97) **The messenger of Allāh has said, "Performing Hajj that is accepted is more virtuous than twenty Rak'at optional prayer**. Whoever walks around the House seven times and performs the two Rak'at prayers thereafter properly Allāh will grant him cover." He (The Messenger of Allāh) did say on the ninth of the month of Dil Hajj and on the tenth of the month of Dil Hajj in Muzdalifa (a place in Makka), what he wanted to say.' I then asked, 'Which one is important thereafter?' The Imam said, 'It is fasting.' "I then asked, 'Why is fasting the last of all in importance?' The Imam said, 'The Messenger of Allāh has said, "Fasting is a shield against the fire."' The narrator has said that the Imam said, 'The best of all things is that for which, if you miss, you do not find an alternative accept going back to achieve it. **Prayer, al-Wilāya and Hajj are not of matters replaceable with their own kind**. On the other hand if fasting is missed on a journey one has the choice to fast on other days as remedy, or compensate for the sin with expiation and no fasting is necessary as a remedy. In the cases of the other four issues there is no alternative for them.' The narrator has said that the Imam then said, 'The topmost, the peak of the issue, the key and the door to it and the pleasure of the Beneficent (Lord) is to obey the Imam properly after knowing him clearly. Allāh, the Most Majestic, the Most Holy, says, "Whoever obeys the Messenger he has obeyed Allāh and whoever turns away from such obedience then you should know that We have not sent you to guard them." (4:80) 'Without recognizing the Divine Authority of the Imam, the deputy of Allāh, no one has the right to receive any reward from Allāh, the Most Majestic, the Most Holy. This is true even though in his lifetime he may stand up in worship the whole night, fast during the day, give all his belongings in charity and perform Hajj every year. So also it is if he does not acknowledge the Divine Authority of his Imam with which all of one's deeds can take place with the guidance of the Imam. Without al-Wilāya, one is not considered of the people of belief.' Thereafter the Imam said, 'Allāh will admit, those of them who do good deeds into paradise through His extra mercy. (صحيح)[1]

2.

عَلِيُّ بْنُ إِبْرَاهِيمَ عَنْ أَبِيهِ وَمُحَمَّدُ بْنِ إِسْمَاعِيلَ عَنِ الْفَضْلِ بْنِ شَاذَانَ جَمِيعاً عَنِ ابْنِ أَبِي عُمَيْرٍ عَنْ عُمَرَ بْنِ أُذَيْنَةَ عَنْ زُرَارَةَ قَالَ كُنْتُ قَاعِداً إِلَى جَنْبِ أَبِي جَعْفَرٍ (عَلَيْهِ السَّلَام) وَهُوَ مُحْتَبٍ مُسْتَقْبِلُ الْكَعْبَةِ فَقَالَ أَمَا إِنَّ النَّظَرَ إِلَيْهَا عِبَادَةٌ فَجَاءَهُ رَجُلٌ مِنْ بَجِيلَةَ يُقَالُ لَهُ عَاصِمُ بْنُ عُمَرَ فَقَالَ لِأَبِي جَعْفَرٍ (عَلَيْهِ السَّلَام) إِنَّ كَعْبَ الْأَحْبَارِ كَانَ يَقُولُ إِنَّ الْكَعْبَةَ تَسْجُدُ لِبَيْتِ الْمَقْدِسِ فِي كُلِّ غَدَاةٍ فَقَالَ أَبُو جَعْفَرٍ (عَلَيْهِ السَّلَام) فَمَا تَقُولُ فِيمَا قَالَ كَعْبٌ فَقَالَ صَدَقَ الْقَوْلُ مَا قَالَ كَعْبٌ فَقَالَ أَبُو جَعْفَرٍ (عَلَيْهِ السَّلَام) كَذَبْتَ وَكَذَبَ كَعْبُ الْأَحْبَارِ مَعَكَ وَغَضِبَ قَالَ زُرَارَةُ مَا رَأَيْتُهُ اسْتَقْبَلَ أَحَداً بِقَوْلِ كَذَبْتَ غَيْرَهُ ثُمَّ قَالَ مَا خَلَقَ اللهُ عَزَّ وَجَلَّ بُقْعَةً فِي الْأَرْضِ أَحَبَّ إِلَيْهِ مِنْهَا ثُمَّ أَوْمَأَ بِيَدِهِ نَحْوَ الْكَعْبَةِ وَلَا أَكْرَمَ عَلَى اللهِ عَزَّ وَجَلَّ مِنْهَا لَهَا حَرَّمَ اللهُ الْأَشْهُرَ الْحُرُمَ فِي كِتَابِهِ

---

[1] *Al-Kāfi, v2, ch13, h5*

يَوْمَ خَلَقَ السَّمَاوَاتِ وَالأَرْضَ ثَلاثَةٌ مُتَوَالِيَةٌ لِلْحَجِّ شَوَّالٌ وَذُو الْقَعْدَةِ وَذُو الْحِجَّةِ وَشَهْرٌ مُفْرَدٌ لِلْعُمْرَةِ وَهُوَ رَجَبٌ

Ali b. Ibrahim has narrated from his father and Muḥammad b. Isma'il from af-Fadf b. Shadhan all from b. abu 'Umayr from 'Umar b. 'Udhaynah from Zurāra who has said the following: "I, once, was sitting near abu Ja'far, (عليه السلام), while he was sitting in an Ihtiba' position (holding one's knees against one's belly with one's arms or a piece of cloth) facing al-Ka'bah. He (the Imam) said, 'Looking at al-Ka'bah is an act of worship.' At this time a man from Bajilah people who was called 'Asem b. 'Umar came to abu Ja'far, (عليه السلام), and said, 'Ka'b al-Ahbar would say, "Al-Ka'bah every morning prostrates before al-Bayt al-Maqdis (the holy house in Jerusalem)."' Abu Ja'far, (عليه السلام), then asked, 'What do you say about what Ka'b has said?' He (the man) replied, 'He has spoken the truth, the word is what Ka'b has said.' Abu Ja'far, (عليه السلام), then said, 'You have spoken lies. Ka'b al-Ahbar has spoken lies along with you.' He (the Imam) became angry. Zurāra has said, 'I never found him (the Imam) facing someone say, "You speak lies" except him (this man).' He (the Imam) then said, 'Allāh, the Most Majestic, the Most Glorious, has not created any site on earth more beloved to Him than al-Ka'bah.' He (the Imam) then pointed with his hand to al-Ka'bah and said, 'There is not anything more graceful before Allāh, the Most Majestic, the Most Glorious, than al-Ka'bah. For this (al-Ka'bah) Allāh made the sacred months, in His book, on the day He created the skies and earth. Of these months, three are consecutive: the months of Shawwal, Dhu al-Qa'dah and Dhu al-Hajjah, and one is alone for performing 'Umrah (and it is) the month of Rajab.'"

(حسن كالصحيح)[2]

3.

---

[2] *Al-Kāfi, v4, ch23, h1*

وَبِهَذَا الْإِسْنَادِ عَنِ ابْنِ أَبِي عُمَيْرٍ عَنْ مُعَاوِيَةَ بْنِ عَمَّارٍ عَنْ أَبِي عَبْدِ اللهِ (عَلَيْهِ السَّلَام) قَالَ إِنَّ للهِ تَبَارَكَ وَتَعَالَى حَوْلَ الْكَعْبَةِ عِشْرِينَ وَمِائَةَ رَحْمَةٍ مِنْهَا سِتُّونَ لِلطَّائِفِينَ وَأَرْبَعُونَ لِلْمُصَلِّينَ وَعِشْرُونَ لِلنَّاظِرِينَ

It is narrated from him (narrator of previous Hadīth) from b. abu 'Umayr from Mu'awiyah b. 'Ammar who has said the following: "Abu 'Abd Allāh, (عليه السلام), has said that Allāh, the most Blessed, the most High, has one hundred twenty blessings around al-Ka'bah of which sixty are for those who perform Tawaf, forty for those who perform salat (prayer) and twenty for those who look at al-Ka'bah.'" (حسن كالصحيح)[3]

4.

عَلِيُّ بْنُ إِبْرَاهِيمَ عَنْ أَبِيهِ عَنِ ابْنِ أَبِي عُمَيْرٍ عَنْ أَبِي عَبْدِ اللهِ الْخَزَّازِ عَنْ أَبِي عَبْدِ اللهِ (عَلَيْهِ السَّلَام) قَالَ إِنَّ لِلْكَعْبَةِ لَلَحْظَةً فِي كُلِّ يَوْمٍ يُغْفَرُ لِمَنْ طَافَ بِهَا أَوْ حَنَّ قَلْبُهُ إِلَيْهَا أَوْ حَبَسَهُ عَنْهَا عُذْرٌ

Ali b. Ibrahim has narrated from his father from b. abu 'Umayr from abu 'Abd Allāh al-Khazzaz who has said the following: "Abu 'Abd Allāh, (عليه السلام), has said that for al-Ka'bah, there is a moment every day in which forgiveness is granted to those who perform Tawaf around it, or whose hearts incline toward it or are prevented from visiting it for a good reason." (مجهول)[4]

5.

عَلِيُّ بْنُ إِبْرَاهِيمَ عَنْ أَبِيهِ عَنْ حَمَّادِ بْنِ عِيسَى عَنْ حَرِيزٍ عَنْ أَبِي عَبْدِ اللهِ (عَلَيْهِ السَّلَام) قَالَ النَّظَرُ إِلَى الْكَعْبَةِ عِبَادَةٌ وَالنَّظَرُ إِلَى الْوَالِدَيْنِ عِبَادَةٌ وَالنَّظَرُ إِلَى الْإِمَامِ عِبَادَةٌ وَقَالَ مَنْ نَظَرَ إِلَى الْكَعْبَةِ كُتِبَتْ لَهُ حَسَنَةٌ وَمُحِيَتْ عَنْهُ عَشْرُ سَيِّئَاتٍ

---

[3] *Al-Kāfi, v4, ch23, h2*

[4] *Al-Kāfi, v4, ch23, h3*

Ali b. Ibrahim has narrated from his father from Hammad b. 'Isa from Hariz who has said the following: "Abu 'Abd Allāh, (عليه السلام), has said that looking at al-Ka'bah is an act of worship; looking at parents is an act of worship; and looking at the Imam is an act of worship. For one's looking at al- Ka'bah, one good deed is written for him and ten of his bad deeds are deleted." (حسن)[5]

6.

مُحَمَّدُ بْنُ يَحْيَى عَنْ أَحْمَدَ بْنِ مُحَمَّدٍ عَنِ ابْنِ أَبِي عُمَيْرٍ عَنْ عَلِيِّ بْنِ عَبْدِ الْعَزِيزِ عَنْ أَبِي عَبْدِ اللهِ (عَلَيْهِ السَّلَامِ) قَالَ مَنْ نَظَرَ إِلَى الْكَعْبَةِ بِمَعْرِفَةٍ فَعَرَفَ مِنْ حَقِّنَا وَحُرْمَتِنَا مِثْلَ الَّذِي عَرَفَ مِنْ حَقِّهَا وَحُرْمَتِهَا غَفَرَ اللهُ لَهُ ذُنُوبَهُ وَكَفَاهُ هَمَّ الدُّنْيَا وَالْآخِرَةِ

Muhammad b. Yahya has narrated from Ahmad b. Muḥammad from b. abu 'Umayr from 'Alī b. 'Abd al-'Aziz who has said the following: "Abu 'Abd Allāh, (عليه السلام), has said that Allāh forgives one's sins and suffices him in this world and in the next life, if he looks at al-Ka'bah with proper understanding and then recognizes our rights and sanctity just as his recognition of the rights and sanctity of al-Ka'bah." (مجهول)[6]

7.

عَلِيُّ بْنُ إِبْرَاهِيمَ عَنْ أَبِيهِ عَنْ عَمْرِو بْنِ عُثْمَانَ الْخَزَّازِ عَنْ عَلِيِّ بْنِ عَبْدِ اللهِ الْبَجَلِيِّ عَنْ خَالِدٍ الْقَلَانِسِيِّ عَنْ أَبِي عَبْدِ اللهِ (عَلَيْهِ السَّلَامِ) قَالَ قَالَ عَلِيُّ بْنُ الْحُسَيْنِ (عَلَيْهِمَا السَّلَامِ) حُجُّوا وَاعْتَمِرُوا تَصِحَّ أَبْدَانُكُمْ وَتَتَّسِعْ أَرْزَاقُكُمْ وَتُكْفَوْنَ مَئُونَاتِ عِيَالِكُمْ وَقَالَ الْحَاجُّ مَغْفُورٌ لَهُ وَمَوْجُوبٌ لَهُ الْجَنَّةُ وَمُسْتَأْنَفٌ لَهُ الْعَمَلُ وَمَحْفُوظٌ فِي أَهْلِهِ وَمَالِهِ

---

[5] *Al-Kafi, v4, ch23, h5*

[6] *Al-Kāfi, v4, ch23, h6*

Ali b. Ibrahim has narrated from his father from 'Amr b. ' Uthman af-Khazzaz from Afi b. ' Abd Allāh al-Bajaliy, from Khalid al- Qalanisiy who has said the following: "Abu 'Abd Allāh, (عليه السلام), has said that 'Alī b. Al-Husayn, (عليه السلام), has said, 'Perform 'Umrah and Hajj, your bodies will become healthy, your sustenance increase and you will have sufficient for the expenses of your families.' He (the Imam) said, 'One who performs Hajj is forgiven, paradise is necessary, he resumes his deeds and he is safe and sound as well as his family and properties.'" (مجهول)[7]

8.

عَلِيٌّ عَنْ أَبِيهِ عَنِ ابْنِ أَبِي عُمَيْرٍ عَنْ مُعَاوِيَةَ بْنِ عَمَّارٍ قَالَ قَالَ أَبُو عَبْدِ اللهِ (عَلَيْهِ السَّلَام) الْحُجَّاجُ يَصْدُرُونَ عَلَى ثَلاثَةِ أَصْنَافٍ صِنْفٌ يُعْتَقُ مِنَ النَّارِ وَصِنْفٌ يَخْرُجُ مِنْ ذُنُوبِهِ كَهَيْئَةِ يَوْمَ وَلَدَتْهُ أُمُّهُ وَصِنْفٌ يُحْفَظُ فِي أَهْلِهِ وَمَالِهِ فَذَاكَ أَدْنَى مَا يَرْجِعُ بِهِ الْحَاجُّ

Ali b. Ibrahim has narrated from his father from b. abu 'Umayr from Mu'awiyah b. 'Ammar who has said the following: "Abu 'Abd Allāh, (عليه السلام), has said, 'Pilgrims (al-Hujjaj) are of three categories. Those in one group are set free from hellfire, the other group are made free of sins like their freedom from sin on the day their mother gave birth to them, and the third group consists of those who receive protection for their families and properties and this is the minimum benefit with which pilgrims return home.'" (حسن)[8]

9.

أَبُو عَلِيٍّ الأَشْعَرِيُّ عَنْ مُحَمَّدِ بْنِ عَبْدِ الْجَبَّارِ عَنْ صَفْوَانَ بْنِ يَحْيَى عَنْ عَبْدِ اللهِ بْنِ يَحْيَى الْكَاهِلِيِّ قَالَ سَمِعْتُ أَبَا عَبْدِ اللهِ (عَلَيْهِ السَّلَام) يَقُولُ وَيَذْكُرُ الْحَجَّ فَقَالَ قَالَ رَسُولُ اللهِ (صلّى اللهُ عَلَيْهِ وَآلِهِ) هُوَ أَحَدُ الْجِهَادَيْنِ هُوَ جِهَادُ الضُّعَفَاءِ وَنَحْنُ الضُّعَفَاءُ أَمَا إِنَّهُ لَيْسَ شَيْءٌ أَفْضَلَ مِنَ الْحَجِّ إِلاَّ الصَّلاةُ وَفِي الْحَجِّ لَهَاهُنَا

[7] *Al-Kāfi, v4, ch28, h1*

[8] *Al-Kāfi, v4, ch28, h6*

صَلاةٌ وَلَيْسَ فِي الصَّلاةِ قِبَلَكُمْ حَجٌّ لا تَدَعِ الْحَجَّ وَأَنْتَ تَقْدِرُ عَلَيْهِ أَ مَا تَرَى أَنَّهُ يَشْعَثُ رَأْسُكَ وَيَقْشَفُ فِيهِ جِلْدُكَ وَيَمْتَنِعُ فِيهِ مِنَ النَّظَرِ إِلَى النِّسَاءِ وَإِنَّا نَحْنُ لَهَاهُنَا وَنَحْنُ قَرِيبٌ وَلَنَا مِيَاهٌ مُتَّصِلَةٌ مَا نَبْلُغُ الْحَجَّ حَتَّى يَشُقَّ عَلَيْنَا فَكَيْفَ أَنْتُمْ فِي بُعْدِ الْبِلادِ وَمَا مِنْ مَلِكٍ وَلا سُوقَةٍ يَصِلُ إِلَى الْحَجِّ إِلاَّ بِمَشَقَّةٍ فِي تَغْيِيرِ مَطْعَمٍ أَوْ مَشْرَبٍ أَوْ رِيحٍ أَوْ شَمْسٍ لا يَسْتَطِيعُ رَدَّهَا وَذَلِكَ قَوْلُهُ عَزَّ وَجَلَّ وَتَحْمِلُ أَثْقالَكُمْ إِلى بَلَدٍ لَمْ تَكُونُوا بالِغِيهِ إِلاَّ بِشِقِّ الْأَنْفُسِ إِنَّ رَبَّكُمْ لَرَؤُفٌ رَحِيمٌ

Abu ʿAlī al-Ash'ariy has narrated from Muḥammad b. ʿ Abd al-Jabbar from Safwan b. Yahya from ʿ Abd Allāh b. Yahya al-Kahiliy who has said the following: "I once heard abu 'Abd Allāh, (عليه السلام), speaking of Hajj, say, 'The Messenger of Allāh, (صلى الله عليه وآله وسلم), has said, "It (Hajj) is one of the two kinds of Jihad (striving for a cause). This is the Jihad for the weak ones and we are the weak ones. However, no other thing is better than Hajj except salat (prayer). In Hajj nowadays is salat (prayer) and there was no salat (prayer) in Hajj before you. Do not ignore Hajj when you are able to perform it. Consider how your hairs become dusty during performing Hajj and your skin rough and you abstain from looking at women. We are here and near. We have water but still arrive (in Makkah) for Hajj with a great deal of difficulty. The case of those who live far away from Makkah is much more difficult. All kings and subjects arrive (in Makkah) for Hajj after facing a great deal of difficulties, such as changes in their diet, water, air and sun, which they cannot avoid. This is in the words of Allāh, the Most Majestic, the Most Glorious, 'They carry your loads to a town that you could only do so with causing a great deal of hardships to souls. Your Lord is compassionate and kind.''' (16:7) (حسن)[9]

10.

مُحَمَّدُ بْنُ إِسْمَاعِيلَ عَنِ الْفَضْلِ بْنِ شَاذَانَ عَنْ حَمَّادِ بْنِ عِيسَى عَنْ رِبْعِيِّ بْنِ عَبْدِ اللهِ عَنِ الْفُضَيْلِ بْنِ يَسَارٍ قَالَ سَمِعْتُ أَبَا جَعْفَرٍ (عَلَيْهِ السَّلَامِ) يَقُولُ قَالَ رَسُولُ اللهِ (صَلَّى اللهُ عَلَيْهِ وَآلِهِ) لا يُحَالِفُ الْفَقْرُ وَالْحُمَّى مُدْمِنَ الْحَجِّ وَالْعُمْرَةِ

[9] *Al-Kafi, v4, ch28, h7*

Muhammad b. Isma'il has narrated from al-Fadl b. Shadhan from Hammad b. 'Isa from Rib'iy b. 'Abd Allāh from al-Fudayl b. Yasar who has said the following: "I heard abu Ja'far, (عليه السلام), say, 'The Messenger of Allāh, (صلى الله عليه وآله وسلم), has said, "Chronic poverty and fever cannot come with al-Hajj and al-'Umrah. (مجهول كالصحيح)[10]

11.

مُحَمَّدُ بْنُ يَحْيَى عَنْ عَلِيِّ بْنِ إِسْمَاعِيلَ عَنْ عَلِيِّ بْنِ الْحَكَمِ عَنْ جَعْفَرِ بْنِ عِمْرَانَ عَنْ أَبِي بَصِيرٍ عَنْ أَبِي عَبْدِ اللهِ (عَلَيْهِ السَّلاَم) قَالَ الْحَجُّ وَالْعُمْرَةُ سُوقَانِ مِنْ أَسْوَاقِ الآخِرَةِ اللاَّزِمُ لَهُمَا فِي ضَمَانِ اللهِ إِنْ أَبْقَاهُ أَدَّاهُ إِلَى عِيَالِهِ وَإِنْ أَمَاتَهُ أَدْخَلَهُ الْجَنَّةَ

Muhammad b. Yahya has narrated from 'Alī b. Isma'il from 'Alī b. al-Hakam from Ja'far b. 'Imran from abu Basir who has said the following: "Abu 'Abd Allāh, (عليه السلام), has said that al-Hajj and al-'Umrah are two market places (that deal with the merchandise) of the next life. Those who attach themselves to these two are part of the undertaking of Allāh. He returns them to their families if He decides to keep them living, or admits them in paradise if He decides to cause them to die." (مجهول)[11]

12.

عَلِيُّ بْنُ إِبْرَاهِيمَ عَنْ أَبِيهِ عَنِ ابْنِ فَضَّالٍ عَنِ الرِّضَا (عَلَيْهِ السَّلاَم) قَالَ سَمِعْتُهُ يَقُولُ مَا وَقَفَ أَحَدٌ فِي تِلْكَ الْجِبَالِ إِلاَّ اسْتُجِيبَ لَهُ فَأَمَّا الْمُؤْمِنُونَ فَيُسْتَجَابُ لَهُمْ فِي آخِرَتِهِمْ وَأَمَّا الْكُفَّارُ فَيُسْتَجَابُ لَهُمْ فِي دُنْيَاهُمْ

Ali b. Ibrahim has narrated from his father from b. Faddal who has said the following: "I once heard al-Rida, (عليه السلام), say, 'No one has stood in those hills without their

---

[10] *Al-Kāfi, v4, ch28, h8*

[11] *Al-Kāfi, v4, ch28, h13*

prayers answered. The believing people's prayers are answered in the matters of their next life, and the unbeliever's prayers are answered in their worldly matters.' (حسن أو موثق)[12]

13.

عَلِيُّ بْنُ إِبْرَاهِيمَ عَنْ أَبِيهِ عَنِ ابْنِ أَبِي عُمَيْرٍ عَنْ أَبِي أَيُّوبَ عَنْ أَبِي حَمْزَةَ الثُّمَالِيِّ قَالَ قَالَ رَجُلٌ لِعَلِيِّ بْنِ الْحُسَيْنِ (عَلَيْهِما السَّلاَم) تَرَكْتَ الْجِهَادَ وَخُشُونَتَهُ وَلَزِمْتَ الْحَجَّ وَلِينَهُ قَالَ وَكَانَ مُتَّكِئاً فَجَلَسَ وَقَالَ وَيْحَكَ أَ مَا بَلَغَكَ مَا قَالَ رَسُولُ اللهِ (صلّى اللهُ عَلَيْهِ وَآلِه) فِي حَجَّةِ الْوَدَاعِ إِنَّهُ لَمَّا وَقَفَ بِعَرَفَةَ وَهَمَّتِ الشَّمْسُ أَنْ تَغِيبَ قَالَ رَسُولُ اللهِ (صلّى اللهُ عَلَيْهِ وَآلِه) يَا بِلاَلُ قُلْ لِلنَّاسِ فَلْيُنْصِتُوا فَلَمَّا نَصَتُوا قَالَ رَسُولُ اللهِ (صلّى اللهُ عَلَيْهِ وَآلِه) إِنَّ رَبَّكُمْ تَطَوَّلَ عَلَيْكُمْ فِي هَذَا الْيَوْمِ فَغَفَرَ لِمُحْسِنِكُمْ وَشَفَّعَ مُحْسِنَكُمْ فِي مُسِيئِكُمْ فَأَفِيضُوا مَغْفُوراً لَكُمْ قَالَ وَزَادَ غَيْرُ الثُّمَالِيِّ أَنَّهُ قَالَ إِلاَّ أَهْلَ التَّبِعَاتِ فَإِنَّ اللهَ عَدْلٌ يَأْخُذُ لِلضَّعِيفِ مِنَ الْقَوِيِّ فَلَمَّا كَانَتْ لَيْلَةُ جَمْعٍ لَمْ يَزَلْ يُنَاجِي رَبَّهُ وَيَسْأَلُهُ لأَهْلِ التَّبِعَاتِ فَلَمَّا وَقَفَ بِجَمْعٍ قَالَ لِبِلاَلٍ قُلْ لِلنَّاسِ فَلْيُنْصِتُوا فَلَمَّا نَصَتُوا قَالَ إِنَّ رَبَّكُمْ تَطَوَّلَ عَلَيْكُمْ فِي هَذَا الْيَوْمِ فَغَفَرَ لِمُحْسِنِكُمْ وَشَفَّعَ مُحْسِنَكُمْ فِي مُسِيئِكُمْ فَأَفِيضُوا مَغْفُوراً لَكُمْ وَضَمِنَ لأَهْلِ التَّبِعَاتِ مِنْ عِنْدِهِ الرِّضَا

Ali b. Ibrahim has narrated from his father from b. abu 'Umayr from abu Ayyub from abu Hamzah al-Thumafiy who has said the following: "A man once said to 'Alī b. al-Husayn, (عليه السلام), 'You have given up Jihad because it is harsh, but you have attached yourself to Hajj because it is comfortable.' He (the Imam) who was leaning sat up straight and said, 'Fie upon you. Have you not heard what the Messenger of Allāh, (صلى الله عليه وآله وسلم), said during his farewell pilgrimage during his stay in 'Arafat, and it was about sunset. The Messenger of Allāh said, 'O Bilal, ask people to remain silent.' When people became silent the Messenger of Allāh said, 'Your Lord has granted you favors on this day. He has granted forgiveness to the individuals of good deeds, and has made the ones of good deed to intercede for the ones of evil deeds. You can leave now with your sins forgiven.' Narrators other than abu Hamzah al-Thumaliy have mentioned that the Imam additionally said, 'Except those who are of

[12] *Al-Kāfi, v4, ch28, h19*

individuals of al-Tabi'at (acts that require investigation).' Allāh is just. He brings to justice the stronger ones who wrong the weaker ones. On the night of al-Jam' he continued quietly speaking to his Lord and asked Him for forgiveness for the individuals of al-Tabi'at. When he stayed in Jam' he said to Bilal, 'You should ask people to remain silent.' When people became silent he (the Messenger of Allāh) said, 'Your Lord has granted you favors on this day. He has forgiven the individuals of good deeds among you. He has made the individuals of good deeds among you to intercede on behalf of the individuals of evil deeds. You now may leave with your sins forgiven and He has made an undertaking in favor of the individuals of al- Tabi'at (people liable for the rights of others) to be happy with them.' (حسن)[13]

14.

عَلِيٌّ عَنْ أَبِيهِ وَمُحَمَّدُ بْنُ إِسْمَاعِيلَ عَنِ الْفَضْلِ بْنِ شَاذَانَ عَنِ ابْنِ أَبِي عُمَيْرٍ عَنْ مُعَاوِيَةَ بْنِ عَمَّارٍ قَالَ لَمَّا أَفَاضَ رَسُولُ اللهِ (صلَّى اللهُ عَلَيْهِ وَآلِه) تَلَقَّاهُ أَعْرَابِيٌّ بِالأَبْطَح فَقَالَ يَا رَسُولَ اللهِ إِنِّي خَرَجْتُ أُرِيدُ الْحَجَّ فَعَاقَنِي وَأَنَا رَجُلٌ مَيِّلٌ يَعْنِي كَثِيرَ الْمَالِ فَمُرْنِي أَصْنَعُ فِي مَالِي مَا أَبْلُغُ بِهِ مَا يَبْلُغُ بِهِ الْحَاجُّ قَالَ فَالْتَفَتَ رَسُولُ اللهِ (صلَّى اللهُ عَلَيْهِ وَآلِه) إِلَى أَبِي قُبَيْسٍ فَقَالَ لَوْ أَنَّ أَبَا قُبَيْسٍ لَكَ زِنَتَهُ ذَهَبَةٌ حَمْرَاءُ أَنْفَقْتَهُ فِي سَبِيلِ اللهِ مَا بَلَغْتَ مَا بَلَغَ الْحَاجُّ

Ali has narrated from his father and Muḥammad b. Isma'il from al-Fadl b. Shadhan from b. abu 'Umayr from Mu'awiyah b. 'Ammar who has said the following: "He (the Imam) has said, that when the Messenger of Allāh, (صلى الله عليه وآله وسلم), left an Arab came to him in al- Abtah and said, 'O Messenger of Allāh, I wanted to perform Hajj but something prevented me. I am a wealthy person. Command me to do something with my wealth that benefits me like the benefit of performing Hajj. The Messenger of Allāh then looked to abu Qubays hill and said, "Even if you spend an amount of

---

[13] *Al-Kafi, v4, ch28, h24*

gold equal to the weight of abu Qubays hill for the cause of Allāh, you will not gain the benefit of Hajj.'" (حسن كالصحيح)[14]

15.

مُحَمَّدُ بْنُ يَحْيَى عَنْ أَحْمَدَ بْنِ مُحَمَّدِ بْنِ عِيسَى عَنْ مُحَمَّدِ بْنِ إِسْمَاعِيلَ عَنْ أَبِي إِسْمَاعِيلَ السَّرَّاجِ عَنْ هَارُونَ بْنِ خَارِجَةَ قَالَ سَمِعْتُ أَبَا عَبْدِ اللهِ (عَلَيْهِ السَّلامُ) يَقُولُ مَنْ دُفِنَ فِي الْحَرَمِ أَمِنَ مِنَ الْفَزَعِ الْأَكْبَرِ فَقُلْتُ لَهُ مِنْ بَرِّ النَّاسِ وَفَاجِرِهِمْ قَالَ مِنْ بَرِّ النَّاسِ وَفَاجِرِهِمْ

Muhammad b. Yahya has narrated from Ahmad b. Muḥammad b. 'Isa from Muḥammad b. Isma'il from abu Isma'il al-Sarraj from Harun b. Kharijah who has said the following: "I once heard abu 'Abd Allāh, (عليه السلام), say, 'One who is buried in al-Haram is immune from the great terrifying event.' I (the narrator) asked him, 'Does it apply to both people of good and evil deeds?' He (the Imam) replied, 'Yes, it applies to both kinds of people.' (صحيح)[15]

16.

عَلِيُّ بْنُ إِبْرَاهِيمَ عَنْ أَبِيهِ عَنِ ابْنِ أَبِي عُمَيْرٍ عَنْ بَعْضِ أَصْحَابِهِ عَنْ عُمَرَ بْنِ يَزِيدَ قَالَ سَمِعْتُ أَبَا عَبْدِ اللهِ (عَلَيْهِ السَّلامُ) يَقُولُ حَجَّةٌ أَفْضَلُ مِنْ عِتْقِ سَبْعِينَ رَقَبَةً فَقُلْتُ مَا يَعْدِلُ الْحَجَّ شَيْءٌ قَالَ مَا يَعْدِلُهُ شَيْءٌ وَلَدِرْهَمٌ وَاحِدٌ فِي الْحَجِّ أَفْضَلُ مِنْ أَلْفَيْ أَلْفِ دِرْهَمٍ فِيمَا سِوَاهُ مِنْ سَبِيلِ اللهِ ثُمَّ قَالَ لَهُ خَرَجْتُ عَلَى نَيِّفٍ وَسَبْعِينَ بَعِيراً وَبِضْعَ عَشْرَةَ دَابَّةً وَلَقَدِ اشْتَرَيْتُ سُوداً أُكَثِّرُ بِهَا الْعَدَدَ وَلَقَدْ آذَانِي أَكْلُ الْخَلِّ وَالزَّيْتِ حَتَّى إِنَّ حَمِيدَةَ أَمَرَتْ بِدَجَاجَةٍ فَشُوِيَتْ فَرَجَعَتْ إِلَيَّ نَفْسِي

Ali b. Ibrahim has narrated from his father from b. abu 'Umayr from certain individuals of his people from 'Umar b. Yazid who has said the following: "I heard

---

[14] *Al-Kāfi, v4, ch28, h25*

[15] *Al-Kāfi, v4, ch28, h26*

abu 'Abd Allāh, (عليه السلام), say, 'Al-Hajj is better than setting free of seventy slaves/ I then asked, 'Is there anything equal to al-Hajj?' He (the Imam) replied, 'No other thing is equal to al- Hajj. Spending one dirham for al-Hajj is better than spending two million dirhams for the cause of Allāh, which is other than al-Hajj. He (the Imam) then said, 'I left for al-Hajj and there were seventy camels and ten or so horses. I had purchased slaves to increase the number. Eating vinegar with oil had made me upset. Hamidah had ordered to roast a chicken that made me feel better."' (حسن)[16]

17.

عَلِيٌّ عَنْ أَبِيهِ عَنِ ابْنِ أَبِي عُمَيْرٍ عَنْ حُسَيْنٍ الْأَحْمَسِيِّ عَنْ أَبِي بَصِيرٍ قَالَ قَالَ أَبُو عَبْدِ اللهِ (عَلَيْهِ السَّلَامُ) حَجَّةٌ خَيْرٌ مِنْ بَيْتٍ مَمْلُوءٍ ذَهَباً يُتَصَدَّقُ بِهِ حَتَّى يَفْنَى

Ali b. Ibrahim has narrated from his father from b. abu 'Umayr from Husayn al-Ahmasiy from abu Basir who has said the following: "Abu 'Abd Allāh, (عليه السلام), has said, 'One Hajj is better than spending a whole house full of gold in charity until it is finished."' (حسن)[17]

18.

عَلِيٌّ عَنْ أَبِيهِ عَنِ ابْنِ أَبِي عُمَيْرٍ عَنْ رِبْعِيِّ بْنِ عَبْدِ اللهِ عَنِ الْفُضَيْلِ قَالَ سَمِعْتُ أَبَا جَعْفَرٍ (عَلَيْهِ السَّلَامُ) يَقُولُ لَا وَرَبِّ هَذِهِ الْبَنِيَّةِ لَا يُخَالِفُ مُدْمِنَ الْحَجِّ بِهَذَا الْبَيْتِ حُمَّى وَلَا فَقْرٌ أَبَداً

Ali b. Ibrahim has narrated from his father from b. abu 'Umayr from Rib'iy b. 'Abd Allāh from al-Fudayl who has said the following: "I heard abu Ja'far, (عليه السلام), say, 'I

---

[16] *Al-Kāfi, v4, ch28, h31*

[17] *Al-Kāfi, v4, ch28, h32*

swear by the Lord of this House that one constantly visiting this House does not suffer from fever and poverty.''' (حسن)[18]

19.

عِدَّةٌ مِنْ أَصْحَابِنَا عَنْ سَهْلِ بْنِ زِيَادٍ وَأَحْمَدَ بْنِ مُحَمَّدٍ جَمِيعاً عَنْ أَحْمَدَ بْنِ مُحَمَّدِ بْنِ أَبِي نَصْرٍ عَنْ مُحَمَّدِ بْنِ عَبْدِ اللهِ قَالَ قُلْتُ لِلرِّضَا (عَلَيْهِ السَّلَام) جُعِلْتُ فِدَاكَ إِنَّ أَبِي حَدَّثَنِي عَنْ آبَائِكَ (عَلَيْهِم السَّلَام) أَنَّهُ قِيلَ لِبَعْضِهِمْ إِنَّ فِي بِلَادِنَا مَوْضِعَ رِبَاطٍ يُقَالُ لَهُ قَزْوِينُ وَعَدُوّاً يُقَالُ لَهُ الدَّيْلَمُ فَهَلْ مِنْ جِهَادٍ أَوْ هَلْ مِنْ رِبَاطٍ فَقَالَ عَلَيْكُمْ بِهَذَا الْبَيْتِ فَحُجُّوهُ ثُمَّ قَالَ فَأَعَادَ عَلَيْهِ الْحَدِيثَ ثَلَاثَ مَرَّاتٍ كُلَّ ذَلِكَ يَقُولُ عَلَيْكُمْ بِهَذَا الْبَيْتِ فَحُجُّوهُ ثُمَّ قَالَ فِي الثَّالِثَةِ أَ مَا يَرْضَى أَحَدُكُمْ أَنْ يَكُونَ فِي بَيْتِهِ يُنْفِقُ عَلَى عِيَالِهِ يَنْتَظِرُ أَمْرَنَا فَإِنْ أَدْرَكَهُ كَانَ كَمَنْ شَهِدَ مَعَ رَسُولِ اللهِ (صَلَّى اللهُ عَلَيْهِ وَآلِهِ) بَدْراً وَإِنْ لَمْ يُدْرِكْهُ كَانَ كَمَنْ كَانَ مَعَ قَائِمِنَا فِي فُسْطَاطِهِ هَكَذَا وَهَكَذَا وَجَمَعَ بَيْنَ سَبَّابَتَيْهِ فَقَالَ أَبُو الْحَسَنِ (عَلَيْهِ السَّلَام) صَدَقَ هُوَ عَلَى مَا ذَكَرَ

A number of our people have narrated from Sahl b. Ziyad and Ahmad b. Muḥammad all from Ahmad b. Muḥammad b. abu Nasr from Muḥammad b. 'Abd Allāh who has said the following: "I once said to al-Rida, (عليه السلام), 'I pray to Allāh to keep my soul in service for your cause. My father has narrated to me from your ancestors, (عليه السلام), that it was said to one of them, 'In our country there is a station for travelers called Qazvin and enemies called al-Daylam. Is it obligatory to fight and arm (ourselves)?' He (the Imam) replied, 'You must not ignore this House and must not miss performing Hajj.' He (the narrator) has said that the question was repeated three times. Each time he (the Imam) said, 'You must not ignore this House and must not miss performing Hajj.' After the last time he (the Imam) said, 'Why should one of you not love to spend on his family at home waiting for the rise of one from us with Divine Authority? If he finds him, it is as if he has joined the Messenger of Allāh, (صلى الله عليه وآله وسلم), in the battle of Badr. If he does not find, him it will be as if he is standing in the tent of al-Qa'im from us like this and this.' He placed his two fingers

---

[18] *Al-Kafi, v4, ch28, h33*

side by side. Abu al- Hassan, (عليه السلام), then said, 'He has spoken the truth in what he has narrated.'" (مجهول)[19]

20.

ابْنُ أَبِي عُمَيْرٍ عَنْ هِشَامِ بْنِ الْحَكَمِ عَنْ أَبِي عَبْدِ اللهِ (عَلَيْهِ السَّلامُ) قَالَ مَا مِنْ سَفَرٍ أَبْلَغَ فِي لَحْمٍ وَلا دَمٍ وَلا جِلْدٍ وَلا شَعْرٍ مِنْ سَفَرِ مَكَّةَ وَمَا أَحَدٌ يَبْلُغُهُ حَتَّى تَنَالَهُ الْمَشَقَّةُ

b. abu 'Umayr has narrated from Hisham b. al-Hakam who has said the following: "Abu 'Abd Allāh, (عليه السلام), has said that no other journey affects one's flesh, blood, skin and hair more than the journey to Makkah. No one reaches it (the journey) without facing hardships. (حسن كالصحيح)[20]

21.

عَلِيُّ بْنُ إِبْرَاهِيمَ عَنْ أَبِيهِ عَنِ ابْنِ أَبِي عُمَيْرٍ عَنِ ابْنِ سِنَانٍ عَنْ أَبِي عَبْدِ اللهِ (عَلَيْهِ السَّلامُ) قَالَ مَنْ مَاتَ فِي طَرِيقِ مَكَّةَ ذَاهِباً أَوْ جَائِياً أَمِنَ مِنَ الْفَزَعِ الأَكْبَرِ يَوْمَ الْقِيَامَةِ

Ali b. Ibrahim has narrated from his father from b. abu ' Umayr from b. Sinan who has said the following: "Abu 'Abd Allāh, (عليه السلام), has said that if one dies on the way to or from Makkah, he receives immunity against the terror of the Day of Judgment." (حسن)[21]

22.

---

[19] *Al-Kāfi, v4, ch28, h34*

[20] *Al-Kāfi, v4, ch28, h41*

[21] *Al-Kāfi, v4, ch28, h45*

أَحْمَدُ بْنُ مُحَمَّدٍ عَنِ الْحَسَنِ بْنِ عَلِيٍّ عَنْ يُونُسَ بْنِ يَعْقُوبَ عَنْ عُمَرَ بْنِ يَزِيدَ عَنْ أَبِي عَبْدِ اللَّهِ (عَلَيْهِ السَّلَام) قَالَ حَجَّ رَسُولُ اللَّهِ (صلَّى اللَّهُ عَلَيْهِ وَآلِهِ) عِشْرِينَ حَجَّةً

Ahmad b. Muḥammad has narrated from al-Hassan b. ʿAlī from Yunus b. Ya'qub from 'Umar b. Yazid who has said the following: "Abu 'Abd Allāh, (عليه السلام), has said that the Messenger of Allāh, (صلى الله عليه وآله وسلم), performed Hajj a total of twenty times." (موثق)[22]

23.

أَبُو عَلِيٍّ الْأَشْعَرِيُّ عَنْ مُحَمَّدِ بْنِ عَبْدِ الْجَبَّارِ عَنْ صَفْوَانَ بْنِ يَحْيَى عَنْ ذَرِيحٍ الْمُحَارِبِيِّ عَنْ أَبِي عَبْدِ اللَّهِ (عَلَيْهِ السَّلَام) قَالَ مَنْ مَاتَ وَلَمْ يَحُجَّ حَجَّةَ الْإِسْلَامِ لَمْ يَمْنَعْهُ مِنْ ذَلِكَ حَاجَةٌ تُجْحِفُ بِهِ أَوْ مَرَضٌ لا يُطِيقُ فِيهِ الْحَجَّ أَوْ سُلْطَانٌ يَمْنَعُهُ فَلْيَمُتْ يَهُودِيّاً أَوْ نَصْرَانِيّاً

Abu ʿAlī al-Ash'ariy has narrated from Muḥammad b. 'Abd al-Jabbar from Safwan b. Yahya from Dharih al-Muharibiy who has said the following: "Abu 'Abd Allāh, (عليه السلام), has said that one who dies without performing Hajjahta al-Islam when nothing such as poverty, illness with which he could not perform al-Hajj, or the ruling authorities prevent him from performing al-Hajj, he dies as a Jew or as a Christian.'" (صحيح)[23]

24.

حُمَيْدُ بْنُ زِيَادٍ عَنِ الْحَسَنِ بْنِ مُحَمَّدِ بْنِ سَمَاعَةَ عَنْ أَحْمَدَ بْنِ الْحَسَنِ الْمِيثَمِيِّ عَنْ أَبَانِ بْنِ عُثْمَانَ عَنْ أَبِي بَصِيرٍ قَالَ سَمِعْتُ أَبَا عَبْدِ اللَّهِ (عَلَيْهِ السَّلَام) يَقُولُ مَنْ مَاتَ وَهُوَ صَحِيحٌ مُوسِرٌ لَمْ يَحُجَّ فَهُوَ مِمَّنْ قَالَ اللَّهُ

[22] *Al-Kāfi, v4, ch27, h3*

[23] *Al-Kāfi, v4, ch31, h1*

عَزَّ وَجَلَّ وَنَحْشُرُهُ يَوْمَ الْقِيَامَةِ أَعْمى قَالَ قُلْتُ سُبْحَانَ اللهِ أَعْمى قَالَ نَعَمْ إِنَّ اللهَ عَزَّ وَجَلَّ أَعْمَاهُ عَنْ طَرِيقِ الْحَقِّ

Humayd b. Ziyad has narrated from al-Hassan b. Muḥammad b. Sama'ah from Ahmad b. al-Hassan al-Mithamiy from Aban b. 'Uthman from abu Basir who has said the following: "I heard abu 'Abd Allāh, (عليه السلام), say, 'If one dies without performing al-Hajj when in good health and wealthy, he is one of those about whom Allāh, the Most Majestic, the Most Glorious, has said, 'We will, on the Day of Judgment, raise him blind.' (20:124) I (the narrator) then said, 'Allāh is free of all defects. Will he be raised blind?' He (the Imam) said, 'Yes, blind he will be raised. Allāh, the Most Majestic, the Most Glorious, has turned him blind toward the true path.' (موثق)[24]

25.

عَلِيُّ بْنُ إِبْرَاهِيمَ عَنْ أَبِيهِ عَنِ ابْنِ أَبِي عُمَيْرٍ عَنْ مُعَاوِيَةَ بْنِ عَمَّارٍ وَجَمِيلِ بْنِ صَالِحٍ عَنْ أَبِي عَبْدِ اللهِ (عَلَيْهِ السَّلَامِ) قَالَ لَمَّا طَافَ آدَمُ بِالْبَيْتِ وَانْتَهَى إِلَى الْمُلْتَزَمِ قَالَ لَهُ جَبْرَئِيلُ (عَلَيْهِ السَّلَامِ) يَا آدَمُ أَقِرَّ لِرَبِّكَ بِذُنُوبِكَ فِي هَذَا الْمَكَانِ قَالَ فَوَقَفَ آدَمُ (عَلَيْهِ السَّلَامِ) فَقَالَ يَا رَبِّ إِنَّ لِكُلِّ عَامِلٍ أَجْراً وَقَدْ عَمِلْتُ فَمَا أَجْرِي فَأَوْحَى اللهُ عَزَّ وَجَلَّ إِلَيْهِ يَا آدَمُ قَدْ غَفَرْتُ ذَنْبَكَ قَالَ يَا رَبِّ وَلِوُلْدِي أَوْ لِذُرِّيَّتِي فَأَوْحَى اللهُ عَزَّ وَجَلَّ إِلَيْهِ يَا آدَمُ مَنْ جَاءَ مِنْ ذُرِّيَّتِكَ إِلَى هَذَا الْمَكَانِ وَأَقَرَّ بِذُنُوبِهِ وَتَابَ كَمَا تُبْتَ ثُمَّ اسْتَغْفَرَ غَفَرْتُ لَهُ

Ali b. Ibrahim has narrated from his father from b. abu 'Umayr from Mu'awiyah b. 'Ammar and Jamil b. Salih who has said the following: "Abu 'Abd Allāh, (عليه السلام), has said that when Adam performed Tawaf around the House and ended by al-Multazam, Jibril said to him, "O Adam, (you must) confess your sins before your Lord at this place." He (the Imam) has said, 'Adam stood there and said, "O Lord, every worker has wages. I have worked. What are my wages?" Allāh, the Most Majestic, the Most Glorious, sent wahy (revelation) that said, "I have forgiven your

---

[24] *Al-Kāfi, v4, ch31, h6*

sin." He then asked, "O Lord, what will happen to my offspring and descendents?" Allāh, the Most Majestic, the Most Glorious, then sent revelation saying, "Whoever of your offspring will come to this place, confess his sins and return as you returned (repented), then ask for forgiveness, I will forgive." (حسن)[25]

26.

عَلِيٌّ عَنْ أَبِيهِ عَنِ ابْنِ أَبِي عُمَيْرٍ عَنْ مُعَاوِيَةَ بْنِ عَمَّارٍ عَنْ أَبِي عَبْدِ اللهِ (عَلَيْهِ السَّلَامُ) قَالَ لَمَّا أَفَاضَ آدَمُ مِنْ مِنًى تَلَقَّتْهُ الْمَلَائِكَةُ فَقَالُوا يَا آدَمُ بُرَّ حَجُّكَ أَمَا إِنَّهُ قَدْ حَجَجْنَا هَذَا الْبَيْتَ قَبْلَ أَنْ تَحُجَّهُ بِأَلْفَيْ عَامٍ

Ali has narrated from his father from b. abu 'Umayr from Mu'awiyah b. 'Ammar who has said the following: "Abu 'Abd Allāh, (عليه السلام), has said that when Adam left Mina (for Makkah), the angels met him saying, "Good for you is your Hajj; however, we have performed Hajj around this House two thousand years before your Hajj.'"
(حسن)[26]

27.

عَلِيٌّ عَنْ أَبِيهِ عَنْ حَمَّادِ بْنِ عِيسَى عَنِ الْحُسَيْنِ بْنِ الْمُخْتَارِ عَنْ أَبِي بَصِيرٍ قَالَ سَمِعْتُ أَبَا جَعْفَرٍ (عَلَيْهِ السَّلَامُ) يَقُولُ مَرَّ مُوسَى بْنُ عِمْرَانَ فِي سَبْعِينَ نَبِيّاً عَلَى فِجَاجِ الرَّوْحَاءِ عَلَيْهِمُ الْعَبَاءُ الْقَطَوَانِيَّةُ يَقُولُ لَبَّيْكَ عَبْدُكَ ابْنُ عَبْدِكَ

Ali has narrated from his father from Hammad b. 'Isa from al-Husayn b. al-Mukhtar from abu Basir who has said the following: "I once heard abu Ja'far, (عليه السلام), say, 'Moses, son of 'Imran, passed by the wide road in al- Rawha' (a place between al-Madinah and Makkah), along with seventy prophets dressed with gowns made in al-

---

[25] *Al-Kafi, v4, ch4, h3*

[26] *Al-Kāfi, v4, ch4, h4*

Qatwan, near al-Kufa, Iraq, saying, "Here I am to obey Your command O Lord, Your servant, son of Your servant.'" (حسن موثق)[27]

28.

عَلِيُّ بْنُ إِبْرَاهِيمَ عَنْ أَبِيهِ عَنِ ابْنِ فَضَّالٍ عَنْ عَلِيِّ بْنِ عُقْبَةَ عَنْ أَبِيهِ عَنْ زُرَارَةَ عَنْ أَبِي جَعْفَرٍ (عَلَيْهِ السَّلَام) أَنَّ سُلَيْمَانَ بْنَ دَاوُدَ حَجَّ الْبَيْتَ فِي الْجِنِّ وَالإِنْسِ وَالطَّيْرِ وَالرِّيَاحِ وَكَسَا الْبَيْتَ الْقَبَاطِيَّ

Ali b. Ibrahim has narrated from his father from b. Faddal from 'Alī b. 'Uqbah, from his father from Zurāra who has said the following: "Abu Ja'far, (عليه السلام), has said, 'Sulayman son of Dawud (Solomon son of David) performed Hajj along with Jinn, man, bird and wind, wearing a Coptic gown.'" (حسن موثق)[28]

29.

مُحَمَّدُ بْنُ يَحْيَى عَنْ أَحْمَدَ بْنِ مُحَمَّدٍ عَنِ ابْنِ مَحْبُوبٍ عَنْ عَلِيِّ بْنِ رِئَابٍ عَنْ أَبِي عُبَيْدَةَ وَزُرَارَةَ جَمِيعاً عَنْ ابي جعفر (عَلَيْهِ السَّلام) قَالَ لَمَّا قُتِلَ الْحُسَيْنُ (عَلَيْهِ السَّلام) أَرْسَلَ مُحَمَّدُ بْنُ الْحَنَفِيَّةِ إِلَى عَلِيِّ بن الحسين (عَلَيْهِمَا السَّلام) فَخَلا بِهِ فَقَالَ لَهُ يَا ابْنَ أَخِي قَدْ عَلِمْتَ أَنَّ رَسُولَ الله (صَلَّى اللهُ عَلَيْهِ وَآلِه) دَفَعَ الْوَصِيَّةَ وَالامَامَةَ مِنْ بَعْدِهِ إِلَى أَمِيرِ الْمُؤْمِنِينَ (عَلَيْهِ السَّلام) ثُمَّ إِلَى الْحَسَنِ (عَلَيْهِ السَّلام) ثُمَّ إِلَى الْحُسَيْنِ (عَلَيْهِ السَّلام) وَقَدْ قُتِلَ أَبُوكَ رَضِيَ الله عَنْهُ وَصَلَّى عَلَى رُوحِهِ وَلَمْ يُوصِ وَأَنَا عَمُّكَ وَصِنْوُ أَبِيكَ وَوِلادَتِي مِنْ علي (عَلَيْهِ السَّلام) فِي سِنِّي وَقَدِيمِي أَحَقُّ بِهَا مِنْكَ فِي حَدَاثَتِكَ فَلا تُنَازِعْنِي فِي الْوَصِيَّةِ وَالامَامَةِ وَلا تُحَاجَّنِي فَقَالَ لَهُ عَلِيُّ بن الحسين (عَلَيْهِمَا السَّلام) يَا عَمِّ اتَّقِ الله وَلا تَدَّعِ مَا لَيْسَ لَكَ بِحَقٍّ إِنِّي أَعِظُكَ أَنْ تَكُونَ مِنَ الْجَاهِلِينَ إِنَّ أَبِي يَا عَمِّ صَلَوَاتُ الله عَلَيْهِ أَوْصَى إِلَيَّ قَبْلَ أَنْ يَتَوَجَّهَ إِلَى الْعِرَاقِ وَعَهِدَ إِلَيَّ فِي ذَلِكَ قَبْلَ أَنْ يُسْتَشْهَدَ بِسَاعَةٍ وَهَذَا سِلاحُ رَسُولِ الله (صَلَّى اللهُ عَلَيْهِ وَآلِه) عِنْدِي فَلا تَتَعَرَّضْ لِهَذَا فَإِنِّي أَخَافُ عَلَيْكَ نَقْصَ الْعُمُرِ وَتَشَتُّتَ الْحَالِ إِنَّ الله عَزَّ وَجَلَّ جَعَلَ الْوَصِيَّةَ وَالامَامَةَ فِي عَقِبِ الْحُسَيْنِ (عَلَيْهِ السَّلام) فَإِذَا أَرَدْتَ أَنْ تَعْلَمَ ذَلِكَ فَانْطَلِقْ بِنَا إِلَى الْحَجَرِ الاسْوَدِ حَتَّى نَتَحَاكَمَ إِلَيْهِ وَنَسْأَلَهُ عَنْ ذَلِكَ قَالَ أَبُو جَعْفَرٍ (عَلَيْهِ

---

[27] *Al-Kāfi, v4, ch8, h3*

[28] *Al-Kāfi, v4, ch8, h6*

السَّلام) وَكَانَ الْكَلامُ بَيْنَهُمَا بِمَكَّةَ فَانْطَلَقَا حَتَّى أَتَيَا الْحَجَرَ الاسْوَدَ فَقَالَ عَلِيُّ بْنُ الْحُسَيْنِ لِمُحَمَّدِ بْنِ الْحَنَفِيَّةِ ابْدَأْ أَنْتَ فَابْتَهِلْ إِلَى اللهِ عَزَّ وَجَلَّ وَسَلْهُ أَنْ يُنْطِقَ لَكَ الْحَجَرَ ثُمَّ سَلْ فَابْتَهَلَ مُحَمَّدٌ فِي الدُّعَاءِ وَسَأَلَ اللهَ ثُمَّ دَعَا الْحَجَرَ فَلَمْ يُجِبْهُ فَقَالَ عَلِيُّ بن الحسين (عَلَيْهِما السَّلام) يَا عَمِّ لَوْ كُنْتَ وَصِيّاً وَإِمَاماً لاجَابَكَ قَالَ لَهُ مُحَمَّدٌ فَادْعُ اللهَ أَنْتَ يَا ابْنَ أَخِي وَسَلْهُ فَدَعَا اللهَ عَلِيُّ بن الحسين (عَلَيْهِما السَّلام) بِمَا أَرَادَ ثُمَّ قَالَ أَسْأَلُكَ بِالَّذِي جَعَلَ فِيكَ مِيثَاقَ الانْبِيَاءِ وَمِيثَاقَ الاوْصِيَاءِ وَمِيثَاقَ النَّاسِ أَجْمَعِينَ لَمَّا أَخْبَرْتَنَا مَنِ الْوَصِيُّ وَالامَامُ بَعْدَ الْحُسَيْنِ بن علي (عَلَيْهِما السَّلام) قَالَ فَتَحَرَّكَ الْحَجَرُ حَتَّى كَادَ أَنْ يَزُولَ عَنْ مَوْضِعِهِ ثُمَّ أَنْطَقَهُ اللهُ عَزَّ وَجَلَّ بِلِسَانٍ عَرَبِيٍّ مُبِينٍ فَقَالَ اللهُمَّ إِنَّ الْوَصِيَّةَ وَالامَامَةَ بَعْدَ الْحُسَيْنِ بن علي (عَلَيْهِما السَّلام) إِلَى عَلِيِّ بْنِ الْحُسَيْنِ بْنِ عَلِيِّ بْنِ أَبِي طَالِبٍ وَابْنِ فَاطِمَةَ بِنْتِ رَسُولِ اللهِ (صَلَّى اللهُ عَلَيْهِ وَآلِه) قَالَ فَانْصَرَفَ مُحَمَّدُ بْنُ عَلِيٍّ وَهُوَ يَتَوَلَّى عَلِيَّ بْنَ الْحُسَيْنِ (عَلَيْهِما السَّلام)

Muhammad b. Yahya has narrated from Ahmad b. Muḥammad from b. Mahbub from 'Alī b. Ri'ab from abu 'Ubayda and Zurara from abu Ja'far (عليه السلام) who has said the following. "When al-Husayn (عليه السلام) was martyred, Muḥammad b. al-Hanafiya asked 'Alī b. al-Husayn (عليه السلام) for a private meeting. In the meeting he said, "O son of my brother, you know that the Messenger of Allāh (s.a) delivered the task of al-Wasiyya, (the executor-ship of the will) and al-Imamat, (Leadership with Divine Authority) thereafter it was delivered to al-Hassan (عليه السلام) and then to al-Husayn (عليه السلام). Your father, may Allāh be pleased with him has been murdered, may Allāh grant blessing up on his soul, and he did make any will. I am your uncle and equal in status to your father and I am a son of 'Alī (عليه السلام). Because of being older in age I am more deserving of the the position of Imamat considering that you are younger than me. Therefore, you should not dispute with me about al-Wasiyya, the will and Imamat, leadership and should argue with me about it." 'Alī b. al-Husayn (عليه السلام) said, "O uncle, be pious before Allāh and do not claim in what you have no right. I advise not to be of the ignorant people. In fact, my father (عليه السلام), O my uncle, appointed me as the executor of his will before his leaving for Iraq. He made such covenant with me just an hour before his becoming a martyr. This is the Armament of the Messenger of Allāh with me. You then should not dislocate them. I am afraid for you of a shorter life and quandary of conditions. Allāh, the Most Majestic, the Most gracious, has placed al-Wasiyya, and Imamat in the descendants of al-Husayn (عليه السلام). **If you would like to know it we can go near the**

Blackstone and fro judgment and ask it about the issue." Abu Ja'far (عليه السلام) has said that the issue came up between them in Makka and they went near the Blackstone. 'Alī b. al-Husayn (عليه السلام) said to Muḥammad al-Hanafiya, "You begin first and pray to Allāh, the Most Majestic, the Most gracious, and ask Him to make the Blackstone speak to you and then ask your question." Muḥammad then pleaded in his prayer and asked Allāh and then ask the Blackstone about the disputed issue but there was no answer. 'Alī **b. al-Husayn** (عليه السلام) **said**, "**O uncle, had you been the Executor of the will and the Imam it would have answered your question**. Muḥammad then said, "Now you pray to Allāh, O son of my brother and ask your question. Alin b. al-Husayn (عليه السلام) prayed to Allāh for what he wanted then addressing the Blackstone said, "I ask you for the sake of the One Who placed the covenant of the prophets in you, as well as the covenant of the executors of the will and the covenant of all the peole. You must tell us who the Wasiyy and Imam after al-Husayn (عليه السلام)?" **The narrator has said that the Blackstone began to shake so much that it almost camme out of its place**. **Allāh**, **the Most Majestic**, **the Most gracious**, **then made it to speak in clear Arabic language and said**, "**O Lord, al-Wasiyya and Imamat after al-Husayn** (عليه السلام) **b**. '**Alī is for** '**Alī b**. **al-Husayn b**. '**Alī ab**. **abu Talib and b**. **Fatima** (عليه السلام) **daughter of the the Messenger of Allāh**." The narrator has said that Muḥammad 'Alī (عليه السلام) returned back and he acknowledged 'Alī b. al-Husayn (عليه السلام) to be his Wali (Leadership with Divine Authority)." 'Alī b. Ibrahim has narrated from his father from Hammad b. 'Isa from Hariz from Zurara from abu Ja'far (عليه السلام) the same Hadīth. (صحيح)[29]

30.

[29] *Al-Kafi, v1, ch81, h5*

عَلِيُّ بْنُ مُحَمَّدٍ عَنْ مُحَمَّدِ بْنِ عَلِيِّ بْنِ إِبْرَاهِيمَ عَنْ أَبِي عَبْدِ اللهِ بْنِ صَالِحٍ أَنَّهُ رَآهُ عِنْدَ الْحَجَرِ الاسْوَدِ وَالنَّاسُ يَتَجَاذَبُونَ عَلَيْهِ وَهُوَ يَقُولُ مَا بِهَذَا أُمِرُوا

Ali b. Muḥammad has narrated from Muḥammad b. ʻAlī b. Ibrahim from abu ʻAbdAllāh b. Salih who has said the following. "I saw him (the twelfth Imam) near the Black Stone while people were clinging over it. The Imam (عليه السلام) would say, "They are not commanded in this condition (to kiss the Black Stone.)" (صحيح على الظاهر)[30]

31.

حدثنا محمد بن موسى بن المتوكل رضي الله عنه قال: حدثنا عبد الله بن جعفر الحميري، عن محمد بن عثمان العمري رضي الله عنه قال: سمعته يقول: والله إن صاحب هذا الامر ليحضر الموسم كل سنة فيرى الناس ويعرفهم ويرونه ولا يعرفونه

Narrated to us Muḥammad b. Mūsā b. Mutawakkil رضي الله عنه: Narrated to us ʻAbd Allāh b. Ja'far Himyari from Muḥammad b. Uthman al-Amari رضي الله عنه that he said: "The master of this affair shall perform the Hajj rituals every year. Thus he shall see the people and recognize them and they shall (also) see him but will not recognize him." (صحيح)[31]

32.

حدثنا محمد بن موسى بن المتوكل رضي الله عنه قال: حدثنا عبد الله بن جعفر الحميري قال: سألت محمد بن عثمان العمري رضي الله عنه فقلت له: أرأيت صاحب هذا الامر ؟ فقال: نعم وآخر عهدي به عند بيت الله الحرام وهو يقول: " اللهم أنجز لي ما وعدتني."

[30] *Al-Kāfi, v1, ch77, h7*

[31] *Kamal ad-Deen (Ṣaduq), pg. 468*

Narrated to us Muḥammad b. Mūsā b. Mutawakkil رضي الله عنه: Narrated to us 'Abd Allāh b. Ja'far Himyari that:
I asked Muḥammad b. Uthman Amari: "Have you the seen the master of this affair?" He replied: "Yes, and the last time I saw him, he was besides the Holy House of Allāh and praying: O my Lord, fulfill the promise that You made to me." (صحيح)[32]

33.

حدثنا محمد بن موسى بن المتوكل رضي الله عنه قال: حدثنا عبد الله بن جعفر الحميري قال: سمعت محمد بن عثمان العمري رضي الله عنه يقول: رأيته صلوات الله عليه متعلقا بأستار الكعبة في المستجار وهو يقول: " اللهم انتقم لي من أعدائي."

Narrated to us Muḥammad b. Mūsā b. Mutawakkil رضي الله عنه: Narrated to us 'Abd Allāh b. Ja'far Himyari that:
I heard Muḥammad b. Uthman Amari رضي الله عنه say: "I saw His Eminence (عليه السلام) holding the curtain of the Kaaba below the spout and praying: O my Lord, take revenge from my enemies." (صحيح)[33]

---

[32] *Kamal ad-Deen (Ṣaduq), pg. 468*

[33] *Kamal ad-Deen (Ṣaduq), pg. 468*

باب الصوم

Chapter on as-Ṣawm (Fasting)

1.

عَلِيُّ بْنُ إِبْرَاهِيمَ عَنْ أَبِيهِ وَعَبْدِ اللهِ بْنِ الصَّلْتِ جَمِيعاً عَنْ حَمَّادِ بْنِ عِيسَى عَنْ حَرِيزِ بْنِ عَبْدِ اللهِ عَنْ زُرَارَةَ عَنْ أَبِي جَعْفَرٍ (عَلَيهِ السَّلام) قَالَ بُنِيَ الإِسْلامُ عَلَى خَمْسَةِ أَشْيَاءَ عَلَى الصَّلاةِ وَالزَّكَاةِ وَالْحَجِّ وَالصَّوْمِ وَالْوَلايَةِ قَالَ زُرَارَةُ فَقُلْتُ وَأَيُّ شَيْءٍ مِنْ ذَلِكَ أَفْضَلُ فَقَالَ الْوَلايَةُ أَفْضَلُ لأَنَّهَا مِفْتَاحُهُنَّ وَالْوَالِي هُوَ الدَّلِيلُ عَلَيْهِنَّ قُلْتُ ثُمَّ الَّذِي يَلِي ذَلِكَ فِي الْفَضْلِ فَقَالَ الصَّلاةُ إِنَّ رَسُولَ اللهِ (صَلَّى اللهُ عَلَيْهِ وآلِه) قَالَ الصَّلاةُ عَمُودُ دِينِكُمْ قَالَ قُلْتُ ثُمَّ الَّذِي يَلِيهَا فِي الْفَضْلِ قَالَ الزَّكَاةُ لأَنَّهُ قَرَنَهَا بِهَا وَبَدَأَ بِالصَّلاةِ قَبْلَهَا وَقَالَ رَسُولُ اللهِ (صَلَّى اللهُ عَلَيْهِ وآلِه) الزَّكَاةُ تُذْهِبُ الذُّنُوبَ قُلْتُ وَالَّذِي يَلِيهَا فِي الْفَضْلِ قَالَ الْحَجُّ قَالَ اللهُ عَزَّ وَجَلَّ وَللهِ عَلَى النَّاسِ حِجُّ الْبَيْتِ مَنِ اسْتَطَاعَ إِلَيْهِ سَبِيلاً وَمَنْ كَفَرَ فَإِنَّ اللهَ غَنِيٌّ عَنِ الْعَالَمِينَ وَقَالَ رَسُولُ اللهِ (صَلَّى اللهُ عَلَيْهِ وآلِه) لَحَجَّةٌ مَقْبُولَةٌ خَيْرٌ مِنْ عِشْرِينَ صَلاةً نَافِلَةً وَمَنْ طَافَ بِهَذَا الْبَيْتِ طَوَافاً أَحْصَى فِيهِ أُسْبُوعَهُ وَأَحْسَنَ رَكْعَتَيْهِ غَفَرَ اللهُ لَهُ وَقَالَ فِي يَوْمِ عَرَفَةَ وَيَوْمِ الْمُزْدَلِفَةِ مَا قَالَ قُلْتُ فَمَا ذَا يَتْبَعُهُ قَالَ الصَّوْمُ قُلْتُ وَمَا بَالُ الصَّوْمِ صَارَ آخِرَ ذَلِكَ أَجْمَعَ قَالَ قَالَ رَسُولُ اللهِ (صَلَّى اللهُ عَلَيْهِ وآلِه) الصَّوْمُ جُنَّةٌ مِنَ النَّارِ قَالَ ثُمَّ قَالَ إِنَّ أَفْضَلَ الأَشْيَاءِ مَا إِذَا فَاتَكَ لَمْ تَكُنْ مِنْهُ تَوْبَةٌ دُونَ أَنْ تَرْجِعَ إِلَيْهِ فَتُؤَدِّيَهُ بِعَيْنِهِ إِنَّ الصَّلاةَ وَالزَّكَاةَ وَالْحَجَّ وَالْوَلايَةَ لَيْسَ يَقَعُ شَيْءٌ مَكَانَهَا دُونَ أَدَائِهَا وَإِنَّ الصَّوْمَ إِذَا فَاتَكَ أَوْ قَصَّرْتَ أَوْ سَافَرْتَ فِيهِ أَدَّيْتَ مَكَانَهُ أَيَّاماً غَيْرَهَا وَجَزَيْتَ ذَلِكَ الذَّنْبَ بِصَدَقَةٍ وَلا قَضَاءَ عَلَيْكَ وَلَيْسَ مِنْ تِلْكَ الأَرْبَعَةِ شَيْءٌ يُجْزِيكَ مَكَانَهُ غَيْرُهُ قَالَ ثُمَّ قَالَ ذِرْوَةُ الأَمْرِ وَسَنَامُهُ وَمِفْتَاحُهُ وَبَابُ الأَشْيَاءِ وَرِضَا الرَّحْمَنِ الطَّاعَةُ لِلإِمَامِ بَعْدَ مَعْرِفَتِهِ إِنَّ اللهَ عَزَّ وَجَلَّ يَقُولُ مَنْ يُطِعِ الرَّسُولَ فَقَدْ أَطَاعَ اللهَ وَمَنْ تَوَلَّى فَمَا أَرْسَلْنَاكَ عَلَيْهِمْ حَفِيظاً أَمَا لَوْ أَنَّ رَجُلاً قَامَ لَيْلَهُ وَصَامَ نَهَارَهُ وَتَصَدَّقَ بِجَمِيعِ مَالِهِ وَحَجَّ جَمِيعَ دَهْرِهِ وَلَمْ يَعْرِفْ وَلايَةَ وَلِيِّ اللهِ فَيُوَالِيَهُ وَيَكُونَ جَمِيعُ أَعْمَالِهِ بِدَلالَتِهِ إِلَيْهِ مَا كَانَ لَهُ عَلَى

اللہ جَلَّ وَعَزَّ حَقٌّ فِي ثَوَابِهِ وَلاَ كَانَ مِنْ أَهْلِ الإِيمَانِ ثُمَّ قَالَ أُولَئِكَ الْمُحْسِنُ مِنْهُمْ يُدْخِلُهُ اللہ الْجَنَّةَ بِفَضْلِ رَحْمَتِهِ

Ali b. Ibrahim has narrated from his father and 'Abd Allāh b. al-Salt all of them from Hammad b. 'Isa from Hariz b. 'Abd Allāh from Zurara from abu Ja'far (عليه السلام) who has said the following: "Abu Ja'far (عليه السلام) has said, **'Islam is based on five issues. It is based on prayer, charity (al- Zakat), Hajj, Fasting and al-Wilāya.**" Zurara has said, 'I then asked the Imam, "Which of these is more important than the others?"' The Imam said, 'Al-Wilāya is more important. It is the key to the others. The person who possesses Divine Authority is the guide to the other principles.' I then asked, 'Which is the next important?' The Imam said, 'Thereafter is prayer. The Messenger of Allāh has said, "Prayer is the pillar of your religion."' I then asked, 'Which is the next important among them?' The Imam said, 'Al-Zakat is the one thereafter. Allāh has mentioned it next to prayer but He has mentioned prayer first. The Messenger of Allāh has said, "Al-Zakat removes sins."' I then asked, 'Which one is important thereafter?' The Imam said, 'Hajj is important thereafter. Allāh, the Most Majestic, the Most Holy, has said, "It is a duty of the people to Allāh to perform Hajj of the House if they are capable to do so. Whoever rejects it should know that Allāh does not need anyone in the world." (3:97) The messenger of Allāh has said, "Performing Hajj that is accepted is more virtuous than twenty Rak'at optional prayer. Whoever walks around the House seven times and performs the two Rak'at prayers thereafter properly Allāh will grant him cover." He (The Messenger of Allāh) did say on the ninth of the month of Dil Hajj and on the tenth of the month of Dil Hajj in Muzdalifa (a place in Makka), what he wanted to say.' I then asked, **'Which one is important thereafter?' The Imam said, 'It is fasting.' "I then asked, 'Why is fasting the last of all in importance?'** The Imam said, **'The Messenger of Allāh has said, "Fasting is a shield against the fire.'"** The narrator has said that the Imam said, 'The best of all things is that for which, if you miss, you do not find an alternative accept going back to achieve it. Prayer, al-Wilāya and Hajj are not of matters replaceable with their own kind. On the other hand if fasting is missed on a journey one has the choice to fast on other days as remedy, or compensate for the sin with expiation and no fasting is necessary as a remedy. In the cases of the other four issues there is no alternative for them.' The narrator has said that the Imam then said, 'The topmost, the peak of the issue, the key and the door to it and the pleasure of the Beneficent (Lord) is to obey the Imam properly after knowing him clearly. Allāh, the Most Majestic, the Most Holy, says, "Whoever obeys the Messenger he has obeyed Allāh and whoever turns away from such obedience then you should know that We have not sent you to guard them." (4:80) 'Without recognizing the Divine Authority of the Imam, the deputy of Allāh, no one has the right to receive any reward from Allāh, the Most Majestic, the Most Holy. This is true even though in his lifetime he may stand up in worship the whole night, fast during the day, give all his belongings in charity and perform Hajj every year. So also it is if he does not acknowledge the Divine Authority of his Imam with which all of one's deeds can take place with the guidance of the Imam. Without al- Wilāya, one is not considered of the people of belief.' Thereafter the Imam said, 'Allāh will admit, those of them who do good deeds into paradise through His extra mercy. (صحيح)[1]

2.

عَلِيُّ بْنُ إِبْرَاهِيمَ بْنِ هَاشِمٍ عَنْ أَبِيهِ عَنْ حَمَّادِ بْنِ عِيسَى عَنْ حَرِيزٍ عَنْ زُرَارَةَ عَنْ أَبِي جَعْفَرٍ (عَلَيْهِ السَّلَام) قَالَ بُنِيَ الإِسْلامُ عَلَى خَمْسَةِ أَشْيَاءَ عَلَى الصَّلاةِ وَالزَّكَاةِ وَالْحَجِّ وَالصَّوْمِ وَالْوَلايَةِ وَقَالَ رَسُولُ الله (صلَّى اللهُ عَلَيْهِ وَآلِه) الصَّوْمُ جُنَّةٌ مِنَ النَّارِ

Ali b. Ibrahim b. Hashim has narrated from his father from Hammad b. 'Isa from Hariz from Zurāra who has said the following: "Abu Ja'far, (عليه السلام), has said, 'Islam is founded on five isssues. It is founded on Salat (prayer), zakat, al-Hajj, Fasting and

---

[1] *Al-Kafi, v2, ch13, h5*

al-Wilāyat (belief in Divine Authority of 'A'immah). The Messenger of Allāh has said, 'Fasting is a shield against the fire of hell." (حسن)[2]

3.

مُحَمَّدُ بْنِ يَحْيَى عَنْ أَحْمَدَ بْنِ مُحَمَّدِ بْنِ عِيسَى عَنِ ابْنِ فَضَّالٍ عَنْ ثَعْلَبَةَ عَنْ عَلِيِّ بْنِ عَبْدِ الْعَزِيزِ قَالَ قَالَ لِي أَبُو عَبْدِ اللهِ (عَلَيْهِ السَّلاَمُ) أَ لاَ أُخْبِرُكَ بِأَصْلِ الإِسْلاَمِ وَفَرْعِهِ وَذِرْوَتِهِ وَسَنَامِهِ قُلْتُ بَلَى قَالَ أَصْلُهُ الصَّلاَةُ وَفَرْعُهُ الزَّكَاةُ وَذِرْوَتُهُ وَسَنَامُهُ الْجِهَادُ فِي سَبِيلِ اللهِ أَ لاَ أُخْبِرُكَ بِأَبْوَابِ الْخَيْرِ إِنَّ الصَّوْمَ جُنَّةٌ

Muhammad b. Yahya has narrated from Ahmad b. Muḥammad b. 'Isa from b. Faddal from Tha'labah from 'Alī b. 'Abd al-'Aziz who has said the following: "Abu 'Abd Allāh, (عليه السلام), once asked me, 'Should I tell you what the root, the branch, the peak and the highest point of Islam is?' I replied, 'Please, do so.' He said, 'The root of Islam is salat (prayer), its branch is zakat, and its peak and highest point is al-Jihad in the way of Allāh. Should I tell you about the doors to goodness? Fasting certainly is a shield. (مجهول)[3]

4.

مُحَمَّدُ بْنُ إِسْمَاعِيلَ عَنِ الْفَضْلِ بْنِ شَاذَانَ عَنِ ابْنِ أَبِي عُمَيْرٍ عَنْ مُعَاوِيَةَ بْنِ عُثْمَانَ عَنْ إِسْمَاعِيلَ بْنِ يَسَارٍ قَالَ قَالَ أَبُو عَبْدِ اللهِ (عَلَيْهِ السَّلاَمُ) قَالَ أَبِي إِنَّ الرَّجُلَ لَيَصُومُ يَوْماً تَطَوُّعاً يُرِيدُ مَا عِنْدَ اللهِ عَزَّ وَجَلَّ فَيُدْخِلُهُ اللهُ بِهِ الْجَنَّةَ

Muhammad b. Isma'il has narrated from al-Fadl b. Shadhan from b. abu 'Umayr from Mu'awiyah b. 'Uthman from Isma'il b. Yasar who has said the following: "Abu 'Abd Allāh, (عليه السلام), has said, 'My father has said, "When a person completes a day of

---

[2] *Al-Kāfi, v4, ch1, h1*

[3] *Al-Kāfi, v4, ch1, h3*

optional fasting for the sake of Allāh, the Most Majestic, the Most Glorious, Allāh admits him in Paradise.' (مجهول)[4]

5.

عَلِيُّ بْنُ إِبْرَاهِيمَ عَنْ أَبِيهِ عَنِ ابْنِ أَبِي عُمَيْرٍ عَنْ سَلَمَةَ صَاحِبِ السَّابِرِيِّ عَنْ أَبِي الصَّبَّاحِ عَنْ أَبِي عَبْدِ اللَّه (عَلَيْهِ السَّلَام) قَالَ إِنَّ اللَّه تَبَارَكَ وَتَعَالَى يَقُولُ الصَّوْمُ لِي وَأَنَا أَجْزِي عَلَيْهِ

Ali b. Ibrahim has narrated from his father from b. abu 'Umayr from Salamah, Sahib al-Sabiriy from abu al-Sabbah who has said the following: "Abu 'Abd Allāh, (عليه السلام), has said that Allāh, the most Blessed, the most High, has said, 'Fasting is for Me, and I reward for it.'" (مجهول)[5]

6.

عَلِيُّ بْنُ إِبْرَاهِيمَ عَنْ أَبِيهِ عَنِ السَّمَّانِ الأَرْمَنِيِّ عَنْ أَبِي عَبْدِ اللَّه (عَلَيْهِ السَّلَام) قَالَ إِذَا رَأَى الصَّائِمُ قَوْماً يَأْكُلُونَ أَوْ رَجُلاً يَأْكُلُ سَبَّحَتْ كُلُّ شَعْرَةٍ مِنْهُ

Ali b. Ibrahim has narrated from his father from al-Samman al-Armaniy who has said the following: "Abu 'Abd Allāh, (عليه السلام), has said that when a fasting person observes people or a person eating food, every piece of his hair feels a kind of covering (tranquility)." (مجهول)[6]

7.

---

[4] *Al-Kāfi, v4, ch1, h5*

[5] *Al-Kāfi, v4, ch1, h6*

[6] *Al-Kāfi, v4, ch1, h16*

عَلِيُّ بْنُ إِبْرَاهِيمَ عَنْ أَبِيهِ عَنْ عَبْدِ اللهِ بْنِ الْمُغِيرَةِ عَنْ عَمْرٍو الشَّامِيِّ عَنْ أَبِي عَبْدِ اللهِ (عَلَيْهِ السَّلَام) قَالَ إِنَّ عِدَّةَ الشُّهُورِ عِنْدَ اللهِ اثْنَا عَشَرَ شَهْراً فِي كِتَابِ اللهِ يَوْمَ خَلَقَ السَّمَاوَاتِ وَالأَرْضَ فَغُرَّةُ الشُّهُورِ شَهْرُ اللهِ عَزَّ ذِكْرُهُ وَهُوَ شَهْرُ رَمَضَانَ وَقَلْبُ شَهْرِ رَمَضَانَ لَيْلَةُ الْقَدْرِ وَنُزِّلَ الْقُرْآنُ فِي أَوَّلِ لَيْلَةٍ مِنْ شَهْرِ رَمَضَانَ فَاسْتَقْبِلِ الشَّهْرَ بِالْقُرْآنِ

Ali b. Ibrahim has narrated from his father from ' Abd Allāh b. al-Mughirah from 'Amr al-Shamiy who has said the following: "Abu 'Abd Allāh, (عليه السلام), has said that the number of months before Allāh is twelve in Allāh's Book, from the day He created the heavens and earth. In front of the months is the month of Allāh, whose mention is most majestic, and that is the month of Ramadan. The heart of the month of Ramadan is the night of al-Qadr (destiny). The Holy Qur'ān came during the first night of the month of Ramadan; thus, the month is welcomed with the Holy Qur'ān." (مجهول)[7]

8.

مُحَمَّدُ بْنُ يَحْيَى وَغَيْرُهُ عَنْ أَحْمَدَ بْنِ مُحَمَّدِ بْنِ عِيسَى عَنِ الْحَسَنِ بْنِ مَحْبُوبٍ عَنْ أَبِي أَيُّوبَ عَنْ أَبِي الْوَرْدِ عَنْ أَبِي جَعْفَرٍ (عَلَيْهِ السَّلَام) قَالَ خَطَبَ رَسُولُ اللهِ (صَلَّى اللهُ عَلَيْهِ وَآلِه) النَّاسَ فِي آخِرِ جُمُعَةٍ مِنْ شَعْبَانَ فَحَمِدَ اللهَ وَأَثْنَى عَلَيْهِ ثُمَّ قَالَ أَيُّهَا النَّاسُ إِنَّهُ قَدْ أَظَلَّكُمْ شَهْرٌ فِيهِ لَيْلَةٌ خَيْرٌ مِنْ أَلْفِ شَهْرٍ وَهُوَ شَهْرُ رَمَضَانَ فَرَضَ اللهُ صِيَامَهُ وَجَعَلَ قِيَامَ لَيْلَةٍ فِيهِ بِتَطَوُّعِ صَلَاةٍ كَتَطَوُّعِ صَلَاةِ سَبْعِينَ لَيْلَةً فِيمَا سِوَاهُ مِنَ الشُّهُورِ وَجَعَلَ لِمَنْ تَطَوَّعَ فِيهِ بِخَصْلَةٍ مِنْ خِصَالِ الْخَيْرِ وَالْبِرِّ كَأَجْرِ مَنْ أَدَّى فَرِيضَةً مِنْ فَرَائِضِ اللهِ عَزَّ وَجَلَّ وَمَنْ أَدَّى فِيهِ فَرِيضَةً مِنْ فَرَائِضِ اللهِ كَانَ كَمَنْ أَدَّى سَبْعِينَ فَرِيضَةً مِنْ فَرَائِضِ اللهِ فِيمَا سِوَاهُ مِنَ الشُّهُورِ وَهُوَ شَهْرُ الصَّبْرِ وَإِنَّ الصَّبْرَ ثَوَابُهُ الْجَنَّةُ وَشَهْرُ الْمُوَاسَاةِ وَهُوَ شَهْرٌ يَزِيدُ اللهُ فِي رِزْقِ الْمُؤْمِنِ فِيهِ وَمَنْ فَطَّرَ فِيهِ مُؤْمِناً صَائِماً كَانَ لَهُ بِذَلِكَ عِنْدَ اللهِ عِتْقُ رَقَبَةٍ وَمَغْفِرَةٌ لِذُنُوبِهِ فِيمَا مَضَى قِيلَ يَا رَسُولَ اللهِ لَيْسَ كُلُّنَا يَقْدِرُ عَلَى أَنْ يُفَطِّرَ صَائِماً فَقَالَ إِنَّ اللهَ كَرِيمٌ يُعْطِي هَذَا الثَّوَابَ لِمَنْ لَمْ يَقْدِرْ إِلَّا عَلَى مَذْقَةٍ مِنْ لَبَنٍ يُفَطِّرُ بِهَا صَائِماً أَوْ شَرْبَةٍ مِنْ مَاءٍ عَذْبٍ أَوْ تَمَرَاتٍ لا يَقْدِرُ عَلَى أَكْثَرَ مِنْ ذَلِكَ وَمَنْ خَفَّفَ فِيهِ عَنْ مَمْلُوكِهِ خَفَّفَ اللهُ عَنْهُ حِسَابَهُ وَهُوَ شَهْرٌ أَوَّلُهُ رَحْمَةٌ وَأَوْسَطُهُ مَغْفِرَةٌ وَآخِرُهُ الإِجَابَةُ وَالْعِتْقُ مِنَ النَّارِ وَلا غِنَى بِكُمْ عَنْ أَرْبَعِ خِصَالٍ خَصْلَتَيْنِ

---

[7] *Al-Kāfi, v4, ch2, h1*

تُرْضُونَ اللهَ بِهِمَا وَخَصْلَتَيْنِ لا غِنَى بِكُمْ عَنْهُمَا فَأَمَّا اللَّتَانِ تُرْضُونَ اللهَ عَزَّ وَجَلَّ بِهِمَا فَشَهَادَةُ أَنْ لا إِلَهَ إِلاَّ اللهُ وَأَنَّ مُحَمَّداً رَسُولُ اللهِ وَأَمَّا اللَّتَانِ لا غِنَى بِكُمْ عَنْهُمَا فَتَسْأَلُونَ اللهَ فِيهِ حَوَائِجَكُمْ وَالْجَنَّةَ وَتَسْأَلُونَ الْعَافِيَةَ وَتَعُوذُونَ بِهِ مِنَ النَّارِ

Muhammad b. Yahya and people other than him have narrated from Ahmad b. Muḥammad b. 'Isa from al-Hassan b. Mahbub, from abu Ayyub from abu al-Ward, who has said the following: "Abu Ja'far, (عليه السلام), has said, 'Once, the Messenger of Allāh, (صلى الله عليه وآله وسلم), delivered a speech on the last Friday of the month of Sha'ban. He thanked Allāh, praised Him, and then said, "O people, a month is upon you when there is a night that is better than one thousand months. That month is the month of Ramadan. Allāh has made fasting obligatory in the month of Ramadan. He has made one night in it wherein performing optional salat (prayer) is equal in reward to seventy nights of performing salat (prayer) in other months. For performing one good and virtuous deed voluntarily in it, He has assigned a reward equal to that for fulfilling an obligation toward Allāh, the Most Majestic, the Most Glorious. For fulfilling an obligation toward Allāh in this month, He has assigned a reward equal to that for fulfilling seventy obligations toward Allāh in other months. It is the month of patience, and the reward for patience is Paradise. It is the month of cooperation. In this month, Allāh increases the sustenance of the believing people. If one serves food for a fasting person at the end of a fasting day, Allāh counts it equal in reward to setting free a slave and forgiveness of his sins of the past." It was said, "O Messenger of Allāh, not every one of us is able to serve food to a fasting person at the end of a fasting day." The Messenger of Allāh, (صلى الله عليه وآله وسلم), said, "Allāh is gracious, He grants such reward even for serving some milk mixed with water or some sweet water or a few pieces of dates, if he is unable to do more than this. For one's easing off the tasks for His servants to perform, Allāh eases off his accountabilities. The beginning of this month is mercy and kindness, its middle is forgiveness, and its end is acceptance and freedom from the fire. You must have four characteristics during this month. With two of these characteristics, you will please Allāh, but without the other two, you cannot have anything. The two with which you will please Allāh is your testimony. 'No one deserves worship besides Allāh, and Muḥammad is the Messenger of Allāh.' The other two are asking Him to meet your needs and for Paradise, and asking Him to grant you good health and protection against hell fire.' (حسن)[8]

9.

مُحَمَّدُ بْنُ يَحْيَى عَنْ أَحْمَدَ بْنِ مُحَمَّدٍ وَمُحَمَّدِ بْنِ الْحُسَيْنِ عَنْ مُحَمَّدِ بْنِ يَحْيَى الْخَثْعَمِيِّ عَنْ غِيَاثِ بْنِ إِبْرَاهِيمَ عَنْ أَبِي عَبْدِ اللهِ عَنْ أَبِيهِ (عَلَيْهِمَا السَّلاَمُ) قَالَ قَالَ أَمِيرُ الْمُؤْمِنِينَ صَلَوَاتُ اللهِ عَلَيْهِ لاَ تَقُولُوا رَمَضَانَ وَلَكِنْ قُولُوا شَهْرُ رَمَضَانَ فَإِنَّكُمْ لاَ تَدْرُونَ مَا رَمَضَانُ

Muhammad b. Yahya has narrated from Ahmad b. Muḥammad and Muḥammad b. al-Husayn from Muḥammad b. Yahya al- Khath'amiy form Ghiyath b. Ibrahim who has said the following: "Abu ' Abd Allāh, has narrated from his father, (عليه السلام), who has said that 'Amir al- Mu'minin, (عليه السلام), has said, 'Do not say, "Ramadan." Say the month of Ramadan; you do not know what Ramadan is.' (موثق)[9]

10.

عَلِيُّ بْنُ إِبْرَاهِيمَ عَنْ أَبِيهِ عَنِ ابْنِ أَبِي عُمَيْرٍ عَنْ حَمَّادِ بْنِ عُثْمَانَ عَنْ مُحَمَّدِ بْنِ مُسْلِمٍ قَالَ قَالَ أَبُو عَبْدِ اللهِ (عَلَيْهِ السَّلاَمُ) إِذَا صُمْتَ فَلْيَصُمْ سَمْعُكَ وَبَصَرُكَ وَشَعْرُكَ وَجِلْدُكَ وَعَدَّدَ أَشْيَاءَ غَيْرَ هَذَا وَقَالَ لاَ يَكُونُ يَوْمُ صَوْمِكَ كَيَوْمِ فِطْرِكَ

Ali b. Ibrahim has narrated from his father from b. abu 'Umayr from Hammad b. 'Uthman from Muḥammad b. Muslim who has said the following: "Abu ' Abd Allāh, (عليه السلام), has said, 'When you fast, your ears, eyes, hairs and skin must also fast . .

---

[8] *Al-Kāfi, v4, ch2, h4*

[9] *Al-Kāfi, v4, ch4, h1*

counting other things also, the Imam said that 'the day of your fast should not be just like any other day." (حسن)[10]

11.

أَحْمَدُ بْنُ مُحَمَّدٍ عَنْ عَلِيِّ بْنِ الْحُسَيْنِ عَنْ مُحَمَّدِ بْنِ عُبَيْدٍ عَنْ عُبَيْدِ بْنِ هَارُونَ قَالَ حَدَّثَنَا أَبُو يَزِيدَ عَنْ حُصَيْنٍ عَنْ أَبِي عَبْدِ اللهِ (عَلَيْهِ السَّلَامِ) قَالَ قَالَ أَمِيرُ الْمُؤْمِنِينَ (صلَّى اللهُ عَلَيْهِ وَآلِه) عَلَيْكُمْ فِي شَهْرِ رَمَضَانَ بِكَثْرَةِ الاسْتِغْفَارِ وَالدُّعَاءِ فَأَمَّا الدُّعَاءُ فَيُدْفَعُ بِهِ عَنْكُمُ الْبَلَاءُ وَأَمَّا الاسْتِغْفَارُ فَيَمْحَى ذُنُوبَكُمْ

Ahmad b. Muḥammad has narrated from 'Alī b. al-Husayn from Muḥammad b. 'Ubayd from 'Ubayd b. Harun who has said that abu Yazid narrated to us from Husayn who has said the following: "Abu 'Abd Allāh, (عليه السلام), has said that 'Amir al-Mu'minin, (عليه السلام), has said, 'In the month of Ramadan you should increase asking forgiveness from Allāh and offering prayer before Him. Prayers repel misfortunes, and asking forgiveness deletes your sins.'" (مجهول)[11]

12.

عَلِيُّ بْنُ إِبْرَاهِيمَ عَنْ أَبِيهِ عَنِ ابْنِ أَبِي عُمَيْرٍ عَنْ مَنْصُورِ بْنِ يُونُسَ عَنْ أَبِي بَصِيرٍ قَالَ سَمِعْتُ أَبَا عَبْدِ اللهِ (عَلَيْهِ السَّلَامِ) يَقُولُ الْكَذِبَةُ تَنْقُضُ الْوُضُوءَ وَتُفَطِّرُ الصَّائِمَ قَالَ قُلْتُ هَلَكْنَا قَالَ لَيْسَ حَيْثُ تَذْهَبُ إِنَّمَا ذَلِكَ الْكَذِبُ عَلَى اللهِ عَزَّ وَجَلَّ وَعَلَى رَسُولِهِ وَعَلَى الْأَئِمَّةِ ع.

Ali b. Ibrahim has narrated from his father from b. abu 'Umayr from Mansur b. Yunus from abu Basir who has said the following: "I heard abu 'Abd Allāh, (عليه السلام), say, 'Speaking lies invalidates Wudu' and fasting.' I (the narrator) then said, 'We are destroyed.' He (the Imam) said, 'It is not the way you think it is. It means speaking

---

[10] *Al-Kafi, v4, ch11, h1*

[11] *Al-Kafi, v4, ch11, h7*

lies against Allāh, the Most Majestic, the Most Glorious, His Messenger and 'A'immah, (عليه السلام).'" (حسن أو موثق)[12]

13.

عَلِيُّ بْنُ إِبْرَاهِيمَ عَنْ أَبِيهِ وَمُحَمَّدُ بْنُ يَحْيَى عَنْ أَحْمَدَ بْنِ مُحَمَّدٍ جَمِيعاً عَنِ ابْنِ أَبِي عُمَيْرٍ عَنْ حَمَّادِ بْنِ عُثْمَانَ عَنِ الْحَلَبِيِّ عَنْ أَبِي عَبْدِ اللهِ (عَلَيْهِ السَّلاَم) أَنَّهُ سُئِلَ عَنْ رَجُلٍ نَسِيَ فَأَكَلَ وَشَرِبَ ثُمَّ ذَكَرَ قَالَ لا يُفْطِرْ إِنَّمَا هُوَ شَيْءٌ رَزَقَهُ اللهُ عَزَّ وَجَلَّ فَلْيُتِمَّ صَوْمَهُ

Ali b. Ibrahim has narrated from his father from and Muḥammad b. Yahya has narrated from Ahmad b. Muḥammad all from b. abu 'Umayr from Hammad b. 'Uthaman from al-Halabiy who has said the following: "I once asked abu ' Abd Allāh, (عليه السلام), about a man who because of forgetfulness eats and drinks and then remembers. He (the Imam) said, 'His fast is not destroyed. It was something Allāh, most Majestic, most Glorious, granted him. He is required to complete his fast (of that day).'" (صحيح)[13]

14.

عَلِيُّ بْنُ إِبْرَاهِيمَ عَنْ أَبِيهِ عَنِ ابْنِ أَبِي عُمَيْرٍ عَنْ حَمَّادٍ عَنِ الْحَلَبِيِّ عَنْ أَبِي عَبْدِ اللهِ (عَلَيْهِ السَّلاَم) قَالَ إِنَّا نَأْمُرُ صِبْيَانَنَا بِالصِّيَامِ إِذَا كَانُوا بَنِي سَبْعِ سِنِينَ بِمَا أَطَاقُوا مِنْ صِيَامِ الْيَوْمِ فَإِنْ كَانَ إِلَى نِصْفِ النَّهَارِ وَأَكْثَرَ مِنْ ذَلِكَ أَوْ أَقَلَّ فَإِذَا غَلَبَهُمُ الْعَطَشُ وَالْغَرَثُ أَفْطَرُوا حَتَّى يَتَعَوَّدُوا الصَّوْمَ وَيُطِيقُوهُ فَمُرُوا صِبْيَانَكُمْ إِذَا كَانُوا أَبْنَاءَ تِسْعِ سِنِينَ بِمَا أَطَاقُوا مِنْ صِيَامٍ فَإِذَا غَلَبَهُمُ الْعَطَشُ أَفْطَرُوا

Ali b. Ibrahim has narrated from his father [from b. abu ' Umayr] from Hammad from al-Halabiy who has said the following: "Abu ' Abd Allāh, (عليه السلام), has said, 'We

[12] *Al-Kāfi, v4, ch11, h10*

[13] *Al-Kāfi, v2, ch21, h1*

command our children, when they are seven years old, to fast as long as they can. In midday or more if thirst increases, they stop fasting so they develop endurance. You should command your children to fast, when they are nine years old, for as long as they can fast. When thirst increases they can stop fasting.'" (حسن)[14]

15.

عَلِيُّ بْنُ إِبْرَاهِيمَ عَنْ أَبِيهِ عَنْ حَمَّادِ بْنِ عِيسَى عَنْ شُعَيْبٍ عَنْ أَبِي بَصِيرٍ عَنْ أَبِي عَبْدِ اللهِ (عَلَيْهِ السَّلَامِ) قَالَ سَأَلْتُهُ عَنِ السَّحُورِ لِمَنْ أَرَادَ الصَّوْمَ أَ وَاجِبٌ هُوَ عَلَيْهِ فَقَالَ لَا بَأْسَ بِأَنْ لَا يَتَسَحَّرَ إِنْ شَاءَ وَأَمَّا فِي شَهْرِ رَمَضَانَ فَإِنَّهُ أَفْضَلُ أَنْ يَتَسَحَّرَ نُحِبُّ أَنْ لَا يُتْرَكَ فِي شَهْرِ رَمَضَانَ

Ali b. Ibrahim has narrated from his father from Hammad b. 'Isa from Shu'ayb from abu Basir who has said the following: "I asked abu ' Abd Allāh, (عليه السلام), about breakfast before dawn, in the case of one who likes to fast whether it is obligatory or not. The Imam replied, 'It is fine if one likes not to have breakfast before dawn. However, in the month of Ramadan, it is better. We love not to ignore it in the month of Ramadan.'" (حسن)[15]

---

[14] *Al-Kāfi, v4, ch45, h1*

[15] *Al-Kāfi, v4, ch14, h1*

باب الفضائل اليوم الجمعة

Chapter on the virtues of the Day of Jum'ah

1.

حدثنا أبي رضي الله عنه قال: حدثنا سعد بن عبد الله، عن يعقوب بن يزيد، عن محمد بن أبي عمير، عن غير واحد، عن أبي عبد الله عليه السلام قال: السبت لنا، والاحد لشيعتنا، والاثنين لاعدائنا، والثلثاء لبني امية، والاربعاء يوم شرب الدواء، والخميس تقضى فيه الحوائج، والجمعة للتنظف والتطيب، وهو عيد المسلمين وهو أفضل من الفطر والاضحى، ويوم الغدير أفضل الاعياد، وهو ثامن عشر من ذي الحجة وكان يوم الجمعة، ويخرج قائمنا أهل البيت يوم الجمعة، ويقوم القيامة يوم الجمعة، وما من عمل يوم الجمعة أفضل من الصلاة على محمد وآله

(The compiler of the book narrated) that his father - may God be pleased with him - narrated that Sa'ed b. 'Abd Allāh quoted Yaqoob b. Yazid, on the authority of Muḥammad b. Abi Umayr, on the authority of some other people that Aba 'Abd Allāh as-Ṣādiq (عليه السلام) said, "Saturdays are for us. Sundays are for our followers. Mondays are for our enemies. Tuesdays are for the Umayyads. Wednesdays are the days for taking medicine. Thursdays are for taking care of your needs. Fridays are for leaning up and putting on perfume. Fridays are the holidays for the Muslims. They are even better than the Eid ul-Fitr and Eid ul-Azha. The Day of Eid ul-Qadir is the noblest of the holidays. It is on the eighteenth day of the month of Dhul-Hijja. Our Riser (عجل الله تعالى فرجه) - the Riser (عجل الله تعالى فرجه) from the Members of the Holy Household - will rise on a Friday. The Resurrection Day will be on a Friday. No deeds are better on Fridays than sending God's Blessings upon Muḥammad (صلى الله عليه وآله وسلم) and his Household." (صحيح)[1]

2.

مُحَمَّدُ بْنُ يَحْيَى عَنْ أَحْمَدَ بْنِ مُحَمَّدٍ عَنْ حَمَّادِ بْنِ عِيسَى عَنِ الْحُسَيْنِ بْنِ الْمُخْتَارِ عَنْ أَبِي بَصِيرٍ قَالَ سَمِعْتُ أَبَا جَعْفَرٍ (عَلَيْهِ السَّلام) يَقُولُ مَا طَلَعَتِ الشَّمْسُ بِيَوْمٍ أَفْضَلَ مِنْ يَوْمِ الْجُمُعَةِ

Muhammad b. Yahya has narrated from Ahmad b. Muḥammad from Hammad b. 'Isa from al-Husayn b. al-Mukhtar from abu Basir who has said the following: "I heard abu Ja'far, (عليه السلام), saying, 'The sun does not shine on anything (other days) more excellent than Friday." (موثق)[2]

3.

عَنْهُ عَنْ أَحْمَدَ بْنِ مُحَمَّدٍ عَنِ الْحُسَيْنِ بْنِ سَعِيدٍ عَنِ النَّضْرِ بْنِ سُوَيْدٍ عَنْ عَبْدِ اللهِ بْنِ سِنَانٍ عَنْ حَفْصِ بْنِ الْبَخْتَرِيِّ عَنْ مُحَمَّدِ بْنِ مُسْلِمٍ عَنْ أَبِي جَعْفَرٍ (عَلَيْهِ السَّلام) قَالَ إِذَا كَانَ يَوْمُ الْجُمُعَةِ نَزَلَ الْمَلَائِكَةُ الْمُقَرَّبُونَ مَعَهُمْ قَرَاطِيسُ مِنْ فِضَّةٍ وَأَقْلَامٌ مِنْ ذَهَبٍ فَيَجْلِسُونَ عَلَى أَبْوَابِ الْمَسْجِدِ عَلَى كَرَاسِيَّ مِنْ نُورٍ فَيَكْتُبُونَ النَّاسَ عَلَى مَنَازِلِهِمُ الْأَوَّلَ وَالثَّانِيَ حَتَّى يَخْرُجَ الْإِمَامُ فَإِذَا خَرَجَ الْإِمَامُ طَوَوْا صُحُفَهُمْ وَلَا يَهْبِطُونَ فِي شَيْءٍ مِنَ الْأَيَّامِ إِلَّا فِي يَوْمِ الْجُمُعَةِ يَعْنِي الْمَلَائِكَةَ الْمُقَرَّبِينَ

---

[1] *Al-Khiṣal, ch49, h5*

[2] *Al-Kāfi, v3, ch66, h1*

It is a narration from him (narrator of previous Hadīth) by Ahmad b. Muḥammad from al-Husayn b. Sa'id from al-Nadr b. al- Suwayd from 'Abd Allāh b. Sinan from Hafs al-Bakhtariy from Muḥammad b. Muslim who has said the following: "Abu Ja'far, (عليه السلام), has said, 'On Fridays, prominent angels come down with paper of silver and pens of gold and sit on the doors of Masjids on chairs of light and write people according to their grades such as first, second . . . until the Imam (prayer leader) comes out. When he comes out they (angels) roll up their pages and do not descend again until next Friday.'" (صحيح)[3]

4.

أَحْمَدُ عَنِ الْحُسَيْنِ عَنِ النَّضْرِ بْنِ سُوَيْدٍ عَنْ عَبْدِ اللهِ بْنِ سِنَانٍ عَنْ أَبِي عَبْدِ اللهِ (عَلَيْهِ السَّلام) قَالَ كَانَ رَسُولُ اللهِ (صلّى اللهُ عَلَيْهِ وَآلِهِ) يَسْتَحِبُّ إِذَا دَخَلَ وَإِذَا خَرَجَ فِي الشِّتَاءِ أَنْ يَكُونَ ذَلِكَ فِي لَيْلَةِ الْجُمُعَةِ وَقَالَ أَبُو عَبْدِ اللهِ (عَلَيْهِ السَّلام) إِنَّ اللهَ اخْتَارَ مِنْ كُلِّ شَيْءٍ شَيْئاً فَاخْتَارَ مِنَ الأَيَّامِ يَوْمَ الْجُمُعَةِ

Ahmad has narrated from al-Husayn from al-Nadr b. al-Suwayd from 'Abd Allāh b. Sinan who has said the following: "Abu 'Abd Allāh, (عليه السلام), has said, 'The Messenger of Allāh loved it, when traveling or coming home in winter, to be on Friday nights.' Abu 'Abd Allāh, (عليه السلام), has also said, 'Allāh has chosen something from everything. From days He has chosen Friday.'" (صحيح)[4]

5.

وَعَنْهُ عَنِ النَّضْرِ عَنْ عَبْدِ اللهِ بْنِ سِنَانٍ عَنْ أَبِي عَبْدِ اللهِ (عَلَيْهِ السَّلام) قَالَ السَّاعَةُ الَّتِي يُسْتَجَابُ فِيهَا الدُّعَاءُ يَوْمَ الْجُمُعَةِ مَا بَيْنَ فَرَاغِ الإِمَامِ مِنَ الْخُطْبَةِ إِلَى أَنْ يَسْتَوِيَ النَّاسُ فِي الصُّفُوفِ وَسَاعَةٌ أُخْرَى مِنْ آخِرِ النَّهَارِ إِلَى غُرُوبِ الشَّمْسِ

---

[3] *Al-Kāfi, v3, ch66, h2*

[4] *Al-Kāfi, v3, ch66, h3*

The narrator of previous Hadīth has also narrated from al-Nadr from 'Abd Allāh b. Sinan who has said the following: "Abu 'Abd Allāh, (عليه السلام), has said, 'The hour of Friday wherein prayers are answered is the time when the prayer leader completes the sermons, until people get ready in rows for Salah (prayer). The other hour is the time at the end of the day to sunset.'" (صحيح)[5]

6.

مُحَمَّدُ بْنُ يَحْيَى عَنْ عَبْدِ اللهِ بْنِ مُحَمَّدٍ عَنْ عَلِيِّ بْنِ الْحَكَمِ عَنْ أَبَانٍ عَنْ أَبِي عَبْدِ اللهِ (عَلَيْهِ السَّلام) قَالَ إِنَّ لِلْجُمُعَةِ حَقّاً وَحُرْمَةً فَإِيَّاكَ أَنْ تُضَيِّعَ أَوْ تُقَصِّرَ فِي شَيْءٍ مِنْ عِبَادَةِ اللهِ وَالتَّقَرُّبِ إِلَيْهِ بِالْعَمَلِ الصَّالِحِ وَتَرْكِ الْمَحَارِمِ كُلِّهَا فَإِنَّ اللهَ يُضَاعِفُ فِيهِ الْحَسَنَاتِ وَيَمْحُو فِيهِ السَّيِّئَاتِ وَيَرْفَعُ فِيهِ الدَّرَجَاتِ قَالَ وَذَكَرَ أَنَّ يَوْمَهُ مِثْلُ لَيْلَتِهِ فَإِنِ اسْتَطَعْتَ أَنْ تُحْيِيَهَا بِالصَّلاةِ وَالدُّعَاءِ فَافْعَلْ فَإِنَّ رَبَّكَ يَنْزِلُ فِي أَوَّلِ لَيْلَةِ الْجُمُعَةِ إِلَى سَمَاءِ الدُّنْيَا فَيُضَاعِفُ فِيهِ الْحَسَنَاتِ وَيَمْحُو فِيهِ السَّيِّئَاتِ وَإِنَّ اللهَ وَاسِعٌ كَرِيمٌ

Muhammad b. Yahya has narrated from 'Abd Allāh b. Muḥammad from 'Alī b. al-Hakam from Aban who has said the following: "Abu 'Abd Allāh, (عليه السلام), has said, 'For Friday there are rights and respect, you must not fail to observe them or have shortcomings in worshipping Allāh or in striving to become nearer to Him through good deeds and through refraining from all prohibited matters. Allāh on this day increases good deeds, obliterates bad deeds and raises degrees of excellence.' The narrator has said that the Imam then said, 'Friday night is like its day. If you can, stay awake all night in Salah (prayer) and supplication; your Lord in the beginning of Friday night (commands an angel who) descends to the first heaven, (he) increases good deeds, obliterates bad deeds and Allāh's kindness is vast and graceful.' (مجهول)[6]

---

[5] *Al-Kāfi, v3, ch66, h4*

[6] *Al-Kāfi, v3, ch66, h6*

7.

مُحَمَّدُ بْنُ يَحْيَى عَنْ مُحَمَّدِ بْنِ مُوسَى عَنِ الْعَبَّاسِ بْنِ مَعْرُوفٍ عَنِ ابْنِ أَبِي نَجْرَانَ عَنْ عَبْدِ اللهِ بْنِ سِنَانٍ عَنِ ابْنِ أَبِي يَعْفُورٍ عَنْ أَبِي حَمْزَةَ عَنْ أَبِي جَعْفَرٍ (عَلَيْهِ السَّلام) قَالَ قَالَ لَهُ رَجُلٌ كَيْفَ سُمِّيَتِ الْجُمُعَةُ قَالَ إِنَّ اللهَ عَزَّ وَجَلَّ جَمَعَ فِيهَا خَلْقَهُ لِوَلَايَةِ مُحَمَّدٍ وَوَصِيِّهِ فِي الْمِيثَاقِ فَسَمَّاهُ يَوْمَ الْجُمُعَةِ لِجَمْعِهِ فِيهِ خَلْقَهُ

Muhammad b. Yahya has narrated from Muḥammad b. Mūsā from al-‘ Abbas b. The Ma’ruf from b. abu Najran from ‘Abd Allāh b. Sinan from b. abu Ya‘fur from abu Hamzah who has said the following: “Abu Ja’far, (عليه السلام), has said, in answer to a question, ’How was Friday called Friday?’ The Imam said, ’Allāh, the Most Majestic, the Most Glorious, brought His creatures under the Divine Authority of Muhammad, (عليه السلام), and the Executor of his will during “the divine Covenant session”, and that session was called “al-Jumu‘ah” (the assembly) because of His calling His creatures together.’” (مجهول)[7]

8.

مُحَمَّدُ بْنُ يَحْيَى عَنْ مُحَمَّدِ بْنِ الْحُسَيْنِ عَنْ عَلِيِّ بْنِ النُّعْمَانِ عَنْ عُمَرَ بْنِ يَزِيدَ عَنْ جَابِرٍ عَنْ أَبِي جَعْفَرٍ (عَلَيْهِ السَّلام) قَالَ سُئِلَ عَنْ يَوْمِ الْجُمُعَةِ وَلَيْلَتِهَا فَقَالَ لَيْلَتُهَا غَرَّاءُ وَيَوْمُهَا يَوْمٌ زَاهِرٌ وَلَيْسَ عَلَى الْأَرْضِ يَوْمٌ تَغْرُبُ فِيهِ الشَّمْسُ أَكْثَرَ مُعَافًى مِنَ النَّارِ مِنْهُ مَنْ مَاتَ يَوْمَ الْجُمُعَةِ عَارِفاً بِحَقِّ أَهْلِ هَذَا الْبَيْتِ كَتَبَ اللهُ لَهُ بَرَاءَةً مِنَ النَّارِ وَبَرَاءَةً مِنَ الْعَذَابِ وَمَنْ مَاتَ لَيْلَةَ الْجُمُعَةِ أُعْتِقَ مِنَ النَّارِ

Muhammad b. Yahya has narrated from Muḥammad b. al-Husayn from ‘Alī b. al-Nu‘man from ‘Umar b. Yazid from Jabir who has said the following: “Someone asked abu Ja’far, (عليه السلام), about Friday and its night. The Imam replied, ’Friday night is the finest; its day is brilliant. There is no other day in which sunset takes place with as many rescued from the fire as is on Friday. If one dies on Friday while fully acknowledging the rights of Ahl al-Bayt (people of this house), Allāh writes for him

[7] *Al-Kāfi, v3, ch66, h7*

the certificate of freedom from the fire and punishment. If one dies on a Friday night, he is set free from the fire.' (صحيح)[8]

9.

مُحَمَّدُ بْنُ يَحْيَى عَنْ أَحْمَدَ بْنِ مُحَمَّدٍ عَنْ مُحَمَّدِ بْنِ خَالِدٍ عَنِ النَّضْرِ بْنِ سُوَيْدٍ عَنْ عَبْدِ اللهِ بْنِ سِنَانٍ قَالَ قَالَ أَبُو عَبْدِ اللهِ (عَلَيْهِ السَّلام) فَضَّلَ اللهُ الْجُمُعَةَ عَلَى غَيْرِهَا مِنَ الأَيَّامِ وَإِنَّ الْجِنَانَ لَتُزَخْرَفُ وَتُزَيَّنُ يَوْمَ الْجُمُعَةِ لِمَنْ أَتَاهَا وَإِنَّكُمْ تَتَسَابَقُونَ إِلَى الْجَنَّةِ عَلَى قَدْرِ سَبْقِكُمْ إِلَى الْجُمُعَةِ وَإِنَّ أَبْوَابَ السَّمَاءِ لَتُفَتَّحُ لِصُعُودِ أَعْمَالِ الْعِبَادِ

Muhammad b. Yahya has narrated from Ahmad b. Muḥammad from Muḥammad b. Khalid from al-Nadr b. al-Suwayd from 'Abd Allāh b. Sinan who has said the following: "Abu 'Abd Allāh, (عليه السلام), has said, 'Allāh has given excellence to Friday over other days. On Friday, decoration and beautification takes place in paradise for those who attend it (Friday). You race to paradise proportionate to the degree of your attending Friday. On Friday the doors of heavens open for the deeds of servants (of Allāh).''' (صحيح)[9]

10.

عَلِيُّ بْنُ إِبْرَاهِيمَ عَنْ مُحَمَّدِ بْنِ عِيسَى عَنْ يُونُسَ بْنِ عَبْدِ الرَّحْمَنِ عَنْ هِشَامِ بْنِ الْحَكَمِ قَالَ قَالَ أَبُو عَبْدِ اللهِ (عَلَيْهِ السَّلام) لِيَتَزَيَّنْ أَحَدُكُمْ يَوْمَ الْجُمُعَةِ يَغْتَسِلُ وَيَتَطَيَّبُ وَيُسَرِّحُ لِحْيَتَهُ وَيَلْبَسُ أَنْظَفَ ثِيَابِهِ وَلْيَتَهَيَّأْ لِلْجُمُعَةِ وَلْيَكُنْ عَلَيْهِ فِي ذَلِكَ الْيَوْمِ السَّكِينَةُ وَالْوَقَارُ وَلْيُحْسِنْ عِبَادَةَ رَبِّهِ وَلْيَفْعَلِ الْخَيْرَ مَا اسْتَطَاعَ فَإِنَّ اللهَ يَطَّلِعُ عَلَى أَهْلِ الأَرْضِ لِيُضَاعِفَ الْحَسَنَاتِ

---

[8] *Al-Kafi, v3, ch66, h8*

[9] *Al-Kafi, v3, ch66, h9*

Ali b. Ibrahim has narrated from Muḥammad b. 'Isa from Yunus b. 'Abd al-Rahman from Hisham b. al-Hakam who has said the following: "Abu 'Abd Allāh, (عليه السلام), has said, 'Everyone of you should take a shower, apply fragrance, comb your beard, dress up in your best dress and prepare himself for Friday. On that day, he should be serene and dignified. He should make his worshipping his Lord to be the best and do as much good as he can; Allāh watches over the people of earth to double their good deeds.''' (صحيح)[10]

11.

مُحَمَّدُ بْنُ يَحْيَى عَنْ أَحْمَدَ بْنِ مُحَمَّدٍ عَنِ الْحُسَيْنِ بْنِ سَعِيدٍ عَنْ مُحَمَّدِ بْنِ الْحُصَيْنِ عَنْ عُمَرَ الْجُرْجَانِيِّ عَنْ مُحَمَّدِ بْنِ الْعَلَاءِ عَنْ أَبِي عَبْدِ اللهِ (عَلَيْهِ السَّلام) قَالَ سَمِعْتُهُ يَقُولُ مَنْ أَخَذَ مِنْ شَارِبِهِ وَقَلَّمَ مِنْ أَظْفَارِهِ يَوْمَ الْجُمُعَةِ ثُمَّ قَالَ بِسْمِ اللهِ عَلَى سُنَّةِ مُحَمَّدٍ وَآلِ مُحَمَّدٍ كَتَبَ اللهُ لَهُ بِكُلِّ شَعْرَةٍ وَكُلِّ قُلَامَةٍ عِتْقَ رَقَبَةٍ وَلَمْ يَمْرَضْ مَرَضاً يُصِيبُهُ إِلَّا مَرَضَ الْمَوْتِ

Muhammad b. Yahya has narrated from Ahmad b. Muḥammad from al-Husayn b. Sa'id from Muḥammad b. al-Husayn from 'Umar al-Jurjaniy from Muḥammad b. al-'Ala' who has said the following: "I heard abu 'Abd Allāh, (عليه السلام), say, 'One may, on Friday trim his mustache and fingernails. In so doing if one says, " (I do this) in the name of Allāh and because of the Sunnah (traditions) of the Holy Prophet, Muhammad, and his family," Allāh writes for him for every hair and piece of fingernail a reward equal to freeing a slave. He will not become ill to a harmful degree except the illness that causes his death.''' (مجهول)[11]

12.

[10] *Al-Kafi, v3, ch67, h1*

[11] *Al-Kafi, v3, ch67, h2*

مُحَمَّدُ بْنُ يَحْيَى عَنْ مُحَمَّدِ بْنِ الْحُسَيْنِ عَنْ صَفْوَانَ بْنِ يَحْيَى عَنْ مَنْصُورِ بْنِ حَازِمٍ عَنْ أَبِي عَبْدِ اللهِ (عَلَيْهِ السَّلام) قَالَ الْغُسْلُ يَوْمَ الْجُمُعَةِ عَلَى الرِّجَالِ وَالنِّسَاءِ فِي الْحَضَرِ وَعَلَى الرِّجَالِ فِي السَّفَرِ

Muhammad b. Yahya has narrated from Muḥammad b. al-Husayn from Safwan b. Yahya from Mansur b. Hazim who has said the following: "Abu 'Abd Allāh, (عليه السلام), has said, 'Both men and women should take a shower on Friday when at home. On the journey men should take a shower on Friday.'" (صحيح)[12]

13.

عَلِيُّ بْنُ إِبْرَاهِيمَ عَنْ أَبِيهِ عَنْ حَمَّادِ بْنِ عِيسَى عَنْ حَرِيزٍ عَنْ زُرَارَةَ قَالَ قَالَ أَبُو جَعْفَرٍ (عَلَيْهِ السَّلام) لا تَدَعِ الْغُسْلَ يَوْمَ الْجُمُعَةِ فَإِنَّهُ سُنَّةٌ وَشَمَّ الطِّيبَ وَالْبَسْ صَالِحَ ثِيَابِكَ وَلْيَكُنْ فَرَاغُكَ مِنَ الْغُسْلِ قَبْلَ الزَّوَالِ فَإِذَا زَالَتْ فَقُمْ وَعَلَيْكَ السَّكِينَةَ وَالْوَقَارَ وَقَالَ الْغُسْلُ وَاجِبٌ يَوْمَ الْجُمُعَةِ

Ali b. Ibrahim has narrated from his father from Hammad b. 'Isa from Hariz from Zurāra who has narrated the following: "Abu Ja'far, (عليه السلام), has said, 'You must not ignore Ghusl (bath) on Friday; it is a sunnah. You should use perfumes, dress up in you proper dress and you should complete your Ghusl (bath) before noontime. At Zawal (declining of the sun toward the west at noontime) rise up with calmness and dignity for prayer.' He (the Imam) said, 'Ghusl (bath) on Friday is obligatory.'" (حسن)[13]

14.

مُحَمَّدُ بْنُ إِسْمَاعِيلَ عَنِ الْفَضْلِ بْنِ شَاذَانَ عَنِ ابْنِ أَبِي عُمَيْرٍ عَنْ حَفْصِ بْنِ الْبَخْتَرِيِّ عَنْ أَبِي عَبْدِ اللهِ (عَلَيْهِ السَّلام) قَالَ أَخْذُ الشَّارِبِ وَالأَظْفَارِ مِنَ الْجُمُعَةِ إِلَى الْجُمُعَةِ أَمَانٌ مِنَ الْجُذَامِ

---

[12] *Al-Kafi, v3, ch67, h3*

[13] *Al-Kafi, v3, ch67, h4*

Muhammad b. 'Isma'il has narrated from al-Fadl b. Shadhan from b. abu 'Umayr from Hafs b. al-Bakhtariy who has said the following: "Abu 'Abd Allāh, (عليه السلام), has said, 'Trimming one's mustache, and fingernails every Friday is protection against leprosy.'" (مجهول كالصحيح)[14]

15.

عَلِيُّ بْنُ إِبْرَاهِيمَ عَنْ أَبِيهِ عَنْ عَبْدِ اللهِ بْنِ الْمُغِيرَةِ عَنْ جَمِيلٍ عَنْ مُحَمَّدِ بْنِ مُسْلِمٍ عَنْ أَبِي جَعْفَرٍ (عَلَيْهِ السَّلَامُ) قَالَ إِنَّ اللهَ أَكْرَمَ بِالْجُمُعَةِ الْمُؤْمِنِينَ فَسَنَّهَا رَسُولُ اللهِ (صَلَّى اللهُ عَلَيْهِ وَآلِهِ) بِشَارَةً لَهُمْ وَالْمُنَافِقِينَ تَوْبِيخاً لِلْمُنَافِقِينَ وَلاَ يَنْبَغِي تَرْكُهَا فَمَنْ تَرَكَهَا مُتَعَمِّداً فَلاَ صَلَاةَ لَهُ

Ali b. Ibrahim has narrated from his father from 'Abd Allāh b. al-Mughirah from Jamil from Muḥammad b. Muslim who has said the following: "Abu Ja'far, (عليه السلام), has said, 'Allāh has granted honor to the believers by means of sending (Surah (chapter) of al-Jumu'ah). The Messenger of Allāh established it a Sunnah (noble tradition) and good news for them. He sent al-Munafiqun to reprimand the hypocrites. It is not proper to omit it. Salah (prayer) of one who willfully omits it is not valid.'" (حسن)[15]

16.

الْحُسَيْنُ بْنُ مُحَمَّدٍ عَنْ عَبْدِ اللهِ بْنِ عَامِرٍ عَنْ عَلِيِّ بْنِ مَهْزِيَارَ عَنِ النَّضْرِ بْنِ سُوَيْدٍ عَنْ عَبْدِ اللهِ بْنِ سِنَانٍ عَنْ أَبِي عَبْدِ اللهِ (عَلَيْهِ السَّلَامُ) قَالَ تَقُولُ فِي آخِرِ سَجْدَةٍ مِنَ النَّوَافِلِ بَعْدَ الْمَغْرِبِ لَيْلَةَ الْجُمُعَةِ اللهُمَّ إِنِّي أَسْأَلُكَ بِوَجْهِكَ الْكَرِيمِ وَاسْمِكَ الْعَظِيمِ أَنْ تُصَلِّيَ عَلَى مُحَمَّدٍ وَآلِ مُحَمَّدٍ وَأَنْ تَغْفِرَ لِي ذَنْبِيَ الْعَظِيمَ سَبْعاً

---

[14] *Al-Kāfi, v3, ch67, h7*

[15] *Al-Kāfi, v3, ch71, h4*

Al-Husayn b. Muḥammad has narrated from ‘Abd Allāh b. ‘Amir from ‘Alī b. Mahziyar from al-Nadr b. al-Suwayd from ‘Abd Allāh b. Sinan who has said the following: “Abu ‘Abd Allāh, (عليه السلام), has said that on Friday night after optional Salah (prayer), after Maghrib (soon after sunset) Salah (prayer) one should say, ‘O Lord, I appeal to You through Your gracious face and great name. “Allāhumma Salli ‘Ala Muḥammad wa ‘Ali Muḥammad (O Allāh grant Muḥammad and his family a compensation worthy of their serving Your cause,)” Forgive my great sin’- seven times.” (صحيح)[16]

---

[16] *Al-Kafi, v3, ch75, h1*

باب الاجتماعي

Chapter on Sociality

These Hadīths display the akhlaq/social etiquette one should have amongst the people

1.

مُحَمَّدُ بْنُ إِسْمَاعِيلَ عَنِ الْفَضْلِ بْنِ شَاذَانَ وَأَبُو عَلِيٍّ الْأَشْعَرِيُّ عَنْ مُحَمَّدِ بْنِ عَبْدِ الْجَبَّارِ جَمِيعاً عَنْ صَفْوَانَ بْنِ يَحْيَى عَنْ مُعَاوِيَةَ بْنِ وَهْبٍ قَالَ قُلْتُ لِأَبِي عَبْدِ اللهِ (عَلَيهِ السَّلام) كَيْفَ يَنْبَغِي لَنَا أَنْ نَصْنَعَ فِيمَا بَيْنَنَا وَبَيْنَ قَوْمِنَا وَفِيمَا بَيْنَنَا وَبَيْنَ خُلَطَائِنَا مِنَ النَّاسِ قَالَ فَقَالَ تُؤَدُّونَ الْأَمَانَةَ إِلَيْهِمْ وَتُقِيمُونَ الشَّهَادَةَ لَهُمْ وَعَلَيْهِمْ وَتَعُودُونَ مَرْضَاهُمْ وَتَشْهَدُونَ جَنَائِزَهُمْ

Muhammad b. Isma'il has narrated from al-Fadl b. Shadhan and Abu 'Alī al- Ash'ari from Muḥammad b. 'Abd al-Jabbar from Safwan b. Yahya from Mu'awiyah b. Wahab who has said the following: "Once I asked abu 'Abd Allāh (عليه السلام) 'What is the proper way to deal with ourselves, our people, our associates and the people in general?' The Imam said, 'You must return their trust, present your testimony for and against them, visit them during their illness and attend their funerals.'" (صحيح)[1]

---

[1] *Al-Kāfi, v2, ch1, h2*

2.

مُحَمَّدُ بْنُ يَحْيَى عَنْ أَحْمَدَ بْنِ مُحَمَّدٍ عَنْ عَلِيِّ بْنِ الْحَكَمِ عَنْ مُعَاوِيَةَ بْنِ وَهْبٍ قَالَ قُلْتُ لَهُ كَيْفَ يَنْبَغِي لَنَا أَنْ نَصْنَعَ فِيمَا بَيْنَنَا وَبَيْنَ قَوْمِنَا وَبَيْنَ خُلَطَائِنَا مِنَ النَّاسِ مِمَّنْ لَيْسُوا عَلَى أَمْرِنَا قَالَ تَنْظُرُونَ إِلَى أَئِمَّتِكُمُ الَّذِينَ تَقْتَدُونَ بِهِمْ فَتَصْنَعُونَ مَا يَصْنَعُونَ فَوَ اللَّهِ إِنَّهُمْ لَيَعُودُونَ مَرْضَاهُمْ وَيَشْهَدُونَ جَنَائِزَهُمْ وَيُقِيمُونَ الشَّهَادَةَ لَهُمْ وَعَلَيْهِمْ وَيُؤَدُّونَ الْأَمَانَةَ إِلَيْهِمْ

Muhammad b. Yahya has narrated from Ahmad b. Muḥammad from ʿAlī b. al-Hakam from Mu'awiyah b. Wahab who has said the following: "Once I asked the Imam (عليه السلام) 'What is the proper way to deal with ourselves and our people, our associates of the people who do not believe as we do?' The Imam said, 'Look to your 'A'immah (plural of Imam) whom you follow and do what they do. By Allāh, they, ('A'immah) visit their sick people, attend their funerals, present their testimony for and against them and return their trust.'" (صحيح)[2]

3.

أَبُو عَلِيٍّ الْأَشْعَرِيُّ عَنْ مُحَمَّدِ بْنِ عَبْدِ الْجَبَّارِ وَمُحَمَّدُ بْنُ إِسْمَاعِيلَ عَنِ الْفَضْلِ بْنِ شَاذَانَ جَمِيعاً عَنْ صَفْوَانَ بْنِ يَحْيَى عَنْ أَبِي أُسَامَةَ زَيْدٍ الشَّحَّامِ قَالَ قَالَ لِي أَبُو عَبْدِ اللَّهِ (عَلَيهِ السَّلام) اقْرَأْ عَلَى مَنْ تَرَى أَنَّهُ يُطِيعُنِي مِنْهُمْ وَيَأْخُذُ بِقَوْلِيَ السَّلَامَ وَأُوصِيكُمْ بِتَقْوَى اللَّهِ عَزَّ وَجَلَّ وَالْوَرَعِ فِي دِينِكُمْ وَالِاجْتِهَادِ لِلَّهِ وَصِدْقِ الْحَدِيثِ وَأَدَاءِ الْأَمَانَةِ وَطُولِ السُّجُودِ وَحُسْنِ الْجِوَارِ فَبِهَذَا جَاءَ مُحَمَّدٌ (صَلَّى اللهُ عَلَيهِ وآلِه) أَدُّوا الْأَمَانَةَ إِلَى مَنِ ائْتَمَنَكُمْ عَلَيْهَا بَرّاً أَوْ فَاجِراً فَإِنَّ رَسُولَ اللَّهِ (صَلَّى اللهُ عَلَيهِ وآلِه) كَانَ يَأْمُرُ بِأَدَاءِ الْخَيْطِ وَالْمِخْيَطِ صِلُوا عَشَائِرَكُمْ وَاشْهَدُوا جَنَائِزَهُمْ وَعُودُوا مَرْضَاهُمْ وَأَدُّوا حُقُوقَهُمْ فَإِنَّ الرَّجُلَ مِنْكُمْ إِذَا وَرِعَ فِي دِينِهِ وَصَدَقَ الْحَدِيثَ وَأَدَّى الْأَمَانَةَ وَحَسُنَ خُلُقُهُ مَعَ النَّاسِ قِيلَ هَذَا جَعْفَرِيٌّ فَيَسُرُّنِي ذَلِكَ وَيَدْخُلُ عَلَيَّ مِنْهُ السُّرُورُ وَقِيلَ هَذَا أَدَبُ جَعْفَرٍ وَإِذَا كَانَ عَلَى غَيْرِ ذَلِكَ دَخَلَ عَلَيَّ بَلَاؤُهُ وَعَارُهُ وَقِيلَ هَذَا أَدَبُ جَعْفَرٍ فَوَ اللَّهِ لَحَدَّثَنِي أَبِي (عَلَيهِ السَّلام) أَنَّ الرَّجُلَ كَانَ يَكُونُ فِي الْقَبِيلَةِ مِنْ شِيعَةِ عَلِيٍّ (عَلَيهِ السَّلام) فَيَكُونُ زَيْنَهَا آدَاهُمْ لِلْأَمَانَةِ وَأَقْضَاهُمْ

[2] *Al-Kāfi, v2, ch1, h4*

لِلْحُقُوقِ وَأَصْدَقَهُمْ لِلْحَدِيثِ إِلَيْهِ وَصَايَاهُمْ وَوَدَائِعُهُمْ تُسْأَلُ الْعَشِيرَةُ عَنْهُ فَتَقُولُ مَنْ مِثْلُ فُلانٍ إِنَّهُ لَآدَانَا لِلأَمَانَةِ وَأَصْدَقُنَا لِلْحَدِيثِ

Abu 'Alī al-Ash'ari has narrated from Muḥammad b. 'Abd al-Jabbar from Safwan b. Yahya from abu 'Usamah Zayd al-Shahham who has said the following: "Once abu 'Abd Allāh (عليه السلام) said to me, 'Convey greetings of peace from me to all that you will see of those who obey me and uphold my words. Tell them that I enjoin upon you to be pious before Allāh, the Most Majestic, the Most Holy, to restraint yourselves from the worldly attractions (sins) in the matters of your religion, to work hard, to maintain truthfulness in your words, keep your trust, perform long prostrations, and to maintain good neighborly relations. This is what Muḥammad (عليه السلام) has brought (from Allāh). Return the trust to those who have entrusted you, whether they are virtuous people or evildoers. The Messenger of Allāh would command to return the needle and swing thread. Maintain good relations with the people of your tribe, attend their funerals, visit their sick people, and fulfill your obligations toward them. If one of you maintains restraint in the worldly attractions (sins) in the matters of his religion, is truthful in his words, keeps his trust, has acquired proper moral discipline to behave toward people, it will be said about him, 'This is a Ja'fari (follower of Ja'far b. Muhammad, recipient of divine supreme covenant)', and this will bring me joy and delight and they will say, 'This is the discipline of Ja'far.' If otherwise, its misfortune and disgrace will trouble me and they will say, 'This is the behavior of Ja'far. 'By Allāh my father spoke to me about a man who lived with a Shi'a (followers) of 'Alī (عليه السلام) tribe whose beauty was in his keeping his trust, fulfilling his obligations, and his being the most truthful in his words. With him they would keep their important documents and valuables. If one were to ask people of the tribe about him, they would ask, "Who is like him? He is the most trusted one in safekeeping of valuables and the most truthful in his words.'" (صحيح)[3]

---

[3] *Al-Kāfi, v2, ch1, h4*

4.

عِدَّةٌ مِنْ أَصْحَابِنَا عَنْ أَحْمَدَ بْنِ مُحَمَّدِ بْنِ خَالِدٍ عَنْ إِسْمَاعِيلَ بْنِ مِهْرَانَ عَنْ مُحَمَّدِ بْنِ حَفْصٍ عَنْ أَبِي الرَّبِيعِ الشَّامِيِّ قَالَ دَخَلْتُ عَلَى أَبِي عَبْدِ اللهِ (عَلَيهِ السَّلام) وَالْبَيْتُ غَاصٌّ بِأَهْلِهِ فِيهِ الْخُرَاسَانِيُّ وَالشَّامِيُّ وَمِنْ أَهْلِ الآفَاقِ فَلَمْ أَجِدْ مَوْضِعاً أَقْعُدُ فِيهِ فَجَلَسَ أَبُو عَبْدِ اللهِ (عَلَيهِ السَّلام) وَكَانَ مُتَّكِئاً ثُمَّ قَالَ يَا شِيعَةَ آلِ مُحَمَّدٍ اعْلَمُوا أَنَّهُ لَيْسَ مِنَّا مَنْ لَمْ يَمْلِكْ نَفْسَهُ عِنْدَ غَضَبِهِ وَمَنْ لَمْ يُحْسِنْ صُحْبَةَ مَنْ صَحِبَهُ وَمُخَالَقَةَ مَنْ خَالَقَهُ وَمُرَافَقَةَ مَنْ رَافَقَهُ وَمُجَاوَرَةَ مَنْ جَاوَرَهُ وَمُمَالَحَةَ مَنْ مَالَحَهُ يَا شِيعَةَ آلِ مُحَمَّدٍ اتَّقُوا اللهَ مَا اسْتَطَعْتُمْ وَلا حَوْلَ وَلا قُوَّةَ إِلا بِاللهِ

A number of our people have narrated from Ahmad b. Muḥammad b. Khalid from Isma'il b. Mehran from Muḥammad b. Hafs from abu al-Rabi' al-Shami who has said the following: "Once I went in the presence of abu 'Abd Allāh (عليه السلام) and the house was full of people. There were people from Khurasan, from al-Sham and from various horizons and I could not find a place to sit. Abu 'Abd Allāh (عليه السلام) sat in his place and he was leaning against a pillow. He said, 'O Shi'a (followers) of the family of Muḥammad (عليه السلام) bear in mind that one who is not able to control his soul when angry is not from us, and so also is one who does not better his association with his associates, show proper behavior with those who exercise proper behavior, befriend those who befriend him, provide protection to those who protect him, observe proper table manners with those who share with him the table. O Shi'a (followers) of the family of Muḥammad (عليه السلام) be pious before Allāh to the best of your abilities. There are no means and no power without Allāh.'" (مجهول)[4]

5.

عَلِيُّ بْنُ إِبْرَاهِيمَ عَنْ أَبِيهِ عَنِ ابْنِ أَبِي عُمَيْرٍ عَمَّنْ ذَكَرَهُ عَنْ أَبِي عَبْدِ اللهِ (عَلَيهِ السَّلام) فِي قَوْلِ اللهِ عَزَّ وَجَلَّ إِنَّا نَرَاكَ مِنَ الْمُحْسِنِينَ قَالَ كَانَ يُوَسِّعُ الْمَجْلِسَ وَيَسْتَقْرِضُ لِلْمُحْتَاجِ وَيُعِينُ الضَّعِيفَ

[4] *Al-Kāfi, v2, ch2, h2*

Ali b. Ibrahim has narrated from his father from b. abu 'Umayr from those whom he has mentioned (in his book) from abu 'Abd Allāh (عليه السلام) who has said the following: "About the words of Allāh, the Most Majestic, the Most Holy, 'We believe you to be a righteous person,' (12:36) the Imam said, 'He would make room for others in a gathering, lend money to the needy and assist the weak.'" (حسن)[5]

6.

قَالَ وَسَمِعْتُ أَبَا عَبْدِ الله (عَلَيهِ السَّلام) يَقُولُ حُبُّ الأَبْرَارِ لِلأَبْرَارِ ثَوَابٌ لِلأَبْرَارِ وَحُبُّ الْفُجَّارِ لِلأَبْرَارِ فَضِيلَةٌ لِلأَبْرَارِ وَبُغْضُ الْفُجَّارِ لِلأَبْرَارِ زَيْنٌ لِلأَبْرَارِ وَبُغْضُ الأَبْرَارِ لِلْفُجَّارِ خِزْيٌ عَلَى الْفُجَّارِ

He has also said, 'I heard abu 'Abd Allāh (عليه السلام) saying: "The virtuous ones' love of other virtuous ones is a rewarding deed for them. Indecent ones loving the virtuous ones is a credit for the virtuous ones. Indecent ones' hating the virtuous ones beautifies the virtuous ones. Virtuous one's hating the indecent ones is a loss to the indecent ones." (صحيح على الظاهر)[6]

7.

مُحَمَّدُ بْنُ يَحْيَى عَنْ أَحْمَدَ بْنِ مُحَمَّدٍ وَعَلِيُّ بْنُ إِبْرَاهِيمَ عَنْ أَبِيهِ جَمِيعاً عَنِ ابْنِ مَحْبُوبٍ عَنْ هِشَامِ بْنِ سَالِمٍ عَنْ أَبِي بَصِيرٍ عَنْ أَبِي جَعْفَرٍ (عَلَيهِ السَّلام) قَالَ إِنَّ أَعْرَابِيّاً مِنْ بَنِي تَمِيمٍ أَتَى النَّبِيَّ (صَلَّى اللهُ عَلَيْهِ وآلِه) فَقَالَ لَهُ أَوْصِنِي فَكَانَ مِمَّا أَوْصَاهُ تَحَبَّبْ إِلَى النَّاسِ يُحِبُّوكَ

Muhammad b. Yahya has narrated from Ahmad b. Muḥammad and 'Alī b. Ibrahim has narrated from his father all from b. Mahbub from Hisham b. Salim from abu Basir

---

[5] *Al-Kāfi, v2, ch2, h3*

[6] *Al-Kāfi, v2, ch4, h6*

from abu Ja'far (عليه السلام) who has said the following: "Once an Arab man came to the Holy Prophet and said, 'Instinct me with good advice.' Of the good advice to him was: 'Love people, they will love you.'" (صحيح)[7]

8.

عِدَّةٌ مِنْ أَصْحَابِنَا عَنْ أَحْمَدَ بْنِ مُحَمَّدِ بْنِ خَالِدٍ عَنْ عُثْمَانَ بْنِ عِيسَى عَنْ سَمَاعَةَ عَنْ أَبِي عَبْدِ اللهِ (عَلَيهِ السَّلام) قَالَ مُجَامَلَةُ النَّاسِ ثُلُثُ الْعَقْلِ

A number of our people have narrated from Ahmad b. Muḥammad b. Khalid from 'Uthman b. 'Isa from Sama'a from abu 'Abd Allāh (عليه السلام) who has said the following: "Dealing with people in a graceful manner is one third of (the power) reason." (موثق)[8]

9.

أَحْمَدُ بْنُ مُحَمَّدِ بْنِ خَالِدٍ وَمُحَمَّدُ بْنُ يَحْيَى عَنْ أَحْمَدَ بْنِ مُحَمَّدِ بْنِ عِيسَى جَمِيعاً عَنْ عَلِيِّ بْنِ الْحَكَمِ عَنْ هِشَامِ بْنِ سَالِمٍ عَنْ أَبِي عَبْدِ اللهِ (عَلَيهِ السَّلام) قَالَ إِذَا أَحْبَبْتَ رَجُلاً فَأَخْبِرْهُ بِذَلِكَ فَإِنَّهُ أَثْبَتُ لِلْمَوَدَّةِ بَيْنَكُمَا

Ahmad b. Khalid and Muḥammad b. Yahya have narrated from Ahmad b. Muḥammad b. 'Isa all from 'Alī b. al-Hakam from Hisham b. Salim from abu 'Abd Allāh (عليه السلام) who has said the following: "When you love a man(as a brother), tell him about it; it strengthens your love for one another." (صحيح)[9]

---

[7] *Al-Kāfi, v2, ch5, h1*

[8] *Al-Kāfi, v2, ch5, h2*

[9] *Al-Kāfi, v2, ch6, h2*

10.

عِدَّةٌ مِنْ أَصْحَابِنَا عَنْ سَهْلِ بْنِ زِيَادٍ عَنْ عَبْدِ الرَّحْمَنِ بْنِ أَبِي نَجْرَانَ عَنْ عَاصِمِ بْنِ حُمَيْدٍ عَنْ مُحَمَّدِ بْنِ مُسْلِمٍ عَنْ أَبِي جَعْفَرٍ (عَلَيهِ السَّلام) قَالَ كَانَ سَلْمَانُ رَحِمَهُ اللهُ يَقُولُ أَفْشُوا سَلامَ اللهِ فَإِنَّ سَلامَ اللهِ لا يَنَالُ الظَّالِمِينَ

A number of our people have narrated from Sahl b. Ziyad from 'Abd al- Rahman b. abu Najran from 'Asim b. Hamid from Muḥammad b. Muslim from abu Ja'far (عليه السلام) who has said the following: "Salman, May Allāh grant him favors, would say, 'Offer the greeting of peace from Allāh openly; the unjust do not receive the greeting of peace from Allāh.'" (موثق)[10]

11.

عَنْهُ عَنِ ابْنِ فَضَّالٍ عَنْ مُعَاوِيَةَ بْنِ وَهْبٍ عَنْ أَبِي عَبْدِ اللهِ (عَلَيهِ السَّلام) قَالَ إِنَّ اللهَ عَزَّ وَجَلَّ قَالَ إِنَّ الْبَخِيلَ مَنْ يَبْخَلُ بِالسَّلامِ

It is narrated from him (narrator of the Hadīth above) from b. Faddal from Mu'awiyah b. Wahab from abu 'Abd Allāh (عليه السلام) who has said the following: "Allāh, the Most Majestic, the Most Holy, has said, 'Really stingy is one who is stingy in offering the greeting of peace.'" (صحيح)[11]

12.

عِدَّةٌ مِنْ أَصْحَابِنَا عَنْ أَحْمَدَ بْنِ مُحَمَّدٍ عَنْ عُثْمَانَ بْنِ عِيسَى عَنْ هَارُونَ بْنِ خَارِجَةَ عَنْ أَبِي عَبْدِ اللهِ (عَلَيهِ السَّلام) قَالَ مِنَ التَّوَاضُعِ أَنْ تُسَلِّمَ عَلَى مَنْ لَقِيتَ

---

[10] *Al-Kāfi, v2, ch7, h4*

[11] *Al-Kāfi, v2, ch7, h6*

A number of our people have narrated from Ahmad b. Muḥammad from ‘Uthman b. ‘Isa from Harun b. Kharijah from abu ‘Abd Allāh (عليه السلام) who has said the following: “It is of humility to offer the greeting of peace to whomever you meet.” (صحيح)[12]

13.

عَلِيُّ بْنُ إِبْرَاهِيمَ عَنْ أَبِيهِ عَنِ ابْنِ أَبِي عُمَيْرٍ عَنِ ابْنِ أُذَيْنَةَ عَنْ زُرَارَةَ عَنْ أَبِي جَعْفَرٍ (عَلَيهِ السَّلام) قَالَ دَخَلَ يَهُودِيٌّ عَلَى رَسُولِ الله (صَلَّى اللهُ عَلَيْهِ وآلِه) وَعَائِشَةُ عِنْدَهُ فَقَالَ السَّامُ عَلَيْكُمْ فَقَالَ رَسُولُ الله (صَلَّى اللهُ عَلَيْهِ وآلِه) عَلَيْكُمْ ثُمَّ دَخَلَ آخَرُ فَقَالَ مِثْلَ ذَلِكَ فَرَدَّ عَلَيْهِ كَمَا رَدَّ عَلَى صَاحِبِهِ ثُمَّ دَخَلَ آخَرُ فَقَالَ مِثْلَ ذَلِكَ فَرَدَّ رَسُولُ الله (صَلَّى اللهُ عَلَيْهِ وآلِه) كَمَا رَدَّ عَلَى صَاحِبَيْهِ فَغَضِبَتْ عَائِشَةُ فَقَالَتْ عَلَيْكُمُ السَّامُ وَالْغَضَبُ وَاللَّعْنَةُ يَا مَعْشَرَ الْيَهُودِ يَا إِخْوَةَ الْقِرَدَةِ وَالْخَنَازِيرِ فَقَالَ لَهَا رَسُولُ الله (صَلَّى اللهُ عَلَيْهِ وآلِه) يَا عَائِشَةُ إِنَّ الْفُحْشَ لَوْ كَانَ مُمَثَّلاً لَكَانَ مِثَالَ سَوْءٍ إِنَّ الرِّفْقَ لَمْ يُوضَعْ عَلَى شَيْءٍ قَطُّ إِلا زَانَهُ وَلَمْ يُرْفَعْ عَنْهُ قَطُّ إِلا شَانَهُ قَالَتْ يَا رَسُولَ الله أَ مَا سَمِعْتَ إِلَى قَوْلِهِمُ السَّامُ عَلَيْكُمْ فَقَالَ بَلَى أَ مَا سَمِعْتِ مَا رَدَدْتُ عَلَيْهِمْ قُلْتُ عَلَيْكُمْ فَإِذَا سَلَّمَ عَلَيْكُمْ مُسْلِمٌ فَقُولُوا سَلامٌ عَلَيْكُمْ وَإِذَا سَلَّمَ عَلَيْكُمْ كَافِرٌ فَقُولُوا عَلَيْكَ

Ali b. Ibrahim has narrated from his father from b. abu ‘Umayr from b. ‘Udhaynah from Zurara from abu Ja’far (عليه السلام) who has said the following: “Once, a Jewish person went in the presence of the Messenger of Allāh while ‘A’ishah was with him. The Jewish person said, ‘Sam ‘Alaykum instead of ‘ Salamun ‘Alaykum. ’ The Messenger of Allah said, Alaykum. ’ Then another Jewish person came and said the same thing as the one before and the Messenger of Allāh responded just as before. Then a third Jewish person came. He also said what the other two had said before and the Messenger of Allāh responded just as that to the other two before. ‘A’ishah became angry and said, Alaykum al-Sam (wrath and condemnation) O Jewish group, brethren of monkeys and swine.’ The Messenger of Allāh said to her, ‘O ‘A’ishah, if name-calling were to appear with a shape and form it would have a very evil shape.

---

[12] *Al-Kāfi, v2, ch7, h12*

Wherever gentleness is placed it beautifies it and removing it is only to make it despised. ' "'A'ishah then asked, 'O the Messenger of Allāh, did you not hear their words: 'al-Sam Alaykuml' The Messenger of Allāh said, 'I heard them but did you not note what I said? I said, 'Alaykum'. Whenever a Muslim offers you the greeting of peace say, ' Salamun 'Alaykum,' but when a non-Muslim says something in their manners, just say, Alaykum', meaning the same to you.' (حسن)[13]

14.

مُحَمَّدُ بْنُ يَحْيَى عَنْ أَحْمَدَ بْنِ مُحَمَّدٍ وَعَلِيُّ بْنُ إِبْرَاهِيمَ عَنْ أَبِيهِ جَمِيعاً عَنِ ابْنِ مَحْبُوبٍ عَنْ عَبْدِ اللهِ بْنِ سِنَانٍ قَالَ قَالَ لِي أَبُو عَبْدِ اللهِ (عَلَيهِ السَّلام) إِنَّ مِنْ إِجْلَالِ اللهِ عَزَّ وَجَلَّ إِجْلَالَ الشَّيْخِ الْكَبِيرِ

Muhammad b. Yahya has narrated from Ahmad b. Muḥammad and 'Alī b. Ibrahim has narrated from his father all from b. Mahbub from 'Abd Allāh b. Sinan who has said the following: "Abu 'Abd Allāh (عليه السلام) has said, 'It is of honoring Allāh, the Most Majestic, the Most Holy, to honor a Muslim man advanced in age.'" (صحيح)[14]

15.

مُحَمَّدُ بْنُ يَحْيَى عَنْ أَحْمَدَ بْنِ مُحَمَّدِ بْنِ عِيسَى عَنِ الْحَسَنِ بْنِ مَحْبُوبٍ عَنْ مَالِكِ بْنِ عَطِيَّةَ عَنْ أَبِي بَصِيرٍ عَنْ أَبِي عَبْدِ اللهِ (عَلَيهِ السَّلام) قَالَ إِذَا كَانَ الْقَوْمُ ثَلَاثَةً فَلَا يَتَنَاجَى مِنْهُمُ اثْنَانِ دُونَ صَاحِبِهِمَا فَإِنَّ فِي ذَلِكَ مَا يُحْزِنُهُ وَيُؤْذِيهِ

Muhammad b. Yahya has narrated from Ahmad b. Muḥammad b. 'Isa from al-Hassan b. Mahbub from Malik b. 'Atiyyah from abu Basir from abu 'Abd Allāh (عليه السلام)

---

[13] *Al-Kāfi, v2, ch11, h1*

[14] *Al-Kāfi, v2, ch16, h1*

who has said the following: "Out of three people, two of them should not hold a private conversation because it saddens and hurts the feelings of the third." (صحيح)[15]

16.

مُحَمَّدُ بْنُ يَحْيَى عَنْ أَحْمَدَ بْنِ مُحَمَّدِ بْنِ عِيسَى عَنْ مُعَمَّرِ بْنِ خَلادٍ قَالَ سَأَلْتُ أَبَا الْحَسَنِ (عَلَيهِ السَّلام) فَقُلْتُ جُعِلْتُ فِدَاكَ الرَّجُلُ يَكُونُ مَعَ الْقَوْمِ فَيَجْرِي بَيْنَهُمْ كَلامٌ يَمْزَحُونَ وَيَضْحَكُونَ فَقَالَ لا بَأْسَ مَا لَمْ يَكُنْ فَظَنَنْتُ أَنَّهُ عَنَى الْفُحْشَ ثُمَّ قَالَ إِنَّ رَسُولَ اللهِ (صَلَّى اللهُ عَلَيْهِ وآلِه) كَانَ يَأْتِيهِ الأَعْرَابِيُّ فَيُهْدِي لَهُ الْهَدِيَّةَ ثُمَّ يَقُولُ مَكَانَهُ أَعْطِنَا ثَمَنَ هَدِيَّتِنَا فَيَضْحَكُ رَسُولُ اللهِ (صَلَّى اللهُ عَلَيْهِ وآلِه) وَكَانَ إِذَا اغْتَمَّ يَقُولُ مَا فَعَلَ الأَعْرَابِيُّ لَيْتَهُ أَتَانَا

Muhammad b. Yahya has narrated from Ahmad b. Muḥammad b. 'Isa from Mu'ammar b. Khallad who has said the following: "Once I asked abu al-Hassan (عليه السلام) 'May Allāh keep my soul in service for your cause, can a man be with a people who speak and laugh at funny stories?' The Imam said, 'It is not an offense if there is not that.' I (the narrator) then thought ' that ' was his signal to indecent acts. The Imam then said, 'Arabs would come to the Messenger of Allāh and bring him gifts and then say, "Pay us for our gifts." The Messenger of Allāh would laugh. When he felt sad he would say, "What happened to the Arab man? I wish he comes by.' (صحيح)[16]

17.

عَنْهُ عَنْ أَبِيهِ عَنِ ابْنِ أَبِي عُمَيْرٍ عَمَّنْ حَدَّثَهُ عَنْ أَبِي عَبْدِ اللهِ (عَلَيهِ السَّلام) قَالَ إِذَا أَحْبَبْتَ رَجُلاً فَلا تُمَازِحْهُ وَلا تُمَارِهِ

---

[15] *Al-Kafi, v2, ch20, h1*

[16] *Al-Kafi, v2, ch23, h1*

It is narrated from him (narrator of the Hadīth above) from b. abu 'Umayr from those whom he has mentioned (in his book) from abu 'Abd Allāh (عليه السلام) who has said the following: "If you love a person, do not play jokes on him and do not argue with him." (حسن)[17]

18.

عَنْهُ عَنِ النَّهِيكِيِّ عَنْ إِبْرَاهِيمَ بْنِ عَبْدِ الْحَمِيدِ عَنِ الْحَكَمِ الْخَيَّاطِ قَالَ قَالَ أَبُو عَبْدِ اللهِ (عَلَيهِ السَّلام) حُسْنُ الْجِوَارِ يَعْمُرُ الدِّيَارَ وَيَزِيدُ فِي الأَعْمَارِ

It is narrated from him (narrator of the Hadīth above) from al-Nahiki from Ibrahim b. 'Abd al-Hamid from al-Hakam al-Khayyat who has said the following: "Abu 'Abd Allāh (عليه السلام) has said, 'Maintaining good neighborly relations increases the development of the country and one's life span.'" (مجهول كالحسن)[18]

19.

أَبُو عَلِيٍّ الأَشْعَرِيُّ عَنِ الْحَسَنِ بْنِ عَلِيٍّ الْكُوفِيِّ عَنْ عُبَيْسِ بْنِ هِشَامٍ عَنْ مُعَاوِيَةَ بْنِ عَمَّارٍ عَنْ أَبِي عَبْدِ اللهِ (عَلَيهِ السَّلام) قَالَ قَالَ رَسُولُ اللهِ (صَلَّى اللهُ عَلَيْهِ وآلِه) حُسْنُ الْجِوَارِ يَعْمُرُ الدِّيَارَ وَيُنْسِئُ فِي الأَعْمَارِ

Abu 'Alī al-Ash'ari has narrated from al-Hassan b. 'Alī al-Kufi from 'Uthman bays b. Hisham from Mu'awiyah b. 'Ammar from abu 'Abd Allāh (عليه السلام) who has said the following: "The Messenger of Allāh has said, 'Maintaining good neighborly relations develops the country and extends one's lifespan.'" (صحيح)[19]

---

[17] *Al-Kāfi, v2, ch23, h9*

[18] *Al-Kāfi, v2, ch24, h8*

[19] *Al-Kāfi, v2, ch24, h10*

20.

وَعَنْهُ عَنْ أَبِيهِ عَنِ ابْنِ أَبِي عُمَيْرٍ عَنْ جَمِيلِ بْنِ دَرَّاجٍ عَنْ أَبِي جَعْفَرٍ (عَلَيهِ السَّلام) قَالَ حَدُّ الْجِوَارِ أَرْبَعُونَ دَاراً مِنْ كُلِّ جَانِبٍ مِنْ بَيْنِ يَدَيْهِ وَمِنْ خَلْفِهِ وَعَنْ يَمِينِهِ وَعَنْ شِمَالِهِ

It is narrated from him (narrator of the Hadīth above) from his father from b. abu 'Umayr from Jamil b. Darraj from abu Ja'far (عليه السلام) who has said the following: "The limits of a neighborhood are forty houses on all sides, front, back, right and left." (حسن)[20]

21.

مُحَمَّدُ بْنُ يَحْيَى عَنْ أَحْمَدَ بْنِ مُحَمَّدٍ عَنِ الْوَشَّاءِ عَنْ جَمِيلِ بْنِ دَرَّاجٍ عَنْ أَبِي عَبْدِ الله (عَلَيهِ السَّلام) قَالَ كَانَ رَسُولُ الله (صَلَّى اللهُ عَلَيْهِ وآلِه) يُقَسِّمُ لَحَظَاتِهِ بَيْنَ أَصْحَابِهِ فَيَنْظُرُ إِلَى ذَا وَيَنْظُرُ إِلَى ذَا بِالسَّوِيَّةِ قَالَ وَلَمْ يَبْسُطْ رَسُولُ الله (صَلَّى اللهُ عَلَيْهِ وآلِه) رِجْلَيْهِ بَيْنَ أَصْحَابِهِ قَطُّ وَإِنْ كَانَ لَيُصَافِحُهُ الرَّجُلُ فَمَا يَتْرُكُ رَسُولُ الله (صَلَّى اللهُ عَلَيْهِ وآلِه) يَدَهُ مِنْ يَدِهِ حَتَّى يَكُونَ هُوَ التَّارِكَ فَلَمَّا فَطَنُوا لِذَلِكَ كَانَ الرَّجُلُ إِذَا صَافَحَهُ قَالَ بِيَدِهِ فَنَزَعَهَا مِنْ يَدِهِ

Muhammad b. Yahya has narrated from Ahmad b. Muḥammad from al- Washsha' from Jamil b. Darraj from abu 'Abd Allāh (عليه السلام) who has said the following: "The Messenger of Allāh would look to every one of his companions in equal proportions of time. He would look to this and then to that person. The Messenger of Allāh was never seen stretching his legs in a gathering of his companions. When he would shake hands, with a person, the Messenger of Allāh would not pull back his hand before the other man. When they noticed it thereafter a man shaking hands with him would pull his hand away quickly. (صحيح)[21]

---

[20] *Al-Kāfi, v2, ch25, h2*

[21] *Al-Kāfi, v2, ch28, h1*

باب العلم الغيب

Chapter on the Hidden Knowledge

Often times we are asked whether the Prophets or A'immah had 'Ilm al-Ghayb, and if so, then to what extent, the Hadīths below answer these questions.

1.

عَلِيُّ بْنُ إِبْرَاهِيمَ عَنْ صَالِحِ بْنِ السِّنْدِيِّ عَنْ جَعْفَرِ بْنِ بَشِيرٍ عَنْ ضُرَيْسٍ قَالَ سَمِعْتُ أَبَا جَعْفَرٍ (عَلَيْهِ السَّلام)
يَقُولُ إِنَّ للهِ عَزَّ وَجَلَّ عِلْمَيْنِ عِلْمٌ مَبْذُولٌ وَعِلْمٌ مَكْفُوفٌ فَأَمَّا الْمَبْذُولُ فَإِنَّهُ لَيْسَ مِنْ شَيْءٍ تَعْلَمُهُ الْمَلائِكَةُ
وَالرُّسُلُ إِلا نَحْنُ نَعْلَمُهُ وَأَمَّا الْمَكْفُوفُ فَهُوَ الَّذِي عِنْدَ اللهِ عَزَّ وَجَلَّ فِي أُمِّ الْكِتَابِ إِذَا خَرَجَ نَفَذَ

Ali b. Ibrahim has narrated from Salih b. al-Sindi from Ja'far b. Bashir from Durays who has said that he heard abu Ja'far (عليه السلام) say the following. "Allāh, the Most Holy, the Most High, has two kinds of knowledge. One kind is that which is granted and the kind is that which I withheld. Of the one which, is granted, nothing is known to the angels and the Messengers, but only we know it. The one which is withheld is the kind that is before Allāh, the Most Holy, the Most High in the original Book. When it appears it permeates." (مجهول)[1]

2.

أَبُو عَلِيٍّ الاشْعَرِيُّ عَنْ مُحَمَّدِ بْنِ عَبْدِ الْجَبَّارِ عَنْ مُحَمَّدِ بْنِ إِسْمَاعِيلَ عَنْ عَلِيِّ بْنِ النُّعْمَانِ عَنْ سُوَيْدٍ الْقَلاءِ عَنْ أَبِي أَيُّوبَ عَنْ أَبِي بَصِيرٍ عَنْ ابي جعفر (عَلَيْهِ السَّلام) قَالَ إِنَّ لله عَزَّ وَجَلَّ عِلْمَيْنِ عِلْمٌ لا يَعْلَمُهُ إِلا هُوَ وَعِلْمٌ عَلَّمَهُ مَلائِكَتَهُ وَرُسُلَهُ فَمَا عَلَّمَهُ مَلائِكَتَهُ وَرُسُلَهُ (عَلَيْهِ السَّلام) فَنَحْنُ نَعْلَمُهُ

Abu 'Alī al-Ash'ari has narrated from Muḥammad b. 'Abd al-Jabber from Muḥammad b. Isma'il from 'Alī b. al-Nu'man from Suwayd al-Qalla from abu Ayyub from abu Basir from abu Ja'far (عليه السلام) who has said the following. "Allāh, the Most Holy, the Most High, has two kinds of knowledge. One kind of knowledge is that which no one knows except He. The other kind is that which He has taught to the His angels and His messengers. Whatever His angels and Messengers have learned we know it." (صحيح)[2]

3.

مُحَمَّدُ بْنُ يَحْيَى عَنْ أَحْمَدَ بْنِ مُحَمَّدٍ عَنِ الْحُسَيْنِ بْنِ سَعِيدٍ عَنِ النَّضْرِ بْنِ سُوَيْدٍ عَنْ يَحْيَى الْحَلَبِيِّ عَنْ ذَرِيحٍ الْمُحَارِبِيِّ قَالَ قَالَ لِي أَبُو عَبْدِ الله (عَلَيْهِ السَّلام) يَا ذَرِيحُ لَوْ لا أَنَّا نَزْدَادُ لانْفَدْنَا

Muhammad b. Yabya has narrated from Ahmad b. Muḥammad from al-Husayn b. Sa'id from an-Nadr b. Suwayd from Yahya al-Halabi from Dharih al-Muharibi who

---

[1] *Al-Kāfi, v1, ch44, h3*

[2] *Al-Kāfi, v1, ch44, h4*

has said that abu ‘AbdAllāh (عليه السلام) has said to him the following. “O Dharih, “Would we not receive (new knowledge) we will diminish (in knowledge).” (صحيح)[3]

4.

مُحَمَّدُ بْنُ يَحْيَى عَنْ أَحْمَدَ بْنِ مُحَمَّدٍ عَنِ ابْنِ أَبِي نَصْرٍ عَنْ ثَعْلَبَةَ عَنْ زُرَارَةَ قَالَ سَمِعْتُ أَبَا جَعْفَرٍ (عَلَيْهِ السَّلام) يَقُولُ لَوْ لا أَنَّا نَزْدَادُ لانْفَدْنَا قَالَ قُلْتُ تَزْدَادُونَ شَيْئاً لا يَعْلَمُهُ رَسُولُ الله (صَلَّى اللهُ عَلَيْهِ وَآلِه) قَالَ أَمَا إِنَّهُ إِذَا كَانَ ذَلِكَ عُرِضَ عَلَى رَسُولِ الله (صَلَّى اللهُ عَلَيْهِ وَآلِه) ثُمَّ عَلَى الائِمَّةِ ثُمَّ انْتَهَى الامْرُ إِلَيْنَا

Muhammad b. Yahya has narrated from Ahmad b. Muḥammad from abu Nasr from Tha‘labah from Zurāra who has said that he heard abu Ja‘far (عليه السلام) say the following. “Would we not receive additional (knowledge) we would diminish (in knowledge).” The narrator has said that he asked the Imams (عليه السلام) “Do receive additional something that the Messenger of Allāh does not know?” The Imam (عليه السلام) said, “The fact of the matter is that when that happens, it is presented to the Messenger of Allāh then to the Imams and then it reaches us.” (صحيح)[4]

5.

عَلِيُّ بْنُ إِبْرَاهِيمَ عَنْ مُحَمَّدِ بْنِ عِيسَى عَنْ يُونُسَ بْنِ عَبْدِ الرَّحْمَنِ عَنْ بَعْضِ أَصْحَابِهِ عَنْ أَبِي عَبْدِ الله (عَلَيْهِ السَّلام) قَالَ لَيْسَ يَخْرُجُ شَيْءٌ مِنْ عِنْدِ الله عَزَّ وَجَلَّ حَتَّى يَبْدَأَ بِرَسُولِ الله (صَلَّى اللهُ عَلَيْهِ وَآلِه) ثُمَّ بِأَمِيرِ الْمُؤْمِنِينَ (عَلَيْهِ السَّلام) ثُمَّ بِوَاحِدٍ بَعْدَ وَاحِدٍ لِكَيْلا يَكُونَ آخِرُنَا أَعْلَمَ مِنْ أَوَّلِنَا

Ali b. Ibrahim has narrated from Muḥammad b. ‘Isa from Yunus b. ‘Abd al-Rahman from some of his people from abu ‘AbdAllāh (عليه السلام) who has said the following. “Nothing comes from Allāh, the Most Holy, the Most High, except that first it

[3] *Al-Kāfi, v1, ch43, h2*

[4] *Al-Kāfi, v1, ch43, h3*

begins with the Messenger of Allāh then Amir al-Mu'minin 'Alī (عليه السلام) then the Imams one after the other so that the last us would not be more knowledgeable than the first of us." (مرسل)[5]

6.

عِدَّةٌ مِنْ أَصْحَابِنَا عَنْ أَحْمَدَ بْنِ مُحَمَّدِ بْنِ عِيسَى عَنْ مُعَمَّرِ بْنِ خَلادٍ قَالَ سَأَلَ أَبَا الْحَسَنِ (عَلَيْهِ السَّلام) رَجُلٌ مِنْ أَهْلِ فَارِسَ فَقَالَ لَهُ أَ تَعْلَمُونَ الْغَيْبَ فَقَالَ قَالَ أَبُو جَعْفَرٍ (عَلَيْهِ السَّلام) يُبْسَطُ لَنَا الْعِلْمُ فَنَعْلَمُ وَيُقْبَضُ عَنَّا فَلا نَعْلَمُ وَقَالَ سِرُّ اللهِ عَزَّ وَجَلَّ أَسَرَّهُ إِلَى جَبْرَئِيلَ (عَلَيْهِ السَّلام) وَأَسَرَّهُ جَبْرَئِيلُ إِلَى مُحَمَّدٍ (صَلَّى اللهُ عَلَيْهِ وَآلِهِ) وَأَسَرَّهُ مُحَمَّدٌ إِلَى مَنْ شَاءَ اللهُ

A number of our people has narrated from Ahmad b. Muḥammad b. 'Isa from Mu'ammar b. Khallad who has said that a man from Persia asked abu al-Hassan (عليه السلام) the following. "Do you know al-Ghayb (the hidden facts)?" The Imam (عليه السلام) said, "abu Ja'far (عليه السلام) has said, 'It opens to us then we know it and it is withheld from us then we do not know." The Imam (عليه السلام) then said, "It is the secret of Allāh, the Most Holy, the Most High, who has secretly given to Jibril and Jibril has secretly given to Muḥammad and Muḥammad has secretly given to whoever Allāh wished." (صحيح)[6]

7.

عَنْ أَبِيهِ عَنِ ابْنِ أَبِي عُمَيْرٍ عَنِ ابْنِ أُذَيْنَةَ عَنْ زُرَارَةَ عَنْ ابي جعفر)عَلَيْهِ السَّلام (قَالَ نَزَلَ جَبْرَئِيلُ)عَلَيْهِ السَّلام (عَلَى رَسُولِ الله)صَلَّى اللهُ عَلَيْهِ وَآلِهِ (بِرُمَّانَتَيْنِ مِنَ الْجَنَّةِ فَأَعْطَاهُ إِيَّاهُمَا فَأَكَلَ وَاحِدَةً وَكَسَرَ الاخْرَى بِنِصْفَيْنِ فَأَعْطَى عَلِيّاً)عَلَيْهِ السَّلام (نِصْفَهَا فَأَكَلَهَا فَقَالَ يَا عَلِيُّ أَمَّا الرُّمَّانَةُ الاولَى الَّتِي أَكَلْتُهَا فَالنُّبُوَّةُ لَيْسَ لَكَ فِيهَا شَيْءٌ وَأَمَّا الاخْرَى فَهُوَ الْعِلْمُ فَأَنْتَ شَرِيكِي فِيهِ

[5] *Al-Kāfi, v1, ch43, h4*

[6] *Al-Kāfi, v1, ch45, h1*

Ali has narrated from his father from b. abu 'Umayr from b. 'Udhaynah from Zurāra from abu Ja'far (عليه السلام) who has said the following. "Once Jibril brought from Paradise two pieces of pomegranate to the Messenger of Allāh and brought him two pieces of pomegranates. The Messenger of Allāh ate one of them and broke the other one into two pieces. He then ate one half and gave the other half to 'Alī (عليه السلام) who also ate it (عليه السلام). The Messenger of Allāh said, "The first one that I ate was prophet-hood. There is no share in it for you. The other one is knowledge in which you are my partner. (حسن)[7]

8.

أَحْمَدُ بْنُ مُحَمَّدٍ عَنْ مُحَمَّدِ بْنِ الْحَسَنِ عَنْ عَبَّادِ بْنِ سُلَيْمَانَ عَنْ مُحَمَّدِ بْنِ سُلَيْمَانَ عَنْ أَبِيهِ عَنْ سَدِيرٍ قَالَ كُنْتُ أَنَا وَأَبُو بَصِيرٍ وَيَحْيَى الْبَزَّازُ وَدَاوُدُ بْنُ كَثِيرٍ فِي مَجْلِسِ أَبِي عَبْدِ اللهِ (عَلَيْهِ السَّلام) إِذْ خَرَجَ إِلَيْنَا وَهُوَ مُغْضَبٌ فَلَمَّا أَخَذَ مَجْلِسَهُ قَالَ يَا عَجَباً لاقْوَامٍ يَزْعُمُونَ أَنَّا نَعْلَمُ الْغَيْبَ مَا يَعْلَمُ الْغَيْبَ إِلا اللهُ عَزَّ وَجَلَّ لَقَدْ هَمَمْتُ بِضَرْبِ جَارِيَتِي فُلانَةَ فَهَرَبَتْ مِنِّي فَمَا عَلِمْتُ فِي أَيِّ بُيُوتِ الدَّارِ هِيَ قَالَ سَدِيرٌ فَلَمَّا أَنْ قَامَ مِنْ مَجْلِسِهِ وَصَارَ فِي مَنْزِلِهِ دَخَلْتُ أَنَا وَأَبُو بَصِيرٍ وَمُيَسِّرٌ وَقُلْنَا لَهُ جُعِلْنَا فِدَاكَ سَمِعْنَاكَ وَأَنْتَ تَقُولُ كَذَا وَكَذَا فِي أَمْرِ جَارِيَتِكَ وَنَحْنُ نَعْلَمُ أَنَّكَ تَعْلَمُ عِلْماً كَثِيراً وَلا نَنْسُبُكَ إِلَى عِلْمِ الْغَيْبِ قَالَ فَقَالَ يَا سَدِيرُ أَ لَمْ تَقْرَأِ الْقُرْآنَ قُلْتُ بَلَى قَالَ فَهَلْ وَجَدْتَ فِيمَا قَرَأْتَ مِنْ كِتَابِ اللهِ عَزَّ وَجَلَّ قَالَ الَّذِي عِنْدَهُ عِلْمٌ مِنَ الْكِتابِ أَنَا آتِيكَ بِهِ قَبْلَ أَنْ يَرْتَدَّ إِلَيْكَ طَرْفُكَ قَالَ قُلْتُ جُعِلْتُ فِدَاكَ قَدْ قَرَأْتُهُ قَالَ فَهَلْ عَرَفْتَ الرَّجُلَ وَهَلْ عَلِمْتَ مَا كَانَ عِنْدَهُ مِنْ عِلْمِ الْكِتَابِ قَالَ قُلْتُ أَخْبِرْنِي بِهِ قَالَ قَدْرُ قَطْرَةٍ مِنَ الْمَاءِ فِي الْبَحْرِ الاخْضَرِ فَمَا يَكُونُ ذَلِكَ مِنْ عِلْمِ الْكِتَابِ قَالَ قُلْتُ جُعِلْتُ فِدَاكَ مَا أَقَلَّ هَذَا فَقَالَ يَا سَدِيرُ مَا أَكْثَرَ هَذَا أَنْ يَنْسِبَهُ اللهُ عَزَّ وَجَلَّ إِلَى الْعِلْمِ الَّذِي أُخْبِرُكَ بِهِ يَا سَدِيرُ فَهَلْ وَجَدْتَ فِيمَا قَرَأْتَ مِنْ كِتَابِ اللهِ عَزَّ وَجَلَّ أَيْضاً قُلْ كَفى بِاللهِ شَهِيداً بَيْنِي وَبَيْنَكُمْ وَمَنْ عِنْدَهُ عِلْمُ الْكِتابِ قَالَ قُلْتُ قَدْ قَرَأْتُهُ جُعِلْتُ فِدَاكَ قَالَ أَ فَمَنْ عِنْدَهُ عِلْمُ الْكِتَابِ كُلِّهِ أَفْهَمُ أَمْ مَنْ عِنْدَهُ عِلْمُ الْكِتَابِ بَعْضُهُ قُلْتُ لا بَلْ مَنْ عِنْدَهُ عِلْمُ الْكِتَابِ كُلُّهُ قَالَ فَأَوْمَأَ بِيَدِهِ إِلَى صَدْرِهِ وَقَالَ عِلْمُ الْكِتَابِ وَاللهِ كُلُّهُ عِنْدَنَا عِلْمُ الْكِتَابِ وَاللهِ كُلُّهُ عِنْدَنَا

---

[7] *Al-Kāfi, v1, ch49, h2*

Ahmad b. Muḥammad has narrated from Muḥammad b. al-Hassan from 'Abbad b. Sulayman from Muḥammad b. Sulayman from his father from Sadir who has said that he, abu Basir, Yahya al-Bazzaz and Dawud b. Kathir were in the presence of abu 'AbdAllāh (عليه السلام). The Imam (عليه السلام) came to us while he was angry. When he settled in his seat he then said, "How strange is it that certain people think we know the hidden facts. No one knows the hidden things except Allāh, the Most Holy, the Most High. I thought to discipline our house maid, so and so, and could not find in which quarter she was." Sadir has said, "When the meeting was over and the Imam (عليه السلام) went home, I, abu Basir and Muyassir went to his house. We said to him, "May Allāh take our souls in service for your cause, we heard you say so and so about the matter of your house maid but we know that you have a great deal of knowledge. We do not say that you possess the knowledge of (al-Ghayb) hidden facts." The narrator has said that the Imam (عليه السلام) said, "O Sadir, Do you not read the Holy Qur'ān?" I said, "Yes, I do read the Holy Qur'ān." The Imam (عليه السلام) then asked, "In your reading have you found the following words of Allāh, the Most Holy, the Most High? "The one who had knowledge from the Book said, "I can bring it to you before you even blink your eye. . ." (27:40) The narrator has said that he said that he has read those words. The Imam (عليه السلام) asked, "Do you know who the man is? Do you know how much knowledge of the Book he had?" The narrator has said that he asked the Imams (عليه السلام) "Please tell me about his knowledge." The Imam (عليه السلام) said, "His knowledge of the Book was like one drop compared to the green ocean (Atlantic). The narrator has said that he said, "May Allāh take my soul in service for your cause, that is very little.." The Imam (عليه السلام) then said, "O Sadir, say, "What a great knowledge is that when Allāh, the Most Holy, the Most High, would ascribe to a knowledge that I am about to speak of to you. Have you found in the book of Allāh, the Most Holy, the Most High, the following. "Say, "God and those who have the knowledge of the Book are sufficient witness (to my prophethood)." (13:43) The narrator has said that he said to the Imams (عليه السلام), "Yes. "May Allāh take my soul in service for your cause, I have read it." The Imam (عليه السلام) then said, "Is the knowledge of one who possesses the knowledge of the whole book greater or that of the one who possesses some knowledge of the Book?" I said, "The knowledge of one who possesses the knolwedge of the whole book is greater." The narrator has said that the Imam (عليه السلام) pointing to his chest said, "The knowledge of the whole Book, I swear by Allāh, is with us. The knowledge of the whole Book, I swear by Allāh, is with us." (مجهول)[8]

9.

أَحْمَدُ بْنُ مُحَمَّدٍ عَنْ مُحَمَّدِ بْنِ الْحَسَنِ عَنْ أَحْمَدَ بْنِ الْحَسَنِ بْنِ عَلِيٍّ عَنْ عَمْرِو بْنِ سَعِيدٍ عَنْ مُصَدِّقِ بْنِ صَدَقَةَ عَنْ عَمَّارٍ السَّابَاطِيِّ قَالَ سَأَلْتُ أَبَا عَبْدِ اللَّهِ (عَلَيْهِ السَّلام) عَنِ الامَامِ يَعْلَمُ الْغَيْبَ فَقَالَ لا وَلَكِنْ إِذَا أَرَادَ أَنْ يَعْلَمَ الشَّيْءَ أَعْلَمَهُ اللَّهُ ذَلِكَ

Ahmad b. Muḥammad has narrated from Muḥammad b. al-Hassan from Ahmad b. a1-Hassan b. ʿAlī from ʿAmr b. Saʿid from Musaddiq b. Sadaqa from ʿAmmar al-Sabati who has said that he asked abu ʿAbdAllāh (عليه السلام) the following. "Dose the Imam have the knowledge of the hidden facts?" The Imam (عليه السلام) said, "No, he does not have such knowledge but if he would like to know about a thing Allāh grants him such knowledge." (موثق)[9]

10.

مُحَمَّدُ بْنُ يَحْيَى عَنْ عِمْرَانَ بْنِ مُوسَى عَنْ مُوسَى بْنِ جَعْفَرٍ عَنْ عَمْرِو بْنِ سَعِيدٍ الْمَدَائِنِيِّ عَنْ أَبِي عُبَيْدَةَ الْمَدَائِنِيِّ عَنْ أَبِي عَبْدِ اللَّهِ (عَلَيْهِ السَّلام) قَالَ إِذَا أَرَادَ الامَامُ أَنْ يَعْلَمَ شَيْئاً أَعْلَمَهُ اللَّهُ ذَلِكَ

Muhammad b. Yahya has narrated from ʿUmrah b. Mūsā from Mūsā b. Jaʿfar from ʿAmr b. Saʿid al-Mada'ini from abu ʿUbayda al-Mada'ini from abu ʿAbdAllāh (عليه

[8] *Al-Kāfi, v1, ch45, h3*

[9] *Al-Kāfi, v1, ch45, h4*

(السلام) who has said the following. "When the Imam (عليه السلام) would will to know something Allāh will grant him such knowledge." (مجهول)[10]

11.

مُحَمَّدُ بْنُ يَحْيَى عَنْ أَحْمَدَ بْنِ مُحَمَّدٍ عَنْ مُحَمَّدِ بْنِ إِسْمَاعِيلَ عَنْ عَمِّهِ حَمْزَةَ بْنِ بَزِيعٍ عَنْ عَلِيٍّ السَّائِيُّ عَنْ أَبِي الْحَسَنِ الْأَوَّلِ مُوسَى (عَلَيْهِ السَّلَام) قَالَ قَالَ مَبْلَغُ عِلْمِنَا عَلَى ثَلَاثَةِ وُجُوهٍ مَاضٍ وَغَابِرٍ وَحَادِثٍ فَأَمَّا الْمَاضِي فَمُفَسَّرٌ وَأَمَّا الْغَابِرُ فَمَزْبُورٌ وَأَمَّا الْحَادِثُ فَقَذْفٌ فِي الْقُلُوبِ وَنَقْرٌ فِي الْأَسْمَاعِ وَهُوَ أَفْضَلُ عِلْمِنَا وَلَا نَبِيَّ بَعْدَ نَبِيِّنَا

Muhammad b. Yahya has narrated from Ahmad b. Muhammad from Muhammad b. Isma'il from his paternal uncle Hamzah b. Bazi' from 'Alī as-Sa'I from abu al-Hassan, the first, Mūsā (عليه السلام) who has said the folloowing. "The totality of our knowledge is of three aspects. Knowledge of the past, future and that coming into being. The knowledge of the past is that which is interpreted. The knowledg eot he future is that which is written and the knowledge of that which come into being is the kind that is thrown into the hearts and is heard by the ears and this is best aspect of our knowledge and there is no prophet after our Holy Prophet صلى الله عليه وآله وسلم." (صحيح على الظاهر)[11]

12.

قَالَ: أَخْبَرَنِي الْحُسَيْنِ بْنِ أَحْمَدَ بْنِ الْمُغِيرَةِ قَالَ: أَخْبَرَنِي أَبُو مُحَمَّدٍ حَيْدَرِ بْنِ مُحَمَّدٍ السَّمَرْقَنْدِي قَالَ: أَخْبَرَنِي أَبُو عَمْرٍو مُحَمَّدُ بْنُ عَمْرِو الْكَشِّي قَالَ: حَدَّثَنَا حَمْدَوِيهِ بْنُ نَصِيرٍ قَالَ: حَدَّثَنَا يَعْقُوبُ بْنُ يَزِيدَ، عَنِ ابْنِ أَبِي عُمَيْرٍ، عَنِ ابْنِ الْمُغِيرَةِ قَالَ: كُنْتُ أَنَا وَيَحْيَى بْنِ عَبْدِ اللَّهِ بْنِ الْحَسَنِ عِنْدَ أَبِي الْحَسَنِ عَلَيْهِ السَّلَامِ فَقَالَ لَهُ يَحْيَى، جُعِلْتُ فِدَاكَ إِنَّهُمْ يَزْعُمُونَ أَنَّكَ تَعْلَمُ الْغَيْبَ، فَقَالَ: سُبْحَانَ اللَّهِ، ضَعْ يَدَكَ عَلَى رَأْسِي فَوَاللَّهِ مَا بَقِيَتْ شَعْرَةٌ فِيهِ وَ [لَا] فِي جَسَدِي إِلَّا قَامَتْ، ثُمَّ قَالَ: لَا وَاللَّهِ مَا هِيَ إِلَّا وِرَاثَةٌ عَنْ رَسُولِ اللَّهِ صَلَّى اللَّهُ عَلَيْهِ وَآلِهِ

---

[10] Al Kafi, v1, ch46, h3

[11] Al-Kafi, v1, ch50, h1

He said: I have been informed by al-Husayn b. Ahmad b. al-Mughairah, who reported from Abu Muḥammad Haider b. Muḥammad al-Samarqandi, who reported from Abu Amru Muḥammad b. Amru al-Kashi, who reported from Hamdawayh b. Naseer, who reported from Ya'qoob b. Yazeed, who reported from b. Abi Umayr, who reported from b. al-Mughairah who said: Yahya b. ʿAbd Allāh b. al-Hasan and I were with Abul Hasan, (عليه السلام), and Yahya asked him: "May I be your ransom, they think that you have the knowledge of the unseen (Ilmul Ghaib)." He said: "Glory be to Allāh! Place your hand over my head." When I did that, every hair in my head and on my body stood on its end. Then he said: "No, By Allāh, it is nothing but what we have inherited from the Prophet (صلى الله عليه وآله وسلم)."[12]

---

[12] *Al-Amālī (Mufīd), ch3, h5*

باب التعصب

Chapter on Racism

Unfortunately, a common polemic brought against the Shi'a is that they are racists because of a few misunderstood Hadīths, although those Hadīths have proper explanations, this chapter will be dedicated to the absolute prohibition on exercising racial discrimination, which in turn destroys the notion of racism from Shi'a Hadīths

1.

مُحَمَّدُ بْنُ يَحْيَى عَنْ أَحْمَدَ بْنِ مُحَمَّدِ بْنِ عِيسَى عَنْ عَلِيِّ بْنِ الْحَكَمِ عَنْ دَاوُدَ بْنِ النُّعْمَانِ عَنْ مَنْصُورِ بْنِ حَازِمٍ عَنْ أَبِي عَبْدِ الله (عَلَيهِ السَّلام) قَالَ مَنْ تَعَصَّبَ أَوْ تُعُصِّبَ لَهُ فَقَدْ خَلَعَ رِبْقَةَ الإِيمَانِ مِنْ عُنُقِهِ.

Muhammad b. Yahya has narrated from Ahmad b. Muḥammad b. 'Isa from 'Alī b. al-Hakam from Dawud b. al-Nu'man from Mansur b. Hazim from abu 'Abd Allāh (عليه السلام) who has said the following: "Whoever exercises racial discrimination or it is exercised for him, he has taken off the collar of belief from his neck." (صحيح)[1]

---

[1] *Al-Kafi, v2, ch123, h1*

2.

عَلِيُّ بْنُ إِبْرَاهِيمَ عَنْ أَبِيهِ عَنِ ابْنِ أَبِي عُمَيْرٍ عَنْ هِشَامِ بْنِ سَالِمٍ وَدُرُسْتَ بْنِ أَبِي مَنْصُورٍ عَنْ أَبِي عَبْدِ اللَّهِ (عَلَيهِ السَّلام) قَالَ قَالَ رَسُولُ اللَّهِ (صَلَّى اللَّهُ عَلَيْهِ وآلِه) مَنْ تَعَصَّبَ أَوْ تُعُصِّبَ لَهُ فَقَدْ خَلَعَ رِبْقَ الْإِيمَانِ مِنْ عُنُقِهِ

Ali b. Ibrahim has narrated from his father from b. abu 'Umayr from Hisham b. Salim and Drust b. abu Mansur from abu 'Abd Allāh (عليه السلام) who has said the following: "The Messenger of Allāh has said, 'Whoever practices racial discrimination or it is practiced for him has removed the collar of belief from his neck.'" (حسن كالصحيح)[2]

3.

أَبُو عَلِيٍّ الْأَشْعَرِيُّ عَنْ مُحَمَّدِ بْنِ عَبْدِ الْجَبَّارِ عَنْ صَفْوَانَ بْنِ يَحْيَى عَنْ خَضِرٍ عَنْ مُحَمَّدِ بْنِ مُسْلِمٍ عَنْ أَبِي عَبْدِ اللَّهِ (عَلَيهِ السَّلام) قَالَ مَنْ تَعَصَّبَ عَصَبَهُ اللَّهُ بِعِصَابَةٍ مِنْ نَارٍ

Abu 'Alī al-Ash'ari has narrated from Muḥammad b. 'Abd al-Jabbar from Safwan b. Yahya from Khudr from Muḥammad b. Muslim from abu 'Abd Allāh (عليه السلام) who has said the following: "On the Day of Judgment Allāh will join those who practice racial discrimination with a race in fire." (مجهول)[3]

4.

عِدَّةٌ مِنْ أَصْحَابِنَا عَنْ أَحْمَدَ بْنِ مُحَمَّدِ بْنِ خَالِدٍ عَنْ أَحْمَدَ بْنِ مُحَمَّدِ بْنِ أَبِي نَصْرٍ عَنْ صَفْوَانَ بْنِ مِهْرَانَ عَنْ عَامِرِ بْنِ السِّمْطِ عَنْ حَبِيبِ بْنِ أَبِي ثَابِتٍ عَنْ عَلِيِّ بْنِ الْحُسَيْنِ (عَلَيهِما السَّلام) قَالَ لَمْ يَدْخُلِ الْجَنَّةَ حَمِيَّةٌ

---

[2] *Al-Kāfi, v2, ch123, h2*

[3] *Al-Kāfi, v2, ch123, h4*

غَيْرُ حَمِيَّةِ حَمْزَةَ بْنِ عَبْدِ الْمُطَّلِبِ وَذَلِكَ حِينَ أَسْلَمَ غَضَباً لِلنَّبِيِّ (صَلَّى اللهُ عَلَيْهِ وآلِه) فِي حَدِيثِ السَّلَى الَّذِي أُلْقِيَ عَلَى النَّبِيِّ (صَلَّى اللهُ عَلَيْهِ وآلِه)

A number of our people have narrated from Ahmad b. Muḥammad b. Khalid from Ahmad b. Muḥammad b. abu Nasr from Safwan b. Mehran from 'Amir b. al-Simt from Habib b. abu Thabit from 'Alī b. al-Husayn (عليه السلام) who has said the following: "Tribal and racist feelings will not enter paradise except that of Hamza b. 'Abd al-Muttalib. When he accepted Islam he expressed such angered feelings over the story of the contents of a camel's stomach poured over the Holy Prophet." (مجهول)[4]

5.

عَنْهُ عَنْ أَبِيهِ عَنْ فَضَالَةَ عَنْ دَاوُدَ بْنِ فَرْقَدٍ عَنْ أَبِي عَبْدِ اللهِ (عَلَيهِ السَّلام) قَالَ إِنَّ الْمَلَائِكَةَ كَانُوا يَحْسَبُونَ أَنَّ إِبْلِيسَ مِنْهُمْ وَكَانَ فِي عِلْمِ اللهِ أَنَّهُ لَيْسَ مِنْهُمْ فَاسْتَخْرَجَ مَا فِي نَفْسِهِ بِالْحَمِيَّةِ وَالْغَضَبِ فَقَالَ خَلَقْتَنِي مِنْ نَارٍ وَخَلَقْتَهُ مِنْ طِينٍ

It is narrated from him (narrator of the Hadīth above) from his father from Fadalah from Dawud b. Farqad from abu 'Abd Allāh (عليه السلام) who has said the following: "The angels thought that Satan was one of them. In the knowledge of Allāh he was not one of them. He (Satan) let out that which was in his soul with racist feelings and anger saying, 'You have created me from fire and You created him from clay.'" (صحيح)[5]

6.

عَلِيُّ بْنُ إِبْرَاهِيمَ عَنْ أَبِيهِ وَعَلِيُّ بْنُ مُحَمَّدٍ الْقَاسَانِيِّ عَنِ الْقَاسِمِ بْنِ مُحَمَّدٍ عَنِ الْمِنْقَرِيِّ عَنْ عَبْدِ الرَّزَّاقِ عَنْ مَعْمَرٍ عَنِ الزُّهْرِيِّ قَالَ سُئِلَ عَلِيُّ بْنُ الْحُسَيْنِ (عَلَيهما السَّلام) عَنِ الْعَصَبِيَّةِ فَقَالَ الْعَصَبِيَّةُ الَّتِي يَأْثَمُ عَلَيْهَا

---

[4] *Al-Kāfi, v2, ch123, h5*

[5] *Al-Kāfi, v2, ch123, h6*

صَاحِبِهَا أَنْ يَرَى الرَّجُلُ شِرَارَ قَوْمِهِ خَيْراً مِنْ خِيَارِ قَوْمٍ آخَرِينَ وَلَيْسَ مِنَ الْعَصَبِيَّةِ أَنْ يُحِبَّ الرَّجُلُ قَوْمَهُ وَلَكِنْ مِنَ الْعَصَبِيَّةِ أَنْ يُعِينَ قَوْمَهُ عَلَى الظُّلْمِ.

Ali b. Ibrahim has narrated from his father and 'Alī b. Muḥammad al-Qasani from al-Qasim b. Muḥammad from al-Minqari from 'Abd al-Razzaq from Mu'ammar from al-Zuhri who has said the following: "Once, 'Alī b. al-Husayn (عليه السلام) was asked about racist feelings. He said, 'The racist feeling that is a sin is the one that makes a person call the evil doers of his own people better than the virtuous individuals of the other people. A man's loving his own people is not racism but it is a sin to help one's own people to commit injustice." (ضعيف)[6]

(The following Hadīth is quite long , however it is one of favorite Hadīths and demonstrates that discrimination based off of race has absolutely no place in the Islam on The Messenger of Allāh(صلى الله عليه وآله وسلم))

7.

مُحَمَّدُ بْنُ يَحْيَى عَنْ أَحْمَدَ بْنِ مُحَمَّدِ بْنِ عِيسَى عَنِ الْحَسَنِ بْنِ مَحْبُوبٍ عَنْ مَالِكِ بْنِ عَطِيَّةَ عَنْ أَبِي حَمْزَةَ الثُّمَالِيِّ قَالَ كُنْتُ عِنْدَ أَبِي جَعْفَرٍ (عَلَيْهِ السَّلام) إِذِ اسْتَأْذَنَ عَلَيْهِ رَجُلٌ فَأَذِنَ لَهُ فَدَخَلَ عَلَيْهِ فَسَلَّمَ فَرَحَّبَ بِهِ أَبُو جَعْفَرٍ (عَلَيْهِ السَّلام) وَأَدْنَاهُ وَسَاءَلَهُ فَقَالَ الرَّجُلُ جُعِلْتُ فِدَاكَ إِنِّي خَطَبْتُ إِلَى مَوْلاكَ فُلانِ بْنِ أَبِي رَافِعٍ ابْنَتَهُ فُلانَةَ فَرَدَّنِي وَرَغِبَ عَنِّي وَازْدَرَأَنِي لِدَمَامَتِي وَحَاجَتِي وَغُرْبَتِي وَقَدْ دَخَلَنِي مِنْ ذَلِكَ غَضَاضَةٌ هَجْمَةٌ غُضَّ لَهَا قَلْبِي تَمَنَّيْتُ عِنْدَهَا الْمَوْتَ فَقَالَ أَبُو جَعْفَرٍ (عَلَيْهِ السَّلام) اذْهَبْ فَأَنْتَ رَسُولِي إِلَيْهِ وَقُلْ لَهُ يَقُولُ لَكَ مُحَمَّدُ بْنُ عَلِيِّ بْنِ الْحُسَيْنِ بْنِ عَلِيِّ بْنِ أَبِي طَالِبٍ (عَلَيْهِ السَّلام) زَوِّجْ مُنْجِحَ بْنَ رَبَاحٍ مَوْلايَ ابْنَتَكَ فُلانَةَ وَلا تَرُدَّهُ قَالَ أَبُو حَمْزَةَ فَوَثَبَ الرَّجُلُ فَرِحاً مُسْرِعاً بِرِسَالَةِ أَبِي جَعْفَرٍ (عَلَيْهِ السَّلام) فَلَمَّا أَنْ تَوَارَى الرَّجُلُ قَالَ أَبُو جَعْفَرٍ (عَلَيْهِ السَّلام) إِنَّ رَجُلاً كَانَ مِنْ أَهْلِ الْيَمَامَةِ يُقَالُ لَهُ جُوَيْبِرٌ أَتَى رَسُولَ اللهِ (صَلَّى اللهُ عَلَيْهِ وَآلِهِ) مُنْتَجِعاً لِلإِسْلامِ فَأَسْلَمَ وَحَسُنَ إِسْلامُهُ وَكَانَ رَجُلاً قَصِيراً دَمِيماً مُحْتَاجاً عَارِياً وَكَانَ مِنْ قِبَاحِ السُّودَانِ فَضَمَّهُ

[6] Al-Kāfi, v2, ch123, h7

رَسُولُ اللهِ (صَلَّى اللهُ عَلَيْهِ وَآلِه) لِحَالِ غُرْبَتِهِ وَعَرَاهُ وَكَانَ يُجْرِي عَلَيْهِ طَعَامَهُ صَاعاً مِنْ تَمْرٍ بِالصَّاعِ الأَوَّلِ وَكَسَاهُ شَمْلَتَيْنِ وَأَمَرَهُ أَنْ يَلْزَمَ الْمَسْجِدَ وَيَرْقُدَ فِيهِ بِاللَّيْلِ فَمَكَثَ بِذَلِكَ مَا شَاءَ اللهُ حَتَّى كَثُرَ الْغُرَبَاءُ مِمَّنْ يَدْخُلُ فِي الإِسْلامِ مِنْ أَهْلِ الْحَاجَةِ بِالْمَدِينَةِ وَضَاقَ بِهِمُ الْمَسْجِدُ فَأَوْحَى اللهُ عَزَّ وَجَلَّ إِلَى نَبِيِّهِ (صَلَّى اللهُ عَلَيْهِ وَآلِه) أَنْ طَهِّرْ مَسْجِدَكَ وَأَخْرِجْ مِنَ الْمَسْجِدِ مَنْ يَرْقُدُ فِيهِ بِاللَّيْلِ وَمُرْ بِسَدِّ أَبْوَابِ مَنْ كَانَ لَهُ فِي مَسْجِدِكَ بَابٌ إِلا بَابَ عَلِيٍّ (عَلَيْهِ السَّلام) وَمَسْكَنَ فَاطِمَةَ (عَلَيْهَا السَّلام) وَلا يَمُرَّنَّ فِيهِ جُنُبٌ وَلا يَرْقُدْ فِيهِ غَرِيبٌ قَالَ فَأَمَرَ رَسُولُ اللهِ (صَلَّى اللهُ عَلَيْهِ وَآلِه) بِسَدِّ أَبْوَابِهِمْ إِلا بَابَ عَلِيٍّ (عَلَيْهِ السَّلام) وَأَقَرَّ مَسْكَنَ فَاطِمَةَ (عَلَيْهَا السَّلام) عَلَى حَالِهِ قَالَ ثُمَّ إِنَّ رَسُولَ اللهِ (صَلَّى اللهُ عَلَيْهِ وَآلِه) أَمَرَ أَنْ يُتَّخَذَ لِلْمُسْلِمِينَ سَقِيفَةٌ فَعُمِلَتْ لَهُمْ وَهِيَ الصُّفَّةُ ثُمَّ أَمَرَ الْغُرَبَاءَ وَالْمَسَاكِينَ أَنْ يَظَلُّوا فِيهَا نَهَارَهُمْ وَلَيْلَهُمْ فَنَزَلُوهَا وَاجْتَمَعُوا فِيهَا فَكَانَ رَسُولُ اللهِ (صَلَّى اللهُ عَلَيْهِ وَآلِه) يَتَعَاهَدُهُمْ بِالْبُرِّ وَالتَّمْرِ وَالشَّعِيرِ وَالزَّبِيبِ إِذَا كَانَ عِنْدَهُ وَكَانَ الْمُسْلِمُونَ يَتَعَاهَدُونَهُمْ وَيَرِقُّونَ عَلَيْهِمْ لِرِقَّةِ رَسُولِ اللهِ (صَلَّى اللهُ عَلَيْهِ وَآلِه) وَيَصْرِفُونَ صَدَقَاتِهِمْ إِلَيْهِمْ فَإِنَّ رَسُولَ اللهِ (صَلَّى اللهُ عَلَيْهِ وَآلِه) نَظَرَ إِلَى جُوَيْبِرٍ ذَاتَ يَوْمٍ بِرَحْمَةٍ مِنْهُ لَهُ وَرِقَّةٍ عَلَيْهِ فَقَالَ لَهُ يَا جُوَيْبِرُ لَوْ تَزَوَّجْتَ امْرَأَةً فَعَفَفْتَ بِهَا فَرْجَكَ وَأَعَانَتْكَ عَلَى دُنْيَاكَ وَآخِرَتِكَ فَقَالَ لَهُ جُوَيْبِرٌ يَا رَسُولَ اللهِ بِأَبِي أَنْتَ وَأُمِّي مَنْ يَرْغَبُ فِيَّ فَوَ اللهِ مَا مِنْ حَسَبٍ وَلا نَسَبٍ وَلا مَالٍ وَلا جَمَالٍ فَأَيَّةُ امْرَأَةٍ تَرْغَبُ فِيَّ فَقَالَ لَهُ رَسُولُ اللهِ (صَلَّى اللهُ عَلَيْهِ وَآلِه) يَا جُوَيْبِرُ إِنَّ اللهَ قَدْ وَضَعَ بِالإِسْلامِ مَنْ كَانَ فِي الْجَاهِلِيَّةِ شَرِيفاً وَشَرَّفَ بِالإِسْلامِ مَنْ كَانَ فِي الْجَاهِلِيَّةِ وَضِيعاً وَأَعَزَّ بِالإِسْلامِ مَنْ كَانَ فِي الْجَاهِلِيَّةِ ذَلِيلا وَأَذْهَبَ بِالإِسْلامِ مَا كَانَ مِنْ نَخْوَةِ الْجَاهِلِيَّةِ وَتَفَاخُرِهَا بِعَشَائِرِهَا وَبَاسِقِ أَنْسَابِهَا فَالنَّاسُ الْيَوْمَ كُلُّهُمْ أَبْيَضُهُمْ وَأَسْوَدُهُمْ وَقُرَشِيُّهُمْ وَعَرَبِيُّهُمْ وَعَجَمِيُّهُمْ مِنْ آدَمَ وَإِنَّ آدَمَ خَلَقَهُ اللهُ مِنْ طِينٍ وَإِنَّ أَحَبَّ النَّاسِ إِلَى اللهِ عَزَّ وَجَلَّ يَوْمَ الْقِيَامَةِ أَطْوَعُهُمْ لَهُ وَأَتْقَاهُمْ وَمَا أَعْلَمُ يَا جُوَيْبِرُ لأَحَدٍ مِنَ الْمُسْلِمِينَ عَلَيْكَ الْيَوْمَ فَضْلا إِلا لِمَنْ كَانَ أَتْقَى للهِ مِنْكَ وَأَطْوَعَ ثُمَّ قَالَ لَهُ. انْطَلِقْ يَا جُوَيْبِرُ إِلَى زِيَادِ بْنِ لَبِيدٍ فَإِنَّهُ مِنْ أَشْرَفِ بَنِي بَيَاضَةَ حَسَباً فِيهِمْ فَقُلْ لَهُ إِنِّي رَسُولُ رَسُولِ اللهِ إِلَيْكَ وَهُوَ يَقُولُ لَكَ زَوِّجْ جُوَيْبِراً ابْنَتَكَ الذَّلْفَاءَ قَالَ فَانْطَلَقَ جُوَيْبِرٌ بِرِسَالَةِ رَسُولِ اللهِ (صَلَّى اللهُ عَلَيْهِ وَآلِه) إِلَى زِيَادِ بْنِ لَبِيدٍ وَهُوَ فِي مَنْزِلِهِ وَجَمَاعَةٌ مِنْ قَوْمِهِ عِنْدَهُ فَاسْتَأْذَنَ فَأُعْلِمَ فَأَذِنَ لَهُ فَدَخَلَ وَسَلَّمَ عَلَيْهِ ثُمَّ قَالَ يَا زِيَادَ بْنَ لَبِيدٍ إِنِّي رَسُولُ رَسُولِ اللهِ إِلَيْكَ فِي حَاجَةٍ لِي فَأَبُوحُ بِهَا أَمْ أُسِرُّهَا إِلَيْكَ فَقَالَ لَهُ زِيَادٌ بَلْ بُحْ بِهَا فَإِنَّ ذَلِكَ شَرَفٌ لِي وَفَخْرٌ فَقَالَ لَهُ جُوَيْبِرٌ إِنَّ رَسُولَ اللهِ (صَلَّى اللهُ عَلَيْهِ وَآلِه) يَقُولُ لَكَ زَوِّجْ جُوَيْبِراً ابْنَتَكَ الذَّلْفَاءَ فَقَالَ لَهُ زِيَادٌ أَرَسُولُ اللهِ أَرْسَلَكَ إِلَيَّ بِهَذَا فَقَالَ لَهُ نَعَمْ مَا كُنْتُ لأَكْذِبَ عَلَى رَسُولِ اللهِ (صَلَّى اللهُ عَلَيْهِ وَآلِه) فَقَالَ لَهُ زِيَادٌ إِنَّا لا نُزَوِّجُ فَتَيَاتِنَا إِلا أَكْفَاءَنَا مِنَ الأَنْصَارِ فَانْصَرِفْ يَا جُوَيْبِرُ حَتَّى أَلْقَى رَسُولَ اللهِ (صَلَّى اللهُ عَلَيْهِ وَآلِه) فَأُخْبِرَهُ بِعُذْرِي فَانْصَرَفَ جُوَيْبِرٌ وَهُوَ يَقُولُ وَاللهِ مَا بِهَذَا نَزَلَ الْقُرْآنُ وَلا بِهَذَا ظَهَرَتْ نُبُوَّةُ مُحَمَّدٍ (صَلَّى اللهُ عَلَيْهِ وَآلِه) فَسَمِعَتْ مَقَالَتَهُ الذَّلْفَاءُ بِنْتُ زِيَادٍ وَهِيَ فِي خِدْرِهَا فَأَرْسَلَتْ إِلَى أَبِيهَا ادْخُلْ إِلَيَّ فَدَخَلَ إِلَيْهَا فَقَالَتْ لَهُ مَا هَذَا الْكَلامُ الَّذِي سَمِعْتُهُ مِنْكَ تُحَاوِرُ بِهِ جُوَيْبِراً فَقَالَ لَهَا ذَكَرَ لِي أَنَّ رَسُولَ اللهِ (صَلَّى اللهُ عَلَيْهِ وَآلِه) أَرْسَلَهُ وَقَالَ يَقُولُ لَكَ رَسُولُ اللهِ (صَلَّى اللهُ عَلَيْهِ وَآلِه) زَوِّجْ جُوَيْبِراً ابْنَتَكَ الذَّلْفَاءَ فَقَالَتْ لَهُ وَاللهِ مَا كَانَ جُوَيْبِرٌ لِيَكْذِبَ عَلَى رَسُولِ اللهِ (صَلَّى اللهُ عَلَيْهِ وَآلِه) بِحَضْرَتِهِ فَابْعَثِ الآنَ رَسُولا يَرُدُّ عَلَيْكَ جُوَيْبِراً فَبَعَثَ زِيَادٌ

رَسُولا فَلحِق جُوَيْبِراً فَقَالَ لَهُ زِيَادٌ يَا جُوَيْبِرُ مَرْحَباً بِكَ اطْمَئِنَّ حَتَّى أَعُودَ إِلَيْكَ ثُمَّ انْطَلَقَ زِيَادٌ إِلَى رَسُولِ اللهِ (صَلَّى اللهُ عَلَيْهِ وَآلِه) فَقَالَ لَهُ بِأَبِي أَنْتَ وَأُمِّي إِنَّ جُوَيْبِراً أَتَانِي بِرِسَالَتِكَ وَقَالَ إِنَّ رَسُولَ اللهِ (صَلَّى اللهُ عَلَيْهِ وَآلِه) يَقُولُ لَكَ زَوِّجْ جُوَيْبِراً ابْنَتَكَ الذَّلْفَاءَ فَلَمْ أَلِنْ لَهُ بِالْقَوْلِ وَرَأَيْتُ لِقَاءَكَ وَنَحْنُ لا نَتَزَوَّجُ إِلا أَكْفَاءَنَا مِنَ الأَنْصَارِ فَقَالَ لَهُ رَسُولُ اللهِ (صَلَّى اللهُ عَلَيْهِ وَآلِه) يَا زِيَادُ جُوَيْبِرٌ مُؤْمِنٌ وَالْمُؤْمِنُ كُفْوٌ لِلْمُؤْمِنَةِ وَالْمُسْلِمُ كُفْوٌ لِلْمُسْلِمَةِ فَزَوِّجْهُ يَا زِيَادُ وَلا تَرْغَبْ عَنْهُ قَالَ فَرَجَعَ زِيَادٌ إِلَى مَنْزِلِهِ وَدَخَلَ عَلَى ابْنَتِهِ فَقَالَ لَهَا مَا سَمِعَهُ مِنْ رَسُولِ اللهِ (صَلَّى اللهُ عَلَيْهِ وَآلِه) فَقَالَتْ لَهُ إِنَّكَ إِنْ عَصَيْتَ رَسُولَ اللهِ (صَلَّى اللهُ عَلَيْهِ وَآلِه) كَفَرْتَ فَزَوِّجْ جُوَيْبِراً فَخَرَجَ زِيَادٌ فَأَخَذَ بِيَدِ جُوَيْبِرٍ ثُمَّ أَخْرَجَهُ إِلَى قَوْمِهِ فَزَوَّجَهُ عَلَى سُنَّةِ اللهِ وَسُنَّةِ رَسُولِهِ (صَلَّى اللهُ عَلَيْهِ وَآلِه) وَضَمِنَ صَدَاقَهُ قَالَ فَجَهَّزَهَا زِيَادٌ وَهَيَّئُوهَا ثُمَّ. أَرْسَلُوا إِلَى جُوَيْبِرٍ فَقَالُوا لَهُ أَلَكَ مَنْزِلٌ فَنَسُوقَهَا إِلَيْكَ فَقَالَ وَاللهِ مَا لِي مِنْ مَنْزِلٍ قَالَ فَهَيَّئُوهَا وَهَيَّئُوا لَهَا مَنْزِلا وَهَيَّئُوا فِيهِ فِرَاشاً وَمَتَاعاً وَكَسَوْا جُوَيْبِراً ثَوْبَيْنِ وَأُدْخِلَتِ الذَّلْفَاءُ فِي بَيْتِهَا وَأُدْخِلَ جُوَيْبِرٌ عَلَيْهَا مُعْتِماً فَلَمَّا رَآهَا نَظَرَ إِلَى بَيْتٍ وَمَتَاعٍ وَرِيحٍ طَيِّبَةٍ قَامَ إِلَى زَاوِيَةِ الْبَيْتِ فَلَمْ يَزَلْ تَالِياً لِلْقُرْآنِ رَاكِعاً وَسَاجِداً حَتَّى طَلَعَ الْفَجْرُ فَلَمَّا سَمِعَ النِّدَاءَ خَرَجَ وَخَرَجَتْ زَوْجَتُهُ إِلَى الصَّلاةِ فَتَوَضَّأَتْ وَصَلَّتِ الصُّبْحَ فَسُئِلَتْ هَلْ مَسَّكِ فَقَالَتْ مَا زَالَ تَالِياً لِلْقُرْآنِ وَرَاكِعاً وَسَاجِداً حَتَّى سَمِعَ النِّدَاءَ فَخَرَجَ فَلَمَّا كَانَتِ اللَّيْلَةُ الثَّانِيَةُ فَعَلَ مِثْلَ ذَلِكَ وَأَخْفَوْا ذَلِكَ مِنْ زِيَادٍ فَلَمَّا كَانَ الْيَوْمُ الثَّالِثُ فَعَلَ مِثْلَ ذَلِكَ فَأُخْبِرَ بِذَلِكَ أَبُوهَا فَانْطَلَقَ إِلَى رَسُولِ اللهِ (صَلَّى اللهُ عَلَيْهِ وَآلِه) فَقَالَ لَهُ بِأَبِي أَنْتَ وَأُمِّي يَا رَسُولَ اللهِ أَمَرْتَنِي بِتَزْوِيجِ جُوَيْبِرٍ وَلا وَاللهِ مَا كَانَ مِنْ مَنَاكِحِنَا وَلَكِنْ طَاعَتُكَ أَوْجَبَتْ عَلَيَّ تَزْوِيجَهُ فَقَالَ لَهُ النَّبِيُّ (صَلَّى اللهُ عَلَيْهِ وَآلِه) فَمَا الَّذِي أَنْكَرْتُمْ مِنْهُ قَالَ إِنَّا هَيَّأْنَا لَهُ بَيْتاً وَمَتَاعاً وَأُدْخِلَتِ ابْنَتِي الْبَيْتَ وَأُدْخِلَ مَعَهَا مُعْتِماً فَمَا كَلَّمَهَا وَلا نَظَرَ إِلَيْهَا وَلا دَنَا مِنْهَا بَلْ قَامَ إِلَى زَاوِيَةِ الْبَيْتِ فَلَمْ يَزَلْ تَالِياً لِلْقُرْآنِ رَاكِعاً وَسَاجِداً حَتَّى سَمِعَ النِّدَاءَ فَخَرَجَ ثُمَّ فَعَلَ مِثْلَ ذَلِكَ فِي اللَّيْلَةِ الثَّانِيَةِ وَمِثْلَ ذَلِكَ فِي الثَّالِثَةِ وَلَمْ يَدْنُ مِنْهَا وَلَمْ يُكَلِّمْهَا إِلَى أَنْ جِئْتُكَ وَمَا نَرَاهُ يُرِيدُ النِّسَاءَ فَانْظُرْ فِي أَمْرِنَا فَانْصَرَفَ زِيَادٌ وَبَعَثَ رَسُولُ اللهِ (صَلَّى اللهُ عَلَيْهِ وَآلِه) إِلَى جُوَيْبِرٍ فَقَالَ لَهُ أَمَا تَقْرَبُ النِّسَاءَ فَقَالَ لَهُ جُوَيْبِرٌ أَوَمَا أَنَا بِفَحْلٍ بَلَى يَا رَسُولَ اللهِ إِنِّي لَشَبِقٌ نَهِمٌ إِلَى النِّسَاءِ فَقَالَ لَهُ رَسُولُ اللهِ (صَلَّى اللهُ عَلَيْهِ وَآلِه) قَدْ خُبِّرْتُ بِخِلافِ مَا وَصَفْتَ بِهِ نَفْسَكَ قَدْ ذُكِرَ لِي أَنَّهُمْ هَيَّئُوا لَكَ بَيْتاً وَفِرَاشاً وَمَتَاعاً وَأُدْخِلَتْ عَلَيْكَ فَتَاةٌ حَسْنَاءُ عَطِرَةٌ وَأَتَيْتَ مُعْتِماً فَلَمْ تَنْظُرْ إِلَيْهَا وَلَمْ تُكَلِّمْهَا وَلَمْ تَدْنُ مِنْهَا فَمَا دَهَاكَ إِذَنْ فَقَالَ لَهُ جُوَيْبِرٌ يَا رَسُولَ اللهِ دَخَلْتُ بَيْتاً وَاسِعاً وَرَأَيْتُ فِرَاشاً وَمَتَاعاً وَفَتَاةً حَسْنَاءَ عَطِرَةً وَذَكَرْتُ حَالِيَ الَّتِي كُنْتُ عَلَيْهَا وَغُرْبَتِي وَحَاجَتِي وَوَضِيعَتِي وَكِسْوَتِي مَعَ الْغُرَبَاءِ وَالْمَسَاكِينِ فَأَحْبَبْتُ إِذْ أَوْلانِي اللهُ ذَلِكَ أَنْ أَشْكُرَهُ عَلَى مَا أَعْطَانِي وَأَتَقَرَّبُ إِلَيْهِ بِحَقِيقَةِ الشُّكْرِ فَنَهَضْتُ إِلَى جَانِبِ الْبَيْتِ فَلَمْ أَزَلْ فِي صَلاتِي تَالِياً لِلْقُرْآنِ رَاكِعاً وَسَاجِداً أَشْكُرُ اللهَ حَتَّى سَمِعْتُ النِّدَاءَ فَخَرَجْتُ فَلَمَّا أَصْبَحْتُ رَأَيْتُ أَنْ أَصُومَ ذَلِكَ الْيَوْمَ فَفَعَلْتُ ذَلِكَ ثَلاثَةَ أَيَّامٍ وَلَيَالِيَهَا وَرَأَيْتُ ذَلِكَ فِي جَنْبِ مَا أَعْطَانِي اللهُ يَسِيراً وَلَكِنِّي سَأُرْضِيهَا وَأُرْضِيهِمُ اللَّيْلَةَ إِنْ شَاءَ اللهُ فَأَرْسَلَ رَسُولُ اللهِ (صَلَّى اللهُ عَلَيْهِ وَآلِه) إِلَى زِيَادٍ فَأَتَاهُ فَأَعْلَمَهُ مَا قَالَ جُوَيْبِرٌ فَطَابَتْ أَنْفُسُهُمْ قَالَ وَوَفَى لَهَا جُوَيْبِرٌ بِمَا قَالَ ثُمَّ إِنَّ رَسُولَ اللهِ (صَلَّى اللهُ عَلَيْهِ وَآلِه) خَرَجَ فِي غَزْوَةٍ لَهُ وَمَعَهُ جُوَيْبِرٌ فَاسْتُشْهِدَ رَحِمَهُ اللهُ تَعَالَى فَمَا كَانَ فِي الأَنْصَارِ أَيِّمٌ أَنْفَقُ مِنْهَا بَعْدَ جُوَيْبِرٍ

Muhammad b. Yahya has narrated from Ahmad b. Muḥammad b. 'Isa from al-Hassan b. Mahbub from Malik b. 'Atiyyah from abu Hamzah al-Thumaliy who has said the following: "I once was with abu Ja'far when a man asked permission for a meeting. He came in and offered Salam (the phrase of offering greeting of peace). Abu Ja'far, (عليه السلام), said welcome to him, gave him a place nearby and asked about his condition. The man said, I pray to Allāh to keep my soul in service for your cause, I proposed marriage to your Mawla', so and so b. abu Rafi' for his daughter so and so but he refused, turned away from me, considered me worthless, because of my ugliness, poverty and alienation, which attacked and broke my heart and I wished death to approach me.' Abu Ja'far, (عليه السلام), said, 'You must go; you are my messenger to him and say to him that Muḥammad b. 'Alī b. al-Husayn and b. 'Alī b. abu Talib says, "You must give your daughter so and so in marriage to my Mawla' Munjih b. Rabah and do not refuse."' Abu Hamzah has said that the man jumped out with joy with the letter from abu Ja'far, (عليه السلام). When he left abu Ja'far, (عليه السلام), said, 'There was a man from the people of Yamamah called Juwayabir who came to the Messenger of Allāh, (صلى الله عليه وآله وسلم), seeking success through Islam. He became a Muslim and a good Muslim. He was of short height, ugly looking, poor, naked and he was of the ugly looking people of Sudan. The Messenger of Allāh associated with him closely because of his alienation and nakedness and had assigned one Sa' of dates by the measure of the first Sa' food for him, clothed him with two pieces of sheets, commanded him to stay in Masjid and sleep there during the night. He lived that way as long as Allāh wanted until the number of emigrants grew of those who accepted Islam of the poor people in al-Madinah and the Masjid became smaller and congested. Allāh, most Majestic, most Glorious, sent revelation to His holy prophet, to clean the Masjid, move from it those who slept there in the night, commanded to block all doors that opened to the Masjid except the door of 'Alī and the door to the living-quarter of Fatimah, (عليها السلام) . Everyone after sexual relation and before Ghusl (bath) was barred from entering the Masjid, and no alien could sleep in the Masjid. So the Messenger of Allāh commanded to blocking all doors that opened to the Masjid except the door of Ali, and allowed the door of the living-quarter of Fatimah, (عليها السلام) , to remain as they were before.' He (the Imam) said, 'The Messenger of Allāh, (صلى الله عليه وآله وسلم), then commanded to build a canopy for the Muslims which was built and that was the platform or the edge. He (the Messenger of Allāh) then commanded the emigrants and the poor ones to stay there for the night and days. They made it their home and gathered therein. The Messenger of Allāh, (صلى الله عليه وآله وسلم), would come to see them, bring for them wheat, dates, barley and raisins whenever available. The Muslims sympathized with them because the Messenger of Allāh sympathized with them and spent their charity on them. The Messenger of Allāh one day looked at Juwayabir with kindness and sympathy and said to him, "I wish you to get married with a woman to safeguard your chastity and receive help for your worldly affairs as well as those of the hereafter." Juwayabir then said, "O Messenger of Allāh, I pray to Allāh to keep my soul and the souls of my parents in service for your cause, who will want me? By Allāh, I do not have any good position and social standing, or wealth, or physical beauty. No woman will ever pay attention to me." The Messenger of Allāh then said, "O Juwayabir, Allāh by means of Islam has removed those who were called noble in pre-Islamic time of darkness and ignorance and has honored them with Islam. To those who did not have any social position before Islam, Allāh has granted honor as well as to those who were considered low in the time of ignorance. With Islam He has removed the pride of the time of ignorance and people's expressing pride because of tribes and strong genealogy. Today (we say) all people, white and black, those from Quraysh, Arab, non- Arab are all from Adam, and Adam was created by Allāh from clay. The most beloved in the sight of Allāh, most Majestic, most Glorious, on the Day of Judgment will be those who are most obedient to Him and most pious before Him. O Juwayabir, I do not see any of the Muslims as better than you except because of his being more pious and more obedient to Allāh than you."' He (the Messenger of Allāh) said, 'O Juwayabir, you must go to Ziyad b. Labid; he is an honorable man of the tribe of Bayadah, due to social standards and say to him, "I am the messenger of the Messenger of Allāh to you and the Messenger of Allāh says, 'You must give your daughter al-Dhalfa' in marriage to Juwayabir."" He (the Imam) said that Juwayabir left with the message from the Messenger of Allāh, (صلى الله عليه وآله وسلم), to Ziyad b. Labid when he was at home with a group from his people. Juwayabir asked permission. He was informed and permission was granted. He entered and offered his greeting of peace, then said, 'I am a messenger from the Messenger of Allāh to you for a certain issue: if you like I can convey it to you in private or if you want I can say it in public.' He said, 'Say it in public; it is an honor for me and a privilege.' Juwayabir said, 'The Messenger of Allāh says to you, "You must give your daughter al-Dhalfa' in marriage to Juwayabir."' Ziyad then asked him, 'Has the Messenger of Allāh sent you with this?' Juwayabir replied, 'Yes, I never want to speak a lie against the Messenger of Allāh.' Ziyad said, 'We do not give our young girls in marriage to anyone, unless he is a good match for us of the people of al-Ansar (people of al-Madinah); so you must go back, O Juwayabir, until I meet the Messenger of Allāh and inform him of my excuse.' Juwayabir returned back saying, 'By Allāh, this is not what the Qur'ān is all about or Prophet Muhammad, (صلى الله عليه وآله وسلم), has appeared for it.' Al-Dhalfa', daughter of Ziyad in her living-quarter heard what Juwayabir said. She sent someone to her father to ask him to come to her room and he went to her. She asked, 'What were the words that I heard you spoke to Juwayabir?' He said to her, 'He told me that the Messenger of Allāh had sent him and he (the Messenger of Allāh) said, "You must give your daughter, al-Dhalfa' in marriage to Juwayabir."' She then said, 'By Allāh Juwayabir cannot lie against the Messenger of Allāh, (صلى الله عليه وآله وسلم), in his presence. You must now send a messenger to call him back.' Ziyad sent a messenger to call Juwayabir and approached him and said. 'O Juwayabir, you are welcome. You must not be worried and wait until I come back.' Ziyad went to the Messenger of Allāh and said, 'I pray to Allāh to keep my soul and the souls of my parents in service for your cause, Juwayabir has brought your message to me that says, "The Messenger of Allāh commands you to give your daughter al-Dhalfa' in marriage to Juwayabir." I was not so soft speaking to him. We do not give our young women in marriage to anyone except to our match of al-Ansar (people of al-Madinah).' The Messenger of Allāh said to him, 'O Ziyad, Juwayabir is a believing person. A believing man is a match of a believing woman. A Muslim is a match of a female Muslim. Therefore you must give her in marriage to him. O Ziyad, you must give her in marriage to him and you must not refuse.' He (the Imam) said that Ziyad returned back to his home, went to his daughter and said to her what he had heard from the Messenger of Allāh, (صلى الله عليه وآله وسلم), She said to him, 'If you disobey the Messenger of Allāh, you will become an unbeliever, so you must give in marriage to Juwayabir.' Ziyad came out, held the hand of Juwayabir, took him before his people, gave her to him in marriage according to the tradition of Allāh and the tradition of the Messenger of Allāh and took responsibility of mahr (dower). He (the Imam) has said, 'They prepared al-Dhalfa' for her wedding, sent for Juwayabir and asked him, 'Do you have any house so we escort her to your house?' he replied, 'No, by Allāh, I do not have any house.' He (the Imam) said, 'They prepared her for her wedding, prepared for them a house, furnishings, household necessities, dressed Juwayabir with two dresses, brought al-Dhalfa' to her house, and admitted Juwayabir also there. Juwayabir went in the house after al-'Isha' Salat (prayer). He looked at the house, the furnishings, the sweet smelling fragrance, thus, he moved to a corner of the house and began to recite from the Qur'ān, in Ruku' (bowing down on one's knees) and in Sajdah (prostration) until it was dawn. He heard the call for Salat (prayer), so he went out for Salat (prayer) as well as his wife. She made wudu and performed Salat (prayer) of the morning and she was asked about being touched. She replied, 'He continued reciting the Qur'ān in Ruku ' and Sajdah until the call for Salat (prayer) was said then he went out.' In the second night he did just as he had done the night before but they did not tell it to Ziyad. In the third night he again did as he had done before, then her father was informed. He went to the Messenger of Allāh and said, 'I pray to Allāh to keep my soul and the souls of my parents in service for your cause, O Messenger of Allāh, you commanded me to give my daughter in marriage to Juwayabir and by Allāh we did not want to do so; but obedience to you made it necessary on us to do so.' The Holy Prophet, (صلى الله عليه وآله وسلم), asked, 'What is it that you disliked about him?' he replied, 'We prepared a house for him with furnishings, household necessities, sent my daughter to that house, he also was admitted there after al- 'Isha ' Salat (prayer) but he did not speak to her, did not look at her and did not go close to her, instead he stood in one corner of the house, continued reciting al-Qur'ān, in Ruku' and Sajdah (prostration) until the call for Salat (prayer) was said. He went out for Salat (prayer); he did it again in the second, and in the third nights. He did not go close to her and did not speak to her until the time of my coming to you. We did not find him to be interested in women. Please look into our problem.' Ziyad went back and the Messenger of Allāh sent for Juwayabir and asked him, 'Is it the case that you do not go close to women?' Juwayabir replied, 'A male person I am O Messenger of Allāh and I indeed have intense desire and passion for women.' The Messenger of Allāh said, to him, 'I am informed otherwise about what you are telling to me. I am told that they prepared for you a house, furnishings, the necessities of a household and she was brought to you in that house, a beautiful young woman and rich with sweet smelling perfumes. You went after performing your al-'Isha ' Salat (prayer) but did not look at her, did not speak to her, and did not go close to her. What was your wisdom in it?' Juwayabir replied, 'O Messenger of Allāh, when I entered the vast house, saw the furnishings, the household necessities, the young beautiful girl, rich in sweet smelling perfumes, remembered my condition in which I lived, my alienation, my poverty, and lowliness, my clothes with the emigrants and the destitute people; I then loved at first to thank Allāh for what He had given to me and tried to become closer to Him. I then went to one corner of the house and continued in Salat (prayer) reciting al-Qur'ān in Ruku ' (bowing down on one's knees) and Sajdah (prostration) thanking Allāh until I heard the call for Salat (prayer), then I went out. In the day I decided to fast that day and did so for three days and nights and I thought to do that for what Allāh had given to me although my thanks were very little, however, I will make her happy and make them happy tonight, by the will of Allāh.' The Messenger of Allāh then sent a message to Ziyad who came to the Messenger of Allāh and he (the Messenger of Allāh) informed him about Juwayabir. They became delighted. Juwayabir kept his promise. Thereafter, the Messenger of Allāh went out for an armed expedition, Juwayabir was with him and he became a martyr, may Allāh, most High grant him mercy. In the community of al-Ansar (people of al-Madinah) there was no single woman in such a great demand than her (al-Dhalfa') after Juwayabir.'"

(صحيح)[7]

---

[7] *Al-Kāfi, v5, ch21, h1*

باب الايمان ابو طالب

Chapter on the Faith of Abu Talib

Amongst the opposition are those who challenge the faith of the noble companion Abu Talib, the following Hadīths not only testify to the belief of Abu Talib, but they also demonstrate his great virtue

1.

عَلِيُّ بْنُ إِبْرَاهِيمَ عَنْ أَبِيهِ عَنِ ابْنِ أَبِي عُمَيْرٍ عَنْ هِشَامِ بْنِ سَالِمٍ عَنْ أَبِي عَبْدِ اللهِ (عَلَيْهِ السَّلام) قَالَ إِنَّ مَثَلَ
أَبِي طَالِبٍ مَثَلُ أَصْحَابِ الْكَهْفِ أَسَرُّوا الايمَانَ وَأَظْهَرُوا الشِّرْكَ فَآتَاهُمُ اللهُ أَجْرَهُمْ مَرَّتَيْنِ

Ali b. Ibrahim has narrated from his father from b. abu 'Umayr from Hisham b. Salim from abu 'AbdAllāh (عليه السلام) who has said the following. "The case of abu Talib islike the case of the people of the cave who hid their faith and expressed polytheism. Allāh gave them twice as much reward." (حسن)[1]

2.

---

[1] *Al-Kafi, v1, ch111, h28*

لحسين بن محمد ومحمد بن يحيى، عن أحمد بن إسحاق، عن بكر بن محمد الازدي، عن إسحاق بن جعفر، عن ابيه (عليه السلام) قال: قيل له: إنهم يزعمون أن أبا طالب كان كافرا؟ فقال: كذبوا كيف يكون كافرا وهو يقول: ألم تعلموا أنا وجدنا محمدا * نبيا كموسى خط في أول الكتب وفي حديث آخر كيف يكون أبوطالب كافرا وهو يقول: لقد علموا أن ابننا لا مكذب * لدينا ولا يعبأ بقيل الاباطل (1) وأبيض يستسقى الغمام بوجهه * ثمال اليتامى عصمة

Al-Husayn b. Muḥammad and Muḥammad b. Yahya have narrated from Ahmad b. Ishaq from Bakr b. Muḥammad al-Azdi from Ishaq b. Ja'far from his father (عليه السلام) who has said the following. "They think that abu Talib was an unbeliever. They speak lies, how could he be an unbeliever when he would say such worlds as herein below. "Do they not know that we found Muḥammad as a prophet like Mūsā (Moses) whose name is written in the ancient books." In another Hadīth he has said, "How could abu Talib be an unbeliever when he would say, "They certainly know that our child is not a liar to us and the false words are not paid any attention to. The (beautiful) white face that prays for rain from the clouds, is the helper of the orphans and the protector of the widows." (صحيح)[2]

3.

عَلِيُّ بْنُ إِبْرَاهِيمَ عَنْ أَبِيهِ عَنِ ابْنِ أَبِي عُمَيْرٍ عَنْ هِشَامِ بْنِ الْحَكَمِ عَنْ أَبِي عَبْدِ اللهِ (عَلَيْهِ السَّلام) قَالَ بَيْنَا النَّبِيُّ (صَلَّى اللهُ عَلَيْهِ وَآلِه) فِي الْمَسْجِدِ الْحَرَامِ وَعَلَيْهِ ثِيَابٌ لَهُ جُدُدٌ فَأَلْقَى الْمُشْرِكُونَ عَلَيْهِ سَلَى نَاقَةٍ فَمَلَئُوا ثِيَابَهُ بِهَا فَدَخَلَهُ مِنْ ذَلِكَ مَا شَاءَ اللهُ فَذَهَبَ إِلَى أَبِي طَالِبٍ فَقَالَ لَهُ يَا عَمِّ كَيْفَ تَرَى حَسَبِي فِيكُمْ فَقَالَ لَهُ وَمَا ذَاكَ يَا ابْنَ أَخِي فَأَخْبَرَهُ الْخَبَرَ فَدَعَا أَبُو طَالِبٍ حَمْزَةَ وَأَخَذَ السَّيْفَ وَقَالَ لِحَمْزَةَ خُذِ السَّلَى ثُمَّ تَوَجَّهَ إِلَى الْقَوْمِ وَالنَّبِيُّ مَعَهُ فَأَتَى قُرَيْشاً وَهُمْ حَوْلَ الْكَعْبَةِ فَلَمَّا رَأَوْهُ عَرَفُوا الشَّرَّ فِي وَجْهِهِ ثُمَّ قَالَ لِحَمْزَةَ أَمِرَّ السَّلَى عَلَى سِبَالِهِمْ فَفَعَلَ ذَلِكَ حَتَّى أَتَى عَلَى آخِرِهِمْ ثُمَّ الْتَفَتَ أَبُو طَالِبٍ إِلَى النَّبِيِّ (صَلَّى اللهُ عَلَيْهِ وَآلِه) فَقَالَ يَا ابْنَ أَخِي هَذَا حَسَبُكَ فِينَا

[2] *Al-Kāfi, v1, ch111, h29*

Ali b. Ibrahim has narrated from his father from b. abu 'Umayr from Hisham b. al-Hakam from abu 'AbdAllāh (عليه السلام) who has said the following. "Once when the Holy Prophet (s.a) in the sacred Mosque wearing new clothes the pagans threw the contents of the stomach of camel on him and his new clothes was messed up. Allāh knows how hard it was for him. He went to abu Talib and asked, "How is mannerism and discipline among you?" He asked what is the matter, O son of my brother?" The Holy Prophet (s.a) informed him of the incident. Abu Talib called Hamza and pickup a sword. He asked Hamza to pick up the stomach of the camel and they came to the peole along with the Holy Prophet (s.a). They found people of Quraysh around the Ka'ba. When the saw him they read trouble from his face. Abu Talib asked Hamza to level of the contents of camel stomach against everyone's mustache and Hamza did so to the last person. Abu Talib then turned to the Holy Prophet (s.a) and said, "Son of my brother, this is how much we value your mannerism and discipline (face such great risk)." (حسن كالصحيح)[3]

4.

عَلِيٌّ عَنْ أَبِيهِ عَنِ ابْنِ أَبِي نَصْرٍ عَنْ إِبْرَاهِيمَ بْنِ مُحَمَّدٍ الاشْعَرِيِّ عَنْ عُبَيْدِ بْنِ زُرَارَةَ عَنْ أَبِي عَبْدِ اللهِ (عَلَيْهِ السَّلام) قَالَ لَمَّا تُوُفِّيَ أَبُو طَالِبٍ نَزَلَ جَبْرَئِيلُ عَلَى رَسُولِ اللهِ (صَلَّى اللهُ عَلَيْهِ وَآلِه) فَقَالَ يَا مُحَمَّدُ اخْرُجْ مِنْ مَكَّةَ فَلَيْسَ لَكَ فِيهَا نَاصِرٌ وَثَارَتْ قُرَيْشٌ بِالنَّبِيِّ (صَلَّى اللهُ عَلَيْهِ وَآلِه) فَخَرَجَ هَارِباً حَتَّى جَاءَ إِلَى جَبَلٍ بِمَكَّةَ يُقَالُ لَهُ الْحَجُونُ فَصَارَ إِلَيْهِ

Ali has narrated from his father from b. abu Nasr from Ibrahim b. Muḥammad al-Ash'ari from 'Ubayd b. Zurara from abu 'AbdAllāh (عليه السلام) who has said the following. "When abu Talib (عليه السلام) passed away, Jibril came to the Messenger of Allāh and said, "O Muhammad, migrate from Makka. There is no one to help you. Qurash revolted against the Holy Prophet (s.a) and came out of Makka running away

---

[3] *Al-Kafi, v1, ch111, h30*

until he reach one of the mountains of Makka. Called al-Hajun. He went there." (حسن كالصحيح)[4]

5.

عَلِيُّ بْنُ مُحَمَّدِ بْنِ عَبْدِ اللهِ وَمُحَمَّدُ بْنُ يَحْيَى عَنْ مُحَمَّدِ بْنِ عَبْدِ اللهِ رَفَعَهُ عَنْ أَبِي عَبْدِ اللهِ (عَلَيْهِ السَّلام) قَالَ إِنَّ أَبَا طَالِبٍ أَسْلَمَ بِحِسَابِ الْجُمَّلِ قَالَ بِكُلِّ لِسَانٍ

Ali b. Muḥammad b. 'AbdAllāh and Muḥammad b.yh have narrated from Muḥammad b. 'AbdAllāh who in a in a marfu' manner has narrated it from abu 'AbdAllāh (عليه السلام) who has said the following. "Abu Talib acknowledged Islam through the expression of (al-Jummal). (It is a system wherein each letter of the alphabet is given a certain numerical and instead of a letter its numeric value is used for secrecy or other reasons.)"[5]

6.

مُحَمَّدُ بْنُ يَحْيَى عَنْ سَعْدِ بْنِ عَبْدِ اللهِ عَنْ جَمَاعَةٍ مِنْ أَصْحَابِنَا عَنْ أَحْمَدَ بْنِ هِلَالٍ عَنْ أُمَيَّةَ بْنِ عَلِيٍّ الْقَيْسِيِّ قَالَ حَدَّثَنِي دُرُسْتُ بْنُ أَبِي مَنْصُورٍ أَنَّهُ سَأَلَ أَبَا الْحَسَنِ الاوَّلَ (عَلَيْهِ السَّلام) أَكَانَ رَسُولُ اللهِ (صَلَّى اللهُ عَلَيْهِ وَآلِه) مَحْجُوجاً بِأَبِي طَالِبٍ فَقَالَ لا وَلَكِنَّهُ كَانَ مُسْتَوْدَعاً لِلْوَصَايَا فَدَفَعَهَا إِلَيْهِ (صَلَّى اللهُ عَلَيْهِ وَآلِه) قَالَ قُلْتُ فَدَفَعَ إِلَيْهِ الْوَصَايَا عَلَى أَنَّهُ مَحْجُوجٌ بِهِ فَقَالَ لَوْ كَانَ مَحْجُوجاً بِهِ مَا دَفَعَ إِلَيْهِ الْوَصِيَّةَ قَالَ فَقُلْتُ فَمَا كَانَ حَالُ أَبِي طَالِبٍ قَالَ أَقَرَّ بِالنَّبِيِّ وَبِمَا جَاءَ بِهِ وَدَفَعَ إِلَيْهِ الْوَصَايَا وَمَاتَ مِنْ يَوْمِهِ

Muhammad b. Yahya has narrated from Sa'd b. 'AbdAllāh from a group of our people from Ahmad b. Hilal from 'Umayya b. 'Alī al-Qaysi who has said that narrated to me Durust b. abu Mansur who has said the following. " I once asked abu

[4] *Al-Kāfi, v1, ch111, h31*

[5] *Al-Kāfi, v1, ch111, h32*

al-Hassan (عليه السلام), 'Did the Messenger of Allāh receive any authority from abu Talib (عليه السلام) ?" The Imam (عليه السلام) said, "No, but abu Talib was the trustee of certain (items) that he delivered to the Holy Prophet ." I then asked, "What was the condition of abu Talib?" The Imam (عليه السلام) Imam said, " He acknowledged the Holy Prophet and his Divine message. He delivered to him the (Items of) will and died on that day." (ضعيف)[6]

[6] *Al-Kāfi, v1, ch111, h18*

باب النكاح

Chapter on an-Nikāḥ (Marriage)

1.

حُمَيْدُ بْنُ زِيَادٍ عَنِ الْحَسَنِ بْنِ مُحَمَّدِ بْنِ سَمَاعَةَ عَنْ عَلِيِّ بْنِ الْحَسَنِ بْنِ رِبَاطٍ عَنْ حَبِيبٍ الْخَثْعَمِيِّ عَنِ ابْنِ أَبِي يَعْفُورٍ عَنْ أَبِي عَبْدِ اللهِ (عَلَيْهِ السَّلام) قَالَ قُلْتُ لَهُ إِنِّي أُرِيدُ أَنْ أَتَزَوَّجَ امْرَأَةً وَإِنَّ أَبَوَيَّ أَرَادَا غَيْرَهَا قَالَ تَزَوَّجِ الَّتِي هَوِيتَ وَدَعِ الَّتِي يَهْوَى أَبَوَاكَ

Humayd b. Ziyad has narrated from al-Hassan b. Muḥammad b. Sama'ah from al-Hassan Ribat from Habib ai-Khath'amiy from b. abu Ya'fur who has said the foiiowing: "I once said to abu ' Abd Allāh, (عليه السلام), 'I want to marry with a woman but my father wants another one. He (the Imam) said, 'Marry the one you love, not the one your parents love.'" (موثق)[1]

2.

[1] Al-Kafi, v5, ch65, h1

محمد بن يحيى، عن أحمد بن محمد بن عيسى، عن علي بن الحكم، عن صفوان بن مهران، عن أبي عبد الله (عليه السلام) قال: قال رسول الله (صلى الله عليه وآله): تزوجوا وزوجوا ألا فمن حظ امرء مسلم إنفاق قيمة أيمة (2) وما من شئ أحب إلى الله عز وجل من بيت يعمر في الاسلام بالنكاح وما من شئ أبغض إلى الله عز وجل من بيت يخرب في الاسلام بالفرقة - يعني الطلاق - ثم قال أبو عبد الله (عليه السلام): إن الله عز وجل إنما وكد في الطلاق وكرر فيه القول من بغضه الفرقة

Muhammad b. Yahya has narrated from Ahmad b. Muḥammad b. 'Isa from 'Alī b. al-Hakam from Safwan b. Mehran who has said the following: "Abu 'Abd Allāh, (عليه السلام), has said that the Messenger of Allāh, (صلى الله عليه وآله وسلم), has said, 'It is of the share of good fortune of a Muslim that female members of his family find marriage early on and there is nothing more beloved to Allāh, most Majestic, most Glorious, than a home that is established in Islam with marriage and there is nothing more hated to Allāh, most Majestic, most Glorious, than a home that is destroyed in Islam because of division, - divorce.' Abu 'Abd Allāh, (عليه السلام), then said, 'Allāh, most Majestic, most Glorious, has stressed on His hating divorce in repeated ways because of His extreme dislike of division.'" (صحيح)[2]

3.

عِدَّةٌ مِنْ أَصْحَابِنَا عَنْ أَحْمَدَ بْنِ مُحَمَّدٍ عَنِ ابْنِ فَضَّالٍ عَنِ ابْنِ الْقَدَّاحِ قَالَ قَالَ أَبُو عَبْدِ اللهِ (عَلَيْهِ السَّلام) رَكْعَتَانِ يُصَلِّيهِمَا الْمُتَزَوِّجُ أَفْضَلُ مِنْ سَبْعِينَ رَكْعَةً يُصَلِّيهَا أَعْزَبُ. عِدَّةٌ مِنْ أَصْحَابِنَا عَنْ سَهْلِ بْنِ زِيَادٍ عَنْ جَعْفَرِ بْنِ مُحَمَّدٍ الْأَشْعَرِيِّ عَنِ ابْنِ الْقَدَّاحِ عَنْ أَبِي عَبْدِ اللهِ (عَلَيْهِ السَّلام) مِثْلَهُ

A number of our people have narrated from Ahmad b. Muḥammad from b. Faddal from b. al-Qaddah who has said the following: "Abu ' Abd Allāh, (عليه السلام), has said, 'Two Rak'at Salat (prayer) performed by a married person is more virtuous than seventy Rak'at Salat (prayer) performed by a non-married person.'" "A number of

[2] *Al-Kāfi, v5, ch8, h1*

our people have narrated from Sahl b. Ziyad from Ja'far b. Muḥammad al-Ash'ariy from b. al-Qaddah from abu 'Abd Allāh, (عليه السلام), a similar Hadīth." (موثق)[3]

4.

مُحَمَّدُ بْنُ إِسْمَاعِيلَ عَنِ الْفَضْلِ بْنِ شَاذَانَ عَنْ صَفْوَانَ بْنِ يَحْيَى عَنْ أَبِي الْحَسَنِ عَلِيِّ بْنِ مُوسَى الرِّضَا (عَلَيْهِ السَّلام) قَالَ مَا أَفَادَ عَبْدٌ فَائِدَةً خَيْراً مِنْ زَوْجَةٍ صَالِحَةٍ إِذَا رَآهَا سَرَّتْهُ وَإِذَا غَابَ عَنْهَا حَفِظَتْهُ فِي نَفْسِهَا وَمَالِهِ

Muhammad b. 'Isma'il has narrated from al-Fadl b. Shadhan from Safwan b. Yahya who has said the following: "Abu al-Hassan, al-Rida', (عليه السلام), has said, 'A servant (of Allāh) never gains a benefit better than a virtuous wife who gives him joy when he looks to her and who protects his interest in his absence.'" (مجهول كالصحيح)[4]

5.

مُحَمَّدُ بْنُ يَحْيَى عَنْ أَحْمَدَ بْنِ مُحَمَّدٍ عَنْ مُحَمَّدِ بْنِ إِسْمَاعِيلَ عَنْ حَنَانِ بْنِ سَدِيرٍ عَنْ أَبِيهِ عَنْ أَبِي جَعْفَرٍ (عَلَيْهِ السَّلام) قَالَ قَالَ رَسُولُ اللهِ (صَلَّى اللهُ عَلَيْهِ وَآلِه) إِنَّ مِنَ الْقِسْمِ الْمُصْلِحِ لِلْمَرْءِ الْمُسْلِمِ أَنْ يَكُونَ لَهُ الْمَرْأَةُ إِذَا نَظَرَ إِلَيْهَا سَرَّتْهُ وَإِذَا غَابَ عَنْهَا حَفِظَتْهُ وَإِذَا أَمَرَهَا أَطَاعَتْهُ

Muhammad b. Yahya has narrated from Ahmad b. Muḥammad from 'Isma'il b. Hanan b. Sadir from his father who has said the following: "Abu Ja'far, (عليه السلام), has said that the Messenger of Allāh, (صلى الله عليه وآله وسلم), has said, 'Of the shares forming the well-being of a Muslim one is a wife who makes him delightful when he looks at her and in his absence protects his interests and obeys his orders.'" (حسن أو موثق)[5]

---

[3] *Al-Kāfi, v5, ch9, h1*

[4] *Al-Kāfi, v5, ch7, h3*

[5] *Al-Kāfi, v5, ch7, h5*

6.

عَلِيُّ بْنُ إِبْرَاهِيمَ عَنْ أَبِيهِ عَنِ ابْنِ أَبِي عُمَيْرٍ عَنْ أَبَانِ بْنِ عُثْمَانَ عَنْ حَرِيزٍ عَنْ وَلِيدِ بْنِ صَبِيحٍ عَنْ أَبِي عَبْدِ اللهِ (عَلَيْهِ السَّلام) قَالَ مَنْ تَرَكَ التَّزْوِيجَ مَخَافَةَ الْعَيْلَةِ فَقَدْ أَسَاءَ بِاللهِ الظَّنَّ

Ali b. Ibrahim has narrated from his father from b. abu 'Umayr from Aban b. 'Uthman from Hariz from Walid b. Sabih who has said the following: "One who neglects marriage for fear of failure to feed his family has become distrustful of Allāh."' (حسن)[6]

7.

مُحَمَّدُ بْنُ يَحْيَى عَنْ أَحْمَدَ وَعَبْدِ اللهِ ابْنَيْ مُحَمَّدِ بْنِ عِيسَى عَنْ عَلِيِّ بْنِ الْحَكَمِ عَنْ هِشَامِ بْنِ سَالِمٍ عَنْ أَبِي عَبْدِ اللهِ (عَلَيْهِ السَّلام) قَالَ جَاءَ رَجُلٌ إِلَى النَّبِيِّ (صَلَّى اللهُ عَلَيْهِ وَآلِهِ) فَشَكَا إِلَيْهِ الْحَاجَةَ فَقَالَ تَزَوَّجْ فَتَزَوَّجَ فَوُسِّعَ عَلَيْهِ

Muhammad b. Yahya has narrated from Ahmad and 'Abd Allāh sons of Muḥammad b. 'Isa from 'Alī b. al-Hakam from Hisham b. Salim who has said the following: "Abu 'Abd Allāh, (عليه السلام), has said, 'Once a man came to the Holy Prophet, (صلى الله عليه وآله وسلم), and complained about his financial condition. He (the Messenger of Allāh) told him to become married and he did so after which he became affluent.'" (صحيح)[7]

8.

[6] *Al-Kafi, v5, ch10, h1*

[7] *Al-Kafi, v5, ch10, h2*

عِدَّةٌ مِنْ أَصْحَابِنَا عَنْ أَحْمَدَ بْنِ مُحَمَّدٍ عَنْ عُثْمَانَ بْنِ عِيسَى عَنْ سَمَاعَةَ بْنِ مِهْرَانَ عَنْ أَبِي عَبْدِ اللهِ (عَلَيْهِ السَّلام) قَالَ مَنْ زَوَّجَ أَعْزَبَ كَانَ مِمَّنْ يَنْظُرُ اللهُ عَزَّ وَجَلَّ إِلَيْهِ يَوْمَ الْقِيَامَةِ

A number of our people have narrated from Ahmad b. Muḥammad from 'Uthman b. 'Isa from Sama'ah b. Mehran who has said the following: "Abu 'Abd Allāh, (عليه السلام), has said, 'One who arranges a marriage for an unmarried person is of those to whom Allāh, most Majestic, most Glorious, will look on Day of Judgment.'" (موثق)[8]

9.

عِدَّةٌ مِنْ أَصْحَابِنَا عَنْ سَهْلِ بْنِ زِيَادٍ وَمُحَمَّدُ بْنُ يَحْيَى عَنْ أَحْمَدَ بْنِ مُحَمَّدِ بْنِ عِيسَى وَعَلِيُّ بْنُ إِبْرَاهِيمَ عَنْ أَبِيهِ جَمِيعاً عَنِ الْحَسَنِ بْنِ مَحْبُوبٍ عَنْ عَلِيِّ بْنِ رِئَابٍ عَنْ أَبِي حَمْزَةَ قَالَ سَمِعْتُ جَابِرَ بْنَ عَبْدِ اللهِ يَقُولُ كُنَّا عِنْدَ النَّبِيِّ (صَلَّى اللهُ عَلَيْهِ وَآلِهِ) فَقَالَ إِنَّ خَيْرَ نِسَائِكُمُ الْوَلُودُ الْوَدُودُ الْعَفِيفَةُ الْعَزِيزَةُ فِي أَهْلِهَا الذَّلِيلَةُ مَعَ بَعْلِهَا الْمُتَبَرِّجَةُ مَعَ زَوْجِهَا الْحَصَانُ عَلَى غَيْرِهِ الَّتِي تَسْمَعُ قَوْلَهُ وَتُطِيعُ أَمْرَهُ وَإِذَا خَلا بِهَا بَذَلَتْ لَهُ مَا يُرِيدُ مِنْهَا وَلَمْ تَبَذَّلْ كَتَبَذُّلِ الرَّجُلِ

A number of our people have narrated from Sahl b. Ziyad and Muḥammad b. Yahya has narrated from Ahmad b. 'Isa and 'Alī b. Ibrahim has narrated from his father from all from al-Hassan b. Mahbub from 'Alī b. Ri'ab from abu Hamzah who has said the following: "I once heard Jabir b. 'Abd Allāh saying, 'Once we were with the Holy Prophet, (صلى الله عليه وآله وسلم), when he said, "The best of your women are the child bearing, loving and chaste who are dear at home, humble with her husband, showing her beauty to her husband, fortressed from strangers, who listens to his words and obeys his orders and in private offers to him what he wants and she does not display vulgar manners as man does.' (صحيح)[9]

---

[8] *Al-Kāfi, v5, ch10, h2*

[9] *Al-Kāfi, v5, ch4, h1*

10.

عِدَّةٌ مِنْ أَصْحَابِنَا عَنْ أَحْمَدَ بْنِ مُحَمَّدِ بْنِ خَالِدٍ الْبَرْقِيِّ عَنْ أَحْمَدَ بْنِ مُحَمَّدِ بْنِ أَبِي نَصْرٍ عَنْ حَمَّادِ بْنِ عُثْمَانَ عَنْ أَبِي بَصِيرٍ عَنْ أَبِي عَبْدِ اللهِ (عَلَيْهِ السَّلام) قَالَ خَيْرُ نِسَائِكُمُ الَّتِي إِذَا خَلَتْ مَعَ زَوْجِهَا خَلَعَتْ لَهُ دِرْعَ الْحَيَاءِ وَإِذَا لَبِسَتْ لَبِسَتْ مَعَهُ دِرْعَ الْحَيَاءِ

A number of our people have narrated from Ahmad b. Muḥammad b. Khalid al-Barqiy from Ahmad b. abu Nasr from Hammad b. 'Isa from abu Basir who has said the following: "Abu 'Abd Allāh, (عليه السلام), has said, 'The best of your women are those who in privacy removes the shield of shyness before her husband and when dressed up dresses with him the shield of shyness.'" (صحيح)[10]

11.

عِدَّةٌ مِنْ أَصْحَابِنَا عَنْ أَحْمَدَ بْنِ مُحَمَّدٍ الْبَرْقِيِّ عَنْ إِسْمَاعِيلَ بْنِ مِهْرَانَ عَنْ سُلَيْمَانَ الْجَعْفَرِيِّ عَنْ أَبِي الْحَسَنِ الرِّضَا (عَلَيْهِ السَّلام) قَالَ قَالَ أَمِيرُ الْمُؤْمِنِينَ (عَلَيْهِ السَّلام) خَيْرُ نِسَائِكُمُ الْخَمْسُ قِيلَ يَا أَمِيرَ الْمُؤْمِنِينَ وَمَا الْخَمْسُ قَالَ الْهَيِّنَةُ اللَّيِّنَةُ الْمُؤَاتِيَةُ الَّتِي إِذَا غَضِبَ زَوْجُهَا لَمْ تَكْتَحِلْ بِغُمْضٍ حَتَّى يَرْضَى وَإِذَا غَابَ عَنْهَا زَوْجُهَا حَفِظَتْهُ فِي غَيْبَتِهِ فَتِلْكَ عَامِلٌ مِنْ عُمَّالِ اللهِ وَعَامِلُ اللهِ لا يَخِيبُ

A number of our people have narrated from Ahmad b. Muḥammad from al-Barqiy from 'Isma'il b. Mehran from Sulayman al- Ja'fariy who has said the following: "Abu al-Hassan al-Rida', (عليه السلام), has said that 'Amir al-Mu'minin, (عليه السلام), has said, 'The best of your women are five.' It was asked, 'O 'Amir al-Mu'minin what kind of five are they?' He (the Imam) replied, 'Simple, nice and suitable, when her husband becomes angry, does not neglect him until he is pleased, and when he is absent she

[10] *Al-Kāfi, v5, ch4, h2*

protects him in his absence and that is a worker from Allāh and the worker from Allāh does not fail.'" (صحيح)[11]

12.

مُحَمَّدُ بْنُ يَحْيَى عَنْ أَحْمَدَ بْنِ مُحَمَّدٍ عَنِ ابْنِ مَحْبُوبٍ عَنْ جَمِيلِ بْنِ صَالِحٍ عَنْ فُضَيْلِ بْنِ يَسَارٍ عَنْ أَبِي عَبْدِ اللهِ (عَلَيْهِ السَّلام) قَالَ لا يَتَزَوَّجِ الْمُؤْمِنُ النَّاصِبَةَ الْمَعْرُوفَةَ بِذَلِكَ

Muhammad b. Yahya has narrated from Ahmad b. Muḥammad from b. Mahbub from Jamil b. Salih from Fudayl b. Yasar who has said the following: "Abu 'Abd Allāh, (عليه السلام), has said, 'A believer must not marry one who is hostile(nasab) to 'A'immah, (عليه السلام), and his hostility is well known.'" (صحيح)[12]

13.

أَبُو عَلِيٍّ الأَشْعَرِيُّ عَنْ مُحَمَّدِ بْنِ عَبْدِ الْجَبَّارِ عَنْ صَفْوَانَ بْنِ يَحْيَى عَنْ إِسْحَاقَ بْنِ عَمَّارٍ قَالَ قُلْتُ لأَبِي عَبْدِ اللهِ (عَلَيْهِ السَّلام) مَا حَقُّ الْمَرْأَةِ عَلَى زَوْجِهَا الَّذِي إِذَا فَعَلَهُ كَانَ مُحْسِناً قَالَ يُشْبِعُهَا وَيَكْسُوهَا وَإِنْ جَهِلَتْ غَفَرَ لَهَا وَقَالَ أَبُو عَبْدِ اللهِ (عَلَيْهِ السَّلام) كَانَتِ امْرَأَةٌ عِنْدَ أَبِي (عَلَيْهِ السَّلام) تُؤْذِيهِ فَيَغْفِرُ لَهَا

Abu 'Alī al-Ash'ariy has narrated from Muḥammad b. 'Abd al-Jabbar from Safwan b. Yahya from Ishaq b. 'Ammar who has said the following: "I once asked abu 'Abd Allāh, (عليه السلام), about the right of woman on her husband for which when he yields is a man of good deeds. He (the Imam) said, 'He must provide her sufficient food, clothes and forgive her if she acted ignorantly.' Abu 'Abd Allāh, (عليه السلام), has said,

[11] *Al-Kafi, v5, ch4, h5*

[12] *Al-Kafi, v5, ch27, h3*

'My father had a woman who would disappoint him (the Imam) but he would forgive her.''' (موثق)[13]

14.

حُمَيْدُ بْنُ زِيَادٍ عَنِ الْحَسَنِ بْنِ مُحَمَّدِ بْنِ سَمَاعَةَ عَنْ غَيْرِ وَاحِدٍ عَنْ أَبَانٍ عَنْ أَبِي مَرْيَمَ عَنْ أَبِي جَعْفَرٍ (عَلَيْهِ السَّلام) قَالَ قَالَ رَسُولُ اللهِ (صَلَّى اللهُ عَلَيْهِ وَآلِه) أَيَضْرِبُ أَحَدُكُمُ الْمَرْأَةَ ثُمَّ يَظَلُّ مُعَانِقَهَا

Humayd b. Ziyad has narrated from al-Hassan b. Muḥammad b. Sama'ah from more than one person from Aban from abu Maryam who has said the folio wing: "Abu Ja'far, (عليه السلام), has said that the Messenger of Allāh, (صلى الله عليه وآله وسلم), has said, 'How can one of you hurt the woman whom he continues to embrace? (موثق)[14]

15

عَلِيُّ بْنُ إِبْرَاهِيمَ عَنْ أَبِيهِ عَنِ ابْنِ أَبِي عُمَيْرٍ عَنْ حَمَّادِ بْنِ عُثْمَانَ عَنِ الْحَلَبِيِّ عَنْ أَبِي عَبْدِ اللهِ (عَلَيْهِ السَّلام) قَالَ الْكَادُّ عَلَى عِيَالِهِ كَالْمُجَاهِدِ فِي سَبِيلِ اللهِ

Ali b. Ibrahim has narrated from his father from b. abu 'Umayr from Hammad b. 'Uthman from af-Halabiy who has said the following: "Abu ' Abd Allāh, (عليه السلام), has said, 'A person working hard for his family is like Mujahid (fighter) for the cause of Allāh. ''' (حسن)[15]

16.

---

[13] *Al-Kāfi, v5, ch152, h1*

[14] *Al-Kāfi, v5, ch151, h1*

[15] *Al-Kāfi, v5, ch13, h1*

عَلِيُّ بْنُ إِبْرَاهِيمَ بْنِ هَاشِمٍ عَنْ أَبِيهِ عَنْ مُحَمَّدِ بْنِ أَبِي عُمَيْرٍ عَنْ إِسْحَاقَ بْنِ عَمَّارٍ قَالَ قَالَ أَبُو عَبْدِ اللهِ (عَلَيْهِ السَّلام) مِنْ أَخْلَاقِ الْأَنْبِيَاءِ صَلَّى اللهُ عَلَيْهِمْ حُبُّ النِّسَاءِ

Ali b. Ibrahim b. Hashim has narrated from his father from Muḥammad b. abu 'Umayr from Ishaq b. 'Ammar who has said the following: "Abu ' Abd Allāh, (عليه السلام), has said, 'Love for women is of the moral manners of the prophets.'" (حسن أو موثق)[16]

17.

مُحَمَّدُ بْنُ يَحْيَى الْعَطَّارُ عَنْ عَبْدِ اللهِ بْنِ مُحَمَّدٍ عَنْ عَلِيِّ بْنِ الْحَكَمِ عَنْ أَبَانِ بْنِ عُثْمَانَ عَنْ عُمَرَ بْنِ يَزِيدَ عَنْ أَبِي عَبْدِ اللهِ (عَلَيْهِ السَّلام) قَالَ مَا أَظُنُّ رَجُلا يَزْدَادُ فِي الْإِيمَانِ خَيْراً إِلا ازْدَادَ حُبّاً لِلنِّسَاءِ

Muhammad b. Yahya al-' Attar has narrated from 'Abd Allāh b. Muḥammad from 'Alī b. al-Hakam from Aban b. 'Uthman from 'Umar b. Yazid who has said the following: "Abu 'Abd Allāh, (عليه السلام), has said, 'I do not think a man can increase anything good in his belief except that he increases his love for women.'" (مجهول)[17]

18.

مُحَمَّدُ بْنُ يَحْيَى عَنْ أَحْمَدَ بْنِ مُحَمَّدِ بْنِ عِيسَى عَنْ مُعَمَّرِ بْنِ خَلادٍ قَالَ سَمِعْتُ عَلِيَّ بْنَ مُوسَى الرِّضَا (عَلَيْهِ السَّلام) يَقُولُ ثَلَاثٌ مِنْ سُنَنِ الْمُرْسَلِينَ الْعِطْرُ وَأَخْذُ الشَّعْرِ وَكَثْرَةُ الطَّرُوقَةِ

Muhammad b. Yahya has narrated from Ahmad b. Muḥammad b. 'Isa from Mu'ammar b. Khallad who has said the following: "I once heard al-Rida', (عليه السلام),

[16] *Al-Kāfi, v5, ch1, h1*

[17] *Al-Kāfi, v5, ch1, h2*

saying, 'Three things are of the traditions of the Messengers (of Allāh): use of perfume, trimming hairs and ampleness of (relation in) marriage.'" (صحيح)[18]

19.

عَلِيُّ بْنُ إِبْرَاهِيمَ عَنْ أَبِيهِ عَنِ ابْنِ أَبِي عُمَيْرٍ عَنْ حَفْصِ بْنِ الْبَخْتَرِيِّ عَنْ أَبِي عَبْدِ اللهِ (عَلَيْهِ السَّلام) قَالَ قَالَ رَسُولُ اللهِ (صَلَّى اللهُ عَلَيْهِ وَآلِه) مَا أُحِبُّ مِنْ دُنْيَاكُمْ إِلا النِّسَاءَ وَالطِّيبَ

Ali b. Ibrahim has narrated from his father from b. abu 'Umayr from Hafs b. al-Bakhtariy who has said the following: "Abu 'Abd Allāh, (عليه السلام), has said that the Messenger of Allāh, (صلى الله عليه وآله وسلم), has said, 'I do not love anything from your world except women and perfume.'" (حسن)[19]

20.

أَحْمَدُ بْنُ مُحَمَّدٍ عَنْ عَلِيِّ بْنِ الْحَكَمِ عَنْ مُعَاوِيَةَ بْنِ وَهْبٍ عَنْ أَبِي عَبْدِ اللهِ (عَلَيْهِ السَّلام) قَالَ زَوَّجَ رَسُولُ اللهِ (صَلَّى اللهُ عَلَيْهِ وَآلِه) عَلِيّاً فَاطِمَةَ (عَلَيْهَا السَّلام) عَلَى دِرْعٍ حُطَمِيَّةٍ وَكَانَ فِرَاشُهَا إِهَابَ كَبْشٍ يَجْعَلانِ الصُّوفَ إِذَا اضْطَجَعَا تَحْتَ جُنُوبِهِمَا

Ahmad b. Muḥammad has narrated from 'Alī b. al-Hakam from Mu'awiyah b. Wahab who has said the following: "Abu 'Abd Allāh, (عليه السلام), has said, 'The Messenger of Allāh, (صلى الله عليه وآله وسلم), arranged marriage of 'Alī and Fatimah, (عليه السلام), with a mahr (dower) from a shield made by Hatmiyah and their bed was made of the hide of ram and when sleeping they would turn its fury face under their side.'" (صحيح)[20]

---

[18] *Al-Kāfi, v5, ch1, h3*

[19] *Al-Kāfi, v5, ch1, h6*

[20] *Al-Kāfi, v5, ch46, h3*

21.

حَدَّثَنَا أَبُو الحَسَن مُحَمَّدِ بْنِ عَلِيِّ بْنِ لِشاه بِمَرْوَرُودَ قالَ: حَدَّثَنا أَبُوالعَبّاس أَحْمَدِ بْنِ المُظَفَّرِ بْنِ الحُسَيْنِ قالَ: حَدَّثَنا أَبُوعَبْدِ اللّه مُحَمَّدِ بْنِ زَكَرِيَّا البَصْرِيِّ قالَ: حَدَّثَني مُحَمَّدِ بْنِ سابِق قالَ: حَدَّثَنا عَلِيِّ بْنِ مُوسَى بْنِ جَعْفَر عَلَيْهِ السَّلامُ قالَ: حَدَّثَني أَبي، عَن أَبيهِ جَعْفَر بْنِ مُحَمَّد عَلَيْهِ السَّلامُ عَنْ أَبيهِ، عَن جَدِّهِ عَلَيْهِ السَّلامُ قالَ: قالَ عَلِيّ بْن أَبي طالب عَلَيْهِ السَّلامُ: لَقَدْ هَمَمْتُ بِتَزْوِيجِ فاطِمَةَ ابْنَةَ مُحَمَّدٍ صَلَّى اللهُ عَلَيْهِ وَآلِهِ وَلَمْ أَتَجَرَّأْ أَنْ أَذْكُرَ ذَلِكَ لِلنَّبِيِّ وَإِنَّ ذَلِكَ لَيَخْتَلِجُ فِي صَدْرِي لَيْلِي وَنَهَارِي حَتَّى دَخَلْتُ عَلَى رَسُولِ اللَّهِ صَلَّى اللهُ عَلَيْهِ وَآلِهِ فَقالَ: يا عَلِيُّ. قُلْتُ: لَبَّيْكَ يَا رَسُولَ اللّهِ. قالَ: هَلْ لَكَ فِي التَّزْوِيجِ؟ قُلْتُ: رَسُولُ اللّهِ أَعْلَمُ. وَإِذا هُوَ يُرِيدُ أَنْ يُزَوِّجَني بَعْضَ نِساءِ قُرَيْشٍ، وَإِنِّي لَخائِفٌ عَلَى فَوْتِ فاطِمَةَ، فَمَا شَعَرْتُ بِشَيْءٍ إِذْ أَتانِي رَسُولُ رَسُولِ اللّهِ صَلَّى اللهُ عَلَيْهِ وَآلِهِ فَقالَ لِي: أَجِبِ النَّبِيَ صَلَّى اللهُ عَلَيْهِ وَآلِهِ وَأَسْرِعْ، فَما رَأَيْنا رَسُولَ اللّهِ صَلَّى اللهُ عَلَيْهِ وَآلِهِ أَشَدَّ فَرَحاً مِنْهُ الْيَوْمَ. قالَ: فَأَتَيْتُهُ مُسْرِعاً، فَإِذا هُوَ فِي حُجْرَةِ أُمِّ سَلَمَةَ. فَلَمَّا نَظَرَ إِلَيَّ تَهَلَّلَ وَجْهُهُ فَرَحاً وَتَبَسَّمَ حَتَّى نَظَرْتُ إِلَى بَياضِ أَسْنانِهِ يَبْرُقُ. فَقالَ: أَبْشِرْ يَا عَلِيُّ، فَإِنَّ اللّهَ عَزَّ وَجَلَّ قَدْ كَفاني مَا قَدْ كانَ أَهَمَّني مِنْ أَمْرِ تَزْوِيجِكَ. فَقُلْتُ: وَكَيْفَ ذَلِكَ يَا رَسُولَ اللّهِ؟ قالَ: أَتانِي جَبْرَئِيلُ وَمَعَهُ مِنْ سُنْبُلِ الْجَنَّةِ وَقَرَنْفُلِها فَناوَلَنِيهِمَا فَأَخَذْتُهُمَا وَشَمَمْتُهُما فَقُلْتُ: مَا سَبَبُ هَذَا السُّنْبُلِ وَالْقَرَنْفُلِ؟ فَقالَ: إِنَّ اللّهَ تَبارَكَ وَتَعالَى أَمَرَ سُكّانَ الْجِنانِ مِنَ الْمَلائِكَةِ وَمَنْ فِيهَا أَنْ يُزَيِّنُوا الْجِنانَ كُلَّهَا بِمَغارِسِها وَأَشْجارِها وَثِمارِها وَقُصُورِها، وَأَمَرَ رِيحَها فَهَبَّتْ بِأَنْواعِ الْعِطْرِ وَالطِّيبِ، وَأَمَرَ حُورَ عِينِها بِالْقِراءَةِ فِيهَا بِسُورَةِ طه وَطَواسِينَ وَيس وَحمعسق. ثُمَّ نادَى مُنادٍ مِنْ تَحْتِ الْعَرْشِ أَلا إِنَّ الْيَوْمَ يَوْمُ وَلِيمَةِ عَلِيِّ بْنِ أَبِي طالِبٍ عَلَيْهِ السَّلامُ. أَلا إِنِّي أُشْهِدُكُمْ أَنِّي قَدْ زَوَّجْتُ فاطِمَةَ بِنْتَ مُحَمَّدٍ مِنْ عَلِيِّ بْنِ أَبِي طالِبٍ رِضَى مِنِّي بَعْضُهُما لِبَعْضٍ.ثُمَّ بَعَثَ اللّهُ تَبارَكَ وَتَعالَى سَحابَةً بَيْضاءَ فَقَطَرَتْ عَلَيْهِمْ مِنْ لُؤْلُئِها وَزَبَرْجَدِها وَيَواقِيتِها وَقامَتِ الْمَلائِكَةُ فَنَثَرَتْ مِنْ سُنْبُلِ الْجَنَّةِ وَقَرَنْفُلِها هَذا مِمَّا نَثَرَتِ الْمَلائِكَةُ ثُمَّ أَمَرَ اللّهُ تَبارَكَ وَتَعالَى مَلَكاً مِنْ مَلائِكَةِ الْجَنَّةِ يُقالُ لَهُ راحِيلُ وَلَيْسَ فِي الْمَلائِكَةِ أَبْلَغُ مِنْهُ فَقالَ اخْطُبْ يا راحِيلُ فَخَطَبَ بِخُطْبَةٍ لَمْ يَسْمَعْ بِمِثْلِها أَهْلُ السَّماءِ وَلا أَهْلُ الأَرْضِ ثُمَّ نادَى مُنادٍ أَلا يا مَلائِكَتِي وَسُكّانَ جَنَّتِي بارِكُوا عَلَى عَلِيِّ بْنِ أَبِي طالِبٍ حَبِيبِ مُحَمَّدٍ وَفاطِمَةَ بِنْتِ مُحَمَّدٍ فَقَدْ بارَكْتُ عَلَيْهِما أَلا إِنِّي قَدْ زَوَّجْتُ أَحَبَّ النِّساءِ إِلَيَّ مِنْ أَحَبِّ الرِّجالِ إِلَيَّ بَعْدَ النَّبِيِّينَ وَالْمُرْسَلِينَ فَقالَ راحِيلُ الْمَلَكُ يا رَبِّ وَما بَرَكَتُكَ فِيهِما بِأَكْثَرَ مِمَّا رَأَيْنا لَهُما فِي جِنانِكَ وَدارِكَ فَقالَ عَزَّ وَجَلَّ يا راحِيلُ إِنَّ مِنْ بَرَكَتِي عَلَيْهِما أَنْ أَجْمَعَهُما عَلَى مَحَبَّتِي وَأَجْعَلَهُما حُجَّةً عَلَى خَلْقِي وَعِزَّتِي وَجَلالِي لاخْلُقَنَّ مِنْهُما خَلْقاً وَلانْشِئَنَّ مِنْهُما ذُرِّيَّةً أَجْعَلُهُمْ خُزّانِي فِي أَرْضِي وَمَعادِنَ لِعِلْمِي وَدُعاةً إِلَى دِينِي بِهِمْ أَحْتَجُّ عَلَى خَلْقِي بَعْدَ النَّبِيِّينَ وَالْمُرْسَلِينَ فَأَبْشِرْ يا عَلِيُّ فَإِنَّ اللّهَ عَزَّ وَجَلَّ أَكْرَمَكَ كَرامَةً لَمْ يُكْرِمْ بِمِثْلِها أَحَداً وَقَدْ زَوَّجْتُكَ ابْنَتِي فاطِمَةَ عَلَى ما زَوَّجَكَ الرَّحْمنُ وَقَدْ رَضِيتُ لَها بِما رَضِيَ اللّهُ لَها فَدُونَكَ أَهْلَكَ فَإِنَّكَ أَحَقُّ بِها مِنِّي وَلَقَدْ أَخْبَرَنِي جَبْرَئِيلُ عَلَيْهِ السَّلامُ أَنَّ الْجَنَّةَ مُشْتاقَةٌ إِلَيْكُما وَلَوْ لا

أَنَّ اللَّهَ عَزَّ وَجَلَّ قَدَّرَ أَنْ يُخْرِجَ مِنْكُمَا مَا يَتَّخِذُهُ عَلَى الْخَلْقِ حُجَّةً لاجَابَ فِيكُمَا الْجَنَّةَ وَأَهْلَهَا فَنِعْمَ الأَخُ أَنْتَ وَنِعْمَ الْخَتَنُ أَنْتَ وَنِعْمَ الصَّاحِبُ أَنْتَ وَكَفَاكَ بِرِضَى اللَّهِ رِضًى قَالَ عَلِيٌّ عَلَيْهِ السَّلامُ فَقُلْتُ يَا رَسُولَ اللَّهِ بَلَغَ مِنْ قَدْرِي حَتَّى إِنِّي ذُكِرْتُ فِي الْجَنَّةِ وَزَوَّجَنِي اللَّهُ فِي مَلائِكَتِهِ فَقَالَ إِنَّ اللَّهَ عَزَّ وَجَلَّ إِذَا أَكْرَمَ وَلِيَّهُ وَأَحَبَّهُ أَكْرَمَهُ بِمَا لا عَيْنٌ رَأَتْ وَلا أُذُنٌ سَمِعَتْ فَحَبَاهَا اللَّهُ لَكَ يَا عَلِيُّ فَقَالَ عَلِيٌّ عَلَيْهِ السَّلامُ رَبِّ أَوْزِعْنِي أَنْ أَشْكُرَ نِعْمَتَكَ الَّتِي أَنْعَمْتَ عَلَيَّ فَقَالَ رَسُولُ اللَّهِ صَلَّى اللَّهُ عَلَيْهِ وَآلِهِ آمِينَ.حَدَّثَنِي بِهذَا الْحَدِيث عَلِيُّ بْنِ أَحْمَدِ بْنِ مُحَمَّدِ بْنِ عِمْران الدَّقَّاق رَضِيَ اللهُ عَنْهُ قالَ: حَدَّثَنَا أَحْمَدِ بْنِ يَحْيَى بن زَكَرِيَّا القَطَّانُ قالَ: حَدَّثَنَا أَبُو مُحَمَّد بَكْرِ بْنِ عَبْدِاللَّه بْنِ حَبِيبٍ قالَ: حَدَّثَنَا أَحْمَدِ بْنِ الحارِثِ قالَ: حَدَّثَنَا أَبُو مُعاوِيَة، عَنِ الأَعْمَشِ، عَنْ جَعْفَرِ بْنِ مُحَمَّد، عَنْ أَبِيهِ عَنْ جَدِّهِ، عَنْ أَبِيهِ، عَنْ عَلِيِّ بْنِ أَبِي طالِب عَلَيْهِ السَّلامُ قالَ لَقَدْ همـمتهممت بتزويج فاطِمَة عَلَيْهَا السَّلامُ وَلامْ◌َجتر؟ أَن أذكر ذٰلِكَ لرسول اللَّه وَذكر الْحَدِيث مِثْلَهُ سَواء. وَلِهذَا الْحَدِيث طَرِيق آخِرَ قَدْ أَخْرَجْتُه فِي مَدِينَة العِلْمُ

Abul Hassan Muḥammad b. ʿAlī b. al-Shah in Marvrood narrated that Abul Abbas Ahmad b. Al-Mudhaffar b. Al-Hussein quoted on the authority of Abu ʿAbd Allāh Muḥammad b. Zakariya al-Basri, on the authority of Muḥammad b. Sabiq, on the authority of ʿAlī b. Mūsā b. Ja'far (al-Reza) (عليه السلام) on the authority of his father (Imam Kazim) (عليه السلام), on the authority of his grandfather (عليه السلام), on the authority of ʿAlī b. Abi Talib (عليه السلام), "When I decided to get married, I did not dare to tell God's Prophet (صلى الله عليه وآله وسلم). This issue was on my mind for many days and nights until one day I went to see God's Prophet (صلى الله عليه وآله وسلم) and he (صلى الله عليه وآله وسلم) said, "O Ali!" I said, "Prophet of God! Yes." He (صلى الله عليه وآله وسلم) said, "Are you interested in getting married?" I said, "God's Prophet (صلى الله عليه وآله وسلم) knows best." I thought that God's Prophet (صلى الله عليه وآله وسلم) would marry off one of the women from the Quraysh tribe to me. I was worried that I might lose the chance to marry (the Blessed Lady) Fatima. I did not understand what happened and God's Prophet (صلى الله عليه وآله وسلم) called me in. I went to see him in the house of Umm Salama. When he (صلى الله عليه وآله وسلم) saw me his face got bright and he smiled such that his white teeth were shining. He (صلى الله عليه وآله وسلم) told me, "O Ali! Here are the glad tidings. The Blessed the Sublime God took care of the issue of your marriage which was on my mind." I asked, "O Prophet of God! What is the result?" He (صلى الله عليه وآله وسلم) said, "Gabriel descended to me and gave me some heavenly hyacinth and clove gillyflower. I took them and smelled them and said, O Gabriel! What is the occasion for bringing me this hyacinth and gillyflower? He (صلى الله عليه وآله وسلم) said, "The Blessed the Sublime God has ordered all the angels and others residing in Paradise to decorate all the trees, rivers, fruits and palaces in Heaven. He has ordered the winds to blow there with the scent of various perfumes. He has ordered the houri-eyed ones to recite the Chapters of Ta-Ha (No. 20) the three chapters beginning with Ta-Sin (al-Shu'ara, al-Naml, and al-Qasas -No. 26,27,28-) and the chapter of Ya-Sin (No. 36) and the chapter of Ha Mim Ayn Sin Qaf (al-Shura, No.42). The Honorable the Exalted God has ordered the callers to call out, 'Verily, today is the banquet of 'Alī b. Abi-Talib. Bear witness that I marry off (the Blessed Lady) Fatima, the daughter of Muhammad, to 'Alī b. Abi Talib. I am pleased with this. These two are one from the other.'"Then, Almighty God sent a white cloud to pour down some of its pearls, aquamarine, and corundum. The angels then dispersed hyacinth and gillyflower of Paradise. Then, the Blessed the Sublime God ordered one of the angels of Paradise called Rahil -who has no other equal in eloquence among the angels- to read the marriage contract. Then Rahil recited such a marriage contract which no one from the heavens and the Earth had recited before. Then God ordered one of the angels to call out, 'O My angels and the residents of My Paradise! Express congratulations to the beloved friend of Muḥammad 'Alī b. Abi Talib and the daughter of Muḥammad - (the Blessed Lady) Fatima. I have established Blessings for them.'" Rahil said, "O Lord! Are not Your Blessings for them more than what we saw for them in Paradise and considering their rank?" The Honorable the Exalted God said, "O Rahil! Amongst My Blessings for them is My own Love with which I unite them, and establish them as My Proofs for My creatures. I swear by My Honor and Majesty that I will create from them descendants whom I will make My Treasures on My Earth, and as Mines of My Wisdom. By them I will provide My Proofs after My Prophets and Messengers.""O Ali! Then give me glad tidings! I will marry off my daughter (the Blessed Lady) Fatima to you as the Merciful God did. For her I am pleased with what God is pleased with. Now take the hands of your spouse as you deserve her more than I do. Gabriel informed me that Paradise and its residents are eager to see you two. Had not the Blessed the Sublime God planned to create Proofs for His creatures from your generation, He would have fulfilled the request of the residents of Paradise regarding you. How good a brother, a groom and a companion you are. God's Pleasure suffices for you. It is better than anyone else's pleasure." Then 'Alī (عليه السلام) said, "O my Lord! Enable me to be grateful for Thy favours, which thou hast bestowed on me..." Then God's Prophet (صلى الله عليه وآله وسلم) said, "Amin!"The same tradition was narrated by 'Alī b. Ahmad b. Muḥammad b. Imran ad-Daqqaq - may God be pleased with him, on the authority of Ahmad b. Yahya al-Zakariya al-Qattan, on the authority of Abu Muḥammad Bakr b. 'Abd Allāh b. HAbib on the authority of Ahmad b. al-Harith, on the authority of Abu Mo'awiya, on the authority of al-A'amesh, on the authority of Ja'far b. Muḥammad (as-Ṣādiq) (عليه السلام), on the authority of his father (عليه السلام), on the authority of his grandfather (عليه السلام), on the authority of his father (عليه السلام) that 'Alī b. Abi Talib (عليه السلام) said, "I had decided to marry (the Blessed Lady) Fatima (عليها السلام) but did not dare tell this to God's Prophet (صلى الله عليه وآله وسلم)." The rest is as it was narrated before.This tradition has also been narrated in a different way which I have stated in my book Madinatul-Ilm. (معتبر)[21]

22.

مُحَمَّدُ بْنُ يَحْيَى عَنْ أَحْمَدَ بْنِ مُحَمَّدِ بْنِ عِيسَى عَنِ الْحَسَنِ بْنِ مَحْبُوبٍ عَنْ مَالِكِ بْنِ عَطِيَّةَ عَنْ أَبِي حَمْزَةَ الثُّمَالِيِّ قَالَ كُنْتُ عِنْدَ أَبِي جَعْفَرٍ (عَلَيْهِ السَّلام) إِذِ اسْتَأْذَنَ عَلَيْهِ رَجُلٌ فَأَذِنَ لَهُ فَدَخَلَ عَلَيْهِ فَسَلَّمَ فَرَحَّبَ بِهِ أَبُو جَعْفَرٍ (عَلَيْهِ السَّلام) وَأَدْنَاهُ وَسَاءَلَهُ فَقَالَ الرَّجُلُ جُعِلْتُ فِدَاكَ إِنِّي خَطَبْتُ إِلَى مَوْلَاكَ فُلَانِ بْنِ أَبِي رَافِعٍ ابْنَتَهُ فُلَانَةَ فَرَدَّنِي وَرَغِبَ عَنِّي وَازْدَرَأَنِي لِدَمَامَتِي وَحَاجَتِي وَغُرْبَتِي وَقَدْ دَخَلَنِي مِنْ ذَلِكَ غَضَاضَةٌ هَجْمَةٌ غُضَّ لَهَا قَلْبِي تَمَنَّيْتُ عِنْدَهَا الْمَوْتَ فَقَالَ أَبُو جَعْفَرٍ (عَلَيْهِ السَّلام) اذْهَبْ فَأَنْتَ رَسُولِي إِلَيْهِ وَقُلْ لَهُ يَقُولُ لَكَ مُحَمَّدُ بْنُ عَلِيِّ بْنِ الْحُسَيْنِ بْنِ عَلِيِّ بْنِ أَبِي طَالِبٍ (عَلَيْهِ السَّلام) زَوِّجْ مُنْجِحَ بْنَ رَبَاحٍ مَوْلَايَ ابْنَتَكَ فُلَانَةَ وَلا تَرُدَّهُ قَالَ أَبُو حَمْزَةَ فَوَثَبَ الرَّجُلُ فَرِحاً مُسْرِعاً بِرِسَالَةِ أَبِي جَعْفَرٍ (عَلَيْهِ السَّلام) فَلَمَّا أَنْ تَوَارَى الرَّجُلُ قَالَ أَبُو جَعْفَرٍ (عَلَيْهِ السَّلام) إِنَّ رَجُلا كَانَ مِنْ أَهْلِ الْيَمَامَةِ يُقَالُ لَهُ جُوَيْبِرٌ أَتَى رَسُولَ اللهِ (صَلَّى اللهُ عَلَيْهِ وَآلِه) مُنْتَجِعاً لِلإِسْلامِ فَأَسْلَمَ وَحَسُنَ إِسْلامُهُ وَكَانَ رَجُلا قَصِيراً دَمِيماً مُحْتَاجاً عَارِياً وَكَانَ مِنْ قِبَاحِ السُّودَانِ فَضَمَّهُ رَسُولُ اللهِ (صَلَّى اللهُ عَلَيْهِ وَآلِه) لِحَالِ غُرْبَتِهِ وَعَرَاهُ وَكَانَ يُجْرِي عَلَيْهِ طَعَامَهُ صَاعاً مِنْ تَمْرٍ بِالصَّاعِ الأَوَّلِ وَكَسَاهُ شَمْلَتَيْنِ وَأَمَرَهُ أَنْ يَلْزَمَ الْمَسْجِدَ وَيَرْقُدَ فِيهِ بِاللَّيْلِ فَمَكَثَ بِذَلِكَ مَا شَاءَ اللهُ حَتَّى كَثُرَ الْغُرَبَاءُ مِمَّنْ

---

[21] *'Uyūn Akhbār al-Riḍā, v1, ch21, h1*

يَدْخُلُ فِي الإسْلامِ مِنْ أَهْلِ الْحَاجَةِ بِالْمَدِينَةِ وَضَاقَ بِهِمُ الْمَسْجِدُ فَأَوْحَى اللهُ عَزَّ وَجَلَّ إِلَى نَبِيِّهِ (صَلَّى اللهُ عَلَيْهِ وَآلِه) أَنْ طَهِّرْ مَسْجِدَكَ وَأَخْرِجْ مِنَ الْمَسْجِدِ مَنْ يَرْقُدُ فِيهِ بِاللَّيْلِ وَمُرْ بِسَدِّ أَبْوَابِ مَنْ كَانَ لَهُ فِي مَسْجِدِكَ بَابٌ إِلا بَابَ عَلِيٍّ (عَلَيْهِ السَّلام) وَمَسْكَنَ فَاطِمَةَ (عَلَيْهَا السَّلام) وَلا يَمُرَّنَّ فِيهِ جُنُبٌ وَلا يَرْقُدْ فِيهِ غَرِيبٌ قَالَ فَأَمَرَ رَسُولُ اللهِ (صَلَّى اللهُ عَلَيْهِ وَآلِه) بِسَدِّ أَبْوَابِهِمْ إِلا بَابَ عَلِيٍّ (عَلَيْهِ السَّلام) وَأَقَرَّ مَسْكَنَ فَاطِمَةَ (عَلَيْهَا السَّلام) عَلَى حَالِهِ قَالَ ثُمَّ إِنَّ رَسُولَ اللهِ (صَلَّى اللهُ عَلَيْهِ وَآلِه) أَمَرَ أَنْ يُتَّخَذَ لِلْمُسْلِمِينَ سَقِيفَةٌ فَعُمِلَتْ لَهُمْ وَهِيَ الصُّفَّةُ ثُمَّ أَمَرَ الْغُرَبَاءَ وَالْمَسَاكِينَ أَنْ يَظَلُّوا فِيهَا نَهَارَهُمْ وَلَيْلَهُمْ فَنَزَلُوهَا وَاجْتَمَعُوا فِيهَا فَكَانَ رَسُولُ اللهِ (صَلَّى اللهُ عَلَيْهِ وَآلِه) يَتَعَاهَدُهُمْ بِالْبُرِّ وَالتَّمْرِ وَالشَّعِيرِ وَالزَّبِيبِ إِذَا كَانَ عِنْدَهُ وَكَانَ الْمُسْلِمُونَ يَتَعَاهَدُونَهُمْ وَيَرِقُّونَ عَلَيْهِمْ لِرِقَّةِ رَسُولِ اللهِ (صَلَّى اللهُ عَلَيْهِ وَآلِه) وَيَصْرِفُونَ صَدَقَاتِهِمْ إِلَيْهِمْ فَإِنَّ رَسُولَ اللهِ (صَلَّى اللهُ عَلَيْهِ وَآلِه) نَظَرَ إِلَى جُوَيْبِرٍ ذَاتَ يَوْمٍ بِرَحْمَةٍ مِنْهُ لَهُ وَرِقَّةٍ عَلَيْهِ فَقَالَ لَهُ يَا جُوَيْبِرُ لَوْ تَزَوَّجْتَ امْرَأَةً فَعَفَفْتَ بِهَا فَرْجَكَ وَأَعَانَتْكَ عَلَى دُنْيَاكَ وَآخِرَتِكَ فَقَالَ لَهُ جُوَيْبِرٌ يَا رَسُولَ اللهِ بِأَبِي أَنْتَ وَأُمِّي مَنْ يَرْغَبُ فِيَّ فَوَ اللهِ مَا مِنْ حَسَبٍ وَلا نَسَبٍ وَلا مَالٍ وَلا جَمَالٍ فَأَيَّةُ امْرَأَةٍ تَرْغَبُ فِيَّ فَقَالَ لَهُ رَسُولُ اللهِ (صَلَّى اللهُ عَلَيْهِ وَآلِه) يَا جُوَيْبِرُ إِنَّ اللهَ قَدْ وَضَعَ بِالإسْلامِ مَنْ كَانَ فِي الْجَاهِلِيَّةِ شَرِيفاً وَشَرَّفَ بِالإسْلامِ مَنْ كَانَ فِي الْجَاهِلِيَّةِ وَضِيعاً وَأَعَزَّ بِالإسْلامِ مَنْ كَانَ فِي الْجَاهِلِيَّةِ ذَلِيلا وَأَذْهَبَ بِالإسْلامِ مَا كَانَ مِنْ نَخْوَةِ الْجَاهِلِيَّةِ وَتَفَاخُرِهَا بِعَشَائِرِهَا وَبَاسِقِ أَنْسَابِهَا فَالنَّاسُ الْيَوْمَ كُلُّهُمْ أَبْيَضُهُمْ وَأَسْوَدُهُمْ وَقُرَشِيُّهُمْ وَعَرَبِيُّهُمْ وَعَجَمِيُّهُمْ مِنْ آدَمَ وَإِنَّ آدَمَ خَلَقَهُ اللهُ مِنْ طِينٍ وَإِنَّ أَحَبَّ النَّاسِ إِلَى اللهِ عَزَّ وَجَلَّ يَوْمَ الْقِيَامَةِ أَطْوَعُهُمْ لَهُ وَأَتْقَاهُمْ وَمَا أَعْلَمُ يَا جُوَيْبِرُ لأحَدٍ مِنَ الْمُسْلِمِينَ عَلَيْكَ الْيَوْمَ فَضْلا إِلا لِمَنْ كَانَ أَتْقَى لِلَّهِ مِنْكَ وَأَطْوَعَ ثُمَّ قَالَ لَهُ. انْطَلِقْ يَا جُوَيْبِرُ إِلَى زِيَادِ بْنِ لَبِيدٍ فَإِنَّهُ مِنْ أَشْرَفِ بَنِي بَيَاضَةَ حَسَباً فِيهِمْ فَقُلْ لَهُ إِنِّي رَسُولُ رَسُولِ اللهِ إِلَيْكَ وَهُوَ يَقُولُ لَكَ زَوِّجْ جُوَيْبِراً ابْنَتَكَ الذَّلْفَاءَ قَالَ فَانْطَلَقَ جُوَيْبِرٌ بِرِسَالَةِ رَسُولِ اللهِ (صَلَّى اللهُ عَلَيْهِ وَآلِه) إِلَى زِيَادِ بْنِ لَبِيدٍ وَهُوَ فِي مَنْزِلِهِ وَجَمَاعَةٌ مِنْ قَوْمِهِ عِنْدَهُ فَاسْتَأْذَنَ فَأُعْلِمَ فَأَذِنَ لَهُ فَدَخَلَ وَسَلَّمَ عَلَيْهِ ثُمَّ قَالَ يَا زِيَادَ بْنَ لَبِيدٍ إِنِّي رَسُولُ رَسُولِ اللهِ إِلَيْكَ فِي حَاجَةٍ لِي فَأَبُوحُ بِهَا أَمْ أُسِرُّهَا إِلَيْكَ فَقَالَ لَهُ زِيَادٌ بَلْ بُحْ بِهَا فَإِنَّ ذَلِكَ شَرَفٌ لِي وَفَخْرٌ فَقَالَ لَهُ جُوَيْبِرٌ إِنَّ رَسُولَ اللهِ (صَلَّى اللهُ عَلَيْهِ وَآلِه) يَقُولُ لَكَ زَوِّجْ جُوَيْبِراً ابْنَتَكَ الذَّلْفَاءَ فَقَالَ لَهُ زِيَادٌ أَرَسُولُ اللهِ أَرْسَلَكَ إِلَيَّ بِهَذَا فَقَالَ لَهُ نَعَمْ مَا كُنْتُ لأكْذِبَ عَلَى رَسُولِ اللهِ (صَلَّى اللهُ عَلَيْهِ وَآلِه) فَقَالَ لَهُ زِيَادٌ إِنَّا لا نُزَوِّجُ فَتَيَاتِنَا إِلا أَكْفَاءَنَا مِنَ الأنْصَارِ فَانْصَرِفْ يَا جُوَيْبِرُ حَتَّى أَلْقَى رَسُولَ اللهِ (صَلَّى اللهُ عَلَيْهِ وَآلِه) فَأُخْبِرَهُ بِعُذْرِي فَانْصَرَفَ جُوَيْبِرٌ وَهُوَ يَقُولُ وَاللهِ مَا بِهَذَا نَزَلَ الْقُرْآنُ وَلا بِهَذَا ظَهَرَتْ نُبُوَّةُ مُحَمَّدٍ (صَلَّى اللهُ عَلَيْهِ وَآلِه) فَسَمِعَتْ مَقَالَتَهُ الذَّلْفَاءُ بِنْتُ زِيَادٍ وَهِيَ فِي خِدْرِهَا فَأَرْسَلَتْ إِلَى أَبِيهَا ادْخُلْ إِلَيَّ فَدَخَلَ إِلَيْهَا فَقَالَتْ لَهُ مَا هَذَا الْكَلامُ الَّذِي سَمِعْتُهُ مِنْكَ تُحَاوِرُ بِهِ جُوَيْبِراً فَقَالَ لَهَا ذَكَرَ لِي أَنَّ رَسُولَ اللهِ (صَلَّى اللهُ عَلَيْهِ وَآلِه) أَرْسَلَهُ وَقَالَ يَقُولُ لَكَ رَسُولُ اللهِ (صَلَّى اللهُ عَلَيْهِ وَآلِه) زَوِّجْ جُوَيْبِراً ابْنَتَكَ الذَّلْفَاءَ فَقَالَتْ لَهُ وَاللهِ مَا كَانَ جُوَيْبِرٌ لِيَكْذِبَ عَلَى رَسُولِ اللهِ (صَلَّى اللهُ عَلَيْهِ وَآلِه) بِحَضْرَتِهِ فَابْعَثِ الآنَ رَسُولا يَرُدُّ عَلَيْكَ جُوَيْبِراً فَبَعَثَ زِيَادٌ رَسُولا فَلَحِقَ جُوَيْبِراً فَقَالَ لَهُ زِيَادٌ يَا جُوَيْبِرُ مَرْحَباً بِكَ اطْمَئِنَّ حَتَّى أَعُودَ إِلَيْكَ ثُمَّ انْطَلَقَ زِيَادٌ إِلَى رَسُولِ اللهِ (صَلَّى اللهُ عَلَيْهِ وَآلِه) فَقَالَ لَهُ بِأَبِي أَنْتَ وَأُمِّي إِنَّ جُوَيْبِراً أَتَانِي بِرِسَالَتِكَ وَقَالَ إِنَّ رَسُولَ اللهِ (صَلَّى اللهُ عَلَيْهِ

وَآلِه) يقُولُ لَكَ زَوِّجْ جُوَيْبِراً ابْنَتَكَ الذَّلْفَاءَ فَلَمْ أَلِنْ لَهُ بِالْقَوْلِ وَرَأَيْتُ لِقَاءَكَ وَنَحْنُ لا نَتَزَوَّجُ إلا أكْفَاءَنَا مِنَ الأنْصَارِ فَقَالَ لَهُ رَسُولُ اللهِ (صَلَّى اللهُ عَلَيْهِ وَآلِه) يَا زِيَادُ جُوَيْبِرٌ مُؤْمِنٌ وَالْمُؤْمِنُ كُفْؤٌ لِلْمُؤْمِنَةِ وَالْمُسْلِمُ كُفْؤٌ لِلْمُسْلِمَةِ فَزَوِّجْهُ يَا زِيَادُ وَلا تَرْغَبْ عَنْهُ قَالَ فَرَجَعَ زِيَادٌ إِلَى مَنْزِلِهِ وَدَخَلَ عَلَى ابْنَتِهِ فَقَالَ لَهَا مَا سَمِعَهُ مِنْ رَسُولِ اللهِ (صَلَّى اللهُ عَلَيْهِ وَآلِه) فَقَالَتْ لَهُ إِنَّكَ إِنْ عَصَيْتَ رَسُولَ اللهِ (صَلَّى اللهُ عَلَيْهِ وَآلِه) كَفَرْتَ فَزَوِّجْ جُوَيْبِراً فَخَرَجَ زِيَادٌ فَأَخَذَ بِيَدِ جُوَيْبِرٍ ثُمَّ أَخْرَجَهُ إِلَى قَوْمِهِ فَزَوَّجَهُ عَلَى سُنَّةِ اللهِ وَسُنَّةِ رَسُولِهِ (صَلَّى اللهُ عَلَيْهِ وَآلِه) وَضَمِنَ صَدَاقَهُ قَالَ فَجَهَّزَهَا زِيَادٌ وَهَيَّئُوهَا ثُمَّ أَرْسَلُوا إِلَى جُوَيْبِرٍ فَقَالُوا لَهُ أَلَكَ مَنْزِلٌ فَنَسُوقَهَا إِلَيْكَ فَقَالَ وَاللهِ مَا لِي مِنْ مَنْزِلٍ قَالَ فَهَيَّئُوهَا وَهَيَّئُوا لَهَا مَنْزِلا وَهَيَّئُوا فِيهِ فِرَاشاً وَمَتَاعاً وَكَسَوْا جُوَيْبِراً ثَوْبَيْنِ وَأُدْخِلَتِ الذَّلْفَاءُ فِي بَيْتِهَا وَأُدْخِلَ جُوَيْبِرٌ عَلَيْهَا مُعَتِّماً فَلَمَّا رَآهَا نَظَرَ إِلَى بَيْتٍ وَمَتَاعٍ وَرِيحٍ طَيِّبَةٍ قَامَ إِلَى زَاوِيَةِ الْبَيْتِ فَلَمْ يَزَلْ تَالِياً لِلْقُرْآنِ رَاكِعاً وَسَاجِداً حَتَّى طَلَعَ الْفَجْرُ فَلَمَّا سَمِعَ النِّدَاءَ خَرَجَ وَخَرَجَتْ زَوْجَتُهُ إِلَى الصَّلاةِ فَتَوَضَّأَتْ وَصَلَّتِ الصُّبْحَ فَسُئِلَتْ هَلْ مَسَّكِ فَقَالَتْ مَا زَالَ تَالِياً لِلْقُرْآنِ وَرَاكِعاً وَسَاجِداً حَتَّى سَمِعَ النِّدَاءَ فَخَرَجَ فَلَمَّا كَانَتِ اللَّيْلَةُ الثَّانِيَةُ فَعَلَ مِثْلَ ذَلِكَ وَأَخْفَوْا ذَلِكَ مِنْ زِيَادٍ فَلَمَّا كَانَ الْيَوْمُ الثَّالِثُ فَعَلَ مِثْلَ ذَلِكَ فَأُخْبِرَ بِذَلِكَ أَبُوهَا فَانْطَلَقَ إِلَى رَسُولِ اللهِ (صَلَّى اللهُ عَلَيْهِ وَآلِه) فَقَالَ لَهُ بِأَبِي أَنْتَ وَأُمِّي يَا رَسُولَ اللهِ أَمَرْتَنِي بِتَزْوِيجِ جُوَيْبِرٍ وَلا وَاللهِ مَا كَانَ مِنْ مَنَاكِحِنَا وَلَكِنْ طَاعَتُكَ أَوْجَبَتْ عَلَيَّ تَزْوِيجَهُ فَقَالَ لَهُ النَّبِيُّ (صَلَّى اللهُ عَلَيْهِ وَآلِه) فَمَا الَّذِي أَنْكَرْتُمْ مِنْهُ قَالَ إِنَّا هَيَّأْنَا لَهُ بَيْتاً وَمَتَاعاً وَأُدْخِلَتِ ابْنَتِي الْبَيْتَ وَأُدْخِلَ مَعَهَا مُعَتِّماً فَمَا كَلَّمَهَا وَلا نَظَرَ إِلَيْهَا وَلا دَنَا مِنْهَا بَلْ قَامَ إِلَى زَاوِيَةِ الْبَيْتِ فَلَمْ يَزَلْ تَالِياً لِلْقُرْآنِ رَاكِعاً وَسَاجِداً حَتَّى سَمِعَ النِّدَاءَ فَخَرَجَ ثُمَّ فَعَلَ مِثْلَ ذَلِكَ فِي اللَّيْلَةِ الثَّانِيَةِ وَمِثْلَ ذَلِكَ فِي الثَّالِثَةِ وَلَمْ يَدْنُ مِنْهَا وَلَمْ يُكَلِّمْهَا إِلَى أَنْ جِئْتُكَ وَمَا نَرَاهُ يُرِيدُ النِّسَاءَ فَانْظُرْ فِي أَمْرِنَا فَانْصَرَفَ زِيَادٌ وَبَعَثَ رَسُولُ اللهِ (صَلَّى اللهُ عَلَيْهِ وَآلِه) إِلَى جُوَيْبِرٍ فَقَالَ لَهُ أَمَا تَقْرَبُ النِّسَاءَ فَقَالَ لَهُ جُوَيْبِرٌ أَوَمَا أَنَا بِفَحْلٍ بَلَى يَا رَسُولَ اللهِ إِنِّي لَشَبِقٌ نَهِمٌ إِلَى النِّسَاءِ فَقَالَ لَهُ رَسُولُ اللهِ (صَلَّى اللهُ عَلَيْهِ وَآلِه) قَدْ خُبِّرْتُ بِخِلافِ مَا وَصَفْتَ بِهِ نَفْسَكَ قَدْ ذُكِرَ لِي أَنَّهُمْ هَيَّئُوا لَكَ بَيْتاً وَفِرَاشاً وَمَتَاعاً وَأُدْخِلَتْ عَلَيْكَ فَتَاةٌ حَسْنَاءُ عَطِرَةٌ وَأَتَيْتَ مُعَتِّماً فَلَمْ تَنْظُرْ إِلَيْهَا وَلَمْ تُكَلِّمْهَا وَلَمْ تَدْنُ مِنْهَا فَمَا دَهَاكَ إِذَنْ فَقَالَ لَهُ جُوَيْبِرٌ يَا رَسُولَ اللهِ دَخَلْتُ بَيْتاً وَاسِعاً وَرَأَيْتُ فِرَاشاً وَمَتَاعاً وَفَتَاةً حَسْنَاءَ عَطِرَةً وَذَكَرْتُ حَالِيَ الَّتِي كُنْتُ عَلَيْهَا وَغُرْبَتِي وَحَاجَتِي وَوَضِيعَتِي وَكِسْوَتِي مَعَ الْغُرَبَاءِ وَالْمَسَاكِينِ فَأَحْبَبْتُ إِذْ أَوْلانِي اللهُ ذَلِكَ أَنْ أَشْكُرَهُ عَلَى مَا أَعْطَانِي وَأَتَقَرَّبَ إِلَيْهِ بِحَقِيقَةِ الشُّكْرِ فَنَهَضْتُ إِلَى جَانِبِ الْبَيْتِ فَلَمْ أَزَلْ فِي صَلاتِي تَالِياً لِلْقُرْآنِ رَاكِعاً وَسَاجِداً أَشْكُرُ اللهَ حَتَّى سَمِعْتُ النِّدَاءَ فَخَرَجْتُ فَلَمَّا أَصْبَحْتُ رَأَيْتُ أَنْ أَصُومَ ذَلِكَ الْيَوْمَ فَفَعَلْتُ ذَلِكَ ثَلاثَةَ أَيَّامٍ وَلَيَالِيَهَا وَرَأَيْتُ ذَلِكَ فِي جَنْبِ مَا أَعْطَانِي اللهُ يَسِيراً وَلَكِنِّي سَأُرْضِيهَا وَأُرْضِيهِمُ اللَّيْلَةَ إِنْ شَاءَ اللهُ فَأَرْسَلَ رَسُولُ اللهِ (صَلَّى اللهُ عَلَيْهِ وَآلِه) إِلَى زِيَادٍ فَأَتَاهُ فَأَعْلَمَهُ مَا قَالَ جُوَيْبِرٌ فَطَابَتْ أَنْفُسُهُمْ قَالَ وَوَفَى لَهَا جُوَيْبِرٌ بِمَا قَالَ ثُمَّ إِنَّ رَسُولَ اللهِ (صَلَّى اللهُ عَلَيْهِ وَآلِه) خَرَجَ فِي غَزْوَةٍ لَهُ وَمَعَهُ جُوَيْبِرٌ فَاسْتُشْهِدَ رَحِمَهُ اللهُ تَعَالَى فَمَا كَانَ فِي الأنْصَارِ أَيِّمٌ أَنْفَقُ مِنْهَا بَعْدَ جُوَيْبِرٍ

Muhammad b. Yahya has narrated from Ahmad b. Muḥammad b. 'Isa from al-Hassan b. Mahbub from Malik b. 'Atiyyah from abu Hamzah al-Thumaliy who has said the following: "I once was with abu Ja'far when a man asked permission for a meeting. He came in and offered Salam (the phrase of offering greeting of peace). Abu Ja'far, (عليه السلام), said welcome to him, gave him a place nearby and asked about his condition. The man said, T pray to Allāh to keep my soul in service for your cause, I proposed marriage to your Mawla', so and so b. abu Rafi' for his daughter so and so but he refused, turned away from me, considered me worthless, because of my ugliness, poverty and alienation, which attacked and broke my heart and I wished death to approach me.' Abu Ja'far, (عليه السلام), said, 'You must go; you are my messenger to him and say to him that Muḥammad b. 'Alī b. al-Husayn and b. 'Alī b. abu Talib says, "You must give your daughter so and so in marriage to my Mawla' Munjih b. Rabah and do not refuse."' Abu Hamzah has said that the man jumped out with joy with the letter from abu Ja'far, (عليه السلام). When he left abu Ja'far, (عليه السلام), said, 'There was a man from the people of Yamamah called Juwayabir who came to the Messenger of Allāh, (صلى الله عليه وآله وسلم), seeking success through Islam. He became a Muslim and a good Muslim. He was of short height, ugly looking, poor, naked and he was of the ugly looking people of Sudan. The Messenger of Allāh associated with him closely because of his alienation and nakedness and had assigned one Sa' of dates by the measure of the first Sa' food for him, clothed him with two pieces of sheets, commanded him to stay in Masjid and sleep there during the night. He lived that way as long as Allāh wanted until the number of emigrants grew of those who accepted Islam of the poor people in al-Madinah and the Masjid became smaller and congested. Allāh, most Majestic, most Glorious, sent revelation to His holy prophet, to clean the Masjid, move from it those who slept there in the night, commanded to block all doors that opened to the Masjid except the door of 'Alī and the door to the living-quarter of Fatimah, (عليها السلام) . Everyone after sexual relation and before Ghusl (bath) was barred from entering the Masjid, and no alien could sleep in the Masjid. So the Messenger of Allāh commanded to blocking all doors that opened to the Masjid except the door of Ali, and allowed the door of the living-quarter of Fatimah, (عليها السلام) , to remain as they were before.' He (the Imam) said, 'The Messenger of Allāh,

(صلى الله عليه وآله وسلم), then commanded to build a canopy for the Muslims which was built and that was the platform or the edge. He (the Messenger of Allāh) then commanded the emigrants and the poor ones to stay there for the night and days. They made it their home and gathered therein. The Messenger of Allāh, (صلى الله عليه وآله وسلم), would come to see them, bring for them wheat, dates, barley and raisins whenever available. The Muslims sympathized with them because the Messenger of Allāh sympathized with them and spent their charity on them. The Messenger of Allāh one day looked at Juwayabir with kindness and sympathy and said to him, "I wish you to get married with a woman to safeguard your chastity and receive help for your worldly affairs as well as those of the hereafter." Juwayabir then said, "O Messenger of Allāh, I pray to Allāh to keep my soul and the souls of my parents in service for your cause, who will want me? By Allāh, I do not have any good position and social standing, or wealth, or physical beauty. No woman will ever pay attention to me." The Messenger of Allāh then said, "O Juwayabir, Allāh by means of Islam has removed those who were called noble in pre-Islamic time of darkness and ignorance and has honored them with Islam. To those who did not have any social position before Islam, Allāh has granted honor as well as to those who were considered low in the time of ignorance. With Islam He has removed the pride of the time of ignorance and people's expressing pride because of tribes and strong genealogy. Today (we say) all people, white and black, those from Quraysh, Arab, non- Arab are all from Adam, and Adam was created by Allāh from clay. The most beloved in the sight of Allāh, most Majestic, most Glorious, on the Day of Judgment will be those who are most obedient to Him and most pious before Him. O Juwayabir, I do not see any of the Muslims as better than you except because of his being more pious and more obedient to Allāh than you.'" He (the Messenger of Allāh) said, 'O Juwayabir, you must go to Ziyad b. Labid; he is an honorable man of the tribe of Bayadah, due to social standards and say to him, "I am the messenger of the Messenger of Allāh to you and the Messenger of Allāh says, 'You must give your daughter al-Dhalfa' in marriage to Juwayabir."'" He (the Imam) said that Juwayabir left with the message from the Messenger of Allāh, (صلى الله عليه وآله وسلم), to Ziyad b. Labid when he was at home with a group from his people. Juwayabir asked permission. He was informed and permission was granted. He entered and offered his greeting of peace, then said, 'I am a messenger from the Messenger of Allāh to you for a certain issue: if you like I can convey it to you in private or if you want I can say it in public.' He said, 'Say it in public; it is an honor for me and a privilege.' Juwayabir said, 'The Messenger of Allāh says to you, "You must give your daughter al-Dhalfa' in marriage to Juwayabir."' Ziyad then asked him, 'Has the Messenger of Allāh sent you with this?' Juwayabir replied, 'Yes, I never want to speak a lie against the Messenger of Allāh.' Ziyad said, 'We do not give our young girls in marriage to anyone, unless he is a good match for us of the people of al-Ansar (people of al-Madinah); so you must go back, O Juwayabir, until I meet the Messenger of Allāh and inform him of my excuse.' Juwayabir returned back saying, 'By Allāh, this is not what the Qur'ān is all about or Prophet Muhammad, (صلى الله عليه وآله وسلم), has appeared for it.' Al-Dhalfa', daughter of Ziyad in her living-quarter heard what Juwayabir said. She sent someone to her father to ask him to come to her room and he went to her. She asked, 'What were the words that I heard you spoke to Juwayabir?' He said to her, 'He told me that the Messenger of Allāh had sent him and he (the Messenger of Allāh) said, "You must give your daughter, al-Dhalfa' in marriage to Juwayabir."' She then said, 'By Allāh Juwayabir cannot lie against the Messenger of Allāh, (صلى الله عليه وآله وسلم), in his presence. You must now send a messenger to call him back.' Ziyad sent a messenger to call Juwayabir and approached him and said. 'O Juwayabir, you are welcome. You must not be worried and wait until I come back.' Ziyad went to the Messenger of Allāh and said, 'I pray to Allāh to keep my soul and the souls of my parents in service for your cause, Juwayabir has brought your message to me that says, "The Messenger of Allāh commands you to give your daughter al-Dhalfa' in marriage to Juwayabir." I was not so soft speaking to him. We do not give our young women in marriage to anyone except to our match of al-Ansar (people of al-Madinah).' The Messenger of Allāh said to him, 'O Ziyad, Juwayabir is a believing person. A believing man is a match of a believing woman. A Muslim is a match of a female Muslim. Therefore you must give her in marriage to him. O Ziyad, you must give her in marriage to him and you must not refuse.' He (the Imam) said that Ziyad returned back to his home, went to his daughter and said to her what he had heard from the Messenger of Allāh, (صلى الله عليه وآله وسلم), She said to him, 'If you disobey the Messenger of Allāh, you will become an unbeliever, so you must give in marriage to Juwayabir.' Ziyad came out, held the hand of Juwayabir, took him before his people, gave her to him in marriage according to the tradition of Allāh and the tradition of the Messenger of Allāh and took responsibility of mahr (dower). He (the Imam) has said, 'They prepared al-Dhalfa' for her wedding, sent for Juwayabir and asked him, 'Do you have any house so we escort her to your house?' he replied, 'No, by Allāh, I do not have any house.' He (the Imam) said, 'They prepared her for her wedding, prepared for them a house, furnishings, household necessities, dressed Juwayabir with two dresses, brought al-Dhalfa' to her house, and admitted Juwayabir also there. Juwayabir went in the house after al-'Isha' Salat (prayer). He looked at the house, the furnishings, the sweet smelling fragrance, thus, he moved to a corner of the house and began to recite from the Qur'ān, in Ruku' (bowing down on one's knees) and in Sajdah (prostration) until it was dawn. He heard the call for Salat (prayer), so he went out for Salat (prayer) as well as his wife. She made wudu and performed Salat (prayer) of the morning and she was asked about being touched. She replied, 'He continued reciting the Qur'ān in Ruku ' and Sajdah until the call for Salat (prayer) was said then he went out.' In the second night he did just as he had done the night before but they did not tell it to Ziyad. In the third night he again did as he had done before, then her father was informed. He went to the Messenger of Allāh and said, 'I pray to Allāh to keep my soul and the souls of my parents in service for your cause, O Messenger of Allāh, you commanded me to give my daughter in marriage to Juwayabir and by Allāh we did not want to do so; but obedience to you made it necessary on us to do so.' The Holy Prophet, (صلى الله عليه وآله وسلم), asked, 'What is it that you disliked about him?' he replied, 'We prepared a house for him with furnishings, household necessities, sent my daughter to that house, he also was admitted there after al- 'Isha ' Salat (prayer) but he did not speak to her, did not look at her and did not go close to her, instead he stood in one corner of the house, continued reciting al-Qur'ān, in Ruku' and Sajdah (prostration) until the call for Salat (prayer) was said. He went out for Salat (prayer); he did it again in the second, and in the third nights. He did not go close to her and did not speak to her until the time of my coming to you. We did not find him to be interested in women. Please look into our problem.' Ziyad went back and the Messenger of Allāh sent for Juwayabir and asked him, 'Is it the case that you do not go close to women?' Juwayabir replied, 'A male person I am O Messenger of Allāh and I indeed have intense desire and passion for women.' The Messenger of Allāh said, to him, 'I am informed otherwise about what you are telling to me. I am told that they prepared for you a house, furnishings, the necessities of a household and she was brought to you in that house, a beautiful young woman and rich with sweet smelling perfumes. You went after performing your al-'Isha ' Salat (prayer) but did not look at her, did not speak to her, and did not go close to her. What was your wisdom in it?' Juwayabir replied, 'O Messenger of Allāh, when I entered the vast house, saw the furnishings, the household necessities, the young beautiful girl, rich in sweet smelling perfumes, remembered my condition in which I lived, my alienation, my poverty, and lowliness, my clothes with the emigrants and the destitute people; I then loved at first to thank Allāh for what He had given to me and tried to become closer to Him. I then went to one corner of the house and continued in Salat (prayer) reciting al-Qur'ān in Ruku ' (bowing down on one's knees) and Sajdah (prostration) thanking Allāh until I heard the call for Salat (prayer), then I went out. In the day I decided to fast that day and did so for three days and nights and I thought to do that for what Allāh had given to me although my thanks were very little, however, I will make her happy and make them happy tonight, by the will of Allāh.' The Messenger of Allāh then sent a message to Ziyad who came to the Messenger of Allāh and he (the Messenger of Allāh) informed him about Juwayabir. They became delighted. Juwayabir kept his promise. Thereafter, the Messenger of Allāh went out for an armed expedition, Juwayabir was with him and he became a martyr, may Allāh, most High grant him mercy. In the community of al-Ansar (people of al-Madinah) there was no single woman in such a great demand than her (al-Dhalfa') after Juwayabir.'"

(صحيح)[22]

---

[22] *Al-Kāfi, v5, ch21, h1*

باب الشيخين

Chapter on the Two Shaykhs[1] (Abu Bakr and Umar)

1.

حَنَانٌ عَنْ أَبِيهِ عَنْ أَبِي جَعْفَرٍ (عليه السلام) قَالَ قُلْتُ لَهُ مَا كَانَ وُلْدُ يَعْقُوبَ أَنْبِيَاءَ قَالَ لَا وَ لَكِنَّهُمْ كَانُوا أَسْبَاطَ أَوْلَادِ الْأَنْبِيَاءِ وَ لَمْ يَكُنْ يُفَارِقُوا الدُّنْيَا إِلَّا سُعَدَاءَ تَابُوا وَ تَذَكَّرُوا مَا صَنَعُوا وَ إِنَّ الشَّيْخَيْنِ فَارَقَا الدُّنْيَا وَ لَمْ يَتُوبَا وَ لَمْ يَتَذَكَّرَا مَا صَنَعَا بِأَمِيرِ الْمُؤْمِنِينَ (عليه السلام) فَعَلَيْهِمَا لَعْنَةُ اللَّهِ وَ الْمَلَائِكَةِ وَ النَّاسِ أَجْمَعِينَ

Hanaan, from his father, who has said: Abu Ja'far (عليه السلام) said, when I said to him, 'What were the children of Yaqoub (عليه السلام), Prophets (عليه السلام)?' He said: 'No, but they were the grandchildren of the children of the Prophets (عليه السلام), and they did not depart from the world except as happy, repentant, and remembered what they had done, and the two old men (Abu Bakr and Umar – Shaykhayn) departed from the world, and they never remembered what they had done with Amir al- Mu'minin (عليه

[1] The term "Shaykhayn" is most commonly used for Abu Bakr and Umar, it is not a statement of praise, but rather means "The two old men"

(السلام), so upon these two be the Curses of Allāh (تبارك و طائلة), and the Angels, and the people altogether'. (حسن أو موثق)[2]

2.

عَنْهُ عَنْ أَحْمَدَ بْنِ مُحَمَّدٍ عَنْ أَبِي يَحْيَى الْوَاسِطِيِّ عَنْ عَجْلَانَ أَبِي صَالِحٍ قَالَ دَخَلَ رَجُلٌ عَلَى أَبِي عَبْدِ اللَّهِ (عليه السلام) فَقَالَ لَهُ جُعِلْتُ فِدَاكَ هَذِهِ قُبَّةُ آدَمَ (عليه السلام) قَالَ نَعَمْ وَ لِلَّهِ قِبَابٌ كَثِيرَةٌ أَلَا إِنَّ خَلْفَ مَغْرِبِكُمْ هَذَا تِسْعَةٌ وَ ثَلَاثُونَ مَغْرِباً أَرْضاً بَيْضَاءَ مَمْلُوَّةً خَلْقاً يَسْتَضِيئُونَ بِنُورِهِ لَمْ يَعْصُوا اللَّهَ عَزَّ وَ جَلَّ طَرْفَةَ عَيْنٍ مَا يَدْرُونَ خُلِقَ آدَمُ أَمْ لَمْ يُخْلَقْ يَبْرَءُونَ مِنْ فُلَانٍ وَ فُلَانٍ

From him, from Ahmad b. Muhammad, from Abu Yahya Al-Wasity, from Ajlaan Abu Salih who said: A man came up to Abu 'AbdAllāh (عليه السلام), so he said to him, 'May I be sacrificed for you. This here (the sky) is the dome of Adam (عليه السلام)?' He said: 'Yes. By Allāh (تبارك و طائلة), there are numerous domes. Indeed! Behind this West of yours are thirty-nine (other) in the West, white lands filled with creatures illuminated by its light. They have never disobeyed Allāh (تبارك و طائلة) even for the blink of an eye. These creatures are not aware of the creation of Adam (عليه السلام), but they are distancing themselves (Tabarra) from so and so and so and so (Abu Bakr and Umar)'. (صحيح)[3]

3.

عَلِيُّ بْنُ إِبْرَاهِيمَ عَنْ أَبِيهِ عَنْ حَنَانِ بْنِ سَدِيرٍ وَ مُحَمَّدُ بْنُ يَحْيَى عَنْ أَحْمَدَ بْنِ مُحَمَّدٍ عَنْ مُحَمَّدِ بْنِ إِسْمَاعِيلَ عَنْ حَنَانِ بْنِ سَدِيرٍ عَنْ أَبِيهِ قَالَ سَأَلْتُ أَبَا جَعْفَرٍ (عليه السلام) عَنْهُمَا فَقَالَ يَا أَبَا الْفَضْلِ مَا تَسْأَلُنِي عَنْهُمَا فَوَ اللَّهِ مَا مَاتَ مِنَّا مَيِّتٌ قَطُّ إِلَّا سَاخِطاً عَلَيْهِمَا وَ مَا مِنَّا الْيَوْمَ إِلَّا سَاخِطاً عَلَيْهِمَا يُوصِي بِذَلِكَ الْكَبِيرُ مِنَّا الصَّغِيرَ إِنَّهُمَا ظَلَمَانَا حَقَّنَا وَ مَنَعَانَا فَيْئَنَا وَ كَانَا أَوَّلَ مَنْ رَكِبَ أَعْنَاقَنَا وَ بَثَقَا عَلَيْنَا بَثْقاً فِي الْإِسْلَامِ لَا يُسْكَرُ

---

[2] *Al-Kafi, v8, h343*

[3] *Al-Kafi, v8, h301*

أَبداً حَتَّى يَقُومَ قَائِمُنَا أَوْ يَتَكَلَّمَ مُتَكَلِّمُنَا ثُمَّ قَالَ أَمَا وَ اللَّهِ لَوْ قَدْ قَامَ قَائِمُنَا أَوْ تَكَلَّمَ مُتَكَلِّمُنَا لَأَبْدَى مِنْ أُمُورِهِمَا مَا كَانَ يُكْتَمُ وَ لَكَتَمَ مِنْ أُمُورِهِمَا مَا كَانَ يُظْهَرُ وَ اللَّهِ مَا أُسِّسَتْ مِنْ بَلِيَّةٍ وَ لَا قَضِيَّةٍ تَجْرِي عَلَيْنَا أَهْلَ الْبَيْتِ إِلَّا هُمَا أَسَّسَا أَوَّلَهَا فَعَلَيْهِمَا لَعْنَةُ اللَّهِ وَ الْمَلَائِكَةِ وَ النَّاسِ أَجْمَعِينَ

Ali b. Ibrahim, from his father, from hanaan b. Sudeyr, and Muḥammad b. Yahya, from Ahmad b. Muhammad, from Muḥammad b. Ismail, from Hanaan b. Sudeyr, from his father who said: I asked Abu Ja'far (عليه السلام) about the two (Abu Bakr and Umar), so he said: 'O Abu Al-Fazl, don't ask me about these two, for by Allāh (تبارك و طائلة), no one from among us passes away at all except being angry against these two, and there is none from us today except that he is angry at them. The old ones bequeath it to the young ones from us. These two have been unjust to us for our rights, and prevented us from our Fey (Spoils of War – Khums), and first one rode upon our necks, and caused damage to us with a damage in Al-Islam which can never be repaired ever until our Qa'im (عجل الله تعالى فرجه) makes a stand and speaks our speech'. Then he said; 'But, by Allāh (تبارك و طائلة), when our Qa'im (عجل الله تعالى فرجه) makes a stand, or speaks our speech, he will expose the matters of these two of what they had concealed, and conceal from their matters what they used to make apparent. By Allāh (تبارك و طائلة), nothing has afflicted us from the afflictions, and what has passed of the difficulties against us, the People of the Household, except that these two laid the foundations of it at first place, so against these two are the Curses of Allāh (تبارك و طائلة), and the Angels, and the people altogether'. (حسن أو موثق)[4]

4.

مُحَمَّدُ بْنُ أَحْمَدَ الْقُمِّيُّ عَنْ عَمِّهِ عَبْدِ اللَّهِ بْنِ الصَّلْتِ عَنْ يُونُسَ بْنِ عَبْدِ الرَّحْمَنِ عَنْ عَبْدِ اللَّهِ بْنِ سِنَانٍ عَنْ حُسَيْنٍ الْجَمَّالِ عَنْ أَبِي عَبْدِ اللَّهِ (عليه السلام) فِي قَوْلِ اللَّهِ تَبَارَكَ وَ تَعَالَى رَبَّنا أَرِنَا الَّذَيْنِ أَضَلَّانا مِنَ الْجِنِّ وَ الْإِنْسِ نَجْعَلْهُما تَحْتَ أَقْدامِنا لِيَكُونا مِنَ الْأَسْفَلِينَ قَالَ هُمَا ثُمَّ قَالَ وَ كَانَ فُلَانٌ شَيْطَاناً

[4] *Al-Kafi, v8, h340*

Muhammad b. Ahmad Al-Qummy, from his uncle 'Abd Allāh b. Al-Salt, from Yunus b. Abdul Rahman, from 'Abd Allāh b. Sinan, from Husayn Al-Jamal, who has reported the following: Abu 'AbdAllāh (عليه السلام) regarding the Statement of Allāh (تبارك و طائلة) Blessed and High: "[41:29] Our Lord! show us those who led us astray from among the jinn and the men that we may trample them under our feet so that they may be of the lowest", he said: 'Those two (Abu Bakr and Umar)'. Then said: 'And that one (Umar) was a Satan (لعنة الله عليه)'. (صحيح)[5]

5.

يُونُسُ عَنْ سَوْرَةَ بْنِ كُلَيْبٍ عَنْ أَبِي عَبْدِ اللَّهِ (عليه السلام) فِي قَوْلِ اللَّهِ تَبَارَكَ وَ تَعَالَى رَبَّنا أَرِنَا الَّذَيْنِ أَضَلَّانا مِنَ الْجِنِّ وَ الْإِنْسِ نَجْعَلْهُما تَحْتَ أَقْدامِنا لِيَكُونا مِنَ الْأَسْفَلِينَ قَالَ يَا سَوْرَةُ هُمَا وَ اللَّهِ هُمَا ثَلَاثاً وَ اللَّهِ يَا سَوْرَةُ إِنَّا لَخُزَّانُ عِلْمِ اللَّهِ فِي السَّمَاءِ وَ إِنَّا لَخُزَّانُ عِلْمِ اللَّهِ فِي الْأَرْضِ

Yunus, from Sowrat b. Kuleyb, who has reported the following: Abu 'AbdAllāh (عليه السلام) regarding the statement of Allāh (تبارك و طائلة) Blessed and High: "[41:29] Our Lord! show us those who led us astray from among the jinn and the men that we may trample them under our feet so that they may be of the lowest", he said: 'O Sowrat! Those two (Abu Bakr and Umar), by Allāh (تبارك و طائلة) those two (Abu Bakr and Umar) three times over. By Allāh (تبارك و طائلة), O Sowrat, we are the Treasurers of the Knowledge of Allāh (تبارك و طائلة) in the sky and we are the Treasurers of the Knowledge of Allāh (تبارك و طائلة) in the earth'. (مجهول)[6]

6.

---

[5] *Al-Kāfi, v8, h522*

[6] *Al-Kāfi, v8, h523*

عَلِيُّ بْنُ إِبْرَاهِيمَ عَنْ أَبِيهِ وَ مُحَمَّدُ بْنُ إِسْمَاعِيلَ وَ غَيْرُهُ عَنْ مَنْصُورِ بْنِ يُونُسَ عَنِ ابْنِ أُذَيْنَةَ عَنْ عَبْدِ اللَّهِ بْنِ النَّجَاشِيِّ قَالَ سَمِعْتُ أَبَا عَبْدِ اللَّهِ (عليه السلام) يَقُولُ فِي قَوْلِ اللَّهِ عَزَّ وَ جَلَّ أُولئِكَ الَّذِينَ يَعْلَمُ اللَّهُ ما فِي قُلُوبِهِمْ فَأَعْرِضْ عَنْهُمْ وَ عِظْهُمْ وَ قُلْ لَهُمْ فِي أَنْفُسِهِمْ قَوْلًا بَلِيغاً يَعْنِي وَ اللَّهِ فُلَاناً وَ فُلَاناً وَ ما أَرْسَلْنا مِنْ رَسُولٍ إِلَّا لِيُطاعَ بِإِذْنِ اللَّهِ وَ لَوْ أَنَّهُمْ إِذْ ظَلَمُوا أَنْفُسَهُمْ جاؤُكَ فَاسْتَغْفَرُوا اللَّهَ وَ اسْتَغْفَرَ لَهُمُ الرَّسُولُ لَوَجَدُوا اللَّهَ تَوَّاباً رَحِيماً يَعْنِي وَ اللَّهِ النَّبِيَّ (صلى الله عليه وآله) وَ عَلِيّاً (عليه السلام) مِمَّا صَنَعُوا أَيْ لَوْ جَاءُوكَ بِهَا يَا عَلِيُّ فَاسْتَغْفَرُوا اللَّهَ مِمَّا صَنَعُوا وَ اسْتَغْفَرَ لَهُمُ الرَّسُولُ لَوَجَدُوا اللَّهَ تَوَّاباً رَحِيماً فَلا وَ رَبِّكَ لا يُؤْمِنُونَ حَتَّى يُحَكِّمُوكَ فِيما شَجَرَ بَيْنَهُمْ فَقَالَ أَبُو عَبْدِ اللَّهِ (عليه السلام) هُوَ وَ اللَّهِ عَلِيٌّ بِعَيْنِهِ ثُمَّ لا يَجِدُوا فِي أَنْفُسِهِمْ حَرَجاً مِمَّا قَضَيْتَ عَلَى لِسَانِكَ يَا رَسُولَ اللَّهِ يَعْنِي بِهِ مِنْ وَلَايَةِ عَلِيٍّ وَ يُسَلِّمُوا تَسْلِيماً لِعَلِيٍّ

Ali b. Ibrahim, from his father, and Muḥammad b. Ismail, and someone else, from Mansour b. Yunus, from b. Azina, from 'Abd Allāh b. Najjashy who said: I heard Abu 'AbdAllāh (عليه السلام) saying regarding the Statement of Allāh (تبارك و طائلة) Mighty and Majestic: "[4:63] These are they of whom Allāh knows what is in their hearts; therefore turn aside from them and admonish them, and speak to them effectual words concerning themselves", Meaning, by Allāh (تبارك و طائلة), so and so and so and so (Abu Bakr and Umar). "[4:64] And We did not send any messenger but that he should be obeyed by Allāh's permission; and had they, when they were unjust to themselves, come to you and asked forgiveness of Allāh and the Messenger had (also) asked forgiveness for them, they would have found Allāh Oft-returning (to mercy), Merciful", Meaning, by Allāh (تبارك و طائلة), the Prophet (صلى الله عليه وآله وسلم) and 'Alī (عليه السلام) due to what they had done to him. Yes, had they come to you with it, O 'Alī (عليه السلام), and asked forgiveness of Allāh and the Messenger had (also) asked forgiveness for them, they would have found Allāh Oft-returning (to mercy), Merciful. "[4:65] But no! by your Lord! they do not believe (in reality) until they make you a judge of that which has become a matter of disagreement among them". So Abu 'AbdAllāh (عليه السلام) said: 'By Allāh (تبارك و طائلة), it is 'Alī (عليه السلام) who is Meant by it. and then do not find any straightness in their hearts as to what you have decided, upon your tongue, O Messenger of Allāh (صلى الله عليه وآله وسلم), Meaning by it the Wilāya of 'Alī (عليه السلام) and submit with entire submission to 'Alī (عليه السلام)'. (صحيح)[7]

7.

محمد بن مسعود، عن علي بن الحسن، عن عباس بن عامر، عن أبان بن عثمان، عن زرارة، عن أبي جعفر عليه السلام: أن المهدي مولى عثمان أتى فبايع أمير المؤمنين و محمد بن أبي بكر جالس، قال أبايعك على أن الأمر كان لك أولا و أبرأ من فلان و فلان و فلان، فبايعه

Muhammad b. Masud from 'Alī b. al-Hasan from Abbas b. A'mir from Aban b. Uthman from Zurara from Abi Ja'far عليه السلام who said: al-Mahdi the client of Uthman came to pledge allegiance to the Commander of the Faithful [Ali] while Muḥammad b. Abi Bakr was seated. He [al-Mahdi] said: I pledge allegiance to you that the matter [Khilafa] was for you from the start and I disassociate myself from Fulan(Abu Bakr), Fulan(Umar), and Fulan(Uthman), then he pledged allegiance to him. (معتبر)[8]

8.

حمدويه بن نصير، عن محمد بن عيسى، عن محمد بن أبي عمير، عن عمر بن أذينة، عن زرارة بن أعين، عن أبي جعفر عليه السلام: أن محمد بن أبي بكر بايع عليا عليه السلام على البراءة من أبيه

Hamduwayh b. Nusayr from Muḥammad b. Isa from Muḥammad b. Abi Umayr from Umar b. Udhayna from Zurara b. A'yan from Abi Ja'far عليه السلام that:

[7] *Al-Kāfi, v8, h525*

[8] *Rijal al-Kashshi, h166*

Muḥammad b. Abi Bakr gave the pledge of allegiance to 'Alī عليه السلام upon the condition of disassociating from his father [Abu Bakr]. (معتبر)[9]

9.

مُحَمَّدُ بْنُ يَحْيَى عَنْ أَحْمَدَ بْنِ مُحَمَّدِ بْنِ عِيسَى عَنِ الْحُسَيْنِ بْنِ سَعِيدٍ عَنْ سُلَيْمَانَ الْجَعْفَرِيِّ قَالَ سَمِعْتُ أَبَا الْحَسَنِ (عليه السلام) يَقُولُ فِي قَوْلِ اللَّهِ تَبَارَكَ وَ تَعَالَى إِذْ يُبَيِّتُونَ ما لا يَرْضى مِنَ الْقَوْلِ قَالَ يَعْنِي فُلَاناً وَ فُلَاناً وَ أَبَا عُبَيْدَةَ بْنَ الْجَرَّاحِ

Muhammad b. Yahya, from Ahmad b. Muḥammad b. Isa, from Al-Husayn b. Saeed, from Suleyman Al-Ja'fary who said: I heard Abu Al-Hasan (عليه السلام) saying regarding the Statement of Allāh (تبارك و طائلة) Blessed and High: "[4:108] They seek to hide from men and seek not to hide from Allāh. He is with them when by night they hold discourse displeasing unto Him", he said: 'It means so and so and so and so (Abu Bakr and Umar), and Abu Ubeyda b. Al-Jarrah'. (صحيح)[10]

10.

عِدَّةٌ مِنْ أَصْحَابِنَا عَنْ سَهْلِ بْنِ زِيَادٍ عَنْ إِسْمَاعِيلَ بْنِ مِهْرَانَ عَنْ مُحَمَّدِ بْنِ مَنْصُورٍ الْخُزَاعِيِّ عَنْ عَلِيِّ بْنِ سُوَيْدٍ وَ مُحَمَّدُ بْنُ يَحْيَى عَنْ مُحَمَّدِ بْنِ الْحُسَيْنِ عَنْ مُحَمَّدِ بْنِ إِسْمَاعِيلَ بْنِ بَزِيعٍ عَنْ عَمِّهِ حَمْزَةَ بْنِ بَزِيعٍ عَنْ عَلِيِّ بْنِ سُوَيْدٍ وَ الْحَسَنُ بْنُ مُحَمَّدٍ عَنْ مُحَمَّدِ بْنِ أَحْمَدَ النَّهْدِيِّ عَنْ إِسْمَاعِيلَ بْنِ مِهْرَانَ عَنْ مُحَمَّدِ بْنِ مَنْصُورٍ عَنْ عَلِيِّ بْنِ سُوَيْدٍ قَالَ كَتَبْتُ إِلَى أَبِي الْحَسَنِ مُوسَى (عليه السلام) وَ هُوَ فِي الْحَبْسِ كِتَاباً أَسْأَلُهُ عَنْ حَالِهِ وَ عَنْ مَسَائِلَ كَثِيرَةٍ فَاحْتَبَسَ الْجَوَابُ عَلَيَّ أَشْهُراً ثُمَّ أَجَابَنِي بِجَوَابٍ هَذِهِ نُسْخَتُهُ بِسْمِ اللَّهِ الرَّحْمَنِ الرَّحِيمِ الْحَمْدُ لِلَّهِ الْعَلِيِّ الْعَظِيمِ الَّذِي بِعَظَمَتِهِ وَ نُورِهِ أَبْصَرَ قُلُوبَ الْمُؤْمِنِينَ وَ بِعَظَمَتِهِ وَ نُورِهِ عَادَاهُ الْجَاهِلُونَ وَ بِعَظَمَتِهِ وَ نُورِهِ ابْتَغَى مَنْ فِي السَّمَاوَاتِ وَ مَنْ فِي الْأَرْضِ إِلَيْهِ الْوَسِيلَةَ بِالْأَعْمَالِ الْمُخْتَلِفَةِ وَ الْأَدْيَانِ الْمُتَضَادَّةِ فَمُصِيبٌ وَ مُخْطِئٌ وَ ضَالٌّ وَ مُهْتَدٍ وَ سَمِيعٌ وَ أَصَمُّ وَ بَصِيرٌ وَ أَعْمَى حَيْرَانُ فَالْحَمْدُ لِلَّهِ الَّذِي عَرَفَ وَ

---

[9] *Rijal al-Kashshi, h114*

[10] *Al-Kāfi, v8, h524*

وَصَف دِينَهُ مُحَمَّدٌ (صلى الله عليه وآله) أَمَّا بَعْدُ فَإِنَّكَ امْرُؤٌ أَنْزَلَكَ اللَّهُ مِنْ آلِ مُحَمَّدٍ بِمَنْزِلَةٍ خَاصَّةٍ وَ حَفِظَ مَوَدَّةَ مَا اسْتَرْعَاكَ مِنْ دِينِهِ وَ مَا أَلْهَمَكَ مِنْ رُشْدِكَ وَ بَصَّرَكَ مِنْ أَمْرِ دِينِكَ بِتَفْضِيلِكَ إِيَّاهُمْ وَ بِرَدِّكَ الْأُمُورَ إِلَيْهِمْ كَتَبْتَ تَسْأَلُنِي عَنْ أُمُورٍ كُنْتُ مِنْهَا فِي تَقِيَّةٍ وَ مِنْ كِتْمَانِهَا فِي سَعَةٍ فَلَمَّا انْقَضَى سُلْطَانُ الْجَبَابِرَةِ وَ جَاءَ سُلْطَانُ ذِي السُّلْطَانِ الْعَظِيمِ بِفِرَاقِ الدُّنْيَا الْمَذْمُومَةِ إِلَى أَهْلِهَا الْعُتَاةِ عَلَى خَالِقِهِمْ رَأَيْتُ أَنْ أُفَسِّرَ لَكَ مَا سَأَلْتَنِي عَنْهُ مَخَافَةَ أَنْ يَدْخُلَ الْحَيْرَةُ عَلَى ضُعَفَاءِ شِيعَتِنَا مِنْ قِبَلِ جَهَالَتِهِمْ فَاتَّقِ اللَّهَ عَزَّ ذِكْرُهُ وَ خُصَّ لِذَلِكَ الْأَمْرِ أَهْلَهُ وَ احْذَرْ أَنْ تَكُونَ سَبَبَ بَلِيَّةٍ عَلَى الْأَوْصِيَاءِ أَوْ حَارِشاً عَلَيْهِمْ بِإِفْشَاءِ مَا اسْتَوْدَعْتُكَ وَ إِظْهَارِ مَا اسْتَكْتَمْتُكَ وَ لَنْ تَفْعَلَ إِنْ شَاءَ اللَّهُ إِنَّ أَوَّلَ مَا أُنْهِي إِلَيْكَ أَنِّي أَنْعَى إِلَيْكَ نَفْسِي فِي لَيَالِيَّ هَذِهِ غَيْرَ جَازِعٍ وَ لَا نَادِمٍ وَ لَا شَاكٍّ فِيمَا هُوَ كَائِنٌ مِمَّا قَدْ قَضَى اللَّهُ عَزَّ وَ جَلَّ وَ حَتَمَ فَاسْتَمْسِكْ بِعُرْوَةِ الدِّينِ آلِ مُحَمَّدٍ وَ الْعُرْوَةِ الْوُثْقَى الْوَصِيِّ بَعْدَ الْوَصِيِّ وَ الْمُسَالَمَةِ لَهُمْ وَ الرِّضَا بِمَا قَالُوا وَ لَا تَلْتَمِسْ دِينَ مَنْ لَيْسَ مِنْ شِيعَتِكَ وَ لَا تُحِبَّنَّ دِينَهُمْ فَإِنَّهُمُ الْخَائِنُونَ الَّذِينَ خَانُوا اللَّهَ وَ رَسُولَهُ وَ خَانُوا أَمَانَاتِهِمْ وَ تَدْرِي مَا خَانُوا أَمَانَاتِهِمُ ائْتُمِنُوا عَلَى كِتَابِ اللَّهِ فَحَرَّفُوهُ وَ بَدَّلُوهُ وَ دُلُّوا عَلَى وُلَاةِ الْأَمْرِ مِنْهُمْ فَانْصَرَفُوا عَنْهُمْ فَأَذَاقَهُمُ اللَّهُ لِبَاسَ الْجُوعِ وَ الْخَوْفِ بِمَا كَانُوا يَصْنَعُونَ وَ سَأَلْتَ عَنْ رَجُلَيْنِ اغْتَصَبَا رَجُلًا مَالًا كَانَ يُنْفِقُهُ عَلَى الْفُقَرَاءِ وَ الْمَسَاكِينِ وَ أَبْنَاءِ السَّبِيلِ وَ فِي سَبِيلِ اللَّهِ فَلَمَّا اغْتَصَبَاهُ ذَلِكَ لَمْ يَرْضَيَا حَيْثُ غَصَبَاهُ حَتَّى حَمَّلَاهُ إِيَّاهُ كُرْهاً فَوْقَ رَقَبَتِهِ إِلَى مَنَازِلِهِمَا فَلَمَّا أَحْرَزَاهُ تَوَلَّيَا إِنْفَاقَهُ أَ يَبْلُغَانِ بِذَلِكَ كُفْراً فَلَعَمْرِي لَقَدْ نَافَقَا قَبْلَ ذَلِكَ وَ رَدَّا عَلَى اللَّهِ عَزَّ وَ جَلَّ كَلَامَهُ وَ هَزِئَا بِرَسُولِهِ (صلى الله عليه وآله) وَ هُمَا الْكَافِرَانِ عَلَيْهِمَا لَعْنَةُ اللَّهِ وَ الْمَلَائِكَةِ وَ النَّاسِ أَجْمَعِينَ وَ اللَّهِ مَا دَخَلَ قَلْبَ أَحَدٍ مِنْهُمَا شَيْءٌ مِنَ الْإِيمَانِ مُنْذُ خُرُوجِهِمَا مِنْ حَالَتَيْهِمَا وَ مَا ازْدَادَا إِلَّا شَكّاً كَانَا خَدَّاعَيْنِ مُرْتَابَيْنِ مُنَافِقَيْنِ حَتَّى تَوَفَّتْهُمَا مَلَائِكَةُ الْعَذَابِ إِلَى مَحَلِّ الْخِزْيِ فِي دَارِ الْمُقَامِ وَ سَأَلْتَ عَمَّنْ حَضَرَ ذَلِكَ الرَّجُلَ وَ هُوَ يُغْصَبُ مَالُهُ وَ يُوضَعُ عَلَى رَقَبَتِهِ مِنْهُمْ عَارِفٌ وَ مُنْكِرٌ فَأُولَئِكَ أَهْلُ الرِّدَّةِ الْأُولَى مِنْ هَذِهِ الْأُمَّةِ فَعَلَيْهِمْ لَعْنَةُ اللَّهِ وَ الْمَلَائِكَةِ وَ النَّاسِ أَجْمَعِينَ وَ سَأَلْتَ عَنْ مَبْلَغِ عِلْمِنَا وَ هُوَ عَلَى ثَلَاثَةِ وُجُوهٍ مَاضٍ وَ غَابِرٌ وَ حَادِثٌ فَأَمَّا الْمَاضِي فَمُفَسَّرٌ وَ أَمَّا الْغَابِرُ فَمَزْبُورٌ وَ أَمَّا الْحَادِثُ فَقَذْفٌ فِي الْقُلُوبِ وَ نَقْرٌ فِي الْأَسْمَاعِ وَ هُوَ أَفْضَلُ عِلْمِنَا وَ لَا نَبِيَّ بَعْدَ نَبِيِّنَا مُحَمَّدٍ (صلى الله عليه وآله) وَ سَأَلْتَ عَنْ أُمَّهَاتِ أَوْلَادِهِمْ وَ عَنْ نِكَاحِهِمْ وَ عَنْ طَلَاقِهِمْ فَأَمَّا أُمَّهَاتُ أَوْلَادِهِمْ فَهُنَّ عَوَاهِرُ إِلَى يَوْمِ الْقِيَامَةِ نِكَاحٌ بِغَيْرِ وَلِيٍّ وَ طَلَاقٌ فِي غَيْرِ عِدَّةٍ وَ أَمَّا مَنْ دَخَلَ فِي دَعْوَتِنَا فَقَدْ هَدَمَ إِيمَانُهُ ضَلَالَهُ وَ يَقِينُهُ شَكَّهُ وَ سَأَلْتَ عَنِ الزَّكَاةِ فِيهِمْ فَمَا كَانَ مِنَ الزَّكَاةِ فَأَنْتُمْ أَحَقُّ بِهِ لِأَنَّا قَدْ حَلَّلْنَا ذَلِكَ لَكُمْ مَنْ كَانَ مِنْكُمْ وَ أَيْنَ كَانَ وَ سَأَلْتَ عَنِ الضُّعَفَاءِ فَالضَّعِيفُ مَنْ لَمْ يُرْفَعْ إِلَيْهِ حُجَّةٌ وَ لَمْ يَعْرِفِ الِاخْتِلَافَ فَإِذَا عَرَفَ الِاخْتِلَافَ فَلَيْسَ بِضَعِيفٍ وَ سَأَلْتَ عَنِ الشَّهَادَاتِ لَهُمْ فَأَقِمِ الشَّهَادَةَ لِلَّهِ عَزَّ وَ جَلَّ وَ لَوْ عَلَى نَفْسِكَ وَ الْوَالِدَيْنِ وَ الْأَقْرَبِينَ فِيمَا بَيْنَكَ وَ بَيْنَهُمْ فَإِنْ خِفْتَ عَلَى أَخِيكَ ضَيْماً فَلَا وَ ادْعُ إِلَى شَرَائِطِ اللَّهِ عَزَّ ذِكْرُهُ بِمَعْرِفَتِنَا مَنْ رَجَوْتَ إِجَابَتَهُ وَ لَا تَحَصَّنْ بِحِصْنِ رِيَاءٍ وَ وَالِ آلَ مُحَمَّدٍ وَ لَا تَقُلْ لِمَا بَلَغَكَ عَنَّا وَ نُسِبَ إِلَيْنَا هَذَا بَاطِلٌ وَ إِنْ كُنْتَ تَعْرِفُ مِنَّا خِلَافَهُ فَإِنَّكَ لَا تَدْرِي لِمَا قُلْنَاهُ وَ عَلَى أَيِّ وَجْهٍ وَصَفْنَاهُ آمِنْ بِمَا أُخْبِرُكَ وَ لَا تُفْشِ مَا اسْتَكْتَمْنَاكَ مِنْ خَبَرِكَ إِنَّ مِنْ وَاجِبِ حَقِّ أَخِيكَ أَنْ لَا تَكْتُمَهُ شَيْئاً تَنْفَعُهُ بِهِ لِأَمْرِ دُنْيَاهُ وَ آخِرَتِهِ وَ لَا تَحْقِدَ عَلَيْهِ وَ إِنْ أَسَاءَ وَ أَجِبْ دَعْوَتَهُ إِذَا دَعَاكَ وَ لَا تُخَلِّ بَيْنَهُ وَ بَيْنَ عَدُوِّهِ مِنَ النَّاسِ وَ إِنْ

كَانَ أَقْرَبَ إِلَيْهِ مِنْكَ وَ عُدْهُ فِي مَرَضِهِ لَيْسَ مِنْ أَخْلَاقِ الْمُؤْمِنِينَ الْغِشُّ وَ لَا الْأَذَى وَ لَا الْخِيَانَةُ وَ لَا الْكِبْرُ وَ لَا الْخَنَا وَ لَا الْفُحْشُ وَ لَا الْأَمْرُ بِهِ فَإِذَا رَأَيْتَ الْمُشَوَّهَ الْأَعْرَابِيَّ فِي جَحْفَلٍ جَرَّارٍ فَانْتَظِرْ فَرَجَكَ وَ لِشِيعَتِكَ الْمُؤْمِنِينَ وَ إِذَا انْكَسَفَتِ الشَّمْسُ فَارْفَعْ بَصَرَكَ إِلَى السَّمَاءِ وَ انْظُرْ مَا فَعَلَ اللَّهُ عَزَّ وَ جَلَّ بِالْمُجْرِمِينَ فَقَدْ فَسَّرْتُ لَكَ جُمَلًا مُجْمَلًا وَ صَلَّى اللَّهُ عَلَى مُحَمَّدٍ وَ آلِهِ الْأَخْيَارِ

A number of our companions, from Sahl b. Ziyad, from Ismail b. Mahraan, from Muḥammad b. Mansour Al-Khuzai'e, from 'Alī b. Suweyd and Muḥammad b. Yahya, from Muḥammad b. Al-Husayn, from Muḥammad b. Ismail b. Yazi'e, from his uncle Hamza b. Yazi'e, from 'Alī b. Suweyd and Al-Hassan Biin Muhammad, from Muḥammad b. Ahmad Al-Nahdy, from Ismail b. Mahraan, from Muḥammad b. Mansour, from 'Alī b. Suweyd who said: 'I wrote to Abu Al-Hassan Mūsā (عليه السلام) whilst he was in the solitary confinement. I wrote asking him about his condition and about numerous matters. The answer did not come for months, then he answered me by an answer and this is its copy: - In the Name of Allāh (تبارك و طائلة) the Beneficent, the Merciful. Praise be to the High, the Magnificent. It is by His Greatness and His Light the hearts of the 'الْمُؤْمِنِينَ' (believers) achieve vision, and by His Greatness and His Light, (whereas) the ignorant ones are inimical to Him , and by His Greatness and His Light crave the ones in the heavens and in the earth and to Him is the Means by the different deeds and the contradictory Religions. So the rightful, and the mistaken, and the stray, and the guided, and the hearing, and the deaf, and the seeing, and the blind ones are perplexed. So the Praise Belongs to Allāh (تبارك و طائلة) Whose Religion was recognised and described by Messenger of Allāh (صلى الله عليه وآله وسلم). Having said that, you are of the people whom Allāh (تبارك و طائلة) has Blessed by Sending the Progeny of Messenger of Allāh (صلى الله عليه وآله وسلم) (towards you and) and by special status, and Preserved the cordiality which attracted you to His Religion, and what He has Inspired from your guidance and your vision from the matters of your Religion that you give preference to them and are referring your matters to them. You wrote to me asking me about matters which I was observing dissimulation in and concealed them for a while. So when the authority of the tyrant passed by, and there came the authority of the One with Great Authority, by my departing from the world which has been condemned by its inhabitants who have hardened themselves against their Creator, I saw that I could explain to you what you had asked me about, fearing that our weak Shiites may enter into confusion because of the ignorance which is in front of them. So fear Allāh (تبارك و طائلة), Mighty is His Mention, and single out for these matters, its deserving ones, and be cautious that you should become a reason for the calamities against the successors or provoking (people) against them by publicising what I am entrusting you with and exposing what I have told you to conceal, and Allāh (تبارك و طائلة) Willing, you will not do this. Firstly what I would like to inform you is that you should mourn for myself in this very night without remorse and no complaints, for what is to transpire is from what Allāh (تبارك و طائلة) Mighty and Majestic has Ordained and is inevitable. So attach yourself to the Handle of the Progeny of Messenger of Allāh (صلى الله عليه وآله وسلم), and the Firmest Handle of the successor after the successor, and the submission to them and be pleased with what they say, and do not seek Religion from the ones who are not from your Shiites, and do not love their Religion, for they are traitors who have betrayed Allāh (تبارك و طائلة) and His Messenger of Allāh (صلى الله عليه وآله وسلم), and betrayed their trusts. And do you know how they betrayed their trusts? They were entrusted with the Book of Allāh (تبارك و طائلة) so they distorted it and changed it, and evidenced it upon the rulers among them. So stay away from them. Allāh (تبارك و طائلة) has Made them to Taste the clothing of the hunger, and the fear due to what they had done. **And you asked about two men (Abu Bakr and Umar) who usurped the wealth of a man which he used to spend upon the poor and the needy and the traveller in need, and in the Way of Allāh (تبارك و طائلة). So when they usurped that, they were not happy until they made him carry it unwillingly upon his ride to their own homes. When they undertook to be in charge of its spending, and so reached infidelity by doing that. By my life, they had become hypocrites before that and rejected against Allāh (تبارك و طائلة) His Words, and mocked at His Messenger of Allāh (صلى الله عليه وآله وسلم), and they were both infidels. May Allāh (تبارك و طائلة) Curse them, and the Angels, and the people altogether. By Allāh (تبارك و طائلة), the 'Eman' (belief) did not enter into the heart of any one of them since their coming out from their condition (Kufr), and it did not**

increase them in anything except for doubts. They were deceivers, sceptical, hypocrites until they both died and the Angels of Punishment took them to the place of disgrace in the eternal abode. And you asked about those who were in the presence of that man whilst he was usurping his wealth and placed it upon his ride, and there were among them who knew about it and denied it. So those (Abu Bakr and Umar) are the first apostates from this community, and so may the Curse of Allāh (تبارك و طائلة) and the Angels and all the people be upon them. And you asked about extent of our Knowledge, and it is upon three aspects. The past, and the future, and the newly recurring. So as for the past, it has been explained, and as for the future, it has been written down, and as for that which is newly occurring, so it gets imprinted upon the hearts, and resonated in the ears, and it is the highest of our Knowledge, and there is no Prophet (عليه السلام) after our Prophet (صلى الله عليه وآله وسلم). And you asked about the mothers of their children (the followers of those two), and about their marriages, and about their divorces. So, as for the mothers of their children, they are prostitutes up to the Day of Judgement, having married without a guardian (Wali's consent), and going through divorces without (completing the) waiting periods. And as for the one who enters into our Invitation (call to Wilāya), so his 'Eman' demolishes his misguidance, and so does his 'Yaqeen' conviction (demolish) his doubts. And you asked about the Zakaat among them. So, there was nothing from the Zakaat (for them), as you are more deserving of it, because we have made that to be lawful for you, and those who are from you wherever they may be. And you asked about the weak. So the weak is the one who cannot argue against (the batil) and he does not understand the differences, for if he understands the difference, then he is not with the weakness. You asked about the 'الشَّهَادَاتِ' testimonies for them. So establish the testimony for the sake of Allāh (تبارك و طائلة), even if it is against your own-self, and the parents and the relatives in what is between you and them. So if you fear injustice against your brother, don't (be part of it). And call to the Law of Allāh (تبارك و طائلة), as He has (placed those) in our recognition (Ma'rifat). The one who hopes would be Answered and do not barricade yourself by the fort of hypocrisy. And befriend the Progeny of Messenger of Allāh

(صلى الله عليه وآله وسلم) and do not speak of what reaches you from us, and ascribe to us that 'this is false', and you may know something from us which is against it, for you do not know why we may have said it, and upon which perspective we may have described it. Believe in what I inform you and do not publicise what I have told you to conceal from what I inform you. It is from the obligatory right of your brother that you do not conceal anything from him which might benefit him in the affairs of the world and the Hereafter. And do not hold a grudge against him and not to hurt him, and answer his call when he calls you and do not leave him alone between him and his enemies from the people even though they may be closer to you than him, and support him in his illness. It is not from etiquettes of the 'الْمُؤْمِنِينَ' Believers, the defrauding, and the injuring, and the treachery, and the arrogance, and the vulgarities, and the immoralities, and the commanding for such things. So if you were to see the deformed Bedouin in legions (large armies), so wait for your relief (Al-Qa'im (عجل الله تعالى فرجه)), and for your Shiites, the believers, and when the sun rises, raise your vision to the sky and look at what Allāh (تبارك و طائلة) has Done with the criminals. So I have explained to you all of this in summary. And send greetings upon Messenger of Allāh (صلى الله عليه وآله وسلم) and his Progeny, the righteous'. (صحيح)[11]

11.

عَلِيُّ بْنُ إِبْرَاهِيمَ عَنْ أَبِيهِ عَنِ ابْنِ مَحْبُوبٍ عَنْ عَلِيِّ بْنِ رِئَابٍ وَ يَعْقُوبَ السَّرَّاجِ عَنْ أَبِي عَبْدِ اللَّهِ (عليه السلام) أَنَّ أَمِيرَ الْمُؤْمِنِينَ (عليه السلام) لَمَّا بُويِعَ بَعْدَ مَقْتَلِ عُثْمَانَ صَعِدَ الْمِنْبَرَ فَقَالَ الْحَمْدُ لِلَّهِ الَّذِي عَلَا فَاسْتَعْلَى وَ دَنَا فَتَعَالَى وَ ارْتَفَعَ فَوْقَ كُلِّ مَنْظَرٍ وَ أَشْهَدُ أَنْ لَا إِلَهَ إِلَّا اللَّهُ وَحْدَهُ لَا شَرِيكَ لَهُ وَ أَشْهَدُ أَنَّ مُحَمَّداً عَبْدُهُ وَ رَسُولُهُ خَاتَمُ النَّبِيِّينَ وَ حُجَّةُ اللَّهِ عَلَى الْعَالَمِينَ مُصَدِّقاً لِلرُّسُلِ الْأَوَّلِينَ وَ كَانَ بِالْمُؤْمِنِينَ رَءُوفاً رَحِيماً فَصَلَّى اللَّهُ وَ مَلَائِكَتُهُ عَلَيْهِ وَ عَلَى آلِهِ أَمَّا بَعْدُ أَيُّهَا النَّاسُ فَإِنَّ الْبَغْيَ يَقُودُ أَصْحَابَهُ إِلَى النَّارِ وَ إِنَّ أَوَّلَ مَنْ بَغَى عَلَى اللَّهِ جَلَّ ذِكْرُهُ عَنَاقُ بِنْتُ آدَمَ وَ أَوَّلَ قَتِيلٍ قَتَلَهُ اللَّهُ عَنَاقُ وَ كَانَ مَجْلِسُهَا جَرِيباً [مِنَ الْأَرْضِ] فِي جَرِيبٍ وَ كَانَ لَهَا عِشْرُونَ إِصْبَعاً فِي كُلِّ إِصْبَعٍ ظُفُرَانِ مِثْلُ الْمِنْجَلَيْنِ فَسَلَّطَ اللَّهُ عَزَّ وَ جَلَّ عَلَيْهَا أَسَداً كَالْفِيلِ وَ ذِئْباً كَالْبَعِيرِ وَ نَسْراً مِثْلَ الْبَغْلِ فَقَتَلُوهَا وَ قَدْ قَتَلَ اللَّهُ الْجَبَابِرَةَ عَلَى أَفْضَلِ أَحْوَالِهِمْ وَ آمَنِ مَا كَانُوا وَ

[11] *Al-Kāfi, v8, h95*

أَمَاتَ هَامَانَ وَ أَهْلَكَ فِرْعَوْنَ وَ قَدْ قُتِلَ عُثْمَانُ أَلَا وَ إِنَّ بَلِيَّتَكُمْ قَدْ عَادَتْ كَهَيْئَتِهَا يَوْمَ بَعَثَ اللَّهُ نَبِيَّهُ (صلى الله عليه وآله) وَ الَّذِي بَعَثَهُ بِالْحَقِّ لَتُبَلْبَلُنَّ بَلْبَلَةً وَ لَتُغَرْبَلُنَّ غَرْبَلَةً وَ لَتُسَاطُنَّ سَوْطَةَ الْقِدْرِ حَتَّى يَعُودَ أَسْفَلُكُمْ أَعْلَاكُمْ وَ أَعْلَاكُمْ أَسْفَلَكُمْ وَ لَيَسْبِقَنَّ سَابِقُونَ كَانُوا قَصَّرُ ا وَ لَيُقَصِّرَنَّ وَ سَبِقَاُونَ كَانُوا سَبَقُوا وَ اللَّهِ مَا كَتَمْتُ وَشْمَةً وَ لَا كَذَبْتُ كِذْبَةً وَ لَقَدْ نُبِّئْتُ بِهَذَا الْمَقَامِ وَ هَذَا الْيَوْمِ أَلَا وَ إِنَّ الْخَطَايَا خَيْلٌ شُمُسٌ حُمِلَ عَلَيْهَا أَهْلُهَا وَ خُلِعَتْ لُجُمُهَا فَتَقَحَّمَتْ بِهِمْ فِي النَّارِ أَلَا وَ إِنَّ التَّقْوَى مَطَايَا ذُلُلٌ حُمِلَ عَلَيْهَا أَهْلُهَا وَ أُعْطُوا أَزِمَّتَهَا فَأَوْرَدَتْهُمُ الْجَنَّةَ وَ فُتِحَتْ لَهُمْ أَبْوَابُهَا وَ وَجَدُوا رِيحَهَا وَ طِيبَهَا وَ قِيلَ لَهُمْ ادْخُلُوها بِسَلامٍ آمِنِينَ أَلَا وَ قَدْ سَبَقَنِي إِلَى هَذَا الْأَمْرِ مَنْ لَمْ أُشْرِكْهُ فِيهِ وَ مَنْ لَمْ أَهَبْهُ لَهُ وَ مَنْ لَيْسَتْ لَهُ مِنْهُ نَوْبَةٌ إِلَّا بِنَبِيٍّ يُبْعَثُ أَلَا وَ لَا نَبِيَّ بَعْدَ مُحَمَّدٍ (صلى الله عليه وآله) أَشْرَفَ مِنْهُ عَلَى شَفَا جُرُفٍ هَارٍ فَانْهَارَ بِهِ فِي نَارِ جَهَنَّمَ حَقٌّ وَ بَاطِلٌ وَ لِكُلٍّ أَهْلٌ فَلَئِنْ أَمِرَ الْبَاطِلُ لَقَدِيماً فَعَلَ وَ لَئِنْ قَلَّ الْحَقُّ فَلَرُبَّمَا وَ لَعَلَّ وَ لَقَلَّمَا أَدْبَرَ شَيْءٌ فَأَقْبَلَ وَ لَئِنْ رُدَّ عَلَيْكُمْ أَمْرُكُمْ أَنَّكُمْ سُعَدَاءُ وَ مَا عَلَيَّ إِلَّا الْجُهْدُ وَ إِنِّي لَأَخْشَى أَنْ تَكُونُوا عَلَى فَتْرَةٍ مِلْتُمْ عَنِّي مَيْلَةً كُنْتُمْ فِيهَا عِنْدِي غَيْرَ مَحْمُودِي الرَّأْيِ وَ لَوْ أَشَاءُ لَقُلْتُ عَفَا اللَّهُ عَمَّا سَلَفَ سَبَقَ فِيهِ الرَّجُلَانِ وَ قَامَ الثَّالِثُ كَالْغُرَابِ هَمُّهُ بَطْنُهُ وَيْلَهُ لَوْ قُصَّ جَنَاحَاهُ وَ قُطِعَ رَأْسُهُ كَانَ خَيْراً لَهُ شُغِلَ عَنِ الْجَنَّةِ وَ النَّارُ أَمَامَهُ ثَلَاثَةٌ وَ اثْنَانِ خَمْسَةٌ لَيْسَ لَهُمْ سَادِسٌ مَلَكٌ يَطِيرُ بِجَنَاحَيْهِ وَ نَبِيٌّ أَخَذَ اللَّهُ بِضَبْعَيْهِ وَ سَاعٍ مُجْتَهِدٌ وَ طَالِبٌ يَرْجُو وَ مُقَصِّرٌ فِي النَّارِ الْيَمِينُ وَ الشِّمَالُ مَضَلَّةٌ وَ الطَّرِيقُ الْوُسْطَى هِيَ الْجَادَّةُ عَلَيْهَا يَأْتِي الْكِتَابُ وَ آثَارُ النُّبُوَّةِ هَلَكَ مَنِ ادَّعَى وَ خَابَ مَنِ افْتَرَى إِنَّ اللَّهَ أَدَّبَ هَذِهِ الْأُمَّةَ بِالسَّيْفِ وَ السَّوْطِ وَ لَيْسَ لِأَحَدٍ عِنْدَ الْإِمَامِ فِيهِمَا هَوَادَةٌ فَاسْتَتِرُوا فِي بُيُوتِكُمْ وَ أَصْلِحُوا ذَاتَ بَيْنِكُمْ وَ التَّوْبَةُ مِنْ وَرَائِكُمْ مَنْ أَبْدَى صَفْحَتَهُ لِلْحَقِّ هَلَكَ

Ali b. Ibrahim, from his father, from b. Mahboub, from 'Alī b. Ra'ab abd Yaqoub Al-Sarraaj who has said: Abu 'AbdAllāh (عليه السلام) has narrated that: 'Amir al-Mu'minin (عليه السلام), when they had pledged allegiance to him after the killing of Usman, ascended the Pulpit, so he said: 'Praise be to Allāh (تبارك و طائلة) Who is High and thus all is in His possession and He is Closer than any in the view. And I hereby testify that there is no god but Allāh (تبارك و طائلة), One with no associates to Him , and I testify that Messenger of Allāh (صلى الله عليه وآله وسلم) is His servant and His Messenger, the last of the Prophets (عليه السلام) and a Proof over the worlds, a ratification for the former Prophets (عليه السلام) and was kind and merciful to the Believers. The Angels sent 'salam' greetings of peace upon him and upon his Progeny. Having said that, O you people! The transgression (indecency) places its owner into the Fire, and the first one to transgression (commit indecency) against Allāh (تبارك و طائلة) Majestic is His Remembrance was Onaq the daughter of Adam (عليه السلام), and the first one who was killed, whom Allāh (تبارك و طائلة) Killed was Onaq. And the area that she occupied when seated upon the ground measured one square acre (Jarib) of the land, and she had twenty fingers and on each of her fingers were two nails like two sickles. So Allāh (تبارك و طائلة) Mighty and Majestic Made her to be overcome by a lion which was like an elephant (in size), and a wolf which was like a camel (in size), and an eagle like a mule (in size). So they killed her. And Allāh (تبارك و طائلة) had Killed the tyrants in their best conditions, and gave Safety to those who used to be (oppressed). And He Made Hannaan to die, and destroyed the Pharaoh (لعنة الله عليه), and He has Killed Usman. Indeed! Your misfortunes have returned to what they were on the day Allāh (تبارك و طائلة) Sent His Prophet (صلى الله عليه وآله وسلم). By the One Who Sent him by the truth, you will be confused with a (severe) confusion and be sifted with a (severe) sifting, and stirred and turned like the contents of a frying pan until your underside becomes your upper side and your upper side becomes your underside. The ones who used to be with the shortcomings will become the foremost ones, and those who used to be the foremost ones would become the people with shortcomings. By Allāh (تبارك و طائلة)! I have neither concealed, nor blocked, nor lied a lie, and I have been foretold about this place and this day. Indeed! And the sins are like uncontrollable horses which carry its riders, with its harnesses removed, plunging into the Fire. Indeed! And the piety is like a humble ride which takes its rider, along with its rein, to the Paradise, and its Doors will be opened up for them, and they will find its aroma and goodness. And it will be said to them: 'Enter it in peace and security'. Indeed! The ones who had no association with it has preceded me to this command (Caliphate), and the ones to whom it had not been Granted to, and the ones for whom there was no chance from it except if they were to be Prophets (عليه السلام) who had been Sent. And indeed! There is no Prophet (عليه السلام) to be after Messenger of Allāh (صلى الله عليه وآله وسلم) who is more noble than him (عليه السلام) over the intercession on the brink of the Fire. So they will fall with by it (their lies) in the Fire of Hell. Truth as well as falsehood, for each of them are its people. The matter of falsehood is a very old one and has been active. And if the truth is less (in practice) it is because of 'if' and 'maybe'. And it is rare that if a thing gone away comes back, and if your command (Caliphate) returns to you, you would be pleased, and it is not on me except for the striving, and I am afraid that you all will end up being on the nature of your nation (away) from me, the nation that you were in beforehand and would not have a praiseworthy opinion in my sight, and if I so desire to I would say: 'May Allāh (تبارك و طائلة) Forgive what was in the past'. Two men preceded me with regards to it (Caliphate), and the third one stood up like the Raven. His main concern was his stomach. Woe be unto him! Had his wings been clipped and his head cut-off, it would have been better for him. He was distracted from the Paradise and the Hell was in front of him. Three and two make five, there is no sixth of them – An Angel who files by his wings, and a Prophet (عليه السلام) whom Allāh (تبارك و طائلة) has Grabbed by his (عليه السلام) shoulders (Given him Divine Status), and a diligent seeker (momin), and a hopeful student, and a reducer (Muqassir) are in the Fire. The right and the left are misleading, whereas the middle path is the street on which you will come across the Book and the effects of the Prophet-hood. Destroyed is the one who makes a claim, and disillusioned is the one who fabricates that Allāh (تبارك و طائلة) Disciplined this community by the sword and the whip, and there is no leniency for either of them with the Imam (عليه السلام). So, hide in your homes and mend your relationships in between yourselves and the repentance is behind you all. The one who turned his cheek (opposed the Imam (عليه السلام)) to the truth is destroyed. (حسن)[12]

12.

مُحَمَّدُ بْنُ يَحْيَى عَنْ مُحَمَّدِ بْنِ الْحُسَيْنِ عَنِ الْحَجَّالِ عَنْ عَبْدِ الصَّمَدِ بْنِ بَشِيرٍ عَنْ حَسَّانَ الْجَمَّالِ قَالَ حَمَلْتُ أَبَا عَبْدِ اللَّهِ (عَلَيْهِ السَّلَام) مِنَ الْمَدِينَةِ إِلَى مَكَّةَ فَلَمَّا انْتَهَيْنَا إِلَى مَسْجِدِ الْغَدِيرِ نَظَرَ إِلَى مَيْسَرَةِ الْمَسْجِدِ فَقَالَ ذَلِكَ مَوْضِعُ قَدَمِ رَسُولِ اللَّهِ (صلَّى اللَّهُ عَلَيْهِ وَآلِه) حَيْثُ قَالَ مَنْ كُنْتُ مَوْلَاهُ فَعَلِيٌّ مَوْلَاهُ ثُمَّ نَظَرَ إِلَى الْجَانِبِ الْآخَرِ فَقَالَ ذَلِكَ مَوْضِعُ فُسْطَاطِ أَبِي فُلَانٍ وَفُلَانٍ وَسَالِمٍ مَوْلَى أَبِي حُذَيْفَةَ وَأَبِي عُبَيْدَةَ الْجَرَّاحِ فَلَمَّا أَنْ رَأَوْهُ رَافِعاً يَدَيْهِ قَالَ بَعْضُهُمْ لِبَعْضٍ انْظُرُوا إِلَى عَيْنَيْهِ تَدُورُ كَأَنَّهُمَا عَيْنَا مَجْنُونٍ فَنَزَلَ جَبْرَئِيلُ (عَلَيْهِ السَّلَام) بِهَذِهِ الْآيَةِ وَإِنْ يَكادُ الَّذِينَ كَفَرُوا لَيُزْلِقُونَكَ بِأَبْصارِهِمْ لَمَّا سَمِعُوا الذِّكْرَ وَيَقُولُونَ إِنَّهُ لَمَجْنُونٌ وَما هُوَ إِلَّا ذِكْرٌ لِلْعالَمِينَ

---

[12] *Al-Kāfi, v8, h23*

Muhammad b. Yahya has narrated from Muḥammad b. al-Husayn form al-Hajjal from 'Abd al-Samad b. Bashir from Hassan al- Jammal who has said the following: "I once provided transportation for abu 'Abd Allāh, (عليه السلام), from al-Madinah to Makkah. When we arrived at Masjid of al-Ghadir Khum, he looked to the left side of the Masjid and said this. 'That is the place where the Messenger of Allāh, (صلى الله عليه وآله وسلم), set foot when he (the Messenger of Allāh) said, "On whoever I have Divine Authority, 'Alī also has Divine Authority." He then looked to the other side and said, 'That is the place for the tent of abu so(Abu Bakr) and so(Umar) and Salim Mawla' abu Hudhayfah and abu 'Ubayda al-Jarrah, who on seeing him raising his hands, said to each other, "Look at his eyes turning like the eyes of an insane person." Jibril at this time came with this verse of the Holy Qur'ān, "The disbelievers almost make you slip up, by their piercing eyes when they hear (passages) of the Qur'ān and say that he is an insane person. It (Qur'ān) is not anything other than good advice from the Lord of the worlds."' (54:50-51) " (صحيح على الظاهر)[13]

13.

عَلِيُّ بْنُ إِبْرَاهِيمَ عَنْ أَبِيهِ عَنِ ابْنِ أَبِي عُمَيْرٍ عَنْ حَمَّادِ بْنِ عُثْمَانَ عَنِ الْحَلَبِيِّ عَنْ أَبِي عَبْدِ اللَّه (عَلَيْهِ الْسَّلام) قَالَ لَمَّا مَاتَ عَبْدُ اللَّه بْنُ أُبَيِّ بْنِ سَلُولٍ حَضَرَ النَّبِيُّ (صلّى اللَّهُ عَلَيْهِ وَآلِه) جِنَازَتَهُ فَقَالَ عُمَرُ لِرَسُولِ اللَّه (صلّى اللَّهُ عَلَيْهِ وَآلِه) يَا رَسُولَ اللَّه أَ لَمْ يَنْهَكَ اللَّه أَنْ تَقُومَ عَلَى قَبْرِهِ فَسَكَتَ فَقَالَ يَا رَسُولَ اللَّه أَ لَمْ يَنْهَكَ اللَّه أَنْ تَقُومَ عَلَى قَبْرِهِ فَقَالَ لَهُ وَيْلَكَ وَمَا يُدْرِيكَ مَا قُلْتُ إِنِّي قُلْتُ اللَّهُمَّ احْشُ جَوْفَهُ نَاراً وَامْلأْ قَبْرَهُ نَاراً وَأَصْلِهِ نَاراً قَالَ أَبُو عَبْدِ اللَّه (عَلَيْهِ الْسَّلام) فَأَبْدَى مِنْ رَسُولِ اللَّه مَا كَانَ يَكْرَهُ

Ali b. Ibrahim has narrated from his father from b. abu 'Umayr from Hammad b. 'Isa from af-Halabiy who has said the following: "Abu 'Abd Allāh, (عليه السلام), has said, 'When 'Abd Allāh b. 'Ubay b. Salul died, the Holy prophet attended his funeral. 'Umar said to the Messenger of Allāh, "O Messenger of Allāh, has Allāh not forbidden you from standing on his grave?" He (the Messenger of Allāh) remained

---

[13] *Al-Kāfi, v4, ch225, h2*

silent. He ('Umar) said, "O Messenger of Allāh, has Allāh not forbidden you from standing on his grave?" He (the Messenger of Allāh) said, 'Fie upon you, how you could tell what I say? I said, "O Lord, fill his belly with fire, fill his grave with fire and make him feel the heat of fire."' Abu 'Abd Allāh, (عليه السلام), then said, 'He made the Messenger of Allāh to expose what he disliked.'" (حسن)[14]

14.

عَلِيُّ بْنُ مُحَمَّدِ بْنِ عَبْدِ اللهِ عَنْ بَعْضِ أَصْحَابِنَا أَظُنُّهُ السَّيَّارِيَّ عَنْ عَلِيِّ بْنِ أَسْبَاطٍ قَالَ لَمَّا وَرَدَ أَبُو الْحَسَنِ مُوسَى (عَلَيْهِ السَّلام) عَلَى الْمَهْدِيِّ رَآهُ يَرُدُّ الْمَظَالِمَ فَقَالَ يَا أَمِيرَ الْمُؤْمِنِينَ مَا بَالُ مَظْلِمَتِنَا لا تُرَدُّ فَقَالَ لَهُ وَمَا ذَاكَ يَا أَبَا الْحَسَنِ قَالَ إِنَّ اللهَ تَبَارَكَ وَتَعَالَى لَمَّا فَتَحَ عَلَى نَبِيِّهِ (صَلَّى اللهُ عَلَيْهِ وَآلِه) فَدَكاً وَمَا وَالاهَا لَمْ يُوجَفْ عَلَيْهِ بِخَيْلٍ وَلا رِكَابٍ فَأَنْزَلَ اللهُ عَلَى نَبِيِّهِ (صَلَّى اللهُ عَلَيْهِ وَآلِه) وَآتِ ذَا الْقُرْبَى حَقَّهُ فَلَمْ يَدْرِ رَسُولُ اللهِ (صَلَّى اللهُ عَلَيْهِ وَآلِه) مَنْ هُمْ فَرَاجَعَ فِي ذَلِكَ جَبْرَئِيلَ وَرَاجَعَ جَبْرَئِيلُ (عَلَيْهِ السَّلام) رَبَّهُ فَأَوْحَى اللهُ إِلَيْهِ أَنِ ادْفَعْ فَدَكاً إِلَى فَاطِمَةَ (عليها السلام) فَدَعَاهَا رَسُولُ اللهِ (صَلَّى اللهُ عَلَيْهِ وَآلِه) فَقَالَ لَهَا يَا فَاطِمَةُ إِنَّ اللهَ أَمَرَنِي أَنْ أَدْفَعَ إِلَيْكِ فَدَكاً فَقَالَتْ قَدْ قَبِلْتُ يَا رَسُولَ اللهِ مِنَ اللهِ وَمِنْكَ فَلَمْ يَزَلْ وُكَلاؤُهَا فِيهَا حَيَاةَ رَسُولِ اللهِ (صَلَّى اللهُ عَلَيْهِ وَآلِه) فَلَمَّا وُلِّيَ أَبُو بَكْرٍ أَخْرَجَ عَنْهَا وُكَلاءَهَا فَأَتَتْهُ فَسَأَلَتْهُ أَنْ يَرُدَّهَا عَلَيْهَا فَقَالَ لَهَا ائْتِينِي بِأَسْوَدَ أَوْ أَحْمَرَ يَشْهَدُ لَكِ بِذَلِكِ فَجَاءَتْ بِأَمِيرِ الْمُؤْمِنِينَ (عَلَيْهِ السَّلام) وَأُمِّ أَيْمَنَ فَشَهِدَا لَهَا فَكَتَبَ لَهَا بِتَرْكِ التَّعَرُّضِ فَخَرَجَتْ وَالْكِتَابُ مَعَهَا فَلَقِيَهَا عُمَرُ فَقَالَ مَا هَذَا مَعَكِ يَا بِنْتَ مُحَمَّدٍ قَالَتْ كِتَابٌ كَتَبَهُ لِيَ ابْنُ أَبِي قُحَافَةَ قَالَ أَرِينِيهِ فَأَبَتْ فَانْتَزَعَهُ مِنْ يَدِهَا وَنَظَرَ فِيهِ ثُمَّ تَفَلَ فِيهِ وَمَحَاهُ وَخَرَقَهُ فَقَالَ لَهَا هَذَا لَمْ يُوجِفْ عَلَيْهِ أَبُوكِ بِخَيْلٍ وَلا رِكَابٍ فَضَعِي الْحِبَالَ فِي رِقَابِنَا فَقَالَ لَهُ الْمَهْدِيُّ يَا أَبَا الْحَسَنِ حُدَّهَا لِي فَقَالَ حَدٌّ مِنْهَا جَبَلُ أُحُدٍ وَحَدٌّ مِنْهَا عَرِيشُ مِصْرَ وَحَدٌّ مِنْهَا سِيفُ الْبَحْرِ وَحَدٌّ مِنْهَا دُومَةُ الْجَنْدَلِ فَقَالَ لَهُ كُلُّ هَذَا قَالَ نَعَمْ يَا أَمِيرَ الْمُؤْمِنِينَ هَذَا كُلُّهُ إِنَّ هَذَا كُلَّهُ مِمَّا لَمْ يُوجِفْ عَلَى أَهْلِهِ رَسُولُ اللهِ (صَلَّى اللهُ عَلَيْهِ وَآلِه) بِخَيْلٍ وَلا رِكَابٍ فَقَالَ كَثِيرٌ وَأَنْظُرُ فِيهِ

Ali b. Muḥammad b. 'AbdAllāh has narrated from Certain persons of our people that I thinks is al-Sayyari from 'Alī b. Asbat who has said the following. "In one of the meetings of abu al-Hassan Mūsā (عليه السلام) with al-Mahdi (one of 'Abbassid ruler) the Imam found him paying reparations (for the damages caused to people). The Imam

[14] *Al-Kafi, v3, ch58, h1*

(عليه السلام) said, "O Amir al-Mu'minin, what has happened to the reparations due to us?" He then asked, "What damage is caused to you O abu al-Hassan ?" He (the Imam (عليه السلام) said, "Allāh, the Holy, the Most High, granted victory to His Holy Prophet (s.a) and the land of Fadak and its surrounding areas came under his control without any armed struggle Allāh sent a message to His the Holy Prophet (s.a). It said, "Give the relatives their rights." The Messenger of Allāh did not know who they were. He turned to Jibril to find out and Jibril turned to his Lord for the answer. Allāh then sent revelation to him to give possession of Fadak to Fatima (عليه السلام). Thereupon, the Messenger of Allāh called Fatima and said to her. "O Fatima (عليه السلام) Allāh has commanded me to give possession of Fadak to you. She then said, " O the Messenger of Allāh, I have accepted the offer from Allāh and from you." Thereafter her representatives lived there during the life time of the Messenger of Allāh. When abu Bakr took control he expelled her representatives therefrom. She went to abu Bakr and asked him to reverse his decision and return Fadak to her but he said to Fatima (عليه السلام), "Bring to a black or white to testify that Fadak belonged to you." Fatima (عليه السلام) brought Amir al-Mu'minin 'Alī (عليه السلام) and 'Umm Ayman who both testified in favor of Fatima (عليه السلام). He then wrote, "Fatima must not be disturbed in the matters of Fadak." Fatima then left with the document. On the way 'Umar came from the opposite direction and asked, "What is it in your hand O daughter of Muhammad?" Fatima (عليه السلام) said, "It is a document that b. abu Quhafa has written for me." He said, "Show it to me." Fatima refused to hand it over to him but he snatched it away from her hand and read it. He then spit on it wiped out its writing and tore it into pieces. He said, "This was not captured by forces of the camels and horses of your father so that you can tie the rope around our necks." Al-Mahdi said, "O abu al-Hassan define for me the boundaries of Fadak." The Imam (عليه السلام) said, "On one side it borders the mountain of 'Uhud. On the other side is 'Arish Misr. Also it borders Sayf al-Bahr and on one of its sides is Dawmat al-Jandal." Then he asked the Imams, "Is that all?" He said, "Yes, O Amir al-Mu'minin, this is all that came to the Messenger of Allāh without the use of the forces of the camels and horses." He said, "This is a large area but I will look into it. (مجهول)[15]

15.

يَحْيَى عَنْ عَبْدِ اللَّهِ بْنِ مُسْكَانَ عَنْ ضُرَيْسٍ قَالَ تَمَارَى النَّاسُ عِنْدَ أَبِي جَعْفَرٍ (عليه السلام) فَقَالَ بَعْضُهُمْ حَرْبُ عَلِيٍّ شَرٌّ مِنْ حَرْبِ رَسُولِ اللَّهِ (صلى الله عليه وآله) وَ قَالَ بَعْضُهُمْ حَرْبُ رَسُولِ اللَّهِ (صلى الله عليه وآله) شَرٌّ مِنْ حَرْبِ عَلِيٍّ (عليه السلام) قَالَ فَسَمِعَهُمْ أَبُو جَعْفَرٍ (عليه السلام) فَقَالَ مَا تَقُولُونَ فَقَالُوا أَصْلَحَكَ اللَّهُ تَمَارَيْنَا فِي حَرْبِ رَسُولِ اللَّهِ (صلى الله عليه وآله) وَ فِي حَرْبِ عَلِيٍّ (عليه السلام) فَقَالَ بَعْضُنَا حَرْبُ عَلِيٍّ (عليه السلام) شَرٌّ مِنْ حَرْبِ رَسُولِ اللَّهِ (صلى الله عليه وآله) وَ قَالَ بَعْضُنَا حَرْبُ رَسُولِ اللَّهِ (صلى الله عليه وآله) شَرٌّ مِنْ حَرْبِ عَلِيٍّ (عليه السلام) فَقَالَ أَبُو جَعْفَرٍ (عليه السلام) لَا بَلْ حَرْبُ عَلِيٍّ (عليه السلام) شَرٌّ مِنْ حَرْبِ رَسُولِ اللَّهِ (صلى الله عليه وآله) فَقُلْتُ لَهُ جُعِلْتُ فِدَاكَ أَ حَرْبُ عَلِيٍّ (عليه السلام) شَرٌّ مِنْ حَرْبِ رَسُولِ اللَّهِ (صلى الله عليه وآله) قَالَ نَعَمْ وَ سَأُخْبِرُكَ عَنْ ذَلِكَ إِنَّ حَرْبَ رَسُولِ اللَّهِ (صلى الله عليه وآله) لَمْ يُقِرُّوا بِالْإِسْلَامِ وَ إِنَّ حَرْبَ عَلِيٍّ (عليه السلام) أَقَرُّوا بِالْإِسْلَامِ ثُمَّ جَحَدُوهُ

Yahya, from Abdulah b. Muskaan, from Zureys who said: The people disputed in the presence of Abu Ja'far (عليه السلام). So some of them said, 'The wars fought by 'Alī (عليه السلام) were (against a people) more evil than the wars fought by the Messenger of Allāh (صلى الله عليه وآله وسلم), and some of them said, 'The wars fought by the Messenger of Allāh (صلى الله عليه وآله وسلم) were (against a people) more evil than the wars fought by 'Alī (عليه السلام)'. He (the narrator) said, 'So Abu Ja'far listened to them and said: 'What are you all saying?' So they said, 'May Allāh (تبارك و تعالى) keep you well, we are disputing with regards to the wars of the Messenger of Allāh (صلى الله عليه وآله وسلم) and the wars of 'Alī (عليه السلام). Some of us are saying that the wars of 'Alī (عليه السلام) were (against a people) more evil than the wars fought by the Messenger of Allāh (صلى الله عليه وآله وسلم), whilst some of us are saying that the wars fought by the Messenger were (against a people) more evil than the wars fought by 'Alī (عليه السلام)'. So Abu Ja'far (عليه السلام) said: 'No! But, the wars of 'Alī (عليه السلام) were (against a people) more evil than the wars of

[15] *Al-Kāfi, v1, ch130, h5*

the Messenger of Allāh (صلى الله عليه وآله وسلم)'. So I said to him, 'May I be sacrificed for you, the wars of 'Alī (عليه السلام) were (against a people) more evil than the wars of the Messenger of Allāh (صلى الله عليه وآله وسلم)?' He said: 'Yes, and I shall inform you about that. The Messenger fought wars (against a people) who did not accept Al-Islam, and that the wars of 'Alī (عليه السلام) were (against a people) who accepted Al-Islam, then fought against him'. (صحيح على الظاهر)[16]

---

[16] *Al-Kāfi, v8, h353*

Miscellaneous

This is a chapter dedicated to the Hadīths I came across, but could not find enough similar Hadīths to form an independent chapter

1.

مُحَمَّدُ بْنُ يَحْيَى عَنْ أَحْمَدَ بْنِ مُحَمَّدِ بْنِ عِيسَى عَنِ الْحَسَنِ بْنِ مَحْبُوبٍ عَنْ مُعَاوِيَةَ بْنِ وَهْبٍ قَالَ سَمِعْتُ أَبَا عَبْدِ اللهِ (عَلَيهِ السَّلام) يَقُولُ إِذَا تَابَ الْعَبْدُ تَوْبَةً نَصُوحاً أَحَبَّهُ اللهُ فَسَتَرَ عَلَيْهِ فِي الدُّنْيَا وَالآخِرَةِ فَقُلْتُ وَكَيْفَ يَسْتُرُ عَلَيْهِ قَالَ يُنْسِي مَلَكَيْهِ مَا كَتَبَا عَلَيْهِ مِنَ الذُّنُوبِ وَيُوحِي إِلَى جَوَارِحِهِ اكْتُمِي عَلَيْهِ ذُنُوبَهُ وَيُوحِي إِلَى بِقَاعِ الأَرْضِ اكْتُمِي مَا كَانَ يَعْمَلُ عَلَيْكِ مِنَ الذُّنُوبِ فَيَلْقَى اللهَ حِينَ يَلْقَاهُ وَلَيْسَ شَيْءٌ يَشْهَدُ عَلَيْهِ بِشَيْءٍ مِنَ الذُّنُوبِ

Muhammad b. Yahya has narrated from Ahmad b. Muḥammad b. 'Isa from al-Hassan b. Mahbub from Mu'awiyah b. Wahab who has said the following: "I heard abu 'Abd Allāh (عليه السلام) saying, 'When a servant (of Allāh) repents in the form of the repentance of Nasuh (sincere advise to one's soul, or name of a person who repented in the real sense), Allāh then loves him, covers and protects him in this world and in the next life.' 1 then asked, 'How will He cover him?' The Imam said, 'He will make the two angels forget what they have written against him. He will inspire the parts of his body to hide his sins and the places of earth to hide the sins that he had committed thereat. Allāh will meet him while there will be nothing to testify anything against him.''' (صحيح)[1]

2.

عَلِيُّ بْنُ إِبْرَاهِيمَ عَنْ أَبِيهِ عَنِ ابْنِ أَبِي عُمَيْرٍ عَنْ أَبِي أَيُّوبَ عَنْ أَبِي بَصِيرٍ قَالَ قُلْتُ لأَبِي عَبْدِ الله (عَلَيهِ السَّلام) يا أَيُّهَا الَّذِينَ آمَنُوا تُوبُوا إِلَى الله تَوْبَةً نَصُوحاً قَالَ هُوَ الذَّنْبُ الَّذِي لا يَعُودُ فِيهِ أَبَداً قُلْتُ وَأَيُّنَا لَمْ يَعُدْ فَقَالَ يَا أَبَا مُحَمَّدٍ إِنَّ الله يُحِبُّ مِنْ عِبَادِهِ الْمُفَتَّنَ التَّوَّابَ

Ali b. Ibrahim has narrated from his father from b. abu 'Umayr from abu Ayyub from abu Basir who has said the following: "Once I asked abu 'Abd Allāh (عليه السلام) about the words of Allāh, the Most Majestic, the Most Holy, 'Believers, turn to Allāh in repentance, "In a Nasuh manner," with the intention of never repeating the same sin.' (66:8) The Imam said, 'It is the sin that one never repeats.' I then asked, 'Who among us does not repeat?' The Imam said, 'O abu Muhammad, of His servants Allāh loves those who are put to trial and the ones who repent very often.''' (حسن كالصحيح)[2]

3.

مُحَمَّدُ بْنُ يَحْيَى عَنْ أَحْمَدَ بْنِ مُحَمَّدٍ عَنِ ابْنِ مَحْبُوبٍ عَنِ الْعَلاءِ عَنْ مُحَمَّدِ بْنِ مُسْلِمٍ عَنْ أَبِي جَعْفَرٍ (عَلَيهِ السَّلام) قَالَ يَا مُحَمَّدَ بْنَ مُسْلِمٍ ذُنُوبُ الْمُؤْمِنِ إِذَا تَابَ مِنْهَا مَغْفُورَةٌ لَهُ فَلْيَعْمَلِ الْمُؤْمِنُ لِمَا يَسْتَأْنِفُ بَعْدَ التَّوْبَةِ وَالْمَغْفِرَةِ أَمَا وَالله إِنَّهَا لَيْسَتْ إِلا لأَهْلِ الإِيمَانِ قُلْتُ فَإِنْ عَادَ بَعْدَ التَّوْبَةِ وَالإِسْتِغْفَارِ مِنَ الذُّنُوبِ وَعَادَ فِي التَّوْبَةِ فَقَالَ يَا مُحَمَّدَ بْنَ مُسْلِمٍ أَ تَرَى الْعَبْدَ الْمُؤْمِنَ يَنْدَمُ عَلَى ذَنْبِهِ وَيَسْتَغْفِرُ مِنْهُ وَيَتُوبُ ثُمَّ لا يَقْبَلُ الله تَوْبَتَهُ قُلْتُ فَإِنَّهُ فَعَلَ ذَلِكَ مِرَاراً يُذْنِبُ ثُمَّ يَتُوبُ وَيَسْتَغْفِرُ الله فَقَالَ كُلَّمَا عَادَ الْمُؤْمِنُ بِالإِسْتِغْفَارِ وَالتَّوْبَةِ عَادَ الله عَلَيْهِ بِالْمَغْفِرَةِ وَإِنَّ الله غَفُورٌ رَحِيمٌ يَقْبَلُ التَّوْبَةَ وَيَعْفُو عَنِ السَّيِّئَاتِ فَإِيَّاكَ أَنْ تُقَنِّطَ الْمُؤْمِنِينَ مِنْ رَحْمَةِ الله

---

[1] *Al-Kāfi, v2, ch191, h1*

[2] *Al-Kāfi, v2, ch191, h4*

Muhammad b. Yahya has narrated from Ahmad b. Muḥammad from b. Mahbub from al-'Ala' from Muḥammad b. Muslim from abu Ja'far (عليه السلام) who has said the following: "Once abu Ja'far (عليه السلام) said, 'O Muḥammad b. Muslim, if believing people repent for their sins they will be forgiven. Believing people must resume their good deeds after repentance and forgiveness. By Allāh, this is only for the believers.' I then asked, 'What if he goes back to sin after repenting and asking for forgiveness and repents again?' The Imam said, 'O Muḥammad b. Muslim, do you think a believing servant (of Allāh) regrets his sins, asks forgiveness and repents but Allāh does not accept his repentance?' I said, 'He, however, has done it many times. He sins, repents and asks forgiveness (from Allāh).' The Imam said, 'Whenever a believing servant (of Allāh) returns back for repentance and pleas for forgiveness, Allāh returns to him with forgiveness; Allāh is forgiving and merciful. He accepts repentance and effaces the evil deeds. You must never cause a believer to lose hope in the favor and mercy of Allāh.'" (صحيح)[3]

4.

عَنْهُ عَنْ أَبِيهِ عَنِ ابْنِ أَبِي عُمَيْرٍ وَأَبُو عَلِيٍّ الأَشْعَرِيُّ عَنْ مُحَمَّدِ بْنِ عَبْدِ الْجَبَّارِ عَنْ صَفْوَانَ عَنْ أَبِي أَيُّوبَ عَنْ أَبِي بَصِيرٍ عَنْ أَبِي عَبْدِ اللهِ (عَلَيهِ السَّلام) قَالَ مَنْ عَمِلَ سَيِّئَةً أُجِّلَ فِيهَا سَبْعَ سَاعَاتٍ مِنَ النَّهَارِ فَإِنْ قَالَ أَسْتَغْفِرُ اللهَ الَّذِي لا إِلَهَ إِلا هُوَ الْحَيُّ الْقَيُّومُ ثَلاثَ مَرَّاتٍ لَمْ تُكْتَبْ عَلَيْهِ

It is narrated from him (narrator of the Hadīth above) from his father from b. abu 'Umayr and Abu 'Alī al-Ash'ari from Muḥammad b. 'Abd al-Jabbar from Safwan from abu Ayyub from abu Basir from abu 'Abd Allāh (عليه السلام) who has said the following: "If one commits a sin he is given seven hours respite during the day. If he says, 'I ask forgiveness from Allāh, besides Whom no one deserves to be worshipped.

---

[3] *Al-Kāfi, v2, ch191, h6*

Who is living and controls all things, - three times - no sin will be written against him.'" (صحيح)[4]

5.

مُحَمَّدُ بْنُ يَحْيَى عَنْ أَحْمَدَ بْنِ مُحَمَّدِ بْنِ عِيسَى عَنْ عَلِيِّ بْنِ الْحَكَمِ عَنْ فَضْلِ بْنِ عُثْمَانَ الْمُرَادِيِّ قَالَ سَمِعْتُ أَبَا عَبْدِ اللَّهِ (عَلَيهِ السَّلام) يَقُولُ قَالَ رَسُولُ اللَّهِ (صَلَّى اللَّهُ عَلَيْهِ وآلِه) أَرْبَعٌ مَنْ كُنَّ فِيهِ لَمْ يَهْلِكْ عَلَى اللَّهِ بَعْدَهُنَّ إِلا هَالِكٌ يَهُمُّ الْعَبْدُ بِالْحَسَنَةِ فَيَعْمَلُهَا فَإِنْ هُوَ لَمْ يَعْمَلْهَا كَتَبَ اللَّهُ لَهُ حَسَنَةً بِحُسْنِ نِيَّتِهِ وَإِنْ هُوَ عَمِلَهَا كَتَبَ اللَّهُ لَهُ عَشْراً وَيَهُمُّ بِالسَّيِّئَةِ أَنْ يَعْمَلَهَا فَإِنْ لَمْ يَعْمَلْهَا لَمْ يُكْتَبْ عَلَيْهِ شَيْءٌ وَإِنْ هُوَ عَمِلَهَا أُجِّلَ سَبْعَ سَاعَاتٍ وَقَالَ صَاحِبُ الْحَسَنَاتِ لِصَاحِبِ السَّيِّئَاتِ وَهُوَ صَاحِبُ الشِّمَالِ لا تَعْجَلْ عَسَى أَنْ يُتْبِعَهَا بِحَسَنَةٍ تَمْحُوهَا فَإِنَّ اللَّهَ عَزَّ وَجَلَّ يَقُولُ إِنَّ الْحَسَنَاتِ يُذْهِبْنَ السَّيِّئَاتِ أَوِ الإسْتِغْفَارِ فَإِنْ هُوَ قَالَ أَسْتَغْفِرُ اللَّهَ الَّذِي لا إِلَهَ إِلا هُوَ عَالِمَ الْغَيْبِ وَالشَّهَادَةِ الْعَزِيزَ الْحَكِيمَ الْغَفُورَ الرَّحِيمَ ذَا الْجَلالِ وَالإكْرَامِ وَأَتُوبُ إِلَيْهِ لَمْ يُكْتَبْ عَلَيْهِ شَيْءٌ وَإِنْ مَضَتْ سَبْعُ سَاعَاتٍ وَلَمْ يُتْبِعْهَا بِحَسَنَةٍ وَاسْتِغْفَارٍ قَالَ صَاحِبُ الْحَسَنَاتِ لِصَاحِبِ السَّيِّئَاتِ اكْتُبْ عَلَى الشَّقِيِّ الْمَحْرُومِ

Muhammad b. Yahya has narrated from Ahmad b. Muḥammad b. 'Isa from 'Alī b. al-Hakam from Fadl b. 'Uthman al-Muradi who has said the following: "I heard abu 'Abd Allāh (عليه السلام) saying, 'The Messenger of Allāh has said, 'If four things are found in a person Allāh will not allow his destruction to take place unless he is one of those doomed to destruction: (1) a servant (of Allāh) intends to perform a good deed and actually does it, (2) even if he does not do it Allāh still writes for him one good deed because of his good intention, but if he actually does perform it Allāh will write ten good deeds for him. (3) One may intend to commit an evil deed and if he does not do it nothing will be written against him, however, (4) if he does commit such act he will be given seven hours. The angel for the good deeds will say to the one for the evil deeds who is on the left side, 'Do not hurry, perhaps he may perform a good deed that will cancel the evil deed as Allāh, the Most Majestic, the Most Holy, says, 'The good deeds remove the bad deeds,' (11:115) if he may say, 'I ask forgiveness from

---

[4] *Al-Kāfi, v2, ch192, h2*

Allāh, besides whom no one deserves to be worshipped. He knows the unseen and the manifest, He is the most majestic, the most wise, the forgiving, the merciful, glorious and honorable and 1 turn in repentance to Him,' nothing will be written against him. If seven hours pass, and he performs no good deed or repentance the angel for the good deeds will say to the one for the evil deeds, 'Write it down against the wicked and deprived one that he is.'" (صحيح)[5]

6.

عِدَّةٌ مِنْ أَصْحَابِنَا عَنْ أَحْمَدَ بْنِ مُحَمَّدٍ عَنِ ابْنِ مَحْبُوبٍ عَنْ جَمِيلِ بْنِ صَالِحٍ عَنْ أَبِي عَبْدِ اللهِ (عَلَيْهِ السَّلام) فِي قَوْلِ اللهِ عَزَّ وَجَلَّ رَبَّنا آتِنا فِي الدُّنْيا حَسَنَةً وَفِي الْآخِرَةِ حَسَنَةً رِضْوَانُ اللهِ وَالْجَنَّةُ فِي الْآخِرَةِ وَالْمَعَاشُ وَحُسْنُ الْخُلُقِ فِي الدُّنْيَا

A number of our people have narrated from Ahmad b. Muḥammad from b. Mahbub from Jamil b. Salih who has said the following: "About the words of Allāh, most Majestic, most Glorious, 'O Lord, grant us good in this world and in the next world', abu 'Abd Allāh, (عليه السلام), has said, 'It is Allāh's happiness with one, paradise in the next life, good living and excellent moral manners in this world.'" (صحيح)[6]

7.

مُحَمَّدُ بْنُ يَحْيَى عَنْ أَحْمَدَ بْنِ مُحَمَّدِ بْنِ عِيسَى وَعَلِيُّ بْنُ إِبْرَاهِيمَ عَنْ أَبِيهِ جَمِيعاً عَنِ ابْنِ مَحْبُوبٍ عَنْ أَبِي مُحَمَّدٍ الْوَابِشِيِّ وَإِبْرَاهِيمَ بْنِ مِهْزَمٍ عَنْ إِسْحَاقَ بْنِ عَمَّارٍ قَالَ سَمِعْتُ أَبَا عَبْدِ اللهِ (عَلَيْهِ السَّلام) يَقُولُ إِنَّ رَسُولَ اللهِ (صَلَّى اللهُ عَلَيْهِ وَآلِهِ) صَلَّى بِالنَّاسِ الصُّبْحَ فَنَظَرَ إِلَى شَابٍّ فِي الْمَسْجِدِ وَهُوَ يُخْفِقُ وَيَهْوِي بِرَأْسِهِ مُصْفَرّاً لَوْنُهُ قَدْ نَحَفَ جِسْمُهُ وَغَارَتْ عَيْنَاهُ فِي رَأْسِهِ فَقَالَ لَهُ رَسُولُ اللهِ (صَلَّى اللهُ عَلَيْهِ وَآلِهِ) كَيْفَ أَصْبَحْتَ يَا فُلانُ قَالَ أَصْبَحْتُ يَا رَسُولَ اللهِ مُوقِناً فَعَجِبَ رَسُولُ اللهِ (صَلَّى اللهُ عَلَيْهِ وَآلِهِ) مِنْ قَوْلِهِ وَقَالَ إِنَّ لِكُلِّ

---

[5] Al-Kafi, v2, ch190, h4

[6] Al-Kafi, v5, ch3, h2

يَقِينٍ حَقِيقَةً فَمَا حَقِيقَةُ يَقِينِكَ فَقَالَ إِنَّ يَقِينِي يَا رَسُولَ اللهِ هُوَ الَّذِي أَحْزَنَنِي وَأَسْهَرَ لَيْلِي وَأَظْمَأَ هَوَاجِرِي فَعَزَفَتْ نَفْسِي عَنِ الدُّنْيَا وَمَا فِيهَا حَتَّى كَأَنِّي أَنْظُرُ إِلَى عَرْشِ رَبِّي وَقَدْ نُصِبَ لِلْحِسَابِ وَحُشِرَ الْخَلَائِقُ لِذَلِكَ وَأَنَا فِيهِمْ وَكَأَنِّي أَنْظُرُ إِلَى أَهْلِ الْجَنَّةِ يَتَنَعَّمُونَ فِي الْجَنَّةِ وَيَتَعَارَفُونَ وَعَلَى الْأَرَائِكِ مُتَّكِئُونَ وَكَأَنِّي أَنْظُرُ إِلَى أَهْلِ النَّارِ وَهُمْ فِيهَا مُعَذَّبُونَ مُصْطَرِخُونَ وَكَأَنِّي الْآنَ أَسْمَعُ زَفِيرَ النَّارِ يَدُورُ فِي مَسَامِعِي فَقَالَ رَسُولُ اللهِ (صَلَّى اللهُ عَلَيْهِ وآلِه) لأَصْحَابِهِ هَذَا عَبْدٌ نَوَّرَ اللهُ قَلْبَهُ بِالإِيمَانِ ثُمَّ قَالَ لَهُ الْزَمْ مَا أَنْتَ عَلَيْهِ فَقَالَ الشَّابُّ ادْعُ اللهَ لِي يَا رَسُولَ اللهِ أَنْ أُرْزَقَ الشَّهَادَةَ مَعَكَ فَدَعَا لَهُ رَسُولُ اللهِ (صَلَّى اللهُ عَلَيْهِ وآلِه) فَلَمْ يَلْبَثْ أَنْ خَرَجَ فِي بَعْضِ غَزَوَاتِ النَّبِيِّ (صَلَّى اللهُ عَلَيْهِ وآلِه) فَاسْتُشْهِدَ بَعْدَ تِسْعَةِ نَفَرٍ وَكَانَ هُوَ الْعَاشِرَ

Muhammad b. Yahya has narrated from Ahmad b. Muḥammad b. 'Isa and 'Alī b. Ibrahim has narrated from his father all from b. Mahbub from abu Muḥammad al-Wabishi and Ibrahim b. Mehzam from Ishaq b. 'Ammar who has said the following: "I heard abu 'Abd Allāh (عليه السلام) saying, 'Once the Messenger of Allāh after leading the morningprayer for the people looked at a young man in the Mosque whose head hung down. He looked pale and slim and his eyes sunk into his head. The Messenger of Allāh asked, 'O so and so, how is your morning?' He (the young man) replied, 'This morning, I, O Messenger of Allāh, am in a condition of certainty. The messenger of Allāh admired him for his words and he said, 'For everything there is an essence. What is the essence of your certainty?' The young man said, 'My certainty, O Messenger of Allāh, is that which has made me depressed. It has kept me awake all night and to endure thirst during the day. My soul is withdrawn from the world and the things in it, so much so, as if I am looking at the Throne of my Lord that is established to call everyone to Judgment, all creatures are resurrected and I am among them. It is as if I am looking at the people of paradise who enjoy therein being introduced to each other while leaning against raised couches. It is also as if I am looking at the people of hell wherein they suffer and cry for help. Right now, it is as if I hear the roaring of the fire. It is striking against my ears.' The Messenger of Allāh said to his companions, 'This is a servant of Allāh whose heart He has brightened up with belief.' He (the Messenger of Allāh) said to him (the young man), 'Keep up with what you are in (condition of your belief).' The young man said, 'Pray to Allāh for me, O Messenger of Allāh, to grant me martyrdom (while working hard in support of your cause) along with you.' The Messenger of Allāh prayed for him. Not very long thereafter he joined the prophet in an armed expedition and he was the tenth man to become a martyr.'" (موثق)[7]

8.

ابْنُ مَحْبُوبٍ عَنْ أَبِي أَيُّوبَ عَنْ عَبْدِ الْمُؤْمِنِ الْأَنْصَارِيِّ عَنْ أَبِي جَعْفَرٍ (عليه السلام) قَالَ إِنَّ اللَّهَ تَبَارَكَ وَ تَعَالَى أَعْطَى الْمُؤْمِنَ ثَلَاثَ خِصَالٍ الْعِزَّ فِي الدُّنْيَا وَ الْآخِرَةِ وَ الْفَلْجَ فِي الدُّنْيَا وَ الْآخِرَةِ وَ الْمَهَابَةَ فِي صُدُورِ الظَّالِمِينَ

b. Mahboub, from Abu Ayyub, from Abdul Momin Al-Ansary, who has narrated: Abu Ja'far (عليه السلام) having said that: 'Allāh (تبارك و طائلة) has Granted three characteristics to the Believer – the honour in the world and the Hereafter, and the success in the world and the Hereafter, and the prestige in front of the unjust ones'. (حسن)[8]

9.

أبي رحمه الله قال حدثنا سعد بن عبد الله عن أحمد بن محمد بن عيسى عن علي بن الحكم عن عبد الله بن سنان قال سألت أبا عبد الله جعفر بن محمد الصادق ع فقلت الملائكة أفضل أم بنو آدم فقال قال أمير المؤمنين علي بن أبي طالب ع إن الله عز و جل ركب في الملائكة عقلا بلا شهوة و ركب في البهائم شهوة بلا عقل و ركب في بني آدم كليهما فمن غلب عقله شهوته فهو خير من الملائكة و من غلبت شهوته عقله فهو شر من البهائم

From `Abd Allāh b. Sinān said, I asked Abā `Abd Allāh, Ja`far b. Muḥammad al-Sādiq (عليه السلام), I (narrator) said: "Are the angels better (*afDal*) or the children of Adam? So he (عليه السلام)said that Amīr al-Mu'minīn, `Alī b. Abī al-Tālib said: "Verily, Allāh (عَزَّ وَ جَلَّ)has composed in angels *'aql* (intellect) and no desire, and he composed

[7] *Al-Kāfi, v2, ch27, h2*

[8] *Al-Kāfi, v8, h310*

in beasts desire and no intellect, and he composed in the children of Adam both (*'aql* and desire). So whoever (lets) *'aql* overcome his desires, he will be than the angels, and whoever (lets) his desires overcome his *'aql*, he is will be worse than the beasts" (صحيح)[9]

10.

حمدويه، عن اليقطيني، عن يونس قال: العبد الصالح عليه السلام: يا يونس ارفق بهم، فإن كلامك يدق عليهم قال: قلت: إنهم يقولون لي: زنديق، قال لي: ما يضرك أن تكون في يديك لؤلؤة فيقول لك الناس: هي حصاة، وما كان ينفعك إذا كان في يدك حصاة فيقول الناس: هي لؤلؤة

Hamduwayh from al-Yaqtini from Yunus who said: the Righteous Servant عليه السلام said: O Yunus – be more lenient towards them for your words are hard-hitting on them, I said: but they consider me a Zindiq, he said to me: what will it affect you if you have in your hands a pearl but the people say to you: it is a stone, and what will it benefit you if you have in your hand a stone but the people say: it is a pearl! (معتبر)[10]

11.

قال: أخبرني أبو الحسين محمد بن المظفر البزاز قال: حدثنا أبو القاسم عبد الملك بن علي الدهان قال: حدثنا أبو الحسن علي بن الحسن، عن الحسن بن بشير، عن أسعد بن سعيد، عن جابر قال: سمع أمير المؤمنين علي بن أبي طالب عليه السلام رجلا يشتم قنبرا وقد رام قنبر أن يرد عليه، فناداه أمير المؤمنين علي عليه السلام: مهلا يا قنبر، دع شاتمك مهانا ترض الرحمن، وتسخط الشيطان، وتعاقب عدوك. فوالذي فلق الحبة وبرأ النسمة ما أرضى المؤمن ربه بمثل الحلم، ولا أسخط الشيطان بمثل الصمت، ولا عوقب الأحمق بمثل السكوت عنه

---

[9] *Ilal al-Sharai, v1, ch6, h1*

[10] *Rijal al-Kashshi, h927*

He said: Abdul Husayn Muḥammad b.al-Muzaffar al-Bazzaz, reported to me from Abul Qasim Abdul Malik b. 'Ali al-Dahhan, who reported from Abul Hasan 'Ali b. al-Hasan, from al-Hasan b. Bashir, from As'ad b. Saeed from Jabir who said: Once, Amirul Mu'mineen 'Ali b. Abi Talib, (عليه السلام) heard someone abusing Qambar, and Qambar was about to answer back. So, Amirul Mu'mineen 'Ali, (عليه السلام), called out to Qambar: "Take it easy O, Qambar! Leave the one who abuses you to be ashamed of himself, so that Allāh is pleased and Satan is resentful and your adversary is punished. For, By He Who, split the grain and created the breathing man, nothing from a believer pleases His Sustainer better than forbearance; and nothing makes Satan more indignant than the silence; and the fool is best punished when totally ignored."[11]

12.

أَحْمَدُ بْنُ عَبْدِ اللهِ عَنْ جَدِّهِ عَنْ مُحَمَّدِ بْنِ عَلِيٍّ عَنْ مُحَمَّدِ بْنِ الْفُضَيْلِ عَنْ عَبْدِ الرَّحْمَنِ بْنِ زَيْدٍ عَنْ أَبِي عَبْدِ اللهِ (عَلَيْهِ السَّلاَمِ) قَالَ قَالَ رَسُولُ اللهِ (صلَّى اللهُ عَلَيْهِ وَآلِهِ) أَرْضُ الْقِيَامَةِ نَارٌ مَا خَلاَ ظِلَّ الْمُؤْمِنِ فَإِنَّ صَدَقَتَهُ تُظِلُّهُ

Ahmad b. 'Abd Allāh has narrated from his grandfather from Muḥammad b. 'Alī from Muḥammad b. al-Fudayl from 'Abd al- Rahman b. Zayd who has said the following: "Abu 'Abd Allāh, (عليه السلام), has said that the Messenger of Allāh, (صلى الله عليه وآله وسلم), has said, 'The land on the Day of Judgment is all fire except the shadow of a believing person. His charity provides him shadow.'" (مجهول)[12]

13.

[11] *Al-Amālī (Mufid), ch2, h1*

[12] *Al-Kāfi, v4, ch1, h6*

عَلِيُّ بْنُ إِبْرَاهِيمَ عَنْ أَبِيهِ عَنِ ابْنِ أَبِي عُمَيْرٍ عَنْ عَبْدِ اللهِ بْنِ سِنَانٍ عَنْ أَبِي عَبْدِ اللهِ (عَلَيْهِ السَّلاَمُ) قَالَ سَمِعْتُهُ يَقُولُ يُسْتَحَبُّ لِلْمَرِيضِ أَنْ يُعْطِيَ السَّائِلَ بِيَدِهِ وَيَأْمُرَ السَّائِلَ أَنْ يَدْعُوَ لَهُ

Ali b. Ibrahim has narrated from his father from b. abu 'Umayr from 'Abd Allāh b. Sinan who has said the following: "Abu 'Abd Allāh, (عليه السلام), has said that it is preferable for a person suffering from illness to give charity with his own hand to one who asks for charity, then ask him to pray for him." (حسن)[13]

14.

مُحَمَّدُ بْنُ يَحْيَى عَنْ أَحْمَدَ بْنِ مُحَمَّدِ بْنِ عِيسَى عَنِ ابْنِ أَبِي عُمَيْرٍ عَنْ جَمِيلِ بْنِ دَرَّاجٍ قَالَ سَأَلْتُ أَبَا عَبْدِ اللهِ (عَلَيهِ السَّلام) عَنِ الإِيمَانِ فَقَالَ شَهَادَةُ أَنْ لا إِلَهَ إِلا اللهُ وَأَنَّ مُحَمَّداً رَسُولُ اللهِ قَالَ قُلْتُ أَ لَيْسَ هَذَا عَمَلٌ قَالَ بَلَى قُلْتُ فَالْعَمَلُ مِنَ الإِيمَانِ قَالَ لا يَثْبُتُ لَهُ الإِيمَانُ إِلا بِالْعَمَلِ وَالْعَمَلُ مِنْهُ

Muhammad b. Yahya has narrated from Ahmad b. Muḥammad b. 'Isa from b. abu 'Umayr from Jamil b. Darraj who has said the following: "I asked abu 'Abd Allāh (عليه السلام) about belief. He said, 'It is to testify that no one deserves to be worshipped except Allāh and that Muḥammad (عليه السلام) is the Messenger of Allāh.' I asked, 'Is it not a deed?' He said, 'Yes, it is a deed.' 1 then asked, 'Is deed of belief?' He said, 'One's belief does not take any root without deed and deed is from belief.'" (صحيح)[14]

15.

عَلِيُّ بْنُ إِبْرَاهِيمَ عَنْ أَبِيهِ وَمُحَمَّدُ بْنُ إِسْمَاعِيلَ عَنِ الْفَضْلِ بْنِ شَاذَانَ جَمِيعاً عَنِ ابْنِ أَبِي عُمَيْرٍ عَنْ حَفْصِ بْنِ الْبَخْتَرِيِّ عَنْ أَبِي عَبْدِ اللهِ (عَلَيهِ السَّلام) قَالَ لا تُكَرِّهُوا إِلَى أَنْفُسِكُمُ الْعِبَادَةَ

[13] *Al-Kāfi, v4, ch1, h9*

[14] *Al-Kāfi, v2, ch18, h6*

Ali b. Ibrahim has narrated from his father and Muḥammad b. Isma'il from Fadl b. Shadhan all from b. abu 'Umayr from Hafs b. al-Bakhtari from abu 'Abd Allāh (عليه السلام) who has said the following: "Abu 'Abd Allāh (عليه السلام) has said, 'Do not cause your souls to dislike worship.' (حسن كالصحيح)[15]

16.

مُحَمَّدُ بْنُ يَحْيَى عَنْ أَحْمَدَ بْنِ مُحَمَّدِ بْنِ عِيسَى عَنْ مُحَمَّدِ بْنِ إِسْمَاعِيلَ عَنْ حَنَانِ بْنِ سَدِيرٍ قَالَ سَمِعْتُ أَبَا عَبْدِ اللهِ (عَلَيهِ السَّلام) يَقُولُ إِنَّ اللهَ عَزَّ وَجَلَّ إِذَا أَحَبَّ عَبْداً فَعَمِلَ عَمَلاً قَلِيلاً جَزَاهُ بِالْقَلِيلِ الْكَثِيرَ وَلَمْ يَتَعَاظَمْهُ أَنْ يَجْزِيَ بِالْقَلِيلِ الْكَثِيرَ لَ

Muhammad b. Yahya has narrated from Ahmad b. Muḥammad b. 'Isa from Muḥammad b. Isma'il from Hanan b. Sadir who has said the following: "I heard abu 'Abd Allāh (عليه السلام) saying, 'When Allāh, the Most Majestic, the Most Holy, loves any (of His) servants who have done a little good deed, He grants him a great reward for his little deeds. He does not consider granting a great reward, for a little deed, a difficult thing at all.'" (موثق)[16]

17.

مُحَمَّدُ بْنُ يَحْيَى عَنْ أَحْمَدَ بْنِ مُحَمَّدِ بْنِ عِيسَى عَنْ مُعَمَّرِ بْنِ خَلادٍ عَنْ أَبِي الْحَسَنِ (عَلَيهِ السَّلام) أَنَّهُ ذَكَرَ رَجُلاً فَقَالَ إِنَّهُ يُحِبُّ الرِّئَاسَةَ فَقَالَ مَا ذِئْبَانِ ضَارِيَانِ فِي غَنَمٍ قَدْ تَفَرَّقَ رِعَاؤُهَا بِأَضَرَّ فِي دِينِ الْمُسْلِمِ مِنَ الرِّئَاسَةِ

Muhammad b. Yahya has narrated from Ahmad b. Muḥammad b. 'Isa from Mu'ammar b. Khallad from abu al-Hassan (عليه السلام) who has said the following: "It was mentioned before the Imam that a certain man loves to have leadership. The

---

[15] *Al-Kāfi, v2, ch45, h2*

[16] *Al-Kāfi, v2, ch45, h3*

Imam said, 'Two fierce wolves in a flock of sheep, whose shepherd is far away, are not more harmful to the flock than seeking leadership to a Muslim's religion is.'" (صحيح)[17]

18.

عَلِيُّ بْنُ إِبْرَاهِيمَ عَنْ مُحَمَّدِ بْنِ عِيسَى عَنْ يُونُسَ عَنِ الْعَلَاءِ عَنْ مُحَمَّدِ بْنِ مُسْلِمٍ قَالَ سَمِعْتُ أَبَا عَبْدِ اللَّه (عَلَيهِ السَّلام) يَقُولُ أَ تَرَى لا أَعْرِفُ خِيَارَكُمْ مِنْ شِرَارِكُمْ بَلَى وَاللَّه وَإِنَّ شِرَارَكُمْ مَنْ أَحَبَّ أَنْ يُوطَأَ عَقِبُهُ إِنَّهُ لا بُدَّ مِنْ كَذَّابٍ أَوْ عَاجِزِ الرَّأْيِ

Ali b. Ibrahim has narrated from Muḥammad b. 'Isa from Yunus from al-'Ala' from Muḥammad b. Muslim who has said the following: "I heard abu 'Abd Allāh (عليه السلام) asking, 'Do you think I do not distinguish the bad from good among you? Yes, by Allāh, the bad ones among you are those who love people walking behind him. Such a person is inevitably a liar or a helpless one (due to his ignorance) in his opinion.'" (صحيح)[18]

19.

عَلِيُّ بْنُ إِبْرَاهِيمَ عَنْ أَبِيهِ عَنِ ابْنِ أَبِي عُمَيْرٍ عَنْ هِشَامِ بْنِ سَالِمٍ عَنِ ابْنِ أَبِي يَعْفُورٍ عَنْ أَبِي عَبْدِ اللَّه (عَلَيهِ السَّلام) قَالَ إِنَّ مِنْ أَعْظَمِ النَّاسِ حَسْرَةً يَوْمَ الْقِيَامَةِ مَنْ وَصَفَ عَدْلاً ثُمَّ خَالَفَهُ إِلَى غَيْرِهِ

Ali b. Ibrahim has narrated from his father from b. abu 'Umayr from Hisham b. Salim from b. abu Ya'fur from abu 'Abd Allāh (عليه السلام) who has said the following: "Of the

[17] *Al-Kāfi, v2, ch117, h1*

[18] *Al-Kāfi, v2, ch117, h8*

people who, on the Day of Judgment, will regret the most is one who preaches justice but himself does not yield to justice." (حسن كالصحيح)[19]

20.

عَلِيُّ بْنُ إِبْرَاهِيمَ عَنْ صَالِحِ بْنِ السِّنْدِيِّ عَنْ جَعْفَرِ بْنِ بَشِيرٍ عَنْ عَمَّارِ بْنِ مَرْوَانَ قَالَ قَالَ أَبُو عَبْدِ اللهِ (عَلَيهِ السَّلام) لا تُمَارِيَنَّ حَلِيماً وَلا سَفِيهاً فَإِنَّ الْحَلِيمَ يَقْلِيكَ وَالسَّفِيهَ يُؤْذِيكَ

Ali b. Ibrahim has narrated from Salih b. al-Sindy from Ja'far b. Bashir from 'Ammar b. Marwan who has said the following: "Abu 'Abd Allāh (عليه السلام) has said, 'Do not engage in a disputation against either a forbearing or a thoughtless person; a forbearing person turns into your foe and a thoughtless person will hurt you.'" (مجهول)[20]

21.

مُحَمَّدُ بْنُ يَحْيَى عَنْ أَحْمَدَ بْنِ مُحَمَّدِ بْنِ عِيسَى عَنِ ابْنِ مَحْبُوبٍ عَنْ عَنْبَسَةَ الْعَابِدِ عَنْ أَبِي عَبْدِ اللهِ (عَلَيهِ السَّلام) قَالَ إِيَّاكُمْ وَالْخُصُومَةَ فَإِنَّهَا تَشْغَلُ الْقَلْبَ وَتُورِثُ النِّفَاقَ وَتَكْسِبُ الضَّغَائِنَ

Muhammad b. Yahya has narrated from Ahmad b. Muḥammad b. 'Isa from b. Mahbub from 'Anbasah al-'Abid from abu 'Abd Allāh (عليه السلام) who has said the following: "Beware of quarreling; it occupies the heart, causes hypocrisy and brings in hatred." (صحيح)[21]

22.

---

[19] *Al-Kāfi, v2, ch119, h3*

[20] *Al-Kafi, v2, ch120, h4*

[21] *Al-Kāfi, v2, ch120, h8*

حَدَّثَنِي مُحَمَّدُ بْنُ الْحَسَنِ عَنْ مُحَمَّدِ بْنِ الْحَسَنِ الصَّفَّارِ قَالَ حَدَّثَنِي أَحْمَدُ بْنُ إِسْحَاقَ بْنِ سَعِيدٍ عَنْ بَكْرِ بْنِ مُحَمَّدٍ الْأَزْدِيِّ عَنْ أَبِي عَبْدِ اللَّهِ ع قَالَ: تَجْلِسُونَ وَ تَتَحَدَّثُونَ قَالَ قُلْتُ نَعَمْ قَالَ إِنَّ تِلْكَ الْمَجَالِسَ أُحِبُّهَا فَأَحْيُوا أَمْرَنَا إِنَّهُ مَنْ ذَكَرَنَا وَ ذَكَرْنَا عِنْدَهُ فَخَرَجَ مِنْ عَيْنِهِ مِثْلُ جَنَاحِ الذُّبَابِهِ غَفَرَ اللَّهُ ذُنُوبَهُ وَ لَوْ كَانَتْ أَكْثَرَ مِنْ زَبَدِ الْبَحْرِ

It was narrated to me by Muḥammad b. al-Hassan from Muḥammad b. al-Hassan al-Saffar who said it was narrated to me by Ahmad b. Ishaq b. Sa'eed from Bakr b. Muḥammad al-Azdi from Abi Abdillah (عليه السلام) who said: I like those gatherings in which our commands are enlivened. One who is discussing about us or if any of the people hearing him shed a tear equal to the size of the wing of a fly Allāh will forgive his sins even if those sins are more than an ocean." (صحيح)[22]

23.

عَلِيُّ بْنُ إِبْرَاهِيمَ عَنْ أَبِيهِ وَ مُحَمَّدُ بْنُ إِسْمَاعِيلَ عَنِ الْفَضْلِ بْنِ شَاذَانَ جَمِيعاً عَنِ ابْنِ أَبِي عُمَيْرٍ عَنْ هِشَامِ بْنِ الْحَكَمِ عَنْ أَبِي عَبْدِ اللَّهِ (عليه السلام) قَالَ مِنَ السَّعَادَةِ سَعَةُ الْمَنْزِلِ

Ali b. Ibrahim has narrated from his father from and Muḥammad b. 'Isma'il has narrated from al-Fadl b. Shadhan from all from b. abu 'Umayr from Hisham b. al-Hakam who has said the following: "Abu 'Abd Allāh, (عليه السلام), has said, 'Spaciousness of the house is of one's good fortune.'" (حسن كالصحيح)[23]

24.

[22] *Thawab al-A'māl wa 'iqāb al-A'māl, ch426, h1*

[23] *al-Kāfi, v6, ch64, h1*

أَبُو عَلِيٍّ الْأَشْعَرِيُّ عَنْ مُحَمَّدِ بْنِ عَبْدِ الْجَبَّارِ عَنِ ابْنِ فَضَّالٍ عَنْ عَلِيِّ بْنِ عُقْبَةَ عَنْ أَبِيهِ عَنْ مُيَسِّرٍ قَالَ ذُكِرَ الْغَضَبُ عِنْدَ أَبِي جَعْفَرٍ (عَلَيْهِ السَّلام) فَقَالَ إِنَّ الرَّجُلَ لَيَغْضَبُ فَمَا يَرْضَى حَتَّى يَدْخُلَ النَّارَ فَأَيُّمَا رَجُلٍ غَضِبَ عَلَى قَوْمٍ وَهُوَ قَائِمٌ فَلْيَجْلِسْ مِنْ فَوْرِهِ ذَلِكَ فَإِنَّهُ سَيَذْهَبُ عَنْهُ رِجْزُ الشَّيْطَانِ وَأَيُّمَا رَجُلٍ غَضِبَ عَلَى ذِي رَحِمٍ فَلْيَدْنُ مِنْهُ فَلْيَمَسَّهُ فَإِنَّ الرَّحِمَ إِذَا مُسَّتْ سَكَنَتْ

Abu ʿAlī al-Ashʿari has narrated from Muḥammad b. ʿAbd al-Jabbar from b. Faddal from ʿAlī b. ʿUqbah from his father from Muyassir who has said the following: "Once anger was mentioned before abu Jaʿ far (عليه السلام) and he said, 'Once a man is angered (unless something is done to control it) he will never become happy until he enters the fire. Therefore, whoever becomes angry with people if he is standing must sit down immediately. The filth of Satan goes away from him. Whenever one becomes angry with a relative he should reach out and touch him; when kinship is touched, it calms down.'" (حسن)[24]

25.

عَلِيُّ بْنُ إِبْرَاهِيمَ عَنْ مُحَمَّدِ بْنِ عِيسَى عَنْ يُونُسَ عَنْ دَاوُدَ بْنِ فَرْقَدٍ قَالَ قَالَ أَبُو عَبْدِ الله (عَلَيْهِ السَّلام) الْغَضَبُ مِفْتَاحُ كُلِّ شَرٍّ

Ali b. Ibrahim has narrated from Muḥammad b. ʿIsa from Yunus from Dawud b. Farqad who has said the following: "Abu ʿAbd Allāh (عليه السلام) has said, 'Anger is the key to all evil.'" (صحيح)[25]

26.

---

[24] al-Kāfī, v2, ch121, h2

[25] al-Kāfī, v2, ch121, h3

مُحَمَّدُ بْنُ يَحْيَى عَنْ أَحْمَدَ بْنِ مُحَمَّدِ بْنِ عِيسَى عَنِ ابْنِ مَحْبُوبٍ عَنْ إِسْحَاقَ بْنِ عَمَّارٍ قَالَ سَمِعْتُ أَبَا عَبْدِ الله
(عَلَيْهِ السَّلام) يَقُولُ إِنَّ فِي التَّوْرَاةِ مَكْتُوباً يَا ابْنَ آدَمَ اذْكُرْنِي حِينَ تَغْضَبُ أَذْكُرْكَ عِنْدَ غَضَبِي فَلَا أَمْحَقُكَ
فِيمَنْ أَمْحَقُ وَإِذَا ظُلِمْتَ بِمَظْلِمَةٍ فَارْضَ بِانْتِصَارِي لَكَ فَإِنَّ انْتِصَارِي لَكَ خَيْرٌ مِنِ انْتِصَارِكَ لِنَفْسِكَ

Muhammad b. Yahya has narrated from Ahmad b. Muḥammad b. 'Isa from b. Mahbub from Ishaq b. ' Ammar who has said the following: "I heard abu 'Abd Allāh (عليه السلام) saying, 'It is written in the Torah: "Remember Me when you are angry so I remember you when I am angry and will not efface you along with those whom I will blot out. When injustice is done to you, accept My support; My support for you is better than your support for yourself.'" (موثق)[26]

27.

مُحَمَّدُ بْنُ يَحْيَى عَنْ أَحْمَدَ بْنِ مُحَمَّدٍ عَنِ ابْنِ مَحْبُوبٍ عَنِ الْعَلَاءِ بْنِ رَزِينٍ عَنْ مُحَمَّدِ بْنِ مُسْلِمٍ قَالَ قَالَ أَبُو
جَعْفَرٍ (عَلَيْهِ السَّلام) إِنَّ الرَّجُلَ لَيَأْتِي بِأَيِّ بَادِرَةٍ فَيَكْفُرُ وَإِنَّ الْحَسَدَ لَيَأْكُلُ الإِيمَانَ كَمَا تَأْكُلُ النَّارُ الْحَطَبَ

Muhammad b. Yahya has narrated from Ahmad b. Muḥammad from b. Mahbub from al-'Ala' b. Razin from Muḥammad b. Muslim who has said the following: "Abu Ja'far (عليه السلام) has said, 'The man may hastily commit any evil deed and then (gradually) turn in disbelief, however, envy consumes belief (immediately) just as fire consumes firewood." (صحيح)[27]

28.

عَلِيُّ بْنُ إِبْرَاهِيمَ عَنْ مُحَمَّدِ بْنِ عِيسَى عَنْ يُونُسَ عَنْ مُعَاوِيَةَ بْنِ وَهْبٍ قَالَ قَالَ أَبُو عَبْدِ الله (عَلَيْهِ السَّلام)
آفَةُ الدِّينِ الْحَسَدُ وَالْعُجْبُ وَالْفَخْرُ

---

[26] al-Kāfi, v2, ch121, h10
[27] al-Kāfi, v2, ch122, h1

Ali b. Ibrahim has narrated from Muḥammad b. 'Isa from Yunus from Mu'awiyah b. Wahab who has said the following: "Abu 'Abd Allāh (عليه السلام) has said, 'Among the tragedies for religion is envy, feeling self- important and proud.'" (صحيح)[28]

29.

عِدَّةٌ مِنْ أَصْحَابِنَا عَنْ أَحْمَدَ بْنِ أَبِي عَبْدِ اللهِ عَنْ عُثْمَانَ بْنِ عِيسَى عَنِ الْعَلَاءِ بْنِ الْفُضَيْلِ عَنْ أَبِي عَبْدِ اللهِ (عَلَيهِ السَّلام) قَالَ قَالَ أَبُو جَعْفَرٍ (عَلَيهِ السَّلام) الْعِزُّ رِدَاءُ اللهِ وَالْكِبْرُ إِزَارُهُ فَمَنْ تَنَاوَلَ شَيْئاً مِنْهُ أَكَبَّهُ اللهُ فِي جَهَنَّمَ

A number of our people have narrated from Ahmad b. abu 'Abd Allāh from 'Uthman b. 'Isa from al-'Ala' b. al-Fudayl from abu 'Abd Allāh (عليه السلام) who has said the following: "Abu Ja'far (عليه السلام) has said, 'Majesty is the gown of Allāh and pride is His loin clothe, therefore, whoever holds to any of these, Allāh will throw him in hell.'" (موثق)[29]

30.

عَلِيُّ بْنُ إِبْرَاهِيمَ عَنْ مُحَمَّدِ بْنِ عِيسَى عَنْ يُونُسَ عَنْ أَبِي أَيُّوبَ عَنْ مُحَمَّدِ بْنِ مُسْلِمٍ عَنْ أَحَدِهِمَا (عَلَيهِمَا السَّلام) قَالَ لَا يَدْخُلُ الْجَنَّةَ مَنْ كَانَ فِي قَلْبِهِ مِثْقَالُ حَبَّةٍ مِنْ خَرْدَلٍ مِنَ الْكِبْرِ قَالَ فَاسْتَرْجَعْتُ فَقَالَ مَا لَكَ تَسْتَرْجِعُ قُلْتُ لِمَا سَمِعْتُ مِنْكَ فَقَالَ لَيْسَ حَيْثُ تَذْهَبُ إِنَّمَا أَعْنِي الْجُحُودَ إِنَّمَا هُوَ الْجُحُودُ

Ali b. Ibrahim has narrated from Muḥammad b. 'Isa from Yunus from abu Ayyub from Muḥammad b. Muslim from one of them (two Imam) who has said the following: "Whoever has an amount of arrogance in his heart of the size of a mustard

---

[28] *al-Kafi, v2, ch122, h5*

[29] *al-Kāfi, v2, ch124, h3*

seed, he will not be able to enter paradise." I then expressed astonishment saying, 'To Allāh we belong and to Him we return!' The Imam asked, 'What has made you astonish?' I said, 'I have not heard such Hadīth from you.' The Imam said, 'It is not the way you have thought. I meant thereby denial and rejection; it (arrogance) is rejection.'" (صحيح)[30]

31.

أَبُو عَلِيٍّ الْأَشْعَرِيُّ عَنْ مُحَمَّدِ بْنِ عَبْدِ الْجَبَّارِ عَنِ ابْنِ فَضَّالٍ عَنْ عَلِيِّ بْنِ عُقْبَةَ عَنْ أَيُّوبَ بْنِ الْحُرِّ عَنْ عَبْدِ الْأَعْلَى عَنْ أَبِي عَبْدِ اللَّهِ (عَلَيهِ السَّلَام) قَالَ الْكِبْرُ أَنْ تَغْمِصَ النَّاسَ وَتَسْفَهَ الْحَقَّ

Abu 'Alī al-Ash'ari has narrated from Muḥammad b. 'Abd al-Jabbar from b. Faddal from 'Alī b. 'Uqbah from Ayyub b. al-Hurr from 'Abd al-'Ala' from abu 'Abd Allāh (عليه السلام) who has said the following: "Arrogance is when one belittles the people and calls the truth foolishness." (مجهول كالحسن)[31]

32.

عَلِيُّ بْنُ إِبْرَاهِيمَ عَنْ أَبِيهِ عَنِ ابْنِ أَبِي عُمَيْرٍ عَنْ بَعْضِ أَصْحَابِهِ عَنْ أَبِي عَبْدِ اللَّهِ (عَلَيهِ السَّلَام) قَالَ مَا مِنْ عَبْدٍ إِلَّا وَفِي رَأْسِهِ حَكَمَةٌ وَمَلَكٌ يُمْسِكُهَا فَإِذَا تَكَبَّرَ قَالَ لَهُ اتَّضِعْ وَضَعَكَ اللَّهُ فَلَا يَزَالُ أَعْظَمَ النَّاسِ فِي نَفْسِهِ وَأَصْغَرَ النَّاسِ فِي أَعْيُنِ النَّاسِ وَإِذَا تَوَاضَعَ رَفَعَهُ اللَّهُ عَزَّ وَجَلَّ ثُمَّ قَالَ لَهُ انْتَعِشْ نَعَشَكَ اللَّهُ فَلَا يَزَالُ أَصْغَرَ النَّاسِ فِي نَفْسِهِ وَأَرْفَعَ النَّاسِ فِي أَعْيُنِ النَّاسِ

Ali b. Ibrahim has narrated from his father from b. abu 'Umayr from certain individuals of his people from abu 'Abd Allāh (عليه السلام) who has said the following: "Every servant (of Allāh) has in his head a certain degree of wisdom being held

---

[30] *al-Kāfi, v2, ch124, h7*

[31] *al-Kāfi, v2, ch124, h8*

therein by an angel. When he expresses arrogance the angel says, 'Be humble, may Allāh bring you low.' Thereafter he thinks himself to be the greatest of people but in the eyes of the people he remains the lowest of all. When he behaves humbly, Allāh, the Most Majestic, the Most Holy, lifts him up. The angel then says, 'Be lofty, may Allāh grant you dignity.' He thereafter remains the lowest of all people before his own soul and the most dignified in the eyes of people.'" (حسن كالصحيح)[32]

33.

عَلِيُّ بْنُ إِبْرَاهِيمَ عَنْ أَبِيهِ عَنِ ابْنِ أَبِي عُمَيْرٍ عَنْ عَبْدِ الرَّحْمَنِ بْنِ الْحَجَّاجِ عَنْ أَبِي عَبْدِ اللهِ (عَلَيهِ السَّلام) قَالَ إِنَّ الرَّجُلَ لَيُذْنِبُ الذَّنْبَ فَيَنْدَمُ عَلَيْهِ وَيَعْمَلُ الْعَمَلَ فَيَسُرُّهُ ذَلِكَ فَيَتَرَاخَى عَنْ حَالِهِ تِلْكَ فَلأَنْ يَكُونَ عَلَى حَالِهِ تِلْكَ خَيْرٌ لَهُ مِمَّا دَخَلَ فِيهِ

Ali b. Ibrahim has narrated from his father from b. abu 'Umayr from 'Abd al-Rahman b. al-Hajjaj from abu 'Abd Allāh (عليه السلام) who has said the following: "A man sins and then feels regretful. He then does a good deed that gives him happiness (feeling of self-importance). He then weakens. His being in a condition (regretful) is better than what he finds himself in (after a good deed with feeling of self-importance)." (حسن كالصحيح)[33]

34.

عَلِيُّ بْنُ إِبْرَاهِيمَ عَنْ مُحَمَّدِ بْنِ عِيسَى عَنْ يُونُسَ عَنْ عَبْدِ الرَّحْمَنِ بْنِ الْحَجَّاجِ قَالَ قُلْتُ لأَبِي عَبْدِ اللهِ (عَلَيهِ السَّلام) الرَّجُلُ يَعْمَلُ الْعَمَلَ وَهُوَ خَائِفٌ مُشْفِقٌ ثُمَّ يَعْمَلُ شَيْئاً مِنَ الْبِرِّ فَيَدْخُلُهُ شِبْهُ الْعُجْبِ بِهِ فَقَالَ هُوَ فِي حَالِهِ الأُولَى وَهُوَ خَائِفٌ أَحْسَنُ حَالاً مِنْهُ فِي حَالِ عُجْبِهِ

---

[32] *al-Kāfi, v2, ch124, h16*

[33] *al-Kāfi, v2, ch125, h4*

Ali b. Ibrahim has narrated from Muḥammad b. 'Isa from Yunus from 'Abd al-Rahman b. al-Hajjaj who has said the following: "Once I asked abu 'Abd Allāh (عليه السلام) 'A man performs a deed and he is fearful and worried. Then he performs a good deed that gives him a feeling of self- importance.' The Imam said, 'His being in a fearful condition is better than his having a feeling of self-importance.'" (كالصحيح)[34]

35.

عَنْهُ عَنْ أَبِيهِ عَنْ عُثْمَانَ بْنِ عِيسَى عَنْ أَبِي أَيُّوبَ عَنْ مُحَمَّدِ بْنِ مُسْلِمٍ عَنْ أَبِي جَعْفَرٍ (عَلَيهِ السَّلام) قَالَ مَا ذِئْبَانِ ضَارِيَانِ فِي غَنَمٍ لَيْسَ لَهَا رَاعٍ هَذَا فِي أَوَّلِهَا وَهَذَا فِي آخِرِهَا بِأَسْرَعَ فِيهَا مِنْ حُبِّ الْمَالِ وَالشَّرَفِ فِي دِينِ الْمُؤْمِنِ

It is narrated from him (narrator of the Hadīth above) from his father from 'Uthman b. 'Isa from abu Ayyub from Muḥammad b. Muslim from abu Ja'far (عليه السلام) who has said the following: "No two fierce wolves in a flock of sheep without a shepherd, one wolf on either side is as quick (to destroy them) as the love of property and honor (popularity) is to destroy the religion of a believer." (حسن موثق كالصحيح)[35]

36.

مُحَمَّدُ بْنُ يَحْيَى عَنْ أَحْمَدَ بْنِ مُحَمَّدِ بْنِ عِيسَى عَنْ مُحَمَّدِ بْنِ يَحْيَى الْخَزَّازِ عَنْ غِيَاثِ بْنِ إِبْرَاهِيمَ عَنْ أَبِي عَبْدِ اللهِ (عَلَيهِ السَّلام) قَالَ إِنَّ الشَّيْطَانَ يُدِيرُ ابْنَ آدَمَ فِي كُلِّ شَيْءٍ فَإِذَا أَعْيَاهُ جَثَمَ لَهُ عِنْدَ الْمَالِ فَأَخَذَ بِرَقَبَتِهِ.

Muhammad b. Yahya has narrated from Ahmad b. Muḥammad b. 'Isa from Muḥammad b. Yahya al-Khazzaz from Ghiyath b. Ibrahim from abu 'Abd Allāh (عليه السلام) who has said the following: "Satan circles around the children of Adam in every

[34] *al-Kāfi, v2, ch125, h7*

[35] *al-Kāfi, v2, ch126, h3*

(evil) matter (to make him sin), when he is frustrated (man did not sin) he ambushes him through his (love of) property and holds him (man) through such love by his neck." (موثق)[36]

37.

عَنْهُ عَنْ أَحْمَدَ بْنِ مُحَمَّدٍ عَنْ عَلِيِّ بْنِ النُّعْمَانِ عَنْ أَبِي أُسَامَةَ زَيْدٍ عَنْ أَبِي عَبْدِ اللهِ (عَلَيهِ السَّلام) قَالَ قَالَ رَسُولُ اللهِ (صَلَّى اللهُ عَلَيْهِ وآلِه) مَنْ لَمْ يَتَعَزَّ بِعَزَاءِ اللهِ تَقَطَّعَتْ نَفْسُهُ حَسَرَاتٍ عَلَى الدُّنْيَا وَمَنْ أَتْبَعَ بَصَرَهُ مَا فِي أَيْدِي النَّاسِ كَثُرَ هَمُّهُ وَلَمْ يَشْفِ غَيْظَهُ وَمَنْ لَمْ يَرَ للهِ عَزَّ وَجَلَّ عَلَيْهِ نِعْمَةً إِلا فِي مَطْعَمٍ أَوْ مَشْرَبٍ أَوْ مَلْبَسٍ فَقَدْ قَصُرَ عَمَلُهُ وَدَنَا عَذَابُهُ.

It is narrated from him (narrator of the Hadīth above) from Ahmad b. Muḥammad from 'Alī b. al-Nu'man from abu 'Usamah Zayd from abu 'Abd Allāh (عليه السلام) who has said the following: "The Messenger of Allāh has said, 'One who is not comforted and satisfied with relief from Allāh, his soul will be torn in pieces due to his sorrow for the world. One who follows his eyes to what is in the hands of the people, his depressed condition will increase and his anguish will not cease. One who does not appreciate Allāh's bounties, besides food, drinks and clothes, his deeds fall short and his suffering draws near." (صحيح)[37]

38.

عَلِيُّ بْنُ إِبْرَاهِيمَ عَنْ أَبِيهِ عَنِ ابْنِ أَبِي عُمَيْرٍ عَنْ هِشَامِ بْنِ سَالِمٍ عَنْ أَبِي عَبْدِ اللهِ (عَلَيهِ السَّلام) قَالَ مَا فَتَحَ اللهُ عَلَى عَبْدٍ بَاباً مِنْ أَمْرِ الدُّنْيَا إِلا فَتَحَ اللهُ عَلَيْهِ مِنَ الْحِرْصِ مِثْلَهُ

---

[36]*al-Kāfi, v2, ch126, h4*

[37]*al-Kāfi, v2, ch126, h5*

Ali b. Ibrahim has narrated from his father from b. abu ‘Umayr from Hisham b. Salim from abu ‘Abd Allāh (عليه السلام) who has said the following: “With every door to the worldly affairs that Allāh opens to a servant. He also opens a door of greed to him.” (حسن كالصحيح)[38]

39.

حمدويه، عن محمد بن عيسى بن عبيد و يعقوب بن يزيد، عن ابن أبي عمير، عن أبي العباس البقباق عن أبي عبد الله عليه السلام أنه قال: أربعة أحب الناس إلي أحياء و أمواتا، بريد بن معاوية العجلي و زرارة بن أعين و محمد بن مسلم و أبو جعفر الأحول، أحب الناس إلي أحياء و أمواتا

Hamduwayh from Muḥammad b. Isa b. Ubayd and Yaqub b. Yazid from b. Abi Umayr from Abi al-Abbas al-Baqbaq from Abi Abdillah عليه السلام who said: The most beloved persons to me – whether alive or dead – are four: Burayd b. Muawiya al-Ijli, Zurara b. A’yan, Muḥammad b. Muslim and Abu Ja’far al-Ahwal. They are the most beloved persons to me – alive or dead. (معتبر)[39]

40.

حدثنا أبي رضي الله عنه قال: حدثنا سعد بن عبد الله، عن أحمد بن أبي عبد الله البرقي. عن أبيه محمد بن خالد، عن صفوان بن يحيى، عن أبي أيوب الخزاز. عن محمد بن مسلم وغيره، عن أبي عبد الله عليه السلام قال: قال رسول الله صلى الله عليه وآله:اغد عالما أو متعلما أو أحب العلماء، ولا تكن رابعا فتهلك ببغضهم

My father from Sa’d from al-Barqi from his father from Safwan from al-Khazzaz from Muḥammad b. Muslim and others apart from him from Abi Abdillah عليه السلام who said: the messenger of Allāh صلى الله عليه وآله said: start the day either as a scholar or as a

[38] *al-Kāfi, v2, ch126, h12*

[39] *Rijal al-Kashshi, h438*

student or loving the scholars and do not be a fourth for you will perish because of your hatred towards them (i.e. the scholars). (معتبر)[40]

41.

عِدَّةٌ مِنْ أَصْحَابِنَا عَنْ أَحْمَدَ بْنِ مُحَمَّدِ بْنِ خَالِدٍ عَنْ عُثْمَانَ بْنِ عِيسَى عَنْ سَمَاعَةَ عَنْ أَبِي بَصِيرٍ عَنْ أَبِي عَبْدِ اللَّهِ (عَلَيهِ السَّلام) قَالَ إِنَّ النَّبِيَّ (صَلَّى اللهُ عَلَيْهِ وآلِه) بَيْنَا هُوَ ذَاتَ يَوْمٍ عِنْدَ عَائِشَةَ إِذَا اسْتَأْذَنَ عَلَيْهِ رَجُلٌ فَقَالَ رَسُولُ اللَّهِ (صَلَّى اللهُ عَلَيْهِ وآلِه) بِئْسَ أَخُو الْعَشِيرَةِ فَقَامَتْ عَائِشَةُ فَدَخَلَتِ الْبَيْتَ وَأَذِنَ رَسُولُ اللَّهِ (صَلَّى اللهُ عَلَيْهِ وآلِه) لِلرَّجُلِ فَلَمَّا دَخَلَ أَقْبَلَ عَلَيْهِ بِوَجْهِهِ وَبِشْرُهُ إِلَيْهِ يُحَدِّثُهُ حَتَّى إِذَا فَرَغَ وَخَرَجَ مِنْ عِنْدِهِ قَالَتْ عَائِشَةُ يَا رَسُولَ اللَّهِ بَيْنَا أَنْتَ تَذْكُرُ هَذَا الرَّجُلَ بِمَا ذَكَرْتَهُ بِهِ إِذْ أَقْبَلْتَ عَلَيْهِ بِوَجْهِكَ وَبِشْرِكَ فَقَالَ رَسُولُ اللَّهِ (صَلَّى اللهُ عَلَيْهِ وآلِه) عِنْدَ ذَلِكَ إِنَّ مِنْ شَرِّ عِبَادِ اللَّهِ مَنْ تُكْرَهُ مُجَالَسَتُهُ لِفُحْشِهِ

A number of our people have narrated from Ahmad b. Muḥammad b. Khalid from ‘Uthman b. ‘Isa from Sama’a from abu Basir from abu ‘Abd Allāh (عليه السلام) who has said the following: “One day, when the Holy Prophet was with ‘A’ishah, a man asked permission to meet him. The Messenger of Allāh said, ‘What an evil fellow from the tribe!’ ‘A’ishah then went to her chamber and the Holy Prophet granted permission to the man for a meeting. When he came in, the Holy Prophet met him cheerfully, politely speaking to him until the meeting was over and the man left. ‘A’ishah then asked, ‘O Messenger of Allāh, a while ago you said about the man what you said and then you met him in such a cheerful and polite manner! ’ The Messenger of Allāh said, ‘Of the most evil among the servants (of Allāh) is one whose meeting is disliked because of his using obscene language.’” (موثق)[41]

42.

---

[40] Al-Khiṣāl, ch90, h3

[41] Al-Kafi, v2, ch132, h1

مُحَمَّدُ بْنُ يَحْيَى عَنْ أَحْمَدَ بْنِ مُحَمَّدِ بْنِ عِيسَى عَنِ الْحَسَنِ بْنِ مَحْبُوبٍ عَنْ هِشَامِ بْنِ سَالِمٍ عَنْ أَبِي حَمْزَةَ الثُّمَالِيِّ قَالَ قَالَ عَلِيُّ بْنُ الْحُسَيْنِ (عَلَيهِما السَّلام) عَجَباً لِلْمُتَكَبِّرِ الْفَخُورِ الَّذِي كَانَ بِالأَمْسِ نُطْفَةً ثُمَّ هُوَ غَداً جِيفَةٌ

Muhammad b. Yahya has narrated from Ahmad b. Muḥammad b. 'Isa from al-Hassan b. Mahbub from Hisham b. Salim from abu Hamza al-Thumali who has said the following: "Ali b. al-Husayn (عليه السلام) has said, 'It is astonishing how one who yesterday was only a sperm and tomorrow will turn into a carcass displays arrogance and boastfulness.'" (صحيح)[42]

43.

مُحَمَّدُ بْنُ يَحْيَى عَنْ أَحْمَدَ بْنِ مُحَمَّدِ بْنِ عِيسَى عَنِ الْحُسَيْنِ بْنِ سَعِيدٍ عَنْ إِبْرَاهِيمَ بْنِ عَبْدِ الْحَمِيدِ عَنِ الْوَلِيدِ بْنِ صَبِيحٍ عَنْ أَبِي عَبْدِ اللهِ (عَلَيهِ السَّلام) قَالَ مَا مِنْ مَظْلِمَةٍ أَشَدَّ مِنْ مَظْلِمَةٍ لا يَجِدُ صَاحِبُهَا عَلَيْهَا عَوْناً إِلا اللهَ عَزَّ وَجَلَّ

Muhammad b. Yahya has narrated from Ahmad b. Muḥammad b. 'Isa from al-Husayn b. Sa'id from Ibrahim b. 'Abd al-Hamid from al-Walid b. Sabiyh from abu 'Abd Allāh (عليه السلام) who has said the following: "No injustice is more severe than the one against which the oppressed cannot find any support except Allāh, the Most Majestic, the Most Holy." (موثق)[43]

44.

مُحَمَّدُ بْنُ يَحْيَى عَنْ أَحْمَدَ بْنِ مُحَمَّدِ بْنِ عِيسَى عَنْ مُحَمَّدِ بْنِ عِيسَى عَنْ مَنْصُورٍ عَنْ هِشَامِ بْنِ سَالِمٍ عَنْ أَبِي عَبْدِ اللهِ (عَلَيهِ السَّلام) قَالَ قَالَ رَسُولُ اللهِ (صَلَّى اللهُ عَلَيْهِ وآلِه) اتَّقُوا الظُّلْمَ فَإِنَّهُ ظُلُمَاتُ يَوْمِ الْقِيَامَةِ

[42] *Al-Kāfi, v2, ch134, h1*

[43] *Al-Kāfi, v2, ch136, h4*

Muhammad b. Yahya has narrated from Ahmad b. Muḥammad b. 'Isa from Muḥammad b. 'Isa from Mansur from Hisham b. Salim from abu 'Abd Allāh (عليه السلام) who has said the following: "The Messenger of Allāh has said, 'Be afraid of doing injustice; on the Day of Judgment there will be much darkness.'" (صحيح)[44]

45.

عِدَّةٌ مِنْ أَصْحَابِنَا عَنْ أَحْمَدَ بْنِ مُحَمَّدٍ عَنْ عَلِيِّ بْنِ الْحَكَمِ عَنْ هِشَامِ بْنِ سَالِمٍ قَالَ سَمِعْتُ أَبَا عَبْدِ اللهِ (عَلَيهِ السَّلام) يَقُولُ إِنَّ الْعَبْدَ لَيَكُونُ مَظْلُوماً فَمَا يَزَالُ يَدْعُو حَتَّى يَكُونَ ظَالِماً

A number of our people have narrated from Ahmad b. Muḥammad from 'Alī b. al-Hakam from Hisham b. Salim who has said the following: "I heard abu 'Abd Allāh (عليه السلام) saying, 'A servant (of Allāh) may become oppressed and continues praying against the oppressor until he himself becomes an oppressor (for excessive praying against him).'" (صحيح)[45]

46.

عَنْهُ عَنْ عُثْمَانَ بْنِ عِيسَى عَنِ ابْنِ مُسْكَانَ عَنْ مُحَمَّدِ بْنِ مُسْلِمٍ عَنْ أَبِي جَعْفَرٍ (عَلَيهِ السَّلام) قَالَ إِنَّ اللهَ عَزَّ وَجَلَّ جَعَلَ لِلشَّرِّ أَقْفَالاً وَجَعَلَ مَفَاتِيحَ تِلْكَ الأَقْفَالِ الشَّرَابَ وَالْكَذِبُ شَرٌّ مِنَ الشَّرَابِ

It is narrated from him (narrator of the Hadīth above) from 'Uthman b. 'Isa from b. Muskan from Muḥammad b. Muslim from abu Ja'far (عليه السلام) who has said the

---

[44] *Al-Kāfi, v2, ch136, h11*

[45] *Al-Kāfi, v2, ch136, h17*

following: "Allāh, the Most Majestic, the Most Holy, has created certain locks for evil. He has made wine the key to those locks. Lying is more evil than wine." (موثق)[46]

47.

عَلِيُّ بْنُ إِبْرَاهِيمَ عَنْ أَبِيهِ عَنِ ابْنِ أَبِي عُمَيْرٍ عَنْ عَبْدِ الرَّحْمَنِ بْنِ الْحَجَّاجِ قَالَ قُلْتُ لأَبِي عَبْدِ اللهِ (عَلَيهِ السَّلام) الْكَذَّابُ هُوَ الَّذِي يَكْذِبُ فِي الشَّيْءِ قَالَ لا مَا مِنْ أَحَدٍ إِلا يَكُونُ ذَلِكَ مِنْهُ وَلَكِنَّ الْمَطْبُوعَ عَلَى الْكَذِبِ

Ali b. Ibrahim has narrated from his father from b. abu 'Umayr from 'Abd al-Rahman b. al-Hajjaj who has said the following: "Once I asked abu 'Abd Allāh (عليه السلام) 'Is a liar one who lies about something?' The Imam said, 'No, there is no one who does not do so. It is those in whom lying becomes a thing of second nature.'" (حسن كالصحيح)[47]

48.

عَنْهُ عَنْ أَحْمَدَ عَنِ الْحَسَنِ بْنِ مَحْبُوبٍ عَنْ مَالِكِ بْنِ عَطِيَّةَ عَنْ أَبِي عُبَيْدَةَ عَنْ أَبِي جَعْفَرٍ (عَلَيهِ السَّلام) قَالَ فِي كِتَابِ عَلِيٍّ (عَلَيهِ السَّلام) ثَلاثُ خِصَالٍ لا يَمُوتُ صَاحِبُهُنَّ أَبَداً حَتَّى يَرَى وَبَالَهُنَّ الْبَغْيُ وَقَطِيعَةُ الرَّحِمِ وَالْيَمِينُ الْكَاذِبَةُ يُبَارِزُ اللهَ بِهَا وَإِنَّ أَعْجَلَ الطَّاعَةِ ثَوَاباً لَصِلَةُ الرَّحِمِ وَإِنَّ الْقَوْمَ لَيَكُونُونَ فُجَّاراً فَيَتَوَاصَلُونَ فَتَنْمِي أَمْوَالُهُمْ وَيُثْرُونَ وَإِنَّ الْيَمِينَ الْكَاذِبَةَ وَقَطِيعَةَ الرَّحِمِ لَتَذَرَانِ الدِّيَارَ بَلاقِعَ مِنْ أَهْلِهَا وَتَنْقُلُ الرَّحِمَ وَإِنَّ نَقْلَ الرَّحِمِ انْقِطَاعُ النَّسْلِ

It is narrated from him (narrator of the Hadīth above) from Ahmad from al- Hassan b. Mahbub from Malik b. 'Atiyyah from abu 'Ubaydah from abu Ja'far (عليه السلام) who has said the following: "It is written in the book of 'Alī (عليه السلام) 'There are three characteristics, that if found in anyone, he will never die before suffering their

[46] *Al-Kāfi, v2, ch139, h3*

[47] *Al-Kāfi, v2, ch139, h12*

consequences: treachery, failing to maintain good relations with relatives and taking a false oath to oppose Allāh thereby. Of the acts of obedience with the quickest best result is to maintain good relations with relatives. A people may happen to be unjust in their affairs but maintain good relations with relatives, their wealth increases and they grow rich. False oath and failing to maintain good relations with relatives can leave a town in mins, empty of the inhabitants and transform the family. Transformation of family is discontinuation of the lineage and reproduction.'" (صحيح)[48]

49.

مُحَمَّدُ بْنُ يَحْيَى عَنْ أَحْمَدَ بْنِ مُحَمَّدٍ عَنِ ابْنِ مَحْبُوبٍ عَنْ هِشَامِ بْنِ سَالِمٍ قَالَ سَمِعْتُ أَبَا عَبْدِ اللهِ (عَلَيهِ السَّلام) يَقُولُ قَالَ اللهُ عَزَّ وَجَلَّ لِيَأْذَنْ بِحَرْبٍ مِنِّي مَنْ آذَى عَبْدِيَ الْمُؤْمِنَ وَلْيَأْمَنْ غَضَبِي مَنْ أَكْرَمَ عَبْدِيَ الْمُؤْمِنَ وَلَوْ لَمْ يَكُنْ مِنْ خَلْقِي فِي الأَرْضِ فِيمَا بَيْنَ الْمَشْرِقِ وَالْمَغْرِبِ إِلا مُؤْمِنٌ وَاحِدٌ مَعَ إِمَامٍ عَادِلٍ لاسْتَغْنَيْتُ بِعِبَادَتِهِمَا عَنْ جَمِيعِ مَا خَلَقْتُ فِي أَرْضِي وَلَقَامَتْ سَبْعُ سَمَاوَاتٍ وَأَرَضِينَ بِهِمَا وَلَجَعَلْتُ لَهُمَا مِنْ إِيمَانِهِمَا أُنْساً لا يَحْتَاجَانِ إِلَى أُنْسِ سِوَاهُمَا

Muhammad b. Yahya has narrated from Ahmad b. Muḥammad from b. Mahbub from Hisham b. Salim who has said the following: "I heard abu 'Abd Allāh (عليه السلام) saying, 'Allāh, the Most Majestic, the Most Holy, has said, "He who causes suffering to the believers has declared war against Me. He who respects and honors My believing servant should have no fear of My anger. Had there been no other creature on earth between the West and the East, except a believer with a just Imam, I would have been free of want (reason for My granting rewards) with their worship, from all that I have created on earth. The seven heavens and earths would remain up in their service and, out of their belief, I provide them company with which they did not need company from anyone besides themselves.'" (صحيح)[49]

---

[48] *Al-Kāfi, v2, ch142, h4*

[49] *Al-Kāfi, v2, ch145, h1*

50.

عِدَّةٌ مِنْ أَصْحَابِنَا عَنْ أَحْمَدَ بْنِ مُحَمَّدِ بْنِ خَالِدٍ عَنْ إِسْمَاعِيلَ بْنِ مِهْرَانَ عَنْ أَبِي سَعِيدٍ الْقَمَّاطِ عَنْ أَبَانِ بْنِ تَغْلِبَ عَنْ أَبِي جَعْفَرٍ (عَلَيهِ السَّلام) قَالَ لَمَّا أُسْرِيَ بِالنَّبِيِّ (صَلَّى اللهُ عَلَيْهِ وآلِه) قَالَ يَا رَبِّ مَا حَالُ الْمُؤْمِنِ عِنْدَكَ قَالَ يَا مُحَمَّدُ مَنْ أَهَانَ لِي وَلِيّاً فَقَدْ بَارَزَنِي بِالْمُحَارَبَةِ وَأَنَا أَسْرَعُ شَيْءٍ إِلَى نُصْرَةِ أَوْلِيَائِي وَمَا تَرَدَّدْتُ عَنْ شَيْءٍ أَنَا فَاعِلُهُ كَتَرَدُّدِي عَنْ وَفَاةِ الْمُؤْمِنِ يَكْرَهُ الْمَوْتَ وَأَكْرَهُ مَسَاءَتَهُ وَإِنَّ مِنْ عِبَادِيَ الْمُؤْمِنِينَ مَنْ لا يُصْلِحُهُ إِلا الْغِنَى وَلَوْ صَرَفْتُهُ إِلَى غَيْرِ ذَلِكَ لَهَلَكَ وَإِنَّ مِنْ عِبَادِيَ الْمُؤْمِنِينَ مَنْ لا يُصْلِحُهُ إِلا الْفَقْرُ وَلَوْ صَرَفْتُهُ إِلَى غَيْرِ ذَلِكَ لَهَلَكَ وَمَا يَتَقَرَّبُ إِلَيَّ عَبْدٌ مِنْ عِبَادِي بِشَيْءٍ أَحَبَّ إِلَيَّ مِمَّا افْتَرَضْتُ عَلَيْهِ وَإِنَّهُ لَيَتَقَرَّبُ إِلَيَّ بِالنَّافِلَةِ حَتَّى أُحِبَّهُ فَإِذَا أَحْبَبْتُهُ كُنْتُ إِذاً سَمْعَهُ الَّذِي يَسْمَعُ بِهِ وَبَصَرَهُ الَّذِي يُبْصِرُ بِهِ وَلِسَانَهُ الَّذِي يَنْطِقُ بِهِ وَيَدَهُ الَّتِي يَبْطِشُ بِهَا إِنْ دَعَانِي أَجَبْتُهُ وَإِنْ سَأَلَنِي أَعْطَيْتُهُ.

A number of our people have narrated from Ahmad b. Muḥammad b. Khalid from Isma'il b. Mehran from abu Sa'id al-Qammat from Aban b. Taghlib from abu Ja'far (عليه السلام) who has said the following: "When the Holy Prophet was taken to visit the heavens, he asked, 'O Lord, how is the condition of the believers before you?' He (Allāh) said, 'O Muhammad, whoever insults any of My friends has declared war against Me. I am the quickest to help My friends. I have not hesitated in any of My acts as much as I do at the time of the death of a believer who dislikes death and I dislike to disappoint him. Of My believing servants there are those who do not perform well without wealth and if I change his condition he is destroyed. Also among My believing servants are those who do not perform well unless they are poor and, if I change their condition to something else, they are destroyed. For seeking nearness to Me there is no better means for My servant than to fulfill what 1 have made obligatory for them and that he should seek nearness to Me through performing optional acts of worship so I will love him. When I will love him I will be his ears with which he will hear, his eyes with which he will see, his tongue with which he will speak and his hands with which he will perform his activities. Whenever he prays I will answer him and, whenever he asks a favor, I will grant him.'" (صحيح)[50]

---

[50] *Al-Kāfi, v2, ch145, h8*

51.

عَلِيُّ بْنُ إِبْرَاهِيمَ عَنْ أَبِيهِ عَنِ ابْنِ أَبِي عُمَيْرٍ عَنْ بَعْضِ أَصْحَابِهِ عَنْ أَبِي عَبْدِ اللهِ (عَلَيهِ السَّلام) قَالَ مَنِ اسْتَذَلَّ مُؤْمِناً وَاسْتَحْقَرَهُ لِقِلَّةِ ذَاتِ يَدِهِ وَلِفَقْرِهِ شَهَرَهُ اللهُ يَوْمَ الْقِيَامَةِ عَلَى رُءُوسِ الْخَلَائِقِ

Ali b. Ibrahim has narrated from his father from b. abu 'Umayr from certain individuals of his people from abu 'Abd Allāh (عليه السلام) who has said the following: "Whoever looks down upon a believer or belittles him because of his small resources or poverty, on the Day of Judgment Allāh will make (his disgrace) public to all creatures." (حسن كالصحيح)[51]

52.

عَلِيُّ بْنُ إِبْرَاهِيمَ عَنْ مُحَمَّدِ بْنِ عِيسَى عَنْ يُونُسَ عَنْ مُعَاوِيَةَ عَنْ أَبِي عَبْدِ اللهِ (عَلَيهِ السَّلام) قَالَ قَالَ رَسُولُ اللهِ (صَلَّى اللهُ عَلَيْهِ وآلِه) لَقَدْ أَسْرَى رَبِّي بِي فَأَوْحَى إِلَيَّ مِنْ وَرَاءِ الْحِجَابِ مَا أَوْحَى وَشَافَهَنِي إِلَى أَنْ قَالَ لِي يَا مُحَمَّدُ مَنْ أَذَلَّ لِي وَلِيّاً فَقَدْ أَرْصَدَنِي بِالْمُحَارَبَةِ وَمَنْ حَارَبَنِي حَارَبْتُهُ قُلْتُ يَا رَبِّ وَمَنْ وَلِيُّكَ هَذَا فَقَدْ عَلِمْتُ أَنَّ مَنْ حَارَبَكَ حَارَبْتَهُ قَالَ لِي ذَاكَ مَنْ أَخَذْتُ مِيثَاقَهُ لَكَ وَلِوَصِيِّكَ وَلِذُرِّيَّتِكُمَا بِالْوَلَايَةِ

Ali b. Ibrahim has narrated from Muhammad b. 'Isa from Yunus from Mu'awiyah from abu 'Abd Allāh (عليه السلام) who has said the following: "The Messenger of Allāh has said, 'My Lord took me for a journey and revealed to me from behind the curtain whatever He wanted to reveal, and spoke to me vocally and said to me, "O Muhammad, whoever insults any of My friends has waged a war against Me. Whoever fights Me, I fight him." I then said, 'O Lord, who is this friend of Yours? I have learned that whoever fights You, You fight him.' He said to me, 'This friend is the one with whom I have made a covenant, that he must accept your Divine

[51] *Al-Kafi, v2, ch145, h9*

Authority and Guardianship, the Divine Authority and Guardianship of the executor of your will and the Divine Authority and Guardianship of the descendents of both of you.''' (صحيح)[52]

53.

عِدَّةٌ مِنْ أَصْحَابِنَا عَنْ أَحْمَدَ بْنِ مُحَمَّدِ بْنِ خَالِدٍ عَنْ عَلِيِّ بْنِ الْحَكَمِ عَنْ عَبْدِ اللهِ بْنِ بُكَيْرٍ عَنْ زُرَارَةَ عَنْ أَبِي جَعْفَرٍ (عَلَيهِ السَّلام) قَالَ إِنَّ أَقْرَبَ مَا يَكُونُ الْعَبْدُ إِلَى الْكُفْرِ أَنْ يُوَاخِيَ الرَّجُلُ الرَّجُلَ عَلَى الدِّينِ فَيُحْصِيَ عَلَيْهِ عَثَرَاتِهِ وَزَلاتِهِ لِيُعَنِّفَهُ بِهَا يَوْماً مَا

A number of our people have narrated from Ahmad b. Muḥammad b. Khalid from 'Alī b. al-Hakam from 'Abd Allāh b. Bukayr from Zurara from abu Ja'far (عليه السلام) who has said the following: "Abu Ja'far (عليه السلام) has said, 'A servant (of Allāh) is closest to disbelief when he assumes brotherhood (in belief) with a man and then begins to count his mistakes and slips so he can one day use them against him.''' (موثق كالصحيح)[53]

54.

عَنْهُ عَنِ الْحَجَّالِ عَنْ عَاصِمِ بْنِ حُمَيْدٍ عَنْ أَبِي بَصِيرٍ عَنْ أَبِي جَعْفَرٍ (عَلَيهِ السَّلام) قَالَ قَالَ رَسُولُ اللهِ (صَلَّى اللهُ عَلَيْهِ وآلِه) يَا مَعْشَرَ مَنْ أَسْلَمَ بِلِسَانِهِ وَلَمْ يُسْلِمْ بِقَلْبِهِ لا تَتَبَّعُوا عَثَرَاتِ الْمُسْلِمِينَ فَإِنَّهُ مَنْ تَتَبَّعَ عَثَرَاتِ الْمُسْلِمِينَ تَتَبَّعَ اللهُ عَثْرَتَهُ وَمَنْ تَتَبَّعَ اللهُ عَثْرَتَهُ يَفْضَحْهُ

It is narrated from him (narrator of the Hadīth above) from al-Hajjal from 'Asim b. Humayd from abu Basir from abu Ja'far (عليه السلام) who has said the following: "The Messenger of Allāh has said, 'O group of people who have accepted Islam with their

---

[52] *Al-Kāfi, v2, ch145, h10*

[53] *Al-Kāfi, v2, ch146, h3*

tongue and not yet with their heart, do not seek to search into the privacies of the Muslims to find faults in them; Allāh will then do the same to them and to whomever Allāh will do such a thing. He will bring disgrace upon him.'" (صحيح)[54]

55.

عَلِيُّ بْنُ إِبْرَاهِيمَ عَنْ أَبِيهِ عَنِ ابْنِ أَبِي عُمَيْرٍ عَنْ بَعْضِ أَصْحَابِهِ عَنْ أَبِي عَبْدِ اللهِ (عَلَيهِ السَّلام) قَالَ مَنْ قَالَ فِي مُؤْمِنٍ مَا رَأَتْهُ عَيْنَاهُ وَسَمِعَتْهُ أُذُنَاهُ فَهُوَ مِنَ الَّذِينَ قَالَ اللهُ عَزَّ وَجَلَّ إِنَّ الَّذِينَ يُحِبُّونَ أَنْ تَشِيعَ الْفَاحِشَةُ فِي الَّذِينَ آمَنُوا لَهُمْ عَذابٌ أَلِيمٌ

Ali b. Ibrahim has narrated from his father from b. abu 'Umayr from certain individuals of his people from abu 'Abd Allāh (عليه السلام) who has said the following: "Whoever says something about a believer that has not seen with his eyes and has not heard with his ears is then considered among those about whom Allāh, the Most Majestic, the Most Holy, has said, 'Those who like to publicize indecency among the believers will face painful torment in this world and in the life to come. . . .'" (24:19) (حسن كالصحيح)[55]

56.

عَلِيُّ بْنُ إِبْرَاهِيمَ عَنْ مُحَمَّدِ بْنِ عِيسَى عَنْ يُونُسَ عَنِ ابْنِ مُسْكَانَ عَنْ أَبِي بَصِيرٍ عَنْ أَبِي عَبْدِ اللهِ (عَلَيهِ السَّلام) قَالَ أَيُّمَا رَجُلٍ مِنْ شِيعَتِنَا أَتَى رَجُلاً مِنْ إِخْوَانِهِ فَاسْتَعَانَ بِهِ فِي حَاجَتِهِ فَلَمْ يُعِنْهُ وَهُوَ يَقْدِرُ إِلا ابْتَلاهُ اللهُ بِأَنْ يَقْضِيَ حَوَائِجَ غَيْرِهِ مِنْ أَعْدَائِنَا يُعَذِّبُهُ اللهُ عَلَيْهَا يَوْمَ الْقِيَامَةِ

Ali b. Ibrahim has narrated from Muḥammad b. 'Isa from Yunus from b. Muskan from abu Basir from abu 'Abd Allāh (عليه السلام) who has said the following: "If anyone

---

[54] *Al-Kāfi, v2, ch146, h4*

[55] *Al-Kāfi, v2, ch148, h2*

of our Shi'a (followers) comes to his brother (in belief) for help and does not help him while he is able to help, Allāh will make him help other people of our enemies and on the Day of Judgment Allāh will punish him for such help." (صحيح)[56]

57.

أحمد بن زياد بن جعفر الهمداني، عن علي بن إبراهيم بن هاشم، عن محمد بن عيسى بن عبيد، عن إبراهيم بن محمد الهمداني قال: قلت للرضا عليه السلام: يا ابن رسول الله أخبرني عن زرارة هل كان يعرف حق أبيك؟ فقال عليه السلام: نعم، فقلت له: فلم بعث ابنه عبيدا ليتعرف الخبر إلى من أوصى الصادق جعفر بن محمد عليهما السلام؟ فقال: إن زرارة كان يعرف أمر أبي عليه السلام، ونص أبيه عليه، وإنما بعث ابنه ليتعرف من أبي هل يجوز له أن يرفع التقية في إظهار أمره، ونص أبيه عليه؟ وأنه لما أبطأ عنه طولب باظهار قوله في أبي عليه السلام، فلم يحب أن يقدم على ذلك دون أمره فرفع المصحف وقال: اللهم إن إمامي من أثبت هذا المصحف إمامته من ولد جعفر بن محمد عليهما السلام

Ahmad b. Ziyad b. Ja`far al-Hamdani from 'Alī b. Ibrahim b. Hashim from Muḥammad b. Isa b. Ubayd from Ibrahim b. Muḥammad al-Hamdani who said: I said to al-Rida عليه السلام: O the son of the messenger of Allāh inform me about Zurara – did he know of the right of your father [al-Kadhim to be the Imam]? He عليه السلام said: yes he did. I said: then why did he send his son Ubayd to investigate the question of the succession to al-Ṣādiq Ja`far b. Muhammad? He said: Zurara knew of the affair of my father [his Imama] and the designation of his father [al-Ṣādiq] to him, he only sent his son to know from my father [al-Kadhim] whether it was permitted for him to lift the Taqiyya in announcing the affair [Imama] and the designation of his father to him. When the answer delayed he was asked to declare his opinion about my father but he did not wish to proceed in doing so without his instruction so he raised the Mushaf and said: O Allāh my Imam is the one whose Imama this Mushaf establishes among the sons of Ja`far b. Muḥammad عليهما السلام (معتبر)[57]

---

[56] *Al-Kāfi, v2, ch156, h2*

[57] *Kamal ad-Deen (Ṣaduq), pg. 103*

58.

عَلِيُّ بْنُ إِبْرَاهِيمَ عَنْ أَبِيهِ عَنِ ابْنِ أَبِي عُمَيْرٍ عَنْ عَلِيِّ بْنِ يَقْطِينٍ عَنْ أَبِي الْحَسَنِ مُوسَى (عَلَيهِ السَّلام) قَالَ قُلْتُ لَهُ إِنِّي قَدْ أَشْفَقْتُ مِنْ دَعْوَةِ أَبِي عَبْدِ اللهِ (عَلَيهِ السَّلام) عَلَى يَقْطِينٍ وَمَا وَلَدَ فَقَالَ يَا أَبَا الْحَسَنِ لَيْسَ حَيْثُ تَذْهَبُ إِنَّمَا الْمُؤْمِنُ فِي صُلْبِ الْكَافِرِ بِمَنْزِلَةِ الْحَصَاةِ فِي اللَّبِنَةِ يَجِيءُ الْمَطَرُ فَيَغْسِلُ اللَّبِنَةَ وَلا يَضُرُّ الْحَصَاةَ شَيْئاً

Ali b. Ibrahim from his father from b. Abi Umayr from 'Alī b. Yaqtin from Abi al-Hasan Mūsā عليه السلام. He [Ali b. Yaqtin] said: I said to him: I am fearful because of the supplication of Abi Abdillah عليه السلام against Yaqtin and his off-spring, so he [the Imam] said: O Aba al-Hasan [Ali b. Yaqtin] it is not as you think, verily the believer who arises from the back-bone [lineage] of a disbeliever is like the stone in a clay brick, when rain comes it washes away the clay [dissolves it to mud] but does not harm the stone in any way. (حسن كالصحيح)[58]

59.

حمدويه و إبراهيم ابنا نصير، عن أيوب، عن صفوان، عن معاوية بن عمار و غير واحد، عن أبي عبد الله عليه السلام قال: كان عمار بن ياسر و محمد بن أبي بكر لا يرضيان أن يعصي الله عز و جل

Hamduwayh b. Nusayr and Ibrahim b. Nusayr from Ayyub from Safwan from Mu`awiya b. Ammar and more than one from Abi Abdillah عليه السلام who said: Ammar b. Yasir and Muḥammad b. Abi Bakr could never tolerate that Allāh Mighty and Majestic be disobeyed. (معتبر)[59]

[58] *Al-Kāfi, v2, ch7, h2*

[59] *Rijal al-Kashshi, h112*

60.

أَبِي رَحِمَهُ اَللَّهُ قَالَ حَدَّثَنِي عَبْدُ اَللَّهِ بْنُ جَعْفَرٍ عَنْ أَحْمَدَ بْنِ مُحَمَّدٍ عَنِ اِبْنِ أَبِي نَجْرَانَ قَالَ سَمِعْتُ أَبَا اَلْحَسَنِ ع يَقُولُ مَنْ عَادَى شِيعَتَنَا فَقَدْ عَادَانَا وَ مَنْ وَالاَهُمْ فَقَدْ وَالاَنَا لِأَنَّهُمْ مِنَّا خُلِقُوا مِنْ طِينَتِنَا مَنْ أَحَبَّهُمْ فَهُوَ مِنَّا وَ مَنْ أَبْغَضَهُمْ فَلَيْسَ مِنَّا شِيعَتُنَا يَنْظُرُونَ بِنُورِ اَللَّهِ وَ يَتَقَلَّبُونَ فِي رَحْمَةِ اَللَّهِ وَ يَفُوزُونَ بِكَرَامَةِ اَللَّهِ مَا مِنْ أَحَدٍ مِنْ شِيعَتِنَا يَمْرَضُ إِلاَّ مَرِضْنَا لِمَرَضِهِ وَ لاَ اِغْتَمَّ إِلاَّ اِغْتَمَمْنَا لِغَمِّهِ وَ لاَ يَفْرَحُ إِلاَّ فَرِحْنَا لِفَرَحِهِ وَ لاَ يَغِيبُ عَنَّا أَحَدٌ مِنْ شِيعَتِنَا أَيْنَ كَانَ فِي شَرْقِ اَلْأَرْضِ أَوْ غَرْبِهَا وَ مَنْ تَرَكَ مِنْ شِيعَتِنَا دَيْناً فَهُوَ عَلَيْنَا وَ مَنْ تَرَكَ مِنْهُمْ مَالاً فَهُوَ لِوَرَثَتِهِ شِيعَتُنَا اَلَّذِينَ يُقِيمُونَ اَلصَّلاَةَ وَ يُؤْتُونَ اَلزَّكَاةَ وَ يَحُجُّونَ اَلْبَيْتَ اَلْحَرَامَ وَ يَصُومُونَ شَهْرَ رَمَضَانَ وَ يُوَالُونَ أَهْلَ اَلْبَيْتِ وَ يَتَبَرَّءُونَ مِنْ أَعْدَائِهِمْ[مِنْ أَعْدَائِنَا] أُولَئِكَ أَهْلُ اَلْإِيمَانِ وَ اَلتُّقَى وَ أَهْلُ اَلْوَرَعِ وَ اَلتَّقْوَى وَ مَنْ رَدَّ عَلَيْهِمْ فَقَدْ رَدَّ عَلَى اَللَّهِ وَ مَنْ طَعَنَ عَلَيْهِمْ فَقَدْ طَعَنَ عَلَى اَللَّهِ لِأَنَّهُمْ عِبَادُ اَللَّهِ حَقّاً وَ أَوْلِيَاؤُهُ صِدْقاً وَ اَللَّهِ إِنَّ أَحَدَهُمْ لَيَشْفَعُ فِي مِثْلِ رَبِيعَةَ وَ مُضَرَ فَيُشَفِّعُهُ اَللَّهُ تَعَالَى فِيهِمْ لِكَرَامَتِهِ عَلَى اَللَّهِ عَزَّ وَ جَلَّ

From b. Abī Najrān said, I heard Abā al-Hasan (عليه السلام)and he said: "Whoever hates our shī`ahs, has certainly hated us, and whoever follows them, has certainly followed us, because they are from us, and they are created from our clay. Whoever loves them has loved us, and whoever hates them is not from us. Our Shī`ahs see through the *nūr*(light) of Allāh, and they turn (move) in the mercy of Allāh, and triumph in the honor of Allāh. No one from our shī`ahs becomes ill except that we become ill due to his illness, they do not become sad, except that we are sad for his sadness. And they are not happy except that we are happy for his happiness, and nothing is concealed from us that is (concealed) from one of our shī`ahs, whether it is in the east or the west of the earth. And the debt that is left from our shī`ahs is our debt, and whoever leaves it from them the fortune is left to his heir. Our shī`ahs are those who establish prayer, give zakāh, go on pilgrimage to *Bayt al-Harām*, fast in the month of RamaDān, follow the Ahl al-Bayt (عليهم السلام)and do bara'a from their (عليهم السلام)enemies [from our enemies], they are the people of *Imān* (faith), taqwa, the people of *wara'a* (piety) and *taqwa.* And whoever rejects them has certainly rejected Allāh, and whoever disputes with them, has certainly disputed with Allāh, because they are the true slaves of Allāh, and the genuine patrons of Allāh. By Allāh, Verily, each one of them will be able to intercede for as many (people as) *RAbi'ah* (a tribe) and *MuDar* (a tribe), so Allāh (accepts) the intercession for them due to his honor with/to Allāh (عزَّ وَ جَلَّ)" . (صحيح)[60]

61.

عنه عن علي بن أسباط عن عيينة بياع القصب عن أبي عبد الله ع قال و الله لنعم الاسم الذي منحكم الله ما دمتم تأخذون بقولنا و لا تكذبون علينا قال و قال لي أبو عبد الله ع هذا القول إني كنت خبرته أن رجلا قال لي إياك أن تكون رافضيا

Abu `Abd Allāh (عليه السلام) said: 'By Allāh, Allāh has bestowed this name(Rafidah) as a blessing, as long as you take our sayings and do not (attribute) lies upon us.' Abu `Abd Allāh (عليه السلام) said to me this statement I told him that a man said to me 'Beware of being a Rafidah' (موثق)[61]

62.

عنه عن يعقوب بن يزيد عن صفوان بن يحيى عن أبي أسامة زيد الشحام عن أبي الجارود قال أصم الله أذنيه كما أعمى عينيه إن لم يكن سمع أبا جعفر ع يقول إن فلانا سمانا باسم قال و ما ذاك الاسم قال سمانا الرافضة فقال أبو جعفر ع بيده إلى صدره و أنا من الرافضة و هو مني قالها ثلاثا

May Allāh make deaf his ears as he has blinded his eyes if he did not hear Abaa Ja`far (عليه السلام) say so-and-so called us a name. He said: 'And what is this name?' He said: 'He calls us Rafidah.' So Abu Ja`far (عليه السلام) put his hand on his chest and said three times: 'I am from the Rafidah and he is from me'. (موثق)[62]

---

[60] *Ṣifāt al-Shī'a, h5*

[61] *Al-Mahasin, pg. 157*

[62] *Al-Mahasin, pg. 157*

63.

مُحَمَّدُ بْنُ يَحْيَى عَنْ أَحْمَدَ بْنِ مُحَمَّدٍ عَنْ مُحَمَّدِ بْنِ خَالِدٍ عَنْ سَعْدِ بْنِ سَعْدٍ عَنْ أَبِي الْحَسَنِ الرِّضَا (عَلَيْهِ السَّلام) قَالَ سَأَلْتُهُ عَنْ قَوْلِ أَمِيرِ الْمُؤْمِنِينَ صَلَوَاتُ اللهِ عَلَيْهِ وَاللهِ لأَلْفُ ضَرْبَةٍ بِالسَّيْفِ أَهْوَنُ مِنْ مَوْتٍ عَلَى فِرَاشٍ قَالَ فِي سَبِيلِ اللهِ

Muhammad b. Yahya has narrated from Ahmad b. Muhammad from Muḥammad b. Khalid from Sa'd b. Sa'd who has said the following: "I once asked abu al-Hassan al-Rida, (عليه السلام), about the words of Amir al-Mu'minin, (عليه السلام), 'I swear by Allāh, enduring one thousand strikes by the sword is easier than dying on the bed.' He (the Imam) said, 'It means 'for the cause of Allāh.''' (صحيح)[63]

64.

مُحَمَّدُ بْنُ يَحْيَى عَنْ أَحْمَدَ بْنِ مُحَمَّدٍ عَنِ الْحُسَيْنِ بْنِ سَعِيدٍ عَنْ عَلِيِّ بْنِ النُّعْمَانِ عَنْ عَبْدِ اللهِ بْنِ مُسْكَانَ عَنْ سَدِيرٍ قَالَ كُنَّا عِنْدَ أَبِي جَعْفَرٍ (عليه السلام) فَذَكَرْنَا مَا أَحْدَثَ النَّاسُ بَعْدَ نَبِيِّهِمْ (صلى الله عليه وآله) وَ اسْتِذْلَالَهُمْ أَمِيرَ الْمُؤْمِنِينَ (عليه السلام) فَقَالَ رَجُلٌ مِنَ الْقَوْمِ أَصْلَحَكَ اللَّهُ فَأَيْنَ كَانَ عِزُّ بَنِي هَاشِمٍ وَ مَا كَانُوا فِيهِ مِنَ الْعَدَدِ فَقَالَ أَبُو جَعْفَرٍ (عليه السلام) وَ مَنْ كَانَ بَقِيَ مِنْ بَنِي هَاشِمٍ إِنَّمَا كَانَ جَعْفَرٌ وَ حَمْزَةُ فَمَضَيَا وَ بَقِيَ مَعَهُ رَجُلَانِ ضَعِيفَانِ ذَلِيلَانِ حَدِيثَا عَهْدٍ بِالْإِسْلَامِ عَبَّاسٌ وَ عَقِيلٌ وَ كَانَا مِنَ الطُّلَقَاءِ أَمَا وَ اللَّهِ لَوْ أَنَّ حَمْزَةَ وَ جَعْفَراً كَانَا بِحَضْرَتِهِمَا مَا وَصَلَا إِلَى مَا وَصَلَا إِلَيْهِ وَ لَوْ كَانَا شَاهِدَيْهِمَا لَأَتْلَفَا نَفْسَيْهِمَا

Muhammad b. yahya, from Ahmad b. Muhammad, from Al-Husayn b. Saeed, from 'Alī b. Al-No'man, from 'Abd Allāh b. Muskaan, from Sudeyr who said: We were in the presence of Abu Ja'far (عليه السلام), so we mentioned what the people had done after their Prophet (صلى الله عليه وآله وسلم), and their humiliating Amir al- Mu'minin (عليه السلام). So a man from the people said, 'May Allāh (تبارك و طائلة) Keep you well, so where were the strong ones of the Clan of Hashim (عليه السلام) and what was their number?' So Abu

[63] *Al-Kafi, v5, ch25, h1*

Ja'far (عليه السلام) said: 'And from those ones of the Clan of Hashim (عليه السلام) that remained were Ja'far (عليه السلام) and Hamza (عليه السلام) who had passed away (martyred), and there remained with them two men who were weak, disgraceful, new ones in the era of Al-Islam, Abbas and Aqeel who were from the freed ones. By Allāh (تبارك و طائلة)! If Hamza (عليه السلام) and Ja'far (عليه السلام) were present among them, they would not have achieved what they achieved. And had they seen them (عليه السلام) two, they would not have damaged themselves'. (حسن)[64]

65.

عَنْهُ عَنْ أَحْمَدَ بْنِ مُحَمَّدٍ عَنِ ابْنِ فَضَّالٍ عَنْ عَلِيِّ بْنِ عُقْبَةَ بَيَّاعِ الْأَكْسِيَةِ عَنْ أَبِي عَبْدِ اللهِ (عَلَيهِ السَّلام) قَالَ إِنَّ الْمُؤْمِنَ لَيُذْنِبُ الذَّنْبَ فَيُذَكَّرُ بَعْدَ عِشْرِينَ سَنَةً فَيَسْتَغْفِرُ اللهَ مِنْهُ فَيَغْفِرُ لَهُ وَإِنَّمَا يُذَكِّرُهُ لِيَغْفِرَ لَهُ وَإِنَّ الْكَافِرَ لَيُذْنِبُ الذَّنْبَ فَيَنْسَاهُ مِنْ سَاعَتِهِ

It is narrated from him (narrator of the Hadīth above) from Ahmad b. Muḥammad from b. Faddal from 'Alī b. 'Uqbah Bayya' al-Aksiyah from abu 'Abd Allāh (عليه السلام) who has said the following: "A believer commits a sin and remembers it after twenty years, then he pleads before Allāh for forgiveness, He still forgives him. He is made to remember so He may forgive him. An unbeliever commits a sin and forgets it within the same hour.' (موثق)[65]

66.

عَلِيُّ بْنُ إِبْرَاهِيمَ عَنْ أَبِيهِ عَنْ حَمَّادِ بْنِ عِيسَى عَنْ حَرِيزٍ عَنْ زُرَارَةَ عَنْ أَبِي جَعْفَرٍ (عَلَيهِ السَّلام) قَالَ قَالَ أَحَبُّ الْأَعْمَالِ إِلَى اللهِ عَزَّ وَجَلَّ مَا دَاوَمَ عَلَيْهِ الْعَبْدُ وَإِنْ قَلَّ

---

[64] *Al-Kāfi, v8, h216*

[65] *Al-Kāfi, v2, ch192, h6*

Ali b. Ibrahim has narrated from his father from Hammad b. 'Isa from Hariz from Zurara from abu Ja'far (عليه السلام) who has said the following: "Abu Ja'far (عليه السلام) has said, 'The most beloved deed in the sight of Allāh, the Most Majestic, the Most Holy, is that which is continued even though it is very little.'" (حسن كالصحيح)[66]

67.

عَلِيُّ بْنُ إِبْرَاهِيمَ عَنْ أَبِيهِ عَنْ حَمَّادِ بْنِ عِيسَى عَنْ إِبْرَاهِيمَ بْنِ عُمَرَ الْيَمَانِيِّ عَنْ أَبِي الْحَسَنِ الْمَاضِي (صَلَّى اللهُ عَلَيْهِ وآلِه) قَالَ لَيْسَ مِنَّا مَنْ لَمْ يُحَاسِبْ نَفْسَهُ فِي كُلِّ يَوْمٍ فَإِنْ عَمِلَ حَسَناً اسْتَزَادَ اللهَ وَإِنْ عَمِلَ سَيِّئاً اسْتَغْفَرَ اللهَ مِنْهُ وَتَابَ إِلَيْهِ.

Ali b. Ibrahim has narrated from his father from Hammad b. 'Isa from Ibrahim b. 'Umar al-Yamani from abu al-Hassan (Ali b. al-Husayn) (عليه السلام) who has said the following: "One who does not evaluate his deeds every day is not one of us. One must evaluate his deeds and pray to Allāh to increase his good deeds, plead for forgiveness to Allāh due to one's committing evil deeds and turn to Him in repentance." (حسن)[67]

68.

جماعة، عن أبي جعفر محمد بن علي بن الحسين بن موسى بن بابويه وأبي عبدالله الحسين بن علي أخيه عن أبوجعفر محمد بن علي الاسود رحمه الله قال: سألني علي بن الحسن بن موسى بن بابويه رضي الله عنه بعد موت محمد بن عثمان العمري قدس سره أن أسأل أبا القاسم الروحي قدس الله روحه أن يسأل مولانا صاحب الزمان عليه السلام أن يدعو الله أن يرزقه ولدا ذكرا قال: فسألته فأنهى ذلك، ثم أخبرني بعد ذلك بثلاثة أيام أنه قد دعا لعلي بن الحسين رحمه الله فإنه سيولد له ولد مبارك ينفع الله به، وبعده أولاد ... قال: فولد لعلي بن الحسين رضي الله عنه تلك السنة إبنه محمد بن علي وبعده أولاد ... قال أبو جعفر بن بابويه:

---

[66] *Al-Kāfi, v2, ch41, h2*

[67] *Al-Kāfi, v2, ch203, h2*

وكان أبو جعفر محمد بن علي الأسود كثيرا ما يقول لي – إذا رآني أختلف إلى مجلس شيخنا محمد بن الحسن بن الوليد رضي الله عنه وأرغب في كتب العلم وحفظه – ليس بعجب أن تكون لك هذه الرغبة في العلم وأنت ولدت بدعاء الإمام عليه السلامعليه السلام

A large number from Abi Ja'far Muḥammad b. 'Alī b. al-Husayn b. Mūsā b. Babawayh and his brother Abi AbdAllāh al-Husayn b. 'Alī both of them from Abu Ja'far Muḥammad b. 'Alī al-Aswad رحمه الله who said: 'Alī b. al-Husayn b. Mūsā b. Babawayh رضي الله عنه asked me – after the death of Muḥammad b. Uthman al-Amri قدس سره – to request Aba al-Qasim al-Ruhi قدس سره to implore our Leader the Master of the Age عليه السلام to supplicate to Allāh that He grant him a male child. He [al-Aswad] says: I asked him [al-Ruhi] but he refused it. Then he informed me after three days that he [the Imam] had supplicated for 'Alī b. al-Husayn رحمه الله and 'will be born to him a blessed son through whom Allāh will benefit many and after him other sons'. He [al-Aswad] said: Muḥammad b. 'Alī was born to 'Alī b. al-Husayn رضي الله عنه that same year and after him other children ... Abu Ja'far b. Babawayh (al-Ṣaduq) said: Abu Ja'far Muḥammad b. 'Alī al-Aswad would always say to me – when he sees me going to the study session of our Shaykh Muḥammad b. al-Hasan b. al-Walid رضي الله عنه and after observing my motivation for studying the books of knowledge and gaining mastery over them: it is not strange that you have this desire for knowledge for you were born because of the supplication of the Imam عليه السلام. (معتبر)[68]

69.

وبهذا الاسناد قال: قال أمير المؤمنين عليه السلام: الرجال ثلاثة: عاقل وأحمق وفاجر ، فالعاقل الدين شريعته، والحلم طبيعته، والرأي سجيته، وإن سئل أجاب، وإن تكلم أصاب، وإن سمع وعى، وإن حدث صدق، وإن اطمأن إليه أحد وفى، والاحمق إن استنبه بجميل غفل، وإن استنزل عن حسن نزل، وإن حمل على جهل جهل، وإن حدث كذب، لا يفقه وإن فقه لا يتفقه، والفاجر إن ائتمنته خانك، وإن صاحبته شانك وإن وثقت به لم ينصحك

[68] *Al-Ghayba (Tusi), pg. 343*

And with these same documents he narrated that the Commander of the Faithful Imam ʿAlī (عليه السلام) said, "Men are of three types: intelligent, stupid and corrupt. For the intelligent, religion is his way; patience is his nature, and thinking is in his character. If questioned, he will respond. If he talks, he says the right words. If he listens, he perceives. If he speaks, he tells the truth. If someone trusts him, he will be loyal to him. However, if you direct a stupid person to the good, he will neglect it. If he is directed away from the good, he will follow. If he is guided towards ignorance, he becomes ignorant. If he talks, he lies. He doesn't understand. Even if you try to make him understand, he will not understand. And a corrupt person is such that if you entrust him with something, he will cheat you. If you become his companion, he will debase you. And if you trust him in some affairs, he will not be sincere to you." (موثق)[69]

70.

عَلِيُّ بْنُ إِبْرَاهِيمَ عَنْ أَبِيهِ عَنِ ابْنِ أَبِي عُمَيْرٍ عَنْ هِشَامِ بْنِ سَالِمٍ عَنْ أَبِي عَبْدِ اللَّهِ (عليه السلام) قَالَ اللَّحْمُ بِاللَّبَنِ مَرَقُ الْأَنْبِيَاءِ (عليهم السلام)

Ali b. Ibrahim has narrated from his father from b. abu ' Umayr from Hisham b. Salim who has said the following: "Abu 'Abd Allāh, (عليه السلام), has said, 'Meat with milk is the sauce of Prophets, (عليهم السلام) '" (حسن)[70]

71.

---

[69] *Al-Khiṣāl, ch76, h2*

[70] *Al-Kāfi, v6, ch66, h1*

عَلِيُّ بْنُ إِبْرَاهِيمَ عَنْ أَبِيهِ عَنِ ابْنِ أَبِي عُمَيْرٍ عَنْ حَمَّادٍ عَنْ مُحَمَّدِ بْنِ مُسْلِمٍ قَالَ قُلْتُ لأَبِي جَعْفَرٍ (عَلَيْهِ السَّلام) قَوْلُ اللهِ عَزَّ وَجَلَّ وَاللَّيْلِ إِذا يَغْشى وَالنَّجْمِ إِذا هَوى وَمَا أَشْبَهَ ذَلِكَ فَقَالَ إِنَّ للهِ عَزَّ وَجَلَّ أَنْ يُقْسِمَ مِنْ خَلْقِهِ بِمَا شَاءَ وَلَيْسَ لِخَلْقِهِ أَنْ يُقْسِمُوا إِلا بِهِ

Ali b. Ibrahim has narrated from his father from b. abu 'Umayr from Hammad from Muḥammad b. Muslim who has narrated the following: "This is about the meaning of the words of Allāh, most Majestic, most Glorious. . . I swear by the night when it becomes dark. . .' (92:2) and '. . . I swear by the star when it descends down' (52:2) and so on. Abu Ja'far, (عليه السلام), has said, 'Allāh, most Majestic, most Glorious, swears by anything of His creatures as He wants but His creatures can only swear and take oath by Allāh.'" (حسن)[71]

72.

عِدَّةٌ مِنْ أَصْحَابِنَا عَنْ أَحْمَدَ بْنِ مُحَمَّدٍ عَنْ عُثْمَانَ بْنِ عِيسَى عَنْ أَبِي أَيُّوبَ الْخَزَّازِ قَالَ سَمِعْتُ أَبَا عَبْدِ اللهِ (عَلَيْهِ السَّلام) يَقُولُ لا تَحْلِفُوا بِاللهِ صَادِقِينَ وَلا كَاذِبِينَ فَإِنَّهُ عَزَّ وَجَلَّ يَقُولُ وَلا تَجْعَلُوا اللهَ عُرْضَةً لأَيْمانِكُمْ

A number of our people have narrated from Ahmad b. Muḥammad from 'Uthman b. 'Isa from abu Ayyub al-Khazzaz who has said the following: "I once heard abu ' Abd Allāh, (عليه السلام), saying, 'Do not swear by Allāh, regardless, you are truthful or not truthful; Allāh, most Majestic, most Glorious, says, "Do not swear by Allāh unnecessarily."' (2:224)" (موثق)[72]

73.

[71] *Al-Kāfi, v7, ch14, h1*

[72] *Al-Kāfi, v7, ch1, h1*

عَلِيُّ بْنُ إِبْرَاهِيمَ عَنْ أَبِيهِ عَنْ عَمْرِو بْنِ عُثْمَانَ عَنْ عَبْدِ اللهِ بْنِ سِنَانٍ عَنْ أَبِي عَبْدِ اللهِ (عَلَيْهِ السَّلام) قَالَ اجْتَمَعَ الْحَوَارِيُّونَ إِلَى عِيسَى (عَلَيْهِ السَّلام) فَقَالُوا لَهُ يَا مُعَلِّمَ الْخَيْرِ أَرْشِدْنَا فَقَالَ لَهُمْ إِنَّ مُوسَى نَبِيَّ اللهِ أَمَرَكُمْ أَنْ لا تَحْلِفُوا بِاللهِ كَاذِبِينَ وَأَنَا آمُرُكُمْ أَنْ لا تَحْلِفُوا بِاللهِ كَاذِبِينَ وَلا صَادِقِينَ

Ali b. Ibrahim has narrated from his father from ‘Amr b. ‘Uthman from ‘Abd Allāh b. Sinan who has said the following: “Abu ‘Abd Allāh, (عليه السلام), has said that the disciples gathered around Jesus, (عليه السلام), and said, ‘O teacher of good, give us advice.’ He said to them, ‘Musa, the Prophet of Allāh has commanded you not to swear by Allāh falsely, but I command you not to swear by Allāh, regardless, you are truthful or false.’” (حسن)[73]

74.

عِدَّةٌ مِنْ أَصْحَابِنَا عَنْ أَحْمَدَ بْنِ مُحَمَّدِ بْنِ خَالِدٍ عَنْ يَحْيَى بْنِ إِبْرَاهِيمَ عَنْ أَبِيهِ عَنْ أَبِي سَلامٍ الْمُتَعَبِّدِ أَنَّهُ سَمِعَ أَبَا عَبْدِ اللهِ (عَلَيْهِ السَّلام) يَقُولُ لِسَدِيرٍ يَا سَدِيرُ مَنْ حَلَفَ بِاللهِ كَاذِباً كَفَرَ وَمَنْ حَلَفَ بِاللهِ صَادِقاً أَثِمَ إِنَّ اللهَ عَزَّ وَجَلَّ يَقُولُ وَلا تَجْعَلُوا اللهَ عُرْضَةً لأَيْمَانِكُمْ

A number of our people have narrated from Ahmad b. Muḥammad b. Khalid from Yahya b. Ibrahim from his father from abu Salam al-Salam al-Muta‘abbid who has said the following: “I once heard abu ‘Abd Allāh, (عليه السلام), saying to Sadir, ‘O Sadir, one who swears by Allāh, most Majestic, most Glorious, falsely as well as one who swears by Allāh truthfully has sinned; Allāh, most Majestic, most Glorious, says, ‘Do not swear by Allāh, unless you are obligated.’ (2:224)” (مجهول)[74]

75.

---

[73] *Al-Kāfi, v7, ch1, h3*

[74] *Al-Kāfi, v7, ch1, h4*

مُحَمَّدُ بْنُ يَحْيَى عَنْ أَحْمَدَ بْنِ مُحَمَّدِ بْنِ عِيسَى عَنْ أَحْمَدَ بْنِ مُحَمَّدِ بْنِ أَبِي نَصْرٍ قَالَ قَالَ أَبُو الْحَسَنِ الرِّضَا (عَلَيهِ السَّلام) مِنْ عَلامَاتِ الْفِقْهِ الْحِلْمُ وَالْعِلْمُ وَالصَّمْتُ إِنَّ الصَّمْتَ بَابٌ مِنْ أَبْوَابِ الْحِكْمَةِ إِنَّ الصَّمْتَ يَكْسِبُ الْمَحَبَّةَ إِنَّهُ دَلِيلٌ عَلَى كُلِّ خَيْرٍ

Muhammad b. Yahya has narrated from Ahmad b. Muḥammad b. 'Isa from Ahmad b. Muḥammad b. abu Nasr who has said the following: "Abu al-Hassan al-Rida (عليه السلام) has said, 'Of the signs of one's intelligence is forbearance, knowledge and silence. Silence is one of the doors of wisdom. Silence earns love and it, certainly, is the guide to all good.'" (صحيح)[75]

76.

عَنْهُ عَنِ الْحَسَنِ بْنِ مَحْبُوبٍ عَنْ عَبْدِ اللهِ بْنِ سِنَانٍ عَنْ أَبِي حَمْزَةَ قَالَ سَمِعْتُ أَبَا جَعْفَرٍ (عَلَيهِ السَّلام) يَقُولُ إِنَّمَا شِيعَتُنَا الْخُرْسُ

It is narrated from him (narrator of the Hadīth above) from al-Hassan b. Mahbub from 'Abd Allāh b. Sinan from abu Hamza who has said the following: "I heard abu Ja'far (عليه السلام) saying, 'Our Shi'a (followers) are just (like) mute people (do not speak uselessly).'" (صحيح)[76]

77.

عَنْهُ عَنِ الْحَسَنِ بْنِ مَحْبُوبٍ عَنْ أَبِي عَلِيٍّ الْجَوَّانِيِّ قَالَ شَهِدْتُ أَبَا عَبْدِ اللهِ (عَلَيهِ السَّلام) وَهُوَ يَقُولُ لِمَوْلَى لَهُ يُقَالُ لَهُ سَالِمٌ وَوَضَعَ يَدَهُ عَلَى شَفَتَيْهِ وَقَالَ يَا سَالِمُ احْفَظْ لِسَانَكَ تَسْلَمْ وَلا تَحْمِلِ النَّاسَ عَلَى رِقَابِنَا

---

[75] *Al-Kafi, v3, ch56, h1*

[76] *Al-Kafi, v3, ch56, h2*

It is narrated from him (narrator of the Hadīth above) from al-Hassan b. Mahbub from abu ʻAlī al-Jawwani who has said the following: "I saw abu 'Abd Allāh (عليه السلام) speaking to one of his slaves called Salim, placing his hands over his (slaves) mouth, 'O Salim, control your tongue and you will have peace and do not load people over our necks.'" (مجهول)[77]

78.

عَنْهُ عَنْ عُثْمَانَ بْنِ عِيسَى قَالَ حَضَرْتُ أَبَا الْحَسَنِ صَلَوَاتُ اللهِ عَلَيْهِ وَقَالَ لَهُ رَجُلٌ أَوْصِنِي فَقَالَ لَهُ احْفَظْ لِسَانَكَ تُعَزَّ وَلَا تُمَكِّنِ النَّاسَ مِنْ قِيَادِكَ فَتُذِلَّ رَقَبَتَكَ

It is narrated from him (narrator of the Hadīth above) from 'Uthman b. 'Isa who has said the following: "Once I was in the presence of abu al-Hassan (عليه السلام) and a man said, 'Please teach me good advice.' The Imam said, 'Control your tongue and you will be respected and do not allow people to lead you to humiliation.'" (موثق)[78]

79.

يُونُسَ عَنْ مُثَنًّى عَنْ أَبِي بَصِيرٍ قَالَ سَمِعْتُ أَبَا جَعْفَرٍ (عَلَيهِ السَّلام) يَقُولُ كَانَ أَبُو ذَرٍّ رَحِمَهُ اللهُ يَقُولُ يَا مُبْتَغِيَ الْعِلْمِ إِنَّ هَذَا اللِّسَانَ مِفْتَاحُ خَيْرٍ وَمِفْتَاحُ شَرٍّ فَاخْتِمْ عَلَى لِسَانِكَ كَمَا تَخْتِمُ عَلَى ذَهَبِكَ وَوَرِقِكَ

Yunus has narrated from Muthanna from abu Basir who has said the following: "I heard abu Ja'far (عليه السلام) saying, abu Dhar may Allāh grant him blessings, would say, 'O you who seek knowledge, this tongues is the key to both good and evil. Seal your tongue as you would seal your gold and silver.'" (حسن)[79]

---

[77] *Al-Kāfi, v3, ch56, h3*

[78] *Al-Kafi, v3, ch56, h4*

[79] *Al-Kāfi, v3, ch56, h10*

80.

مُحَمَّدُ بْنُ يَحْيَى عَنْ أَحْمَدَ بْنِ مُحَمَّدِ بْنِ عِيسَى وَعَلِيُّ بْنُ إِبْرَاهِيمَ عَنْ أَبِيهِ جَمِيعاً عَنِ الْحَسَنِ بْنِ مَحْبُوبٍ عَنْ
أَبِي وَلَادٍ الْحَنَّاطِ قَالَ سَأَلْتُ أَبَا عَبْدِ الله (عَلَيهِ السَّلام) عَنْ قَوْلِ الله عَزَّ وَجَلَّ وَبِالْوَالِدَيْنِ إِحْسَاناً مَا هَذَا
الإِحْسَانُ فَقَالَ الإِحْسَانُ أَنْ تُحْسِنَ صُحْبَتَهُمَا وَأَنْ لَا تُكَلِّفَهُمَا أَنْ يَسْأَلَاكَ شَيْئاً مِمَّا يُحْتَاجَانِ إِلَيْهِ وَإِنْ كَانَا
مُسْتَغْنِيَيْنِ أَ لَيْسَ يَقُولُ الله عَزَّ وَجَلَّ لَنْ تَنَالُوا الْبِرَّ حَتَّى تُنْفِقُوا مِمَّا تُحِبُّونَ قَالَ ثُمَّ قَالَ أَبُو عَبْدِ الله (عَلَيهِ
السَّلام) وَأَمَّا قَوْلُ الله عَزَّ وَجَلَّ إِمَّا يَبْلُغَنَّ عِنْدَكَ الْكِبَرَ أَحَدُهُمَا أَوْ كِلَاهُمَا فَلَا تَقُلْ لَهُمَا أُفٍّ وَلَا تَنْهَرْهُمَا قَالَ
إِنْ أَضْجَرَاكَ فَلَا تَقُلْ لَهُمَا أُفٍّ وَلَا تَنْهَرْهُمَا إِنْ ضَرَبَاكَ قَالَ وَقُلْ لَهُمَا قَوْلاً كَرِيماً قَالَ إِنْ ضَرَبَاكَ فَقُلْ لَهُمَا غَفَرَ
الله لَكُمَا فَذَلِكَ مِنْكَ قَوْلٌ كَرِيمٌ قَالَ وَاخْفِضْ لَهُمَا جَنَاحَ الذُّلِّ مِنَ الرَّحْمَةِ قَالَ لَا تَمْلَأْ عَيْنَيْكَ مِنَ النَّظَرِ إِلَيْهِمَا
إِلَّا بِرَحْمَةٍ وَرِقَّةٍ وَلَا تَرْفَعْ صَوْتَكَ فَوْقَ أَصْوَاتِهِمَا وَلَا يَدَكَ فَوْقَ أَيْدِيهِمَا وَلَا تَقَدَّمْ قُدَّامَهُمَا

Muhammad b. Yahya has narrated from Ahmad b. Muḥammad b. 'Isa and 'Alī b. Ibrahim from his father all from al-Hassan b. Mahbub from abu Wallad al-Hannat who has said the following: "I asked abu 'Abd Allāh (عليه السلام) about the meaning of 'kindness' in the words of Allāh, the Most Majestic, the Most Holy, '. . . and that you must be kind to your parents. . . .' (17:23) The Imam said, 'It means to behave with them in a good manner, not to make them ask you for help, even though they are self-sufficient. Allāh, the Most Majestic, the Most Holy, has said, "You can never have extended virtue and righteousness unless you spend part of what you dearly love for the cause of Allāh.'" (3:92) "The narrator has said that the Imam then said, 'The words of Allāh, the Most Majestic, the Most Holy, "If either or both of your parents should become advanced in age, do not express to them words which show your slightest disappointment. Never shout at them but always speak to them with kindness," (17:23) if they say harsh words to you, do not say 'Uff (expression of disappointment) to them, and do not shout at them if they beat you. Allāh has said, 'Speak kind words to them.' The Imam said, 'If they beat you say to them, "May Allāh forgive you," and this will be the kind and noble word from you.' Allāh has said, "Be humble and merciful toward them. . . ." (17:24) The Imam said, 'Do not have an eyeful look at them except with kindness and tender heart, do not raise your voice over their voice or your hands over their hands and do not walk in front of them.'" (صحيح)[80]

81.

عَلِيُّ بْنُ إِبْرَاهِيمَ عَنْ أَبِيهِ عَنِ ابْنِ أَبِي عُمَيْرٍ عَنْ سَيْفٍ عَنْ أَبِي عَبْدِ اللهِ (عَلَيهِ السَّلام) قَالَ يَأْتِي يَوْمَ الْقِيَامَةِ شَيْءٌ مِثْلُ الْكُبَّةِ فَيَدْفَعُ فِي ظَهْرِ الْمُؤْمِنِ فَيُدْخِلُهُ الْجَنَّةَ فَيُقَالُ هَذَا الْبِرُّ

Ali b. Ibrahim has narrated from his father from b. abu 'Umayr from Sayf from abu 'Abd Allāh (عليه السلام) who has said the following: "On the Day of Judgment something will suddenly come behind the believer, rush him forward and admit him in paradise. It will be said, 'This is kindness.'" (حسن كالصحيح)[81]

82.

مُحَمَّدُ بْنُ يَحْيَى عَنْ أَحْمَدَ بْنِ مُحَمَّدِ بْنِ عِيسَى عَنْ مُعَمَّرِ بْنِ خَلادٍ قَالَ قُلْتُ لأَبِي الْحَسَنِ الرِّضَا (عَلَيهِ السَّلام) أَدْعُو لِوَالِدَيَّ إِذَا كَانَا لا يَعْرِفَانِ الْحَقَّ قَالَ ادْعُ لَهُمَا وَتَصَدَّقْ عَنْهُمَا وَإِنْ كَانَا حَيَّيْنِ لا يَعْرِفَانِ الْحَقَّ فَدَارِهِمَا فَإِنَّ رَسُولَ اللهِ (صَلَّى اللهُ عَلَيهِ وآلِه) قَالَ إِنَّ اللهَ بَعَثَنِي بِالرَّحْمَةِ لا بِالْعُقُوقِ

Muhammad b. Yahya has narrated from Ahmad b. Muḥammad b. 'Isa from Mu'ammar b. Khallad who has said the following: "I asked abu al-Hassan al-Rida (عليه السلام) 'Can I pray for my parents who do not know the truth?' The Imam said, 'Pray for them and give charity on their behalf. If they are living and do not know the truth, be kind to them; the Messenger of Allāh has said, "Allāh has sent me with (message of) kindness and not to punish."'" (صحيح)[82]

---

[80] *Al-Kāfi, v2, ch69, h1*

[81] *Al-Kāfi, v2, ch69, h3*

[82] *Al-Kāfi, v2, ch69, h8*

83.

عَلِيُّ بْنُ إِبْرَاهِيمَ عَنْ أَبِيهِ عَنِ ابْنِ أَبِي عُمَيْرٍ عَنْ هِشَامِ بْنِ سَالِمٍ عَنْ أَبِي عَبْدِ اللَّه (عَلَيهِ السَّلام) قَالَ جَاءَ رَجُلٌ إِلَى النَّبِيِّ (صَلَّى اللَّهُ عَلَيْهِ وآلِه) فَقَالَ يَا رَسُولَ اللَّه مَنْ أَبَرُّ قَالَ أُمَّكَ قَالَ ثُمَّ مَنْ قَالَ أُمَّكَ قَالَ ثُمَّ مَنْ قَالَ أُمَّكَ قَالَ ثُمَّ مَنْ قَالَ أَبَاكَ

Ali b. Ibrahim has narrated from his father from b. abu 'Umayr from Hisham b. Salim from abu 'Abd Allāh who has said the following: "Once a man came to the Holy Prophet and said, 'O Messenger of Allāh, to whom should I be kind?' The Messenger of Allāh said, 'Be kind to your mother.' The man asked, 'Then whom?' The Messenger of Allāh said, 'Your mother.' The man asked, 'Then whom?' The Messenger of Allāh said, 'Your mother.' The man asked, 'Then whom?' The Messenger of Allāh said, "Be kind to your father." (حسن كالصحيح)[83]

84.

مُحَمَّدُ بْنُ يَحْيَى عَنْ أَحْمَدَ بْنِ مُحَمَّدِ بْنِ عِيسَى عَنْ عَلِيِّ بْنِ الْحَكَمِ عَنْ سَيْفِ بْنِ عَمِيرَةَ عَنْ عَبْدِ اللَّه بْنِ مُسْكَانَ عَنْ إِبْرَاهِيمَ بْنِ شُعَيْبٍ قَالَ قُلْتُ لأَبِي عَبْدِ اللَّه (عَلَيهِ السَّلام) إِنَّ أَبِي قَدْ كَبِرَ جِدّاً وَضَعُفَ فَنَحْنُ نَحْمِلُه إِذَا أَرَادَ الْحَاجَةَ فَقَالَ إِنِ اسْتَطَعْتَ أَنْ تَلِيَ ذَلِكَ مِنْه فَافْعَلْ وَلَقِّمْه بِيَدِكَ فَإِنَّه جُنَّةٌ لَكَ غَداً

Muhammad b. Yahya has narrated from Ahmad b. Muḥammad b. 'Isa from 'Alī b. al-Hakam from Sayf b. 'Amirah from 'Abd Allāh b. Muskan from Ibrahim b. Shu'ayb who has said the following: "Once I said to abu 'Abd Allāh (عليه السلام) 'My father has become very old and weak. We pick him up and help him for the restrooms.' The

[83] Al-Kāfi, v2, ch69, h9

Imam said, 'If you can, you should do all of this for him and feed him with your own hand; it is paradise for you tomorrow. ''' (مجهول)[84]

85.

مُحَمَّدُ بْنُ الْحَسَنِ وَعَلِيُّ بْنُ مُحَمَّدٍ عَنْ سَهْلِ بْنِ زِيَادٍ وَمُحَمَّدُ بْنُ يَحْيَى عَنْ أَحْمَدَ بْنِ مُحَمَّدٍ جَمِيعاً عَنْ جَعْفَرِ بْنِ مُحَمَّدٍ الاشْعَرِيِّ عَنْ عَبْدِ اللهِ بْنِ مَيْمُونٍ الْقَدَّاحِ وَعَلِيُّ بْنُ إِبْرَاهِيمَ عَنْ أَبِيهِ عَنْ حَمَّادِ بْنِ عِيسَى عَنِ الْقَدَّاحِ عَنْ أَبِي عَبْدِ اللهِ (عَلَيْهِ السَّلام) قَالَ قَالَ رَسُولُ اللهِ (صَلَّى اللهُ عَلَيْهِ وَآلِه) مَنْ سَلَكَ طَرِيقاً يَطْلُبُ فِيهِ عِلْماً سَلَكَ اللهُ بِهِ طَرِيقاً إِلَى الْجَنَّةِ وَإِنَّ الْمَلائِكَةَ لَتَضَعُ أَجْنِحَتَهَا لِطَالِبِ الْعِلْمِ رِضًا بِهِ وَإِنَّهُ يَسْتَغْفِرُ لِطَالِبِ الْعِلْمِ مَنْ فِي السَّمَاءِ وَمَنْ فِي الارْضِ حَتَّى الْحُوتِ فِي الْبَحْرِ وَفَضْلُ الْعَالِمِ عَلَى الْعَابِدِ كَفَضْلِ الْقَمَرِ عَلَى سَائِرِ النُّجُومِ لَيْلَةَ الْبَدْرِ وَإِنَّ الْعُلَمَاءَ وَرَثَةُ الانْبِيَاءِ إِنَّ الانْبِيَاءَ لَمْ يُوَرِّثُوا دِينَاراً وَلا دِرْهَماً وَلَكِنْ وَرَّثُوا الْعِلْمَ فَمَنْ أَخَذَ مِنْهُ أَخَذَ بِحَظٍّ وَافِرٍ

Muhammad b. al-Hasan and Ali b. Muhammad from Sahl b. Ziyad; Muhammad b. Yahya from Ahmad b. Muhammad – all together from Ja'far b. Muhammad al-Ash'ari from Abdallah b. Maymun al-Qaddah; Ali b. Ibrahim from his father from Hammad b. Isa from al-Qaddah from Abi Abdillah عليه السلام who said: the messenger of Allāh صلى الله عليه وآله said: whoever treads a path seeking knowledge Allāh makes him tread a path to heaven. The angels lay down their wings for the seeker of knowledge being pleased with him. They do seek forgiveness for the seeker of knowledge whatsoever is in heaven and whatsoever is on earth even the fish in the sea. The merit of the scholar over the worshipper is like the excellence of the moon over the rest of the stars on a full-moon night. The scholars are the inheritors of the prophets, the prophets do not leave behind silver or gold coins rather they leave behind knowledge so whomsoever partakes of it then he has obtained a fortunate share. (معتبر) [85]

---

[84] *Al-Kāfi, v2, ch69, h13*

[85] *Al-Kāfi, v2, ch36, h2*

86.

عِدَّةٌ مِنْ أَصْحَابِنَا عَنْ أَحْمَدَ بْنِ مُحَمَّدٍ عَنِ ابْنِ فَضَّالٍ عَنْ عَاصِمِ بْنِ حُمَيْدٍ عَنْ أَبِي حَمْزَةَ الثُّمَالِيِّ عَنْ أَبِي جَعْفَرٍ
(عَلَيْهِ السَّلَام) قَالَ خَطَبَ رَسُولُ الله (صَلَّى اللهُ عَلَيْهِ وَآلِه) فِي حَجَّةِ الْوَدَاعِ فَقَالَ يَا أَيُّهَا النَّاسُ وَاللهِ مَا مِنْ
شَيْءٍ يُقَرِّبُكُمْ مِنَ الْجَنَّةِ وَيُبَاعِدُكُمْ مِنَ النَّارِ إِلَّا وَقَدْ أَمَرْتُكُمْ بِهِ وَمَا مِنْ شَيْءٍ يُقَرِّبُكُمْ مِنَ النَّارِ وَيُبَاعِدُكُمْ مِنَ الْجَنَّةِ
إِلَّا وَقَدْ نَهَيْتُكُمْ عَنْهُ أَلَا وَإِنَّ الرُّوحَ الْأَمِينَ نَفَثَ فِي رُوعِي أَنَّهُ لَنْ تَمُوتَ نَفْسٌ حَتَّى تَسْتَكْمِلَ رِزْقَهَا فَاتَّقُوا الله
وَأَجْمِلُوا فِي الطَّلَبِ وَلَا يَحْمِلْ أَحَدَكُمُ اسْتِبْطَاءُ شَيْءٍ مِنَ الرِّزْقِ أَنْ يَطْلُبَهُ بِغَيْرِ حِلِّهِ فَإِنَّهُ لَا يُدْرَكُ مَا عِنْدَ الله
إِلَّا بِطَاعَتِهِ

A number of our people have narrated from Ahmad b. Muhammad from b. Fadal
from 'Asim b. Humayd from abu Hamza al-Thumali from abu Ja'far (عليه السلام) who
has said the following: "The Messenger of Allāh addressed the people during his
farewell (last) visit to Makka, 'O people, I swear by Allāh, everything that can take
you closer to paradise and farther away from hell I have commanded you all to follow.
Everything that may take you closer to hell and farther away from paradise I have
prohibited you to do. You must know that the trusted spirit has inspired me that no
soul dies before his supply of sustenance is completely exhausted. Be pious before
Allāh and do your best in search of means of sustenance. Do not allow laziness to
overcome you in your search to make a living, or lead you to make a living through
improper means; nothing is achievable from what is with Allāh except through
obedience to Him.'" (موثق كالصحيح)[86]

---

[86] Al-Kāfi, v2, ch36, h2

بِسْمِ ٱللَّهِ ٱلرَّحْمٰنِ ٱلرَّحِيمِ

للّهُمّ كُنْ لِوَلِيّكَ الحُجّةِ ابْنِ الحَسَنِ

صَلَوَاتُكَ عَلَيْهِ وَعَلَى آبَائِهِ

فِي هذِهِ السَّاعَةِ وَفي كُلّ سَاعَةٍ

وَلِيّاً وَحَافِظاً

وَقَائِداً وَنَاصِراً

وَدَلِيلاً وَعَيْناً

حَتَّى تُسْكِنَهُ أَرْضَكَ طَوْعاً

وَتُمَتّعَهُ فِيهَا طَوِيلاً.

ٱللّٰهُمَّ صَلِّ عَلَىٰ مُحَمَّدٍ وَآلِ مُحَمَّدٍ وَعَجِّلْ فَرَجَهُمْ وَٱلْعَنْ أَعْدَاءَهُمْ

Concluding Remarks

All praise is due to Allāh (طبرقة وتعالى), The Majestic, and Sublime, the one who enabl this sinful servant to pen this compilation, although it has many short-comings and most definitely can be improved upon, I pray that it is accepted by Allāh (طبرقة وتعالى), his Messenger (صلى الله عليه وآله وسلم), and the Ulu l-Amr (عليهم السلام) as an act of obedienc I also hope that the reader may have found this compilation to be of benefit to them, and hope that they refer back to the blessed aHadīth of the Ahl al-Bayt (عليهم السلام) in every step on their life and pray that we may be raised together under the banner of Muhammad wa A'l Muhammad. Lastly, I would like to conclude this work with a Du'a for the re-appearance of the Imam of our time.

Made in the USA
Monee, IL
20 July 2025

21481920R00295